THIRD EDITION

WESTERN CIVILIZATION

Volume I: To 1715

THIRD EDITION

WESTERN CIVILIZATION

Volume I: To 1715

JACKSON J. SPIELVOGEL

The Pennsylvania State University

WEST PUBLISHING COMPANY

MINNEAPOLIS/ST. PAUL
NEW YORK
LOS ANGELES
SAN FRANCISCO

Production Credits

COPYEDITING Patricia Lewis
DESIGN Diane Beasley
COMPOSITION Carlisle Communications
DUMMY ARTIST Techarts
ARTWORK Maryland Cartographics
INDEX Patricia Lewis
PERMISSIONS Lynn Reichel
COVER ILLUSTRATION *October: Ploughing and Sowing* from *Book of Hours,* Victoria and Albert Museum, London. Bridgeman Art Library/Art Resource, NY

COPYRIGHT © 1991, 1994 By West Publishing Company
COPYRIGHT © 1997 By West Publishing Company
610 Opperman Drive
P.O. Box 64526
St. Paul, MN 55164-0526

Library of Congress Cataloging-in-Publication Data

Spielvogel, Jackson J., 1939–
   Western civilization / Jackson J. Spielvogel.—3rd ed.
      p.   cm.
   Includes bibliographical references and index.
   ISBN 0-314-09674-4 (comprehensive hbk.).—ISBN
0-314-20533-0 (pbk. v. I : to 1715).—ISBN 0-314-20526-8
(pbk. v. II : since
1550).—ISBN 0-314-20523-3 (pbk. v. A : to 1550).—ISBN
0-314-20524-1 (pbk. v. B : 1300 to 1815),—ISBN
0-314-20525-X (pbk. v. C : since 1789).—ISBN
0-314-20527-6 (pbk. since 1300)
   1. Civilization, Western—History. I. Title.
CB245.S63 1997
909′.09812—dc20   96-30605
                                                    CIP

West's Commitment to the Environment

In 1906, West Publishing Company began recycling materials left over from the production of books. This began a tradition of efficient and responsible use of resources. Today, 100% of our legal bound volumes are printed on acid-free, recycled paper consisting of 50% new fibers. West recycles nearly 27,700,000 pounds of scrap paper annually—the equivalent of 229,300 trees. Since the 1960s, West has devised ways to capture and recycle waste inks, solvents, oils, and vapors created in the printing process. We also recycle plastics of all kinds, wood, glass, corrugated cardboard, and batteries, and have eliminated the use of polystyrene book packaging. We at West are proud of the longevity and the scope of our commitment to the environment.

West pocket parts and advance sheets are printed on recyclable paper and can be collected and recycled with newspapers. Staples do not have to be removed. Bound volumes can be recycled after removing the cover.

Production, Prepress, Printing and Binding by West Publishing Company.

Photo Credits

CHAPTER 1

2 © Will and Deni McIntyre/Photo Researchers, Inc.; **5** © François Ducasse/Photo Researchers, Inc.; **8** © British Museum, London, reproduced by Courtesy of the Trustees of the British Museum; **9** Akkad, *Stele of Naram-Sin,* Musee du Louvre, © Photo R.M.N.; **12** Robert Harding Picture Library; **14** Samuel Kramer, *The Sumerians,* University of Chicago Press, 1963, © University of Chicago Press; **18** Babylonian, *Stele of Hammurabi,* Musee du Louvre, © Photo R.M.N.; **23** Pair Statue of King Mycerinus and His Queen; From Giza, Dynasty IV, 2599–1571 B.C., Slate Schist, 54 1/2 in.; Harvard MFA Expedition. Courtesy, Museum of Fine Arts, Boston; **26** © Will and Deni McIntyre/Photo Researchers, Inc.; **29** Egyptian Museum, Cairo; **30** © John and Anne Abbott, New York; **32** © Brian Brake/Photo Researchers, Inc.; **33** Erich Lessing/Art Resource, NY; **34** © Adam Woolfitt/Robert Harding Picture Library

CHAPTER 2

38 © British Museum, London, reproduced by Courtesy of the Trustees of the British Museum; **41** © British Museum, London, reproduced by Courtesy of the Trustees of the British Museum; **43** © Ronald Sheridan/Ancient Art and Architecture; **44** © Marcello Bertinetti/Photo Researchers, Inc.; **48** © British Museum, London, reproduced by Courtesy of the Trustees of the British Museum; **50** Erich Lessing/Art Resource, NY; **53** © British Museum, London, reproduced by Courtesy of the Trustees of the British Museum; **54** Hirmer Fotoarchiv, Munich; **58** © G. Dagli Orti; **60** *Archers of the Persian Guard,* Musee du Louvre, © Photo R.M.N.

continued following index

About the Author

Jackson J. Spielvogel is associate professor of history at The Pennsylvania State University. He received his Ph.D. from The Ohio State University, where he specialized in Reformation history under Harold J. Grimm. His articles and reviews have appeared in such journals as Moreana, Journal of General Education, Catholic Historical Review, Archiv für Reformationsgeschichte, and American Historical Review. He has also contributed chapters or articles to The Social History of the Reformation, The Holy Roman Empire: A Dictionary Handbook, Simon Wiesenthal Center Annual of Holocaust Studies, and Utopian Studies. His work has been supported by fellowships from the Fulbright Foundation and the Foundation for Reformation Research. At Penn State, he helped inaugurate the Western civilization courses as well as a popular course on Nazi Germany. His book Hitler and Nazi Germany was published in 1987 (third edition, 1996). He is the co-author (with William Duiker) of World History, published in January 1994. Professor Spielvogel has won three major university-wide teaching awards. During the year 1988–1989, he held the Penn State Teaching Fellowship, the university's most prestigious teaching award. In 1996, he won the Dean Arthur Ray Warnock Award for Outstanding Faculty Member.

◆

To Diane,
whose love and support made it all possible

Contents

CHAPTER 4

✦✦✦✦✦✦✦✦✦✦✦

The Hellenistic World   104

CHAPTER 5

✦✦✦✦✦✦✦✦✦✦✦

The Roman Republic   132

CHAPTER 6

✦✦✦✦✦✦✦✦✦✦✦

The Roman Empire   170

CHAPTER 7

The Passing of the Roman World and the Emergence of Medieval Civilization   206

CHAPTER 8

European Civilization in the Early Middle Ages, 750–1000   244

CHAPTER 9

The Recovery and Growth of European Society in the High Middle Ages   278

CHAPTER *10*

A New World of Cities and Kingdoms   306

CHAPTER *11*

Crusades and Culture in the High Middle Ages   342

CHAPTER *12*

The Late Middle Ages: Crisis and Disintegration in the Fourteenth Century   376

CHAPTER *16*

◆◆◆◆◆◆◆◆◆◆◆

Response to Crisis: State Building and the Search for Order in the Seventeenth Century   528

CHAPTER *17*

◆◆◆◆◆◆◆◆◆◆◆

Toward a New Heaven and a New Earth: The Scientific Revolution and the Emergence of Modern Science   570

Documents

We are grateful to the authors and publishers acknowledged here for their permission to reprint copyrighted material. We have made every reasonable effort to identify copyright owners of materials in the boxed documents. If any information is found to be incomplete, we will gladly make whatever additional acknowledgements might be necessary.

Maps

Chronologies

Preface

We are often reminded how important it is to understand today's world if we are to deal with our growing number of challenges. And yet that understanding will be incomplete if we in the Western world do not comprehend the meaning of Western civilization and the role Western civilization has played in the world. For all of our modern progress, we still greatly reflect our religious traditions, our political systems and theories, our economic and social structures, and our cultural heritage. I have written this history of Western civilization to assist a new generation of students in learning more about the past that has helped create them and the world in which they live.

As a teacher of Western civilization courses at a major university, I have become aware of the tendency of many textbooks to simplify the content of Western civilization courses by emphasizing an intellectual perspective or political perspective or, most recently, a social perspective, often at the expense of sufficient details in a chronological framework. This approach is confusing to students whose high school social studies programs have often neglected a systematic study of Western civilization. I have attempted to write a well-balanced work in which the political, economic, social, religious, intellectual, cultural, and military aspects of Western civilization have been integrated into a chronologically ordered synthesis. I have been especially aware of the need to integrate the latest research on social history and women's history into each chapter of the book rather than isolating it either in lengthy topical chapters, which confuse the student by interrupting the chronological narrative, or in separate sections that appear at periodic intervals between chapters. If the results of the new social and women's history are to be taken seriously, they must be fully integrated into the basic narrative itself.

Another purpose in writing this history of Western civilization has been to put the story back in history. That story is an exciting one; yet many textbooks, often the product of several authors with different writing styles, fail to capture the imagination of their readers.

Narrative history effectively transmits the knowledge of the past and is the form that best aids remembrance. At the same time, I have not overlooked the need for the kind of historical analysis that makes students aware that historians often disagree in their interpretations of the past.

To enliven the past and let readers see for themselves the materials that historians use to create their pictures of the past, I have included in each chapter primary sources (boxed documents) they are keyed to the discussion in the text. The documents include examples of the religious, artistic, intellectual, social, economic, and political aspects of Western life. Such varied sources as a Roman banquet menu, a student fight song in twentieth-century Britain, letters exchanged between a husband on the battle front and his wife in World War I, the Declaration of the Rights of Woman and the Citizen in the French Revolution, and a debate in the Reformation era all reveal in a vivid fashion what Western civilization meant to the individual men and women who shaped it by their activities.

Each chapter has a lengthy introduction and conclusion to help maintain the continuity of the narrative and to provide a synthesis of important themes. For the third edition, I have added anecdotes to the introductions in order to convey more dramatically the major theme or themes of each chapter. Detailed chronologies reinforce the events discussed in the text while timelines at the beginning of each chapter, new to the third edition, enable students to see at a glance the major developments of an era. An annotated bibliography at the end of each chapter reviews the most recent literature on each period and also gives references to some of the older, "classic" works in each field. Extensive maps and illustrations serve to deepen the reader's understanding of the text. To facilitate understanding of cultural movements, illustrations of artistic works discussed in the text are placed next to the discussions.

As preparation for the revision of *Western Civilization*, I reexamined the entire book and analyzed the com-ments and reviews of many colleagues who have found the book to be a useful instrument for introducing their students to the history of Western civilization. In making revisions for the third edition, I sought to build upon the strengths of the first and second editions and, above all, to maintain the balance, synthesis, and narrative qualities that characterized those editions. To keep up with the ever-growing body of historical scholarship, new or revised material has been added throughout the book on many topics, including, for example, early human beings in the Neolithic and Paleolithic eras; civilization in Mesopotamia and Egypt; early Greece; Sparta; women in the Hellenistic kingdoms; the Roman Republic; women and sexual attitudes in early Christianity; the world of Islam; medieval guilds; the crusades; the artistic Renaissance; the English Reformation; the age of expansion and discovery; women and witchcraft; art in the seventeenth century; the "Women's Question" in the Enlightenment; neoclassicism and David; women in the French Revolution and Napoleonic eras; the last years of Napoleon; public health in the nineteenth century; John Stuart Mill and liberalism; Imperial Russia; the emergence of Canada; the Dada movement; the Holocaust; the Korean War; the Cuban Missile Crisis; and Western politics, society, and culture since 1970. Throughout the revising process, I also worked to craft a book that I hope students will continue to find very readable. Headings and subheadings in every chapter were revised to give students a more vivid introduction to the content of the chapters.

To provide a more logical arrangement of the material, I also made organizational changes in Chapters 5, 6, 7, 8, 12, 13, 15, 16, 17, 18, 20, 22, 23, 27, and 30. Chapters 24 and 25 were reduced in length and completely reorganized on a chronological basis and are now entitled "Mass Society in an 'Age of Progress,' 1871–1894" and "An Age of Modernity and Anxiety, 1894–1914." Moreover, all "Suggestions for Further Reading" at the end of each chapter were updated, and new illustrations were added to every chapter.

The enthusiastic response to the primary sources (boxed documents) led me to evaluate the content of each document carefully and add a number of new documents throughout the text, including such subjects as "A New Autonomy for Women in Hellenistic Society," "The Achievements of Charlemagne," "Women in Medieval Thought," "The Letters of Isabella d'Este," "Hobbes and Locke: Two Views of Political Authority," "British Victory at Quebec," "A Victim of the Reign of Terror," "Bismarck and the Welfare of the Workers," and "Women in the Factories." For the third edition,

the maps have been revised where needed and, as in the second edition, are carefully keyed to all text references. New maps have also been added, including "Trading Routes and Products in the Roman Empire," "Pilgrimage Routes in the Middle Ages," and "The Death Camps of the Holocaust."

Because courses in Western civilization at American and Canadian colleges and universities follow different chronological divisions, a one-volume edition, two two-volume editions, and a three-volume edition of this text are being made available to fit the needs of instructors. Teaching and learning ancillaries include the following:

For Instructors: Instructor's Manual with Test Bank; map acetates and commentary; computerized test items; Western Civilization video library; videodiscs with maps, still images, video clips, and music; slide set with commentary, and color slides of all maps.

For Students: Study Guide, Document Exercise Workbook, Workbook, Primary Source Reader, Student Study Tips Booklet (shrink-wrapped free with the text at the request of instructors), and Computerized Study Guide.

For Both: CD-ROM and Web site.

Acknowledgments

I began to teach at age five in my family's grape arbor. By the age of ten, I wanted to know and understand everything in the world so I set out to memorize our entire set of encyclopedia volumes. At seventeen, as editor of the high school yearbook, I chose "Patterns" as its theme. With that as my early history, followed by twenty rich years of teaching, writing, and family nurturing, it seemed quite natural to accept the challenge of writing a history of Western civilization as I approached that period in life often described as the age of wisdom. Although I see this writing adventure as part of the natural unfolding of my life, I gratefully acknowledge that without the generosity of many others, it would not have been possible.

David Redles gave generously of his time and ideas, especially for Chapters 29 and 30. Chris Colin provided research on the history of music, while Laurie Batitto, Alex Spencer, Stephen Maloney, Shaun Mason, Peter Angelos, and Fred Schooley offered valuable editorial assistance. I deeply appreciate the valuable technical assistance provided by Dayton Coles. I am also thankful to the thousands of students whose questions and responses have caused me to see many aspects of Western civilization in new ways.

My ability to undertake a project of this magnitude was in part due to the outstanding European history teachers that I had as both an undergraduate and a graduate student. These included Kent Forster (modern Europe) and Robert W. Green (early modern Europe) at The Pennsylvania State University; and Franklin Pegues (medieval), Andreas Dorpalen (modern Germany), William MacDonald (ancient), and Harold J. Grimm (Renaissance and Reformation) at The Ohio State University. These teachers provided me with profound insights into Western civilization and also taught me by their examples that learning only becomes true understanding when it is accompanied by compassion, humility, and open-mindedness.

Thanks to West Publishing Company's comprehensive review process, many historians were asked to evaluate my manuscript and review the first and second editions. I am grateful to the following for the innumerable suggestions that have greatly improved my work:

Gerald Anderson
North Dakota State University

Letizia Argenteri
University of San Diego

Roy A. Austensen
Illinois State University

James A. Baer
Northern Virginia Community College—Alexandria

James T. Baker
Western Kentucky University

Patrick Bass
Morningside College

John F. Battick
University of Maine

Frederic J. Baumgartner
Virginia Polytechnic Institute

Phillip N. Bebb
Ohio University

Anthony Bedford
Modesto Junior College

F. E. Beemon
Middle Tennessee State University

Leonard R. Berlanstein
University of Virginia

Douglas T. Bisson
Belmont University

Stephen H. Blumm
Montgomery County Community College

Hugh S. Bonar
California State University

Werner Braatz
University of Wisconsin—Oshkosh

Alfred S. Bradford
University of Missouri

Maryann E. Brink
College of William & Mary

Blaine T. Browne
Broward Community College

J. Holden Camp, Jr.,
Hillyer College, University of Hartford

Elizabeth Carney
Clemson University

Eric H. Cline
Xavier University

Robert Cole
Utah State University

William J. Connell
Rutgers University

Nancy Conradt
College of DuPage

Marc Cooper
Southwest Missouri State

Richard A. Cosgrove
University of Arizona

David A. Crain
South Dakota State University

Michael F. Doyle
Ocean County College

James W. Ermatinger
University of Nebraska—Kearney

Porter Ewing
Los Angeles City College

Carla Falkner
Northeast Mississippi Community College

Steven Fanning
University of Illinois—Chicago

Ellsworth Faris
California State University—Chico

Gary B. Ferngren
Oregon State University

Mary Helen Finnerty
Westchester Community College

A. Z. Freeman
Robinson College

Frank J. Frost
University of California—Santa Barbara

Frank Garosi
California State University—Sacramento

Richard M. Golden
University of North Texas

Manuel G. Gonzales
Diablo Valley College

Amy G. Gordon
Denison University

Richard J. Grace
Providence College

Hanns Gross
Loyola University

John F. Guilmartin
Ohio State University

Jeffrey S. Hamilton
Gustavus Adolphus College

J. Drew Harrington
Western Kentucky University

James Harrison
Siena College

A. J. Heisserer
University of Oklahoma

Shirley Hickson
North Greenville College

Martha L. Hildreth
University of Nevada

Boyd H. Hill, Jr.
University of Colorado—Boulder

Michael Hofstetter
Bethany College

Donald C. Holsinger
Seattle Pacific University

Frank L. Holt
University of Houston

Paul Hughes
Sussex County Community College

Richard A. Jackson
University of Houston

Fred Jewell
Harding University

Jenny M. Jochens
Towson State University

William M. Johnston
University of Massachusetts

Jeffrey A. Kaufmann
Muscatine Community College

David O. Kieft
University of Minnesota

Patricia Killen
Pacific Lutheran University

William E. Kinsella, Jr.
Northern Virginia Community College—Annandale

James M. Kittelson
Ohio State University

Cynthia Kosso
Northern Arizona University

Harold Marcuse
University of California—Santa Barbara

Mavis Mate
University of Oregon

T. Ronald Melton
Brewton Parker College

Jack Allen Meyer
University of South Carolina

Eugene W. Miller, Jr.
The Pennsylvania State University—Hazleton

Thomas M. Mulhern
University of North Dakota

Pierce Mullen
Montana State University

Frederick I. Murphy
Western Kentucky University

William M. Murray
University of South Florida

Otto M. Nelson
Texas Tech University

Sam Nelson
Willmar Community College

John A. Nichols
Slippery Rock University

Lisa Nofzinger
Albuquerque Technical Vocational Institute

Donald Ostrowski
Harvard University

James O. Overfield
University of Vermont

Matthew L. Panczyk
Bergen Community College

Kathleen Parrow
Black Hills State University

Carla Rahn Phillips
University of Minnesota

Keith Pickus
Wichita State University

Linda J. Piper
University of Georgia

Janet Polasky
University of New Hampshire

Charles A. Povlovich
California State University—Fullerton

Nancy Rachels
Hillsborough Community College

Jerome V. Reel, Jr.
Clemson University

Joseph Robertson
Gadsden State Community College

Jonathan Roth
San Jose State University

Constance M. Rousseau
Providence College

Julius R. Ruff
Marquette University

Richard Saller
University of Chicago

Magdalena Sanchez
Texas Christian University

Jack Schanfield
Suffolk County Community College

Roger Schlesinger
Washington State University

Joanne Schneider
Rhode Island College

Thomas C. Schunk
University of Wisconsin—Oshkosh

Kyle C. Sessions
Illinois State University

Linda Simmons
Northern Virginia Community College—Manassas

Donald V. Sippel
Rhode Island College

John W. Steinberg
Georgia Southern University

Paul W. Strait
Florida State University

James E. Straukamp
California State University—Sacramento

Brian E. Strayer
Andrews University

Fred Suppe
Ball State University

Roger Tate
Somerset Community College

Tom Taylor
Seattle University

Jack W. Thacker
Western Kentucky University

Thomas Turley
Santa Clara University

John G. Tuthill
University of Guam

Maarten Ultee
University of Alabama

Donna L. Van Raaphorst
Cuyahoga Community College

Allen M. Ward
University of Connecticut

Richard D. Weigel
Western Kentucky University

Michael Weiss
Linn-Benton Community College

Arthur H. Williamson
*California State University—
Sacramento*

Judith T. Wozniak
Cleveland State University

Walter J. Wussow
University of Wisconsin—Eau Claire

Edwin M. Yamauchi
Miami University

The editors at West Publishing Company have been both helpful and congenial at all times. Their flexible policies allowed the creative freedom that a writer cherishes. I especially wish to thank Clark Baxter, whose faith in my ability to do this project was inspiring. His clever wit, good insight, and friendship have added much depth to our working relationship. Linda Poirier and Patricia MacDonald were always helpful with their insightful analyses and organization of many practical details. Members of the the West production team— Kara ZumBahlen, Amy Gabriel, and Peter Krall—were as cooperative as they were competent. John Och's artful cover designs greatly enhanced the appearance of the book. Pat Lewis, an outstanding copy editor, taught me much about the fine points of the English language. Lynn Reichel provided valuable assistance in obtaining permissions for the boxed documents. I appreciate the professional and personal relationships that I have shared with the West "family."

Above all, I thank my family for their support. The gifts of love, laughter, and patience from my daughters, Jennifer and Kathryn, my sons Eric and Christian, and my daughters-in-law, Liz and Michele were invaluable. My wife and best friend, Diane, provided me with editorial assistance, wise counsel, and the loving support that made it possible for me to complete a project of this magnitude. I could not have written the book without her.

Introduction to Students of Western Civilization

Civilization, as historians define it, first emerged between 5,000 and 6,000 years ago when people began to live in organized communities with distinct political, military, economic, and social structures. Religious, intellectual, and artistic activities also assumed important roles in these early societies. The focus of this book is on Western civilization, a civilization that for most of its history has been identified with the continent of Europe. Its origins, however, go back to the Mediterranean basin, including lands in North Africa, and the Near East as well as Europe itself. Moreover, the spread of Europeans abroad led to the development of offshoots of Western civilization in other parts of the world.

Because civilized life includes all the deeds and experiences of people organized in communities, the history of a civilization must encompass a series of studies. An examination of Western civilization requires us to study the political, economic, social, military, cultural, intellectual, and religious aspects that make up the life of that civilization and show how they are interrelated. In so doing, we need also at times to focus on some of the unique features of Western civilization. Certainly, science played a crucial role in the development of modern Western civilization. Although such societies as those of the Greeks, the Romans, and medieval Europeans were based largely on a belief in the existence of a spiritual order, Western civilization experienced a dramatic departure to a natural or material view of the universe in the seventeenth-century Scientific Revolution. Science and technology have been important in the growth of a modern and largely secular Western civilization, although antecedents to scientific development also existed in Greek, Islamic, and medieval thought and practice.

Many historians have also viewed the concept of political liberty, the fundamental value of every individual, and the creation of a rational outlook, based on a system of logical, analytical thought, as unique aspects of Western civilization. Of course, Western civilization has also witnessed the frightening negation of liberty, individualism, and reason. Racism, violence, world wars,

totalitarianism—these, too, must form part of the story. Finally, regardless of our concentration on Western civilization and its characteristics, we need to take into account that other civilizations have influenced Western civilization and it, in turn, has affected the development of other civilizations.

In our examination of Western civilization, we need also to be aware of the dating of time. In recording the past, historians try to determine the exact time when events occurred. World War II in Europe, for example, began on September 1, 1939, when Hitler sent German troops into Poland, and ended on May 7, 1945, when Germany surrendered. By using dates, historians can place events in order and try to determine the development of patterns over periods of time.

If someone asked you when you were born, you would reply with a number, such as 1978. In the United States, we would all accept that number without question because it is part of the dating system followed in the Western world (Europe and the Western Hemisphere). In this system, events are dated by counting backward or forward from the birth of Christ (assumed to be the year 1). An event that took place 400 years before the birth of Christ would be dated 400 B.C. (before Christ). Dates after the birth of Christ are labeled A.D. These letters stand for the Latin words *anno Domini*, which mean "in the year of the lord." Thus, an event that took place 250 years after the birth of Christ is written A.D. 250, or in the year of the lord 250. It can also be written as 250, just as you would not give your birth year as A.D. 1978, but simply 1978.

Historians also make use of other terms to refer to time. A decade is 10 years; a century is 100 years; and a millennium is 1,000 years. The phrase fourth century B.C. refers to the fourth period of 100 years counting backward from 1, the assumed date of the birth of Christ. Since the first century B.C. would be the years 100 B.C. to 1 B.C., the fourth century B.C. would be the years 400 B.C. to 301 B.C. We could say, then, that an event in 350 B.C. took place in the fourth century B.C.

The phrase fourth century A.D. refers to the fourth period of 100 years after the birth of Christ. Since the first period of 100 years would be the years 1 to 100, the fourth period or fourth century would be the years 301 to 400. We could say, then, for example, that an event in 350 took place in the fourth century. Likewise, the first millennium B.C. refers to the years 1000 B.C. to 1 B.C.; the second millennium A.D. refers to the years 1001 to 2000.

Some historians now prefer to use the abbreviations B.C.E. ("before the common era") and C.E. ("common era") instead of B.C. and A.D. This is especially true of world historians who prefer to use symbols that are not so Western or Christian oriented. The dates, of course, remain the same. Thus, 1950 B.C.E. and 1950 B.C. would be the same year. In keeping with current usage by many historians of Western civilization, this book will use the terms B.C. and A.D.

The dating of events can also vary from people to people. Most people in the Western world use the Western calendar, also known as the Gregorian calendar after Pope Gregory XIII who refined it in 1582. The Hebrew calendar, on the other hand, uses a different system in which the year 1 is the equivalent of the Western year 3760 B.C., considered by Jews to be the date of the creation of the world. Thus, the Western year 2000 will be the year 5760 on the Jewish calendar. The Islamic calendar begins year 1 on the day Muhammad fled Mecca, which is the year 622 on the Western calendar.

THIRD EDITION

WESTERN CIVILIZATION

CHAPTER

1

The Ancient Near East: The First Civilizations

In 1849, a daring young Englishman made a hazardous journey into the deserts and swamps of southern Iraq. Moving south down the banks of the Euphrates River while braving high winds and temperatures that reached 120 degrees Fahrenheit, William Loftus led a small expedition in search of the roots of civilization. As he said, "From our childhood we have been led to regard this place as the cradle of the human race."

Guided by native Arabs into the southernmost reaches of Iraq, Loftus and his small group of explorers were soon overwhelmed by what they saw. He wrote, "I know of nothing more exciting or impressive than the first sight of one of these great piles, looming in solitary grandeur from the surrounding plains and marshes." One of these piles, known to the natives as the mound of Warka, contained the ruins of Uruk, one of the first cities in the world and part of the world's first civilization.

Southern Iraq, known to ancient peoples as Mesopotamia, was one of four areas in the world where civilization began. In the fertile valleys of the Tigris and Euphrates, the Nile, the Indus, and the Yellow River, in Mesopotamia, Egypt, India, and China, intensive agriculture became capable of supporting large groups of people. In these regions the first civilizations were born. The beginnings of Western civilization can be traced back to the ancient Near East, where people in Mesopotamia and Egypt developed organized societies and created the ideas and institutions that we associate with civilization. The later Greeks and Romans, who played such a crucial role in the development of Western civilization, were themselves nourished and influenced by these older societies in the Near East. It is appropriate, therefore, to begin our story of Western civilization in the ancient Near East with the early civilizations of Mesopotamia and Egypt. Before considering them, however, we must briefly examine humankind's prehistory and observe how human beings made the shift from hunting and gathering to agricultural communities and ultimately to cities and civilization.

Early Dynastic
Age of Sumerian city-states

Construction of
Stonehenge

Babylonian Kingdom

Hittite Empire

Emergence of
Egyptian civilization

Egypt—Old Kingdom

Egypt—Middle Kingdom

Egypt—New Kingdom

Beginning of cuneiform

Great Pyramid

Code of Hammurabi

Akhenaten's religious upheaval

The First Humans

Historians rely mostly on documents to create their pictures of the past, but no written records exist for the prehistory of humankind. In their absence, the story of early humanity depends upon archaeological and, more recently, biological information, which anthropologists and archaeologists use to formulate theories about our early past.

Although modern science has given us more precise methods for examining prehistory, much of our understanding of early humans still relies upon considerable conjecture. Given the rate of new discoveries, the following account of the current theory of early human life might well be changed in a few years. As the great British archaeologist Louis Leakey reminded us years ago: "Theories on prehistory and early man constantly change as new evidence comes to light."

The earliest humanlike creatures—known as hominids—lived in Africa as long as three to four million years ago. Known as Australopithecines, they flourished in East and South Africa and were the first hominids to make simple stone tools. The oldest known stone tool—a knife blade that is probably 2.6 million years old—was found in Africa.

A second stage in early human development occurred around 1.5 million years ago when *Homo erectus* ("upright human being") emerged. *Homo erectus* made use of larger and more varied tools and was the first hominid to leave Africa and move into both Europe and Asia.

Around 250,000 years ago, a third—and crucial—stage in human development began with the emergence of *Homo sapiens* ("wise human being"). By 100,000 B.C.,

two groups of *Homo sapiens* had developed. One type was the Neanderthal, whose remains were first found in the Neander valley in Germany. Their remains have since been found in both Europe and the Middle East and have been dated to between 100,000 and 30,000 B.C. Neanderthals relied on a variety of stone tools and were the first early people to bury their dead. Some scientists maintain that burial of the dead indicates a belief in an afterlife. Neanderthals in Europe made clothes from the skins of animals that they had killed for food.

The first anatomically modern humans, known as *Homo sapiens sapiens* ("wise, wise human being"), appeared in Africa between 200,000 and 150,000 years ago. Recent evidence indicates that they began to spread outside Africa around 100,000 years ago. Map 1.1 on p. 4 shows probable dates for different movements, although many of these are still controversial. By 30,000 B.C., *Homo sapiens sapiens* had replaced the Neanderthals, who had largely become extinct.

The movement of the first modern humans was rarely deliberate. Groups of people advanced beyond their old hunting grounds at a rate of only two or three miles per generation. This was enough, however, to populate the world in some tens of thousands of years. Based on recent evidence, some scholars have suggested that such advanced human creatures may have emerged independently in different parts of the world, rather than in Africa alone. In any case, by 10,000 B.C., members of the *Homo sapiens sapiens* species could be found throughout the world. By that time, it was the only human species left. All humans today, be they Europeans, Australian aborigines, or Africans, belong to the same subspecies of human being.

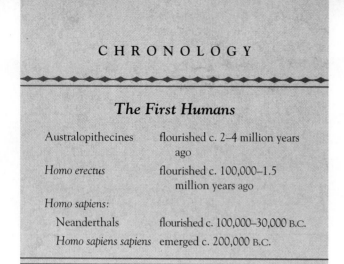
The Hunter-Gatherers of the Old Stone Age

One of the basic distinguishing features of the human species is the ability to make tools. The earliest tools were made of stone, and the term *Paleolithic* (Greek for "Old Stone") Age is used to designate this early period of human history (c. 2,500,000–10,000 B.C.)

For hundreds of thousands of years, humans relied on hunting and gathering for their daily food. Paleolithic peoples had a close relationship with the world around them, and over a period of time, they came to know what animals to hunt and what plants to eat. They did not know how to grow crops or raise animals, however.

They gathered wild nuts, berries, fruits, and a variety of wild grains and green plants. Around the world, they hunted and consumed various animals, including buffalo, horses, bison, wild goats, and reindeer. In coastal areas, fish provided a rich source of food.

The hunting of animals and the gathering of wild plants no doubt led to certain patterns of living. Archaeologists and anthropologists have speculated that Paleolithic people lived in small bands of twenty or thirty people. They were nomadic (they moved from place to place) since they had no choice but to follow animal migrations and vegetation cycles. Hunting depended upon careful observation of animal behavior patterns and required a group effort to have any real chance of success. Over the years, tools became more refined and more useful. The invention of the spear, and later the bow and arrow, made hunting considerably easier. Harpoons and fishhooks made of bone increased the catch of fish.

Both men and women were responsible for finding food—the chief work of Paleolithic people. Since women bore and raised the children, they generally stayed close to the camps, but they played an important role in acquiring food, gathering berries, nuts, and grains. Men hunted the wild animals, an activity that took them far from camp. Because both men and women played important roles in providing for the band's

❧ **Map 1.1** The Spread of *Homo Sapiens Sapiens*.

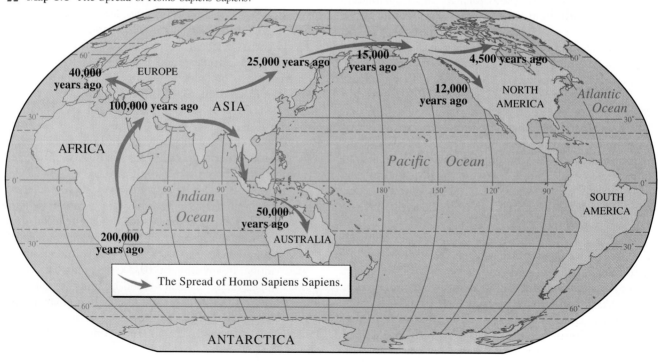

survival, scientists have argued that a rough equality existed between men and women. Indeed, some speculate that both men and women made the decisions that affected the activities of the Paleolithic band.

These groups of Paleolithic people, especially those who lived in cold climates, found shelter in caves. Over time, they created new types of shelter as well. Perhaps the most common was a simple structure of wood poles or sticks covered with animal hides. Where wood was scarce, Paleolithic hunter-gatherers might use the bones of mammoths to build frames that were then covered with animal hides. The systematic use of fire, which archaeologists believe began around 500,000 years ago, made it possible for the caves and human-made structures to have a source of light and heat. Fire also enabled early humans to cook their food, making it better tasting, longer lasting, and, in the case of some plants, such as wild grain, easier to chew and digest.

The making of tools and the use of fire—two important technological innovations of Paleolithic peoples—remind us how crucial the ability to adapt was to human survival. Changing physical conditions during periodic ice ages posed a considerable threat to human existence. Paleolithic peoples used their technological innovations—such as the ability to make tools and use fire—to change their physical environment. By working together, they found a way to survive. And by passing on their common practices, skills, and material products to their children, they ensured that later generations, too, could survive in a harsh environment.

But Paleolithic peoples did more than just survive. The cave paintings of large animals found in southwestern France and northern Spain bear witness to the cultural activity of Paleolithic peoples. A cave discovered in southern France in 1994 contains more than three hundred paintings of lions, oxen, owls, panthers, and other animals. Most of these are animals that Paleolithic people did not hunt, which suggests that the paintings were made for religious or even decorative purposes.

The Agricultural Revolution, c. 10,000–4000 B.C.

The end of the last ice age around 10,000 B.C. was followed by what is called the Neolithic Revolution; that is, the revolution that occurred in the New Stone Age (the word *Neolithic* is Greek for "New Stone.") The name New Stone Age is misleading, however. Although Neolithic peoples made a new type of polished stone

◆ **Paleolithic Cave Painting.** Cave paintings of large animals provide good examples of the cultural creativity of Paleolithic peoples. This scene is part of a large underground chamber found accidentally in 1940 at Lascaux, France, by some boys looking for their dog. This work is dated around 15,000 B.C.

axes, this was not the major change that occurred after 10,000 B.C.

The real change was the shift from hunting animals and gathering plants for sustenance to producing food by systematic agriculture. The planting of grains and vegetables provided a regular supply of food while the taming of animals, such as goats, cattle, pigs, and sheep, added a steady source of meat, milk, and fibers such as wool for clothing. Larger animals could also be used as beasts of burden. The growing of crops and the taming of food-producing animals created a new relationship between humans and nature. Historians like to speak of this as an agricultural revolution. Revolutionary change is dramatic and requires great effort, but the ability to acquire food on a regular basis gave humans greater control over their environment. It also enabled them to give up their nomadic ways of life and begin to live in settled communities.

The shift to food producing from hunting and gathering was not as sudden as was once believed, however. The Mesolithic period ("Middle Stone Age," c. 10,000–7000 B.C.) saw a gradual transition from the old food-gathering and hunting economy to a food-producing one and witnessed a gradual domestication of animals as well. Likewise, the movement toward the use of plants and their seeds as an important source of nourishment was also not sudden. Evidence seems to support the possibility that some Paleolithic hunters and gatherers had already grown crops to supplement their traditional sources of food.

In fact, historians are not certain where systematic agriculture first began. It probably developed independently between 8000 and 7000 B.C. in four different areas of the world. In each of these areas, different plants were cultivated: wheat, barley, and lentils in the Near East, rice and millet in southern Asia, millet and yams in western Africa, and beans, potatoes, and corn in the middle Americas. In the Near East as elsewhere, the Neolithic agricultural revolution needed a favorable environment. The upland areas above the Fertile Crescent (present-day northern Iraq and southern Turkey) were initially more conducive to systematic farming than the river valleys. This region received the necessary rainfall and was the home of two wild plant (barley, wheat) and four wild animal (pigs, cows, goats, sheep) species that came to be domesticated for human use.

The growing of crops on a regular basis gave rise to more permanent settlements, which historians refer to as Neolithic farming villages or towns. One of the oldest known agricultural villages was Jericho, in Palestine near the Dead Sea. Jericho existed by 8000 B.C. and by 7000 B.C. covered several acres. It had a wall several feet thick that enclosed houses made of sun-dried bricks. Çatal Hüyük, located in modern-day Turkey, was an even larger community. Its walls enclosed thirty-two acres, and its population probably reached six thousand inhabitants during its high point from 6700 to 5700 B.C. People lived in simple mudbrick houses that were built so close to one another that there were few streets. To get to their homes, people had to walk along the rooftops

and then enter the house through a hole in the roof.

Archaeologists have discovered twelve cultivated products in Çatal Hüyük, including fruits, nuts, and three kinds of wheat. People grew their own food and stored it in storerooms in their homes. Domesticated animals, especially cattle, yielded meat, milk, and hides. Hunting scenes on the walls would indicate that the people of Çatal Hüyük hunted as well, but unlike earlier hunter-gatherers, they no longer relied on hunting to survive. Food surpluses also made it possible for people to do things other than farming. Some people became artisans and made weapons and jewelry that were traded with neighboring peoples, thus opening the inhabitants of Çatal Hüyük to the wider world around them.

Religious shrines housing figures of gods and goddesses have been found at Çatal Hüyük, as have a number of female statuettes. Molded with noticeably large breasts and buttocks, these "earth mothers" perhaps symbolically represented the fertility of both "our mother" earth and human mothers. Both the shrines and the statues point to the growing role of religion in the lives of these Neolithic people.

The Neolithic agricultural revolution had far-reaching consequences. Once people settled in villages or towns, they built houses for protection and other structures for the storage of goods. As organized communities stored food and accumulated material goods, they began to engage in trade. In the Near East, for example,

❖ **Map 1.2** The Development of Agriculture.

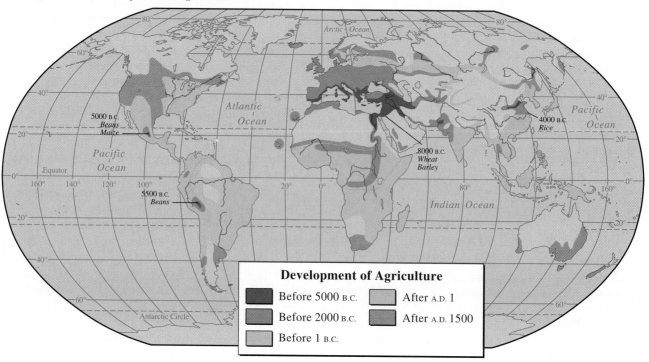

the new communities exchanged such objects as shells, flint, and semiprecious stones. People also began to specialize in certain crafts, and a division of labor developed. Pottery was made from clay and baked in a fire to make it hard. The pots were used for cooking and to store grains. Woven baskets were also used for storage. Stone tools became refined as flint blades were used to make sickles and hoes for use in the fields. In the course of the Neolithic Age, many of the food plants still in use today came to be cultivated. Moreover, vegetable fibers from such plants as flax and cotton were used to make thread that was woven into cloth.

The change to systematic agriculture in the Neolithic Age also had consequences for the relationship between men and women. Men assumed the primary responsibility for working in the fields and herding animals, jobs that kept them away from the home. Women remained behind, caring for the children and weaving clothes, making cheese from milk, and performing other tasks that required considerable labor in one place. In time, as work outside the home was increasingly perceived as more important than work done at home, men came to play the more dominant role in society, a basic pattern that would persist until our own times.

Other patterns set in the Neolithic Age also proved to be enduring elements of human history. Fixed dwellings, domesticated animals, regular farming, a division of labor, men holding power, all of these are part of the human story. For all of our scientific and technological progress, human survival still depends on the growing and storing of food, an accomplishment of people in the Neolithic Age. The Neolithic Revolution was truly a turning point in human history.

Between 4000 and 3000 B.C., significant technical developments began to transform the Neolithic towns. The invention of writing (see Writing later in this chapter) enabled records to be kept while the use of metals marked a new level of human control over the environment and its resources. Already, before 4000 B.C., craftsmen had discovered that metal-bearing rocks could be heated to liquefy metals, which could then be cast in molds to produce tools and weapons that were more useful than stone instruments. Although copper was the first metal to be utilized in producing tools, after 4000 B.C., craftsmen in western Asia discovered that a combination of copper and tin produced bronze, a much harder and more durable metal than copper. Its widespread use has led historians to speak of a Bronze Age from around 3000 to 1200 B.C., when bronze was increasingly replaced by iron.

At first, Neolithic settlements were hardly more than villages. But as their inhabitants mastered the art of farming, they gradually began to give birth to more complex human societies. As wealth increased, such societies began to develop armies and to build walled cities. By the beginning of the Bronze Age, the concentration of larger numbers of people in the river valleys of Mesopotamia and Egypt was leading to a whole new pattern for human life.

The Emergence of Civilization

As we have seen, early human beings formed small groups that developed a simple culture that enabled them to survive. As human societies grew and developed greater complexity, a new form of human existence— called civilization—came into being. A civilization is a complex culture in which large numbers of human beings share a number of common elements. Historians have identified a number of basic characteristics of civilization, most of which are evident in the Mesopotamian and Egyptian civilizations. These include (1) an urban revolution: cities became the focal points for political, economic, social, cultural, and religious development; (2) a distinct religious structure: the gods were deemed crucial to the community's success, and professional priestly classes, as stewards of the gods' property, regulated relations with the gods; (3) new political and military structures: an organized government bureaucracy arose to meet the administrative demands of the growing population while armies were organized to gain land and power; (4) a new social structure based on economic power: while kings and an upper class of priests, political leaders, and warriors dominated, there also existed a large group of free men (farmers, artisans, craftsmen) and at the very bottom, socially, a class of slaves; (5) the development of writing: kings, priests, merchants, and artisans used writing to keep records; (6) new forms of significant artistic and intellectual activity, such as monumental architectural structures, usually religious, occupied a prominent place in urban environments; and (7) the development of more complexity in a material sense: capital was accumulated and metals smelted to produce a variety of material objects.

Why early civilizations developed remains difficult to explain. Since civilizations developed independently in India, China, Mesopotamia, and Egypt, can general causes be identified that would explain why all of these civilizations emerged? A number of possible explanations of the beginning of civilization have been suggested. A theory of challenge and response maintains that challenges forced human beings to make efforts that resulted in the rise of civilization. Some scholars

✦ **The "Royal Standard" of Ur.** This series of panels is from the "Royal Standard" of Ur, a box dating from c. 2700 B.C. and discovered in a stone tomb from the royal cemetery of the Sumerian city-state of Ur. These scenes from the box depict the activities of the king and his court after a military victory. In the top panel, the king and his court drink wine while at the right a musician plays a bull-headed harp. The middle panel shows bulls, rams, and fish being brought to the banquet hall. The bottom panel shows booty from the king's victory.

have adhered to a material explanation. Material forces, such as the growth of food surpluses, made possible the specialization of labor and development of large communities with bureaucratic organization. But the area of the Fertile Crescent, in which Mesopotamian civilization emerged, was not naturally conducive to agriculture. Abundant food could only be produced with a massive human effort to carefully manage the water, an effort that created the need for organization and bureaucratic control and led to civilized cities. Some historians have argued that nonmaterial forces, primarily religious, provided the sense of unity and purpose that made such organized activities possible. Finally, some scholars doubt that we are capable of ever discovering the actual causes of early civilization.

Civilization in Mesopotamia

The Greeks spoke of the river valley between the Tigris and Euphrates Rivers as Mesopotamia, the land "between the rivers." The region receives little rain, but the soil of the plain of southern Mesopotamia was enlarged and enriched over the years by layers of silt deposited by the two rivers. In late spring, the Tigris and Euphrates overflow their banks and deposit their fertile silt, but since this flooding depends upon the melting of snows in the upland mountains where the rivers begin, it is irregular and sometimes catastrophic. In such circum-

stances, farming could be accomplished only with human intervention in the form of irrigation and drainage ditches. A complex system was required to control the flow of the rivers and produce the crops. Large-scale irrigation made possible the expansion of agriculture in this region, and the abundant food provided the material base for the emergence of civilization in Mesopotamia.

The City-States of Ancient Mesopotamia

The creators of Mesopotamian civilization were the Sumerians, a people whose origins remain unclear. By 3000 B.C., they had established a number of independent cities in southern Mesopotamia, including Eridu, Ur, Uruk, Umma, and Lagash. As the cities grew larger, they came to exercise political and economic control over the surrounding countryside, forming city-states. These city-states were the basic units of Sumerian civilization.

Sumerian cities were surrounded by walls. Uruk, for example, occupied an area of approximately a thousand acres encircled by a wall six miles long with defense towers located every thirty to thirty-five feet along the wall. City dwellings, built of sun-dried bricks, included both the small flats of peasants and the larger dwellings of the civic and priestly officials. Although Mesopotamia had little stone or wood for building purposes, it did have plenty of mud. Mudbricks, easily shaped by hand, were left to bake in the hot sun until they were hard enough to use for building. People in Mesopotamia were remarkably inventive with mudbricks, inventing the arch and the dome and constructing some of the largest brick buildings in the world. Mudbricks are still used in rural areas of the Middle East today.

The most prominent building in a Sumerian city was the temple, which was dedicated to the chief god or goddess of the city and often built atop a massive stepped tower called a ziggurat. The Sumerians believed that the gods and goddesses owned the cities, and much wealth was used to build temples as well as elaborate houses for the priests and priestesses who served the gods. Priests and priestesses, who supervised the temples and their property, had much power. The temples owned much of the city land and livestock and served not only as the physical center of the city, but also its economic and political center.

In fact, historians believe that in the early stages of the city-states, priests and priestesses played an important role in ruling. The Sumerians believed that the gods ruled the cities, making the state a theocracy (government by a divine authority). Eventually, however, ruling power passed into the hands of worldly figures known as kings.

Sumerians viewed kingship as divine in origin—kings, they believed, derived their power from the gods and were the agents of the gods. Regardless of their origins, kings had power—they led armies, initiated legislation, supervised the building of public works, provided courts, and organized workers for the irrigation projects upon which Mesopotamian agriculture depended. The army, the government bureaucracy, and the priests and priestesses all aided the kings in their rule. Befitting their power, Sumerian kings lived in large palaces with their wives and children.

The economy of the Sumerian city-states was primarily agricultural, but commerce and industry became important as well. The people of Mesopotamia produced woolen textiles, pottery, and the metalwork for which they were especially well known. Foreign trade, which was primarily a royal monopoly, could be extensive. Royal officials imported luxury items, such as copper and tin, aromatic woods, and fruit trees, in exchange for dried fish, wool, barley, wheat, and the metal goods produced by Mesopotamian craftsmen. Traders traveled by land to the eastern Mediterranean in the west and by sea to India in the east. The invention of the wheel around 3000 B.C. led to carts with wheels that made the transport of goods easier.

Sumerian city-states contained three major social groups—nobles, commoners, and slaves. Nobles included royal and priestly officials and their families. Commoners included the nobles' clients who worked for the palace and temple estates and other free citizens who worked as farmers, merchants, fishermen, scribes, and craftsmen. Probably 90 percent or more of the population were farmers. They could exchange their crops for the goods of the artisans in free town markets. Slaves belonged to palace officials, who used them mostly in building projects; temple officials, who used mostly female slaves to weave cloth and grind grain; and rich landowners, who used them for farming and domestic work.

Empires in Ancient Mesopotamia

As the number of Sumerian city-states grew and the states expanded, new conflicts arose as city-state fought city-state for control of land and water. During the Early Dynastic Age (3000–2340 B.C.), the fortunes of various cities rose and fell over the centuries. The constant wars, with their burning and sacking of cities, left many Sumerians in deep despair, as is evident in this Sumerian poem from the city of Ur: "Ur is destroyed, bitter is its lament. The country's blood now fills its holes like hot bronze in a mould. Bodies dissolve like fat in the sun. Our temple is destroyed, the gods have abandoned us, like migrating birds. Smoke lies on our city like a shroud." Attempts to control all of Sumer tended to fail until Lugalzaggisi, the king of Umma, succeeded in defeating Lagash, Uruk, and Ur and became ruler of all Sumer. But his success proved short-lived.

Located on the flat, open land of Mesopotamia, the Sumerian city-states were also vulnerable to invasion.

◆ **Stele of Naram-Sin, King of Akkad.** This sculpture in pink sandstone, dated c. 2250 B.C., is from the period of Akkadian hegemony in Mesopotamia. The sculpture depicts Naram-Sin, the fourth monarch of the dynasty founded by Sargon, leading his forces to the top of a mountain. The stele commemorates the defeat of a hill tribe in western Iran.

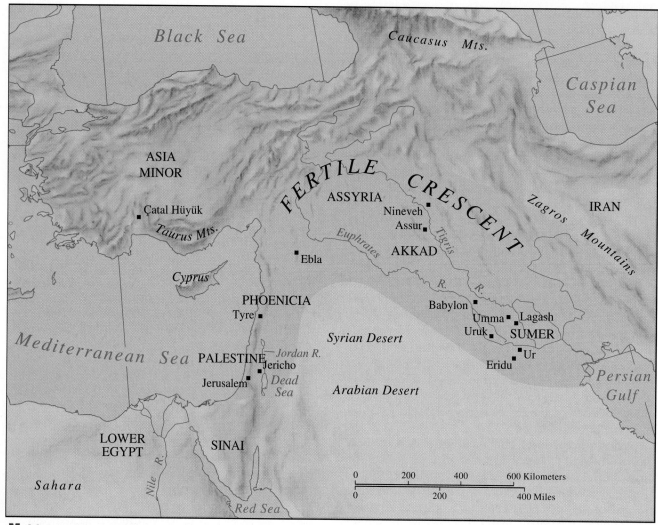

⚒ **Map 1.3** The Ancient Near East.

To the north of the Sumerian city-states were the Akkadians. We call them a Semitic people because of the type of language they spoke (see Table 1.1). Around 2340 B.C., Sargon, leader of the Akkadians, defeated the army of Lugalzaggisi and established a new dynastic empire. Sargon's empire, including all of Mesopotamia as well as lands westward to the Mediterranean, inspired generations of Near Eastern leaders to emulate his accomplishment. Despite a period of economic growth, prosperity, and cultural flowering, Sargon's successors were ultimately unable to preserve his empire, however. Attacks from neighboring hill peoples caused the Akkadian empire to fall by 2100 B.C.

One of Sargon's claims was that he had conquered a prosperous state called Ebla. In the 1960s and 1970s,

archaeologists uncovered ancient Ebla in modern Syria. Excavations revealed that Ebla had been a well-organized city-state possessing a rich and complex urban culture. With a large population, it flourished from 2600 to 2250 B.C. and apparently controlled an extensive area northwest of Mesopotamia. The discovery of 20,000 clay tablets written in a version of Sumerian cuneiform (see Writing later in this chapter) provided important sources of information about this hitherto unknown community.

HAMMURABI AND THE BABYLONIAN EMPIRE

The end of the Akkadian empire brought a return to independent city-states in Mesopotamia until Ur-Nammu of Ur succeeded in reunifying much of Mesopotamia. The Third Dynasty of Ur (c. 2112–2000 B.C.) that he established witnessed a final flowering of Sumerian culture. The economy flourished, and new temples and canals were built. In addition to promulgating the first known comprehensive law code in Sumer, Ur-Nammu developed an efficient system of monthly obligations levied on major Sumerian and Akkadian provinces. Invasion by nomadic tribes, a perennial problem in Mesopotamian history, proved disastrous for the Third Dynasty of Ur, however. After a lengthy period of fighting and confusion, the sixth king of the Amorite dynasty—Hammurabi—managed to establish power. Under Hammurabi, the Amorites or Old Babylonians, a large group of Semitic-speaking seminomads, created a new empire.

Hammurabi (1792–1750 B.C.) had a well-disciplined army of foot soldiers who carried axes, spears, and copper or bronze daggers. He learned to divide his opponents and subdue them one by one. Using such methods, he gained control of Sumer and Akkad and reunified Mesopotamia almost to the old borders established by Sargon of Akkad. After his conquests, Hammurabi called himself "the sun of Babylon, the king who has made the four quarters of the world subservient," and established a new capital at Babylon, north of Akkad.

Hammurabi, the man of war, was also a man of peace. He followed in the footsteps of previous conquerors by assimilating Mesopotamian culture with the result that Sumerian ways continued to exist despite the end of the Sumerians as a political entity. A collection of his letters, found by archaeologists, reveals that the king took a strong interest even in trivial matters. He built temples, defensive walls, and irrigation canals, encouraged trade, and fostered an economic revival. Hammu-

CHRONOLOGY

Chief Events in Mesopotamian History

Sumerian city-states: Early	
Dynastic Age	c. 3000–2340 B.C.
Sargon's empire	c. 2340–2100 B.C.
Third Dynasty of Ur	c. 2112–2000 B.C.
Hammurabi's reign	1792–1750 B.C.
Invasion by Kassites	c. 1550 B.C.

rabi is best known, though, for his law code, which provides considerable insight into social conditions in Mesopotamia (see Daily Life in Mesopotamia later in this chapter). Hammurabi left his dynasty strong enough that it survived until the 1550s B.C. when the Kassites from the northeast took over.

Mesopotamian Culture

A spiritual worldview was of fundamental importance to Mesopotamian culture. In Mesopotamia, the gods were living realities who affected all aspects of life. It was crucial, therefore, that the correct hierarchies be observed. Leaders could prepare armies for war, but success really depended on a favorable relationship with the gods. This helps to explain the importance of the priestly class and the reason why even the kings took great care to dedicate offerings and monuments to the gods. The records of these dedications are among our earliest historical documents.

THE IMPORTANCE OF RELIGION

The Mesopotamians viewed their city-states as earthly copies of a divine model and order. Each city-state was sacred since it was linked to a god or goddess. Hence, Nippur, the earliest center of Sumerian religion, was dedicated to Enlil, god of wind, and Babylon to Marduk, who supplanted Enlil in Babylonian myth. Nannar, a moon god, was the owner of Ur. Moreover, located at the heart of each major city-state was a temple complex. Occupying several acres, this sacred area consisted of a ziggurat with a temple at the top dedicated to the god or goddess who owned the city. The temple complex was the true center of the community. The main god or goddess dwelt there symbolically in the form of a statue, and the ceremony of dedication included a ritual that

---

❖❖❖❖❖❖❖❖❖❖❖❖❖❖❖❖❖❖❖❖❖❖

❖ Table 1.1   *Some Semitic Languages*

Assyrian
Akkadian
Aramaic
Babylonian
Canaanitic
Phoenician
Syriac
Arabic
Hebrew

Note: Languages in italic type are no longer spoken.

♦ **Ziggurat at Ur.** This ziggurat, located at Ur, is rectangular in shape, not square like later ones. The ziggurat was located in the temple complex, which was at the heart of the city and occupied several acres. At the top of the ziggurat was a temple dedicated to the god believed to own the city. The god was thought to dwell symbolically at the temple complex in the form of a statue, and a ritual performed during the ceremony of dedication supposedly linked the statue to the god, thus harnessing the god's power for the city.

linked the statue to the god or goddess and thus supposedly harnessed the power of the deity for the city's benefit. Considerable wealth was poured into the construction of temples as well as other buildings used for the residences of priests and priestesses who served the gods. Although the gods literally owned the city, the temple complex used only part of the land and rented out the remainder. Essentially, the temples dominated individual and commercial life, indicating the close relationship of religion to Mesopotamian culture.

The physical environment had an obvious impact on the Mesopotamian view of the universe. Ferocious floods, heavy downpours, scorching winds, and oppressive humidity were all part of the Mesopotamian climate. These conditions and resulting famines easily convinced Mesopotamians that this world was controlled by supernatural forces and that the days of human beings "are numbered; whatever he may do, he is but wind," as *The Epic of Gilgamesh* laments (see Mesopotamian Literature later in this chapter). In the presence of nature, Mesopotamians could easily feel helpless, as this poem relates:

> *The rampant flood which no man can oppose,*
> *Which shakes the heavens and causes earth to tremble,*
> *In an appalling blanket folds mother and child,*
> *Beats down the canebrake's full luxuriant greenery,*
> *And drowns the harvest in its time of ripeness.*
>
> *Rising waters, grievous to eyes of man,*
> *All-powerful flood, which forces the embankments*
> *And mows down mighty trees,*
> *Frenzied storm, tearing all things in massed confusion*
> *With it in hurtling speed.[1]*

The Mesopotamians discerned cosmic rhythms in the universe and accepted its order, but perceived that it was not completely safe because of the presence of willful, powerful cosmic forces that they identified with gods and goddesses.

With its numerous gods and goddesses animating all aspects of the universe, Mesopotamian religion was polytheistic in nature. The four most important deities were An, Enlil, Enki, and Ninhursaga. An was the god of the sky and hence the most important force in the universe. Since his basic essence was authority, he was also viewed as the source or active principle of all authority, including the earthly power of rulers and fathers alike. In one myth, the gods address him thus:

> *What you have ordered comes true!*
> *The utterance of prince and lord is but what you have ordered, do agree with.*
> *O An! your great command takes precedence, who could gainsay it?*
> *O father of the gods, your command, the very foundations of heaven and earth, what god could spurn it?[2]*

Enlil, god of wind, was considered the second greatest power of the visible universe. In charge of the wind and thus an expression of the legitimate use of force, Enlil became the symbol of the proper use of force on earth as well. But the wind included not only the moist winds of spring that brought fertility to the soil, but also the destructive storms. This other side of Enlil inspired a justifiable fear of him, as this Mesopotamian hymn reveals:

> *What has he planned? . . .*
> *What is in my father's heart?*
> *What is in Enlil's holy mind?*
> *What has he planned against me in his holy mind?*
> *A net he spread: the net of an enemy; a snare he set: the snare of an enemy.*
> *He has stirred up the waters and will catch the fishes, he has cast his net, and will bring down the birds too.[3]*

Enki was god of the earth. Since the earth was the source of life-giving waters, Enki was also god of rivers, wells, and canals. More generally, he represented the waters of creativity and was responsible for inventions and crafts. Ninhursaga began as a goddess associated with soil, mountains, and vegetation. Eventually, however, she was worshiped as a mother goddess, a "mother of all children," who manifested her power by giving birth to kings and conferring the royal insignia upon them.

A Creation Myth: "Let Man Carry the Labor-Basket of the Gods"

This selection is taken from Atrahasis, a Mesopotamian poem probably composed early in the second millennium B.C. It is a myth that relates the creation, destruction, and regeneration of the human race. In this excerpt, the gods create human beings to do the physical labor—digging canals—that they have grown to detest.

Atrahasis

When the gods, like man,
    bore the work, carried the labor-basket—
    the labor-basket of the great gods—
    the work was heavy, much was the distress. . . .
Forty more years
    they bore the labor night and day.
They wearied, complained,
    grumbled in the workpits.
"Let us confront the throne-bearer
    that he may remove from us our heavy labor.
Come on, let us confuse him in his dwelling,
Enlil, the counselor of the gods, the hero,
    come on, let us confuse him in his dwelling. . . ."

[After the lesser gods who are digging the canals rebel against Enlil, who rules the surface of the earth, he agrees to create human beings to do the physical labor for the lesser gods.]

"While [Nintu the birth-goddess] is present,
    let the birth-goddess create the offspring,
    let man bear the labor-basket of the gods."

They called the goddess and asked her,
    the midwife of the gods, wise Mami:
"You are the birth-goddess, creatress of man.
Create lullu-man, let him bear the yoke.
Let him bear the yoke, the work of Enlil;
    let man carry the labor-basket of the gods. . . ."
At the new moon, the seventh day, and the full moon,
    he set up a purifying bath.
We-ila, who had rationality,
    they slaughtered in their assembly.
With his flesh and blood
Nintu mixed the clay.
Till the end of days they hear the drum [heartbeat].
From the flesh of the god there was spirit.
She proclaimed "alive" as its sign.
For the sake of not-forgetting there was a spirit.
After she had mixed the clay,
    she called the Anunnaki, the great gods.
The Igigi, the great gods,
    cast their spittle on the clay.
Mami opened her mouth
    and said to the great gods,
"You commanded me a task—
I have completed it.
You slaughtered a god together with his rationality.
I have removed your heavy labor,
    have placed your labor-basket on man.
You raised a cry for mankind;
I have loosened your yoke, have established freedom."

Although these four deities ranked supreme, there were numerous gods and goddesses below them. One group included astral deities, the powers in the lesser cosmic elements, who were all grandchildren and great-grandchildren of An. These included Utu, god of the sun, the moon god Nannar, and Inanna, goddess of the morning and evening star as well as of war and rain. Unlike humans, these and the various other gods and goddesses were divine and immortal.

Human beings' relationship with the gods was based on subservience since, according to Sumerian myth, human beings were created to do the manual labor the gods were unwilling to do for themselves (see the box above). Moreover, humans were insecure because they could never be sure what the gods would do. But humans did make attempts to circumvent or relieve their anxiety by discovering the intentions of the gods and by trying to influence them as well; these efforts gave rise to the development of the arts of divination.

Their importance is evident in that texts on divination are the largest single category of Akkadian literature.

Divination took a variety of forms. A common form, at least for kings and priests who could afford it, involved killing animals, such as sheep or goats, and examining their livers or other organs. Supposedly, features seen in the organs of the sacrificed animals foretold events to come. Thus, one handbook states that if the animal organ has shape x, then the outcome of the military campaign will be y. Private individuals relied on cheaper divinatory techniques. These included interpreting patterns of smoke from burning incense or the pattern formed when oil was poured into water. Even the throw of dice could be used to foretell events. These methods of divination were based on the principle that a human request would evoke a divine response.

These methods were eventually superseded by intuitive ones that were based on the belief that divine purpose was everywhere and hence accessible. The new

	I	II	III	IV	V		I	II	III	IV	V
1						10					
2						11					
3						12					
4						13					
5						14					
6						15					
7						16					
8						17					
9						18					

◆ **The Development of the Cuneiform System of Writing.** This table shows the evolution of eighteen representative signs from c. 3000 B.C. to 600 B.C. Examples: No. 1 is a picture of a star. The sign for star also meant heaven, sky, or god. No. 11 is a picture of a stream of water. The sign for water was also used for the word "in" since the Sumerian words for "water" and "in" sounded alike. No. 12 combines a picture of a head emphasizing the mouth with the sign for water. The compound sign represents a Sumerian word meaning to eat.

intuitive techniques included the interpretation of dreams and the examination of facial and bodily characteristics for omens. Rulers used more elaborate intuitive methods, primarily astrological ones, to read the skies to see what was coming. Horoscopic astrology, based on determining the specific heavenly influences at the time of one's birth, also came to be used.

The Mesopotamian arts of divination arose out of the desire to discover the purposes of the gods. If people could decipher the signs that foretold events, the events would be predictable and humans could act wisely. But the Mesopotamians also developed cultic arts to influence good powers (gods and goddesses) whose decisions could determine human destiny and to ward off evil powers (demons). These cultic arts included ritualistic formulas, such as spells against evil spirits, and prayers or hymns to the gods to win their positive influence. Since only the priests knew the precise rituals, it is not hard to understand the important role they exercised in a society dominated by a belief in the reality of spiritual powers.

WRITING

The realization of writing's great potential was another aspect of Mesopotamian culture. The oldest written Mesopotamian texts date to around 3000 B.C.

The Sumerians used a cuneiform ("wedge-shaped") system of writing. Using a reed stylus, they made wedge-shaped impressions on clay tablets, which were then baked or dried in the sun. Once dried, these tablets were virtually indestructible, and the several hundred

≶ A Sumerian Schoolboy ≶

This document is a Sumerian essay narrating the daily activities of a schoolboy, written by a teacher as a copying exercise for pupils. The schoolboy experiences numerous trials and tribulations, including being beaten ("caned") for improper behavior. Scribal schools came into being in Sumer around 2500 B.C.

A Sumerian Essay for Schoolboys

"Schoolboy, where did you go from earliest day?"

"I went to school."

"What did you do in school?"

"I read my tablet, wrote it, finished it; then my prepared lines were prepared for me and in the afternoon, my hand copies were prepared for me."

Upon the school's dismissal, I went home, entered the house, there was my father sitting. I spoke to my father of my hand copies, then read the tablet to him, and my father was pleased; truly I found favor with my father.

"I am thirsty, give me drink, I am hungry, give me bread, wash my feet, set up the bed, I want to go to sleep; wake me early in the morning, I must not be late, or my teacher will cane me."

When I awoke early in the morning, I faced my mother, and said to her: "Give me my lunch, I want to go to school. . . ."

My mother gave me two "rolls," I went to school.

In the tablet-house, the monitor said to me: "Why are you late?" I was afraid, my heart beat fast. I entered before my teacher, took my place.

My "school-father" read my tablet to me, said "The . . . is cut off," caned me. . . .

Who was in charge of drawing said "Why when I was not here did you stand up?" caned me.

Who was in charge of the gate said "Why when I was not here did you go out?" caned me. . . .

My teacher said "Your hand is not good," caned me.

[At this point, the student decides he needs help and suggests to his father that he invite his teacher home for dinner. The father does so, thanks the teacher, and treats him to a feast and gifts. The teacher now responds to the student.]

Young man, because you did not neglect my word, did not forsake it,

May you reach the pinnacle of the scribal art, achieve it completely

Because you gave me that which you were by no means obliged to give,

You presented me with a gift over and above my earnings, have shown me great honor, may Nidaba, the queen of the guardian deities, be your guardian deity.

May she show favor to your fashioned reed,

May she take all evil from your hand copies.

Of your brothers, may you be their leader,

Of your companions, may you be their chief,

May you rank the highest of all the schoolboys.

thousand that have been found so far have been a valuable source of information for modern scholars. Originally, Sumerian writing was pictographic. Scribes drew pictures or representations of concrete objects. Each sign represented a word identical in meaning to the object pictured, although pictures could also represent more than the actual object. Hence, the pictograph for boomerang meant not only boomerang, but also to throw and to throw down. The pictographic system proved cumbersome, however, and the characters were gradually simplified and stylized, and their pictographic nature gave way to conventionalized signs that symbolized ideas. The sign for star could be used to mean heaven, sky, or god. The next major step in simplification was the development of phonetization in which characters or signs were used to represent sounds. Thus, the character for water was also used to mean "in," since the Sumerian words for "water" and "in" sounded similar. With a phonetic system, the scribes could now represent words for which there were no pictographs, making possible the written expression of abstract ideas. Eventually, the scribes devised a simplified phonetic system containing fundamental groups of symbols that stood for syllables and could be combined to form words.

Sumerian was the chief spoken and written language of Mesopotamia and the surrounding areas in the third millennium, but it was replaced in the second millennium by Akkadian. After 2500 B.C., Sumerian cuneiform was adapted by Semitic-speaking peoples (as seen in Old Akkadian) for their own written languages. Eventually, two dialects of Old Akkadian were used in Mesopotamia, Assyrian in the north and Babylonian in the south.

Mesopotamian peoples used writing primarily for record keeping. The most common cuneiform tablets record transactions of daily life: tallies of cattle kept by herdsmen for their owners, production figures, lists of taxes and wage payments, accounts, contracts, and court decisions dealing with business matters. There are also monumental texts, documents that were intended to last forever, such as inscriptions etched in stone on statues and royal buildings.

Still another category of cuneiform inscriptions includes a large body of basic texts produced for teaching purposes (see the box on p. 15). Schools for scribes were in operation by 2500 B.C. They were necessary because considerable time was needed to master the cuneiform system of writing. The primary goal of scribal education was to produce professionally trained scribes for careers in the temples and palaces, the military, and government service. Pupils were male and primarily from wealthy families. Gradually, the schools became important centers for culture since Mesopotamian literature was utilized for instructional purposes. Moreover, new literary productions came out of the scribal schools.

MESOPOTAMIAN LITERATURE

Although many fragments of Mesopotamian literary works remain, the most famous piece of Mesopotamian literature was *The Epic of Gilgamesh*. This epic poem, Sumerian in origin but preserved in Akkadian, records the exploits of a legendary king of Uruk. Gilgamesh, wise, strong, and perfect in body, part man, part god, abused the citizens of Uruk:

> "Gilgamesh sounds the tocsin for his amusement," the people complained, "his arrogance has no bounds by day or night. No son is left with his father, for Gilgamesh takes them all, even the children. . . . His lust leaves no virgin to her lover, neither the warrior's daughter nor the wife of the noble. . . ."[4]

The citizens asked the gods to send a competitor to oppose Gilgamesh and keep him busy. The gods comply and send a hairy, barbaric beast named Enkidu whom Gilgamesh tries to weaken by sending a prostitute to seduce him. When Enkidu finally comes to Uruk, he and Gilgamesh engage in a fierce struggle that neither can win. The two become fast friends and set off in pursuit of heroic deeds. Ishtar (Sumerian Inanna), goddess of love, attempts to seduce Gilgamesh, but he refuses her advances. In anger, she convinces her father Anu (Sumerian An) to send a Bull of Heaven to kill Gilgamesh and Enkidu. They manage to kill the bull instead,

however, and the gods decide that in return one of them must die. Enlil, god of wind, rules for Enkidu, and he falls ill and dies, much to the prolonged grief of Gilgamesh. Gilgamesh experiences the pain of mortality and enters upon a search for the secret of immortality. He finds the man who had been granted "everlasting life" by the gods, Utnapishtim. The latter tells him the story of how he survived the Great Flood sent by the gods to destroy humankind (see the box on p. 17). Regretting what they had done, the gods bestowed immortality upon Utnapishtim. The latter now passes the secret on to Gilgamesh and instructs him to dive to the bottom of a river and find a certain plant that gives the power to grow younger. Although Gilgamesh finds the plant, a snake snatches it away before he can eat it. Gilgamesh remains mortal. The desire for immortality, one of humankind's great searches, ends in complete frustration. "Everlasting life," as this Mesopotamian epic makes clear, is only for the gods.

MATHEMATICS AND ASTRONOMY

The Mesopotamians made outstanding achievements in mathematics and astronomy. In math, they devised a number system based on 60, using combinations of 6 and 10 for practical solutions. They used the processes of multiplication and division and compiled tables for the computation of interest. The Mesopotamians also developed a sense of place value; that is, the value of a number depends on where it stands relative to other numbers. Geometry was utilized for practical purposes, such as measuring fields and building projects. In astronomy, the Mesopotamians made use of units of 60 and charted the chief heavenly constellations. Their calendar was based on twelve lunar months and was brought into harmony with the solar year by adding an extra month from time to time.

Daily Life in Mesopotamia

Remarkable insight into the daily life of Mesopotamia, at least for its later period, is provided in a famous document from the Babylonia of Hammurabi. As we have seen, people in Mesopotamian society viewed themselves as subservient to the gods and believed humans were at the mercy of the gods' arbitrary decisions. To counter their insecurity, the Mesopotamians not only developed the arts of divination to fathom the wishes of the gods, but also relieved some anxiety by establishing codes that regulated their relationships with each other. These law codes became an integral part of

⇒ The Great Flood ⇐

The great epic poem of Mesopotamian literature, The Epic of Gilgamesh, includes an account by Utnapishtim (a Mesopotamian version of the later biblical Noah), who had built a ship and survived the flood unleashed by the gods to destroy humankind. This selection recounts how the god Ea advised Utnapishtim to build a boat and how he came to land his boat at the end of the flood. In this section, Utnapishtim is telling his story to Gilgamesh.

The Epic of Gilgamesh

"In those days the world teemed, the people multiplied, the world bellowed like a wild bull, and the great god was aroused by the clamor. Enlil heard the clamor and he said to the gods in council, 'The uproar of mankind is intolerable and sleep is no longer possible by reason of the babel.' So the gods agreed to exterminate mankind. Enlil did this, but Ea [Sumerian Enki, god of the waters] because of his oath warned me in a dream. . . . 'tear down your house and build a boat, abandon possessions and look for life, despise worldly goods and save your soul alive. Tear down your house, I say, and build a boat. . . . then take up into the boat the seed of all living creatures. . . .' [Utnapishtim did as he was told and then the destruction came.]

"For six days and six nights the winds blew, torrent and tempest and flood overwhelmed the world, tempest and flood raged together like warring hosts. When the seventh day dawned the storm from the south subsided, the sea grew calm, the flood was stilled; I looked at the face of the world and there was silence, all mankind was turned to clay. The surface of the sea stretched as flat as a rooftop; I opened a hatch and the light fell on my face. Then I bowed low, I sat down and I wept, the tears streamed down my face, for on every side was the waste of water. I looked for land in vain, but fourteen leagues distant there appeared a mountain, and there the boat grounded; on the mountain of Nisir the boat held fast, she held fast and did not budge. . . . When the seventh day dawned I loosed a dove and let her go. She flew away, but finding no resting-place she returned. Then I loosed a swallow, and she flew away but finding no resting-place she returned. I loosed a raven, she saw that the waters had retreated, she ate, she flew around, she cawed, and she did not come back. Then I threw everything open to the four winds, I made a sacrifice and poured out a libation on the mountain top."

Mesopotamian society. Although there were early Sumerian law codes, the best-preserved Mesopotamian compilation was that of Hammurabi (see the box on p. 19).

Since Babylonian society had no public prosecutors, private individuals were responsible for bringing charges before a court of law. To ensure that accusations of wrongdoing were not brought lightly, the accuser in cases of murder was responsible for proving his case against the defendant. If the accuser could not, he was put to death. Providing false testimony in a murder case was also punished by death.

The Code of Hammurabi reveals a society with a system of strict justice. Penalties for criminal offenses were severe and varied by class. According to the code, there were three social classes in Babylonia: an upper class of nobles, which included government officials, priests, and warriors; a class of freemen comprised of merchants, artisans, professionals, and wealthier farmers; and a lower class of slaves, who, though oppressed, did possess some rights. An offense against a member of the

upper class was punished with considerably more severity than the same offense against a member of a lower class. Moreover, the principle of retaliation ("an eye for an eye, a tooth for a tooth") was fundamental to this system of justice. It was applied in cases where members of the upper class committed criminal offenses against their own social equals. But for offenses against members of the lower classes, a money payment was made instead. Hence, "If a seignior has knocked out the tooth of a seignior of his own rank, they shall knock out his tooth. If he has knocked out a commoner's tooth, he shall pay one-third mina of silver."

It appears that Mesopotamian society, like all others, had its share of crime. Burglary was common and punishments were stern. If a person stole goods belonging to the temples or the state, he was put to death and so was the person receiving the stolen goods. If the private property of citizens was stolen, the thief had to make a tenfold restitution. If he could not afford to, he was put to death. Since the mudbrick construction of

◆ **Stele of Hammurabi (Code of Hammurabi, King of Babylonia).** Although the Sumerians compiled earlier law codes, Hammurabi's code was the most famous in early Mesopotamian history. The code recognized three social classes in Babylonia (nobles, freemen, and slaves) and included laws dealing with marriage and divorce, job performance, punishments for crime, and even sexual relations. The upper section of the stele depicts Hammurabi standing in front of the seated sun god Shamash who orders the king to record the law. The lower section contains the actual code.

Mesopotamian homes made them easily vulnerable to robbery by digging holes in the walls, robbers, if caught in the act, "shall be put to death in front of that breach" and walled in. An offender caught attempting to loot a burning house was to be "thrown into that fire." These practices gave legal support to what people would ordinarily do anyway under those circumstances.

Hammurabi's code took seriously the responsibilities of public officials. The governor of an area and city officials were expected to catch burglars. If they failed to do so, officials in the district where the crime was committed had to replace the lost property. If murderers were not found, the officials had to pay a fine to the relatives of the murdered person. Soldiers were likewise expected to fulfill their duties and responsibilities for the order and maintenance of the state. If a soldier hired a substitute to fight for him, he was put to death, and the substitute was given control of his estate. Laws also sheltered ordinary soldiers from the wrongful actions of their officers. An officer who forced someone to join his army, took the goods of his soldiers, or wronged them seriously was executed.

Proper performance of work was also furthered by the law code, in what virtually amount to consumer protection laws. Builders were held responsible for the buildings they constructed. If a house collapsed and caused the death of the owner, the builder was put to death. If the collapse caused the death of the son of the owner, the son of the builder was put to death. If goods were destroyed by the collapse, they must be replaced and the house itself reconstructed at the builder's expense.

Slavery was a common feature of Mesopotamian society. Slaves were obtained from numerous sources. Some were war captives; others were criminals or debtors. Crimes, such as striking one's older brother and kicking one's mother, were punished by condemnation to slavery. The head of a household could pay his debts by selling both his children and wife into slavery, although usually only for a specified period of years. He himself could be condemned to slavery if he defaulted on his loans. Slaves were used in temples, in the royal buildings, and in the homes of private citizens. Most temple slaves were women who did domestic chores, such as cooking and weaving. Royal slaves were used to construct buildings and fortifications. The slaves of private citizens mostly performed domestic duties. Laws were harsh for slaves who tried to escape or disobeyed. Hence, "If a male slave has said to his master, 'You are not my master,' his master shall prove him to be his slave and cut off his ear." Despite such harshness, slaves in Mesopotamia also possessed a number of privileges (at least, for slaves), such as being able to hold property, participate in business, marry free men or women (the children of such unions were free), and purchase their freedom.

The number of laws in Hammurabi's code dedicated to land tenure and commerce reveal the importance of agriculture and trade in the Mesopotamian economy.

⇒ The Code of Hammurabi ⇐

Hammurabi's code is the most complete, although not the earliest, Mesopotamian law code. It was inscribed on a stone stele topped by a bas-relief picturing Hammurabi receiving the inspiration for the law code from the sun god Shamash, who was also the god of justice. The law code emphasizes the principle of retribution ("an eye for an eye") and punishments that vary according to social status. Punishments could be severe. Marriage and family affairs also play a large role in the code. The following examples illustrate these concerns.

The Code of Hammurabi

25. If fire broke out in a seignior's [the translator used the word seignior to designate any free man of the upper class] house and a seignior, who went to extinguish it, cast his eye on the goods of the owner of the house and has appropriated the goods of the owner of the house, that seignior shall be thrown into that fire.

129. If the wife of a seignior has been caught while lying with another man, they shall bind them and throw them into the water. If the husband of the woman wishes to spare his wife, then the king in turn may spare his subject.

131. If a seignior's wife was accused by her husband, but she was not caught while lying with another man, she shall make affirmation by god and return to her house.

196. If a seignior has destroyed the eye of a member of the aristocracy, they shall destroy his eye.

198. If he has destroyed the eye of a commoner or broken the bone of a commoner, he shall pay one mina of silver.

199. If he has destroyed the eye of a seignior's slave or broken the bone of a seignior's slave, he shall pay one-half his value.

209. If a seignior struck another seignior's daughter and has caused her to have a miscarriage, he shall pay ten shekels of silver for her fetus.

210. If that woman has died, they shall put his daughter to death.

211. If by a blow he has caused a commoner's daughter to have a miscarriage, he shall pay five shekels of silver.

212. If that woman has died, he shall pay one-half mina of silver.

213. If he struck a seignior's female slave and has caused her to have a miscarriage, he shall pay two shekels of silver.

214. If that female slave has died, he shall pay one-third mina of silver.

Numerous laws dealt with questions of landholding, such as the establishment of conditions for renting farmland and the division of produce between tenants and their landlords. Tenant farming was the basis of Mesopotamian agriculture. Tenant farmers paid their annual rent in crops rather than money. Laws concerning land use and irrigation were especially strict, an indication of the danger of declining crop yields if the land were used incompetently. If landowners and tenants failed to keep dikes in good repair or to control water flow properly and thus caused damage to others' crops, they were required to pay for the grain that was destroyed. If they could not pay, they were sold into slavery and their goods sold and the proceeds divided among the injured parties.

Commercial activity was carefully regulated. Rates of interest on loans were watched closely. If the lender raised his rate of interest after a loan was made, he lost the entire amount of the loan. The Code of Hammurabi even specified the precise wages of laborers and artisans, such as brickmakers and jewelers.

The largest number of laws in the Code of Hammurabi were dedicated to marriage and the family. Parents arranged marriages for their children. After marriage, the parties involved signed a marriage contract; without it, no one was considered legally married. While the husband provided a bridal payment, the woman's parents were responsible for a dowry to the new husband. Dowries were carefully monitored and were governed by specific regulations.

As in many patriarchal societies, women possessed far fewer privileges and rights in the married relationship than men. A woman's place was in the home, and failure to fulfill her expected duties was grounds for divorce. If she was not able to bear children, her husband could divorce her, but he did have to return the

⧽ *Significance of the Nile River and the Pharaoh* ⧽

Two of the most important sources of life for the ancient Egyptians were the Nile River and the pharaoh. Egyptians perceived that the Nile River made possible the abundant food that was a major source of their well-being. This Hymn to the Nile, *probably from the nineteenth and twentieth dynasties in the New Kingdom, expresses the gratitude Egyptians felt for the Nile.*

Hymn to the Nile

*Hail to you, O Nile, that issues from the earth and comes
    to keep Egypt alive! . . .
He that waters the meadows which Re created, in order to
    keep every kid alive.
He that makes to drink the desert and the place distant
    from water: that is his dew coming down from
    heaven. . . .
The lord of fishes, he who makes the marsh-birds to go up-
    stream. . . .
He who makes barley and brings emmer into being, that he
    may make the temples festive.
If he is sluggish, then nostrils are stopped up, and every-
    body is poor. . . .
When he rises, then the land is in jubilation, then every
    belly is in joy, every backbone takes on laughter, and
    every tooth is exposed.
The bringer of good, rich in provisions, creator of all good,
    lord of majesty, sweet of fragrance. . . .*

*He who makes every beloved tree to grow, without lack of
    them.*

The Egyptian king, or pharaoh, was viewed as a god and the absolute ruler of Egypt. His significance and the gratitude of the Egyptian people for his existence are evident in this hymn from the reign of Sesotris III (c. 1880–1840 B.C.).

Hymn to the Pharaoh

*He has come unto us that he may carry away Upper
    Egypt; the double diadem [crown of Upper and Lower
    Egypt] has rested on his head.
He has come unto us and has united the Two Lands; he
    has mingled the reed with the bee [symbols of Lower and
    Upper Egypt].
He has come unto us and has brought the Black Land under
    his sway; he has apportioned to himself the Red Land.
He has come unto us and has taken the Two Lands under his
    protection; he has given peace to the Two Riverbanks.
He has come unto us and has made Egypt to live; he has
    banished its suffering.
He has come unto us and has made the people to live; he
    has caused the throat of the subjects to breathe. . . .
He has come unto us and has done battle for his bound-
    aries; he has delivered them that were robbed.*

dowry to the woman's family. If his wife tried to leave home to engage in business, thus neglecting her house, her husband could divorce her and did not have to repay the dowry. Furthermore, if his wife was a "gadabout, . . . neglecting her house [and] humiliating her husband," she could be drowned. We do know that in practice not all women remained at home. Some worked in business and were especially prominent in running taverns.

Women were guaranteed some rights, however. If a woman was divorced without good reason, she received the dowry back. A woman could seek divorce and get her dowry back if her husband was unable to show that she had done anything wrong. In theory, a wife was guaranteed the use of her husband's legal property in the event of his death. The mother also chose to which son an inheritance would be passed.

Sexual relations were strictly regulated as well. Husbands, but not wives, were permitted sexual activity

outside marriage. A wife caught committing adultery was pitched into the river, although her husband could ask the king to pardon her. Incest was strictly forbidden. If a father committed incestuous relations with his daughter, he would be banished. Incest between a son and his mother resulted in both being burned.

Fathers ruled their children as well as their wives. Obedience was duly expected: "If a son has struck his father, they shall cut off his hand." If a son committed a serious enough offense, his father could disinherit him, although fathers were not permitted to disinherit their sons arbitrarily. Obviously, Hammurabi's law code covered virtually every aspect of people's lives. Although some legal scholars have recently questioned the extent to which these laws were actually employed in Babylonian jurisprudence, the Code of Hammurabi provides us a priceless glimpse of the values of this early society.

*E*gyptian Civilization: "The Gift of the Nile"

Although contemporaneous with Mesopotamia, civilization in Egypt evolved along somewhat different lines. Of central importance to the development of Egyptian civilization was the Nile River. That the Egyptian people recognized its significance is apparent in this Hymn to the Nile (see the box on p. 20): "The bringer of food, rich in provisions, creator of all good, lord of majesty, sweet of fragrance. ... He who ... fills the magazines, makes the granaries wide, and gives things to the poor. He who makes every beloved tree to grow. ..."[5] Egypt, like Mesopotamia, was a river civilization.

The Nile is a unique river, beginning in the heart of Africa and coursing northward for thousands of miles. It is the longest river in the world. The Nile was responsible for creating an area several miles wide on both banks of the river that was fertile and capable of producing abundant harvests. The "miracle" of the Nile was its annual flooding. The river rose in the summer from rains in central Africa, crested in Egypt in September and October, and left a deposit of silt that created an area of rich soil. The Egyptians called this fertile land, which was dark in color from the silt and the lush crops

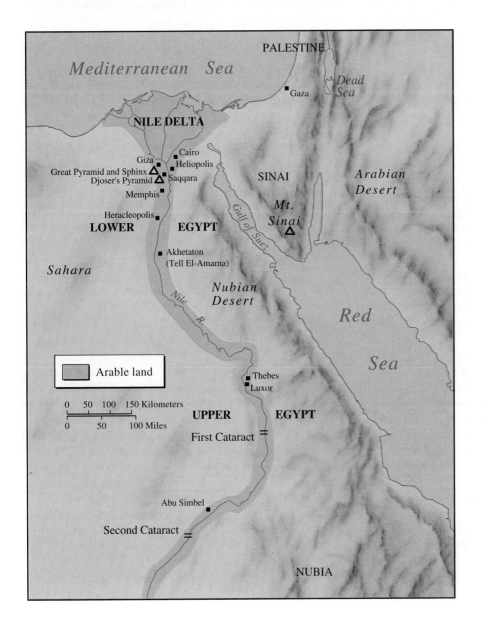

Map 1.4 Ancient Egypt.

that grew on it, the "Black Land." Beyond these narrow strips of fertile fields lay the deserts (the "Red Land").

Unlike Mesopotamia's rivers, the flooding of the Nile was gradual and usually predictable, and the river itself was seen as life enhancing, not life threatening. Although a system of organized irrigation was still necessary, the small villages along the Nile could make the effort without the massive state intervention that was required in Mesopotamia. Egyptian civilization, consequently, tended to remain more rural with many small population centers congregated along a narrow band on both sides of the Nile. About one hundred miles before it empties into the Mediterranean, the river splits into two major branches, forming the delta, a triangular-shaped territory called Lower Egypt to distinguish it from Upper Egypt, the land upstream to the south. Egypt's important cities developed at the tip of the delta. Even today, most of Egypt's 58 million people are crowded along the banks of the Nile River.

The surpluses of food that Egyptian farmers grew in the fertile Nile valley made Egypt prosperous. But the Nile also served as unifying factor in Egyptian history. In ancient times, the Nile was the fastest way to travel through the land, making both transportation and communication easier. Winds from the north pushed sailboats south, and the current of the Nile carried them north. Often when they headed downstream (or north), people used long poles or paddles to propel their boats forward.

Unlike Mesopotamia, which was subject to constant invasion, Egypt was blessed by natural barriers that fostered isolation, protected it from invasion, and gave it a sense of security. These barriers included the deserts to the west and east, the cataracts (rapids) on the southern part of the Nile, which made defense relatively easy, and the Mediterranean Sea to the north. These barriers, however, did not prevent the development of trade. Indeed, there is evidence of very early trade between Egypt and Mesopotamia itself.

In essence, Egyptian geography and topography played important roles in the early history of the country. The regularity of the Nile floods and the relative isolation of the Egyptians created a sense of security and a feeling of changelessness. To the ancient Egyptians, when the Nile flooded each year, "the fields laugh and people's faces light up." Unlike people in Mesopotamia, Egyptians faced life with a spirit of confidence in the stability of things. Egyptian civilization was characterized by a remarkable degree of continuity over thousands of years. It was certainly no accident that Egyptians believed in cyclical rather than linear progress. Like the daily cycles of the sun and the annual overflow of the Nile, Egyptian kings, too, reaffirmed the basic, unchanging principles of justice at the beginning of each new cycle of rule.

The Old and Middle Kingdoms

The basic framework for the study of Egyptian history was provided by Manetho, an Egyptian priest and historian who lived in the early third century B.C. He divided Egyptian history into thirty-one dynasties of kings. Based on Manetho and other king lists, modern historians have divided Egyptian history into three major periods known as the Old Kingdom, Middle Kingdom, and New Kingdom. These were periods of long-term stability characterized by strong monarchical authority, competent bureaucracy, freedom from invasion, much construction of temples and pyramids, and considerable intellectual and cultural activity. But between the periods of stability were ages of political chaos known as the Intermediate periods, which were characterized by weak political structures and rivalry for leadership, invasions, a decline in building activity, and a restructuring of society.

THE OLD KINGDOM

According to the Egyptians' own tradition, their land consisted initially of numerous populated areas ruled by tribal chieftains. Around 3100 B.C., during the Thinite or Early Dynastic period, the first Egyptian royal dynasty, under a king called Menes, united both Upper and Lower Egypt into a single kingdom. Henceforth, the king would be called "King of Upper and King of Lower Egypt," and the royal crown would be a double diadem, signifying the unification of all Egypt. Just as the Nile served to unite Upper and Lower Egypt physically, kingship served to unite the two areas politically.

The Old Kingdom encompassed the third through sixth dynasties of Egyptian kings, lasting from around 2700 to 2200 B.C. It was an age of prosperity and splendor, made visible in the construction of the greatest and largest pyramids in Egypt's history. The capital of the Old Kingdom was located at Memphis, south of the delta.

Kingship was a divine institution in ancient Egypt and formed part of a universal cosmic scheme (see the box on p. 20): "What is the king of Upper and Lower Egypt? He is a god by whose dealings one lives, the father and mother of all men, alone by himself, without an equal."[6] In obeying their king, subjects helped to maintain the cosmic order. A breakdown in royal power could only mean that citizens were offending divinity and weakening the universal structure. Among the various titles of Egyptian kings, that of pharaoh (originally meaning "great house" or "palace") became most common during the period of the New Kingdom (see Chaos and a New Order later in this chapter).

Although they possessed absolute power, Egyptian kings were not supposed to rule arbitrarily, but according to set principles. The chief principle was called *Ma'at*, a spiritual precept that conveyed the idea of truth and justice, but especially right order and harmony. To ancient Egyptians, this fundamental order and harmony had existed throughout the universe since the beginning of time. Pharaohs were the divine instruments who maintained this order and harmony and were themselves subject to it.

Although theoretically absolute in their power, in practice Egyptian kings did not rule alone. Initially, administrative tasks were performed by members of the king's family, but by the fourth dynasty a bureaucracy with regular procedures had developed. Especially important was the office of vizier, "steward of the whole land." Directly responsible to the king, the vizier was in charge of the bureaucracy with its numerous departments, such as police, justice, river transport, and public works. Agriculture and the treasury were the most important departments. Agriculture was, of course, the backbone of Egyptian prosperity, and the treasury collected the taxes that were paid in kind. A careful assessment of land and tenants was undertaken to establish the tax base.

For administrative purposes, Egypt was divided into provinces or nomes, as they were later called by the Greeks—twenty-two in Upper and twenty in Lower Egypt. A governor, called by the Greeks a nomarch, was head of each nome and was responsible to the king and vizier. Nomarchs, however, tended to build up large holdings of land and power within their nomes, creating a potential rivalry with the pharaohs. Of special importance to the administration of the state was a vast bureaucracy of scribes who kept records of everything. Armed with the knowledge of writing and reading, they were highly regarded and considered themselves a superior class of men. Their high standard of living reflected their exalted status.

THE MIDDLE KINGDOM

Despite the theory of divine order, the Old Kingdom eventually collapsed, ushering in an Intermediate period

◆ **Pair Statue of King Menkaure and His Queen.** The period designated as the Old Kingdom began approximately four centuries after Egypt's unification (c. 3100 B.C.) and lasted until approximately 2200 B.C. During this period, Egypt's greatest and largest pyramids were constructed. The kings (eventually called "pharaohs") were regarded as gods, divine instruments who maintained the fundamental order and harmony of the universe and wielded absolute power. This statue depicts King Menkaure and his queen (Dynasty IV).

of chaos (c. 2200–2050 B.C.). A so-called prophet named Nefer-Rohu (Neferti) described the scene:

This land is so damaged that there is no one who is concerned with it, no one who speaks, no one who weeps. . . . The sun disc is covered over. It will not shine so that people may see. . . . The rivers of Egypt are empty, so that the water is crossed on foot. Men seek for water for the

◆◆◆◆◆◆◆◆◆◆◆◆◆◆◆◆◆◆◆

The Egyptians

Thinite Period or Early Dynastic (dynasties 1–2)	c. 3100–2700 B.C.
Old Kingdom (dynasties 3–6)	c. 2700–2200 B.C.
First Intermediate Period (dynasties 7–10)	c. 2200–2050 B.C.
Middle Kingdom (dynasties 11–12)	c. 2050–1652 B.C.
Second Intermediate Period (dynasties 13–17)	c. 1652–1567 B.C.
New Kingdom (dynasties 18–20)	c. 1567–1085 B.C.
Post-empire (dynasties 21–31)	1085–30 B.C.

ships to sail on it. . . . This land is helter-skelter, and no one knows the result that will come about, which is hidden from speech, sight, or hearing.[7]

Several problems overwhelmed the Old Kingdom. Nomarchs grew in power as their positions became virtually hereditary over time. Consequently, the nomes became more independent and central authority was weakened. Loyalty to the nome replaced loyalty to the pharaoh. Famines, stemming from crop failures as a result of low Nile flooding, caused economic decline. During this First Intermediate Period of chaos, new centers of power even established rival dynasties, such as those at Heracleopolis near Lower Egypt and Thebes in Upper Egypt. Finally, the king of Thebes, Mentuhotep, defeated the ruler of Heracleopolis and achieved the reunification of all Egypt, thus beginning the Middle Kingdom, a new period of stability lasting from 2050 to 1652 B.C.

Much of the Middle Kingdom's history centered around the twelfth dynasty founded by Amenemhet I, a vizier who established himself and his successors as pharaohs. Egyptians later portrayed the Middle Kingdom as a golden age, a clear indication of its stability. Several factors contributed to its vitality. The nome structure was reorganized. The boundaries of each nome were now settled precisely, and the obligations of the nomes to the state were clearly delineated. Nomarchs were confirmed as hereditary officeholders but with the understanding that their duties must be performed faithfully. These included the collection of taxes for the state and the recruitment of labor forces for royal projects, such as stone quarrying. A new system of co-regency, in which the pharaoh took his son as a co-ruler to prepare him for governing and preclude succession problems, added to the vigor of the Middle Kingdom.

The Middle Kingdom was characterized by a new concern of the pharaohs for the people. In the Old Kingdom, the pharaoh had been viewed as an inaccessible god-king. Now he was portrayed as the shepherd of his people with the responsibility to build public works and provide for the public welfare. As one pharaoh expressed it: "He [a particular god] created me as one who should do that which he had done, and to carry out that which he commanded should be done. He appointed me herdsman of this land, for he knew who would keep it in order for him."[8]

As confirmation of its newfound strength, Egypt embarked upon a period of expansion. Lower Nubia was conquered, and fortresses were built to protect the new southern frontier. The government also sent military expeditions into Palestine and Syria. Although they did not remain there, this campaign marks the beginning of Egyptian imperialism in those areas.

Social and Economic Structures

Egyptian society had a simple structure in the Old and Middle Kingdoms; basically, it was organized along hierarchical lines with the god-king at the top. The king was surrounded by an upper class of nobles and priests who participated in the elaborate rituals of life that surrounded the pharaoh. This ruling class ran the government and managed its own landed estates, which provided much of its wealth.

Below the upper classes were merchants and artisans. Within Egypt, merchants engaged in an active trade up and down the Nile as well as in town and village markets. Barter was the primary means by which goods were exchanged. Some merchants also engaged in international trade; they were sent by the king to Crete and Syria where they obtained wood and other products. Expeditions traveled into Nubia for ivory and down the Red Sea to Punt for incense and spices. Egyptian artisans displayed unusually high standards of craftsmanship and physical beauty, while producing an incredible variety of goods: stone dishes; beautifully painted boxes made of clay; wooden furniture, especially of Lebanon cedar; gold, silver, and copper tools and containers; paper and rope made of papyrus; and linen clothes.

By far, the largest number of people in Egypt simply worked the land. In theory, the king owned all the land, but granted out portions of it to his subjects. Large sections were in the possession of nobles and the temple complexes. Moreover, although free farmers who owned their own land had once existed, by the end of the Old Kingdom, this group had disappeared. Most of the lower classes were serfs or common people bound to the land who cultivated the estates. They paid taxes in the form of crops to the king, nobles, and priests, lived in small villages or towns, and provided military service and labor for building projects.

The Culture of Egypt

Egypt produced a culture that dazzled and overawed its later conquerors. The Egyptians' technical achievements alone, especially visible in the construction of the pyramids, demonstrated a measure of skill unique to the world of that time. To the Egyptians, all of these achievements were part of a cosmic order suffused with the presence of the divine.

SPIRITUAL LIFE IN EGYPTIAN SOCIETY

It is misleading to speak of religion in Egyptian society. The Egyptians had no word for religion, because it was an inseparable element of the entire world order to which Egyptian society belonged. In the Old Kingdom, a document called the Memphite Theology portrayed Ptah as the creator-god who had held an image of the universe in his mind and brought the entire universe into being by speaking the word. Ptah was embodied in every fiber of that universe, including Egypt. Egypt, then, belonged to the universal cosmic scheme, and the pharaoh was the divine being whose function was to maintain its stability within that cosmic order.

The Egyptians possessed a remarkable number of gods associated with heavenly bodies and natural forces. Two groups, sun gods and land gods, came to have special prominence, hardly unusual in view of the importance of the sun, the river, and the fertile land along its banks to Egypt's well-being. The sun was the source of life and hence worthy of worship. A sun cult developed, especially at Heliopolis, now a suburb of modern Cairo. The sun god took on different forms and names, depending on his specific function. He was worshiped as Atum in human form; as Khepra in the form of a scarab beetle, since it was believed that the sun, like the scarab, came forth out of its own substance; and as Re, who had a human body but the head of a falcon. In this last

embodiment, he was also identified with the god Horus. Later, in the New Kingdom, Re became associated with Amon, an air god of Thebes, as Amon-Re. The pharaoh took the title of "Son of Re," since he was regarded as the earthly embodiment of Re.

River and land deities included Osiris and Isis with their child Horus, who was related to the Nile and to the sun as well. Osiris became especially important as a symbol of resurrection or rebirth. A famous Egyptian myth told of the struggle between Osiris, who brought civilization to Egypt, and his evil brother Seth, who killed him, cut his body into fourteen parts, and tossed them into the Nile River. Osiris's faithful wife Isis found the pieces and, with help from other gods, restored Osiris to life. Their son Horus avenged his father by castrating Seth. As a symbol of resurrection and judge of the dead, Osiris took on an important role for the Egyptians. By identifying with Osiris, one could hope to gain new life, just as Osiris had done. The dead, embalmed and mummified, were placed in tombs (in the case of kings, in pyramidal tombs), given the name of Osiris, and, by a process of magical identification, became Osiris. Like Osiris, they could then be reborn. The flood of the Nile and the new life it brought to Egypt were symbolized by Isis gathering all of Osiris's parts together and celebrated each spring in the festival of the new land.

Later Egyptian spiritual practice developed an emphasis on morality by stressing Osiris's role as judge of the dead. The dead were asked to give an account of their earthly deeds to show whether they deserved a reward. Other means were also employed to gain immortality. As seen in the *Book of the Dead*, magical incantations were used to ensure a favorable journey to a happy afterlife. Specific instructions were given on what to do when confronted by the judge of the dead. These instructions had two aspects. The negative confession gave a detailed list of what one had not done:

> What is said on reaching the Broad-Hall of the Two Justices [the place of the next-world judgment], absolving X [the name and title of the deceased] of every sin which he had committed, . . .
>
> I have not committed evil against men.
> I have not mistreated cattle.
> I have not committed sin in the place of truth [temple or burial place].
> I have not blasphemed a god. . . .
> I have not done violence to a poor man.
> I have not done that which the gods abominate.
> I have not defamed a slave to his superior.

I have not made anyone sick.
I have not made anyone weep.
I have not killed. . . .
I have not caused anyone suffering. . . .
I have not had sexual relations with a boy.
I have not defiled myself. . . .
I have not driven cattle away from their pasturage. . . .
I have not built a dam against running water. . . .
I have not driven away the cattle of the god's property.[9]

Later the supplicant made a speech listing his good actions: "I have done that which men said and that with which gods are content. . . . I have given bread to the hungry, water to the thirsty, clothing to the naked, and a ferry-boat to him who was marooned. I have provided divine offerings for the gods and mortuary offerings for the dead."[10]

At first the Osiris cult was reserved for the very wealthy who could afford to take expensive measures to preserve the body after death. During the Middle Kingdom, however, the cult became "democratized"— extended to all Egyptians who aspired to an afterlife. This is particularly evident in the magical formulas called Coffin Texts that were inscribed on the wooden coffins of less wealthy Egyptians to ensure that the deceased would pass to a blessed afterlife.

THE PYRAMIDS

One of the great achievements of Egyptian civilization, the building of pyramids, occurred in the time of the Old Kingdom. Pyramids were not built in isolation but as part of a larger complex dedicated to the dead, in effect, a city of the dead. The area included a large pyramid for the king's burial, smaller pyramids for his family, and mastabas, rectangular structures with flat roofs as tombs for the pharaoh's noble officials. The tombs were well prepared for their residents. The rooms were furnished and stocked with numerous supplies, including chairs, boats, chests, weapons, games, dishes, and a variety of food. The Egyptians believed that human beings had two bodies, a physical one and a spiritual one, which they called the *ka*. If the physical body was properly preserved (hence mummification) and the tomb furnished with all the various objects of regular life, the *ka* could return and continue its life despite the death of the physical body.

To preserve the physical body after death, the Egyptians practiced mummification, a process of slowly drying a dead body to prevent it from rotting. special workshops, run by priests, performed this procedure, primarily for the wealthy families who could afford it. Workers first removed the liver, lungs, stomach, and

◆ **The Great Pyramid of Giza.**
The three pyramids at Giza, across the Nile River from Cairo, are the most famous in Egypt. Pyramids served as tombs for both the king and his immediate family. The largest of the three pyramids at Giza is the Great Pyramid of Khufu.

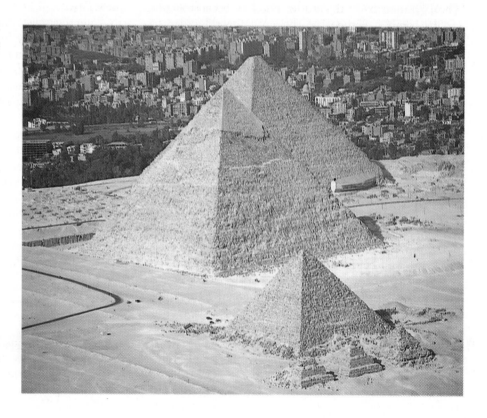

intestines and placed them in four special jars that were put in the tomb with the mummy. The priests also removed the brain by extracting it through the nose. They then covered the corpse with a natural salt that absorbed the body's water. Later, they filled the body with spices and wrapped it with layers of linen soaked in resin. At the end of the process, which took about seventy days, a lifelike mask was placed over the head and shoulders of the mummy, which was then sealed in a case and placed in its tomb.

Pyramids were tombs for the mummified bodies of pharaohs. The first pyramid was built in the third dynasty during the reign of King Djoser. The architect Imhotep, a priest of Heliopolis, the center dedicated to the sun cult, was responsible for the step pyramid at Saqqara. Beginning with Djoser, wives and immediate families of the kings were buried in pyramids, nobles and officials in mastabas.

The first real pyramid, in which each side was filled in to make an even surface, was constructed in the fourth dynasty around 2600 B.C. by King Snefru who built three pyramids. But the largest and most magnificent of all was built under Snefru's son Khufu. Constructed at Giza around 2540 B.C., the famous Great Pyramid covers thirteen acres, measures 756 feet at each side of its base, and stands 481 feet high. Its four sides are almost precisely oriented to the four points of the compass.

The building of the Great Pyramid was an enormous construction project that used limestone blocks as well as granite from Upper Egypt. The Greek historian Herodotus (see Chapter 3) reported the tradition that it took 100,000 Egyptians twenty years to build the great pyramid. But Herodotus wrote two thousand years after the event, and considerable controversy and speculation still surround the construction of the Great Pyramid, especially in view of the precision with which it was built. The stone slabs on the outside of the Great Pyramid, for example, fit so closely side by side that a hair cannot be pushed into the joints between them. The Great Pyramid still stands as a symbol of the power of Egyptian kings of the Old Kingdom. No later pyramid ever matched its size or splendor. But an Egyptian pyramid was not just the king's tomb; it was also an important symbol of royal power. It could be seen for miles away as a visible reminder of the glory and might of the ruler who was a living god on earth.

ART AND WRITING

Commissioned by kings or nobles for use in temples and tombs, Egyptian art was largely functional. Wall paint-

ings and statues of gods and kings in temples served a strictly spiritual purpose. They were an integral part of the performance of ritual, which was thought necessary to preserve the cosmic order and hence the well-being of Egypt. Likewise, the mural scenes and sculptured figures found in the tombs had a specific function. They were supposed to aid the journey of the deceased into the afterworld. Although placed there to assist the dead, these works of art have proved valuable to us by providing glimpses of Egyptian daily life. Peasants are shown plowing the fields and harvesting their abundant crops. Nobles hunt and fish, and their banquets are pictured in graphic detail.

Egyptian art was also formulaic. Artists and sculptors were expected to observe a strict canon of proportions that determined both form and presentation. This canon gave Egyptian art a distinctive appearance for thousands of years. Especially characteristic was the convention of combining the profile, semiprofile, and frontal views of the human body in relief work and painting in order to represent each part of the body accurately. This fashion created an art that was highly stylized, yet still allowed distinctive features to be displayed.

Writing emerged in Egypt during the first two dynasties. It was the Greeks who later labeled Egyptian writing hieroglyphics, meaning "priest-carvings" or "sacred writings." Hieroglyphs were sacred characters used as picture signs that depicted objects and had a sacred value at the same time. Although hieroglyphs were later simplified for writing purposes into two scripts, they never developed into an alphabet. Egyptian hieroglyphs were initially carved in stone, but later the two simplified scripts were written on papyrus, a paper made from the papyrus reed that grew along the Nile. Most of the ancient Egyptian literature that has come down to us was written on papyrus rolls and wooden tablets. The most popular literature consisted of adventure stories about the deeds of historical kings and famous men. The so-called Wisdom Texts were the most highly regarded pieces of literature. Written in the form of instructions from a father to his son, they provided sound advice based on tradition and worldly experience.

Chaos and a New Order: The New Kingdom

In contrast to the twelfth dynasty, the thirteenth exhibited considerable instability, foreshadowing the Second Intermediate Period (c. 1652–1567 B.C.). An incursion into the delta region by a people known as the Hyksos initiated this second age of chaos. The Hyksos were part

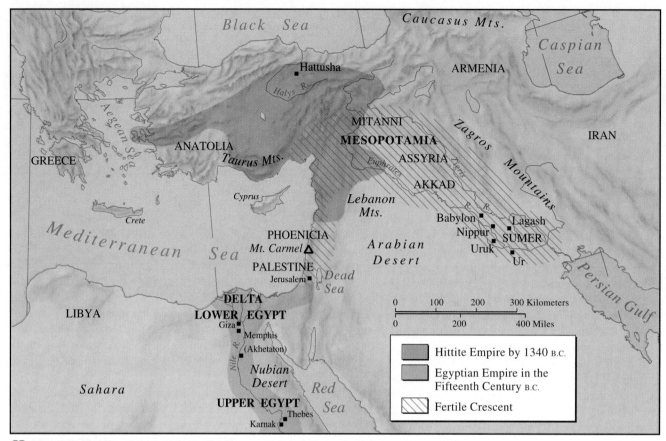

■ **Map 1.5** The Egyptian and Hittite Empires.

of a larger group of peoples who spoke Semitic languages and originally lived in the Arabian peninsula. Some of these Semitic-speaking peoples had moved into northern Mesopotamia as well as Syria and Palestine. The Hyksos infiltrated Egypt in the seventeenth century B.C. and came to dominate much of Egypt during the Second Intermediate Period. Other peoples, such as the Nubians in the south, took advantage of Egypt's problems to free themselves from Egyptian control. However, the presence of the Hyksos was not entirely negative for Egypt. They introduced Egypt to Bronze Age technology by teaching the Egyptians how to make bronze for use in new agricultural tools and weapons. More significantly, the Hyksos introduced new aspects of warfare to Egypt, including the horse-drawn war chariot, a heavier sword, and the compound bow. Eventually, the Egyptians made use of their new weapons to throw off Hyksos domination.

It was the pharaoh Ahmose I who managed to defeat and expel the Hyksos from Egypt. He reunited Egypt,

founded the eighteenth dynasty, established the New Kingdom (c. 1567–1085 B.C.), and launched the Egyptians along a new militaristic and imperialistic path. A more professional army was developed. Viziers, who were in charge of the state bureaucracy, were now chosen only from the ranks of military commanders.

During the period of the New Kingdom, Egypt became the most powerful state in the ancient Near East. Tuthmosis III (c. 1480–c. 1450 B.C.) led seventeen military campaigns into Syria and Palestine and even reached the Euphrates. Palestine and Syria were occupied, and local native princes were permitted to rule, but under Egyptian suzerainty. The sons of these princes were brought to Egypt as hostages to ensure cooperation. Tuthmosis also led his armies westward into Libya. Egypt was no longer content to remain in isolation but pursued an active political and diplomatic policy.

The new Egyptian imperial state reached its height during the reign of Amenhotep III (c. 1412–1375 B.C.), the great-grandson of Tuthmosis III. The achievements of the empire were made visible in the construction of magnificent new buildings and temples. Especially famous were the temple centers at Karnak and Luxor and the seventy-foot high statues of Amenhotep III in front of the mortuary temples along the Nile.

Egyptian conquests in its imperialistic age brought significant changes to the government of Egypt. Although the pharaoh was still viewed as a god, he lost a significant amount of real power to three strong institutions—the army, the royal bureaucracy, and the priesthoods. Conquests had greatly strengthened army commanders who had grown accustomed to acting autonomously while abroad. With the pharaohs frequently absent on military campaigns, the royal bureaucracy experienced a tremendous growth in independent power. Finally, the priesthoods, such as those of Re at Heliopolis, Ptah at Memphis, and especially Amon-Re at Thebes, became rich and powerful. Gifts of conquered lands enabled the temples to accumulate vast estates and numerous slaves. The priesthood at Amon-Re had, in fact, become the chief land and capital owner in Egypt.

By the end of his reign, Amenhotep III faced a growing military challenge from a people known as the Hittites (see The Impact of the Indo-Europeans later in this chapter). His son, Amenhotep IV (c. 1364–1347 B.C.), proved even less able to deal with this threat and lost Syria and Palestine to the Hittites. In large part, Amenhotep's failure to respond favorably to foreign challenges was due to his preoccupation with a religious revolution that he had initiated in Egypt.

Amenhotep introduced the worship of Aton, god of the sun disk, as the chief god (see the box on p. 30) and pursued his worship with great enthusiasm. Changing his own name to Akhenaten ("It is well with Aton"), the pharaoh closed the temples of other gods and especially endeavored to lessen the power of Amon-Re and his priesthood at Thebes. Akhenaten strove to reduce their influence by replacing Thebes as the capital of Egypt with Akhetaton ("dedicated to Aton"), a new city located near modern Tell-el-Amarna, two hundred miles north of Thebes.

Akhenaten's attempt at religious change proved to be a failure. It was too much to ask Egyptians to ignore their traditional ways and beliefs, especially since they saw the destruction of the old gods as subversive of the very cosmic order upon which Egypt's survival and continuing prosperity depended. Moreover, the priesthood at Thebes was unalterably opposed to the changes because of the implications for their position. Akhenaten's changes were soon undone after his death by those

◆ **Amenhotep IV (Akhenaten).** During the New Kingdom, the reign of Amenhotep IV was one of religious change. In place of the various deities worshiped by the Egyptians, Amenhotep introduced Aton, god of the sun disk, as the chief god.

who influenced his successor, the boy-pharaoh Tutankhamon (1347–1338 B.C.). Tutankhamon returned the government to Thebes and restored the old gods. The Aton experiment had failed to take hold, and the eighteenth dynasty itself came to an end with the rise to power of a military officer and vizier, Horemhab, who assumed the kingship in 1333 B.C.

The nineteenth dynasty managed to restore Egyptian power one more time. Under Rameses II (c. 1279–1213 B.C.), the Egyptians regained control of Palestine but were unable to reestablish the borders of their earlier empire. New invasions in the thirteenth century by the "Sea Peoples," as the Egyptians called them, destroyed Egyptian power in Palestine and drove the Egyptians back within their old frontiers. The days of Egyptian empire were ended, and the New Kingdom itself expired with the end of the twentieth dynasty in 1085 B.C. For the next thousand years, despite periodic revivals of strength, Egypt was dominated by Libyans, Nubians,

⇒ Akhenaten's Hymn to Aton ⇐

Amenhotep IV, more commonly known as Akhenaten, created a religious upheaval in Egypt by introducing the worship of Aton, god of the sun disk, as the chief god. Akhenaten's attitude to Aton is seen in this hymn. Some authorities have noted a similarity in spirit and wording to the 104th Psalm of the Old Testament.

Hymn to Aton

Your rays suckle every meadow.
When you rise, they live, they grow for you.
You make the seasons in order to rear all that you have
    made,
The winter to cool them,
And the heat that they may taste you.
You have made the distant sky in order to rise therein,
In order to see all that you do make.
While you were alone,
Rising in your form as the living Aton,
Appearing, shining, withdrawing or approaching,
You made millions of forms of yourself alone.

Cities, towns, fields, road, and river—
Every eye beholds you over against them,
For you are the Aton of the day over the earth. . . .
The world came into being by your hand,
According as you have made them.
When you have risen they live,
When you set they die.
You are lifetime your own self,
For one lives only through you.
Eyes are fixed on beauty until you set.
All work is laid aside when you set in the west.
But when you rise again,
Everything is made to flourish for the king . . .
Since you did found the earth
And raise them up for your son,
Who came forth from your body: the King of Upper and
    Lower Egypt, . . . Akh-en-Aton, . . . and the
Chief Wife of the King . . . Nefert-iti, living and
    youthful forever and ever.

Persians, and finally Macedonians after the conquest of Alexander the Great (see Chapter 4). In the first century B.C., Egypt became a province in Rome's mighty empire. Egypt continued, however, to influence its con-querors by the richness of its heritage and the awesome magnificence of its physical remains.

Daily Life in Ancient Egypt

The spiritual preoccupations of the Egyptians did not lead them to practice asceticism in the hope of a better life in the next world. Ancient Egyptians had a very positive attitude toward daily life on earth. The Egyptian's home was his castle, and he followed the advice of the wisdom literature, which suggested people marry young and establish a home and family. Monogamy was the general rule, although a husband was allowed to keep additional wives if his first wife was childless. Pharaohs, of course, were entitled to harems. The queen was acknowledged, however, as the Great Wife with a status higher than that of the other wives. The husband was master in the house, but wives were very much respected and in charge of the household and education of the children. From a book of wise sayings (which the Egyptians called "instructions") came this advice:

> If you are a man of standing, you should found your household and love your wife at home as is fitting. Fill her belly; clothe her back. Ointment is the prescription for her body. Make her heart glad as long as you live. She is a profitable field for her lord. You should not contend

◆ **Temple of Rameses II at Abu Simbel.** After being driven out of Palestine and Syria by the Hittites during the reign of Amenhotep IV, Egypt grew to power one final time under Rameses II (c. 1279-1213). He succeeded in reconquering Palestine, but was unable to restore the boundaries of the previous empire. The massive temple of Rameses II, located at Abu Simbel, was carved out of a cliff of Nubian sandstone. The giant statues represent Rameses II. The smaller figures at his feet are members of his family.

⇒ A Father's Advice ⇐

Upper-class Egyptians enjoyed compiling collections of wise sayings to provide guidance for leading an upright and successful life. This excerpt is taken from "The Instruction of the Vizier Ptah-hotep" and dates from around 2450 B.C. The vizier was the pharaoh's chief official. In this selection, Ptah-hotep advises his son on how to be a successful official.

The Instruction of the Vizier Ptah-hotep

Then he said to his son:

Let not your heart be puffed-up because of your knowledge; be not confident because you are a wise man. Take counsel with the ignorant as well as the wise. The full limits of skill cannot be attained, and there is no skilled man equipped to his full advantage. Good speech is more hidden than the emerald, but it may be found with maidservants at the grindstones. . . .

If you are a leader commanding the affairs of the multitude, seek out for yourself every beneficial deed, until it may be that your own affairs are without wrong. Justice is great, and its appropriateness is lasting; it has been disturbed since the time of him who made it, whereas there is punishment for him who passes over its laws. It is the right path before him who knows nothing. Wrongdoing has never brought its undertaking into port. It may be that it is fraud that gains riches, but the strength of justice is that it lasts . . . .

If you are a man of intimacy, whom one great man sends to another, be thoroughly reliable when he sends you. Carry out the errand for him as he has spoken. Do not be reserved about what is said to you, and beware of any act of forgetfulness. Grasp hold of truth, and do not exceed it. Mere gratification is by no means to be repeated. Struggle against making words worse, thus making one great man hostile to another through vulgar speech. . . .

If you are a man of standing and found a household and produce a son who is pleasing to god, if he is correct and inclines toward your ways and listens to your instruction, while his manners in your house are fitting, and if he takes care of your property as it should be, seek out for him every useful action. He is your son, . . . you should not cut your heart off from him.

But a man's seed often creates enmity. If he goes astray and transgresses your plans and does not carry out your instruction, so that his manners in your household are wretched, and he rebels against all that you say, while his mouth runs on in the most wretched talk, quite apart from his experience, while he possesses nothing, you should cast him off: he is not your son at all. He was not really born to you. Thus you enslave him entirely according to his own speech. He is one whom god has condemned in the very womb. . . .

with her at law, and keep her far from gaining control. . . . Let her heart be soothed through what may accrue to you; it means keeping her long in your house.[11]

Women did have equal legal rights with men. Their property and inheritance remained in their hands, even in marriage. Although most careers and public offices were closed to women, some did operate businesses. Peasant women worked long hours in the fields and at numerous domestic tasks. Upper-class women could function as priestesses, and a queen even became pharaoh in her own right. This was Hatshepsut in the New Kingdom. She served as regent for her stepson Thutmosis III, but assumed the throne for herself and remained in power until her death. Since pharaohs were almost always male, Hatshepsut's official statues show her clothed and bearded like a king. She was addressed as "His Majesty." That Hatshepsut was aware of her unusual position is evident from an inscription she had

placed on one of her temples. It read: "Now my heart turns to and fro, in thinking what will the people say, they who shall see my monument in after years, and shall speak of what I have done."

Little is known about marital arrangements and ceremonies although it does appear that marriages were arranged by parents. The primary concerns were family and property, and clearly the chief purpose of marriage was to produce children, especially sons (see the box above). From the New Kingdom came this piece of wisdom: "Take to yourself a wife while you are [still] a youth, that she may produce a son for you."[12] Only sons could carry on the family name. Daughters were not slighted, however. Numerous tomb paintings show the close and affectionate relationship parents had with both sons and daughters. Although marriages were arranged, some of the surviving love poems from ancient Egypt would indicate an element of romance in some marriages. Here is the lament of a lovesick boy for his

♦ Statue of Hatshepsut. Wife of Thutmose II, Hatshepsut served as regent for her stepson Thutmose III after her husband's death. In 1473 B.C., however, she proclaimed herself pharaoh. This red granite statue shows her as a woman, although most official statues portrayed her dressed and bearded like a king.

"sister" (lovers referred to each other as "brother" and "sister", although the practice of brother-sister marriage in the Egyptian royal family probably reached down into the general population as well):

Seven days to yesterday I have not seen the sister,
  and a sickness has invaded me;
My body has become heavy,
  And I am forgetful of my own self.
If the chief physicians come to me,
  My heart is not content with their remedies . . . .
What will revive me is to say to me: "Here she is!"
  Her name is what will lift me up. . . .
My health is her coming in from outside:
  When I see her, then I am well.[13]

Marriages could and did end in divorce, which was allowed, apparently with compensation for the wife. Adultery, however, was strictly prohibited with stiff punishments, especially for women who could have their noses cut off or be burned at the stake.

Under normal circumstances, Egypt was blessed by a material abundance that not only kept its entire population fed, but also enabled its upper classes to lead a life of gracious leisure. These wealthy families had attractive homes located on walled estates. Much energy was devoted to the garden, which contained fruit trees and vegetables, as well as tree-lined paths and pools for the family's leisure time.

Tomb paintings indicate that the upper classes participated in numerous banquets where guests were lavishly fed and entertained. Although some people obviously got drunk, a collection of "instructions" advises more circumspect behavior:

> If you are one of those sitting at the table of one greater than yourself, take what he may give, when it is set before your nose. You should gaze at what is before you. . . . Let your face be cast down until he addresses you, and you should speak only when he addresses you. Laugh after he laughs, and it will be very pleasing to his heart and what you may do will be pleasing to the heart.[14]

The same collection of "instructions" warns that when one has been invited to a party, "beware of approaching the women. It does not go well with the place where that is done."[15]

Entertainment, especially music, was a regular feature of parties. The Egyptians used an astonishing variety of instruments: drums, tambourines, flutes, trumpets, and a variety of stringed instruments that were plucked rather than played with a bow. Singers, accompanying themselves on lute or harp, presented songs in praise of the host's generosity and, judging from the words of this Middle Kingdom song, of dedication to enjoying life while one could: "Follow your desire, as long as you shall live. Put myrrh upon your head and clothing of fine linen upon you . . . . Set an increase to your good things; let not your heart flag. Follow your desire and your good. Fulfill your needs upon earth, after the command of your heart . . . ."[16]

Judging from the paintings in their tombs, the upper classes found a myriad of ways to entertain themselves as well. Fowling in the stands of papyrus reeds that grew along the riverbanks was a favorite pastime. Using a reed skiff, the huntsman used a boomerang to bring down his prey, much to the delight of his family who accompanied him. Once the waterfowl was downed,

Egyptian families used trained retriever cats to swim out into the water and bring back the birds. The hunting of animals was only for the men. The hunters rode in chariots and used dogs to pursue antelope, gazelles, and other creatures who were shot with bows and arrows. Indoor activities included board games among other things. The earliest known board games in the world have been found in Egyptian tombs. Many are made of wood decorated with ivory or ebony. The games played on them involved moving pieces on the boards according to the roll of the dice. We know considerably less about the activities of the lower classes, but we can be sure that they did not have the leisurely lifestyle of their social superiors.

On the Fringes of Civilization

Our story of the beginnings of Western civilization has been dominated so far by Mesopotamia and Egypt. But significant developments were also taking place on the fringes of these civilizations. Farming had spread into the Balkan peninsula of Europe by 6500 B.C., and by 4000 B.C., it was well established in southern France, central Europe, and the coastal regions of the Mediterranean. Although migrating farmers from the Near East may have brought some farming techniques into Europe, historians now believe that the Neolithic peoples of Europe domesticated animals and began to farm largely on their own.

One outstanding feature of late Neolithic Europe was the building of megalithic structures. Megalith is Greek for "large stone." Radiocarbon dating, a technique that allows scientists to determine the age of objects, shows that the first megalithic structures were built around 4000 B.C., more then a thousand years before the great pyramids were built in Egypt. Between 3200 and 1500 B.C., standing stones that were placed in circles or lined up in rows were erected throughout the British Isles and northwestern France. Other megalithic constructions have been found as far north as Scandinavia and as far south as the islands of Corsica, Sardinia, and Malta. Some archaeologists have demonstrated that the stone circles were used as observatories to detect not only such simple astronomical phenomena as midwinter and midsummer sunrises, but also such sophisticated observations as the major and minor standstills of the moon.

By far, the most famous of these megalithic constructions is Stonehenge in England. Stonehenge consists of a series of concentric rings of standing stones. Its construction sometime between 2100 and 1900 B.C. was no small accomplishment. The eighty bluestones used at

✦ **A Hunting Scene.** A favorite pastime of the Egyptian upper classes was hunting waterfowl in the stands of papyrus reeds that grew along the riverbanks. This tomb painting shows a wealthy Egyptian with members of his family hunting geese with throwsticks.

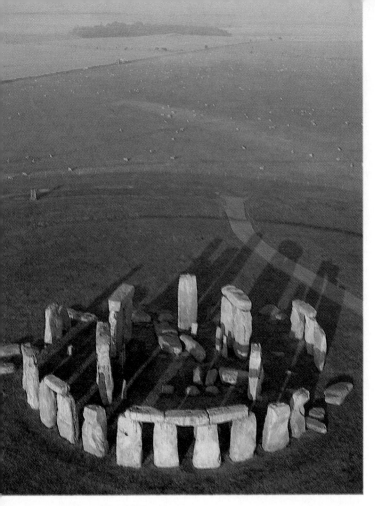

◆ **Stonehenge.** The Bronze Age in northwestern Europe is known for its "megaliths," or large standing stones. Between 3200 and 1500 B.C., standing stones that were placed in circles or lined up in rows were erected throughout the British Isles and northwestern France. By far, the most famous of these megalithic constructions was Stonehenge in England.

Table 1.2). It has been suggested that the original Indo-European–speaking peoples were based somewhere in the steppe region north of the Black Sea or in southwestern Asia, in modern Iran or Afghanistan. Although there had been earlier migrations, around 2000 B.C. they began major nomadic movements into Europe (including present-day Italy and Greece), India, and the Near East. The Indo-Europeans who moved into Asia Minor and Anatolia (modern Turkey) coalesced with the native peoples to form the Hittite kingdom around 1750 B.C. with its capital at Hattusha (Bogazköy in modern Turkey).

The Hittites began to spread outward around 1600 B.C., but it was not until the reign of Suppiluliumas (c. 1380–1340 B.C.) that the Hittites established a real empire. He destroyed the power of the Mitanni kingdom, which had been created by the Hurrians and was allied with the Egyptians, and then conquered Syria. For the next hundred years, the Hittites were in conflict with Egypt until the Egyptian pharaoh Rameses II made a remarkable nonaggression treaty that stabilized relations between Egypt and the Hittites. The end of Hittite power came around 1200 B.C. when the Sea Peoples struck at both Egypt and the Hittite empire. Egypt managed to keep the invaders out but remained weakened thereafter. The Hittite Empire was destroyed, however. By 1190 B.C., Hittite power was at an end.

At its height, the Hittite Empire demonstrated an interesting ability to assimilate other cultures to create its own. In languages, literature, art, law, and religion, the Hittites borrowed much from Mesopotamian tradition as well as from the native peoples that they had subdued. Their law code, for example, though less harsh,

Stonehenge weigh four tons each and were transported to the site from their original source 135 miles away. Like other megalithic structures, Stonehenge indicates a remarkable awareness of astronomy on the part of its builders, as well as an impressive coordination of workers.

The Impact of the Indo-Europeans

For many historians, both the details of construction and the purpose of the megalithic structures of Europe remain a mystery. Also puzzling is the role of the Indo-European people. The term *Indo-European* refers to people who used a language derived from a single parent tongue. Indo-European languages include Greek, Latin, Persian, Sanskrit, and the Germanic languages (see

❖ **Table 1.2** *Some Indo-European Languages*

Subfamily	Languages
Indo–Iranian	*Sanskrit*; Persian
Balto–Slavic	Russian, Serbo-Croatian, Czech, Polish, Lithuanian
Hellenic	Greek
Italic	*Latin*, romance languages (French, Italian, Spanish, Portuguese, Romanian)
Celtic	Irish, Gaelic
Germanic	Swedish, Danish, Norwegian, German, Dutch, English

Note: Languages in italic type are no longer spoken.

reflected the influence of Mesopotamia. Hittite religion combined Indo-European deities and Mesopotamian gods. Recent scholarship has stressed the important role of the Hittites in transmitting Mesopotamian culture, as they transformed it, to later Western civilization in the Mediterranean area, especially to the Mycenaean Greeks.

Conclusion

The foundation stones for the building of Western civilization were laid by the Mesopotamians and the Egyptians. They developed cities and struggled with the problems of organized states. They developed writing to keep records and created literature. They constructed monumental architecture to please their gods, symbolize their power, and preserve their culture for all time. They developed new political, military, social, and religious structures to deal with the basic problems of human existence and organization. These first literate civilizations left detailed records that allow us to view how they grappled with three of the fundamental problems that humans have pondered: the nature of human relationships, the nature of the universe, and the role of divine forces in that cosmos. Although later peoples in Western civilization would provide different answers from those of the Mesopotamians and Egyptians, it was they who first posed the questions, gave answers, and wrote them down. Human memory begins with these two civilizations.

By the middle of the second millennium B.C., much of the creative impulse of the Mesopotamian and Egyptian civilizations was beginning to wane. The invasion of the Sea Peoples around 1200 B.C. ushered in a whole new pattern of petty states and new kingdoms that would lead to the largest empires the ancient Near East had seen.

NOTES

1. Quoted in Thorkild Jacobsen, "Mesopotamia," in Henri Frankfort et al., *Before Philosophy* (Baltimore, 1949), p. 139.
2. Quoted in Thorkild Jacobsen, *The Treasures of Darkness: A History of Mesopotamian Religion* (New Haven, Conn., 1976), p. 97.
3. Ibid., pp. 101–2.
4. *The Epic of Gilgamesh*, trans. N. K. Sandars (London, 1972), p. 62.
5. James B. Pritchard, *Ancient Near Eastern Texts*, 3d ed. (Princeton, N.J., 1969), p. 372.
6. Quoted in Milton Covensky, *The Ancient Near Eastern Tradition* (New York, 1966), p. 51.
7. Pritchard, *Ancient Near Eastern Texts*, p. 445.
8. Quoted in B. G. Trigger, B. J. Kemp, D. O'Connor, and A. B. Lloyd, *Ancient Egypt: A Social History* (Cambridge, 1983), p. 74.
9. Pritchard, *Ancient Near Eastern Texts*, p. 34.
10. Ibid., p. 36.
11. Ibid., p. 413.
12. Ibid., p. 420.
13. Quoted in John A. Wilson, *The Culture of Ancient Egypt* (Chicago, 1956), p. 264.
14. Pritchard, *Ancient Near Eastern Texts*, p. 412.
15. Ibid., p. 413.
16. Ibid., p. 467.

SUGGESTIONS FOR FURTHER READING

For a beautifully illustrated introduction to the ancient world, see *Past Worlds: The Times Atlas of Archaeology* (Maplewood, N.J., 1988), written by an international group of scholars. A similar kind of guide with more elaborate historical discussions is provided by A. Cotterell, ed., *The Penguin Encyclopedia of Ancient Civilization* (London, 1980). A detailed history of the ancient world with chapters written by different specialists is available in the twelve volumes of *The Cambridge Ancient History*, now in its third edition. A less detailed but sound survey can be found in C. G. Starr, *A History of the Ancient World*, 4th ed. (New York, 1991). The following works are of considerable value in examining the prehistory of humankind: M. N. Cohen, *The Food Crisis in Prehistory: Overpopulation and the Origins of Agriculture* (New Haven, Conn., 1977); R. Leakey, *The Making of Mankind* (London, 1981); P. Mellars and C. Stringer, *The Human Revolution* (Edinburgh, 1989); J. Mellaert, *The Neolithic of the Near East* (New York, 1976); T. Champion, C. Gamble, S. Shennan, and A. Whittle, *Prehistoric Europe* (London, 1984); A. Whittle, *Neolithic Europe: A Survey* (Cambridge, 1985); D. O. Henry, *From Foraging to Agriculture* (Philadelphia, 1989); C. Renfrew, *Before Civilization: The Radiocarbon Revolution and Prehistoric Europe* (London, 1973); and C. Redman, *The Rise of Civilization* (San Francisco, 1978). For a specialized study of the role of women in early human society, see F. Dahlberg, ed., *Woman the Gatherer* (New Haven, Conn., 1981).

A fascinating introduction to the world of ancient Near Eastern studies can be found in W. D. Jones, *Venus and Sothis: How the Ancient Near East Was Rediscovered* (Chicago, 1982). A very competent general survey primarily of the political history of Mesopotamia and Egypt is W. W. Hallo and W. K. Simpson, *The Ancient Near East: A History* (New York, 1971). Also valuable are A. B. Knapp, *The History and Culture of Ancient Western Asia and Egypt* (Chicago, 1987); C. Burney, *The Ancient Near East* (Ithaca, N.Y., 1977); W. von Soden, *The Ancient Orient: An Introduction to the Study of the Ancient Near East* (Grand Rapids, Mich., 1994); and

H. J. Nissen, *The Early History of the Ancient Near East, 9000–2000* B.C. (Chicago, 1988). H. W. F. Saggs, *Babylonians* (Norman, Okla., 1995) provides an overview of the peoples of ancient Mesopotamia. The fundamental collection of translated documents from the ancient Near East is J. B. Pritchard, *Ancient Near Eastern Texts*, 3d ed. with supplement (Princeton, N.J., 1969). For a good translation of *The Epic of Gilgamesh*, see the edition by N. K. Sandars (London, 1972).

General works on ancient Mesopotamia include A. L. Oppenheim, *Ancient Mesopotamia*, 2d ed. (Chicago, 1977); S. Lloyd, *The Archaeology of Mesopotamia*, rev. ed. (London, 1984); and G. Roux, *Ancient Iraq* (Harmondsworth, 1966). The world of the Sumerians has been well described in S. N. Kramer, *The Sumerians* (Chicago, 1963) and *History Begins at Sumer* (New York, 1959). Kramer's book *Sumerian Mythology* (New York, 1961) is a study of Sumer's spiritual and literary achievement in the third millennium B.C. See also the recent summary of the historical and archaeological evidence by H. Crawford, *Sumer and the Sumerians* (Cambridge, 1991). On Ebla, see P. Matthiae, *Ebla: An Empire Rediscovered* (London, 1980). The fundamental work on the spiritual perspective of ancient Mesopotamia is T. Jacobsen, *The Treasures of Darkness: A History of Mesopotamian Religion* (New Haven, Conn., 1976). On art, see S. Lloyd, *The Art of the Ancient Near East* (New York, 1961).

For a good introduction to ancient Egypt, see the beautifully illustrated work by J. Baines and J. Málek, *The Cultural Atlas of the World: Ancient Egypt* (Alexandria, Va., 1991). Other general surveys include C. Hobson, *The World of the Pharaohs* (New York, 1987); and C. Aldred, *The Egyptians* (London, 1984). For an interesting introduction to Egyptian history, see B. J. Kemp, *Ancient Egypt* (London, 1989). A new approach is attempted in B. G. Trigger, B. J. Kemp, D. O'Connor, and A. B. Lloyd, *Ancient Egypt: A Social History* (Cambridge, 1983). On Akhenaten and his religious changes, see D. Redford, *Akhenaten: The Heretic King* (Princeton, N.J., 1984). Egyptian religion is covered in H. Frankfort,

Ancient Egyptian Religion (New York, 1948), a brief but superb study; and J. Cerney, *Ancient Egyptian Religion* (New York, 1979). The importance of the afterlife in Egyptian civilization is examined in A. Spencer, *Death in Ancient Egypt* (Harmondsworth, 1982). On culture in general, see J. A. Wilson, *The Culture of Ancient Egypt* (Chicago, 1956). The leading authority on the pyramids is I. E. S. Edwards, *The Pyramids of Egypt*, rev. ed. (Harmondsworth, 1976). On art, see H. Schäfer, *The Principles of Egyptian Art* (Oxford, 1974). There are many examples of Egyptian literature in M. Lichtheim, *Ancient Egyptian Literature*, 3 vols. (Berkeley, 1973–80). An important new study on women is G. Robins, *Women in Ancient Egypt* (Cambridge, Mass., 1993).

Daily life in ancient Egypt can be examined in J. White, *Everyday Life in Ancient Egypt* (London, 1963); P. Montet, *Everyday Life in Egypt in the Days of Ramses the Great*, trans. A. R. Maxwell-Hyslop (New York, 1974); and T. G. H. James, *Pharaoh's People: Scenes from Life in Imperial Egypt* (London, 1984).

On the Sea Peoples, see the standard work by N. Sandars, *The Sea Peoples: Warriors of the Ancient Mediterranean* (London, 1978). A good introductory survey on the Hittites can be found in O. R. Gurney, *The Hittites*, 2d ed. (Harmondsworth, 1981). See also J. Macqueen, *The Hittites and Their Contemporaries in Asia Minor* (New York, 1986). On the Hyksos, see J. Van Seters, *The Hyksos: A New Investigation* (New Haven, Conn., 1966).

The Ancient Near East: Peoples and Empires

Around 971 B.C., Solomon came to the throne of Israel, a small state in western Asia. He was lacking in military prowess, but excelled in many other ways. Through trade and a series of foreign alliances, he became a well-known figure in the ancient Near East. But he was especially famed for another of his qualities. When confronted with two women who each claimed that the child before them was her natural child, Solomon ordered his servant to cut the child in half and give half to each woman. The first woman objected: "Please, my lord, give her the living baby! Don't kill him!" The second woman replied, "Neither I nor you shall have him. Cut him in two!" Then Solomon rendered his judgment: "Give the living baby to the first woman. Do not kill him; she is his mother." According to the biblical account, "when all Israel heard the verdict the king had given, they held the king in awe, because they saw that he had wisdom from God to administer justice." Outside Israel, too, the fame of Solomon spread far. But how was the king of such a small nation able to achieve such renown? And how was such a small nation able to survive for as long as it did in a Near East dominated by mighty empires?

The destruction of the Hittite kingdom and the weakening of Egypt around 1200 B.C. temporarily left no dominant powers in the Near East, allowing a patchwork of petty kingdoms and city-states to emerge, especially in the area of Syria and Palestine. One of these small states, the Hebrew nation, has played a role in Western civilization completely disproportionate to its size. The Hebrews were a minor factor in the politics of the ancient Near East, but their spiritual heritage—in the form of the Judaeo-Christian view of life—is one of the basic pillars of Western civilization.

The small states did not last, however. Ever since the first city-states had arisen in the Near East around 3000 B.C., there had been an ongoing movement toward the creation of larger territorial states with more sophisticated systems of control. This pro-

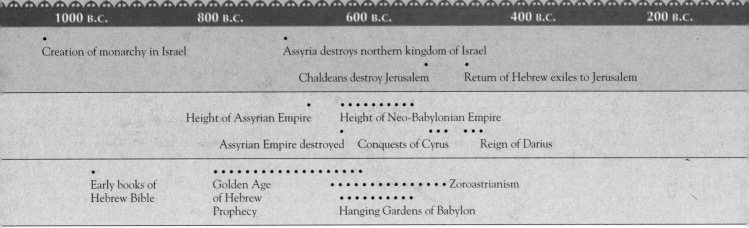

Creation of monarchy in Israel

Assyria destroys northern kingdom of Israel

Chaldeans destroy Jerusalem

Return of Hebrew exiles to Jerusalem

Height of Assyrian Empire

Height of Neo-Babylonian Empire

Assyrian Empire destroyed

Conquests of Cyrus

Reign of Darius

Early books of
Hebrew Bible

Golden Age
of Hebrew
Prophecy

Zoroastrianism

Hanging Gardens of Babylon

cess reached a high point in the first millennium B.C. with the appearance of empires that embraced the entire Near East. Between 1000 and 500 B.C., the Assyrians, Chaldeans, and Persians all created empires that encompassed either large areas or all of the ancient Near East. Each had impressive and grandiose capital cities that emphasized the power and wealth of its rulers. Each brought peace and order for a period of time by employing new administrative techniques. Each eventually fell to other conquerors. In the long run, these large empires had less impact on Western civilization than the Hebrew people. In human history, the power of ideas is often more significant than the power of empires.

The Hebrews: "The Children of Israel"

The Hebrews were a Semitic-speaking people who had a tradition concerning their origins and history that was eventually written down as part of the Jewish Bible, known to Christians as the Old Testament. Historians do not agree on the extent to which the early books of the Jewish Bible reflect the true history of the early Hebrews. The Hebrews' own tradition states that they were descendants of the patriarch Abraham who had migrated from Mesopotamia to the land of Palestine, where they became identified as the "Children of Israel." This migration of a Semitic people, a common occurrence in the ancient Near East, probably took place around 1800 B.C.

The Hebrews were a nomadic people, organized along tribal lines in clans, who followed a lifestyle based on grazing flocks and herds rather than farming. They continued these practices in Palestine and made no effort to form a political state. According to tradition, a drought in Palestine caused many Hebrews to migrate to Egypt where they lived peacefully until they were enslaved by pharaohs who used them as laborers on their numerous building projects. They remained in bondage until Moses led his people out of Egypt in the well-known "exodus." Some historians believe this would have occurred in the first half of the thirteenth century B.C. The Hebrews then wandered for many years in the desert until they entered Palestine (possibly around 1220 B.C.). Organized in twelve tribes, they became embroiled in conflict with the Philistines, a people who had settled in the coastal area of Palestine but were beginning to move into the inland areas. Leaders called judges assumed the leadership of the Hebrews in these conflicts. Around 1000 B.C., under the pressure of the ongoing struggle with the Philistines, the Hebrews embarked upon the establishment of a monarchy.

Political Aspirations and Frustrations

The creation of a monarchy, first accomplished by Saul (c. 1020–1000 B.C.), was not an easy task because many Hebrews were still accustomed to tribal life and tribal organization. Saul achieved some success in the ongoing struggle with the Philistines but committed suicide after a defeat by his enemies. After a brief period of anarchy, one of Saul's lieutenants, David (c. 1000–971 B.C.), reunited the Hebrews, defeated the Philistines, and

The Hebrews

Migration of Hebrews to Palestine	c. 1800 B.C.
Exodus from Egypt	Between 1300 and 1200 B.C.
Saul—first king	c. 1020–1000 B.C.
King David	c. 1000–971 B.C.
King Solomon	c. 971–931 B.C.
Northern kingdom of Israel destroyed by Assyria	722 B.C.
Fall of southern kingdom of Judah to Chaldeans; destruction of Jerusalem	586 B.C.
Return of exiles to Jerusalem	538 B.C.

established control over all of Palestine. The city of Jerusalem was conquered and made into the capital of a united kingdom. David's conquests accelerated the integration of the formerly nomadic Hebrews into a more settled community based on farming and urban life. Centralized political organization was replacing the independent ways of the twelve Hebrew tribes.

David's son Solomon (c. 971–931 B.C.) did even more to strengthen royal power. He expanded the political and military establishments and was especially active in extending the trading activities of the Hebrews. Solomon is best known for his building projects, including a large palace with state offices and forts for the protection of trade routes. Of all his new construction projects, the most famous was the Temple in the city of Jerusalem. The Hebrews viewed the Temple as the symbolic center of their religion, and hence of the Hebrew kingdom itself. The Temple now housed the Ark of the Covenant, the holy chest containing the sacred relics of the Hebrew religion and, symbolically, the throne of the invisible God of Israel. Under Solomon, ancient Israel was at the height of its power, but his efforts to centralize royal power along the lines of Mesopotamian despotism led to dissatisfaction among his subjects, who believed that his actions threatened the old Hebrew tribal ties.

After Solomon's death, the tension between the northern and southern Hebrew tribes led to the establishment of two separate kingdoms—a kingdom of Israel, composed of the ten northern tribes with its capital at Samaria, and a southern kingdom of Judah, consisting of two tribes with its capital at Jerusalem. The northern kingdom of Israel, especially under King Ahab (869–850 B.C.), joined other petty Syrian states to stop temporarily the onslaught of the Assyrians, who had consolidated their kingdom to the northeast (see The Assyrian Empire later in this chapter). But the power of Israel declined after Ahab, and by the end of the ninth century, the kingdom of Israel was forced to pay tribute to powerful Assyria. In the next century, the kingdom itself was destroyed. The Assyrians overran the northern kingdom, destroyed the capital of Samaria in 722 B.C., and deported many Hebrews to other parts of the Assyrian Empire. These dispersed Hebrews (the "ten lost tribes") merged with neighboring peoples and gradually lost their identity.

Map 2.1 Palestine in the First Millennium B.C.

The southern kingdom of Judah was also forced to pay tribute to Assyria but managed to survive as an independent state as Assyrian power declined. A new enemy, however, appeared on the horizon. The Chaldeans, allied with the Medes from Iran, brought the final destruction of Assyria. Under King Nebuchadnezzar, the Chaldeans then conquered the kingdom of Judah and completely destroyed Jerusalem in 586 B.C. Many upper-class Hebrews were sent into exile to Babylonia, the memory of which is still evoked in the stirring words of Psalm 137:

> By the rivers of Babylon, we sat and wept when we
> remembered Zion. . . .
> How can we sing the songs of the Lord while in a foreign
> land?
> If I forgot you, O Jerusalem, may my right hand forget its
> skill.
> May my tongue cling to the roof of my mouth if I do not
> remember you, if I do not consider Jerusalem my
> highest joy.[1]

But the Babylonian captivity of the Hebrew people did not last. Upon the destruction of the Chaldean kingdom by a new set of conquerors, the Persians, the Hebrews were allowed to return to Jerusalem and rebuild their city and the Temple. The revived kingdom of Judah remained under Persian control until the conquests of Alexander the Great in the fourth century B.C. The people of Judah survived, eventually becoming known as the Jews and giving their name to Judaism, the religion of Yahweh, the Jewish god.

The Spiritual Dimensions of Israel

The spiritual perspective of the Hebrews evolved over a period of time. Early Hebrews probably worshiped many gods, including nature spirits dwelling in trees and rocks. Yahweh first appears as the god of one Hebrew tribe— the Midian. By the time they had returned to Palestine from their captivity in Egypt, many Hebrews had made a commitment to Yahweh as their only god. But it was not until after the Babylonian captivity of the Jews (the sixth century B.C.) that pure monotheism, or the belief that there is only one God for all peoples, became standard.

"I AM THE LORD YOUR GOD": RULER OF THE WORLD

According to the Hebrew conception, there is but one God, whom the Hebrews called Yahweh. God is the

◆ **The King of Israel Pays Tribute to the King of Assyria.** By the end of the ninth century B.C., the kingdom of Israel had been forced to pay tribute to the Assyrian Empire. The Assyrians overran the kingdom in 722 B.C. and destroyed the capital city of Samaria. In this scene from a black obelisk, Jehu, king of Israel, is shown paying tribute to the king of Assyria.

creator of the world and everything in it. Indeed, Yahweh means "he causes to be." To the Hebrews, the gods of all other peoples were simply idols. The Hebrew god ruled the world; he was subject to nothing. All peoples were his servants, whether they knew it or not. This God was also transcendent. He had created nature, but was not in nature. The stars, moon, rivers, wind, and other natural phenomena were not divinities or suffused with divinity, as other peoples of the ancient Near East believed, but God's handiwork. All of God's creations could be admired for their awesome beauty, but not worshiped as god.

This omnipotent creator of the universe was not removed from the life he had created, however, but was a just and good God who expected goodness from his people. If they did not obey his will, they would be punished. But he was also a God of mercy and love: "The Lord is gracious and compassionate, slow to anger and rich in love. The Lord is good to all; he has compassion on all he has made."[2]

Each person was important in the Hebrew spiritual perspective. Possessed of moral freedom, he or she had the ability to choose between good and evil. But an important condition was attached to this freedom. People could not simply establish their own ethical standards. Through Moses and other holy men, God had made known his commandments, his ideals of behavior.

The Covenant and the Law: The Book of Exodus

During the Exodus from Egypt, the Hebrews supposedly made their covenant with Yahweh. They agreed to obey their God and follow his law. In return, Yahweh promised to take special care of his chosen people. This selection from the Book of Exodus describes the making of the covenant and God's commandments to the Hebrews.

Exodus 19: 1–8

In the third month after the Israelites left Egypt—on the very day—they came to the Desert of Sinai. After they set out from Rephidim, they entered the desert of Sinai, and Israel camped there in the desert in front of the mountain. Then Moses went up to God, and the Lord, called to him from the mountain, and said, "This is what you are to say to the house of Jacob and what you are to tell the people of Israel: 'You yourselves have seen what I did to Egypt, and how I carried you on eagles' wings and brought you to myself. Now if you obey me fully and keep my covenant, then out of all nations you will be my treasured possession. Although the whole earth is mine, you will be for me a kingdom of priests and a holy nation.' These are the words you are to speak to the Israelites." So Moses went back and summoned the elders of the people and set before them all the words the Lord had commanded him to speak. The people all responded together, "We will do everything the Lord has said." So Moses brought their answer back to the Lord.

Exodus 20: 1–17

And God spoke all these words, "I am the lord your God, who brought you out of Egypt, out of the land of slavery. You shall have no other gods before me. You shall not make for yourself an idol in the form of anything in heaven above or on the earth beneath or in the waters below. You shall not bow down to them or worship them; for I, the Lord your God, am a jealous God, punishing the children for the sin of the fathers to the third and fourth generation of those who hate, but showing love to a thousand generations of those who love me and keep my commandments. You shall not misuse the name of the Lord your God, for the Lord will not hold anyone guiltless who misuses his name. Remember the Sabbath day by keeping it holy. Six days you shall labor and do all your work, but the seventh day is a Sabbath to the Lord your God. On it you shall not do any work, neither you, nor your son or daughter, nor your manservant or maidservant, not your animals, nor the alien within your gates. For in six days the Lord made the heavens and the earth, the sea, and all that is in them, but he rested on the seventh day. Therefore the Lord blessed the Sabbath day and made it holy. Honor your father and your mother, so that you may live long in the land the Lord your God is giving you. You shall not murder, You shall not commit adultery. You shall not steal. You shall not give false testimony against your neighbor. You shall not covet your neighbor's house. You shall not covet your neighbor's wife, or his manservant or maidservant, his ox or donkey, or anything that belongs to your neighbor.

If people chose to ignore the good, then suffering and evil would follow. Each individual ultimately bore responsibility for his or her decisions. Despite the powerful dimensions of God as creator and sustainer of the universe, the Hebrew message also emphasized that each person could have a personal relationship with this powerful being. As the psalmist sang: "My help comes from the Lord, the Maker of heaven and earth. He will not let your foot slip—he who watches over you will not slumber."[3]

The chief source of information about Israel's spiritual conceptions is the Hebrew Bible or the Old Testament of the Christian Bible. Its purpose was to teach the Hebrews the essential beliefs about the God of Israel after the Babylonian captivity of the Jews and their dispersal. But it also provides an unusual collection of Hebrew literature, since it contains hymns (the Psalms), adages (Proverbs), folk tales, literary romances, love lyrics (Book of Solomon), and, of course, a great deal of history.

The basic core of the Hebrew Bible consists of works written before the Babylonian captivity of the Jews, probably around 950 B.C. The first five books (known as the Pentateuch), which range from the beginning of the world until the Hebrews arrived in Palestine, constitute the Torah, or law code, governing the lives of worshipers and their relations to one another and to the non-Jewish population. The Hebrew Bible also includes historical books, which describe Jewish attempts to develop institutions by which they could observe the law properly, and the words of the prophets (see "You Only Have I Chosen": Covenant, Law, and Prophets below). The Hebrew Bible focuses on one basic theme—the necessity for the Hebrews to obey their God.

"YOU ONLY HAVE I CHOSEN:" COVENANT, LAW, AND PROPHETS

Three aspects of the Hebrew religious tradition had special significance: the covenant, the law, and the prophets. The Hebrews believed that during the exodus from Egypt, when Moses led his people out of bondage into the promised land, a special event occurred that determined the Hebrew experience for all time. According to tradition, God entered into a covenant or contract with the tribes of Israel who believed that Yahweh had spoken to them through Moses (see the box on p. 42). The Hebrews promised to obey Yahweh and follow his law. In return, Yahweh promised to take special care of his chosen people, "a peculiar treasure unto me above all people."

This covenant between Yahweh and his chosen people could be fulfilled, however, only by Hebrew obedience to the law of God. Law became a crucial element of the Hebrew world and had a number of different dimensions. In some instances, it set forth specific requirements, such as payments for offenses. Most important, since the major characteristic of God was his goodness, ethical concerns stood at the center of the law. Sometimes these took the form of specific standards of moral behavior: "You shall not murder. You shall not commit adultery. You shall not steal."[4] But these concerns were also expressed in decrees that regulated the economic, social, and political life of the community since God's laws of morality applied to all areas of life. These laws made no class distinctions and

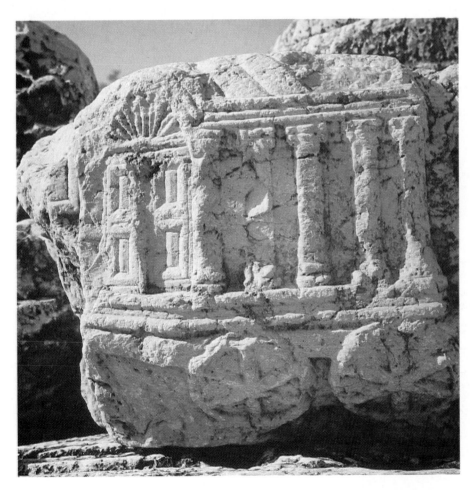

◆ **A Representation of the Ark of the Covenant.** The most famous project carried out under King Solomon was the building of the Temple of Jerusalem. Within the Temple the Israelites placed the Ark of the Covenant, the holy chest that contained the sacred relics of the Hebrew faith. The Ark was also considered to be the throne of the invisible God on earth. This representation of the Ark, believed to be one of the earliest, is from a second-century A.D. synagogue at Capernaum.

emphasized the protection of the poor, widows, orphans, and slaves.

The Hebrews believed that certain religious leaders or "holy men," called prophets, were sent by God to serve as his voice to his people. The prophets preached, whether invited to or not, and did not hesitate to say whatever pleased them, even if it displeased the established authorities. In the ninth century B.C., the prophets were particularly vociferous about the tendency of the Hebrews to accept other gods, chiefly the fertility and earth gods of other peoples in Palestine. They warned of the terrible retribution that God would exact from the Hebrews if they did not keep the covenant to remain faithful to him alone and just in their dealings with one another (see the box on p. 45).

The golden age of prophecy began in the mid-eighth century and continued during the time when the He-

✦ **Mount Sinai.** According to their tradition, the Hebrews entered into a covenant with God while wandering in the desert after leaving Egypt. They promised to worship only Yahweh and to obey his laws. A part of these laws is the Decalogue (the Ten Commandments), received by the prophet Moses on Mount Sinai, which is pictured in the photograph.

brews were threatened by Assyrian and Chaldean conquerors. The words of these reforming prophets were written down and are part of the Hebrew Bible. These "men of God" went through the land warning the Hebrews that they had failed to keep God's commandments and would be punished for breaking the covenant: "I will punish you for all your iniquities." Amos prophesied the fall of the northern kingdom of Israel to Assyria; twenty years later Isaiah said the kingdom of Judah too would fall; and two hundred years later, Jeremiah said that Jerusalem would be crushed by the Babylonians.

But the prophets did not just spread doom and gloom. Once the disasters had occurred as they foretold and many Hebrews had been taken into exile, the prophets offered a new message of hope. Fearful that the Hebrew exiles might accept the conqueror's gods out of desperation and despair, the prophets tried to kindle optimism by changing their basic message. Since the Hebrews had been punished for their sins and had repented of their evil ways, God would forgive them and extend his kindness again toward his chosen people. Israel, they proclaimed, would be reborn out of the ashes, a prophecy seemingly fulfilled in 538 B.C. when the Persians allowed the Hebrews to return to the kingdom of Judah and reestablish the Temple in the city of Jerusalem.

Out of the words of the prophets came new concepts that enriched the Hebrew tradition and Western civilization, including a notion of universalism and a yearning for social justice. Although Hebrew religious practices gave Jews a sense of separateness from other peoples, the prophets transcended this by embracing a concern for all humanity. All nations would someday come to the God of Israel: "all the earth shall worship you." A universal community of all people under God would someday be established by Israel's effort. This vision encompassed the elimination of war and the establishment of peace for all the nations of the world. In the words of the prophet Isaiah: "He will judge between the nations and will settle disputes for many people. They will beat their swords into plowshares and their spears into pruning hooks. Nation will not take up sword against nation, nor will they train for war anymore."[5]

The change in Israel's social structure from a classless tribal society to a monarchical state with class differences produced outcries by the prophets against social injustice. They condemned the rich for causing the poor to suffer, denounced luxuries as worthless, and threatened Israel with prophecies of dire punishments for these sins. God's command was to live justly, share with

The Hebrew Prophets: Micah, Isaiah, and Amos

The Hebrew prophets warned the Hebrew people that they must obey God's commandments or face being punished for breaking their covenant with God. These selections from the prophets Micah, Isaiah, and Amos make clear that God's punishment would fall upon the Hebrews for their sins. Even the Assyrians, as Isaiah indicated, would be used as God's instrument to punish them.

Micah 6: 9–16

Listen! The Lord is calling to the city—and to fear your name is wisdom—"Heed the rod and the One who appointed it. Am I still to forget, O wicked house, your ill-gotten treasures. . .? Shall I acquit a man with dishonest scales, with a bag of false weights? Her rich men are violent; her people are liars and their tongues speak deceitfully. Therefore, I have begun to destroy you, to ruin you because of your sins. You will eat but not be satisfied; your stomach will still be empty. You will store up but save nothing, because what you save I will give to the sword. You will plant but not harvest: you will press olives but not use the oil on yourselves, you will crush grapes but not drink the wine. . . .Therefore I will give you over to ruin and your people to derision; you will bear the scorn of the nations.

Isaiah 10: 1–6

Woe to those who make unjust laws, to those who issue oppressive decrees, to deprive the poor of their rights and withhold justice from the oppressed of my people, making their prey and robbing the fatherless. What will you do on the day of reckoning, when disaster comes from afar? To whom will you run for help? Where will you leave your riches? Nothing will remain but to cringe among the captives or fall among the slain. Yet for all this, his anger is not turned away, his hand is still upraised. "Woe to the Assyrian, the rod of my anger, in whose hand is the club of my wrath! I send him against a godless nation, I dispatch him against a people who anger me, to seize loot and snatch plunder, and to trample them down like mud in the streets."

Amos 3: 1–2

Hear this word the Lord has spoken against you, O people of Israel—against the whole family I brought up out of Egypt: "You only have I chosen of all the families of the earth; therefore, I will punish you for all your sins."

one's neighbors, care for the poor and the unfortunate, and act with compassion. When God's command was not followed, the social fabric of the community was threatened. These proclamations by Israel's prophets became a source for Western ideals of social justice, even if they have never been very perfectly realized.

UNIQUENESS OF THE HEBREW RELIGION IN THE NEAR EAST

The Hebrew religion was unique compared to the religions of other people in the ancient Near East. The Hebrews' belief that there is only one God for all peoples (a true monotheism) most dramatically separates them from all the others. But the Hebrews also differed in other significant ways. In virtually every religion in the ancient Near East, priests alone (and occasionally rulers) had access to the gods and their desires. In the Hebrew tradition, God's wishes, although communicated to the people through a series of special holy men, had all been written down. No Jewish spiritual leader could claim that he alone knew God's will. It was accessible to anyone who could read Hebrew. Judaism was a religion initially of the spoken word and eventually of the written word. Finally, although the Hebrew prophets eventually developed a sense of universalism, the demands of the Hebrew religion (the need to obey their God) encouraged a separation between Jews and their non-Jewish neighbors. Unlike most other peoples of the Near East, Jews could not simply be amalgamated into a community by accepting the gods of their conquerors and their neighbors. To remain faithful to the demands of their God, they might even have to refuse loyalty to political leaders.

The Social Structure of the Hebrews

Originally, the Hebrews had been organized along tribal lines. As they settled in Palestine, tribal organization broke down, and a new social structure had evolved by the time of the monarchy as the Hebrews settled in towns and villages. Although historians warn that the

Hebrews did not develop social classes in the modern sense of self-conscious groups opposed to one another, there were conspicuous "divisions of the population."

The "men of rank and influence" formed a special group of considerable importance in Hebrew society. This group included officials of the king, military officers, civil officials, and governors. Although simply servants to the kings, they held a privileged position in the society at large. These men of position, who were often synonymous with the heads of the great families, were most numerous in the capital cities, Samaria and Jerusalem. The common people, sometimes called "people of the land," remained a body of free people having basic civil rights. Their livelihood came mostly from the land and from various crafts. These peasants and craftsmen sold their own produce and products directly to buyers in markets in their local town or village squares, thus eliminating middlemen or traders. There was no real merchant class in ancient Israel. Commerce was carried on by foreigners, such as the Phoenicians. Not until the Diaspora, when Jews became scattered throughout the ancient world after their exile to Babylon, did they become merchants.

As was customary in the ancient Near East, Hebrews possessed slaves. Hebrew law permitted Hebrews to buy both male and female slaves of foreign birth or children of resident aliens. Hebrews themselves could be enslaved to other Hebrews, but only temporarily: "If you buy a Hebrew servant, he is to serve you for six years. But in the seventh year, he shall go free, without paying anything."[6] When Hebrews were enslaved, it was usually because they or a relative had been too poor to repay a debt. Thieves who could not repay what they had stolen were also sold as slaves to compensate the victim.

The number of domestic slaves in ancient Israel seems small, especially in comparison to later Greece and Rome. A family of substance might have one or two. Although slaves belonged to their masters and could be used as they wished, Hebrew law afforded slaves some protection. If the owner caused bodily injury, the slave would be freed. If a slave was beaten to death, the owner would be punished. Domestic slaves were usually regarded as part of the family and were protected and cared for accordingly. There are even examples of slaves inheriting their master's estate or marrying into a family and gaining freedom as a result.

The state also possessed slaves, who were obtained primarily as prisoners of war. These slaves either worked in the temples or for the kings. Solomon, for example, used slaves in mines, his building projects, and the big commercial and industrial enterprises run by the royal authority.

The family was the central social institution in Hebrew life and consisted of those connected by common blood and a common living place. A family living in one house could comprise husband and wife, married sons and their wives, and their children. The Hebrew family was patriarchal. The husband-father was master of his wife and possessed absolute authority over his children, including the power of life and death. The closeness of family ties was a remnant of tribal life, but the shift to a settled life in towns and villages affected the family. The old patriarchal system broke down. Fewer people could remain in one small house. Married sons now moved out of their father's house and into their own. Moreover, by the eighth century B.C., wage earners replaced domestic slaves and servants, and the old extended family with master, children, grandchildren, and servants living in one house passed away. These changes also weakened the authority of the head of the family. Fathers no longer had the power of life and death over their children, and the right of judgment for children's misdeeds was put in the hands of the town elders.

Marriage was an important aspect of Hebrew family life. In ancient Israel, under the judges and the monarchy, polygamy was an accepted form of marriage, especially for kings and wealthier citizens. Hebrew law limited kings to eighteen wives and subjects to four. In practice, only kings could afford a large harem. When others had more than one wife, it was usually because they desired more children; the first wife, for example, might be unable to have children or have produced only daughters.

Many Hebrews, however, believed that monogamy was the preferred form of marriage. Wives were honored for their faithfulness and dedication to their husbands. The Book of Proverbs in the Hebrew Bible provides a picture of what Hebrews considered a perfect wife:

> A wife of noble character who can find? She is worth far
> more than rubies.
> Her husband has full confidence in her and lacks nothing
> of value.
> She brings him good, not harm, all the days of her life.
> She selects wool and flax and works with eager hands.
> She is like the merchant ships, bringing her food from afar.
> She gets up while it is still dark; she provides food for her
> family and portions for her servant girls.
> She considers a field and buys it; out of her earnings she
> plants a vineyard.

*She sets about her work vigorously; her arms are strong for
  her tasks.*

*She sees that her trading is profitable, and her lamp does
  not go out at night.*

*In her hand she holds the distaff and grasps the spindle
  with her fingers.*

*She opens her arms to the poor and extends her hands to
  the needy. . . .*

*She makes linen garments and sells them, and supplies the
  merchants with sashes.*

*She is clothed with strength and dignity; she can laugh at
  the days to come.*

*She speaks with wisdom, and faithful instruction is on her
  tongue.*

*She watches over the affairs of her household, and does not
  eat the bread of idleness.*

*Her children arise and call her blessed; her husband also,
  and he praises her.*[7]

Women were greatly valued, but their work was obviously never done.

It should not surprise us to learn that a married woman was subject to her husband's authority. Unlike the Mesopotamians, the Hebrews did not develop the custom of a dowry from the bride's parents. They did, however, have a practice whereby the bridegroom's family paid a sum of money to the bride's family, not as a purchase price as such, but apparently as compensation to the family for the loss of their daughter. A married woman left her parents' home, lived with her husband's family, and became a member of their clan. Her children also belonged to the husband's clan.

Since boys and girls were married at a relatively young age, parents took the responsibility for matchmaking. Although marriages occurred between persons of different families and even with foreign women, it was customary to find marriage partners within one's own clan or extended family. Indeed, marriages between first cousins were frequently arranged.

In ancient Israel, divorce was readily available for the husband, but not for the wife. Although divorce was easy—a husband simply drew up a divorce writ—there is no evidence to suggest that it was very common. In any case, infidelity, could be costly. A man committed no crime by having sex with prostitutes, but adultery with a married woman was punishable by death. Wives were expected to remain faithful to their husbands.

The primary goal of marriage was to produce children. They were the "crown of man," and sons, in particular, were desired. Daughters would eventually leave the family house, but sons carried on the family line. Mothers were in charge of the early education of children, especially in regard to basic moral principles. As boys matured, their fathers took over responsibility for their education, which remained largely informal. This included religious instruction as well as general education for life. The rod was not spared as a matter of principle. Since trades were usually hereditary, fathers also provided their sons' occupational education. As one rabbi stated, "He who does not teach his son a useful trade is bringing him up to be a thief."[8] Additional education for boys came from priests, whose sacred mission was to instruct people in the Torah, or law code of ancient Israel. An organized school system was not established until much later, possibly in the second century B.C. The only education girls received was from their mothers who taught them the basic fundamentals of how to be good wives, mothers, and housekeepers.

The Neighbors of the Hebrews

The Hebrews were not the only people who settled in the area of Palestine. The Philistines, who invaded from the sea, established five towns on the coastal plain of Palestine. They settled down as farmers and eventually entered into conflict with the Hebrews. While the Philistines were newcomers to the area, the Phoenicians had resided there for some time, but now found themselves with a new independence. A Semitic-speaking people, the Phoenicians resided along the Mediterranean coast on a narrow band of land 120 miles long. They had rebuilt their major cities, Byblos, Tyre, and Sidon, after destruction by the Sea Peoples. Their newfound political independence helped the Phoenicians expand the trade that was already the foundation of their prosperity. In fact, Byblos had been the principal distribution center for Egyptian papyrus outside Egypt (the Greek word for book, *biblos*, is derived from the name Byblos).

The chief cities of Phoenicia—Byblos, Tyre, and Sidon—were ports on the eastern Mediterranean, but they also served as distribution centers for the lands to the east in Mesopotamia. The Phoenicians themselves produced a number of goods for foreign markets, including purple dye, glass, wine, and lumber from the famous cedars of Lebanon. In addition, the Phoenicians improved their ships and became the great international sea traders of the ancient Near East. They chartered new routes, not only in the Mediterranean, but also in the Atlantic Ocean where they reached Britain and sailed south along the west coast of Africa. The Phoenicians

✦ **Phoenician Plaque.** The Phoenicians were a Semitic-speaking people dwelling in ancient Palestine who became the predominant sea traders of the ancient Near East. Ivory was one of the favorite materials of Phoenician artists of the eighth and ninth centuries B.C. This ivory plaque inlaid with glass stones shows a lioness attacking a slave boy.

established a number of colonies in the western Mediterranean, including settlements in southern Spain, Sicily, and Sardinia. Most of the Phoenician colonies were trading stations, not places where Phoenicians brought their families and settled permanently. A major exception was Carthage, the Phoenicians' most famous colony, located on the North African coast.

Culturally, the Phoenicians are best known as transmitters. Instead of using pictographs or signs to represent whole words and syllables as the Mesopotamians and Egyptians did, the Phoenicians simplified their writing by using twenty-two different signs to represent the sounds of their speech. These twenty-two characters or letters could be used to spell out all the words in the Phoenician language. Although the Phoenicians were not the only people to invent an alphabet, theirs would have special significance because it was eventually passed on to the Greeks. From the Greek alphabet was derived the Roman alphabet that we still use today. The Phoenicians achieved much while independent, but they ultimately fell subject to the Assyrians, Chaldeans, and Persians.

The Assyrian Empire

The existence of independent states in Palestine was only possible because of the power vacuum existing in the ancient Near East after the destruction of the Hittite kingdom and the weakening of the Egyptian empire. But this condition did not last, as new empires soon arose and came to dominate vast stretches of the ancient Near East. The first of these empires emerged in Assyria, an area whose location on the upper Tigris River brought it into both cultural and political contact with Mesopotamia.

Although close to Mesopotamia, Assyria, with its hills and adequate, if not ample, rainfall, had a different terrain and climate. The Assyrians were a Semitic-speaking people, akin to the Akkadians in Mesopotamia. For much of their early history, the Assyrians were vassals of foreign rulers. From about 1650 to 1360 B.C., the Hurrian kingdom of Mitanni dominated Assyria (see Chapter 1). The Assyrians finally became independent when the Hittites destroyed the kingdom of Mitanni; we read in Hittite documents from about 1360 B.C. of the emergence of the "king of the land of Assyria." For the next 250 years, the Assyrians experienced alternate expansion and decline until the reassertion of Assyrian power under Tiglath-pileser I (c. 1115–1077 B.C.). He was a brutal conqueror whose policy of deliberate terror set a pattern for later Assyrian rulers.

The Assyrian empire created by Tiglath-pileser was unable to maintain its strength after his death. A new phase of expansion did not begin until the ninth century with the conquests of Shalmaneser III (858–824 B.C.), who marched westward into Palestine and southward into Babylonia. Yet Assyrian power did not go unchallenged. The almost continuous warfare on these new frontiers did not end until Assyria reestablished control over Babylonia and completely subdued Palestine. By 700 B.C., the Assyrian Empire had reached the height of its power and included Mesopotamia, Elam, parts of the Iranian plateau, sections of Asia Minor, Syria, Palestine, and Egypt down to Thebes.

Ashurbanipal (669–626 B.C.) was one of the strongest Assyrian rulers, but it was already becoming apparent during his reign that the Assyrian Empire was greatly overextended. Other problems plagued the empire as well. Internal strife intensified as powerful Assyrian nobles gained control of vast territories and waged their own private military campaigns. Moreover, subject peoples greatly resented Assyrian rule. The hatred that the Babylonians felt after the brutal Assyrian sack of the city of Babylon in 689 B.C., for example, led them to rebel during the reign of Ashurbanipal. As Ashurbanipal became mired in Babylonian affairs, Egypt freed itself from Assyrian control. Soon after Ashurbanipal's reign, the Assyrian Empire began to disintegrate rapidly. The capital city of Nineveh fell to a coalition of Chaldeans and Medes (see The Neo-Babylonian Empire later in this chapter) in 612 B.C., and in 605 B.C., the rest of the empire was finally divided between the coalition powers.

At its height, the Assyrian Empire was ruled by kings whose power was considered absolute. Officially, kings served as viceregents of the god Ashur, the chief Assyrian deity. But it is clear that by the first millennium B.C. Assyrian kings viewed themselves as sole rulers in their own right. Although the king was considered absolute, certain taboos conditioned the exercise of royal power. Normally, only the superintendent of the palace had direct access to his exalted majesty. Others could approach the king, but only if the astrological omens were favorable. Basically, omens, whether favorable or unfavorable, determined when government business could be carried on and international affairs pursued.

During its period of expansion, the Assyrian Empire came to be well organized. Especially by the eighth century, greater control over the resources of the empire had been put in the hands of the king by the development of new provincial arrangements. Governorships held by nobles on a hereditary basis were eliminated, and a new hierarchy of local officials, directly responsible to the king, was instituted. The Assyrians also developed an efficient system of communication to administer their empire more effectively. A network of posting stages that used relays of horses (mules or donkeys in mountainous terrain) to carry messages was established throughout the empire. The system was so effective that a provincial governor anywhere in the empire (except Egypt) could send a question and receive an answer from the king in his palace within a week. The Assyrians were also known for developing an efficient intelligence network. By using spies, they were able to gain inside information about places they planned to attack.

At the beginning of the first millennium B.C., the Assyrians had a reputation as a mighty military machine. In large part, this was because of the topography of the region. Assyria had no natural boundaries; its

✖ Map 2.2 The Assyrian and Neo-Babylonian Empires.

pasture lands lay open to invaders. After their experiences in the third and second millennia, the Assyrians felt the need for a strong military to protect themselves. To prevent invasions, they decided to expand into areas from which they traditionally had been attacked. That expansion, of course, led to a need for further expansion to protect the newly occupied territories. We could say that their quest for security led the Assyrians to a large empire. The Assyrian rulers claimed that their expansion was a divine mission; it was the will of their god Ashur.

The ability of the Assyrians to conquer and maintain an empire was due to a combination of factors. Over many years of practice, the Assyrians developed good military leaders and fighters. They were able to enlist and deploy troops numbering in the hundreds of thousands, although most campaigns were not on such a large scale. In 845 B.C., Shalmaneser III led an army of 120,000 men across the Euphrates on a campaign. Size alone was not decisive, however. The Assyrian army was extremely well organized and disciplined. It included a standing army of infantrymen as its core, accompanied by cavalrymen and horse-drawn war chariots that were used as mobile platforms for shooting arrows. The army also included specialized units, such as a pioneer corps

◆ **Ashurbanipal Destroys an Elamite City.** Assyria was the first great empire to gain control over the ancient Near East in the first millennium B.C. The Assyrians had a highly efficient and well-organized military machine, capable of fighting under a variety of conditions. This relief depicts the army of King Ashurbanipal sacking an Elamite city in 647 B.C. Shown at the top are Assyrian soldiers destroying the city walls while below soldiers carry off the spoils of war.

The Assyrian Military Machine

The Assyrians won a reputation for having a mighty military machine. They were able to use a variety of military tactics and were successful whether they were employing guerrilla warfare, fighting set battles, or laying siege to cities. In these three selections, Assyrian kings describe their military conquests.

King Sennacherib (704–681 B.C.) Describes a Battle with the Elamites in 691

At the command of the god Ashur, the great Lord, I rushed upon the enemy like the approach of a hurricane. . . . I put them to rout and turned them back. I transfixed the troops of the enemy with javelins and arrows. . . . I cut their throats like sheep. . . .My prancing steeds, trained to harness, plunged into their welling blood as into a river; the wheels of my battle chariot were bespattered with blood and filth. I filled the plain with the corpses of their warriors like herbage. . . .As to the sheikhs of the Chaldeans, panic from my onslaught overwhelmed them like a demon. They abandoned their tents and fled for their lives, crushing the corpses of their troop as they went. . . . In their terror they passed scalding urine and voided their excrement into their chariots.

King Sennacherib Describes His Siege of Jerusalem (701 B.C.)

As to Hezekiah, the Jew, he did not submit to my yoke, I laid siege to 46 of his strong cities, walled forts and to the countless small villages in their vicinity, and conquered them by means of well-stamped earth-ramps, and battering-rams brought thus near to the walls combined with the attack by foot soldiers, using mines, breeches as well as sapper work. I drove out of them 200,150 people, young and old, male and female, horses, mules, donkeys, camels, big and small cattle beyond counting, and considered them booty. Himself I made a prisoner in Jerusalem, his royal residence, like a bird in a cage. I surrounded him with earthwork in order to molest those who were leaving his city's gate.

King Ashurbanipal (669–626 B.C.) Describes His Treatment of Conquered Babylon

I tore out the tongues of those whose slanderous mouths had uttered blasphemies against my god Ashur and had plotted against me, his god-fearing prince; I defeated them completely. The others, I smashed alive with the very same statues of protective deities with which they had smashed my own grandfather Sennacherib—now finally as a belated burial sacrifice for his soul. I fed their corpses, cut into small pieces, to dogs, pigs, . . . vultures, the birds of the sky and also to the fish of the ocean. After I had performed this and thus made quiet again the hearts of the great gods, my lords, I removed the corpses of those whom the pestilence had felled, whose leftovers after the dogs and pigs had fed on them were obstructing the streets, filling the places of Babylon, and of those who had lost their lives through the terrible famine.

that made smooth tracks for the wagons and chariots and constructed pontoon bridges over rivers for the movement of troops. Other specialized military personnel included language interpreters, intelligence officers, and scribes who kept a record of the booty. Moreover, the Assyrians had the advantage of having the first large armies equipped with iron weapons. The Hittites (see Chapter 1) had been the first to develop iron metallurgy, but iron came to be used extensively only after new methods for hardening it came into common use after 1000 B.C.

Another factor in the army's success was its ability to use different kinds of military tactics (see the box above).

The Assyrian army was capable of fighting guerrilla warfare in the mountains and set battles on open ground as well as laying siege to cities. The Assyrians were especially renowned for their siege warfare. They made efficient use of heavy, wheeled siege towers and armored battering rams. Sappers were organized to dig tunnels to undermine the foundations of walls and cause them to collapse. The besieging Assyrian armies learned to cut off supplies so effectively that if a city did not fall to them, the inhabitants could be starved into submission.

A final factor in the effectiveness of the Assyrian military machine was its ability to create a climate of terror as an instrument of warfare. The Assyrians became famous for their terror tactics, although some historians believe their policies were no worse than other Near Eastern conquerors. As a matter of regular policy, the Assyrians laid waste the land in which they were fighting, smashing dams, looting and destroying towns, setting crops on fire, and cutting down trees, particularly fruit trees. The Assyrians were especially known for committing atrocities on their captives. King Ashurnasirpal recorded this account of his treatment of prisoners:

> 3000 of their combat troops I felled with weapons. . . . Many of the captives taken from them I burned in a fire. Many I took alive; from some of these I cut off their hands to the wrist, from others I cut off their noses, ears, and fingers; I put out the eyes of many of the soldiers. . . . I burned their young men and women to death.

After conquering another city, the same king wrote: "I fixed up a pile of corpses in front of the city's gate. I flayed the nobles, as many as had rebelled, and spread their skins out on the piles. . . . I flayed many within my land and spread their skins out on the walls."[9] (Obviously, not a king to play games with!) It should be noted that this policy of extreme cruelty to prisoners was not used against all enemies, but was primarily reserved for those who were already part of the empire and then rebelled against Assyrian rule.

Many prisoners of newly conquered territories were deported from their native lands to Assyria. They were generally well treated, since they were useful to the Assyrians. Usually, communities and families were deported en masse. They were sent to work as skilled labor in cities, to farm in rural areas, and to repopulate sections that had been decimated by warfare. It has been estimated that over a period of three centuries between four and five million people were deported to Assyria, resulting in a population that was very racially and linguistically mixed. In fact, in some major Assyrian cities, ethnic Assyrians were a minority, overwhelmed by Aramaeans (a Semitic-speaking people who lived in what is now eastern Syria), Egyptians, Hebrews, Phoenicians, Medes, and others.

Assyrian Society and Culture

The Assyrians were not fearful of mixing with other peoples. In fact, Assyrian deportation policies created a polyglot society in which ethnic differences were not very important. What gave identity to the Assyrians themselves was their language, although even that was akin to that of their southern neighbors in Babylonia who also spoke a Semitic language. Religion was also a cohesive force. Assyria was literally, "the land of Ashur," a reference to its chief god. The king, as the human representative of the god Ashur, provided a final unifying focus.

Little is certain about Assyrian social stratification. By the end of the second millennium B.C., society was composed of two distinct groups, the free and nonfree (slave) with gradations of status among the free men. By the first millennium, however, it appears that royal officials, who owed their position to the favor of the king, made up the leading group of free men. Moreover, at the bottom of the social scale, the distinction between free and slave had become blurred because large numbers of peasants had lost their old land rights and had been reduced to serfdom.

Agriculture formed the principal basis of Assyrian life. Assyria was a land of farming villages with relatively few significant cities, especially in comparison to Mesopotamia. Unlike Mesopotamia, where farming required the minute organization of large numbers of people to control irrigation, Assyrian farms received sufficient moisture from regular rainfall.

Trade was second to agriculture in economic importance. Internal trade depended on a system that used metals, such as gold, silver, copper, and bronze, as a medium of exchange. Various agricultural products also served as a form of payment or exchange. Because of their geographical location, the Assyrians served as middlemen and participated in an international trade in which they imported timber, wine, and precious metals and stones while exporting textiles produced in palaces, temples, and private villas. In the first millennium, however, the levying of tribute from various parts of the empire diminished the need for international trade.

The culture of the Assyrian Empire was essentially hybrid in nature. The Assyrians assimilated much of Mesopotamian civilization and saw themselves as guardians of Sumerian and Babylonian culture. Ashurbanipal, for example, amassed a large library at Nineveh that included the available works of Mesopotamian history. Assyrian religion reflected this assimilation of other cultures as well. Although the Assyrians had their own national god Ashur as their chief deity, virtually all of their remaining gods and goddesses were Mesopotamian.

Among the best-known objects of Assyrian art are the relief sculptures found in the royal palaces in three of the Assyrian capital cities, Nimrud, Nineveh, and Khorsabad. These reliefs, which were begun during the

✦ **King Ashurbanipal's Lion Hunt.** This relief, sculptured on alabaster as a decoration for the northern palace in Nineveh, depicts King Ashurbanipal engaged in a lion hunt.

The relief sculpture, one of the best known forms of Assyrian art, ironically reached its high point under Ashurbanipal at the same time that the Assyrian Empire began to disintegrate.

reign of Ashurnasirpal in the ninth century and reached their high point in the reign of Ashurbanipal in the seventh century, depicted two different kinds of subject matter: ritual or ceremonial scenes revolving around the person of the king and scenes of hunting and war. The latter show realistic action scenes of the king and his warriors engaged in battle or hunting animals, especially lions. These reliefs depict a strongly masculine world where discipline, brute force, and toughness are the enduring values, indeed, the very values of the Assyrian military monarchy.

The Neo-Babylonian Empire

The Chaldeans, a Semitic-speaking people, had gained ascendancy in Babylonia by the seventh century and came to form the chief resistance to Assyrian control of Mesopotamia. The Chaldean king Nabopolassar (625–605 B.C.), who joined forces with the Medes to capture the Assyrian capital Nineveh in 612 B.C., was responsible for establishing a new Babylonian monarchy. But it was his son Nebuchadnezzar II (605–562 B.C.) who achieved the final defeat of the Assyrian Empire. Under his rule, the Chaldeans defeated Egypt to gain control of Syria and Palestine, destroyed Jerusalem, carried the Jews into exile in Babylon, and in the process regained for Babylonia a position as the leading power in the ancient Near East.

During Nebuchadnezzar's reign, Babylonia was renowned for a prosperity based upon lush agricultural lands, lucrative trade routes running through Mesopotamia, and industries, especially its much-desired textiles and metals. Nebuchadnezzar rebuilt Babylon as the center of his empire, giving it a reputation as one of the great cities of the ancient world. Babylon was surrounded by great walls, eight miles in length, encircled by a moat filled by the Euphrates River. The Ishtar Gate opened onto a Triumphal Way that led to the sacred precincts of Marduk, the chief Babylonian god. Babylon was adorned with temples and palaces; most famous of all were the Hanging Gardens, known as one of the Seven Wonders of the ancient world. These were supposedly built to satisfy Nebuchadnezzar's wife, a princess from the land of Media, who missed the mountains of her homeland. A series of terraces led to a plateau, an artificial mountain, at the top of which grew the lush gardens irrigated by water piped to the top. From a distance the gardens appeared to be suspended in air.

The splendor of the Neo-Babylonian Empire proved to be short-lived. Nabonidus (555–539 B.C.) was the last of the Chaldean dynasty. He had a great interest in history and encouraged scholars to collect Sumerian texts and study the Sumerian language. But his policies aroused considerable internal dissent. Among other things, Nabonidus tried to replace Marduk with the moon god Sin, an insult to the Babylonians. When Babylon fell to the Persian conqueror Cyrus in 539 B.C.,

✦ **Ishtar Gate of Babylon.** The Chaldeans formed the chief resistance to Assyrian control of Mesopotamia. Under Nebuchadnezzar II, the Chaldeans finally succeeded in destroying the Assyrian Empire. Nebuchadnezzar rebuilt Babylon as the center of his empire and adorned it with such architectural wonders as the Ishtar Gate, which opened onto the Triumphal Way. This picture shows the west wall of the inner gatehouse of the Ishtar Gate.

the Babylonians welcomed him as a liberator, clearly indicating their disaffection with Nabonidus's rule.

The Persian Empire

The Persians were an Indo-European–speaking people related to the Medes. Both peoples are first mentioned in Assyrian documents in the ninth century B.C. and probably formed part of the great waves of Indo-European migrations into the Mediterranean, the Near East, and India. The Persians lived to the southeast of the Medes, who occupied the western Iranian plateau south of the Caspian Sea. Although crops were grown, lack of moisture made these lands more suitable for pasture. The Medes, in particular, were famous throughout the Near East for the quality of the horses they bred. Primarily nomadic, both Medes and Persians were organized in tribes or clans. Both peoples were led by petty kings assisted by a group of warriors who formed a class of nobles. Their populations also included both free and unfree people who worked the land, craftsmen, and slaves.

By 735 B.C., the Medes had begun to form a confederation of the various tribes, and sometime at the beginning of the seventh century, they became unified under a monarchy. The Persians did likewise under the so-called Achaemenid dynasty established in Persis in

southern Iran. About fifty years later, the Persians were made subject to the Medes. The Medes now constituted a powerful state and joined the Babylonians in attacking the Assyrians. After the capture of Nineveh in 612 B.C., King Cyaxares established a Median empire.

Cyrus the Great (559–530 B.C.)

In 559 B.C., Cyrus became the leader of the Persians, united them under his rule, and went on the offensive against the Medes. In 550 B.C., he overcame the Median king Astyages and established Persian control over Media, making it the first Persian satrapy or province. The conquest of Media brought Cyrus into confrontation with the three surviving powers of the ancient Near East—Lydia, Babylonia, and Egypt. Only the last would escape his conquest.

In the northwest, the Halys River formed the boundary between the old Median empire Cyrus had subdued and the kingdom of Lydia under King Croesus, whose wealth was legendary. The defeat of the Medes by Cyrus led Croesus to attempt to recover his former lands east of the Halys River. Cyrus marched west to meet this challenge, defeated Croesus decisively in 547 B.C., and occupied the Lydian capital of Sardis. Lydia was made into another Persian satrapy. The conquest of Lydia in western Asia Minor brought the Persians into their first contact with the Greeks settled on the Ionian coast. The Greek city-states had been subjects of Lydia, but had been allowed to keep their own institutions and had grown rich from the commercial opportunities in Lydia. Cyrus's forces easily conquered the Ionian Greek city-states, which were then placed under the control of local tyrants loyal to Cyrus.

While a Persian army took care of the Ionian Greeks, Cyrus turned his attention eastward where he felt his power threatened by barbaric nomadic tribes. He subdued the eastern part of the Iranian plateau and then moved into Sogdia, a territory between the Oxus and Jaxartes Rivers. He even advanced into the western part of India. His eastern conquests doubled the territory, but not the wealth or population, of the growing Persian Empire. He did gain more soldiers, however, and was now able to turn on the powerful state to his south, the Neo-Babylonian Empire.

In 539 B.C., he entered Mesopotamia and easily captured Babylon (see the box on p. 55). The disgust of the Babylonians with their king Nabonidus led them to welcome Cyrus as a hero. Cyrus showed remarkable restraint and wisdom after his conquest. Babylonia was made into a Persian province under a Persian satrap, but

⋟ The Fall of Babylon ⋞

Under the Chaldeans, Babylon became the center of an empire and gained a reputation as one of the great cities of the ancient world. But the Neo-Babylonian Empire failed to last, and Babylon fell to the Persian forces under King Cyrus in 539 B.C. In his history of the Persian Wars, the ancient Greek historian Herodotus described how Cyrus supposedly captured Babylon.

Herodotus, *The Persian Wars*

Cyrus, with the first approach of the ensuing spring, marched forward against Babylon. The Babylonians, encamped without their walls, awaited his coming. A battle was fought at a short distance from the city, in which the Babylonians were defeated by the Persian king, whereupon they withdrew within their defenses. Here they shut themselves up, and made light of his siege, having laid in a store of provisions for many years in preparation against this attack; for when they saw Cyrus conquering nation after nation, they were convinced that he would never stop, and that their turn would come at last.

Cyrus was now reduced to great perplexity, as time went on and he made no progress against the place. In this distress either some one made the suggestion to him, or he thought himself of a plan, which he proceeded to put in execution. He placed a portion of his army at the point where the river enters the city and another body at the back of the place where it issues forth, with orders to march into the town by the bed of the stream, as soon as the water became shallow enough: he then himself drew off with the unwarlike portion of his host, and made for the place where Nitocris [supposedly a queen of Babylon] dug the basin for the river, where he did exactly what she had done formerly: he turned the Euphrates by a canal into the basin, which was then a marsh, on which the river sank to such an extent that the natural bed of the stream became fordable. Hereupon the Persians who had been left for the purpose at Babylon by the river-side entered the stream, which had now sunk so as to reach about midway up a man's thigh, and thus got into the town. Had the Babylonians been apprised of what Cyrus was about, or had they noticed their danger, they would not have allowed the entrance of the Persians within the city, which was what ruined them utterly, but would have made fast all the street-gates which gave upon the river, and mounting upon the walls along both sides of the stream, would so have caught the enemy as it were in a trap. But, as it was, the Persians came upon them by surprise and so took the city. Owing to the vast size of the place, the inhabitants of the central parts (as the residents at Babylon declare) long after the outer portions of the town were taken, knew nothing of what had chanced, but as they were engaged in a festival, continued dancing and revelling until they learned the capture but too certainly. Such, then, were the circumstances of the first taking of Babylon.

many government officials were kept in their positions. Cyrus took the title "King of All, Great King, Mighty King, King of Babylon, King of the Land of Sumer and Akkad, King of the Four Rims (of the Earth), the Son of Cambyses the Great King, King of Anshan,"[10] and insisted that he stood in the ancient, unbroken line of Babylonian kings. By appealing to the vanity of the Babylonians, he won their loyalty. Cyrus also undid the destructive work of Nabonidus. He returned the statues of gods that the Babylonian ruler had brought to Babylon from various cities and temples throughout Babylonia. Temples were restored and the rightful worship of Marduk was reestablished. Cyrus also issued an edict permitting the Jews, who had been brought to Babylon in the reign of Nebuchadnezzar, to return to Jerusalem with their sacred temple objects and to rebuild their Temple as well.

From 538 to 530 B.C., Cyrus consolidated his empire. Among other things, he constructed forts, especially in the northeastern part of his empire, to protect against nomadic incursions. It was in the northeast that he undertook his last campaign. In 530 B.C., he marched into the territory of the Massagetae where he was killed in battle.

To his contemporaries, Cyrus the Great was deserving of his epithet. The Greek historian Herodotus recounted that the Persians viewed him as a "father," a ruler who was "gentle, and procured them all manner of goods."[11] Certainly, Cyrus must have been an unusual ruler for his time, a man who demonstrated considerable wisdom and compassion in the conquest and organization of his empire. Cyrus attempted—successfully—to obtain the favor of the priesthoods in his conquered lands by restoring temples and permitting a wide degree of reli-

The Empires

The Assyrians	
Domination of Assyria by	
kingdom of Mitanni	c. 1650–1360 B.C.
Assyrian independence	c. 1360 B.C.
Tiglath-pileser I	c. 1115–1077 B.C.
Conquests of Shalmaneser III	858–824 B.C.
Height of power	700 B.C.
Ashurbanipal	669–626 B.C.
Capture of Nineveh	612 B.C.
Assyrian Empire destroyed	605 B.C.
The Chaldeans	
Ascendancy in Babylonia	600s B.C.
Nabopolassar establishes	
Neo-Babylonian monarchy	625–605 B.C.
Height of empire under	
King Nebuchadnezzar II	605–562 B.C.
Fall of Babylon	539 B.C.
The Persians	
Unification under	
Achaemenid dynasty	600s B.C.
Persian control over Medes	550 B.C.
Conquests of Cyrus the Great	559–530 B.C.
Cambyses and conquest	
of Egypt	530–522 B.C.
Reign of Dairus	521–486 B.C.

gious toleration. He won approval by using not only Persians, but also native peoples as government officials in their own states. He allowed Medes to be military commanders. Unlike the Assyrian rulers of an earlier empire, he had a reputation for mercy. Medes, Babylonians, and Jews all accepted him as their legitimate ruler. Some peoples, such as the Greeks and Jews, portrayed him as a great leader and peacemaker. Indeed, the Jews regarded him as the anointed one of God: "I am the Lord who says of Cyrus, 'He is my shepherd and will accomplish all that I please'; he will say of Jerusalem, 'Let it be rebuilt'; and of the temple, 'Let its foundations be laid.' This is what the Lord says to his anointed, to Cyrus, whose right hand I take hold of to subdue nations

before him."[12] Cyrus had a genuine respect for ancient civilizations—in building his palaces, he made use of Assyrian, Babylonian, Egyptian, and Lydian practices. Indeed, Cyrus had a sense that he was creating a "world empire" that included peoples who had ancient and venerable traditions and institutions.

Expanding the Empire

In 538 B.C., Cyrus had installed his son Cambyses as king in Babylon while he returned to the Persian homeland. Upon his father's death in 530 B.C., Cambyses took over power as the Great King. Four years later, he undertook the invasion of Egypt, the only kingdom in the Near East not yet brought under Persian control. Aided by the Phoenician fleet, he defeated and captured the pharaoh and the Egyptian forces. Egypt was made into a satrapy with Memphis as its capital. In the summer of 525 B.C., Cambyses took the title of pharaoh.

After the death of Cambyses in 522, Darius, a young member of a collateral branch of the Achaemenid ruling family, emerged as Great King after a year of intense civil war. Once in charge, Darius (521–486 B.C.) turned to the task of strengthening the empire. He codified Egyptian law and built a canal to link the Red Sea and the Mediterranean. A campaign into western India led to the creation of a new Persian province that extended to the Indus River. Darius also moved into Europe proper conquering Thrace and making the Macedonian king a vassal. A revolt of the Ionian Greek cities in 499 B.C. resulted in temporary freedom for these communities in western Asia Minor. Aid from the Greek mainland, most notably from Athens, led to a brief invasion of Lydia by the Ionians and the burning of Sardis, center of the Lydian satrapy. This event led to Darius's involvement with the mainland Greeks. After reestablishing control of the Ionian Greek cities, Darius undertook an invasion of the Greek mainland, which culminated in the famous Athenian victory in the Battle of Marathon in 490 B.C. (see Chapter 3).

Governing the Empire

Although the Greeks viewed their struggle with the Persians as crucial to their survival, the Persians saw it as a minor episode on their western frontier. By the reign of Darius, the Persians had created the largest empire the world had yet seen. It included not only all the old centers of power in the Near East, Egypt, Mesopotamia, and Assyria, but also extended into Thrace and Asia Minor in the west and into India in the east.

For administrative purposes, the empire had been divided into approximately twenty provinces called satrapies. Each province was ruled by a governor or satrap, literally a "protector of the Kingdom." Although Darius had not introduced the system of satrapies, he did see that it was organized more rationally. He also created a sensible system for calculating the tribute that each satrapy owed to the central government. Instead of contributions based on local practices, Darius determined the levies on the basis of the productive capacity of each satrapy, resulting in a fixed annual sum. Satrapies also provided soldiers for the royal army. Satraps had both civil and military duties. They collected tributes, were responsible for justice and security, raised military levies, and normally commanded the military forces within their satrapies. In terms of real power, the satraps were miniature kings who established courts imitative of the Great King's.

From the time of Darius on, satraps were men of Persian descent. The major satrapies were given to princes of the king's family, and their position became essentially hereditary. The minor satrapies were placed in the hands of Persian nobles. Their offices, too, tended to pass from father to son. The hereditary nature of the governors' offices made it necessary to provide some checks on their power. Consequently, some historians think that there were officials at the satrapal courts, such as secretaries and generals in charge of the garrison, who reported directly to the Great King, keeping him informed of what was going on within the various satrapal governments. It is also possible that an official known as the "king's eye" or "king's messenger" made annual inspections of each satrapy.

An efficient system of communication was considered crucial to sustain the Persian Empire. Roads were maintained to facilitate the rapid transit of military and government personnel. One in particular, the so-called Royal Road, stretched from Sardis, the center of Lydia in Asia Minor, to Susa, the chief capital of the Persian Empire. Like the Assyrians, the Persians established

✖ Map 2.3 The Persian Empire at the Time of Darius.

staging posts equipped with fresh horses for the king's messengers. Moreover, trunk roads off the Royal Road linked important cities like Memphis to the capital at Susa.

In this vast administrative system, the Persian king occupied an exalted position. Although not considered to be a god as was the Egyptian pharaoh, he was nevertheless the elect one or regent of the Persian god Ahuramazda (see Persian Religion later in this chapter). All subjects were the king's servants, and he was the source of all justice, possessing the power of life and death over everyone. Persian kings were largely secluded and not easily available. They resided in a series of splendid palaces. Darius especially was a palace builder on a grand scale. His description of the construction of a palace in the chief Persian capital of Susa demonstrated what a truly international empire Persia was:

> This is the . . . palace which at Susa I built. From afar its ornamentation was brought. . . . The cedar timber was brought from a mountain named Lebanon; the Assyrians brought it to Babylon, and from Babylon the Carians and Ionians brought it to Susa. Teakwood was brought from Gandara and from Carmania. The gold which was used here was brought from Sardis and from Bactria. The stone—lapis lazuli and carnelian—was brought from Sogdiana. . . . The silver and copper were brought from Egypt. The ornamentation with which the wall was adorned was brought from Ionia. The ivory was brought from Ethiopia, from India, and from Arachosia. The stone pillars were brought from . . . Elam. The artisans who dressed the stone were Ionians and Sardians. The goldsmiths who wrought the gold were Medes and Egyptians. . . . Those who worked the baked brick (with figures) were Babylonians. The men who adorned the wall were Medes and Egyptians. At Susa here a splendid work was ordered; very splendid did it turn out.[13]

But Darius was unhappy with Susa. He did not really consider it his homeland, and it was oppressively hot in the summer months. He built another residence at Persepolis, a new capital located to the east of the old one and at a higher elevation.

The policies of Darius also tended to widen the gap between the king and his subjects. As the Great King himself said of all his subjects: "what was said to them by me, night and day it was done."[14] Over a period of time, the Great Kings in their greed came to hoard immense quantities of gold and silver in the various treasuries located in the capital cities. Both their hoarding of wealth and their later overtaxation of their subjects are seen as crucial factors in the ultimate weakening of the Persian Empire (see the box on p. 59).

In its heyday, however, the empire stood supreme, and much of its power depended upon the military. By the time of Darius, the Persian monarchs had created a standing army of professional soldiers. This army was truly international in character, composed of contingents from the various peoples who made up the empire.

✦ **Darius, the Great King.** Darius ruled the Persian Empire from 521 to 486 B.C. He is shown here on his throne in Persepolis, a new capital city that he built. In his right hand, Darius holds the royal staff. In his left hand, he grasps a lotus blossom with two buds, a symbol of royalty.

A Dinner of the Persian King

The Persian kings lived in luxury as a result of their conquests and ability to levy taxes from their conquered subjects. In this selection we read a description of how a Persian king dined with his numerous guests.

Athenaeus, *The Deipnosophists*, IV: 145–46

Heracleides of Cumae, author of the *Persian History* writes in the second book of the work entitled *Equipment*: "All who attend upon the Persian kings when they dine first bathe themselves and then serve in white clothes, and spend nearly half the day on preparations for the dinner. Of those who are invited to eat with the king, some dine outdoors, in full sight of anyone who wishes to look on; others dine indoors in the king's company. Yet even these do not eat in his presence, for there are two rooms opposite each other, in one of which the king has his meal, in the other the invited guests. The king can see them through the curtain at the door, but they cannot see him. Sometimes, however, on the occasion of a public holiday, all dine in a single room with the king, in the great hall. And whenever the king commands a symposium [drinking-bout following the dinner] which he does often, he has about a dozen companions at the drinking. When they have finished dinner, that is the king by himself, the guests in the other room, these fellow-drinkers are summoned by one of the eunuchs; and entering they drink with him, though even they do not have the same wine; moreover, they sit on the floor, while he reclines on a couch supported by feet of gold, and they depart after having drunk to excess. In most cases the king breakfasts and dines alone, but sometimes his wife and some of his sons dine with him. And throughout the dinner his concubines sing and play the lyre; one of them is the soloist, the others sing in chorus. And so, Heracleides continues, the 'king's dinner,' as it is called, will appear prodigal to one who merely hears about it, but when one examines it carefully it will be found to have been got up with economy and even with parsimony; and the same is true of the dinners among other Persians in high station. For one thousand animals are slaughtered daily for the king; these comprise horses, camels, oxen, asses, deer, and most of the small animals; many birds are also consumed, including Arabian ostriches—and the creature is large—geese, and cocks. And of all these only moderate portions are served to each of the king's guests, and each of them may carry home whatever he leaves untouched at the meal. But the greater part of these meats and other foods are taken out into the courtyard for the body-guard and light-armed troopers maintained by the king; there they divide all the half-eaten remnants of meat and bread and share them in equal portions. . . ."

At its core was a cavalry force of 10,000 and an elite infantry force of 10,000 Medes and Persians known as the Immortals because they were never allowed to fall below 10,000 in number. When one was killed, he was immediately replaced. These Immortals enjoyed special privileges. When out on a campaign, they were accompanied by their concubines and servants in wagons. Their own special food was brought along on camels, which the Persians used as pack animals. On a major campaign, the size of the Persian army could be enormous.

The Persians made effective use of their cavalry, especially for operating behind enemy lines and breaking up lines of communication. When the army fought on level ground, the cavalry would ride up near the enemy lines, shoot their arrows, throw their spears, and then wheel away before they could be harmed. The infantry were armed with wicker shields, spears, and bows and arrows. Generally, the infantry advanced on the enemy, set up their wicker shields as a protective barrier, and then fired arrows at the enemy from behind them. Not until the arrows were used up did they engage in hand-to-hand combat. The Persian navy consisted of ships from subject states, including the Phoenicians, Egyptians, Anatolians, and Ionian Greeks.

Persian Religion

Of all the Persians' cultural contributions, the most original was their religion. The popular religion of the Iranians before the advent of Zoroastrianism in the sixth century focused on the worship of the powers of nature, such as the sun, moon, fire, and winds. Mithra was an especially popular god of light and war who came to be viewed as a sun god. The people worshiped and sacrificed to these powers of nature with the aid of priests, known as Magi.

Zoroaster was a semilegendary figure who, according to Persian tradition, was born in 660 B.C. After a period of wandering and solitude, he experienced revelations that caused him to be revered as a prophet of the "true religion." It is difficult to know what Zoroaster's original teachings were since the sacred book of Zoroastrianism, the *Zend Avesta*, was not written down until the third century A.D. Scholars believe, however, that the earliest section of the *Zend Avesta*, known as the *Yasna*, consisting of seventeen hymns or gathas, contains the actual writings of Zoroaster. This enables us to piece together his message.

Zoroaster did not introduce a new god but taught that Ahuramazda, who had long been one of the Iranians' deities, was the only god and that his religion was the

✦ **Archers of the Persian Guard.** One of the main pillars supporting the Persian Empire was the military. This frieze, composed of enamel brick, depicts members of the famous infantry force known as the Immortals, so-called because their number was never allowed to drop below 10,000. Those killed would be replaced immediately. They carry the standard lance and bow and arrow of the infantry.

only perfect one. Ahuramazda (the "Wise Lord") was the supreme deity who brought all things into being:

This I ask of You, O Ahuramazda; answer me well:
Who at the Creation was the first father of Justice?—
Who assigned their path to the sun and the stars?—
Who decreed the waxing and waning of the moon, if it
  was not You?— . . .
Who has fixed the earth below, and the heaven above with
  its clouds that it might not be moved?—
Who has appointed the waters and the green things upon
  the earth?—
Who has harnessed to the wind and the clouds their
  steeds?— . . .
Thus do I strive to recognize in You, O Wise One,
Together with the Holy Spirit, the Creator of all things.[15]

According to Zoroaster, Ahuramazda also possessed abstract qualities or states that all humans should aspire to, such as Good Thought, Right, and Piety. Although Ahuramazda was supreme, he was not unopposed. Right is opposed by the Lie, Truth by Falsehood, Life by Death. At the beginning of the world, the good spirit of Ahuramazda was opposed by the evil spirit (in later Zoroastrianism, the evil spirit is identified with Ahriman). Although it appears that Zoroaster saw it as simply natural that where there is good, there will be evil, later followers had a tendency to make these abstractions concrete and overemphasize the reality of an evil spirit. Humans also played a role in this cosmic struggle between good and evil. Ahuramazda, the creator, gave all humans free will and the power to choose between right and wrong. The good man chooses the right way of Ahuramazda. Zoroaster taught that there would be an end to the struggle between good and evil. Ahuramazda would eventually triumph, and at the last judgment at the end of the world, the final separation of good and evil would occur. Zoroaster also provided for individual judgment as well. Each soul faced a final evaluation of its actions. If a person had performed good deeds, he or she would achieve paradise, the "House of Song" or the "Kingdom of Good Thought"; if evil deeds, then the soul would be thrown into an abyss, the "House of Worst Thought," where it would experience future ages of darkness, torment, and misery.

The spread of Zoroastrianism was due to its acceptance by the Great Kings of Persia. The inscriptions of Darius make clear that he believed Ahuramazda was the only god. Although he mentions "other gods that are," he gives them no role whatever in the scheme of things.

Although Darius himself may have been a monotheist, as the kings and Magi, or priests, of Persia propagated Zoroaster's teachings on Ahuramazda, dramatic changes occurred. Zoroastrianism lost its monotheistic emphasis, and the old nature worship resurfaced. Hence, Persian religion returned to polytheism with Ahuramazda becoming only the chief of a number of gods of light. Mithra, the sun god, became a helper of Ahuramazda and later, in Roman times, the source of another religion. Persian kings were also very tolerant of other religions, and gods and goddesses of those religions tended to make their way into the Persian pantheon. Moreover, Zoroaster's teachings, as frequently happens to the ideas of founders of religions, acquired concrete forms that he had never originally intended. The struggle between good and evil was taken beyond the abstractions of Zoroaster into a strong ethical dualism. The spirit of evil became an actual being who had to be warded off by the use of spells and incantations. Descriptions of the last judgment came to be filled with minute physical details. Some historians believe that Zoroastrianism, with its emphasis on good and evil, a final judgment, and individual judgment of souls, had an impact on Christianity, a religion that eventually surpassed it in significance.

Conclusion

Around 1200 B.C., the decline of the Hittites and Egyptians had created a power vacuum that allowed a number of small states to emerge and flourish temporarily. All of them were eventually overshadowed by the rise of the great empires of the Assyrians, Chaldeans, and Persians. The Assyrian Empire was the first to unite almost all of the ancient Near East. Even larger, however, was the empire of the Great Kings of Persia. Although it owed much to the administrative organization created by the Assyrians, the Persian Empire had its own peculiar strengths. Persian rule was tolerant as well as efficient. Conquered peoples were allowed to keep their own religions, customs, and methods of doing business. The many years of peace that the Persian Empire brought to the Near East facilitated trade and the general well-being of its peoples. It is no wonder that many Near Eastern peoples expressed their gratitude for being subjects of the Great Kings of Persia.

The Hebrews were one of these peoples. They created no empire and were dominated by the Assyrians, Chaldeans, and Persians. Nevertheless, they left a spiritual legacy that influenced much of the later development of Western civilization. The evolution of Hebrew monotheism created in Judaism one of the world's greatest religions; it influenced the development of both Christianity and Islam. When we speak of the Judaeo-Christian heritage of Western civilization, we refer not only to the concept of monotheism, but also to ideas of

law, morality, and social justice that have become important parts of Western culture.

On the western fringes of the Persian Empire, another relatively small group of people, the Greeks, were creating cultural and political ideals that would also have an important impact on Western civilization. It is to the Greeks that we must now turn.

NOTES

1. Psalms 137: 1, 4–6.
2. Psalms 145: 8–9.
3. Psalms 121: 2–3.
4. Exodus 20: 13–15.
5. Isaiah 2: 4.
6. Exodus 21: 2.
7. Proverbs 31: 10–20, 24–28.
8. Quoted in Roland de Vaux, *Ancient Israel: Its Life and Institutions* (New York, 1961), p. 49.
9. Quoted in H. W. F. Saggs, *The Might That Was Assyria* (London, 1984), pp. 261–62.

10. Quoted in J. M. Cook, *The Persian Empire* (New York, 1983), p. 32.
11. Herodotus, *The Persian Wars*, trans. George Rawlinson (New York, 1942), p. 257.
12. Isaiah 44: 28; 45: 1.
13. Quoted in A. T. Olmstead, *History of the Persian Empire* (Chicago, 1948), p. 168.
14. Quoted in Cook, *The Persian Empire*, p. 76.
15. Yasna 44: 3–4, 7, as quoted in A. C. Bouquet, *Sacred Books of the World* (Harmondsworth, 1954), pp. 111–12.

SUGGESTIONS FOR FURTHER READING

There is an enormous literature on ancient Israel. Two good studies on the archaeological aspects are Y. Aharoni, *The Archaeology of the Land of Israel* (Philadelphia, 1982); and W. F. Albright, *The Archaeology of Palestine* (Harmondsworth, 1949). For historical narratives, see especially J. Bright, *A History of Israel*, 3d ed. (Philadelphia, 1981), a fundamental study; W. F. Albright, *The Biblical Period from Abraham to Ezra* (New York, 1963), a concise summary; J. M. Miller and J. H. Hayes, *A History of Ancient Israel and Judah* (Philadelphia, 1986); the well-done survey by M. Grant, *The History of Ancient Israel* (New York, 1984); and H. Shanks, *Ancient Israel: A Short History from Abraham to the Roman Destruction of the Temple* (Englewood Cliffs, N.J., 1988). For a new perspective, see N. P. Lemche, *Ancient Israel: A New History of Israelite Society* (Sheffield, 1988). A brief summary of Hebrew history and thought can be found in J. H. Hexter, *The Judaeo-Christian Tradition* (New York, 1966). R. de Vaux, *Ancient Israel: Its Life and*

Institutions (New York, 1961) is especially good on the social institutions of ancient Israel.

For general studies on the religion of the Hebrews, see Y. Kaufmann, *The Religion of Israel* (Chicago, 1960); and H. Ringgren, *Israelite Religion* (London, 1966). On the covenant and law, see D. R. Hillers, *Covenant: The History of a Biblical Idea* (Baltimore, 1969). The role of the prophets is examined in J. Lindblom, *Prophecy in Ancient Israel* (Oxford, 1962); and R. B. Y. Scott, *The Relevance of the Prophets* (New York, 1968).

For a good account of Phoenician domestic and overseas expansion, see D. Harden, *The Phoenicians*, rev. ed. (Harmondsworth, 1980). On the development of the alphabet, see D. Diringer, *The Alphabet* (London, 1975).

A detailed account of Assyrian political, economic, social, military, and cultural history is H. W. F. Saggs, *The Might That Was Assyria* (London, 1984). The same author has also written an account of daily life entitled *Everyday Life in Babylonia and Assyria* (London, 1965).

A. T. Olmstead, *History of Assyria* (Chicago, 1975) is a basic survey of the Assyrian Empire. Information from the Assyrians themselves can be found in A. Grayson, *Assyrian and Babylonian Chronicles* (New York, 1975). On one aspect of Assyrian culture, see R. D. Barnett, *Assyrian Sculpture* (Toronto, 1975). The Neo-Babylonian Empire can be examined in J. Oates, *Babylon* (London, 1979); and H. W. F. Saggs, *Babylonians* (Norman, Okla., 1995).

The classic work on the Persian Empire is A. T. Olmstead, *History of the Persian Empire* (Chicago, 1948), but a recent work by J. M. Cook, *The Persian Empire* (New York, 1983), provides new material and fresh interpretations. Also of value are B. Dicks, *The Ancient Persians* (Newton Abbott, 1979); R. Frye, *The Heritage of Persia* (Cleveland, 1963); and W. Cullican, *The Medes and the Persians* (New York, 1965). On the history of Zoroastrianism, see especially R. C. Zaehner, *The Dawn and Twilight of Zoroastrianism* (London, 1961). Also helpful is M. Boyce, *Zoroastrians: Their Religious Beliefs and Practices* (London, 1979).

CHAPTER

3

The Civilization of the Greeks

In 431 B.C., war erupted in Greece as two very different Greek city-states—Athens and Sparta—fought for domination of the Greek world. The people of Athens felt secure behind their walls and in the first winter of the war held a public funeral to honor those who had died in battle. On the day of the ceremony, the citizens of Athens joined in a procession, with the relatives of the dead wailing for their loved ones. As was the custom in Athens, one leading citizen was asked to address the crowd, and on this day it was Pericles who spoke to the people. He talked about the greatness of Athens and reminded the Athenians of the strength of their political system. "Our constitution," he said, "is called a democracy because power is in the hands not of a minority but of the whole people. When it is a question of settling private disputes, everyone is equal before the law. Just as our political life is free and open, so is our day-to-day life in our relations with each other. . . . Here each individual is interested not only in his own affairs but in the affairs of the state as well."

In this famous Funeral Oration, Pericles gave voice to the ideal of democracy and the importance of the individual. It was the Greeks who created the intellectual foundations of our Western heritage. They asked some basic questions about human life that still dominate our own intellectual pursuits: What is the nature of the universe? What is the purpose of human existence? What is our relationship to divine forces? What constitutes a community? What constitutes a state? What is true education? What are the true sources of law? What is truth itself and how do we realize it? The Greeks not only gave answers to these questions; they proceeded to create a system of logical, analytical thought in order to examine them. This rational outlook has remained an important feature of Western civilization.

The story of ancient Greek civilization is a remarkable one that begins with the first arrival of the Greeks around 2000 B.C. By the eighth century B.C., the characteristic institution of ancient Greek life, the

Mycenaean Greece

Age of Greek Expansion

Dark Age

Classical Age

Reforms • • • • •
in Sparta   • Cleisthenes' reforms
             Battle of •   • • Great
             Marathon   Peloponnesian War

• •
Homer   Parthenon • • • Plato and
                                            Aristotle
Greek drama (Aeschylus, Sophocles, Euripides) • • • • • •

polis *or city-state, had emerged. Greek civilization flourished and reached its height in the classical era of the fifth century* B.C., *which has come to be closely identified with the achievements of Athenian democracy. But the inability of the Greek states to end their fratricidal warfare eventually helped to bring about the conquest of Greece by the Macedonian king Philip II and thus to bring the Greek world of independent city-states to an end.*

Early Greece

Geography played an important role in the evolution of Greek history. Compared to the landmasses of Mesopotamia and Egypt, Greece occupied a small area. It was a mountainous peninsula that encompassed only 45,000 square miles of territory, about the size of the state of Louisiana. The mountains and the sea played especially significant roles in the development of Greek history. Much of Greece consists of small plains and river valleys surrounded by mountain ranges 8,000–10,000 feet high. The mountainous terrain had the effect of isolating Greeks from one another. Consequently, Greek communities tended to follow their own separate paths and develop their own way of life. Over a period of time, these communities became attached to their independence and were only too willing to fight one another to gain advantage. No doubt the small size of these independent Greek communities fostered participation in political affairs and unique cultural expressions, but the rivalry among these communities also led to the internecine warfare that ultimately devastated Greek society.

The sea also influenced the evolution of Greek society. Greece had a long seacoast, dotted by bays and inlets that provided numerous harbors. The Greeks also inhabited a number of islands to the west, south, and particularly the east of the Greek mainland. It is no accident that the Greeks became seafarers who sailed out into the Aegean and the Mediterranean Seas first to make contact with the outside world and later to establish colonies that would spread Greek civilization throughout the Mediterranean world.

Greek topography helped to determine the major territories into which Greece was ultimately divided. South of the Gulf of Corinth was the Peloponnesus, virtually an island as seen on a map. Consisting mostly of hills, mountains, and small valleys, the Peloponnesus was the location of Sparta, as well as the site of Olympia where the famous athletic games were held. Northeast of the Peloponnesus was the Attic peninsula (or Attica), the home of Athens, hemmed in by mountains to the north and west and surrounded by the sea to the south and east. Northwest of Attica was Boeotia in central Greece with its chief city of Thebes. To the north of Boeotia was Thessaly, which contained the largest plains and became a great producer of grain and horses. To the north of Thessaly lay Macedonia, which was not of much importance in Greek history until the Greeks, by their own fratricidal warfare, opened the door to invasion by the Macedonian king Philip II in 338 B.C.

Minoan Crete

By 2800 B.C., a Bronze Age civilization that used metals, especially bronze, in the construction of weapons had been established in the area of the Aegean Sea. The early Bronze Age settlements on the Greek mainland, created by non-Greek-speaking peoples, were overshadowed by another Bronze Age civilization on the large island of Crete, southeast of the Greek mainland.

The civilization of Minoan Crete was first discovered by the English archaeologist, Arthur Evans, who named it *Minoan* after Minos, the legendary king of Crete. Evans's excavations on Crete at the beginning of the twentieth century led to the discovery of an enormous palace complex at Knossus near modern Heracleion. The remains revealed a rich and prosperous culture with Knossus as the probable center of a far-ranging "sea empire," probably largely commercial in nature. Since Evans found few military fortifications for the defense of Knossus itself, he assumed that Minoan Crete had a strong navy. We do know from archaeological remains

that the people of Minoan Crete were accustomed to sea travel and had made contact with the more advanced civilization of Egypt. Egyptian products have been found in Crete and Cretan products in Egypt.

The civilization of the Minoan Cretans reached its height between 2000 and 1450 B.C. The palace at Knossus, the royal seat of the kings, demonstrates the obvious prosperity and power of this civilization. It was an elaborate structure built around a central courtyard and included numerous private living rooms for the royal family and workshops for making decorated vases, small sculptures, such as ivory figurines, and jewelry. Even bathrooms, with elaborate drains, formed part of the complex. The rooms were decorated with frescoes in bright colors showing sporting events and naturalistic scenes that have led some to assume that the Cretans

Map 3.1 Classical Greece.

◆ **The Minoan Sport of Bull Leaping.** Minoan bull games were held on festival days in the great palaces on the island of Crete. As seen in this fresco from the east wing of the palace at Knossus, women and men acrobats (the man in red) somersaulted over the back of the bull. Another person waited behind the bull to catch the leapers.

had a great love of nature. Storerooms in the palace held enormous jars of oil, wine, and grain, presumably paid as taxes in kind to the king. The kings were apparently assisted by a large bureaucracy that kept detailed records of the payments.

The centers of Minoan civilization on Crete suffered a sudden and catastrophic collapse around 1450 B.C. The cause of this destruction has been vigorously debated. Some historians believe that a tsunami triggered by a powerful volcanic eruption on the island of Thera was responsible for the devastation. Most historians, however, maintain that the destruction was the result of invasion and pillage by mainland Greeks known as the Mycenaeans.

The Mycenaean Greeks

The term *Mycenaean* is derived from Mycenae, a remarkable fortified site first excavated by the amateur German archaeologist, Heinrich Schliemann. In a series of shaft graves, Schliemann discovered an incredible collection of gold masks, cups, jewelry, bronze weapons, and pottery, all belonging to the Mycenaean Greek civilization, which flourished between 1600 and 1100 B.C.

The Mycenaean Greeks were part of the Indo-European family of peoples (see Chapter 1) who spread from their original location into southern and western Europe, India, and Iran. One group entered the territory of Greece from the north around 1900 B.C. From the evidence of pottery, archaeologists have argued that, over a period of time, these Indo-European–speaking invaders managed to gain control of the Greek mainland and develop a civilization.

Mycenaean culture reached its high point between 1400 and 1200 B.C. It is especially noted for its fortified palace-centers, which were built on hills surrounded by gigantic stone walls. While the royal families lived within the walls of these complexes, the civilian populations lived in scattered locations outside the walls. Among the noticeable features of these Mycenaean centers were the tombs where members of the royal families were buried. Known as *tholos* tombs, they were built into hillsides. An entryway led into a circular tomb chamber constructed of cut stone blocks in a domed shape that resembled a beehive in appearance.

Mycenaean civilization consisted of a number of powerful monarchies centered in the palace complexes, such as those found at Mycenae, Tiryns, Pylos, Thebes, and Orchomenos. These various centers of power probably formed a loose confederacy of independent states with Mycenae the strongest. According to tablets written in an early form of Greek script called Linear B, a Mycenaean king used the title of *wanax*. Next in importance to the king were commanders of the army, priests, and bureaucrats who kept careful records. The free citizenry included peasants, soldiers, and artisans with the lowest rung of the social ladder consisting of serfs and slaves. The latter were often victims of war, such as the five hundred women listed as slaves from Asia who worked at Pylos collecting and preparing flax for weaving clothes.

The Mycenaeans were, above all, a warrior people who prided themselves on their heroic deeds in battle.

◆ **The So-Called Death Mask of Agamemnon.** This death mask of thin gold was one of the first objects found by Heinrich Schliemann in his excavation of a series of shaft graves at Mycenae. Schliemann claimed that he had found the mask of Agamemnon, king of Mycenae in Homer's *Iliad*. The excited archaeologist wrote to the king of Greece: "Today I have looked on the face of Agamemnon."

Unlike Cretan frescoes, Mycenaean wall murals often show war and hunting scenes, the natural occupations of a warrior aristocracy. Archaeological evidence also indicates that the Mycenaean monarchies developed an extensive commercial network. Mycenaean pottery has been found throughout the Mediterranean basin, in Syria and Egypt to the east and Sicily and southern Italy to the west. But some scholars believe that the Mycenaeans, led by Mycenae itself, also spread outward militarily, conquering Crete and making it part of the Mycenaean world. Some of the Aegean islands also fell subject to Mycenaean control. The most famous of all the Mycenaeans' supposed military adventures has come down to us in the epic poetry of Homer (see the discussion of Homer in the next section). Did the Mycenaeans, led by Agamemnon, king of Mycenae, sack the city of Troy on the northwestern coast of Asia Minor around 1250 B.C.? Since the excavations of Heinrich Schliemann, begun in 1870, scholars have debated this question. Many do believe in the basic authenticity of the Homerian legend, even if the details have become shrouded in mystery.

By the late thirteenth century, Mycenaean Greece was showing signs of serious trouble. Mycenae itself was torched around 1190 B.C., reinhabited, and finally abandoned around 1125 B.C. Other Mycenaean centers show similar patterns of destruction. By 1100 B.C., the Mycenaean culture was coming to an end.

Modern scholars have proposed a number of theories to explain the collapse of Mycenaean civilization. According to the Greeks' own legend, their mainland was invaded from the north by another Greek-speaking people who were less civilized than the Mycenaeans. Called the Dorians, these invaders supposedly destroyed the old centers of Mycenaean power and ultimately established themselves in the Peloponnesus. But there is little archaeological evidence to support the idea of massive Dorian invasions. Other historians argue that internal conflict among the Mycenaean kings and major earthquakes were more important factors in the Mycenaean decline. What is certain is that by 1100 B.C., the Greek world had entered a new period of considerable insecurity.

The Greeks in a Dark Age (c. 1100–c. 750 B.C.)

After the collapse of Mycenaean civilization, Greece entered a difficult era of declining population and falling food production. Moreover, we have few records to help us reconstruct what happened in this period. Because of the difficult conditions and our lack of knowledge about the period, historians refer to it as a Dark Age. Not until 850 B.C. did farming revive. At the same time, some new developments were forming the basis for a revived Greece.

During the Dark Age, large numbers of Greeks left the mainland and migrated across the Aegean Sea to various islands, and especially to the western shores of Asia Minor, a strip of territory that came to be called Ionia. Based on their dialect, the Greeks who resided there were called Ionians. Two other major groups of Greeks settled in established parts of Greece. The Aeolian Greeks who were located in northern and central Greece colonized the large island of Lesbos and the adjacent territory of the mainland. The Dorians established themselves in southwestern Greece, especially in the Peloponnesus, as well as on some of the southern Aegean islands, including Crete.

Other important activities occurred in this Dark Age as well. There was a revival of some trade and some economic activity besides agriculture. Iron replaced bronze in the construction of weapons, making them affordable for more people. And farming tools made of iron helped to reverse the decline in food production. At some point in the eighth century B.C., the Greeks adopted the Phoenician alphabet to give themselves a new system of writing. By reducing all words to a combination of twenty-four letters (both consonants and vowels), the Greeks made learning to read and write simpler. Finally, near the very end of this so-called Dark Age appeared the work of Homer, who has come to be viewed as one of the truly great poets of all time.

Homer

The origins of the *Iliad* and the *Odyssey*, the first great epics of early Greece, are to be found in the oral tradition of reciting poems recounting the deeds of heroes of the Mycenaean age. It is generally assumed that early in the eighth century B.C., Homer made use of these oral traditions to compose the *Iliad*, his epic of the Trojan War. The war was caused by an act of Paris, a prince of Troy. By kidnapping Helen, wife of the king of the Greek state of Sparta, he outraged all the Greeks. Under the leadership of the Spartan king's brother, Agamemnon of Mycenae, the Greeks attacked Troy. Ten years later, the Greeks finally won and sacked the city.

But the *Iliad* is not so much the story of the war itself as it is the tale of the Greek hero Achilles and how the "wrath of Achilles" led to disaster. As is true of all great

♦ **The Dragging of Hector's Body by Achilles.** This late sixth-century Athenian vase depicts Achilles dragging Hector's body around the city of Troy, a scene taken from Homer's *Iliad*. The *Iliad* is Homer's masterpiece, and though many scholars doubt its historical accuracy, this work (and the *Odyssey*) were important to later Greeks as a means of teaching the aristocratic values of courage and honor.

literature, the *Iliad* abounds in universal lessons. Underlying them all is the clear message, as one commentator has observed, that "men will still come and go like the generations of leaves in the forest; that he will still be weak, and the gods strong and incalculable; that the quality of a man matters more than his achievement; that violence and recklessness will still lead to disaster, and that this will fall on the innocent as well as on the guilty."[1]

Although the *Odyssey* has long been considered Homer's other masterpiece, some scholars believe that it was composed later than the *Iliad* and was probably not the work of Homer. The *Odyssey* is an epic romance that recounts the journeys of one of the Greek heroes,

Odysseus, after the fall of Troy and his ultimate return to his wife. But there is a larger vision here as well: the testing of the heroic stature of Odysseus until, by both cunning and patience, he prevails. In the course of this testing, the underlying moral message is "that virtue is a better policy than vice."[2]

The *Iliad* and the *Odyssey* supposedly describe the heroes of the Mycenaean age of the thirteenth century B.C. However, there is considerable debate about their usefulness as historical documents. Since the epics were probably composed in the eighth century B.C., some historians believe that they really describe social conditions of that century, while others believe that they reveal the circumstances of the Dark Age itself in the tenth and ninth centuries. Still others have argued that the epics may incorporate elements from different periods. If we do accept these works as indicative of the Dark Age, what kind of society do they describe?

Homeric Greece was a society based on agriculture in which a landed warrior-aristocracy controlled much wealth and exercised considerable power. Kings were regarded as simply first among equals and ruled kingdoms petty in size and power compared to the Mycenaean Greek monarchies. Homer's kings were assisted in ruling by a council of nobles who were free to give advice contrary to the king and even to disobey his commands. There was also an assembly of commoners, consisting in wartime of all soldiers and in peacetime of all who lived near the king's residence. The king and the council of nobles brought only major questions to the assembly, which did not debate but simply made decisions by acclamation. There is no doubt that Homer's society was divided along class lines with the warrior-aristocrats as the dominant group. Homer's world reflects the values of aristocratic heroes.

This, of course, explains the importance of Homer to later generations of Greeks. Homer did not so much record history; he made it. The Greeks regarded the *Iliad* and the *Odyssey* as authentic history and as the work of one poet, Homer. These masterpieces gave to the Greeks an ideal past with a legendary age of heroes and came to be used as standard texts for the education of generations of Greek males. As one Athenian stated, "My father was anxious to see me develop into a good man . . . and as a means to this end he compelled me to memorize all of Homer."[3] The values Homer inculcated were essentially the aristocratic values of courage and honor (see the box on p. 71). It was important to strive for the excellence befitting a hero, which the Greeks called *arete*. In the warrior-aristocratic world of Homer, *arete* is won in a struggle or contest. In his willingness to

fight, the hero protects his family and friends, preserves and expands his own honor and that of his family, and earns his reputation. To a later generation of Greek males, these heroic values formed the core of aristocratic virtue, a fact that explains the tremendous popularity of Homer as an educational tool. Homer gave to the Greeks one universally known model of heroism, honor, and nobility. But in time, as a new world of city-states emerged in Greece, new values of cooperation and community also transformed what Greeks learned from Homer.

The World of the Greek City-States (c. 750–c. 500 B.C.)

In the eighth century B.C., Greek civilization burst forth with new energies, beginning the period that historians have called the Archaic Age of Greece. Two major developments stand out in this era: the evolution of the *polis*, or city-state, as the central institution in Greek life and the Greeks' colonization of the Mediterranean and Black Seas.

The *Polis*

The origins of the Greek *polis* (plural *poleis*) are not very clear. It developed slowly during the Dark Age following the upheavals that brought a close to the Mycenaean age and by the eighth century B.C. had emerged as a truly unique and fundamental institution in Greek society. In the most basic sense, a *polis* could be defined as a small but autonomous political unit in which all major political, social, and religious activities were carried out at one central location.

In a physical sense, the *polis* encompassed a town or city or even a village and its surrounding countryside. But the town or city or village served as the focus or central point where the citizens of the *polis* could assemble for political, social, and religious activities. In some *poleis*, this central meeting point was a hill, like the Acropolis at Athens, which could serve as a place of refuge during an attack and later in some sites came to be the religious center on which temples and public monuments were erected. Below the acropolis would be an agora, an open space that served both as a place where citizens could assemble and as a market. Citizens resided in town and country alike, but the town remained the center of political activity.

Poleis could vary greatly in size, from a few square miles to a few hundred square miles. The larger ones

Homer's Ideal of Excellence

The Iliad *and the* Odyssey, *which the Greeks believed were both written by Homer, were used as basic texts for the education of Greeks for hundreds of years in antiquity. This passage from the* Iliad, *describing a conversation between Hector, prince of Troy, and his wife Andromache, illustrates the Greek ideal of gaining honor through combat. At the end of the passage, Homer also reveals the Greek attitude toward women.*

Homer, *Iliad*

Hector looked at his son and smiled, but said nothing. Andromache, bursting into tears, went up to him and put her hand in his. "Hector," she said, "you are possessed. This bravery of yours will be your end. You do not think of your little boy or your unhappy wife, whom you will make a widow soon. Some day the Achaeans [Greeks] are bound to kill you in a massed attack. And when I lose you I might as well be dead. . . . I have no father, no mother, now. . . . I had seven brothers too at home. In one day all of them went down to Hades' House. The great Achilles of the swift feet killed them all. . . ."

"So you, Hector, are father and mother and brother to me, as well as my beloved husband. Have pity on me now; stay here on the tower; and do not make your boy an orphan and your wife a widow. . . ."

"All that, my dear," said the great Hector of the glittering helmet, "is surely my concern. But if I hid myself like a coward and refused to fight, I could never face the Trojans and the Trojan ladies in their trailing gowns.

Besides, it would go against the grain, for I have trained myself always, like a good soldier, to take my place in the front line and win glory for my father and myself. . . ."

As he finished, glorious Hector held out his arms to take his boy. But the child shrank back with a cry to the bosom of his girdled nurse, alarmed by his father's appearance. He was frightened by the bronze of the helmet and the horsehair plume that he saw nodding grimly down at him. His father and his lady mother had to laugh. But noble Hector quickly took his helmet off and put the dazzling thing on the ground. Then he kissed his son, dandled him in his arms, and prayed to Zeus and the other gods: "Zeus; and you other gods, grant that this boy of mind may be, like me, pre-eminent in Troy; as strong and brave as I; a mighty king of Ilium. May people say, when he comes back from battle, 'Here is a better man than his father.' Let him bring home the bloodstained armor of the enemy he has killed, and make his mother happy."

Hector handed the boy to his wife, who took him to her fragrant breast. She was smiling through her tears, and when her husband saw this he was moved. He stroked her with his hand and said: "My dear, I beg you not to be too much distressed. No one is going to send me down to Hades before my proper time. But Fate is a thing that no man born of woman, coward or hero, can escape. Go home now, and attend to your own work, the loom and the spindle, and see that the maidservants get on with theirs. War is men's business; and this war is the business of every man in Ilium, myself above all."

---

were the product of consolidation. The territory of Attica, for example, had once had twelve *poleis*, but eventually became a single *polis* (Athens) through a process of amalgamation. Athens grew to have a population of more than 300,000 by the fifth century B.C., with an adult male citizen body of about 43,000. Most *poleis* were considerably smaller than Athens, however, consisting of a few hundred to several thousand people.

The *polis* was much more than just a political institution. It was, above all, a community of citizens in which all political, economic, social, cultural, and religious activities were focused. As a community, the *polis* consisted of citizens with political rights (adult males), citizens with no political rights (women and children), and noncitizens (slaves and resident aliens). All citizens of a *polis* possessed the same fundamental rights, but these rights were coupled with responsibilities. The Greek philosopher Aristotle argued that the citizen did not just belong to himself; "we must rather regard every citizen as belonging to the state." The unity of citizens was important and often meant that states would take an active role in directing the patterns of life.

The system of the *polis* also relied on local patriotism, which was encouraged by the veneration of a god or goddess as patron of the community. But there was also a negative side to local patriotism. It tended to foster mutual suspicion and divide Greece into a large number of tiny sovereign units. In times of emergency, some of the Greek states managed to shed their rivalries and cooperate against an outside enemy. But freedom of the *polis* often came first, and in the long run, the division of Greece into fiercely patriotic sovereign units helped to bring about its ruin. The cultural unity of the Greeks, reinforced by a common language and common gods, did not mean much politically.

The development of the *polis* was paralleled by the emergence of a new military system. Greek fighting had previously been dominated by aristocratic cavalrymen, who reveled in individual duels with enemy soldiers. But by the end of the eighth century and beginning of the seventh century B.C., a new military order based on hoplites came into being. Hoplites were heavily armed infantrymen, who wore bronze or leather helmets, breastplates, and greaves (shin guards). Each carried a round shield, short sword, and a thrusting spear about nine feet long. Hoplites advanced into battle as a unit,

shoulder to shoulder, forming a phalanx (a rectangular formation) in tight order, usually eight ranks deep. As long as the hoplites kept their order, were not out-flanked, and did not break, they either secured victory or, at the very least, suffered no harm. The phalanx was easily routed, however, if it broke its order. The safety of the phalanx depended, above all, on the solidarity and discipline of its members.

The hoplite force, which apparently developed first in the Peloponnesus, had political as well as military repercussions. The aristocratic cavalry was now out-dated. Since each hoplite provided his own armor, men of property, both aristocrats and small farmers, made up the new phalanx. Initially, this created a bond between the aristocrats and peasants, which minimized class conflict and enabled the aristocrats to dominate their societies. In the long run, however, those who could become hoplites and fight for the state could also challenge aristocratic control.

◆ **The Hoplite Forces.** The Greek hoplites were infantrymen equipped with large round shields and long thrusting spears. In battle they advanced in tight phalanx formation and were dangerous opponents as long as this formation remained unbroken. This vase painting of the seventh century B.C. shows two groups of hoplite warriors engaged in battle. The piper on the left is leading another line of soldiers preparing to enter the fray.

Colonization and the Growth of Trade

Greek expansion overseas was another major development of the Archaic Age. Between 750 and 550 B.C., the Greek people left their homeland in large numbers to settle in distant lands. One reason for the exodus was the poverty and land hunger created by the growing gulf between rich and poor, between wealthy landed aristocrats who seized more and more land and the peasants who lost their land. The land problem was intensified by overpopulation. The growing division in some Greek communities caused the ruling classes to look with favor upon the migration of discontented elements to new lands. Throughout history, colonization has always been a safety valve to release potentially revolutionary pressures. Trade, too, was a factor in the development of colonization. By the eighth century B.C., Greeks were producing dyed woolen fabrics and pottery, and these goods, along with olive oil and wine, were playing important roles in a growing commerce. Some colonies were established in places ideal for trade and at locations where important raw materials, such as metals, could be obtained. Greek tyrants (see Tyranny in the Greek *Polis* later in this chapter) proved especially eager to win the approval of merchants and traders by establishing new colonies.

Greek colonies varied in purpose and organization. Some were simply trading posts or centers for the transshipment of goods to Greece. Most were larger settlements that included good agricultural land taken from the native populations found in those areas. Each colony was founded as a *polis* and was usually independent of the mother *polis* (hence, the word *metropolis*) that had established it. Indeed, the use of the word *colony* is misleading in describing Greek expansion. Although the mother *polis* created a colony to further its interests, invariably the colony saw itself as an independent entity. Its links to the mother city were not political, but were based on sharing common social, economic, and especially religious practices.

In the western Mediterranean, new Greek settlements were established along the coastline of southern Italy, such as the cities of Tarentum and Neapolis (Naples). So many Greek communities were established in southern Italy that the Romans later called it *Magna Graecia* ("Great Greece"). An important city was founded at Syracuse in eastern Sicily in 734 B.C. by the city-state of Corinth, one of the most active Greek states in establishing colonies. Greek settlements were also established in southern France (Massilia; modern Marseilles), eastern Spain, and northern Africa west of Egypt.

To the north, the Greeks set up colonies in Thrace, where they sought good agricultural lands to grow grains. Greeks also settled along the shores of the Black Sea and secured the approaches to it with cities on the Hellespont and Bosphorus, most notably Byzantium, site of the later Constantinople (Istanbul). A trading post was established in Egypt, giving the Greeks access to both the products and the advanced culture of the east.

The establishment of these settlements over such a wide area had important effects. For one thing, they contributed to the diffusion of culture as the Greeks spread their culture throughout the Mediterranean basin. The later Romans, after all, made their first contact with the Greeks through the settlements in southern Italy. In addition, colonization led to increased trade and industry. The Greeks sent their pottery, wine, and olive oil to these areas; in return, they received grains and metals from the west and fish, timber, wheat, metals, and slaves from the Black Sea region. The expansion of trade and industry created a new group of rich men in many *poleis* who desired political privileges commensurate with their wealth, but found them impossible to gain because of the power of the ruling aristocrats. The desire for change on the part of this group soon led to political crisis in many Greek states.

Tyranny in the Greek Polis

When the *polis* emerged as an important institution in Greece in the eighth century, monarchical power waned, and kings virtually disappeared in most Greek states or survived only as ceremonial figures with little or no real power. Instead, political power passed into the hands of local aristocracies. But increasing divisions between rich and poor and the aspirations of newly rising industrial and commercial groups in Greek *poleis* opened the door to the rise of tyrants in the seventh and sixth centuries B.C. They were not necessarily oppressive or wicked as our word *tyrant* connotes. Greek tyrants were rulers who came to power in an unconstitutional way; a tyrant was not subject to the law. Many who became tyrants were actually aristocrats who opposed the control of the ruling aristocratic factions in their cities. The support for the tyrants, however, came from the new rich who had made their money in trade and industry and the poor peasants. Both groups were opposed to the domination of political power by aristocratic oligarchies.

Tyrants usually achieved power by a local coup d'etat and maintained it by using mercenary soldiers. Once in power, they promoted public works projects, such as the

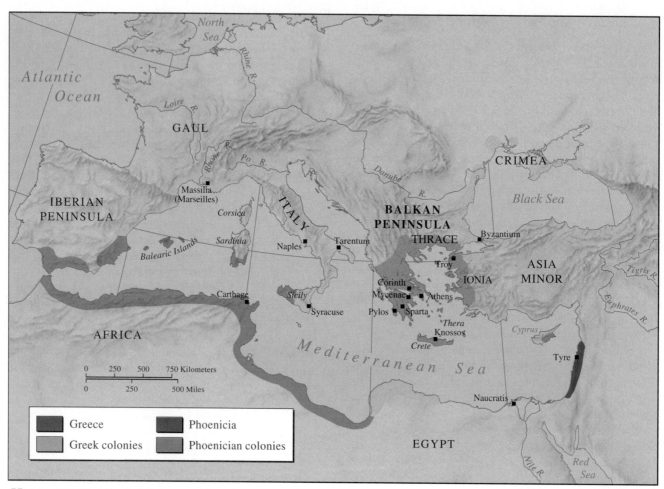

✵ Map 3.2 The Greek Colonies in the Archaic Age.

construction of new marketplaces, temples, and walls, that not only glorified the city but also enhanced their own popularity. Tyrants also favored the interests of merchants and traders by encouraging the founding of new colonies, developing new coinage, and establishing new systems of weights and measures. In many instances, they added to the prosperity of their cities. By their patronage of the arts, they encouraged cultural development.

Despite these achievements, tyranny was largely extinguished by the end of the sixth century B.C. The children and grandchildren of tyrants, who tended to be corrupted by their inherited power and wealth, often became cruel and unjust rulers, making tyranny no longer seem such a desirable institution. Its very nature as a system outside the law seemed contradictory to the ideal of law in a Greek community. Tyranny did not last, but it played a significant role in the evolution of Greek history. The rule of narrow aristocratic oligarchies was

destroyed. Once the tyrants were eliminated, the door was opened to the participation of new and more people in the affairs of the community. Although this trend culminated in the development of democracy in some communities, in other states expanded oligarchies of one kind or another managed to remain in power. Greek states exhibited considerable variety in their governmental structures; this can perhaps best be seen by examining the two most famous and most powerful Greek city-states, Sparta and Athens.

Sparta

The Greeks of Sparta and Athens spoke different dialects and developed different political systems. The Spartans sought stability and conformity and emphasized order. The Athenians allowed for individual differences and stressed freedom. Although the two states shared a common heritage, their differences grew so large in their own minds that they were ultimately willing to engage in a life-and-death struggle to support their separate realities. When they did so, the entire Greek world was the real loser.

Sparta had been a monarchy in Mycenaean and Homeric times. After emerging out of the Dark Age, it remained a monarchy, but one with two kings whose powers were limited by a strong council and assembly. The Spartan constitution underwent dramatic changes, however, as a result of Sparta's imperialism.

Located in the southeastern Peloponnesus, Sparta, like other Greek states, was faced with a problem of land hunger. Rather than solving this problem by colonization, Sparta looked for land nearby and, beginning around 740 B.C., undertook the conquest of neighboring Messenia despite its larger size and population. Messenia possessed a large, fertile plain ideal for growing grain. After its conquest, Sparta subjected the Messenians, although greatly outnumbered by them (7 to 1), to serfdom. Known as helots, they were bound to the land for Sparta's benefit. Initially, this imperialistic venture had little apparent effect on Sparta. In the eighth and even seventh centuries B.C., Sparta still appears to have been a culturally vibrant state. But in the seventh century, the Messenians revolted. Although Sparta succeeded in quelling the revolt, the struggle was so long and hard that the Spartans made a conscious decision to renounce the amenities of civilized life and create a military state so that they could dominate Messenia for ages to come.

After 600 B.C., the Spartans instituted a series of reforms that are associated with the name of the lawgiver Lycurgus (see the box on p. 76). Although historians are not sure of his historicity, there is no doubt about the results of these reforms. By the end of the sixth century B.C., Sparta had been transformed into a perpetual military camp.

The lives of Spartans were now rigidly organized. At birth, each child was examined by state officials who decided whether it was fit to live. Those judged unfit were exposed to die. Boys were taken from their mothers at the age of seven and put under control of the state. They lived in military-like barracks, where they were subjected to harsh discipline to make them tough and given an education that stressed military training and obedience to authority. At twenty, Spartan males were enrolled in the army for regular military service. Although allowed to marry, they continued to live in the military barracks. All meals were eaten in public dining halls with fellow soldiers. Meals were simple; the famous Spartan black broth consisted of a piece of pork boiled in blood, salt, and vinegar, causing a visitor who ate in a public mess to remark that he now understood why Spartans were not afraid to die. At thirty, Spartan males were recognized as mature and allowed to vote in the assembly and live at home, but they remained in military service until the age of sixty.

While their husbands remained in military barracks until age thirty, Spartan women lived at home. Because of this separation, Spartan women had greater freedom of movement and greater power in the household than was common for women elsewhere in Greece. They were encouraged to exercise and remain fit to bear and raise healthy children. Like the men, Spartan women engaged in athletic exercises in the nude. At solemn feasts, the young women would march naked in processions, and in the presence of the young men, they would sing songs about those who had showed special gallantry or cowardice on the battlefield. Many Spartan women upheld the strict Spartan values, expecting their husbands and sons to be brave in war. The story is told that as a Spartan mother was burying her son, an old woman came up to her and said, "You poor woman, what a misfortune." "No," replied the other, "because I bore him so that he might die for Sparta and that is what has happened, as I wished."[4] Another Spartan woman saw her son off to war by telling him to come back carrying his shield or carried on it.

The Spartan social structure was rigidly organized. At the summit were the *Spartiates*—full Spartan citizens. Each Spartan citizen owned a piece of land, worked by the Messenian helots, to provide economic sustenance. With their material needs provided for them, Spartan citizens could dedicate themselves to their duties as a ruling class. Below the *Spartiates* were the *perioeci*. Though free, they did not possess the privileges of citizenship and served as small merchants and craftsmen. They were subject to military duty, however. At the bottom of the social scale were the helots, perpetually bound to the land. They were assigned to the lands of the Spartan citizens. The helots farmed the land and gave their masters one-half of the produce. A secret police force lived among them and was permitted to kill any helot considered dangerous. To legalize this murder, the state officially declared war on the helots at the beginning of each year.

The so-called Lycurgan reforms also reorganized the Spartan government. The political structure combined monarchical, aristocratic, and democratic elements. The executive branch of the Spartan state originally consisted of two kings from different families. They were primarily responsible for military affairs and served as

The Lycurgan Reforms

In order to maintain their control over the conquered Messenians, the Spartans instituted the reforms that created their military state. In this account of the supposed lawgiver Lycurgus, the Greek historian Plutarch discusses the effect of these reforms on the treatment and education of boys.

Plutarch, *Lycurgus*

Lycurgus was of another mind; he would not have masters brought out of the market for his young Spartans, . . . nor was it lawful, indeed, for the father himself to breed up the children after his own fancy; but as soon as they were seven years old they were to be enrolled in certain companies and classes, where they all lived under the same order and discipline, doing their exercises and taking their play together. Of these, he who showed the most conduct and courage was made captain; they had their eyes always upon him, obeyed his orders, and underwent patiently whatsoever punishment he inflicted; so that the whole course of their eduction was one continued exercise of a ready and perfect obedience. The old men, too, were spectators of their performances, and often raised quarrels and disputes among them, to have a good opportunity of finding out their different characters, and of seeing which would be valiant, which a coward, when they should come to more dangerous encounters. Reading and writing they gave them just enough to serve their turn; their chief care was to make them good subjects, and to reach them to endure pain and conquer in battle. To this end, as they grew in years, their discipline was proportionately increased; their heads were close-clipped, they were accustomed to go barefoot, and for the most part to play naked.

After they were twelve years old, they were no longer allowed to wear any undergarments, they had one coat to serve them a year; their bodies were hard and dry, with but little acquaintance of baths and unguents; these human indulgences they were allowed only on some few particular days in the year. They lodged together in little bands upon beds made of the rushes which grew by the banks of the river Eurotas, which they were to break off with their hands with a knife; if it were winter, they mingled some thistledown with their rushes, which it was thought had the property of giving warmth. But the time they were come to this age there was not any of the more hopeful boys who had not a lover to bear him company. The old men, too, had an eye upon them, coming often to the grounds to hear and see them contend either in wit or strength with one another, and this as seriously . . . as if they were their fathers, their tutors, or their magistrates; so that there scarcely was any time or place without some one present to put them in mind of their duty, and punish them if they had neglected it.

[Spartan boys were also encouraged to steal their food.] They stole, too, all other meat they could lay their hands on, looking out and watching all opportunities, when people were asleep or more careless than usual. If they were caught, they were not only punished with whipping, but hunger, too, being reduced to their ordinary allowance, which was but very slender, and so contrived on purpose, that they might set about to help themselves, and be forced to exercise their energy and address. This was the principal design of their hard fare.

---

the leaders of the Spartan army on its campaigns. Moreover, the kings served as the supreme priests within the state religion and had some role in foreign policy. Probably in the early eighth century, the domestic role of the kings was superseded by a college of five *ephors*. Elected annually, their duties included supervising the education of youth and the conduct of all citizens. They also served as judges in all civil cases.

The Spartan constitution contained an aristocratic element in the form of a body called the *gerousia*, a council of old men. It consisted of twenty-eight citizens over the age of sixty, who were elected for life, and the two kings. Although the *gerousia* helped the *ephors*

manage public affairs, its primary task was to determine the issues that would be presented to the assembly of citizens. It also acted as a judicial body, primarily in criminal cases. The democratic element of the state was in an assembly of all male citizens called the *apella*. The *apella* did not debate, but only voted on the issues put before it by the *gerousia*. The assembly also elected the *ephors* and *gerousia*.

To guarantee the continuity of their new military state, the Spartans deliberately turned their backs on outside society and cultural amenities. Foreigners were discouraged from visiting Sparta to prevent the importation of novel ideas. Nor were Spartans, except for military reasons, encouraged to travel abroad where they might pick up new ideas. Trade and commerce were likewise minimized. Spartan citizens were discouraged from pursuing philosophy, literature, the arts, or any subject that might foster novel thoughts dangerous to the stability of the state. Eventually, however, for reasons of security, the Spartans were forced to wage war outside the Peloponnesus. When they did go abroad, Spartan leaders often failed to follow the Spartan ideal and succumbed to the allure of wealth and power. Their behavior seemed to confirm the wisdom of restricting their travel as much as possible.

In the sixth century, Sparta used its military might and the fear it inspired to gain greater control of the Peloponnesus by organizing an alliance of almost all the Peloponnesian states. Sparta's strength enabled it to dominate this Peloponnesian League and determine its policies.

By 500 B.C., the Spartans had organized a powerful military state that maintained order and stability in the Peloponnesus. Of course, this was achieved at great cost, especially the loss of freedom, not only for the Messenians, their subject peoples, but also for the Spartans themselves. It is doubtful that the Spartans saw it that way, however. Raised from early childhood to believe that total loyalty to the Spartan state was the basic reason for existence, the Spartans viewed their strength as justification for their militaristic ideals and regimented society.

Athens

By 700 B.C., Athens had established a unified *polis* on the peninsula of Attica. Although early Athens had been ruled by a monarchy, by the seventh century B.C., it had fallen under the control of its aristocrats. They possessed the best land and controlled political and religious life by means of a council of nobles called the Areopagus, assisted by a board of nine archons. Since the archons served only one year and entered the Areopagus afterward, the latter body held the real power. Although there was an *ecclesia* or assembly of full citizens, it possessed few powers.

Near the end of the seventh century B.C., Athens was experiencing political and social discontent stemming from the development of rival factions within the aristocracy and serious economic problems. A codification of the laws about 621 B.C. by the archon Draco failed to stop the unrest. Increasing numbers of Athenian farmers found themselves sold into slavery when they were unable to repay the loans they had borrowed

from their aristocratic neighbors, pledging themselves as collateral. Repeatedly, revolutionary cries for cancellation of debts and a redistribution of land were heard. As we have seen, it was precisely this kind of economic and social crisis that produced tyrannies in other *poleis*.

Hoping to avoid tyranny, the ruling Athenian aristocrats responded to this crisis by choosing Solon, a liberally minded aristocrat, as sole archon in 594 B.C. and giving him full power to make reforms. Solon's reforms dealt with both the economic and political problems. He canceled all current land debts, outlawed new loans based on humans as collateral, and freed people who had fallen into slavery for debt. He refused, however, to carry out the redistribution of the land and hence failed to deal with the basic cause of the economic crisis. This failure, however, was overshadowed by other economic steps that ultimately led to increased prosperity for Athens. These included devising new weights and measures, enacting a less severe law code, encouraging the growth of olive trees and the export of olive oil, and attracting foreign artisans by offering them citizenship—all steps that helped Athens achieve increased commercial and industrial prosperity in the following decades.

Like his economic reforms, Solon's political measures were also a compromise. While by no means eliminating the power of the aristocracy, they opened the door to the participation of new people, especially the non-aristocratic wealthy, into the government. Solon now divided all Athenian citizens into four classes on the basis of wealth. Only men in the first two classes (the wealthiest classes) could hold the archonship and be members of the Areopagus. Men in the third class could be elected to a new council of 400 called the *boule,* whose function was to prepare the agenda for the assembly. The fourth (and poorest) class, though not allowed to hold any political offices, could now vote in the assembly. All four classes could also sit in the new popular court (the *heliaea*) instituted by Solon to hear appeals from cases tried before the archons.

Solon's reforms, though popular, did not truly solve Athens's problems. Aristocratic factions continued to vie for power, and the poorer peasants resented Solon's failure to institute land redistribution. Internal strife finally led to the very institution Solon had hoped to avoid—tyranny. Pisistratus, an aristocrat and a distant relative of Solon, seized power in 560 B.C. and made himself a tyrant. Although driven into exile twice after his initial coup d'etat, he used mercenary soldiers to reestablish his tyranny in 546 B.C. and remained in power until his death in 527 B.C.

Pisistratus did not tamper very much with the constitution. The assembly, councils, and courts continued to function while he made sure that his supporters were elected as magistrates and to the councils. Pisistratus curried favor with an ambitious building program, aimed at beautifying the city. To encourage patriotic unity, he introduced new public festivals, such as the one to honor Dionysus, god of wine, while old festivals, such as the Panathenaia, celebrated in honor of the patron goddess Athena, were expanded and made more appealing to the public. Pursuing a foreign policy that aided Athenian trade, Pisistratus remained popular with the mercantile and industrial classes.

Pisistratus's mild tyranny had been popular with many Athenians, but the policies of his son Hippias eventually (527–510 B.C.) produced a reaction. With the help of Spartan troops under their ambitious and active King Cleomenes I, the Athenians sent Hippias into exile and ended the tyranny. Although the aristocrats attempted, with Spartan help, to reestablish an aristocratic oligarchy, Cleisthenes, a liberal aristocrat, opposed this plan and, with the backing of the Athenian people, gained the upper hand in 508 B.C. The reforms of Cleisthenes now established the basis for Athenian democracy.

A major aim of Cleisthenes' reforms was to weaken the power of traditional localities and regions, which had provided the foundation for aristocratic strength. He made the deme—a small territorial unit—the basic

unit of Athenian political life. Citizens were now those people who were enrolled in the demes, which ultimately numbered about 170. The residents of the demes were grouped into ten new tribes instead of the traditional four. Each tribe contained demes located in the country districts of Attica, the coastal areas, and Athens. The new tribes thus contained a cross section of the population and reflected all of Attica, a move that diminished local interests and increased loyalty to the *polis.* Cleisthenes' ten new tribes were then linked to a new council of 500 that replaced Solon's council of 400. Each of the ten tribes chose fifty members by lot each year for the new council. No one was allowed to serve more than two years (and then not in succession) on the council. It prepared the business that would be handled by the assembly and was responsible for the administration of both foreign and financial affairs. The assembly of all the citizens had final authority in the passing of laws after debate; thus, Cleisthenes' reforms had reinforced the assembly's central role in the Athenian political system.

The reforms of Cleisthenes created the foundations for Athenian democracy. More changes would come in the fifth century when the Athenians themselves would begin to use the word *democracy* to describe their system. By 500 B.C., Athens was more united than it had been and was on the verge of playing a more important role in Greek affairs.

Greek Culture in the Archaic Age

The period after the Dark Age, as we have seen, was one of economic growth, social upheaval, and political change. It witnessed a revitalization of Greek life that is also evident in Greek art and literature. Some aspects of archaic Greek culture, such as pottery and sculpture, were especially influenced by the East. Greek sculpture, particularly that of the Ionian Greek settlements in western Asia Minor, demonstrates the impact of the considerably older Egyptian civilization. There we first see the life-size stone statues of young male nudes known as *kouros* figures. The *kouros* bears considerable resemblance to Egyptian statues of the New Kingdom. The figures are not realistic, but stiff, with a slight smile; one leg is advanced ahead of the other, and the arms are held rigidly at the sides of the body.

Greek literature of the seventh century is perhaps best known for its lyric poetry. The lyric is considerably shorter than epic poetry (such as Homer's) and focuses on personal emotions, usually the power of love and its impact on human lives. Later Greeks acknowledged

Sappho as their greatest female lyric poet (see the box on p. 80). Born in the seventh century, Sappho lived on the island of Lesbos in the Aegean Sea, where she taught music and poetry to her young charges. Many of her poems are love songs to her female students. Our word *lesbian* is derived from Sappho's island of Lesbos. Sappho, like many upper-class Greeks, accepted that homosexual and heterosexual feelings could exist in the same individual. Sappho was both a wife and a mother who also wrote poems about love between men and women.

Archaic Greece is also known for poets who reflected the lifestyles of both aristocrats and peasants. Although trade and industry were growing, most people still lived off the land. A wide gulf, however, separated the wealthy aristocrat with his large landed estates from the poor peasants and small farmers who eked out their existence as best they could. Hesiod, a poet from Boeotia in central Greece who lived around 700 B.C., wrote a lengthy epic poem entitled *Works and Days*. Himself a farmer, Hesiod reflected the values of his nonaristocratic society. He distrusted aristocrats and looked down upon what he considered the aristocratic emphasis on pride and war. One of his aims was to show that the gods punished injustice:

> But there are some who till the fields of pride
> And work at evil deeds; Zeus marks them out,
> And often, all the city suffers for
> Their wicked schemes, and on these men, from heaven
> The son of Kronos [Zeus] sends great punishments,
> Both plague and famine, and the people die.
> Their wives are barren, and their villages
> Dwindle, according to the plan of Zeus.
> At other times the son of Kronos will
> Destroy their army, or will snatch away
> Their city wall, or all their ships at sea.
> You lords, take notice of this punishment.
> The deathless gods are never far away;
> They mark the crooked judges who grind down
> Their fellow-men and do not fear the gods.

The way to success was to work: "Famine and blight do not beset the just, who till their well-worked fields and feast. The earth supports them lavishly." *Works and Days* is the first paean to work in Western literature.

In his poem, Hesiod gave a calendar for the farmer's work. In fall, one ploughs and plants the main crop of grain. In fall and winter, he builds wagons, cuts wood, and makes ploughs and other tools. He harvests the

◆ **Kouros.** This statue of a young male nude is dated around 600 B.C., making it an early example of *kouros* sculpture. The role these statues played in the Greek world is not known. The most common belief is that since they were placed in temples (along with companion figures of young women, known as *korai*), they were meant to be representations of the faithful dedicated to the gods.

grain in early May, and threshes and stores it in July. In the heat of summer comes time to relax: "Exhausting summertime has come. The goats are very fat, and wine is very good. . . . Then may I sit in shade and drink the shining wine, and eat my fill." But soon it is time to harvest the grapes and make the wine for next year. No sooner is that done than it is time to begin the cycle anew and plough and plant. Hesiod emphasized the importance of two things to the farmer's success. It

⪦ The Lyric Poetry of Sappho ⪧

These love poems are examples of the work of Sappho of Lesbos, regarded as one of Greece's greatest lyric poets. She wrote directly about her personal world of emotions. Sappho is an unusual figure, an independent woman in a world dominated by males. Her attitude toward the Trojan War, as seen in the poem To Anaktoria, is quite different from that found in Homer's Iliad.

Sappho, To Anaktoria, Now a Soldier's Wife in Lydia

Some say cavalry and some would claim
infantry or a fleet of long oars
is the supreme sight on the black earth.
    I say it is

the girl you love. And easily proved.
Did not Helen, who was queen of mortal
beauty, choose as first among mankind
    the very scourge

of Trojan honor? Haunted by Love
she forgot kinsmen, her own dear child
and wandered off to a remote country.
    O weak and fitful

woman bending before any man:
so Anaktoria, although you are
far, do not forget your loving friends.
    And I for one

would rather listen to your soft step
and see your radiant face—than watch
all the dazzling horsemen and armored
    hoplites of Lydia.

To Atthis

So I shall never see Atthis again,
and really I long to be dead,
although she too cried bitterly

when she left and she said to me,
"Ah, what a nightmare we've suffered.
Sappho, I swear I go unwillingly."

And I answered, "Go, and be happy.
But remember me, for surely you
know how I worshipped you. If not,

then I want you to remember all
the exquisite days we too shared;
how when near me you would adorn

your hanging locks with violets and
tiny roses and your sapling throat
with necklets of a hundred blossoms;

how your young flesh was rich with kingly
myrrh as you leaned near my breasts on
the soft couch where delicate girls

served us all an Ionian could desire;
how we went to every hill, brook,
and holy place, and when early spring

filled the woods with noises of birds
and a choir of nightingales—we two
in solitude were wandering there."

depended, first of all, on proper respect for and treatment of divine forces: "Please the gods with incense and libations, when you go to bed, and when the holy light returns, that they may favor you, with gracious hearts and spirits, so that you may buy the lands of other men, and they may not buy yours." But success depended on more than prayer; therefore:

. . . you must learn to organize your work
So you may have full barns at harvest time.
From working, men grow rich in flocks and gold

And dearer to the deathless gods. In work
There is no shame; shame is in idleness.
And if you work, the lazy man will soon
Envy your wealth: a rich man can become
Famous and good. No matter what your luck,
To work is better; turn your foolish mind
From other men's possessions to your own,
And earn your living, as I tell you to.[5]

To Hesiod, hard work and honesty were the keys to success.

Theognis of Megara described a way of life considerably different from Hesiod's. Theognis was an aristocrat who lived and wrote primarily in the sixth century B.C. Because of revolutionary upheaval, he, like other aristocrats in sixth-century *poleis*, lost his position and probably his wealth. Sent into exile, he became a bitter man. In his poetry, he portrayed aristocrats as the only good people who are distinguished from others by their natural intelligence, virtue, honor, and moderation. The lower classes or common people were by nature bad and debased:

> Only a fool does favors for the base;
> You'd do as well to sow the grey salt sea.
> No crop of corn would come up from the deep,
> No gratitude, no favors from the base.
> The scum are never sated. If you slip,
> Just once, their former friendship melts away.
> But put a gentleman once in your debt,
> You have a friend for life; he won't forget.

Aristocrats, then, should associate only with other aristocrats: "avoid low company, mix only with the better sort of men. . . . from them you will learn goodness. Men of little worth will spoil the natural virtue of your birth."

The poems of Theognis show clearly the political views and biases of a typical sixth-century aristocrat. It should not surprise us to learn that some of his poems were used to extoll the aristocratic perspective. Some of his poems were also used as drinking songs, especially at symposia. The symposium (*symposion*) was an important part of aristocratic social life. The participants (men only) ate, drank wine, played games, enjoyed such entertainments as dancing and singing, and engaged in contests to see who could compose the best poetry or even the best philosophical argument. Drunkenness was not the goal of the party, as Theognis makes clear in one of his poems: "To drink too much is bad, but if you would drink wisely, you'd find wine not bad, but good." Pleasure was acceptable: "Let's give our hearts to banqueting, while we can still find pleasure in delightful things. For glorious youth goes by as fast as thought."[6] These last lines catch the air of delight, of enjoying life to the full that made the symposium important to the aristocratic class.

The High Point of Greek Civilization: Classical Greece

Classical Greece is the name given to the period of Greek history from around 500 B.C. to the conquest of

CHRONOLOGY

The Persian Wars

Persian control of Greek cities in western Asia Minor	By 546 B.C.
Rebellion of Greek cities in Asia Minor	499–494 B.C.
Battle of Marathon	490 B.C.
Xerxes invades Greece	480–479 B.C.
Battles of Thermopylae and Salamis	480 B.C.
Battles of Plataea and Mycale	479 B.C.

Greece by the Macedonian king Philip II in 338 B.C. It was a period of brilliant achievement, much of it associated with the flowering of democracy in Athens under the leadership of Pericles. Many of the lasting contributions of the Greeks to Western civilization occurred during this period. The age began with a mighty confrontation between the Greek states and the mammoth Persian Empire.

The Challenge of Persia

Archaic Greece had the luxury of developing its civilization without an external threat to its freedom of action. But as Greek civilization grew and expanded throughout the Mediterranean, it was inevitable that it would come into contact with the Persian Empire to the east. In his play *The Persians*, the Greek playwright Aeschylus reflected what some Greeks perceived to be the essential difference between themselves and the Persians. The Persian queen, curious to find out more about the Athenians, asks: "Who commands them? Who is shepherd of their host?" The chorus responds: "They are slaves to none, nor are they subject."[7] Thus, at least some Greeks saw the struggle with the Persians as a contest between freedom and slavery.

The Ionian Greek cities in western Asia Minor had already fallen subject to the Persian Empire by the mid-sixth century B.C. (see Chapter 2). But the Greek cities were restless under Persian tyranny, and a revolt of the Ionian cities, led by the tyrant Aristagoras of Miletus, broke out against the Persians in 499 B.C. Aristagoras sought aid from the mainland Greeks. The Spartans refused, but the Athenians sent twenty ships and helped the Milesians capture and burn Sardis, the

Persian capital of the Lydian satrapy. The success was temporary, however, and the Persians managed to sack Miletus and reestablish control. By 494 B.C., the rebellion had been suppressed. The Persian ruler Darius now decided to attack the mainland Greeks, in part, no doubt, to gain revenge for the Athenian action, but also to expand his empire westward. In 490 B.C., a Persian expedition was sent to Greece.

The Persians sailed across the Aegean, captured Eretria on the island of Euboea across from Attica, and then transferred their army to the plain of Marathon, only twenty-six miles from Athens. The Athenians requested aid from the Spartans, who complied, but arrived too late for the decisive battle at Marathon. The Athenians, aided by the Plataeans (from a neighboring town in Boeotia), confronted the Persians without additional assistance. The two armies were quite different.

The Persians with their light-armed troops were more mobile and flexible and relied heavily on missiles; the Greek hoplites were armed with heavy shields and relied on spear thrusts at close range. The Athenians and Plataeans were clearly outnumbered, but went on the attack anyway and defeated the Persians decisively (see the box on p. 83). The Persians did not mount another attack against mainland Greece for ten years. Although a minor defeat to the Persians, the Battle of Marathon was of great importance to the Athenians, who had proven that the Persians could be beaten.

In the meantime, Athens had acquired a new leader, Themistocles, who persuaded his fellow citizens to pursue a new military policy, namely, the development of a navy. The Athenians used a new vein of silver from Laurium to finance the construction of ships and new port facilities. By 480 B.C., Athens had produced a navy

Map 3.3 The Persian Wars.

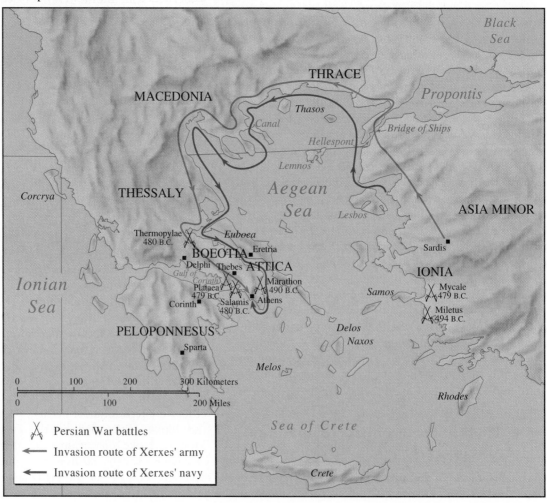

➤ The Battle of Marathon ⬅

The Battle of Marathon (490 B.C.) was an important event in the struggle between the Greeks and Persians. The defeat of the mighty Persians gave Athenian confidence a tremendous boost. In his History of Persian Wars, *the Greek historian Herodotus gave an account of this momentous battle.*

Herodotus, *History of the Persian Wars*

So when the battle was set in array, and the victims showed themselves favorable, instantly the Athenians, so soon as they were let go, charged the barbarians at a run. Now the distance between the two armies was little short of a mile. The Persians, therefore, when they saw the Greeks coming on at speed, made ready to receive them, although it seemed to them that the Athenians were bereft of their senses, and bent upon their own destruction; for they saw a mere handful of men coming on at a run without either horsemen or archers. Such was the opinion of the barbarians; but the Athenians in close array fell upon them, and fought in a manner worthy of being recorded. They were the first of the Greeks, so far as I know, who introduced the custom of charging the enemy at a run, and they were likewise the first who dared to look upon the Median garb, and to face men clad in that fashion. Until this

time the very name of the Medes had been a terror to the Greeks to hear.

The two armies fought together on the plain of Marathon for a length of time; and in the mid battle, where the Persians themselves and the Sacae had their place, the barbarians were victorious, and broke and pursued the Greeks into the inner country; but on the two wings the Athenians and the Plataeans defeated the enemy. Having so done, they suffered the routed barbarians to fly at their ease, and joining the two wings in one, fell upon those who had broken their own centre, and fought and conquered them. These likewise fled, and now the Athenians hung upon the runaways and cut them down, chasing them all the way to the shore, on reaching which they laid hold of the ships and called for fire. . . .

After the full of the moon 2,000 Lacedaemonians [Spartans] came to Athens. So eager had they been to arrive in time, that they took but three days to reach Attica from Sparta. They came, however, too late for the battle; yet, as they had a longing to behold the Medes, they continued their march to Marathon and there viewed the slain. Then, after giving the Athenians all praise for their achievement, they departed and returned home.

of about 200 vessels, primarily triremes (ships with three banks of oars).

A revolt in Egypt, compounded by the death of Darius in 486, kept the Persians from mounting another attack on Greece. Xerxes, the new Persian monarch, was bent on revenge and expansion, however. After first securing Egypt and then spending several years in preparation, he renewed the invasion of Greece. Some of the Greeks prepared by forming a defensive league under Spartan leadership, although many Greek states remained neutral; some even fought on the Persian side.

Xerxes and the Persians undertook their invasion in 480 B.C. Their military forces were massive: close to 150,000 troops, almost 700 naval ships, and hundreds of supply ships to feed their large army. The Persians crossed the Hellespont by a bridge of ships and then moved through Thrace and Macedonia on their way into Greece. The Greek plan, as it evolved, was to fight a delaying action at the pass of Thermopylae along the main road from Thessaly into Boeotia, probably to give

the Greek fleet of 300 ships at Artemisium, off northern Euboea, the chance to fight the Persian fleet. The Greeks knew that the Persian army depended on the fleet for supplies. A Greek force numbering close to 9,000, under the leadership of the Spartan King Leonidas and his contingent of 300 Spartans, managed to hold the Persian army for two days until a Greek traitor told the Persians how to use a mountain path to outflank the Greek force. Although some of the Greeks retreated when they became aware of the Persian movement, King Leonidas and the 300 Spartans fought to the last man.

The Athenians, now threatened by the onslaught of the Persian forces, decided to abandon Athens and evacuated the population of Attica to the offshore island of Salamis. Meanwhile the Greek fleet remained in the straits off Salamis while the Persians sacked and burned Athens. The Peloponnesians wanted the Greeks to retreat to the Peloponnesus and the Greek ships to move to the isthmus as well. Themistocles' refusal and

CHRONOLOGY

━━━━◆◆◆◆◆◆◆◆◆◆◆◆◆◆◆◆◆◆━━━━

Events between the Persian Wars and the Great Peloponnesian War

Delian League created	478–477 B.C.
Victory over Persians in southern Asia Minor	469 B.C.
Ostracism of Cimon	461 B.C.
Curtailment of Areopagus	461 B.C.
Beginning of First Peloponnesian War	c. 460 B.C.
Treasury of Delian League moved to Athens	454 B.C.
Peace with Persia	449 B.C.
Thirty Years' Peace and end of First Peloponnesian War	445 B.C.

his threat to withdraw the Athenian ships altogether if a fight was not made forced the ships to remain and set up the naval Battle of Salamis. Although the Greeks were outnumbered, they managed to outmaneuver the Persian fleet (mostly Phoenicians and Ionians) and decisively defeated them. The Persians still had their army and much of their fleet intact, but Xerxes, frightened at the prospect of another Ionian revolt, decided to return to Asia. He left a Persian force in Thessaly under his general Mardonius.

Early in 479 B.C., the Greeks formed the largest Greek army seen up to that time. The Athenians forced the Spartans to move north of the Peloponnesus and take on the Persians at Plataea, northwest of Attica, where the Greek forces decisively defeated the Persian army. The remnants of the Persian forces returned to Asia. At the same time, the Greeks destroyed much of the Persian fleet in a naval battle at Mycale in Ionia. The Greeks were overjoyed at their victory, but remained cautious. Would the Persians try again?

The Growth of an Athenian Empire

After the defeat of the Persians, some Greeks perceived the need for an offensive policy that would free the Ionian Greek cities in Asia Minor and push the Persians out of the Aegean Sea. The Spartans, always fearful of foreign entanglements, withdrew from the leadership role they had assumed in Greek affairs. Athens stepped

in to provide new leadership against the Persians by forming a confederation called the Delian League.

Organized in the winter of 478/477 B.C., the Delian League was dominated by the Athenians from the beginning. Its main headquarters was the island of Delos, sacred to the Ionian Greeks, but its chief officials, including the treasurers and commanders of the fleet, were Athenians. Athens also provided 100 of the league's 300 ships. While the larger states in the league, such as Lesbos, Samos, and Chios, contributed ships, the smaller communities made payments in money.

Under the leadership of the Athenians, the Delian League pursued the attack against the Persian Empire. Virtually all of the Greek states in the Aegean were liberated from Persian control, and the Persian fleet and army were decisively defeated in 469 B.C. in southern Asia Minor. Arguing that the Persian threat was now over, some members of the Delian League wished to withdraw. Naxos did so in 470 and Thasos in 465 B.C. The Athenians responded vigorously. They attacked both states, destroyed their walls, took over their fleets, eliminated their liberty, and forced them to pay tribute. "No secession" became Athenian policy. The Delian League was rapidly becoming an instrument of Athenian imperialism and the nucleus of an Athenian empire.

THE AGE OF PERICLES

At home, Athenians favored the new imperial policy. One of the chief benefits, a prosperous economy, was only too apparent. Revenues from the Delian League were used to finance building projects that provided Athenians with many construction jobs. Moreover, ships of the Delian League were manned with Athenian rowers, thus creating another sizable group of Athenians who benefited from the empire. Nevertheless, despite agreement on the new empire, considerable squabbling on other issues divided conservative and liberal factions in domestic Athenian politics. The conservative party, led by Cimon, favored more privileges for the property-owning classes and a pro-Spartan foreign policy. The liberal faction was led by Ephialtes, the successor to Themistocles, and a newcomer, a young aristocrat named Pericles. The liberals favored further changes in the direction of democracy and severing the ties with Sparta in order to expand Athenian power in Greece. In 461 B.C., the liberal faction triumphed. Cimon was sent into exile, and the powers of the council of the Areopagus were curtailed. Athens embarked upon both the growth of democracy at home and the expansion of its new empire abroad. Both policies were guided by Pericles, who was a dominant figure in Athenian politics until 429 B.C. This period of Athenian and Greek history, which historians have subsequently labeled the age of Pericles, witnessed the height of Athenian power and the culmination of its brilliance as a civilization.

In the age of Pericles, the Athenians became deeply attached to their democratic system. The sovereignty of the people was embodied in the assembly (*ecclesia*), which consisted of all male citizens over eighteen years of age. In the 440s, that was probably a group of about 43,000. Meetings of the assembly were held four times a year on the hillside of the Pnyx, east of the Acropolis. Not all attended, and the number present seldom exceeded 6,000. The assembly passed all laws and made final decisions on war and foreign policy. Although anyone could speak, usually only respected leaders did so, a feat that required considerable speaking ability in such a large crowd. Pericles expanded the Athenians' involvement in their democracy (see the box on p. 86). Lower-class citizens were now eligible for public offices formerly closed to them. Pericles also introduced state pay for officeholders, including the widely held jury duty. This meant that poor citizens could now afford to participate in public affairs.

The reforms of Cleisthenes had introduced the council of 500 elected by lot from the ten tribes. It prepared the agenda for the assembly and made recommendations for action. Thus the council served as a control on the assembly. The council was divided into ten smaller groups of fifty called prytanies. Each prytany held office for one-tenth of the year to supervise the execution of the laws passed by the assembly.

Routine administration of public affairs was handled by a large body of city magistrates, usually chosen by lot without regard to class. The general directors of policy, a board of ten officials known as generals (*strategoi*), were elected by public vote and were usually wealthy aristocrats, even though the people were free to select otherwise. The generals could be reelected, enabling individual leaders to play an important political role. Pericles, for example, was elected to the generalship thirty times between 461 and 429 B.C. But all public officials were subject to scrutiny and could be deposed from office if they lost the people's confidence. After 488 B.C., the Athenians began to make use of an instrument first devised by Cleisthenes to protect the citizenry against overly ambitious politicians. Called ostracism, this practice enabled the members of the assembly to write on a broken pottery fragment (*ostrakon*) the name of the person they most disliked or considered most

harmful to the *polis*. Frequently, this was a person whose policy, approved at first by the assembly, had failed. A person who received a majority (if at least 6,000 votes were cast) was exiled for ten years, although the practical Athenians often recalled a man from exile if they needed him. Aristides, for example, was recalled in 480 B.C., just two years after he was ostracized, in order to fight the Persians.

The Athenian pursuit of democracy at home was coupled with increasing imperialism abroad as Athens

◆ **Pericles: Roman Copy of Fifth-Century Bronze Original.** Pericles dominated Athenian politics from 461 B.C. until 429 B.C. In addition to increasing the Athenians' participation in their own democratic system, he also pursued an imperialistic policy, expanding the Athenian Empire both on the Greek mainland and abroad. Largely with funds taken from the treasury of the Delian League, Pericles also initiated a number of beautification projects for Athens.

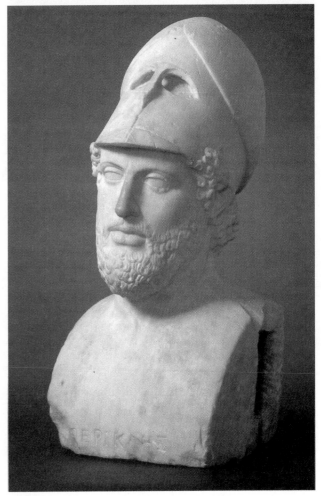

Athenian Democracy: The Funeral Oration of Pericles

In his History of the Peloponnesian War, *the Greek historian Thucydides presented his reconstruction of the eulogy given by Pericles in the winter of 431/430 B.C. to honor the Athenians killed in the first campaigns of the Great Peloponnesian War. It is a magnificent, idealized description of the Athenian democracy at its height.*

Thucydides, *History of the Peloponnesian War*

Our constitution is called a democracy because power is in the hands not of a minority but of the whole people. When it is a question of settling private disputes, everyone is equal before the law; when it is a quesiton of putting one person before another in positions of public responsibility, what counts is not membership of a particular class, but the actual ability which the man possesses. No one, so long as he has it in him to be of service to the state, is kept in political obscurity because of poverty. And, just as our political life is free and open, so is our day-to-day life in our relations with each other. We do not get into a state with our next-door neighbor if he enjoys himself in his own way, nor do we give him the kind of black looks which, though they do no real harm, still do hurt people's feeling. We are free and tolerant in our private lives; but in public affairs we keep to the law. This is because it commands our deep respect.

We give our obedience to those whom we put in positions of authority, and we obey the laws themselves, especially those which are for the protection of the oppressed, and those unwritten laws which it is an acknowledged shame to break. . . . Here each individual is interested not only in his own affairs but in the affairs of the state as well: even those who are mostly occupied with their own business are extremely well-informed on general politics—this is a peculiarity of ours: we do not say that a man who takes no interest in politics is a man who minds his own business; we say that he has no business here at all. We Athenians, in our own persons, take our decisions on polity or submit them to proper discussions: for we do not think that there is an incompatibility between words and deeds; the worst thing is to rush into action before the consequences have been properly debated. . . . Taking everything together then, I declare that our city is an education to Greece, and I declare that in my opinion each single one of our citizens, in all the manifold aspects of life, is able to show himself the rightful lord and owner of his own person and do this, moreover, with exceptional grace and exceptional versatility. And to show that this is no empty boasting for the present occasion, but real tangible fact, you have only to consider the power which our city possesses and which has been won by those very qualities which I have mentioned.

---

attempted to create both a land empire in Greece and a maritime empire in the Aegean. As we have seen, after 470 B.C., Athenian policies had the effect of converting the voluntary allies of the Delian League into the involuntary subjects of an Athenian naval empire. After 462 B.C., Athens attempted to expand its empire on the Greek mainland as well. The creation of a land empire, however, overextended the Athenians and involved them in a series of skirmishes with Sparta and its allies called the First Peloponnesian War (c. 460–445 B.C.). After a series of defeats in 445 B.C., the land empire of Athens disintegrated, and Athens agreed to a Thirty Years' Peace with the Spartans in the following year. Athens consented to give up most of its land empire, and in return, Sparta recognized the existence of Athens' maritime empire.

While building its land empire, Athens continued its offensive against Persia and at the same time tightened its control over the Delian League. Citing the threat of the Persian fleet in the Aegean, the Athenians moved the treasury of the league from the island of Delos to Athens itself in 454 B.C. Members were, in effect, charged a fee (tribute) for the Athenian claim of protection. Pericles also used the treasury money of the league, without the approval of its members, to build new temples in Athens, a clear indication that the Delian League had become the Athenian empire. Henceforth, any protest by a league state against the tribute imposed by Athens could be heard only before an Athenian court. However, Athenian imperialism, pursued both in Greece and abroad, took its toll. Pericles recognized the dangers of Athenian exhaustion and sought a lull; peace was made with Persia in 449 B.C. and, as we have seen, with Sparta in 445 B.C. After 445 B.C., the Athenians had a breathing space in which to beautify Athens and enjoy the fruits of empire, but it was not long before all Greece was confronted with a new and prolonged struggle.

The Great Peloponnesian War (431–404 B.C.)

After the Thirty Years' Peace in 445 B.C., the Greek world seemed to accept that it was divided into two major camps: Sparta and its Peloponnesian League and the Athenian maritime empire. It was not long before the rivalry between the two erupted again into war.

In his classic *History of the Peloponnesian War*, the great Greek historian Thucydides pointed out that the fundamental, long-range cause of the Peloponnesian War was the fear that Athens and its empire inspired in Sparta (see the box on p. 88). The Spartans were especially concerned that Athens would use its superior naval power to weaken Sparta's control of the Peloponnesian League. The immediate causes of the war involved conflicts between Corinth and Athens and between Athens and Megara. When these two allies of Sparta threatened that they would withdraw from the Peloponnesian League if Sparta did not back them, the Spartans sent an ultimatum to Athens: if the Athenians did not back down in their disputes with Corinth and Megara, it would mean war. The Athenians refused to compromise when Pericles convinced them that if they accepted Sparta's ultimatum, they would be admitting that Sparta was the dominant power in Greece.

At the beginning of the war in 431 B.C., both sides believed they had winning strategies. The Athenian plan was based on the navy. The citizens of Attica would be brought in behind the protective walls of Athens and the port of Piraeus, while the overseas empire and the navy would keep them supplied. Pericles knew perfectly well that the Spartans and their allies could beat the Athenians in pitched battles, which, of course, formed the focus of the Spartan strategy. The Spartans and their allies invaded Attica and ravaged the fields and orchards, hoping that the Athenians would send out their army to fight beyond the walls. But Pericles was convinced that Athens was secure behind its walls and retaliated by sending out naval excursions to ravage the seacoast of the Peloponnesus. In the second year of the war, however, a plague devastated the crowded city of Athens and wiped out possibly one-third of the Athenian population. Pericles himself died the following year (429 B.C.), a severe loss to Athens. Dominance now passed to Cleon, leader of the war party, who was opposed by Nicias, head of a conservative faction that favored peace. Despite the losses from the plague, the Athenians fought on in a struggle that witnessed numerous instances of futile destruction. Cleon achieved some successes for the Athenians; Brasi-

das came to be a dynamic general for the Spartans. At the Battle of Amphipolis in 422 B.C., both generals were killed and the new Athenian leader Nicias negotiated the Peace of Nicias (421 B.C.). Although both parties agreed to keep the peace for fifty years, the truce did not really solve the problems that had caused the war in the first place.

A second phase of the war began only six years after the fifty-year truce began. This phase was initiated by Alcibiades, a nephew of Pericles. Elected to the generalship in 420 B.C., he proved to be a poor choice because of his recklessness and self-seeking. In 415 B.C., he convinced the Athenians to invade the island of Sicily, arguing that its conquest would give the Athenians a strong source of support to carry on a lengthy war. But the expedition was ill-fated. Alcibiades himself was removed from leadership of the expedition on a charge of profaning the religious mysteries. Rather than stand trial, he fled to Sparta and advised them how to defeat Athens by getting help from Persia and assembling a

◆ **Greek Trireme.** The trireme became the standard warship of ancient Greece. Highly maneuverable, fast, and outfitted with metal prows, Greek triremes were especially effective at ramming enemy ships. This photo shows the *Olympias*, a trireme reconstructed by the Greek navy.

⇒ *The Significance of the Great Peloponnesian War* ⇐

In his History of the Peloponnesian War, Thucydides gave a detailed account of the origins, course, and effects of the Great Peloponnesian War. Thucydides was an Athenian general who was banished from Athens for failing to win an important battle against the Spartans. Near the beginning of his history, he discussed the significance of this war to the Greeks and its underlying cause.

Thucydides, *History of the Peloponnesian War*

The greatest war in the past was the Persian War; yet in this war the decision was reached quickly as a result of two naval battles and two battles on land. The Peloponnesian War, on the other hand, not only lasted for a long time, but throughout its course brought with it unprecedented suffering for Hellas. Never before had so many cities been captured and then devastated, whether by foreign armies or by the Hellenic Powers themselves; never had there been so many exiles; never such loss of life—both in the actual warfare and in internal revolutions. Old stories of past prodigies, which had not found much confirmation in recent experience, now became credible. Wide areas, for instance, were affected by violent earthquakes; there were more frequent eclipses of the sun than had ever been recorded before; in various parts of the country there were extensive droughts followed by famine; and there was the plague which did more harm and destroyed more life than almost any other single factor. All of these calamities fell together upon the Hellenes after the outbreak of war.

War began when the Athenians and the Peloponnesians broke the Thirty Years Truce which had been made after the capture of Euboea. As to the reasons why they broke the truce, I propose first to give an account of the causes of complaint which they had against each other and of the specific instances where their interests clashed: this is in order that there should be no doubt in anyone's mind about what led to this great war falling upon the Hellenes. But the real reason for the war is, in my opinion, most likely to be disguised by such an argument. What made war inevitable was the growth of Athenian power and the fear which this caused in Sparta.

navy with ships and money supplied by the Persians. The Spartans later followed his advice.

In the meantime, the Athenians pursued the Sicilian policy. A "great expedition" consisting of 5,000 Athenian hoplites was sent out in 415 B.C. and reinforced in 413 B.C. by an even larger army of Athenians and allies. All was in vain. The Athenians failed to take Syracuse and were captured during their retreat. All of the Athenians were killed or sold into slavery. These heavy losses at Syracuse had immediate domestic repercussions. The democracy was weakened and an aristocratic oligarchy was temporarily established (411–410 B.C.).

Despite the disaster, the Athenians refused to give up, but raised new armies and sent out new fleets. The final crushing blow came, however, in 405 B.C., when the Athenian fleet was destroyed at Aegospotami on the Hellespont. Athens was besieged and surrendered in 404 B.C. Its walls were torn down, the navy disbanded, and the Athenian empire destroyed. The great war was finally over.

THE DECLINE OF THE GREEK STATES (404–338 B.C.)

The next seventy years of Greek history are a tale of continuing warfare among the Greeks with the leading roles shifting among Sparta, Athens, and a new Greek power, the city-state of Thebes. After the defeat of Athens in 404 B.C., the Spartans established their own control over Greece. The Athenian empire was dissolved. Oligarchies, headed by local *decarchies* (ten-man boards) in cooperation with Spartan garrisons, were placed in control of the states "liberated" from Athenian imperialism. But oligarchical control proved ineffective, especially in Athens where the ruling oligarchical faction of thirty, set up by the Spartans, earned their nickname of "Thirty Tyrants" by executing about 1,500 of their democratic opponents. This led to a reaction in which the Athenians were able to reestablish their democracy in 403 B.C. They also rebuilt their navy and again became an importance force in the Greek world.

To maintain its newly organized leadership in Greek affairs, Sparta encouraged a Panhellenic crusade against the Persians as a common enemy. The Persians had taken advantage of the Greeks' internal struggle to reimpose their control over the Greek states in western Asia Minor. The Spartans, under King Agesilaus, led a Greek expedition into Asia Minor in 396 B.C. But the Persians had learned the lessons of Greek politics and offered financial support to Athens, Thebes, and other Greek states to oppose Spartan power within Greece itself, thus beginning a new war, the Corinthian War

(395–387 B.C.). The war ended when the Greek states, weary of the struggles, accepted the King's Peace dictated by the Great King of Persia.

The city-state of Thebes, in Boeotia north of Athens, now began to exert its influence. Under their leader Epaminondas, the Thebans dramatically defeated the Spartan army at the Battle of Leuctra in 371 B.C. Spartan power declined, to be replaced by the ascendancy of the Thebans. But Theban power was short-lived. After the death of Epaminondas in the Battle of Mantinea in 362 B.C., the Thebans could no longer dominate Greek politics. And yet the Greek states continued their petty wars, seemingly oblivious to the growing danger to the north where King Philip II of Macedonia was developing a unified state that would finally end the destructive fratricide of the Greek states by imposing Macedonian authority.

The Culture of Classical Greece

Classical Greece saw a period of remarkable intellectual and cultural growth throughout the Greek world. Historians agree, however, that Periclean Athens was the most important center of classical Greek culture. Indeed, the eighteenth-century French philosopher and writer Voltaire listed the Athens of Pericles as one of four happy ages "when the arts were brought to perfection and which, marking an era of the greatness of the human mind, are an example to posterity."[8]

THE BIRTH OF HISTORY

History as we know it, as the systematic analysis of past events, was a Greek creation. Herodotus (c. 484–c. 425 B.C.), an Ionian Greek from Asia Minor, has rightly been

Map 3.4 The Great Peloponnesian War (431–404 B.C.).

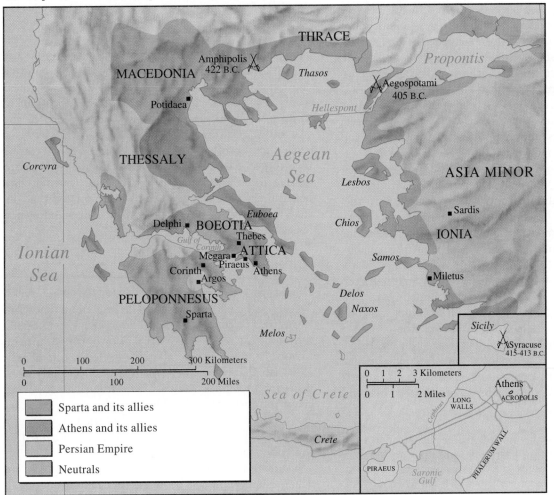

called the "father of history" since his *History of the Persian Wars* is usually regarded as the first real history in Western civilization. It is indeed the earliest lengthy Greek prose work to have survived intact. The Greek word *historia* (from which we derive our word *history*) means "research" or "investigation," and it is in the opening line of Herodotus's *History* that we find the first recorded use of the word:

> These are the researches [*historia*] of Herodotus of Halicarnassus, which he publishes, in the hope of thereby preserving from decay the remembrance of what men have done, and of preventing the great and wonderful actions of the Greeks and the Barbarians from losing their due meed of glory; and withal to put on record what were their ground of feud.[9]

The central theme of Herodotus's work is the conflict between the Greeks and the Persians, which he viewed as a struggle between Greek freedom and oriental despotism. Herodotus felt it important, however, to discuss the histories of all the peoples involved in the Persian Wars and thus provides considerable background information. All of book two, for example (there are nine books in the *History*), is devoted to a discussion of Egyptian history, customs, traditions, and geography. His account demonstrates a remarkable range of interests, including geography, politics, social structures, economics, religion, and even psychology. Herodotus traveled extensively for his information and was dependent for his sources on what we today would call oral history. Although he was a master storyteller and sometimes included considerable fanciful material, Herodotus was also capable of exhibiting a critical attitude toward the materials he used. Regardless of its weaknesses, Herodotus's *History* is an important source of information on the Persians and certainly our chief source on the Persian Wars themselves.

Thucydides (c. 460–c. 400 B.C.) was, by far, the better historian; in fact, historians consider him the greatest historian of the ancient world. Thucydides was an Athenian and a participant in the Peloponnesian War. He had been elected a general, but a defeat in battle led the fickle Athenian assembly to send him into exile, which gave him the opportunity to write his *History of the Peloponnesian War*. In the book, he described his own activities in the war:

> I lived through the whole of it, being of an age to understand what was happening, and I put my mind to the subject so as to get an accurate view of it. It happened, too, that I was banished from my country for twenty years after my command at Amphipolis [424 B.C.]; I saw what was being done on both sides, particularly on the Peloponnesian side, because of my exile, and this leisure gave me rather exceptional facilities for looking into things.[10]

Some scholars regard Thucydides as the first modern historian. Unlike Herodotus, Thucydides was not concerned with underlying divine forces or gods as explanatory causal factors in history. He saw war and politics in purely rational terms, as the activities of human beings. He examined the long-range and immediate causes of the Peloponnesian War in a clear, methodical, objective fashion. Thucydides placed much emphasis on accuracy and the precision of his facts. As he stated:

> And with regard to my factual reporting of the events of the war I have made it a principle not to write down the first story that came my way, and not even to be guided by my own general impressions; either I was present myself at the events which I have described or else I heard of them from eyewitnesses whose reports I have checked with as much thoroughness as possible.[11]

Thucydides also provided remarkable insight into the human condition. He believed that human nature was a constant: "It will be enough for me, however, if these words of mine are judged useful by those who want to understand clearly the events which happened in the past and which (human nature being what it is) will, at some time or other and in much the same ways, be repeated in the future."[12] He was not so naive as to believe in an exact repetition of events, but felt that political situations recur in similar fashion and that the study of history is of great value in understanding the present.

GREEK DRAMA

Drama, as we know it, was created by the Greeks. Tragedy was clearly intended to do more than entertain. It was used to educate citizens and was supported by the state for that reason. Its origins, however, are unclear. Many historians assume that it developed out of religious ritual, and its performance was certainly connected to religious festivals. In Athens, tragedy was given its initial form by Thespis, who wrote tragedies that were performed at the festival of the City Dionysia (see Greek Religion later in this chapter) instituted by the tyrant Pisistratus in the 530s B.C.

Drama was a city-state event; the issues it raised were deemed important to the lives of citizens. A series of plays would be performed outdoors in the daytime over the course of several days. Greek tragedy adhered to a rather stable form. Three males who wore masks acted all the parts (including the female roles). A chorus (also male) spoke the important lines that explained what was going on. Action was very limited, since the emphasis was on the story and its meaning. Content was generally based on myths or legends that the audience already knew. In fact, early Greek tragedy derived many of its themes and its basic preoccupation with the sufferings of the tragic hero from Homer.

Aeschylus (525–456 B.C.) is the first tragedian whose plays are known to us. He had fought at the battles of Marathon and Salamis and considered his participation there a greater achievement than his plays. Although he wrote ninety tragedies, only seven have survived. As was customary in Greek tragedy, his plots are simple, and the characters are primarily embodiments of a single passion. The entire drama focuses on a single tragic event and its meaning. At the City Dionysia, Greek tragedies were supposed to be presented in a trilogy (a set of three plays) built around a common theme. The only complete trilogy we possess, called the *Oresteia,* was composed by Aeschylus. The theme of this trilogy is derived from Homer. Agamemnon, the king of Mycenae, returns a hero from the defeat of Troy. His wife Clytemnestra revenges the sacrificial death of her daughter Iphigenia by murdering Agamemnon, who had been responsible for Iphigenia's death. In the second play of the trilogy, Agamemnon's son Orestes avenges his father by killing his mother. Orestes is now pursued by the avenging furies who torment him for killing his mother. Evil acts breed evil acts and suffering is one's lot, suggests Aeschylus. But Orestes is put on trial and acquitted by Athena, the patron goddess of Athens. Personal vendetta has been eliminated and law has prevailed. Reason has triumphed over the forces of evil.

Sophocles (c. 496–406 B.C.) added a third actor to his plays and diminished the role of the chorus. Only 7 of his 123 plays have survived. Probably his most famous play, considered by the Greek philosopher Aristotle to be the best example of tragedy, was *Oedipus the King.* The oracle of Apollo foretells that a man (Oedipus) will kill his own father and marry his mother. Despite all attempts at prevention, the tragic events occur. Although it appears that Oedipus suffered the fate determined by the gods, Oedipus also accepts that he himself as a free man must bear responsibility for his actions: "It was Apollo, friends, Apollo, that brought this bitter bitterness, my sorrows to completion. But the hand that struck me was none but my own."[13]

✦ **The Theater at Epidaurus.** Drama in ancient Greece was designed to do more than simply entertain. Tragedy generally had an educational function, while comedy examined contemporary issues and was used to attack or satirize prominent individuals. This photo shows the theater at Epidaurus in the eastern Peloponnesus. It held 18,000 onlookers for the theatrical presentations and athletic games that were part of the religious festivals dedicated to Asclepius, the god of healing.

The third outstanding Athenian tragedian, Euripides (c. 485–406 B.C.), moved beyond his predecessors in creating more realistic characters. His plots also became more complex with a greater interest in real-life situations. Perhaps the greatest of all his plays was *The Bacchae,* which dealt with the introduction of the hysterical rites associated with Dionysus, god of wine. Euripides is often seen as a skeptic, who questioned traditional moral and religious values. Was *The Bacchae* a criticism of the gods' traditional behavior? Euripides was also critical of the traditional view that war was glorious. He portrayed war as brutal and barbaric and expressed deep compassion for the women and children who suffered from it.

Greek tragedies dealt with universal themes still relevant to our day. They probed such problems as the nature of good and evil, the conflict between spiritual values and the demands of the state or family, the rights of the individual, the nature of divine forces, and the nature of human beings. Over and over again, the tragic lesson was repeated: humans were free and yet could

❧ Athenian Comedy: Sex as an Antiwar Instrument ❧

Greek comedy became a regular feature of the dramatic presentations at the festival of Dionysus in Athens beginning in 488/487 B.C. Aristophanes used his comedies to present political messages, and especially to express his antiwar sentiments. The plot of Lysistrata centers on a sex strike by wives in order to get their husbands to end the Peloponnesian War. In this scene from the play, Lysistrata (whose name means "she who dissolves the armies") has the women take a special oath.

Aristophanes, *Lysistrata*

LYSISTRATA: Lampito: all of you women: come, touch the bowl, and repeat after me: *I WILL HAVE NOTHING TO DO WITH MY HUSBAND OR MY LOVER*

KALONIKE: I will have nothing to do with my husband or my lover

LYSISTRATA: *THOUGH HE COME TO ME IN PITIABLE CONDITION*

KALONIKE: Though he come to me in pitiable condition (Oh, Lysistrata! This is killing me!)

LYSISTRATA: *I WILL STAY IN MY HOUSE UNTOUCHABLE*

KALONIKE: I will stay in my house untouchable

LYSISTRATA: *IN MY THINNEST SAFFRON SILK*

KALONIKE: In my thinnest saffron silk

LYSISTRATA: *AND MAKE HIM LONG FOR ME.*

KALONIKE: And make him long for me.

LYSISTRATA: *I WILL NOT GIVE MYSELF*

KALONIKE: I will not give myself

LYSISTRATA: *AND IF HE CONSTRAINS ME*

KALONIKE: And if he constrains me

LYSISTRATA: *I WILL BE AS COLD AS ICE AND NEVER MOVE*

KALONIKE: I will be as cold as ice and never move

LYSISTRATA: *I WILL NOT LIFT MY SLIPPERS TOWARD THE CEILING*

KALONIKE: I will not lift my slippers toward the ceiling

LYSISTRATA: *OR CROUCH ON ALL FOURS LIKE THE LIONESS IN THE CARVING*

KALONIKE: Or crouch on all fours like the lioness in the carving

LYSISTRATA: *AND IF I KEEP THIS OATH LET ME DRINK FROM THIS BOWL*

KALONIKE: And if I keep this oath let me drink from this bowl

LYSISTRATA: *IF NOT, LET MY OWN BOWL BE FILLED WITH WATER.*

KALONIKE: If not, let my own bowl be filled with water.

LYSISTRATA: You have all sworn?

MYRRHINE: We have.

operate only within limitations imposed by the gods. The real task was to cultivate the balance and moderation that led to awareness of one's true position. But the pride in human accomplishment and independence is real. As the chorus chants in Sophocles' *Antigone:* "Is there anything more wonderful on earth, our marvellous planet, than the miracle of man?"[14]

Competitions for Greek comedy developed later than those for tragedy. We first see comedies organized at the festival of Dionysus in Athens in 488/487 B.C. The plays of Aristophanes (c. 450–c. 385 B.C.), who used both grotesque masks and obscene jokes to entertain the Athenian audience, are examples of Old Comedy. But comedy in Athens was also more clearly political than tragedy. It was used to attack or savagely satirize both politicians and intellectuals. In *The Clouds,* for example, Aristophanes characterized the philosopher Socrates as the operator of a thought factory where people could learn deceitful ways to handle other people. Later plays gave up the element of personal attack and featured contemporary issues. Of special importance to Aristophanes was his opposition to the Peloponnesian War. *Lysistrata,* performed in 411 B.C., at a time when Athens was in serious danger of losing the war, had a comic but effective message against the war (see the box above).

THE ARTS: THE CLASSICAL IDEAL

The arts of the Western world have been largely dominated by the artistic standards established by the Greeks of the classical period. Classical Greek art did not aim at experimentation for experiment's sake, but was concerned with expressing eternally true ideals. Its subject matter was basically the human being, but expressed harmoniously as an object of great beauty. The classic style, based on the ideals of reason, moderation, symmetry, balance, and harmony in all things, was meant to civilize the emotions.

In architecture the most important form was the temple dedicated to a god or goddess. Since Greek religious ceremonies were held at altars in the open air, temples were not used to enclose the faithful, as modern churches are. At the center of Greek temples were walled rooms that housed the statues of deities and treasuries in which gifts to the gods and goddesses were safeguarded. These central rooms were surrounded, however, by a screen of columns that make Greek temples open structures rather than closed ones. The columns were originally made of wood, but changed to limestone in the seventh century and to marble in the fifth century B.C. The most significant formal element in Greek temples was the shape and size of the columns in combination with the features above and below the column. The Doric order, evolved first in the Dorian Peloponnesus, consisted of thick, fluted columns with simple capitals resting directly on a platform without a base. Above the capitals was a fairly complex entablature. The Greeks considered the Doric order grave, dignified, and masculine. The Ionic style was first devel-

oped in western Asia Minor and consisted of slender columns with a more elaborate base and volute or spiral-shaped capitals. The Greeks characterized the Ionic order as slender, elegant, and feminine in principle. Corinthian columns, with their more detailed capitals modeled after acanthus leaves, came later, near the end of the fifth century B.C.

It is in fifth-century Athens that some of the finest examples of Greek classical architecture were built. The development of Athenian architecture was aided tremendously by the massive rebuilding program funded from the treasury of the Delian League and instituted almost a half-century after the Persians destroyed Athens in the Persian Wars. New buildings were erected in the agora, but especially important was a series of constructions on the Acropolis begun in 448 B.C., which included a monumental entrance gate, a temple to Athena Nike (the Bringer of Victory), and the Erechtheum, a multilevel temple. These temples honored the gods and heroes who protected Athens. The most famous building, regarded as the greatest example of the classical Greek temple, was the Parthenon, built between 447 and 432 B.C. The master builders Ictinus and

◆ **Doric, Ionic and Corinthian Orders.** The illustration depicts the Doric, Ionic, and Corinthian orders of columns. The size and shape of a column constituted one of the most important aspects of Greek temple architecture. The Doric order, with plain capitals and no base, developed first in the

Dorian Peloponnesus and was rather simple in comparison to the slender Ionic column, which had an elaborate base and spiral-shaped capitals, and the Corinthian column, which featured leaf-shaped capitals.

The Parthenon. The arts in classical Greece were designed to express the eternal ideals of reason, moderation, symmetry, balance, and harmony. In architecture, the most important form was the temple, and the classical example of this kind of architecture is the Parthenon, built between 447 and 432 B.C. The Parthenon, located on the Acropolis, was dedicated to Athena, the patron goddess of the city, but it also served as a shining example of the power and wealth of the Athenian Empire.

Callicrates directed the construction of this temple, which was consecrated to Athena, the patron goddess of Athens. We could say, however, that the Parthenon, an expression of Athenian enthusiasm, was also dedicated to the glory of Athens and the Athenians. The Parthenon typifies the principles of classical architecture: the search for calmness, clarity, and freedom from superfluous detail. The individual parts of the temple were constructed in accordance with certain mathematical ratios also found in natural phenomena. The concern of the architects with these laws of proportion is paralleled by the attempt of Greek philosophers to understand the general laws underlying nature.

Greek sculpture also developed a classic style that differed significantly from the artificial stiffness of the *kouros* figure of the archaic period. Statues of the male nude, the favorite subject of Greek sculptors, now exhibited more relaxed attitudes; their faces were self-assured; their bodies flexible and smooth-muscled. Although the figures possessed natural features that made them lifelike, Greek sculptors sought to achieve not realism, but a standard of ideal beauty. Polyclitus, a fifth-century sculptor, authored a treatise (now lost) on a canon of proportions that he illustrated in a work known as the *Doryphoros*. His theory maintained that the use of ideal proportions, based on mathematical ratios found in nature, could produce an ideal human form, beautiful in its perfected and refined features. This search for ideal beauty was the dominant feature of the classical standard in sculpture.

THE GREEK LOVE OF WISDOM

Philosophy is a Greek word that originally meant "love of wisdom." Although influenced by the cosmology and theology of the Near East, early Greek philosophers went their own way in seeking "wisdom." They were concerned with the development of critical or rational thought about the nature of the universe and the place of divine forces and souls in it.

Much of early Greek philosophy focused on the attempt to explain the universe on the basis of unifying principles. Thales of Miletus, an Ionian Greek who lived around 600 B.C., postulated the unity of the universe. All things were linked by water as the basic substance. Another Ionian Greek, Pythagoras (c. 580–c. 490 B.C.), taught that the essence of the universe could be found in music and number. These early Greek philosophers may have eliminated the role of the gods as they were portrayed in Greek myths, but they did not eliminate divinity itself from the world, tending instead to identify it with the underlying, unchanging forces that govern the universe.

Another major preoccupation of the so-called pre-Socratic philosophers (Greek philosophers before Socrates) was the nature of reality. Some philosophers saw change as the only reality, while others took the opposite view that all change is merely an illusion of the senses. Empedocles (c. 493–c. 433 B.C.) arrived at a compromise, believing that there are four basic substances: earth, air, fire, and water. They are unchanging, but their interaction makes up the physical universe and produces the appearance of change.

Many Greeks, however, were simply not interested in speculations on the nature of the universe or reality. The Sophists were a group of philosophical teachers in the fifth century who rejected such speculation as foolish; they argued that to understand the universe was simply beyond the reach of the human mind. It was more important for individuals to improve themselves, so the only worthwhile object of study was human behavior. The Sophists were wandering scholars who sold their services as professional teachers to the young men of Greece, especially those of Athens. The Sophists stressed the importance of rhetoric (the art of persuasive speaking) in winning debates and swaying an audience, a skill that was especially valuable in democratic Athens. The Sophists tended to be skeptics who questioned the traditional values of their societies. Their skepticism was often intertwined with relativism, the idea that there are no absolute values or beliefs. There was, for example, no absolute right or wrong—what was right for one individual might be wrong for another. Consequently, true wisdom consisted of being able to perceive one's own good and to pursue its acquisition. Many people, however, viewed the Sophists as harmful to the traditional values of society and especially dangerous to the values of young people.

In classical Greece, Athens became the foremost intellectual and artistic center. Its reputation is perhaps strongest of all in philosophy. After all, Socrates, Plato, and Aristotle raised basic questions that have been debated for two thousand years; these are still largely the same philosophical questions we wrestle with today.

Socrates (469–399 B.C.) left no writings, but we know about him from his pupils, especially his most famous one, Plato. By occupation, Socrates was a stonemason, but his true love was philosophy. He taught a number of pupils, but not for pay, since he believed that the goal of education was only to improve the individual. He made use of a teaching method that is still known by his name. The "Socratic method" utilizes a question-and-answer technique to lead pupils to see things for themselves by using their own reason. Socrates believed that all real knowledge is within each person; only critical examination was needed to call it forth. This was the real task of philosophy since "the unexamined life is not worth living."

Socrates' questioning of authority and public demonstrations of others' lack of knowledge led him into trouble. Athens had had a tradition of free thought and inquiry, but defeat in the Peloponnesian War had created an environment intolerant of open debate and soul-searching. Socrates was accused and convicted of corrupting the youth of Athens by his teaching. An Athenian jury sentenced him to death (see the box on p. 96).

One of Socrates' disciples was Plato (c. 429–347 B.C.), considered by many the greatest philosopher of Western civilization. Unlike his master Socrates, who wrote nothing, Plato wrote a great deal. In his dialogues, he used Socrates as his chief philosophical debater.

Plato's philosophical thought focused on the essence of reality and was centered in the concept of Ideas or ideal Forms. According to Plato, a higher world of eternal, unchanging Ideas or Forms has always existed. To know these Forms is to know truth. These ideal Forms constitute reality and can only be apprehended by a trained mind, which, of course, is the goal of philosophy. The objects that we perceive with our senses are simply reflections of the ideal Forms. Hence, they are shadows while reality is found in the Forms themselves.

Plato's ideas of government were set out in his dialogue entitled *The Republic*. Based on his experience in Athens, Plato had come to distrust the workings of democracy. It was obvious to Plato that individuals could not attain an ethical life unless they lived in a just and rational state. Plato's search for the just state led him to construct an ideal state. *The Republic* is often considered the first major work of utopian literature. In his ideal state, the population was divided into three

◆ **Doryphoros.** This statue, known as the *Doryphoros*, or spear-carrier, is by the fifth-century sculptor Polyclitus, who believed it illustrated the ideal proportions of the human figure. Classical Greek sculpture moved away from the stiffness of the *kouros* figure, but retained the young male nude as the favorite subject matter. The statues became more lifelike, with relaxed poses and flexible, smooth-muscled bodies. The aim of sculpture, however, was not simply realism, but rather the expression of ideal beauty.

≽ The Death of Socrates ≼

In his dialogue entitled the Phaedo, *Plato gave an account of the death of his teacher. Socrates had been charged with corrupting the youth of Athens and was sentenced to death by an Athenian jury. He died by drinking poison (hemlock) as described in this scene. Some historians, however, have questioned whether the effects of hemlock are as gentle as portrayed here.*

Plato, *Phaedo*

At this Crito made a sign to his servant, who was standing near by. The servant went out and after spending a considerable time returned with the man who was to administer the poison; he was carrying it ready prepared in a cup. When Socrates saw him he said: "Well, my good fellow, you understand these things; what ought I to do?"

"Just drink it," he said, "and then walk about until you feel a weight in your legs, and then lie down. Then it will act of its own accord. . . ."

Up till this time most of us had been fairly successful in keeping back our tears; but when we saw that he was drinking, that he had actually drunk it, we could do so no longer; in spite of myself the tears came pouring out, so that I covered my face and wept broken-heartedly—not for him, but for my own calamity in losing such a friend. . . . Socrates ∴ . . said:

"Really, my friends, what a way to behave! Why, that was my main reason for sending away the women, to prevent this sort of disturbance; because I am told that one should make one's end in a tranquil frame of mind. Calm yourselves and try to be brave."

This made us feel ashamed, and we controlled our tears. Socrates walked about, and presently, saying that his legs were heavy, lay down on his back—that was what the man recommended. The man. . .kept his hand upon Socrates, and after a little while examined his feet and legs; then pinched his foot hard and asked if he felt it. Socrates said no. Then he did the same to his legs; and moving gradually upwards in this way let us see that he was getting cold and numb. Presently he felt him again and said that when it reached the heart, Socrates would be gone.

The coldness was spreading about as far as his waist when Socrates uncovered his face—for he had covered it up—and said (they were his last words): "Crito, we ought to offer a cock to Asclepius [the god of healing]. See to it, and don't forget."

"No, it shall be done," said Crito. "Are you sure that there is nothing else?"

Socrates made no reply to this question, but after a little while he stirred; and when the man uncovered him, his eyes were fixed. When Crito saw this, he closed the mouth and eyes.

Such . . . was the end of our comrade, who was, we may fairly say, of all those whom we knew in our time, the bravest and also the wisest and most upright man.

---

basic groups. At the top was an upper class, a ruling elite, the famous philosopher-kings: "Unless either philosophers become kings in their countries or those who are now called kings and rulers come to be sufficiently inspired with a genuine desire for wisdom; unless, that is to say, political power and philosophy meet together . . . there can be no rest from troubles . . . for states, nor yet, as I believe, for all mankind."[15] The second group were those who showed courage; they would be the warriors who protected the society. All the rest made up the masses, essentially people driven, not by wisdom or courage, but by desire for material things. They would be the producers of society—the artisans, tradesmen, and farmers.

In Plato's ideal state, each group fulfilled its assigned role, creating a society that functioned harmoniously. The needs of the community, rather than the happiness of the individual, were Plato's concern, and he focused on the need for the guardians or rulers, above all, to be removed from any concerns for wealth or prestige so that they could strive for what was best for the community. To rid the guardians of these desires, Plato urged that they live together, forgoing both private property and family life. Plato believed that women, too, could be rulers; in this, he departed radically from the actual practices of the Greek states.

Plato established a school at Athens known as the Academy. One of his pupils, who studied there for twenty years, was Aristotle (384–322 B.C.), who later became a tutor to Alexander the Great. Aristotle differed significantly from his teacher in that he did not accept Plato's theory of ideal Forms. He, like Plato, believed in universal principles or forms, but he believed that form and matter were inseparable. By examining individual objects, we can perceive their form and arrive at universal principles, but they do not exist as a separate higher world of reality beyond material things, but are a part of things themselves. Aristotle's interests, then, lay in analyzing and classifying things based on thorough research and investigation. His interests were wide-ranging, and he wrote treatises on an enormous number of subjects: ethics, logic, politics, poetry, astronomy, geology, biology, and physics.

Like Plato, Aristotle wished for an effective form of government that would rationally direct human affairs. Unlike Plato, he did not seek an ideal state based on embodiment of an ideal Form of justice, but tried to find the best form of government by a rational examination of existing governments. For his *Politics*, Aristotle examined the constitutions of 158 states and arrived at general categories for organizing governments. He identified three good forms of government: monarchy, aristocracy, and constitutional government. But based on his examination, he warned that monarchy can easily turn into tyranny, aristocracy into oligarchy, and constitutional government into radical democracy or anarchy. He favored constitutional government as the best form for most people.

With Aristotle's death, the great age of classical Greek philosophy came to an end. By 322 B.C., the world of the small city-state was also coming to a close, and a time for new empires had arrived. Philosophical thought began to move into new channels.

Greek Religion

The emphasis on rationalism and the role of human beings in Greek literature and thought might lead some to believe that a spiritual perspective was not important to the Greeks. This is simply not true. Even Plato, the greatest of the philosophers, though skeptical of popular religious manifestations, believed in a divine principle. Greek religion was intricately connected to every aspect of daily life; it was both social and practical. Public festivals, which originated from religious practices, served specific functions: boys were prepared to be warriors, girls to be mothers. Especially dangerous activities, such as seafaring, required numerous rituals because the people involved needed special protection. Since religion was related to every aspect of life, citizens had to have a proper attitude to the gods. Religion was a civic cult necessary for the well-being of the state. Temples dedicated to a god or goddess were the major buildings of Greek society. Much misunderstanding about the role of Greek religion arises because, unlike Christianity, Greek religion did not require belief in a body of doctrine. There were no sacred books, such as the Bible. Proper ritual rather than belief was the crucial element of Greek religion. It had no official body of priests enunciating dogma and controlling religious matters. Although there were priests and priestesses to care for certain religious shrines, most religious ceremonies were led by civilians serving as priests, and priesthoods were civic offices.

The epic poetry of Homer contained a coherent theogony, or genealogy of the gods, that served to give a definite structure to Greek religion. Over a period of time, all Greeks accepted a common Olympian religion. There were twelve chief gods who supposedly lived on Mount Olympus, the highest mountain in Greece. Among the twelve were Zeus, the chief deity and father of the gods; Athena, goddess of wisdom and crafts; Apollo, god of the sun and poetry; Aphrodite, goddess of love; and Poseidon, brother of Zeus and god of the seas and earthquakes.

Greek mythology was closely related to the gods and goddesses of Greek religion, although it also included stories of heroes and heroines. Through the works of Homer and Hesiod, gods were seen as human in their activities, but also superhuman in that they were immortal. While the mythic stories were often entertaining, they also served a number of purposes: they could explain phenomena, such as thunderbolts (from Zeus); they could serve a political function, such as legitimizing control of a particular territory; they could define relationships, such as those between men and women, or between humans and gods; and they could preserve the history of names and great events. They could also be very confusing since the many variants of the stories often conflicted with each other.

The twelve Olympian gods were common to all Greeks, who thus shared a basic polytheistic religion. Each *polis* usually singled out one of the twelve Olympians as a guardian deity of its community. Athena was the patron goddess of Athens, for example. But each *polis* also had its own local deities who remained important to the community as a whole, and each family had patron gods as well. Since it was desirable to have the gods look favorably upon one's activities, ritual assumed enormous proportions in Greek religion. Prayers were often combined with gifts to the gods based on the principle, "I give so that you [the gods] will give [in return]." Some prayers directly reflected this mutual benefit: "Protect our city. I believe that what I say is in

✦ **The Temple of Apollo at Delphi.** Oracles were sacred shrines dedicated to a god or goddess who revealed the future. The oracle of Apollo at Delphi was the most famous in the Greek world. Seen here are the restored columns of the temple of Apollo in its magnificent natural setting. After an earthquake destroyed the first temple in 373 B.C., it was rebuilt on the same plan.

our common interest. For a flourishing city honors the gods." Ritual meant sacrifices, whether of animals or agricultural products. Animal victims were burned on an altar in front of a temple or on a small altar in front of a home. The Greeks maintained religious calendars (lists of sacrifices) specifying what a god or goddess should receive and on what day it should be offered. The father made sacrifices for the family, officials did so for the state.

Festivals were also developed as a way to honor the gods and goddesses. Some of these (the Panhellenic celebrations) came to have international significance and were held at special locations, such as those dedicated to the worship of Zeus at Olympia; to Poseidon at the Isthmus of Corinth; and to Apollo at Delphi. The great festivals incorporated numerous events in honor of the gods, including athletic competitions to which all Greeks were invited. The first such games were held at the Olympic festival in 776 B.C. and then held every four years thereafter to honor Zeus. Initially, the Olympic contests consisted of foot races and wrestling, but later, boxing, javelin throwing, and various other contests were added. Competitions were always between individuals, not groups.

Individual *poleis* also held religious festivals on a regular basis. At Athens, the most splendid was the Great Panathenaia, begun in the early sixth century and held every four years in July. Dedicated to the patron goddess Athena, the highlight of the festival was a great procession of the entire community through the city. But as with all great religious festivals, the Great Panathenaia also included dancing and singing, choruses of men and women, torch races, and athletic and musical contests. At the festival of Dionysus, known as the City Dionysia, tragedies and comedies were presented as part of the festival.

As another practical side of Greek religion, Greeks wanted to know the will of the gods. There were seers who obtained omens from dreams, the flight of birds, or the entrails of sacrificial animals. But perhaps the most famous method of divining the will of the gods was the use of the oracle, a sacred shrine dedicated to a god or goddess who revealed the future. The most famous was the oracle of Apollo at Delphi, located on the side of Mount Parnassus, overlooking the Gulf of Corinth. At Delphi, a priestess listened to questions while in a state of ecstasy that was believed to be induced by Apollo. Her responses were interpreted by the priests and given in verse form to the person asking questions. Representatives of states and individuals traveled to Delphi to consult the oracle of Apollo. States might inquire whether they should undertake a military expedition; individuals might raise such questions as, "Heracleidas asks the god whether he will have offspring from the wife he has now." Responses were often enigmatic and could be interpreted more than one way. Croesus, the king of Lydia in Asia Minor who was known for his incredible wealth, sent messengers to the oracle at Delphi, asking "whether he shall go to war with the Persians." The oracle replied that if Croesus attacked the Persians, he would destroy a mighty empire. Overjoyed to hear these words, Croesus made war on the Persians but was crushed by his enemy. A mighty empire—that of Croesus—was destroyed.

Greek religion, centered in ritual and a formal relationship with the gods, tended to lack a strong emotional component. It also offered little or no certain hope of life after death for most people. As a result, the Greeks sometimes turned to mystery religions, which included initiation into secret rites that promised a more emotional involvement with spiritual forces and a greater hope of immortality. The most important mysteries were those of the Eleusinian cult connected with the myth of Demeter. This was a fertility cult in which participants felt reborn and gained some hope for life after death. The Orphic cultists, who considered themselves followers of the legendary singer Orpheus, believed in cycles of reincarnation since the human soul had become trapped in the physical body. Their aim was to liberate the soul from its confinement.

Daily Life in Classical Athens

The Greek city-state was, above all, a male community: only adult male citizens took part in public life. In Athens, this meant the exclusion of women, slaves, and foreign residents, or roughly 85 percent of the total population of Attica. In the fifth century, Athens had the largest population of all the Greek city-states. There were probably 150,000 citizens, of whom about 43,000 were adult males who exercised political power. Resident foreigners, known as metics, numbered about 35,000. In return for registering with the authorities and paying a small tax, metics received the protection of the laws. They were also subject to some of the responsibilities of citizens, namely, military service and the funding of festivals. Metics were usually loyal to Athens, and some, in fact, became prosperous through industry, trade, or banking. A few even became citizens. The remaining social group, the slaves, numbered around 100,000.

Slavery was a common institution in the ancient world. Owners of slaves in Athens were permitted to treat their slaves as they wished, although it was obviously not to their advantage to be overly harsh. Economic necessity dictated the desirability of owning at least one slave, although the very poor in Athens did not own any. A soldier on campaign usually took along one slave to carry his armor. The really wealthy might own large numbers, but those who did usually employed them in industry. Most often, slaves in Athens performed domestic tasks, such as being cooks and maids, or worked in the fields. Few peasants could afford more than one or two. Other slaves worked as unskilled and skilled labor. Slaves who worked in public construction were paid the same as metics or citizens. Some slaves were able to save their earnings and eventually buy their freedom. In many ways, as some historians have argued, although Athens was a slave-owning society, the economy was not dependent on the use of slaves. Slavery in most instances was a substitute for wage labor, which was frowned upon by most freedom-loving Athenians. Only in one area of economic life did the Athenians have a real slave economy, and that was in the silver mines of Laurium.

The Athenian economy was largely agricultural, but highly diversified as well. Agriculture consisted of growing grains, vegetables, and fruit trees for local consumption; vines and olive trees for wine and olive oil, which were exportable products; and the grazing of sheep and goats for wool and milk products. Given the size of the population in Attica and the lack of abundant fertile land, Athens had to import between 50 and 80 percent of its grain, a staple in the Athenian diet. Trade was thus highly important to the Athenian economy. The building of the port at Piraeus and the Long Walls (a series of defensive walls four and one-half miles long connecting Athens and Piraeus) created the physical conditions that made Athens the leading trade center in the fifth-century Greek world.

Athens did not have large numbers of craftsmen, but they were important to the economy. Athens was the chief producer of high-quality painted pottery in the fifth century. Other crafts had moved beyond the small workshop into the factory through the use of slave labor. The shield factory of Lysias, for example, employed 120 slaves. Public works projects also provided considerable livelihood for Athenians. The building program of Pericles, financed from the Delian League treasury, made possible the hiring of both skilled and unskilled labor. This labor force was mixed, consisting of free Athenians, foreign residents, and slaves. All were paid the same wages. The mining of silver was also important to the Athenian economy, especially the new vein discovered at Laurium early in the fifth century. The state leased concessions to private entrepreneurs who used gangs of slaves in the mines. Profits were enormous, both for the state and for the individuals who bought the concessions, as well as for the suppliers of labor. Nicias, who provided a labor force of 1,000 slaves, made a 33 percent return on his capital investment. In fact, given the pitiful working conditions, many slaves did not survive more than three years working in the mines. Even at that, an investor could still make money by simply buying new slaves rather than caring for the old ones.

The Athenian lifestyle was basically simple. Athenian houses were furnished with necessities bought from craftsmen, such as beds, couches, tables, chests, pottery, stools, baskets, and cooking utensils. Clothes and blankets were made at home by wives and slaves. The Athenian diet was rather plain. Basic foods consisted of barley, wheat, millet, lentils, grapes, figs, olives, almonds, bread made at home, vegetables, eggs, fish, cheese, and chicken. Olive oil was widely used, not only for eating, but for lighting lamps, and rubbing on the body after washing and exercise. Although country houses kept animals, they were used for reasons other than their flesh: oxen for ploughing, sheep for wool, and goats for milk and cheese. Meat was consumed only on special occasions, such as festivals when animals were sacrificed and the cooked meat then eaten.

The family was an important institution in ancient Athens. It was composed of husband, wife, and children (a nuclear family), although other dependent relatives and slaves were regarded as part of the family because of its economic unity. The family's primary social function was to produce new citizens. Strict laws of the fifth century had stipulated that a citizen must be the off-spring of a legally acknowledged marriage between two Athenian citizens whose parents were also citizens. By law, property was divided by lot among all the surviving

✦ Women in the Loom Room. In Athens, women were considered to be citizens and could participate in religious cults and festivals, but they had no rights and were barred from any political activity. Women were thought to belong in the house, caring for the children and the needs of the household. A principal activity of Greek women was the making of clothes. This vase shows two women working on a warp-weighted loom.

sons; as a result, marriages were usually sought within a close circle of relatives so as to preserve the family property. The family also served to protect and enclose women.

Women were citizens who could participate in most religious cults and festivals, but were otherwise excluded from public life. They could not own property beyond personal items and always had a male guardian: if unmarried, a father or male relative; if married, a husband; if widowed, a son or male relative.

The function of the Athenian woman as wife was very clear. Her foremost obligation was to bear children, especially male children who would preserve the family line. The marriage formula that Athenians used put it succinctly: "I give this woman for the procreation of legitimate children." Secondly, a wife was to take care of her family and her house, either doing the household work herself or supervising the slaves who did the actual work (see the box on p. 101).

Women were kept under strict control. Since they were married at fourteen or fifteen, they were taught about their responsibilities at an early age. Although many managed to learn to read and play musical instruments, they were often cut off from any formal education. And women were expected to remain at home out of sight unless they attended funerals or festivals, such as the women's festival of Thesmophoria. If they left the house, they were to be accompanied. A woman working alone in public was either poverty-stricken or not a citizen.

Women in Athens served males in other ways as well. Prostitution (both male and female) flourished in classical Athens. Most female prostitutes were slaves in brothels run as a business or trade by an Athenian citizen. Another class of prostitutes in Athenian society occupied a more favorable position; these more refined courtesans were known as *hetairai*, literally "female companions." Usually ex-slaves or foreign residents, these women were more sophisticated than ordinary prostitutes and were known for their intellectual and musical achievements as well as their physical ones. Athenian males continued the aristocratic practice of the symposium, the sophisticated drinking party, where *hetairai* were often present. Symposia were held in the men's dining rooms and wives were not present. *Hetairai* danced, played musical instruments, and provided entertainment, including sex. Some *hetairai* achieved fortune and considerable renown. Aspasia was certainly the most famous. A friend of Socrates and known for her learning, she was the mistress of Pericles and eventually became his common-law wife.

➤ *Household Management and the Role of the Athenian Wife* ⧫

In fifth-century Athens, a woman's place was in the home. She had two major responsibilities: the bearing and raising of children and the management of the household. In his dialogue on estate management, Xenophon relates the instructions of an Attican gentleman to his new wife.

Xenophon, *Oeconomicus*

[Ischomachus addresses his new wife] For it seems to me, dear, that the gods with great discernment have coupled together male and female, as they are called, chiefly in order that they may form a perfect partnership in mutual service. For, in the first place that the various species of living creatures may not fail, they are joined in wedlock for the production of children. Secondly, offspring to support them in old age is provided by this union, to human beings, at any rate. Thirdly, human beings live not in the open air, like beasts, but obviously need shelter. Nevertheless, those who mean to win stores to fill the covered place, have need of someone to work at the open-air occupations; since ploughing, sowing, planting and grazing are all such open-air employments; and these supply the needful food. . . . For he

made the man's body and mind more capable of enduring cold and heat, and journeys and campaigns; and therefore imposed on him the outdoor tasks. To the woman, since he had made her body less capable of such endurance, I take it that God has assigned the indoor tasks. And knowing that he had created in the woman and had imposed on her the nourishment of the infants, he meted out to her a larger portion of affection for newborn babes than to the man. . . .

Your duty will be to remain indoors and send out those servants whose work is outside, and superintend those who are to work indoors, and to receive the incomings, and distribute so much of them as must be spent, and watch over so much as is to be kept in store, and take care that the sun laid by for a year be not spent in a month. And when wool is brought to you, you must see that cloaks are made for those that want them. You must see too that the dry corn is in good condition for making food. One of the duties that fall to you, however, will perhaps seem rather thankless: you will have to see that any servant who is ill is cared for.

Male homosexuality was also a prominent feature of classical Athens. It was widely practiced and certainly tolerated. Athenian law disfranchised a citizen who had prostituted his body to another male, but nothing was done to males who engaged in homosexual love with male prostitutes or other adult males for love or pleasure. The law did not eliminate male prostitution, but assured that male prostitutes would be foreigners, not Athenian citizens.

The Greek homosexual ideal was a relationship between a mature man and a young male. It is likely that this was an aristocratic ideal and not one practiced by the common people. While the relationship was frequently physical, the Greeks also viewed it as educational. The older male (the "lover") won the love of his "beloved" by his value as a teacher and by the devotion he demonstrated in training his charge. In a sense, this love relationship was seen as a way of initiating young males into the male world of political and military dominance. The Greeks did not feel that the coexistence of homosexual and heterosexual predilections created any special problems for individuals or their society.

Conclusion

The civilization of the ancient Greeks was the fountainhead of Western culture. Socrates, Plato, and Aristotle established the foundations of Western philosophy. Herodotus and Thucydides created the discipline of history. Our literary forms are largely derived from Greek poetry and drama. Greek notions of harmony, proportion, and beauty have remained the touchstones for all subsequent Western art. A rational method of inquiry, so important to modern science, was conceived in ancient Greece. Many of our political terms are Greek in origin, and so too are our concepts of the rights and duties of citizenship, especially as they were conceived in Athens, the first great democracy the world had seen. Especially during their classical period, the Greeks raised and debated the fundamental questions about the purpose of human existence, the structure of human society, and the nature of the universe that have concerned Western thinkers ever since.

All of these achievements came from a group of small city-states in ancient Greece. And yet Greek civilization also contains an element of tragedy. For all of their brilliant accomplishments, the Greeks were unable to rise above the divisions and rivalries that caused them to fight each other and undermine their own civilization. Of course, their contributions to Western civilization have outlived their political struggles, but in studying the Greeks and seeing what went wrong, we can come to appreciate one of the remaining challenges of Western civilization.

NOTES

1. H. D. F. Kitto, *The Greeks* (Harmondsworth, 1951), p. 64.
2. Homer, *Odyssey*, trans. E. V. Rieu (Harmondsworth, 1946), p. 337.
3. Xenophon, *Symposium*, trans. O. J. Todd (Cambridge, Mass., 1968), III, 5.
4. These words from Plutarch are quoted in E. Fantham, H. P. Foley, N. B. Kampen, S. B. Pomeroy, and H. A. Shapiro, *Women in the Classical World* (New York, 1994), p. 64.
5. Hesiod, *Works and Days*, trans. Dorothea Wender (Harmondsworth, 1973), pp. (in order of quotations) 66, 77, 69, 73, 71, 68.
6. Theognis, *Elegies*, trans. Dorothea Wender (Harmondsworth, 1973), pp. (in order of quotations), 118, 100, 98, 114, 131.
7. Aeschylus, *The Persians*, in *The Complete Greek Tragedies*, vol. 1, ed. David Grene and Richmond Lattimore (Chicago, 1959), p. 229.

8. Voltaire, *The Age of Louis XIV*, trans. Martyn Pollack (London, 1926), p. 1.
9. Herodotus, *The Persian Wars*, trans. George Rawlinson (New York, 1942), p. 3.
10. Thucydides, *The Peloponnesian War*, trans. Rex Warner (Harmondsworth, 1954), p. 324.
11. Ibid., p. 24.
12. Ibid.
13. Sophocles, *Oedipus the King*, trans. David Grene (Chicago, 1959), pp. 68–69.
14. Sophocles, *Antigone*, trans. Don Taylor (London, 1986), p. 146.
15. Plato, *The Republic*, trans. F. M. Cornford (New York, 1945), pp. 178–79.

SUGGESTIONS FOR FURTHER READING

The standard one-volume reference work for Greek history remains J. B. Bury and R. Meiggs, *A History of Greece to the Death of Alexander the Great*, 4th ed. (New York, 1975). Other good, general introductions to Greek history include *The Oxford History of the Classical World*, ed. J. Boardman, J. Griffin, and O. Murray (Oxford, 1986), pp. 19–314; N. G. L. Hammond, *A History of Greece to 322 B.C.*, 3d ed. (Oxford, 1986); A. Andrewes, *Greek Society* (Harmondsworth, 1975); and two brief works, H. D. F. Kitto, *The Greeks* (Harmondsworth, 1951); and R. Sowerby, *The Greeks* (London, 1995). For a general survey of economic and social aspects, see P. Naquet, *Economic and Social History of Ancient Greece: An Introduction* (Berkeley, 1978). Warfare is covered in F. Adcock, *The Greek and Macedonian Art of War* (Berkeley, 1957).

Early Greek history is examined in O. Murray, *Early Greece* (London, 1980); M. I. Finley, *Early Greece: The Bronze and Archaic Ages*, 2d ed. (New York, 1982); L. W. Taylor, *The Mycenaeans*, rev. ed. (London, 1983); and J. T. Hooker, *Mycenaean Greece* (New York, 1976). For Dark Age Greece, see A. M. Snodgrass, *The Dark Age of Greece* (Edinburgh, 1971). For good introductions to Homer and the Homeric problem, see J. Griffin, *Homer* (Oxford, 1980); and D. Page, *History and the Homeric Iliad* (Berkeley, 1959). On Homer and his world, see the modern classic by M. I. Finley, *The World of Odysseus*, 2d ed. (New York, 1979).

General works on archaic Greece include A. M. Snodgrass, *Archaic Greece* (London, 1980); W. G. Forrest, *The Emergence of Greek Democracy* (London, 1966); and M. Grant, *The Rise of the Greeks* (London, 1987). Economic and social history of the period is covered in C. Starr, *The Economic and Social Growth of Early Greece, 800–500 B.C.* (Oxford, 1977). On colonization, see J. Boardman, *The Greeks Overseas*, rev. ed. (Baltimore, 1980). The best work on tyranny is A. Andrewes, *The Greek Tyrants* (New York, 1963). On the culture of archaic Greece, see A. R. Burn, *The World of Hesiod* (London, 1936); and A. J. Podlecki, *The Early Greek Poets and Their Themes* (Vancouver, 1984). See also the work of translation by W. Barnstone, *Greek Lyric Poetry* (New York, 1962). The best histories of Sparta are W. Forrest, *A History of Sparta, 950–121 B.C.*, 2d ed. (London, 1980); and P. A. Cartledge, *Sparta and Laconia: A Regional History, 1300–362 B.C.* (London, 1979). On early Athens, see the still valuable A. Jones, *Athenian Democracy* (London, 1957); and R. Osborne, *Demos* (New York, 1985). The Persian Wars are examined in A. Burn, *Persia and the Greeks: The Defense of the West*, rev. ed. (Stanford, 1984).

A general history of classical Greece can be found in S. Hornblower, *The Greek World, 479–323 B.C.* (London, 1983); and J. K. Davies, *Democracy and Classical Greece* (London, 1978). Economic aspects are examined in R. Hopper, *Trade and Industry in Classical Greece* (London, 1979). Valuable works on Athens include R. Garner, *Law and Society in Classical Athens* (New York, 1987); W. R. Connor, *The New Politicians of Fifth-Century Athens* (Princeton, 1971); D. Kagan, *Pericles of Athens and the Birth of Democracy* (New York, 1991); and P. J. Rhodes, *The Athenian Boule* (Oxford, 1985). On the development of the Athenian empire, see R. Meiggs, *The Athenian Empire* (Oxford, 1975); and the recent work by M. F. McGregor, *The Athenians and Their Empire* (Vancouver, 1987). A provocative view of male politics in fifth-century Athens can be found in E. C. Keuls, *The Reign of the Phallus: Sexual Politics in Ancient Athens* (New York, 1985). The best way to examine the Great Peloponnesian War is to read the work of Thucydides, *History of the Peloponnesian War*, trans. Rex Warner (Harmondsworth, 1954). A detailed study has been done in the four books by D. Kagan, *Outbreak of the Peloponnesian War* (Ithaca, N.Y., 1969); *The Archidamian War* (Ithaca, N.Y., 1974); *The Peace of Nicias and the Sicilian Expedition* (Ithaca, N.Y., 1981); and *The Fall of the Athenian Empire* (Ithaca, N.Y., 1987). On fourth-century Athens, see J. Ober, *Mass and Elite in Democratic Athens* (Princeton, 1989).

For a comprehensive history of Greek art, see M. Robertson, *A History of Greek Art*, 2 vols. (Cambridge, 1975). A good, brief study is J. Boardman, *Greek Art* (London, 1985). On sculpture, see G. M. A. Richter, *Sculpture and Sculptors of the Greeks* (Oxford, 1971). A basic survey of architecture is H. W. Lawrence, *Greek Architecture*, rev. ed. (Harmondsworth, 1983). For another aspect of Greek architecture, see J. Coulton, *Greek Architects at Work* (London, 1977). On Greek drama, see the general work by A. Lesky, *History of Greek Literature* (London, 1966). More specialized studies include K. Reinhardt, *Sophocles* (Oxford, 1978); the classic *Euripides and His Age* (Oxford, 1965) by G. Murray; and A. W. Pickard-Cambridge, *The Dramatic Festivals of Athens*, 2d ed. (Oxford, 1968). For sound studies of Greek history writing, see J. A. S. Evans, *Herodotus* (Boston, Mass., 1982); and K. Dover, *Thucydides* (Oxford, 1973). On Greek philosophy, a detailed study is available in W. K. C. Guthrie, *A History of Greek Philosophy*, 6 vols. (Cambridge, 1962–81). Individual works include J. Barnes, *Aristotle* (Oxford, 1982), primarily on his scientific and logical works; J. Findlay, *Plato and Platonism* (New York, 1978); and A. Taylor, *Socrates* (New York, 1933).

A short, general study of Greek religion is W. Guthrie, *The Greeks and Their Gods* (Boston, 1965). Other works of value are W. Burkert, *Greek Religion*, trans. J. Raffan (Cambridge, Mass., 1985); C. Seltman, *The Twelve Olympians* (New York, 1960); M. P. Nilsson, *Greek Popular Religion* (New York, 1940); J. D. Mikalson, *Athenian Popular Religion* (Chapel Hill, N.C., 1983); and H. W. Parke, *Greek Oracles* (London, 1967). E. R. Dodds, *The Greeks and the Irrational* (Berkeley, 1951), examines the role of the supernatural in Greek life.

For general accounts of daily life in classical Athens, see T. B. L. Webster, *Everyday Life in Classical Athens* (London, 1969); and M. and C. Quennell, *Everyday Things in Ancient Greece* (London, 1954). On the family and women, see W. K. Lacey, *The Family in Classical Greece* (London, 1968); S. C. Humphreys, *The Family, Women and Death* (London, 1983); S. B. Pomeroy, *Goddesses, Whores, Wives, and Slaves* (New York, 1975), the best general book on women; and E. Fantham, H. P. Foley, N. B. Kampen, S. B. Pomeroy, and H. A. Shapiro, *Women in the Classical World* (New York, 1994). On slavery, see M. I. Finley, ed., *Slavery in Classical Antiquity* (Cambridge, 1960); and Y. Garlan, *Slavery in Ancient Greece* (Ithaca, N.Y., 1988). On homosexuality, see K. J. Dover, *Greek Homosexuality* (London, 1978); and E. Cantarella, *Bisexuality in the Ancient World* (New Haven, Conn., 1992).

CHAPTER
4

The Hellenistic World

In 334 B.C., Alexander the Great led an army of Greeks and Macedonians into western Asia to launch his attack on the Persian Empire. Years of campaigning resulted in the complete defeat of the Persians, and in 327 B.C. Alexander and his troops pushed east into India. But two more years of fighting in an exotic and difficult terrain exhausted his troops, who rebelled and refused to go on. Reluctantly, Alexander turned back, leading his men across the arid lands of southern Iran. Conditions in the desert were appalling; the blazing sun and lack of water led to thousands of deaths. At one point, when a group of his soldiers found a little water, they scooped it up in a helmet and gave it to Alexander. Then, according to Arrian, an ancient Greek historian, Alexander, "with a word of thanks for the gift, took the helmet and, in full view of his troops, poured the water on the ground. So extraordinary was the effect of this action that the water wasted by Alexander was as good as a drink for every man in the army." Ever the great military leader, Alexander had found yet another way to inspire his troops.

Alexander the Great was the son of King Philip II of Macedonia, who in 338 B.C. defeated the Greeks and established his control over the Greek peninsula. After Philip's death, Alexander became king and led the Macedonians and Greeks on a spectacular conquest of the Persian Empire and opened the door to the spread of Greek culture throughout the ancient Near East. Greek settlers poured into the lands of the ancient Near East as bureaucrats, traders, soldiers, and scholars. Alexander's triumph created a new series of kingdoms that blended together the achievements of the eastern world with the cultural outlook and attitudes of the Greeks. We use the term Hellenistic to designate this new order. The Hellenistic world was the world of Greeks and non-Greek easterners, and it resulted, in its own way, in a remarkable series of accomplishments that are sometimes underestimated. They form the story of this chapter.

Philip II conquers Greece ●········   The Hellenistic monarchies ●·····················

····· Conquests of Alexander the Great   Roman conquests in the east, c. ●···················

Death of Alexander ●   Seleucids gain control of Judaea ●

Battle of Ipsus ●   Uprising of Judas Maccabaeus ●

········●········· Philosophy (Epicurus and Zeno)   ·········● Writing of history (Polybius)

Poetry ●···········
(Theocritus)   ·················● Science (Archimedes)

The Rise of Macedonia and the End of Hellenic Civilization

While the Greek city-states were continuing to fight each other, to their north a new and ultimately powerful kingdom was emerging in its own right. Although a Greek-speaking people, the Macedonians were viewed as barbarians by their southern neighbors, the Greeks. The Macedonians were mostly rural folk and were organized in tribes, not city-states. Not until the end of the fifth century B.C., during the reign of King Archelaus (c. 413–399 B.C.), did Macedonia emerge as an important kingdom. But his reign was followed by decades of repeated foreign invasions and internal strife until King Philip II (359–336 B.C.) took control and turned Macedonia into the chief power of the Greek world.

Philip had spent three years as a hostage in Thebes, where he had gained a great admiration for Greek culture and absorbed the latest Greek military developments. Philip understood the importance of having an efficient army if Macedonia was to be a strong state. He was aware that the Greek states, in the course of their struggles with each other, had come to rely too much on mercenaries. Philip used Macedonian countrymen, sturdy peasants and shepherds, as the core of his phalanx of infantrymen. From the gold mines of Mount Pangaeus, he obtained the wealth to pay these soldiers and establish a standing professional army. The Macedonian phalanx was also armed with longer thrusting spears and supported by strong cavalry contingents that served to break the opposing line of battle and create disorder in the enemy's ranks. Philip's new army defeated the Illyrians to the west and the Thracians to the north and

east, took Amphipolis from the Athenians, and was then drawn into the Greeks' interstate conflicts.

The reactions within the Greek world to Philip's growing strength and expansion were mixed. Many

✦ **Philip II.** Although he often seems overshadowed by the exploits of his son Alexander, Philip II made Alexander's conquests possible. Having unified Macedonia, Philip built a powerful standing army from his Macedonian subjects and defeated the Greek city-states allied against him in 338 B.C. He then imposed order on the Greek peninsula and demanded that the Greek states aid him in his planned invasion of Persia. Before he could move against the Persians, however, Philip was assassinated. This silver coin depicts the Macedonian king.

⇒ Demosthenes Condemns Philip of Macedonia ⇐

Among the Greeks, Demosthenes, above all, reacted strongly to the growing strength and expansionary policies of the Macedonian king Philip II. Demosthenes delivered a series of orations to the Athenian assembly in which he pictured Philip as a ruthless and barbaric man. This excerpt is from the Third Philippic, probably delivered in 341 B.C.

Demosthenes, *The Third Philippic*

I observe, however, that all men, and you first of all, have conceded to him something which has been the occasion of every war that the Greeks have ever waged. And what is that? The power of doing what he likes, of calmly plundering and stripping the Greeks one by one, and of attacking their cities and reducing them to slavery. Yet your hegemony in Greece lasted seventy-three years, that of Sparta twenty-nine, and in these later times Thebes too gained some sort of authority after the battle of Leuctra. But neither to you nor to the Thebans nor to the Lacedaemonians [Spartans] did the Greeks ever yet, men of Athens, concede the right of unrestricted action, or anything like it. On the contrary, when you, or rather the Athenians of that day, were thought to be showing a want of consideration in dealing with others, all felt it their duty, even those who had no grievance against them, to go to war in support of those who had been in-

jured. . . . Yet all the faults committed by the Lacedaemonians in those thirty years, and by our ancestors in their seventy years of supremacy, are fewer, men of Athens, than the wrongs which Philip has done to the Greeks in the thirteen incomplete years in which he has been coming to the top—or rather, they are not a fraction of them. . . . Ay, and you know this also, that the wrongs which the Greeks suffered from the Lacedaemonians or from us, they suffered at all events at the hands of true-born sons of Greece, and they might have been regarded as the acts of a legitimate son, born to great possessions, who should be guilty of some fault or error in the management of his estate: so far he would deserve blame and reproach, yet it could not be said that it was not one of the blood, not the lawful heir who was acting thus. But if some slave or supposititious bastard had wasted and squandered what he had no right to, heavens! how much more monstrous and exasperating all would have called it! Yet they have no such qualms about Philip and his present conduct, though he is not only no Greek, nor related to the Greeks, but not even a barbarian from any place that can be named with honor, but a pestilent knave from Macedonia, whence it was never yet possible to buy a decent slave.

Athenians, especially the orator Demosthenes, came to have a strong distrust of the Macedonian leader's intentions. Demosthenes delivered a series of orations, known as the Philippics, in which he portrayed Philip as ruthless, deceitful, treacherous, and barbaric and called upon the Athenians to undertake a struggle against him (see the box above). Other Athenians, such as the philosopher Isocrates, viewed Philip as a savior who would rescue the Greeks from themselves by uniting them and organizing the entire Greek world in a crusade against the common enemy, the Persians.

Demosthenes' repeated calls for action, combined with Philip's rapid expansion, finally spurred Athens into action. Allied with Thebes and some other smaller states, Athens fought the Macedonians at the Battle of Chaeronea, near Thebes, in 338 B.C. The Macedonian army crushed the Greek allies, and Philip was now free to consolidate his control over the Greek peninsula. While Thebes was punished severely, Athens was treated leniently out of respect for its past and expected

cooperation in the future. The Greek states were joined together in an alliance that we call the Corinthian League because they met at Corinth. Though based on the principle of self-governing, independent states, the league did have an army and a council. Philip of Macedon was recognized as *hegemon* (leader) of the league and its army. Moreover, Macedonian garrisons were stationed at strategic locations in Greece. Although Philip allowed the Greek city-states autonomy in domestic affairs, he retained the general direction of their foreign affairs. Many Greeks still objected to being subject to the less civilized master from the north, but Philip insisted that the Greek states end their bitter rivalries and cooperate with him in a war against Persia.

Before Philip could undertake his invasion of Asia, however, he was assassinated, leaving the task to his son Alexander. Although Alexander justly deserves credit for the destruction of the Persian Empire, it was Philip who really paved the way for the conquest. He had unified Macedonia, created a powerful military machine, and subdued the Greeks. He did for the Greeks what the Greeks had not been able to do for themselves.

The Conquests of Alexander the Great

Alexander was only twenty when he became king of Macedonia. In only twelve years, he achieved so much that he has since been called Alexander the Great. The illustrious conqueror was, in many ways, prepared for kingship by his father. Philip had allowed Alexander to act as regent while he was away, had taken him along on military campaigns, and indeed, at the important Battle of Chaeronea, had given him control of the cavalry. After his father's assassination, Alexander moved quickly to assert his authority, securing the Macedonian frontiers and smothering a rebellion in Greece. He then turned to his father's dream, the invasion of the Persian Empire.

There is no doubt that Alexander was taking a chance in attacking the Persian Empire. Although weakened in some respects, it was still a strong state. Alexander's fleet was inferior to the Persian navy, which drew its ships from the Phoenicians and other coastal peoples of western Asia, and his finances were shaky at best. His army would have to live off the countryside and win quick victories to gain the resources needed to continue the struggle. In the spring of 334 B.C., Alexander entered Asia Minor with an army of some 37,000 men. About half were Macedonians, the rest being Greeks and other allies. The cavalry, which would play an important role as a striking force, numbered about 5,000. The army was accompanied by architects, engineers, historians, and scientists, a clear indication of Alexander's grand vision and positive expectations at the beginning of his campaign.

His first confrontation with the Persians, at the battle at the Granicus River in 334 B.C., almost cost him his life, but resulted in a major victory. By the spring of 333 B.C., the entire western half of Asia Minor was in Alexander's hands, and the Ionian Greek cities of western Asia Minor had been "liberated" from the Persian oppressor. Not all of them wished to be liberated and regarded Alexander simply as their new master. There is evidence that they were hardly "free and autonomous" as Alexander claimed.

Meanwhile, the Persian king Darius III mobilized his forces to stop Alexander's army. Although the Persian troops outnumbered Alexander's, the Battle of Issus was fought on a narrow field that canceled the advantage of superior numbers and resulted in another Macedonian

success. The Persian cause was certainly not helped when Darius made a spectacular exit from the battlefield before it was even clear who would be victorious. After his victory at Issus in 333 B.C., Alexander laid siege to the port cities of Tyre and Gaza to prevent Persian control of the sea. Egypt surrendered without a fight, and by the winter of 332, Syria, Palestine, and Egypt were under Alexander's domination. He took the traditional title of pharaoh of Egypt and was hailed as the "son of Amon," to the Greeks the equivalent of being called the son of Zeus. Alexander also built the first of a series of cities named after him (Alexandria) to be the Greek administrative capital of Egypt. It became (and remains today) one of Egypt's and the Mediterranean world's most important cities.

In the meantime, Darius indicated his willingness to make a peace settlement, offering to cede all land west

♦ **Bust of Alexander the Great.** This bust of Alexander the Great is a Roman copy of the head of a statue, possibly by Lysippus. Although he aspired to be another Achilles, the tragic hero of Homer's *Iliad*, Alexander also sought more divine honors. He claimed to be descended from Heracles, a Greek hero worshiped as a god, and as pharaoh of Egypt, he gained recognition as a living deity.

�֎ **Map 4.1** The Conquests of Alexander the Great.

of the Euphrates River to Alexander. Alexander refused and renewed the offensive. He moved now into the territory of the ancient Near Eastern kingdoms and fought the decisive battle with the Persians at Gaugamela, not far from Babylon, in the summer of 331. At Gaugamela, Alexander's men were clearly outnumbered by the Persian forces, which had established the battle site on a broad, open plain where their war chariots could maneuver to best advantage. Alexander was able to break through the center of the Persian line with his heavy cavalry, followed by the infantry. The battle turned into a rout, although Darius managed to escape. After his victory at Gaugamela, Alexander entered Babylon and then proceeded to the Persian capitals at Susa and Persepolis where he acquired the Persian treasuries and took possession of vast quantities of gold and silver (see the box on p. 110). By 330, Alexander was again on the march, pursuing Darius. After Darius was killed by one of his own men, Alexander took the title and office of the Great King of the Persians. But he was not content to rest with the spoils of the Persian Empire. Over the next three years he

moved east and northeast, as far as modern Pakistan. By the summer of 327 B.C., he had entered India, where he experienced a number of difficult campaigns. Weary of campaigning year after year, his soldiers mutinied and refused to go further. Alexander surrendered to their demands and agreed to return, leading his troops through southern Iran across the Gedrosian Desert, where they suffered heavy losses from appalling desert conditions. Alexander and the remnant of his army went to Susa and then Babylon, where he planned more campaigns. But in June 323 B.C., weakened from wounds, fever, and probably excessive alcohol, he died at the young age of thirty-two.

Alexander's Ideals

Alexander is one of the most puzzling great figures in history. Historians relying on the same sources give vastly different pictures of him. Some portray him as an idealistic visionary and others as a ruthless Machiavellian. How did Alexander the Great view himself? We know that he sought to imitate Achilles, the hero of

Homer's *Iliad*, destroyer of Hector and Troy. He also claimed to be descended from Heracles, the Greek hero who came to be worshiped as a god. No doubt, Alexander aspired to divine honors; as pharaoh of Egypt, he became a living god according to Egyptian tradition and at one point even sent instructions to the Greek cities to "vote him a god."

Some historians have argued that Alexander believed in an ideal of universal humanity. As evidence they cite the fact that he urged his soldiers to marry native women, and at Susa in 324 B.C. he celebrated the marriages of 10,000 of them en masse to native women. Alexander himself married easterners—Stateira, daughter of Darius, and Roxane, the daughter of a Bactrian baron. Was Alexander pursuing a lofty ideal or was he simply looking for a realistic way to unify his newly won domains? Early on in his conquests, he adopted features of Persian rule. He called himself the Great King and asked his subjects to bow before him in the Persian fashion. He wore Persian dress, used Persians as administrators, and trained native youths in Macedonian military methods. His fellow Macedonians objected to these trappings of oriental despotism and the equal treatment he accorded Persians. Some even went so far as to attempt his assassination. But Alexander must have felt a need to fuse the Macedonian-Greeks and the Persians into a ruling class that would enable him to

C H R O N O L O G Y

The Rise of Macedonia and the Conquests of Alexander

Reign of Philip II	359–336 B.C.
Battle of Chaeronea; Philip II conquers Greece	338 B.C.
Reign of Alexander the Great	336–323 B.C.
Alexander invades Asia; Battle of Granicus River	334 B.C.
Battle of Issus	333 B.C.
Battle of Gaugamela	331 B.C.
Fall of Persepolis, the Persian capital	330 B.C.
Alexander enters India	327 B.C.
Death of Alexander	323 B.C.

control such an extensive empire. One is left with the impression that he aspired to autocratic monarchy rather than a lofty vision of the unity of humankind.

Alexander's Legacy

Regardless of his ideals, motives, or views about himself, one fact stands out: Alexander truly created a new age,

◆ **Alexander and Darius at the Battle of Issus.** This late Hellenistic mosaic from Pompeii depicts the battle between Alexander and Darius III, king of Persia, at Issus in 333 B.C. Alexander landed his forces in western Asia Minor in 334 B.C. to begin his Persian campaign and first met Darius at Issus where the narrow field made the greater numbers of the Persians useless.

➤ The Destruction of the Persian Palace at Persepolis ➤

After Alexander's decisive victory at Gaugamela, he advanced into Persia where he captured the chief Persian cities. At Persepolis, he burned the Persian grand palace to the ground. The ancient historians Arrian and Diodorus of Sicily gave different explanations of this act: one argues that it was a deliberate act of revenge for the Persian invasion of Greece in the fifth century, the other that the burning resulted from a wild drinking party. Modern historians do not agree on which version is more plausible. Arrian was a Greek-speaking Roman senator of the second century A.D. Diodorus of Sicily lived in the first century B.C.

Arrian, *The Life of Alexander the Great*

Thence he marched to Persepolis with such rapidity that the garrison had no time to plunder the city's treasure before his arrival. He also captured the treasure of Cyrus the First at Pasargadae. . . . He burnt the palace of the Persian kings, though this act was against the advice of Parmenio, who urged him to spare it for various reasons, chiefly because it was hardly wise to destroy what was now his own property, and because the Asians would, in his opinion, be less willing to support him if he seemed bent merely upon passing through their country as a conqueror rather than upon ruling it securely as a king. Alexander's answer was that he wished to punish the Persians for their invasion of Greece; his present act was retribution for the destruction of Athens, the burning of the temples, and all the other crimes they had committed against the Greeks.

Diodorus of Sicily, *Library of History*

Alexander held games in honor of his victories. He performed costly sacrifices to the gods and entertained his friends bountifully. While they were feasting and the drinking was far advanced, as they began to be drunken a madness took possession of the minds of the intoxicated guests. At this point one of the women present, Thaïs by name and Attic by origin, said that for Alexander it would be the finest of all his feats in Asia if he joined them in a triumphal procession, set fire to the palaces, and permitted women's hands in a minute to extinguish the famed accomplishments of the Persians. This was said to men who were still young and giddy with wine, and so, as would be expected someone shouted out to form the procession and light torches, and urged all to take vengeance for the destruction of the Greek temples. Others took up the cry and said that this was a deed worthy of Alexander alone. When the king had caught fire at their words, all leaped up from their couches and passed the word along to form a victory procession in honor of Dionysus [god of wine and religious ecstasy].

Promptly many torches were gathered. Female musicians were present at the banquet, so the king led them all out for the procession to the sound of voices and flutes and pipes, Thaïs the courtesan leading the whole performance. She was the first, after the king, to hurl her blazing torch into the palace. As the others all did the same, immediately the entire palace area was consumed, so great was the conflagration. It was most remarkable that the impious act of Xerxes, king of the Persians, against the acropolis at Athens should have been repaid in kind after many years by one woman, a citizen of the land which had suffered it, and in sport.

---

the Hellenistic era. The word *Hellenistic* is derived from a Greek word meaning "to imitate Greeks." It is an appropriate way, then, to describe an age that saw the extension of the Greek language and ideas to the non-Greek world of the ancient Near East. Alexander's destruction of the Persian monarchy had extended Greco-Macedonian rule over an enormous area. It brought vast quantities of gold and silver to Macedonia and Greece, stimulating their economies, and created opportunities for Greek engineers, intellectuals, merchants, soldiers, and administrators. While the Greeks on the mainland might remain committed to the ideals of their city-states, those who followed Alexander and his successors participated in a new political unity based on the principle of monarchy. Alexander had transformed his army from a Macedonian force into an international one, owing loyalty only to himself. His successors used force to establish military monarchies that dominated the Hellenistic world after his death. Autocratic power, based on military strength and pretensions of divine rule, became a regular feature of those Hellenistic monarchies and was part of Alexander's political legacy to the Hellenistic world.

But Alexander also left a cultural legacy. As a result of his conquests, Greek language, art, architecture, and literature spread throughout the Near East. The urban centers of the Hellenistic age, many founded by Alexander and his successors, became springboards for the diffusion of Greek culture. Alexander had established a number of cities and military colonies named Alexandria to guard strategic points and supervise wide areas. Most of the settlers were Greek mercenaries. It has been estimated that, in the course of his campaigns, Alexander summoned some 60,000 to 65,000 additional mercenaries from Greece, at least 36,000 of whom took up residence in the garrisons and new cities. While the Greeks spread their culture in the east, they were also inevitably influenced by eastern ways. Thus, Alexander's legacy included one of the basic characteristics of the Hellenistic world: the clash and fusion of different cultures.

Some historians have suggested that Alexander overextended the Greco-Macedonian world by his conquests. They argue that the Greeks and Macedonians did not possess the resources to govern either efficiently or for the long run and that in trying to do so they weakened the Greek world and opened the door to Roman conquest. Probably so. In any case, the creation of an empire was part of Alexander's chief legacy. His vision of empire no doubt inspired the Romans, who were, of course, the real heirs of Alexander's legacy.

The World of the Hellenistic Kingdoms

The united empire that Alexander created by his conquests disintegrated soon after his death. An attempt to create a system of joint rule by Alexander's weak-minded half-brother and infant son under a regency of the most important Macedonian generals failed. All too soon, these military leaders were engaged in a struggle for power. By 301 B.C., after the Battle of Ipsus, any hope of unity was dead, and eventually four Hellenistic kingdoms emerged as the successors to Alexander: Macedonia under the Antigonid dynasty, Syria and the East under the Seleucids, the Attalid kingdom of Pergamum, and Egypt under the Ptolemies.

Map 4.2 The World of the Hellenistic Kingdoms.

gonids viewed control of Greece as essential to their power, but did not see outright conquest as necessary. Macedonia was, of course, also important to the Greeks. As one ancient commentator noted, "It is in the interest of the Greeks that the Macedonian dominion should be humbled for long, but by no means that it should be destroyed. For in that case . . . they would very soon experience the lawless violence of the Thracians and Gauls, as they had on more than one occasion."[1] But the Greeks, like the Macedonians, eventually fell subject to Roman power.

Another Hellenistic monarchy was founded by the Alexandrian general Seleucus, who established the Seleucid dynasty of Syria. This was the largest of the Hellenistic kingdoms and controlled much of the old Persian Empire from Turkey in the west to India in the east, although the Seleucids found it increasingly difficult to maintain control of the eastern territories. Moreover, a third Hellenistic kingdom came into being by freeing itself from the Seleucids. This was the kingdom of Pergamum in western Asia Minor under the Attalid dynasty. It was Pergamum that brought the Romans into the area by seeking their aid first against the Antigonids and then against the Seleucids. This led to the Roman defeat of Antiochus III, probably the strongest of the Seleucid monarchs, in 191 B.C. The Seleucids declined thereafter until their small remaining territory was made a Roman province in 63 B.C. Seventy years before that, the last of the Attalid dynasty had bequeathed his kingdom to Rome in his will.

The fourth Hellenistic monarchy was Egypt, which had come under the control of Ptolemy, another Macedonian general. Named governor of Egypt after Alexander's death, Ptolemy had established himself as king by 305 B.C., creating the Ptolemaic dynasty of pharaohs. Hellenistic Egypt lasted longer than all the other Hellenistic monarchies; it was not until the reign of Cleopatra VII, who allied herself with the wrong side in the Roman civil wars (see Chapter 5), that Egypt fell to the Romans in 30 B.C.

Hellenistic Monarchies

The Hellenistic monarchies created a semblance of stability for several centuries, even though Hellenistic kings refused to accept the new status quo and periodically engaged in wars to alter it. At the same time, an underlying strain always existed between the new Greco-Macedonian ruling class and the native populations. Together these factors created a certain degree of tension that was never truly ended until the vibrant

◆ **A Gaul and His Wife: Monument to the Victory of a Hellenistic King.** After the death of Alexander, the empire he had created collapsed, and four Hellenistic kingdoms arose in its place. Warfare continued to be of importance to these kingdoms, as it was through warfare that they were created, maintained, and expanded. They did not just fight among themselves, however; they also faced foreign enemies, such as the Gauls, who first entered the Hellenistic world in 279 B.C. This statue of a Gaulish chieftain and his wife was part of a larger monument erected to commemorate the victory of Attalus I of Pergamum over the Gauls, a victory that gave Pergamum control over much of Asia Minor.

In Macedonia, the struggles for power led to the extermination of Alexander the Great's dynasty. Not until 276 B.C. did Antigonus Gonatus, the grandson of one of Alexander's generals, succeed in establishing the Antigonid dynasty as rulers of Macedonia. The Anti-

Roman state to the west stepped in and imposed a new order.

The Hellenistic kingdoms shared a common political system that represented a break with their Greek past. With the exception of the Spartan kings, monarchy had not been a regular feature of classical Greek life. To the Greeks, monarchy was an institution for barbarians, associated in their minds with people like the Persians. While they retained democratic forms of government in their cities, at the same time the Greeks of the Hellenistic world were forced to accept monarchy as a new fact of political life.

The power of Hellenistic kings was despotic. "The king's will is right" was a basic operating principle. Only in Macedonia were there remnants of old constitutional forms that might have placed limits on the king's power, but even there they failed to be important. In addition to a council to assist the king personally, Hellenistic monarchs had a government bureaucracy to execute their wishes. Both the Seleucids and Ptolemies utilized previous administrative frameworks. The Seleucid kingdom was divided into provinces similar to the Persians' satrapies (see Chapter 2), and the Ptolemies used the system of the pharaohs (see Chapter 1), which came to be called "nomes" (from the Greek word for district).

Both the Seleucid and Ptolemaic dynasties excluded natives from important administrative positions. Contrary to Alexander the Great's plan to fuse Greeks and easterners, Hellenistic monarchs relied only on Greeks and Macedonians to form the new ruling class. It has been estimated that in the Seleucid kingdom, for example, only 2.5 percent of the people in authority were non-Greek, and most of them were commanders of local military units. Those who did advance to important administrative posts had learned Greek (all government business was transacted in Greek) and had become hellenized in a cultural sense. The policy of excluding non-Greeks from leadership positions, it should be added, was not due to the incompetence of the natives, but to the determination of the Greek ruling class to maintain its privileged position. It was the Greco-Macedonian ruling class that provided the only unity in the Hellenistic world.

Since the Hellenistic monarchs created and maintained their kingdoms by military force, warfare continued to be an integral part of the Hellenistic world. The size of armies increased dramatically with some Hellenistic kings raising forces of 68,000 troops or more for a single encounter. Unable to recruit adequate forces from their cities, the Hellenistic monarchs frequently made use of mercenaries. The phalanx or heavily armed infantry with long spears (lengthened by this time to eighteen feet) and the cavalry still formed the core of the Hellenistic forces.

Though the familiar phalanx was retained, Hellenistic warfare saw some innovations. Most noticeable were the elephants, "the tanks of ancient warfare," which were especially prominent in the army of the Seleucids who procured theirs from India and the Ptolemies who obtained them from North Africa. But even more important, since armies quickly learned tricks that neutralized the elephants, was the development of new siege machinery, especially the catapult and siege towers. In classical times, cities with good walls were virtually impregnable; Alexander and later Hellenistic rulers could capture cities by using their new equipment.

Hellenistic Cities

Cities played an especially important role in the Hellenistic kingdoms. Throughout his conquests, Alexander had founded a series of new cities and military settlements, and Hellenistic kings did likewise. The Seleucids, in particular, created more than sixty. The new population centers varied considerably in size and importance. Military settlements were meant to maintain order and might consist of only a few hundred men heavily dependent upon the king. But there were also new independent cities with thousands of inhabitants. Alexandria in Egypt was the largest city in the Mediterranean region by the first century B.C.

Hellenistic rulers encouraged this massive spread of Greek colonists to the Near East because of their intrinsic value to the new monarchies. Greeks (and Macedonians) provided not only a recruiting ground for the army, but also a pool of civilian administrators and workers who would contribute to economic development. Even architects, engineers, dramatists, and actors were in demand in the new Greek cities. Many Greeks and Macedonians were quick to see the advantages of moving to the new urban centers and gladly sought their fortunes in the Near East. Greeks of all backgrounds joined the exodus, at least until around 250 B.C. when the outpouring began to slow significantly.

Within the Hellenistic cities, the culture was primarily Greek. Based on the dialect used in Athens, a common Greek language called *koiné* ("common tongue") developed. Used by Greek administrators, merchants, and literary people, *koiné* transcended all the old Greek dialects. Moreover, the political institutions of the cities were modeled after those of the Greek *polis*. Greeks of the classical period would easily have recognized the

◆ **Greek War Elephants.** Some of the armies in the Hellenistic world made use of elephants obtained from North Africa and India. Pictured on this Italian plate is a Greek war elephant that was brought to the Mediterranean by one of Alexander's successors. The battle fortress on the back of the elephant was a Greek innovation.

councils, magistracies, assemblies, and codes of law. The physical layout of the new cities was likewise modeled after those of the Greek homeland. Using the traditional rectilinear grid, cities were laid out with stoas (porticoes), temples, altars (some were quite elaborate), and stone theaters. Many amenities, such as a regular water supply and public lavatories, were also available.

Many of the new urban centers were completely dominated by Greeks while the native populations remained cut off from all civic institutions. The Greeks commissioned purely Greek sculpture, read literature of the classical period, and had separate law courts for themselves. Complaints from resentful natives have been recorded. An Egyptian camel-driver, for example, complained bitterly that he was not paid regularly because he did "not know how to behave like a Greek." Not only was it difficult for easterners to enter the ranks of the ruling class, but those who did so had to become thoroughly hellenized. This often required alienation from one's own culture and led to humiliating experiences.

The Greeks' belief in their own cultural superiority provided an easy rationalization for their political dominance of the eastern cities. But Greek control of the new cities was also necessary because the kings frequently used the cities as instruments of government, enabling them to rule considerable territory without an extensive bureaucracy. At the same time, for security reasons, the Greeks needed the support of the kings. After all, the Hellenistic cities were islands of Greek culture in a sea of non-Greeks. The relationship between rulers and cities, therefore, was a symbiotic one that bore serious consequences for the cities.

In their political system, religious practices, and city architecture, the Greeks tried to recreate the *polis* of their homeland in their new cities. But it was no longer possible to do so. The new cities were not autonomous entities and soon found themselves dependent upon the power of the Hellenistic monarchies. Although the kings did not rule the cities directly, they restricted their freedom in other ways. Cities knew they could not conduct an independent foreign policy and did not try to do so. The kings also demanded tribute, which could be a heavy burden.

A noticeable feature of the Hellenistic cities was the increasing control of the rich over urban affairs. Alexander and his successors had encouraged the practice of democracy in both old and new Greek cities: all had a council, magistrates, and, most important, a popular assembly that enabled the people to exercise control over political life. But by 300 B.C., the wealthy citizens in Greek communities were using their money to ingratiate themselves with their communities and to make their communities dependent upon them. Patronage by the wealthy was, of course, not new to Greek cities, but it increased in both volume and frequency. Furthermore, it enabled the rich to dominate the magistracies with the acquiescence of the citizenry who expected further beneficence from the wealthy in exchange. By the third century B.C., the power of the magistrates and councils was surpassing that of the popular assemblies, a clear indication of a shift from democracy to oligarchy, or the rule of a wealthy elite.

But the increasing power of the wealthy and the growing gap between rich and poor gave rise to class conflict and even calls for social revolution, usually couched in the familiar demands for the redistribution of land and the cancellation of debts. Such appeals were heard more frequently on the Greek mainland than in the rest of the Hellenistic world. But such appeals rarely led to successful revolutions, and Roman entry into the Hellenistic world put an end to them altogether. The Romans made it clear that they supported wealthy oligarchies at the expense of the poor.

The Greek cities of the Hellenistic era were the chief agents for the spread of Hellenic culture in the Near East, as far, in fact, as modern Afghanistan and India. These Greek cities were also remarkably vibrant despite their subordination to the Hellenistic monarchies and persisted in being a focal point for the loyalty of their citizens. Their continuing vitality is perhaps most evident on the Greek mainland where the Greek cities formed two important leagues, the Aetolian League in central Greece and the Achaean League in the Peloponnesus. Both leagues concentrated their efforts on foreign policy, and neither was dominated by a single city as the Delian League had been by Athens and the Peloponnesian League by Sparta in the fifth century B.C. (see Chapter 3). One of the goals of the Achaean League, however, was to expel the Macedonians and restore the Greeks' "ancestral freedom." It succeeded only briefly, for time was running out on the viability of small cities. The Hellenistic monarchies had already demonstrated that they were more powerful than the cities, and the Romans were, after all, waiting in the wings.

Economic Trends

Agriculture was still of primary importance to both the native populations and the new Greek cities of the Hellenistic world. The Greek cities continued their old agrarian patterns. A well-defined citizen body owned land and worked it with the assistance of slaves. But their farms were isolated units in a vast area of land ultimately owned by the king or assigned to large estate owners and worked by native peasants dwelling in villages. Overall, then, neither agricultural patterns nor methods of production underwent significant changes.

There were some improvements, however. New irrigation canals were constructed, especially in Egypt where the Ptolemies were active in land reclamation. The irrigation of the Fayum in Egypt created a large expanse of land that was used primarily by the Greek settlers. Fully 50 percent of the villages that developed there had Greek names. New fruits and crops were also introduced. The Greeks were especially active in introducing grapevines and olive trees wherever they could.

Few new products or manufacturing methods were introduced in the Hellenistic world. The most famous invention was the "Archimedean screw," which was a mechanism used to pump water out of mines or into irrigation trenches. Many historians believe that the availability of cheap labor worked against the invention of labor-saving machines. Most articles were produced by individual craftsmen or small-scale operations consisting of an owner and a few slaves. It should be noted, however, that both royal and city governments in the Hellenistic era also became involved in manufacturing as a state enterprise. In Egypt, the Ptolemies experimented with state factories for the production of oil and textiles. State factories at Pergamum produced textiles and parchment. Slaves were used as the chief source of labor in these factories. The city of Miletus owned textile factories worked by slaves and became the center of the woolen industry in the Hellenistic world.

But although products and methods of production were much the same, the centers of manufacturing shifted significantly in the Hellenistic era. Industry spread from Greece to the east—especially to Asia Minor, Rhodes, and Egypt. New textile centers were set up at Pergamum, while glass and silver crafts were developed in Syria. And leading all cities in manufacturing was Alexandria in Egypt, which became the center for the production of parchment, textiles, linens, oil, metalwork, and glass.

Commerce experienced considerable expansion in the Hellenistic era. Indeed, it was trade that tied much of the Hellenistic world together. Commercial traffic was furthered by the decline in the number of political barriers. Although Hellenistic monarchs still fought wars, the conquests of Alexander and the policies of his successors made possible greater trade between east and west. Technical improvements were minor, but still helpful. Harbors underwent extensive work, especially the building of breakwaters to protect them. Manuals, such as *On Harbors* by Timosthenes, provided aid in navigation. While real improvements in roads would await the Romans, trade routes between east and west were facilitated by the Hellenistic kingdoms. Two major trade routes were used to connect the east with the Mediterranean world. The central route was the major one and led by sea from India to the Persian Gulf, up the Tigris River to Seleucia on the Tigris, which replaced Babylon as the center for waterborne traffic from the Persian Gulf and overland caravan routes as well. Overland routes from Seleucia then led to Antioch and Ephesus. A southern route wound its way from India by sea but went around Arabia and up the Red Sea to Petra or later Berenice. Caravan routes then led overland to Coptos on the Nile, thence to Alexandria and the Mediterranean.

An incredible variety of products were traded: gold and silver from Spain; tin from Cornwall and Brittany; iron from northern Armenia; salt from Asia Minor; balsam from Jericho; timber from Macedonia; purple dye from Tyre; ebony, gems, ivory, and spices from India; frankincense (used on altars) from Arabia; slaves from Thrace, Syria, and Asia Minor; silk from Cos; fine wines from Syria and western Asia Minor; olive oil from Athens; and numerous exquisite foodstuffs, such as the famous prunes of Damascus. The greatest trade, however, was in the basic staple of life—grain. The great exporting areas were Egypt, Sicily, and the Black Sea region, while Rhodes and Delos served as the major depots for the international grain trade.

Trade in the Hellenistic world was greatly facilitated by the development of a money economy in the east, a product of Alexander's conquests and the Greek colonization encouraged by the Seleucid dynasty. Alexander had confiscated enormous quantities of gold and silver from the Persian treasuries, much of which was coined or recoined in Greek mints for further circulation. The Alexander drachma was based on the Attic standard and came to be used in Macedonia, parts of Greece, Asia Minor, and the Seleucid kingdom. Although Egypt continued to use a Phoenician standard, the simplification of coinage to two basic international standards facilitated commercial activity. So too did the development of banks by states, cities, and private individuals; these banks took in money on deposit and provided loans for commercial enterprises.

Hellenistic Society

One of the more noticeable features of social life in the Hellenistic world was the emergence of new opportunities for women—at least for upper-class women. No doubt this was related to the changes in Hellenistic society itself, since the subordination of the cities to the kings altered the way men related to their *polis* and to each other. Some historians maintain that the visible role of Hellenistic queens may also have contributed to a new model for upper-class women.

New Opportunities for Upper-Class Women

The creation of the Hellenistic monarchies, which represented a considerable departure from the world of the city-state, gave new scope to the role played by the monarchs' wives, the Hellenistic queens. In Macedonia, a pattern of alliances between mothers and sons provided openings for women to take an active role in politics, especially in political intrigue. In Egypt, opportunities for royal women were even greater since the Ptolemaic rulers reverted to an Egyptian custom of kings marrying their own sisters. Of the first eight Ptolemaic rulers, four wed their sisters. Ptolemy II and his sister-wife Arsinoë II were both worshiped as gods in their lifetimes. Arsinoë played an energetic role in government and was involved in the expansion of the Egyptian navy. She was also the first Egyptian queen whose portrait appeared on coins with her husband. Hellenistic queens also showed an intense interest in culture. They wrote poems, collected art, and corresponded with intellectuals.

But it is important to remember the limitations on the power of Hellenistic queens. In the final analysis, they were still largely dependent upon a male world for their status. Their power was usually derived from their position as regents for underage sons or as wives or mothers, especially if their husbands or sons were weak rulers. Moreover, the traditional pattern in which male guardians arranged marriages to further diplomatic and military alliances persisted. If it suited them, kings were not averse to ousting their queens for political reasons.

Of course, Hellenistic queens constituted only a very small number of women, but their status undoubtedly had some impact on the prestige of upper-class women in general. The most notable gains for upper-class women came in the economic area. Documents show increasing numbers of women involved in managing slaves, selling property, and even making loans. Even then, legal contracts in which women were involved had to include their official male guardians, although in numerous instances these men no longer played an important function but were only listed to satisfy legal requirements. Only in Sparta were women allowed to own land and manage their own economic affairs. As many of their husbands were absent or even died in war, many Spartan women became noticeably wealthy. It has been estimated that 40 percent of the Spartan land was owned by females. Some Spartan women even entered their racehorses in the competitions at the Olympic games, in part perhaps to make others aware of their affluence.

Spartan women, however, were an exception, especially on the Greek mainland. Women in Athens, for example, still remained highly restricted and supervised.

The Hellenistic World 117

Although a few philosophers welcomed female participation in men's affairs, many philosophers rejected equality between men and women and asserted that the traditional roles of wives and mothers were most satisfying for women.

But the opinions of philosophers did not prevent upper-class women from making gains in areas other than the economic sphere (see the box on p. 118). New possibilities for females arose when women in some areas of the Hellenistic world were allowed to pursue education in the traditional fields of literature, music, and even athletics. Education, then, provided new opportunities for women: female poets appeared again in the third century, and there are instances of women involved in both scholarly and artistic pursuits.

Some wealthy aristocratic women even became politically active in the running of their cities. In the second century B.C., a number of cities passed decrees honoring women for their services to their communities. Cyme, in Asia Minor, for example, paid homage to Archippe for her enormous financial contributions. In return, some women were given political rights and in a few instances were even allowed to hold office as city magistrates. But often economic motives were attached to this generosity. When Phile of Priene was made a magistrate of her city, it was probably with the understanding that she would donate funds for public works. Once in office, she did build an aqueduct and reservoir for the community.

In some areas of the Hellenistic world, especially outside Greece, the legal status of Greek women gradually improved, although one could hardly describe the changes as dramatic. In Egypt, for example, Greek women could petition the government or police without a guardian but still needed guardians for everything else. Married women's rights were expanded by contractual limitations on a husband's freedom for sexual activity outside the marriage. Some marriage contracts even provided equal opportunities for husbands and wives to divorce each other.

These improvements in the position of females were, of course, largely restricted to upper-class women. A harsher reality existed for a large group of women condemned to the practice of prostitution. The practice of infanticide or exposing unwanted children to die was one source of prostitutes. Inscriptional evidence indicates that small families were common in the Hellenistic world; boys were preferred and rarely was more than one daughter raised. Hence girls were more commonly subjected to infanticide. Some of these infants exposed

✦ **Portrait of Queen Arsinoë II.** Arsinoë II, sister and wife of King Ptolemy II, played an active role in Egyptian political affairs. This statue from around 270–240 B.C. shows the queen in the traditional style of a pharaoh.

to die were gathered up by eager entrepreneurs and raised to be slave prostitutes. Only the more beautiful and lucky prostitutes came to be the companions (the *hetairai*) of upper-class men.

⋟ A New Autonomy for Women ⋞

There were noticeable gains for upper-class women in Hellenistic society. But even in the lives of ordinary women, a new assertiveness came to the fore despite the continuing domination of society by men. The first selection is taken from the letter of a wife to her husband, complaining about his failure to return home. In the second selection, a father complains that his daughter has abandoned him, contrary to Egyptian law providing that children who have been properly raised should support their parents.

Letter from Isias to Hephaistion, 168 B.C.

If you are well and other things are going right, it would accord with the prayer that I make continually to the gods. I myself and the child and all the household are in good health and think of you always. When I received your letter from Horos, in which you announce that you are in detention in the Serapeum at Memphis, for the news that you are well I straightway thanked the gods, but about your not coming home, when all the others who had been secluded there have come, I am ill-pleased, because after having piloted myself and your child through such bad times and been driven to every extremity owing to the price of wheat, I thought that now at least, with you at home, I should enjoy some respite, whereas you have not even thought of coming home nor given any regard to our circumstances, remembering how I was in want of everything while you were still here, not to mention this long lapse of time and these critical days, during which you have sent us nothing. As, moreover, Horos who delivered the letter has brought news of your having been released from detention, I am thoroughly ill-pleased. Notwithstanding, as your mother also is annoyed, for her sake as well as for mine please return to the city, if nothing more pressing holds you back. You will do me a favor by taking care of your bodily health. Farewell.

Letter from Ktesikles to King Ptolemy, 220 B.C.

I am wronged by Dionysios and by Nike my daughter. For though I raised her, my own daughter, and educated her and brought her to maturity, when I was stricken with bodily ill-health and was losing my eyesight, she was not minded to furnish me with any of the necessities of life. When I sought to obtain justice from her in Alexandria, she begged my pardon, and in the eighteenth year she swore me a written royal oath to give me each month twenty drachmas, which she was to earn by her own bodily labor. . . . But now corrupted by Dionysios, who is a comic actor, she does not do for me anything of what was in the written oath, despising my weakness and ill-health. I beg you, therefore, o king, not to allow me to be wronged by my daughter and by Dionysios the actor who corrupted her, but to order Diophanes the strategus [a provincial administrator] to summon them and hear us out; and if I am speaking the truth, let Diophanes deal with her corrupter as seems good to him and compel my daughter Nike to do justice to me. If this is done I shall no longer be wronged but by fleeing to you, O King, I shall obtain justice.

The Role of Slavery

The Hellenistic world witnessed the migration of large numbers of people from one area to another. Greeks and Macedonians, of course, went into the Hellenistic kingdoms of the east as administrators, mercenaries, engineers, scholars, artists, teachers, and merchants. Moreover, significantly large numbers of non-Greeks moved around for economic and military purposes. But the largest number of uprooted people were slaves. Although statistics on slavery in antiquity are almost completely lacking, we do know that the number of slaves was significant while slavery itself was viewed as a normal part of life in the Hellenistic world and in antiquity in general.

Slaves were obtained from four chief sources: the children of slaves; children who were sold by their parents or abandoned to perish; persons kidnapped by pirates; and, perhaps the largest source of all, prisoners of war. Delos, a major trade center, could handle 10,000 slaves a day in its markets. Although slaves came from everywhere, Thracians and Syrians were most numerous. Slaves varied in price; Macedonians, Thracians, and Italians drew the highest prices.

Slaves were put to work in numerous ways in the Hellenistic world. States employed slaves as servants for

≫ *Treatment of Slaves in the Egyptian Gold Mines* ≪

Slavery was a common practice throughout antiquity. In both classical Greece and the Hellenistic world, the worst-treated slaves were those who worked in the mines. The Egyptians were especially notorious for their treatment of slaves in the gold mines in Nubia, described in this account by Diodorus of Sicily who lived in the first century B.C. *His account was based on the now lost work of the second-century writer Agatharchides.*

Diodorus of Sicily, *Library of History*

And those who have been condemned in this way—and they are a great multitude and are all bound in chains—work at their task unceasingly both by day and throughout the entire night, enjoying no respite and being carefully cut off from any means of escape; since guards of foreign soldiers who speak a language different from theirs stand watch over them, so that not a man, either by conversation or by some contact of a friendly nature, is able to corrupt one of his keepers. . . . And the entire operations are in charge of a skilled worker who distinguishes the stone and points it out to the laborers; and of those who are assigned to this unfortunate task the physically strongest break the quartz-rock with iron hammers, applying no skill to the task but only force, and cutting tunnels through the stone, not in a straight line but wherever the seam of gleaming rock may lead. Now these men, working in darkness as they do because of the bending and winding of the passages, carry lamps bound on their foreheads; and since much of the time they change the position of their bodies to follow the particular character of the stone they throw the blocks,

as they cut them out, on the ground, and at this task they labor without ceasing beneath the sternness and blows of an overseer.

The boys there who have not yet come to maturity, entering through the tunnels into the galleries formed by the removal of the rock, laboriously gather up the rock as it is cast down piece by piece and carry it out into the open to the place outside the entrance. Then those who are above thirty years of age take this quarried stone from them and with iron pestles pound a specified amount of it in stone mortars, until they have worked it down to the size of a vetch. Thereupon the women and older men receive from them the rock of this size and cast it into mills of which a number stand there in a row, and taking their places in groups of two or three at the spoke or handle of each mill they grind it until they have worked down the amount given them to the consistency of the finest flour. And since no opportunity is afforded any of them to care for his body and they have no garment to cover their shame, no man can look upon the unfortunate wretches without feeling pity for them because of the exceeding hardships they suffer. For no leniency or respite of any kind is given to any man who is sick, or maimed or aged, or in the case of a woman for her weakness, but all without exception are compelled by blows to persevere in their labors, until through ill-treatment they die in the midst of their tortures. Consequently the poor unfortunates believe, because their punishment is so excessively severe, that the future will always be more terrible than the present and therefore look forward to death as more to be desired than life.

government officials and in government-run industries, such as weaving. Most slaves were used in domestic service, farming, and mines, but the situation could vary from state to state. Egypt had no slave class in the countryside, nor was there much domestic slavery, except in Alexandria. But the Egyptians did use slave labor in state-run textile factories and made especially brutal use of them in mining operations (see the box above). Women were also sold as slaves to be concubines for Greek and Macedonian soldiers and civilians.

The effects of slavery could also be important. The employment of large numbers of slaves in the Hellenistic kingdoms contributed to the hellenizing process.

Slaves working in homes, farms, or factories had opportunities to absorb Greek ways. This is especially evident in the case of the slave-wives of Hellenistic soldiers.

The Transformation of Education

In the Hellenistic world, education underwent a significant transformation. In the classical period of Greek history, education had been largely left to private enterprise. Greek cities now began to supervise education in new ways. The Greek gymnasium, which had been primarily an athletic institution, evolved into a secondary school. The curriculum centered on music, physical exercise, and literature, especially the poetry of Homer. Wealthy individuals often provided the money for the schools and also specified how it should be spent. An inscription from the city of Teos in Asia Minor specified that Polythroos "gave 34,000 drachmas, . . . for there to be appointed each year . . . three grammar-masters to teach the boys and the girls; . . . for two gymnastics-masters to be appointed, . . . for a lyre—or harp—player to be appointed . . . he will teach music and lyre—or harp—playing to the children. . . ."[2]

The school in Teos, was an exception, however, in that education was usually for upper-class male children. An official known as gymnasiarch served as the actual head of a gymnasium. Essentially, this was a civic position of considerable prestige. He was not paid and was expected to provide money for sacrifices, competitions, entertainment, and even school repairs. Many cities passed decrees awarding praise and a "gold crown" to the gymnasiarch for his "munificence towards the people." The educational year culminated with various musical, academic, and athletic contests in which students competed for the honor of having their names inscribed on a victory column.

Hellenistic kings also served as patrons of gymnasia, recognizing their importance in training youths who might serve later as administrators of the state. The institution of the gymnasium played a significant role in the diffusion of Greek culture throughout the Hellenistic world. Whether an upper-class Greek youth lived on the Greek mainland, in Alexandria, or in another city in the east, he could imbibe Greek culture and maintain that sense of superiority that characterized the Greek overlords of the Hellenistic kingdoms.

Culture in the Hellenistic World

Although the Hellenistic kingdoms encompassed tremendous territorial areas and many diverse peoples, the Greeks provided a sense of unity as a result of the diffusion of Greek culture throughout the Hellenistic world. The Hellenistic era was a period of considerable cultural accomplishment in many areas—literature, art, science, medicine, and philosophy. Although these achievements occurred throughout the Hellenistic world, certain centers, especially the great Hellenistic cities of Alexandria and Pergamum, stood out. In both cities, cultural developments were encouraged by the rulers themselves. Of course, the patronage of culture was not a new phenomenon, as the cities of classical Greece illustrate, but rich Hellenistic kings had considerably greater resources with which to make contributions to cultural life.

The Ptolemies in Egypt made Alexandria an especially important cultural center. The library became the largest in ancient times with over 500,000 scrolls. The museum (literally, "temple of the Muses") created a favorable environment for scholarly research. Alexandria became home to poets, writers, philosophers, and scientists—scholars of all kinds. The library encouraged the systematic study of language and literature. As a result of patronage from the Attalid dynasty, Pergamum, the greatest city in Asia Minor, also became a leading cultural center that attracted both scholars and artists. Its library was second only to that of Alexandria.

New Directions in Literature and Art

The Hellenistic age produced an enormous quantity of literature, most of which has not survived. Literary talent was held in high esteem by Hellenistic monarchs who were inclined to subsidize literary people on a grand scale. The Ptolemaic rulers of Egypt were particularly lavish. The combination of their largess and the famous library drew a host of scholars and authors to Alexandria, including a circle of poets. Theocritus (c. 315–250 B.C.) was originally a native of the island of Sicily. He wrote "little poems" or idylls dealing with erotic themes, lovers' complaints, and, above all, pastoral themes expressing his love of nature and his appreciation of nature's beauties (see the box on p. 121). In writing short poems, Theocritus was following the advice of Greek literary scholars who argued that Homer could never be superseded and urged writers to stick to well-composed, short poems instead. But Apollonius of Rhodes (born c. 295 B.C.) ignored this advice and wrote an epic called the *Argonautica*, which recounts the story of Jason's search for the Golden Fleece. Although he was not a particularly good storyteller, Apollonius did produce a remarkably sympathetic portrait of Medea's love for Jason: "Time and again she darted a bright glance at Jason. All else was forgotten. Her heart, brimful of this new agony, throbbed within her and overflowed with the sweetness of the pain. . . . Such was the fire of Love, stealthy but all-consuming, that swept through Medea's heart."[3]

In the Hellenistic era, Athens remained the theatrical center of the Greek world. While little remained of tragedy, a New Comedy developed, which completely rejected political themes and sought only to entertain

❧ The Pastoral Idyll of Theocritus ❧

Little is known of the poet Theocritus (c. 315-250 B.C.). Born in Syracuse on the island of Sicily, he also lived in Miletus, Cos, and Alexandria. He is best known as the creator of pastoral idylls that portray his great love of nature. This selection is from the famous Seventh Idyll (called the "queen of pastorals"), which describes a delightful day on the island of Cos.

Theocritus, The Seventh Idyll

*This I sang, and Lykidas laughed
again pleasantly, and gave me his stick
in fellowship of the Muses,
and turned left, taking the road
to Pyxa, but Eukritos
and handsome Amyntas and I
turned off at Phrasidamos's
and happily laid ourselves down
on beds of sweet grass and vine-leaves,
freshly picked. Overhead, many elms
and poplars rustled, and nearby
the sacred waters splashed down
from the Nymphs' cave. Brown cicadas
shrilled from the shady branches,
and far off the tree-frog whined*

*in the heavy underbrush.
Lark and finches sang, doves crooned,
and bees hummed about the spring.
Everything smelled of rich summer
and rich fruits. Pears lay at our feet,
apples in plenty rolled beside us,
and branches loaded down with plums
bent to the ground. And we broke
the four-year seals on the wine-jars.
Nymphs of Kastalia that live
on the slopes of Parnassos, tell me,
was it such a cup old Chiron
offered Herakles in Pholos'
rocky cave? Was it a drink like this
set Polyphemos dancing,
that mighty shepherd who grazed
his flocks beside the Anapos
and pelted ships with mountains—
such nectar as you mixed for us,
you Nymphs, that day by the altar
of Demeter of the Harvest?
May I plant the great winnowing-fan
another time in her grain-heaps,
while she stands and smiles at us
with wheat-sheaves and poppies in her hand.*

and amuse. The Athenian playwright Menander (c. 342–291 B.C.) was perhaps the best representative of New Comedy. Plots were simple: typically, a hero falls in love with a not-really-so-bad prostitute who turns out eventually to be the long-lost daughter of a rich neighbor. The hero marries her and they live happily ever after.

The Hellenistic period saw a great outpouring of historical and biographical literature. Much of it had a narrow focus, such as histories of Greek cities or districts. The chief historian of the Hellenistic age was Polybius (c. 203–c. 120 B.C.), a Greek who lived for some years in Rome. He is regarded by many historians as second only to Thucydides among Greek historians. His major work consisted of forty books narrating the history of the "inhabited Mediterranean world" from 221 to 146 B.C. Only the first five books are extant although long extracts from the rest of the books

survive. His history focuses on the growth of Rome from a city-state to a world empire. It is apparent that Polybius understood the significance of the Romans' achievement. He followed Thucydides in seeking rational motives for historical events. He also approached his sources critically and used firsthand accounts. In his eagerness for accuracy, he even undertook journeys to visit the sites of battles personally.

In addition to being patrons of literary talent, the Hellenistic monarchs were eager to spend their money to beautify and adorn the cities within their states. The founding of new cities and the rebuilding of old ones provided numerous opportunities for Greek architects and sculptors. Hellenistic architects laid out their new cities on the rectilinear grid model first used by Hippodamus of Miletus in the fifth century B.C. The buildings of the Greek homeland—gymnasia, baths, theaters, and, of course, temples—lined the streets of these cities.

✦ **Laocoön and His Sons.** Three sculptors from Pergamum created this famous piece. This version is probably a Roman copy of the original. The scene illustrates an episode from the Trojan War when the gods sent serpents into Troy to kill the Trojan priest Laocoön and his sons. The intense struggles of the figures are reflected in the pained expressions on their faces.

Most noticeable in the construction of temples was the use of the more ornate Corinthian order (see Chapter 3), which became especially popular during the Hellenistic era.

Sculptors were patronized by Hellenistic kings and rich citizens. Thousands of statues, many paid for by the people honored, were erected in towns and cities all over the Hellenistic world. Hellenistic sculptors traveled throughout this world, attracted by the material rewards offered by wealthy patrons. As a result, although distinct styles developed in Alexandria, Rhodes, and Pergamum, Hellenistic sculpture was characterized by a considerable degree of uniformity. While maintaining the technical skill of the classical period, Hellenistic sculptors moved away from the idealism of fifth-century classicism to a more emotional and realistic art, seen in numerous statues of old women, drunks, and little children at play. The interest in realism also produced excellent portraits, especially of rulers on coins.

A Golden Age of Science and Medicine

The Hellenistic era witnessed a more conscious separation of science from philosophy. In classical Greece, what we would call the physical and life sciences had been divisions of philosophical inquiry. Nevertheless, the Greeks, by the time of Aristotle, had already established an important principle of scientific investigation, empirical research or systematic observation as the basis for generalization. In the Hellenistic age, the sciences tended to be studied in their own right. While Athens remained the philosophical center, Alexandria and Pergamum, the two leading cultural centers of the Hellenistic world, played a significant role in the development of Hellenistic science. Alexandria, in particular, with its library and museum, provided a focus for these activities.

One of the traditional areas of Greek science was astronomy, and two Alexandrian scholars continued this exploration. Aristarchus of Samos (c. 310–230 B.C.) authored a work on the sizes of the sun and moon and their distances from earth and also presented a heliocentric view of the universe; that is, that the sun and the fixed stars remain stationary while the earth rotates around the sun in a circular orbit. He also argued that the earth rotates around its own axis. This view was not widely accepted, and most scholars clung to the earlier geocentric view of the Greeks, which held that the earth was at the center of the universe.

Another Alexandrian scholar with an interest in astronomy was Eratosthenes (c. 275–194 B.C.). He became head of the library at Alexandria and was active in many disciplines, writing works on poetry, philosophy, mathematics, and the history of comedy. His most interesting achievement, however, was his calculation of the earth's circumference using simple geometry. He arrived at a figure of 24,675 miles, an estimate that was within 200 miles of the actual figure. Eratosthenes also proposed that the oceans constituted a single body of water and that Europe, Asia, and Africa formed a single large island. He wrote a handbook of geography that one historian has labeled "the first scientific description of the world."

A third Alexandrian scholar was Euclid, who lived around 300 B.C. He established a school in Alexandria but is primarily known for his work entitled the *Elements*. This was a systematic organization of the fundamental elements of geometry as they had already been worked out; it became the standard textbook of plane geometry and was used up to modern times.

By far the most famous of the scientists of the Hellenistic period, Archimedes of Syracuse (287–212 B.C.), came from the western Mediterranean region. Archimedes was especially important for his work on the geometry of spheres and cylinders, for establishing the value of the mathematical constant pi, and for creating the science of hydrostatics. Archimedes was also a practical inventor. He may have devised the so-called Archimedean screw used to pump water out of mines and to lift irrigation water as well as a compound pulley for transporting heavy weights. During the Roman siege of his native city of Syracuse, he constructed a number of devices to thwart the attackers. According to Plutarch's account, the Romans became so frightened "that if they did but see a little rope or a piece of wood from the wall, instantly crying out, that there it was again, Archimedes was about to let fly some engine at them, they turned their backs and fled."[4] Archimedes' accomplishments inspired a wealth of semilegendary stories. Supposedly, he discovered specific gravity by observing the water he displaced in his bath and became so excited by his realization that he jumped out of the water and ran home naked, shouting, "Eureka" ("I have found it"). He is said to have emphasized the importance of levers by proclaiming to the king of Syracuse: "Give me a lever and a place to stand on and I will move the earth." The king was so impressed that he encouraged Archimedes to lower his sights and build defensive weapons instead.

Historians have observed that most Hellenistic scientists made little effort to translate their abstract scientific knowledge into applied technology or the creation of labor-saving devices. Many have argued that cheap labor, whether slave or low-paid free men and women, provided no incentive for developing labor-saving devices. Others have pointed to the contempt that upper-class Greeks (who, after all, had the leisure to be scientists and philosophers) had for manual labor and crafts. The ancient author Plutarch expressed the belief that even Archimedes himself shared this attitude:

Yet Archimedes possessed so high a spirit, so profound a soul, and such treasures of scientific knowledge, that though these inventions had now obtained him the

♦ **Old Market Woman.** Greek architects and sculptors were highly valued throughout the Hellenistic world, as kings undertook projects to beautify the cities of their kingdoms. The sculptors of this period no longer tried to capture ideal beauty in their sculpture, a quest that characterized Greek classicism, but moved toward a more emotional and realistic art. This statue of an old market woman is typical of this new trend in art.

renown of more than human sagacity, he yet would not deign to leave behind him any commentary or writing on such subjects; but, repudiating as sordid and ignoble the whole trade of engineering, and every sort of art that lends itself to mere use and profit, he placed his whole affection and ambition in those purer speculations where there can be no reference to the vulgar needs of life. . . .[5]

Regardless of the reasons for the failure to develop a technological revolution, there was one field in which practical applications of scientific knowledge were encouraged: military science. The Hellenistic kings were quite ready to employ military technicians to work on

❧ *Miraculous Cures* ❧

Although all gods and goddesses were believed to have healing powers, special curative powers were attributed to Asclepius, the god of healing. A cult of supernatural healing came to be associated with him. Dreams that people experienced when they slept in a sanctuary dedicated to Asclepius supposedly had curative powers, as these texts demonstrate.

Texts on the Miraculous Cures at Epidaurus

A man with the fingers of his hand paralyzed except for one came as a suppliant to the god, and when he saw the tablets in the sanctuary he would not believe the cures and was rather contemptuous of the inscriptions, but when he went to sleep he saw a vision: he thought that as he was playing dice below the sanctuary and was about to throw the dice, the god appeared, sprang on his hand and stretched out his fingers, and when the god moved away, the man thought he bent his hand and stretched out the fingers one by one, when he had straightened them all out, the god asked him whether he still did not believe the inscriptions on the tablets in the sanctuary, and the man said he did. The god said: "Since previously you would not believe them, although they are not incredible, in future let [your name] be 'Incredulous.'" When day came he went away cured.

Ambrosia from Athens, blind in one eye. She came as a suppliant to the god, and as she walked about the sanctuary she ridiculed some of the cures as being incredible and impossible, that persons who were lame and blind should be restored to health merely by seeing a dream. But when she went to sleep she saw a vision: she thought the god was standing next to her and saying that he would restore her to health, but she must dedicate in the sanctuary as a reward a silver pig, as a memorial of her stupidity. Having said this he split open the diseased eye and poured in a medicine. When day came she went away cured.

siege towers, grappling-engines, and new forms of catapults.

The scientific foundations of medicine also made considerable strides in the Hellenistic period, especially at Alexandria. This represents a continuation from the fifth century when Hippocrates, a contemporary of Socrates, is credited with having been the "first to separate medicine from philosophy" by stressing natural explanations and natural cures for disease. Herophilus and Erasistratus, both well-known physicians, were active in Alexandria in the first half of the third century B.C. Both were interested in anatomy and used dissection and vivisection (the dissection of living bodies) to expand their knowledge, or so the Roman author Celsus claimed:

> Moreover, as pains, and also various kinds of diseases, arise in the more internal parts, they hold that no one can apply remedies for these who is ignorant about the parts themselves; hence it becomes necessary to lay open the bodies of the dead and to scrutinize their viscera and intestines. They hold that Herophilus and Erasistratus did this in the best way by far, when they laid open men whilst alive—criminals received out of prison from the kings—and whilst these were still breathing, observed parts which beforehand nature had concealed, their position, color, shape, size, arrangement, hardness, softness, smoothness, relation, processes and depressions of each, and whether any part is inserted into or is received into another.[6]

Herophilus added significantly to the understanding of the brain, eye, liver, and the reproductive and nervous systems. Erasistratus made discoveries in the process of digestion, clarified the distinction between sensory and motor nerves, and theorized on the flow of blood through the veins without, however, arriving at an understanding of the circulation of the blood through the body. After these two, the reputation of Alexandrian doctors began to decline, and by the second century B.C., according to the historian Polybius, they were no longer to be trusted: "Not a few invalids indeed who had nothing serious the matter with them have before now come very near losing their lives by entrusting themselves to these physicians, impressed by their rhetorical powers."[7]

It would be misleading to think of medicine in the Hellenistic world only in terms of scientific advances. Alongside these developments, a wide range of alternative methods of healing continued to exist. These included magical practices, such as the use of amulets to cast off evil spirits, herbal remedies, and the healing powers of deities, especially those of Asclepius, the god of healing (see the box on p. 124).

Philosophy: New Schools of Thought

While Alexandria and Pergamum became the renowned cultural centers of the Hellenistic world, Athens remained the prime center for philosophy. After Alexander the Great, the home of Socrates, Plato, and Aristotle continued to attract the most illustrious philosophers from the Greek world who chose to establish their schools there. While Plato's Academy and Aristotle's Lyceum continued to exist and attract some students, new schools of philosophical thought (the Epicureans and Stoics) reinforced Athens's reputation as a philosophical center.

Epicurus (341–270 B.C.), the founder of Epicureanism, established a school in Athens near the end of the fourth century B.C. Epicurus's famous belief in a doctrine of "pleasure" began with his view of the world. While he did not deny the existence of the gods, he did not believe they played any active role in the world. The universe ran on its own. This left human beings free to follow self-interest as a basic motivating force. Happiness was the goal of life, and the means to achieve it was the pursuit of pleasure, the only true good. But the pursuit of pleasure was not meant in a physical, hedonistic sense:

> When, therefore, we maintain that pleasure is the end, we do not mean the pleasures of profligates and those that consist in sensuality, as is supposed by some who are either ignorant or disagree with us or do not understand, but freedom from pain in the body and from trouble in the mind. For it is not continuous drinkings and revellings, nor the satisfaction of lusts, nor the enjoyment of fish and other luxuries of the wealthy table, which produce a pleasant life, but sober reasoning, searching out the motives for all choice and avoidance, and banishing mere opinions, to which are due the greatest disturbance of the spirit.

Pleasure was not satisfying one's desire in an active, gluttonous fashion, but freedom from emotional turmoil, freedom from worry, the freedom that came from a mind at rest. To achieve this passive pleasure, one had to free oneself from public activity: "We must release ourselves from the prison of affairs and politics." They were too strenuous to give peace of mind. But this was not a

◆ **Portrait of Epicurus.** Epicurus was the founder of the Epicurean school of philosophy, which became very popular during the Hellenistic period. He maintained an "atomic" theory of the universe—that the only things that exist are atoms moving through the void—and an ethical theory based upon the pursuit of pleasure.

renunciation of all social life, for to Epicurus, a life could only be complete when it was centered on the basic ideal of friendship: "Of all the things which wisdom acquires to produce the blessedness of the complete life, far the greatest is the possession of friendship."[8] Epicurus's own life in Athens was an embodiment of his teachings. He and his family created their own private community where they could pursue their ideal of true happiness.

Epicureanism was eventually overshadowed by another school of thought known as Stoicism, which became the most popular philosophy of the Hellenistic world and later flourished in the Roman Empire as well. It was the product of a teacher named Zeno (335–263 B.C.), who came to Athens and began to teach in a public colonnade known as the Painted Portico (the *Stoa Poikile*—hence Stoicism). Like Epicureanism, Stoicism was concerned with how individuals find happiness. But Stoics took a radically different approach to the problem. To them, happiness, the supreme good, could be found only in virtue, which meant essentially living in harmony with the will of God: "And this very thing constitutes the virtue of the happy man and the smooth current of life, when all actions promote the harmony of the spirit dwelling in the individual man with the will of him who orders the universe."[9] One achieved happiness by choosing to follow the will of God through the free exercise of one's own will. To the Stoics, the will of God was the same thing as the will of nature since nature was simply a manifestation or expression of God. "Living according to nature," therefore, meant following the will of God or the natural laws that God established to run the universe.

Virtuous living, then, was living in accordance with the laws of nature or submitting to the will of God (see the box above). This led to the acceptance of whatever one received in life since God's will for us was by its very nature good. By accepting God's law, people mastered themselves and gained inner peace. Life's problems could not disturb such individuals, and they could bear whatever life offered (hence our word "stoic"). The Stoics did not believe that it was difficult to know the will of God. This knowledge could be derived through the senses, or what the Stoics called the "perception conveying direct apprehension." Sense perceptions of overwhelming strength had to be a revelation of God's standards.

Unlike Epicureans, Stoics did not believe in the need to separate oneself from the world and politics. Public service was regarded as noble. The real Stoic was a good citizen and could even be a good government official. Since Stoics believed that a divine principle was present throughout the universe, each human being also contained a divine spark. This led to a belief in the oneness of humanity. The world constituted a single society of equal human beings. Although not equal in the outer world, the divine spark in each meant that all were free to follow God's will (what was best for each individual). All persons then, even slaves, though unfree in body, were equal at the level of the soul.

Epicureanism and especially Stoicism appealed to large numbers of people in the Hellenistic world. Both of these philosophies focused primarily on the problem of human happiness. Their popularity would suggest a fundamental change in the character of the Greek lifestyle. In the classical Greek world, the happiness of individuals and the meaning of life were closely associated with the life of the *polis*. One found fulfillment within the community. In the Hellenistic kingdoms, although the *polis* continued to exist, the sense that one could find satisfaction and fulfillment through life in the *polis* had weakened. Not only did individuals seek new philosophies that offered personal happiness, but in the cosmopolitan world of the Hellenistic states with their mixtures of peoples, a new openness to thoughts of universality could also emerge. For some people, Stoicism embodied this larger sense of community. The appeal of new philosophies in the Hellenistic era can also be explained by the apparent decline in certain aspects of traditional religion, which we can see by examining the status of Hellenistic religion.

Religion in the Hellenistic World

When the Greeks spread throughout the Hellenistic kingdoms of the Near East, they took their gods with them. Hellenistic cities increased the number of public festivals and celebrated them with great magnificence. The priesthoods tied to the civic cults were still desirable to the leading citizens who competed to purchase these offices. But over a period of time, there was a noticeable decline in the vitality of the traditional Greek Olympian religion. Much of Greek religion had always revolved around ritual, but the civic cults based on the traditional gods no longer seemed sufficient to satisfy people's emotional needs. Then, too, the breakdown of the old commitment to the *polis* brought insecurity and changes that the civic cults, tied to the traditional Greek *polis,* seemed unable to meet. The spread of ruler cults was yet another sign of the weakening of the traditional Greek civic cults.

The Hellenistic kings who established themselves after Alexander were eager to buttress their power with religious support. The new royal families all embraced a traditional Greek Olympian god or goddess as a protector. The Antigonid dynasty of Macedonia asserted that they were descendants of the demigod Heracles. While the Seleucids of Syria adopted Apollo and the Attalids Athena as their "ancestors," the Egyptian Ptolemies dedicated themselves to the cult of Dionysus.

But the cults of these patron gods were soon overshadowed by ruler cults devoted to the worship of the Hellenistic kings themselves, both dead and living, as gods. Although there are earlier isolated examples of such a practice among the Greeks, Alexander's success, combined with the traditions of the Near East where god kings were not unknown, inspired the widespread institution of such cults in the Hellenistic kingdoms. Ptolemy I of Egypt had created a cult of Alexander by 285 B.C. and was himself proclaimed a god by his son upon his death in 283 B.C. Later, the Ptolemies added their own names to the official cult while still alive. The divinization of living Seleucids did not take place until the end of the third century, while the Attalids of Pergamum were never acknowledged as divine while alive. The Antigonids refused to be gods, whether dead or alive. As their founders intended, the ruler cults added to the authority and legitimacy of the Hellenistic dynasties.

Greek cities on the mainland likewise instituted religious cults dedicated to living rulers. In fact, they seemed particularly eager to pay homage to rulers who could affect their lives, thus demonstrating the close relationship between political and religious motivations in the establishment of ruler cults. Indeed, the Athenians sang the following hymn to honor Demetrius, the king of Macedonia:

> Something august he seems, all his friends about him, and he himself in their midst, his friends the stars, even as he is the sun. O son of the most mighty god Poseidon and of Aphrodite, hail! For other gods are either far away, or have not ears, or are not, or heed us not at all; but you we can see in very presence, not in wood and not in stone, but in truth. And so we pray to you.[10]

One wonders what the hymn really meant to people since it expresses doubts about the efficacy of the traditional gods.

The decline in traditional Greek religion left the Greeks receptive to the numerous religious cults of the eastern world. The Greeks were always tolerant of other existing religious institutions. Hence in the Hellenistic cities of the Near East, the traditional civic cults of their own gods, ruler cults, and foreign cults existed side by side. Alexandria had cults of the traditional Greek gods, Alexander and the Ptolemies, Egyptian deities, such as Isis and Horus, the Babylonian Astarte, and the Syrian Atargatis. This medley of cults existed in Greek cities everywhere, whether large or small. While the Greeks maintained their own cults out of pride, at the same time there was a movement toward syncretism or the fusing of one god with another as a manifestation of different forms of the same underlying divine force. Moreover, the strongest appeal of eastern religions to the Greeks came from the mystery religions. What was the source of their attraction?

The normal forms of religious worship in Hellenistic communities had lost some of their appeal. Ruler cults and patron gods could obviously be viewed as politically motivated. The practices of traditional, ritualized Greek religion in the civic cults seemed increasingly meaningless. For many people, the search for personal meaning remained unfulfilled. People sought alternatives. Among educated Greeks, the philosophies of Epicureanism and especially Stoicism offered help. Another source of solace came in the form of mystery religions.

Mystery cults, with their secret initiations and promises of individual salvation, were, of course, not new to the Greek world; we have already seen the Eleusinian mysteries in Attica, for example (see Chapter 3). But the Greeks were also strongly influenced by eastern mystery cults, such as those of Egypt, which offered a distinct advantage over the Greek mystery religions.

◆ **The Cult of Isis.** The cult of Isis was one of the most popular mystery religions in the Hellenistic world. This fresco from Herculaneum in Italy depicts a religious ceremony in front of the temple of Isis. At the top, a priest holds a golden vessel while below him another priest leads the worshipers with a staff. A third priest fans the flames at the altar.

The latter had usually been connected to specific locations (such as Eleusis), which meant that a would-be initiate had to undertake a pilgrimage in order to participate in the rites. In contrast, the eastern mystery religions were readily available since temples to their gods and goddesses were located throughout the Greek cities of the east.

All of the mystery religions were based on the same fundamental premises. Individuals could pursue a path to salvation and the achievement of eternal life by being initiated into a union with a savior god or goddess who had died and risen again. The ritual of initiation, by which the seeker identified with the god or goddess, was, no doubt, a highly emotional experience.

The Egyptian cults of Isis and Serapis were the most popular of the mystery religions. The cult of Isis was very ancient, but became truly universal in Hellenistic times, as seen in this inscription from one of her Egyptian temples: "The Syrians call her Astarte, Artemis, and Anaia; ... the Thracians, the Mother of the Gods; the

Greeks, Hera of the mighty throne, and Aphrodite, good Hestia, Rheia, and Demeter; the Egyptians Thiouis, for you alone are all the other goddesses named by the nations."[11] Isis was the goddess of women, marriage, and children, as one of her hymns states: "I am she whom women call goddess. I ordained that women should be loved by men: I brought wife and husband together, and invented the marriage contract. I ordained that women should bear children. . . ."[12] Isis was portrayed as the giver of civilization who had brought laws and letters to all humankind. The cult of Serapis emerged during the reign of the first Ptolemaic rulers of Egypt. The worship of Serapis was centered in Alexandria, but he also became a universal deity whose worship spread throughout the Hellenistic world. The cults of both Isis and Serapis offered a precious commodity to their initiates—the promise of eternal life. In many ways, the mystery religions of the Hellenistic era helped to pave the way for the coming and the success of Christianity (see Chapter 6).

There were other spiritual manifestations in the Hellenistic era as well. Some people spoke of *Tyche* or Fortune as a deified force that affected lives. Others became involved in the practice of astrology, which proved to be highly popular in the Hellenistic era. Although influenced by Babylonian astronomy, astrology as an organized system was a product of Hellenistic times. The first astrological handbooks appeared in Ptolemaic Egypt in the second century B.C. Astrology was considered a spiritual science by its practitioners, who adhered to the Greek belief that the heavens operated in a regular and predictable fashion. Future events could be foretold by an understanding of heavenly movements ("as above, so below"), and the lives of individuals were affected by the position of the planets and heavenly constellations at the time of their birth. Since astrologers believed their system was a product of divine wisdom, astrology could and did serve as a substitute for religion. The Stoics found much value in astrology, and some of the Alexandrian scientists found nothing incompatible in their interests in both astrology and astronomy.

The Jews in the Hellenistic World

In observing the similarities among their gods and goddesses, Greeks and easterners tended to assume they were the same beings with different names, giving rise to a process of syncretism. But a special position was occupied in the Hellenistic world by the Hebrews, whose monotheistic religion was exclusive and did not permit this kind of fusion of spiritual beings.

The Jewish kingdom of Judaea was ruled by the Ptolemies until it fell under the control of the Seleucids by 200 B.C. Initially, this led to little change. There was some inclination to hellenization, but also a strong reaction against it that led to greater Jewish orthodoxy. In the reign of the Seleucid king Antiochus IV (175–163 B.C.), conflict erupted in Judaea. Hellenistic monarchs were generally tolerant of all religions, but problems with Rome prompted Antiochus to try to impose more cultural and religious unity throughout his kingdom. When he sent troops to Jerusalem and seized the Temple, he sparked a Jewish uprising led by Judas Maccabaeus (164 B.C.). The rebels succeeded in recapturing the Temple, a joyous event that has been celebrated every year since in the Jewish holiday of Hanukkah, the Festival of Light. Although the conflict in Judaea continued, the Seleucids ultimately made concessions and allowed the Jews considerable freedom.

But since the Diaspora (see Chapter 2), large numbers of Jews no longer lived in Judaea. There was a large Jewish population in Egypt, particularly in Alexandria, as well as Jewish settlements throughout the cities of Asia Minor and Syria. In each city, Jews generally set up a synagogue and formed a private association for worship as other foreigners did. But some city authorities also allowed the Jews to form a political corporation that gave them greater rights than other resident aliens. Most importantly, they gained the privilege to live by their own laws and their own judicial system. The Jews were not really interested in citizenship in the cities in which they resided since full citizenship meant worship of the city's gods, an anathema to Jews who believed only in Yahweh.

Residence in Greek cities, however, did lead many Jews to adopt the Greek language and some aspects of Greek culture. In the third century B.C., Jews in Alexandria translated the Hebrew Bible into Greek. Services in some synagogues were held in Greek, and a number of Jews also took Greek names.

Conclusion

Although historians used to view the Hellenistic era as a period of stagnation after the brilliant Greek civilization of the fifth century B.C., our survey of the Hellenistic world has shown the weakness of that position. The Hellenistic period was, in its own way, a vibrant one. New cities arose and flourished. New philosophical ideas captured the minds of many. Significant achievements occurred in art, literature, and science. Greek culture spread throughout the Near East and made an impact wherever it was carried. In some areas of the Hellenistic world, queens played an active role in political life, and many upper-class women found new avenues for expressing themselves.

But serious problems remained. Hellenistic kings continued to engage in inconclusive wars. The gulf between rich and poor was indeed great. Much of the formal culture was the special preserve of the Greek conquerors whose attitude of superiority kept them largely separated from the native masses of the Hellenistic kingdoms. Although the Hellenistic world achieved a degree of political stability, by the late third century B.C. signs of decline were beginning to multiply. Some of the more farsighted perhaps realized the danger presented to the Hellenistic world by the growing power of Rome. The Romans would ultimately inherit Alexander's empire, and we must now turn to them and try to understand what made them such successful conquerors.

NOTES

1. Polybius, *The Histories*, trans. W. R. Paton (Cambridge, Mass., 1960), XVIII, 37, 8–10.
2. Roger S. Bagnall and Peter Derow, *Greek Historical Documents: The Hellenistic Period* (Chico, Calif., 1981), p. 113.
3. Apollonius of Rhodes, *The Voyage of Argo,* trans. E. V. Rieu (Baltimore, 1959), p. 117.
4. Plutarch, *Life of Marcellus,* trans. John Dryden (New York, n.d.), p. 378.
5. Ibid.

6. Celsus, *De Medicina,* trans. W. G. Spencer (Cambridge, Mass., 1935), Prooemium 23–24.

7. Polybius, *The Histories,* XII, 25d, 5.

8. *Epicurus: The Extant Remains,* trans. Cyril Bailey (Oxford, 1926), pp. (in order of quotations) 89–91, 115, 101.

9. Diogenes Laertius, *Life of Zeno,* vol. 2, trans.

R. D. Hicks (London, 1925), p. 195.

10. Athenaeus, *The Deipnosophistae,* trans. Charles B. Gulick (Cambridge, Mass., 1929), VI, 253d–e.

11. Quoted in C. Bradford Welles, *Alexander and the Hellenistic World* (Toronto, 1970), p. 197.

12. Quoted in W. W. Tarn, *Hellenistic Civilization* (London, 1930), p. 324.

SUGGESTIONS FOR FURTHER READING

For a general introduction to the Hellenistic era, see J. Boardman, J. Griffin, and O. Murray, eds., *The Oxford History of the Classical World* (Oxford, 1986), pp. 315–85. A brief, but excellent guide to recent trends in scholarship on the Hellenistic era can be found in C. Starr, *Past and Future in Ancient History* (Lanham, Md., 1987), pp. 19–32. The best general survey is F. W. Walbank, *The Hellenistic World* (Cambridge, Mass., 1993). Other studies include C. B. Welles, *Alexander and the Hellenistic World* (Toronto, 1970); W. W. Tarn and G. T. Griffith, *Hellenistic Civilization,* 3d ed. (London, 1952); M. Grant, *From Alexander to Cleopatra: The Hellenistic World* (London, 1982); and P. Green, *Alexander to Actium: The Historic Evolution of the Hellenistic Age* (Berkeley, 1990). There are good collections of sources in translation in M. M. Austin, *The Hellenistic World from Alexander to the Roman Conquest* (Cambridge, 1981); R. S. Bagnall and P. Derow, *Greek Historical Documents: The Hellenistic Period* (Chico, Calif., 1981); and S. M. Burstein, *The Hellenistic Age from the Battle of Ipsos to the Death of Kleopatra VII* (Cambridge, 1985).

For a good introduction to the early history of Macedonia, see E. N. Borza, *In the Shadow of Olympus: The Emergence of Macedon* (Princeton, N.J., 1990); and R. M. Errington, *A History of Macedonia* (Berkeley, 1990). Philip of Macedon is covered well in G. L. Cawkwell, *Philip of Macedon* (London, 1978); and N. Hammond and G. Griffith, *A History of Macedonia,* vol. 2, *550–336* B.C. (Oxford, 1979). There are considerable differences of opinion on Alexander the Great. Good biographies include R. L. Fox, *Alexander the Great* (London, 1973); J. R. Hamilton, *Alexander the Great* (London, 1973); N. G. L. Hammond, *Alexander the Great* (London, 1981); and P. Green, *Alexander of Macedon* (Berkeley, 1991).

Studies on the various Hellenistic monarchies include N. G. L. Hammond and F. W. Walbank, *A History of Macedonia,* vol. 3, *336–167* B.C. (Oxford, 1988); H. I. Bell, *Egypt from Alexander the Great to the Arab Conquest* (Oxford, 1948); E. V. Hansen, *The Attalids of Pergamum,* 2d ed. (Ithaca, N.Y., 1971); R. E. Allen, *The Attalid Kingdom* (Oxford, 1983); and O. Morkholm, *Antiochus IV of Syria* (Copenhagen, 1966) on one of the Seleucid rulers. The limits of hellenization are discussed in A. D. Momigliano, *Alien Wisdom: The Limits of Hellenization* (Cambridge, 1975); M. Hengel, *Judaism and Hellenism* (London, 1974); and V. Tcherikover, *Hellenistic Civilization and the Jews* (Philadelphia, 1959). On Hellenistic military developments, see W. W. Tarn, *Hellenistic Military and Naval Developments* (Cambridge, 1930); G. T. Griffith, *Mercenaries of the Hellenistic World* (Cambridge, 1935); and B. Bar-Kochva, *The Seleucid Army* (Cambridge, 1976).

A good survey of Hellenistic cities can be found in A. H. M. Jones, *The Greek City from Alexander to Justinian* (Oxford, 1940). Alexandria is covered in P. M. Fraser, *Ptolemaic Alexandria* (Oxford, 1972). On the contributions of the rich to their cities, see A. R. Hands, *Charities and Social Aid in Greece and Rome* (London, 1968). On economic and social trends, see M. I. Finley, *The Ancient Economy,* 2d ed. (London, 1985); and the classic and still indispensable M. I. Rostovtzeff, *Social and Economic History of the Hellenistic World,* 3 vols., 2d ed. (Oxford, 1953).

Hellenistic women are examined in two works by S. B. Pomeroy, *Goddesses, Whores, Wives, and Slaves* (New York, 1975), pp. 120–48, and *Women in Hellenistic Egypt* (New York, 1984). Slavery is examined in W. L. Westermann, *The Slave-Systems of Greek and Roman Antiquity* (Philadelphia, 1955). The classic work on education is H. I. Marrou, *A History of Education in Antiquity* (London, 1956).

For a general introduction to Hellenistic culture, see M. Hadas, *Hellenistic Culture: Fusion and Diffusion* (New York, 1959); and J. Onians, *Art and Thought in the Hellenistic Age* (London, 1979). On art, see J. J. Pollitt, *Art in the Hellenistic Age* (New York, 1986). The best general survey of Hellenistic philosophy is A. A. Long, *Hellenistic Philosophy: Stoics, Epicureans, Skeptics,* 2d ed. (London, 1986). A superb work on Hellenistic science is G. E. R. Lloyd, *Greek Science after Aristotle* (London, 1973). A good survey of Hellenistic literature is A.

Lesky, *A History of Greek Literature* (London, 1966), pp. 642–806.

On various facets of Hellenistic religion, see L. Martin, *Hellenistic Religions: An Introduction* (New York, 1987); and R. E. Witt, *Isis in the Graeco-Roman World* (London, 1971). The best introduction to astrology is now S. J. Tester, *A History of Western Astrology* (Wolfeboro, N. H., 1987).

On the entry of Rome into the Hellenistic world, see the basic work by E. S. Gruen, *The Hellenistic World and the Coming of Rome,* 2 vols. (Berkeley, 1984).

CHAPTER
5

The Roman Republic

Early Roman history is filled with legendary stories that tell of the heroes who made Rome great. One of the best known is the story of Horatius at the bridge. Threatened by attack from the neighboring Etruscans, Roman farmers abandoned their fields and moved into the city, where they would be protected by the walls. One weak point in the Roman defenses, however, was a wooden bridge over the Tiber River. Horatius was on guard at the bridge when a sudden assault by the Etruscans caused many Roman troops to throw down their weapons and flee. Horatius urged them to make a stand at the bridge to protect Rome; when they hesitated, as a last resort he told them to destroy the bridge behind him while he held the Etruscans back. Astonished at the sight of a single defender, the confused Etruscans threw their spears at Horatius who caught them on his shield and barred the way. By the time the Etruscans had regrouped and were about to overwhelm the lone defender, the Roman soldiers brought down the bridge. When Horatius heard the bridge crash into the river behind him, he dove fully armed into the water and swam safely to the other side through a hail of arrows. Rome had been saved by the courageous act of a Roman who knew his duty and was determined to carry it out. Courage, duty, determination—these qualities would also serve the many Romans who believed that it was their mission to rule nations and peoples.

In the first millennium B.C., a group of Latin-speaking people established a small community on the plain of Latium on the Italian peninsula. This community, called Rome, was merely one of numerous Latin-speaking communities in Latium, and the Latin speakers, in turn, constituted only some of the many peoples in Italy. Roman history is basically the story of the Romans' conquest of the plain of Latium, then Italy, and finally the entire Mediterranean world. Why were the Romans able to do this? Scholars do not really know all the answers. The Romans made the right decisions at the right time, which is to say

Republic begins

Conquest of the Mediterranean

Conquest of Italy

Decline and collapse of the Republic

Struggle of the orders

Reforms of the Gracchi brothers

Twelve Tables

Caesar as dictator

Plays of Plautus

Poems of Catullus

Plays of Terence

Works of Cicero

the Romans were a people distinguished by a high degree of political wisdom.

The Romans were also a practical people. Unlike the Greeks, who reserved their citizenship for small, select groups, the Romans often offered their citizenship to the peoples they conquered, thus laying the basis for a strong, integrated empire. The Romans also did not hesitate to borrow ideas and culture from the Greeks. Roman strength lay in government, law, and engineering. The Romans knew how to govern people, establish legal structures, and construct the roads that took them to the ends of the known world. Throughout their empire, they carried their law, their political institutions, their engineering skills, and their Latin language. And even after the Romans were gone, those same gifts continued to play an important role in the continuing saga of Western civilization.

Early Rome and the Etruscans

There is still considerable uncertainty about the nature of the prehistoric peoples who lived in Italy. We do know that Indo-European peoples moved into Italy during the second half of the second millennium B.C. By the first millennium B.C., other peoples had also settled in Italy—the two most notable being the Greeks and the Etruscans. Before examining these peoples, however, we need to consider the influence geography had on the historical development of the peoples on the Italian peninsula.

Geography of the Italian Peninsula

Italy is a peninsula extending about 750 miles from north to south. It is not very wide, however, averaging about 120 miles across. The Alps in the north form a natural barrier although numerous passes did permit peoples to cross into northern Italy. The Apennines are not as high as the Alps, but connect with the Alps in northwest Italy and then traverse the peninsula from north to south, forming a ridge down the middle that divides west from east. Nevertheless, Italy is left with some fairly large fertile plains ideal for farming, especially on the western side of the Apennines. Most important were the Po valley in the north, probably the most fertile agricultural area; the plain of Latium, on which Rome was located; and Campania to the south of Latium. To the east of the Italian peninsula is the Adriatic Sea and to the west the Tyrrhenian Sea with the nearby large islands of Corsica and Sardinia. Sicily lies just west of the toe of the boot-shaped peninsula.

While geography alone did not determine the course of Roman development, it did have an impact on Roman history. Although the Apennines bisected Italy, they were less rugged than the mountain ranges of Greece and did not divide the peninsula into many small isolated communities. Italy also possessed considerably more productive agricultural land than Greece, enabling it to support a large population. Rome's location was favorable from a geographical point of view. Located eighteen miles inland on the Tiber River, Rome had access to the sea and was yet far enough inland to be safe from pirates. Built on the famous seven hills, it was easily defended. Situated where the Tiber could be readily forded, Rome became a natural crossing point for north-south traffic in western Italy. All in all, Rome had a good central location in Italy from which to expand.

Moreover, the Italian peninsula juts into the Mediterranean, making it an important crossroads between the western and eastern Mediterranean. Once Rome had unified Italy, involvement in Mediterranean affairs was natural. And after the Romans had conquered their Mediterranean empire, Italy's central location made their task of governing that empire considerably less difficult.

✖ **Map 5.1** Ancient Italy and the City of Rome (inset).

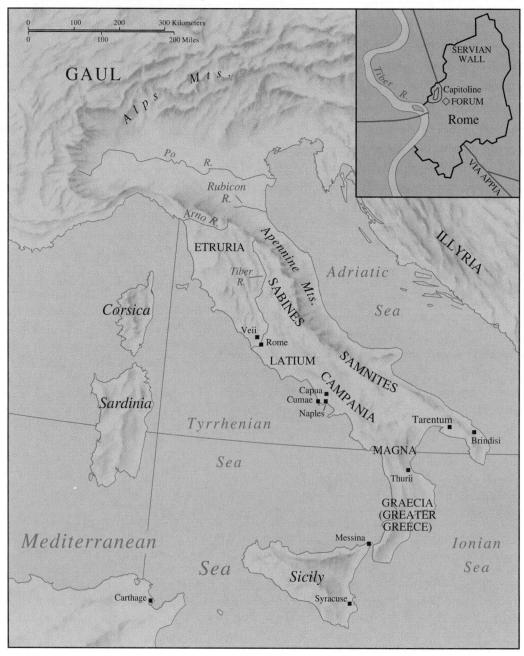

The Greeks

The Greeks arrived on the Italian peninsula in large numbers during the age of Greek colonization (750–550 B.C.—see Chapter 3). Initially, the Greeks settled in southern Italy. They founded Cumae in the Bay of Naples, Naples itself (Neapolis), and Tarentum and then crept around the coast and up the peninsula as far as Brindisi (Brundisium). The eastern two-thirds of Sicily was also occupied by the Greeks. In establishing their colonies, the Greeks planned permanent communities, secured the coastal plains for agriculture, and built walled cities with harbors to carry on trade. Ultimately, the Greeks had considerable influence on Italy, particularly the Etruscan cities and Rome. They cultivated the olive and the vine, passed on their alphabetic system of writing, and provided artistic and cultural models through their sculpture, architecture, and literature. Indeed, many historians view Roman culture as a continuation of Greek culture. While Greek influence initially touched Rome indirectly through the Etruscans, the Roman conquest of southern Italy and Sicily brought them into direct contact with the Greeks. Later, in the second century B.C., the Roman conquest of Greece completed the Greek cultural domination of Rome.

The Etruscans

The initial development of Rome was influenced most by a people known as the Etruscans. The Etruscans were located north of Rome in Etruria. They were a city-dwelling people who established their towns in commanding positions and fortified them with walls. Their pottery reflected considerable Greek influence. Numerous inscriptions in tombs show that the Etruscans adopted alphabetic writing from the Greeks before 600 B.C.

The origins of the Etruscans are not clear. Were they native Italians or, like the Greeks in Italy, were they immigrants from the east? The debate about their ancestry began in the ancient world. One Greek historian, Herodotus, maintained that the Etruscans stemmed from Asia Minor, while another, Dionysius of Halicarnassus, argued for Italian origins. The most obvious arguments for a non-Italic origin include their language, which is non-Indo-European, and their use of Near Eastern religious customs, such as divination (see Chapter 1). Many scholars now believe that the archaeological evidence is best interpreted as showing an unbroken

✦ **Etruscan Married Couple.** This sculpture, dating from 550 B.C., depicts a wealthy Etruscan married couple reclining on a couch. The Etruscans greatly influenced the early development of Rome and had an impact on Roman religion, Roman sporting events, and military institutions.

evolution from earlier native, non-Indo-European–speaking peoples known as the Villanovans.

After 650 B.C., the Etruscans expanded in Italy and became the dominant cultural and economic force in a number of areas. To the north, they moved into north-central Italy, including the Po valley. To the south, according to Roman tradition and archaeological evidence, they controlled Rome and possibly all of Latium. From Latium they moved south into Campania, founded a settlement at Capua, and came into direct contact with Greek colonists in southern Italy. They also encountered the Greeks in naval conflicts. Around 535 B.C., the Etruscans joined with the Carthaginians to defeat the Greeks in a battle off the island of Corsica, but were later routed by the Greeks in a naval battle off Cumae around 480 B.C. By this time, Etruscan power was on the decline. By 400 B.C., they had been limited to Etruria itself and later were invaded by the Gauls and then conquered by the Romans. The Etruscans, then, reached the height of their power in the sixth century B.C. Nevertheless, they had had an impact. By transforming villages into towns and cities, they brought urbanization to northern and central Italy (the Greeks brought urbanization to southern Italy). Rome was, of course, the Etruscans' most famous product, and it is now time to examine that city's early history.

Early Rome

According to Roman legend, Rome was founded by the twin brothers, Romulus and Remus, in 753 B.C. Of course, the Romans invented this story to provide a noble ancestry for their city. After all, the twins' father was supposed to have been the god Mars, the most important deity in early Roman religion. Archaeologists have found, however, that by the eighth century there was a settlement consisting of huts on the tops of Rome's hills. The early Romans, basically a pastoral people, spoke Latin, which, like Greek, belongs to the Indo-European family of languages (see the table in Chapter 1). The Roman historical tradition also maintained that early Rome (753–509 B.C.) had been under the control of seven kings and that two of the last three had been Etruscans. Some historians believe that the king list, with the exception of Romulus as the first, may have some historical accuracy. What is certain is that Rome did fall under the influence of the Etruscans for about a hundred years during the period of the kings. The Etruscans found Rome a pastoral community but left it a city.

Etruscan influence on Rome appears to have begun around 625 B.C. The Etruscans were responsible for draining the area of the Forum and inaugurating its use as a public arena. By the beginning of the sixth century, under Etruscan influence, Rome began to emerge as an actual city. The Etruscans were responsible for an outstanding building program. They constructed the first roadbed of the chief street through Rome—the Sacred Way—before 575 B.C. and oversaw the development of temples, markets, shops, streets, and houses. By 509 B.C., supposedly when the monarchy was overthrown, a new Rome had emerged, essentially a product of the fusion of Etruscan and native Roman elements.

The Etruscans had an impact on Roman civilization in numerous ways—both small and large. Etruscan dress—the toga and short cloak—was adopted by the Romans. The insignia of the Etruscan kings became the insignia of Roman magistrates in the Republic. Most impressive was the *fasces*, an axe surrounded by a bundle of rods used as a symbol for the power to scourge and execute, hence to rule. In the Republic, the consuls as chief magistrates were preceded by twelve lictors bearing the *fasces*. The Romans were also indebted to the Etruscans for the alphabet. The Etruscan alphabet was derived from the Greeks although historians are unsure whether it came from the Greek settlements in Italy or the mainland Greeks. The Latin alphabet was a modification of the Greek-derived Etruscan one.

The Etruscans are also thought to have had an impact on the Roman military. Rome's greatness, of course, was based on military power, and the basis of Roman military organization probably was borrowed from the Etruscans. The Etruscans had adopted the Greek hoplite shield, body armor, and weapons and made them standard equipment by the sixth century B.C. With this came a shift from reliance on cavalry, normally the preserve of aristocrats, to the hoplite infantry.

The Romans traditionally associated the end of both monarchy and Etruscan domination with the rape of Lucretia, a Roman noblewoman of great virtue. Raped by a son of the king, Lucretia informed her father, husband, and their friends what had happened and then committed suicide, "rather than be an example of unchastity to other wives," as an ancient Roman historian put it. Lucretia became the model Roman woman: a faithful wife and a pure and courageous woman who chose death rather than be seen as lacking in virtue. In revenge, the Roman nobles drove the king and his family from Rome and established a republican form of government, which ushered in the era of the Republic. According to the Romans of the late Republic, all this occurred in 509 B.C. Though interesting, the story has little historical foundation. It is more likely that the overthrow of the monarchy was accomplished by nobles who experienced a loss of power because of the shift from cavalry to heavy-armed infantry during the reign of Servius Tullius, the next-to-last king. The overthrow was not a patriotic uprising, but an attempt by Roman nobles to maintain their position of power. Some scholars have even argued that the continuation of Etruscan influence at Rome into the fifth century necessitates dating the beginning of the Roman Republic to around 475 B.C., but most historians remain committed to a date close to the traditional 509 B.C.

The Roman Republic (c. 509–264 B.C.)

The transition from monarchy to republican government was not an easy one. Rome felt threatened by enemies from every direction and, in the process of meeting these threats, embarked on a course of military expansion that led to the conquest of the entire Italian peninsula (see The Roman Conquest of Italy later in this chapter). During this period of expansion in Italy, the Roman Republic developed political institutions that were, in many ways, determined by the social divisions that existed within the community.

The Roman State

In politics and law, as in conquest, the Romans took a practical approach. They did not concern themselves with the construction of an ideal government, but instead fashioned political institutions in response to problems as they arose. Hence it is important to remember that the political institutions we will discuss evolved over a period of centuries.

POLITICAL INSTITUTIONS

The Romans had a clear concept of executive authority that was embodied in their word *imperium*, or "the right to command." Invested with *imperium*, the chief magistrates of the Roman state exercised a supreme power that was circumscribed only by extraneous means—officials held office for a limited term and could be tried for offenses committed in office once their term ended. While political institutions changed, the concept of *imperium* did not, and it is the one factor that gives Roman constitutional history continuity and unity.

The chief executive officers of the Roman Republic who possessed *imperium* were the consuls and praetors. Two consuls who were chosen annually administered the government and led the Roman army into battle. In 366 B.C., a new office, that of the praetor, was created. The praetor also possessed *imperium* and could govern Rome when the consuls were away from the city and could also lead armies. The praetor's primary function, however, was the execution of justice. He was in charge of the *ius civile*, or the civil law as it applied to Roman citizens. In 242 B.C., reflecting Rome's growth, another praetor was added to judge cases in which one or both parties were noncitizens.

As Rome expanded into the Mediterranean, additional praetors were established to govern the newly conquered provinces (two in 227, two more in 197 B.C.). But as the number of provinces continued to grow, the Romans devised a new system in which ex-consuls and ex-praetors who had served their one-year terms were given the title of proconsul and propraetor, respectively, and sent out as provincial governors. This demonstrates once again the Romans' practical solution to an immediate problem. It was reasonable to assume that officials with governmental experience would make good provincial administrators, although this was not always true in practice due to the opportunities for financial corruption in the provinces.

Periodically, the Republic also created an extraordinary executive. In an emergency the consuls would

♦ **Lictors with *Fasces*.** Pictured are lictors bearing the *fasces*, an axe surrounded by a bundle of rods tied with a red thong, an insignia borrowed from the Etruscan kings. The *fasces* was a symbol of the power to rule, and the consuls, the chief executives of the Roman Republic, were always preceded by twelve lictors bearing the *fasces*.

resign, and a dictator with unlimited power would be chosen to run the state. This office was supposed to last only for the duration of the emergency, the usual limit being six months. The Roman state also had administrative officials with various specialized duties. Quaestors were assigned to assist consuls and praetors in the administration of financial affairs. Aediles supervised the public games and watched over the grain supply of the city, a major problem for a rapidly growing urban community that came to rely on imported grain to feed its population. Censors were chosen every five years with the chief responsibility of making an assessment of the population on the basis of age and property for purposes of taxes, military service, and officeholding.

The Roman senate came to hold an especially important position in the Roman Republic. The senate or council of elders was a select group of about 300 men who served for life. The senate was not a legislative body and could only advise the magistrates. This advice of the senate (called *senatus consultum*) was not taken lightly, however, and by the third century B.C. had virtually the force of law. No doubt the prestige of the senate's members furthered this development. But it also helped that the senate met continuously, while the chief magistrates changed annually and the popular assemblies operated slowly and met only periodically.

The Roman Republic possessed a number of popular assemblies. The earliest assembly, known as the *comitia curiata*, went back to the monarchical period and fell into disuse during the Republic. By far the most important was the *comitia centuriata* (the centuriate assembly), essentially the Roman army functioning in its political role. Organized by classes based on wealth, it was structured in such a way that the wealthiest citizens always had a majority. The centuriate assembly elected the chief magistrates and passed laws. It is important to remember, however, that the Romans passed few statutory laws and simply left much activity to magisterial authority. As a result of the struggle between the orders, a third assembly, the *concilium plebis* or plebeian assembly, came into being in 471 B.C. This assembly came to be paralleled by a *comitia tributa* (tribal assembly)—an assembly of the whole people organized in tribes.

SOCIAL ORGANIZATION

The family was the basis of Roman society. At its head was the *paterfamilias* who theoretically had unlimited power over his family. In the early Republic, for example, it is claimed that he had the right to put his children to death, although this actually occurred in very few instances. With the *paterfamilias* at the head, the family resembled a kind of miniature state within the state. When a father died, his sons became heads of their own families. Since many families had the same name, a new social unit known as the *gens* or clan was instituted. The clan became very important later in Roman history.

Closely associated with the clan and family was the practice of clientage. Clients constituted a dependent class, people who did not have the means to protect themselves or their families without the assistance of a patron. The patron, usually a wealthy member of the upper classes, gave protection and especially legal assistance to his clients. In return, clients provided their patrons with certain services, such as field labor, military assistance, and, especially important in the Republic, votes in the assemblies. The mutual obligations between patrons and clients were not sanctioned by law, but by custom and religion, and even become hereditary.

The most noticeable element in the social organization of early Rome was the division between two groups—the patricians and the plebeians. The word *patrician* is derived from *patres*—the fathers—as the members of the Roman senate were called. The patrician class in Rome consisted of those families who were descended from the original senators appointed during the period of the kings. Their initial prominence was probably due to their wealth as great landowners. Thus, patricians constituted an aristocratic governing class. What particularly distinguished the patricians was their possession of certain religious privileges that enabled them to control the government. They alone had mastery of the religious calendar and knew on what days legal or political business could be conducted. Only they could be consuls, other magistrates, and senators. Through their patronage of large numbers of dependent clients, they could control the centuriate assembly and many other facets of Roman life. The plebeians constituted the considerably larger group of "independent, unprivileged, poorer and vulnerable men" as well as nonpatrician large landowners, less wealthy landholders, craftsmen, merchants, and small farmers. Although they were citizens, they did not possess the same rights as the patricians and at the beginning of the fifth century B.C. began a struggle to rectify that situation. The plebeians who led the struggle for plebeian rights were large landowners who were equal in wealth to many patricians and, therefore, considered themselves equally qualified to enjoy their privileges.

THE STRUGGLE OF THE ORDERS

The constitutional struggle between the orders also resulted in innovations in Roman political institutions. Although we do not know the specific grievances, two major problems that existed in the fifth century probably fueled the struggle between the patricians and the plebeians. No doubt the chief issue was power, specifically, the patrician monopoly and the plebeian lack of it. Both patricians and plebeians could vote, but only the patricians could be elected to governmental offices. Both had the right to make legal contracts and marriages, but intermarriage between patricians and plebeians was forbidden. The wealthy plebeians wanted political equality with the patricians, namely, the right to hold office, and social equality in the form of the right of intermarriage.

The plebeians used their numerical strength and military importance to force the issue by withdrawing physically from the state. This first secession of the plebs (the traditional date is 494 B.C.) would be imitated later.

It was a successful tactic that forced the patricians, who by themselves could not defend Rome, to make compromises. Two new officials known as tribunes of the plebs were instituted (later the number was raised to five and then ten); they were given the power to protect plebeians against arrest by patrician magistrates. The tribunes were considered sacrosanct—sacred to the gods—and any person who harmed a tribune could be executed by the plebeians without a trial. Moreover, after a new popular assembly for plebeians only, called the *concilium plebis* (council of the plebs), was created in 471 B.C., the tribunes became responsible for convoking and placing proposals before it. If adopted, they became *plebiscita* ("it is the opinion of the plebs"), but they were binding only on the plebeians, not the patricians. Nevertheless, the plebeian council gave the plebeians political leverage and virtually made them a legal corporation or a state within the state.

The next step for the plebeians involved the law. The plebeians came to realize that if they were to increase their power, they needed knowledge of the law and the legal and governmental procedures carefully guarded by the patricians. Due to plebeian pressure, a special commission of ten officials known as the *decemviri* ("ten men") was created with the task of regularizing and publishing the laws. This action resulted in the publication of the Twelve Tables of Law in 450 B.C., which included, among other things, the legal procedures for going to court; provisions on family, women, and divorce; regulations concerning private property; rules governing relationships and injuries to others; and a provision prohibiting intermarriage between patricians and plebeians (see the box on p. 140). This publication of the laws produced further agitation from the plebeians between 450 and 445 since they could now see how disadvantaged they were. In particular, they demanded the right of intermarriage and admission to the chief magistracies, especially the consulship. In 445 B.C., the *lex Canuleia* allowed patricians and plebeians to intermarry. Once this was permitted, the division between the two groups became less important. The solidarity of the patrician class against plebeian gains began to falter. But it was not until 367 B.C. that the consulship was opened to plebeians. The Licinian-Sextian laws stipulated that one consul could now be a plebeian. From 366 to 361 B.C., however, only two plebeians were elected to the consulship, and from 361 to 340, only three, a clear indication that only the most prominent plebeian families could obtain the office. In 342 B.C., another law stipulated that both consuls could be plebeians, while

CHRONOLOGY

The Struggle of the Orders

First secession of the plebeians; creation of tribunes of the plebs	494 B.C.
Creation of *concilium plebis* (plebeian assembly)	471 B.C.
Publication of the Twelve Tables of Law	451–450 B.C.
Lex Canuleia: Right of plebeians to marry patricians	445 B.C.
Licinian-Sextian laws: One consul may be a plebeian	367 B.C.
Both consuls may be plebeians; one must be	342 B.C.
Chief priesthoods opened to the plebeians	300 B.C.
Lex Hortensia: Laws passed by plebeian assembly are binding on all Romans	287 B.C.

one had to be. In 300 B.C., all religious offices were opened to the plebeians as well, so that patrician monopoly over the Roman state religion was eliminated.

The chief landmark in Roman constitutional history—and the climax of the struggle between the orders—came in 287 B.C. with the *lex Hortensia*. Henceforth, all *plebiscita* passed by the plebeian assembly had the force of law and were binding on the entire community, both plebeians and patricians. Moreover, unlike the laws passed by the centuriate assembly, these *plebiscita* did not need the approval of the senate.

The struggle between the orders, then, had a significant impact on the development of the Roman constitution. Plebeians could hold the highest offices of state, they could intermarry with the patricians, and they could help pass laws binding on the entire Roman community. Although the struggle had been long, the Romans had handled it by compromise, not violent revolution. Theoretically, by 287 B.C. all Roman citizens were equal under the law, and all could strive for political office. But in reality, as a result of the right of intermarriage, a select number of patrician and plebeian families formed a new senatorial aristocracy called the

The Twelve Tables

In 451 B.C., plebeian pressure led to the creation of a special commission of ten men who were responsible for codifying Rome's laws and making them public. In so doing, the plebeians hoped that they could restrict the arbitrary power of the patrician magistrates who alone had access to the laws. The Twelve Tables represent the first formal codification of Roman laws and customs. The laws dealt with litigation procedures, debt, family relations, property, and other matters of public and sacred law. The Twelve Tables were considered a landmark in the development of Roman law and until the time of Cicero remained one of the fundamental texts memorized by Roman school-boys. The code was inscribed on bronze plaques, which eventually were destroyed. These selections are taken from reconstructions of the code preserved in later writers.

Selections from the Twelve Tables

Table III: Execution; Law of Debt

When a debt has been acknowledged, or judgment about the matter has been pronounced in court, thirty days must be the legitimate time of grace. After that, the debtor may be arrested by laying on of hands. Bring him into court. If he does not satisfy the judgment, or no one in court offers himself as surety in his behalf, the creditor may take the defaulter with him. He may bind him either in stocks or in fetters. . . .

Unless they make a settlement, debtors shall be held in bond for sixty days. During that time they shall be brought before the praetor's court in the meeting place on three successive market days, and the amount for which they are judged liable shall be announced; on the third market day they shall suffer capital punishment or be delivered up for sale abroad, across the Tiber.

Table IV: Rights of Head of Family

Quickly kill . . . a dreadfully deformed child.

If a father three times surrenders a son for sale, the son shall be free from the father.

A child born ten months after the father's death will not be admitted into legal inheritance.

Table V: Guardianship; Succession

Females shall remain in guardianship even when they have attained their majority.

If a man is raving mad, rightful authority over his person and chattels shall belong to his agnates [nearest male relatives] or to his clansmen.

A spendthrift is forbidden to exercise administration over his owns goods . . . . A person who, being insane or a spendthirft, is prohibited from administering his own goods shall be under trusteeship of agnates.

Table VII: Rights concerning Land

Branches of a tree may be lopped off all round to a height of more than 15 feet . . . . Should a tree on a neighbor's farm be bent crooked by a wind and lean over your farm, action may be taken for removal of that tree.

It is permitted to gather up fruit falling down on another man's farm.

Table VIII: Torts or Delicts

If any person has sung or composed against another person a song such as was causing slander or insult to another, he shall be clubbed to death.

If a person has maimed another's limb, let there be retaliation in kind unless he makes agreement for settlement with him.

Any person who destroys by burning any building or heap of corn deposited alongside a house shall be bound, scourged, and put to death by burning at the stake, provided that he has committed the said misdeed with malice aforethought, but if he shall have committed it by accident, that is, by negligence, it is ordained that he repair the damage, or, if he be too poor to be competent for such punishment, he shall receive a lighter chastisement.

Table IX: Public Law

The penalty shall be capital punishment for a judge or arbiter legally appointed who has been found guilty of recieving a bribe for giving a decision.

Table XI: Supplementary Laws

Intermarriage shall not take place between plebeians and patricians.

nobiles, which came to dominate the political offices. The Roman Republic had not become a democracy.

The Roman Conquest of Italy

At the beginning of the Republic, Rome was surrounded by enemies, including the Etruscans to the north and the Sabines, Volscians, and Aequi to the east and south. A more immediate threat was posed by the Latin communities on the plain of Latium. After the expulsion of the Etruscan kings, a league of Latin allies formed that challenged Roman leadership in Latium. But in 493 B.C., the Romans established an alliance with the Latin communities, which provided for a common defense of Latium.

Rome was under constant pressure from its neighbors for the next hundred years. If we are to believe Livy, one of the chief ancient sources for the history of the early Roman Republic, Rome was engaged in almost continuous warfare with the Volscians, Sabines, Aequi, and others. One of Rome's important victories came in 396 B.C., when, according to tradition, the Etruscan city of Veii fell to the Romans, supposedly after a ten-year siege.

In his account of these years, the historian Livy provided a detailed narrative of Roman efforts. Many of Livy's stories were legendary in character and indeed were modeled after events in Greek history. His account of the 306 members of the Fabii clan who were ambushed by the Etruscans but stood their ground and died to the last man fulfilling their duty is very reminiscent of the stand of the 300 Spartans at Thermopylae (see Chapter 3). The ten-year siege of Veii corresponds to Homer's account of Troy. But Livy, writing in the first century B.C., used such stories to teach Romans the moral values and virtues that had made Rome great. These included tenacity, duty, courage, and especially discipline (see the box on p. 142). Indeed, Livy recounted stories of military leaders who executed their own sons for leaving their place in battle, a serious offense since the success of the hoplite infantry depended on maintaining a precise order. These stories had little basis in fact, but like the story of George Washington and the cherry tree in American history, they provided mythical images to reinforce Roman patriotism.

The Roman success at Veii proved to be short-lived. In 387 B.C., the Celts, known to the Romans as the Gauls, a people from north of the Alps who had previously moved into northern Italy, defeated the Romans in a battle outside Rome. The Gauls conquered

CHRONOLOGY

The Roman Conquest of Italy

Alliance with Latin states	493 B.C.
Fall of Veii	396 B.C.
Sack of Rome by the Gauls	387 B.C.
Latin revolt	340–338 B.C.
Creation of the Roman confederation	338 B.C.
First Samnite War	343–341 B.C.
Second Samnite War	326–304 B.C.
Third Samnite War	298–290 B.C.
Pyrrhic War	281–267 B.C.

Rome, sacked large parts of the city, and probably left only after the Romans had paid an indemnity. Rome was left in shambles. But Roman tenacity won out. The city was rebuilt, although haphazardly, and with new determination the Romans began again.

In 340 B.C., however, Rome had to deal with a revolt of the Latin states in Latium, which had come to resent Rome's increasing domination of their alliance. The Romans crushed the revolt and established complete supremacy in Latium, inaugurating a new system that ultimately became the basis for organizing the entire Italian peninsula: the Roman confederation, formed in 338 B.C. Under this system, Rome established treaties with the defeated members of the Latin League that linked these communities to Rome in one of three ways. In the first category, which included only five or six privileged states, all the citizens were given full Roman citizenship. A second category of communities acquired municipal status, which entitled their citizens to make legal contracts and intermarry with Romans, but not to vote or hold office in Rome. The remaining communities were made allies and bound to Rome by special treaties specifying their relations with Rome. All three categories of states remained largely autonomous in their domestic affairs, but were required to provide soldiers for Rome. In the Roman confederation, Rome created a system that could be expanded, as it eventually was, to the rest of Italy. Moreover, the Romans did not regard the status of the conquered states as permanent. Loyal allies could improve their status and even have hopes of becoming Roman citizens. Thus, the Romans had found a way to give conquered states a stake in Rome's success.

⋙ Cincinnatus Saves Rome: A Roman Morality Tale ⋘

There is perhaps no better account of how the virtues of duty and simplicity enabled good Roman citizens to prevail during the travails of the fifth century B.C. than Livy's account of Cincinnatus. He was chosen dictator, supposedly in 457 B.C., to defend Rome against the attacks of the Aequi. The position of dictator was a temporary expedient used only in emergencies; the consuls would resign, and a leader with unlimited power would be appointed for a limited period (usually six months). In this account, Cincinnatus did his duty, defeated the Aequi, and returned to his simple farm in just fifteen days.

Livy, *The Early History of Rome*

The city was thrown into a state of turmoil, and the general alarm was as great as if Rome herself were surrounded. Nautius was sent for, but it was quickly decided that he was not the man to inspire full confidence; the situation evidently called for a dictator, and, with no dissenting voice, Lucius Quinctius Cincinnatus was named for the post.

Now I would solicit the particular attention of those numerous people who imagine that money is everything in this world, and that rank and ability are inseparable from wealth: let them observe that Cincinnatus, the one man in whom Rome reposed all her hope of survival, was at that moment working a little three-acre farm . . . west of the Tiber, just opposite the spot where the shipyards are today. A mission from the city found him at work on his land—digging a ditch, maybe, or ploughing. Greetings were exchanged, and he was asked—with a prayer for divine blessing on himself and his country—to put on his toga and hear the Senate's instructions. This naturally surprised him, and, asking if all were well, he told his wife Racilia to run to their cottage and fetch his toga. The toga was brought, and wiping the grimy sweat from his hands and face he put it on; at once the envoys from the city saluted him, with congratulations, as Dictator, invited him to enter Rome, and informed him of the terrible danger of Municius's army. A state vessel was waiting for him on the river, and on the city bank he was welcomed by his three sons who had come to meet him, then by other kinsmen and friends, and finally by nearly the whole body of senators. Closely attended by all these people and preceded by his lictors he was then escorted to his residence through streets lined with great crowds of common folk who, be it said, were by no means so pleased to see the new Dictator, as they thought his power excessive and dreaded the way in which he was likely to use it.

[Cincinnatus proceeds to raise an army, march out, and defeat the Aequi.]

In Rome the Senate was convened by Quintus Fabius the City Prefect, and a decree was passed inviting Cincinnatus to enter in triumph with his troops. The chariot he rode in was preceded by the enemy commanders and the military standards, and followed by his army loaded with its spoils. . . . Cincinnatus finally resigned after holding office for fifteen days, having originally accepted it for a period of six months.

Even before they had crushed the Latin League, the Romans had entered into renewed conflict with a very stubborn opponent, the Samnites, resulting in the three Samnite Wars (343–290 B.C.). The Samnites were a hill people from the central Apennines. In the fifth century, some of them had moved into Campania where they had forced out the Etruscans and settled down, becoming known as the Oscans. But in the fourth century B.C., the position of the Oscans was threatened by a second wave of Samnites. The Oscans asked Rome for help, and in the first two Samnite Wars (343–341 and 326–304 B.C.), the Romans fought only to protect Campania and, of course, themselves. Although successful, the Romans made a critical change in policy when they concluded that the only sure way to protect themselves was to control the Samnites; therefore, a Third Samnite War (298–290 B.C.) broke out. Rome was victorious and incorporated Campania and the Samnite states of central Italy into an expanded Roman confederation as Italian allies. These communities agreed to provide military aid (cavalry and infantry soldiers) to Rome and to allow Rome to control their foreign policy. Otherwise, they were free to govern themselves and maintain their own laws and political institutions. Though internally free, the "allies" were ringed with colonies of Roman veterans settled on confiscated land and knew that if they showed any signs of disloyalty to Rome, a Roman army would quickly appear to show them the error of their ways.

The conquest of the Samnites gave Rome considerable control over a large part of Italy and also brought it into direct contact with the Greek communities of southern Italy. While the Greek cities had occupied the coastal plains, they did not control the interior, so attacks by the native populations were rather frequent. In 282 B.C., the Greek city of Thurii, attacked by the Bruttians, asked Rome for help. Rome agreed knowing full well the possible consequences of becoming involved in hostilities in southern Italy. Rome's aid to Thurii aroused anxiety among the other Greek cities, especially Tarentum, the most powerful of the Greek states on the southern Italian peninsula. Consequently, when a Roman fleet appeared off Tarentum, the Tarentines attacked and sank it. The result was the Pyrrhic War (281–267 B.C.).

Tarentum and the other Greek communities were primarily commercial cities and possessed no standing armies. They were accustomed to hiring mercenaries to fight their battles for them. Consequently, they bought the aid of King Pyrrhus of Epirus (approximately modern-day Epirus in Greece), who crossed the Adriatic with 20,000 troops and defeated the Romans twice. In both battles, however, Pyrrhus experienced heavy losses, leading him to comment that one more victory would ruin him (hence our phrase "Pyrrhic victory"). After a diversion to Sicily, Pyrrhus came back for one more battle with the Romans, and this time was decisively defeated by 267 B.C. The Romans completed their conquest of southern Italy and added the Greek states to the Roman confederation. Their relationship to Rome, also determined by treaties, was the same as the Italian allies, except that the Greeks were required to furnish naval assistance—warships and sailors—instead of infantry and cavalry. After crushing the remaining Etruscan states to the north, Rome had conquered all of Italy, except the extreme north, by 264 B.C.

In the course of their expansion throughout Italy, the Romans had pursued consistent policies that help to explain their success. The Romans excelled in making the correct diplomatic decisions; they were superb diplomats. While firm and even cruel when necessary—rebellions were crushed without mercy—they were also shrewd in extending their citizenship and allowing autonomy in domestic affairs. Their conquest of Italy could hardly be said to be the result of a direct policy of expansion. Much of it was opportunistic. The Romans did not hesitate to act once they felt their security threatened. And surrounded by potential enemies, Rome in a sense never felt secure. The Romans were not only good soldiers, but persistent ones. The loss of an army or a fleet did not cause them to quit, but spurred them on to build new armies and new fleets. Finally, the Romans had a practical sense of strategy. As they conquered, they settled Romans and Latins in new

communities outside Latium. By 264 B.C., the Romans had established colonies—fortified towns—at all strategic locations. By building roads to these settlements and connecting them, the Romans assured themselves of an impressive military and communications network that enabled them to rule effectively and efficiently. By insisting upon military service from the allies in the Roman confederation, Rome essentially mobilized the entire military manpower of all Italy for its wars.

Thus, by 264 B.C., Rome had united all of Italy, except the Po valley, into the Roman confederation. Each city and its inhabitants were bound to Rome by a treaty, which specified the terms of the alliance. Although Rome demanded military service from all communities and determined their foreign policy, they were still allowed to have their own municipal freedom with their own magistrates. The Roman confederation brought unity to Italy on the eve of Rome's struggle with

◆ **King Pyrrhus.** By sinking a Roman fleet off its coast, the Greek city of Tarentum initiated the Pyrrhic War. The Tarentines bought the aid of King Pyrrhus of Epirus, who defeated the Romans in their first two encounters, but not without suffering heavy losses. In their third battle, in which the Romans stampeded Pyrrhus's war elephants into his own troops, Rome was victorious. Pictured is a marble bust of Pyrrhus found at Herculaneum.

Carthage. It proved to be an important factor in the Romans' victory over this powerful enemy.

The Roman Conquest of the Mediterranean (264–133 B.C.)

After their conquest of the Italian peninsula, the Romans found themselves face-to-face with a formidable Mediterranean power—Carthage. Founded around 800 B.C. by Phoenicians from Tyre, Carthage was located in a

✦ **A Roman Legionary.** The Roman legionaries, with their legendary courage and tenacity, made possible the creation of the Roman Empire. This picture shows a bronze figure of a Roman legionary in full dress at the height of the empire in the second century A.D. The soldier's cuirass is constructed of overlapping metal bands.

favorable position for commanding Mediterranean trade routes and had become an important commercial center. It had become politically and militarily strong as well. Around 600 B.C. Carthage took the lead in heading off Greek colonists in the western Mediterranean and in a series of wars lasting about three centuries ejected the Greeks from most of the Spanish coast, reducing them for the most part to Sicily and southern Italy. By the third century B.C., the Carthaginian empire included the coast of North Africa, southern Spain, Sardinia, Corsica, and western Sicily. With its monopoly of western Mediterranean trade, Carthage was the largest and richest state in the area. Although it possessed a fine navy, its army was not as formidable, usually being made up of mercenaries or men drafted from the local area. Both were hard to control. The officers, however, constituted a professional military class and were experienced, especially in comparison to the Romans who relied on annually appointed magistrates as commanders.

In its relations with Italy, Carthage had relied on diplomacy rather than warfare. In the fourth century B.C., when the Romans had acquired a fairly large seafront, Carthage had offered them two successive treaties and supplemented these with a military alliance against Pyrrhus in 279 B.C., although it appears that neither Carthage nor Rome provided military help to the other. Yet Rome was apparently apprehensive about Carthaginian encroachment on the Italian coast for the Romans had stipulated in each of the three treaties with Carthage that the latter must not establish a permanent foothold on Italian soil. As late as 264 B.C., a war between Rome and Carthage seemed to be far away, and it took a number of circumstances to bring the conflict on.

The Struggle with Carthage

The treaties between Rome and Carthage had made no attempt to define precisely their respective spheres of influence on Sicily since the Romans at that time had no important interest in the island. But an unforeseen situation arose at Messana (modern Messina)—a city that commanded the straits between Italy and Sicily—that became the immediate cause of war. Since 289 B.C., Messana had been controlled by a group of mercenaries from Campania called the Mamertines. In 264 B.C., Messana was besieged by Hiero, the king of Syracuse. The Mamertines sought help first from Carthage and then from the Romans. The Romans hesitated, knowing this was their first commitment outside Italy and was

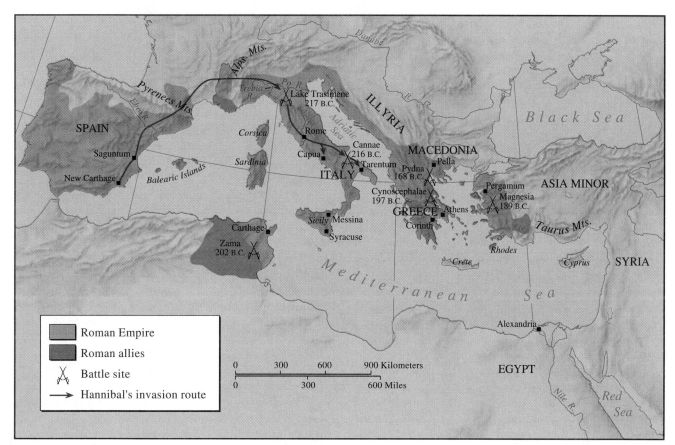

Map 5.2 Roman Conquests in the Mediterranean (264–133 B.C.).

likely to involve them in a struggle with Carthage. But the Romans also perceived the strategic importance of Messana and Sicily to the security of southern Italy and sent a detachment of troops to Messana. The Carthaginians, who had also sent an army there, fled, but considered the Roman action just cause for war. Both states shipped reinforcements to Sicily and the First Punic War began.

Both sides sought to conquer Sicily. The Romans perceived that the war would be long and drawn out if they could not supplement their land operations with a navy. But building ships and finding admirals to sail them proved to be difficult. The Roman fleet suffered severe losses in both battles and storms, but Rome showed its tenacity once again. In a storm in 253 B.C., Rome lost 284 ships out of a fleet of 364. Within three months, the Romans had constructed 220 new ships. The Carthaginian problem, on the other hand, lay in finding enough mercenaries to continue the fight. After a long struggle in which both sides lost battles in North

Africa and Sicily, a Roman fleet defeated the Carthaginian navy off Drepana near Sicily in 242 B.C. The cities of western Sicily that had been controlled by Carthage capitulated. Carthage sued for peace and the war ended in 241 B.C. Carthage gave up all rights to Sicily and had to pay an indemnity. Three years later, Rome took advantage of Carthage's problems with its mercenaries to seize the islands of Sardinia and Corsica. This act so angered the Carthaginians that, according to one story, their leading general, Hamilcar Barca, made his nine-year-old son swear that he would hate Rome ever after. The son's name was Hannibal.

Between the wars, Carthage made an unexpected recovery under the leadership of the general who had been briefly successful in Sicily in the First Punic War—Hamilcar Barca. Hamilcar extended Carthage's domains in Spain to compensate for the territory lost to Rome. The primary objective of this new empire was to find fresh sources of revenue to make up for the recent war losses. Carthage was especially successful in this

Rome's Struggle with Carthage

Military alliance with Carthage	279 B.C.
First Punic War	264–241 B.C.
Rome seizes Corsica and Sardinia	238 B.C.
Second Punic War	218–201 B.C.
Battle of Cannae	216 B.C.
Scipio completes seizure of Spain	206 B.C.
Battle of Zama	202 B.C.
Third Punic War	149–146 B.C.
Destruction of Carthage	146 B.C.

regard, benefiting tremendously from the copper and silver mines in southern Spain. Another purpose in creating the Spanish empire was to get manpower for Carthage. The Spanish natives made great soldiers, being physically strong and possessing excellent swords. Hamilcar and his successors proceeded to build up a formidable land army in the event of a second war with Rome, because they realized that Carthage's success depended upon defeating Rome on land. In 221 B.C., Hannibal, Hamilcar Barca's twenty-five-year-old son, took over direction of Carthaginian policy. Within three years, Rome and Carthage were again at war.

Carthage and Rome had agreed to divide Spain into respective spheres of influence. Although Saguntum was located in the Carthaginian sphere, Rome made an alliance with the city and encouraged its inhabitants in anti-Carthaginian activities. Thoroughly provoked by the Roman action, Hannibal attacked Saguntum, and the Romans declared war on Carthage in 218 B.C. This time the Carthaginian strategy aimed at bringing the war home to the Romans and defeating them in their own backyard. In an amazing march, Hannibal crossed the Alps with an army of 30,000–40,000 men and 6,000 horses and elephants and advanced into northern Italy. After defeating the Romans at the Trebia River, he added thousands of Gauls to his army and proceeded into central Italy. At Lake Trasimene in Etruria, he again defeated the Romans. In desperation, the Romans elected as consul Quintus Fabius Maximus who became known as the "Delayer" because of his tactics of following and delaying Hannibal's army without risking a pitched battle. Hannibal hoped to destroy the Roman confederation and win Italian cities away from Rome. The policy failed initially; virtually all remained loyal to Rome.

In 216 B.C., the Romans decided to meet Hannibal head on. It was a serious mistake. At Cannae, Hannibal's forces decimated a Roman army, killing as many as 40,000. Now at last, some of the southern Italian cities rebelled against Roman rule and went over to Hannibal. Rome seemed on the brink of disaster but refused to give up and raised yet another army.

Rome gradually recovered. Although Hannibal remained free to roam in Italy, he had neither the men nor the equipment to lay siege to the major cities, including Rome itself. The Romans began to reconquer some of the rebellious Italian cities. More important, the Romans pursued a Spanish strategy that aimed at undermining the Carthaginian empire in Spain. Publius Cornelius Scipio, later known as Scipio Africanus, was given command of the Roman forces in Spain even though he was too young to hold the position legally. But he was a brilliant general who learned from Hannibal's tactics and by 206 B.C. had pushed the Carthaginians out of Spain.

The Romans then took the war directly to Carthage. Late in 204 B.C., Scipio led a Roman army from Sicily into North Africa and forced the Carthaginians to recall Hannibal from Italy. At the Battle of Zama in 202 B.C., Scipio decisively defeated Hannibal and the Carthaginian forces, and the war was over. By the peace treaty signed in 201, Carthage lost Spain, agreed to pay an indemnity, and promised not to go to war without Rome's permission. Spain, like Sicily, Corsica, and Sardinia earlier, was made into a Roman province ruled by a governor who possessed full *imperium*. The inhabitants were now Roman subjects required to pay tribute to their new masters. By 201 B.C., Carthage was no longer a great state, and Rome had become the dominant power in the western Mediterranean.

But some Romans wanted even more. A number of prominent Romans, especially the conservative politician Cato, advocated the complete destruction of Carthage. Cato ended every speech he made to the senate with the words, "And I think Carthage must be destroyed." When the Carthaginians technically broke their peace treaty with Rome by going to war against one of Rome's North African allies who had been encroaching on Carthage's home territory, the Romans declared war. Led by Scipio Aemilianus, the younger Africanus, Roman forces undertook their third and last

The Destruction of Carthage

The Romans used a technical breach of Carthage's peace treaty with Rome as a pretext to undertake a third and final war with Carthage (149–146 B.C.). Although Carthage posed no real threat to Rome's security, the Romans still remembered the traumatic experiences of the Second Punic War when Hannibal had ravaged much of their homeland. The hardliners gained the upper hand in the senate and called for the complete destruction of Carthage. The city was razed, the survivors sold into slavery, and the land turned into a province. In this passage, the historian Appian of Alexandria describes the final destruction of Carthage by the Romans under the command of Scipio Aemilianus.

Appian, *Roman History*

Then came new scenes of horror. The fire spread and carried everything down, and the soldiers did not wait to destroy the buildings little by little, but pulled them all down together So the crashing grew louder, and many fell with the stones into the midst dead. Others were seen still living, especially old men, women, and young children who had hidden in the inmost nooks of the houses, some of them wounded, some more or less burned, and uttering horrible cries. Still others, thrust out and falling from such a height with the stones, timbers, and fire, were torn asunder into all kinds of horrible shapes, crushed and mangled. Nor was this the end of their miseries, for the street cleaners, who were removing the rubbish with axes, mattocks, and boathooks, and making the roads passable, tossed with these instruments the dead and the living together into holes in the ground, sweeping them along like sticks and stones or turning them over with their iron tools, and man was used for filling up a ditch. Some were thrown in head foremost, while their legs, sticking out of the ground, writhed a long time. Others fell with their feed downward and their heads above the ground. Horses ran over them, crushing their faces and skulls, not purposely on the part of the riders, but in their headlong haste. Nor did the street cleaners either do these things on purpose; but the press of war, the glory of approaching victory, the rush of the soldiery, the confused noise of heralds and trumpeters all round, the tribunes and centurions changing guard and marching the cohorts here and there—all together made everybody frantic and heedless of the spectacle before their eyes.

Six days and nights were consumed in this kind of turmoil, the soldiers being changed so that they might not be worn out with toil, slaughter, lack of sleep, and these horrid sights. . . .

Scipio, beholding this city, which had flourished 700 years from its foundation and had ruled over so many lands, islands, and seas, as rich in arms and fleets, elephants, and money as the mightiest empires, but far surpassing them in hardihood and high spirit . . . now come to its end in total destruction—Scipio, beholding this spectacle, is said to have shed tears and publicly lamented the fortune of the enemy. After meditating by himself a long time and reflecting on the inevitable fall of cities, nations, and empires, as well as of individuals, upon the fate of Troy, that once proud city, upon the fate of the Assyrian, the Median, and afterwards of the great Persian empire, and, most recently of all, of the splendid empire of Macedon, either voluntarily or otherwise the words of the poet [Homer, *Iliad*] escaped his lips:

The day shall come in which our sacred Troy
And Priam, and the people over whom
Spear-bearing Priam rules, shall perish all.

Being asked by Polybius in familiar conversation (for Polybius had been his tutor) what he meant by using these words, Polybius says that he did not hesitate frankly to name his own country, for whose fate he feared when he considered the mutability of human affairs. And Polybius wrote this down just as he heard it.

war with Carthage (149–146 B.C.). This time, Carthage was no match for the Romans, who in 146 B.C. seized this opportunity to carry out the final destruction of Carthage (see the box above). The territory of Carthage was made a province called Africa.

The Eastern Mediterranean

Roman involvement with the Hellenistic states of the eastern Mediterranean began indirectly in 219 B.C. when Rome sent soldiers across the Adriatic into Illyria to

CHRONOLOGY

◆◆◆◆◆◆◆◆◆◆◆◆◆◆◆◆◆◆◆◆◆◆◆◆◆◆◆◆◆◆◆◆◆◆

Rome and the Eastern Mediterranean

First Macedonian War	215–205 B.C.
Second Macedonian War	200–197 B.C.
Battle of Cynoscephalae	197 B.C.
Proclamation of Greek freedom	196 B.C.
Syrian War	192–189 B.C.
Battle of Magnesia—defeat of Antiochus III	189 B.C.
Third Macedonian War	171–167 B.C.
Battle of Pydna	168 B.C.
Fourth Macedonian War	149–148 B.C.

suppress pirates who were harassing commercial ships in the Adriatic. Philip V, king of Macedonia (221–179 B.C.), was disturbed by Roman entry into an area he considered his own sphere of influence. In revenge, Philip made an alliance with Hannibal after the Roman loss at Cannae, although he did not provide any real assistance to the Carthaginians. The Romans, in turn, made an alliance with the Greek Aetolian League, a move that pulled Rome into the world of Hellenistic politics. But Rome was preoccupied with the Carthaginians and agreed to a separate peace with Philip of Macedonia in 205 B.C., thus ending the so-called First Macedonian War.

After the defeat of Carthage, some Romans advocated punishing Macedonia for its alliance with Hannibal. Despite their war weariness, the Romans undertook the Second Macedonian War (200–197 B.C.) in alliance with both the Achaean and Aetolian Leagues of Greek states. At Cynoscephalae in Thessaly in 197 B.C., the Roman legions met and defeated the Macedonian phalanx. Philip was forced to pay a small indemnity, and in 196 B.C. the Romans announced the freedom of all the Greek states. The Romans, however, expected the Greeks to behave as if they were clients in the domestic system of clientage. When they did not, Roman policy changed.

The Aetolian League was especially unhappy with the Roman peace. Although an ally of Rome, it felt that it had achieved no real gains from fighting on Rome's side against the Macedonian king. Consequently, the league allied itself with the Seleucid ruler, Antiochus III (223–187 B.C.). Antiochus had far-flung ambitions that

included control of Thrace to gain a foothold in Europe. The Romans had no intention of allowing Antiochus to become established in Greece and again went to war— the Syrian War (192–189 B.C.). Rome first defeated an army of the Aetolians and Antiochus in 191 B.C. and in 189 routed the forces of Antiochus at the Battle of Magnesia. Antiochus was forced to pay a large indemnity and to transfer his lands in Asia Minor to a Roman ally, the kingdom of Pergamum. The Romans took no lands for themselves.

Meanwhile, the Romans found it impossible to extricate themselves from Greek affairs. Greek states were constantly appealing to Rome against the encroachment of the Macedonians. When Philip's son Perseus continued what the Romans considered to be anti-Roman policies, Rome again declared war on Macedonia and inaugurated the Third Macedonian War (171–167 B.C.). At Pydna in 168 B.C., Perseus and the Macedonians were decisively defeated. Macedonia was split into four republics, but was not annexed. The Romans confiscated the Macedonian treasury and enslaved many people. Imperialism could be profitable; in 167 B.C., the Romans eliminated the payment of direct property taxes by Roman citizens. The spoils of war had made them unnecessary.

The Roman settlement after the Third Macedonian War failed to last, however. After a revolt, the Romans fought a brief and final Fourth Macedonian War (149–148 B.C.). Macedonia was now made a Roman province. The Greeks, especially the Achaean League, also rose in revolt against Rome's restrictive policies and were decisively defeated. The city of Corinth, leader of the revolt, was destroyed in 146 B.C. to teach the Greeks a lesson. Greece was placed under the control of the provincial governor of Macedonia rather than being made a separate province. Rome was now master of the Mediterranean Sea.

The Nature of Roman Imperialism

Rome's empire was built in three stages: the conquest of Italy, the conflict with Carthage and expansion into the western Mediterranean, and the involvement with and domination of the Hellenistic kingdoms in the eastern Mediterranean. The Romans did not possess a master plan for the creation of an empire. Much of their expansion was opportunistic; once involved in a situation that threatened their security, the Romans did not hesitate to act. And the more they expanded, the more threats to their security appeared on the horizon, involving them in yet more conflicts. Indeed, the Romans liked to portray themselves as declaring war only for defensive reasons or to protect allies. That is only part of the story, however. It is likely, as some historians have recently suggested, that at some point a group of Roman aristocratic leaders emerged who favored expansion both for the glory it offered and for the economic benefits it provided. Certainly, by the second century B.C., aristocratic senators perceived new opportunities for lucrative foreign commands, enormous spoils of war, and an abundant supply of slave labor for their growing landed estates. By that same time, as the destruction of Corinth and Carthage indicates, Roman imperialism had become more arrogant and brutal as well. Rome's foreign success also had enormous repercussions for the internal development of the Roman Republic.

Society and Culture in the Roman Republic

One of the most noticeable characteristics of Roman society and culture is the impact of the Greeks. The Romans had experienced Greek influence early on, indirectly through the Etruscans and directly through the Greek cities in southern Italy. By the end of the third century B.C., however, Greek civilization played an ever-increasing role in Roman culture. Greek ambassadors, merchants, and artists traveled to Rome and spread Greek thought and practices. After their conquest of the Hellenistic kingdoms, Roman military commanders shipped Greek manuscripts and art back to Rome. Multitudes of educated Greek slaves were used in Roman households. Virtually every area of Roman life, from literature and philosophy to religion and education, was affected by Greek models. Rich Romans hired Greek tutors and sent their sons to Athens to study. As the Roman poet Horace said, "captive Greece took captive her rude conqueror." Greek thought captivated the less sophisticated Roman minds, and the Romans became willing transmitters of Greek culture—not, however, without some resistance from Romans who had nothing but contempt for Greek politics and feared the end of old Roman values. Even those who favored Greek culture, such as Scipio Aemilianus, blamed the Greeks for Rome's new vices, including luxury and homosexual practices.

Roman Religion

Every aspect of Roman society was permeated with religion. The main feature of early Roman religion was its animism or the belief that spirits or living forces dwell in all the objects of the natural world. Gradually, the Romans came to identify such spiritual forces with gods, but worshiped them without images or temples. The early triad of chief divinities consisted of Mars, Jupiter, and Quirinus worshiped at open-air altars on the hill called the Quirinal.

The Etruscans made a major impact on Roman religion. They introduced the personalization of the gods, so that Roman deities were now presented in human form with statues or visual images housed in temples. The Etruscans introduced a sky god similar to the Greek Zeus and, during the period of Etruscan kingship, built a huge temple to this Jupiter. A new triad of chief deities emerged consisting of Jupiter, Juno, the patron goddess of women, and Minerva, the goddess of craftsmen. Jupiter Optimus Maximus (best and greatest) became the patron deity of Rome and assumed a central place in the religious life of the city. As Rome developed and came into contact with other peoples and gods, the community simply adopted new deities. Hence, the Greek Hermes became the Roman Mercury and the Greek Demeter, Ceres. Apollo and Asclepius, both gods of healing, were added directly to the Roman pantheon. The Romans also took over the enormous body of Greek mythology as well. By the end of the third century B.C., a rather complete amalgamation of Greek and Roman religion had occurred. In general, the Romans were very tolerant of new religious cults and only occasionally outlawed them. The most prominent example occurred in 186 B.C. when authorities curtailed the orgiastic cult of Bacchus (Dionysus), charging that it posed a threat to public morals and that its secret societies were fomenting anti-Roman conspiracies.

Roman religion focused on the worship of the gods for a very practical reason—human beings were thought to be totally dependent upon them. The Romans expressed this dependency in contractual terms. If a man followed the correct ritual in worship, then the gods would act favorably toward him; if they granted his request, he must make an offering in gratitude; if a man failed to observe proper ritual, he could expect to be punished. Not morality, but the exact performance of ritual was crucial to establishing a right relationship with the gods. What was true for individuals was also valid for the state. It also had to observe correct ritual in order to receive its reward. Accurate performance of ritual was consequently important, and the Romans established a college of priests or pontiffs to carry out that responsibility. Initially three in number, by the first century B.C., they had increased to sixteen. The pontiffs were in charge of what the Romans called the *ius*

✦ **Temple of Portunus.** The Romans considered the proper worship of the gods an important element of their success. Typical of Roman religious architecture was the small urban temple located in the midst of a crowded commercial center. Pictured here is a rectangular temple built in Rome in the late second or early first century B.C. and dedicated to Portunus, the god of harbors. The temple was located in the cattle market close to the Tiber River.

overcome all the nations of the world, because we have realized that the world is directed and governed by the gods."[1] Religion and politics obviously went hand in hand to the Romans, despite the abuses of the late Republic in the first century B.C. when politicians frequently manipulated religion in the interests of politics.

In addition to the college of pontiffs, a college of augurs existed whose responsibility was to interpret the signs (auspices) or warnings that the gods gave to men. Before every important act of state, a magistrate with *imperium* took the auspices to make sure the gods approved. The Romans attributed great importance to this—if the omens were unfavorable, then the act was invalid or the planned action was not auspicious. As Cicero later commented, the augurs had "the highest and most important authority in the State" because "no act of any magistrate at home or in the field can have any validity for any person without their authority."[2] Auspices were taken by observing the flights of birds, lightning and other natural phenomena, and the behavior of certain animals.

Just as the state had an official cult, so too did families. Because the family was regarded as a small state within the state, it had its own household cults, which included Janus, the spirit of the doorway; Vesta, goddess of the hearth; and the Penates, the spirits of the storehouse. Here, too, proper ritual was important, and it was the responsibility of the *paterfamilias* as head of the family to ensure the religious obligations were properly fulfilled. One of the most important ceremonies involved purification. In his manual *On Agriculture*, Marcus Cato the Elder spelled out the proper ritual for purification of a landed estate. The ceremony included these words:

> Father Mars [god of vegetation as well as war], I beg and entreat you to be of good will and favorable to me and to our house and household, for which purpose I have ordered the swine-sheep-bull procession to be led around my land and fields and farm. And [I beg] that you will check, thrust back, and avert diseases seen and unseen, crop failure and crop destruction, sudden losses and storms, and that you will permit the annual crops, the grain crops, the vineyards, and tree and vine slips to grow and turn out well. And [that you] keep safe the shepherds and the flocks and give good health and strength to me and to our house and household: with these purposes in view . . . receive the honor of this suckling swine-sheep-bull sacrifice.[3]

divinum (divine law) or, in other words, of maintaining the right relationship between the state and the gods. The pontiffs then were really officials of the state; in effect, they were the heads of the religious department of state. They performed all public religious acts and supervised magistrates in the correct ritual for public political acts. If the rituals were performed correctly, then the Romans would obtain the "peace of the gods." No doubt, the Roman success in creating an empire was a visible confirmation of divine favor. As Cicero, the first-century politician and writer, claimed, "We have

Proper observance of the ritual was so crucial that any error necessitated a repetition of the entire ritual.

Religious festivals were an important part of Roman religious practice. There were two kinds: public festivals ordained and paid for by the state and private festivals celebrated by individuals and families. Public festivals included annual ones, such as the Lupercalia, and irregular ones that were held upon the occasion of a victory or emergency of some kind. By the mid-second century B.C., six public festivals were celebrated annually, each lasting several days.

The practice of holding games also grew out of religious festivals. The games were inaugurated in honor of Jupiter Optimus Maximus, but had become annual events by 366 B.C. In the late Republic, both the number of games and the number of days they lasted were increased. Consequently, state funds became inadequate for the magnificence expected, and the aediles, who were in charge of the games and hoped to use their office as a stepping-stone to higher political offices, paid additional expenses out of their own pockets. Originally, the games consisted of chariot racing in the Circus Maximus; later, animal hunts and theatrical performances were added. In the empire, gladiatorial contests would become the primary focus.

Education: The Importance of Rhetoric

The Romans did not possess a system of public education. In the early Republic, education consisted of training in the various skills needed by a Roman citizen and was done within the context of the family. Boys were expected to master the basic elements of farming,

develop the physical skills needed to be good soldiers, learn the traditions of the state through the legends of heroic Roman ancestors, and become acquainted with public affairs. Girls were supposed to learn the skills needed to be good wives and mothers. Every upper-class Roman boy or girl was expected to learn to read.

Through contact with the Greek world, Roman education took on new ideals in the third and second centuries B.C. The wealthy classes wanted their children exposed to Greek studies and were especially attracted to the training in rhetoric and philosophy that would prepare their sons for a successful public career. For upper-class males, rhetoric—or the art of persuasive speaking—was an especially important part of their education. To pursue a public career, they needed to learn good speaking skills that would enable them to win elections and lawsuits in the court. By winning lawsuits, a person could make a name for himself and build political support.

Since knowledge of Greek was a crucial ingredient in education, schools taught by professional teachers emerged to supply this need. Those who could afford to might provide Greek tutors for their children, but less well endowed families could turn to private schools where most of the instructors were educated slaves or freedmen, usually of Greek origin. After several years of primary instruction, whose aim was simply to teach the basics of reading, writing, and arithmetic, the pupil went to a secondary school run by a *grammaticus* or grammarian. These schools had a standard curriculum based on the liberal arts: literature, dialectic (logic), arithmetic,

◆ **Schoolmaster and Pupils.** By the third and second centuries B.C., wealthy Romans sought to prepare their sons for successful public careers by a thorough education in rhetoric and philosophy. Pictured here is a Roman teacher with his two pupils who are reading from papyrus scrolls.

geometry, astronomy, and music. The core of the liberal arts and the curriculum, however, was Greek literature. As a result, by the second and first centuries B.C., educated Romans had become increasingly bilingual.

The Growth of Slavery

While slavery was a common institution throughout the ancient world, no people possessed more slaves or relied so much on slave labor as the Romans eventually did. Before the third century B.C., a small Roman farmer might possess one or two slaves who would help farm his few acres and perform domestic chores. These slaves would most likely be from Italy and be regarded as part of the family household. Only the very rich would have large numbers of slaves.

The Roman conquest of the Mediterranean brought a drastic change in the use of slaves. Large numbers of foreign slaves were brought back to Italy. During the Republic, then, the chief source of slaves was from capture in war, followed by piracy. Of course, the children of slaves also became slaves. While some Roman generals brought back slaves to be sold to benefit the public treasury, ambitious generals of the first century, such as Pompey and Caesar, made personal fortunes by treating slaves captured by their armies as private property.

Slaves were used in many ways in Roman society. The rich, of course, owned the most and the best. In the late Republic, it became a badge of prestige to be attended by many slaves. Greeks were in much demand as tutors, musicians, doctors, and artists. Roman businessmen would employ them as shop assistants or craftsmen. Slaves were also used as farm laborers; the large landed estates known as *latifundia* were worked by huge gangs of slaves living in pitiful conditions. Cato the Elder argued that it was cheaper to work slaves to death and then replace them than to treat them well. Many slaves of all nationalities were used as menial household workers, such as cooks, valets, waiters, cleaners, and gardeners. Roads, aqueducts, and other public facilities were constructed by contractors utilizing slave labor. The total number of slaves is difficult to judge— estimates range from two to four free men to every slave.

It is also difficult to generalize about the treatment of Roman slaves. There are numerous instances of humane treatment by masters and situations where slaves even protected their owners from danger out of gratitude and esteem. But slaves were also subject to severe punishments, torture, abuse, and hard labor that drove some to run away or even revolt against their owners. The Republic had stringent laws against aiding a runaway slave. The murder of a master by a slave might mean the execution of all the other household slaves. Near the end of the second century B.C., large-scale slave revolts occurred in Sicily where enormous gangs of slaves were subjected to horrible working conditions on large landed estates. Slaves were branded, beaten, fed inadequately, worked in chains, and housed at night in underground prisons. It took three years (from 135 to 132 B.C.) to crush a revolt of 70,000 slaves, and the great revolt on Sicily (104–101 B.C.) involved most of the island and took a Roman army of 17,000 men to suppress it. The most famous revolt on the Italian peninsula occurred in 73 B.C. Led by a Thracian gladiator named Spartacus, the revolt broke out in southern Italy and involved 70,000 slaves. Spartacus managed to defeat several Roman armies before he was finally trapped and killed in southern Italy in 71 B.C. Six thousand of his followers were crucified, the traditional form of execution for slaves.

The Roman Family

At the heart of the Roman social structure stood the family, headed by the *paterfamilias*—the dominant male. The household also included the wife, sons with their wives and children, unmarried daughters, and slaves. As we have seen, a family was virtually a small state within the state, and the power of the *paterfamilias* was parallel to that of the state magistrates over citizens. Like the Greeks, Roman males believed that the weakness of the female sex necessitated male guardians (see the box on p. 153). The *paterfamilias* exercised that authority; upon his death, sons or the nearest male relatives assumed the role of guardians. By the late Republic, however, although the rights of male guardians remained legally in effect, upper-class women found numerous ways to circumvent the power of their guardians.

Fathers arranged the marriages of daughters, although there are instances of mothers and daughters having influence on the choice. In the Republic, women married *cum manu*, "with legal control" passing from father to husband. By the mid-first century B.C., the dominant practice had changed to *sine manu*, "without legal control," which meant that married daughters officially remained within the father's legal power. Since the fathers of most married women were dead, not being in the "legal control" of a husband made possible independent property rights that forceful women could translate into considerable power within the household and outside it. Traditionally, Roman marriages were intended to

❧ Cato the Elder on Women ❧

During the Second Punic War, the Romans enacted the Oppian Law, which limited the amount of gold women could possess and restricted their dress and use of carriages. In 195 B.C., an attempt to repeal the law was made, and women demonstrated in the streets on behalf of the effort. According to the Roman historian Livy, the conservative Roman official Cato the Elder spoke against repeal and against the women favoring it. Although the words are probably not Cato's own, they do reflect a traditional male Roman attitude toward women.

Livy, *The History of Rome*

"If each of us, citizens, had determined to assert his rights and dignity as a husband with respect to his own spouse, we should have less trouble with the sex as a whole; as it is, our liberty, destroyed at home by female violence, even here in the Forum is crushed and trodden underfoot, and because we have not kept them individually under control, we dread them collectively. . . . But from no class is there not the greatest danger if you permit them meetings and gatherings and secret consultations. . . ."

"Our ancestors permitted no women to conduct even personal business without a guardian to intervene in her behalf; they wished them to be under the control of fathers, brothers, husbands; we (Heaven help us!) allow them now even to interfere in public affairs, yes, and to visit the Forum and our informal and formal sessions.

What else are they doing now on the streets and at the corners except urging the bill of the tribunes and voting for the repeal of the law? Give loose rein to their uncontrollable nature and to this untamed creature and expect that they will themselves set bounds to their license; unless you act, this is the least of the things enjoined upon women by custom or law and to which they submit with a feeling of injustice. It is complete liberty or rather, if we wish to speak the truth, complete license that they desire."

"If they win in this, what will they not attempt? Review all the laws with which your forefathers restrained their license and made them subject to their husbands; even with all these bonds you can scarcely control them. What of this? If you suffer them to seize these bonds one by one and wrench themselves free and finally to be placed on a parity with their husbands, do you think you will be able to endure them? The moment they begin to be your equals, they will be your superiors. . . ."

"Now they publicly address other women's husbands, and, what is more serious, they beg for a law and votes, and from various men they get what they ask. In matters affecting yourself, your property, your children, you, Sir, can be importuned; once the law has ceased to set a limit to your wife's expenditures you will never set it yourself. Do not think, citizens, that the situation which existed before the law was passed will ever return. . . ."

---

be for life, but divorce was introduced in the third century and became relatively easy to obtain since either party could initiate it and no one needed to prove the breakdown of the marriage. Divorce became especially prevalent in the first century B.C.—a period of political turmoil—when marriages were used to cement political alliances.

Some parents in upper-class families provided education for their daughters. Some had private tutors and others may have gone to primary schools. But, at the age when boys were entering secondary schools, girls were pushed into marriage. The legal minimum age was twelve, although fourteen was a more common age in practice. Although some Roman doctors warned that early pregnancies could be dangerous to young girls, early marriages persisted due to the desire to benefit

from dowries as soon as possible and the reality of early mortality. A good example is Tullia, Cicero's beloved daughter. She was married at sixteen, widowed at twenty-two, remarried one year later, divorced at twenty-eight, remarried at twenty-nine, and divorced at thirty-three. She died at thirty-four, not unusual for females in Roman society.

In contrast to upper-class Athenian women, Roman upper-class women were not segregated from males in the home. Wives were appreciated as enjoyable company and were at the center of household social life. Women talked to visitors and were free to shop, visit friends, and go to games, temples, and theaters. Nevertheless, they were not allowed to participate in public life, although there are examples of women exerting considerable political influence through their husbands.

✦ **A Roman Lady.** Roman women, especially those of the upper class, developed comparatively more freedom than women in classical Athens despite the persistent male belief that women required guardianship. This mural decoration was found in the remains of a villa destroyed by the eruption of Mount Vesuvius.

The Evolution of Roman Law

One of Rome's chief gifts to the Mediterranean world of its day and to succeeding generations of Western civilization was its development of law. After the Twelve Tables of 450 B.C., there was no complete codification of Roman law until that of the Byzantine emperor Justinian in the sixth century A.D. (see Chapter 7). The Twelve Tables, although inappropriate for later times, were never officially abrogated and were still memorized by schoolboys in the first century B.C. Civil law (*ius civile*) derived from the Twelve Tables proved inadequate for later Roman needs, however, and gave way to corrections and additions by the praetors. Upon taking office, a praetor issued an edict listing his guidelines for dealing with different kinds of legal cases. Although as a member of the Roman ruling class the praetor was knowledgeable in law, he also relied on Roman jurists for advice in preparing his edicts. These jurists were not professional lawyers, but amateur law experts, who helped to determine the law through the use of precedents, not theory. Their interpretations, often embodied

in the edicts of the praetors, created a body of legal principles.

In 242 B.C., the Romans appointed a second praetor who was responsible for examining suits between a Roman and a non-Roman as well as between two non-Romans. The Romans found that although some of their rules of law could be used in these cases, special rules were often needed. These rules gave rise to a body of law known as the *ius gentium*—the law of nations—defined by the Romans as "that part of the law which we apply both to ourselves and to foreigners." But the influence of Greek philosophy, primarily Stoicism, led Romans in the late Republic to develop the idea of *ius naturale*—the law of nature—or universal divine law derived from right reason. The Romans came to view their *ius gentium* as derived from or identical to this *ius naturale*, thus giving Roman jurists a philosophical justification for systematizing Roman law according to basic principles.

The Development of Literature and Art

The Romans produced little literature before the third century B.C. The Latin literature that emerged in that century was strongly influenced by Greek models. In drama, for example, Latin translations of Greek plays for presentation at the public festivals in Rome introduced Romans to the world of Greek theater. The demand for plays at public festivals eventually led to a growing number of native playwrights. The best known were Plautus and Terence.

Plautus (c. 254–184 B.C.) used plots from Greek New Comedy (see Chapter 4) for his own plays (see the box on p. 155). The actors wore Greek costumes and Greek masks and portrayed the same stock characters: dirty old men, clever slaves, prostitutes, and young men in love, whose pains are recounted in this brief excerpt:

> *Not the throes of all mankind*
> *Equal my distracted mind.*
> *I strain and I toss*
> *On a passionate cross:*
> *Love's goad makes me reel,*
> *I whirl on Love's wheel,*
> *In a swoon of despair*
> *Hurried here, hurried there—*
> *Torn asunder, I am blind*
> *With a cloud upon my mind.*[4]

While indebted to the Greeks, Plautus managed to infuse his plays with his own earthy Latin quality,

Roman Comedy

This excerpt is a scene from one of the plays of Plautus. While Plautus made use of Greek New Comedy, his devious plots and earthiness were original. His farcical humor and buffoonery made his plays exceedingly popular, especially with the masses. This excerpt is from Miles Gloriosus *("The Swaggering Soldier"). This opening scene features a pompous general and a parasitical bootlicker. Plautus loved to create fantastic names for his characters. Pyrgopolynices means "Often victorious over fortresses" and Artotrogus means "Bread eater."*

Plautus, *The Swaggering Soldier*

PYRGOPOLYNICES: My shield, there—have it burnished brighter than the bright splendor of the sun on any summer's day. Next time I have occasion to use it in the press of battle, it must flash defiance into the eyes of the opposing foe. My sword, too, I see, is pining for attention; poor chap, he's quite disheartened and cast down, hanging idly at my side so long; he's simply itching to get at an enemy and carve him into little pieces. . . . Where's Artotrogus?

ARTOTROGUS: Here, at his master's heels, close to his hero, his brave, his blessed, his royal, his doughty warrior—whose valor Mars himself could hardly challenge or outshine.

PYRGOPOLYNICES [*reminiscent*]: Ay—what of the man whose life I saved on the Curculionean field, where the enemy was led by Bumbomachides Clytomestoridysarchides, a grandson of Neptune?

ARTOTROGUS: I remember it well. I remember his golden armor, and how you scattered his legions with a puff of breath, like a wind sweeping up leaves or lifting the thatch form a roof.

PYRGOPOLYNICES [*modestly*]: It was nothing much, after all.

ARTOTROGUS: Oh, to be sure, nothing to the many more famous deeds you did—[aside] or never did. [He comes down, leaving the captain attending to his men.] If anyone ever saw a bigger liar or more conceited braggart than this one, he can have me for keeps. . . . The only thing to be said for him is, his cook makes a marvellous olive salad. . . .

PYRGOPOLYNICES [*missing him*]: Where have you got to, Artotrogus?

ARTOTROGUS [*obsequiously*]: Here I am sir. I was thinking about that elephant in India, and how you broke his ulna with a single blow of your fist.

PYRGOPOLYNICES: His ulna, was it?

ARTOTROGUS: His femur, I should have said.

PYRGOPOLYNICES: It was only a light blow, too.

ARTOTROGUS: By Jove, yes, if you had really hit him, your arm would have smashed through the animal's hide, bones, and guts.

PYRGOPOLYNICES [*modestly*]: I'd rather not talk about it, really.

incorporating elements that appealed to the Romans: drunkenness, gluttony, and womanizing. Plautus wrote for the masses and became a very popular playwright in Rome.

A second playwright of distinction was Terence (185–159 B.C.), who was born in Carthage and brought to Rome as a slave by a Roman senator who freed him. Terence died at an early age after he had written six plays. He also used plots from Greek New Comedy, but his plays contained less slapstick than those of Plautus. Terence was more concerned with the subtle portrayal of character and the artistry of his language. His refined Latin style appealed more to a cultivated audience than to the masses. In the prologue to *The Brothers*, he stated:

> The author . . . takes it as a high compliment if he can win the approval of men who themselves find favor with you all and with the general public, men whose services in war, in peace, and in your private affairs, are given at the right moment, without ostentation, to be available for each one of you.[5]

As this quotation indicates, Terence really wrote for Rome's aristocracy.

Latin prose works developed later than poetry and playwriting and were often the products of Rome's ruling elite. These upper classes were interested in history because it could be a means of exalting their ideals and in oratory because it could be an important instrument for effective statecraft. Hence, their emphasis in writing

✦ **Roman Theater: Rehearsal of a Greek Play.** This mosaic found at Pompeii shows Roman actors preparing to present a Greek play. The seated figure is the chorus master who observes two actors dancing to the music of a pipe.

prose was on works of a practical value. This is a prominent feature of the oldest existing work of Latin prose, Cato the Elder's treatise *On Agriculture*. In effect, this was a technical manual reminiscent of the practical handbooks produced in the Hellenistic world.

Despite their attraction to the Greek world, Romans were generally repelled by much of Greek philosophy with the exception of Stoicism. The latter's emphasis on virtuous conduct and performance of duty (see Chapter 4) fit well with Roman ideals and the practical bent of the Roman character. Panaetius of Rhodes (c. 180–111 B.C.), whose works helped introduce Stoicism to the Romans, proved especially popular.

The Romans were also dependent on the Greeks for artistic inspiration. During the third and second centuries B.C., they adopted many features of the Hellenistic style of art (see Chapter 4). The Romans excelled in architecture, a highly practical art. In addition to their justly famous highways, they built bridges and aqueducts making use of the arch. They also developed a new technique by using concrete in construction projects. Its utilization enabled them to erect giant amphitheaters, public baths, and the high-rise tenement buildings that housed Rome's exploding population in the late second and first centuries B.C.

The Romans developed a taste for Greek statues, which they placed not only in public buildings, but in their private houses. When demand outstripped the

supply of original works, reproductions of Greek statues became fashionable. The Romans' own portrait sculpture was characterized by an intense realism that included even unpleasant physical details.

Values and Attitudes

By their very nature, the Romans were a conservative people. They were very concerned about maintaining the *mos maiorum*, the customs or traditions of their ancestors. The Romans emphasized parental authority and, above all, their obligations to the state. The highest virtue was *pietas*—the dutiful execution of one's obligations to one's fellow citizens, to the gods, and to the state.

By the second century B.C., however, the creation of an empire had begun to weaken the old values. The Romans began to place greater stress on affluence, status, and material possessions. There was also more emphasis on individualism and less on collective well-being, on the old public spirit that had served Rome so well. Those who worried about the decline of the old values blamed it on different causes. Some felt that after the destruction of Carthage, the Romans no longer had any strong enemies to challenge them. Others believed that the Romans had simply been overwhelmed by the affluence created by the new empire. And finally, there were those who blamed everything on the Greeks for importing ideas and practices baneful to the Romans.

Of course, Romans responded differently to the changes brought by the creation of an empire. Two examples from the second century demonstrate this well. Marcus Cato the Elder (234–149 B.C.) was a Roman praetor, consul, and member of the ruling class who became censor in 184. Cato scorned the "Greeklings"—people who followed Greek ways and read Greek philosophy and literature. He even introduced a decree to force all Greek philosophers to leave Rome. He wrote to his son:

> I shall speak about those Greek fellows in their proper place, son Marcus, and point out the results of my enquiries at Athens, and convince you what benefit comes from dipping into their literature, and not making a close study of it. They are a quite worthless people, and an intractable one, and you must consider my words prophetic. When that race gives us its literature it will corrupt all things. . . .[6]

But Cato was not stupid. He not only learned Greek himself but also allowed his own son to study in Athens.

He knew only too well that, like it or not, Greek was becoming a necessity for Roman political life.

Scipio Aemilianus (185–129 B.C.) was a member of a patrician family and a brilliant general who easily achieved the top offices of the Roman state. Scipio was also concerned about the traditional Roman values, but he was much more inclined to accept Rome's growing urbanization as it became the center of the Mediterranean world and was consequently more open to the Greeks as well. He was a philhellene—an admirer of Greek philosophy and literature. He created the so-called Scipionic circle, a group of intellectuals dedicated to Greek thought, which included Polybius, Terence, and Panaetius. While desirous of maintaining old Roman virtues, Scipio was well aware that the acquisition of an empire had created a new world with new demands and values.

The Decline and Fall of the Roman Republic (133–31 B.C.)

By the mid-second century B.C., Roman domination of the Mediterranean Sea was well established. Yet the process of creating an empire had weakened and threatened the internal stability of Rome. This internal instability characterizes the period of Roman history from 133 until 31 B.C., when the armies of Octavian defeated Mark Antony and stood supreme over the Roman world. By that time, the constitution of the Roman Republic was in shambles (see the box on p. 158).

Background: Social, Economic, and Political Problems

By the second century B.C., the senate had become the effective governing body of the Roman state. It had achieved this position not by constitutional enactment but through its own initiative—not through law, but by custom. It comprised some 300 men, drawn primarily from the landed aristocracy; they remained senators for life and held the chief magistracies of the Republic. During the wars of the third and second centuries, the senate came to exercise enormous power. It directed the wars and took control of both foreign and domestic policy, including financial affairs. The *senatus consultum*, or advice of the senate to the consuls, had come to have the force of law.

Moreover, the magistracies and senate were increasingly controlled by a relatively select circle of wealthy and powerful families—both patrician and plebeian—

✦ **Appian Way.** Because of their practical-minded nature, the Romans excelled in certain arts, especially architecture. In addition to aqueducts, amphitheaters, and tenement buildings, the Romans constructed a series of highways that traversed the Roman world and linked it together. Pictured here is the Appian Way, constructed by the censor Appius Claudius in 312 B.C. This highway connected Rome to Capua through the Pontine plain.

called the *nobiles* ("nobles") The *nobiles* were essentially the men whose families were elected to the more important political offices of the Republic. In the hundred years from 233 to 133 B.C., 80 percent of the consuls came from twenty-six families; moreover, 50 percent came from only ten families. Hence, the *nobiles* constituted a governing oligarchy that managed, through landed wealth, patronage, and intimidation, to maintain its hold over the magistracies and senate and thus guide the destiny of Rome while running the state in its own interests. When a new man—called a *novus homo*—did win a consulship, he and his descendants became members of this select oligarchy. The *nobiles* and other aristocrats also tended to split into various allied groups, strengthened by intermarriage for the political advantage of the families.

By the end of the second century B.C., two types of aristocratic leaders called the *optimates* ("the best men") and the *populares* ("favoring the people") became prominent. These were not political parties or even individual cliques, but leaders who followed two different approaches to politics. *Optimates* and *populares* were terms

The Decline of the Roman Republic

Although Rome stood supreme over the Mediterranean world by 133 B.C., the internal structure of the Republic began to disintegrate. Over the next hundred years, the Republic was afflicted with mob violence, assassinations, civil wars, and unscrupulous politicians who seized every opportunity to advance their own interests. The Roman historian Sallust (86–35 B.C.), who lived through many of these crises, reflected upon the causes of Rome's problems. In this selection, he discusses the moral decline that set in after the destruction of Carthage in 146 B.C.

Sallust, The War with Catiline

Accordingly, good morals were culvatied at home and in the field; [in the early Republic] there was the greatest harmony and little or no avarice; justice and honesty prevailed among them, thanks not so much to laws as to nature. Quarrels, discord, and strife were reserved for their enemies; citizen vied with citizen only for the prize of merit. They were lavish in their offerings to the gods, frugal in the home, loyal to their friends. By practicing these two qualities, boldness in warfare and justice when peace came, they watched over themselves and their country. In proof of these statements, I present this convincing evidence, firstly, in time of war punishment was more often inflicted for attacking the enemy contrary to orders, or for withdrawing too tardily when recalled from the field, than for venturing to abandon the standards or to give ground under stress; and secondly, in time of peace they ruled by kindness rather fear, and when wronged preferred forgiveness to vengeance.

But when our country had grown great through toil and the practice of justice, when great kings had been vanquished in war, savage tribes and mighty peoples subdued by force of arms, when Carthage, the rival of Rome's sway, had perished root and branch, and all seas and lands were open, then Fortune began to grow cruel and to bring confusion into all our affairs. Those who had found it easy to bear hardships and dangers, anxiety and adversity, found leisure and wealth, desirable under other circumstances, a burden and a curse. Hence the lust for power first, then for money, grew upon them; these were, I may say, the root of all evils. For avarice destroyed honor, integrity, and all other noble qualities; taught in their place insolence, cruelty, to neglect the gods, to set a price on everything. Ambition drove many men to become false; to have one thought locked in the breast, another ready on the tongue; to value friendships and enmities not on their merits but by the standard of self-interest, and to show a good front rather than a good heart. At first these vices grew slowly, from time to time they were punished; finally, when the disease had spread like a deadly plague, the state was changed and a government second to none in justice and excellence became cruel and intolerable.

---

of political rhetoric that were used by individuals within the aristocracy against fellow aristocratic rivals to distinguish one set of tactics from another. The *optimates* tended to be the *nobiles* who currently controlled the senate and wished to maintain their oligarchical privileges, while the *populares* were usually other ambitious aristocrats who used the peoples' assemblies, especially the *concilium plebis* as instruments to break the domination of the *optimates*. Although politicians of both types pursued their own political ambitions, they may also have believed some of their own rhetoric—that a traditional oligarchy on the one hand or a leadership more concerned with the desires of nonaristocrats on the other was best for Rome. In any case, the conflicts between these two types of aristocratic leaders and their supporters engulfed the first century in political turmoil.

Another social group in Rome also became entangled in this political turmoil—the *equites* or equestrians, a name derived from the fact that they had once formed Rome's cavalry. Many equestrians had become extremely wealthy through a variety of means, often related to the creation of the empire. Some, for example, were private contractors who derived their wealth from government contracts for the collection of taxes, the outfitting of armies, and the construction of fleets and public works. In 218 B.C., the senate enacted a law that forbade senators to bid for state contracts or engage in commerce. The law effectively barred the equestrians from high office, since to serve in the senate they would have to give up their livelihoods. By the end of the second century B.C., the equestrians were seeking real political power commensurate with their financial stake in the empire. They would play an important role in the political turmoil that brought an end to the Republic.

Of course, both equestrians and *nobiles* formed only a tiny minority of the Roman people. The backbone of the Roman state and army had traditionally been the small farmers who tilled their little plots of land and made up the chief source of recruits for the army. But economic changes that began in the period of the Punic Wars increasingly undermined the position of that group. This occurred for several reasons. Their lands had been severely damaged during the Second Punic War when Hannibal invaded Italy. Moreover, in order to win the wars, Rome had to increase the term of military service from two to six years. The Roman army was never meant to serve in distant wars, but was called out for the "war season," after which the soldiers returned to their farms. Now when the soldiers returned home after many years of service abroad, they found their farms so deteriorated that they chose to sell out instead of remaining on the land. By this time, capitalistic agriculture was also increasing rapidly. Landed aristocrats had been able to develop large estates (called *latifundia*) by taking over state-owned land and by buying out small peasant owners. These large estates relied on slave and tenant labor and frequently concentrated on cash crops, such as grapes for wine, olives, and sheep for wool, which small farmers could not afford to do. Thus, the rise of *latifundia* contributed to the decline in the number of small citizen farmers. Since the latter group traditionally formed the basis of the Roman army—Romans only conscripted people with a financial stake in the community—the number of men available for military service declined. Many of the newly landless men stayed in the countryside, finding agricultural work as best they could. Some of them, however, drifted to the cities, especially Rome, forming a large class of day laborers who possessed no property. This new class of urban proletariat formed a highly unstable mass with the potential for much trouble in depressed times. Thus, Rome's economic, social, and political problems were serious and needed attention. In 133 B.C., a member of the aristocracy proposed a solution that infuriated his fellow aristocrats.

The Reforms of Tiberius and Gaius Gracchus

Tiberius Gracchus (163–133 B.C.) was a member of the *nobiles* who ruled Rome. Although concerned with the immediate problem of a shortage of military recruits, Tiberius believed that the underlying cause of Rome's problems was the decline of the small farmers. Tiberius was not a revolutionary, and his proposals for reform, drafted with the help of several prominent senators, were essentially conservative; he was looking backward to what had constituted the foundation of Rome's greatness.

Tiberius Gracchus was elected one of the tribunes of the plebs for 133 B.C. Without consulting the senate, where he knew his rivals would oppose his proposal, Tiberius took his legislation directly to the *concilium plebis* or plebeian assembly. After some effort, his land-reform bill was passed. It placed limits on the amount of state-owned land that could be held by any Roman and stipulated that the public land reclaimed in this fashion should be given to landless Romans on a permanent lease at low rent. Tiberius believed this measure would restore the small farmers and reinvigorate the traditional system. His law also established a land commission to redistribute the land. Many senators, themselves large landowners whose estates included large tracts of public land, opposed this reform, which would also have created a large mass of clients loyal to Tiberius among the rural voters. When Tiberius decided to run again for the office of tribune, a group of senators, fearful that his appeal to such a large bloc of voters would make him and his supporters even more powerful, took the law into their own hands and assassinated him. The land commission continued to divide the large estates, although its work was slowed after 129 B.C., when the senate deprived the commission of its judicial power. The land reform of Tiberius had not failed (thousands of small allotments had been made), but the use of political violence—the breaking of the law by the people sworn to uphold it—to prevent Tiberius from reaping the political rewards of his reform was an ominous omen for the Republic.

The efforts of Tiberius Gracchus were continued by his brother Gaius, elected tribune for both 123 and 122 B.C. Gaius broadened his reform program to appeal to more people disenchanted with the current senatorial leadership. He restored the old judicial powers of the land commission and appealed to the small farmers by quickening the pace of land redistribution. To win the support of the *equites*, he replaced the senators on the jury courts that tried provincial governors accused of extortion with members of the equestrian order and opened the new province of Asia to equestrian tax collectors. Thus, Gaius gave the *equites* two instruments of public power: control over the jury courts that often tried provincial governors, and provincial taxation. An-

The Decline and Fall of the Republic

Reforms of Tiberius Gracchus	133 B.C.
Reforms of Gaius Gracchus	123–122 B.C.
Jugurthine War	111–105 B.C.
Marius: First consulship	107 B.C.
Marius: Consecutive consulships	104–100 B.C.
Italian or Social War	90–88 B.C.
Sulla's march on Rome	88 B.C.
Sulla as dictator	82–79 B.C.
Pompey's command in Spain	77–71 B.C.
Campaign of Crassus against Spartacus	73–71 B.C.
Consulship of Crassus and Pompey	70 B.C.
First Triumvirate (Caesar, Pompey, Crassus)	60 B.C.
Caesar in Gaul	59–49 B.C.
Crassus and Pompey as consuls	55 B.C.
Crassus killed by Parthians	53 B.C.
Caesar crosses the Rubicon	49 B.C.
Battle of Pharsalus; Pompey killed in Egypt	48 B.C.
End of civil war	45 B.C.
Caesar as dictator	47–44 B.C.
Second Triumvirate (Octavian, Antony, Marcus Lepidus); Cicero killed	43 B.C.
Caesar's assassins defeated at Philippi	42 B.C.
Octavian defeats Antony at Actium	31 B.C.

ultimum (a final decree of the senate), which virtually gave the consuls the right to use martial law against Gaius and his followers. As a result, the reformer and many of his friends were killed in 121 B.C.

The attempts of the Gracchi brothers to bring reforms by using the tribuneship and *concilium plebis* created a popular alternative to the power of the *optimates* in the magistracies and senate. No doubt both sides felt justified in their positions: the *populares* believed they needed to bypass the senate to break the domination of their rivals within the senatorial aristocracy, while the *optimates* thought that the popular leaders were aspirants to tyranny who were using the masses to further their own ambitions. Although there may have been an element of truth on both sides, the unwillingness to compromise and the willingness to resort to assassination and constitutionally dubious expedients simply opened the door to more instability and further violence.

Marius and the New Roman Army

In the closing years of the second century B.C., a series of military disasters gave rise to a fresh outburst of popular anger against the old leaders of the senate and resulted in the rise of Marius (157–86 B.C.).

Marius came to prominence during the war in North Africa against Jugurtha and the Numidians. The senate had badly bungled the war effort. Marius had served as legate to the senatorial-appointed commanding general Metellus, but quarreled with his superior, returned to Rome, and ran for the consulship with "win the war" as his campaign slogan. Despite being a *novus homo*—a "new man"—from the equestrian order, Marius won and became a consul for 107 B.C. The plebeian assembly then voted to give Marius command of the army in Africa, a definite encroachment on the senate's right to conduct wars. Generals no longer needed to be loyal to the senate.

Marius brought the Jugurthine War to a successful conclusion and was then called upon to defeat the Celtic tribes (or Gauls, as the Romans called them), who had annihilated a Roman army and threatened an invasion of Italy. Marius was made consul for five years, from 104 to 100 B.C., raised a new army, and decisively defeated the Celts, leaving him in a position of personal ascendancy in Rome.

In raising a new army, Marius initiated military reforms that proved to have drastic consequences. The Roman army had traditionally been a conscript army of small landholders. Marius recruited volunteers from both the urban and the rural proletariat who possessed

other law appealed to the Roman proletariat by establishing government subsidies that enabled grain to be sold at below market prices. Finally, Gaius proposed legislation that would have made all Latin allies Roman citizens. Although this legislation probably failed to pass, this offer of Roman citizenship was widely popular throughout Italy, but not among Romans who feared that their privileges would be diluted by such a large influx of new citizens.

Despite his efforts, Gaius was not reelected to the tribuneship for a third year. Fellow senators, hostile to his reforms and fearful of his growing popularity, made use of a constitutional innovation, a *senatus consultum* no property. These volunteers swore an oath of loyalty to the general, not the senate, and thus inaugurated a professional-type army that might no longer be subject to the state. Moreover, to recruit these men, a general would promise them land, so generals had to play politics to get legislation passed that would provide the land for their veterans. In 100 B.C., for example, while still consul, Marius entered into an alliance with a tribune, Saturninus, to gain land for his soldiers through legislation in the plebeian assembly. Complications arose, however, and the senate passed a final decree requesting Marius as consul to put down Saturninus. Marius did so, apparently putting the senate's call for order ahead of his previous alliance with the tribune. Soon after, Marius retired from politics. But he left a powerful legacy. He had created a new system of military recruitment that placed much power in the hands of the individual generals. By using his army to crush Saturninus, he had shown how this army could be used to save the Republic. His action had another implication as well—such an army could also be used to destroy the Republic. Roman republican politics was entering a new and potentially dangerous stage.

The Role of Sulla

After almost a decade of relative quiet, the Roman Republic was threatened with another crisis—the Italian War (90–88 B.C.). This war resulted from Rome's unwillingness to deal constructively with the complaints of its Italian allies. These allies had fought loyally on Rome's side, but felt they had not shared sufficiently in the lands and bonuses given to Roman veterans. In 90 B.C., the Italians rebelled and formed their own confederation. Two years of bitter fighting left Italy devastated and took an enormous number of lives. The Romans managed to end the rebellion, but only by granting full rights of Roman citizenship to all free Italians. "Rome was now Italy, and Italy Rome."[7] This influx of new voters into the tribal and plebeian assemblies drastically altered the voting power structure in favor of the *populares* who had earlier favored enfranchisement of the Italians.

During this war, a new figure began to emerge into prominence—Lucius Cornelius Sulla (138–78 B.C.), a member of the *nobiles*. Sulla had been made consul for 88 B.C. and been given command by the senate of the war against Mithridates, the king of Pontus in Asia Minor, who had rebelled against Roman power. However, Marius, who had retired from Roman politics, now returned to the scene. The plebeian assembly, contradicting the senate's wishes, transferred command of the

war against Mithridates to Marius. Considering this action illegal, Sulla marched on Rome with his army. Marius fled and Sulla reestablished his command. It was the first time a Roman consul had used his forces against fellow Roman citizens. After Sulla left again for the east, Marius joined forces with the consul Cinna, marched on Rome, seized control of the government, outlawed Sulla, and killed many of Sulla's supporters. Civil war had become a fact of life in Roman politics.

Marius soon died, but Cinna continued to use his forces to remain as consul. His control, however, really depended upon the fortunes of Sulla and his army. After defeating Mithridates in the east, Sulla returned to Rome, crushed the armies opposing him in Italy, and seized Rome itself in 82 B.C. He forced the senate to grant him the title of dictator to "reconstitute the Republic." After conducting a reign of terror to wipe out all opposition, Sulla revised the constitution to restore power to the hands of the senate. He eliminated most of the powers of the popular assemblies and the tribunes of the plebs and restored the senators to the jury courts. He also enlarged the senate by adding men of the equestrian order. In 79 B.C., believing that he had restored the traditional Republic governed by a powerful senate, he resigned his office of dictator, retired, and soon died, leaving a power vacuum. But his real legacy was quite different from what he had intended. His example of how an army could be used to seize power would prove most attractive to ambitious men.

The Death of the Republic

For the next fifty years, Roman history would be characterized by two important features: the jostling for power by a number of powerful individuals and the civil wars generated by their conflicts. Not long after Sulla's attempts to revive senatorial power, the senate made two extraordinary military appointments that raised to prominence two very strong personalities—Crassus (c. 112–53 B.C.) and Pompey (106–48 B.C.). Crassus had fought for Sulla and had also become extremely rich—it was said that he owned most of Rome. In 73 B.C., the senate gave Crassus a military command against the slave rebellion led by Spartacus, which he successfully completed. Pompey had also fought for Sulla and was given an important military command in Spain in 77 B.C. When he returned in 71 B.C., he was hailed as a military hero.

Despite their jealousy of one another, Pompey and Crassus joined forces and were elected consuls for 70 B.C. Although both men had been Sulla's supporters, they undid his work. They restored the power of the tribunes

◆ **Pompey.** A popular and powerful figure of the late Republic, Pompey was a successful general who joined with Caesar and Crassus in a coalition known as the First Triumvirate in order to secure his reorganization of the east and to obtain lands for his veterans. Later, he opposed Caesar during the civil war of 49-45 B.C. Pictured is a marble copy of an earlier sculpted head of Pompey.

and helped put *equites* back on the jury courts, thereby reviving the *populares* as a path to political power.

With their power reestablished by this action, friendly plebeian tribunes now proposed legislation that gave two important military commands to Pompey. In 67 B.C., he cleared the Mediterranean Sea of the pirates who were harassing Roman commerce. After this success, he was put in charge of the campaign against Mithridates, who felt he could take advantage of Rome's internal troubles to pursue his plans of conquest. Pompey defeated Mithridates and reorganized the east, winning immense success and prestige as well as enormous wealth. When he returned to Rome, he disbanded his army, expecting the senate would automatically ratify his eastern settlement and give land to his veterans. But new forces and new personalities had risen to prominence during his absence, and his requests encountered complications.

Marcus Tullius Cicero (106–43 B.C.) was one of these new personalities. A "new man" from the equestrian order and the first of his family to achieve the consulship, Cicero made a name for himself as a lawyer, using his outstanding oratorical skills to defend people accused of crimes and to prosecute others, including a corrupt provincial governor (see the box on p. 163). He became consul in 63 B.C. and upheld the interests of the senate.

While consul, he added to his reputation by acting forcefully to suppress a political conspiracy led by a desperate and bankrupt aristocrat named Catiline. Cicero was one of the few prominent politicians who attempted to analyze the problems of the Republic systematically. He believed in a "concord of the orders," meaning the cooperation of the equestrians and senators. In effect, Cicero harkened back to the days of collective rule, a time when political leaders were motivated to work together for the good of the Roman state. But collective rule was no longer meaningful to ambitious men seeking personal power. Cicero himself had few military skills and could not command an army. He realized that the senate needed the support of a powerful general if the concord of the orders were to be made a reality. In 62 B.C., he saw Pompey as that man. But a large element in the senate felt Pompey had become too powerful, and they now refused to grant his wishes after his return from the east. This same element in the senate treated Julius Caesar in a similar fashion when he returned from Spain. That turned out to be a big mistake.

Julius Caesar (100–44 B.C.) had been a spokesman for the *populares* from the beginning of his political career, an alliance that ran in the family—Marius was his uncle by marriage. Caesar pursued political power by appealing to many of the same groups who had supported Marius. After serving as aedile and praetor, he sought a military command and was sent to Spain. He returned from

◆ **Cicero.** The great orator Marcus Tullius Cicero, whose writings provide much information about politics and upper-class life, rose to the highest offices in the Republic due to his oratorical skills. He was a supporter of the senate and wished to establish a "concord of the orders," or cooperative rule by the equestrians and the senators.

Exploitation of the Provinces

As the Romans expanded their territory outside Italy, conquered lands were made provinces. These possessions were clearly distinguished from Italy in that their inhabitants were forced to pay tribute to the Roman state. Eventually, the senate came to control the appointment of the governors who administered the provinces. By the first century B.C., many provincial governors used their provinces to amass enormous fortunes through extortion, confiscation of property, and bribery. Although governors could be prosecuted after their term of office, the senators who served as judges often protected the accused who were members of their own class. Cicero successfully prosecuted Verres, the corrupt governor of Sicily, and thereby gained prominence as a politician. This excerpt is taken from one of his speeches against Verres.

Cicero, Against Verres

But nowhere did he multiply and magnify the memorials and the proofs of all his evil qualities so thoroughly as in his governorship of Sicily; which island for the space of three years he devastated and ruined so effectually that nothing can restore it to its former condition, and it hardly seems possible that a long lapse of years and a succession of upright governors can in time bring it a partial revival of prosperity. So long as Verres was governing it, its people were protected neither by their own laws, nor by the decrees of the Roman Senate, nor by the rights that belong to all nations alike. . . .

For the space of three years, the law awarded nothing to anybody unless Verres chose to agree; and nothing was so undoubtedly inherited from a man's father or grandfather that the courts would not cancel his right to it, if Verres asked them to do so. Countless sums of money, under a new and unprincipled regulation, were wrung from the purses of the farmers; our most loyal allies were treated as if they were national enemies; Roman citizens were tortured and executed like slaves; the guiltiest criminals bought their legal acquittal, while the most honorable, and honest men would be prosecuted in absence, and condemned and banished unheard; strongly fortified harbors, mighty and well-defended cities, were left open to the assaults of pirates and buccaneers; Sicilian soldiers and sailors, our allies and our friends, were starved to death; fine fleets, splendidly equipped, were to the great disgrace of our nation destroyed and lost to us. Famous and ancient works of art, some of them the gifts of wealthy kings, who intended them to adorn the cities where they stood, others the gifts of Roman generals, who gave or restored them to the communities of Sicily in the hour of victory—this same governor stripped and despoiled every one of them. Nor was it only the civic statues and works of art that he treated thus; he also pillaged the holiest and most venerated sanctuaries. . . . As to his adulteries and the like vile offenses, a sense of decency makes me afraid to repeat the tale of his acts of wanton wickedness: and besides, I would not wish, by repeating it, to add to the calamities of those who have not been suffered to save their children and their wives from outrage at the hands of this lecherous scoundrel. Is it alleged that he did these things so secretly that they were not known everywhere? I do not believe that one human being lives, who has heard the name of Verres spoken and cannot also repeat the tale of his evil doings.

Spain in 60 B.C. and requested a special dispensation so that he could both celebrate a triumph with his troops and run for the consulship, which would place him in the highest rank within the senate. Rival senators blocked his request. Consequently, Caesar joined with two fellow senators, Crassus and Pompey, who were also being stymied by the senate. Historians call their coalition the First Triumvirate. Though others had made political deals before, the combined wealth and power of these three men was enormous, enabling them to dominate the political scene. Caesar was elected consul for 59 B.C. and used the popular assemblies to achieve the basic aims of the triumvirs: Pompey received his eastern settlement and lands for his veterans; equestrian allies of Crassus were given a reduction on tax contracts for which they had overbid; and Caesar was granted a special military command in Gaul (modern France, Belgium, and parts of the Netherlands) for five years.

Caesar did so well in Gaul that Crassus and Pompey realized anew the value of military command. They became consuls again for 55 B.C. and garnered more benefits for the coalition: Caesar was given a five-year extension in Gaul; Crassus a command in Syria; and Pompey one in Spain. When Crassus was killed in battle in 53 B.C., his death left two powerful men with armies in direct competition. Caesar had used his time in Gaul to gain fame and military experience. He had waged numerous campaigns, costing the lives, it has been estimated, of almost two million men, women, and children. But his wars had also enabled him to amass enough booty and slaves to pay off all of the debts he had accumulated in gaining political offices. Moreover, he now had an army of seasoned veterans who were loyal to him. No doubt, most senators would have preferred both Pompey and Caesar to lay down their commands and give up their armies. Since both refused, the leading senators fastened on Pompey as the least harmful to their cause and voted for Caesar to lay down his command and return as a private citizen to Rome. Such a step was intolerable to Caesar since it would leave him totally vulnerable to his enemies. He chose to keep his army and moved into Italy by crossing the Rubicon, the river that formed the southern boundary of his province on January 10, 49 B.C. In bringing his army into Italy, he guaranteed a civil war between his forces and those of Pompey and his allies. At the Battle of Pharsalus in 48 B.C., Caesar's veterans carried the day against Pompey's forces. The defeated Pompey fled to Egypt where the king was one of his foreign clients, but one of the king's advisers had Pompey killed. The war continued, however, since some of the senators on his side, including Cato the Younger, had recruited new

◆ **Caesar.** Conqueror of Gaul and member of the First Triumvirate, Julius Caesar is perhaps the best-known figure of the late Republic. Caesar became dictator of Rome in 47 B.C. and, after his victories in the civil war, was made dictator for life. Some members of the senate who resented his power assassinated him in 44 B.C. Pictured is a marble copy of a bust of Caesar.

troops. After victories in North Africa and Spain, Caesar returned triumphant to Rome in 45 B.C.

No doubt Caesar realized that the old order of unfettered political competition could not be saved. He was unwilling to take the title of king, which was intensely disliked by the Roman upper classes, but he had no intention of giving up his control. Caesar had officially been made dictator in 47 B.C., and in 44 B.C. he was made dictator for life. He continued to hold elections for offices, but saw to it that his supporters chose the people he recommended. As Rome's new ruler, he quickly instituted a number of ambitious reforms. He increased the senate to 900 members by filling it with many of his followers. He granted citizenship to a number of people in the provinces who had provided assistance to him. By establishing colonies of Roman citizens in North Africa, Gaul, and Spain, he initiated a process of romanization in those areas. He tried to reorganize the administrative structures of cities in Italy in order to create some sense of rational order in their government. Caesar was a generous victor and pardoned many of the republican leaders who had opposed him, allowing them to return to Rome. He also reformed the calendar by introducing the Egyptian solar year of 365 days (with later changes in 1582, it became the basis of our own calendar). He planned much more in the way of building projects and military adventures in the east, but was not able to carry them out. In 44 B.C., a group of leading senators who resented his domination assassinated him, believing that the old republican system would now return (see the box on p. 166). In truth, however, they had set the stage for another civil war that delivered the final death blow to the Republic.

A new struggle for power soon ensued. Caesar's heir, his grandnephew Octavian, though only nineteen, took command of some of Caesar's legions and made himself into a player of substantial importance. After forcing the senate to name him consul, he joined forces with Mark Antony, Caesar's ally and assistant, and Marcus Lepidus, who had been commander of Caesar's cavalry. Together, the three formed the Second Triumvirate, which was legally empowered to rule Rome. Their first act was to restore Sulla's policy of proscription, as described by the ancient historian Appian:

As soon as they were on their own, the three drew up a list of those who were to die. They put on the list, both then and later, those of whom they were suspicious because of their ability, as well as their personal enemies, trading with each other for the lives of their own relations and friends. They decreed death and confiscation of property for about 300 senators and 2,000 eques-

Map 5.3 Roman Dominions in the Late Republic, 31 B.C.

trians, among them their own brothers and uncles, as well as senior officers serving under them who had had cause to offend them or their own colleagues.[8]

In addition to proscribing their enemies at home (Cicero was one of those killed), the three commanders pursued Caesar's assassins, who had meanwhile raised an army, and defeated them at Philippi in Macedonia. Lepidus was soon shunted aside, and Octavian and Antony then divided the Roman world between them—Octavian taking the west and Antony the east. But the empire of the Romans, large as it was, was still too small for two masters, and Octavian and Antony eventually came into conflict. Antony allied himself with the Egyptian queen Cleopatra VII, with whom, like Caesar before him, he fell deeply in love. Octavian began a propaganda campaign, accusing Antony of catering to Cleopatra and giving away Roman territory to this

"whore of the east." Finally, at the Battle of Actium in Greece in 31 B.C., Octavian's forces smashed the army and navy of Antony and Cleopatra. Both fled to Egypt where, according to the Roman historian Florus, they committed suicide a year later:

> Antony was the first to commit suicide, by the sword. Cleopatra threw herself at Octavian's feet, and tried her best to attract his gaze: in vain, for his self-control was impervious to her beauty. It was not her life she was after, for that had already been granted, but a portion of her kingdom. When she realized this was hopeless and that she had been earmarked to feature in Octavian's triumph in Rome, she took advantage of her guard's carelessness to get herself into the mausoleum, as the royal tomb is called. Once there, she put on the royal robes which she was accustomed to wear, and lay down in a richly perfumed coffin beside her Antony. Then she applied poisonous snakes to her veins and passed into death as though into a sleep.[9]

The Assassination of Julius Caesar

When it quickly became apparent that Julius Caesar had no intention of restoring the Republic as they conceived it, about sixty senators, many of them his friends or pardoned enemies, formed a conspiracy to assassinate the dictator. It was led by Gaius Cassius and Marcus Brutus, who naively imagined that this act would restore the traditional Republic. The conspirators set the Ides of March (March 15) 44 B.C., as the date for the assassination. Caesar was in the midst of preparations for a campaign in the eastern part of the empire. Although warned about a plot against his life, he chose to disregard it. This account of Caesar's death is taken from his biography by the Greek writer Plutarch.

Plutarch, *Life of Caesar*

Fate, however, is to all appearance more unavoidable than unexpected. For many strange prodigies and apparitions are said to have been observed shortly before this event. . . . One finds it also related by many that a soothsayer bade him [Caesar] prepare for some great danger on the Ides of March. When this day was come, Caesar, as he went to the senate, met this soothsayer, and said to him mockingly, "The Ides of March are come," who answered him calmly, "Yes, they are come, but they are not past. . . . "

All these things might happen by chance. But the place which was destined for the scene of this murder, in which the senate met that day, was the same in which Pompey's statue stood, and was one of the edifices which Pompey had raised and dedicated with his theater to the use of the public, plainly showing that there was something of a supernatural influence which guided the action and ordered it to that particular place. Cassius, just before the act, is said to have looked toward Pompey's statue, and silently implored his assistance. . . . When Caesar entered, the senate stood up to show their respect to him, and of Brutus's confederates, some came about his chair and stood behind it, others met him, pretending to add their petitions to those of Tillius Cimber, in behalf of his brother, who was in exile; and they followed him with their joint applications till he came to his seat. When he sat down, he refused to comply with their requests, and upon their urging him further began to reproach them severely for their demand, when Tillius, laying hold of his robe with both his hands, pulled it down from his neck, which was the signal for the assault. Casca gave him the first cut in the neck, which was not mortal nor dangerous, as coming from one who at the beginning of such a bold action was probably very much disturbed; Caesar immediately turned about, and laid his hand upon the dagger and kept hold of it. And both of them at the same time cried out, he that received the blow, in Latin, "Vile Casca, what does this mean?" and he that gave it, in Greek to his brother, "Brother, help!" Upon this first onset, those who were not privy to the design were astonished, and their horror and amazement at what they saw were so great that they dared not fly nor assist Caesar, nor so much as speak a word. But those who came prepared for the business enclosed him on every side, with their naked daggers in their hands. Which way soever he turned he met with blows, and saw their swords leveled at his face and eyes, and was encompassed like a wild beast in the toils on every side. For it had been agreed they should each of them make a thrust at him, and flesh themselves with his blood: for which reason Brutus also gave him one stab in the groin. Some say that he fought and resisted all the rest, shifting his body to avoid the blows, and calling out for help, but that when he saw Brutus's sword drawn, he covered his face with his robe and submitted, letting himself fall, whether it were by chance or that he was pushed in that direction by his murderers, at the foot of the pedestal on which Pompey's statue stood, and which was thus wetted with his blood. So that Pompey himself seemed to have presided, as it were, over the revenge done upon his adversary, who lay here at his feet, and breathed out his soul through his multitude of wounds, for they say he received three-and-twenty. And the conspirators themselves were many of them wounded by each other while they all leveled their blows at the same person.

Octavian, at the age of thirty-two, stood supreme over the Roman world. The civil wars had ended. And so had the Republic.

Literature in the Late Republic

The last century of the Roman Republic had witnessed the completion of the union of Greek and

Roman culture in a truly Greco-Roman civilization. After all, Greek was the language not only of Greece but of the entire eastern Mediterranean Hellenistic world, which Rome had conquered. Moreover, educated, upper-class Romans spoke Greek fluently. The influence of Greece would continue to be felt in the development of Latin literature.

In the last century of the Republic, the Romans began to produce a new poetry, less dependent on epic themes and more inclined to personal expression. Latin poets were now able to use various Greek forms to express their own feelings about people, social and political life, and love. The finest example is the work of Catullus (c. 87–54 B.C.), the "best lyric poet" Rome produced and one of the greatest in world literature.

Like most of the great Roman writers of the first century B.C., Catullus was not from Rome. He grew up in northern Italy, but came to Rome where he belonged to a group of carefree, youthful aristocrats. He became a master at adapting and refining Greek forms of poetry to express emotions. He wrote a variety of poems on, among other things, political figures, social customs, the use of language, the death of his brother, and the travails of love. Catullus became infatuated with Clodia, the promiscuous sister of a tribune and wife of a provincial governor, and addressed a number of poems to her (he called her Lesbia), describing his passionate love and hatred for her (Clodia had many other lovers besides Catullus):

> Lesbia for ever on me rails;
> To talk of me, she never fails.
> Now, hang me, but for all her art
> I find that I have gained her heart.
> My proof is this: I plainly see
> The case is just the same with me;
> I curse her every hour sincerely,
> Yet, hang me, but I love her dearly.[10]

The ability of Catullus to express in simple fashion his intense feelings and curiosity about himself and his world had a noticeable impact on later Latin poets.

Another important poet of the late Republic was Lucretius (c. 94–55 B.C.), who followed an old Greek tradition of expounding philosophy in the form of poetry. Although Stoicism was the Greek school of philosophy that the Romans found most congenial, the philosophy of Epicurus also enjoyed a period of intense popularity between 60 and 40 B.C. No doubt, Lucretius's lengthy poem, *On the Nature of the Universe,* played an important role in furthering that philosophy. In this work, Lucretius attempted to set out poetically Epicu-

rus's idea that the world and all its creatures had been created by an accidental combination of atoms and not by the operation of divine forces. Two themes are repeated: divine forces have no effect on us, and death is of no real consequence since the soul like the body is material and after death also dissolves into atoms. Lucretius was especially adept at using vivid imagery. Describing the movement of atoms in the void, he said:

> Observe what happens when sunbeams are admitted into a building and shed light on its shadowy places. You will see a multitude of tiny particles mingling in a multitude of ways in the empty space within the light of the beam, as though contending in everlasting conflict, rushing into battle rank upon rank with never a moment's pause in a rapid sequence of unions and disunions.[11]

If the gods and death are of no significance, how then are we to lead our lives? Lucretius's Epicurean argument that a simple life free of political worries was the highest good ran counter to Roman ideals, but had an obvious appeal to Romans sick of the civil discord of the first century B.C.

The development of Roman prose was greatly aided by the practice of oratory. Romans had great respect for oratory since the ability to persuade people in public debate meant success in politics. Oratory was brought to perfection in a literary fashion by Cicero, the best exemplar of the literary and intellectual interests of the elite of the late Republic and, indeed, the greatest prose writer of that period. For Cicero, oratory was not simply skillful speaking. An orator was a statesman, a man who achieved his highest goal by pursuing an active life in public affairs.

Later, when the turmoil of the late Republic forced him into semiretirement politically, Cicero turned his attention to writing philosophical treatises. He was not an original thinker, but performed a valuable service for Roman society by popularizing and making understandable the works of Greek philosophers. In his philosophical works, Cicero, more than anyone else, transmitted the classical intellectual heritage to the Western world.

Cicero's original contributions to Western thought came in the field of politics. His works *On the Laws* and *On the Republic* provided fresh insights into political thought. His emphasis on the need to pursue an active life to benefit and improve humankind would greatly influence the later Italian Renaissance. Cicero's correspondence, especially his letters to his friend and adviser Atticus, are a font of information about politics and society in the last century of the Republic.

Rome's upper classes continued to have a strong interest in history. The best-known historian of the late

Republic is Sallust (86–35 B.C.), who established an approach to historical studies that influenced later Roman historians. Sallust, who served as governor of the province of Africa, was on Caesar's side in the civil war and after Caesar's death went into retirement and turned to the writing of history. His two extant works are the *War with Jugurtha*, which discusses the Roman war with the African king from 112–105 B.C., and the *War with Catiline*, an account of the conspiracy of the disaffected aristocrat Catiline, whom Cicero had opposed during his consulship in 63 B.C.

Sallust modeled his style after that of the Greek historian Thucydides, whose historical work experienced a sudden wave of popularity in the later 50s and 40s B.C. Sallust's works expressed his belief that the most important causative factor in Roman history was the moral degeneration of Roman society, which he attributed to the lack of a strong enemy after Carthage and the corrupting influence of the Greeks (see the box on p. 158).

Brief mention should also be made of the historical writing of Julius Caesar. Most famous is the *Commentaries on the Gallic War*, an account of his conquest of Gaul between 58 and 51 B.C. The work was published in 51 B.C., at a time when Caesar was afraid that his political enemies would take advantage of his absence from the Roman scene. Although the *Commentaries* served a partisan purpose by defending his actions in Gaul, Caesar presented his material in straightforward, concise prose with objective detachment. He referred to himself in the third person and, as the following passage indicates, was not averse to extolling his own bravery:

> Caesar saw that the situation was critical, and there was no reserve to throw in. He snatched a shield from a soldier in the rear—he had not brought one himself—and moved to the front line; he called upon the centurions by name, encouraged the men to advance, and directed them to open their lines out to give freer play to their swords. His coming inspired the men with hope and gave them new heart. Even in a desperate situation each man was anxious to do his utmost when his general was looking on, and the enemy's onset was somewhat slowed down.[12]

Caesar's work reminds us that some of the best prose of the late Republic was written by politicans who were concerned with enhancing their own position in a world of civil conflict.

Conclusion

In the eighth and seventh centuries B.C., the pastoral community of Rome emerged as an actual city. Between 509 and 264 B.C., the expansion of this city led to the union of almost all of Italy under Rome's control. Even more dramatically, between 264 and 133 B.C., Rome expanded to the west and east and became master of the Mediterranean Sea.

After 133 B.C., however, Rome's republican institutions proved inadequate for the task of ruling an empire. In the breakdown that ensued, ambitious individuals saw opportunities for power unparalleled in Roman history and succumbed to the temptations. After a series of bloody civil wars, peace was finally achieved when Octavian defeated Antony and Cleopatra. Octavian's real task was at hand: to create a new system of government that seemed to preserve the Republic while establishing the basis for a new order that would rule the empire in an orderly fashion. Octavian proved equal to the task of establishing a Roman imperial state.

NOTES

1. Quoted in Chester Starr, *Past and Future in Ancient History* (Lanham, Md., 1987), pp. 38–39.
2. Cicero, *Laws*, trans. C. W. Keyes (Cambridge, Mass., 1966), II, xii, 31.
3. Cato the Censor, *On Farming*, trans. Ernest Brehaut (New York, 1933), CXLI.
4. Quoted in J. Wright Duff, *A Literary History of Rome* (London, 1960), pp. 136–37.
5. Terence, *The Comedies*, trans. Betty Radice (Harmondsworth, 1976), p. 339.
6. Pliny, *Natural History*, trans. W. H. S. Jones (Cambridge, Mass., 1963), XXIX, vii.
7. Mary Beard and Michael Crawford, *Rome in the Late Republic* (London, 1985), p. 3.
8. Appian, *Roman History: The Civil Wars*, trans. H. White (Cambridge, Mass., 1961), IV, ii, 149–151.
9. Florus, *Epitome of Roman History*, trans. E. S. Forster (Cambridge, Mass., 1960), II, xxii, 327.
10. Michael Grant, ed., *Roman Readings* (Harmondsworth, 1958), p. 86.
11. Lucretius, *On the Nature of the Universe*, trans. Ronald Latham (Harmondsworth, 1951), p. 63.
12. Julius Caesar, *The Gallic War and Other Writings*, trans. Moses Hadas (New York, 1957), 2:25, pp. 52–53.

SUGGESTIONS FOR FURTHER READING

For a general account of the Roman Republic, see J. Boardman, J. Griffin, and O. Murray, eds., *The Oxford History of the Classical World* (Oxford, 1986), pp. 384–523. A brief, but excellent guide to recent trends in scholarship on the Roman Republic can be found in C. Starr, *Past and Future in Ancient History* (Lanham, Md., 1987), pp. 33–45. A standard one-volume reference is M. Cary and H. H. Scullard, *A History of Rome down to the Reign of Constantine*, 3d ed. (New York, 1975). Good surveys of Roman history include M. H. Crawford, *The Roman Republic*, 2d ed. (Cambridge, Mass., 1993); H. H. Scullard, *History of the Roman World 753–146 B.C.*, 4th ed. (London, 1978), and *From the Gracchi to Nero*, 4th ed. (London, 1976); and A. Kamm, *The Romans* (London, 1995). For a beautifully illustrated survey, see J. F. Drinkwater and A. Drummond, *The World of the Romans* (New York, 1993). A good collection of source materials in translation is contained in N. Lewis and M. Reinhold, eds., *Roman Civilization*, vol. 1 (New York, 1951). The history of early Rome is well covered in R. M. Ogilvie, *Early Rome and the Etruscans* (London, 1976). Good works on the Etruscans include M. Pallottino, *The Etruscans*, rev. ed. (Bloomington, Ind., 1975); and M. Grant, *The Etruscans* (New York, 1980).

A general work, heavily political, on Rome's impact on Italy is E. T. Salmon, *The Making of Roman Italy* (London, 1983). Other aspects of the impact of Roman expansion on Italy are examined in P. A. Brunt, *Italian Manpower* (Oxford, 1971).

Aspects of the Roman political structure can be studied in A. N. Sherwin-White, *The Roman Citizenship*, 2d ed. (Oxford, 1973). On Roman military practices, see F. Adcock, *The Roman Art of War under the Republic*, rev. ed. (Cambridge, Mass., 1963). Changes in Rome's economic life can be examined in K. Hopkins, *Conquerors and Slaves* (Cambridge, 1978); and J. H. D'Arms, *Commerce and Social Standing in Ancient Rome* (Cambridge, Mass., 1981). On the Roman social structure, see G. Alfoeldy, *The Social History of Rome* (London, 1985).

A general account of Rome's expansion in the Mediterranean world is provided by R. M. Errington, *The Dawn of Empire: Rome's Rise to World Power* (Ithaca, N.Y., 1971). The best work on Carthage is B. H. Warmington, *Carthage*, rev. ed. (London, 1969). On one aspect of Rome's struggle with Carthage, see the detailed study by J. Lazenby, *Hannibal's War: A Military History of the Second Punic War* (Warminster, 1978). Especially important works on Roman expansion and imperialism include W. V. Harris, *War and Imperialism in Republican Rome* (Oxford, 1979); and E. Badian, *Roman Imperialism in the Late Republic* (Oxford, 1968). On Roman expansion in the eastern Mediterranean, see the work by A. N. Sherwin-White, *Roman Foreign Policy in the Greek East* (London, 1984).

Roman religion can be examined in J. Liebeschuetz, *Continuity and Change in Roman Religion* (Oxford, 1979); and H. H. Scullard, *Festivals and Ceremonies of the Roman Republic* (Ithaca, N.Y., 1981). General studies of daily life in Rome include F. Dupont, *Daily Life in Ancient Rome* (Oxford, 1994); and J. Balsdon, *Life and Leisure in Ancient Rome* (New York, 1969). Roman women are examined in J. Balsdon, *Roman Women*, rev. ed., (London, 1974); S. Pomeroy, *Goddesses, Whores, Wives, and Slaves: Women in Classical Antiquity* (New York, 1976), pp. 149–89; J. F. Gardner, *Women in Roman Law and Society* (Bloomington, Ind., 1986); and S. Dixon, *The Roman Mother* (Norman, Okla., 1988). On various aspects of Roman law, see H. F. Jolowicz and B. Nicholas, *Historical Introduction to Roman Law* (Cambridge, 1972). On slavery and its consequences, see K. R. Bradley, *Slavery and Rebellion in the Roman World, 140 B.C.–70 B.C.* (Bloomington, Ind., 1989). For a brief and readable survey of Latin literature, see R. M. Ogilvie, *Roman Literature and Society* (Harmondsworth, 1980). There are good translations of Terence by B. Radice and Plautus by E. F. Watling in the Penguin Classics series. On Roman art and architecture, see A. Boethius, *Etruscan and Early Roman Architecture* (Harmondsworth, 1978); and G. Richter, *Ancient Italy* (Ann Arbor, 1955).

An excellent account of basic problems in the history of the late Republic can be found in M. Beard and M. H. Crawford, *Rome in the Late Republic* (London, 1985). The classic work on the fall of the Republic is R. Syme, *The Roman Revolution* (Oxford, 1960). A more recent work is E. S. Gruen, *The Last Generation of the Roman Republic* (Berkeley, 1974). Also valuable are P. A. Brunt, *Social Conflicts in the Roman Republic* (London, 1971); and C. Nicolet, *The World of the Citizen in Republican Rome* (London, 1980). Numerous biographies provide many details on the politics of the period. Especially worthwhile are A. H. Bernstein, *Tiberius Sempronius Gracchus: Tradition and Apostasy* (Ithaca, N.Y., 1978); D. Stockton, *The Gracchi* (Oxford, 1979); M. Gelzer, *Caesar: Politician and Statesman* (London, 1968); R. Seager, *Pompey: A Political Biography* (Berkeley, 1980); A. Ward, *Marcus Crassus and the Late Roman Republic* (Columbia, Mo., 1977); and D. Stockton, *Cicero: A Political Biography* (London, 1971).

CHAPTER

6

The Roman Empire

With the victories of Octavian, peace finally settled upon the Roman world. Although there would still be occasional civil conflict, the new imperial state constructed by Octavian experienced a period of remarkable stability for the next two hundred years. The Romans imposed their peace upon the largest empire established in antiquity. Indeed, Rome's writers proclaimed that "by heaven's will my Rome shall be capital of the world."[1] To the Romans, their divine mission was clearly to rule nations and peoples. Hadrian, one of the emperors of the second century A.D., was but one of many Roman rulers who believed in Rome's mission. He was a strong and intelligent ruler who took his responsibilities quite seriously. Between 121 and 132, he visited all of the provinces in the empire. According to his Roman biographer, Aelius Spartianus, "hardly any emperor ever traveled with such speed over so much territory." When he arrived in a province, Hadrian dealt firsthand with any problems and bestowed many favors on the local population. He also worked to establish the boundaries of the provinces and provide for their defense. New fortifications, such as the eighty-mile-long Hadrian's Wall across northern Britain, were built to defend the borders. Hadrian insisted on rigid discipline for frontier armies and demanded that the soldiers be kept in training, "just as if war were imminent." He also tried to lead by personal example; according to his biographer, he spent time with the troops and "cheerfully ate out of doors such camp food as bacon, cheese, and vinegar." Moreover, he "would walk as much as twenty miles fully armed."

By the third century A.D., however, Rome's ability to rule nations and people began to weaken as the Roman Empire began to experience renewed civil war, economic chaos, and invasions. Although order was reestablished by the end of the third and beginning of the fourth centuries, Rome's decline was halted only temporarily. In the meantime, the growth of Christianity, one of the remarkable success stories of Western civilization, led to the emergence of a vi-

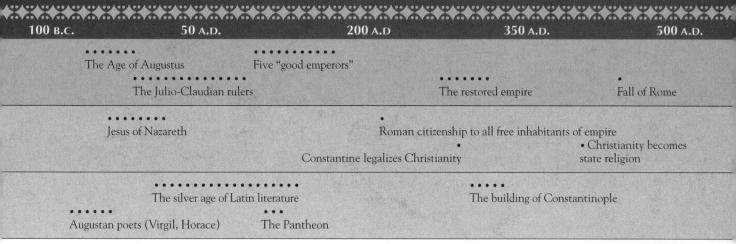

The Age of Augustus — Five "good emperors"

The Julio-Claudian rulers — The restored empire — Fall of Rome

Jesus of Nazareth — Roman citizenship to all free inhabitants of empire

Constantine legalizes Christianity — Christianity becomes state religion

The silver age of Latin literature — The building of Constantinople

Augustan poets (Virgil, Horace) — The Pantheon

brant and powerful institution that picked up the pieces left by Rome's collapse and provided the civilizing core for a new medieval civilization.

The Age of Augustus (31 B.C.–A.D. 14)

In 27 B.C., Octavian proclaimed the "restoration of the Republic." He understood the need to appease the senatorial ruling class and realized from the experience of Julius Caesar that he could not exercise power too openly. Only traditional republican forms would satisfy the senatorial aristocracy. At the same time, Octavian was aware that the Republic could not be fully restored and managed to arrive at a compromise that worked, at least during his lifetime. In 27 B.C., the senate awarded him the title of Augustus—"the revered one." He preferred the title *princeps,* meaning chief citizen or first among equals. The system of rule that Augustus established is sometimes called the principate, conveying the idea of a constitutional monarch as co-ruler with the senate. But while Augustus worked to maintain this appearance, in reality, power was heavily weighted in favor of the *princeps.* After the devastating political chaos of the late Republic, it should come as no surprise that the position of *princeps* eventually became that of an absolute monarch.

The New Constitutional Order

In the new constitutional order that Augustus created, the basic governmental structure consisted of a *princeps* (Augustus) and an aristocratic senate. Augustus retained the senate as the chief deliberative body of the Roman state. Its decrees, screened in advance by the *princeps,* now had the effect of law. The senate officially controlled disbursements from the public treasury and served as a high court of justice. Despite its powers, however, the senate was not a full and equal partner with the *princeps.*

The title of *princeps*—first citizen of the state—carried no power in itself. Nevertheless, while Augustus wished to avoid the appearance of absolute authority, he had no intention of giving up his control. Initially, the legal foundation for Augustus's power came from the office of consul, which he held each year beginning in 31 B.C.; this gave him *imperium* or the right to command (see Chapter 5). This lasted until 23 B.C., when Augustus gave up the consulship and was granted a greater proconsular or *maius imperium*—a greater *imperium* than all others. The consulship was now unnecessary. Moreover, very probably in 23 B.C., Augustus was accorded the *tribunicia potestas,* the power of a tribune, without actually holding the office itself. This power enabled him to propose laws and veto any item of public business. Periodically, he also assumed the power of *censor,* which permitted him to revise the citizenship lists and the roll of senators. In 12 B.C., Augustus was also elected *pontifex maximus* or chief pontiff, head of the official state religion. While officials continued to be elected, Augustus's authority ensured that his candidates for offices usually won. This situation caused participation in elections to decline. Consequently, the popular assemblies, shorn of any real role in elections and increasingly overshadowed by the senate's decrees, gradually declined in importance.

By observing proper legal forms for his power, Augustus proved to be highly popular. As the Roman historian

✦ **Augustus.** Octavian, Caesar's adopted son, emerged victorious from the civil conflict that rocked the Republic after Caesar's assassination. Augustus operated through a number of legal formalities to ensure that control of the Roman state rested firmly in his hands. This marble statue from Prima Porta depicts the *princeps* Augustus.

Tacitus commented, "Indeed, he attracted everybody's goodwill by the enjoyable gift of peace. . . . Opposition did not exist."[2] No doubt, the ending of the civil wars had greatly bolstered Augustus's popularity (see the box on p. 174). At the same time, his continuing control of the army, while making possible the Roman peace, was a crucial source of his power.

The Army

The peace of the Roman Empire depended on the army and so did the security of the *princeps*. While primarily responsible for guarding the frontiers of the empire, the army was also used to maintain domestic order within the provinces. Moreover, the army played an important social role. It was an agent of upward mobility for both officers and recruits and provided impetus for romanization wherever the legions were stationed. The colonies of veterans established by Augustus throughout the empire proved especially valuable in romanizing the provinces.

After the Battle of Actium in 31 B.C., Augustus reorganized the army. He maintained a standing army of twenty-eight legions. Since each legion at full strength numbered 5,400 soldiers, the Roman Empire had an army of about 150,000 men, certainly not large either by modern standards or in terms of the size of the empire itself (the population of the empire was probably close to 50 million). Roman legionaries served twenty years and were recruited only from the citizenry and, under Augustus, largely from Italy. Augustus also maintained a large contingent of auxiliary forces enlisted from the subject peoples. They served as both light-armed troops and cavalry and were commanded by Roman officers as well as tribal leaders. The German Arminius, who defeated the Romans in Germany in A.D. 9 (see Roman Provinces and Frontiers later in this chapter), had, in fact, once commanded a cohort of German tribesmen as Roman auxiliaries. During the reign of Augustus, the auxiliaries numbered around 130,000. They were recruited only from noncitizens, served for twenty-four years, and along with their families received citizenship after their terms of service.

Augustus was responsible for establishing the praetorian guard. Although nominally a military reserve, these "9 cohorts of elite troops," roughly 9,000 men, had the important task of guarding the person of the *princeps*. They were recruited from Roman citizens in Italy and served for sixteen years. Eventually, the praetorian guard would play an important role in making and deposing emperors.

The role of the *princeps* as military commander gave rise to a title by which this ruler eventually came to be known. When victorious, a military commander was acclaimed by his troops as *imperator*. Augustus was so acclaimed on a number of occasions. *Imperator* is our word *emperor*. Although such a title was applied to Augustus and his successors, Augustus still preferred to use the title *princeps*. Not until the reign of Vespasian

(69–79) did emperor become the common title for the Roman ruler.

Roman Provinces and Frontiers

During the Republic, as we have seen, the Romans had established control over a number of overseas possessions, which were called provinces. Two praetors were chosen in 227 B.C. to govern the first provinces of Sicily and Sardinia, and two more beginning in 197 for the two Spanish provinces. Eventually, a new system developed in which ex-consuls and ex-praetors had their *imperium* extended (as proconsuls and propraetors) and were then sent out as governors. Under the Republic, the senate supervised the allocation of the provinces.

Augustus inaugurated a new system for governing the provinces. Certain provinces were allotted to the *princeps*, who assigned deputies known as legates to govern them. These legates were from the senatorial class and held office as long as the emperor chose. The remaining provinces were designated as senatorial provinces. They continued to be ruled by proconsuls and propraetors as governors who were appointed annually by lot for one year and reported directly to the senate. Although a dual system of provincial administration seemed to have been created, in reality the greater proconsular *imperium* that had been granted to Augustus gave him the power to overrule the senatorial governors and hence to establish a unified imperial policy. Egypt was treated differently from the other provinces in that the emperor considered it a personal possession and governed it through an equestrian prefect. Because all provincial governors, whether of imperial or senatorial provinces, now received regular salaries, there was less need for the kind of extortion that had characterized provincial administration in the late Republic. In general, although there were still abuses, especially in the area of tax collection, provincial administration under Augustus was more efficient than under the Republic, and provincials were better protected against abuses of power.

Since a governor had relatively few administrative officials to assist him, effective government of the provinces necessitated considerable cooperation from local authorities. By supporting the power of local elites—the upper classes—in return for their cooperation, Roman policy encouraged a substantial degree of self-government and local autonomy in the cities. By fostering municipal life, Rome essentially made cities and city-states the basic units of imperial administration. City councils of leading citizens made for stable

♦ **The Praetorian Guard.** Augustus was responsible for setting up the Praetorian Guard as an imperial bodyguard of elite troops. Pictured in this second-century relief are five members of the Praetorian Guard.

local government, and leading city officials were rewarded for their administrative services with Roman citizenship.

Augustus's frontier policy was not wholly defensive as it is sometimes portrayed. He was not immune to the glories of military conquest and, in fact, added more territory to the Roman Empire than any other single Roman. He did, however, use diplomacy rather than force to retrieve the Roman battle standards seized by the Parthians when they destroyed a Roman force under Crassus in the first century B.C. Augustus also encouraged the establishment of client kingdoms in the east instead of creating new provinces. In effect, Augustus minimized the Roman military presence in the east so that he could use his forces elsewhere. After the final pacification of Spain in 19 B.C., the *princeps* expended his greatest military efforts along the northern frontiers of the Roman Empire. He conquered the central and maritime Alps and then expanded Roman control of the Balkan peninsula up to the Danube River.

The Achievements of Augustus

This excerpt is taken from a text written by Augustus and inscribed on a bronze tablet at Rome. Copies of the text were displayed in stone in many provincial capitals. Called "the most famous ancient inscription," the Res Gestae *of Augustus summarizes his accomplishments in three major areas: his offices, his private expenditures on behalf of the state, and his exploits in war and peace. While factual in approach, it is a highly subjective account.*

Augustus, *Res Gestae*

Below is a copy of the accomplishments of the deified Augustus by which he brought the whole world under the empire of the Roman people, and of the moneys expended by him on the state and the Roman people, as inscribed on two bronze pillars set up in Rome.

1. At the age of nineteen, on my own initiative and at my own expense, I raised an army by means of which I liberated the Republic, which was oppressed by the tyranny of a faction [Mark Antony and his supporters]. . . .

2. Those who assassinated my father [Julius Caesar, his adoptive father] I drove into exile, avenging their crime by due process of law; and afterwards when they waged war against the state, I conquered them twice on the battlefield.

3. I waged many wars throughout the whole world by land and by sea, both civil and foreign, and when victorious I spared all citizens who sought pardon. . . .

5. The dictatorship offered to me . . . by the people and the senate, both in my absence and in my presence, I refused to accept. . . .

9. The senate decreed that vows for my health should be offered up every fifth year by the consuls and priests. In fulfillment of these vows, games were often celebrated during my lifetime, sometimes by the four most distinguished colleges of priests, sometimes by the consuls. Moreover, the whole citizen body, with one accord, both individually and as members of municipalities, prayed continuously for my health at all the shrines. . . .

17. Four times I came to the assistance of the treasury with my own money, transferring to those in charge of the treasury 150,000,000 sesterces. And in the consulship of Marcus Lepidus and Lucius Arruntius I transferred out of my own patrimony 170,000,000 sesterces to the soldiers' bonus fund, which was established on my advice for the purpose of providing bonuses for soldiers who had completed twenty or more years of service. . . .

20. I repaired the Capitol and the theater of Pompey with enormous expenditures on both works, without having my name inscribed on them. I repaired the conduits of the aqueducts which were falling into ruin in many places because of age, and I doubled the capacity of the aqueduct called Marcia by admitting a new spring into its conduit. . . .

22. I gave a gladiatorial show three times in my own name, and five times in the names of my sons or grandsons; at these shows about 10,000 fought. . . .

25. I brought peace to the sea by suppressing the pirates. In that war I turned over to their masters for punishment nearly 30,000 slaves who had run away from their owners and taken up arms against the state. . . .

26. I extended the frontiers of all the provinces of the Roman people on whose boundaries were peoples not subject to our empire. . . .

27. I added Egypt to the empire of the Roman people. . . .

28. I established colonies of soldiers in Africa, Sicily, Macedonia, in both Spanish provinces in Achaea, Asia, Syria, Narbonese Gaul, and Pisidia. Italy, moreover, has twenty-eight colonies established by me, which in my lifetime have grown to be famous and populous. . . .

35. When I held my thirteenth consulship, the senate, the equestrian order, and the entire Roman people gave me the title of "father of the country" and decreed that this title should be inscribed in the vestibule of my house, in the Julian senate house, and in the Augustan Forum on the pedestal of the chariot which was set up in my honor by decree of the senate. At the time I wrote this document I was in my seventh-six year.

�֎ **Map 6.1** The Roman Empire from 14 to 117 (Augustus to Trajan).

The extension of Roman power to the Danube now opened the door for Augustus's major military project—expansion into Germany. After 15 B.C., Roman forces advanced across the Rhine and by 9 B.C. had reached the Elbe River in eastern Germany. By 6 A.D., plans were coordinated for another advance between the Elbe and the Danube. This time, however, the Romans encountered a series of difficulties, including the great catastrophe of 9 A.D. when three Roman legions under Varus were massacred in the Teutoburg Forest by a coalition of German tribes led by Arminius, a German tribal leader who had served in the Roman auxiliary forces and had even received Roman citizenship. Roman historians blamed Varus for the disaster: "He [Varus] entertained the notion that the Germans were a people who were

men only in voice and limbs. . . . With this purpose in mind, he entered the heart of Germany as though he were going among a people enjoying the blessings of peace. . . ."[3] The defeat severely dampened Augustus's enthusiasm for limitless expansion in central Europe. Thereafter, the Romans were content to use the Rhine as the frontier between the Roman province of Gaul and the German tribes to the east. In fact, Augustus's difficulties had convinced him that "the empire should not be extended beyond its present frontiers."[4] Although Augustus had not practiced what he later preached, his defeats in Germany taught him that Rome's power was not unlimited. They also left him devastated; for months he beat his head against a door, shouting "Varus, give me back my legions!"

Augustan Society

Roman society in the Early Empire was characterized by a system of social stratification, inherited from the Republic, in which Roman citizens were divided into three basic classes: the senatorial, equestrian, and lower classes. Although the differences between the classes were more precisely defined during the Early Empire, with each class having its own functions and opportunities, the system was not completely rigid. There were possibilities for mobility from one group to another.

Augustus had accepted the senatorial order as a ruling class for the empire. Senators filled the chief magistracies of the Roman government, held the most important military posts, and governed the provinces. An order of ranks was established by which a member of the senatorial order advanced from minor military and magisterial posts to the most important offices in the state. One needed to possess property worth 1,000,000 sesterces (an unskilled laborer in Rome received 3 sesterces a day; a Roman legionary 900 sesterces a year in pay) to belong to the senatorial order. When Augustus took charge, the senate had over a thousand members. Augustus revised the senatorial list and reduced its size to six hundred, but also added new men from wealthy families throughout Italy. Overall, Augustus was successful in winning the support of the senatorial class for his new order.

The equestrian order, which had played an important role in the conflicts of the first century B.C., was expanded under Augustus and given a share of power in the new imperial state. The equestrian order was open to all Roman citizens of good standing who possessed property valued at 400,000 sesterces. They, too, could now hold military and governmental offices, but the positions open to them were less important than those held by the senatorial order. Like the senators, the equestrians had an order of ranks by which they could proceed from lesser military appointments to administrative positions in the civil service, and finally to one of the chief prefectures, such as commander of the imperial guards, administrator of the grain supply of Rome, or governor of Egypt. At the end of his career, an equestrian might be rewarded by membership in the senatorial order.

Those citizens not of the senatorial or equestrian orders belonged to the lower classes, who obviously constituted the overwhelming majority of the free citizens. The diminution of the power of the Roman assemblies ended whatever political power they may have possessed earlier in the Republic. Many of these people were provided with free grain and public spectacles to keep them from creating disturbances. Nevertheless, by gaining wealth and serving as lower officers in the Roman legions, it was sometimes possible for them to advance to the equestrian order.

Augustus was very concerned about certain aspects of Rome's social health, especially the customs and traditions of the Roman state. One area of great concern was religion. Augustus believed that the civil strife of the first century B.C. had sapped the strength of public religion, which he considered the cornerstone of a strong state. Therefore, he restored traditional priesthoods that had fallen into disuse in the late Republic, rebuilt many ruined temples and shrines, and constructed new ones to honor the Roman gods. Moreover, he insisted upon the careful observance of traditional festivals.

Augustus also instituted a new religious cult that would serve to strengthen the empire. Since the Roman state was intimately tied to Roman religion, an imperial cult served as a unifying instrument for the Roman world. Augustus did not claim to be a god, but he did permit the construction of temples to his deified adoptive father, Julius Caesar. Augustus also permitted the building of temples to Augustus and Roma, the personification of the Roman state. The worship of Augustus and Roma became the foundation of the imperial cult. Its development was furthered when Augustus was acclaimed as a god upon his death.

Augustus's belief that Roman morals had been corrupted during the late Republic led him to initiate social legislation to arrest the decline. He thought that increased luxury had undermined traditional Roman frugality and simplicity and caused a decline in morals, evidenced by easy divorce, a falling birthrate among the upper classes, and lax behavior manifested in hedonistic parties and the love affairs of prominent Romans with fashionable women and elegant boys.

Through his new social legislation, Augustus hoped to restore respectability to the upper classes and reverse the declining birthrate as well. Sumptuary legislation limited expenditures for feasts. Other laws made adultery a criminal offense. In fact, Augustus's own beloved daughter Julia was exiled for adultery, a clear indication that Augustus was deadly serious about his attempt to control the sexual behavior of Rome's upper classes. The tax laws were revised to penalize bachelors, widowers, and married persons who had fewer than three children. The laws were enforced, but there is little evidence that they had much effect.

A Golden Age of Latin Literature

From a cultural point of view, the Augustan Age is closely tied to the late Republic. Some of the great literary talents matured during the final phases of the Republic. Traditionally, Roman aristocrats had attempted to gain prestige and enhance their own reputations by providing financial support for artists and poets. Augustus continued this tradition. He perceived the publicity value of literature and art and became the most important patron of the arts during his principate. The literary accomplishments of the Augustan Age were such that the period has been called the "golden age" of Latin literature.

The most distinguished poet of the Augustan Age was Virgil (70–19 B.C.). The son of a small landholder in northern Italy, he proved to be only the first of a series of literary figures in the Augustan Age who welcomed the rule of Augustus. Virgil's first poems were the *Eclogues*, a series of pastoral poems inspired by the Hellenistic poet, Theocritus of Cos (see Chapter 4). The pastoral images in these poems are a combination of natural observation and imaginary, idealized landscapes. His second major work, the *Georgics*, was a didactic poem on farming modeled after the Greek Hesiod's *Works and Days* (see Chapter 3). The *Georgics* showed Virgil's love of the country, but not without pointing out two other realities—the potential harshness of nature and the destruction wrought by humans, especially in wartime. Therefore, he also extolled Augustus for restoring peace and promised to write an even greater work in his honor. Both the *Eclogues* and *Georgics* used Greek models, but increasingly Virgil infused those models with a distinctly Latin spirit. His poetry sang of the beauties of Italy: "Add thereto all her illustrious cities and the labors wrought in her, all her towns piled high by men's hands on their sheer rocks, and her rivers that glide beneath immemorial walls" and "But neither those Median forests where earth is richest, nor fair Ganges and Hermus turbid with gold, may vie with the praise of Italy. . . . Here is perpetual spring and summer in months not her own."[5]

Virgil's masterpiece was the epic poem, the *Aeneid*, clearly meant to rival the work of Homer and fulfill the promise made to Augustus in the *Georgics*. An explicit connection is made between Troy and Rome. Aeneas, the son of Anchises of Troy, survives the destruction of Troy and eventually settles in Latium; hence, Roman civilization is linked to Greek history. The character of Aeneas is portrayed in terms that remind us of the ideal Roman—his virtues are duty, piety, and faithfulness.

Virgil's overall purpose was to show that Aeneas had fulfilled his mission to establish the Romans in Italy and thereby start Rome on its divine mission to rule the world:

> Let others fashion from bronze more lifelike, breathing
> images—
> For so they shall—and evoke living faces from marble;
> Others excel as orators, others track with their instruments
> The planets circling in heaven and predict when stars will
> appear.
> But, Romans, never forget that government is your
> medium!
> Be this your art:—to practice men in the habit of peace,
> Generosity to the conquered, and firmness against
> aggressors.[6]

As Virgil expressed it, ruling was Rome's gift.

Another prominent Augustan poet was Horace (65–8 B.C.), a friend of Virgil. Horace was the son of a freedman from southern Italy, whose land had been confiscated for being on the wrong side of the civil war. Like Virgil, however, Horace was later provided a farm for his livelihood. He was also close to Augustus and had a strong sense of identification with Italy.

Horace was a very sophisticated writer whose overriding concern seems to have been to point out to his contemporaries the "follies and vices of his age." In the *Satires*, a medley of poems on a variety of subjects, Horace is revealed as a detached observer of human weaknesses. He directed his attacks against movements, not living people, and took on such subjects as sexual immorality, greed, and job dissatisfaction ("How does it happen, Maecenas, that no man alone is content with his lot?"[7]). Horace mostly laughs at the weaknesses of humankind and calls for forbearance: "Supposing my friend has got liquored and wetted my couch . . . is he for such a lapse to be deemed less dear as a friend, or because when hungry he snatched up before me a chicken from my side of the dish?"[8] In his final work, the *Epistles*, Horace used another Greek form—the imaginary letter in verse—to provide a portrait of his friends and society and those things he held most dear: a simple life, good friends, and his beloved countryside.

Ovid (43 B.C.–A.D. 18) was the last of the great poets of the golden age. He came from a wealthy equestrian family and, contrary to his father's wishes, decided to pursue literary studies: "Often my father told me: 'Why this useless endeavor? Homer himself left nothing behind him of worldly wealth.' "[9] Ovid belonged to a privileged group of Roman youths who liked to ridicule

≷ Ovid and the Art of Love ≶

Ovid has been called the last great poet of the Augustan golden age of literature. One of his most famous works was The Art of Love, a guidebook for the seduction of women. Unfortunately for Ovid, the work appeared at a time when Augustus was anxious to improve the morals of the Roman upper class. Augustus considered the poem offensive, and Ovid soon found himself in exile.

Ovid, The Art of Love

Now I'll teach you how to captivate and hold the woman of your choice. This is the most important part of all my lessons. Lovers of every land, lend an attentive ear to my discourse; let goodwill warm your hearts, for I am going to fulfill the promises I made you.

First of all, be quite sure that there isn't a woman who cannot be won, and make up your mind that you will win her. Only you must prepare the ground. Sooner would the birds cease their song in the springtime, or the grasshopper be silent in the summer. . . . than a woman resist the tender wooing of a youthful lover. . . .

Now the first thing you have to do is to get on good terms with the fair one's maid. She can make things easy for you. Find out whether she is fully in her mistress's confidence, and if she knows all about her secret dissipations. Leave no stone unturned to win her over. Once you have her on your side, the rest is easy. . . .

In the first place, it's best to send her a letter, just to pave the way. In it you should tell her how you dote on her; pay her pretty compliments and say all the

nice things lovers always say. . . . Even the gods are moved by the voice of entreaty. And promise, promise, promise. Promises will cost you nothing. Everyone's a millionaire where promises are concerned. . . .

If she refuses your letter and sends it back unread, don't give up; hope for the best and try again. . . .

Don't let your hair stick up in tufts on your head; see that your hair and your beard are decently trimmed. See also that your nails are clean and nicely filed; don't have any hair growing out of your nostrils; take care that your breath is sweet, and don't go about reeking like a billy-goat. All other toilet refinements leave to the women or to perverts. . . .

When you find yourself at a feast where the wine is flowing freely, and where a woman shares the same couch with you, pray to that god whose mysteries are celebrated during the night, that the wine may not overcloud your brain. 'Tis then you may easily hold converse with your mistress in hidden words whereof she will easily divine the meaning. . . .

By subtle flatteries you may be able to steal into her heart, even as the river insensibly overflows the banks which fringe it. Never cease to sing the praises of her face, her hair, her taper fingers and her dainty foot. . . .

Tears too, are a mighty useful resource in the matter of love. They would melt a diamond. Make a point, therefore, of letting your mistress see your face all wet with tears. Howbeit, if you can't manage to squeeze out any tears—and they won't always flow just when you want them to—put your finger in your eyes.

old Roman values. In keeping with the spirit of this group, Ovid wrote a frivolous series of love poems known as the *Amores*. Intended to entertain and shock, they achieved their goal. Ovid's most popular work was the *Metamorphoses*, a series of fifteen complex mythological tales involving transformations of shapes, such as the change of chaos into order. A storehouse of mythological information, the *Metamorphoses* inspired many Western painters, sculptors, and writers, including Shakespeare.

Another of Ovid's works was *The Art of Love*. This was essentially a takeoff on didactic poems. Whereas authors of earlier didactic poems had written guides to farming, hunting, or some such subject, Ovid's work was a handbook on the seduction of women (see the box

above). *The Art of Love* appeared to applaud the loose sexual morals of the Roman upper classes at a time when Augustus was trying to clean up the sexual scene in upper-class Rome. The *princeps* was not pleased. Ovid chose to ignore the wishes of Augustus and paid a price for it. In A.D. 8, he was implicated in a sexual scandal, possibly involving the emperor's daughter Julia. He was banished to a small town on the coast of the Black Sea. Despite appeals, he was never permitted to return to Rome and died in exile.

The most famous Latin prose work of the golden age was written by the historian Livy (59 B.C.–A.D. 17). Livy's masterpiece was the *History of Rome* from the foundation of the city to 9 B.C., written in 142 books. Only 35 of the books have survived, although we do possess brief summaries of the whole work from other authors. Livy was born in northern Italy but also came to live in Rome. He was not involved in public affairs and, though not patronized like Virgil and Horace, did become close to the family of Augustus.

Livy perceived history in terms of moral lessons. He stated in the preface that

> The study of history is the best medicine for a sick mind; for in history you have a record of the infinite variety of human experience plainly set out for all to see; and in that record you can find for yourself and your country both examples and warnings: fine things to take as models, base things, rotten through and through, to avoid.[10]

For Livy, human character was the determining factor in history.

Livy's history celebrated Rome's greatness. He built scene upon scene that not only revealed the character of the chief figures but also demonstrated the virtues that had made Rome great. Of course, he had serious weaknesses as a historian. He was not always concerned about the factual accuracy of his myriad stories and was not overly critical of his sources. But he did tell a good story, and his work remained the standard history of Rome for a long time.

The Augustan Age was a lengthy one. Augustus died in A.D. 14 after dominating the Roman world for forty-five years. He had created a new order while placating the old by restoring and maintaining traditional values, a fitting combination for a leader whose favorite maxim was "make haste slowly." By the time of his death, his new order was so well established that few agitated for an alternative. Indeed, as the Roman historian Tacitus pointed out, "Actium had been won before the younger men were born. Even most of the older generation had come into a world of civil wars. Practically no one had ever seen truly Republican government.... Political equality was a thing of the past; all eyes watched for imperial commands."[11] The Republic was now only a memory and, given its last century of warfare, an unpleasant one at that. The new order was here to stay.

The Early Empire (14–180)

There was no serious opposition to Augustus's choice of his stepson Tiberius as his successor. Although Tiberius was not Augustus's first choice, he had managed to outlive the other relatives whom Augustus would have preferred. The designation of a family member as prin-

CHRONOLOGY

Rulers of the Early Empire

Augustus	31 B.C.–A.D. 14
Julio-Claudian dynasty	
Tiberius	14–37
Caligula	37–41
Claudius	41–54
Nero	54–68
Flavian dynasty	
Vespasian	69–79
Titus	79–81
Domitian	81–96
Five good emperors	
Nerva	96–98
Trajan	98–117
Hadrian	117–138
Antoninus Pius	138–161
Marcus Aurelius	161–180

ceps was tantamount to accepting the principle of dynastic rule, hardly appropriate to the image Augustus had tried to cultivate of the princeps as only the "first citizen of the state." By his actions, Augustus established the Julio-Claudian dynasty; the next four rulers were related either to his own family or to that of his wife Livia.

The Julio-Claudians (14–68) and Flavians (69–96)

The Julio-Claudian rulers varied greatly in ability. Tiberius (14–37) was a competent general and able administrator who tried initially to involve the senate in government. Caligula (37–41) was a grandnephew of Tiberius and great-grandson of Augustus. He exhibited tyrannical behavior and was excessively erratic, probably due to mental instability. Claudius (41–54) had been mistreated by his family because of a physical disability due to partial paralysis, but he was intelligent, well educated, and proved to be a competent administrator. He was followed by Nero (54–68), who was only sixteen when he came to power. Nero's interest in the arts caused him to neglect affairs of state, especially the military, and proved to be his undoing.

The Fate of Cremona in the Year of the Four Emperors

After the death of Nero in A.D. 68, a power struggle ensued that resulted in a year of confusion with four different emperors, each the leader of a field army. Galba replaced Nero and was succeeded, in turn, by Otho who was then defeated by Vitellius. Finally, Vespasian established a new dynasty. Some of the Italian cities suffered greatly in these struggles between Roman legions loyal to their commanders. This excerpt is from Tacitus's account of the destruction of Cremona by the forces that had declared for Vespasian.

Tacitus, *The Histories*

Forty thousand armed men forced their way into the city. . . . Neither rank nor years saved the victims from an indiscriminate orgy in which rape alternated with murder and murder with rape. Graybeards and frail old women, who had no value as loot, were dragged off to raise a laugh. But any full-grown girl or good-looking lad who crossed their path was pulled this way and that in a violent tug-of-war between the would-be captors, and finally drove them to destroy each other. A single looter trailing a hoard of money or temple-offerings of massive gold was often cut to pieces by others who were stronger. Some few turned up their noses at the obvious finds and inflicted flogging and torture on the owners in order to rummage after hidden valuables and dig for buried treasure. In their hands they held firebrands, which, once they had got their spoil away, they wantonly flung into the empty houses and rifled temples. It is not surprising that, in an army of varied tongues and conventions, including Romans, allies and foreigners [auxiliaries], there was a diversity of wild desires, differing conceptions of what was lawful, and nothing barred. Cremona lasted them four days. While all its buildings, sacred and secular, collapsed in flames, only the temple of Melitis [goddess of pestilential vapors] outside the walls remained standing, defended by its position or the power of the divinity.

Several major tendencies emerged during the reigns of the four Julio-Claudians. In general, more and more of the responsibilities that Augustus had given to the senate tended to be taken over by the emperors. It is interesting to observe that both Tiberius and Claudius initially encouraged senators to act more independently but wound up undermining the senate's authority in the long run. Moreover, an imperial bureaucracy was instituted under Claudius. He rationalized the central government by developing bureaucratic departments with talented freedmen as their chiefs. This practice further undermined the authority of the senators since they had previously shared in these responsibilities.

As the Julio-Claudian successors of Augustus began to behave openly like real rulers rather than "first citizens of the state," the opportunity for arbitrary and corrupt acts increased. Caligula, who was mentally unbalanced after an illness, wanted to be hailed as a god and neglected affairs of state while indulging his passions. Nero freely eliminated people he wanted out of the way, including his own mother, whom he had murdered. Without troops, the senators proved unable to oppose these excesses. Only the praetorian guard established by Augustus seemed capable of interfering with these rulers, but did so in a manner that did not bode well for future stability. Caligula proved so capricious that the officers of the praetorian guard hatched a plot and assassinated him before he had ruled for four complete years. Afterward, they chose Claudius, uncle of Caligula, as the next emperor and forced the senate to confirm their act, thereby demonstrating the power of the military units stationed around Rome.

The downfall of the Julio-Claudian dynasty came during the reign of Nero. His early reign had been quite successful. He worked hard and, with the assistance of his childhood tutor, the philosopher Seneca, gave the empire a sound government. But Nero soon tired of his duties and began to pursue other interests, including singing, acting, horse racing, and sexual activities. After Seneca resigned his position in disgust in 62, Nero's rule deteriorated. His obsession for singing and acting in public was greeted with contempt by the senatorial class. At the same time, he aroused animosity by executing a number of prominent figures, including a popular general, on a charge of treason. His actions finally led to a conspiracy, not by the praetorian guard, but by the Roman legions themselves. In 68, Galba, governor of one of the Spanish provinces, rose in revolt and secured the principate for himself. Nero, abandoned by his guards, chose to commit suicide by stabbing himself in the throat after uttering his final words, "What an artist the world is losing in me."

But Galba was not readily accepted by the other provincial armies. The result was a civil war in 69, known as the year of the four emperors (see the box on p. 180). Finally Vespasian, commander of the legions in the east, established himself as sole ruler and his family as a new dynasty known as the Flavians. The significance of the year 69 was summed up precisely by Tacitus when he stated that "a well-hidden secret of the principate had been revealed: it was possible, it seemed, for an emperor to be chosen outside Rome"[12]—chosen, of course, by members of the Roman army.

The accession of Vespasian to the imperial power demonstrated that it was no longer necessary to be descended from an ancient aristocratic family to be emperor. In fact, Vespasian (69–79) was from the equestrian order. Once in control, he managed to reestablish the economy on a sound basis after the extravagances of Nero and the destruction wrought by the civil wars of 69. More importantly, Vespasian had no compunctions whatever about establishing the principle of dynastic succession for the principate. He was followed by his sons Titus (79–81) and Domitian (81–96). The Flavians, especially Domitian, dropped the pretense of the word *princeps* and began to use the title of *imperator*, emperor, freely. While the emperor was rapidly becoming an absolute monarch, the Flavian dynasty itself came to an abrupt end with the assassination of Domitian in 96.

The Five "Good Emperors" (96–180)

Many historians see the *Pax Romana* (the Roman peace) and the prosperity it engendered as the chief benefits of Roman rule during the first and second centuries A.D. These benefits were especially noticeable during the reigns of the five so-called good emperors. These rulers treated the ruling classes with respect, cooperated with the senate, ended arbitrary executions, maintained peace in the empire, and supported domestic policies generally beneficial to the empire. Though absolute monarchs, they were known for their tolerance and diplomacy.

The first of the five good emperors was Nerva (96–98), who was chosen by the senate after the assassination of Domitian. By chance, Nerva and his next three successors had no sons and had to resort to adoption to obtain heirs. As his successor, Nerva chose Trajan, a capable man who was also acceptable to the army, an increasingly important requirement. Trajan (98–117) had been born in Spain to an old Roman family and was the first emperor born outside Italy. Trajan was suc-

✦ **Trajan's Column.** Trajan was the first of the five good emperors to conduct wars of expansion. He established new Roman provinces in both the north and the east. Pictured here is Trajan's column, decorated with spiral reliefs depicting events from his military campaigns in Dacia (modern Romania).

ceeded by his second cousin Hadrian (117–138), who also came from a Roman family that had settled in Spain. Hadrian adopted as his successor Antoninus Pius (138–161), who achieved a reputation as the most beneficent of the five good emperors. Unlike Hadrian, who traveled extensively in the provinces, Antoninus Pius stayed in Rome and made even greater use of the senate. In turn, he adopted Marcus Aurelius (161–180), who has been viewed as a philosopher-king of the sort

◆ **The Emperor Hadrian.** The rule of the five good emperors brought a period of peace and prosperity to the Early Empire. All five treated the ruling classes with respect and implemented beneficial domestic policies. Hadrian was the third of the five good emperors.

The five good emperors extended the scope of imperial administration to areas previously untouched by the imperial government. Nerva introduced and Trajan implemented the institutions called *alimenta*. The alimentary program provided state funds to assist poor parents in raising and educating their children. The emperors were not motivated simply by benevolence since they believed that such assistance would materially aid in creating a larger pool of young men in Italy eligible for military service.

The five good emperors were widely praised by their subjects for their extensive building programs. Trajan and Hadrian were especially active in constructing public works—aqueducts, bridges, roads, and harbor facilities—throughout the provinces and in Rome. Trajan built a new forum in Rome to provide a setting for his celebrated victory column. Hadrian's Pantheon, a temple of "all the gods," is one of the grandest ancient buildings surviving in Rome.

The Roman Empire at Its Height: Frontiers and Provinces

At its height in the second century, the Roman Empire was the greatest state the world had seen, surpassing both the Persian Empire and the Hellenistic empire of Alexander the Great. It covered about 3.5 million square miles, and its population has been estimated at more than 50 million. While the emperors and the imperial administration provided a degree of unity, considerable leeway was given to local customs, and the privileges of Roman citizenship were extended to many people throughout the empire. In A.D. 212, the emperor Caracalla completed the process by giving Roman citizenship to every free inhabitant of the empire. Latin was the language of the western part of the empire while Greek was used in the east. Although Roman culture spread to all parts of the empire, there were limits to romanization since local languages persisted and many of the empire's residents spoke neither Latin nor Greek.

With the exception of Claudius's annexation of Britain, the first-century successors of Augustus had largely followed his advice to curb expansion and remain within the natural frontiers of the empire—the ocean to the west, the rivers in the north, and the desert in the east and south. Two areas prompted special concern. The Rhine-Danube frontier in the north became the most heavily fortified frontier area because of the threat from restless barbarian tribes. In the east, the Romans used a system of client states to serve as a buffer against the troublesome Parthians.

Plato envisioned (see Chapter 3). Marcus Aurelius was highly influenced by Stoicism and wrote his *Meditations*, reflecting the ideal of Stoic duty as a religious concept.

Under the five good emperors, the powers of the emperor continued to expand at the expense of the senate. Increasingly, imperial officials appointed and directed by the emperor took over the running of the government. An imperial civil service, staffed primarily by members of the equestrian order, had begun earlier during the reign of Claudius and now developed further, largely through the efforts of Hadrian. It was he who regularized the appointment of equestrians to the important secretaryships in the imperial bureaucracy.

Although Trajan broke with Augustus's policy of defensive imperialism by extending Roman rule into Dacia (modern Romania), Mesopotamia, and the Sinai peninsula, his conquests represent the high-water mark of Roman expansion. His successors recognized that the empire was overextended and pursued a policy of retrenchment. Hadrian withdrew Roman forces from much of Mesopotamia. Although he retained Dacia and Arabia, he went on the defensive in his frontier policy, reinforcing the fortifications along a line connecting the Rhine and Danube Rivers and building a defensive wall eighty miles long across northern Britain. By the reign of Marcus Aurelius, the vulnerability of the empire had become apparent. Frontiers were stabilized, and the Roman forces were established in permanent bases behind the frontiers. But when one frontier was attacked, troops had to be drawn from other frontiers, leaving them vulnerable to attack. The empire lacked a real strategic reserve, and in the next century its weakness would be ever more apparent.

The Roman army was the primary instrument for the defense of the Roman frontiers. In A.D. 14, it numbered twenty-five legions, but had increased to thirty by the time of Trajan. The auxiliaries were increased correspondingly, making a Roman army of about 400,000 by the end of the second century. Since legionaries had to be Roman citizens, most recruits in Augustus's time were from Italy. But in the course of the first century, the Italians' reluctance to serve in the military led to the recruitment of citizens from the provinces. By the time of Vespasian, 50 percent of the legionaries were non-Italian; by 100, only one in five was Italian. In the second century, more and more recruits came from the frontier provinces rather than from the more romanized ones.

In addition to defense and protection, the Roman army served two other important functions: it was an avenue for social mobility and an agent of romanization. Auxiliary units recruited noncitizens who became Roman citizens after being discharged. Moreover, an army career brought many rewards, especially for those who achieved the rank of centurion. Retired senior centurions, in particular, were viewed as high-ranking citizens upon return to their cities and often served in important municipal posts.

The army also served as an important instrument for romanizing the provinces. Roman military camps became centers for the spread of the Latin language and Roman institutions and ways of thought and conduct. The presence of large numbers of troops and their dependent women and slaves encouraged the development of trade and local production to meet the army's need for supplies. Urban centers developed around army bases or nearby colonies. Many cities along the Rhine had their roots in legionary bases or auxiliary forts. The city of Cologne, for example, grew out of the military colony the Romans called Colonia Agrippinensis.

The administration and cultural life of the Roman Empire depended greatly upon cities and towns. Cities were important to the administration of the empire. A provincial governor's staff was not large, so it was left to local city officials to act as Roman agents in carrying out many government functions, especially those related to taxes. Most towns and cities were not large by modern standards. The largest was Rome, but there were also some large cities in the east: Alexandria in Egypt numbered over 300,000 inhabitants, Ephesus in Asia Minor had 200,000, Antioch in Syria around 150,000. In the west, cities were usually small, with only a few thousand inhabitants. Cities were important in the spread of Roman culture, law, and the Latin language. They were also uniform in physical appearance with similar temples, markets, amphitheaters, and other public buildings.

Magistrates and town councillors chosen from the ranks of the wealthy upper classes directed municipal administration. These municipal offices were unsalaried, but were nevertheless desired by wealthy citizens since the offices conferred prestige and power at the local

◆ **A Rome in Africa.** While serving mostly as a defensive force in the first and second centuries A.D., the Roman army also helped to bring Roman culture and institutions to the provinces. Local production and trade grew up around the military camps to meet the soldiers' needs, and cities often developed from the bases themselves or from colonies located nearby. Pictured are the ruins of Timgad, a Roman city built by Trajan in A.D. 100. Although Timgad was located in the remote mountains of Algeria, it provided all the necessities for what Romans considered civilized urban life.

level as well as Roman citizenship. Roman municipal policy effectively tied the upper classes to Roman rule and ensured that these classes would maintain their control over the rest of the population.

The process of romanization in the provinces was reflected in significant changes in the governing classes of the empire. In the course of the first century, there was a noticeable decline in the number of senators from Italian families. By the end of the second century, Italian senators made up less than 50 percent of the total. Only one senatorial family, that of the Acilii Glabriones, went back to republican times. Increasingly, the Roman senate was being recruited from wealthy provincial equestrian families. The provinces also provided many of the equestrian officials for important administrative positions, as well as legionaries for the Roman army. And beginning with Trajan, the provinces also supplied many of the emperors.

Prosperity in the Early Empire

The Early Empire was a period of considerable prosperity. Internal peace and the use of a single currency throughout all the provinces resulted in unprecedented levels of trade. Merchants from all over the empire came to the chief Italian ports of Puteoli on the Bay of Naples and Ostia at the mouth of the Tiber. Trade, however, extended beyond the Roman boundaries and included even silk goods from China. Already in the first century, the balance of trade tilted heavily against the city of Rome and the western half of the empire. The importation of large quantities of grain to feed the populace of Rome and an incredible quantity of luxury items for the wealthy upper classes in the west led to a steady drain of gold and silver coins from Italy and the west to the eastern part of the empire.

Increased trade helped to stimulate manufacturing. The cities of the east still produced the items made in Hellenistic times (see Chapter 4). The first two centuries of the empire also witnessed the high point of industrial development in Italy. Some industries became concentrated in certain areas, such as bronze work in Capua and pottery in Arretium in Etruria. Other industries, such as brickmaking, were pursued in rural areas as by-products of large landed estates. Much industrial production remained small scale and was done by individual craftsmen, usually freedmen or slaves. In the course of the first century, Italian centers of industry experienced increasing competition from the provinces. Pottery produced in Gaul, for example, began to outsell Italian pottery from Arretium.

Despite the prosperity from trade and commerce, agriculture remained the chief occupation of most people and the underlying basis of Roman prosperity. While the large landed estates called *latifundia* still dominated agriculture, especially in southern and central Italy, small peasant farms persisted, particularly in Etruria and the Po valley. Although large estates concentrating on sheep and cattle raising used slave labor, the lands of some *latifundia* were worked by free tenant farmers called *coloni*. The *colonus* was essentially a sharecropper who paid rent in labor, produce, or sometimes cash.

In considering the prosperity of the Roman world, it is important to remember the enormous gulf between rich and poor underlying it (see the box on p. 186). The development of towns and cities, so important to the creation of any civilization, is based in large degree upon

◆ **The Shipping of Grain.** Trade was an important ingredient in the prosperity of the Early Empire. This tomb painting from Ostia, the port of Rome at the mouth of the Tiber, shows workers loading grain onto the *Isis Giminiana*, a small merchant ship, for shipment upriver to Rome. The captain of the ship stands by the rudder. Next to him is Abascantus, the ship's owner.

Map 6.2 Trade Routes and Products in the Roman Empire, c. 200.

the agricultural surpluses of the countryside. In ancient times, the margin of surplus produced by each farmer was relatively small. Therefore, the upper classes and urban populations had to be supported by the labor of a large number of agricultural producers who never found it easy to produce much more than enough for their own subsistence. In lean years, when there were no surpluses, the townspeople often took what they wanted, leaving little for the peasants.

Roman Culture and Society in the Early Empire

THE SILVER AGE OF LATIN LITERATURE

In the history of Latin literature, the century and a half after Augustus is often labeled the "silver age" to indicate that the literary efforts of the period, while good, were not equal to the high standards of the Augustan "golden age." The popularity of rhetorical training encouraged the use of clever and ornate literary expressions at the expense of original and meaningful content. A good example of this trend can be found in the works of Seneca.

Educated in Rome, Seneca (c. 4 B.C.–A.D. 65) became strongly attached to the philosophy of Stoicism (see Chapter 4). After serving as tutor to Nero, he and Burrus, prefect of the praetorian guard, helped to run the government during the first five years of Nero's reign. Seneca began to withdraw from politics after Nero took a more active role in government. In 65, he was charged with involvement in a conspiracy against Nero and committed suicide at Nero's command.

Seneca was a prolific writer, producing nine tragedies, 124 philosophical letters, seven books of *Natural*

⇒ The Daily Life of an Upper-Class Roman ⇐

There was an enormous gulf between rich and poor in Roman society. The upper classes lived lives of great leisure and luxury in their villas and on their vast estates. Pliny the Younger (62?–113?) was an upper-class Roman who rose to the position of governor of Bithynia in Asia Minor. In this excerpt from one of his letters, Pliny describes a typical day vacationing at one of his Italian villas. Although Pliny owned four villas in Italy, we should note that he did not belong to the ranks of the really rich in Roman society.

Letter of Pliny to Fuscus Salinator

You want to know how I plan the summer days I spend in Tuscany. I wake when I like, usually about sunrise, often earlier but rarely later. My shutters stay closed, for in the stillness and darkness I feel myself surprisingly detached from any distractions and left to myself in freedom. . . . If I have anything on hand I work it out in my head, choosing and correcting the wording, and the amount I achieve depends on the ease or difficulty with which my thoughts can be marshaled and kept in my head. Then I call my secretary, the shutters are opened, and I dictate what I have put into shape; he goes out, is recalled, and again dismissed. Three or four hours after I first wake (but I don't keep to fixed times) I betake myself according to the weather either to the terrace or the covered arcade, work out the rest of my subject, and dictate it. I go for a drive, and spend the time in the same way as when walking or lying down; my powers of concentration do not flag and are in fact refreshed by the change. After a short sleep and another walk I read a Greek or Latin speech aloud and with emphasis, not so much for the sake of my voice as my digestion, though of course both are strengthened by this. Then I have another walk, am oiled, take exercise, and have a bath. If I am dining alone with my wife or with a few friends, a book is read aloud during the meal and afterward we listen to a comedy or some music; then I walk again with the members of my household, some of whom are educated. Thus the evening is prolonged with varied conversations, and even when the days are at their longest, comes to a satisfying end.

Sometimes I vary this routine, for, if I have spent a long time on my couch or taking a walk, after my siesta and reading I go out on horseback instead of a carriage so as to be quicker and take less time. Part of the day is given up to friends who visit me from neighboring towns and sometimes come to my aid with a welcome interruption when I am tired. Occasionally I go hunting, but not without my notebooks so that I shall have something to bring home even if I catch nothing. I also give some time to my tenants (they think it should be more) and the boorishness of their complaints gives fresh zest to our literary interests and the more civilized pursuits of town.

Questions, and a number of philosophical dialogues. In letters written to a young friend, he expressed the basic tenets of Stoicism: living according to nature, accepting events dispassionately as part of the divine plan, and a universal love for all humanity. Thus, "The first thing philosophy promises us is the feeling of fellowship, of belonging to mankind and being members of a community. . . . Philosophy calls for simple living, not for doing penance, and the simple way of life need not be a crude one."[13] Viewed in retrospect, Seneca displays some glaring inconsistencies. While preaching the virtues of simplicity, he amassed a fortune and was ruthless at times in protecting it. His letters show humanity, benevolence, and fortitude, but his sentiments are often undermined by an attempt to be clever with words.

The silver age also produced a work called the *Satyricon*, described by some literary historians as the first picaresque novel in Western literature. It was written by Petronius (?–A.D. 66), probably a former governor of Bithynia who had joined Nero's inner circle as "arbiter of taste": "to the blasé emperor smartness and elegance were restricted to what Petronius had approved."[14] The *Satyricon* is a humorous satire on the excesses of the Roman social scene. Basically, it is the story of a young man and his two male companions who engage in a series of madcap escapades and homosexual antics. The longest surviving episode contains a description of an elaborate and vulgar dinner party given by Trimalchio, a freedman who had become a millionaire through an inheritance from his former master. In Trimalchio, Petronius gave a hilarious, satirical portrait of Rome's new rich (see the box on p. 187).

The greatest historian of the silver age was Tacitus (c. 56–120). His main works included the *Annals* and *Histories*, which presented a narrative account of Roman history from the reign of Tiberius through the assassina-

❧ *Menu from a Roman Banquet* ❧

Wealthy Roman homes contained a formal dining room, scene of the dinner parties that were the chief feature of Roman social life. The banquet usually consisted of three courses: appetizers, main course, and dessert. As this menu from a cookbook by Apicius illustrates, each course included an enormous variety of exotic foods. Banquets lasted an entire evening and were accompanied by entertainment provided by acrobats, musicians, dancers, and even poets. Naturally, the diet of lower-class Romans was considerably simpler, consisting of the traditional staples of bread, olives, and grapes. Poorer Romans ate little meat.

A Sample Banquet Menu

Appetizers
Jellyfish and eggs
Sow's udders stuffed with salted sea urchins
Patina of brains cooked with milk and eggs
Boiled tree fungi with peppered fish-fat sauce
Sea urchins with spices, honey, oil and egg sauce

Main Course
Fallow deer roasted with onion sauce and rue
Jericho dates, raisins, oil, and honey
Boiled ostrich with sweet sauce
Turtle dove boiled in its feathers
Roast Parrot
Dormice stuffed with pork and pine kernels
Ham boiled with figs and bay leaves, rubbed with honey, baked in pastry crust
Flamingo boiled with dates

Dessert
Fricassee of roses with pastry
Stoned dates stuffed with nuts and pine kernels, fried in honey
Hot African sweet-wine cakes with honey

tion of Domitian (14–96). Tacitus believed that history had a moral purpose: "It seems to me a historian's foremost duty to ensure that merit is recorded, and to confront evil deeds and words with the fear of posterity's denunciations."[15] As a member of the senatorial class, Tacitus was disgusted with the abuses of power perpetrated by the emperors. Forced to be silent in the reign of Domitian, he was determined that the "evil deeds" of wicked men would not be forgotten. Many historians believe he went too far in projecting the evils of his own day back into his account of the past. Much of what he ascribes to Tiberius, for example, parallels what happened in the reign of Domitian. Tacitus's work *Germania* is especially important as a source of information about the early Germans. But it too is colored by his attempt to depict the Germans as free men and noble savages as a way of criticizing the supposedly degenerate Roman upper classes.

By the second century A.D., though still influenced by the familiar Greek models, Latin authors were increasingly imitating the great Latin writers of earlier ages. This was true of Tacitus who looked more to Livy and Sallust than to Thucydides and was also evident in the work of Juvenal, the best poet of the silver age.

Juvenal (c. 55–c. 128) wrote five books of *Satires* in which he pilloried the manners and vices of his generation. He attacked the affectations of Roman women, the abuse of slaves, the excesses of emperors, the eastern and Greek immigrants, his own poverty, and the inequities of Roman society. For example: "They demand that the teacher shall mould these tender minds, . . . 'See to it,' you're told, and when the school year's ended, you'll get as much as a jockey makes from a single race."[16] But Juvenal was not a reformer. Though he attacked many vices, he offered no basic critique of his society. He criticized the abuse of slaves, but he did not object to the system of slavery itself.

After Juvenal, Latin literature underwent a noticeable decline in both quantity and quality. Christian writers would revive it, but their concerns would be worlds removed from the Latin authors of the Early Empire.

ART IN THE EARLY EMPIRE

The Romans contributed little that was original to painting and sculpture. Much work was done by Greek artists and craftsmen who adhered to the Roman desire

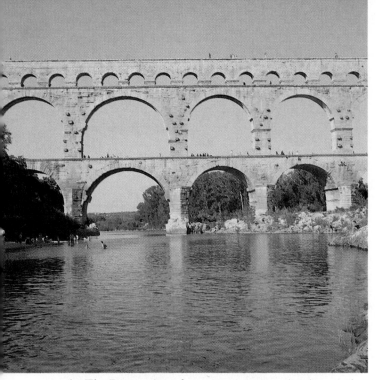

♦ **The Roman Aqueduct.** As engineers and architects, the Romans not only followed Greek models, but also made significant innovations, such as their extensive use of concrete and curvilinear forms. Their engineering skills enabled them to construct the massive Colosseum in Rome, the public baths built under Caracalla, approximately 50,000 miles of roads, and aqueducts, such as this one in southern France known as the Pont du Gard.

for realism and attention to details. Wall paintings and frescoes in the houses of the rich realistically depicted landscapes, portraits, and scenes from mythological stories.

In architecture, the Romans continued to utilize Greek styles and made use of colonnades, rectangular structures, and post and lintel construction. But the Romans were also innovative. They made considerable use of curvilinear forms: the arch, vault, and dome. The Romans were the first people in antiquity to use concrete on a massive scale. By combining concrete and curvilinear forms, they were able to construct massive buildings—public baths, such as those of Caracalla, and amphitheaters, the most famous of which was the Colosseum in Rome, built by the Flavian emperors and capable of seating 50,000 spectators. These large buildings were made possible by Roman engineering skills. These same skills were put to use in constructing roads (the Romans built a network of 50,000 miles of roads throughout their empire), aqueducts (in Rome, almost a dozen aqueducts kept a population of one million supplied with water), and bridges.

IMPERIAL ROME

At the center of the colossal Roman Empire was the ancient city of Rome. Truly a capital city, Rome had the largest population of any city in the empire. It is estimated that its population was close to one million by the time of Augustus and may have been even larger in the second century A.D. For anyone with ambitions, Rome was the place to be. A magnet to many people, Rome was extremely cosmopolitan. Nationalities from all over the empire resided there with entire sections inhabited by specific groups, such as Greeks and Syrians.

Rome was, no doubt, an overcrowded and noisy city. Because of the congestion, cart and wagon traffic was banned from the streets during the day. The noise from the resulting vehicular movement at night often made sleep difficult. Evening pedestrian travel was dangerous. Although Augustus had organized a police force, lone travelers might be assaulted, robbed, and soaked by filth thrown out of the upper-story windows of Rome's massive apartment buildings.

An enormous gulf existed between rich and poor in the city of Rome. While the rich had comfortable villas, the poor lived in apartment blocks called *insulae*, which might be six stories high. Constructed of concrete, they were often poorly built and not infrequently collapsed. The use of wooden beams in the floors and movable stoves, torches, candles, and lamps within the rooms for heat and light made the danger of fire a constant companion. Once started, fires were extremely difficult to put out. The famous conflagration of 64, which Nero was unjustly accused of starting, devastated a good part of the city. Besides the hazards of collapse and fire, living conditions were miserable. High rents forced entire families into one room. In the absence of plumbing and central heating, conditions were so uncomfortable that poorer Romans spent most of their time outdoors in the streets.

Fortunately for these people, Rome boasted public buildings unequaled anywhere in the empire. Its temples, fora, markets, baths, theaters, triumphal arches, governmental buildings, and amphitheaters gave parts of the city an appearance of grandeur and magnificence (see the box on p. 190).

Though the center of a great empire, Rome was also a great parasite. Beginning with Augustus, the emperors accepted responsibility for providing food for the urban populace, with about 200,000 people receiving free grain. Rome needed about six million sacks of grain a year and imported large quantities from its African and Egyptian provinces to meet these requirements. Even with the free grain, conditions were grim for the poor.

Early in the second century A.D., a Roman doctor claimed that rickets was common among the city's children.

In addition to food, entertainment was also provided on a grand scale for the inhabitants of Rome. The poet Juvenal said of the Roman masses: "But nowadays, with no vote to sell, their motto is 'Couldn't care less.' Time was when their vote elected generals, heads of state, commanders of legions: but now they've pulled in their horns, there's only two things that concern them: Bread and Circuses."[17] Public spectacles were provided by the emperor and other state officials as part of the great festivals—most of them religious in origin—celebrated by the state. More than one hundred days a year were given over to these public holidays. The festivals included three major types of entertainment. At the Circus Maximus, horse and chariot races attracted hundreds of thousands, while dramatic and other performances were held in theaters. But the most famous of all the public spectacles were the gladiatorial shows.

THE GLADIATORIAL SHOWS

The gladiatorial shows were an integral part of Roman society. They took place in amphitheaters, with the first permanent one having been constructed at Rome in 29 B.C. Perhaps the most famous was the Flavian amphitheater, called the Colosseum, constructed at Rome under Vespasian and his son Titus to seat 50,000 spectators. Amphitheaters were not limited to the city of Rome but were constructed throughout the empire. In Tunisia alone, which was only a part of the Roman province of Africa, there were more than twenty. They varied greatly in size with capacities ranging from a few thousand to tens of thousands. Considerable resources and ingenuity went into building them, especially in the arrangements for moving wild beasts efficiently into the arena. In most cities and towns, amphitheaters came to be the biggest buildings, rivaled only by the circuses for races and the public baths. As we shall see repeatedly in the course of Western civilization, where a society invests its money gives an idea of its priorities. Since the amphitheater was the primary location for the gladiatorial games, it is fair to say that public slaughter was an important part of Roman culture.

Gladiatorial games were held from dawn to dusk. Their main features were the contests to the death between trained fighters. Most gladiators were slaves or condemned criminals, although some free men lured by the hope of popularity and patronage by wealthy fans participated voluntarily. They were trained for combat in special gladiatorial schools.

Gladiatorial games included other forms of entertainment as well. Criminals of all ages and both sexes were sent into the arena without weapons to face certain death from wild animals who would tear them to pieces.

Map 6.3 Imperial Rome.

The Public Baths of the Roman Empire

The public baths in Rome and other cities played an important role in urban life. Introduced to Rome in the second century B.C. as a result of Greek influence, the number of public baths grew at a rapid pace in the Early Empire as the emperors contributed funds for their construction. The public baths were especially noisy near the end of the afternoon when Romans stopped in after work to use the baths before dinner. The following description is by Lucian, a traveling lecturer who lived in the second century and wrote satirical dialogues in Greek. This selection is take from Hippias, or the Bath.

Lucian, *Hippias, or the Bath*

The building suits the magnitude of the site, accords well with the accepted idea of such an establishment, and shows regard for the principles of lighting. The entrance is high, with a flight of broad steps of which the tread is greater than the pitch, to make them easy to ascend. On entering, one is received into a public hall of good size, with ample accommodations for servants and attendants. On the left are the lounging rooms, also of just the right sort for a bath, attractive, brightly lighted retreats. Then, besides them, a hall, larger than need be for the purposes of a bath, but necessary for the reception of richer persons. Next, capacious locker rooms to undress in, on each side, with a very high and brilliantly lighted hall between them, in which are three swimming pools of cold water; it is finished in Laconian marble, and has two statues of white marble in the ancient style. . . .

On leaving this hall, you come into another which is slightly warmed instead of meeting you at once with fierce heat; it is oblong, and has an apse on each side. Next to it, on the right, is a very bright hall, nicely fitted up for massage. . . . Then near this is another hall, the most beautiful in the world, in which one can stand or sit with comfort, linger without danger, and stroll about with profit. It also is radiant with Phrygian marble clear to the roof. Next comes the hot corridor, faced with Numidian marble. The hall beyond it is very beautiful, full of abundant light and aglow with color like that of purple hangings. It contains three hot tubs.

When you have bathed you need not go back through the same rooms, but can go directly to the cold room thorough a slightly warmed chamber. Everywhere there is copious illumination and full indoor daylight. . . . Why should I go on to tell you of the exercising floor and the cloak rooms? . . . Moreover, it is beautiful with all other marks of thoughtfulness—with two toilets, many exits, and two devices for telling time, a water clock that makes a bellowing sound and a sundial.

Numerous kinds of animal contests were also held: wild beasts against each other, such as bears against buffalo; staged hunts with men shooting safely from behind iron bars; and gladiators in the arena with bulls, tigers, and lions. Reportedly, five thousand beasts were killed in one day of games when the emperor Titus inaugurated the Colosseum in 80 A.D. Enormous resources were invested in capturing and shipping wild animals for slaughter, while whole species were hunted to extinction in parts of the empire.

These bloodthirsty spectacles were highly popular with the Roman people. The Roman historian Tacitus said, "Few indeed are to be found who talk of any other subjects in their homes, and whenever we enter a classroom, what else is the conversation of the youths."[18] But the gladiatorial games served a purpose beyond mere entertainment. The aristocratic statesman Pliny argued that the contests inspired a contempt for pain and death, since even slaves and criminals displayed a love of praise and desire for victory in the arena. More importantly, the gladiatorial games, as well as the other forms of public entertainment, fulfilled both a political and a social function. Certainly, the games served to divert the idle masses from any political unrest. It was said of the emperor Trajan that he understood that although the distribution of grain and money satisfied the individual, spectacles were necessary for the "contentment of the masses."

THE ART OF MEDICINE

Although early Romans had no professional physicians, they still possessed an art of medicine. Early Roman medicine was essentially herbal. The *paterfamilias* would prepare various remedies to heal wounds and cure illnesses. Knowledge of the healing properties of plants was passed down from generation to generation. This traditional herbal medicine continued to be used in the Early Empire. Of course, numerous recipes for nonillnesses, such as remedies to prevent baldness, were also passed on. One such formula consisted of wine, saffron, pepper, vinegar, *laserpicium* (the queen of Roman medicinal plants), and rat dung.

As in other areas of Roman life, Greek influence was also felt in medicine. At the end of the third century B.C., scientific medicine entered the Roman world through professional practitioners from the Hellenistic world. Doctors became fashionable in Rome, although prejudice against them was never completely abandoned. Many were Greek slaves who belonged to the households of large aristocratic families. The first public doctors in Rome were attached to the Roman army. Military practices were then extended to imperial officials and their families in the provinces and included the establishment of public hospitals. Gladiatorial schools had their own resident doctors as well. In fact, one of the most famous physicians, the Greek Galen (129–199), emerged from the ranks of gladiatorial doctors to become court physician to the emperor Marcus Aurelius. Roman scientific medicine also witnessed the development of numerous specialists. For example, Alcon, the famous surgeon of the Flavian age, specialized in bone diseases and hernia operations.

✦ **Interior of the Colosseum of Rome.** The Colosseum was a large amphitheater constructed under the emperor Vespasian and his son Titus. The amphitheaters in which the gladiatorial contests were held varied in size throughout the empire.

ROMAN LAW

The Early Empire experienced great progress in the study and codification of law. The second and early third centuries A.D. witnessed the "classical age of Roman

✦ **The Gladiatorial Games.** Although some gladiators were free men enticed by the possibility of rewards, most were condemned criminals, slaves, or prisoners of war who were trained in special schools. A great gladiator could win his freedom through the games. The more bizarre an event, the more popular it was with the spectators. The fresco pictured here shows a captured tribesman exposed to a wild beast while gladiators are fighting with animals.

law," a period in which a number of great jurists classified and compiled basic legal principles that have proved invaluable to the Western world. Ulpian (d. 228) was one of these jurists. Like others, he emphasized the emperor as the source of law: "What has pleased the emperor has the force of law."

In the "classical age of Roman law," the identification of the *ius gentium* (law of nations) with *ius naturale* (natural law) led to a concept of natural rights. According to the jurist Ulpian, natural rights implied that all men are born equal and should therefore be equal before the law. In practice, however, such a principle was not applied, particularly in the third and later centuries.

The Romans, however, did establish standards of justice, applicable to all people, that included principles that we would immediately recognize. A person was regarded as innocent until proven otherwise. People accused of wrongdoing were allowed to defend themselves before a judge. A judge, in turn, was expected to weigh evidence carefully before arriving at a decision. These principles lived on in Western civilization long after the fall of the Roman Empire.

SLAVES AND THEIR MASTERS

The number of slaves had increased dramatically in the Roman Republic as the empire was expanded through warfare. As a result of this increase, slaves were highly visible in the Early Empire. The households of the rich were filled with slaves. Possessing a large number of slaves was a status symbol; a single residence might include dozens of slaves, serving as hairdressers, footmen, messengers, accountants, secretaries, carpenters, plumbers, librarians, goldsmiths, and doctors as well as ordinary domestic servants. The reliance on slaves, especially as skilled craftsmen, undoubtedly created unemployment among the free population. Some slaves worked at high-status jobs as architects and managers of businesses, while some imperial slaves held positions in the government bureaucracy. Slaves were also used on landed estates.

But the number of slaves probably peaked in the Early Empire. The defensive imperial policies pursued after Augustus led to a decline in the supply of slaves from foreign conquest. Manumission also contributed to the decline in the number of slaves. It had been customary in Rome for "good masters" to free their slaves, especially well-educated ones or good workers. Although freedmen became Roman citizens, they were not given full rights of citizenship. They could vote but not run for office.

Many authors have commented on the supposed advance in humanitarian attitudes toward slaves in the Early Empire, especially in the second century. They argue that the philosophy of Stoicism, with its emphasis on the universality of humanity, had an influence in this direction. Certainly, Seneca stressed the need for kindness to slaves. Very likely, however, the practical Romans were as much, if not more, concerned about the usefulness of their slaves than about any humanitarian attitudes. New laws in the second century moralized more than they actually improved the condition of slaves. Hadrian, for example, forbade the sale of slaves for immoral or gladiatorial purposes. Such laws had little impact, however, on how masters actually treated their slaves. Despite the changes, there were still instances of slaves murdering their owners, and Romans continued to live in unspoken fear of their slaves (see the box on p. 193).

THE UPPER-CLASS ROMAN FAMILY

By the second century A.D., significant changes were occurring in the Roman family. The foundations of the authority of the *paterfamilias* over his family, which had already begun to weaken in the late Republic, were further undermined. The *paterfamilias* no longer had absolute authority over his children; he could no longer sell his children into slavery or have them put to death. Moreover, the husband's absolute authority over his wife also disappeared, a practice that had also begun in the late Republic with the shift to marriage *sine manu* ("without legal control") by which a married daughter remained within her father's legal power (see Chapter 5). In the Early Empire, the idea of male guardianship continued to weaken significantly. Augustus had exempted mothers of three children from guardianship, although he had done so to encourage more prolific marriages. In Hadrian's reign, a married woman no longer needed a guardian to draft her will. By the late second century, though guardianships had not been abolished, they had become a formality.

Upper-class Roman women in the Early Empire had considerable freedom and independence. They had acquired the right to own, inherit, and dispose of property. Upper-class women could attend races, the theater, and events in the amphitheater, although in the latter two places they were forced to sit in separate female sections. Moreover, ladies of rank were still accompanied by maids and companions when they went out. Some women operated businesses, such as shipping firms. Women still could not participate in politics, but the

The Roman Fear of Slaves

The lowest stratum of the Roman population consisted of slaves. They were used extensively in households, and the court, as craftsmen in industrial enterprises, as business managers, and in numerous other ways. Although some historians have argued that slaves were treated more humanely during the Early Empire, these selections by the Roman historian Tacitus and the Roman statesman Pliny indicate that slaves still rebelled against their masters because of mistreatment. Many masters continued to live in fear of their slaves as witnessed by the saying, "As many enemies as you have slaves."

Tacitus, *The Annals of Imperial Rome*

Soon afterward the City Prefect, Lucius Pedanius Secundus, was murdered by one of his slaves [A.D. 61]. Either Pedanius had refused to free the murderer after agreeing to a price, or the slave, in a homosexual infatuation, found competition from his master intolerable. After the murder, ancient custom required that every slave residing under the same roof must be executed. But a crowd gathered, eager to save so many innocent lives; and rioting began. The senate-house was besieged. Inside, there was feeling against excessive severity, but the majority opposed any change. Among the latter was Gaius Cassius Longinus, who when his turn came spoke as follows. . . .

'An ex-consul has been deliberately murdered by a slave in his own home. None of his fellow-slaves prevented or betrayed the murderer, though the senatorial decree threatening the whole household with execution still stands. Exempt them from the penalty if you like. But then, if the City Prefect was not important enough to be immune, who will be? Who will have enough slaves to protect him if Pedanius's four hundred were too few? Who can rely on his household's help if even fear for their own lives does not make them shield us?' [The sentence of death was carried out.]

Pliny the Younger to Acilius

This horrible affair demands more publicity than a letter—Larcius Macedo, a senator and ex-praetor, has fallen a victim to his own slaves. Admittedly he was a cruel and overbearing master, too ready to forget that his father had been a slave, or perhaps too keenly conscious of it. He was taking a bath in his house at Formiae when suddenly he found himself surrounded; one slave seized him by the throat while the others struck his face and hit him in the chest and stomach and—shocking to say—in his private parts. When they thought he was dead they threw him on to the hot pavement, to make sure he was not still alive. Whether unconscious or feigning to be so, he lay there motionless, thus making them believe that he was quite dead. Only then was he carried out, as if he had fainted with the heat, and received by his slaves who had remained faithful, while his concubines ran up, screaming fanatically. Roused by their cries and revived by the cooler air he opened his eyes and made some movement to show that he was alive, it being now safe to do so. The guilty slaves fled, but most of them have been arrested and a search is being made for the others. Macedo was brought back to life with difficulty, but only for a few days; at least he died with the satisfaction of having revenged himself, for he lived to see the same punishment meted out as for murder. There you see the dangers, outrages, and insults to which we are exposed. No master can feel safe because he is kind and considerate; for it is their brutality, not their reasoning capacity, which leads slaves to murder masters.

Early Empire saw a number of important women who influenced politics through their husbands, including Livia, the wife of Augustus, Agrippina, the mother of Nero, and Plotina, the wife of Trajan.

At the end of the first century and beginning of the second, there was a noticeable decline in the number of children among the upper classes, a trend that had already begun in the late Republic. Especially evident was an increase in childless marriages. Despite imperial laws aimed at increasing the number of children, the low birthrate persisted. While infanticide continued to be practiced, upper-class Romans used both contraception and abortion to limit their families. There were numerous techniques for contraception. Though highly touted, amulets, magical formulas, and potions to induce temporary sterility proved ineffective, as did the rhythm method, since Roman medical writers believed that a woman was most fertile just when menstruation was ending. A more dependable practice involved the use of oils, ointments, and soft wool to obstruct the opening of the uterus. Contraceptive techniques for males were also advocated. An early version of a condom involved using the bladder of a goat, but it was prohibitively expensive. Although the medical sources do not mention it, the Romans may also have used the ubiquitous coitus interruptus. Abortion was practiced, either by the use of drugs or by surgical instruments. Ovid chastises Corinna: "Ah, women, why will you thrust and pierce with the instrument, and give dire poisons to your children yet unborn?"[19]

Religion in the Early Empire: The Rise of Christianity

The rise of Christianity marks a fundamental break with the dominant values of the Greco-Roman world. Christian views of God, human beings, and the world were quite different from those of the Greeks and Romans. Nevertheless, to understand the rise of Christianity, we must first examine both the religious environment of the Roman world and the Jewish background from which Christianity emerged.

The Religious World of the Roman Empire

Augustus had taken a number of steps to revive the Roman state religion, which had declined during the turmoil of the late Republic. The official state religion focused on the worship of a pantheon of Greco-Roman gods and goddesses, including Jupiter, Juno, Minerva, and Mars. Observance of proper ritual by state priests theoretically brought the Romans into proper relationship with the gods and guaranteed security, peace, and prosperity. The polytheistic Romans were extremely tolerant of other religions. The Romans allowed the worship of native gods and goddesses throughout their provinces and even adopted some of the local gods. Caligula, for example, approved the cult of the Egyptian Isis (see Chapter 4). In addition, the imperial cult of Roma and Augustus was developed to bolster support for the emperors. After Augustus, those dead emperors deified by the Roman senate were included in the official imperial cult.

In addition to the formal, official religion, the Romans had cults of household and rural spirits whose worship appealed especially to the common people. While giving the Romans a more immediate sense of spiritual contact than they found in the official religion, these cults too failed to satisfy many people. Consequently, some turned to astrology and occult practices to achieve greater understanding of the supernatural world.

The desire for a more emotional spiritual experience also led many people to the mystery religions of the Hellenistic east, which flooded into the western Roman world during the Early Empire. The mystery religions offered secret teachings that supposedly brought special benefits. They promised their followers advantages unavailable through Roman religion: an entry into a higher world of reality and the promise of a future life superior to the present one. They also featured elaborate rituals with deep emotional appeal. By participating in their ceremonies and performing their rites, an adherent could achieve communion with spiritual beings and undergo purification that opened the door to life after death.

Many mystery cults vied for the attention of the Roman world. While the cults of Cybele or the Great Mother and the Egyptian Isis and Serapis had many followers, perhaps the most important mystery cult was Mithraism. Mithras was the chief agent of Ahuramazda, the supreme god of light in Persian Zoroastrianism (see Chapter 2). In the Roman world, Mithra came to be identified with the sun god and was known by his Roman title of the Unconquered Sun. Mithraism had spread rapidly in Rome and the western provinces by the second century A.D. and was especially favored by soldiers who viewed Mithras as their patron deity. It was a religion for men only and featured an initiation ceremony in which devotees were baptized in the blood of a sacrificed bull. Mithraists paid homage to the sun on the first day of the week (Sunday), commemorated the sun's birthday around December 25, and celebrated ceremonial meals. All of these practices had parallels in Christianity.

The Jewish Background

Jesus of Nazareth was a Palestinian Jew who was condemned to death by Pontius Pilate, the procurator of the Roman province of Judaea, which embraced the lands of the old Jewish kingdom of Judah (see Chapter 2). Christianity emerged out of Judaism, and it is to the Jewish political-religious world that we must turn to find the beginnings of Christianity.

In Hellenistic times, the Jewish people had enjoyed considerable independence under their Seleucid rulers (see Chapter 4). Roman involvement with the Jews began in 63 B.C., and by A.D. 6, Judaea had been made a province and placed under the direction of a Roman procurator. But unrest continued, augmented by divisions among the Jews themselves. The Sadducees favored a rigid adherence to Hebrew law, rejected the possibility of personal immortality, and favored cooperation with the Romans. The Pharisees took a more liberal approach to Jewish law, believed in an afterlife, and wanted to liberate Judaea from Roman control. The Essenes were a Jewish sect that lived in a religious community near the Dead Sea. As revealed in the Dead Sea Scrolls, a collection of documents first discovered in 1947, the Essenes, like many other Jews, awaited a Messiah who would save Israel from oppression, usher in the kingdom of God, and establish a true paradise on earth. A fourth group, the Zealots, were militant extremists who advocated the violent overthrow of Roman rule. A Jewish revolt in A.D. 66 was crushed by the Romans four years later. The Jewish Temple in Jerusalem was destroyed, and Roman power once more stood supreme in Judaea.

The Rise of Christianity

In the midst of the confusion and conflict in Judaea, Jesus of Nazareth (c. 6 B.C.–A.D. 30) began his public preaching. Jesus grew up in Galilee, an important center of the militant Zealots. Jesus' message was basically simple. He reassured his fellow Jews that he did not plan to undermine their traditional religion: "Do not think that I have come to abolish the Law or the Prophets; I have not come to abolish them but to fulfill them."[20] According to Jesus, what was important was not strict adherence to the letter of the law and attention to rules and prohibitions, but the transformation of the inner person: "So in everything, do to others what you would have them do to you, for this sums up the Law and the Prophets."[21] God's command was a simple one: to love God and one another: "Love the Lord your God with all your heart and with all your soul and with all your mind and with all your strength. The second is this: Love your neighbor as yourself."[22] In the Sermon on the Mount (see the box on p. 196), Jesus presented the ethical concepts—humility, charity, and brotherly love—that would form the basis for the value system of medieval Western civilization. As we have seen, these were not the values of classical Greco-Roman civilization.

While some people welcomed Jesus as the Messiah who would save Israel from oppression and establish God's kingdom on earth, Jesus spoke of a heavenly kingdom, not an earthly one: "My kingdom is not of this world."[23] Consequently, he disappointed the radicals. At the same time, conservative religious leaders believed Jesus was undermining respect for traditional Jewish religion. To the Roman authorities of Palestine and their local allies, the Nazarene was a potential revolutionary who might transform Jewish expectations of a messianic kingdom into a revolt against Rome. Therefore, Jesus found himself denounced on many sides

◆ **Christ and His Apostles.** Pictured is a fresco from a Roman catacomb depicting Christ and the apostles. Under the leadership of individuals such as Paul of Tarsus, Christianity grew from a small sect within Judaism to a powerful religious force within the empire. Christianity eventually became the official state religion.

and was given over to the Roman authorities. The procurator Pontius Pilate ordered his crucifixion. But that did not solve the problem. A few loyal followers of Jesus spread the story that Jesus had overcome death and had been resurrected. He was then hailed as the "anointed one" or the Messiah who would return and usher in the kingdom of God on earth.

Christianity began, then, as a religious movement within Judaism and was viewed that way by Roman authorities for many decades. Although tradition holds that one of Christ's disciples, Peter, founded the Christian church at Rome, the most important figure in early Christianity after Christ was Paul of Tarsus (c. 5 – c. 67). Paul reached out to non-Jews and transformed Christianity from a Jewish sect into a broader religious movement.

Called the "second founder of Christianity," Paul was a Jewish Roman citizen who had been strongly influenced by Hellenistic Greek culture. He believed that the message of Christ should be preached not only to Jews but to Gentiles (non-Jews) as well. Paul was responsible for founding Christian communities throughout Asia Minor and along the shores of the Aegean.

It was Paul who provided a universal foundation for the spread of Christ's ideas. He taught that Christ was, in effect, a savior-God, the son of God, who had come

⇒ Christian Ideals: The Sermon on the Mount ⇐

Christianity was simply one of many religions competing for attention in the Roman Empire during the first and second centuries. The rise of Christianity marked a fundamental break with the value system of the upper-class elites who dominated the world of classical antiquity. As these excerpts from the Sermon on the Mount in the Gospel of Matthew illustrate, Christians emphasized humility, charity, brotherly love, and a belief in the inner being and a spiritual kingdom superior to this material world. These values and principles were not those of classical Greco-Roman civilization as exemplified in the words and deeds of its leaders.

The Gospel according to Matthew

Now when he saw the crowds, he went up on a mountainside and sat down. His disciples came to him, and he began to teach them saying:

Blessed are the poor in spirit: for theirs is the kingdom of heaven.

Blessed are those who mourn: for they will be comforted.

Blessed are the meek: for they will inherit the earth.

Blessed are those who hunger and thirst for righteousness: for they will be filled.

Blessed are the merciful: for they will be shown mercy.

Blessed are the pure in heart: for they will see God.

Blessed are the peacemakers: for they will be called sons of God.

Blessed are those who are persecuted because of righteousness for theirs is the kingdom of heaven. . . .

You have heard that it was said, 'Eye for eye, and tooth for tooth.' But I tell you, Do not resist an evil person. If someone strikes you on the right cheek, turn to him the other also. . . .

You have heard that it was said, 'Love your neighbor, and hate your enemy.' But I tell you, Love your enemies and pray for those who persecute you. . . .

Do not store up for yourselves treasures on earth, where moth and rust destroy, and where thieves break in and steal. But store up for yourselves treasures in heaven, where moth and rust do not destroy, and where thieves do not break in and steal. For where your treasure is, there you heart will be also. . . .

No one can serve two masters. Either he will hate the one and love the other, or he will be devoted to the one and despise the other. You cannot serve both God and Money.

Therefore I tell you, do not worry about your life, what you will eat or drink; or about your body, what you will wear. Is not life more important than food, and the body more important than clothes? Look at the birds of the air; they do not sow or reap to store away in barns, and yet your heavenly Father feeds them. Are you not much more valuable than they? . . . So do not worry, saying, What shall we eat? or What shall we drink? or What shall we wear? For the pagans run after all these things, and your heavenly Father knows that you need them. But seek first his kingdom and his righteousness, and all these things will be given to you as well.

to earth to save all humans who were basically sinners as a result of Adam's original sin of disobedience against God. By his death, Christ had atoned for the sins of all humans and made it possible for all men and women to experience a new beginning with the potential for individual salvation. By accepting Christ as their savior, they, too, could be saved.

At first, Christianity spread slowly. Although the teachings of early Christianity were mostly disseminated by the preaching of convinced Christians, written materials also appeared. Paul had written a series of letters or epistles outlining Christian beliefs for different Christian communities. Some of Christ's disciples may also have preserved some of the sayings of the master in writing and would have passed on personal memories that became the basis of the written gospels—the "good news" concerning Christ—which attempted to give a

record of Christ's life and teachings and formed the core of the New Testament. Although Jerusalem was the first center of Christianity, its destruction by the Romans in A.D. 70 left individual Christian churches with considerable independence. By 100, Christian churches had been established in most of the major cities of the east and in some places in the western part of the empire. Many early Christians came from the ranks of Hellenized Jews and the Greek-speaking populations of the east. But in the second and third centuries, an increasing number of followers came from Latin-speaking people. A Latin translation of the Greek New Testament that appeared soon after 200 aided this process.

Early Christian groups met in private homes in the evening to share a common meal called an *agape* or love feast and to celebrate what became known as the sacrament of the eucharist or Lord's Supper—the communal celebration of Christ's Last Supper:

> While they were eating, Jesus took bread, gave thanks and broke it, and gave it to the disciples, saying, Take and eat; this is my body. Then he took the cup, gave thanks, and offered it to them, saying, Drink from it, all of you. This is my blood of the covenant, which is poured out for many for the forgiveness of sins.[24]

Early Christian communities were loosely organized, with both men and women playing significant roles. Some women held important positions, often as preachers. Local churches were under the leadership of boards of elders (or presbyters), but by the beginning of the second century, officials known as bishops came to exercise considerable authority over the presbyters. These bishops based their superior position on apostolic succession—as the successors to Christ's original twelve apostles, they were living representatives of Christ's power. As Ignatius of Antioch wrote in 107, "it is clear that we must regard a bishop as the Lord Himself. . . . Your clergy . . . are attuned to their bishop like the strings of a harp, and the result is a hymn of praise to Jesus Christ from minds that are in unison."[25] Bishops were men, a clear indication that by the second century A.D., most Christian communities were following the views of Paul that Christian women should be subject to Christian men.

Although some of the fundamental values of Christianity differed markedly from those of the Greco-Roman world, the Romans initially did not pay much attention to the Christians, whom they regarded at first as simply another sect of Judaism. The structure of the Roman Empire itself aided the growth of Christianity. Christian missionaries, including some of Christ's original twelve disciples or apostles, used Roman roads to travel throughout the empire spreading their "good news."

As time passed, however, the Roman attitude toward Christianity began to change. As we have seen, the Romans were tolerant of other religions except when they threatened public order or public morals. Many Romans came to view Christians as harmful to the order of the Roman state. These views were often based on misperceptions. The practice of the Lord's Supper, for example, led to rumors that Christians practiced horrible crimes, such as the ritualistic murder of children. While we know these rumors are untrue, some Romans believed them and used them to incite people against the Christians during times of crisis. Moreover, because Christians held their meetings in secret and seemed to be connected to Christian groups in other areas, the government could view them as potentially dangerous to the state.

Some Romans felt that Christians were overly exclusive and hence harmful to the community and public order. The Christians did not recognize other gods and therefore abstained from public festivals honoring these deities. Finally, Christians refused to participate in the worship of the state gods and imperial cult. Since the Romans regarded these as important to the state, the Christians' refusal undermined the security of the state and hence constituted an act of treason, punishable by death. It was also proof of atheism (disbelief in the gods) and subject to punishment on those grounds. But to the Christians, who believed there was only one real God, the worship of state gods and the emperors was idolatry and would endanger their own salvation.

Roman persecution of Christians in the first and second centuries was never systematic, but only sporadic and local. Persecution began during the reign of Nero. After the fire that destroyed much of Rome, the emperor used the Christians as scapegoats, accusing them of arson and hatred of the human race and subjecting them to cruel deaths in Rome. In the second century, Christians were largely ignored as harmless.

By the end of the reigns of the five good emperors, Christians still represented a small minority, but one of considerable strength. That strength lay in their conviction of the rightness of their path, a conviction that had been reinforced by the willingness of the first Christians to become martyrs for their faith. As the empire disintegrated in the next three centuries, it would be the Christians who literally picked up the pieces and became the dominant force.

The Terrible Third Century

During the reign of Marcus Aurelius, the last of the five good emperors, a number of natural catastrophes struck Rome. Floods of the Tiber, famine, and plague brought back from the east by the army led to considerable loss of population and a shortage of military manpower. To many Romans, these natural disasters seemed to portend an ominous future for Rome. New problems arose soon after the death of Marcus Aurelius.

Unlike the first four good emperors, who chose capable successors by adopting competent men as their sons, Marcus Aurelius allowed his own son, Commodus (180–192), to become emperor. A cruel man, Commodus was a poor choice, and his assassination led to a brief renewal of civil war until Septimius Severus (193–211), who was born in North Africa and spoke Latin with an accent, used his legions to seize power. Septimius Severus's deathbed admonition to his sons "to pay the soldiers, and ignore everyone else" set the tone for the new dynasty he established. The Severan rulers (193–235) began to create a military monarchy. The army was expanded, soldiers' pay was increased, and military officers were appointed to important government positions.

Military monarchy was followed by military anarchy. For a period of almost fifty years, from 235 to 284, the Roman Empire was mired in the chaos of continual civil war, as contenders for the imperial throne found that bribing soldiers was the primary way to become emperor. In these almost fifty years, there were twenty-two emperors, only two of whom did not meet a violent death. At the same time, the empire was beset by a series of invasions, no doubt exacerbated by the civil wars. In the east, the Sassanid Persians made inroads into Roman territory. A fitting symbol of Rome's decline was the capture of the Roman emperor Valerian (253–260) by the Persians and his death in captivity, an event previously unheard of in Roman history. Germanic tribes also poured into the empire. The Goths overran the Balkans and moved into Greece and Asia Minor. The Franks advanced into Gaul and Spain. The Alemanni even invaded Italy. Moreover, a number of provinces were seized by military commanders who took advantage of the chaotic conditions. It was not until the reign of Aurelian (270–275) that most of the boundaries were restored. Although he abandoned the Danubian province of Dacia, he reconquered Gaul and reestablished order in the east and along the Danube. Grateful citizens hailed him as "restorer of the world."

Invasions, civil wars, and recurrence of the plague came close to causing an economic collapse of the Roman Empire in the third century. The population declined drastically, possibly by as much as one-third. There was a noticeable decline in trade and small industry. The manpower shortage created by the plague affected both military recruiting and the economy. Farm production deteriorated significantly. Fields were ravaged by barbarians, but even more often by the defending Roman armies. Many farmers complained that Roman commanders and their soldiers were confiscating produce and livestock. Provincial governors seemed powerless to stop these depredations, and some even joined in the extortion.

The monetary system began to show signs of collapse as a result of debased coinage and the onset of serious inflation. Gold coins disappeared from circulation and silver coins were diluted. The standard coin—the denarius—was now worth less than 50 percent of its first-century value. After further decline, it was replaced by new coins of even less value. Goods began to replace money as a medium of exchange.

Armies were needed more than ever, but financial strains made it difficult to enlist and pay the necessary soldiers. Whereas in the second century the Roman army had been recruited among the inhabitants of frontier provinces, by the mid-third century, the state had to rely on hiring barbarians to fight under Roman commanders. These soldiers had no understanding of Roman traditions and no real attachment to either the empire or the emperors.

The Restored Empire of the Fourth Century

In the course of the third century, the Roman Empire came near to collapse. At the end of the third and beginning of the fourth centuries, it gained a new lease on life through the efforts of two strong emperors, Diocletian and Constantine, who restored order and stability. This restoration, however, was largely accomplished at the expense of freedom. The Roman Empire was virtually transformed into a new state: the so-called Late Empire, which included a new governmental structure, a rigid economic and social system, and a new state religion—Christianity.

Diocletian and Constantine: Political and Military Reforms

The emperor Diocletian (284–305) created a new administrative system for a restructured empire. The number of provinces was increased to more than one hundred by creating smaller districts superintended by more officials. In turn, the provinces were grouped into twelve dioceses, each headed by an official called a vicar. The twelve dioceses were grouped into four prefectures, each led by a praetorian prefect. The entire Roman Empire was divided into two parts: each part contained two prefectures and was ruled by an "Augustus." Diocletian ruled the east and Maximian, a strong military commander, the west. Each Augustus was assisted by a chief lieutenant or "vice-emperor" called a "Caesar," who theoretically would eventually succeed to the position of Augustus. This new system was called the tetrarchy (rule by four). Diocletian had obviously come to believe that one man was incapable of ruling such an enormous empire, especially in view of the barbarian invasions of the third century. Each of the four tetrarchs—two

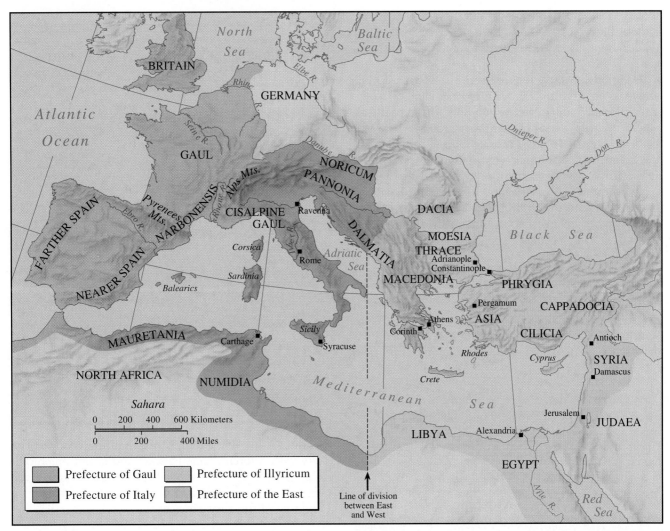

� **Map 6.4** Divisions of the Restored Roman Empire, c. 300.

Augusti and two Caesars—resided in a different administrative capital. Diocletian, for example, established his base at Nicomedia in Bithynia. Despite the appearance of four-man rule, however, it is important to note that Diocletian's military seniority enabled him to claim a higher status and hold the ultimate authority.

Diocletian's system failed to work very well. Soon after his retirement, a new struggle for power ensued. The victory of Constantine (306–337) at the Milvian Bridge north of Rome in 312 led to his control of the entire west. Later, in 324, he managed to establish himself as the sole ruler.

Constantine continued and even expanded the autocratic policies of Diocletian. Under these two rulers, the Roman Empire was transformed into a system where the

emperor had far more personal power than did Augustus, Trajan, or any of the other emperors during the Pax Romana. The emperor, now clothed in jewel-bedecked robes of gold and blue, was seen as a divinely sanctioned monarch whose will was law. Government officials were humble servants required to kneel before the emperor and kiss his robe. The Roman senate was stripped of any power and became simply the city council for Rome.

Diocletian and Constantine greatly strengthened and enlarged the administrative bureaucracies of the Roman Empire. Henceforth, civil and military bureaucracies were sharply separated. Each contained a hierarchy of officials who exercised control at the various levels. The emperor presided over both hierarchies and served as the only link between them. New titles of nobility—

such as *illustres* ("illustrious ones") and *illustrissimi* ("most illustrious ones")—were instituted to dignify the holders of positions in the civil and military bureaucracies.

Additional military reforms were also instituted. The army was enlarged to 500,000 men, including barbarian units. Mobile units were established that could be quickly moved to support frontier troops where the borders were threatened. Although larger, the army was less competent, being made up of Germans and Yugoslavs with less training than the traditional legions.

Constantine was especially interested in building programs despite the strain they placed on the budget. Much of the construction took place in the provinces since Rome had become merely a symbolic capital. It was no longer an imperial administrative center since it was considered too far from the frontiers. Constantine's biggest project was the construction of a new capital city in the east on the site of the Greek city of Byzantium on the shores of the Bosporus. Eventually renamed Constantinople (modern Istanbul), it was developed for defensive reasons; it had an excellent strategic location.

◆ **The Emperor Constantine.** Constantine played an important role in restoring order and stability to the Roman Empire at the beginning of the fourth century. This marble head of Constantine, which is 8 feet, 6 inches high, was part of an enormous seated statue of the emperor in Rome. Constantine used these awe-inspiring statues throughout the empire to build support for imperial policies.

CHRONOLOGY

Chief Events and Rulers of the Late Empire

Commodus	180–192
Military monarchy (Severan dynasty)	193–235
Septimius Severus	193–211
Caracalla	211–217
Military anarchy	235–284
Decius	249–251
Valerian	253–260
Aurelian	270–275
Diocletian	284–305
Constantine	306–337
Edict of Milan	313
Julian	360–363
Valens	364–378
Theodosius "the Great"	378–395
Visigoths sack Rome	410
Vandals sack Rome	455
Odoacer deposes Romulus Augustulus	476

Calling it his "New Rome," Constantine endowed the city with a forum, large palaces, and a vast amphitheater. Constantinople would become the center of the Eastern Roman or Byzantine Empire (see Chapter 7) and one of the great cities of the world.

Diocletian and Constantine: Economic, Social, and Cultural Trends

The political and military reforms of Diocletian and Constantine greatly enlarged two institutions—the army and civil service—that drained most of the public funds. While more revenues were needed to pay for the army and bureaucracy, the population was not growing, so the tax base could not be expanded. Diocletian and Constantine devised new economic and social policies to deal with these financial burdens. Like their political policies, these economic and social policies were all based on coercion and loss of individual freedom (see the box on p. 201).

To fight inflation, in 301 Diocletian resorted to issuing an edict that established maximum wages and prices for the entire empire. It was applied mostly in the east, but despite severe penalties, like most wage and

≋ Compulsory Services in the Late Empire ≋

The political, economic, and social policies of the restored empire under Diocletian and Constantine were based on coercion. This is especially evident in the edicts that forced people to remain in their occupations or in the city magistracies. These excerpts are taken from the Theodosian Code of 438, a compilation of imperial edicts going back to the reign of Constantine. These examples illustrate the plight of city councillors, shipmasters, bakers, and peasants.

Decrees from the Theodosian Code

Since we have learned that the municipal councils are being left deserted by persons who, though subject to them through origin, are requesting military service for themselves through supplications [to the emperor] and are running away to the legions and the various government offices, we order all municipal councils to be advised that if they catch any persons in government service less than twenty years who have either fled from [the duties of] their origin or, rejecting nomination [to municipal office], have enrolled themselves in the military service, they shall drag such person back to the municipal councils.

If any shipmaster by birth becomes captain of a lighter, he shall nonetheless continue right along to remain in the same group in which his parents appear to have been.

No breadmaker or any of his descendants shall be allowed to pass from his service by the union of marriage with private person or with persons of the stage or with persons held bound by the profession of charioteer, even if the assent of all the breadmakers should agree to such action.

Any person whatsoever in whose possession a *colonus* [free tenant farmer] belonging to another is found not only shall restore the said *colonus* to his place of origin but shall also assume the capitation tax on him for the time [that he had him]. And as for *coloni* themselves, it will be proper for such as contemplate flight to be bound with chains to a servile status, so that by virtue of such condemnation to servitude they may be compelled to fulfill the duties that befit free men.

---

price controls, it was unenforceable and failed to work. The decline in circulation of coins led Diocletian to collect taxes and make government payments in produce. Constantine, however, managed to introduce a new gold coin—the solidus—and new silver coins that remained in circulation during his reign.

In the third century, the city councils, which had formed one of the most important administrative units of the empire, had begun to decline. Since the *curiales* (the city councillors) were forced to pay expenses out of their own pockets when the taxes they collected were insufficient, the wealthy no longer wanted to serve in these positions. Diocletian and Constantine responded by issuing edicts that forced the rich to continue in their posts as *curiales*, virtually making the positions hereditary. Some *curiales* realized that their fortunes would be wiped out and fled the cities to escape the clutches of the imperial bureaucracy. If caught, however, they were returned to their cities like runaway slaves and forced to resume their duties.

Coercion came to form the underlying basis for numerous occupations in the Late Roman Empire. To maintain the tax base and keep the empire going despite the shortage of manpower, the emperors issued edicts that forced people to remain in their designated vocations. Hence, basic jobs, such as bakers and shippers, became hereditary.

As the fortunes of the free tenant farmers—the *coloni*—continued to decline, they found themselves bound to the land as well. Large landowners took advantage of depressed agricultural conditions to enlarge their landed estates, which became the forerunners of the manors of the Middle Ages. Free tenant farmers, unable to survive, became dependent on these large estates, and the landlords, anxious to guarantee their supply of labor, gained government cooperation in attaching the *coloni* to their estates. By the time of Constantine, many of the formerly free tenant farmers were becoming a class of serfs, peasants bound to the land.

In addition to facing increased restrictions on their freedom, the lower classes were burdened with enormous taxes since the wealthiest classes in the Late Roman Empire were either exempt from paying taxes or evaded them by bribing the tax collectors. These tax pressures undermined lower-class support for the regime. A fifth-century writer reported that the Roman peasants welcomed the Visigothic invaders of southern Gaul as liberators since the enemy was more lenient to them than the tax collectors.

In general, the economic and social policies of Diocletian and Constantine were based on an unprecedented degree of control and coercion. Though temporarily successful, in the long run such authoritarian policies stifled the very vitality the Late Empire needed to revive its sagging fortunes.

The pagan culture of the Late Empire revealed a decline of vitality as well. The books that have survived are textbooks and manuals that were primarily summaries of past knowledge. There were no figures to compare with the writers of the golden and silver ages of Latin literature. Yet Latin literature did not die. Latin remained the language of the representatives of a Christian culture that was dynamically surging to the forefront of a decaying civilization.

The Growth of Christianity

The sporadic persecution of Christians by the Romans in the first and second centuries had done nothing to stop the growth of Christianity. It had, in fact, served to strengthen Christianity as an institution in the second and third centuries by causing it to shed the loose structure of the first century and move toward a more centralized organization of its various church communities. Crucial to this change was the emerging role of the bishops. While still chosen by the community, bishops began to assume more control, with the bishop serving as leader and the presbyters emerging as clergy subject to the bishop's authority. By the third century, bishops were nominated by the clergy, simply approved by the congregation, and then officially ordained into office. The Christian church was creating a well-defined hierarchical structure in which the bishops and clergy were salaried officers separate from the laity or regular church members.

Christianity grew slowly in the first century, took root in the second, and had spread widely by the third. Why was Christianity able to attract so many followers? Historians are not really sure, but have offered several answers to this question. Certainly, the Christian message had much to offer the Roman world. The promise of salvation, made possible by Christ's death and resurrection, had immense appeal in a world full of suffering and injustice. Christianity seemed to imbue life with a meaning and purpose beyond the simple material things of everyday reality. Secondly, Christianity was not entirely unfamiliar. It could be viewed as simply another eastern mystery religion, offering immortality as the result of the sacrificial death of a savior-god. At the same time, it offered advantages that the other mystery religions lacked. Christ had been a human figure, not a mythological one, such as Isis or Mithras. Moreover, Christianity had universal appeal. Unlike Mithraism, it was not restricted to men. Furthermore, it did not require a difficult or expensive initiation rite as other mystery religions did. Initiation was accomplished simply by baptism—a purification by water—by which one entered into a personal relationship with Christ. In addition, Christianity gave new meaning to life and offered what the Roman state religions could not—a personal relationship with God and a link to higher worlds.

Finally, Christianity fulfilled the human need to belong. Christians formed communities bound to one another in which people could express their love by helping each other and offering assistance to the poor, sick, widows, and orphans. Christianity satisfied the need to belong in a way that the huge, impersonal, and remote Roman Empire could never do.

Christianity proved attractive to all classes. The promise of eternal life was for all—rich, poor, aristocrats, slaves, men, and women. As Paul stated in his Epistle to the Colossians: "And [you] have put on the new self, which is being renewed in knowledge in the image of its Creator. Here there is no Greek nor Jew, circumcised or uncircumcised, barbarian, Scythian, slave or free, but Christ is all, and is in all."[26] Although it did not call for revolution or social upheaval, Christianity emphasized a sense of spiritual equality for all people.

As the Christian church became more organized, two emperors in the third century responded with more systematic persecutions. The emperor Decius (249–251) blamed the Christians for the disasters befalling the Roman Empire in the terrible third century: it was they who had failed to acknowledge the state gods and consequently brought on the gods' retribution against the Romans. Moreover, as the administrative organization of the church grew, Christianity appeared to Decius even more like a state within a state that was undermining the empire. Accordingly, he initiated the first systematic persecution of Christians. All citizens were required to appear before their local magistrates and offer sacrifices to the Roman gods. Christians, of course, refused to do so. Decius's scheme, however, failed to work. Local officials did not cooperate, and Decius's reign was also not that long. The last great persecution was by Diocletian at the beginning of the fourth century, but by then it was too late. Christianity had become too strong to be eradicated by force. Most pagans had come to accept the existence of Christianity.

In the fourth century, Christianity prospered as never before after Constantine became the first Christian emperor. Historians are unsure about when and how he was converted as well as his motives for doing so. According to the traditional story, before a crucial battle, he saw a vision of a Christian cross with the writing, "In this sign you will conquer." Having won the battle, the story goes, Constantine was convinced of the power of the Christian God. Although he was not baptized until the end of his life, in 313 he issued the famous Edict of Milan officially tolerating the existence of Christianity. After Constantine, the emperors were Christian with the exception of Julian (360–363) who tried briefly to restore the traditional Greco-Roman polytheistic religion. But he died in battle, and his reign was too short to make a difference. Under Theodosius "the Great" (378–395), Christianity was made the official religion of the Roman Empire. Once in control, Christian leaders used their influence and power to outlaw pagan religious practices. Christianity had triumphed.

The Fall of the Western Roman Empire

The restored empire of Diocletian and Constantine limped along for more than a century. After Constantine, the empire continued to divide into western and eastern parts. The west came under increasing pressure from invading barbarian forces. The major breakthrough into the Roman Empire came in the second half of the fourth century. Ferocious warriors from Asia, known as Huns, moved into eastern Europe and put pressure on the Germanic Visigoths who in turn moved south and west, crossed the Danube into Roman territory, and settled down as Roman allies. But the Visigoths soon revolted, and the Roman attempt to stop them at Adrianople in 378 led to a crushing defeat and the death of the emperor Valens (364–378).

Increasing numbers of barbarians now crossed the frontiers. In 410, the Visigoths under Alaric sacked Rome. Vandals poured into southern Spain and Africa, Visigoths into Spain and Gaul. The Vandals crossed into Italy from North Africa and sacked Rome in 455. Twenty-one years later, the western emperor Romulus Augustulus (475–476) was deposed, and a series of Germanic kingdoms replaced the Roman Empire in the west while an Eastern Roman Empire continued with its center at Constantinople.

The end of the Roman Empire has given rise to numerous theories that attempt to provide a single, all-encompassing reason for the "decline and fall of the Roman Empire." These include the following: Christianity's emphasis on a spiritual kingdom undermined Roman military virtues and patriotism; traditional Roman values declined as non-Italians gained prominence in the empire; lead poisoning through leaden water pipes and cups caused a mental decline; plague decimated the population; Rome failed to advance technologically because of slavery; and Rome was unable to achieve a workable political system. There may an element of truth in each of these theories, but each of them has also been challenged. History is an intricate web of relationships, causes, and effects. No single explanation will ever suffice to explain historical events. One thing is clear. Weakened by a shortage of manpower, the Roman army in the west was simply not able to fend off the hordes of people invading Italy and Gaul. In contrast, the Eastern Roman Empire, which would survive for another thousand years, remained largely free of invasion.

Conclusion

After a century of internal upheaval, Augustus established a new order that began the Roman Empire, which experienced a lengthy period of peace and prosperity between 14 and 180. During this Pax Romana, trade flourished and the provinces were governed efficiently. In the course of the third century, however, the Roman Empire came near to collapse due to invasions, civil wars, and economic decline. Although the emperors Diocletian and Constantine brought new life to the so-called Late Empire, their efforts only shored up the empire temporarily. In the course of the fifth century, the empire divided into western and eastern parts, and in 476, the Roman Empire in the west came to an end with the ouster of Emperor Romulus Augustulus.

The Roman Empire was the largest empire in antiquity. Using their practical skills, the Romans made achievements in language, law, engineering, and government that were bequeathed to the future. The Romance languages of today (French, Italian, Spanish, Portuguese, and Romanian) are based on Latin. Western practices of impartial justice and trial by jury owe much to Roman law. As great builders, the Romans left monuments to their skills throughout Europe, some of which, such as aqueducts and roads, are still in use today. Aspects of Roman administrative practices survived in the Western world for centuries. The Romans also preserved the intellectual heritage of the ancient world. While we are justified in praising the empire, it is also important to remember its other side: the enormous gulf between rich and poor, the dependence upon enslaved or otherwise subject human beings, the bloodthirsty spectacles in the amphitheaters, and the use of institutionalized terror to maintain the order for which the empire is so often praised. In its last two hundred years, as Christianity spread, a slow transformation of the Roman world took place. The Germanic invasions greatly accelerated this process, and while many aspects of the Roman world would continue, a new civilization was emerging that would carry on yet another stage in the development of Western civilization.

NOTES

1. Livy, *The Early History of Rome*, trans. Aubrey de Sélincourt (Harmondsworth, 1960), p. 35.
2. Tacitus, *The Annals of Imperial Rome*, trans. Michael Grant (Harmondsworth, 1956), p. 30.
3. Velleius Paterculus, *Compendium of Roman History*, trans. Frederick Shipley (Cambridge, Mass., 1967), 2: 117, p. 297.
4. Tacitus, *The Annals of Imperial Rome*, p. 37.
5. Virgil, *Georgics*, in *Virgil's Works*, trans. J. W. Mackail (New York, 1950), pp. 312–13.
6. Virgil, *The Aeneid*, trans. C. Day Lewis (Garden City, N.Y., 1952), p. 154.
7. Horace, *Satires*, in *The Complete Works of Horace*, trans. Lord Dunsany and Michael Oakley (London, 1961), 1.1, p. 139.
8. Ibid., 1.3, p. 151.
9. Ovid, *Tristia*, trans. L. R. Lind (Athens, Ga., 1975), 4.10: 21–22, p. 112.
10. Livy, *The Early History of Rome*, p. 18.
11. Tacitus, *The Annals of Imperial Rome*, p. 31.
12. Tacitus, *The Histories*, trans. Kenneth Wallesley (Harmondsworth, 1964), p. 23.
13. Seneca, *Letters from a Stoic*, trans. Robin Campbell (Harmondsworth, 1969), Letter 5.
14. Tacitus, *The Annals of Imperial Rome*, p. 377.
15. Ibid., p. 147.
16. Juvenal, *The Sixteen Satires*, trans. Peter Green (Harmondsworth, 1967), Satire 7, p. 171.
17. Ibid., Satire 10, p. 207.
18. Tacitus, *A Dialogue on Oratory*, in *The Complete Works of Tacitus*, trans. Alfred Church and William Brodribb (New York, 1942), 29, p. 758.
19. Ovid, *The Amores*, trans. Grant Showerman (Cambridge, Mass., 1963), 2.14: 26–27.
20. Matthew 5: 17.
21. Matthew 7: 12.
22. Mark 12: 30–31.
23. John 18: 36.
24. Matthew 26: 26–28.
25. *Early Christian Writings* (Harmondsworth, 1968), pp. 76–77.
26. Colossians 3: 10–11.

SUGGESTIONS FOR FURTHER READING

For a general account of the Roman Empire, see J. Boardman, J. Griffin, and O. Murray, eds., *The Oxford History of the Classical World* (Oxford, 1986), pp. 531–828. A brief and reliable guide to recent trends in scholarship on the Roman Empire can be found in C. Starr, *Past and Future in Ancient History* (Lanham, Md., 1987), pp. 47–57. Good surveys of the Early Empire include P. Garnsey and R. P. Saller, *The Roman Empire: Economy, Society and Culture* (London, 1987); C. Wells, *The Roman Empire* (Stanford, 1984); J. Wacher, *The Roman Empire* (London, 1987); and F. Millar, *Roman Empire and Its Neighbors*, 2d ed. (London, 1981). An excellent collection of source materials in translation can be found in N. Lewis and M. Reinhold, eds., *Roman Civilization*, vol. 2 (New York, 1955).

Studies of Roman emperors of the first and second centuries include F. Millar and E. Segal, eds., *Caesar Augustus* (Oxford, 1984); R. Seager, *Tiberius* (London,

1972); A. Barrett, *Caligula, The Corruption of Power* (New Haven, Conn., 1990), a new appraisal of Caligula; A. Momigliano, *Claudius, the Emperor and His Achievement,* trans. W. D. Hogarth (Cambridge, 1961); M. Griffin, *Nero: The End of a Dynasty* (London, 1984); and M. Hammond, *The Antonine Monarchy* (Rome, 1959). For brief biographies of all the Roman emperors, see M. Grant, *The Roman Emperors* (New York, 1985). A fundamental work on Roman government and the role of the emperor is F. Millar, *The Emperor in the Roman World* (London, 1977).

There are many specialized studies on various aspects of the administrative, economic, and social conditions in the Early Empire. On the Greek cities in the empire, see A. H. M. Jones, *The Cities of the Eastern Roman Provinces* (Oxford, 1971). On the growth of cities in Italy and the spread of Roman citizenship outside Italy, see A. N. Sherwin White, *The Roman Citizenship,* 2d ed. (Oxford, 1973). A detailed examination of economic matters is T. Frank, *An Economic Survey of Ancient Rome,* vols. 2–5 (Baltimore, 1933–40). See also M. I. Rostovtzeff, *Social and Economic History of the Roman Empire,* 2d ed., 2 vols. (Oxford, 1957); and R. Duncan-Jones, *The Economy of the Roman Empire* (New York, 1982). On social relations in general, see R. MacMullen, *Roman Social Relations, 56 B.C. to A.D. 284* (New Haven, Conn., 1974).

The Roman army is examined in G. Webster, *The Roman Imperial Army of the First and Second Centuries AD,* 2d ed. (London, 1979); L. Keppie, *The Making of the Roman Army* (London, 1984); and J. B. Campbell, *The Emperor and the Roman Army* (Oxford, 1984). On the provinces and Roman foreign policy, see E. N. Luttwak, *The Grand Strategy of the Roman Empire from the First Century A.D. to the Third* (Baltimore, 1976); and S. L. Dyson, *The Creation of the Roman Frontier* (Princeton, 1985).

A good survey of Roman literature can be found in R. M. Ogilvie, *Roman Literature and Society* (Harmondsworth, 1980). More specialized studies include G. Williams, *Change and Decline: Roman Literature in the Early Empire* (Berkeley, 1978); R. O. Lyne, *The Latin Love Poets from Catullus to Horace* (Oxford, 1980); D. A. West and A. J. Woodman, *Poetry and Politics in the Age of Augustus* (New York, 1984); and M. L. W. Laistner, *The Greater Roman Historians* (Berkeley, 1947).

A brief survey of Roman art can be found in J. M. C. Toynbee, *Art of the Romans* (London and New York, 1965). D. E. Strong, *Roman Art* (Harmondsworth,

1976), presents a more detailed account. Architecture is covered in the standard work by J. B. Ward-Perkins, *Roman Imperial Architecture* (Harmondsworth, 1981); and domestic architecture in A. G. McKay, *Houses, Villas and Palaces in the Roman World* (London, 1975).

Various aspects of Roman society are covered in J. P. V. D. Balsdon, *Life and Leisure in Ancient Rome* (London, 1969). See also the essay by P. Veyne on "The Roman Empire" in P. Veyne, ed., *A History of Private Life,* vol. 1 (Cambridge, Mass., 1987). Also useful on urban life is J. E. Stambaugh, *The Ancient Roman City* (Baltimore, 1988). Studies on Roman women include J. P. V. D. Balsdon, *Roman Women: Their History and Habits* (London, 1969); and S. B. Pomeroy, *Goddesses, Whores, Wives and Slaves: Women in Classical Antiquity* (New York, 1975), pp. 149–226. On Roman law, see J. Crook, *Law and Life of Rome* (London, 1967). On slavery, see T. Wiedemann, *Greek and Roman Slavery* (Baltimore, 1981).

An introduction to the problems relating to the religious history of the imperial period is E. R. Dodds, *Pagan and Christian in an Age of Anxiety* (Cambridge, 1965). Useful works on early Christianity include W. A. Meeks, *The First Urban Christians* (New Haven, 1983); W. H. C. Frend, *The Rise of Christianity* (Philadelphia, 1984); and R. MacMullen, *Christianizing the Roman Empire* (New Haven, Conn., 1984).

The classic work on the "decline and fall" of the Roman Empire is Edward Gibbon, *The Decline and Fall of the Roman Empire,* J. B. Bury edition (London, 1909–14). An excellent survey is P. Brown, *The World of Late Antiquity* (London, 1971). Also valuable are A. Cameron, *The Later Roman Empire* (Cambridge, Mass., 1993); and R. MacMullen, *Corruption and the Decline of Rome* (New Haven, Conn., 1988). On the fourth century, see M. Grant, *Constantine the Great: The Man and His Times* (New York, 1993); T. D. Barnes, *The New Empire of Diocletian and Constantine* (Cambridge, Mass., 1982); and S. Williams, *Diocletian and the Roman Recovery* (London, 1985). On economic and social history, including the bureaucracy, see A. H. M. Jones, *The Later Roman Empire,* (Oxford, 1964). Recent studies analyzing the aristocratic circles, the barbarian invasions, and the military problem include E. A. Thompson, *Romans and Barbarians* (Madison, 1982); A. Ferrill, *The Fall of the Roman Empire: The Military Explanation* (London, 1986); and J. M. O'Flynn, *Generalissimos of the Western Roman Empire* (Edmonton, 1983).

CHAPTER
7

The Passing of the Roman World and the Emergence of Medieval Civilization

The period that saw the disintegration of the western part of the Roman Empire also witnessed the emergence of medieval civilization. Scholars know that major historical transitions are never tidy; chaos is often the ground out of which new civilizations are born. The early medieval civilization that arose out of the dissolution of the Western Roman Empire was formed by the coalescence of three major elements: the Germanic peoples who moved into the western empire and established new kingdoms; the continuing attraction of the Greco-Roman cultural legacy; and the Christian church. Christianity was the most distinctive and powerful component of the new medieval civilization. The church assimilated the classical tradition and through its clergy, especially the monks, brought Christianized civilization to the Germanic tribes.

The conversion to Christianity of the pagan leaders of German tribes was sometimes dramatic, at least as it is reported by the sixth-century historian, Gregory of Tours. Clovis, leader of the Franks, married Clotilde, daughter of the king of the Burgundians. She was a Christian, but Clovis refused her pleas to become a Christian, telling her, "Your god can do nothing." But during a battle with the Alemanni, when Clovis's army was close to utter destruction, "He saw the danger; his heart was stirred; and he raised his eyes to heaven, saying, 'Jesus Christ, I beseech the glory of your aid. If you shall grant me victory over these enemies, I will believe in you and be baptized in your name.'" When he had uttered these words, the Alemanni began to flee. Clovis soon became a Christian.

During the time when the Germanic kingdoms were establishing their roots in the west, the eastern part of the old Roman Empire, increasingly Greek in culture, continued to survive as the Byzantine Empire. While serving as a buffer between Europe and the peoples to the east, the Byzantine or Eastern Roman Empire also preserved the intellectual and legal accomplishments of Greek and Roman antiquity. At

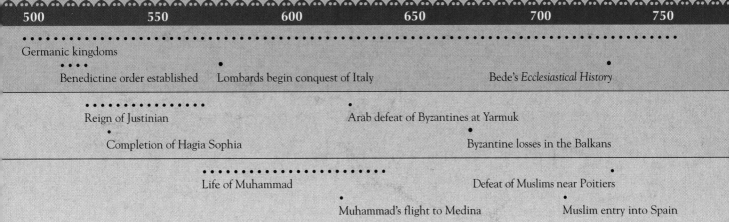

Germanic kingdoms

Benedictine order established   Lombards begin conquest of Italy   Bede's *Ecclesiastical History*

Reign of Justinian   Arab defeat of Byzantines at Yarmuk

Completion of Hagia Sophia   Byzantine losses in the Balkans

Life of Muhammad   Defeat of Muslims near Poitiers

Muhammad's flight to Medina   Muslim entry into Spain

the same time, a new world of Islam emerged in the east; it occupied large parts of the old Roman Empire, preserved much of Greek culture, and created its own flourishing civilization. This chapter, then, largely concerns the heirs of Rome and the new world they created.

The Role and Development of the Christian Church

First officially tolerated in 313 by Emperor Constantine, Christianity had become the predominant religion of the Roman state by the end of the fourth century (see Chapter 6). As the official Roman state disintegrated, the Christian church played an increasingly important role in the new civilization built upon the ruins of the old Roman Empire. We must therefore examine the role and development of the Christian church in order to understand the emergence of medieval civilization.

Organization and Religious Disputes

During the course of the fourth century, the Christian church had undergone significant organizational and structural changes. Although the church had not yet developed a centralized administrative system comparable to the Roman imperial bureaucracy, church government was based on a territorial plan borrowed from Roman administration. For some time, the Christian community in each city had been headed by a bishop, whose area of jurisdiction was known as a bishopric—or diocese. The bishoprics of each Roman province were

clustered together under the direction of an archbishop. The bishops of four great cities, Rome, Jerusalem, Alexandria, and Antioch, held positions of special power in church affairs since the churches in these cities all asserted that they had been founded by the original apostles sent out by Christ. Eventually, the bishop of Rome claimed a position of preeminence above all the other bishops (see The Power of the Pope later in this chapter).

One reason the church needed a more formal organization was the problem of heresy. As Christianity developed and spread, contradictory interpretations of important doctrines emerged. Heresy came to be viewed as a teaching different from the official catholic or universal beliefs of the church. In a world where people were concerned about salvation, the question of whether Christ's nature is divine or human took on great significance. Leaders in both church and state debated these issues, often bitterly. These doctrinal differences also became political issues, creating political factions that actually warred with one another. It is highly unlikely that ordinary people understood what these debates meant.

The two major heresies of the fourth century were Donatism and Arianism. The name Donatist is derived from Donatus, a priest in North Africa, who taught that the sacraments of the church, the channels by which a Christian received God's grace, were not valid if administered by an immoral priest or one who had denied his faith under persecution. Donatus's deviation from traditional teaching on the subject created so much dissension that it came to the attention of the Emperor Constantine, who convened a council of western bishops to denounce it. It was not until 411, however, that the church declared authoritatively that the efficacy of the sacraments was not dependent upon the moral state of the priest administering them as long as the priest had been properly ordained.

Arianism was a product of the followers of Arius, a priest from Alexandria in Egypt. Arius postulated that if Jesus Christ had been human, he must have been created by God and was thus inferior to God the Father. Arius was opposed by Athanasius who argued that Christ was human, but also truly God. Emperor Constantine, disturbed by the controversy, called the first ecumenical council of the church, a meeting composed of representatives from the entire Christian community. The Council of Nicaea, held in 325, condemned Arianism and stated that Christ was of "the same substance" as God: "We believe in one God the Father All-sovereign, maker of all things visible and invisible; And in one Lord Jesus Christ, the Son of God, begotten of the Father, only-begotten, that is, of the substance of the Father, God of God, Light of Light, true God of true God, begotten not made, of one substance with the Father...."[1] The Council of Nicaea did not end the controversy, however; not only did Arianism persist in some parts of the Roman Empire for many years, but more importantly, many of the Germanic Goths who would eventually establish kingdoms in the west converted to Arian Christianity, with important implications for those kingdoms (see The New Kingdoms later in this chapter).

As a result of these fourth-century religious controversies, the Roman emperor came to play an increasingly important role in church affairs. At the same time, such divisions also created a need for leadership within the church and soon led to the elevation of the bishop of Rome to a preeminent position in the affairs of the Christian or Catholic church, at least in the west.

The Power of the Pope

In the early centuries of Christianity, the churches in the larger cities came to have great influence in the administration of the church. It was only natural, then, that the bishops of those cities would also exercise considerable power. One of the far-reaching developments in the history of the Christian church was the emergence of one bishop—that of Rome—as the recognized leader of the western Christian church. This was, by no means, as inevitable as it may seem in retrospect.

The doctrine of Petrine supremacy, based on the belief that the bishops of Rome occupied a preeminent position in the church, was grounded in Scripture. According to the Gospel of Matthew, when Jesus asked his disciples, "Who do you say I am?" Simon Peter answered:

> You are the Christ, the Son of the living God. Jesus replied, Blessed are you, Simon, son of Jonah, for this was not revealed by man, but by my Father in heaven. And I tell you that you are Peter, and on this rock I will build my church, and the gates of hell will not overcome it. I will give you the keys of the kingdom of heaven; whatever you bind on earth will be bound in heaven; and whatever you loose on earth will be loosed in heaven.[2]

According to church tradition, Christ had given the keys to the kingdom of heaven to Peter, who was considered the chief apostle and the first bishop of Rome. Subsequent bishops of Rome were considered Peter's successors and later the "vicars of Christ" on earth. Though this exalted view of the bishops of Rome was by no means accepted by all early Christians, Rome's position as the traditional capital of the Roman Empire served to buttress this claim.

In the fourth and fifth centuries, a series of Roman bishops sought to establish the preeminence of the see of Rome. Damasus, bishop of Rome from 366 to 384, began to address other bishops as "sons" rather than "brothers" in his correspondence with them. By the end of the fourth century, the bishops of Rome were using the title of *papa* or father (our word *pope*). Leo I (440–461) was especially energetic in systematically expounding the doctrine of Petrine supremacy. He portrayed himself as the heir of Peter, whom Christ had chosen to be head of the Christian church. Although western Christians came to accept the bishop of Rome as head of the church, there was certainly no unanimity on the extent of the powers the pope possessed as a result of this position. Nevertheless, the establishment by the fifth century of the superiority of the Roman bishop laid the foundation for later medieval popes, who would claim a direct, centralized control over all Christians based on this primacy.

The Roles of Church and State

Once the Roman emperors became Christians, beginning with Constantine in the early fourth century, they came to play a significant role in the affairs of the church. Although some Roman emperors became Christian for political advantages, all Christian emperors viewed themselves as God's representatives on earth. They not only built churches and influenced the structure of the church's organization, but also became involved in church government and doctrinal controversies. As we have seen, their unwillingness to countenance disunity quickly involved them in the struggles over heresies.

While emperors were busying themselves in church affairs, the spiritual and political vacuum left by the disintegration of the Roman state allowed bishops to play a more active role in imperial government. Increasingly, they served as advisers to Christian Roman emperors. Moreover, as imperial authority declined, bishops often played a noticeably independent political role. A number of powerful bishops had sufficient authority to weather the collapse of the Roman imperial government in the west. Ambrose (c. 339–397) of Milan was an early example of a strong and independent bishop. As a young man, Ambrose entered the Roman imperial service and became governor of the northern Italian province of Emilia with its administrative capital in the city of Milan. In 374, the Christian population of the city proclaimed Ambrose the bishop of Milan. Through his activities and writings, such as his manual on a bishop's administrative responsibilities, Ambrose created an image of the ideal Christian bishop. Among other things, this ideal bishop would defend the independence of the church against the tendency of imperial officials to oversee church policy: "Exalt not yourself, but if you would reign the longer, be subject to God. It is written, God's to God and Caesar's to Caesar. The palace is the Emperor's, the Churches are the Bishop's."[3] When Emperor Theodosius I ordered the massacre of many citizens in Thessalonika for refusing to obey his commands, Ambrose denounced the massacre and refused to allow the emperor to take part in church ceremonies. Theodosius finally agreed to do public penance in the cathedral of Milan for his dastardly deed. Ambrose proved himself a formidable advocate of the position that spiritual authority should take precedence over temporal power, at least in spiritual matters. This emphasis on an independent role for the church made possible the emergence of a dual power structure between church and state that formed one of the most important elements of medieval civilization.

The weakness of the political authorities on the Italian peninsula also contributed to the church's independence in that area. In the German kingdoms (see The New Kingdoms later in this chapter), the kings controlled both churches and bishops. But in Italy a different tradition prevailed, fed by semilegendary accounts of papal deeds. Pope Leo I, for example, supposedly caused Attila the Hun to turn away from Rome in

452. While plague rather than papal persuasion was probably more conducive to Attila's withdrawal, the pope got the credit. Popes, then, played significant political roles in Italy, which only added to their claims of power vis-à-vis the secular authorities. Pope Gelasius I (492–496) could write to the emperor at Constantinople:

> There are two powers, august Emperor, by which this world is ruled from the beginning: the consecrated authority of the bishops, and the royal power. In these matters the priests bear the heavier burden because they will render account, even for rulers of men, at the divine judgment. Besides, most gracious son, you are aware that, although you in your office are the ruler of the human race, nevertheless you devoutly bow your head before those who are leaders in things divine and look to them for the means of your salvation; and in the reception and proper administration of the heavenly sacraments you know that you ought to submit to Christian order rather than take the lead, and in those matters follow their judgment without wanting to subject them to your will.[4]

According to Gelasius, while there were two ruling powers, spiritual and temporal, with different functions, the church was ultimately the higher authority since all men, including emperors, must look to the church "for the means of . . . salvation." Church-state relations would prove to be one of the most important issues of the Middle Ages.

New Patterns of Thought

Many early Christians expressed considerable hostility toward the pagan culture of the classical world. Tertullian (c. 160–c. 225), a Christian writer from Carthage, had proclaimed: "What has Jerusalem to do with Athens, the Church with the Academy, the Christian with the heretic? . . . After Jesus Christ we have no need of speculation, after the Gospel no need of research."[5] To many early Christians, the Bible contained all the knowledge anyone needed.

Others, however, thought it was not possible to separate Christian theological thought from classical traditions and education and encouraged Christians to absorb the classical heritage. As it spread in the eastern Roman world, Christianity adopted Greek as its language. The New Testament was written in Greek. Christians also turned to Greek thought for help in expressing complicated theological concepts. An especially important influence was Neoplatonism, a revival of Platonic thought that reached its high point in the third century A.D. in the work of the pagan philosopher Plotinus (205–270). Plotinus and other Neoplatonists believed that one could use reason to perceive the intimate link between the invisible spiritual world and the visible material world. The human soul, without divine assistance, could achieve union with God—the perfect One. Christian theologians used Neoplatonic concepts to explain doctrines on Christ, especially the distinction between his human and divine natures. In many ways, then, Christianity served to preserve Greco-Roman culture and to keep alive a vision of a past golden age that would later help generate a series of revivals of classical thought in an attempt to recapture that earlier world.

The work of Augustine (354–430) provides one of the best examples of how pagan culture was absorbed in the service of Christianity. Born in North Africa, he was reared by his mother, an ardent Christian. Augustine eventually became a teacher of rhetoric. He went to Rome to teach and then became a professor of rhetoric at Milan in 384.

Augustine's success opened the door to a lucrative career in the imperial bureaucracy if he had wished to pursue it. Throughout his rapid ascent, however, although he had turned his back on Christianity, he had continued to explore spiritual alternatives, including Neoplatonism and a dualist heresy known as Manichae-anism. While in Milan, he came under the influence of the popular bishop Ambrose who encouraged Augustine to return to his mother's religion. After experiencing a profound and moving religious experience, Augustine gave up his teaching position in 386 and went back to North Africa, where he became bishop of Hippo from 396 until his death in 430.

As bishop of Hippo, Augustine did not become an adviser to emperors like his contemporary Ambrose, but produced an enormous outpouring of Christian litera-ture. In his sermons, letters, treatises on dogma, and commentaries on Scripture, Augustine gave reasoned opinions on virtually every aspect of Christian thought. He stressed that while philosophy could bring some understanding, divine revelation was a necessity for perceiving complete truth, an approach to knowledge that became standard in the education of the Middle Ages. Augustine's ideas on free will, grace, and predes-tination helped shape the contours of medieval theology and later had a profound impact on the reformers of the Protestant Reformation of the sixteenth century. In fact, many historians feel that Augustine was the primary intellectual shaper of western Christianity and the most

important formative theologian of Christianity, both Catholic and Protestant, for the next 1,200 years.

His two most famous works are the *Confessions* and *The City of God*. Written in 397, the *Confessions* was a self-portrait not of Augustine's worldly activities, but of the "history of a heart," an account of his own personal and spiritual experiences, written to help others with their search: "To whom do I tell this? not to You, my God; but before You to my own kind, even to that small portion of mankind as may light upon these writings of mine. And to what purpose? that whosoever reads this, may think out of what depths we are to cry unto You. For what is nearer to Your ears than a confessing heart, and a life of faith?"[6] Augustine describes how he struggled throughout his early life to find God until in his thirty-second year he experienced a miraculous conversion (see the box on p. 211). This portrait of an inner journey became a model for an entire genre of autobiographical literature in western society for genera-tions to come.

The City of God, Augustine's other major work, was a profound expression of a Christian philosophy of gov-ernment and history. It was written in response to a line of argument that arose soon after the sack of Rome in 410. Some pagan philosophers maintained that Rome's problems stemmed from the Roman state's recognition of Christianity and abandonment of the old, traditional gods. Augustine argued that Rome's troubles began long before Christianity arose in the empire. In *The City of God*, Augustine theorized on the ideal relations between two kinds of societies existing throughout time—the City of God and the City of the World. The fundamen-tal loyalty of those who loved God was to the City of God, whose ultimate location was the kingdom of heaven. Earthly society would always be insecure and subject to change because of human beings' fallen nature and inclination to sin. Nevertheless, the City of the World was still necessary for it was the duty of rulers to curb the depraved instincts of sinful humans and maintain the peace necessary for Christians to live in the world. Hence, Augustine posited that secular gov-ernment and authority were necessary for the pursuit of the true Christian life on earth; in doing so, he provided a justification for secular political authority that would play an important role in medieval thought.

Augustine was also important in establishing the Christian church's views on sexual desire. Many early Christians had seen celibacy, or complete abstinence from sexual activity, as the surest way to holiness. Augustine, too, believed Christians should reject sex,

⇒ The Confessions of Augustine ⇐

Augustine's spiritual and intellectual autobiography is a revealing self-portrait of the inner struggles of one of the intellectual giants of early Christianity. The first excerpt is taken from Book VIII, in which Augustine describes how he heard a voice from heaven and was converted from his old habits. In the second excerpt from Book IX, Augustine expresses joy and gratitude for his conversion.

Augustine, *The Confessions*

So was I speaking and weeping in the most bitter contrition of my heart, when, lo! I heard from a neighboring house a voice as of boy or girl, I know not, chanting, and oft repeating, "Take up and read; Take up and read." Instantly, my countenance altered, I began to think most intently whether children were wont in any kind of play to sing such words: nor could I remember ever to have heard the like. So checking the torrent of my tears, I arose; interpreting it to be no other than a command from God to open the book, and read the first chapter I should find. For I had heard of Antony, that coming in during the reading of the Gospel, he received the admonition, as if what was being read was spoken to him: Go, sell all that you have, and give to the poor, and you shall have treasure in heaven, and come and follow

me: and by such oracle he was forthwith converted unto You. Eagerly then I returned to the place where Alypius was sitting; for there I had laid the volume of the Apostle when I arose thence. I seized, opened, and in silence read that section on which my eyes first fell: Not in rioting and drunkenness, not in chambering and wantonness, not in strife and envying; but put you on the Lord Jesus Christ, and make not provision for the flesh . . . . No further would I read; nor need I: for instantly at the end of this sentence, by a light as it were of serenity infused into my heart, all the darkness of doubt vanished away. . . .

O Lord I am your servant; I am your servant, and the son of your handmaid: You have broken my bonds in sunder. I will offer to You the sacrifice of praise. Let my heart and my tongue praise You; yea, let all my bones say, O Lord, who is like unto You? Let them say, and answer You me, and say unto my soul, I am your salvation. Who am I, and what am I? What evil have not been either my deeds, or if not my deeds, my words, or if not my words, my will? But You, O Lord, are good and merciful, and your right hand had respect unto the depth of my death, and from the bottom of my heart emptied that abyss of corruption.

but he maintained that many Christians were unable to do so. For them, marriage was a good alternative, but with the understanding that even in marriage sex between a man and woman had to serve a purpose—the procreation of children. It was left to the clergy of the church to uphold the high ideal of celibacy.

Augustine and Ambrose came to be seen as the first of the Latin Fathers of the Catholic church, intellectuals who wrote in Latin and profoundly influenced the development of Christian thought in the west. Another Latin Father was Jerome (345–420), who was born in the Balkans in the Roman province of Dalmatia. He pursued literary studies in Rome and became a master of Latin prose. Jerome had mixed feelings about his love for liberal studies, however, and, like Augustine, experienced a spiritual conversion after which he tried to dedicate himself more fully to Christ. He had a dream in which Christ appeared as his judge: "Asked who and what I was, I replied: 'I am a Christian.' But He who

presided said: 'You lie, you are a follower of Cicero, not of Christ. For where your treasure is, there will your heart be also.' Instantly, I became dumb. . . . Accordingly I made oath and called upon His name, saying: 'Lord, if ever again I possess worldly books [the classics], or if ever again I read such, I have denied You.' " After this dream, Jerome determined to "read the books of God with a zeal greater than I had previously given to the books of men."[7]

Ultimately, Jerome found a compromise by purifying the literature of the pagan world and then using it to further the Christian faith. Eventually, he moved to Palestine and settled in Bethlehem, where he spent the rest of his life settling doctrinal disputes and translating Scripture. Jerome was the greatest scholar among the Latin Fathers, and his extensive knowledge of both Hebrew and Greek enabled him to translate the Old and New Testaments into Latin. In the process, he created the so-called Latin Vulgate, or common text, of the

Scriptures that became the standard edition for the Catholic church in the Middle Ages.

The Beginnings of Monasticism

The spread of Christianity was greatly fostered by the development of monasticism. Although Christian monasticism had its beginnings in the third century, historians have labeled the fourth century the "century of monasticism." A monk (Latin *monachus,* meaning "someone who lives alone") was a person who sought to live a life divorced from the world, cut off from ordinary human society, in order to pursue an ideal of godliness or total dedication to the will of God. During the Middle Ages, monks became responsible for the intellectual,

social, cultural, and even medical needs of the people of Europe.

Christian monasticism developed first in Egypt in a form called eremitical monasticism because it was based on the model of the solitary hermit who forsakes all civilized society to pursue spirituality. Saint Anthony (c. 250–350) has been called the "father of eremitical monasticism." He was a relatively prosperous Egyptian peasant who decided to follow Christ's injunction in the Gospel of Mark: "Go your way, sell whatsoever you have, and give to the poor, and you shall have treasure in heaven: and come, take up the cross, and follow me."[8] Anthony gave away his three hundred acres of land to the poor and went into the desert to pursue his ideal of holiness (see the box on p. 213). Others did

Map 7.1 The Spread of Christianity, A.D. 400–750.

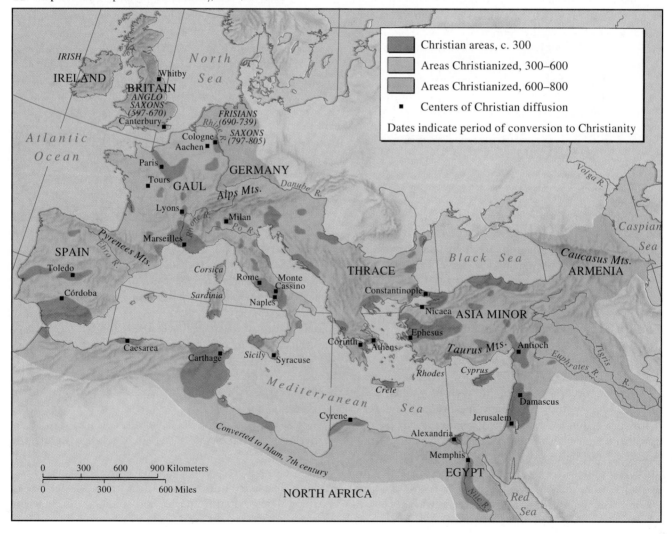

The Life of Saint Anthony

*In the third and early fourth centuries, the lives of martyrs
had provided important models for early Christianity. But
in the course of the fourth century, monks or desert fathers,
who attempted to achieve spiritual perfection through asceticism, the denial of earthly life, and the struggle with demons
became the new spiritual ideal for Christians. Consequently,
spiritual biographies of early monks became a significant new
form of Christian literature. Especially noteworthy was The
Life of Saint Anthony by Saint Athanasius, the defender
of Catholic orthodoxy against the Arians. His work had been
translated into Latin before 386. This excerpt describes how
Anthony fought off the temptations of Satan.*

Athanasius, *The Life of Saint Anthony*

Now when the Enemy [Satan] saw that his craftiness in
this matter was without profit, and that the more he
brought temptation into Saint Anthony, the more
strenuous the saint was in protecting himself against
him with the armor of righteousness, he attacked him
by means of the vigor of early manhood which is bound
up in the nature of our humanity. With the goadings of
passion he sued to trouble him by night, and in the daytime also he would vex him and pain him with the same
to such an extent that even those who saw him knew
from his appearance that he was waging war against the
Adversary. But the more the Evil One brought unto
him filthy and maddening thoughts, the more Saint

Anthony took refuge in prayer and in abundant suppli-
cation, and amid them all he remained wholly chaste.
And the Evil One was working upon him every shameful deed according to his wont, and at length he even
appeared unto Saint Anthony in the form of a woman;
and other things which resembled this he performed
with ease, for such things are a subject for boasting to
him.

But the blessed Anthony knelt down upon his knees
on the ground, and prayed before Him who said, "Before
you criest unto Me, I will answer you," and said, "O my
Lord, this I entreat you. Let not Your love be blotted out
from my mind, and behold, I am, by Your grace, innocent before You." And again the Enemy multiplied in
him the thoughts of lust, until Saint Anthony became
as one who was being burned up, not through the Evil
One, but through his own lusts; but he girded himself
about with the threat of the thought of the Judgment,
and of the torture of Gehenna, and of the worm which
does not die. And while meditating on the thoughts
which could be directed against the Evil One, he prayed
for thoughts which would be hostile to him. Thus, to
the reproach and shame of the Enemy, these things
could not be performed; for he who imagined that he
could be God was made a mock of by a young man, and
he who boasted over flesh and blood was vanquished
by a man who was clothed with flesh. . . .

likewise, often to extremes. Saint Simeon the Stylite
lived in a basket atop a pillar over sixty feet high for
three decades. These spiritual gymnastics established a
new ideal for Christianity. Whereas the early Christian
model had been the martyr who died for the faith and
achieved eternal life in the process, the new ideal was
the monk who died to the world and achieved spiritual
life through denial, asceticism, and mystical experience
of God.

These early monks, however, soon found themselves
unable to live in solitude. Their feats of holiness attracted followers on a wide scale, and as the monastic
ideal spread throughout the east, cenobitic monasticism,
based upon the practice of communal life, soon became
the dominant form. Saint Pachomius (c. 290–346),
regarded as the founder of cenobitic monasticism, organized communities of monks and wrote the first monastic rule for living in communities. He emphasized the

need for obedience and manual labor. It was Saint Basil
(329–379), however, who was the true founder of
Christian monasticism in the eastern world. Born in
Palestine, he visited Egypt and established a community
of monks under one roof since he believed they needed
fellowship and work. Monastic communities soon came
to be seen as the ideal Christian society that could
provide a moral example to the wider society around
them.

The fundamental form of monastic life in the western
Christian church was established by Saint Benedict of
Nursia (c. 480–c. 543). He belonged to a noble Roman
family and received an excellent education. After a
religious experience, he sought hermitic solitude south
of Rome but soon found himself surrounded by followers. Benedict then went to Monte Cassino where he
founded a monastic house, for which he wrote his
famous rule, sometime between 520 and 530. The

◆ **Life of Saint Benedict.** This illustration with its six scenes is from an eleventh-century manuscript of Pope Gregory the Great's *Life of Saint Benedict,* written in 593 or 594. *Top left,* Benedict writes his rule; *top right,* the death of Benedict; *middle left,* his burial; *middle right and bottom left,* scenes of miracles attributed to Saint Benedict's intercession; *bottom right,* Gregory finishes his *Life of Saint Benedict.*

Benedictine rule came to be used by other monastic groups and was crucial to the growth of monasticism in the western Christian world.

Benedict's rule largely rejected the ascetic ideals of eastern monasticism, which had tended to emphasize such practices as fasting and self-inflicted torments (such as living atop pillars for thirty years), in favor of an ideal of moderation. In Chapter 40 of the rule, on the amount of drink a monk should imbibe, this sense of moderation becomes apparent:

> 'Every man has his proper gift from God, one after this manner, another after that.' And therefore it is with some misgiving that we determine the amount of food for someone else. Still, having regard for the weakness of some brothers, we believe that a hemina [a quarter liter] of wine per day will suffice for all. Let those, however, to whom God gives the gift of abstinence, know that they shall have their proper reward. But if either the circumstances of the place, the work, or the heat of summer necessitates more, let it lie in the discretion of the abbot to grant it. But let him take care in all things lest satiety or drunkenness supervene.

At the same time, moderation did not preclude a hard and disciplined existence based on the ideals of poverty, chastity, and obedience.

According to Benedict's rule, each day was divided into a series of activities with primary emphasis upon prayer and manual labor. Physical work of some kind was required of all monks for several hours a day: "Idleness is the enemy of the soul. The brothers, therefore, ought to be engaged at certain times in manual labor. . . ." Peasants, however, were hired to do heavy farm work. At the very heart of community practice was prayer, the proper "Work of God." While this included private meditation and reading, all monks gathered together seven times during the day for common prayer and chanting of psalms. A Benedictine life was a communal one; monks ate, worked, slept, and worshiped together.

Each Benedictine monastery was strictly ruled by an abbot, or "father" of the monastery. Although chosen by his fellow monks, the abbot possessed complete authority over them; unquestioning obedience to the will of the abbot was expected of each monk. However, Benedict urged that the abbot take care "not to teach, ordain, or command anything which is against the law of the Lord" and cautioned him to be moderate: "He should be prudent and considerate in all his commands; and whether the task he enjoins concerns God or the world, let him be discreet and temperate. . . ." Each Benedictine monastery possessed lands that enabled it to be a self-sustaining community, isolated from and independent of the world surrounding it. Within the monastery, however, monks were to fulfill their vow of poverty: "Let all things be common to all, as it is written, lest anyone should say that anything is his own or arrogate it to himself."[9] By the eighth century, Benedictine monasticism had spread throughout the west, where it remained the primary monastic form until the High Middle Ages (see Chapter 9).

Although the original monks were men, women soon followed suit in attempting to withdraw from the world to dedicate themselves to God. Around 320, Saint Pachomius began organizing cenobitic communities that included convents of women. In fact, Pachomius governed a community founded by his sister. The brothers took care of the material needs of the convent but were not permitted to eat there. Relations with the nuns were carefully regulated. The first monastic rule for western women was produced by Caesarius of Arles for his sister in the fifth century. It strongly emphasized a rigid cloistering of female religious to preserve them from dangers. Later in the west, in the seventh and eighth centuries, the growth of double monasteries allowed monks and nuns to reside close by and follow a common rule, often the Benedictine rule, under a common head.

Monasticism played an indispensable role in early medieval civilization. Monks became the new heroes of Christian civilization. Their dedication to God became the highest ideal of Christian life. Moreover, as we shall see later, the monks played an increasingly significant role not only in spreading Christianity to the entire medieval European world, but also in the economy, education, and government of that civilization.

The Germanic Peoples and Their Kingdoms

As we have seen, the first two major elements of early medieval civilization were the Christian church and the Greco-Roman cultural legacy. The third major component came from the contributions of the Germanic peoples. Although our knowledge of early Germanic tribes is scanty, we do know that around 500 B.C., the Germans began to migrate from their northern Scandinavian homeland south into what are now the Baltic states and Germany and east into the fertile lands of Ukraine. Although the Romans had established a series of political frontiers in the western empire, Romans and Germans often came into contact across those boundaries. For some time, the Romans had hired Germanic tribes to fight other Germanic tribes that threatened Rome. Moreover, entire groups of Germans were hired to fight for Rome. Franks and Goths, for example, could even be found fighting in distant provinces as Roman troops.

In the late fourth century, the Germanic tribes came under new pressure when the Huns, a fierce tribe of steppe nomads from Asia (see the box on p. 216), moved into the Black Sea region. They devastated the Germanic Gothic confederation that dominated the region and forced some tribes to move again. One of the largest groups, the Visigoths, crossed the Danube and asked for Roman assistance. Mistreated by the Romans, however, they revolted and, in 378, crushed a Roman army and killed the emperor Valens. The new emperor quickly permitted the Visigoths to settle along the Danube, within the Roman Empire, as allies. But the Visigoths were soon on the move. Under their king Alaric, they moved into Italy and sacked Rome in 410. Then, upon the urging of the emperor, they moved into Spain and southern Gaul as Roman allies.

The Roman experience with the Visigoths established a precedent. The emperors in the first half of the fifth century made alliances with whole groups of Germanic peoples, who settled peacefully in the western part of the empire. The Burgundians settled themselves in much of eastern Gaul, just south of another Germanic tribe called the Alemanni. Only the Vandals remained consistently hostile to the Romans. They sacked parts of Gaul, crossed the Pyrenees Mountains into Spain, and began to establish a Vandal kingdom there. Defeated by incoming Visigoths, the Vandals crossed the Straits of Gibraltar and moved into Roman North Africa by 429. Under King Gaiseric, the Vandals conquered the whole province of Africa. Gaiseric built a fleet and began to harass Sicily and southern Italy. In 455, the Vandals even attacked Rome and sacked it more ferociously than the Visigoths had in 410.

Increasingly, Germanic troops formed the core of the imperial army in the west. The commanders of these armies were also Germans. One such leader finally ended the charade of Roman imperial rule. Odoacer, who had served as master of soldiers, deposed the Roman emperor, Romulus Augustulus, and returned the imperial regalia to Zeno, emperor of the eastern empire at Constantinople. Although Odoacer claimed he would rule as the emperor's regent, in reality he functioned independently, and his lands were also lost to the empire. Zeno was unable to undo Odoacer's actions, but in his desire to act against the German leader, he sent another German tribe, the Ostrogoths, into Italy.

The Ostrogoths were another branch of the Goths who had recovered from a defeat by the Huns in the

⇒ The People of the Huns ⇐

The first selection is a description of the Huns by Ammianus Marcellinus (c. 330–c. 393), who has been called the "last great Roman historian." Ammianus wrote a history of Rome from A.D. 96 to his own day. Only the chapters that deal with the period from 354 to 378 have survived. Historians believe that his account of the Huns is largely based on stereotypes. The second selection is taken from an account by Priscus, an envoy from the Eastern Roman Empire to the court of Attila the Hun. His description of the Huns in 448 is quite different from that of Ammianus Marcellinus.

Ammianus Marcellinus, *The Later Roman Empire*

The people of the Huns . . . are quite abnormally savage. From the moment of their birth they make deep gashes in their children's cheeks, so that when in due course hair appears its growth is checked by the wrinkled scars; as they grow older this gives them the unlovely appearance of beardless eunuchs. They have squat bodies, strong limbs, and thick necks, and are so prodigiously ugly and bent that they might be two-legged animals, or the figures crudely carved from stumps which are seen on the parapets of bridges. Still, their shape, however disagreeable, is human; but their way of life is so rough that they have no use for fire or seasoned food, but live on the roots of wild plants and the half-raw flesh of any sort of animal, which they warm a little by placing it between their thighs and the backs of their horses. They have no buildings to shelter them, but avoid anything of the kind as carefully as we avoid living in the neighborhood of tombs; not so much as a hut thatched with reeds is to be found among them. . . . They wear garments of linen or of the skins of field-mice stitched together, and there is no difference between their clothing whether they are at home or abroad. Once they have put their necks in some dingy shirt they never take it off or change it till it rots and falls to pieces from incessant wear. They have round caps of fur on their heads, and protect their hairy legs with goatskins. Their shapeless shoes are not made on a last and make it hard to walk easily. In consequence they are ill-fitted to fight on foot, and remain glued to their horses, hardy but ugly beasts, on which they sometimes sit like women to perform their everyday business. Buying or selling, eating or drinking, are all done by day or night on horseback, and they even bow forward over their beasts' narrow necks to enjoy a deep and dreamy sleep. . . .

They sometimes fight by challenging their foes to single combat, but when they join battle they advance in packs, uttering their various warcries. Being lightly equipped and very sudden in their movements they can deliberately scatter and gallop about at random, inflicting tremendous slaughter; their extreme nimbleness enables them to force a rampart or pillage an enemy's camp before one catches sight of them. . . . None of them ploughs or ever touches a plough-handle. They have no fixed abode, no home or law or settled manner of life, but wander like refugees with the wagons in which they live. In these their wives weave their filthy clothing, mate with their husbands, and give birth to their children, and rear them to the age of puberty.

Priscus, *An Account of the Court of Attila the Hun*

[We were invited to a banquet with Attila at three o'clock.] When the hour arrived we went to Attila's palace, along with the embassy from the western Romans, and stood on the threshold of the hall in the presence of Attila. The cupbearers gave us a cup, according to the national custom, that we might pray before we sat down. Having tasted the cup, we proceeded to take our seats, all the chairs being ranged along the walls of the room on either side. Attila sat in the middle on a couch; a second couch was set behind him, and from it steps led up to his bed, which was covered with linen sheets and coverlets. . . .

[First the king and his guests pledged one another with the wine.] When this ceremony was over the cupbearers retired and tables, large enough for three or four, or even more, to sit at, were placed next the table of Attila, so that each could take of the food on the dishes without leaving his seat. The attendant of Attila first entered with a dish full of meat, and behind him came the other attendants with bread and other dishes, which they laid on the tables. A luxurious meal, served on silver plate, had been made ready for us and the other guests, but Attila ate nothing but meat on a wooden trencher. In everything else, too, he showed himself temperate; his cup was of wood, while to the guests were given goblets of gold and silver. His dress, too, was quite simple, affecting only to be clean.

Map 7.2 Barbarian Migration and Invasion Routes.

fourth century. Under their king Theodoric (493–526), they proceeded to attack Constantinople. To divert them, Emperor Zeno invited Theodoric to act as his deputy to defeat Odoacer and bring Italy back into the empire. Theodoric accepted the challenge, marched into Italy, killed Odoacer, and then, contrary to Zeno's wishes, established himself as ruler of Italy in 493.

The New Kingdoms

By 500, the Western Roman Empire was being replaced politically by a series of kingdoms ruled by German kings. The pattern of settlement and the fusion of the

Romans and Germans took different forms in the various barbarian kingdoms.

THE OSTROGOTHIC KINGDOM OF ITALY

More than any other successor state, the Ostrogothic kingdom of Italy managed to maintain the Roman tradition of government. The Ostrogothic king Theodoric had received a Roman education while a hostage in Constantinople. After taking control of Italy, he was eager to create a synthesis of Ostrogothic and Roman practices (see the box on p. 218). In addition to maintaining the entire structure of imperial Roman govern-

≽ *Theodoric and Ostrogothic Italy* ≼

The Ostrogothic king Theodoric (493–526), who had been educated in Constantinople, was determined to maintain Roman culture rather than destroy it. His attempt to preserve civilitas *or the traditional Roman civic culture was well expressed in the official letters written in his name by Cassiodorus, who become master of offices in 525. Theodoric's efforts were largely undone by opposition from the Roman nobility and especially by Justinian's reconquest of the Italian peninsula shortly after Theodoric's death.*

Letters of Cassiodorus

King Theodoric to Colossaeus

We delight to entrust our mandates to persons of approved character. . . .

Show forth the justice of the Goths, a nation happily situated for praise, since it is theirs to unite the forethought of the Romans and the virtue of the Barbarians. Remove all ill-planted customs, and impress upon all your subordinates that we would rather that our Treasury lost a suit than that it gained one wrongfully, rather that we lost money than the taxpayer was driven to suicide.

King Theodoric to Unigis, the Sword-Bearer

We delight to live after the law of the Romans, whom we seek to defend with our arms; and we are as much interested in the maintenance of morality as we can possibly be in war. For what profit is there in having removed the turmoil of the Barbarians, unless we live

according to law? . . . Let other kings desire the glory of battles won, of cities taken, of ruins made; our purpose is, God helping us, so to rule that our subjects shall grieve that they did not earlier acquire the blessing of our dominion.

King Theodoric to All the Jews of Genoa

The true mark of *civilitas* is the observance of law. It is this which makes life in communities possible, and which separates man from the brutes. We therefore gladly accede to your request that all the privileges which the foresight of antiquity conferred upon the Jewish customs shall be renewed to you, for in truth it is our great desire that the laws of the ancients shall be kept in force to secure the reverence due to us. Everything which has been found to conduce to *civilitas* should be held fast with enduring devotion.

King Theodoric to All the Goths Settled in Picenum and Samnium

The presence of the Sovereign doubles the sweetness of his gifts, and that man is like one dead whose face is not known to his lord. Come therefore by God's assistance, come all into our presence on the eighth day before the Ides of June [June 6], there solemnly to receive our royal largesse. But let there be no excesses by the way, no plundering the harvest of the cultivators nor trampling down their meadows, since for this cause do we gladly defray the expense of our armies that *civilitas* may be kept intact by armed men.

ment, he established separate systems of rule for the Ostrogoths and Romans. The Italian population lived under Roman law administered by Roman officials. The Ostrogoths were governed by their own customs and their own officials. Nevertheless, while the Roman administrative system was kept intact, the Goths alone controlled the army. Despite the apparent success of this "dual approach," Theodoric's system was unable to keep friction from developing between the Italian population and their Germanic overlords.

Religion proved to be a major source of trouble between Ostrogoths and Romans. The Ostrogoths had

been converted earlier to Christianity, but to Arian Christianity, and consequently were viewed by the Catholic Italians as heretics. Theodoric's rule grew ever harsher as discontent with Ostrogothic domination deepened. In the increasingly suspicious atmosphere, Theodoric even ordered the execution of his own master of offices, the important Catholic philosopher Boethius (see Christianity and Intellectual Life later in this chapter). After Theodoric's death in 526, it quickly became apparent that much of his success had been due to the force of his own personality. His successors soon found themselves face-to-face with opposition from the imperial forces of the Byzantine or Eastern Roman Empire. Under Emperor Justinian (527–565) (see The Reign of Justinian later in this chapter), Byzantine armies reconquered Italy between 535 and 554, devastating much of the peninsula and destroying Rome as one of the great urban centers of the Mediterranean world in the process. The Byzantine reconquest proved ephemeral, however. Another German tribe, the Lombards, invaded Italy in 568 and conquered much of northern and central Italy. Unlike the Ostrogoths, the Lombards were harsh rulers and cared little for Roman structures and traditions. The Lombards' fondness for fighting each other enabled the Byzantines to retain control of some parts of Italy, especially the area around Ravenna, which became the capital of imperial government.

THE VISIGOTHIC KINGDOM OF SPAIN

The Visigothic kingdom in Spain, while surviving longer, demonstrated a number of parallels to the Ostrogothic kingdom of Italy. Both favored coexistence

♦ **The Palace of Theodoric at Ravenna.** The Ostrogothic king Theodoric worked to combine Ostrogothic and Roman practices in his Italian kingdom, whose capital was located at Ravenna. This mosaic on the south wall of the nave of the Basilica of Sant' Apollinare Nuovo in Ravenna depicts Theodoric's palace in his capital city.

between the Roman and German populations; both featured a warrior caste dominating a considerably larger native population; and both inherited and continued to maintain much of the Roman structure of government while largely excluding Romans from power. There were also noticeable differences, however. Perceiving that their Arianism was a stumbling block to good relations, the Visigothic rulers converted to Catholic Christianity in the late sixth century and ended the tension caused by this heresy. Laws preventing intermarriage were dropped, and the Visigothic and Hispano-Roman peoples began to fuse together. A new body of law common to both peoples also developed.

The kingdom possessed one fatal weakness, however—the Visigoths fought constantly over the kingship. The Visigoths had no law of hereditary kingship and no established procedure for choosing new rulers. Church officials tried to help develop a sense of order, as this canon from the Fourth Council of Toledo in 633 illustrates: "No one of us shall dare to seize the kingdom; no one shall arouse sedition among the citizenry; no one shall think of killing the king. . . ." Church decrees failed to stop the feuds, however, and assassinations remained a way of life in Visigothic Spain. In 711, the Visigothic kingdom itself was defeated by Muslim invaders (see The Rise of Islam later in this chapter).

THE FRANKISH KINGDOM

Only one of the German kingdoms on the European continent proved long-lasting—the kingdom of the Franks. The establishment of a Frankish kingdom was closely associated with Clovis (c. 482–511), the leader of one group of Franks who eventually became king of them all.

It is highly significant that Clovis became a Catholic Christian around 500. Unlike many other Germanic peoples who converted first to Arian Christianity, Clovis converted from paganism directly to Catholic Christianity, a move that furthered the development of a society based on the fusion of Gallo-Romans and Germans. Clovis's action had other repercussions as well. He gained the support of the western church and the Roman popes who were only too eager to obtain the friendship of a major Germanic ruler who was a Catholic Christian. The conversion of the king also paved the way for the conversion of the Frankish peoples. Finally, Clovis could justify his expansionary tendencies at the beginning of the sixth century by posing as a defender of the orthodox Christian faith. He defeated the Alemanni in southwest Germany and the Visigoths in southern

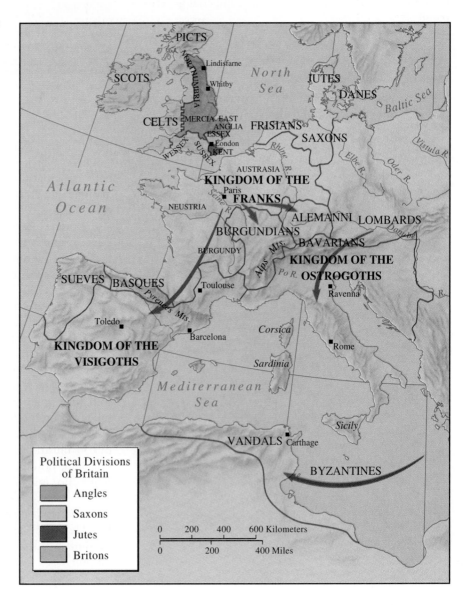

Map 7.3 The New Kingdoms of the Old Western Empire.

Gaul. By 510, Clovis had established a powerful new Frankish kingdom stretching from the Pyrenees in the west to the German lands in the east.

To control his new kingdom, Clovis came to rely on his Frankish followers who ruled in the old Roman city-states under the title of "count." Often these officials were forced to share power with the Gallo-Roman Catholic bishops, producing a gradual fusion of Latin and German cultures with the church serving to preserve the Latin culture. Clovis was also responsible for establishing the Merovingian dynasty, a name derived from Merovech, their semilegendary ancestor. Clovis spent the last years of his life ensuring the survival of his dynasty by killing off relatives who were leaders of other groups of Franks.

After the death of Clovis, his sons divided the newly created kingdom. During the sixth and seventh centuries, the once-united Frankish kingdom came to be partitioned into three major areas: Neustria in northern Gaul; Austrasia, consisting of the ancient Frankish lands on both sides of the Rhine; and the former kingdom of Burgundy. All three were ruled by members of the Merovingian dynasty. Within the three territories, the Merovingian kings were assisted by powerful nobles. Frankish society possessed a ruling class that gradually intermarried with the old Gallo-Roman senatorial class to form a new nobility. These noble families took advantage of their position to strengthen their own lands and wealth at the expense of the monarchy. Within the royal household, the position of *major domus* or mayor of the palace, the chief officer of the king's household, began to overshadow the king. Essentially, both nobles and mayors of the palace were expanding their power at the expense of the kings. In other words, private power was replacing public power.

At the beginning of the eighth century, the most important political development in the Frankish kingdom was the rise of Charles Martel, who served as mayor of the palace of Austrasia beginning in 714. Charles Martel defeated the Muslims near Poitiers in 732 and by the time of his death in 741 had become virtual ruler of the three Merovingian kingdoms. Though he was not king, Charles Martel's dynamic efforts put his family on the verge of creating a new dynasty—the Carolingians—who would establish an even more powerful Frankish state (see Chapter 8).

During the sixth and seventh centuries, the Frankish kingdom witnessed a process of fusion between Gallo-Roman and Frankish cultures and peoples, a process accompanied by a significant decline in Roman standards of civilization and commercial activity. The

✦ **Baptism of Clovis.** The conversion of Clovis to Catholic Christianity was an important factor in gaining papal support for his Frankish kingdom. In this illustration from a medieval manuscript, bishops and nobles look on while Clovis is baptized. One of the nobles holds a crown while a dove, symbol of the Holy Spirit, descends from heaven bringing sacred oil for the ceremony.

Franks were warriors and did little to encourage either urban life or trade. Commerce declined in the interior, though seacoast towns maintained some activity. By 750, Frankish Gaul was basically an agricultural society in which the old Roman villa system of the late empire had continued unimpeded. Institutionally, however, the Roman governmental structure had been replaced by Germanic concepts of kingship and customary law. Although the kingdom had become Catholic Christian, Frankish Christianity was often corrupt and at times bore little resemblance to the ideals of early Christianity. Important church offices, such as those of bishops, came to be controlled by Frankish nobles. In retrospect, we can see that this fusion of Franks, Gallo-Romans, and Christianity in the Frankish kingdom was producing a new culture and a new state. Eventually, as we shall see in the next chapter, it would become a new European civilization.

ANGLO-SAXON ENGLAND

The barbarian pressures on the Western Roman Empire had forced the emperors to withdraw the Roman armies and abandon Britain by the beginning of the fifth century. This opened the door to the Angles and Saxons, Germanic tribes from Denmark and northern

Germany. Although these same peoples had made plundering raids for the past century, the withdrawal of the Roman armies enabled them to make settlements instead. They met with resistance from the Celtic Britons, however, who still controlled the western regions of Cornwall, Wales, and Cumberland at the beginning of the seventh century. The German invaders eventually succeeded in carving out small kingdoms throughout the island, Kent in southeast England being one of them. This wave of German invaders would eventually be converted to Christianity by new groups of Christian missionaries.

The Society of the Germanic Peoples in the New Kingdoms

As the Germans infiltrated the Roman Empire, they were influenced by the Roman society they encountered. Consequently, the Germanic peoples of the fifth, sixth, and seventh centuries were probably quite different from the Germans that the forces of Augustus encountered in the first century A.D. Moreover, there was a meaningful fusion of Roman and German upper classes in the new kingdoms. In Merovingian Frankish lands, upper-class Gallo-Romans intermarried with Frankish nobles to produce a new ruling class. Each influenced the other. Franks constructed Roman-style villas; Gallo-Romans adopted Frankish weapons.

The crucial social bond among the Germanic peoples was the family, especially the extended or patriarchal family of husbands, wives, children, brothers, sisters, cousins, and grandparents. In addition to working the land together and passing it down to succeeding generations, the extended family provided protection, which was sorely needed in the violent atmosphere of Merovingian times.

The German conception of family and kinship affected the way Germanic law treated the problem of crime and punishment. In the Roman system, as in our own, a crime such as murder was considered an offense against society or the state and was handled by a court that heard evidence and arrived at a decision. Germanic law tended to be personal. An injury by one person against another could mean a blood feud in which the family of the injured party took revenge on the kin of the wrongdoer. Feuds could lead to savage acts of revenge, such as hacking off hands or feet, gouging out eyes, or slicing off ears and noses. Since this system had a tendency to get out of control and allow mayhem to

multiply, an alternative system arose that made use of a fine called *wergeld*. This was the amount paid by a wrongdoer to the family of the person he had injured or killed. *Wergeld,* which means "money for a man," was the value of a person in monetary terms. That value varied considerably according to social status. The law of the Salic Franks, which was first written down under Roman influence at the beginning of the sixth century, stated:

> If any one shall have killed a free Frank, or a barbarian living under the Salic law, and it have been proved on him, he shall be sentenced to 8,000 denars. . . .
> But if any one has slain a man who is in the service of the king, he shall be sentenced to 24,000 denars. . . .[10]

An offence against a nobleman obviously cost considerably more than one against a freeman or a slave.

Under German customary law, compurgation and the ordeal were the two most commonly used procedures for determining whether an accused person was guilty and should have to pay *wergeld*. Compurgation was the swearing of an oath by the accused person, backed up by a group of "oathhelpers," numbering twelve or twenty-five, who would also swear that the accused person should be believed. The ordeal functioned in a variety of ways, all of which were based on the principle of divine intervention; divine forces (whether pagan or Christian) would not allow an innocent person to be harmed (see the box on p. 223). The ordeal continued to be used in parts of Europe until the thirteenth century, when the Catholic church finally withdrew its sanction.

THE FRANKISH FAMILY AND MARRIAGE

For the Franks, like other Germanic peoples of the Early Middle Ages, the extended family was at the center of social organization. The Frankish family structure was quite simple. Males were dominant and made all the important decisions. A woman obeyed her father until she married and then fell under the legal domination of her husband. A widow, however, could hold property without a male guardian. In Frankish law, the *wergeld* of a wife of childbearing age—of value because she could bear children—was considerably higher than that of a man. The Salic Law stated: "If any one killed a free woman after she had begun bearing children, he shall be sentenced to 24,000 denars. . . . After she can have no more children, he who kills her shall be sentenced to 8,000 denars. . . ."[11]

⇒ Germanic Customary Law: The Ordeal ⇐

In Germanic customary law, the ordeal came to be a means by which accused persons might clear themselves. Although the ordeal took different forms, all involved a physical trial of some sort, such as holding a red-hot iron. It was believed God would protect the innocent and allow them to come through the ordeal unharmed. This sixth-century account by Gregory of Tours describes an ordeal by hot water.

Gregory of Tours, An Ordeal of Hot Water (c. 580)

An Arian presbyter disputing with a deacon of our religion made venomous assertions against the Son of God and the Holy Ghost, as is the habit of that sect [the Arians]. But when the deacon had discoursed a long time concerning the reasonableness of our faith and the heretic, blinded by the fog of unbelief, continued to reject the truth, . . . the former said: "Why weary ourselves with long discussions? Let acts approve the truth; let a kettle be heated over the fire and someone's ring be thrown into the boiling water. Let him who shall take it from the heated liquid be approved as a follower of the truth, and afterward let the other party be converted to the knowledge of the truth. And do you also understand, O heretic, that this our party will fulfil the conditions with the aid of the Holy Ghost; you shall confess that there is no discordance, no dissimilarity in the Holy Trinity." The heretic consented to the proposition and they separated after appointing the next morning for the trial. But the fervor of faith in which the deacon had first made this suggestion began to cool through the instigation of the enemy. Rising with the dawn he bathed his arm in oil and smeared it with ointment. But nevertheless he made the round of the sacred places and called in prayer on the Lord. . . . About the third hour they met in the market place. The people came together to see the show. A fire was lighted, the kettle was placed upon it, and when it grew very hot the ring was thrown into the boiling water. The deacon invited the heretic to take it out of the water first. But he promptly refused, saying, "You who did propose this trial are the one to take it out." The deacon all of a tremble bared his arm. And when the heretic presbyter saw it besmeared with ointment he cried out: "With magic arts you have thought to protect yourself, that you have made use of these salves, but what you have done will not avail." While they were thus quarreling there came up a deacon from Ravenna named Iacinthus and inquired what the trouble was about. When he learned the truth he drew his arm out from under his robe at once and plunged his right hand into the kettle. Now the ring that had been thrown in was a little thing and very light so that it was thrown about by the water as chaff would be blown about by the wind; and searching for it a long time he found it after about an hour. Meanwhile the flame beneath the kettle blazed up mightily so that the greater heat might make it difficult for the ring to be followed by the hand; but the deacon extracted it at length and suffered no harm, protesting rather that at the bottom the kettle was cold while at the top it was just pleasantly warm. When the heretic beheld this he was greatly confused and audaciously thrust his hand into the kettle saying, "My faith will aid me." As soon as his hand had been thrust in all the flesh was boiled off the bones clear up to the elbow. And so the dispute ended.

Since marriage affected the extended family group, fathers or uncles could arrange marriages for the good of the family without considering their children's wishes. Most important was the engagement ceremony in which a prospective son-in-law made a payment symbolizing the purchase of paternal authority over the bride. The essential feature of the marriage itself involved placing the married couple in bed to achieve their physical union. In first marriages, it was considered important that the wife be a virgin so as to ensure that any children would be the husband's. A virgin symbolized the ability of the bloodline to continue. For this reason, adultery was viewed as pollution of the woman and her offspring, hence poisoning the future. Adulterous wives were severely punished (an adulterous woman could be strangled or even burned alive); adulterous husbands were not. Frankish men were, in fact, accustomed to keeping concubines. Divorce was relatively simple and was initiated primarily by the husband. Divorced wives simply returned to their families. Christianity would eventually make an impact on marriage as well as sexual attitudes (see Chapter 8).

The Development of the Latin Christian Church

The western Christian church, led by the Roman popes, underwent a period of considerable uncertainty in the sixth century. The rulers of the Eastern Roman Empire (see The Byzantine Empire later in this chapter) treated the Roman popes as mere instruments of their imperial policy. While the invasion of the Lombards saved the popes from Byzantine control, Lombard domination seemed a poor alternative. The emergence of a strong pope, Gregory I, known as Gregory the Great and called "the father of the medieval papacy," set the papacy and the Roman Catholic church, as the Christian church of the west came to be called, on an energetic path that enabled the church to play an increasingly prominent role in civilizing the Germans and aiding the emergence of a distinctly new European civilization in the seventh and eighth centuries.

Pope Gregory the Great

As pope, Gregory I (590–604) assumed direction of Rome and its surrounding territories, which had suffered enormously from the Ostrogothic-Byzantine struggle and the Lombard invasion of the sixth century. Gregory described the conditions in a sermon to the people of Rome:

> What Rome herself, once deemed the Mistress of the World, has now become, we see—wasted away with afflictions grievous and many, with the loss of citizens, the assaults of enemies, the frequent fall of ruined buildings. . . . Where is the Senate? Where is the people? The bones are all dissolved, the flesh is consumed, all the pomp of the dignities of this world is gone.[12]

Gregory took charge and made Rome and its surrounding area into an administrative unit that eventually came to be known as the Papal States. While historians disagree about Gregory's motives in establishing papal temporal power, it is important to remember that Gregory was probably only doing what he felt needed to be done: to provide for the defense of Rome against the

Lombards, to establish a government for Rome, and to feed the people. Gregory remained loyal to the empire and continued to address the Byzantine emperor as the rightful ruler of Italy.

Gregory also pursued a policy of extending papal authority over the Christian church in the west. He intervened in ecclesiastical conflicts throughout Italy and corresponded with the Frankish rulers, urging them to reform the church in Gaul. He successfully initiated the efforts of missionaries to convert England to Christianity. In his work, *The Book of Pastoral Care*, Gregory gave detailed advice on how a good bishop should care for his flock.

The Monks and Their Missions

Pope Gregory the Great was especially active in converting the pagan peoples of Germanic Europe. His primary instrument was the monastic movement. Monks turned pagans to the ideals of orthodox Christianity. They also copied Latin works and passed on the legacy of the ancient world to Western civilization in its European stage. Monasticism proved to be the most important "spiritual and cultural force" in medieval Europe.

Moreover, in the fifth, sixth, and seventh centuries, monks turned their conversion efforts to areas not previously part of either the Roman or German world. The British Isles, in particular, became an important center of Christian culture and missionary fervor. After their conversion, the Celts of Ireland and Anglo-Saxons of England created new centers of Christian learning and, in turn, themselves became enthusiastic missionaries. Through these efforts, the monks of Ireland and England made important contributions to the development of Christianity in the Middle Ages.

Ireland had remained a Celtic world outside the boundaries of the Roman Empire and the world of the Germanic invaders. Certainly, the most famous of the Christian missionaries to Ireland in the fifth century was Saint Patrick (c. 390–461). Son of a Romano-British Christian, Patrick was kidnapped as a young man by Irish raiders and kept as a slave in Ireland. After his escape, he became a monk and chose to return to Ireland to convert the Irish to Christianity. Irish tradition ascribes to Patrick the title of "founder of Irish Christianity," a testament to his apparent success.

Since Ireland had not been part of the Roman world and was fairly isolated from the European continent after its conversion, Irish Christianity tended to develop along lines somewhat different from Roman Christianity. Whereas Catholic ecclesiastical structure had followed Roman government models, the absence of these models in Ireland made possible a different pattern of church organization. Rather than bishoprics, monasteries became the fundamental units of church organization, and abbots, the heads of the monasteries, exercised far more control over the Irish church than bishops.

By the sixth century, Irish monasticism was a flourishing institution with its own striking characteristics. It was strongly ascetic. Monks performed strenuous fasts, prayed and meditated frequently under extreme privations, and confessed their sins on a regular basis to their superiors. In fact, Irish monasticism gave rise to the use of penitentials or manuals that provided a guide for examining one's life to see what sins, or offenses against the will of God, one had committed (see the box on p. 226).

Irish monasticism was also characterized by a great love of learning. The Irish eagerly absorbed both Latin and Greek culture and fostered education as a major part of their monastic life. Irish monks were preserving classical Latin at the same time spoken Latin on the continent was being corrupted into new dialects that eventually became the Romance languages, such as Italian, French, and Spanish. Since their interest in education encouraged writing, Irish monasteries produced extraordinary illuminated manuscripts illustrated with abstract geometrical patterns.

Their emphasis on asceticism led many Irish monks to go into voluntary exile. This "exile for the love of God" was not into isolation, however, but into missionary activity. In the Roman Empire, monasteries had been centers where people could withdraw from the world; in contrast, Irish monks became fervid missionaries. Saint Columba (521–597) left Ireland in 565 as a "pilgrim for Christ" and founded a highly influential monastic community on the island of Iona off the coast of Scotland. From there Irish missionaries went to northern England to begin the process of converting the Angles and Saxons. Aidan of Iona, for example, founded the island monastery of Lindisfarne in the Anglo-Saxon kingdom of Northumbria. Lindisfarne, in turn, became a training center for monks who spread out to different parts of Anglo-Saxon England. Meanwhile, other Irish monks traveled to the European continent. Saint Columbanus (c. 530–615) proceeded to Gaul, then Switzerland, and wound up in northern Italy where he established a monastery at Bobbio. New monasteries

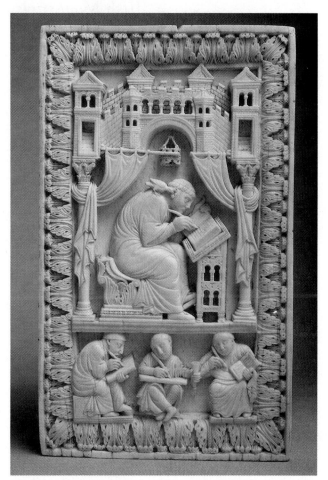

✦ **Pope Gregory I.** Pope Gregory the Great became one of the most important popes of the Early Middle Ages. This tenth-century ivory book cover shows Gregory working at his desk. On his right shoulder is a dove, symbol of the Holy Spirit, which is providing divine inspiration. The lower scene shows a monastic scriptorium or writing room with three monks busy at their work.

founded by the Irish became centers of learning wherever they were located.

At the same time the Irish monks were busy bringing their version of Christianity to the Anglo-Saxons of Britain, Pope Gregory the Great had also set in motion his own effort to convert England to Roman Christianity. His most important agent was Augustine, a monk from Saint Andrew's monastery in Rome, who arrived in England in 597. England at that time had a number of Germanic kingdoms. Augustine went first to Kent where he converted King Ethelbert; thereupon most of the

⇝ *Irish Monasticism and the Penitential* ⇜

*I*rish monasticism became well known for its ascetic practices. Much emphasis was placed on careful examination of conscience to determine if one had committed a sin against God. To facilitate this examination, penitentials were developed that listed possible sins with appropriate penances. Penance usually meant fasting a number of days each week on bread and water. Although these penitentials were eventually used throughout Christendom, they were especially important in Irish Christianity. This excerpt from the Penitential of Cummean, an Irish abbot, was written about 650 and demonstrates a distinctive feature of the penitentials, an acute preoccupation with sexual sins.

The Penitential of Cummean

A bishop who commits fornication shall be degraded and shall do penance for twelve years.

A presbyter or a deacon who commits natural fornication, having previously taken the vow of a monk, shall do penance for seven years. He shall ask pardon every hour; he shall perform a special fast during every week except in the days between Easter and Pentecost.

He who defiles his mother shall do penance for three years, with perpetual pilgrimage.

So shall those who commit sodomy do penance every seven years.

He who merely desires in his mind to commit fornication, but is not able, shall do penance for one year, especially in the three forty-day periods.

He who is willingly polluted during sleep shall arise and sing nine psalms in order, kneeling. On the following day, he shall live on bread and water.

A cleric who commits fornication once shall do penance for one year on bread and water; if he begets a son he shall do penance for seven years as an exile; so also a virgin.

He who loves any woman, but is unaware of any evil beyond a few conversations, shall do penance for forty days.

He who is in a state of matrimony ought to be continent during the three forty-day periods and on Saturday and on Sunday, night and day, and in the two appointed week days [Wednesday and Friday], and after conception, and during the entire menstrual period.

After a birth he shall abstain, if it is a son, for thirty-three [days]; of a daughter, for sixty-six [days].

Boys talking alone and transgressing the regulations of the elders [in the monastery], shall be corrected by three special fasts.

Children who imitate acts of fornication, twenty days; if frequently, forty.

But boys of twenty years who practice masturbation together and confess [shall do penance] twenty or forty days before they take communion.

king's subjects followed suit. Pope Gregory's conversion techniques emphasized persuasion rather than force, and as seen in this excerpt from one of his letters, he was willing to assimilate old pagan practices in order to coax the pagans into the new faith:

> We wish you [Abbot Mellitus] to inform him [Augustine] that we have been giving careful thought to the affairs of the English, and have come to the conclusion that the temples of the idols among that people should on no account be destroyed. The idols are to be destroyed, but the temples themselves are to be aspersed with holy water, altars set up in them, and relics deposited there. For if these temples are well-built, they must be purified from the worship of demons and dedicated to the service of the true God. In this way, we hope that the people,

> seeing that their temples are not destroyed, may abandon their error and, flocking more readily to their accustomed resorts, may come to know and adore the true God.[13]

Likewise, old pagan feasts were to be given new names and incorporated into the Christian calendar: "And since they have a custom of sacrificing many oxen to demons, let some other solemnity be substituted in its place, such as a day of Dedication or the Festivals of the holy martyrs whose relics are enshrined there."[14] No doubt, Gregory was aware that early Christians had done likewise, transforming, for example, Lupercalia day, a Roman invocation of fertility celebrated in mid-February, to Saint Valentine's day in honor of a Christian martyr. The Christian feast of Christmas was held on December 25, the day of the pagan celebration of the winter solstice.

As Roman Christianity spread northward in Britain, it encountered Irish Christianity moving southward. Soon, arguments arose over the differences between Celtic and Roman Christianity, especially over different calendar days for feasts and matters of discipline. The conflict was settled at the Synod of Whitby held in the kingdom of Northumbria in 664. When the king of Northumbria accepted the arguments of the representatives of Roman Christianity, the issue was decided in favor of Roman practices. A gradual fusion of Celtic and Roman Christianity now ensued within a framework of Roman ecclesiastical organization. The archbishop of Canterbury was made the highest ranking church official, and various bishops were subordinated to him. Despite its newfound unity and loyalty to Rome, the English church retained some Celtic features. Most important was the concentration on monastic culture with special emphasis on learning and missionary work. As a result, by 700, the English clergy had become the best trained and most learned in western Europe.

Following the Irish example, English monastic missionaries spread to the European continent to carry on the work of conversion. The most important monk was from Wessex and used the name Boniface (c. 675–754). He undertook the conversion of pagan Germans in Frisia, Bavaria, and Saxony. When Boniface sought papal approval for his missionary activities, the pope made him an archbishop and put him in charge of church reform in the Frankish kingdom. Boniface cooperated with the Frankish leader Charles Martel, and later with his son, in undertaking the regeneration of the Frankish higher clergy. Boniface's efforts also led to closer cooperation between the Franks and the leaders of the Catholic church at Rome. By 740, Saint Boniface, the "Apostle of the Germans," had become the most famous churchman in Europe. Fourteen years later, he was killed while trying to convert the pagan Frisians. Boniface was a brilliant example of the numerous Irish and English monks whose tireless efforts made Europe the bastion of the Roman Catholic faith.

The role of women has frequently been overlooked in the monastic missionary movement and the conversion of the Germanic kingdoms. So-called double monasteries in which monks and nuns lived in separate houses but attended church services together were found in both the English and Frankish kingdoms. The monks and nuns followed a common rule under a common head. Frequently, this leader was an abbess rather than

✦ **The Book of Kells.** The emphasis on education in Irish monasticism led to the production of elaborately illustrated manuscripts. Shown here is the figure of Christ from the Book of Kells, a text believed to have been made by the monks of Iona.

an abbot. Many of these abbesses belonged to royal houses, especially in Anglo-Saxon England. In the kingdom of Northumbria, for example, Saint Hilda founded the monastery of Whitby in 657. As abbess, she was responsible for giving learning an important role in the life of the monastery; five future bishops were educated under her tutelage (see the box on p. 228). For female intellectuals, monasteries offered opportunities for learning not found elsewhere in the society of their day.

Nuns of the seventh and eighth centuries were not always as heavily cloistered as they once had been and were therefore able to play an important role in the spread of Christianity. The great English missionary Boniface relied on nuns in England for books and money. He also asked the abbess of Wimborne to send

⇒ An Anglo-Saxon Abbess: Hilda of Whitby ⇐

Hilda, abbess of the monastery of Whitby, is a good example of the abbesses from royal families in Anglo-Saxon England who played important roles in English monastic institutions. Hilda was especially known for her exemplary life and high regard for learning. This account of her life is taken from Bede, considered by many the first major historian of the Middle Ages.

Bede, *Ecclesiastical History of the English People*
In the following year, that is the year of our Lord 680, Hilda, abbess of the monastery of Whitby, a most religious servant of Christ, passed away to receive the reward of eternal life on the seventeenth of November at the age of sixty-six, after a life full of heavenly deeds. Her life fell into two equal parts, for she spent thirty-three years most nobly in secular occupations, and dedicated the remainder of her life even more nobly to our Lord in the monastic life. She was nobly born, the daughter of Hereric, nephew to King Edwin, with whom she received the Faith and sacraments of Christ through the preaching of Paulinus of blessed memory, first bishop of the Northumbrians, and she preserved this Faith inviolate until she was found worthy to see him in heaven. . . .

When she had ruled this monastery (Heruteu) for some years, constantly occupied in establishing the regular life, she further undertook to found or organize a monastery at a place known as Streaneshalch, and carried out this appointed task with great energy. She established the same regular life as in her former monastery, and taught the observance of justice, devotion, purity, and other virtues, but especially in peace and charity. After the example of the primitive Church, no one there was rich or poor, for everything was held in common, and none possessed any personal property.

So great was her prudence that not only ordinary folk, but kings and princes used to come and ask her advice in their difficulties. Those under her direction were required to make a thorough study of the Scriptures and occupy themselves in good works, in order that many might be found fitted for Holy Orders and the service of God's altar. Subsequently, five bishops were chosen from this monastery—Bosa, Hedda, Oftfor, John, and Wilfrid—all of them men of outstanding merit and holiness. . . .

Christ's servant Abbess Hilda, whom all her acquaintances called Mother because of her wonderful devotion and grace, was not only an example of holy life to members of her own community, for she also brought about the amendment and salvation of many living far distant, who heard the inspiring story of her industry and goodness. . . . When Hilda ruled this monastery for many years, it pleased the Author of our salvation to try her holy soul by a long sickness, in order that, like the Apostle, her strength might be perfected in weakness. She was attacked by a burning fever that racked her continually for six years; but during all this time she never ceased to give thanks to her Maker, or to instruct the flock committed to her both privately and publicly. For her own example taught them all to serve God rightly when in health, and to render thanks to him faithfully when in trouble or bodily weakness. In the seventh year of her illness she suffered interior pains, and her last day came. About dawn she received the Viaticum of the holy Communion, and when she had summoned all the servants of Christ in the monastery, she urged them to maintain the gospel peace among themselves and with others. And while she was still speaking, she joyfully welcomed death, and in the words of our Lord, passed from death to life.

groups of nuns to establish convents in newly converted German lands. A nun named Leoba established the first convent in Germany at Bischofsheim.

It is difficult to assess what Christianity meant to the converted pagans, especially the peasants upon whom the Irish and English monks expended their greatest efforts. As Pope Gregory had recommended, Christian beliefs and values were usually superimposed upon older pagan customs. Though effective in producing quick conversions, it is an open question how much people actually understood of Christian theology. Popular belief tended to focus on God as a judge who needed to be appeased to avert disasters in daily life and gain salvation. Except for the promise of salvation, such an image of God was not all that different from Roman religious practices.

Christianity and Intellectual Life

Invasions and wars destroyed much of the physical foundation of the classical world and its intellectual life. Although the Christian church came to accept classical culture, it was not easy to do so in the world of the barbarian kingdoms. Nevertheless, a number of Christian scholars managed to keep learning alive, even if it meant only preserving a heritage rather than creating new bodies of knowledge.

Boethius and Cassiodorus, two important Christian intellectuals, both served as officials of the Ostrogothic king Theodoric. Boethius (c. 480–524) received the traditional education typical of the Roman aristocracy. He met King Theodoric in 505, became his adviser, and eventually rose to be the highest civil official in Italy. As an example of Roman talent serving a German king, he stands as a symbol of the process of fusion by which the Roman world was transformed to the medieval. Boethius was also a scholar. He translated some of the works of Aristotle into Latin, especially his works on logic, and left an important legacy to the medieval world by providing a systematic Latin vocabulary for the analysis of logic. Boethius's most famous work was written in prison, where he was kept for a year by Theodoric on a charge of treason before being executed. This work, *On the Consolation of Philosophy*, is a dialogue between Boethius and philosophy personified as a woman. Philosophy leads Boethius to a clear understanding of true happiness and the highest good, which she equates with God. These are not achieved by outward conditions, since the person who lives virtuously finds happiness within. Moreover, reason, not faith, enables one to realize the true meaning of happiness. Basically, Boethius was restating Stoic philosophy rather than Christian theology; nevertheless, he presented it eloquently.

Cassiodorus (c. 490–c. 585) also came from an aristocratic Roman family. Whereas Boethius had been concerned with philosophy and theology, Cassiodorus was more interested in history, which he used to reconcile the Romans and Goths by demonstrating how the Goths were attempting to preserve Roman tradition. After the execution of Boethius, Cassiodorus held the position of master of offices to Theodoric. His letters, written while he was secretary to Theodoric, provide us with a major source of information about this period (see the box on p. 218).

The conflicts that erupted after the death of Theodoric led Cassiodorus to withdraw from public life and retire to his landed estates in southern Italy, where he wrote his final work, *Divine and Human Readings*. This was a compendium of the literature of both Christian and pagan antiquity. Cassiodorus accepted the advice of earlier Christian intellectuals to make use of classical works while treasuring the Scriptures above all else: "And therefore, as the blessed Augustine and other very learned Fathers say, secular writings should not be spurned. It is proper, however, . . . to 'meditate in the (divine) law day and night,' for, though a worthy knowledge of some matters is occasionally obtained from secular writings, this law is the source of eternal life."[15]

Cassiodorus continued the tradition of late antiquity of classifying knowledge according to certain subjects. In assembling his compendium of authors, he followed the works of Boethius and other late ancient authors in placing all secular knowledge into the categories of the seven liberal arts, which were divided into two major groups: the *trivium*, consisting of grammar, rhetoric, and dialectic or logic; and the *quadrivium*, consisting of the mathematical subjects of arithmetic, geometry, astronomy, and music. The seven liberal arts would become the cornerstone of education until the seventeenth century.

Isidore of Seville (c. 570–636) was a product of Visigothic Spain. Though not an original thinker, he was especially good at compiling existing knowledge, as his well-known *Etymologiae (Etymologies)* illustrates. This was a twenty-volume compendium of knowledge organized through explanations of the etymology of Latin words. While simplistically incorrect at times ("Man (*homo*) is so called because he was made out of earth (*ex humo*) as is recounted in Genesis."), Isidore still passed on a considerable body of knowledge to medieval people.

The Venerable Bede (c. 672–735) was a scholar and product of Christian Anglo-Saxon England. He entered a monastery at Jarrow as a small boy and remained there most of the rest of his life. Many historians consider Bede the first major historian of the Middle Ages. His *Ecclesiastical History of the English People*, completed in 731, was a product of the remarkable flowering of English ecclesiastical and monastic culture in the eighth century. His work is a history of England that begins with the coming of Christianity to Britain. Although Bede shared the credulity of his age in regard to stories of miracles, he had a remarkable sense of history. He used his sources judiciously to give us our chief source of information about early Anglo-Saxon England (see the box on p. 228). His work was a remarkable accomplishment for a monk from a small corner of England and reflects the high degree of intellectual achievement of England in the eighth century.

The Byzantine Empire

In the fourth century, a noticeable separation between the western and eastern parts of the Roman Empire began to develop (see Chapter 6). In the course of the fifth century, while the Germans moved into the western part of the empire and established their kingdoms, the Roman Empire in the east, centered on Constantinople, continued to exist and even prosper. Though the eastern Roman emperors regarded German rulers, such as Odoacer and Theodoric, as their regents, it was not until the reign of Justinian that an attempt was made to restore Roman institutions and civilization to the entire Mediterranean world.

The Reign of Justinian (527–565)

As the nephew and heir of the previous emperor, Justinian had been well trained in imperial administration. He married Theodora, daughter of a lower-class circus trainer who was said to have been an actress and prostitute. She proved to be a remarkably strong-willed and intelligent woman, who played a crucial role in giving Justinian the determination to crush a revolt against his rule in 532. Justinian was determined to reestablish the Roman Empire in the entire Mediterranean world and began his attempt to reconquer the west within a year after the revolt had failed.

Justinian's army under Belisarius, probably the best general of the late Roman world, presented a formidable force. Belisarius sailed to North Africa and quickly destroyed the Vandals in two major battles. From North Africa, he led his forces onto the Italian peninsula after occupying Sicily in 535. Although he had conquered Italy south of the Po River by 540, the Ostrogoths were given a reprieve when Belisarius had to return east to defend the empire against the Persians. Consequently, the struggle in Italy continued for another twelve years until 552, when the Ostrogoths were defeated and, like the Vandals, became extinct as a separate people. This struggle devastated Italy, which suffered more from

◆ **The Emperor Justinian Surrounded by His Court.** The church of San Vitale at Ravenna contains some of the finest examples of sixth-century Byzantine mosaics. This mosaic depicts the Byzantine emperor Justinian and his court dressed in their elaborate court robes.

Justinian's reconquest than from all of the previous barbarian invasions.

Justinian has been criticized for overextending his resources and bankrupting the empire. Historians now think, however, that a devastating plague in 542 and long-term economic factors were far more damaging to the Eastern Roman Empire than Justinian's conquests. Before he died, Justinian appeared to have achieved his goals. He had restored the imperial Mediterranean world; his empire included Italy, part of Spain, North Africa, Asia Minor, Palestine, and Syria. But the conquest of the western empire proved ephemeral. Only three years after Justinian's death, the Lombards entered Italy. Although the eastern empire maintained the fiction of Italy as a province, its forces were limited to southern and central Italy, Sicily, and coastal areas, such as the territory around Ravenna.

THE CODIFICATION OF ROMAN LAW

Though his conquests proved short-lived, Justinian made a lasting contribution to Western civilization through his codification of Roman law. The eastern empire was heir to a vast quantity of materials connected to the development of Roman law. These included laws passed by the senate and assemblies, legal commentaries of jurists, decisions of praetors, and the edicts of emperors. Justinian had been well trained in imperial government and was well acquainted with Roman law. He wished to codify and simplify this mass of materials, as he explained:

> Therefore, since there is nothing to be found in all things so worthy of attention as the authority of the law, which properly regulates all affairs both divine and human, and expels all injustice; We have found the entire arrangement of the law which has come down to us from the foundation of the City of Rome and the times of Romulus, to be so confused that it is extended to an infinite length and is not within the grasp of human capacity; and hence We were first induced to begin by examining what had been enacted by former most venerated princes, to correct their constitutions, and make them more easily understood; to the end that being included in a single Code, and having had removed all that is superfluous in resemblance and all iniquitous discord, they may afford to all men the ready assistance of their true meaning.[16]

To accomplish his goal, Justinian authorized the jurist Trebonian to make a systematic compilation of imperial edicts. The result was the Code of Law, the first part of the *Corpus Iuris Civilis* (*The Body of Civil Law*), com-

pleted in 529. Four years later, two other parts of the *Corpus* appeared: the *Digest*, a compendium of writings of Roman jurists, and the *Institutes*, a brief summary of the chief principles of Roman law that could be used as a textbook on Roman law. The fourth part of the *Corpus* was the *Novels*, a compilation of the most important new edicts issued during Justinian's reign.

Justinian's codification of Roman law became the basis of imperial law in the Byzantine Empire until its end in 1453. More importantly, however, since it was written in Latin (it was, in fact, the last product of eastern Roman culture to be written in Latin, which was soon replaced by Greek), it was also eventually used in the west and, in fact, became the basis of the legal system of all of continental Europe.

INTELLECTUAL LIFE UNDER JUSTINIAN

The intellectual life of the Eastern Roman Empire was highly influenced by the traditions of classical civilization. Scholars actively strived to preserve the works of the ancient Greeks while basing a great deal of their own literature on classical models. Initially, however, the most outstanding literary achievements of the eastern empire were historical and religious works.

The best known of the early Byzantine historians was Procopius (c. 500–c. 562), court historian during the reign of Justinian. Procopius served as legal assistant and secretary to the great general Belisarius and accompanied him on his wars on behalf of Justinian. Procopius's best historical work, the *Wars*, is a firsthand account of Justinian's wars of reconquest in the western Mediterranean and his wars against the Persians in the east.

CHRONOLOGY

The Byzantine Empire

Protective walls of Theodosius II	408–450
Justinian codifies Roman law	529–533
Reconquest of Italy by the Byzantines	535–554
Completion of Hagia Sophia	537
Attacks on the empire in reign of Heraclius	610–641
Arab defeat of Byzantines at Yarmuk	636
Defeat by the Bulgars; losses in the Balkans	679

�֎ **Map 7.4a** The Byzantine Empire in the Time of Justinian.

✖ **Map 7.4b** Constantinople.

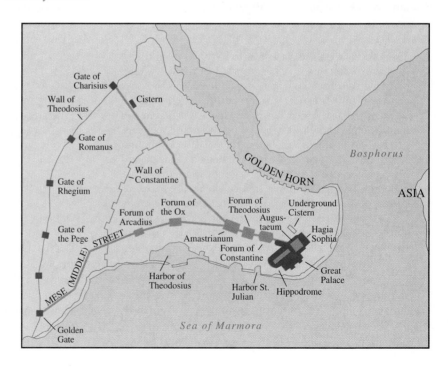

Deliberately modeled after the work of his hero, the Greek historian Thucydides (see Chapter 3), Procopius's narrative features vivid descriptions of battle scenes, clear judgment, and noteworthy objectivity. Procopius also wrote a work that many historians consider mostly scandalous gossip, his infamous *Secret History*. At the beginning of this work, Procopius informed his readers that "What I shall write now follows a different plan, supplementing the previous formal chronicle with a disclosure of what really happened throughout the Roman Empire."[17] What he revealed constituted a scathing attack upon Justinian and his wife Theodora for their alleged misdeeds.

LIFE IN CONSTANTINOPLE: THE EMPEROR'S BUILDING PROGRAM

After the destruction caused by the riots of 532, Justinian rebuilt Constantinople and gave it the appearance it would keep until its sack by the crusaders in 1204 and its capture by the Turks in 1453 (see Chapter 13). With a population estimated in the hundreds of thousands, Constantinople was the largest city in Europe during the Middle Ages. It viewed itself as the center of an empire and a special Christian city. After all, its founder Constantine had dedicated the city with these words: "Oh Christ, ruler and master of the world. To you now I dedicate this subject city, and these scepters and the might of Rome. Protect her; save her from all harm."

Until the twelfth century, Constantinople was the medieval world's greatest commercial center. The city was the chief entrepot for the exchange of products between west and east. Highly desired in Europe were the products of the east: silk from China; spices from southeast Asia and India; jewelry and ivory from India (the latter used by artisans for church items); wheat and furs from southern Russia; and flax and honey from the Balkans. Many of these eastern goods were then shipped to the Mediterranean area and northern Europe. Despite the Germanic incursions, European trade did not entirely end.

Moreover, imported raw materials were used in Constantinople for local industries. During Justinian's reign, silkworms were smuggled from China, and a silk industry began. The state had a monopoly on the production of silk cloth, and the workshops themselves were housed in Constantinople's royal palace complex. European demand for silk cloth made it the city's most lucrative product. It is interesting to note that the upper classes, including emperors and empresses, were not discouraged

✦ **Walls of Constantinople.** Pictured here are the ruins of the walls of Constantinople. From a military perspective, Constantinople was in an ideal strategic location. It was surrounded by water on two sides and protected by massive walls on the third side. The defensive walls, which consisted of a double rampart with 96 towers and a moat outside, were built by Emperor Theodosius II between 413 and 447 and remained impregnable until the city was taken in 1453 by Muslim invaders.

from making money through trade and manufacturing. Indeed, one empress even manufactured perfumes in her bedroom.

Much of Constantinople's appearance in the Early Middle Ages was due to Justinian's program of rebuilding in the sixth century. Earlier, in the mid-fifth century, Emperor Theodosius II (408–450) had constructed an enormous defensive wall to protect the city on its land side. The city was dominated by an immense palace complex, a huge arena known as the Hippodrome, and hundreds of churches. No residential district was particularly fashionable; palaces, tenements, and slums ranged alongside one another. Justinian added many new buildings. His public works projects included roads, bridges, walls, public baths, law courts, and colossal underground reservoirs to hold the city's water supply. He also built hospitals, schools, monasteries, and churches. The latter was his special passion, and in Constantinople alone he built or rebuilt thirty-four of them. His greatest achievement was the famous Hagia Sophia—the church of the Holy Wisdom.

✦ **Interior View of Hagia Sophia.** Pictured here is the interior of the Church of the Holy Wisdom, constructed under Justinian by Anthemius of Tralles and Isidore of Milan. The pulpits and the great plaques bearing inscriptions from the Koran were introduced when the Turks converted this church into a mosque in the fifteenth century.

Completed in 537, Hagia Sophia was designed by a Greek architect who did not use the simple, flat-roofed basilica of western architecture. The center of Hagia Sophia consisted of four enormous piers crowned by an enormous dome, which seemed to be floating in space. This effect was emphasized by Procopius, the court historian, who, at Justinian's request, wrote a treatise on the emperor's building projects: "From the lightness of the building, it does not appear to rest upon a solid foundation, but to cover the place beneath as though it were suspended from heaven by the fabled golden

chain." In part, this impression was created by putting forty-two windows around the base of the dome, which allowed an incredible play of light within the cathedral. Light served to remind the worshipers of God; as Procopius commented:

> Whoever enters there to worship perceives at once that it is not by any human strength or skill, but by the favor of God that this work has been perfected; his mind rises sublime to commune with God, feeling that He cannot be far off, but must especially love to dwell in the place which He has chosen; and this takes place not only when a man sees it for the first time, but it always makes the same impression upon him, as though he had never beheld it before.[18]

As darkness is illumined by invisible light, so too it was believed the world is illumined by invisible spirit.

The royal palace complex, Hagia Sophia, and the Hippodrome were the three greatest buildings in Constantinople. The latter was a huge amphitheater, constructed of brick covered by marble, holding between 40,000 and 60,000 spectators. Although gladiator fights were held there, the main events were the chariot races; twenty-four would usually be presented in one day. The citizens of Constantinople were passionate fans of chariot racing. Successful charioteers were acclaimed as heroes and honored with public statues. Crowds in the Hippodrome also took on political significance. Being a member of the two chief factions of charioteers—the Blues or Greens—was the only real outlet for political expression. Even emperors had to be aware of their demands and attitudes since rioting could threaten even their power. The loss of a race in the Hippodrome frequently resulted in bloody riots.

From Eastern Roman to Byzantine Empire

Although the accomplishments of Justinian's reign had been spectacular, the Eastern Roman Empire was left with serious problems: an empty treasury, a decline in population after the plague, and renewed threats to its frontiers. The seventh century proved to be an important turning point in the history of the Eastern Roman Empire. In the first half of the century, during the reign of Heraclius (610–641), the empire faced attacks from the Persians to the east and the Slavs to the north.

The empire was left exhausted by these struggles. In the midst of them, it had developed a new system of defense by creating a new administrative unit, the *theme*, which combined civilian and military offices in the hands of the same person. Thus, the civil governor was also the military leader of the area. While this innovation helped the empire survive, it also fostered an increased militarization of the empire. By the mid-seventh century, it had become apparent that a restored Mediterranean empire was simply beyond the resources of the eastern empire, which now increasingly turned its back upon the Latin west. A renewed series of external threats in the second half of the seventh century only strengthened this development.

The most serious challenge to the eastern empire was presented by the rise of Islam, which unified the Arab tribes and created a powerful new force that swept through the east (see The Rise of Islam later in this chapter). The defeat of an eastern Roman army at Yarmuk in 636 meant the loss of the provinces of Syria and Palestine. The Arabs also moved into the old Persian Empire and conquered it. Although the Islamic attempt to besiege Constantinople failed, Arabs and eastern Roman forces faced each other along a frontier in southern Asia Minor.

Problems also arose, however, along the northern frontier, especially in the Balkans, where an Asiatic people known as the Bulgars had arrived earlier in the sixth century. In 679, the Bulgars defeated the eastern Roman forces and took possession of the lower Danube valley, creating a strong Bulgarian kingdom.

By the beginning of the eighth century, the Eastern Roman Empire was greatly diminished in size, consisting only of the eastern Balkans and Asia Minor. It was now an eastern Mediterranean state. These external challenges had important internal repercussions as well. By the eighth century, the Eastern Roman Empire had been transformed into what historians call the Byzantine Empire, a civilization with its own unique character that would last until 1453 (Constantinople was built on the site of an older city named Byzantium—hence the term *Byzantine*). What were the characteristics of this Byzantine Empire in the eighth century?

The Byzantine Empire was a Greek state. Justinian's *Body of Civil Law* had been the last official work published in Latin. Increasingly, Latin fell into disuse as Greek became not only the common language of the Byzantine Empire, but its official language as well.

The Byzantine Empire was an orthodox Christian state. Christianity, in fact, had become the foundation stone of the Byzantine state. The empire was built on a faith in Christ that was shared in a profound way by almost all its citizens. An enormous amount of artistic talent was poured into the construction of churches, church ceremonies, and church decoration. Byzantine art was deeply permeated by spiritual principles. The importance of orthodox Christianity to the Byzantines explains why theological disputes took on an exaggerated form. The most famous of these disputes, the so-called iconoclastic controversy, threatened the stability of the empire in the first half of the eighth century.

Beginning in the sixth century, the use of religious images, especially in the form of icons or pictures of sacred figures, became so widespread that charges of idolatry, or the worship of images, began to be heard. The use of images or icons had been justified by the argument that icons were not worshiped, but were simply used to help illiterate people understand their religion. This rationalization failed to stop the iconoclasts, as those who opposed icons were called. Beginning in 730, the Byzantine emperor Leo III (717–741) outlawed the use of icons as worship of images. Severe resistance ensued, especially from monks. Leo III also used the iconoclastic controversy to add to the prestige of the patriarch of Constantinople, the highest church official in the east and second in dignity only to the bishop of Rome. The Roman popes were opposed to the iconoclastic edicts, and their opposition created considerable dissension between the popes and the Byzantine emperors. Late in the eighth century, the Byzantine rulers reversed their stand on the use of images, but not before considerable damage had been done to the unity of the Christian church. Although the final separation between Roman Catholicism and Greek Orthodoxy did not occur until the eleventh century (1054), the iconoclastic controversy was important in moving both sides in that direction.

The Byzantine Empire was characterized by what might be called a permanent war economy. Byzantine emperors maintained the late Roman policy of state regulation of economic affairs. Of course, it was easy to justify; the survival of the empire was dependent upon careful shepherding of economic resources and the maintenance of the army. Thus, the state encouraged agricultural production, regulated the guilds or corporations responsible for industrial production and the various stages of manufacturing, and controlled commerce by making trade in grain and silk, the two most valuable products, government monopolies.

The emperor occupied a crucial position in the Byzantine state. Portrayed as chosen by God, the Byzantine emperor was crowned in sacred ceremonies, and his subjects were expected to prostrate themselves in his presence. His power was considered absolute and limited in practice only by deposition or assassination. The emperor was assisted in his rule by a rather unusual ruling class. Civil servants and high churchmen essentially stemmed from the same ranks of the urban society of Constantinople. They received the same education and often followed the same careers in civil service until they went their separate ways into church and government offices. Their education combined Greek classics with Christian theology, with special emphasis on the importance of Neoplatonic philosophy in Greek Christian theology.

The similar background of the ruling classes, whether clerical or civil, meant that there was no real division between church and state in the Byzantine Empire, a condition symbolized by the divinely chosen emperor, who appointed the patriarch of the church and exercised control over both church and state. The Byzantines believed that God had commanded their state to preserve the true faith—Orthodox Christianity. Emperor, churchmen, and civic officials were all bound together in service to this ideal. It can be said that spiritual values truly held the Byzantine state together.

By 750, it was apparent that two of Rome's heirs, the Germanic kingdoms and the Byzantine Empire, were moving in different directions. Nevertheless, Byzantine influence on the medieval western world was significant. The images of a Roman imperial state that continued to haunt the west had a living reality in the Byzantine state. The legal system of the west came to owe much to Justinian's codification of Roman law. In addition, the Byzantine Empire served in part as a buffer state, protecting the west for a long time from incursions from the east. Although the Byzantine Empire would continue to influence the west until its demise in 1453, it went its own unique way. One of its most bitter enemies was the new power of Islam that erupted out of Arabia in the name of the holy man Muhammad. This third heir of Rome soon controlled large areas of the old Roman Mediterranean area.

The Rise of Islam

The Arabs were a Semitic-speaking people of the Near East who had a long history. They had been mentioned by the Greeks in the fifth century B.C. and even earlier in the Old Testament. In Roman times, the Arabian peninsula seemed less prosperous than previously and came to be dominated by Bedouins, tribes of nomads originally from the northern part of the peninsula. Although some Arabs prospered from trading activities, especially in the north, the majority of the Arabs consisted of poor Bedouins, whose tribes were known for their independence, their warlike qualities, their dedication to their tribal gods, and their dislike for the urban-dwelling Arabs.

◆ **Muhammad on a Camel.** This illustration is from a medieval manuscript of the *Universal History* by Rashid al-Din, a Persian historian. Here Jesus Christ is shown riding on a donkey beside Muhammad who rides on a camel. The purpose of the illustration is to show that while Jesus was accepted as a forerunner of the Prophet, his teachings were superseded by the message of Muhammad.

In the fifth and sixth centuries A.D., urban Arabs became more prominent as new trade routes appeared along the western fringes of the Arabian peninsula. Especially important was the town of Mecca. Though known for its trade, it was more significant as a growing pilgrimage center since it possessed notable shrines, especially the *Ka'ba,* the sanctuary that held the sacred black meteorite. Mecca attracted Bedouins as well, which created conflicts between the independent tribespeople and the increasingly wealthy commercial class. Into this tense world stepped Muhammad, whose spiritual visions would unify the Arab world with a speed no one would have suspected possible.

Muhammad (c. 570–632) was born in Mecca and orphaned at the age of six. He became a caravan manager and eventually married a rich widow who was also his employer. Despite a background of Arabic polytheism, Muhammad arrived at a monotheistic perspective, owing much to the Hebrew and Christian traditions. In his middle years, he began to experience visions inspired by Allah (the Arab word for "God"). Muhammad believed that while Allah had already revealed himself in part through Moses and Jesus—and thus through the Hebrew and Christian traditions—the final revelations were now being given to him. Out of his revelations, which were eventually dictated to secretaries, came the Qu'ran or Koran, the holy scriptures, which contained the guidelines by which a follower of Allah was to live. Like the Christians and Jews, Muslims were a "People of the Book." Muhammad's teachings formed the basis for the religion known as Islam, which means "submission to the will of Allah." Allah was the all-powerful being who had created the universe and everything in it. Humans must subject themselves to Allah if they wished to achieve everlasting life. Those who became his followers were called Muslims, meaning those who practiced Islam. The cardinal principle of the Islamic faith is that there is only one God, Allah, and Muhammad is his Prophet.

Muhammad's first followers came from his own family and clan. The Meccan aristocracy opposed him, fearful of his impact on the traditional idol worship of Arab society. He and his followers were forced to flee from Mecca in 622, a flight known as the Hegira (the day of the flight—September 24, 622—is the first date of the official calendar of Islam). Muhammad and his supporters fled to the rival city of Medina, where they gained additional supporters and managed to unite the townspeople with Bedouin tribes from the surrounding countryside.

Birth of Muhammad	c. 570
Muhammad's flight from Mecca (Hegira)	622
Death of Muhammad	632
Defeat of Byzantines at Yarmuk	636
Seizure of Byzantine provinces of Syria and Egypt	640–642
Defeat of Persians	637–650
Invasion of Spain	710
Arab failure to capture Constantinople	717–718
Defeat of Muslims near Poitiers	732

Muslims saw no separation between political and religious authority. Submission to the will of God meant submission to his Prophet Muhammad. Consequently, Muhammad's political and military skills enabled him to put together a significant force with which he returned to Mecca, conquering the city and converting the townspeople to the new faith. By leading his supporters on successful raids against their enemies, he won prestige and even more followers for his new movement. From Mecca, Muhammad's ideas spread quickly across the Arabian peninsula and within a relatively short time had resulted in both the religious and political union of Arab society.

The rapid spread of Islam among the Arabs was a remarkable phenomenon that has not been fully explained by historians. In a true religious revolution, the Arabs moved from a polytheistic dedication to their tribal gods to a single vision and system in which individuals were tied directly to a monotheistic God. Islam emphasized Allah as an absolute authority. It made a simple, yet apparently powerful appeal to people at all social levels. Both extremes of Arabic society—the fierce independent tribes and the practical-minded merchants—were caught up by the message of Muhammad.

At the heart of Islam was the Koran with its basic message that there is no God but Allah and Muhammad is his Prophet (see the box on p. 238). Essentially, the Koran contains Muhammad's revelations of a heavenly

☙ The Koran and the Spread of the Muslim Faith ❧

The Koran is the sacred book of the Muslims, comparable to the Bible in Christianity. In this selection from Chapter 47, entitled "Muhammad, Revealed at Medina," it is apparent that Islam encourages the spreading of the faith. Believers who died for Allah were promised a garden of paradise quite unlike the arid desert homeland of the Arab warriors.

The Koran: Chapter 47, "Muhammad, Revealed at Medina"

Allah will bring to nothing the deeds of those who disbelieve and debar others from His path. As for the faithful who do good works and believe in what is revealed to Muhammad—which is the truth from their Lord—He will forgive them their sins and ennoble their state.

This, because the unbelievers follow falsehood, while the faithful follow the truth from their Lord. Thus Allah coins their sayings for mankind.

When you meet the unbelievers in the battlefield strike off their heads and, when you have laid them low, bind your captives firmly. Then grant them their freedom or take ransom from them, until War shall lay down her armor.

Thus shall you do. Had Allah willed, He could Himself have punished them; but He has ordained it thus that He might test you, the one by the other.

As for those who are slain in the cause of Allah, he will not allow their works to perish. He will vouchsafe them guidance and ennoble their state; He will admit them to the Paradise He has made known to them.

Believers, if you help Allah, Allah will help you and make you strong. But the unbelievers shall be consigned to perdition. He will bring their deeds to nothing. Because they have opposed His revelations, He will frustrate their works.

Have they never journeyed through the land and seen what was the end of those who have gone before them? Allah destroyed them utterly. A similar fate awaits the unbelievers, because Allah is the protector of the faithful; because the unbelievers have no protector.

Allah will admit those who embrace the true faith and do good works to gardens watered by running streams. The unbelievers take their fill of pleasure and eat as the beasts eat: but Hell shall be their home. . . .

This is the Paradise which the righteous have been promised. There shall flow in it rivers of unpolluted water, and rivers of milk forever fresh; rivers of delectable wine and rivers of clearest honey. They shall eat therein of every fruit and receive forgiveness from their Lord. Is this like the lot of those who shall abide in Hell for ever and drink scalding water which will tear their bowels? . . .

Know that there is no god but Allah. Implore Him to forgive your sins and to forgive the true believers, men and women. Allah knows your busy haunts and resting-places.

book narrated to him by an angelic messenger and written down by secretaries. It comprised 114 suras or chapters. The Koran recorded the beliefs of the Muslims and served as their code of ethics and law.

Islam was a direct and simple faith, emphasizing the need to obey the will of Allah. This meant following a basic ethical code consisting of what are popularly called the "five pillars" of Islam: belief in Allah and Muhammad as his Prophet; standard prayer five times a day and public prayer on Friday at midday to worship Allah; observance of the holy month of Ramadan with fasting from dawn to sunset; making a pilgrimage, if possible, to Mecca in one's lifetime; and giving alms to the poor and unfortunate. The faithful who observed the law were guaranteed a place in an eternal paradise that contained sensuous delights obviously lacking in the midst of the Arabian desert.

Islam was not just a set of religious beliefs, but a way of life as well. After the death of Muhammad, Muslim scholars drew up a law code, called the *Shari'ah*, to provide believers with a set of prescriptions to regulate their daily lives. Much of the law code was drawn from the Koran. Believers were subject to strict behavioral requirements. In addition to the "five pillars," Muslims were forbidden to gamble, to eat pork, to drink alcoholic beverages, and to engage in dishonest behavior. Sexual practices were also strictly regulated. Contacts between unmarried men and women were discouraged, and ideally marriages were to be arranged by the parents. In according with Bedouin custom, males were permitted to have more than one wife, but Muhammed attempted to limit the practice by restricting the number of wives to four.

The Expansion of Islam

The death of Muhammad presented his followers with a dilemma. Although Muhammad had not claimed divine qualities, Muslims saw no separation between political and religious authority. Submission to the will of Allah meant submission to his Prophet Muhammad. According to the Koran, "Whoever obeys the messenger obeys Allah." Muhammad's charismatic authority and political skills had been at the heart of his success. But he never named a successor, and although he had several daughters, he left no sons. In a male-oriented society, who would lead the community of the faithful? Shortly after Muhammad's death, a number of his closest followers selected Abu Bakr, a wealthy merchant from Medina who was Muhammad's father-in-law, as caliph, or temporal leader, of the Islamic community. The selection of Abu Bakr solved the succession problem only temporarily—within a few decades another succession conflict would have permanent effects on Islam.

Muhammad and the early caliphs who succeeded him took up the Arabic tribal custom of the *razzia* or raid against their persecutors. The Koran called this activity "striving in the way of the Lord" or a *jihad*. Although misleadingly called a Holy War, the *jihad* grew out of the Arabic tradition of tribal raids, which were permitted as a way to channel the warlike energies of the Arab tribes. Such aggression was not carried out to convert others since conversion to Islam was purely voluntary. Those who did not convert were required only to submit to Muslim rule and pay taxes.

Once the Arabs had become unified under Muhammad's successor, they began to direct the energy formerly expended upon each other outward against neighboring peoples, thus undertaking a *jihad* on a large scale. The Byzantines and Persians were the first to feel the strength of the newly united Arabs. At Yarmuk in 636, the Muslims defeated the Byzantine army, and by 640 they had taken possession of the province of Syria. To the east, the Arabs defeated the Persian forces in 637 and then went on to conquer the entire Persian Empire by 650. In the meantime, by 642, Egypt and additional parts of North Africa had been added to the new Muslim empire. It has been argued that the earlier Byzantine-Persian conflict had weakened both powers and made their defeats by the Arabs substantially easier.

✦ **Muslims Celebrate the End of Ramadan.** Ramadan is the holy month of Islam during which all Muslims must fast from dawn to sunset. Observance of this holy month is regarded as one of the "five pillars" of the faith. Muhammad instituted the fast during his stay at Medina. It was designed to replace the single Jewish Day of Atonement. This Persian miniature depicts Muslims on horseback celebrating the end of Ramadan.

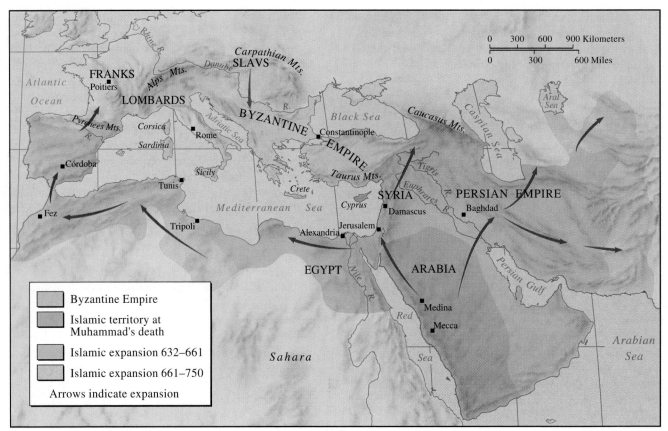

�֎ **Map 7.5** The Expansion of Islam.

Although there is some truth in this assertion, one should not overlook the power of the Arab armies. Led by the caliphs and a series of brilliant generals, the Arabs had put together a large and highly motivated army, whose valor was enhanced by the belief that Muslim warriors were guaranteed a place in paradise if they died in battle.

Early caliphs, ruling from Medina, organized their newly conquered territories into taxpaying provinces. By the mid-seventh century, problems arose again over the succession to the Prophet until Ali, son-in-law of Muhammad, was assassinated and the general Muawiyah reestablished the Umayyad dynasty in 661. This dynasty would rule until it, in turn, was overthrown in 750. As one of its first actions, the Umayyad dynasty moved the capital of the Muslim empire from Medina to Damascus in Syria. This internal dissension over the caliphate created a split in Islam between the Shiítes, or those who accepted only the descendants of Ali, Muhammad's son-in-law, as the true rulers, and the Sunnites, who

claimed that the descendants of the Umayyads were the true caliphs. This seventh-century split in Islam has lasted until the present day.

The internal crisis did not stop the Islamic expansion, however. At the beginning of the eighth century, new attacks were made at both the western and eastern ends of the Mediterranean world. After sweeping across North Africa, the Muslims invaded Germanic Europe by moving into Spain around 710. The Visigothic kingdom, already weakened by internecine warfare, collapsed, and by 725, most of Spain had become a Muslim state with its center at Córdoba. In 732, a Muslim army, making a foray into southern France, was defeated by the army of Charles Martel near Poitiers. Some historians feel that internal exhaustion would have forced the Muslims to retreat anyway.

Meanwhile, in 717, another Muslim force had launched a naval attack on Constantinople in the hope of destroying the Byzantine Empire. The Byzantines were saved by their invention of Greek fire, a petroleum-based compound containing quicklime and sulfur. Since it would burn under water, the Byzantines used the equivalent of modern flamethrowers, blowing Greek fire from tubes against wooden ships with frightening affect. In the spring of 718, the Byzantines destroyed the Muslim fleet and saved the Byzantine Empire and indirectly Christian Europe, since the fall of Constantinople would no doubt have opened the door to Muslim invasion of eastern Europe. The Byzantine Empire and Islam now established an uneasy frontier in southern Asia Minor.

The Arab advance had finally come to an end, but not before the southern and eastern Mediterranean parts of the old Roman Empire had been conquered. Islam had truly become heir to much of the old Roman Empire. The Umayyad dynasty at Damascus now ruled an enormous empire. While expansion had conveyed untold wealth and new ethnic groups into the fold of Islam, it also brought contact with Byzantine and Persian civilization. As a result, the new Arab empire would be influenced by Greek culture as well as the older civilizations of the ancient Near East. The children of the conquerors would be educated in new ways and produce a brilliant culture that would eventually influence western Europe intellectually.

Conclusion

The period from 400 to 750 was both chaotic and creative. Three new entities fell heir to Roman civilization: the German Kingdoms, the Byzantine Empire, and the world of Islam. In the west, Roman elements combined with German and Celtic influences; in the east, Greek and eastern elements of late antiquity were of more consequence. Although the Germanic kingdoms of the west and the Byzantine civilization of the east came to share a common bond in Christianity, it proved incapable of keeping them in harmony politically as the two civilizations continued to move apart. Christianity, however, remained a dominant influence in both civilizations and in the west was especially important as a civilizing agent that brought pagan peoples into a new European civilization that was slowly being born. The rise of Islam, Rome's third heir, resulted in the loss of the southern and eastern Mediterranean worlds of the old Roman Empire to a religious power that was neither Roman nor Christian. The new Islamic empire forced Europe proper back upon itself, and slowly, a new civilization emerged that became the heart of what we know as Western civilization.

NOTES

1. The Creed of Nicaea, in Henry Bettenson, ed., *Documents of the Christian Church* (London, 1963), p. 35.
2. Matthew, 16: 15–19.
3. R. C. Petry, ed., *A History of Christianity: Readings in the History of Early and Medieval Christianity* (Englewood Cliffs, N.J., 1962), p. 70.
4. Brian Pullan, ed., *Sources for the History of Medieval Europe* (Oxford, 1966), p. 46.
5. Tertullian, "The Prescriptions against the Heretics," in *The Library of Christian Classics*, vol. 5, *Early Latin Theology*, ed. and trans. S. L. Greenslade (Philadelphia, 1956), p. 36.
6. Saint Augustine, *The Confessions*, trans. Edward B. Pusey (New York, 1957), p. 22.
7. Anne Fremantle, ed., *A Treasury of Early Christianity* (New York, 1953), p. 91.
8. Mark, 10: 21.
9. Norman F. Cantor, ed., *The Medieval World: 300–1300* (New York, 1963), pp. (in order of quotations) 104, 101, 108, 103.

10. Ernest F. Henderson, *Select Historical Documents of the Middle Ages* (London, 1892), p. 182.
11. Ibid., p. 181.
12. Quoted in Sidney Painter and Brian Tierney, *Western Europe in the Middle Ages, 300–1475* (New York, 1983), p. 106.
13. Bede, *A History of the English Church and People*, trans. Leo Sherley-Price (Harmondsworth, 1968), pp. 86–87.
14. Ibid., p. 87.
15. Cassiodorus, *An Introduction to Divine and Human Readings*, trans. Leslie Jones (New York, 1969), p. 205.
16. Quoted in Cantor, *The Medieval World, 300–1300*, pp. 84–85.
17. Procopius, *Secret History*, trans. Richard Atwater (Ann Arbor, Mich., 1963), p. 3.
18. Procopius, *Buildings of Justinian* (Palestine Pilgrims' Text Society, 1897), pp. (in order of quotations) 9, 6–7, 11.

SUGGESTIONS FOR FURTHER READING

Good general histories of the entire medieval period can be found in S. Painter and B. Tierney, *Western Europe in the Middle Ages, 300–1475* (New York, 1983); E. Peters, *Europe and the Middle Ages*, 2d ed. (Englewood Cliffs, N.J., 1989); and G. Holmes, ed., *The Oxford Illustrated History of Medieval Europe* (Oxford, 1988). For a superb illustrated introduction to medieval civilization, see D. Rice, ed., *The Dark Ages: The Making of European Civilization* (London, 1965); and J. Evans, *The Flowering of the Middle Ages* (London, 1966). For a good general survey of the social history of the Middle Ages, see C. B. Bouchard, *Life and Society in the West: Antiquity and the Middle Ages* (San Diego, 1988). For excellent reference works on medieval history, see H. R. Loyn, *The Middle Ages: A Concise Encyclopedia* (New York, 1989); and J. R. Strayer, ed., *Dictionary of the Middle Ages*, 13 vols. (New York, 1982–1989).

Brief histories of the period covered in this chapter include R. Collins, *Early Medieval Europe, 300–1000* (New York, 1991); M. Grant, *Dawn of the Middle Ages* (New York, 1981), which contains a lively text and excellent illustrations; and J. M. Wallace-Hadrill, *The Barbarian West*, rev. ed. (Oxford, 1985).

For brief, general works on the Christian church, see H. Chadwick, *The Early Church* (Baltimore, 1967); and R. W. Southern, *Western Society and the Church in the Middle Ages* (Baltimore, 1970). Aspects of Christianity in the Roman Empire are covered in E. R. Dodds, *Pagan and Christian in an Age of Anxiety* (New York, 1965). On the relationship of Christian thought to the classical tradition, see H. Chadwick, *Early Christian Thought and the Classical Tradition* (Oxford, 1966); C. N. Cochrane, *Christianity and Classical Culture* (New York, 1957); and R. A. Markus, *Christianity in the Roman World* (London, 1974). On Augustine and Jerome, see P. Brown, *Augustine of Hippo* (Berkeley and Los Angeles, 1969); and J. N. D. Kelly, *Saint Jerome* (London, 1975). A brief, illustrated history of monasticism is G. Zarnecki, *The Monastic Achievement* (New York, 1972). For a more detailed account, see C. H. Lawrence, *Medieval Monasticism* (London, 1984). On Saint Benedict and the Benedictine ideal, see L. von Matt, *Saint Benedict* (London, 1961); and O. Chadwick, *The Making of the Benedictine Ideal* (London, 1981). For women in monas-

tic life, see S. F. Wemple, *Women in Frankish Society: Marriage and the Cloister, 500–900* (Philadelphia, 1981).

For surveys on the German tribes and their migrations, see L. Musset, *The German Invasions* (University Park, Pa., 1975); T. S. Burns, *A History of the Ostrogoths* (Bloomington, Ind., 1984); E. A. Thompson, *The Goths in Spain* (Oxford, 1969); E. James, *The Franks* (Oxford, 1988); and especially H. Wolfram, *The Goths*, trans. T. J. Dunlop (Berkeley, 1988). Also valuable are the revisionist work of W. Goffart, *Barbarians and Romans*, A.D. *418–554: The Techniques of Accommodation* (Princeton, N.J., 1980); and P. Geary, *Before France and Germany* (Oxford, 1988).

A brief survey of the development of the papacy can be found in G. Barraclough, *The Medieval Papacy* (New York, 1968). J. Richards, *The Popes and the Papacy in the Early Middle Ages, 476–752* (Boston, 1979) is a more detailed study of the early papacy. On Pope Gregory the Great, see the biography by J. Richards, *Consul of God: The Life and Times of Gregory the Great* (Boston, 1980). The conversion of Ireland and the significance of Celtic Christianity can be examined in K. Hughes, *The Church in Early Irish Society* (Ithaca, N.Y., 1965). On Irish monasticism, see L. M. Bitel, *Isle of the Saints: Monastic Settlement and Christian Community in Early Ireland* (Ithaca, N.Y., 1990). On Christianity and intellectual life, see the earlier, but still sound work of E. K. Rand, *Founders of the Middle Ages*, reprint ed. (New York, 1957); J. J. O'Donnell, *Cassiodorus* (Berkeley and Los Angeles, 1979); and P. H. Blair, *The World of Bede* (London, 1970). An important aspect of Christian culture is discussed in P. Brown, *The Cult of Saints* (Chicago, 1981).

Brief but good introductions to Byzantine history can be found in H. W. Haussig, *A History of Byzantine Civilization* (New York, 1971); and C. Mango, *Byzantium: The Empire of New Rome* (London, 1980). The best single political history is G. Ostrogorsky, *A History of the Byzantine State*, 2d ed. (New Brunswick, N.J., 1968). Specialized studies include J. W. Barker, *Justinian and the Later Roman Empire* (Madison, Wis., 1966); and W. Kaegi, *Byzantium and the Decline of Rome* (Princeton, N.J., 1968) on the impact of the barbarian invasions on the Eastern Roman Empire. On Justinian, see R. Browning, *Justinian and Theodora*, 2d ed. (London, 1987). On Constantinople, see D. T. Rice, *Constantinople: From Byzantium to Istanbul* (New York, 1965); and P. Sherrard, *Constantinople: Iconography of a Sacred City* (New York, 1965). The role of the Christian church is discussed in J. Hussey, *The Orthodox Church in the Byzantine Empire* (Oxford, 1986).

Good brief surveys of the Islamic Middle East include A. Goldschmidt, Jr., *A Concise History of the Middle East*, 5th ed. (Boulder, Colo., 1995); and S. N. Fisher, *The Middle East: A History*, rev. ed. (New York, 1978). On the rise of Islam, see W. M. Watt, *Muhammad: Prophet and Statesman* (London, 1961); M. Lings, *Muhammad: His Life Based on the Earliest Sources* (New York, 1983); G. E. von Grunebaum, *Classical Islam: A History, 600–1258*, trans. K. Watson (London, 1970); F. Gabrieli, *Muhammad and the Conquests of Islam* (London, 1968); P. Crone and M. Hinds, *God's Caliph: Religious Authority in the First Centuries of Islam* (New York, 1986); and F. Donner, *The Early Islamic Conquests* (Princeton, N.J., 1980).

European Civilization in the Early Middle Ages, 750–1000

In 800, Charlemagne, the king of the Franks, journeyed to Rome to help Pope Leo III, who was barely clinging to power in the face of rebellious Romans. On Christmas Day, Charlemagne and his family, attended by Romans, Franks, and even visitors from the Byzantine Empire, crowded into St. Peter's Basilica to hear mass. Quite unexpectedly, according to a Frankish writer, "as the king rose from praying before the tomb of the blessed apostle Peter, Pope Leo placed a golden crown on his head." In keeping with ancient tradition, the people in the church shouted, "Long life and victory to Charles Augustus, crowned by God the great and pacific Emperor of the Romans." Seemingly, the Roman Empire in the West had been reborn, and Charles had become the first western emperor since 476. But this "Roman emperor" was actually a German king, and he had been crowned by the head of the Western Christian church. In truth, the coronation of Charlemagne was a sign not of the rebirth of the Roman Empire, but of the emergence of a new European civilization.

By the year of Charlemagne's coronation, the contours of this new European civilization were beginning to emerge in western Europe. Increasingly, Europe would become the focus and center of Western civilization. Building upon a fusion of Germanic, classical, and Christian elements, the medieval European world first became visible in the Carolingian Empire of Charlemagne. The agrarian foundations of the eighth and ninth centuries proved inadequate to maintain a large monarchical system, however, and a new political and military order based on the decentralization of political power subsequently evolved to become an integral part of the political world of the Middle Ages.

European civilization began on a shaky and uncertain foundation, however. In the ninth century, Vikings, Magyars, and Muslims posed threats that could easily have stifled the new society. But a vibrant civilization can absorb such challenges, and European civilization did just that. The Vikings and Magyars were assimilated, and recovery slowly began to set in.

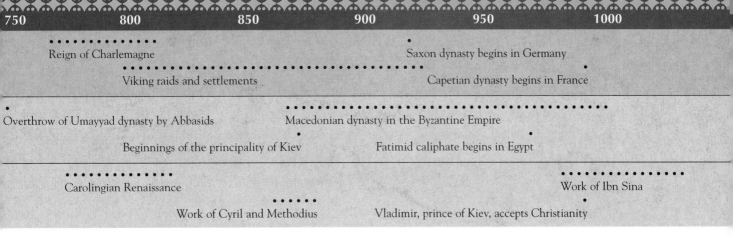

Reign of Charlemagne

Saxon dynasty begins in Germany

Viking raids and settlements

Capetian dynasty begins in France

Overthrow of Umayyad dynasty by Abbasids

Macedonian dynasty in the Byzantine Empire

Beginnings of the principality of Kiev

Fatimid caliphate begins in Egypt

Carolingian Renaissance

Work of Ibn Sina

Work of Cyril and Methodius

Vladimir, prince of Kiev, accepts Christianity

By 1000, European civilization was ready to embark upon a period of dazzling vitality and expansion.

Population and Environment

The number of people in early medieval Europe is a matter of considerable uncertainty. In all probability, the population of the eighth century had still not recovered from the losses caused by the plagues of the sixth and seventh centuries. Historians generally believe that in the Early Middle Ages Europe was a sparsely populated landscape dotted with villages and clusters of villages of farmers and warriors. Although rivers, such as the Loire, Seine, Rhine, Elbe, and Oder, served as major arteries of communication, villages were still separated from one another by forests, swamps, and mountain ridges. Forests, which provided building and heating materials as well as game, continued to dominate the European landscape. In fact, it has been estimated that less than 10 percent of the land was cultivated, a figure so small that some economic historians believe that Europe had difficulty feeding even its small population. Thus, hunting and fishing were necessary to supplement the European diet.

The cultivation of new land proved especially difficult in the Early Middle Ages. Given the crude implements of the time, it was not easy to clear forests and cultivate new land. Moreover, German tribes had for centuries considered trees sacred and resisted cutting them down to clear land for farming. Even conversion to Christianity did not entirely change these attitudes. In addition, the heavy soils of northern Europe were not easily plowed. Agricultural methods also worked against

significant crop yields. Land was allowed to lie fallow (idle) every other year to regain its fertility, but even so it produced low yields. Evidence shows that Frankish estates yielded incredibly low ratios of two measures of grain to one measure of seed. Although climatic patterns show that European weather began to improve around 700 after a centuries-long period of wetter and colder conditions, natural disasters were still a threat, especially since the low yields meant little surplus could be saved for bad times. Drought or too much rain could mean bad harvests, famine, and dietary deficiencies that made people particularly susceptible to a wide range of diseases. This was a period of low life expectancy. One study of Hungarian graves found that of every five skeletons, one was a child below the age of one, and two were children between one and fourteen; more than one in five was a woman below the age of twenty. Overall then, the picture of early medieval Europe is of a relatively small population subsisting on the basis of a limited agricultural economy and leading, in most cases, a precarious existence.

The World of the Carolingians

During the seventh and eighth centuries, within the Frankish kingdom of western Europe, the Carolingian mayors of the palace of Neustria and Austrasia had expanded their power at the expense of the Merovingian dynasty (see Chapter 7). One of these mayors, Charles Martel, provided the military leadership to defend the Frankish kingdom against the Muslims. Pepin, the son of Charles Martel, finally took the logical step of deposing the decadent Merovingians and assum-

The Carolingian Empire

Pepin crowned king of the Franks	751
Pepin's campaigns in Italy	755–756
Reign of Charlemagne	768–814
Campaign in Italy	773–774
Campaign in Spain	778
Conquest of Bavarians	787–788
Charlemagne crowned emperor	800
Final conquest of Saxons	804
Reign of Louis the Pious	814–840
Treaty of Verdun divides Carolingian Empire	843

ing the kingship of the Frankish state for himself and his family.

Emergence of the Carolingian Dynasty

Pepin had hesitated to usurp the throne because the Merovingian rulers had a blood right to be kings. To justify his action, he sought the advice of Pope Zacharias I (741–752), who, for his own political reasons, reassured Pepin:

> Burchard, bishop of Würzburg, and Fulrad, priest and chaplain, were sent [by Pepin] to pope Zacharias to ask his advice in regard to the kings who were then ruling in France, who had the title of king but no real royal authority. The pope replied by these ambassadors that it would be better that he who actually had the power should be called king.[1]

Pepin's actions constituted a papal-approved revolution that created a new form of Frankish kingship. Pepin was crowned king and formally anointed by a representative of the pope with holy oil in imitation of an Old Testament practice. As it was said of David, "Then Samuel took the horn of oil, and anointed him in the midst of his brethren: and the Spirit of the Lord came upon David from that day forward."[2] Only priests had been anointed before, but now so were Frankish kings; the anointing not only symbolized that the kings had been entrusted with a sacred office but also provides yet another example of how a Germanic institution fused with a Christian practice in the Early Middle Ages.

As Pope Zacharias had hoped, the anointing of Pepin (751–768) as the new king of the Franks led to practical benefits for the papacy, including an alliance between the new Frankish king and the Roman popes. The latter were being seriously threatened by the Lombards, who had captured Ravenna, one of the chief remaining centers of Byzantine power in Italy, and now menaced Rome itself. The popes had relied on the Byzantine presence in Italy for military protection. However, because of the Muslim threat and the disagreement between the Roman pontiffs and the Byzantine emperors over the iconoclastic controversy (see Chapter 7), the Byzantines refused papal requests for assistance. Pope Stephen II (752–757) turned to the Franks instead and received promises of aid from the newly crowned Pepin. Pepin made a number of expeditions to Italy, defeated the Lombards, and expanded the church's holdings around Rome by granting lands he conquered in central Italy to the papacy (the so-called Donation of Pepin). This area became known as the Papal States, the papacy's own territorial state in central Italy, which the popes managed to retain until 1870.

Charlemagne and the Carolingian Empire (768–814)

Pepin's death in 768 brought to the throne of the Frankish kingdom his son, a dynamic and powerful ruler known to history as Charles the Great or Charlemagne (from *Carolus magnus* in Latin). Charlemagne was a determined and decisive man, highly intelligent and inquisitive. A fierce warrior, he was also a wise patron of learning and a resolute statesman (see the box on p. 247). He greatly expanded the territory of the Carolingian Empire during his lengthy rule.

EXPANSION OF THE CAROLINGIAN EMPIRE

In the tradition of the Germanic kings, Charlemagne was a determined warrior who undertook fifty-four military campaigns. Even though the Frankish army was relatively small—only 8,000 men gathered each spring for campaigning—supplying it and transporting it to distant areas could still present serious problems. The Frankish army comprised mostly infantry with some cavalry armed with swords and spears.

After ascending the Frankish throne, Charlemagne soon realized that Pepin's arrangements in Italy would not last. In 773, Charlemagne led his army into Italy, crushed the Lombards, and took control of the Lombard

⇒ The Achievements of Charlemagne ⇐

Einhard, the biographer of Charlemagne, was born in the valley of the Main River in Germany about 775. Raised and educated in the monastery of Fulda, an important center of learning, he arrived at the court of Charlemagne in 791 or 792. Although he did not achieve high office under Charlemagne, he served as private secretary to Louis the Pious, Charlemagne's son and successor. Einhard's Life of Charlemagne *was modeled on Suetonius's* Lives of the Caesars, *especially his biography of Augustus. Einhard's work, written between 817 and 830, was the "first medieval biography of a lay figure." In this selection, he discusses some of Charlemagne's accomplishments.*

Einhard, *Life of Charlemagne*

Such are the wars, most skillfully planned and successfully fought, which this most powerful king waged during the forty-seven years of his reign. He so largely increased the Frank kingdom, which was already great and strong when he received it at his father's hands, that more than double its former territory was added to it. . . . He subdued all the wild and barbarous tribes dwelling in Germany between the Rhine and the Vistula, the Ocean and the Danube, all of which speak very much the same language, but differ widely from one another in customs and dress. . . .

He added to the glory of his reign by gaining the good will of several kings and nations; so close, indeed, was the alliance that he contracted with Alfonso, King of Galicia and Asturias, that the latter, when sending letters or ambassadors to Charles, invariably styled himself his man. . . . The Emperors of Constantinople [the Byzantine emperors] sought friendship and alliance with Charles by several embassies; and even when the Greeks [the Byzantines] suspected him of designing to take the empire from them, because of his assumption of the title Emperor, they made a close alliance with him, that he might have no cause of offense. In fact, the power of the Franks was always viewed with a jealous eye, whence the Greek proverb, "Have the Frank for your friend, but not for your neighbor."

This King, who showed himself so great in extending his empire and subduing foreign nations, and was constantly occupied with plans to that end, undertook also very many works calculated to adorn and benefit his kingdom, and brought several of them to completion. Among these, the most deserving of mention are the basilica of the Holy Mother of God at Aix-la-Chapelle, built in the most admirable manner, and a bridge over the Rhine River at Mainz, half a mile long, the breadth of the river at this point. . . . Above all, sacred buildings were the object of his care throughout his whole kingdom; and whenever he found them falling to ruin from age, he commanded the priests and fathers who had charge of them to repair them, and made sure by commissioners that his instructions were obeyed. . . . Thus did Charles defend and increase as well as beautify his kingdom. . . .

He cherished with the greatest fervor and devotion the principles of the Christian religion, which had been instilled into him from infancy. Hence it was that he built the beautiful church at Aix-la-Chapelle, which he adorned with gold and silver and lamps, and with rails and doors of solid brass. He had the columns and marbles for this structure brought from Rome and Ravenna, for he could not find such as were suitable elsewhere. He was a constant worshiper at this church as long as his health permitted, going morning and evening, even after nightfall, besides attending mass. . . .

He was very forward in caring for the poor, so much so that he not only made a point of giving in his own country and his own kingdom, but when he discovered that there were Christians living in poverty in Syria, Egypt, and Africa, at Jerusalem, Alexandria, and Carthage, he had compassion on their wants, and used to send money over the seas to them. . . . He sent great and countless gifts to the popes, and throughout his whole reign the wish that he had nearest at heart was to reestablish the ancient authority of the city of Rome under his care and by his influence, and to defend and protect the Church of St. Peter, and to beautify and enrich it out of his own store above all other churches.

---

state. Although his son was crowned king of Italy, Charlemagne was its real ruler.

Four years after his invasion of Italy, Charlemagne and his forces advanced into northern Spain. This campaign proved to be disappointing; not only did the Basques harass his army as it crossed the Pyrenees on the way home, but they also ambushed and annihilated his rear guard, an event that later gave rise to the epic poem, *The Song of Roland* (see the box on p. 368). Later Charlemagne established the Spanish March, a stretch

✦ **Bronze Equestrian Statue of Charlemagne.** This small bronze statue is believed to represent the emperor Charles the Great. The figure dates from the ninth century, but the horse is a sixteenth-century restoration. The attire on the figure accords with Einhard's account of how Charlemagne dressed.

of territory south of the Pyrenees that was strongly fortified and served as a defensive bulwark against the Muslim forces in Spain.

Charlemagne was considerably more successful with his eastern campaigns into Germany, especially against the Saxons located between the Elbe River and the North Sea. As Einhard, Charlemagne's biographer, recounted it:

> No war ever undertaken by the Frank nation was carried on with such persistence and bitterness, or cost so much labor, because the Saxons, like almost all the tribes of Germany, were a fierce people, given to the worship of devils, and hostile to our religion, and did not consider it dishonorable to transgress and violate all law, human and divine.[3]

Charlemagne's insistence that the Saxons convert to Christianity simply fueled their resistance. Not until

804, after eighteen campaigns, was Saxony finally pacified and added to the Carolingian domain.

In southeastern Germany, Charlemagne invaded the land of the Bavarians in 787 and brought them into his empire by the following year, an expansion that brought him into contact with the southern Slavs and the Avars. The latter disappeared from history after their utter devastation at the hands of Charlemagne's army. Now at its height, Charlemagne's empire covered much of western and central Europe; not until the time of Napoleon in the nineteenth and Hitler in the twentieth century would an empire its size be seen again in Europe.

GOVERNING THE EMPIRE

Charlemagne continued the efforts of his father in organizing the Carolingian kingdom. Since there was no system of public taxation, Charlemagne was highly dependent upon the royal estates for the resources he needed to govern his empire. Food and goods derived from these lands provided support for the king, his household staff, and officials. To keep the nobles in his service, Charlemagne granted part of the royal lands as lifetime holdings to nobles who assisted him.

Besides the household staff, the administration of the empire depended upon the utilization of counts as the king's chief representatives in local areas, although in dangerous border districts officials known as margraves (literally, *mark graf*, count of the border district) were used. Counts were members of the nobility who had already existed under the Merovingians. They had come to control public services in their own lands and thus acted as judges, military leaders, and agents of the king. Gradually, as the rule of the Merovingian kings weakened, many counts had simply attached the royal lands and services performed on behalf of the king to their own family possessions.

In an effort to gain greater control over his kingdom, Charlemagne attempted to limit the power of the counts. They were required to serve outside their own family lands and were moved about periodically rather than being permitted to remain in a county for life. By making the offices appointive, Charlemagne tried to prevent the counts' children from automatically inheriting their offices. Moreover, as another check on the counts, Charlemagne instituted the *missi dominici* ("messengers of the lord king"), two men, one lay lord and one church official, who were sent out to local districts to ensure that the counts were executing the king's wishes. The counts also had assistants, but they were members of their households, not part of a bureaucratic office.

The last point is an important reminder that we should not think of Carolingian government in the modern sense of government offices run by officials committed to an impersonal ideal of state service. The Carolingian system was glaringly inefficient. Great distances had to be covered on horseback, making it impossible for Charlemagne and his household staff to exercise much supervision over local affairs. What held the system together was personal loyalty to the king.

Charlemagne also realized that the Catholic church could provide invaluable assistance in governing his kingdom. By the late seventh century, the system of ecclesiastical government within the Christian church that had been created in the late Roman Empire had largely disintegrated. Church offices were not filled or were often held by grossly unqualified relatives of the royal family. After an impetus for regeneration had come from Saint Boniface (see Chapter 7), both Pepin and his son Charlemagne took up the cause of church reform by creating new bishoprics and archbishoprics, restoring old ones, and seeing to it that the clergy accepted the orders of their superiors and executed their duties. Although the church failed at times to appreciate the degree to which Charlemagne saw himself as its caretaker, the king did gain significant support from the church in return for his efforts.

In examining the governmental machinery of the Carolingian Empire, it is important to realize that Charlemagne's kingdom was held together not by the Christianity that was common to the entire kingdom or by any powerful administrative system, but largely by loyalty to a single ruler who was strong enough to ensure loyalty by force when necessary. By traveling around his kingdom, Charlemagne could directly counter the power of local lords. The Carolingian system worked as long as it had a powerful and energetic ruler like Charlemagne. But even during the last years of Charlemagne's reign, as his energy began to wane, the Carolingian Empire itself began to disintegrate, a process that would continue after his death.

CHARLEMAGNE AS EMPEROR

As Charlemagne's power grew, so too did his prestige as the most powerful Christian ruler; one monk even wrote of his empire as the "kingdom of Europe." Charlemagne acquired a new title—emperor of the Romans—in 800, but substantial controversy surrounds this event, and it can only be understood within the context of the relationship between the papacy and the Frankish monarchs.

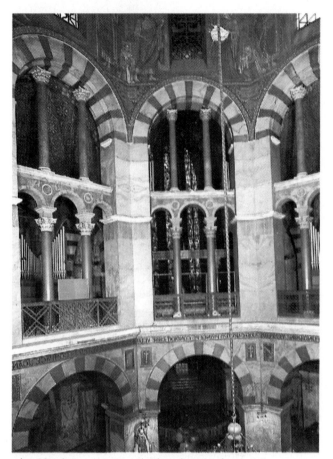

◆ **Charlemagne's Royal Chapel at Aachen.** Construction of the palace chapel at Aachen began in the early 790s. The architect, Odo of Metz, used the church of San Vitale at Ravenna, built almost three centuries earlier by Justinian, as his model. The marble columns were brought from Rome and Ravenna. Charlemagne attended religious services at the chapel on a regular basis.

We have seen the growing alliance between the kingdom of the Franks and the papacy during Pepin's reign. As a result of this alliance and the Donation of Pepin that grew out of it, papal claims to temporal power increased dramatically. In the late eighth century, the pope first brandished a document known as the Donation of Constantine, in which the Emperor Constantine in 313 supposedly gave political control of the western parts of the Roman Empire to the bishop of Rome. The document was not frequently cited, but its very appearance in the eighth century demonstrates that the popes were already interested in boosting their claims to temporal power. Although the document was a forgery, that fact was known to few people, and the

The Donation of Constantine

One of the major documents used by the popes to bolster their claim to temporal power was the Donation of Constantine. Purportedly, this was a fourth-century document in which the Emperor Constantine, in gratitude for being cured of leprosy by Pope Sylvester, had granted complete political supremacy over the western empire to the popes. The document was actually a forgery, probably created in the second half of the eighth century, but was periodically cited by medieval popes until the fifteenth century when the scholar Lorenzo Valla decisively proved its lack of authenticity.

The Donation of Constantine

And when, the blessed Sylvester preaching them, I perceived these things, and learned that by the kindness of St. Peter himself I had been entirely restored to health: I . . . considered it advisable that, as on earth he [Peter] is seen to have been constituted vicar of the Son of God, so the pontiffs, who are the representatives of that same chief of the apostles, should obtain from us and our empire the power of a supremacy greater than the earthly clemency of our imperial serenity is seen to have had conceded to it—we choosing that same prince of the apostles, or his vicars, to be our constant intercessors with God. And, to the extent of our earthly imperial power, we decree that his holy Roman church shall be honored with veneration; and that, more than our empire and earthly throne, the most sacred seat of St. Peter shall be gloriously exalted; we giving to it the imperial power, and dignity of glory, and vigor and honor.

And we ordain and decree that he shall have the supremacy as well over the four chief seats Antioch, Alexandria, Constantinople and Jerusalem, as also over all the churches of God in the whole world. And he who for the time being shall be pontiff of that holy Roman Church shall be more exalted than, and chief over, all the priests of the whole world; and, according to his judgment, everything which is to be provided for the service of God or the stability of the faith of the Christians is to be administered. . . .

In imitation of our own power, in order that for that cause the supreme pontificate may not deteriorate, but may rather be adorned with power and glory even more than is the dignity of an earthly rule: behold we—giving over to the oft-mentioned most blessed pontiff, our father Sylvester the universal pope, as well our palace, as has been said, as also the city of Rome and all the provinces, districts and cities of Italy or of the western regions; and relinquishing them, by our inviolable gift, to the power and sway of himself or the pontiffs his successors—do decree, by this our godlike charter and imperial constitution, that it shall be (so) arranged; and do concede that they (the palaces, provinces, etc.) shall lawfully remain with the holy Roman church.

Wherefore we have perceived it to be fitting that our empire and the power of our kingdom should be transferred and changed to the regions of the East; and that, in the province of Byzantium, in a most fitting place, a city should be built in our name; and that our empire should there be established. For, where the supremacy of priests and the head of the Christian religion has been established by a heavenly Ruler, it is not just that there an earthly ruler should have jurisdiction.

Donation of Constantine was periodically cited by popes throughout the Middle Ages to bolster papal power (see the box above).

Meanwhile, in the course of the second half of the eighth century, the popes increasingly severed their ties with the Byzantine Empire and drew closer to the Frankish kingdom. Charlemagne encouraged this development. In 799, after a rebellion against his authority, Pope Leo III (795–816) managed to escape from Rome and flee to safety at Charlemagne's court. Charlemagne offered assistance, and when he went to Rome in November 800 to settle affairs, he was received by the pope like an emperor. On Christmas Day 800, after mass, Pope Leo placed a crown on Charlemagne's head and proclaimed him emperor of the Romans.

The significance of this imperial coronation has been much debated by historians. We are not even sure whether the pope or Charlemagne initiated the idea or whether Charlemagne was pleased or displeased. His biographer Einhard claimed that "at first [he] had such an aversion that he declared that he would not have set foot in the Church the day that they were conferred, although it was a great feastday, if he could have foreseen the design of the Pope."[4] But Charlemagne also perceived the usefulness of the imperial title; after all, he was now on a level of equality with the Byzantine emperor, a status he did not reject. Moreover, the papacy now had a defender of great stature, although later popes in the Middle Ages would become involved in fierce struggles with emperors over who possessed the higher power.

In any case, Charlemagne's coronation as Roman emperor certainly demonstrated the strength, even after three hundred years, of the concept of an enduring Roman Empire. More importantly, it symbolized the fusion of the Roman, Christian, and Germanic elements that constituted the foundation of European civilization. A Germanic king had been crowned emperor of the Romans by the spiritual leader of Western Christendom. A new civilization had emerged.

The Carolingian Intellectual Renewal

Charlemagne had a strong desire to revive learning in his kingdom, an attitude that stemmed from his own intellectual curiosity as well as the need to provide educated clergy for the church and literate officials for the government. His efforts led to a revival of learning and culture that some historians have labeled a Carolingian Renaissance or "rebirth" of learning.

The term is only partly appropriate, since the Carolingian era is hardly known for outstanding creativity and originality of ideas. Nevertheless, a true revival of classical studies and an attempt to assimilate and preserve Latin and early Christian culture did occur. This goal became a major task of the monasteries, many of which had been established by the Irish and English missionaries of the seventh and eighth centuries (see Chapter 7). By the ninth century, the "work" required of Benedictine monks was the copying of manuscripts. Monasteries established *scriptoria* or writing rooms, where monks copied not only the works of early Christianity, such as the Bible and the treatises of the Church Fathers, but also the works of Latin classical authors. The head of the *scriptorium* became one of the important offices of the monastery.

Following the example of Irish and English monks, their Carolingian counterparts developed new ways of

✦ **The Coronation of Charlemagne.** After a rebellion in 799 forced Pope Leo III to seek refuge at Charlemagne's court, Charlemagne went to Rome to settle the affair. There, on Christmas Day 800, he was crowned emperor of the Romans by the pope. This manuscript illustration shows Leo III placing a crown on Charlemagne's head.

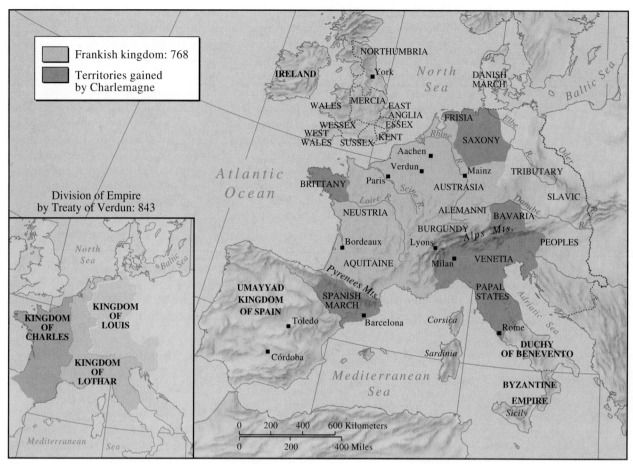

Frankish kingdom: 768

Territories gained
by Charlemagne

Division of Empire
by Treaty of Verdun: 843

N Map 8.1 The Carolingian Empire.

producing books. Their texts were written on pages made of parchment or sheepskin rather than papyrus and then bound in covers decorated with jewels and precious metals. The use of parchment made books very expensive; an entire herd of sheep could be required to make a Bible. (Papyrus was no longer available since Egypt was in Muslim hands, and the west could no longer afford to import it.) Carolingian monastic scribes also developed a new writing style called the Carolingian minuscule. This was really hand printing rather than cursive writing and was far easier to read than the Merovingian cursive script.

The production of illuminated manuscripts in Carolingian monastic *scriptoria* was a crucial factor in the preservation of the ancient legacy. About 8,000 manuscripts, many of them in Carolingian minuscule script, survive from Carolingian times. Virtually 90 percent of the ancient Roman works that we have today exist because they were copied by Carolingian monks. With-

out the work of the medieval monks, there would not have been any later Renaissance or "rebirth" of learning such as occurred in the twelfth and especially the fourteenth and fifteenth centuries.

Charlemagne personally encouraged learning by establishing a palace school and encouraging scholars from all over Europe to come to the Carolingian court. These included men of letters from Italy, Spain, Germany, and Ireland. Best known was Alcuin, called by Einhard the "greatest scholar of that day." He was from the famous school at York that was a product of the great revival of learning in the Anglo-Saxon kingdom of Northumbria. From 782 to 796, while serving at Charlemagne's court as an adviser on ecclesiastical affairs, Alcuin also provided the leadership for the palace school. He concentrated on teaching classical Latin and adopted Cassiodorus's sevenfold division of knowledge known as the liberal arts (see Chapter 7), which became the basis for all later medieval education. All in all, the Carolingian

Renaissance played a crucial role in keeping the classical heritage alive as well as maintaining the intellectual life of the Catholic church.

Life in the Carolingian World

In daily life as well as intellectual life, the newly emerging European world of the Carolingian era witnessed a fusion of Gallo-Roman, Germanic, and Christian practices. The latter in particular seems to have exercised an ever-increasing influence.

THE FAMILY AND MARRIAGE

By Carolingian times, the Catholic church had begun to make a significant impact upon Frankish family life and marital and sexual attitudes. As we have seen, marriages in Frankish society were arranged by fathers or uncles to meet the needs of the extended family. Although wives were expected to be faithful to their husbands, Frankish aristocrats often kept concubines, either slave girls or free women from their estates. Even the "most Christian king" Charlemagne had a number of concubines.

To limit such sexual license, the church increasingly emphasized its role in marriage and attempted to Christianize it. Although marriage was a civil arrangement, priests tried to add their blessings and strengthen the concept of a special marriage ceremony. A local church council in 755 stated that the weddings of all lay people should be public. Moreover, the church tried to serve as the caretaker of marriage by stipulating that a girl over fifteen must give her consent to her guardian's choice of a husband or her marriage was not valid in the eyes of the church.

To stabilize marriages, the church also began to emphasize monogamy and permanence. A Frankish church council in 789 stipulated that marriage was an "indissoluble sacrament" and condemned the practice of concubinage and easy divorce. At first, the church tried to restrict divorce by limiting it for the most part to two cases: the flagrant adultery of the wife or the impotence of the husband. But during the reign of Emperor Louis the Pious (814–840), the church finally established the right to prohibit divorce. Now a man who married was expected to remain with his wife "even though she were sterile, deformed, old, dirty, drunken, a frequenter of bad company, lascivious, vain, greedy, unfaithful, quarrelsome, abusive . . . for when that man was free, he freely engaged himself."[5] This was not easily accepted since monogamy and indissoluble marriages were viewed as

◆ Monk as Copyist. Charlemagne's efforts to revive learning led to what has been called the Carolingian Renaissance. Through their copying of ancient manuscripts, Benedictine monks added an important element to this revival. Shown here at work in this medieval miniature is a monk who is meant to represent Saint Luke, one of the four apostles.

obstacles to the well-established practice of concubinage. It was not until the thirteenth century that divorce was largely stamped out among both the common people and the nobility.

The acceptance and spread of the Catholic church's views on the indissolubility of marriage encouraged the development of the nuclear family at the expense of the extended family. Although the kin was still an influential social and political force, the conjugal unit came to be seen as the basic unit of society. The new practice of young couples establishing their own households brought a dynamic element to European society and contributed to the growth of urban life in the eleventh and twelfth centuries. It also had a significant impact on women (see the box on p. 254). In the extended family, the eldest woman controlled all the other female members; in the nuclear family, the wife was still dominated by her husband, but at least she now had control of her own household and children.

CHRISTIANITY AND SEXUALITY

The early church fathers had stressed that celibacy and complete abstinence from sexual activity constituted an

Advice from a Carolingian Mother

The wife of a Carolingian aristocrat bore numerous responsibilities. She was entrusted with the management of the household and even the administration of extensive landed estates while her husband was absent in the royal service or on a military campaign. A wife was also expected to bear larger numbers of children and to supervise their upbringing. This selection by Dhouda, wife of Bernard, marquis of Septimania (in southern France), is taken from a manual she wrote to instruct her son on his duties to his new lord, King Charles the Bald (840–877).

Dhouda, *Handbook for William*

Direction on your comportment toward your lord.

You have Charles as your lord; you have him as lord because, as I believe, God and your father, Bernard, have chosen him for you to serve at the beginning of your career, in the flower of your youth. Remember that he comes from a great and noble lineage on both sides of his family. Serve him not only so that you please him in obvious ways, but also as one clearheaded in matters of both body and soul. Be steadfastly and completely loyal to him in all things. . . .

This is why, my son, I urge you to keep this loyalty as long as you live, in your body and in your mind. For the advancement that it brings you will be of great value both to you and to those who in turn serve you. May the madness of treachery never, not once, make you offer an angry insult. May it never give rise in your heart to the idea of being disloyal to your lord. There is harsh and shameful talk about men who act in this fashion. I do not think that such will befall you or those who fight alongside you because such an attitude has never shown itself among your ancestors. It has not been seen among them, it is not seen now, and it will not be seen in the future.

Be truthful to your lord, my son William, child of their lineage. Be vigilant, energetic, and offer him ready assistance as I have said here. In every matter of importance to royal power take care to show yourself a man of good judgment—in your own thoughts and in public—to the extent that God gives you strength. Read the sayings and the lives of the holy Fathers who have gone before us. You will there discover how you may serve your lord and be faithful to him in all things. When you understand this, devote yourself to the faithful execution of your lord's commands. Look around as well and observe those who fight for him loyally and constantly. Learn from them how you may serve him. Then, informed by their example, with the help and support of God, you will easily reach the celestial goal I have mentioned above. And may your heavenly Lord God be generous and benevolent toward you. May he keep you safe, be your kind leader and your protector. May he deign to assist you in all your actions and be your constant defender.

ideal state superior to marriage. Subsequently, the early church gradually developed a case for clerical celibacy, although it proved impossible to enforce in the Early Middle Ages.

The early fathers had also emphasized, however, that not all people had the self-discipline to remain celibate. It was thus permissible to marry, as Paul had indicated in his first epistle to the Corinthians: "It is good for a man not to touch a woman. Nevertheless, to avoid fornication, let every man have his own wife, and let every woman have her own husband. . . . I say therefore to the unmarried and widows, It is good for them if they abide even as I. But if they cannot contain, let them marry: for it is better to marry than to burn."[6] The church thus viewed marriage as the lesser of two evils; it was a concession to human weakness and fulfilled the need for companionship, sex, and children. Although marriage was the subject of much debate in the early medieval church, it was generally agreed that marriage gave the right to indulge in sexual intercourse. Sex, then, was permissible within marriage, but only so long as it was used for the sole purpose of procreation, or the begetting of children, not for pleasure.

Since the church developed the tradition that sexual relations between man and wife were only legitimate if done for purposes of procreation, it condemned all forms of contraception. The church also strongly condemned abortion, although its prohibition failed to stop the practice. Various herbal potions, whose formulas were included in writings from Roman and Byzantine doctors, were available to prevent conception or cause abortion. The Catholic church accepted only one way to limit children, by either periodic or total abstinence from intercourse.

The Catholic church's condemnation of sexual activity outside marriage also included homosexuality. Neither Roman religion nor Roman law had recognized any real difference between homosexual and heterosexual eroticism, and the Roman Empire had taken no legal measures against the practice of homosexuality between adults. Later, in the Byzantine Empire, the Emperor Justinian in 538 condemned homosexuality, emphasizing that such practices brought down the wrath of God ("we have provoked Him to anger") and endangered the welfare of the state:

> For because of such crimes, there are famines, earthquakes, and pestilences; wherefore we admonish men to abstain from the aforesaid unlawful acts, that they may not lose their souls.... We order the most illustrious prefect of the capital to arrest those who persist in the aforesaid lawless and impious acts after they have been warned by us, and to inflict on them the extreme punishments, so that the city and the state may not come to harm by reason of such wicked deeds.[7]

Justinian recommended that the guilty parties be punished by castration. Although the church in the Early Middle Ages similarly condemned homosexuality, it also pursued a flexible policy in its treatment of homosexuals. In the Early Middle Ages, homosexuals were treated less harshly than married couples who practiced contraception. Between the seventh and tenth centuries, the Catholic hierarchy did not seem overly concerned with homosexual behavior. The church's policy would not undergo fundamental change until the eleventh century.

NEW ATTITUDES TOWARD CHILDREN

The Catholic church also had an impact upon another aspect of family life—children. The ancient Romans had limited their family size through infanticide, or the exposure of unwanted children, which was accepted in classical society. Romans had then paid much attention to the children chosen to survive, as is especially evident in the education of upper-class children. In the emerging early medieval world, barbarian practices of child rearing became influential. Although the Germans had large families, it is questionable how much they valued their children. As we saw in Chapter 7, the Germanic law codes listed *wergelds*, whose size repre-

sented a crude evaluation of a person's importance. According to a Visigothic code of the mid-seventh century, for example, male children were valued at 60 solidi. At the age of twenty, when they had become warriors, the *wergeld* increased fivefold to 300 solidi, where it remained until the adult male reached fifty, after which it again declined. The value of female children was only one-half that of males, although it also jumped tremendously (to 250 solidi) between the ages of fifteen and forty because of their importance as bearers of children.

Although the Christian church condemned infanticide, it was not able to eliminate the practice, especially among the poor and those who had been seduced and did not want to keep their illegitimate offspring. Nevertheless, priests tried to discourage such practices by encouraging people to abandon their children in churches. Oftentimes, such children were taken in by monasteries and raised to be monks. Following the example of Christ's love for children, monks tended to respect and preserve the virtues of childhood. As children grew older, however, the "master of the boys," who was responsible for their education, thought it necessary to use strict discipline to control what was considered the natural inclination of children to sin, especially by disobeying their elders.

TRAVEL AND HOSPITALITY

Monasteries served another important function in the early medieval world as providers of hospitality. Both monasteries and aristocratic households were expected to provide a place to stay for weary travelers who were ever at risk from thieves or violence of many kinds. Indeed, Burgundian law stipulated that "anyone who refused to offer a visitor shelter and warmth shall pay a fine of three solidi."[8] Hospitality, then, was a sacred duty, and monasteries were especially active in providing it. It was customary for monasteries to have two guest houses, one for the rich and another for the poor. The plan for the monastery of Saint Gall, for example, provided pilgrims and paupers with a house containing benches, two dormitories, and outbuildings. For travelers of high rank, there was a separate guest house with two heated rooms, servants' bedrooms, and stables for horses. One could not always be sure of hospitality, in the Early Middle Ages, however. The famous English missionary to Germany, Saint Boniface, reported that female pilgrims to Rome had been forced to become prostitutes in every town along their route in order to

♦ **Travelers Arriving at an Inn.** Inns provided refuge for the many pilgrims, merchants, and others who traveled Europe's dangerous roads in the Middle Ages. In this illustration, a group of merchants has stopped at an inn, which like most medieval inns provided basic necessities, but not individual beds. Medieval people generally slept in the nude.

obtain their sustenance and reach their goal. The church responded by forbidding females to go on such pilgrimages.

DIET AND HEALTH

For both rich and poor, the fundamental staple of the Carolingian diet was bread. The aristocratic classes, as well as the monks, consumed it in large quantities. Ovens at the monastery of Saint Gall were able to bake a thousand loaves of bread. Sometimes, a gruel made of barley and oats was substituted for bread in the peasant diet.

The upper classes in Carolingian society enjoyed a much more varied diet than the peasants. Pork was the major red meat. Domestic pigs, allowed to run wild in the forests to find their own food, were collected and slaughtered in the fall, then smoked and salted to be eaten during the winter months. Since Carolingian aristocrats were especially fond of roasted meat, hunting wild game became one of their favorite activities. They ate little beef and mutton, however, because cattle were kept as dairy cows and oxen to draw plows while sheep were raised for wool.

Dairy products became prevalent in the Carolingian diet. Milk, which spoiled rapidly, was made into cheese and butter. Chickens were kept for their eggs. Vegetables also formed a crucial part of the diet of both rich and poor. These included legumes, such as beans, peas, and lentils, and roots, such as garlic, onions, and carrots.

The Carolingian diet, especially of the upper classes, was also heavily dependent on honey and spices. Honey was used as a sweetener, both for foods and for many drinks, including wine and ale. Spices included domestic varieties that were grown in home gardens, such as thyme, sage, and chives, and more exotic—and outrageously expensive—varieties imported from the east, such as pepper, cumin, cloves, and cinnamon. Aristocrats were especially fond of spicy dishes, not only for their taste, but as a sign of prestige and wealth; spices were also believed to aid the digestion.

Both gluttony and drunkenness were vices shared by many people in Carolingian society. Monastic rations were greatly enlarged in the eighth century to include a daily allotment of 3.7 pounds of bread (nuns were only permitted 3 pounds), one and one-half quarts of wine or ale, two or three ounces of cheese, and eight ounces of vegetables (four for nuns). These rations provided a total of 6,000 calories a day, and since only heavy and fatty foods—bread, milk, and cheese—were considered nourishing, we begin to understand why some Carolingians were known for their potbellies. Malnutrition, however, remained a widespread problem for common people in this period.

Everyone in Carolingian society, including abbots and monks, drank heavily and often to excess. Taverns became a regular feature of life and were found everywhere: in marketplaces, at pilgrimage centers, and on royal, episcopal, and monastic estates. Drinking contests were not unusual; one penitential stated: "Does drunken bravado encourage you to attempt to out-drink your friends? If so, thirty days fast."

The aristocrats and monks favored wine above all other beverages, and much care was lavished on its production, especially by monasteries. Although ale was considered inferior in some quarters, it was especially popular in the northern and eastern parts of the Carolingian world. Water was also drunk as a beverage, but much care had to be taken to obtain pure sources from wells or clear streams. Monasteries were particularly active in going to the sources of water and building conduits to bring it to the cloister or kitchen fountains.

⇒ Medical Practices in the Early Middle Ages ⇐

A number of medical manuscripts written in Old English have survived from Anglo-Saxon England. Although most of the medical texts date from the tenth to twelfth centuries, scholars believe that they include copies of earlier works and contain older influences as well. As the following selections from three of these treatises illustrate, herbs were the basic materials of the Anglo-Saxon physician (or leech as he was called), and his treatments consequently focused almost entirely on botanical remedies.

The Anglo-Saxon Herbal

Cress (Nasturtium)

1. In case a man's hair falls out, take juice of the wort which one names nasturtium and by another name cress, put it on the nose, the hair shall grow.
2. This wort is not sown but it is produced of itself in springs and in brooks; also it is written that in some lands it will grow against walls.
3. For a sore head, that is for scurf and for itch, take the seed of this same wort and goose grease, pound together, it draws from off the head the whiteness of the scurf.
4. For soreness of the body [indigestion], take this same wort nasturtium and pennyroyal, soak them in water and give to drink; the soreness and the evil departs.

The Leechbook of Bald

Here are wound salves for all wounds and drinks and cleansings of every sort, whether internally or externally. Waybroad beaten and mixed with old lard, the fresh is of no use. Again, a wound salve: take waybroad seed, crush it small, shed it on the wound and soon it will be better.

For a burn, if a man be burned with fire only, take woodruff and lily and brooklime; boil in butter and smear therewith. If a man be burned with a liquid, let him take elm rind and roots of the lily, boil them in milk, smear thereon three times a day. For sunburn, boil in butter tender ivy twigs and smear thereon.

The Peri-Didaxeon

For a Broken Head

For a broken or wounded head which is caused by the humors of the head. Take betony and pound it and lay it on the wound and it will relieve all the pain.

For Sleep

Thus must one do for the man who cannot sleep; take wormwood and rub it into wine or warm water and let the man drink it and soon it will be better with him.

For Sore Hands

This leechcraft is good for sore hands and for sore fingers which is called chilblains. Take white frankincense and silver cinders and brimstone and mingle together, then take oil and add it into this mixture, then warm the hands and smear them with the mixture thus made. Wrap up the hands in a linen cloth.

Water was also used for bathing. Although standards of personal hygiene were not high, medieval people did not ignore cleanliness. A royal palace, such as Charlemagne's, possessed both hot and cold baths. Carolingian aristocrats changed clothes and bathed at least once a week, on Saturdays. The Saturday bath was also a regular practice in many Carolingian monasteries. To monks, bathing more than once a week seemed an unnecessary luxury; to aristocrats, it often seemed desirable.

Bathing was only one of a number of practices used by Carolingian people to avoid and cure illness. Medical practice in Carolingian times stressed the use of medicinal herbs (see the box above) and bleeding. Although the latter was practiced regularly, moderation was frequently recommended. Some advised carefulness as well: "Who dares to undertake a bleeding should see to it that his hand does not tremble."

Physicians were also available when people faced serious illnesses. Many were clerics and monasteries trained their own. Monastic libraries kept medical manuscripts copied from ancient works and grew herbs to provide stocks of medicinal plants. Carolingian medical manuscripts, though deficient in comparison to those of the Byzantines and Arabs, did contain scientific descriptions of illnesses, recipes for medical potions, and even gynecological advice, although monks in particular expended little effort on female medical needs. Some manuals even included instructions for operations, especially for soldiers injured in battle. Some sources clearly demonstrate that there were accurate techniques for amputating gangrenous limbs:

> If you must cut off an unhealthy limb from a healthy body, then do not cut to the limit of the healthy flesh, but cut further into the whole and quick flesh, so that a better and quicker cure may be obtained. When you set fire on the man [ie., cauterize], take leaves of tender leek and grated salt, overlay the places so that the heat of the fire be more quickly drawn away.[9]

Although scholars are not sure whether anesthesia was used for such operations, medieval manuals recommended poppy, mandrake, and henbane for their narcotic properties.

Physicians of the Early Middle Ages supplemented their medicines and natural practices with appeals for otherworldly help. Magical rites and influences were carried over from pagan times since Germanic tribes had used magical medicine for centuries. Physicians recommended that patients wear amulets and charms around their bodies to ward off diseases:

> Procure a little bit of the dung of a wolf, preferably some which contains small bits of bone, and pack it in a tube which the patient may easily wear as an amulet.
> For epilepsy take a nail of a wrecked ship, make it into a bracelet and set therein the bone of a stag's heart taken from its body whilst alive; put it on the left arm; you will be astonished at the result.[10]

But as pagans were converted to Christianity, miraculous healing through the intervention of God, Christ, or the saints soon replaced pagan practices. Medieval chronicles abound with accounts of people healed by touching a saint's body. The use of Christian prayers, written down and used as amulets, however, reminds us that for centuries Christian and pagan medical practices survived side by side.

The Disintegration of the Carolingian Empire: Internal Dissension and New Invasions

The Carolingian Empire began to disintegrate soon after Charlemagne's death. Although Christianity was common to the entire empire, the ideal of Christian unity preached by clerics was not necessarily shared by a Frankish aristocracy accustomed to violence. Even

Charlemagne, near the end of his life, questioned whether the Franks were "truly Christian." Charlemagne's absence from the scene soon made it apparent that he alone had held the empire together. The internal dissension that ensued after his death was a prime factor in the disintegration of the empire.

Internal Dissension

Charlemagne was survived by his son Louis the Pious (814–840). Though a decent man, he was not a strong ruler and was unable to control either the Frankish aristocracy or his own four sons who fought continually. In 843, after their father's death, the three surviving brothers signed the Treaty of Verdun. This agreement divided the Carolingian Empire among them into three major sections: Charles the Bald (843–877) obtained the west Frankish lands, which formed the core of the eventual kingdom of France; Louis the German (843–876) took the eastern lands, which became Germany; and Lothair (840–855) received the title of emperor and a "Middle Kingdom" extending from the North Sea to Italy, including the Netherlands, the Rhineland, and northern Italy. The territories of the Middle Kingdom became a source of incessant struggle between the other two Frankish rulers and their heirs. Indeed, France and Germany would fight over the territories of this Middle Kingdom for centuries.

Although this division of the Carolingian Empire was made for political and not nationalistic reasons (dividing a kingdom among the male heirs was a traditional Frankish custom), it is apparent that two different cultures were beginning to emerge. By the ninth century, inhabitants of the west Frankish area were speaking a Romance language derived from Latin that became French. Eastern Franks spoke a Germanic dialect. The later kingdoms of France and Germany did not yet exist, however. In the ninth century, the frequent struggles among the numerous heirs of the sons of Louis the Pious led to further disintegration of the Carolingian Empire. In the meantime, while powerful aristocrats acquired even more power in their own local territories at the expense of the squabbling Carolingian rulers, the process of disintegration was abetted by external attacks on different parts of the old Carolingian world.

Invasions of the Ninth and Tenth Centuries

Invasions and migrations of peoples were a regular experience for western Europe. The incursion of Germanic peoples had been part of the dissolution of the

Western Roman Empire. The sixth-century Byzantine invasion of Italy had produced not a renewed empire, but more chaos. Later, the *jihad* of the Muslims had ended any Mediterranean unity for Christian peoples. In the ninth and tenth centuries, western Europe was beset by a new wave of invasions of several non-Christian peoples—one old enemy, the Muslims, and two new ones, the Magyars and Vikings. Although battered by these onslaughts, Christian Europe hung on and, with the exception of the Muslims, wound up assimilating the other two peoples into Christian European civilization.

MUSLIMS AND MAGYARS

The first great wave of Muslim expansion had ended at the beginning of the eighth century (see Chapter 7). Gradually, the Muslims built up a series of sea bases in their occupied territories in North Africa, Spain, and southern Gaul and began a new series of attacks in the Mediterranean in the ninth century. They raided the southern coasts of Europe, especially Italy, and even threatened Rome in 843. Their invasion of Sicily in 827 eventually led to a successful occupation of the entire island. Muslim forces also destroyed the Carolingian defenses in northern Spain and conducted forays into southern France. Marauding Muslim bands then set up camps from which they could prey on pilgrims and merchants crossing the Alps.

The Magyars were a people from western Asia. When the Byzantine emperors encouraged them to attack the troublesome Bulgars, the latter in turn encouraged a people known as the Pechenegs to attack the Magyars instead. Consequently, the Magyars, under severe Pecheneg pressure, had moved west into eastern and central Europe by the end of the ninth century. They established themselves on the plains of Hungary and from there made raids into Germany, France, and even Italy, especially between 898 and 920. The Magyars were finally crushed at the Battle of Lechfeld in Germany in 955. At the end of the tenth century, they were

Map 8.2 Invasions of the Ninth and Tenth Centuries.

lation, which limited the resources available, and the emergence of more effective monarchs in Denmark, Norway, and Sweden, which caused some of the freedom-loving Scandinavians to seek escape from the growing order. Other reasons have included the Vikings' great love of adventure and their search for booty and new avenues of trade.

Two features of Viking society help to explain what the Vikings accomplished. First of all, they were warriors. Secondly, they were superb shipbuilders and sailors. Their ships were the best of the period. Long and narrow with beautifully carved arched prows, the Viking dragon ships carried about fifty men. They had both banks of oars and a single great sail. Their shallow draft enabled them to sail up European rivers and attack places at some distance inland. Although Viking raids in the eighth century tended to be small-scale and sporadic, they became more regular and devastating in the ninth. Vikings sacked villages and towns, destroyed churches, and easily defeated small local armies. They were mobile enough that when threatened by a larger force, they simply fled the scene rather then engage in a pitched battle.

Since there were different groups of Scandinavians, Viking expansion varied a great deal. Norwegian Vikings moved into Ireland and western England, while the Danes attacked eastern England, Frisia, and the Rhineland and navigated rivers to enter western Frankish lands. Swedish Vikings dominated the Baltic Sea and progressed into the Slavic areas to the east. Moving into northwest Russia, they went down the rivers of Russia to Novgorod and Kiev and established fortified ports throughout these territories. There they made contact with the Byzantine Empire, either as traders or invaders. They also made contact with Arab traders on the Volga River and Sea of Azov.

Early Viking raids had been carried out largely in the summer; by the mid-ninth century, however, the Northmen had begun to establish winter settlements in Europe from which they could make expeditions to conquer and settle new lands. By 850, groups of Norsemen had settled in Ireland, while the Danes occupied an area known as the Danelaw in northeastern England by 878. Agreeing to accept Christianity, the Danes were eventually assimilated into a larger Anglo-Saxon kingdom. Beginning in 911, the ruler of the western Frankish lands gave one band of Vikings land at the mouth of the Seine River, forming a section of France that ultimately came to be known as Normandy. This policy of settling the Vikings and converting them to Christianity was a

◆ **The Vikings Attack England.** This illustration from an eleventh-century English manuscript depicts a group of armed Vikings invading England. Two ships have already reached the shore, and a few Vikings are shown walking down a long gangplank onto English soil.

converted to Christianity and settled down to establish the kingdom of Hungary.

THE VIKINGS

By far, the most devastating and far-reaching attacks of the time came from the Northmen or Norsemen of Scandinavia, also known to us as the Vikings. The Vikings were a Germanic people based in Scandinavia and constitute, in a sense, the final wave of Germanic migration. Why they did so is not very clear to historians. The most common explanations focus on overpopudeliberate one, since the new inhabitants served as protectors against additional Norsemen attacks.

The Vikings were also daring explorers. After 860, they sailed westward in their long ships across the north Atlantic, reaching Iceland in 874. Erik the Red, a Viking exiled from Iceland, traveled even further west and discovered Greenland in 985. The only known Viking site in North America was found in Newfoundland.

By the tenth century, however, Viking expansion was already drawing to a close. Greater control by the monarchs of Denmark, Norway, and Sweden over their inhabitants and the increasing Christianization of both the Scandinavian kings and peoples tended to inhibit Viking expansion, but not before Viking settlements had been established throughout many parts of Europe. Like the Magyars, the Vikings were also assimilated into European civilization. Once again, Christianity proved a decisive civilizing force in Western civilization in its European form. Europe and Christianity were becoming virtually synonymous.

The Viking raids and settlements also had important political repercussions. The inability of royal authorities to protect their peoples against these incursions caused local populations to turn instead to the local aristocrats who provided security for them. In the process, the landed aristocrats not only increased their strength and prestige but also assumed even more of the functions of local government that had previously belonged to the kings; over time these developments led to a new political and military order.

The Emerging World of Feudalism

The renewed invasions and the disintegration of the Carolingian world led to the emergence of a new type of relationship between free individuals. When governments ceased to be able to defend their subjects, it became important to find some powerful lord who could offer protection in exchange for service. The contract sworn between a lord and his subordinate is the basis of a form of social organization known by later generations of historians as feudalism.

Feudalism contained two component parts: a personal element called vassalage and a property element called the benefice. The practice of vassalage was derived from Germanic society and was based upon a lord attracting followers to himself on certain conditions, primarily military. It was grounded in the practice of the *comitatus*,

the following of a great chief, which was described by the Roman author Tacitus in his *Germania*:

> When they go into battle it is a disgrace for the chief to be surpassed in valor, a disgrace for his followers (*comitatus*) not to equal the valor of the chief. And it is an infamy and a reproach for life to have survived the chief, and returned from the field. To defend, to protect him, to ascribe one's own brave deeds to his renown, is the height of loyalty. The chief fights for victory; his vassals fight for their chief.[11]

In Germanic practice, this relationship between chief and followers was a perfectly honorable one, a relationship between social equals. By the eighth century, one who served a lord in a military capacity was known as a vassal.

Feudalism also contained a property element that was ultimately fused with the personal element of vassalage. In the late Roman Empire, it became customary for great landowners to hire retainers. To provide for the latter's maintenance, the lord provided a grant of land that was known as a benefice (Latin *beneficium*). Under the Carolingian mayors of the palace of the eighth century, the personal element of vassalage developed to

♦ **A Knight's Equipment Showing Saddle and Stirrups.** In return for his fighting skills, a knight received a piece of land from his lord that provided for his economic support. Pictured here is a charging knight with his equipment. The introduction of the high saddle, stirrup, and larger horses allowed horsemen to wear heavier armor and to wield long lances, thereby increasing the importance of the cavalry.

the point where vassals were holding benefices. This emerged out of a king's or lord's need for fighting men, especially the newly developing cavalry. The Frankish army had originally consisted of foot soldiers, dressed in coats of mail and armed with swords. But in the eighth century, a military change began to occur when larger horses were introduced. Earlier, horsemen had been mobile archers and throwers of spears. Eventually they were armored in coats of mail and wielded long lances that enabled them to act as battering rams. For almost five hundred years, warfare in Europe would be dominated by heavily armored cavalry or knights as they came to be called. They came to have the greatest social prestige and formed the backbone of the European aristocracy.

Of course, ample resources were needed to supply a horse, armor, and weapons. Moreover, it took time and much practice to learn to wield these weapons skillfully from a horse. Consequently, lords who wanted military retainers to fight for them had to grant each vassal a benefice, a piece of land that provided the vassal's economic support. In return for the grant of land, the vassal provided his lord with one major service, his fighting skills. In the society of early medieval Europe, where there was little commerce and wealth was based primarily on land, land became the fundamental gift a lord could give to a vassal in return for military service. Hence, what historians later came to call feudalism meant essentially the linking together of the personal element of vassalage with the property element of the benefice.

As the relationship between lord and vassal became more formal, a ceremony emerged to mark the commitment of a man to become a vassal to his lord. To become a vassal, a man performed homage to his lord, as described in this passage from a medieval digest of law and practice:

> The man should put his hands together as a sign of humility, and place them between the two hands of his lord as a token that he vows everything to him and promises faith to him; and the lord should receive him and promise to keep faith with him. Then the man should say: "Sir, I enter your homage and faith and become your man by mouth and hands [i.e., by taking the oath and placing his hands between those of the lord], and I swear and promise to keep faith and loyalty to you against all others, and to guard your rights with all my strength.[12]

Loyalty to one's lord was the chief male virtue. To desert one's leader was an act of cowardice and dishonor.

By the ninth century, the benefice had become known as a fief as it acquired a new characteristic involving the exercise of political power. While a fief was a landed estate held from the lord by a vassal in return for military service, vassals holding such grants of land came to exercise rights of jurisdiction or political and legal authority within these fiefs. As the Carolingian world disintegrated politically under the impact of internal dissension and invasions, an increasing number of powerful lords arose (see the box on p. 263).

Fief-holding also became increasingly complicated as subinfeudation developed. The vassals of a king, who were themselves great lords, might also have vassals who would owe them military service in return for a grant of land from their estates. Those vassals, in turn, might likewise have vassals, who at such a level would be simple knights with barely enough land to provide their equipment. The lord-vassal relationship, then, bound together both greater and lesser landowners. Historians used to speak of a hierarchy with the king at the top, greater lords on the next level, lesser lords on the next, and simple knights at the bottom; however, this was only a model and rarely reflected reality. Such a hierarchy implies a king at the top. The reality in the tenth-century west Frankish kingdom was that the Capetian kings (see New Political Configurations in the Tenth Century later in this chapter) actually controlled no more land than the Ile-de-France, the region around Paris. They possessed little real power over the great lords who held fiefs throughout France.

The lord-vassal relationship at all levels always constituted an honorable relationship between free men and did not imply any sense of servitude. Since kings could no longer provide security in the midst of the breakdown created by the invasions of the ninth century, the system of subinfeudation became ever more widespread. With their rights of jurisdiction, fiefs gave lords virtual possession of the rights of government.

Feudalism was essentially Carolingian; its heartland remained the Frankish lands between the Loire and the Rhine rivers. But it also spread to England, Germany, the Slavic kingdoms of central Europe, and in some form to Italy. It was noticeably weak in Spain and Scandinavia. Feudalism came to be characterized by a set of practices worked out in the course of the tenth century, although they became more prominent after 1000. While we speak of feudalism as a system based on a series of mutual obligations of lord toward vassal and vassal toward lord, it is crucial to remember that such obligations varied considerably from place to place and even from fief to fief. As usual, practice almost always

➤ Lords, Vassals, and Fiefs ⬥

*T*he upheavals of the Early Middle Ages produced a number of new institutions—lordship, vassalage, fiefs. The following selections illustrate two facets of feudalism. The first records the granting of a fief by a lord to a vassal. The second is the classic statement by Bishop Fulbert of Chartres in 1020 on the mutual obligations between lord and vassal.

Record of a Grant Made by Abbot Faritius to Robert, a Knight

Abbot Faritius also granted to Robert, son of William Mauduit, the land of four hides in Weston which his father had held from the former's predecessor, to be held as a fief. And he should do this service for it, to wit: that whenever the church of Abingdon should perform its knight's service he should do the service of half a knight for the same church; that it so say, in castle ward, in military service beyond and on this side of the sea, in giving money in proportion to the knights on the capture of the king, and in the rest of the services which the other knights of the church perform.

Bishop Fulbert of Chartres

Asked to write something concerning the form of fealty, I have noted briefly for you, on the authority of the books, the things which follow. He who swears fealty to his lord ought always to have these six things in memory: what is harmless, safe, honorable, useful, easy, practicable. *Harmless*, that is to say, that he should not injure his lord in his body; *safe*, that he should not injure him by betraying his secrets or the defenses upon which he relies for safety; *honorable*, that he should not injure him in his justice or in other matters that pertain to his honor; *useful*, that he should not injure him in his possessions; *easy* and *practicable*, that that good which his lord is able to do easily he make not difficult, nor that which is practicable he make not impossible to him.

That the faithful vassal should avoid these injuries is certainly proper, but not for this alone does he deserve his holding; for it is not sufficient to abstain from evil, unless what is good is done also. It remains, therefore, that in the same six things mentioned above he should faithfully counsel and aid his lord, if he wishes to be looked upon as worthy of his benefice and to be safe concerning the fealty which he has sworn.

The lord also ought to act toward his faithful vassal reciprocally in all these things. And if he does not do this, he will be justly considered guilty of bad faith, just as the former, if he should be detected in avoiding or consenting to the avoidance of his duties, would be perfidious and perjured.

varied from theory, and the system was far from systematic.

Since the basic objective of feudalism was to provide military support, it is no surprise to learn that the major obligation of a vassal to his lord was to perform military service. In addition to his own personal service, a great lord was also responsible for providing a group of knights for the king's army. Moreover, vassals had to furnish suit at court; this meant a vassal was obliged to appear at his lord's court when summoned, either to give advice to the lord or to sit in judgment in a legal case since the important vassals of a lord were peers and only they could judge each other. Many vassals were also obliged to provide hospitality for their lord when he stayed at a vassal's castle. This obligation was especially important to medieval kings since they tended to be highly itinerant. Finally, vassals were responsible for aids, or financial payments, to the lord upon a number of occasions, among them the knighting of the lord's eldest son, the marriage of his eldest daughter, and the ransom of the lord's person if the lord had been captured (see the box above).

In turn, a lord had responsibilities toward his vassals. His major task was to protect his vassal, either by defending him militarily or by taking his side in a court of law if necessary. The lord was also responsible for the maintenance of the vassal, usually by granting him a fief.

As this system of mutual obligations between lord and vassal evolved, certain practices became common. If a lord acted improperly toward his vassal, the bond between them could be dissolved. Likewise, if a vassal failed to fulfill his vow of loyalty, he was subject to forfeiture of his fief. Upon a vassal's death, his fief theoretically reverted back to the lord since it had been granted to him to use, not to own as a possession. In practice, however, by the tenth century fiefs tended to become hereditary. Following the principle of primogeniture, the eldest son inherited the father's fief. If a

CHRONOLOGY

New Political Configurations of the Tenth Century

The east Franks	
Conrad of Franconia	911–918
Saxon dynasty Henry I	919–936
Otto I	936–973
Defeat of Magyars	955
Coronation as emperor	962
The west Franks	
Election of Hugh Capet as king	987
Anglo-Saxon England	
Alfred the Great, king of Wessex	871–899
Peace with the Danes	885
Reign of King Edgar	959–975

man died without heirs, the lord could once again reclaim the fief.

New Political Configurations in the Tenth Century

In the tenth century, Europe began to recover from the great invasions of the ninth century. The disintegration of the Carolingian Empire and the emergence of great and powerful lords soon produced new political configurations.

In the east Frankish kingdom, the last Carolingian king died in 911. Whereupon, local rulers, especially the powerful dukes (the title of duke is derived from the Latin word *dux*, meaning leader) of the Saxons, Swabians, Bavarians, Thuringians, and Franconians, who exercised much power in their large dukedoms, elected one of their own number, Conrad of Franconia as king of Germany (as we think of it) or of the east Franks (as contemporaries thought of it.) But Conrad did not last long and after his death, the German dukes chose Henry the Fowler, duke of Saxony, as the new king of Germany (919–936). The first of the Saxon dynasty of German kings, Henry was not overly successful in creating a unified east Frankish kingdom. He lacked the resources to impose effective rule over the entire area, although he did begin a practice continued by his successors of using high church officials as administrators.

The best known of the Saxon kings of Germany was Otto I (936–973). He defeated the Magyars at the Battle of Lechfeld in 955 and encouraged an ongoing program of Christianization of both the Slavic and Scandinavian peoples. Even more than his father, he relied on bishops and abbots in governing his kingdom. This practice was in part a response to the tendency of the lay lords to build up their power at the expense of the king. Since the clergy were theoretically celibate, bishops and abbots could not make their offices hereditary, thus allowing the king to maintain more control over them. In the tenth century, Otto's employment of these high church officials as administrators seemed to be a clever move. In the next century, however, it gave rise to a tremendous conflict between the church and emperors over the issue of who should control the clergy.

Otto I also intervened in Italian politics and for his efforts was crowned emperor of the Romans by the pope in 962, reviving a title that had fallen into abeyance with the disintegration of Charlemagne's Carolingian Empire. Once again a pope had conferred the Roman imperial title on a king of the Franks, even though he was a Saxon king of the east Franks. Otto's creation of a new "Roman Empire" in the hands of the east Franks, or Germans as they came to be called, added a tremendous burden to the kingship of Germany. To the difficulties of governing Germany was appended the onerous task of ruling Italy as well. It proved a formidable and ultimately impossible task in the centuries to come.

In the ninth and tenth centuries, the Carolingian kings had little success in controlling the great lords of the west Frankish kingdom. The counts, who were supposed to serve as the chief administrative officials, often paid little attention to the wishes of the Carolingian kings. Some of the counts, such as those of Flanders and Autun (northern Burgundy) regarded themselves as quasi-sovereign hereditary princes. In 987, when the Carolingian king died, the west Frankish nobles and chief prelates of the church chose Hugh Capet, count of Orleans and Paris, as the new king (987–996).

The nobles who elected Hugh Capet did not intend to establish a new royal dynasty. After all, although Hugh was officially king of the west Franks and overlord of the great nobles of the kingdom, his own family controlled only the Ile-de-France, the region around Paris. Other French nobles possessed lands equal to or greater than those of the Capetians and assumed that the king would be content to live off the revenues of his personal lands and not impose any burdensome demands on the nobility. Hugh Capet did succeed in making his position hereditary, however. He asked the nobles, and they agreed, to choose his eldest son Robert as his anointed associate in case Hugh died on a campaign to Spain in 987. And although Hugh Capet could not know it then, the Capetian dynasty would rule the west Frankish kingdom, or France as it came to be known, for centuries. In the late tenth century, however, the territory that would become France was not a unified kingdom, but a loose alliance of powerful lords who treated the king of France as one of themselves. They assisted him only when it was in their own interests to do so.

England's development in the ninth and tenth centuries took a course somewhat different from the west and east Frankish kingdoms. The long struggle of Anglo-Saxon England against the Danish invasions ultimately produced a unified kingdom. Alfred the Great, king of Wessex (871–899), played a crucial role. He defeated a Danish army in 879 and made peace with the Danes in 885. His successors reconquered the areas occupied by the Danes and established a unified Anglo-Saxon monarchy.

By the time of King Edgar (959–975), Anglo-Saxon England had a well-developed and strong monarchical government. Although the kingship was elective, only the descendants of Alfred were chosen for the position.

In the counties or shires, the administrative units into which England was divided, the king was assisted by an agent appointed and controlled by him, the shire-reeve or sheriff. An efficient chancery or writing office was responsible for issuing writs (or royal letters) conveying the king's orders to the sheriffs.

The Manorial System

Feudalism was closely dependent upon the economic system of manorialism. The landholding class of nobles and knights comprised a military elite whose ability to function as warriors depended upon having the leisure time to pursue the arts of war. Landed estates, located on the fiefs given to a vassal by his lord and worked by a dependent peasant class, provided the economic sustenance that made this way of life possible. A manor was simply an agricultural estate operated by a lord and worked by peasants. The manor became the fundamental unit of rural organization in the Middle Ages based on the mutual obligations of lords and peasants. Lords provided protection; peasants gave up their freedom, became tied to the lord's land, and provided labor services for him. The existence of feudalism, then, depended upon manorialism and was, in fact, imposed

◆ **Peasants in the Manorial System.** In the manorial system, peasants were required to provide labor services for their lord. This thirteenth-century illustration shows a group of

English peasants harvesting grain. Overseeing their work is a bailiff, or manager, who supervised the work of the peasants.

upon an already existing manorial system that had emerged in the unsettled conditions of the sixth and seventh centuries.

The basic agricultural unit of the Early Middle Ages was the large estate, which largely continued the Roman practices of the late empire. After the Germanic invasions, estate owners continued to rely on slaves to work the land. But their use gradually declined from the fifth to seventh centuries. Although the Christian church did not try to prohibit slavery, it did encourage the freeing of slaves. Economic considerations were even more important in ending slavery. Landlords found it easier and cheaper to establish slaves on small parcels of land, where they could feed themselves and their families, and to require in exchange that the slaves work the demesne, or lord's land. This decline in the utilization of slaves on large estates (they were still used in households) meant some upward movement for the lowest classes in society.

At the same time, another general tendency was working in the opposite direction. Free peasants were losing their freedom. There were still substantial numbers of free farmers in the late Roman Empire whose numbers were actually augmented by the influx of free German peasants. All too soon, however, these free peasants found themselves in a vulnerable position. In the unsettled circumstances of the Early Middle Ages, small farmers often needed protection or food in a time of bad harvests. Free peasants gave up their freedom to the lords of large landed estates in return for protection and sustenance. While a large class of free peasants continued to exist, increasing numbers of free peasants became serfs. It has been estimated that by the ninth century, 60 percent of the population of western Europe had been reduced to serfdom.

Unlike slaves, serfs could not be bought and sold, but their unfree status made them subject to their lords in a variety of ways. Serfs were required to provide labor services, pay rents, and be subject to the lord's jurisdiction.

Labor services consisted of working the lord's demesne, the land retained by the lord, which might consist of one-third to one-half of the cultivated lands scattered throughout the manor (the rest would have been allotted to the serfs for their maintenance), as well as building barns and digging ditches. Although labor requirements varied from manor to manor and person to person, a common work obligation was three days a week.

Many rents were paid in kind and included a share of every product raised by the serfs. Moreover, serfs paid the lord for the use of the manor's common pasturelands, streams, ponds, and surrounding woodlands. For example, if a tenant fished in the pond or stream on a manor, he turned over part of the catch to his lord. If his cow grazed in the common pasture, he paid a rent in cheese produced from the cow's milk. Serfs were also obliged to pay a tithe (a tenth of their produce) to their local village church.

Map 8.3 A Manor.

⇒ *The Manorial Court* ⇐

The way of life of the medieval lord was made possible by the labors of the serfs on his manor. In addition to his right to collect rents, labor services, and fees from his serfs, the lord also possessed political authority over them, including the right to hold a manorial court to try tenants for crimes and infractions of the manor's rules. This selection, taken from the records of an English manorial court, lists the cases heard, the decisions of the jurors, and the subsequent penalties.

Select Pleas in Manorial Courts

John Sperling complains that Richard of Newmere on the Sunday next before S. Bartholomew's day [August 24] last past with his cattle, horses, and pigs wrongfully destroyed the corn on his (John's) land to his damage to the extent of one thrave of wheat, and to his dishonor to the extent of two shillings; and of this he produces suit. And Richard comes and defends all of it. Therefore let him go to the law six handed [with six companions who will swear to his innocence]. His pledges, Simon Combe and Hugh Frith [like bail bondsmen, pledges stood surety for a person ordered to show up in court or pay a fine].

Hugh Free in mercy [fined] for his beast caught in the lord's garden. Pledges, Walter Hill and William Slipper, Fine 6d. [sixpence].

(The) twelve jurors say that Hugh Cross has right in the bank and hedge about which there was a dispute between him and William White. Therefore let him hold in peace and let William be distrained [forced to comply by seizing his property] for his many trespasses. (Afterwards he made fine for 12d.).

From the whole township of Little Ogbourne, except seven, for not coming to wash the lord's sheep, 6s. 8d. [six shillings, eight pence].

Gilbert Richard's son gives 5s. for license to marry a wife. Pledge, Seaman. Term (for payments), the Purification [February 2].

William Jordan in mercy for bad ploughing on the lord's land. Pledge, Arthur. Fine, 6d.

The parson of the Church is in mercy for his cow caught in the lord's meadow. Pledges, Thomas Ymer and William Coke.

From Martin Shepherd 6d. for the wound that he gave Pekin.

Ragenhilda of Bec. gives 2s. for having married without license. Pledge, William of Primer.

Walter Hull gives 13s. 4d. for license to dwell on the land of the Prior of Harmondsworth so long as he shall live and as a condition finds pledges, to wit, William Slipper, John Bisuthe, Gilbert Bisuthe, Hugh Tree, William Johnson, John Hulle, who undertake that the said Walter shall do to the lord all the services and customs which he would do if he dwelt on the lord's land. . . .

It was presented that Robert Carter's son by night invaded the house of Peter Burgess and in felony threw stones at his door so that the said Peter raised the hue [alarm]. Therefore let the said Robert be committed to prison. Afterwards he made fine with 2s.

All the ploughmen of Great Ogbourne are convicted by the oath of twelve men . . . . because by reason of their default (the land) of the lord is damaged to the amount of 9s. . . . And Walter Reaper is in mercy for concealing (i.e., not giving information as to) the said bad ploughing. Afterwards he made fine with the lord with 1 mark [13 shillings, fourpence].

Lords also possessed a variety of legal rights over their serfs. Serfs were legally bound to the lord's land; they could not leave without his permission. Although free to marry, serfs could not marry anyone outside their manor without the lord's approval. Moreover, due to the decentralization of public power that was part of feudalism, lords sometimes exercised public rights or political authority on their lands. This gave the lord the right to try serfs in his own court, although only for lesser crimes (called "low justice"). In fact, the lord's manorial court provided the only law that most serfs knew (see the box above). Finally, the lord's political authority enabled him to establish monopolies on certain services that provided additional revenues. Serfs could be required to bring their grain to the lord's mill and pay a fee to have it ground into flour. Thus, the rights a lord possessed on his manor gave him virtual control over both the lives and property of his serfs.

The administration of manors varied considerably. If the lord of a manor was a simple knight, he would probably live on the estate and supervise it in person. Great lords possessed many manors and relied on a steward or bailiff to run each estate. We should note that manors were controlled not only by lay lords, but also by monasteries and cathedral churches. Monasteries tended to be far more conscientious about keeping accurate records of their manorial estates than lay lords, and their surveys provide some of the best sources for medieval village life. As for the relationship between manors and villages, it was highly variable. Although a manor and village would often coincide, with a single village constituting a manor, large manors might encompass several villages.

In the Early Middle Ages, whether free or unfree, a vast majority of men and women, possibly as high as 90 percent, worked the land. This period had certainly witnessed a precipitous decline in trade. Coins and jewelry were often hoarded, and at the local level, goods were frequently bartered because so few coins were in circulation. Nevertheless, trade never entirely disappeared. Even in an agrarian society, surplus products could be exchanged at local markets. More significantly, however, both aristocrats and wealthy clerics desired merchandise not produced locally, such as spices, silk cloth, wine, gold, and silver jewelry. It took trade to obtain these items.

Much trade in luxury goods, especially beginning in the ninth century, was with the Byzantine Empire, particularly the city of Constantinople, and the Islamic caliphs of Baghdad. Products from the west included iron, timber, furs, and slaves (many from eastern Europe, including captured Slavs, from whom the modern word *slave* is derived). Traders, often Jews, carried goods by boat on European rivers or on caravans with horses or mules. An Arab geographer of the ninth century left this account of Jewish traders from southern France:

[They] speak Arabic, Persian, Greek, Frankish, Spanish, and Slavonic. They travel from west to east and from east to west, by land and by sea. From the west they bring eunuchs, slave-girls, boys, brocade, castor-skins, marten and other furs, and swords. They take ship from Frankland in the western Mediterranean sea and land at Farama, whence they take their merchandise on camelback to Qulzum. . . . Then they sail on the eastern [Red] Sea from Qulzum, to Al-Jar and Jedda, and onward to Sind, India and China. From China they bring back musk, aloes, camphor, cinnamon, and other products of those parts, and return to Qulzum. Then they transport them to Farama and sail again on the western sea. Some sail with their goods to Constantinople and sell them to the Greeks, and some take them to the king of the Franks and sell them there.[13]

Of course, such caravans were prime targets for thieves and were often plundered. Towns were not needed for such trade, although some ports were frequently utilized. By 900, Italian merchants, especially the Venetians, were entering the trade picture, particularly with the Muslims and Byzantines. Overall, however, compared to the Byzantine Empire or Muslim caliphates, western Europe in the Early Middle Ages was an underdeveloped, predominantly agrarian society and could not begin to match the splendor of either of the other heirs of the Roman Empire.

The Zenith of Byzantine Civilization

In the seventh and eighth centuries, the Byzantine Empire had lost much of its territory to Slavs, Bulgars, and Muslims. By 750, the empire consisted only of Asia Minor, some lands in the Balkans, and the southern coast of Italy. Although Byzantium was beset with internal dissension and invasions in the ninth century, it was able to deal with them and not only endured, but even expanded, reaching its high point in the tenth century, which some historians have called "the golden age of Byzantine civilization."

During the reign of Michael III (842–867), the Byzantine Empire began to experience a revival. Iconoclasm was finally abolished in 843, and reforms were made in education, church life, the military, and the peasant economy. There was a noticeable intellectual renewal. But the Byzantine Empire under Michael was still plagued by persistent problems. The Bulgars mounted new attacks, and the Arabs continued to harass the empire. Moreover, a new church problem with political repercussions erupted over differences between the pope as leader of the western Christian church and the patriarch of Constantinople as leader of the eastern (or Orthodox) Christian church. Patriarch Photius condemned the pope as a heretic for accepting a revised form of the Nicene Creed stating that the Holy Spirit proceeded from the Father and the Son instead of "The Holy Spirit, who proceeds from the Father." A council of eastern bishops followed Photius's wishes and excommunicated the pope, creating the so-called Photian schism. While the differences were later papered over, this controversy served to further the division between the eastern and western Christian churches.

The problems that arose during Michael's reign were effectively dealt with by a new dynasty of Byzantine emperors, known as the Macedonians (867–1081). In

A Western View of the Byzantine Empire

Bishop Liudprand of Cremona undertook diplomatic missions to Constantinople on behalf of two western kings, Berengar of Italy and Otto I of Germany. This selection is taken from his description of his mission to the Byzantine emperor Constantine VII in 949 as an envoy for Berengar, king of Italy from 950 until his overthrow by Otto I of Germany in 964. Liudprand had mixed feelings about Byzantium: admiration, yet also envy and hosility because of its superior wealth.

Liudprand of Cremona, *Antapodosis*

Next to the imperial residence at Constantinople there is a palace of remarkable size and beauty which the Greeks call Magnavra . . . the name being equivalent to "Fresh breeze." In order to receive some Spanish envoys, who had recently arrived, as well as myself . . . , Constantine gave orders that his palace should be got ready. . . .

Before the emperor's seat stood a tree, made of bronze gilded over, whose branches were filled with birds, also made of gilded bronze, which uttered different cries, each according to its varying species. The throne itself was so marvelously fashioned that at one moment it seemed a low structure, and at another it rose high into the air. It was of immense size and was guarded by lions, made either of bronze or of wood covered over with gold, who beat the ground with their tails and gave a dreadful roar with open mouth and quivering tongue. Leaning upon the shoulders of two eunuchs I was brought into the emperor's presence. At my approach the lions began to roar and the birds to cry out, each according to its kind; but I was neither terrified nor surprised, for I had previously made enquiry about all these things from people who were well acquainted with them So after I had three times made obeisance to the emperor with my face upon the ground, I lifted my head, and behold! The man whom just before I had seen sitting on a moderately elevated seat had now changed his raiment and was sitting on the level of the ceiling. How it was done I could not imagine, unless perhaps he was lifted up by some such sort of device as we use for raising the timbers of a wine press. On that occasion he did not address me personally . . . but by the intermediary of a secretary he enquired about Berengar's doings and asked after his health. I made a fitting reply and then, at a nod from the interpreter, left his presence and retired to my lodging.

It would give me some pleasure also to record here what I did then for Berengar. . . . The Spanish envoys . . . had brought handsome gifts from their masters to the emperor Constantine. I for my part had brought nothing from Berengar except a letter and that was full of lies. I was very greatly disturbed and shamed at this and began to consider anxiously what I had better do. In my doubt and perplexity it finally occurred to me that I might offer the gifts, which on my account I had brought for the emperor, as coming from Berengar, and trick out my humble present with fine words. I therefore presented him with nine excellent curaisses, seven excellent shields with gilded bosses, two silver gift cauldrons, some swords, spears and spits, and what was more precious to the emperor than anything, four carzimasia; that being the Greek name for young eunuchs who have had both their testicles and their penis removed. This operation is performed by traders at Verdun, who take the boys into Spain and make a huge profit.

---

general, this dynastic line managed to beat off the external enemies, go over to the offensive, and reestablish domestic order. Supported by the church, the emperors continued to think of the Byzantine Empire as a continuation of the Christian Roman Empire of late antiquity. Although for diplomatic reasons they occasionally recognized the imperial title of western emperors, such as Charlemagne and Otto I, they still regarded them as little more than barbarian parvenus.

The Macedonian emperors could boast of a remarkable number of achievements in the late ninth and tenth centuries. To bolster the military machine, they created new *themes*. Instituted in the early seventh century as a new administrative unit, the *theme* combined civilian and military offices in the hands of the same person. The civil governor was the military leader of the area; the civilian population, consisting primarily of free farmers, served as soldiers. The Macedonian emperors worked to strengthen the farmer-soldiers vis-à-vis the landed aristocrats, who were trying to expand their estates at the expense of the former. The emperors were well aware that the free farmers made up the rank and file of the Byzantine cavalry and provided the military strength of the empire.

The Macedonian emperors fostered a burst of economic prosperity by expanding trade relations with western Europe, especially by selling silks and metalwork. Thanks to this prosperity, the city of Constantinople flourished. Foreign visitors continued to be astounded by its size, wealth, and physical surroundings. To western Europeans, it was the stuff of legends and fables (see the box on p. 269).

In the midst of this prosperity, Byzantine intellectual activity continued to focus on historical chronicles and spiritual works, including hymns and tracts of profound mystical devotion. Nevertheless, Byzantine cultural influence expanded during this period due to the active missionary efforts of eastern Byzantine Christians. Eastern Orthodox Christianity was spread to eastern European peoples, such as the Bulgars and Serbs. Perhaps the greatest missionary success occurred when the prince of Kiev in Russia converted to Christianity in 987 (see The Slavic Peoples of Central and Eastern Europe later in this chapter).

Under the Macedonian rulers, Byzantium enjoyed a strong civil service, talented emperors, and military advances. The Byzantine civil service was staffed by well-educated, competent aristocrats from Constantinople who oversaw the collection of taxes, domestic administration, and foreign policy. At the same time, the Macedonian dynasty produced some truly outstanding emperors skilled in administration and law, such as Leo VI (886–912) and Basil II (976–1025). In the

tenth century, competent emperors combined with a number of talented generals to mobilize the empire's military resources and take the offensive. The Bulgars were defeated, and both the eastern and western parts of Bulgaria were annexed to the empire. The Byzantines went on to add the islands of Crete and Cyprus to the empire and defeat the Muslim forces in Syria, expanding the empire to the upper Euphrates. By the end of the reign of Basil II in 1025, the Byzantine Empire was the largest it had been since the beginning of the seventh century. After Basil's death, however, a new series of dynastic struggles ensued that seriously weakened the state internally and inaugurated a fatal decline.

The Slavic Peoples of Central and Eastern Europe

North of Byzantium and east of the Carolingian Empire lay a spacious plain through which a number of Asiatic nomads, such as the Huns, Bulgars, Avars, and Magyars, had pushed their way westward, terrorizing and plundering the settled peasant communities. Eastern Europe was ravaged by these successive waves of invaders who found it relatively easy to create large empires that, in turn, were overthrown by the next invaders. Over a period of time, the invaders themselves were largely assimilated with the native Slavic peoples of the area.

◆ **Emperor Leo VI.** Under the Macedonian dynasty, the Byzantine Empire achieved economic prosperity through expanded trade and gained new territories from military victories. This mosaic over the western door of the Hagia Sophia in Constantinople depicts the Macedonian emperor Leo VI prostrating himself before Christ. This act of humility symbolized the emperor's function as an intermediary between God and the empire.

The Slavic peoples were originally a single people in central Europe who, through mass migrations and nomadic invaders, were gradually divided into three major groups: the western, southern, and eastern Slavs. In the region east of the east Frankish or Germanic kingdom emerged the Polish and Bohemian kingdoms of the western Slavs. The Germans assumed responsibility for the conversion of these Slavic peoples since German emperors, such as Otto I, considered it their duty to spread Christianity to the barbarians. Of course, it also gave them the opportunity to extend their political authority as well. German missionaries had converted the Czechs in Bohemia by the end of the ninth century, and a bishopric eventually occupied by a Czech bishop was established at Prague in the tenth century. The Slavs in Poland were not converted until the reign of Prince Mieszko (c. 960–992). In 1000, an independent Polish archbishopric was set up at Gniezno by the pope. The non-Slavic kingdom of Hungary, which emerged after the Magyars settled down after their defeat at Lechfeld in 955, was also converted to Christianity by German missionaries. Saint Stephen, king of Hungary from 997 to 1038, facilitated the acceptance of Chris-

tianity by his people. The Poles, Czechs, and Hungarians all accepted Catholic or western Christianity and became closely tied to the Roman Catholic church and its Latin culture.

The southern and eastern Slavic populations largely took a different path because of their proximity to the Byzantine Empire. The Slavic peoples of Moravia were converted to the Eastern Orthodox Christianity of the Byzantine Empire by two Byzantine missionary brothers, Cyril and Methodius, who began their activities in 863. They created a Slavonic (Cyrillic) alphabet, translated the Bible into Slavonic, and developed Slavonic church services. While the southern Slavic peoples accepted Christianity, a split eventually developed between the Croats who accepted the Roman church and the Serbs who remained loyal to eastern Christianity.

Although the Bulgars were originally an Asiatic people who conquered much of the Balkan peninsula, they were eventually absorbed by the larger native south Slavic population. Together, by the ninth century, they formed a largely Slavic Bulgarian kingdom. Although the conversion to Christianity of this state was complicated by the rivalry between the Roman Catholic and

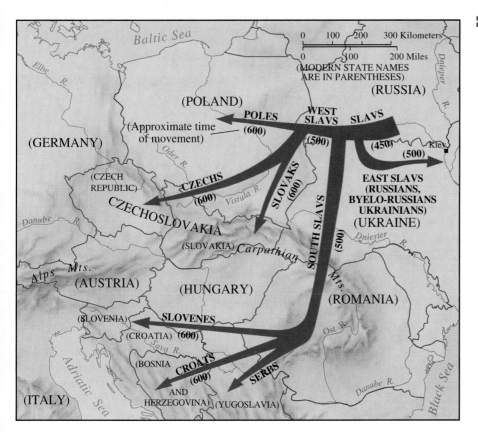

✖ **Map 8.4** The World of the Slavs.

⇒ *A Muslim's Description of the Rus* ⇐

Despite the difficulties that travel presented, early me-dieval civilization did witness some contact among the various cultures. This might occur through trade, diplomacy, or the conquest and migration of peoples. This document is a description of the Swedish Rus who eventually merged with the native Slavic peoples to form the principality of Kiev, commonly regarded as the first Russian state. This account was written by Ibn Fadlan, a Muslim diplomat sent from Baghdad in 921 to a settlement on the Volga River. His com-ments on the filthiness of the Rus reflect the Muslim preoc-cupation with cleanliness.

Ibn Fadlan, Description of the Rus

I saw the Rus folk when they arrived on their trading-mission and settled at the river Atul (Volga). Never had I seen people of more perfect physique. They are tall as date-palms, and reddish in color. They wear neither coat nor kaftan, but each man carried a cape which covers one half of his body, leaving one hand free. No one is ever parted from his axe, sword, and knife. Their swords are Frankish in design, broad, flat, and fluted. Each man has a number of trees, figures, and the like from the finger-nails to the neck. Each woman carried on her bosom a container made of iron, silver, copper or gold—its size and substance depending on her man's wealth. . . .

They [the Rus] are the filthiest of God's creatures. They do not wash after discharging their natural func-tions, neither do they wash their hands after meals. They are as lousy as donkeys. They arrive from their dis-tant river, and there they build big houses on its shores. Ten or twenty of them may live together in one house, and each of them has a couch of his own where he sits and diverts himself with the pretty slave girls whom he had brought along for sale. He will make love with one of them while a comrade looks on; sometimes they in-dulge in a communal orgy, and, if a customer should turn up to buy a girl, the Rus man will not let her go till he has finished with her.

They wash their hands and faces every day in in-credibly filthy water. Every morning the girl brings her master a large bowl of water in which he washes his hands and face and hair, then blows his nose into it and spits into it. When he has finished the girl takes the bowl to his neighbor—who repeats the perfor-mance. Thus the bowl goes the rounds of the entire household. . . .

If one of the Rus folk falls sick they put him in a tent by himself and leave bread and water for him. They do not visit him, however, or speak to him, especially if he is a serf. Should he recover he rejoins the others; if he dies they burn him. But if he happens to be a serf they leave him for the dogs and vultures to devour. If they catch a robber they hang him to a tree until he is torn to shreds by wind and weather. . . .

Eastern Orthodox churches, the Bulgarians eventually accepted the latter. By the end of the ninth century, they embraced the Slavonic church services earlier developed by Cyril and Methodius. The acceptance of Eastern Orthodoxy by the southern Slavic peoples, the Serbs and Bulgarians, meant that their cultural life was also linked to the Byzantine state.

The eastern Slavic peoples, from whom the modern Russians, White (or Byelo-) Russians, and Ukrainians are descended, had settled in the territory of present-day Ukraine and European Russia. There, beginning in the late eighth century, they began to encounter Viking invaders. Swedish Vikings, known to the eastern Slavs as Varangians, moved down the extensive network of rivers into the lands of the eastern Slavs in search of booty and new trade routes. After establishing trading

links with the Byzantine state, the Varangians built trading settlements, became involved in the civil wars among the Slavic peoples, and eventually came to dominate the native peoples, just as their fellow Vikings were doing in parts of western Europe. According to the traditional version of the story, the semilegendary Rurik secured his ruling dynasty in the Slavic settlement of Novgorod in 862. Rurik and his fellow Vikings were called "the Rus," from which the name Russia is de-rived; eventually, that name became attached to the state they founded (see the box above). Although much about Rurik is unclear, it is certain that his follower Oleg (c. 873–913) took up residence in Kiev and created the Rus state or union of east Slavic territories known as the principality of Kiev. Oleg's successors extended their control over the eastern Slavs and expanded the territory of Kiev until it encompassed the lands between the Baltic and Black Seas and the Danube and Volga Rivers. By marrying Slavic wives, the Viking ruling class was gradually assimilated into the Slavic population, a process confirmed by their assumption of Slavic names.

The growth of the principality of Kiev attracted religious missionaries, especially from the Byzantine Empire. One Rus ruler, Vladimir (c. 980–1015), married the Byzantine emperor's sister and officially accepted Christianity for himself and his people in 987. His primary motive was probably not a spiritual one. By all accounts, Vladimir was a cruel and vicious man who believed an established church would be helpful in developing an organized state. From the end of the tenth century on, Byzantine Christianity became the model for Russian religious life, just as Byzantine imperial ideals came to influence the outward forms of Russian political life.

The World of Islam

The Umayyad dynasty of caliphs had established Damascus as the center of an Islamic empire created by Muslim expansion in the seventh and eighth centuries. A revolt led by Abu al-Abbas, a descendant of the uncle of Muhammad, led to the end of the Umayyad dynasty in 750 and the establishment of the Abbasid dynasty, which lasted until 1258. The Abbasid caliphs brought political, economic, and cultural change to the world of Islam. While stressing religious fundamentalism, at the same time they broke down the distinctions between Arab and non-Arab Muslims. All could now hold both civil and military offices. This helped to open Muslim life to the influences of the civilizations they had conquered. In 762, the Abbasids built a new capital city, Baghdad, on the Tigris River far to the east of Damascus. The move eastward allowed Persian influence to come to the fore, encouraging a new cultural orientation. Under the Abbasids, judges, merchants, and government officials, rather than warriors, were viewed as the ideal citizens.

The new Abbasid caliphate experienced a period of splendid rule well into the ninth century. Some of these caliphs are well known, even in the west. Harun-al-Rashed (786–809) was known through the exotic tales of the *Arabian Nights,* which possibly portray the luxurious life at Baghdad during his reign. His son al-Mamun (813–833) was a patron of learning who founded an astronomical observatory and created a foundation for

C H R O N O L O G Y

Byzantium, the Slavs, and the Islamic World

The Byzantine Empire	
Michael III	842–867
Macedonian dynasty	867–1081
Basil II	976–1025
The Slavic peoples of central and eastern Europe	
Establishment of Novgorod	Prob. 862
Cyril and Methodius begin to convert Moravian Slavs	863
Oleg creates principality of Kiev	c. 873–913
Reign of Prince Mieszko—Slavs in Poland converted to Christianity	c. 960–992
Vladimir's conversion to Christianity	987
Saint Stephen, king of Hungary	997–1038
The world of Islam	
Overthrow of Umayyad dynasty by Abbasids	750
Creation of emirate of al-Andalus	756
Harun-al-Rashed	786–809
Establishment of Fatimid caliphate in Egypt	973

translations of classical works. This was also a period of tremendous economic prosperity. After all, the Arabs had conquered many of the richest provinces of the Roman Empire. Baghdad now became the center of an enormous trade empire that extended into Europe, Asia, and Africa, greatly adding to the wealth of the Islamic world.

The late ninth and tenth centuries were a period of political disunity for the Abbasid caliphs, however. By awarding important positions to court favorites, the Abbasids began to undermine the foundations of their own power and become figureheads. Provincial rulers broke away from their control and established independent dynasties. Even earlier, in the eighth century, Spain had been lost when Abd al-Rahman of the Umayyad dynasty had escaped execution and fled there from North Africa. In 756, he seized control of southern Spain and then expanded his power into the center of the peninsula. He took the title of emir, or commander, and set up the emirate of al-Andalus with its center at Córdoba. Under Abd al-Rahman's successors, a unique society developed in which all religions were tolerated. The court also supported writers and artists, creating a brilliant and flourishing culture.

The breakup of the Islamic empire accelerated in the tenth century. A caliphate of the Fatimid family was established in Egypt in 973, and an independent dynasty also operated in North Africa. Despite the political disunity of the Islamic world, however, there was an underlying Islamic civilization based on two common bonds, the Koran and the spread of Arabic.

Islamic Civilization

From the beginning of their empire, Muslim Arabs had demonstrated a willingness to absorb the culture of their conquered territories. The Arabs were truly heirs to the remaining Greco-Roman culture of the Roman Empire. Just as readily, they assimilated Byzantine and Persian culture. In the eighth and ninth centuries, numerous Greek, Syrian, and Persian scientific and philosophical works were translated into Arabic. As the chief language in the southern Mediterranean and the Near East, Arabic became a truly international language.

◆ **Mosque at Córdoba.** The first Great Mosque of Córdoba was built by Abd al-Rahman, founder of the Umayyad dynasty of Spain, in the eighth century. The mosque was later enlarged in the tenth century. Shown here is the interior of the sanctuary with its two levels of arches. Although the Umayyad caliphs of Damascus were overthrown and replaced by the Abbasid dynasty in the eighth century, the independent Umayyad dynasty in Spain lasted until the eleventh century.

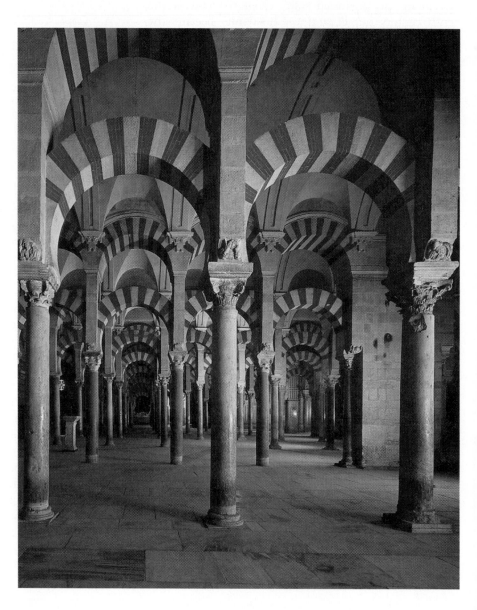

The Muslims created a brilliant urban culture at a time when western Europe was predominantly a rural world of petty villages. This can be seen in such new cities as Baghdad and Cairo, but also in Córdoba, the capital of the Umayyad caliphate in Spain. With a population of possibly 100,000, Córdoba was Europe's largest city after Constantinople. Its library was also the largest in Europe.

Islamic cities had a distinctive physical appearance due to their common use of certain architectural features, such as the pointed arch and traceried windows, and specific kinds of buildings. The latter included palaces and public buildings with fountains and secluded courtyards, mosques for worship, public baths, and bazaars or marketplaces. Muslims embellished their buildings with a unique decorative art that avoided representation of living things because of the commandment that prohibited the making of graven images.

Although Islamic scholars are justly praised for preserving much of classical knowledge for the west, they also made considerable advances of their own. Nowhere is this more true than in their contributions to mathematics and the natural sciences, although early Muslims would have regarded these fields as simply part of the study of philosophy. The list of Muslim achievements in mathematics and astronomy alone is impressive; they adopted and passed on the numerical system of India, added the use of the zero, and created the mathematical discipline of algebra (*al-jebr*). In astronomy, Muslims set up an observatory at Baghdad to study the position of the stars. They were aware that the earth was round and in the ninth century produced a world map based on the tradition of Ptolemy, a Greco-Roman astronomer of the second century A.D. Muslim fleets and caravans opened up new trading routes connecting the Islamic world with other civilizations, and Muslim travelers provide modern readers with their most accurate descriptions of political and social conditions throughout the Middle East.

Muslim scholars also made many new discoveries in optics and chemistry and developed medicine as a field of scientific study. Especially well known was Ibn Sina (Avicenna to the west, 980–1037), who authored a medical encyclopedia that, among other things, emphasized the contagious nature of certain diseases and showed how they could be spread by contaminated water supplies. After its translation into Latin, Avicenna's work became a basic medical textbook for medieval European university students. The achievements of the tenth century were a prelude to the great accomplishments of the eleventh and twelfth centuries. Fortunately for Western civilization, the intellectual and scientific work of the Islamic world was eventually translated and passed on to the underdeveloped and certainly less knowledgeable world of European civilization.

Conclusion

After the turmoil of the disintegration of the Roman Empire and the establishment of the Germanic states, a new European civilization began to emerge slowly in the Early Middle Ages. The coronation of Charlemagne, descendant of a Germanic tribe converted to Christianity, as Roman emperor in 800 symbolized the fusion of the three chief components of the new European civilization: the German tribes, the classical tradition, and Christianity. In the long run, the creation of a western empire fostered the idea of a distinct European identity and marked the shift of power from the south to the north. Italy and the Mediterranean had been the center of the Roman Empire. The lands north of the Alps now became the political center of Europe.

With the disintegration of the Carolingian Empire, new forms of political institutions began to develop in Europe. These were characterized by a decentralization of political power, in which lords exercised legal, administrative, and military power. The practice of feudalism transferred public power into many private hands and seemed to provide the security sorely lacking in a time of weak central government and new invasions by Muslims, Magyars, and Vikings. While Europe struggled, the Byzantine and Islamic worlds continued to prosper and flourish, the brilliance of their urban cultures standing in marked contrast to the underdeveloped rural world of Europe. By 1000, however, that rural world had not only recovered, but was beginning to expand in ways undreamed of by previous generations. Europe stood poised for a giant leap.

NOTES

1. Oliver Thatcher and Edgar McNeal, eds., *A Source Book for Medieval History* (New York, 1905), pp. 37–38.
2. 1 Samuel 16: 13.
3. Einhard, *The Life of Charlemagne*, trans. Samuel Turner (Ann Arbor, Mich., 1960), p. 30.
4. Ibid., p. 57.
5. Quoted in Pierre Riché, *Daily Life in the World of Charlemagne*, trans. Jo Ann McNamara (Philadelphia, 1978), p. 56.
6. 1 Corinthians 7: 1–2, 8–9.
7. Quoted in Derrick Bailey, *Homosexuality and the Western Christian Tradition* (London, 1955), p. 73.
8. Quoted in Paul Veyne, ed., *A History of Private Life*, vol. 1, *From Pagan Rome to Byzantium*, trans. Arthur Goldhammer (Cambridge, Mass., 1987), p. 440.
9. Stanley Rubin, *Medieval English Medicine* (New York, 1974), p. 136.
10. Quoted in Brian Inglis, *A History of Medicine* (New York, 1965), p. 51.
11. Tacitus, *Germany and Its Tribes*, in *The Complete Works of Tacitus*, trans. Alfred Church and William Brodribb (New York, 1942), pp. 715–16.
12. Quoted in Thatcher and McNeal, *A Source Book for Medieval History*, p. 363.
13. Quoted in Bernard Lewis, *The Arabs in History* (London, 1958), p. 90.

SUGGESTIONS FOR FURTHER READING

Surveys of Carolingian Europe include H. Fichtenau, *The Carolingian Empire* (Oxford, 1957); D. Bullough, *The Age of Charlemagne* (New York, 1966); J. Boussard, *The Civilization of Charlemagne*, trans. F. Partridge (New York, 1971); and R. McKitterick, *The Frankish Kingdoms under the Carolingians, 751–987* (London, 1983). On Charlemagne, see H. R. Loyn and J. Percival, *The Reign of Charlemagne* (New York, 1976); the popular biography by R. Winston, *Charlemagne: From the Hammer to the Cross* (Indianapolis, 1954); and R. Folz, *The Coronation of Charlemagne: 25 December 800* (London, 1974). Carolingian political institutions are examined in F. L. Ganshof, *Frankish Institutions under Charlemagne* (Providence, R.I., 1968). On Carolingian culture, see E. S. Duckett, *Alcuin, Friend of Charlemagne* (New York, 1951); and M. L. W. Laistner, *Thought and Letters in Western Europe, 500–900*, rev. ed. (London, 1957).

Various aspects of social life in the Carolingian world are examined in P. Riché, *Daily Life in the World of Charlemagne*, trans. J. A. McNamara (Philadelphia, 1978); M. Rouche, "The Early Middle Ages in the West," in P. Veyne, ed., *A History of Private Life*, (Cambridge, Mass., 1987), 1: 411–549; C. B. Bouchard, *Life and Society in the West: Antiquity and the Middle Ages* (San Diego, 1988), Ch. 5; S. F. Wemple, *Women in Frankish Society: Marriage and the Cloister* (Philadelphia, 1981); and S. Rubin, *Medieval English Medicine* (New York, 1974). On children, see S. Shamar, *Childhood in the Middle Ages*, trans. C. Galai (London, 1992); and J. Boswell, *The Kindness of Strangers* (New York, 1988). On the attitudes toward sexuality in the early Christian church, see the important works by P. Brown, *The Body and Society* (New York, 1988); and E. Pagels, *Adam, Eve, and the Serpent* (New York, 1988).

A good introduction to the problems of the late ninth and tenth centuries can be found in G. Barraclough, *The Crucible of Europe* (Berkeley and Los Angeles, 1976). The Vikings are examined in P. Sawyer, *Kings and Vikings* (London, 1982); F. D. Logan, *The Vikings in History*, 2d ed. (London, 1991); and G. Jones, *A History of the Vikings*, rev. ed. (Oxford, 1984).

Two important introductory works on feudalism are F. L. Ganshof, *Feudalism*, trans. P. Grierson (London, 1952); and the classic work by M. Bloch, *Feudal Society*, trans. L. A. Manyon (London, 1961). Military aspects of feudalism are examined in J. Beeler, *Warfare in Feudal Europe* (Ithaca, N.Y., 1954). There are good studies on early feudalism in the collection by R. F. Cheyette, ed., *Lordship and Community in Medieval Europe* (New York, 1968). Works on the new political configurations that emerged in the tenth century are cited in Chapter 9.

For the economic history of the Early Middle Ages, see G. Duby, *The Early Growth of the European Economy: Warriors and Peasants from the Seventh to the Twelfth Century* (Ithaca, N.Y., 1974). An important work on medieval agriculture is G. Duby, *Rural Economy and Country Life in the Medieval West*, trans. C. Postan (London, 1968). Also worthwhile is B. H. Slicher Van Bath, *The Agrarian History of Western Europe: A.D. 500–1850*, trans. O. Ordish (London, 1963). On population and environment, see E. L. Ladurie, *Times of Feast, Times of Famine* (New York, 1971); and J. C. Russell, *Late Ancient and Medieval Population* (Philadelphia, 1958).

Byzantine civilization in this period is examined in R. Jenkins, *Byzantium: The Imperial Centuries, 610–1071* (New York, 1969); and W. Treadgold, *The Byzantine Revival, 780–842* (Stanford, 1988). D. Obolensky, *The Byzantine Commonwealth* (New York, 1971) examines the impact of the Byzantine Empire upon its neighbors. On the Slavic peoples of central and eastern Europe, see F. Dvornik, *The Making of Central and Eastern Europe* (London, 1949) and *The Slavs in European History and Civilization* (New Brunswick, N.J., 1962); A. P. Vlasto, *The Entry of the Slavs into Christendom* (Cambridge, 1970); and Z. Vana, *The World of the Ancient Slavs* (London, 1983). The world of Islam in this period is discussed in H. Kennedy, *The Prophet and the Age of the Caliphates: The Islamic Near East from the Sixth to the Eleventh Century* (London, 1986); J. Lassner, *The Shaping of Abbasid Rule* (Princeton, N.J. 1980); G. Wiet, *Baghdad: Metropolis of the Abbasid Caliphate*, trans. S. Feiler (Norman, Okla., 1971); and O. Grabar, *The Formation of Islamic Art* (New Haven, Conn., 1971).

CHAPTER

9

The Recovery and Growth of European Society in the High Middle Ages

The new European civilization that had emerged in the ninth and tenth centuries began to come into its own in the eleventh and twelfth centuries as Europeans established new patterns that reached their zenith in the thirteenth century. The High Middle Ages (1000–1300) was a period of recovery and growth for Western civilization, characterized by a greater sense of security and a burst of energy and enthusiasm. Both the Catholic church and the feudal states recovered from the invasions and internal dissension of the Early Middle Ages. New agricultural practices that increased the food supply helped give rise to a commercial and urban revival that, accompanied by a rising population, created new dynamic elements in a formerly static society.

The recovery of the church produced a reform movement that led to exalted claims of papal authority and subsequent conflict with state authorities. At the same time, vigorous papal leadership combined with new dimensions of religious life to make the Catholic church a forceful presence in every area of life. The role of the church in the new European civilization was quite evident in the career of a man named Samson, who became abbot or head of the great English abbey of Bury St. Edmunds in 1182. According to Jocelyn of Brakelond, a monk who assisted him, Abbot Samson was a devout man who wore "undergarments of horsehair and a horsehair shirt." He loved virtue and "abhorred liars, drunkards and talkative folk." His primary concern was the spiritual well-being of his monastery, but he spent much of his time working on problems in the world beyond the abbey walls. Since the monastery had fallen into debt under his predecessors, Abbot Samson toiled tirelessly to recoup the abbey's fortunes by carefully supervising its manors. He also rounded up murderers to stand trial in St. Edmunds and provided knights for the king's army. But his actions were not always tolerant or beneficial. He was instrumental in driving the Jews from the town of St. Edmunds and was not above improving the abbey's possessions at the expense of his

The Investiture Controversy

Innocent III and papal power

Concordat of Worms

Emergence of Franciscans

Election of pope by cardinals

Crusade against the Albigensians

Founding of Cistercians

Expulsion of the Jews from England

Reign of Pope Gregory VII

Emergence of Dominicans

Development of papal curia under Pope Urban II

Fourth Lateran Council

neighbors: "He built up the bank of the fishpond at Babwell so high, for the service of a new mill, that by keeping back the water there is not a man, rich or poor, but has lost his garden and his orchards." The abbot's worldly cares weighed heavily on him, but he had little choice if his abbey were to flourish and fulfill its spiritual and secular functions. But he did have regrets; as he remarked to Jocelyn: "if he could have returned to the circumstances he had enjoyed before he became a monk, he would never have become a monk or an abbot."

People and Land in the High Middle Ages

Although the change probably started before 1000, the period from 1000 to 1300 witnessed an improvement in climate. A small but nevertheless significant rise in temperature made for longer and better growing seasons, especially in areas such as Scandinavia that were affected by cold weather. Some regions even saw the introduction of crops not previously grown there, such as grape vines in southern England.

Although concrete figures are lacking, reasonable calculations exist to warrant one major generalization: Europe experienced a dramatic increase in population after 1000. It has been estimated that the European population virtually doubled between 1000 and 1300, from 38 to 74 million people. As Table 9.1 indicates, the rate of growth tended to vary from region to region. This rise in population was physically evident in the growth of agricultural villages, towns, and cities and the increase in arable land.

Why this dramatic increase in population? Obviously, fertility rates increased sufficiently to gradually outstrip the relatively high mortality rates of medieval society, which were especially acute in infancy and the childhood years. Recent estimates assume a 15 to 20 percent mortality rate for the first year of life and 30 percent before the age of 20. Male mortality rates were highest in the age group 40–59; female mortality rates were highest between 20 and 39. The latter statistic reflects the travails of pregnancy combined with hard work and greater susceptibility to diseases due to childbearing. The greater mortality rate for women in their twenties and thirties, which was even higher than for males engaged in warfare in the same years, led to a population with 20 to 30 percent more men than women.

Traditionally, historians have cited a number of factors to explain the population increase. For one, they attribute it to increased security stemming from more settled and peaceful conditions after the invasions of the Early Middle Ages had stopped. Vikings and Magyars were assimilated and Muslim attacks halted. Although the development of feudalism had created more security, as some have argued, it was still a violent age where feuds and petty wars were a way of life. The decline of slavery may also have been a factor. As it became economically more sound to have people as tenants rather than as slaves, former slaves could marry, have families, and increase the population. Finally, agricultural production increased dramatically after 1000. Although historians are not sure whether this increase was a cause or effect of the population increase, there is no question about its importance. Without such a signifi-

❖❖❖❖❖❖❖❖❖❖❖❖❖❖❖❖❖❖❖❖❖❖❖❖❖❖❖❖❖❖❖

❖ **Table 9.1** *Population Estimates (in millions): 1000 and 1340*

Area	1000	1340
Mediterranean		
Greece and Balkans	5	6
Italy	5	10
Iberia	7	9
Total	17	25
Western and Central Europe		
France and Low Countries	6	19
British Isles	2	5
Germany and Scandinavia	4	11.5
Total	12	35.5
Eastern Europe		
Russia	6	8
Poland	2	3
Hungary	1.5	2
Total	9.5	13
Total	38.5	73.5

Source: J. C. Russell, *The Control of Late Ancient and Medieval Population* (Philadelphia: The American Philosophical Society, 1985) p. 36. Demographic specialists admit that these are merely estimates. Some figures, especially those for eastern Europe, could be radically revised by new research.

cant rise in food supplies, the expansion in population could never have been sustained.

The New Agriculture

In the Early Middle Ages, Europe was overwhelmingly an agricultural society. It continued to be so, more or less, for centuries, even though the High Middle Ages witnessed an upswing in commerce and a revival of town and city life that eventually produced a different kind of Western society. This commercial and urban revival was, of course, dependent upon the food supply, which was dramatically increased by what some have called the "agricultural revolution" of the High Middle Ages. Although some historians have questioned whether these developments deserve to be called a "revolution," significant changes did occur in the way Europeans farmed.

Although the improvement in climate played an underlying role by producing better growing conditions, another important factor in increasing the production of food was the expansion of cultivated or arable land. This was done primarily by clearing forested areas for cultivation. Millions of acres of forests were also cut down to provide timber for fuel, houses, mills, bridges, fortresses,

ships, and charcoal for the iron industry (see the box on p. 282). Eager for land, peasants cut down trees, drained swamps, and, in the area of the Netherlands, even began to reclaim land from the sea. Monks were especially important in expanding the cultivable land. The Cistercians, founded in 1098 (see New Monastic Orders and New Spiritual Ideals later in this chapter), proved particularly ambitious in clearing forests, draining marshes, and plowing new land. By the thirteenth century, Europeans had available a total acreage for farming greater than any used before or since. Once settlers had fully cultivated a given area in western Europe, they tended to move eastward in search of new lands. German settlers crossed the Elbe, Oder, and Vistula Rivers to colonize eastern Europe. They called it a civilizing mission; the native Slavs saw it as an invasion.

Technological changes also furthered the development of agriculture. The Middle Ages witnessed an explosion of labor-saving devices, many of which depended upon the use of iron, which was mined in various areas of Europe and traded to places where it was not found. Iron was in demand to make swords and armor as well as scythes, axeheads, new types of farming implements, such as hoes, and saws, hammers, and nails for building purposes. It was crucial to the development of the heavy-wheeled plow, the *carruca,* which made an enormous impact on medieval agriculture north of the Alps.

The plow of the Mediterranean and Near Eastern worlds had been the *aratum,* a nonwheeled light scratch plow made mostly of wood that was sufficient to break the top layer of the light soils of those areas. It could be pulled by a donkey or single animal. South of the Alps, fields continued to be laid out in the traditional square shape, which facilitated cross plowing with the light wheelless plow. Since a single family could afford its own light plow, the family farm rather than the village remained the basic social unit in the Mediterranean world.

But such a light plow was totally ineffective in the heavy clay soils north of the Alps. The *carruca,* a new heavy-wheeled plow with an iron ploughshare, came into widespread use by the tenth century. It could turn over heavy soils and allow for their drainage. Because of its weight, six or eight oxen were needed to pull it. Oxen were slow, however, and two new inventions for the horse made greater productivity possible. A new horse collar appeared in the tenth century. Although horses were faster than oxen, the amount they could pull with the traditional harness was limited because it tended to choke the horse if it pulled too much weight. The new horse collar distributed the weight around the shoulders and chest rather than the throat and could be used to hitch up a series of horses, enabling them to pull the new heavy plow faster and cultivate more land. The use of the horseshoe, an iron shoe nailed to the horse's hooves, spread in the eleventh and twelfth centuries and provided greater traction and better protection against the rocky and heavy clay soils of northern Europe.

The use of the heavy-wheeled plow also led to cooperative agricultural villages. Since iron was expensive, a heavy-wheeled plow had to be purchased by the entire community. Likewise an individual family could not afford a team of animals so villagers shared their beasts. Moreover, the size and weight of the plow determined that land would be cultivated in long strips to minimize the amount of turning that would have to be done.

Besides using horsepower, the High Middle Ages harnessed the power of water and wind to do jobs formerly done by human or animal power. The watermill, although invented as early as the second century B.C., was not used much in the Roman Empire since it was considered disruptive to the labor of slaves and free wage earners. Not until the High Middle Ages, when the spread of metals made it easier to build, did the watermill become widespread. In 1086, the survey of English land known as the Domesday Book listed 6,000 of them in England. Located along streams, they were used to grind grains for flour. Even dams were constructed to increase waterpower. The development of the cam enabled millwrights to mechanize entire industries; waterpower was used in certain phases of cloth production and to power triphammers for the working of metals.

Where rivers were unavailable or not easily dammed, Europeans developed windmills to yoke the power of the wind. Historians are unsure if windmills were imported into Europe (they were invented in Persia) or designed independently by Europeans. In either case, by the end of the twelfth century, they were beginning to dot the European landscape. The watermill and windmill were the most important devices for the harnessing of power before the invention of the steam engine in the eighteenth century; their spread had revolutionary consequences in enabling Europeans to produce more food.

The shift from a two-field to a three-field system also contributed to the increase in agricultural production. In the Early Middle Ages, it was common to plant one field while allowing another of equal size to lie fallow to regain its fertility. Now estates were divided into three parts. One field was planted in the fall with winter grains, such as rye and wheat, while spring grains, such as oats and barley, and vegetables, such as peas, beans, or lentils, were planted in the second field. The third was

◆ **The Heavy-Wheeled Plow.** The heavy-wheeled plow was an important invention that enabled peasants to turn over the heavy clay soil of northern Europe. This sixteenth-century illumination shows the heavy-wheeled plow pulled by draft horses with collars.

allowed to lie fallow. By rotating their use, only one-third rather than one-half of the land lay fallow at any time. The rotation of crops also prevented the soil from being exhausted so quickly. Grain yields increased to heights that would not be exceeded until the agricultural revolution of the eighteenth century. The three-field system was not adopted everywhere, however. It was not used in Mediterranean lands, and even in northern Europe the two-field and three-field systems existed side by side for centuries.

By the thirteenth century, the growing demand for agricultural produce in the towns and cities led to higher food prices and created new possibilities for growing food for profit. These changes had a significant impact upon the status of the medieval serf.

⇒ *The Elimination of Medieval Forests* ⇐

One of the interesting environmental changes of the Middle Ages was the elimination of millions of acres of forest to create new areas of arable land and to meet the demand for timber, the chief raw material of the High Middle Ages. Timber was used as fuel and to build houses, mills of all kinds, bridges, fortresses, and ships. Incredible quantities of wood were burned to make charcoal for the iron forges. The clearing of the forests not only resulted in environmental damage but caused the price of wood to skyrocket by the thirteenth century. This document from 1140 illustrates the process. Suger, the abbot of Saint-Denis, needed thirty-five-foot beams for the construction of a new church. His master carpenters told him that there were no longer any trees big enough in the area around Paris and he would have to go far afield to find such tall trees. This selection recounts his efforts.

Suger's Search for Wooden Beams

On a certain night, when I had returned from celebrating Matins, I began to think in bed that I myself should go through all the forests of these parts. . . . Quickly disposing of all duties and hurrying up in the early morning, we hastened with our carpenters, and with the measurements of the beams, to the forest called Iveline. When we traversed our possession in the Valley of Chevreuse we summoned . . . the keepers of our own forests as well as men who know about the other woods, and questioned them under oath whether we would find there, no matter with how much trouble, any timbers of that measure. At this they smiled, or rather would have laughed at us if they had dared; they wondered whether we were quite ignorant of the fact that nothing of the kind could be found in the entire region, especially since Milon, the Castellan of Chevreuse . . . . had left nothing unimpaired or untouched that could be used for palisades and bulwarks while he was long subjected to wars both by our Lord the King and Amaury de Montfort. We however—scorning whatever they might say—began, with the courage of our faith as it were, to search through the woods; and toward the first hour we found one timber adequate to the measure. Why say more? By the ninth hour or sooner, we had, through the thickets, the depths of the forest and the dense, thorny tangles, marked down twelve timbers (for so many were necessary) to the astonishment of all. . . .

Owners of landed estates reacted to the new markets for agricultural produce in different ways. Some lords expanded their landholdings but worked the land with free peasants hired for wages. This occurred in the Netherlands as well as in some areas of England, France, and Germany.

Most commonly, however, lords reacted to the new conditions by leasing their demesne land to their serfs. Servile labor services were transformed into money payments or fixed rents. In some places, such as northern Italy and southern France, landlords used a system of sharecropping instead of rents. Serfs worked the land of the lord and shared the crops they grew with him. In either case, the introduction of money payments or sharecropping initiated a process that eventually undermined serfdom. The removal of servile labor conditions converted many unfree serfs into free peasants. Although many peasants still remained economically dependent on their lords, they were no longer legally tied to the land. Naturally, this change also affected the lord's position. The commutation of labor services to money payments transformed serfs into tenants and altered the lord's position from the operator of a manor exercising both political and legal privileges to simply a lessor or collector of rents. The political and legal powers formerly exercised by lords were increasingly reclaimed by the monarchical states.

Overall, then, in the High Middle Ages the old manorial system based on unfree peasants was slowly being transformed into a more flexible system. The new relationships between lords and peasants, however, created social tensions that oftentimes led to local peasant uprisings in the late thirteenth century. The shift from labor services to money payments that transformed the serfs into tenants and their lords into landlords established a much more impersonal relationship based on money. The person-to-person relationship that had characterized manorialism was beginning to disintegrate.

Daily Life of the Peasantry

Since conditions varied from manor to manor and region to region, it is impossible to generalize about the way all European peasants lived in the High Middle Ages. Based on recent studies, however, we can make some generalizations about peasant life on the manors of Europe north of the Alps.

Peasant activities were largely determined by the seasons of the year. Each season brought a new round of tasks appropriate for the time, although some periods were considerably more hectic than others, especially August and September. The basic staple of the peasant diet was bread, so an adequate harvest of grains was crucial to survival in the winter months. A new cycle began in October when peasants prepared the ground for the planting of winter crops. In November came the slaughter of excess livestock since there was usually insufficient fodder to keep animals all winter. The meat would be salted to preserve it for winter use. In February and March, the land was plowed for spring crops—oats, barley, peas, beans, and lentils. Early summer was a comparatively relaxed time, although there was still weeding and sheepshearing to be done. In every season, the peasants worked not only their own land, but also the lord's demesne. They also tended the small gardens attached to their dwellings where they grew the vegetables that made up part of their diet.

But peasants did not face a life of totally unrelieved labor thanks to the feast days or holidays of the Catholic church. Sunday mass, religious feast days, baptisms, marriages, and funerals all were important and brought the peasants into contact with the village church, a crucial part of manorial life. The patron saint of the church was also the patron saint of the village.

THE VILLAGE CHURCH AND FEAST DAYS

The village priest was responsible for the peasant's soul. In the village church, the peasant was baptized as an infant, confirmed in his or her faith, sometimes married, and given the sacrament of Holy Communion as well as the last rites of the church before death (on the sacraments of the church, see Popular Religion in the High Middle Ages later in this chapter). It was the task of the village priest to instruct the peasants in the basic elements of Christianity so that they would gain the Christian's ultimate goal, salvation. But village priests were often barely literate peasants themselves, and it is hard to know how much church doctrine the peasants actually understood. Very likely, they regarded God as an all-powerful force who needed to be appeased by prayer to bring good harvests.

Special events in the peasant's calendar were the feast days commemorating the great events of the Christian faith or the lives of Christian saints or holy persons. The three great feasts of the Catholic church were Christmas (celebrating the birth of Christ), Easter (celebrating the resurrection of Christ), and Pentecost (celebrating the descent of the Holy Spirit on Christ's disciples fifty days

◆ **Peasant Activities.** The life of the European peasant was largely determined by the seasons of the year. The peasants' primary function was labor, and the kind of work they did was determined by the month and the season. In the foreground of this illustration, a herd of sheep is being led out to pasture past a woman milking a cow. Another woman is churning butter in the background.

after his resurrection). Numerous other feasts dedicated to saints or the Virgin Mary, the mother of Christ, were also celebrated, making a total of over fifty days that were essentially holidays (literally holy days). The most elaborate celebrations were often reserved for the feast day of the saint of the local church.

A number of the holidays exhibited a curious blend of paganism and Christianity, which is especially evident in Halloween. In pre-Christian northern Europe, November 1 had been a traditional day for celebrating a feast of the dead. The church made November 1 All Saints' (or Hallows') Day and November 2 All Souls'

Day. Although both were feast days, the real celebration came on All Hallows' Eve, the night before November 1, when people, frequently disguised in masks, lit bonfires and danced around them. Even Christmas, the most special of the Christian feasts, was held on the pagan celebration of the winter solstice. Feasting and drinking began on Christmas Day itself and continued for twelve days until the feast of the Epiphany on January 6. Of course, December and January were also the least busy months in the work cycle of the peasants and offered time for such gaiety and levity.

The village church was not just a religious center. Royal judges held court there and dispensed justice in both civil and criminal cases. Here also petty merchants peddled their goods, and the parish priest made public announcements of messages from both civil and ecclesiastical authorities.

THE PEASANT HOUSEHOLD AND FAMILY

Peasant dwellings were very simple. Peasant cottages had wood frames surrounded by sticks with the space between them filled with straw and rubble and then plastered over with clay. Roofs were simply thatched. By the thirteenth century, richer peasants began building their houses out of stone. The houses of poorer peasants consisted of a single room, but others had at least two rooms—a main room for cooking, eating, and other activities and another room for sleeping. There was little privacy in a medieval household. A hearth in the main room was used for heating and cooking, but since there were few or no windows and no chimney, the smoke from fires in the hearth went out through cracks in the walls or more likely the thatched roof.

Surveys of monastic holdings reveal that the typical peasant household consisted of a husband and wife with two or three children. Due to the high infant mortality rates, more children were born than survived infancy. Males also tended to outnumber females due to the higher mortality rate for females, especially during childbearing years.

Peasant women occupied both an important and a difficult position in manorial society. They were expected to carry and bear children and at the same time fulfill their obligation to labor in the fields. Their ability to manage the household might determine whether a peasant family would starve or survive in difficult times.

Though simple, a peasant's daily diet was potentially nutritious when food was available. The basic staple of the peasant diet, and the medieval diet in general, was bread. While women made the dough for the bread, the loaves were usually baked in community ovens, which were a monopoly of the lord of the manor. Peasant bread was highly nutritious because it contained not only wheat and rye, but also barley, millet, and oats, giving it its dark appearance and very heavy, hard texture. Bread was supplemented by numerous vegetables from the household gardens, cheese from cow's or goat's milk, and, where available, wild game and fish from hunting and fishing. Manorial lords tended to regulate fishing, however, and were especially reluctant to allow peasants to hunt so that game could be reserved for the nobility. Woodlands also provided nuts, berries, and a foraging area for pigs. Fruits, such as apples, pears, and cherries, were also available. Chickens provided eggs and occasionally meat. Peasants usually ate meat only on the great feast days, such as Christmas, Easter, and Pentecost.

Grains were important not only for bread, but also for making ale. In northern European countries, ale was the most common drink of the poor. If records are accurate, enormous quantities of ale were consumed. A monastery in the twelfth century records a daily allotment to the monks of three gallons a day, far above the weekend consumption of many present-day college students. Peasants in the field undoubtedly consumed even more. This high consumption of alcohol might help to explain the large number of accidental deaths recorded in medieval court records.

The Recovery and Reform of the Catholic Church

In the Early Middle Ages, the Catholic church had played a leading role in converting and civilizing first the Germanic invaders and later the Vikings and Magyars. Although highly successful, this had not been accomplished without challenges that undermined the spiritual life of the church itself.

The Problems of Decline

Since the fourth century, the popes of the Catholic church had operated on the basis of their supremacy over the affairs of the church. The popes had also come to exercise more control over the territories in central Italy that came to be known as the Papal States. From the eighth through the tenth century, the papacy was faced with serious problems resulting from Italy's political fragmentation. Byzantine possessions, threats from the Muslims, and the attempts of German emperors to rule northern and central Italy menaced the papacy's own interests in central Italy. As the civil rulers of Rome, the popes came to rely on the powerful noble families of the area for protection. As a result, Roman aristocratic families came to view the papacy as an office worth controlling, and it was not unusual in the ninth and tenth centuries for the heads of aristocratic factions to become popes despite their obvious lack of spiritual qualities. Perhaps the most notorious was Pope John XII, who was made pope in 956 at the age of sixteen and deposed at the age of twenty-three by Emperor Otto I for a series of scandalous crimes and sexual excesses.

The monastic ideal had also suffered during the Early Middle Ages. Benedictine monasteries had sometimes been exemplary centers of Christian living and learning, but the invasions of Vikings, Magyars, and Muslims wreaked havoc with many monastic establishments. Many were obliterated in Ireland, Britain, and France, and many that survived had suffered considerable damage. Discipline declined, as did the monastic reputation for learning and holiness. At the same time, a growing number of monasteries fell under the control of local lords, as did much of the church.

The domination of lay people over the clergy was perhaps inevitable given the chaotic conditions of the Early Middle Ages. The church became increasingly entangled in the evolving feudal system. High officials of the church, such as bishops and abbots, came to hold their offices as fiefs from nobles. As vassals, they were obliged to carry out the usual services, including military obligations. For some, this meant taking up arms, even though a prelate of the church was forbidden to kill; for others, it involved providing a contingent of knights to fight for the lord. Of course, lords assumed the right to choose their own vassals, even when those vassals included bishops and abbots. Since the lords often selected their vassals from other noble families and chose them for political reasons, it could be expected that this secularization of bishops and abbots would lead to a serious decline in the execution of their spiritual responsibilities. An abbot, for example, chosen for political reasons by a lay lord, might care little about monastic discipline. Bishops, in turn, who were responsible for supervising the monasteries in their districts, might pay scant attention to what the monks were doing. Even at the local level, the parish priests often were simply chosen by lords to serve their purposes.

It should come as no surprise then that the standards of clerical behavior declined precipitously. Two problems were especially troublesome: clerical marriage and simony. From early on, the Catholic church had encour-

♦ **Consecration of the Abbey Church of Cluny.** The abbey of Cluny played an important role in revitalizing monasticism. Construction of the third abbey church of Cluny began in 1088. Seven years later, Pope Urban II, himself a former Cluniac monk, consecrated the completed east end of the church. The pope and members of the papal court stand to the left of the altar. To the right are Abbot Hugh and his monks.

aged celibacy as the norm for its clergy. In the Early Middle Ages, however, this policy had become virtually impossible to enforce and was largely ignored. Simony, the sale of church offices, was a logical outcome of a system that had come to view church offices as secular positions and important sources of revenue. Both simony and clerical marriage were increasingly singled out as the symbols of the church's decline stemming from excessive involvement in worldly affairs. A number of people felt the time had come to change this situation.

The Cluniac Reform Movement

Reform of the Catholic church began in Burgundy in eastern France in 910 when Duke William of Aquitaine founded the abbey of Cluny. This was the greatest single religious event of the tenth century. The monastery began with a renewed dedication to the highest spiritual ideals of the Benedictine rule and was fortunate in possessing a series of abbots in the tenth century who exemplified and maintained these ideals. Cluny was deliberately kept independent from any secular control. As Duke William stipulated in his original charter: "It has pleased us also to insert in this document that, from this day, those same monks there congregated shall be subject neither to our yoke, nor to that of our relatives, nor to the sway of the royal might, nor to that of any earthly power."[1] Finally, the new monastery at Cluny tried to eliminate some of the abuses that had crept into religious communities by stressing the need for work, replacing manual labor with the copying of manuscripts, and demanding more community worship and less private prayer.

The Cluniac reform movement sparked an enthusiastic response, first in France and eventually in all of western and central Europe. New monasteries were founded based on Cluniac ideals, and previously existing monasteries rededicated themselves by adopting the Cluniac program. To avoid the lack of supervision that had allowed so much corruption into the monastic movement, all monasteries that became part of the Cluniac system placed themselves under the supervision of Cluny itself. The abbot of Cluny was the only abbot for the hundreds of Cluniac religious houses. Each establishment was headed by a prior who was subordinate to the abbot of Cluny. The latter spent considerable time visiting the various houses to ensure their compliance with the Cluniac regulations. This centralization of control guaranteed rigid discipline and the maintenance of the highest standards in every Cluniac monastery. By the eleventh century, the movement was also beginning to reach beyond monasticism and into the papacy itself, which was in dire need of help.

The Reform of the Papacy

Leo IX (1049–1054) was the first of a series of popes who brought new ideals to their leadership of the church and aspired to a universal reform of Christendom. To ensure the effectiveness of the reform movement, Leo IX instituted structural changes in the government of the church by making regular use of a group of church officials known as cardinals. The word *cardinal* had been used as a title of honor for some of the more important priests in the great churches of Rome. Leo now began to appoint reforming clerics from all over Europe as cardinals and then to use them as his major advisers and administrators. From this time on, cardinals played a major role in the administration of the church. In fact, in 1059, a reform church council at Rome tried to eliminate the interference of both Roman aristocratic factions and emperors in the choice of popes by decreeing that popes should be elected only by the cardinals. The election of popes by the college of cardinals has been Catholic practice ever since.

Strengthening the control of the papacy over the church was one goal of the reform movement. The reformers also wanted to outlaw simony and eliminate violations of clerical celibacy. As a decree of the church stated: "Those who have been advanced to any grade of holy orders, or to any office, through simony, that is, by the payment of money, shall hereafter have no right to officiate in the holy church. . . . Nor shall clergymen who are married say mass or serve the altar in any way."[2] At the same time, papal reformers called for the church's freedom from lay interference in the appointment of church officials. This issue of lay investiture was dramatically taken up by the greatest of the reform popes of the eleventh century, Gregory VII.

Pope Gregory VII (1073–1085) and the Investiture Controversy

One of the reformers named as a cardinal by Leo IX was a monk named Hildebrand. He was a strong personality, who held a passionate conviction about the need for church reform and papal leadership to accomplish it. Elected pope in 1073, he was absolutely certain that he had been chosen by God to reform the church. In pursuit of those aims, Gregory vigorously restated claims of papal power. His dedication to his ideals led him into the Investiture Controversy, one of the great church-state confrontations of the Middle Ages.

There is no doubt that Gregory VII believed that he was truly God's "vicar on earth." While previous popes had been content to accept their authority over the affairs of the church, Gregory asserted that the pope's authority extended over all of Christendom and included the right to depose emperors if they disobeyed his wishes. Gregory's program of reform was directed toward the "freedom of the church." He perceived that a true reform of the church was not possible if secular rulers controlled the appointment of clerical officials. He sought nothing less than the elimination of lay investiture or the practice by which secular rulers both chose and invested their nominees to church offices with the symbols of their office. Only in this way could the church regain its freedom, by which Gregory meant the right of the church to appoint clergy and run its own affairs. If rulers did not accept these "divine" commands, then they could be deposed by the pope acting in his capacity as the vicar of Christ (see the box p. 287). Gregory VII soon found himself in conflict with the king of Germany over these claims. (The king of Germany was also the emperor-designate since it had been accepted by this time that only kings of Germany could be

The "Gregorian Revolution": Papal Claims

In the eleventh century, a dynamic group of cardinals and popes pushed for the "freedom of the church." This came to mean not only papal control over the affairs of the church, but also the elimination of lay investiture. The reformers saw the latter as the chief issue at the heart of lay control of the church. In trying to eliminate it, the reforming popes, especially Gregory VII, extended papal claims to include the right to oversee the secular authorities and, in particular, to depose rulers under certain circumstances. The following selection is from a document that was entered in the papal register in 1075. It consisted of twenty-seven assertions that probably served as headings, or a table of contents, for a collection of ecclesiastical writings that supported the pope's claims.

The Dictates of the Pope

1. That the Roman church was founded by God alone.
2. That the Roman pontiff alone can with right be called universal.
3. That he alone can depose or reinstate bishops.
4. That, in a council, his legate, even if a lower grade, is above all bishops, and can pass sentence of deposition against them.
5. That the pope may depose the absent.
6. That, among other things, we ought not to remain in the same house with those excommunicated by him. . . .
8. That he alone may use the imperial insignia.
9. That of the pope alone all princes shall kiss the feet.
10. That his name alone shall be spoken in the churches.
11. That this is the only name in the world.
12. That it may be permitted to him to depose emperors.
13. That he may be permitted to transfer bishops if need be. . . .
17. That no chapter and no book shall be considered canonical without his authority.
18. That a sentence passed by him may be retracted by no one; and that he himself, alone of all, may retract it.
19. That he himself may be judged by no one.
20. That no one shall dare to condemn one who appeals to the apostolic chair.
21. That to the latter should be referred the more important cases of every church.
22. That the Roman church has never erred; nor will it err to all eternity, the Scripture bearing witness.
23. That the Roman pontiff, if he have been canonically ordained, is undoubtedly made a saint by the merits of St. Peter. . . .
25. That he may depose and reinstate bishops without assembling a synod.
26. That he who is not at peace with the Roman church shall not be considered catholic.
27. That he may absolve subjects from their fealty to wicked men.

emperors, but they did not officially use the title "emperor" until they were crowned by the pope.)

King Henry IV (1056–1106) of Germany was also a determined personality. For many years, German kings had depended upon appointing high-ranking clerics, especially bishops, as their vassals in order to use them as administrators. While to the popes this might seem an infringement on the freedom of the church, it was a simple matter of political expediency to the German king; without the bishops, he could not hope to maintain his own power vis-à-vis the powerful German nobles. At the time they entered their offices, bishops in Germany were invested with two symbols: the *regalia*, or the symbols of temporal office (a scepter), and the *spiritualia*, or the symbols of spiritual office (the ring and crozier, or staff). The kings of Germany had grown accustomed to investing their nominees as bishop with both symbols of office, the temporal and spiritual. In 1075, Pope Gregory issued a decree forbidding important clerics from receiving their spiritual investiture from lay leaders: "We decree that no one of the clergy shall receive the investiture with a bishopric or abbey or church from the hand of an emperor or king or of any lay person. . . ."[3] Henry had no intention of obeying a decree that challenged the very heart of his administration.

The immediate cause of the so-called Investiture Controversy was a disputed election to the bishopric of Milan, an important position because the bishop was also the lay ruler of the city. Control of the bishopric was crucial if the king wished to reestablish German power in northern Italy. Since Milan was considered second only to Rome in importance as a bishopric, papal interest in the office was also keen. Pope and king backed competing candidates for the position.

To gain acceptance of his candidate, the pope threatened the king with excommunication. Excommunication is a censure by which a person is deprived of receiving the sacraments of the church. To counter this threat, the king called a synod or assembly of German bishops, all of whom he had appointed, and had them depose the pope:

> Henry, king not through usurpation but through the holy ordination of God, to Hildebrand, at present not pope but false monk. . . . you . . . have not shunned to rise up against the royal power conferred upon us by God, daring to threaten to divest us of it. As if we have received our kingdom from you! As if the kingdom and the empire were in your and not in God's hand! . . . You, therefore, damned by this curse and by the judgment of all our bishops and by our own, descend and relinquish the apostolic chair which you have usurped . . . I Henry, king by the grace of God, do say unto you, together with all our bishops: Descend, descend, to be damned throughout the ages.[4]

Pope Gregory VII responded by excommunicating the king and freeing his subjects from their allegiance to him. The latter was a clever move. The German nobles were only too eager to diminish the power of a centralized monarchy because of the threat it posed to their own power, and they welcomed this opportunity to rebel against the king. Both the nobles and bishops of Germany agreed to hold a meeting in Germany with the pope to solve the problem, possibly by choosing a new king. Gregory set out for Germany. Henry, realizing the threat to his power, forestalled the pope by traveling to northern Italy, where he met the pope at Canossa in January 1077, admitted his transgressions, and begged for forgiveness and absolution (see the box on p. 289).

Although he made the king wait three days, the pope had no choice but to grant absolution to the penitent sinner and lift the ban of excommunication. This did not end the problem, however. Henry IV returned to Germany, engaged in a fierce struggle to crush the nobles who had rebelled against him, and returned to his old practices. Within three years, pope and king were again locked in combat. This time, Henry responded to the pope's second excommunication by leading an army into Italy. Gregory was forced to leave Rome and died in exile, convinced he had failed.

The struggle continued until a new German king and a new pope achieved a compromise in 1122 known as the Concordat of Worms. Under this agreement, a bishop in Germany was first elected by the cathedral canons, although the king had the right to be present at the election, a clear indication that the king could still influence the final outcome. After election, the nominee paid homage to the king as his lord, who in turn invested him with the symbols of temporal office. A representative of the pope, however, then invested the new bishop with the symbols of his spiritual office.

This struggle between church and state was an important element in the history of Europe in the High Middle Ages. In the Early Middle Ages, popes had been dependent on emperors and had allowed them to exercise considerable authority over church affairs. But a set of new ideals championed by activist cardinals and popes in the eleventh century now supported the "freedom of the church," which meant not only the freedom of the church to control its own affairs, but also extreme claims of papal authority. Not only was the pope superior to all other bishops, but popes now claimed the right to depose kings under certain circumstances. Such papal claims ensured further church-state confrontations.

Christianity and Medieval Civilization

Christianity was an integral part of the fabric of medieval European society and the consciousness of Europe. Papal directives affected the actions of kings and princes alike while Christian teaching and practices touched the economic, social, intellectual, cultural, and daily lives of all Europeans.

Growth of the Papal Monarchy

The popes of the twelfth century did not abandon the reform ideals of Gregory VII, but they were less dogmatic and more inclined to consolidate their power and build a strong administrative system. Although earlier

The Investiture Controversy: The Encounter at Canossa

Perhaps no event in the Investiture Controversy is more dramatic than the encounter between Pope Gregory VII and King Henry IV at Canossa in January 1077. To forestall Gregory's meeting with the German prelates and nobles in Germany, Henry traveled to northern Italy and begged the pope for absolution. The pope granted it since he was bound not to refuse absolution to a penitent sinner. This description is from Gregory's own account.

The Correspondence of Pope Gregory VII:
To the German Princes

Meanwhile we received certain information that the king was on the way to us. Before he entered Italy he sent us word that he would make satisfaction to God and St. Peter and offered to amend his way of life and to continue obedient to us, provided only that he should obtain from us absolution and the apostolic blessing. For a long time we delayed our reply and held long consultations, reproaching him bitterly through messengers back and forth for his outrageous conduct, until finally, of his own accord and without any show of hostility or defiance, he came with a few followers to the fortress of Canossa where we were staying. There, on three successive days, standing before the castle gate, laying aside all royal insignia, barefooted and in coarse attire, he ceased not with many tears to beseech the apostolic help and comfort until all who were present or who had heard the story were so moved by pity and compassion that they pleaded his cause with prayers and tears. All marveled at our unwonted severity, and some even cried out that we were showing, not the seriousness of apostolic authority, but rather the cruelty of a savage tyrant.

At last, overcome by his persistent show of penitence and the urgency of all present, we released him from the bonds of anathema and received him into the grace of Holy Mother Church, accepting from him the guarantees described below, confirmed by the signatures of the abbot of Cluny, of our daughters, the Countess Matilda [countess of Tuscany], and the Countess Adelaide [marchioness of Turin], and other princes, bishops and laymen who seemed to be of service to us.

popes had always claimed great powers, the novelty of the twelfth century was the development of administrative machinery that transformed aspirations into reality. What made the papal centralization of power possible was the maturation of a highly efficient papal curia or papal court, largely the work of Pope Urban II (1088–1099). The Roman curia was divided into a number of specialized divisions, such as a chancery or writing office for documents, a papal chapel, and a treasury. The curia also functioned as a high court of law formulating canon (or church) law and serving as a court of final appeal for all cases touching the church's vast ecclesiastical court system, especially matters dealing with church property, marriages, and oaths. During the twelfth century, the church began to take an active interest in systematizing canon law (see Chapter 11), a crucial step in establishing a centralized administrative system. It is no accident that many of the popes in the twelfth and thirteenth centuries had backgrounds in canon law.

By the twelfth century, the Catholic church possessed a clearly organized hierarchical structure. The pope and papal curia were at the center of the administrative structure. Below them were the bishops since all of Christendom was divided into dioceses under their direction. To be sure, archbishops had larger sees than

bishops and were in principle more powerful than the bishops, but at this time they were unable to exercise any real control over the internal matters of the bishops' dioceses. Theoretically, the bishop chose all priests in his diocese, administered his diocese, and was responsible only to the pope. According to church law, the clergy and laity of a diocese were to elect the bishop. In fact, the elections of bishops were controlled by the most important clerics in a bishop's cathedral, the cathedral canons, although with close royal supervision in England and Germany. The canons chose the new bishop and served as his diocesan administrators.

The development of efficient, centralized administrative machinery supported by an orderly system of canon law was a major foundation for papal authority in the twelfth century. Other factors also contributed to the growing recognition of papal prestige and power. By assuming leadership of the crusades (see Chapter 11), Pope Urban II thrust the papacy into the center of both the spiritual and temporal affairs of Christendom. Moreover, popes exercised their leadership by holding both local and Europe-wide church councils. Councils promulgated reform decrees that brought the new organizational structure and new developments in theology and canon law to dioceses throughout Europe.

In the thirteenth century, the Catholic church reached the height of its political, intellectual, and secular power. The papal monarchy extended its sway over both ecclesiastical and temporal affairs, as was especially evident during the papacy of Pope Innocent III (1198–1216). At the beginning of his pontificate, in a letter to a Tuscan cleric, Innocent made a clear statement of his views on papal supremacy:

> As God, the creator of the universe, set two great lights in the firmament of heaven, the greater light to rule the day, and the lesser light to rule the night so He set two great dignities in the firmament of the universal church, . . . the greater to rule the day, that is, souls, and the lesser to rule the night, that is, bodies. These dignities are the papal authority and the royal power. And just as the moon gets her light from the sun, and is inferior to the sun . . . so the royal power gets the splendor of its dignity from the papal authority.[5]

Although historians do not agree on Innocent's motives, it is apparent that he did, at times, attempt to put this theory into practice by intervening freely in the affairs of European rulers.

Innocent's actions were those of a man who believed that he, the pope, was the supreme judge of European politics. He forced the king of France, Philip Augustus, to take back his wife and queen after Philip had coerced a group of French prelates into annulling his marriage. Innocent did not consider the annulment valid. The pope intervened in German affairs and established his

candidate as emperor. He compelled King John of England to accept his choice for the position of archbishop of Canterbury. The rulers of Aragon and Portugal became vassals to Innocent III, who served as their feudal lord. To achieve his political ends, the pope did not hesitate to use the spiritual weapons at his command, especially excommunication and the interdict. In excommunication, an individual is cut off from the sacraments and deprived of communion with the church. A ruler might ignore excommunication, but an interdict potentially had more serious consequences. An interdict forbade priests to dispense the sacraments of the church in the hope that the people, deprived of the comforts of religion, would exert pressure against their ruler. It was Pope Innocent's interdict that caused King Philip Augustus to restore his Danish wife to her rightful place as queen of France. The frequent use of these spiritual weapons by thirteenth-century popes to fight political battles seemed appropriate at the time but gradually undermined the value of the weapons and the moral authority of the popes. When Innocent's successors chose to utilize the same weapons and pursue his claims of papal supremacy, they had less success.

Pope Innocent III then was a consummate politician in his handling of papal power. He was also concerned about church organization, moral reform, and the purity of the Christian faith. It was Innocent III who called the Fourth Lateran Council of 1215, which defined the sacrament of the Eucharist, decreed annual confession for all Christians, and established detailed regulations for the moral behavior of the clergy. It was also Innocent who approved the foundation of the Franciscans and Dominicans (see Living the Gospel Life later in the chapter), encouraged the nobility of France to massacre the heretical Albigensians of southern France (see Voices of Protest and Intolerance later in the chapter), and proclaimed the fourth crusade.

The popes who succeeded Innocent III in the thirteenth century continued to push papal claims to secular power while perfecting the centralized administrative system that had been created in the eleventh and twelfth centuries. Canon law was refined to underline even more clearly the pope's supremacy over the church. The number of legal cases appealed to the papal court increased dramatically, enhancing the importance of papal administration. The number of papal legates or agents of the pope expanded noticeably, enabling the pope to extend his voice into every area of Europe.

As papal administration expanded, the church required ever-larger revenues. The Papal States, the territories of the church in central Italy, were a major source of income. As temporal lords of these lands, the popes

✦ **Pope Innocent III.** Innocent III was an active and powerful pope during the High Middle Ages. Considering himself the supreme judge of European politics, Innocent III intervened in the affairs of a number of European states. He also approved the creation of the Franciscan and Dominican orders and inaugurated the Fourth Crusade.

had access to rents, tolls, and other fees assessed on the inhabitants. In the thirteenth century, when other traditional sources of income, such as Peter's Pence, an annual tax of a penny a year on every homestead (hearth), proved inadequate, the popes began to tax the clergy on a regular basis. Since monarchs were reluctant to let such large sums of money out of their kingdoms, the popes wisely shared these revenues with them.

New Monastic Orders and New Spiritual Ideals

In the second half of the eleventh century and the first half of the twelfth century, a wave of religious enthusiasm seized Europe. One of its manifestations was the crusades, but another was the spectacular growth of monastic institutions and the development of new monastic orders. Most important was the emergence of the Cistercian order. In 1098, a group of monks, dissatisfied with the lack of strict discipline at their Benedictine monastery, founded a new monastery at Cîteaux in Burgundy (Cistercium in Latin—hence the name of the new order). Cistercian monasticism spread rapidly from southern France into Italy, Spain, England, Germany, and eastern Europe. In 1115, there were five Cistercian houses; by 1150, there were more than three hundred.

The Cistercians emphasized a strict austerity. They ate a simple diet and possessed only a single robe. All decorations were eliminated from their churches and monastic buildings, and no gold or silver ornaments were permitted. The number of hours spent in liturgical services was shortened, leaving more time for private prayer and manual labor. Unlike Benedictine and Cluniac houses, Cistercian monasteries were not supported by peasant labor. To escape from the world, many Cistercians established their monasteries on uninhabited lands, usually wastelands or virgin forests. Since their own manual labor was insufficient to meet the demands of these lands, the Cistercians initiated a separate monastic track for lay brothers from the peasant class. They took monastic vows and participated in common worship, but lived separately from the regular monks and spent most of their time working in the fields and in the industries established by the monks. The Cistercians' attempt to live independently of the world had an ironic result. The hundreds of thousands of acres they opened for agriculture became highly productive. Adopting the technology of their age, including machines powered by water, Cistercians soon were exporting wool and wine from their farms and vineyards. As a result, the Cistercians were incredibly successful in

♦ **Saint Bernard.** One of the most important religious figures of the twelfth century was Saint Bernard of Clairvaux, who advocated a militant expression of Christian ideas while favoring a more personalized understanding of the relationship between humans and God. Here Saint Bernard is shown preaching a sermon to his fellow Cistercians.

creating a widespread "economic empire," and in the process, many of their monasteries became very wealthy.

The Cistercians played a major role in developing a new, activistic spiritual model for twelfth-century Europe. Monasticism had originally been established to isolate a select group of dedicated Christians from the world. A Benedictine monk often spent hours in ritual prayer to honor God. The Cistercian ideal had a different emphasis: "Arise, soldier of Christ, arise! Get up off the ground and return to the battle from which you have fled! Fight more boldly after your flight, and triumph in glory!"[6] These were the words of Saint Bernard of Clairvaux, who more than any other person embodied the new spiritual ideal of Cistercian monasticism.

Bernard of Clairvaux (1090–1153) was the most famous religious figure of the twelfth century (see the box on p. 292). Of noble birth, Bernard joined the Cistercians in 1113 and became abbot of their monastery at Clairvaux. Although well known for his complete dedication to the ascetic ideals of the Cistercians, he also became an active voice outside the monastery. He helped to settle a disputed papal election, preached the need for a new crusade (the second crusade), and even went to Germany to persuade the emperor to join it. At the same time, Bernard gave religious piety a more personal touch when he portrayed Christ, the Virgin Mary, and the saints in more human fashion. In the

A Miracle of Saint Bernard

Saint Bernard of Clairvaux has been called "the most widely respected holy man of the twelfth century." He was an outstanding preacher, wholly dedicated to the service of God. His reputation reportedly influenced many young men to join the Cistercian order. He also inspired a myriad of stories dealing with his miracles.

A Miracle of Saint Bernard

A certain monk, departing from his monastery . . . threw off his habit, and returned to the world at the persuasion of the Devil. And he took a certain parish living; for he was a priest. Because sin is punished with sin, the deserter from his Order lapsed into the vice of lechery. He took a concubine to live with him, as in fact is done by many, and by her he had children.

But as God is merciful and does not wish anyone to perish, it happened that many years after, the blessed abbot [Saint Bernard] was passing through the village in which this same monk was living, and went to stay at his house. The renegade monk recognized him, and received him very reverently, and waited on him devoutly . . . but as yet the abbot did not recognize him.

On the morrow, the holy man said Matins and prepared to be off. But as he could not speak to the priest, since he had got up and gone to the church for Matins, he said to the priest's son "Go, give this message to your master." Now the boy had been born dumb. He obeyed the command and feeling in himself the power of him who had given it, he ran to his father and uttered the words of the Holy Father clearly and exactly. His father, on hearing his son's voice for the first time, wept for joy, and made him repeat the same words . . . and he asked what the abbot had done to him. "He did nothing to me," said the boy, "except to say 'Go and say this to your father.'"

At so evident a miracle the priest repented, and hastened after the holy man and fell at his feet saying "My Lord and Father, I was your monk so-and-so, and at such-and-such a time I ran away from your monastery. I ask your Paternity to allow me to return with you to the monastery, for in your coming God has visited my heart." The saint replied unto him, "Wait for me here, and I will come back quickly when I have done my business, and I will take you with me." But the priest, fearing death (which he had not done before), answered, "Lord, I am afraid of dying before then." But the saint replied, "Know this for certain, that if you die in this condition, and in this resolve, you will find yourself a monk before God."

The saint [eventually] returned and heard that the priest had recently died and been buried. He ordered the tomb to be opened. And when they asked him what he wanted to do, he said, "I want to see if he is lying as a monk or a clerk in his tomb." "As a clerk," they said; "we buried him in his secular habit." But when they had dug up the earth, they found that he was not in the clothes in which they had buried him; but he appeared in all points, tonsure and habit, as a monk. And they all praised God.

Early Middle Ages, these holy figures were most often presented in a majestic manner and viewed as remote from people's lives. Achieving salvation seemed difficult since Christ was portrayed as a stern judge. In his sermons and writings, Bernard described these sacred figures as living human beings to whom people could relate directly. He encouraged an emotional love for Jesus and for the mother of Christ, the Virgin Mary, whom he portrayed as a gentle, loving, kindly intercessor with her Son. The new sentiment is apparent in contemporary depictions of the crucified Christ. He is no longer the triumphant judge, but the suffering son of man.

Men were not the only ones susceptible to the religious fervor of the twelfth century; women were also active participants in the spiritual movements of the age. The number of women joining religious houses increased perceptibly with the spread of the new orders of the twelfth century, although medieval monasticism always remained an overwhelmingly male phenomenon. Even in 1200, there were only about 3,000 nuns in England compared to 14,000 monks. Moreover, male monasteries were larger and better supported financially. The nuns' secondary role stemmed from the church's view of women as subordinate to men. Not allowed to exercise priestly powers, women were dependent on male priests for the sacraments and liturgical services of the church.

In the Early Middle Ages, religious houses for females were frequently founded by queens and governed by abbesses of royal or noble blood, a practice that continued into the High Middle Ages. In tenth- and eleventh-century Germany, for example, some abbesses ruled vast areas of land and summoned knights to war as vassals of the king. One abbess of Quedlinburg minted her own

◆ **Christ as Judge. Christ as Suffering Servant.** In the Early Middle Ages, Christ was often depicted in a majestic, distant manner that seemed to place him far beyond ordinary people. Saint Bernard, however, worked to change this image by emphasizing the human side of Christ and presented him as the suffering man who died for the sins of humans. Pictured here are a mosaic depicting Christ as judge and a manuscript illustration representing Christ as the suffering servant on the cross.

coins, and another, Matilda, served unofficially as regent for her nephew Otto III.

German nuns also possessed a strong intellectual tradition, beginning with Leoba, an eighth-century abbess of Bischofsheim. According to a contemporary monk, she "was so bent on reading that she never laid aside her book except to pray or to strengthen her slight frame with food and sleep." Moreover, "from childhood upward she had studied grammar and the other liberal arts. . . . She zealously read the books of the Old and New Testaments and . . . further added to the rich store of her knowledge by reading the writings of the holy Fathers, the canonical decrees, and the laws of the Church."[7] Better known than Leoba was Hroswitha of Gandersheim from the tenth century. She wrote a number of literary works including six plays using Terence (see Chapter 6) as her model and a contemporary history in verse form.

In the High Middle Ages, most nuns were from the ranks of the landed aristocracy. Convents were convenient for families unable or unwilling to find husbands for their daughters and for aristocratic women who did not wish to marry. Female intellectuals found them a haven for their activities. Most of the learned women of the Middle Ages, especially in Germany, were nuns. This was certainly true of Hildegard of Bingen (1098–1179), who became abbess of a religious house for females at Disibodenberg in western Germany.

Hildegard shared in the religious enthusiasm of the twelfth century. Soon after becoming abbess, she began to write down accounts of the mystical visions she had experienced for years and eventually produced three books. In her most important work, *The Book of Divine Works* (see the box on p. 295), Hildegard presented the universe as a living cosmology in which nature, humanity, divinity, and the cosmos were all interconnected in a harmonious whole. The macrocosm (universe) was one with the microcosm (humankind). Humans, she wrote, were "completely the image of God," and she urged them to be "co-creators with God."[8]

Hildegard gained considerable renown as a mystic and prophet, and popes, emperors, kings, dukes, bishops, abbots, and abbesses eagerly sought her advice. She wrote to them all as an equal and did not hesitate to be critical. To King Henry II of England, she warned, "Look then with fervent zeal at the God who created you. For your heart is full of goodwill to do gladly what is good, except when the filthy habits of humankind rush at you and for a time you became entangled in them. Be resolute and flee those entanglements, beloved son of God, and call out to God!"[9] Hildegard of Bingen was also one of the first important women composers and an important contributor to the body of music known as Gregorian chant or plainsong. Gregorian chant was basically monophonic—a single line of unaccompanied vocal music—set to Latin texts and chanted by groups of monks or nuns during church services. Hildegard excelled in the composition of musical *Sequences*. Her texts are full of rich, mystical imagery, and her music is quite original. Her work is especially remarkable because she succeeded at a time when music in general, and sacred music in particular, was almost exclusively the domain of men.

LIVING THE GOSPEL LIFE

In the thirteenth century, two religious leaders, Saint Francis and Saint Dominic, founded two new religious orders whose members did not remain in the cloister like the monks of the contemplative orders, such as the Benedictines and Cistercians, but rather went out into the secular arena of the towns and countryside to preach the word of God. By their example, the new orders

◆ **A Group of Nuns.** Although still viewed by the medieval church as inferior to men, women were as susceptible to the spiritual fervor of the twelfth century as men, and female monasticism grew accordingly. This miniature shows a group of Flemish nuns listening to the preaching of an abbot, Gilles li Muisis. The nun at the far left wearing a white robe is a novice.

◆ **Saint Francis Preaches to the Birds.** Francis of Assisi was responsible for founding an order of begging friars who ministered to the poor and downtrodden. This illustration from a thirteenth-century panel painting shows the moment in the life of Saint Francis when he preached to the birds.

strove to provide a more personal religious experience for ordinary people.

Saint Francis of Assisi (1182–1226) was born to a wealthy Italian merchant family. He enjoyed fighting in the petty local wars typical of the Italian political scene in the thirteenth century. After having been captured and imprisoned during one of these struggles, he had a series of dramatic spiritual experiences that led him to abandon all worldly goods and material pursuits and to live and preach in poverty, working and begging for his food. His simplicity, joyful nature, and love for others (see the box on p. 296) soon attracted a band of followers, all of whom took vows of absolute poverty, agreeing to reject all property and live by working and begging for their food. Francis drew up a simple rule for his followers that consisted merely of biblical precepts focusing on the need to preach and the importance of poverty. He sought approval for his new rule from Pope Innocent III, who confirmed the new order as the Order of Friars Minor, more commonly known as the Franciscans.

The Franciscans struck a responsive chord in the thirteenth century and became very popular. Many people were obviously disgusted with the worldliness and luxurious lifestyle of many church prelates, including the heads of monastic houses. The Franciscans lived among the people, preaching repentance and aiding the poor. Their calls for a return to the simplicity and

The Mystical Visions of Hildegard of Bingen

Hildegard of Bingen has been called "one of the greatest intellectuals and mystics of the west." She was incredibly prolific. She wrote books on science, theology, philosophy, and medicine; painted a series of images to render her mystical visions in visible form; and composed more than seventy songs. She wrote three books on her visions. This selection is from her third work called The Book of Divine Works. It provides a good example of the spiritual intensity of the twelfth century.

Hildegard of Bingen, The Book of Divine Works
First Vision: On the Origin of Life
Vision One: 1

And I saw within the mystery of God, in the midst of the southern breezes, a wondrously beautiful image. It had a human form, and its countenance was of such beauty and radiance that I could have more easily gazed at the sun than at the face. A broad golden ring circled its head. . . . The figure was wrapped in a garment that shone like the sun. . . . [This "spirit of the macrocosm" then spoke to her:]

I, the highest and fiery power, have kindled every spark of life, and I emit nothing that is deadly. I decide on all reality. With my lofty wings I fly above the globe: With wisdom I have rightly put the universe in order. I, the fiery life of divine essence, am aflame beyond the beauty of the meadows, I gleam in the waters, and I burn in the sun, moon, and stars. With every breeze, as with invisible life that contains everything, I awaken everything to life. The air lives by turning green and being in bloom. The waters flow as if they were alive. The sun lives in its light, and the moon is enkindled, after its disappearance, once again by the light of the sun so

that the moon is again revived. The stars, too, give a clear light with their beaming. I have established pillars that bear the entire globe as well as the power of the winds which, once again, have subordinate wings—so to speak, weaker winds—which through their gentle power resist the mighty winds so that they do not become dangerous. In the same way, too, the body envelops the soul and maintains it so that the soul does not blow away. For just as the breath of the soul strengthens and fortifies the body so that it does not disappear, the more powerful winds, too, revive the surrounding winds so that they can provide their appropriate service.

And thus I remain hidden in every kind of reality as a fiery power. Everything burns because of me in such a way as our breath constantly moves us, like the wind-tossed flame in a fire. All of this lives in its essence, and there is no death in it. For I am life. I am also Reason, which bears within itself the breath of the resounding Word, through which the whole of creation is made. I breathe life into everything so that nothing is mortal in respect to its species. For I am life. . . .

Vision One: 3

And again I heard a voice from heaven saying to me:

God, who created everything, has formed humanity according to the divine image and likeness, and marked in human beings both the higher and the lower creatures. God loved humanity so much that God designated for it the place from which the fallen angel was ejected, intending for human beings all the splendor and honor which that angel lost along with his bliss.

The countenance you are gazing at is an indication of this fact.

---

poverty of the early church, reinforced by their own example, were especially effective.

Unlike other religious orders, the Franciscans lived in the world. They undertook missionary work, first throughout Italy and then to all parts of Europe and even to the Muslim world. The Franciscans had a female component as well, known as the Poor Clares, which was founded by Saint Clare, an aristocratic lady of Assisi who was a great admirer of Francis.

As the Franciscan order grew, it encountered the usual dilemmas of the monastic orders dedicated to poverty. Before his death, Francis had written a new rule confirming absolute poverty but allowing for some governmental structure. Wealthy donors, deeply moved by

the Franciscans' apparent holiness, donated buildings to the order. After Francis's death, the popes allowed friends to hold property for the order so that the Franciscans could establish communities. Soon Francis's goal of absolute poverty was being superseded by new demands that caused a split in the order itself. The "Spiritual Franciscans" favored absolute poverty while the "Conventuals" believed that some communal property was necessary to carry on their study and preaching.

The second new religious order of the thirteenth century arose out of the desire to defend orthodox church teachings from heresy (see Voices of Protest and Intolerance later in the chapter). The Order of Preachers, popularly known as the Dominicans or the Black

Saint Francis: In Praise of Nature

The Canticle of the Sun, *which has been called one of the "first masterpieces of Italian vernacular poetry," was written by Saint Francis of Assisi. It reveals an aspect of Francis's personality that was revered by his contemporaries, his great love of nature. Francis envisioned the world of nature as a mirror in which one could see the reflection of God; hence it was important to treat the natural world with great respect as God's handiwork.*

Francis of Assisi, Canticle of the Sun

Most High, Almighty, good Lord,
Yours be the praise, the glory, the honor,
And all blessing.
To You alone, Most High, are they due,
And no man is worthy
To speak Your Name.

Praise to You, my Lord, for all Your creatures,
Above all Brother Sun
Who brings us the day and lends us his light.
Lovely is he, radiant with great splendor,
And speaks to us of You,
O Most High.

Praise to You, my Lord, for Sister Moon and the stars
Which You have set in the heavens,
Clear, precious, and fair.

Praise to You, my Lord, for Brother Wind,
For air and cloud, for calm and all weather,
By which You support life in all Your creatures.

Praise to You, my Lord, for Sister Water,
Who is so useful and humble,
Precious and pure.

Praise to You, my Lord, for Brother Fire,
By whom You lightest the night;
He is lovely and pleasant, mighty and strong.

Praise to You, my Lord, for our sister Mother Earth
Who sustains and directs us,
And brings forth varied fruits, and colored flowers, and
  plants.

Praise to You, my Lord, for those who pardon one
  another
For love of You, and endure
Sickness and tribulation.
Blessed are they who shall endure it in peace,
For they shall be crowned by You,
O Most High.

Praise to You, my Lord, for our Sister bodily Death
From whom no man living may escape:
Woe to those who die in mortal sin.
Blessed are they who are found in Your most holy will,
For the second death cannot harm them.

Praise and bless my Lord,
Thank Him and serve Him
With great humility.

Friars (the Franciscans were the Grey Friars from the color of their robes), was created through the efforts of a Spanish priest, Dominic de Guzmán (1170–1221). Unlike Francis, Dominic was an intellectual who was particularly appalled by the growth of heretical movements within the church. He came to believe that a new religious order of men who lived lives of apostolic poverty but were learned and capable of preaching effectively would best be able to attack and eliminate heresy. With the approval of Pope Innocent III, the Dominicans became an order of mendicant (begging) friars in 1215.

Like the Franciscans, the Dominicans took a vow of poverty, but did not emphasize it in the same way. Since their chief function was preaching, the Dominicans established schools to provide their friars with training in theology. The Dominicans also created an elaborate system of representative government for their order. As head of the order, the master-general was elected for life but could be deposed for malfeasance in office. The order was divided into provinces, each administered by a provincial prior chosen by all the members. Each prior was assisted by a council of friars composed of the heads of the provincial monastic houses and elected delegates. These councils were active in framing legislation for the order. This system of representative assemblies paralleled the development of parliaments in the secular states of the thirteenth century.

The Franciscans and Dominicans played a significant role in the spiritual life of the thirteenth century, particularly among ordinary Christians. By their poverty, the friars reached people critical of the church's growing wealth. By their effective preaching, they could be heard above the voices of the heretics who had found preaching in the vernacular an avenue to attract followers.

In addition to the friars, the thirteenth century witnessed the development of yet another kind of religious order. Known as Beguines, these were communities of women dwelling together in poverty. They were devout and dedicated to prayer. They begged for their daily support or worked as laundresses in hospitals or at other menial tasks. They did not take religious vows and were free to leave the community at will. Although the Beguines originated in the Low Countries, they eventually became quite strong in the Rhineland area of Germany as well. The church was never quite sure what to do with them, and in the fourteenth century the Beguines ran into serious difficulty with church officials.

Popular Religion in the High Middle Ages

We have witnessed the actions of popes, cardinals, bishops, and monks. We have seen how the church created a papal monarchy in which the pope, assisted by his curia, ran and directed the hierarchical organization of the Catholic church. But what of ordinary clergy and lay people? What were their religious hopes and fears? What were their spiritual aspirations?

The sacramental system of the Catholic church ensured that the church was an integral part of people's lives, from birth to death. In the twelfth century, the system was clarified, as the church finally defined the seven sacraments administered by the clergy. Sacraments were viewed as outward symbols of an inward grace (grace was God's freely given gift that enabled humans to be saved) and were considered imperative for a Christian's salvation. Five sacraments in particular directly affected the lives of medieval Christians. Baptism removed original sin and signified membership in the church proper. The sacrament of marriage dignified the union of two people and made valid the practice of sexual intercourse for the begetting of children. In the Eucharist, bread and wine were believed to be transformed miraculously into the body and blood of Christ. Through the sacrament of penance, Christians received forgiveness for their sins. Finally, the church had a sacrament for death. If possible, a priest administered extreme unction, or the last rites of the church for the dying. Of the remaining two sacraments, holy orders was reserved for the clergy, and confirmation of older children by a bishop did not become a regular practice until the thirteenth century.

Other church practices also played a significant role in the development of medieval Christianity. From its early centuries, the church had recognized men and women who displayed eminent holiness as saints; they held a special position in the spiritual hierarchy that enabled them to act as intercessors before the throne of God. As time passed, their intercessionary powers and ability to protect poor souls made the saints increasingly important at the popular level. Christ's apostles were, of course, universally recognized throughout Europe as saints, but there were also numerous local saints who were of especial significance to a single area, such as Saint Swithun in Winchester, England. New cults developed rapidly, particularly in the intense religious atmosphere of the eleventh and twelfth centuries. The English introduced Saint Nicholas, the patron saint of children, who remains instantly recognizable today through his identification with Santa Claus.

Of all the saints, the Virgin Mary, the mother of Christ, occupied the foremost position in the High Middle Ages. The cult of Mary took on two important aspects. Mary was viewed as the most important mediator with her son Christ, the judge of all sinners. Moreover, from the eleventh century on, with the heightened interest in Jesus as infant, boy, and man, a fascination with Mary as Jesus' human mother became more evident. A sign of Mary's importance is the growing number of churches all over Europe that were dedicated to her in the twelfth and thirteenth centuries. As Mary became more popular, the number of stories about miracles occuring through her intercession also increased dramatically.

Emphasis on the role of the saints was closely tied to the use of relics, which also increased significantly in the High Middle Ages. Relics were usually the bones of saints or objects intimately connected to saints that were considered worthy of veneration by the faithful. A twelfth-century English monk began his description of the abbey's relics by saying that "There is kept there a thing more precious than gold, . . . the right arm of St. Oswald. . . . This we have seen with our own eyes and have kissed, and have handled with our own hands. . . . There are kept here also part of his ribs and of the soil on which he fell."[10] The monk went on to list additional relics possessed by the abbey, which included two pieces of Christ's swaddling clothes, pieces of Christ's manger and part of the five loaves of bread with which Christ fed 5,000 people. Since the holiness of the saint was considered to be inherent in his relics, these objects were believed to be capable of healing people or producing other miracles.

deceased and, of course, by indulgences. Indulgences were granted for charitable contributions and viewing the relics of saints. Although indulgences were not supposed to be taken literally, the church attached a number of years and days to each indulgence, enabling the soul to spend less time in purgatory.

Medieval Christians believed a pilgrimage to a holy shrine was of particular spiritual benefit. The greatest shrine but the most difficult to reach was the Holy City of Jerusalem. On the continent two pilgrim centers were especially popular in the High Middle Ages: Rome, which contained the relics of Saints Peter and Paul, and the town of Santiago de Compostela, supposedly the site of the tomb of the Apostle James. Local attractions, such as shrines dedicated to the Blessed Virgin Mary, also became pilgrimage centers.

✦ **The Gate to Hell.** This twelfth-century miniature depicts the gate of hell as the jaws of a monster filled with sinners and demons. In their sermons, many priests in the tenth and eleventh centuries attempted to frighten their parishioners with vivid images of hell.

✦ **Mass of the Holy Relics.** It was customary for churches that possessed relics to hold a special mass honoring those saints. At that time, the reliquaries would be brought out for the faithful to venerate. The large picture shows the celebration of this special mass of the holy relics. The reliquary is shown on a table to the left. The small pictures illustrate various stages of the mass.

In the High Middle Ages, it became a regular practice of the church to attach indulgences to these relics. An indulgence brought a remission of the temporal punishment due to sin after the sinner had been absolved by a priest. Indulgences were, in turn, closely connected to the church's doctrine of purgatory, which was first clearly defined in the eleventh and twelfth centuries. Purgatory was believed to be a place of punishment in which the soul of the departed could be purified before ascending into heaven. The living could ease that suffering by masses and prayers offered on behalf of the

Voices of Protest and Intolerance

The desire for more personal and deeper religious experience, which characterized the spiritual revival of the High Middle Ages, also led people into directions hostile to the institutional church. From the twelfth century on, religious dissent became a serious problem for the Catholic church.

One form of dissent was anticlericalism. Although some people were orthodox in their religious beliefs, they condemned bishops and priests who failed to live up to the moral standards expected of them. In the mid-twelfth century, Arnold of Brescia, an Italian abbot, abandoned his order to become a popular preacher. A contemporary chronicler observed that "he said things that were entirely consistent with the law accepted by Christian people, but not at all with the life they led."[11] His criticism of the bishop of Brescia's behavior so angered the bishop that Arnold was forced to flee for his life. He went to France where he continued to preach against the excessive wealth and corruption of the church hierarchy. Although such criticism was not heretical, it was considered harmful to the church and the social fabric. Arnold of Brescia was caught and executed by the Emperor Frederick Barbarossa.

Other Christians moved beyond anticlericalism or incorporated it into a larger framework of dissenting thought. Their desire for meaningful religious experience could and did lead to heresy or the holding of religious doctrines different from the orthodox teachings of the church. Since even contemporaries observed that heresies seemed to expand as cities grew in number and size, it may be that the concentration of people in urban areas encouraged the spread of heresy.

The two best-known heresies of the twelfth and thirteenth centuries were Catharism and Waldensianism. The Cathars (the word *Cathar* means "pure") were also called Albigensians after the city of Albi, one of their strongholds in southern France. They believed in a dualist system in which good and evil were separate and distinct (see the box on p. 300). The things of the spirit were good since they were created by a God of light; the things of the world were evil since they were created by Satan, the prince of darkness. Humans, too, were enmeshed in dualism. Their souls, which were good, were trapped in material bodies, which were evil. Jesus was not divine because he had possessed an evil human body. He was merely an emissary of God who was sent to show people the way out of the soul's entrapment. According to the Cathars, the Catholic church, itself a materialistic institution, had nothing to do with God

Map 9.1 Pilgrimage Routes in the Middle Ages.

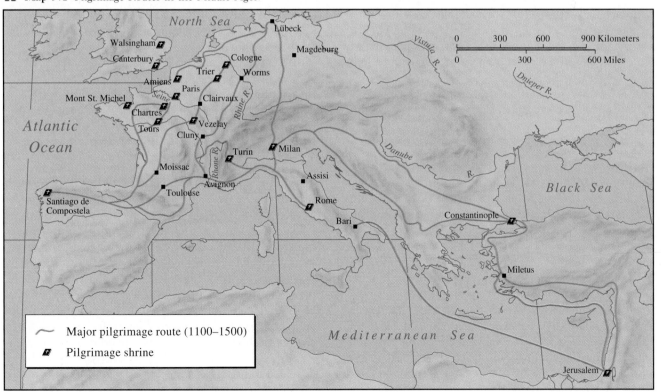

The Albigensians

The Cathars or Albigensians were heretics who were located primarily in southern France. In his determination to eradicate their heresy, Pope Innocent III authorized a crusade by the nobility of northern France against them. Thousands of people were slaughtered, including men, women, and children. One of the crusaders was a young Cistercian monk from the abbey of Vaux-de-Cernay who accompanied the army of Simon of Montfort and wrote a history of the crusade against the Albigensians. This excerpt from his account makes clear his intense feelings against the heretics.

Peter Vaux-de-Cernay,
A History of the Albigensians

It should first be understood that the heretics postulated two creators, to wit, one of the invisible world, whom they called the benign God, and one of the visible world, or the malign god. They ascribed the New Testament to the benign God, the Old Testament to the malign one; the latter book they wholly rejected, except for a few passages which have found their way into the New Testament and which on this account they esteemed worthy of acceptance. . . .

The heretics even affirmed in their secret assemblies that the Christ who was born in terrestrial and visible Bethlehem and crucified in Jerusalem was evil, and that Mary Magdalen was his concubine and the very woman taken in adultery of whom we read in the Gospel; for the good Christ, they said, never ate nor drank nor took on real flesh, and was never of this world, except in a spiritual sense in the body of Paul. . . .

All of these limbs of Antichrist, the first born of Satan, "wicked seed, ungracious children," "speaking lies in hypocrisy," "seducing the hearts of the innocent," corrupted almost the whole province of Narbonne with the poison of their perfidy. They called the Roman Church a "den of thieves" and that harlot of whom we read in Apocalypse. They held as naught the sacraments of the Church to the point of teaching publicly that the water of holy baptism differs not at all from water of a river; that the consecrated bread of the most holy body of Christ is no different from ordinary bread; instilling into the ears of simple folk the blasphemy that the body of Christ, even were it as great as the Alps, would long since have been completely consumed by communicants who partook of it; that confirmation, extreme unction, and confession are trifling and silly matters; and that holy matrimony is nothing else than harlotry, nor can anyone fathering sons and daughters in that state achieve salvation. . . .

Now, it must be understood that certain of the heretics were called the Perfect or the God Men; the others were called the believers of heretics. Those who were called Perfect wore a black mantle; they falsely claimed that they kept themselves chaste; they wholly refused to eat meat, eggs, or cheese; they sought to give the impression of never telling a lie, when they lied constantly, especially concerning God; and they help that one should never for any reason take on oath. Those were called believers of heretics who, while living in the world, did not strive to attain the life of the perfected, but hoped nonetheless to achieve salvation in their faith; they differed, indeed, in their manner of life, but in faith they were at one. Those who were called believers were absorbed in usuries, robberies, murders, sins of the flesh, perjuries, and all sorts of perversities.

and was essentially evil. There was no need to follow its teachings or recognize its authority. Catharism also advocated strict asceticism, including fasting and abstention from sexual relations. Since the spirit had become entrapped in the flesh, the procreation of more children simply forced more souls into evil physical bodies. The Cathars had two levels of practitioners, however. Only a tiny priestly caste, the "perfect ones," adhered to these rigid puritanical standards. The majority of Cathars, the "believers," married and led more relaxed lives. The Cathar movement gained valuable support from important nobles in southern France and northern Italy, especially Raymond IV, count of Toulouse, the chief lord of southern France.

Southern France was home to another heretical sect known as the Waldensians, named after their founder Peter Waldo. He was a wealthy French merchant whose background was quite similar to that of Saint Francis. He, too, experienced moments of religious enlightenment in which he decided to give up all of his material possessions, adopt a life of poverty, and preach to the people in the vernacular. In his sermons, he used biblical texts that emphasized the rejection of material goods and the pursuit of the ideal of apostolic poverty. When the archbishop of Lyons ordered Waldo to stop preaching in public because he had no license to preach, he appealed to the pope. The pope accepted Waldo and his followers' wish to dedicate their lives to poverty, but forbade them to preach without their bishop's consent. The Waldensians refused to give up preaching, however, and defied the church authorities. Their message had a strong appeal in southern France—a region notorious for its inept clerical leadership—where Catharism had also spread. The unwillingness of the Waldensians to accept the church's authority led to their public condemnation as heretics in 1183.

As the parallels and divergences between Waldo and Francis of Assisi suggest, the line between saint and heretic in the High Middle Ages was often a narrow one. Both Francis and Waldo rejected the world and material possessions. Francis became a devoted papal follower and conformed to church authority. Waldo preached the same message of poverty but refused to accept church authority and consequently became a heretic.

The spread of heretical movements in southern France alarmed the church authorities. Pope Innocent III determined to solve the problem, initially by sending preachers to convince the heretics to return to the orthodox Catholic faith. But the preachers had little success, and when the leaders of southern France refused to help, the pope decided to use force. His appeal to the nobles of northern France for a crusade against the heretics fell on receptive ears, especially by nobles eager for adventure, plunder, and gain.

The crusade against the Albigensians, which began in the summer of 1209 and lasted for almost two decades, was a bloody one. Thousands of heretics (and the innocent) were slaughtered, including entire populations of some towns. In Béziers, for example, 7,000 men, women, and children were massacred when they took refuge in the local church. The count of Toulouse and other lords were stripped of their lands.

Southern France was devastated, but Catharism remained. Over a period of years, the church's efforts to devise a method for discovering and dealing with heretics led to the emergence of the papal inquisition. By 1233, Pope Gregory IX (1227–1241) had entrusted both Dominicans and Franciscans with inquisitorial powers that had formerly belonged only to bishops. The Holy Office, as the Inquisition was called, became a formal court whose job it was to ferret out and try heretics. The Dominicans became especially known for their roles as inquisitor-generals.

Gradually, the Holy Office developed its inquisitorial procedure. Anyone could be accused of heresy since the identity of the accuser was not revealed to the indicted heretic. If the accused heretic confessed, he or she was forced to perform public penance and was subjected to punishment, such as flogging; the heretic's property was then confiscated and divided between the secular au-

✦ **Expulsion of Albigensian Heretics.** In 1209, Pope Innocent III authorized a crusade against the heretical Albigensians. In this medieval illustration, French knights are shown expelling Albigensian heretics from the town of Carcassonne near Albi, an Albigensian stronghold in southern France.

thorities and the church. Beginning in 1252, those not confessing voluntarily were subjected to torture. Those who refused to confess and were still considered guilty were turned over to the secular authorities for execution. So also were relapsed heretics—those who confessed, did penance, and then reverted to heresy again. The underlying rationale of the Inquisition was quite simple: if possible, save the heretic's soul; if not, stop the heretic from endangering the souls of others. To the Christians of the thirteenth century who believed that there was only one path to salvation, heresy was a crime against God and against humanity, and force was justified to save souls from damnation. The fanaticism and fear unleashed in the struggle against heretics were also used against others, especially the most well known outgroup of Western society, the Jews.

PERSECUTION OF THE JEWS

The Jews constituted the only religious minority in medieval Europe that was allowed to practice a non-Christian religion. In the Early Middle Ages, Jews were actively involved in trade and crafts. Later, after being excluded from both property holding and trades by the feudal and guild systems, some Jews turned to money-lending as a way to survive, although this was probably true only of a minority. Many historians believe that until the eleventh and twelfth centuries, with some exceptions, Jews were still tolerated relatively well by their Christian neighbors.

There is little certainty about the number of Jews in Europe. England had a relatively small population, probably 2,500 to 3,000, or one-thousandth of the population. There were larger numbers in southern Italy, Spain, France, and Germany. In southern Europe, Jews served an important function as cultural and intellectual intermediaries between the Muslim and Christian worlds.

The religious enthusiasm of the High Middle Ages produced an outburst of intolerance against the supposed enemies of Christianity. Although this was evident in the crusades against the Muslims (see Chapter 11), Christians also took up the search for enemies at home, persecuting Jews in France and the Rhineland at the time of the first crusades. Jews in Speyer, Worms, Mainz, and Cologne were all set upon by bands of Christian crusaders. A contemporary chronicler described how a band of English crusaders who stopped at Lisbon, Portugal, en route to the Holy Land "drove away the pagans and Jews, servants of the king, who dwelt in the city and plundered their property and possessions, and burned their houses; and they then stripped their vineyards, not leaving them so much as a grape or a cluster."[12] Even those who tried to protect the Jews were in danger. When the archbishop of Mainz provided shelter for the Jews, his palace was stormed and he was forced to flee. Prominent Christians came to the Jews' defense. Saint Bernard rushed to Germany in 1144 to halt the attacks on Jews, but even the revered holy man was almost lynched by a mob in Mainz when he tried to stop preachers from attacking the Jews. Popes also came to the Jews' defense by issuing decrees reminding Christians that Jews were not to be persecuted.

By the early twelfth century, kings began to establish the principle that Jews had no legal rights except those granted to them by the king. By the late twelfth century, while issuing decrees of protection, kings were exploiting the Jews in their territories as well as using various expedients to gain possession of their wealth. For example, in England, when a Jew died, the king confiscated one-third of his wealth. Popes also proved to be dubious protectors. Although they condemned the persecutions, they demonstrated their contempt for Jews by punitive legislation. The Fourth Lateran Council in 1215 decreed that Jews must wear distinguishing marks, such as ribbons, yellow badges, and special veils and cloaks to separate themselves from Christians. The same council encouraged the development of Jewish ghettos, or walled enclosures, not to protect the Jews, but to isolate them from Christians. Hence, the provincial council of Breslau in 1267 stated:

> The Polish country is still a young plantation in the body of Christendom [pagans had only recently been converted], in order that the Christian populace be not the more easily infected by the superstitions and the depraved mores of the Jews dwelling among them . . . the Jews . . . shall have their houses either contiguous or adjoining in some segregated location of a city or village, in such manner that the quarter of the Jews be separated from the dwellings of the Christians by a fence, a wall or a moat.[13]

Increasingly, the balance between contempt and toleration tilted toward intolerance and persecution of the Jews.

In the thirteenth century, in the supercharged atmosphere of fear created by the struggle with the heretics, Jews were more and more persecuted (see the box on p. 303). Friars urged action against these "murderers of Christ," referring to the traditional Christian view of the Jews as responsible for the death of Christ, and organized public burnings of Jewish books. Especially prevalent among the masses was the charge that the Jews carried out the ritual murder of small children. The persecutions and the new image of the hated Jew stimulated a tradition of anti-Semitism that proved to be one of Christian Europe's most insidious contributions to the Western heritage.

European kings, who had portrayed themselves as protectors, had so fleeced the Jewish communities of their money by the end of the thirteenth century that they too gave in to the mob fury. Edward I expelled all Jews from England in 1290. The French followed suit in 1306, readmitted them in 1315, and expelled them again in 1322. As this policy spread into central Europe, most northern European Jews were forced to move into Poland as a last refuge.

INTOLERANCE AND HOMOSEXUALITY

The climate of intolerance that characterized thirteenth-century attitudes toward Muslims, heretics, and Jews was also evident toward another minority group, homosexuals. Although the church had condemned homosexuality in the Early Middle Ages, it had not been overly concerned with homosexual behavior, an attitude also prevalent in the secular world. Before the thirteenth century, few laws had been enacted against homosexual activity. Nor did this approach

❧ Treatment of the Jews ❧

The development of new religious sensibilities in the High Middle Ages also had a negative side, the turning of Christians against their supposed enemies. Although the crusades provide the most obvious example, Christians also turned on their supposed enemies, the "murderers of Christ," the Jews. As a result, Jews suffered increased persecution. These three documents show different sides of the picture. The first is Canon 68 of the decrees of the Fourth Lateran Council called by Pope Innocent III in 1215. The decree specifies the need for special dress, one of the ways Christians tried to separate Jews from their community. The second excerpt is a chronicler's account of the most absurd charge levied against the Jews—that they were guilty of the ritual murder of Christian children to obtain Christian blood for the passover service. This charge led to the murder of many Jews. The third document, taken from a list of regulations issued by the city of Avignon, France, illustrates the contempt Christian society held for the Jews.

Canon 68

In some provinces a difference in dress distinguishes the Jews or Saracens from the Christians, but in certain others such a confusion has grown up that they cannot be distinguished by any difference. Thus it happens at times that through error Christians have relations with the women of Jews or Saracens, and Jews or Saracens with Christian women. Therefore, that they may not, under pretext of error of this sort, excuse themselves in the future for the excesses of such prohibited intercourse, we decree that such Jews and Saracens of both sexes in every Christian province and at all times shall be marked off in the eyes of the public from other peoples through the character of their dress. . . .

Moreover, during the last three days before Easter and especially on Good Friday, they shall not go forth in public at all, for the reason that some of them on these very days, as we hear, do not blush to go forth better dressed and are not afraid to mock the Christians who maintain the memory of the most holy Passion by wearing signs of mourning.

The Jews and Ritual Murder of Christian Children

[. . . The eight-year-old-boy] Harold, who is buried in the Church of St. Peter the Apostle, at Gloucester] . . . is said to have been carried away secretly by Jews, in the opinion of many, on Feb. 21, and by them hidden till March 16. On that night, on the sixth of the preceding feast, the Jews of all England coming together as if to circumcise a certain boy, pretend deceitfully that they are about to celebrate the feast [Passover] appointed by law in such case, and deceiving the citizens of Gloucester with the fraud, they tortured the lad placed before them with immense tortures. It is true no Christian was present, or saw or heard the deed, nor have we found that anything was betrayed by any Jew. But a little while after when the whole convent of monks of Gloucester and almost all the citizens of that city, and innumerable persons coming to the spectacle, saw the wounds of the dead body, scars of fire, the thorns fixed on his head, and liquid wax poured into the eyes and face, and touched it with the diligent examination of their hands, those tortures were believed or guessed to have been inflicted on him in that manner. It was clear that they had made him a glorious martyr to Christ, being slain without sin, and having bound his feet and his own girdle, threw him into the river Severn.

The Regulations of Avignon, 1243

Likewise, we declare that Jews or whores shall not dare to touch with their hands either bread or fruit put out for sale, and that if they should do this they must buy what they have touched.

change initially in the High Middle Ages. Prominent figures, both ecclesiastical and lay, were publicly known and accepted as homosexuals. Between 1050 and 1150, especially among the clergy, there developed a whole subculture of men who produced a literature dwelling on male homosexual love.

By the thirteenth century, however, these tolerant attitudes had altered drastically. Some historians connect this change to the century's climate of fear and intolerance against any minority group that deviated from the standards of the majority. A favorite approach of the critics was to identify homosexuals with other detested groups. Homosexuality was portrayed as a regular practice of Muslims and such notorious heretics as the Albigensians. These hostile attitudes became increasingly evident in legislation enacted throughout Europe in the second half of the thirteenth century. As an example, one Spanish edict stated:

> Although we are reluctant to speak of something which is reckless to consider and reckless to perform, terrible sins are nevertheless sometimes committed, and it happens

that one man desires to sin against nature with another. We therefore command that if any commit this sin, once it is proven, both be castrated before the whole populace and on the third day after be hung by the legs until dead, and that their bodies never be taken down.[14]

This law reflected a basic transformation between 1250 and 1300; what had been tolerated in most of Europe was now a criminal act deserving of death.

The legislation against homosexuality commonly referred to it as a "sin against nature." This is precisely the argument developed by Thomas Aquinas (see Chapter 11) who formed Catholic opinion on the subject for centuries to come. In his *Summa Theologica,* Aquinas argued that since the purpose of sex was procreation, it could only be used legitimately in ways that did not exclude this possibility. Hence, homosexuality was "contrary to nature" and a deviation from the natural order established by God. This argument and laws prohibiting homosexual activity on pain of death remained the norm in Europe until the twentieth century.

Conclusion

The new European civilization that had emerged in the Early Middle Ages began to flourish in the High Middle Ages. Climatic improvements that produced better growing conditions, an expansion of cultivated land, and technological changes combined to enable Europe's food supply to increase significantly after 1000. This increase in agricultural production helped sustain a dramatic rise in population that was physically apparent in the expansion of towns and cities.

The Catholic church shared in the challenge of new growth by reforming itself and striking out on a path toward greater papal power, both within the church and over European society. The High Middle Ages witnessed a spiritual renewal that led to numerous and even divergent paths: revived papal leadership, the development of centralized administrative machinery that buttressed papal authority, and new dimensions to the religious life of the clergy and laity. The theology of Saint Bernard, new forms of monasticism, the doctrine of purgatory, and the emergence of a clearly defined sacramental system all seemed to reflect a greater concern for salvation and a greater possibility of achieving it.

The religious enthusiasm of the twelfth century continued well into the thirteenth as new orders of friars gave witness to spiritual growth and passion, but underneath the calm exterior lay seeds of discontent and change. Dissent from church teaching and practices grew, leading to a climate of fear and intolerance as the church responded with inquisitorial procedures to enforce conformity to its teachings. At the same time, papal claims of supremacy over secular authorities were increasingly challenged by the rising power of a new breed of monarchical authorities, who, because of the growth of cities, the revival of trade, and the emergence of a money economy, were now able to hire soldiers and officials to carry out their wishes. It is to this new world of cities and kingdoms that we must now turn.

NOTES

1. Ernest F. Henderson, ed., *Select Historical Documents of the Middle Ages* (London, 1892), p. 332.
2. Oliver J. Thatcher and Edgar H. McNeal, eds., *A Source Book for Medieval History* (New York, 1905), pp. 134–35.
3. Henderson, *Select Historical Documents of the Middle Ages,* p. 365.
4. Ibid., pp. 372–73.
5. Thatcher and McNeal, *A Source Book for Medieval History,* p. 208.
6. Quoted in R. H. C. Davis, *A History of Medieval Europe from Constantine to Saint Louis,* 2d ed. (London and New York, 1988), p. 252.
7. Quoted in Lina Eckenstein, *Woman under Monasticism* (Cambridge, 1896), pp. 136–37.
8. Matthew Fox, ed., *Hildegard of Bingen's Book of Divine Works with Letters and Songs* (Santa Fe, N.M., 1987), p. xiii.
9. Ibid., p. 293.
10. Quoted in Rosalind Brooke and Christopher Brooke, *Popular Religion in the Middle Ages* (London, 1984), p. 19.
11. Quoted in Brooke and Brooke, *Popular Religion in the Middle Ages,* p. 94.
12. Henry T. Riley, ed. and trans., *Memorials of London and London Life in the Thirteenth, Fourteenth and Fifteenth Centuries* (London, 1868), 2:148–49.

13. Quoted in Guido Kisch, *The Jews in Medieval Germany* (Chicago, 1949), p. 293.

14. Quoted in John Boswell, *Christianity, Social Tolerance, and Homosexuality* (Chicago, 1980), p. 288.

SUGGESTIONS FOR FURTHER READING

For a good introduction to this period, see C. N. L. Brooke, *Europe in the Central Middle Ages, 962–1154,* rev. ed. (New York, 1988); and M. Barber, *The Two Cities: Medieval Europe 1050–1320* (London, 1992). On economic conditions, see N. J. G. Pounds, *An Economic History of Medieval Europe* (New York, 1974); and *The Fontana Economic History of Europe,* vol. 1, *The Middle Ages,* ed. C. M. Cipolla (London, 1972). A good short introduction to medieval society is C. Brooke, *The Structure of Medieval Society* (London, 1971). On peasant life, see R. Fossier, *Peasant Life in the Medieval West* (New York, 1988). Technological changes are discussed in L. White, *Medieval Technology and Social Change* (Oxford, 1962); J. Gimpel, *The Medieval Machine* (Harmondsworth, 1976); and J. Langdon, *Horses, Oxen and Technological Innovation* (New York, 1986).

For a good survey of religion in medieval Europe, see B. Hamilton, *Religion in the Medieval West* (London, 1986). On the Cluniac reform movement, see H. E. J. Cowdrey, *The Cluniacs and the Gregorian Reform* (Oxford, 1970); and G. Constable, *Cluniac Studies* (London, 1980). On Europe during the time of the Investiture Controversy, see G. Tellenbach, *Church, State and Christian Society at the Time of the Investiture Controversy* (Oxford, 1948). Also valuable are K. F. Morrison, *Tradition and Authority in the Western Church, 300–1140* (Princeton, N.J., 1969); and B. Tierney, *The Crisis of Church and State: 1050–1300* (Englewood Cliffs, N.J., 1964). On the evolution of papal ideology, see W. Ullmann, *A Short History of the Papacy in the Middle Ages* (London, 1974). For a general survey of church life, see R. W. Southern, *Western Society and the Church in the Middle Ages* (Baltimore, 1970). For a sociohistorical account of the Catholic clergy, see A. Barstow, *Married Priests and the Reforming Papacy* (New York, 1982).

On the papacy in the High Middle Ages, see the general survey by G. Barraclough, *The Medieval Papacy* (New York, 1968); C. Morris, *The Papal Monarchy* (Oxford, 1989); and I. S. Robinson, *The Papacy* (Cambridge, 1990). The papacy of Innocent III is covered in H. Tillmann, *Innocent III* (Amsterdam, 1980). On the

church, see P. Partner, *The Lands of St. Peter* (Berkeley, 1972); and D. P. Waley, *The Papal State in the Thirteenth Century* (London, 1961).

Good works on monasticism include B. Bolton, *The Medieval Reformation* (London, 1983); C. H. Lawrence, *Medieval Monasticism* (London, 1984), a good general account; and H. Leyser, *Hermits and the New Monasticism* (London, 1984). On the Cistercians, see L. J. Lekai, *The Cistercians* (Kent, Ohio, 1977). S. Flanagan, *Hildegard of Bingen* (London, 1989) is a good account of the twelfth-century mystic. The new religious orders of the thirteenth century are examined in R. B. Brooke, *The Coming of the Friars* (New York, 1975). L. K. Little, *Religious Poverty and the Profit Economy in Medieval Europe* (London, 1979) stresses the social context of the development of the mendicant orders. For a good introduction to popular religion in the eleventh and twelfth centuries, see R. and C. N. L. Brooke, *Popular Religion in the Middle Ages* (London, 1984). On miracles, see B. Ward, *Miracles and the Medieval Mind* (London, 1982). The image of women in the secular and religious realms is discussed in P. S. Gold, *The Lady and the Virgin: Image, Attitude and Experience in Twelfth-Century France* (Chicago, 1985).

On dissent and heresy, see M. Lambert, *Medieval Heresy* (New York, 1977); R. I. Moore, *The Origins of European Dissent* (New York, 1977); W. L. Wakefield, *Heresy, Crusade and Inquisition in Southern France, 1100–1250* (Berkeley, 1974); J. Sumption, *The Albigensian Crusade* (London, 1978); and J. Strayer, *The Albigensian Crusades* (New York, 1971). On the Inquisition, see B. Hamilton, *The Medieval Inquisition* (New York, 1981). The persecution of Jews in the thirteenth century can be examined in E. A. Synan, *The Popes and the Jews in the Middle Ages* (New York, 1965); J. Marcus, *The Jew in the Medieval World* (New York, 1972); and J. Cohen, *The Friars and the Jews* (Oxford, 1985); The basic study on intolerance and homosexuality is J. Boswell, *Christianity, Social Tolerance, and Homosexuality* (Chicago, 1980).

CHAPTER
10

A New World of Cities and Kingdoms

By the fifth century A.D., the towns and cities that had been such an integral part of the Roman world began to decline, and the world of the Early Middle Ages became predominantly agricultural. Beginning in the late tenth and early eleventh centuries, however, a renewal of commercial life led to a revival of cities. Old Roman sites came back to life while new towns arose at major crossroads or natural harbors favorable to trading activities. Townspeople themselves were often great enthusiasts for their new way of life. In the twelfth century, William Fitz-Stephen spoke of London as one of the noble cities of the world: "It is happy in the healthiness of its air, in the Christian religion, in the strength of its defenses, the nature of its site, the honor of its citizens, the modesty of its women; pleasant in sports; fruitful of noble men." To Fitz-Stephen, London offered a myriad of opportunities and pleasures. Fairs and markets are held regularly, and "practically anything that man may need is brought daily not only into special places but even into the open squares, and all that can be sold is loudly advertised for sale." Any man, according to Fitz-Stephen, "if he is healthy and not a good-for-nothing, may earn his living expenses and esteem according to his station." Then, too, there are the happy inhabitants of the city: where else has one "ever met such a wonderful show of people this side or the other side of the sea?" Sporting events and leisure activities are available in every season of the year: "In Easter holidays they fight battles on water." In summer, "the youths are exercised in leaping, dancing, shooting, wrestling, casting the stone; the maidens dance as long as they can well see." In winter, "when the great fen, or moor, which waters the walls of the city on the north side, is frozen, many young men play upon the ice; some, striding as wide as they may, do slide swiftly." To Fitz-Stephen, "every convenience for human pleasure is known to be at hand" in London. One would hardly know from his cheerful description that medieval cities faced overcrowded conditions, terrible smells from rotting gar-

Norman conquest of England

Murder of Thomas Becket

Henry II, first of the Plantagenets

Magna Carta

Activities of Eleanor of Aquitaine

The "greater Parliaments" in England

"Saint" Louis IX

First Estates-General in France

Frederick I and the Hohenstaufen dynasty

Mongol conquest of Russia

Frederick II

Election of Rudolf of Habsburg as king of Germany

bage and raw sewage, and the constant threat of epidemics and fires.

By the twelfth and thirteen centuries, both the urban centers and the urban population of Europe were experiencing a dramatic expansion. Although European society in the High Middle Ages remained overwhelmingly agricultural, the growth of trade and cities along with the development of a money economy and new commercial practices and institutions constituted a veritable commercial revolution that affected most of Europe, including its political structures. Commerce, cities, and a money economy helped to undermine feudal institutions while strengthening monarchical authority.

During the High Middle Ages, nobles built innumerable castles that gave a distinctive look to the countryside. Although lords and vassals seemed forever mired in endless petty conflicts, some medieval kings began to exert a centralizing authority and inaugurated the process of developing new kinds of monarchical states. By the thirteenth century, European monarchs were solidifying their governmental institutions in pursuit of greater power.

The New World of Trade and Cities

Medieval Europe was an overwhelmingly agrarian society with most people living in small villages. In the eleventh and twelfth centuries, however, new elements were introduced that began to transform the economic foundation of Western civilization: a revival of trade, considerable expansion in the circulation of money, a restoration of specialized craftsmen and artisans, and the growth and development of towns. These changes were made possible by the new agricultural practices and subsequent increase in food production, which freed part of the European population from the need to produce their own food and allowed diversification in economic functions. Merchants and craftsmen could now buy their necessities.

The Revival of Trade

The revival of commercial activity was a gradual process. Although trade had never completely disappeared in western Europe, the uncertainties and chaotic conditions of the Early Middle Ages caused large-scale trade to decline except for Byzantine contacts with Italy and the Jewish traders who moved back and forth between the Muslim and Christian worlds.

By the end of the tenth century, however, people with both the skills and the products for commercial activity were emerging in Europe (see the box on p. 308). Although most goods were produced for local markets, some items were unique to a particular region and could be sold elsewhere. These included a wide range of goods, such as flax and wool for clothes, wine for drinking and for use at the Catholic mass, salt for preserving food, furs for clothing, hemp for rope, and metals for weapons or tools. Some areas became particularly well known for certain products: England for raw wool, Scandinavia and Germany for iron, and Germany for silver.

The Medieval Merchant

The origins of the merchant class are clouded in uncertainty. Perhaps an occasional runaway serf acquired enough goods to become a wandering peddler and possibly even made enough money to be a flourishing merchant. More likely, however, the merchants' origins are to be found among the younger sons of prosperous farmers who had the capital to set themselves up in business. This excerpt is taken from the life of Godric, a twelfth-century merchant who became a hermit and a saint.

Life of Saint Godric

When the boy had passed his childish years quietly at home; then, as he began to grow to manhood, he began to follow more prudent ways of life, and to learn carefully and persistently the teachings of worldly forethought. Wherefore he chose not to follow the life of a husbandman, but rather to study, learn and exercise the rudiment of more subtle conceptions. For this reason, aspiring to the merchant's trade, he began to follow the peddler's way of life, first learning how to gain in small bargains and things of insignificant price; and thence, while yet a youth, his mind advanced little by little to buy and sell and gain from things of greater expense. For, in his beginnings, he was wont to wander with small wares around the villages and farmsteads of his own neighborhood; but, in process of time, he gradually associated himself by compact with city merchants. Hence, within a brief space of time, the youth who had trudged for many weary hours from village to village, from farm to farm, did so profit by his increase of age and wisdom as to travel with associates of his own age through towns and boroughs, fortresses and cities, to fairs and to all the various booths of the marketplace, in pursuit of his public barter. He went along the highway, neither puffed up by the good testimony of his conscience nor downcast in the nobler part of his soul by the reproach of poverty. . . .

At first, he lived as a peddler for four years in Lincolnshire, going on foot and carrying the smallest wares; then he traveled abroad, first to St. Andrews in Scotland and then for the first time to Rome. On his return, having formed a familiar friendship with certain other young men who were eager for merchandise, he began to launch upon bolder courses, and to coast frequently by sea to the foreign lands that lay around him. Thus, sailing often to and fro between Scotland and Britain, he traded in many different wares and, amid these occupations, learned much worldly wisdom. . . .

Thus aspiring ever higher and higher, and yearning upward with his whole heart, at length his great labors and cares bore much fruit of worldly gain. For he labored not only as a merchant but also as a shipman . . . to Denmark and to Flanders and Scotland; in all which lands he found certain rare, and therefore more precious, wares, which he carried to other parts wherein he knew them to be least familiar, and coveted by the inhabitants beyond the price of gold itself; wherefore he exchanged these wares for others coveted by men of other lands; and thus he traded most freely and assiduously. Hence he made great profit in all his bargains, and gathered much wealth in the sweat of his brow; for he sold dear in one place the wares which he had bought elsewhere at a small price.

Cities in Italy assumed a leading role in the revival of trade. By the end of the eighth century, Venice, on the northeastern coast, had forged close commercial connections with the Byzantine Empire. It developed a mercantile fleet and by the end of the tenth century had become the chief western trading center for Byzantine and Islamic commerce. Venice sent wine, grain, and timber to Constantinople in exchange for silk cloth, which was then peddled to other communities in northern Italy. Other coastal communities in western Italy also opened new trade routes; Genoa and Pisa, for example, ventured into the western Mediterranean despite harassment by Muslim pirates. In the course of the eleventh century, Sardinia, Corsica, and Sicily were liberated from Muslim control; by 1100, the western Mediterranean was relatively safe for Italian commerce.

During the same period, the west had also begun a series of crusades for the "liberation" of the Holy Land from the Muslims (see Chapter 11). Italian merchants benefited from the crusaders' eastern conquests and were able to establish new mercantile settlements in eastern ports. There the merchants obtained silks, sugar, and spices, which they subsequently carried back to Italy and the west. Although these items were not entirely new to western Europe, they were now traded in increasingly large quantities. At the same time, northern Italy began to experience rapid economic growth from the production of high-quality cloth, which was also in demand.

While the northern Italian cities were busy enlarging the scope of commercial activity in the Mediterranean, the towns of Flanders were doing likewise in northern Europe. Flanders, the area along the coast of present-day Belgium and northern France, was known for the production of a much desired high-quality woolen cloth. Flanders's location made it a logical entrepôt for the traders of northern Europe. Merchants from England, Scandinavia, France, and Germany converged there to trade their wares for woolen cloth. England, in particular, became the chief supplier of raw wool for the Flemish woolen industry. Flanders prospered in the eleventh and twelfth centuries, and such Flemish towns as Bruges and Ghent became centers for the trade and manufacture of woolen cloth.

By the twelfth century, both Italy and Flanders had become centers of a revived trade, making it almost inevitable that a regular exchange of goods would eventually develop between these two major centers of northern and southern European trade. The dangers and difficulties of sea travel around western Europe and the expense of overland journeys meant that such an undertaking would not be easy, however. Adding to the difficulties were local lords who felt free to charge tolls to merchants going through their lands and did not hesitate to plunder caravans carrying goods when they needed money.

As trade contacts increased, however, even lords began to see the advantages of encouraging trade. The best example comes from the counts of Champagne in

Map 10.1 Medieval Trade Routes.

✦ The Medieval Fair. The medieval fairs were places where merchants from northern and southern Europe and from the east could meet and exchange their goods. This fifteenth-century illustration depicts the fair of Lendit, which was held in June of every year outside Paris. At the center is the bishop of Paris, who opened the fair by bestowing his blessings on the participants.

northern France who instituted a series of six fairs held annually in the chief towns of their territory. The counts guaranteed the safety of visiting merchants, supervised the trading activities, and, of course, collected a sales tax on all goods exchanged at the fairs. The fairs of Champagne became the largest commercial marketplace in western Europe where the goods of northern Europe could be exchanged for the goods of southern Europe and the east. Northern merchants brought the furs, woolen cloth, tin, hemp, and honey of northern Europe and exchanged them for the cloth and swords of northern Italy and the silks, sugar, and spices of the east. The prosperity of the Champagne fairs caused lords everywhere, both lay and ecclesiastical, to follow their example and establish trading fairs.

As trade increased, coins came to be in demand at fairs and trading markets of all kinds. Without gold mines of its own, western Europe had few gold coins in circulation before the thirteenth century. Silver and copper coins were most frequently used. Many of the silver coins were minted from silver mined in the Harz Mountains of central Germany, where silver had first been discovered at the end of the tenth century. The

silver penny of England—called sterling for its stability—and the pennies of Paris, Tours, and Anjou became the most important coins in circulation in France and England in the twelfth century.

During the thirteenth century, trade continued to expand to the point that historians speak of a commercial revolution, a term that reflects not only the increased volume of goods traded, but also the development of new commercial practices and institutions, many of which were pioneered by Italian merchants. Those of Venice, Genoa, and Pisa, in particular, prospered in the trade of the Mediterranean area.

The goods of thirteenth-century Italian merchants were shipped in galleys, ships with pointed bows that used sails and/or oars. Because of the need to enter small harbors, the galleys were not large and usually hugged the shoreline to avoid the dangers of the open sea. Sailors could navigate by the sun and stars using the astrolabe, which was first developed in the twelfth century and measured the angle of the sun and stars from the horizon, enabling latitude to be calculated. The most daring trade routes of the thirteenth century took a path through the Straits of Gibraltar along the coast of Portugal and France to England and the Low Countries.

The Italian merchants soon discovered that their growing trade required new ways of raising capital and new commercial practices. They formed partnerships in order to raise capital for ships and goods in overseas journeys. The most common form of partnership was the *commenda*, a temporary business partnership in which one partner contributed money while the other supplied labor and time. If the venture was successful, the partners shared the profits. The Italians also developed insurance to protect their investments, although rates were prohibitively high. New methods of credit, such as bills of exchange or notes on credit, were utilized to circumvent the problem of insufficient reserves of money or the inconvenience of exchanging coins in large transactions. It should be noted, however, that the Italians also minted new gold coins that became standards in western Europe. The gold florin of Florence was first struck in 1252; the Venetian gold ducat in 1284.

Matters of finance were complicated by the problem of usury. The church regarded economic activity as an ethical matter and disapproved of usury, which was defined as pure interest on a loan. The church had condemned usury in 1139 and damned usurers as infamous and unworthy of Christian burial. The church's attitude was troublesome, since the lending of money for productive purposes was crucial to the development of commerce, industry, and banking. Consequently, theologians "discovered" rationalizations and merchants found ways to circumvent the church's ban. Most economic historians doubt that usury laws retarded Europe's economic growth, although they may have caused much grief to individual merchants.

Finally, we should note that banking also grew out of mercantile activity. With so many different coins in circulation, professional moneychangers who knew their values and could exchange them were needed. Soon, moneychangers became involved in lending money as well. As merchants accumulated wealth, they were able to hold large deposits of money and function as bankers. The richest and most prominent early banking houses were Italian. All in all, it was the Italians who took the lead in developing the institutions and methods of the new capitalist system. When it came to making money, northern Europeans looked to the Italians as their teachers.

The Growth of Cities

Most importantly, the revival of commerce fostered the development of urban life. Merchants could not function in a society that emphasized the exaction of labor services and attachment to the land. They needed places where they could build warehouses to store their goods for transshipment and dwelling places that could serve as permanent bases. Medieval cities did not develop just anywhere. To meet merchants' needs, cities were located near sources of protection and alongside rivers or major arteries of some kind that provided favorable routes of transportation.

Towns in the economic sense, as centers of population where merchants and artisans practiced their trades and purchased their food from surrounding territories, had greatly declined in the Early Middle Ages, especially in Europe north of the Alps. Old Roman cities continued to exist but experienced great declines in size and population. Many had become the sees or seats of bishops and archbishops or the strongholds of counts and functioned as administrative centers for both church and state. With the revival of trade, merchants began to settle in these old cities, followed by craftsmen or artisans, men who on manors or elsewhere had developed skills and now perceived the opportunity to ply their trade and produce objects that could be sold by the merchants. In the course of the eleventh and twelfth centuries, the old Roman cities came alive with new populations and growth. By 1100, the old areas of these cities had been repopulated; after 1100, the population outgrew the old walls, necessitating the construction of new city walls outside the old.

In the Mediterranean world, cities had survived in a more visible fashion. Spain's Islamic cities had a flourishing urban life, and southern Italy still possessed such thriving cities as Bari, Salerno, Naples, and Amalfi. Although greatly reduced in size, Rome, the old capital of the Roman world, had survived as the center of papal administration. In northern Italy, Venice had already emerged as a town by the end of the eighth century because of its commercial connections to Byzantium.

Beginning in the late tenth century, many new cities or towns were founded, particularly in northern Europe. Usually, a group of merchants established a settlement near some fortified stronghold, such as a castle or monastery. The original meaning of the English "borough" or "burgh" and the German "burg" as a fortress or walled enclosure is still evident in the name of many cities, such as Edinburgh and Nuremberg. Castles were particularly favored since they were usually located along major routes of transportation or at the intersection of two such trade routes; the lords of the castle also offered protection. If the settlement prospered and expanded, new walls were built to protect it.

Most towns were closely tied to their surrounding territories since they were dependent on the countryside for their food supplies. In addition, they were often part of the territory belonging to a lord and were subject to his jurisdiction. Although lords wanted to treat towns and townspeople as they would their vassals and serfs, cities had totally different needs and a different perspective.

The new class of townspeople did not really fit into the traditional society of the Middle Ages. Since they were not lords, they were not subject to the body of customs that applied to lords. They were not really serfs or peasants either and were reluctant to subject themselves to manorial service, although many may originally have come from the ranks of the peasantry of the surrounding countryside. Merchants and artisans needed mobility to trade. Consequently, these townspeople constituted a revolutionary group who needed their own unique laws to meet their requirements. Since the townspeople were profiting from the growth of trade and sale of their products, they were willing to pay to make their own laws and govern themselves. In many instances, lords and kings saw the potential for vast new sources of revenues and were willing to grant (or, more accurately, sell) the liberties the townspeople were beginning to demand.

By 1100, townspeople were obtaining charters of liberties from their territorial lords, either lay or ecclesiastical, that granted them the privileges they wanted. In most cases, they obtained their goal simply by offering some kind of money payment or regular revenue. Most towns gained at least four basic liberties in their charters. These included a testamentary right, the right to bequeath goods and sell property; freedom from military obligation to the lord; written urban law that guaranteed the freedom of the townspeople; and the right to become a free person after residing a year and a day in the town. The last provision made it possible for a runaway serf who could avoid capture to become a free person in a city. While almost all new urban communities gained these elementary liberties, not all obtained the right to govern themselves. Some communities received only partial self-government; the town's charter provided for a provost to serve as the king's (or lord's) agent and collect taxes and administer justice in the community. Other communities, however, were granted many rights of self-government. In 1130, King Henry I granted London a charter that gave the citizens the right to choose their own officials, essentially the right of self-government. Moreover, the Londoners had the right to administer their own courts of law. While taxes were still paid to the king, they were collected by the city's officials, not the king's.

Often urban communities found that their lords were unwilling to grant them all the liberties they wanted, especially self-government. Bishops in cathedral cities were particularly tenacious of their privileges. In these cities, merchants and serfs lived in the same community; to grant freedom meant the loss of the services of the serfs who tilled the fields outside the city. Thus, for a bishop to grant self-government to local officials within his city meant the end of his own authority. Where townspeople experienced difficulty in obtaining privileges, they often swore an oath, forming an association called a commune, and resorted to force against their lay or ecclesiastical lords.

Communes made their first appearance in Italy where, even in the Early Middle Ages, urban communities continued to exist. In northern Italy, in the regions called Tuscany and Lombardy, towns were governed by their bishops, but the nobles whose lands surrounded the cities took an active interest in the towns, whether they lived there or not. Bishops were usually supported by the emperors, who used them as their chief administrators. In the eleventh century, city residents rebelled against the rule of the bishops, swore communal associations with the bishops' noble vassals, and overthrew the authority of the bishops by force. The alliance between town residents and rural nobles was overwhelming, and in the course of the eleventh and twelfth centuries, bishops were shorn of their authority. Communes took over the rights of government and created new offices, such as consuls and city councils, for self-rule. Pisa, Milan, Arezzo, and Genoa all had attained self-government by the end of the eleventh century.

Although communes were also sworn in northern Europe, especially in France and Flanders, townspeople did not have the support of rural nobles. Revolts against lay lords were usually brutally suppressed; those against bishops, as in Laon at the beginning of the twelfth century (see the box on p. 313), were more frequently

◆ **The Fortified Town of Carcassonne.** The expansion of commerce and industry led to an ongoing growth of towns and cities in the High Middle Ages. As seen in this picture of the French town of Carcassonne, medieval towns were surrounded by walls strengthened by defensive towers and punctuated by gates. As is evident here, medieval urban skylines were dominated by towers of all kinds.

The growth of towns and cities was a major aspect of economic life in the High Middle Ages. When townspeople were unable to gain basic liberties for themselves from the lord in whose territory their town was located, they sometimes swore a "commune" to gain these privileges by force. This selection by a contemporary abbot describes the violence that accompanied the formation of a commune at Laon in France in 1116. The bishop of Laon, lord of the town, had granted privileges to the townspeople in return for a large payment. Later he rescinded his grant, thereby angering the citizens.

The Autobiography of Guibert, Abbot of Nogent-sous-Coucy

All the efforts of the prelate and nobles in these days were reserved for fleecing their inferiors. But those inferiors were no longer moved by mere anger, but goaded into a murderous lust for the death of the Bishop and his accomplices and bound themselves by oath to effect their purpose. Now they say that four hundred took the oath. Such a mob could not be secret and when it came to the ears of Anselm toward evening of the holy Sabbath, he sent word to the Bishop, as he was retiring to rest, not to go out to the early morning service, knowing that if he did he must certainly be killed. But he, infatuated with excessive pride said, "Fie, surely I shall not perish at the hands of such. . . ."

The next day, that is, the fifth in Easter week, after midday, as he was engaged in business with Archdeacon Walter about the getting of money, behold there arose a disorderly noise throughout the city, men shouting "Commune!" and again through the middle of the chapel of the Blessed Mary through that door by which the murderers of Gerard had come and gone, there citizens now entered the Bishop's court with swords, battle-axes, bows and hatchets, and carrying clubs and spears, a very great company. As soon as this sudden attack was discovered, the nobles rallied from all sides to the Bishop, having sworn to give him aid against such an onset, if it should occur. . . . [Despite the assistance of the nobles, the commoners were victorious.]

Next the outrageous mob attacking the Bishop and howling before the walls of his palace, he with some who were aiding him fought them off by hurling of stones and shooting of arrows. For he now, as at all times, showed great spirit as a fighter, but because he had wrongly and in vain taken up another sword, by the sword he perished. Therefore, being unable to stand against the reckless assaults of the people, he put on the clothes of one of his servants and flying to the vaults of the church hid himself in a cask, shut up in which with the head fastened on by a faithful follower he thought himself safely hidden. And as they ran hither and thither demanding where, not the Bishop, but the hangdog, was, they seized one of his pages, but through his faithfulness could not get what they wanted. Laying hands on another, they learned from the traitor's nod where to look for him. Entering the vaults therefore, and searching everywhere, at last they found [him]. . . .

[The bishop] therefore, sinner though he was, yet the Lord's anointed, was dragged forth from the cask by the hair, beaten with many blows and brought out into the open air in the narrow lane of the clergy's cloister before the house of the chaplain Godfrey. And as he piteously implored them, ready to take oath that he would henceforth cease to be their Bishop, that he would leave the country, and as they with hardened hearts jeered at him, one named Bernard . . . lifting his battle-axe brutally dashed out the brains of that sacred, though sinner's, head, and he slipping between the hands of those who held him, was dead before he reached the ground stricken by another thwart blow under the eye-sockets and across the middle of the nose. There brought to his end, his legs were cut off and many another wound inflicted. But Thibaut seeing the ring on the finger of the erstwhile prelate and not being able to draw it off, cut off the dead man's finger and took it. And so stripped to his skin he was thrown into a corner in front of his chaplain's house. My God, who shall recount the mocking words that were thrown at him by passersby, as he lay there, and with what clods and stones and dirt his corpse was covered?

successful. When they succeeded, communes received the right to choose their own officials, hold their own courts, and run their own cities. Unlike the towns in Italy, however, where the decline of the emperor's authority ensured that the northern Italian cities could function as self-governing republics, towns in France and England did not become independent city-states, but remained ultimately subject to royal authority.

Medieval cities, then, possessed varying degrees of self-government depending upon the amount of control retained over them by the lord or king in whose territory they were located. Nevertheless, all towns, regardless of the degree of outside control, evolved governmental institutions for running the affairs of the community.

Medieval cities defined citizenship narrowly and accorded it only to males who had been born in the city or had lived there for some time. In many cities, citizens elected members of a city council that bore primary responsibility for running the affairs of the city. City councillors (known as consuls in Italy and southern France) not only enacted legislation but also served as judges and city magistrates. Election of city councillors was by no means democratic. The electoral process was carefully engineered to ensure that only members of the wealthiest and most powerful families, who came to be called the patricians, were elected. They kept the reins of government in their hands despite periodic protests from lesser merchants and artisans.

In the twelfth and thirteenth centuries, cities added some kind of sole executive leader, even if he was only a figurehead. Although the title varied from town to town, this executive officer was frequently called a mayor. Mayors could be appointed by the lord or king or elected by the councillors or citizens. In Italy, the executive came to be known as a *podestá*, literally a person with power. Because of the bitter internal feuds

◆ **Execution of a Criminal.** Violence was a common feature of medieval life. Criminals, if apprehended, were punished quickly and severely. In this illustration, a highwayman caught in the provinces has been brought to Paris for execution by beheading. Public executions were considered a deterrent to crime, although one can surmise from this well-attended event that they were also a form of entertainment.

within their cities, Italians frequently brought in an outsider as an impartial party to be *podestá* and restore order. He was supposed to rule for only one year, but occasionally tried to prolong his tenure. In some areas, especially Italy, guilds also became closely involved in government. In Florence, for example, each of the major guilds supplied a set number of representatives to the city council.

City governments kept close watch over the activities of their community; some historians have used the phrase "municipal socialism" to describe the all-encompassing role played by medieval city governments. To care for the welfare and safety of the community, a government might regulate air and water pollution; provide water barrels and delegate responsibility to people in every section of the town to fight fires, which were an ever-present danger; construct warehouses to stockpile grain in the event of food emergencies; and establish and supervise the standards of weights and measures used in the various local goods and industries. Although violence was a way of life in the Middle Ages, urban crime was not a major problem in the towns of the High Middle Ages. The relatively small size of the communities made it difficult for criminals to operate openly. Nevertheless, medieval urban governments did organize town guards to patrol the streets by night and the city walls by day. People caught committing criminal acts were quickly tried for their offenses. Serious offenses, such as murder, were punished by execution, usually by hanging. Lesser crimes were punished by fines, flogging, or branding.

Whatever their condition or degree of independence, medieval cities remained relatively small in comparison to either ancient or modern cities. In the High Middle Ages, a large trading city would number about 5,000 inhabitants. By 1300, London was the largest city in England with almost 40,000 people. Otherwise, north of the Alps, only a few great centers of commerce, such as Bruges and Ghent, had a population close to 40,000. Italian cities tended to be larger, with Venice, Florence, Genoa, Milan, and Naples numbering almost 100,000. Even the largest European city, however, seemed insignificant alongside the Byzantine capital of Constantinople or the Arab cities of Damascus, Baghdad, and Cairo. For a long time to come, Europe remained predominantly rural. However, the wealth of the cities guaranteed that they would have a significantly disproportionate influence on the political and economic life of Europe. In the long run, the rise of towns and the development of commerce laid the foundations for the eventual transformation of Europe from a rural agricultural society to an urban industrial one.

LIFE IN THE MEDIEVAL CITY

A primary feature of every medieval city was its stone walls, punctuated by a series of defensive towers and gates. Walls were intended to protect urban inhabitants and their dwellings from attack, but they also enabled towns to collect taxes on goods coming into the town and to regulate the flow of both people and goods.

Within the city walls, space was at a premium so almost every inch was tightly filled, giving medieval cities their characteristic appearance of narrow, winding streets with houses crowded against each other. Only town squares, used for selling wares or as places for public executions and the mustering of troops, and vacant areas around churches and palaces provided any kind of open space. Streets, generally left unpaved until the thirteenth century, were narrow with buildings fronting directly on them. To gain more space, inhabitants frequently added balconies or built the second and third stories of their dwellings out over the streets. Since dwellings were constructed mostly of wood before the fourteenth century and candles and wood fires were used for light and heat, the danger of fire was great. Medieval cities burned rapidly once a fire started.

A medieval urban skyline was dominated by the towers of castles and town halls, but especially of churches, whose number was often staggering. At the beginning of the thirteenth century, London had 120 churches. If a city was the center of a bishop's see, a large cathedral would dominate the other buildings and be visible for miles outside the city. Monastic and parish churches added to the number of churches.

Castles were second in importance to churches, but their number varied depending on the location of the cities. Since the Italian landed nobles established their residences in towns near their estates and were not even adverse to engaging in mercantile activities, the towers of their castles dotted the Italian urban skyscape. Although less common, the castles of kings, lords, and bishops were also found in northern cities. Paris, for example, was dominated by two royal castles, the Louvre and Bastille, as well as a small castle for the king's agent.

Churches and castles had a certain number of people attached to them, but the majority of urban residents consisted of merchants involved in trade and artisans active in manufacturing of some kind. Generally, merchants and artisans had their own sections within a city. The merchant area included warehouses, inns, and taverns. Artisan sections were usually divided along craft lines, and each craft had its own street where its activity was pursued.

◆ **Shops in a Medieval Town.** Most urban residents were merchants involved in trade and artisans who manufactured a wide variety of products. Master craftsmen had their workshops in the ground-level rooms of their houses. In this illustration, two well-dressed burghers are touring the shopping districts of a French town. Tailors, furriers, a barber, and a grocer (from left to right) are visible at work in their shops.

Collectively, the merchants and artisans came to be known as burghers or the bourgeoisie, the people of a town living within a walled enclosure (*burgus*, a Latinized version of the German word *burg*). There were, of course, enormous differences within their ranks. Wealthy merchants and struggling artisans were widely separated economically and socially. Nevertheless, as townspeople, they were all legally free, lived under a common town government, and faced the common opposition of the nobles, who, outside Italy, feared that the bourgeoisie were serious rivals for their position at the top of society. These men of money with their freedom to come and go seemed in many ways to threaten the closely ordered rural world of the Middle Ages where everything was supposed to have a fixed place. Kings shared this hostility initially, but quickly perceived the potential for new tax revenues from townspeople that helped the monarchies free themselves from feudal ties and create new systems of government.

The physical environment of medieval cities was not pleasant. They were often dirty and rife with smells from animal and human waste deposited in backyard privies or on the streets (see the box on p. 316). In some places, city governments required citizens to make periodic collections of garbage and waste and cart it outside the

Environmental pollution is not new to the twentieth century. Medieval cities and towns had their own problems with filthy living conditions. This excerpt is taken from an order sent by the king of England to the town of Boutham. It demands rectification of the town's pitiful physical conditions. There is little evidence to indicate that the king's order changed the situation dramatically.

The King's Command to Boutham

To the bailiffs of the abbot of St. Mary's, York, at Boutham. Whereas it is sufficiently evident that the pavement of the said town of Boutham is so very greatly broke up that all and singular passing and going through that town sustain immoderate damages and grievances, and in addition the air is so corrupted and infected by the pigsties situated in the king's highways and in the lanes of that town and by the swine feeding and frequently wandering about in the streets and lanes and by dung and dunghills and many other foul things placed in the streets and lanes, that great repugnance overtakes the king's ministers staying in that town and also others there dwelling and passing through, the advantage of more wholesome air is impeded; the state of men is grievously injured, and other unbearable inconveniences and many other injuries are known to proceed from such corruption, to the nuisance of the king's ministers aforesaid and of others there dwelling and passing through, and to the peril of their lives. . . the king, being unwilling longer to tolerate such great and unbearable defects there, orders the bailiffs to cause the pavement to be suitably repaired within their liberty before All Saints next, and to cause the pigsties, aforesaid streets and lanes to be cleansed from all dung and dunghills, and to cause proclamation to be made throughout their bailiwick forbidding any one, under pain of grievous forfeiture, to cause or permit their swine to feed or wander outside his house in the king's streets or the lanes aforesaid.

---

walls. Atmospheric pollution was also a fact of life, not only from the ubiquitous wood fires, but also from the use of a cheaper fuel, coal, used industrially by lime-burners, brewers, and dyers, as well as poor people who could not afford to purchase wood. The coal most frequently used, surface-mined and "sea" coal, produced ill-smelling, noxious fumes. Although the use of sea coal was prohibited under pain of fine, the laws do not seem to have been enforced.

Cities were also unable to prevent industrial water pollution, especially from the tanning and animal-slaughtering industries. Both industries were forced, however, to locate downstream to avoid polluting the water used by the city upstream. Butchers dumped blood and all remaining waste products from their butchered animals into the river while tanners unloaded tannic acids, dried blood, fat, hair, and the other waste products of their operations. Since tanneries and slaughterhouses existed in virtually every medieval town, rivers rapidly became polluted.

Because of the pollution, cities were not inclined to use the rivers for drinking water but relied instead on wells. Occasionally, communities repaired the system of aqueducts left over from Roman times and sometimes even constructed new ones. Private and public baths also existed in medieval towns, and it is fair to say that standards of hygiene were rather high in the twelfth and thirteenth centuries. Paris, for example, had thirty-two public baths for men and women. City statutes forbade lepers and people with "bad reputations" from using them. This did not prevent public baths from gaining a reputation for permissiveness due to public nudity. One contemporary commented on what occurred in public bathhouses: "Shameful things. Men make a point of staying all night in the public baths and women at the break of day come in and through 'ignorance' find themselves in the men's rooms."[1] Authorities came under increasing pressure to close the bathhouses down, and the great plague of the fourteenth century sealed their fate. The standards of medieval hygiene broke down, and late medieval and early modern European society would prove to be remarkably dirty.

Because of the limited space in medieval towns, houses were narrow, built next to one another, and usually multistoried. In many houses, the shops or workrooms of merchants and craftspeople occupied the ground floor. Inhabitants, who might include husband and wife, children, servants, and apprentices, would live on the upper floors.

For most ordinary merchants and artisans, home life and work life were thus closely intertwined. Merchants and artisans taught their trades to their children and their wives and apprentices; or their children might be apprenticed to another merchant or artisan. Women, in addition to supervising the household, purchasing food and preparing meals, washing clothes, and managing the family finances, were also often expected to help their husbands in their trades. Some women also developed their own trades to earn extra money. Margery Kempe, for example, although the daughter of a mayor and the wife of a wealthy merchant, pursued the trade of brewing ale. When some guild masters died, their widows even carried on their trades. Some women in medieval towns were thus able to lead lives of considerable independence.

INDUSTRY IN MEDIEVAL CITIES

Although peasants in rural villages continued to make many of the items they needed, the revival of trade enabled cities and towns to become important centers for manufacturing a wide range of goods, such as cloth, metalwork, shoes, and leather goods. A host of crafts were carried on in houses located in the narrow streets of the medieval cities. From the twelfth century on, artisans began to organize themselves into guilds, which came to play a leading role in the economic life of the cities.

Originally, guilds were community organizations created by townspeople to meet their common needs and functioned primarily as social and religious fraternities. They gave members a sense of security and companionship, provided financial assistance to the elderly, widows, and orphans, financed religious festivals, and contributed to the building and maintenance of local churches. By acquiring a monopoly on a community's business for the guild's members, they provided economic protection. Since medieval towns were relatively small, there might be only one guild for all merchants and artisans. Gradually, however, merchants separated themselves from the artisans, and by the middle of the thirteenth century, there were individual craft guilds for virtually every craft, such as tanners, carpenters, and bakers, as well as separate guilds for specialized groups of merchants, such as dealers in silk, spices, wool, or banking. Florence alone, for example, had fifty different guilds. Some communities were so comprehensive in covering all trades that they even had guilds for prostitutes.

In addition to their social and religious functions, guilds gradually came to organize and direct almost every aspect of the production process. They established standards for the articles produced, specified the actual methods of production to be used, and even fixed the price at which the finished goods could be sold; the latter in many instances was set in accordance with the church's doctrine of a "just price" based on equitable

bargaining in an open market. Guilds also established the conditions of labor by determining the number of people who could enter a specific trade and the procedure they must follow to do so. A person aspiring to learn a trade first became an apprentice to a master craftsman, usually around the age of ten. Apprentices were not paid, but did receive room and board from their masters. After a specified term of service, usually five to seven years, in which they learned their craft, apprentices became journeymen (or journeywomen, although most were male) who then worked for wages for other masters. Journeymen aspired to become masters as well. To do so, they were expected to produce a "masterpiece," a finished piece in their craft that allowed the master craftsmen of the guild to judge whether the journeymen were qualified to become masters and join the guild. Even if they passed this test, they might still have to serve as journeyman to a master craftsman until they accumulated sufficient capital to open their own

◆ **The Dyeing of Cloth.** The revival of trade encouraged the manufacture of a wide range of goods in towns and cities. During the High Middle Ages, the production of woolen cloth was especially prominent in Flanders and northern Italy. The transformation of raw wool into finished cloth required a large number of different activities. This illustration shows workers in a dyehouse laboring over a hot vat in which pieces of cloth are being dyed.

shop and become masters themselves. In fact, many failed to do so and remained journeymen. Some who were successful did not become masters until they were fairly old.

Craft guilds continued to dominate manufacturing in those industries where raw materials could be acquired locally and the products sold locally. But in those industries that required raw materials from outside the local area to produce high-quality products for growing markets abroad, a new form of industry dependent on large concentrations of capital and unskilled labor began to emerge. Viewed by some observers as the beginning of commercial capitalism, it was particularly evident in the "putting-out" or domestic system used in the production of woolen cloth in both Flanders and northern Italy. An entrepreneur, whose initial capital outlay probably came from commercial activities, bought raw wool and distributed it to workers who carried out the various stages of carding, spinning, weaving, and dyeing to produce a finished piece of woolen cloth. These laborers worked in their own homes and were paid wages. As wage earners, they were dependent upon their employers and the fluctuations in prices for the finished goods that occurred periodically in the international market. The entrepreneur collected the final products and sold the finished cloth, earning a profit that could then be invested in more production. Woolen industries operated by capitalist entrepreneurs in seventeen principal centers in Flanders and northern Europe produced most of the woolen cloth used in northern Europe. An Italian chronicler at the beginning of the fourteenth century estimated that the woolen industry in Florence produced 80,000 pieces of cloth a year and employed 30,000 men, women, and children, usually at pitiful wages.

The Aristocracy of the High Middle Ages

In the High Middle Ages, European society was dominated by a group of men whose primary preoccupation was warfare. King Alfred of England had said that a "well-peopled land" must have "men of prayer, men of war, and men of work," and medieval ideals held to the tripartite division of society into these three basic groups. The "men of war" were the aristocracy who came to form a distinct social group, albeit one with considerable variations in wealth among its members. Nevertheless, they, along with their wives and children, shared a common ethos and a distinctive lifestyle.

The Significance of the Aristocracy

King Alfred's "men of war" were the lords and vassals of medieval society. The lords were the kings, dukes, counts, barons, and viscounts (and even bishops and archbishops) who held extensive lands and considerable political power. They and others formed an aristocracy or nobility that since Carolingian times had consisted of people who exercised real political, economic, and social power. Nobles relied for military help on knights, mounted warriors who fought for them in return for weapons and daily sustenance. Knights were by no means the social equals of nobles; many knights in fact possessed little more than peasants. But in the course of the twelfth and thirteenth centuries, especially in England, France, and Spain, knights improved their social status and joined the ranks of the nobility. In the process, noble and knight came to mean much the same thing, and warfare likewise tended to become a distinguishing characteristic of a nobleman. The great lords and knights came to form a common caste; they were warriors and the institution of knighthood united them. Nevertheless, there were also social divisions among them based on extremes of wealth and landholdings.

Medieval theory maintained that the warlike qualities of the nobility were justified by their role as defenders of society. Knights, however, were also notorious for fighting each other. The Catholic church intervened, and though it could not stop the incessant bloodletting, it did at least try to limit it by instituting the Peace of God. Beginning in the eleventh century, the church encouraged knights to take an oath to respect churches and pilgrimage centers and to refrain from attacking noncombatants, such as clergy, poor people, merchants, and women. It was, of course, permissible to continue killing each other. At the same time, the church initiated the Truce of God, which forbade fighting on Sundays and the primary feast days.

These peace movements did not depend solely upon the pious pronouncements of church leaders and councils. By the end of the eleventh century, Europeans were forming peace associations at the local level in which members took oaths to enforce the Peace and Truce of God; armies were even created to enforce them. In some territories, rulers themselves realized how important it was to minimize private warfare if they were to strengthen their own power. The duke of Normandy, for example, transformed the Peace of God into the Peace of the Duke.

As the church moved to diminish fighting, it also worked to redirect the nobility's warlike energy into different channels, such as crusades against the Muslims (see Chapter 11), and was quite willing to justify violence when used against peace-breakers and especially against the infidel. Hence, being a warrior on behalf of God easily vindicated the nobility's love of war and, in fact, justified their high social status as the defenders of Christian society. The church even furthered this process by steeping knighthood in Christian values. The formal reception of one's arms became a religious ceremony, and weapons were blessed by a priest for Christian service. Throughout the Middle Ages, there remained a constant tension between the ideals of a religion founded on the ideal of peace and the ethos of a nobility based on the love of war.

The Daily Life of the European Nobility

The growth of the European nobility in the High Middle Ages was made visible by an increasing number of castles scattered across the landscape. Although castle architecture varied considerably, castles did possess two common features: they were permanent residences for the noble family, its retainers, and servants, and they were defensible fortifications. The earliest castles were built of wood, but by the eleventh century, they were beginning to be constructed of stone. Initially, the basic castle plan consisted of two parts: a motte, which was an artificial or natural steep-sided hill, and a bailey, an open space adjacent to the motte. Both motte and bailey were then encircled by large stone walls. Built on the motte was the keep, the central citadel of the castle. Constructed of massively thick stone walls, the keep was a large, multistoried building. On the ground floor were the kitchens and stables; the basement housed storerooms for equipment and foodstuffs. Above the ground floor was the great hall, a very large room that served a number of important functions. Here the lord of the castle administered justice and received visitors; here too, the inhabitants of the castle ate and even slept. Smaller rooms might open off the great hall: some bedrooms with huge curtained beds with straw mattresses, latrines, and possibly a chapel. The growing wealth of the High Middle Ages made it possible for the European nobility to improve their standard of living. As nobles sought to buy more luxury goods, such as better clothes, jewelry, and exotic spices, so too did they build more elaborate castles with thicker walls and more stone buildings and towers with more lavishly decorated interiors.

◆ **Castle and Aristocrats.** This illustration from the *Trés Riches Heures* of Jean, duke of Berry, depicts the Chateau of Dourdan, France, and its surrounding lands. In the foreground, elaborately dressed aristocratic men and women are seen amusing themselves.

ARISTOCRATIC WOMEN

Although women could legally hold and inherit property, most women remained under the control of men—of their fathers until they married and of their husbands after they married. Nevertheless, aristocratic women had numerous opportunities for playing important roles. Since the lord was often away at war, on crusade, or at court, the lady of the castle had to manage the estate, a considerable responsibility in view of the fact that households, even of lesser aristocrats, could include large numbers of officials and servants. Keeping financial accounts, both for the household and for the landed estate, alone required considerable financial knowledge. The lady of the castle was also responsible on a regular basis for overseeing the food supply and maintaining all other supplies for the smooth operation of the household.

Childhood ended early for the daughters of aristocrats. Since aristocratic girls were married in their teens (usually at the age of fifteen or sixteen) and were expected by their husbands to assume their responsibilities immediately, the training of girls in a large body of practical knowledge could never start too early. Sent at a young age to the castles of other nobles to be brought up, girls were trained as ladies-in-waiting. The lady of the castle taught them how to sew and weave and instructed them in all the skills needed for running an estate. They also learned some reading and writing, dancing, singing, and how to play musical instruments.

♦ **Aristocratic Lady.** This tapestry depicts a French lady sitting in her garden working on a needlepoint design. She is attended by a lady-in-waiting. Aristocratic wives were expected to oversee the food supply of the castle, supervise the activities of the servants, and at times manage the estate lands.

Although women were expected to be subservient to their husbands (see the box on p. 321), medieval chronicles contain numerous accounts of strong women who advised and sometimes even dominated their husbands. Perhaps the most famous was Eleanor of Aquitaine (c. 1122–1204), heiress to the duchy of Aquitaine in southwestern France. Married to King Louis VII of France, Eleanor accompanied her husband on a crusade, but her alleged affair with her uncle during the crusade led Louis to have their marriage annulled. Eleanor then married Henry, duke of Normandy and count of Anjou, who became King Henry II of England. She took an active role in politics, even assisting her sons in rebelling against Henry in 1173–1174. Imprisoned for her activities, after Henry's death she again assumed an active political life, providing both military and political support for her sons.

Blanche of Castile (1188–1252) was another powerful medieval queen. She became regent while her son Louis IX was a boy and ruled France with a powerful hand during much of the 1220s and 1230s. She repelled the attempt of some rebellious French nobles to seize her son, the young king, and defeated Henry III of England when he tried to incite an uprising in France in order to reconquer Normandy. Blanche's political sense was so astute that even when Louis X came of age he continued to rely on her as his chief adviser. One medieval chronicler gave her the highest compliment he could think of: "she ruled as well as a man."

THE WAY OF THE WARRIOR

At the age of seven or eight, boys were sent either to a clerical school to pursue a religious career or to another nobleman's castle where they prepared for the life of a noble. Their chief lessons were military; they learned how to joust, hunt, ride, and handle weapons properly. Occasionally, aristocrats' sons might also learn the basic fundamentals of reading and writing.

After his apprenticeship in knighthood, at about the age of twenty-one, a young man formally entered the adult world in a ceremony of "knighting." What had been a simple ceremony in the tenth century had grown to elaborate proportions by the twelfth, including a high degree of Christian symbolism. The day before the ceremony, the prospective knight took a bath of purification, was dressed in white, and passed the night in prayer. On the next day, mass was heard before the actual ceremony, in which the sponsor put a sword on the young candidate and struck him on the cheek or neck with an open hand (or later touched him three

Women in Medieval Thought

Whether a nun or the wife of an aristocrat, townsman, or peasant, a woman in the Middle Ages was considered inferior to a man and by nature subject to a man's authority. Although there are a number of examples of strong women who flew in the face of such attitudes, church teachings also reinforced these notions. The first selection from Gratian, the twelfth-century jurist who wrote the first systematic work on canon law, supports this view. The second selection was written by a wealthy fifty-year-old merchant in Paris who wanted to instruct his fifteen-year-old bride on how to be a good wife.

Gratian, *Decretum*

Women should be subject to their men. The natural order for mankind is that women should serve men and children their parents, for it is just that the lesser serve the greater.

The image of God is in man and it is one. Women were drawn from man, who has God's jurisdiction as if he were God's vicar, because he has the image of the one God. Therefore woman is not made in God's image.

Woman's authority is nil; let her in all things be subject to the rule of man. . . . And neither can she teach, nor be a witness, nor give a guarantee, nor sit in judgment.

Adam was beguiled by Eve, not she by him. It is right that he whom woman led into wrongdoing should have her under his direction, so that he may not fail a second time through female-levity.

A Merchant of Paris, On Marriage

I entreat you to keep his linen clean, for this is up to you. Because the care of outside affairs is men's work, a husband must look after these things, and go and come, run here and there in rain, wind, snow, and hail—sometimes wet, sometimes dry, sometimes sweating, other times shivering, badly fed, badly housed, badly shod, badly bedded—and nothing harms him because he is cheered by the anticipation of the care his wife will take of him on his return—of the pleasures, joys, and comforts she will provide, or have provided for him in her presence: to have his shoes off before a good fire, to have his feet washed, to have clean shoes and hose, to be well fed, provided with good drink, well served, well honored, well bedded in white sheets and white nightcaps, well covered with good furs, and comforted with other joys and amusements, intimacies, affections, and secrets about which I am silent. And on the next day fresh linen and garments. . . .

Also keep peace with him. Remember the country proverb that says there are three things that drive a good man from his home: a house with a bad roof, a smoking chimney, and a quarrelsome woman. I beg you, in order to preserve your husband's love and good will, be loving, amiable, and sweet with him. . . . Thus protect and shield your husband from all troubles, give him all the comfort you can think of, wait on him, and have him waited on in your home. . . . If you do what is said here, he will always have his affection and his heart turned toward you and your service, and he will forsake all other homes, all other women, all other help, and all other households.

times on the shoulder with the blade of a sword), possibly signifying the passing of the sponsor's military valor to the new knight. Other Christian elements included the blessing of the knight's sword and the knight's sacred oath to defend the church, widows, orphans, and the weak and to uphold good and pursue evil. This ceremony, like the noble's life itself, managed to combine God and war without any great discomfort or apparent contradiction.

In the eleventh and twelfth centuries, under the influence of the church, an ideal of civilized courtliness called chivalry gradually evolved among the nobility. Chivalry represented a code of ethics that knights were supposed to uphold. In addition to their oath to defend the church and the defenseless, knights were expected to treat captives as honored guests instead of putting them in dungeons. Knightly honor also demanded that unarmed knights should not be attacked. Chivalry also implied that knights should fight only for glory, but this account of a group of English knights by a medieval chronicler reveals another motive for battle: "The whole city was plundered to the last farthing, and then they proceeded to rob all the churches throughout the city, . . . and seizing gold and silver, cloth of all colors, women's ornaments, gold rings, goblets, and precious stones. . . . they all returned to their own lords rich men."[2] Apparently, not all chivalric ideals were taken seriously.

After his formal initiation into the world of warriors, a young man returned home to find himself once again subject to his parents' authority. A special name, *juvenes* (Latin for youths), was given to these young men who had to wait for their fathers to die before they could come into their inheritance and establish their own households. Sometimes, these "young men" were in their thirties or even forties before they were able to do so.

The *juvenes* were left in an awkward position. They were adults with no adult responsibilities. Since they had been trained to be warriors, they naturally gravitated toward military activities and often engaged in the private warfare endemic to the noble class. In the twelfth century, tournaments began to appear as an alternative to the socially destructive fighting that the church was increasingly trying to curb. Initially, tournaments consisted of the "melee," a mock battle in which warriors on horseback fought in open-ended combat. The goal was to take prisoners who would then be ransomed, making success in tournaments a path to considerable gain. Within an eight-month span, the English knight William Marshall made a tour of the tournament circuit, defeated 203 knights, and made so much money that he had to hire two clerks to take care

of it. By the late twelfth century, the "melee" was preceded by the joust or individual combat between two knights. Gradually, the joust became the main part of the tournament. No matter how much the church condemned tournaments, knights themselves continued to see them as an excellent way to train for war. As one knight explained, "a knight cannot distinguish himself in that [war] if he has not trained for it in tourneys. He must have seen his blood flow, heard his teeth crack under fist blows, felt his opponent's weight bear down upon him as he lay on the ground and, after being twenty times unhorsed, have risen twenty times to fight."[3]

Tournaments alone, however, did not satisfy the cravings of young men to participate in the one major activity they had been trained for. The best training for war was battle itself. Bertran de Born, a French nobleman and poet, captured the nobles' love of war:

✦ **The Tournament.** The tournament arose as a socially acceptable alternative to the private warfare that plagued the nobility. This illustration from *The Book of Tourneys* by King

René of Anjou shows knights lined up for a mock battle. At the top red-robed judges and female supporters, seated in boxes, look on.

Not so much joy in sleep have I,
Eating and drinking pleases me less
Than hearing on all sides the cry
"At them!" and horses riderless
Among the woodlands neighing.
And well I like to hear the call
Of "Help!" and see the wounded fall,
Loudly for mercy praying,
And see the dead, both great and small,
Pierced by sharp spearheads one and all.[4]

It is this eagerness to do battle that helps to explain the enthusiasm of the young knights for pursuing their destinies in the crusades of the twelfth and thirteenth centuries (see Chapter 11). What better opportunity to gain glory, rewards, and possibly even salvation itself.

MARRIAGE PATTERNS OF THE ARISTOCRACY

Among aristocrats, marriages were expected to establish alliances with other families, bring new wealth, and provide heirs to carry on the family line. Thus, parents supervised the choice of spouses for their children. One of the most noticeable features of aristocratic marriage patterns was the usually wide discrepancy in the ages of the marital partners. Daughters of nobles married when they were in their teens—usually at fifteen or sixteen. But their husbands might be in their thirties or even forties since *juvenes* did not marry until they came into their inheritances.

The marriage ritual took place first at the door of the local church in a brief ceremony that included the granting of family consent as well as an exchange of vows by the couple to be faithful to each other. This brief ceremony was usually performed in front of witnesses, but the taking of the mutual oath, even without witnesses, still constituted a valid marriage in the eyes of the church. The wedding party then entered the church for a mass and blessing by the priest.

By the twelfth century, the efforts of the church since Carolingian times to end divorce (see Chapter 8) had borne much fruit. As a sacrament, marriage was intended to last for a lifetime and could not be dissolved. In certain cases, however, the church accepted the right of married persons to separate by granting them an annulment or official recognition that their marriage had not been valid in the first place. If it could be established that the couple had not consented to the marriage, that one or the other suffered from a sexual incapacity that prevented the consummation of the marriage, or that the couple were related by blood (more

◆ **Marriage.** Marriage festivities for members of the aristocracy were usually quite elaborate. As seen in this illustration of the marriage of Renaud de Montaubon and Clarisse, daughter of the ruler of Gascogne, after festivities the wedding party would accompany the new couple to their bedroom to prepare them for the physical consummation of their marriage. Only after physical union was a medieval marriage considered valid.

closely than sixth and, after 1215, third cousins), then the church would approve an annulment of their marriage, and the partners would be free to marry again.

The Emergence and Growth of European Kingdoms, 1000–1300

The political organization of Europe had been severely tested by the internal disintegration of the Carolingian Empire and the invasions of the ninth and tenth centuries. The feudal institutions that emerged during that period persisted and, indeed, reached their high point in the eleventh and twelfth centuries. Similarly, the domination of society by the nobility reached its apex in the High Middle Ages. At the same time, kings began, however slowly, the process of extending their power in more effective ways. Out of this growth in the monarchies would eventually come the European kingdoms that dominated much of later European history.

In theory, kings were regarded as the heads of their kingdoms and were expected to lead their vassals and subjects into battle. The king's power, however, was strictly limited. He had to honor the rights and privileges of his vassals and in the case of disputes had to resolve them by principles of established law. If he failed to observe his vassals' rights, they could and did rebel. Weak kings were overthrown or, like later Carolingians, replaced by another ruling dynasty.

In retrospect, however, one can see that kings did possess some sources of power that other influential lords did not. Kings were anointed by holy oil in ceremonies reminiscent of Old Testament precedents; thus, their positions seemed sanctioned by divine favor. War and marriage alliances enabled them to increase their power, and their conquests enabled them to reward their followers with grants of land and bind powerful nobles to them. In the eleventh and twelfth centuries, kings found ways to extend their powers and, by 1200, had begun to develop the administrative machinery of centralized government. The revival of commerce, the growth of cities, and the emergence of a money economy eventually undermined feudalism by enabling monarchs to hire soldiers and officials and to rely less on vassals.

England in the High Middle Ages

At the beginning of the eleventh century, Anglo-Saxon England had fallen subject to Scandinavian control after a successful invasion by the Danes in 1016. King Canute (1016–1035), however, continued English institutions and laws and even supported the Catholic church. His dynastic line proved unable to maintain itself, and in 1042, the Anglo-Saxon line of kings was restored in the person of Edward the Confessor (1042–1066). After his death, the kingship was taken by Harold Godwinson who belonged to one of England's greatest noble families.

A cousin of Edward the Confessor, William of Normandy, laid claim to the throne of England, however, and invaded England in the fall of 1066. The forces of Harold Godwinson and Duke William met at Hastings on October 14, 1066. The Saxon infantry was soundly defeated by the heavily armed Norman knights. Although it was another five years before the Anglo-Saxons were finally pacified, William was crowned king of England at Christmas time in London.

After his conquest, William (1066–1087) treated all of England as a royal possession. Based on the Domesday Book, which William commissioned in 1086 by sending out royal officials to ascertain who owned or held land in tenancy, modern historians have estimated that the Norman royal family took possession of about one-fifth of the land in England as the royal demesne. The remaining English land was held by nobles or the church as fiefs of the king; each of these vassals in turn was responsible for supplying a quota of knights for the royal army. The great landed nobles were allowed to divide their lands among their subvassals however they wished. In 1086, however, by the Oath of Salisbury Plain, William required all subvassals to swear loyalty to him as their king and liege lord. Henceforth, all subvassals owed their primary loyalty to the king rather than to their immediate feudal lords.

Thus, the Norman conquest of England had brought a dramatic change. In Anglo-Saxon England, the king had held limited lands while great families controlled large stretches of land and acted rather independently of the king. In contrast, the Normans established a hierarchy of nobles holding land as fiefs from the king. William of Normandy had manipulated the feudal sys-

✦ **Norman Conquest of England from the Bayeux Tapestry.** The Bayeux tapestry, which consists of woolen embroidery on a linen backing, was made by English needlewomen before 1082 for Bayeux Cathedral. It depicts scenes from the Norman invasion of England. In this segment, the Normans are shown charging the shield wall of the Saxon infantry during the Battle of Hastings.

tem to create a strong, centralized monarchy. Gradually, a process of fusion between the victorious Normans and the defeated Anglo-Saxons created a new England. While the Norman ruling class spoke French, the intermarriage of the Norman-French with the Anglo-Saxon nobility gradually merged Anglo-Saxon and French into a new English language. Political amalgamation also occurred as the Normans adapted existing Anglo-Saxon institutions.

William maintained the Anglo-Saxon administrative system in which counties or shires were divided into hundreds or groups of villages. Within each shire, the sheriff (or shire-reeve) was the chief royal officer responsible for leading the military forces of the county and presiding over the county court. William retained the office but replaced the Anglo-Saxon sheriffs with Normans. William also more fully developed the system of taxation and royal courts begun by the Anglo-Saxon and Danish kings of the tenth and eleventh centuries. Henry I (1100–1135), the last son of William the Conqueror, built on his father's foundation and recruited an efficient group of royal servants who excelled at finding ways to use the courts and tax system to profit the king. Thus, by combining Anglo-Saxon and Norman institutions, the first Norman rulers managed to establish a kingship more powerful than any other monarchy of its time.

The Norman conquest of England had repercussions in France as well. Since the new king of England was still the duke of Normandy, he was both a king (of England) and at the same time a vassal to a king (of France), but a vassal who was now far more powerful than his lord. This connection with France kept England heavily involved in continental affairs throughout the High Middle Ages.

In the twelfth century, the power of the English monarchy was greatly enlarged during the reign of Henry II (1154–1189), the first of the Plantagenet dynasty, who reestablished strong rule after a period of civil war following the death of Henry I. Henry II, however, was not just king of England. He also became lord of Ireland, receiving the homage of several Irish kings after permitting some of his leading noblemen to occupy parts of that island. And he had sizable possessions in France. He was count of Anjou, duke of Normandy, and, through marriage to Eleanor of Aquitaine, duke of Aquitaine as well. Indeed, while theoretically a vassal of the French king, Henry's Angevin empire, as it is called, made him incomparably more powerful than his lord, the king of France.

The reign of Henry II was an important one for the development of the English monarchy. During the pe-

The Growth of the European Kingdoms

England	
King Canute	1016–1035
Battle of Hastings	1066
William the Conqueror	1066–1087
Henry II, first of the Plantagenet dynasty	1154–1189
Murder of Thomas Becket	1170
John	1199–1216
Magna Carta	1215
Edward I	1272–1307
The "greater Parliaments"	1295 and 1297
France	
Louis VI the Fat	1108–1137
Louis VII	1137–1180
Philip II Augustus	1180–1223
Louis IX	1226–1270
Philip IV	1285–1314
First Estates-General	1302
Spain	
Establishment of Portugal	1139
Alfonso X of Castile	1252–1284
Germany, the Empire, and Italy	
Conrad II begins Salian dynasty	1024–1039
Henry III	1039–1056
Henry IV	1056–1106
Frederick I Barbarossa	1152–1190
Lombard League defeats Frederick at Legnano	1176
Henry VI	1190–1197
Frederick II	1212–1250
Charles of Anjou invades southern Italy	1266
Election of Rudolf of Habsburg as king of Germany	1273
Sicilian Vespers	1282
Eastern Europe	
East Prussia given to the Teutonic Knights	1226
Genghis Khan and the rise of the Mongols	c. 1162–1227
Mongol conquest of Russia	1230s
Alexander Nevsky, Prince of Novgorod	c. 1220–1263
Defeat of Germans	1242

riod of civil war following the death of Henry I, the royal income had declined, and the great nobles had become more independent of royal authority. Henry dealt with these problems and was particularly successful in developing administrative and legal institutions that strengthened the royal government.

First of all, Henry continued the development of the exchequer or permanent royal treasury that had begun in the reign of Henry I. Royal officials, known as "barons of the exchequer," received taxes collected by the sheriffs while seated around a table covered by a checkered cloth (hence, exchequer table), which served as a counting device. The barons gave receipts to the sheriffs, while clerks recorded the accounts on sheets of parchment that were then rolled up. These so-called pipe rolls have served as an important source of economic and social information for later historians.

Perhaps even more significant than Henry's financial reforms were his efforts to strengthen the royal courts and his contributions to the development of English common law. Justice had been administered in England by local courts in the counties and hundreds and also in the courts of the various lords. The king's court had been concerned primarily with affairs germane to the king's rights as feudal lord. As overlords of the entire kingdom, however, English kings, beginning with Henry I, had begun to expand matters subject to the king's jurisdiction. In 1166, Henry II issued the Assizes of Clarendon, instructions for his royal justices about to tour England. The Assizes expanded the number of cases to be tried in the king's court by establishing a finding-jury, which was a group of landholders in each hundred who swore an oath to reveal any criminal acts that had taken place in their territory or declare the true owner of disputed or stolen property. Those accused were then brought before the king's justices. The finding-jury was the ancestor of our modern grand jury. Henry also transferred property cases from feudal and county courts to the royal courts and allowed knights to appeal from the courts of their lords to the royal courts. Henry's goals were clear: expanding the jurisdiction of the royal courts extended the king's power and, of course, brought revenues into his coffers. Moreover, since the royal justices were administering law throughout England, a body of common law (law that was common to the whole kingdom) began to develop to replace the customary law used in county and feudal courts, which often varied from place to place. Thus, Henry's systematic approach to law played an important role in developing royal institutions common to the entire kingdom.

Like his continental counterparts, Henry II was also forced to confront the problem of the relationship between church and state. Indeed, the most famous church-state controversy in medieval England arose between Henry and Thomas Becket, archbishop of Canterbury, the highest ranking English cleric. Conflict erupted over whether the king had the right to punish clerics in royal courts and whether legal disputes arising in the English courts could be appealed to the papal court without royal permission. Becket claimed that trying criminous clerics in the royal courts infringed the church's right to try clerics in church courts. Becket had been Henry's chancellor and friend and was a very worldly figure indeed. Henry had appointed Becket as his archbishop expecting complete loyalty, but Becket went through a considerable transformation as archbishop and began to atone for his past worldliness by upholding the rights of the church. Attempts at compromise between the two intense men failed, and after Becket excommunicated some bishops who had supported Henry, the king in exasperation publicly expressed the desire to be rid of Becket. Four knights who had heard the king's words took him literally, went to Canterbury, and murdered the archbishop in the cathedral (see the box on p. 327) on December 29, 1170. Becket the martyr was made a saint three years later, and his tomb at Canterbury became one of the most famous pilgrimage centers of the Middle Ages. Henry did public penance for the act and compromised with the church by allowing the right of appeal from English church courts to the papal court. Despite the compromise, Henry had succeeded overall in building a strong English monarchy.

Toward the end of Henry II's reign, a number of important nobles began to resist his centralizing policies. Although Henry crushed the rebels, baronial discontent could not be as easily contained in the thirteenth century, and open rebellion broke out in the reign of King John (1199–1216). Following in his father's footsteps, John continued the effort to strengthen royal power and proved particularly ingenious at finding novel ways to levy taxes. The barons of England came to resent him deeply. In 1204, John lost Normandy to the French king, Philip Augustus; when John's attempt to reconquer the duchy ended in a devastating defeat, many of the English barons rose in rebellion in 1215. At Runnymeade, John was forced to seal the Magna Carta (the Great Charter) of feudal liberties.

Much of the Magna Carta was aimed at limiting government practices that affected the relations be-

≽ Murder in the Cathedral ≼

*T*he conflict between King Henry II and Thomas Becket, archbishop of Canterbury, was the most dramatic confrontation between church and state in English medieval history. Although Henry did not order the archbishop's murder, he certainly caused it by his reckless public words expressing his desire to be free of Thomas Becket. This excerpt is from a letter by John of Salisbury who served as secretary to Theobald, archbishop of Canterbury, and his successor, Thomas Becket. John was present at the murder of the archbishop in 1170.

John of Salisbury to John of Canterbury, Bishop of Poitiers

The martyr [Becket] stood in the cathedral, before Christ's altar, as we have said, ready to suffer; the hour of slaughter was at hand. When he heard that he was sought—heard the knights who had come for him shouting in the throng of clerks and monks "Where is the archbishop?"—he turned to meet them on the steps which he had almost climbed, and said with steady countenance: "Here am I! What do you want?" One of the knight-assassins flung at him in fury: "That you die now! That you should live longer is impossible." No martyr seems ever to have been more steadfast in his agony than he, . . . and thus, steadfast in speech as in spirit, he replied: "And I am prepared to die for my God, to preserve justice and my church's liberty. If you seek my head, I forbid you on behalf of God almighty and on pain of anathema to do any hurt to any other man, monk, clerk or layman, of high or low degree. Do not involve

them in the punishment, for they have not been involved in the cause: on my head not on theirs be it if any of them have supported the Church in its troubles. I embrace death readily, so long as peace and liberty for the Church follow from the shedding of my blood. . . ." He spoke, and saw that the assassins had drawn their swords; and bowed his head like one in prayer. His last words were "To God and St. Mary and the saints who protect and defend this church, and to the blessed Denis, I commend myself and the church's cause." No one could dwell on what followed without deep sorrow and choking tears. A son's affection forbids me to describe each blow the savage assassins struck, spurning all fear of God, forgetful of all fealty and any human feeling. They defiled the cathedral and the holy season [Christmas] with a bishop's blood and with slaughter; but that was not enough. They sliced off the crown of his head, which had been specially dedicated to God by anointing with holy oil—a fearful thing even to describe; then they used their evil swords, when he was dead, to spill his brain and cruelly scattered it, mixed with blood and bones, over the pavement. . . Through all the agony the martyr's spirit was unconquered, his steadfastness marvellous to observe; he spoke not a word, uttered no cry, let slip no groan, raised no arm nor garment to protect himself from an assailant, but bent his head, which he had laid bare to their swords with wonderful courage, till all might be fulfilled. Motionless he held it, and when at last he fell his body lay straight; and he moved neither hand nor foot.

---

tween the king and his vassals on the one hand and between the king and the church on the other (see the box on p. 328). Some provisions, however, came to have greater significance because of the way they were subsequently interpreted. One in particular stood out; chapter 39 read: "No free man shall be taken or imprisoned or dispossessed, or outlawed, or banished, or in any way destroyed, nor will we go upon him, nor send upon him, except by the legal judgment of his peers or by the law of the land."[5] In 1215, the status of "free man" applied to less than half of the English population, but later this statement was applied to all and in the fourteenth century gave rise to trial by jury. Its emphasis on the need to abide by the "law of the land" in proceeding

against a free person also came to be interpreted as a guarantee of "due process of law" and a protection against arbitrary judgments.

The Magna Carta remains, above all, a quintessential feudal document. Feudal custom had always recognized that the relationship between king and vassals was based on mutual rights and obligations. The Magna Carta gave written recognition to that fact and was used in subsequent years to underscore the concept that the monarch should be limited rather than absolute.

John's successor, Henry III (1216–1272), was weak and unable to control the barons of his realm. The nobles were incapable of cooperating, however, and were crushed by Henry's son, Edward I (1272–1307),

⇒ *Magna Carta* ⇐

After the dismal failure of King John to reconquer Normandy from the French king, some of the English barons rebelled against their king. At Runnymeade in 1215, King John agreed to seal the Magna Carta, the Great Charter of liberties regulating the relationship between the king and his vassals. What made Magna Carta an important historical document was its more general clauses defining rights and liberties. These were later interpreted in broader terms to make them applicable to all the English people.

Magna Carta

John, by the Grace of God, king of England, lord of Ireland, duke of Normandy and Aquitaine, count of Anjou, to the archbisops, bishops, abbots, earls, barons, justiciars, foresters, sheriffs, reeves, servants, and all bailiffs and his faithful people greeting.

1. In the first place we have granted to God, and by this our present charter confirmed, for us and our heirs forever, that the English church shall be free, and shall hold its rights entire and its liberties uninjured. . . . We have granted moreover to all free men of our kingdom for us and our heirs forever all the liberties written below, to be had and holden by themselves and their heirs from us and our heirs.

2. If any of our earls or barons, or others holding from us in chief by military service shall have died, and when he had died his heir shall be of full age and owe relief, he shall have his inheritance by the ancient relief; that is to say, the heir or heirs of an earl for the whole barony of an earl a hundred pounds; the heir or heirs of a baron for a whole barony a hundred pounds; the heir or heirs of a knight, for a whole knight's fee, a hundred shillings at most; and who owes less let him give less according to the ancient custom of fiefs.

3. If moreover the heir of any one of such shall be under age, and shall be in wardship, when he comes of age he shall have his inheritance without relief and without a fine. . . .

12. No scutage or aid shall be imposed in our kingdom except by the common council of our kingdom, except for the ransoming of our body, for the making of our oldest son a knight, and for once marrying our oldest daughter, and for these purposes it shall be only a reasonable aid. . . .

13. And the city of London shall have all its ancient liberties and free customs, as well by land as by water. Moreover, we will and grant that all other cities and boroughs and villages and ports shall have all their liberties and free customs.

14. And for holding a common council of the kingdom concerning the assessment of an aid otherwise than in the three cases mentioned above, or concerning the assessment of a scutage we shall cause to be summoned the archbishops, bishops, abbots, earls, and greater barons by our letters under seal; and besides we shall cause to be summoned generally, by our sheriffs and bailiffs all those who hold from us in chief, for a certain day, that is at the end of forty days at least, and for a certain place; and in all the letters of that summons, we will express the cause of the summons, and when the summons has thus been given the business shall proceed on the appointed day, on the advice of those who shall be present, even if not all of those who were summoned have come. . . .

39. No free man shall be taken or imprisoned or dispossessed, or outlawed, or banished, or in any way destroyed, nor will we go upon him, nor send upon him, except by the legal judgment of his peers or by the law of the land. . . .

60. Moreover, all those customs and franchises mentioned above which we have conceded in our kingdom, and which are to be fulfilled, as far as pertains to us, in respect to our men; all men of our kingdom as well as clergy as laymen, shall observe as far as pertains to them, in respect to their men.

who proved to be a very talented and powerful monarch. Edward began the process of uniting all of the British Isles into a single kingdom. Although Wales was finally conquered and pacified, the attempt to subdue Scotland failed. Edward managed merely to begin a lengthy conflict between England and Scotland that lasted for centuries.

Edward was successful in reestablishing monarchical rights after a period of baronial control. At the same time, the various branches of the administrative machinery of government, which had evolved out of the king's household staff, became increasingly specialized. The barons and chancellor of the exchequer supervised the treasury and financial affairs. Two royal courts emerged: the Court of Common Pleas took responsibility for civil cases, and the Court of King's Bench heard either civil or criminal cases relevant to the king's interest. Finally, during Edward's reign, the role of the English Parliament, an institution of great importance in the development of representative government, also began to be defined.

Parliament in England arose out of the king's need to secure the consent of his barons for extraordinary aids (in effect, new taxes) and to "treat" over important matters of state. Originally, the word *parliament* was applied to meetings of the king's Great Council in which the greater barons and chief prelates of the church met with the king's judges and principal advisers. The Great Council was primarily occupied with judicial affairs. The demand for special subsidies to meet the rising cost of government, however, necessitated impos-

ing a uniform levy on the personal property of all classes. It was easier to collect such levies if these classes gave their consent. This led to the summoning of greater Parliaments, which were called by the king in 1295 and 1297. For them he ordered sheriffs to "cause two knights from the aforesaid county, two citizens from each city in the same county, and two burgesses from each borough . . . to be elected without delay, and to cause them to come to us at the aforesaid time and place."[6] A Parliament, then, came to be composed of two knights from every county and two burgesses from every borough (town) as well as the barons and ecclesiastical lords. Eventually, barons and church lords formed the House of Lords; knights and burgesses, the House of Commons. The Parliaments of Edward I granted taxes, discussed politics, enacted legislation, and handled judicial business. Although still not the important body it would

Map 10.2 England and France in the High Middle Ages: (*left*) England and its French Holdings; (*right*) Growth of the French State.

eventually become, the English Parliament had clearly emerged as an institution by the end of the thirteenth century.

The formation of parliaments was not unique to England, however. Spain and Hungary witnessed their development in the thirteenth century, and the practice soon spread to all of Europe in the fourteenth century. Only the English Parliament, however, eventually grew into a powerful institution capable of limiting the power of the king.

By the beginning of the fourteenth century, England had begun to develop a unique system of national monarchy. The king and his subjects constituted a "community of the realm" in the words of contemporary English jurists. The law of the realm was beginning to be determined not by the king alone, but by the king in consultation with representatives of different groups that constituted the community.

The Growth of the French Kingdom

The Capetian dynasty of French kings emerged at the end of the tenth century. Although they carried the title of kings, there was little reason to believe that the Capetians would ever consolidate their control over the West Frankish kingdom (or France, as we will now call it). The Capetians controlled as the royal domain only the lands around Paris known as the Ile-de-France. Even that was not entirely under their control; in the eleventh century the Capetians struggled unsuccessfully to restrain the nobility in their own territory. As kings of France, the Capetians were formally the overlords of the great lords of France, such as the dukes of Normandy, Brittany, Burgundy, and Aquitaine and the counts of Flanders, Maine, Anjou, Blois, and Toulouse. In reality, however, many were considerably more powerful than the Capetian kings. Thus, it was not a foregone conclusion that the Capetians would be successful in establishing a French monarchy.

The Capetians, however, possessed some advantages. As kings anointed of God in a sacred ceremony, the Catholic church supported them tirelessly. We should also note the incredible luck of the Capetians. Their royal domain was so small and insignificant that most of the great lords were not really tempted to attack it, especially since it was ruled by the divinely anointed king of France. Moreover, the Capetians proved to be a very fertile dynasty. Although the Capetian monarchy of France did not officially become hereditary until 1223, for generation after generation, Capetian kings succeeded in producing sons who could share in ruling and then be elected kings before their fathers died.

In the twelfth century, Louis VI the Fat (1108–1137) and Louis VII (1137–1180) managed to reverse the trend toward loss of control in the royal domain and complete the work of pacifying the Ile-de-France. They also strengthened the royal dynasty by establishing a close alliance with the papacy and gaining church support. Nevertheless, in the eleventh and most of the twelfth centuries, the Capetians did little beyond consolidating their territory in the Ile-de-France. But in doing so, they kept the monarchical principle alive, and in the thirteenth century, the Capetian dynasty began to realize the fruits of its labors.

King Philip II Augustus (1180–1223), Louis VII's son, perceived that the power of the French monarch would never be extended until the Plantagenet power was defeated. After all, Henry II and his sons were not only kings of England, but rulers of the French territories of Normandy, Maine, Anjou, and Aquitaine. Accordingly, Philip II waged war against the Plantagenets, but not until he defeated King John (1199–1216) was he successful in wresting control of Normandy, Maine, Anjou, and Touraine. Through these conquests, Philip quadrupled the income of the French monarchy and greatly enlarged its power.

Philip understood the need to develop centralized institutions of government to rule his new lands. The territories added to the royal domain were divided into bailiwicks, each of which was placed under the jurisdiction of a bailiff or seneschal. Bailiffs were appointed to provinces close to the original royal domain; seneschals to remote provinces. Both royal officials administered justice, collected royal revenues, and served as the king's agents in other matters. Although bailiffs were usually middle-class administrators, seneschals were barons or knights who were able to command royal troops if necessary. Bailiffs, seneschals, and their assistants comprised the beginnings of a French royal bureaucracy in the thirteenth century.

Capetian rulers after Philip II continued to add lands to the royal domain. Although Philip had used military force, other kings used both purchase and marriage to achieve the same end. Much of the thirteenth century was dominated by the man, whom many consider the greatest of the medieval French kings, Louis IX (1226–1270). A deeply religious man, he was later canonized as a saint by the church, an unusual action regardless of the century. "This saintly man loved our lord with all his heart and in all his actions followed His example,"[7] said his contemporary biographer who accompanied the king on a crusade in 1248. Louis was known for his attempts to bring justice to his people and ensure their rights. He sent out royal agents to check on the activities of the bailiffs and seneschals after hearing complaints that they were abusing their power. He was not above hearing complaints personally in a very informal fashion:

> In summer, after hearing mass, the king often went to the wood of Vincennes, where he would sit down with his back against an oak, and make us all sit round him. Those who had any suit to present could come to speak to him without hindrance from an usher or any other person. The king would address them directly, and ask "Is there anyone here who has a case to be settled?" Those who had one would stand up. Then he would say, "Keep silent all of you, and you shall be heard in turn, one after the other." Then he would call Pierre de Fontaines and Geoffroi de Villette, and say to one or other of them: "Settle this case for me." If he saw anything needing correction in what was said by those who spoke on his behalf or on behalf of any other person, he would himself intervene to make the necessary adjustment.[8]

Louis was also responsible for establishing a permanent royal court of justice in Paris whose work was carried on by a regular staff of professional jurists. This court came to be known as the *Parlement* of Paris. Louis made it increasingly difficult for nobles to wage private wars with each other and eventually outlawed the practice. Sharing in the religious sentiments of his age, he played a major role in two of the later crusades (see Chapter 11). Both were failures, and he met his death during an invasion of North Africa.

Although the successors of Saint Louis were more worldly and less saintly, they continued his centralizing policies. Philip IV (1285–1314) was particularly effective in strengthening the French monarchy. The machinery of government became even more specialized. French kings going back to the early Capetians had possessed a household staff for running their affairs. In effect, it was the division and enlargement of this household staff that produced the three major branches of royal administration: a council for advice; a *chambre des comptes* or chamber of accounts for finances; and a *parlement* or royal court. By the beginning of the fourteenth century, the Capetians had created the firm foundations for a royal bureaucracy.

Philip IV was also responsible for bringing the French parliament or Estates-General, a representative assembly, into being. When he became involved in a struggle with the pope (see Chapter 12), Philip summoned representatives of the church, nobility, and towns to meet with him in 1302, inaugurating the Estates-General, the first parliament. The Estates-General proved invaluable to the king since feudal custom had limited the power of kings to make changes contrary to that custom. The Estates-General came to function as an instrument to bolster the king's power since he could ask representatives of the major social classes to change the laws or grant new taxes. Only later did the Estates-General develop the idea that it might control the actions of kings.

Philip's reign was also significant for the growing impact of Roman law (see Chapter 11). Philip's advisers were trained in Roman law and began to view the monarchy not as a feudal monarchy limited in power, but in a new way: "The king of France is emperor in his own kingdom, for he recognizes no superior in temporal affairs." In these words, Philip's advisers exalted an ideal of increased monarchical authority.

In the course of the thirteenth century, the Capetian dynasty had acquired new lands to add to the French royal domain, whether by conquest, purchase, marriage, or inheritance. Although the monarchs tried to impose their authority upon these lands, they also allowed them to keep their own laws and institutions. Not until the French Revolution of the eighteenth century would the French move toward a common pattern for all of France. Despite the lack of institutional uniformity, by the end of the thirteenth century, France was the largest, wealthiest, and best-governed monarchical state in Europe.

Christian Reconquest: The Spanish Kingdoms

Much of Spain had been part of the Islamic world since the eighth century. Muslim Spain had flourished in the Early Middle Ages. Córdoba became a major urban center with a population exceeding 300,000 people. Agriculture prospered, and Spain became known as well for excellent leather, steel, wool, silk, and paper. Beginning in the tenth century, however, the most noticeable feature of Spanish history was the weakening of Muslim power and the beginning of a Christian reconquest that lasted until the final expulsion of the Muslims at the end of the fifteenth century.

By the eleventh century, a number of small Christian kingdoms had become established in northern Spain, namely, Leon, Castile, Navarre, Aragon, and Barcelona. Muslim disunity and the support of French nobles, who were eager to battle the infidel, enabled these Spanish Christian states to take the offensive against the Muslims. By the end of the twelfth century, however, the

Christian reconquest of Spain had slowed considerably. The northern half had been consolidated into the Christian kingdoms of Castile, Navarre, Aragon, and Portugal, which had first emerged as a separate kingdom in 1139. The southern half of Spain remained under the control of the Muslims.

But in the thirteenth century, Aragon, Castile, and Portugal made significant conquests of Muslim territory. Castile subdued most of Andalusia in the south, down to the Atlantic and Mediterranean; at the same time, Aragon conquered Valencia. The Muslims remained ensconced only in the kingdom of Granada in the southeast of the Iberian peninsula, which remained an independent Muslim state.

The Christian conquest of Andalusia meant economic disaster for that region. Hitherto highly urbanized and prosperous, the land became depopulated when skilled workers were driven out of the urban areas. A small group of nobles and knights of the military orders took possession of vast estates that they used for cattle grazing.

To encourage other settlers to move into the newly conquered regions, Spanish kings issued written privileges that guaranteed rule in accordance with the law for most of the communities in their kingdoms. These privileges, or *fueros,* stipulated the punishments for crimes committed within community boundaries and the means for resolving civil disputes. They also established regulations for acquiring citizenship in the community, rules for service in the community militia, and

laws protecting the rights of women and children living within the towns. Kings of the different regions of Spain freely borrowed from the *fueros* of other regions in an effort to develop attractive customs for their towns so that immigrants would be lured into establishing residency there. By the thirteenth century, kings increasingly were required to swear that they would respect these community customs before they were confirmed in office by assemblies of their leading citizens.

The Spanish kingdoms followed no consistent policy in the treatment of the conquered Muslim population. Muslim farmers continued to work the land but were forced to pay very high rents in Aragon. In Castile King Alfonso X (1252–1284), who called himself the "King of Three Religions," encouraged the continued development of a cosmopolitan culture shared by Christians, Jews, and Muslims. Toledo still flourished as an important center of intellectual life.

The Lands of the Holy Roman Empire: Germany and Italy

The Saxon kings of the tenth century had strengthened their hold over the German kingdom and revived the empire of Charlemagne. A new dynasty, known as the Salian kings, began in 1024 with the election of Conrad II (1024–1039) of Franconia. Both Conrad and his successors, Henry III (1039–1056) and Henry IV (1056–1106), managed to create a strong German monarchy and a powerful empire by leading armies into

⚜ Map 10.3 Christian Reconquests in the Western Mediterranean.

Italy. But they also experienced the frustrating difficulties inherent in the position of the German kings.

The great lords of Germany took advantage of the early death of Henry III and the minority of Henry IV to extend their own power at the expense of the latter. The elective nature of the German monarchy posed a problem for the German kings. While some dynasties were strong enough for their members to be elected regularly, the great lords who were the electors did at times deliberately choose otherwise. It was to their advantage to select a weak king.

To compensate for their weaknesses, German kings had come to rely upon their ability to control the church and select bishops and abbots whom they could then use as their royal administrators. The Investiture Controversy, however, had weakened the king's ability to use church officials in this way.

The German kings also tried to bolster their power by using their position as emperors to exploit the resources of Italy. The German king and emperor Otto III (983–1002), for example, spent much of his time pursuing an imperial ideal by residing in Rome and attempting to make it the capital of his empire. After his death in 1002, there was no central political authority in Italy. While important nobles struggled to dominate northern Italy, central Italy remained under the control of the Papal States. In southern Italy, the Lombard dukes, Muslims, and Byzantines seemed to be in constant conflict.

In the latter half of the eleventh century, the arrival of a group of Norman adventurers dramatically altered the southern Italian political scene. Robert the Guiscard (the cunning), his brothers, and a band of fellow Norman knights conquered much of southern Italy, and Robert was recognized by the pope as duke of Apulia and Calabria. His brother Roger was given the task of subduing Muslim Sicily, which he accomplished in 1091 after a thirty-year struggle. The Normans in southern Italy demonstrated astute diplomatic and military abilities. They adapted existing institutions to their benefit and developed well-organized and centralized states in southern Italy and Sicily. Roger II, the son of Roger of Sicily, was crowned king of Sicily by the pope in 1130, proving that lordship could be transformed into kingship. By the end of the twelfth century, the Norman kingdom was one of the most powerful in Europe as well as one of the most fascinating. A melting pot of Christian, Jewish, and Muslim culture, the state issued its official documents in Latin, Greek, and Arabic.

The Norman kingdom in southern Italy was beyond any claims of the German kings, but the wealthy cities

◆ Otto III. The German king and emperor Otto III spent much of his reign pursuing the imperial ideal of making Rome the capital of his empire. In his gospel book, Otto III sits in majesty on his throne surrounded by temporal and spiritual officials.

of northern Italy, which by the twelfth century had become virtually independent after overthrowing the rule of their bishops, were a tempting prize to the German kings who never entirely gave up their dreams of a restored empire. No German dynasty proved more susceptible to the allure of this dream than the Hohenstaufens.

In 1152, Frederick I (1152–1190), known as Barbarossa or Redbeard to the Italians, a powerful lord from the Swabian house of Hohenstaufen, was chosen as king. In need of adequate resources to reestablish his control over the German princes, Frederick chose to pursue an Italian policy to build a base for regular revenues. Frederick's plan was to create a new kind of empire. Previous German kings had focused on building a strong German kingdom, to which Italy might be added as an appendage. To Frederick, Germany was simply a feudal monarchy; his chief revenues would come from Italy as the center of a "holy empire," as he called it (hence the term *Holy Roman Empire*). Consequently, Frederick permitted his cousin Henry the Lion, duke of Saxony and Bavaria, to expand and act independently in much of Germany. Frederick's only request of the princes was that they recognize him as their overlord. In compensation, Frederick turned his efforts toward the south and marched an army into northern Italy, where he was immediately victorious. His victory proved short-lived, however. The papacy was opposed to imperial expansion, fearing that the emperor intended to include Rome and the Papal States in his empire. The cities of northern Italy were also unwilling to submit to Frederick's authority and formed an alliance known as the Lombard League. With the support of the papacy, the league defeated the forces of Emperor Frederick at Legnano in 1176. Frederick had no alternative but to negotiate a truce and return to Germany, a time he spent profitably by breaking the power of his cousin Henry the Lion. Later, he returned to Italy and arranged a settlement with the northern Italian cities by which they retained their independence in return for an annual payment to the emperor. Frederick now had the

financial base he had sought. Moreover, by marrying his son (who became Henry VI, 1190–1197) to the heiress of the Norman kingdom of southern Italy, Frederick seemed to be creating the foundation for making the Holy Roman Empire a reality. After Frederick's death, Henry VI's control of Germany and both northern and southern Italy made him the strongest European ruler since Charlemagne. The longevity of medieval empires was always highly dependent upon the strength of the ruler, however. When Henry VI died prematurely, his son was only two; Henry's empire soon collapsed.

The death of Henry VI brought to the throne his son, Frederick II, the most brilliant of the Hohenstaufen rulers. King of Sicily in 1198, king of Germany in 1212, and crowned emperor in 1220, Frederick II was a truly remarkable man who awed his contemporaries (see the box on p. 335). Frederick had been raised in Sicily with its diverse peoples, languages, and religions. His court brought together a brilliant array of lawyers, poets, artists, and scientists, and he himself took a deep

Map 10.4 The Holy Roman Empire.

The Deeds of Emperor Frederick II

Frederick II, king of Germany and Sicily and would-be ruler of all Italy, was viewed even by contemporaries as one of the most unusual rulers of his time. This account of his "idiosyncracies" is by Salimbene de Adam, a Franciscan friar, whose Chronicle is one of the "richest sources of information" about medieval life in thirteenth-century Italy. He was, however, also known to be notoriously biased against Frederick II.

Salimbene de Adam, Chronicle

Note that Frederick almost always enjoyed having discord with the Church and fighting her on all sides, although she had nourished him, defended him, and raised him up. He held the true faith to be worthless. He was a cunning, crafty man, avaricious, lecherous, and malicious, easily given to wrath.

At times, however, Frederick was a worthy man, and when he wished to show his good, courtly side, he could be witty, charming, urbane, and industrious. He was adept at writing and singing, and was well-versed in the art of writing lyrics and songs. He was a handsome, well-formed man of medium height. I myself saw him and, at one time, loved him. For he once wrote Brother Elias, Minister General of the Friars Minor, on my behalf asking him to return me to my father. He also could speak many and various languages. In short, if he had been a good Catholic and had loved God, the Church, and his own soul, he would scarcely have had an equal as an emperor in the world. . . .

Now, it is necessary to speak of Frederick's idiosyncracies.

His first idiosyncracy is that he had the thumb of a certain notary cut off because he had written his name in a way different from the way the Emperor desired. . . .

His second idiosyncracy was that he wanted to discover what language a child would use when he grew up if he had never heard anyone speak. Therefore, he placed some infants in the care of wet-nurses, commanding them to bathe and suckle the children, but by no means ever to speak to or fondle them. For he wanted to discover whether they would speak Hebrew, the first language, or Greek, Latin, Arabic, or the language of their parents. But he labored in vain, because all of the infants died. . . .

Furthermore, Frederick had many other idiosyncracies: idle curiosity, lack of faith, perversity, tyranny, and accursedness, some of which I have written about in another chronicle. Once, for example, he sealed up a live man in a cask and kept him there until he died in order to prove that the soul totally perished with the body. . . . For Frederick was an Epicurean, and so he and the learned men of his court searched out whatever Biblical passage they could find to prove that there is no life after death. . . .

This sixth example of Frederick's idiosyncracy and idle curiosity . . . was that he fed two men a fine meal, and he sent one to bed to sleep, the other out hunting. And that evening he had both men disemboweled in his presence, in order to determine which one had digested his food the best. The decisions by his doctors went to the man who had slept after the meal. . . .

I have heard and known many other idiosyncracies of Frederick, but I keep quiet for the sake of brevity, and because reporting so many of the Emperor's foolish notions is tedious to me.

interest in their work. He was by no means a devout Christian by contemporary standards but had no fear of papal threats and proved extremely tolerant of Muslim rulers. He was not adverse to using Muslim mercenaries, and it was said that he kept a harem of Muslim women for his enjoyment.

Until 1220, Frederick spent much time in Germany; once he left in 1220, he rarely returned. He basically gave the German princes full control of their territories, voluntarily surrendering any real power over Germany to keep it quiet while he pursued his main goal, the establishment of a strong centralized state in Italy dominated by his kingdom in Sicily. He turned Sicily into the best-organized state in Europe, establishing a strong centralized government staffed by bureaucrats under his absolute authority as "supreme legislator and judge." Frederick's major task was to gain control of northern Italy. In reaching to extend his power in Italy, he became involved in a deadly struggle with the popes, who realized that a single ruler of northern and southern Italy meant the end of papal secular power in central Italy. The northern Italian cities were also unwilling to give up their freedom. The pope logically allied himself with the northern Italian cities, which re-created the Lombard League that had defeated Frederick Barbarossa a century earlier. While popes were intermittently excommunicating him, Frederick waged a bitter struggle in northern Italy, winning many battles but ultimately losing the war. After his death in 1250, the remaining Hohenstaufens were obliterated, and the papacy stood supreme over the ashes of a failed Hohenstaufen empire.

Frederick's preoccupation with the creation of an empire in Italy left Germany in confusion and chaos until 1273 when the major German princes, serving as electors, chose an insignificant German noble, Rudolf of Habsburg, as the new German king. This ended the political chaos in Germany; but in choosing a weak king, the princes were ensuring that the German monarchy would remain impotent and incapable of reestablishing a centralized monarchical state. Rudolf realized the weakness of his position and reacted by taking advantage of his office to acquire territory for his own family. He perceived that in the long run this was the only way to strengthen his standing. Through his efforts, the Habsburgs acquired the duchies of Austria, which eventually became the chief foundation for the power of the Habsburg dynasty.

The German electoral princes, however, saw the dangers of allowing any one family to become overly strong and deliberately elected kings from other families, thus ensuring that the German kings would remain feeble. Some of these kings marched into Italy to be crowned emperor, but in truth, the failure of the Hohenstaufens had led to a situation where his exalted majesty, the German king and Holy Roman Emperor, had no real power over either Germany or Italy. Unlike France, England, and even Spain, neither Germany nor Italy created a unified national monarchy in the Middle Ages. Both became geographical designations for loose confederations of hundreds of petty, independent states under the vague direction of king or emperor. In fact, neither Germany nor Italy would become united until the nineteenth century.

Following the death of Frederick II, Italy fell into considerable political confusion. While the papacy remained in control of much of central Italy, the defeat of imperial power left the cities and towns of northern Italy independent of any other authority. Gradually, the larger ones began to emerge as strong city-states. After defeating Pisa in 1284, Genoa came to dominate its immediate region. Florence assumed the leadership of Tuscany while Milan, under the guidance of the Visconti family, took control of the Lombard region. With its great commercial wealth, the republic of Venice dominated the northeastern part of the peninsula.

The papacy was determined to crush Hohenstaufen rule in southern Italy. Eventually, the popes turned to France and offered the kingdom of Sicily to the brother of King Louis IX, Charles of Anjou, who invaded southern Italy in 1266 and defeated two Hohenstaufen claimants to become king of Sicily. But he did not last long. As a result of the uprising known as the Sicilian Vespers in 1282, the king of Aragon seized the island of Sicily while the Angevins remained in control of a kingdom in southern Italy, now known as the kingdom of Naples.

New Kingdoms in Northern and Eastern Europe

The Scandinavian countries of northern Europe had little political organization before 1000. Although monks traveled as missionaries to the northern lands as early as 826, it was not until the second half of the tenth and the first half of the eleventh centuries that the three Scandinavian kingdoms—Denmark, Norway, and Sweden—emerged with a noticeable political structure. At the same time, the three kingdoms were converted to Christianity by kings who believed that an organized church was a necessary accompaniment to an organized state. Although the old pagan religion held on, especially in Sweden, by the twelfth century Christianity had been widely accepted. Its adoption, however, did not eliminate the warlike tendencies of the Scandinavians. Not only did the three kingdoms fight each other in the eleventh and twelfth centuries, but rival families were in regular conflict over the throne in each state. This period also witnessed the growth of a powerful noble landowning class.

To the south, in eastern Europe, Hungary, which had been a Christian state since 1000, remained relatively stable throughout the High Middle Ages, but the history of Poland and Russia was far more turbulent. In the thirteenth century, eastern Europe was beset by two groups of invaders, the Teutonic Knights from the west and the Mongols from the east.

In the late tenth and early eleventh centuries, the Polish ruler, Boleslav the Brave (992–1025), constructed a larger kingdom by extending his authority across the Oder in the west, down into Bohemia to the south, and eastward to Kiev. After his death, the kingdom fell apart, however, with the central part persisting as a separate state, but with no natural frontiers. Consequently, German settlers encroached on its territory on a regular basis, leading to considerable intermarriage between Slavs and Germans. The Oder River became a crucial dividing line. West of the Oder, the Germanic language predominated; east of it, the Slavic language did. Instability and shifting boundaries would remain a fundamental characteristic of Polish history well into the twentieth century.

During the thirteenth century, relations between the Germans and the Slavs of eastern Europe worsened due to the aggression of the Teutonic Knights. The Teutonic Knights had been founded near the end of the twelfth century to protect the Christian Holy Land. In the early thirteenth century, however, these Christian knights found greater opportunity to the east of Germany where they attacked the pagan Slavs. East Prussia was given to the military order in 1226, and five years later, the knights moved beyond the Vistula where they waged war against the Slavs for another thirty years. By the end

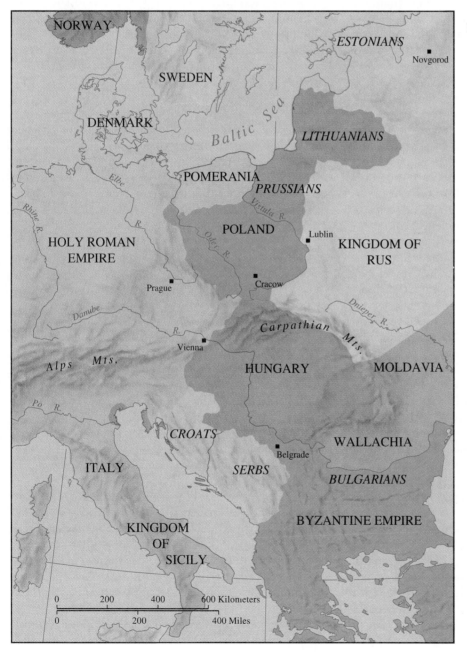

Map 10.5 Northern and Eastern Europe.

of the thirteenth century, Prussia had become German and Christian as the pagan Slavs were forced to convert (see the box on p. 339).

RUSSIA IN THE ELEVENTH AND TWELFTH CENTURIES

The Kiev Rus state, which had become formally Christian in 987, prospered considerably afterward, reaching its high point in the first half of the eleventh century. The city of Kiev was fairly populous, numbering perhaps 20,000 to 30,000 inhabitants, making it larger than any contemporary Christian city in western Europe. The principality of Kiev also maintained rather close contact with the states of western Europe. Indeed, the ruling dynasty of Kiev arranged marriages with the royal families of France, Germany, and Norway, among others.

Kievan society was dominated by a noble class of landowners known as the boyars, who represented a mixture of Scandinavian (Rus) descendants and chiefs of the old Slavonic tribes. Though mostly free, the peasants worked hard and long hours. Kievan merchants maintained regular trade with Scandinavia to the north and the Islamic and Byzantine worlds to the south.

After the mid-eleventh century, the principality of Kiev began to experience serious problems. The members of the ruling dynasty seemed unwilling and unable to work together, which led to constant fighting and destructive civil wars. New invasions by Asiatic nomadic tribes caused political disruption and increasingly cut off Rus traders from the Black Sea, their major outlet to the Byzantine and Islamic worlds. Competition from Italian merchants, especially in the luxury trade of the Black Sea, hurt commercial prosperity as well. By the twelfth century, the principality of Kiev began to disintegrate into a number of constituent parts. One of these was Novgorod, which freed itself from Kiev's control in 1136 and established a prosperous city republic based on trade with German merchants, especially from the north German city of Lübeck. Other cities also emerged in their own right. Moscow, for example, is first mentioned in a chronicle in 1147. The sack of Kiev by north Russian princes in 1169 brought an inglorious end to the first Russian state.

The fundamental civilizing and unifying force of early Russia was the Christian church. The Russian church imitated the liturgy and organization of the Byzantine Empire, whose Eastern Orthodox priests had converted the Kievan Rus to Christianity at the end of the tenth century. Until 1037, when the principality of Kiev made the Russian church self-governing, the metropolitan or head of the Russian church was obedient to the patriarch of Constantinople, the leading authority of the Eastern Christian church.

The Russian church became known for its rigid religious orthodoxy. Only a few basic religious works had been translated into Slavonic for use in Russia, which meant that the Kievan Rus had little awareness of the controversial religious literature of the Christian faith and the ancient works on which it was based. Perhaps as a result, the Russian church tended to view religious issues as matters of faith and rarely questioned the few religious authorities that had been translated into Slavonic. Although Christianity provided a common bond between Russian and European civilization, Russia's religious development guaranteed an even closer affinity between Russian and Byzantine civilization.

THE MONGOL INVASIONS

During the thirteenth century, Russia was cut off even more from western Europe by a new group of invaders, the Mongols. As we have seen, central and eastern Europe had periodically been subject to invasions from fierce Asiatic nomads, such as the Huns, Avars, Bulgars, and Magyars. The last to enter the scene, the Mongols were at the same time the most effective and affected a larger area than any of the earlier groups.

The Mongols were a nomadic people living in the mountains of central Asia. They were illiterate, but tough fighters. In the early thirteenth century, a resourceful leader, Genghis Khan (c. 1162–1227), succeeded in uniting the Mongol tribes and created a powerful military force. Genghis Khan was succeeded by equally competent sons and grandsons.

The Mongols exploded upon the scene in the thirteenth century. They advanced eastward, conquering China and eventually Korea. They moved westward against the Islamic empire as well. Persia fell by 1233, and by 1258, they had conquered Baghdad and destroyed the Abbasid caliphate. But the Mongols were not invincible, as seen by their defeat in Palestine in 1260 by the Mamluks.

Beginning in the 1230s, the Mongols moved into Europe. They conquered Russia, advanced into Poland and Hungary, and destroyed a force of Poles and Teutonic Knights in Silesia in 1241. Europe then seemingly got lucky when the Mongol hordes turned back because of internal fighting over the succession to the Great Khan. While it appears that western and southern Europe were fortunate in escaping the wrath of the Mongols, it is also possible that the Mongols had reached the limits of their expansion. In the east they

Ethnic Cleansing in Eastern Europe

One of the most important migrations in the High Middle Ages was the movement of Germans and people from the Low Countries—all of them Christians—into central and eastern Europe. This push to the east was often accompanied by a considerable slaughter of the native Slavs, who were not Christian. One of the leaders in this effort was Albert the Bear, ruler of the lands that came to be known as Brandenburg. This description of Albert's activities is taken from an account of the German expansion to the east by Helmold, a priest from Bosau.

Helmold, *The Chronicle of the Slavs*

At that time Albert, the margrave whose by-name is the Bear, held eastern Slavia. By the favor of God he also prospered splendidly in the portion of his lot; for he brought under his sway all the country of the Brizani, the Stoderani, and the many tribes dwelling along the Havel and the Elbe, and he curbed the rebellious ones among them. In the end, as the Slavs gradually decreased in number, he sent to Utrecht and to places lying on the Rhine, to those, moreover, who live by the ocean and suffer the violence of the sea—namely, Hollanders, Zeelanders, Flemings—and he brought large numbers of them and had them live in the strongholds and villages of the Slavs. The bishopric of Brandenburg, and likewise that of Havelberg, was greatly strengthened by the coming of the foreigners, because the churches multiplied and the income from the tithes grew enormously. At the same time foreigners from Holland also began to settle on the southern bank of the Elbe; the Hollanders received all the swamp and open country together with many cities and villages from the city Salzwedel clear to the Bohemian woodland. These lands, indeed, the Saxons are said to have occupied of old—namely in the time of the Ottos—as can be seen from the ancient levees that had been constructed along the banks of the Elbe. But afterward, when the Slavs got the upper hand, the Saxons were killed and the land has been held by the Slavs down to our own times. Now, however, because God gave plentiful aid and victory to our duke and to the other princes, the Slavs have been everywhere crushed and driven out. A people strong and without number have come from the bounds of the ocean, and taken possession of the territories of the Slavs. They have built cities and churches and have grown in riches beyond all estimation.

---

were having problems in the jungles of Vietnam and Cambodia. It is doubtful that their cavalry, even with the aid of acquired siege techniques, could have toppled the fortified castles and cities of Europe. Moreover, the Mongol conquests were motivated by little more than plunder and the wish to conquer. To rule their new possessions, they borrowed administrative techniques and administrators from the conquered people. Over the long run, the Mongols left little of any real importance, although their occupation of Russia certainly had some negative effect on that land.

RUSSIA UNDER MONGOL DOMINATION

The Mongols, who occupied the territories known as Russia, were part of an immense empire stretching back across Asia. They were not numerous enough to settle the vast Russian lands, but were content to rule directly an area along the lower Volga and north of the Caspian and Black Seas to Kiev and rule indirectly elsewhere. In the latter territories, Russian princes were required to pay tribute to the Mongol overlords.

One Russian prince soon emerged as more visible and powerful than the others. Alexander Nevsky (c. 1220–1263), prince of Novgorod, defeated a German invading army at Lake Peipus in northwestern Russia in 1242. His cooperation with the Mongols, which included denouncing his own brother and crushing native tax revolts, won him their favor. The khan, the acknowledged leader of the western part of the Mongol empire, rewarded Alexander Nevsky with the title of grandprince, enabling his descendants to become the princes of Moscow and eventually leaders of all Russia.

There is considerable historical debate over the effect Mongol rule had on the Russian people. No doubt the Mongols had some impact, especially in passing on to the Russian princes some very practical skills, such as how to make use of an enemy's military practices, how to secure lines of communication over great distances, and how to siphon off heavy taxes. But it is questionable whether the Mongols had a serious impact on the Russian character since the Russian church remained the dominant influence on that aspect of Russian culture.

The Growth of Medieval Monarchies

As our political survey of Europe has revealed, by the end of the thirteenth century, most of the monarchies of western Europe had reversed the decentralizing tendencies of feudalism in favor of an increased centralization of power in the hands of kings and princes. By extending the power of the royal courts at the expense of feudal courts, by expanding royal treasuries, and by establishing a chancery or secretariat to handle the increased volume of business, rulers became more and more capable of providing the central focus of public power. At the same time, the universities were producing trained lawyers and officials who staffed the new administrative offices (see Chapter 11). Frederick II even established his own university at Naples just to supply lawyers for the bureaucracy in his southern Italian kingdom. The strength of these new monarchical institutions meant that while medieval Europe might still think of itself as an international body of Christendom, regional patterns were becoming increasingly important. It also made it more difficult for rulers to conquer other territories and integrate them into their own lands.

Moreover, as governments became more centralized and kings extended their authority beyond the vassalage of the feudal system, both vassals and new subjects attempted to limit the authority of kings by law to avoid the arbitrary exercise of power. In order to maintain internal stability and gain support for foreign wars, kings acceded to these demands by granting charters to cities and nobles that stipulated limits to the royal power. The Magna Carta of 1215 was the most famous example, but there are others as well. Parliaments, too, brought more subjects into the affairs of kings.

Conclusion

The period from 1000 to 1300 was a very dynamic one in the development of Western civilization. It witnessed economic, social, and political changes that some historians believe set European civilization on a path that lasted until the eighteenth century when the Industrial Revolution created a new pattern. The revival of trade, the expansion of towns and cities, and the development of a money economy did not mean the end of a predominantly rural European society, but they did open the door to new ways to make a living and new opportunities for people to expand and enrich their lives. Eventually, they created the foundations for the development of a predominantly urban industrial society.

The nobles, whose warlike attitudes were rationalized by labeling them the defenders of Christian society, continued to dominate the medieval world politically, economically, and socially. But quietly and surely, within this world of castles and private power, kings gradually began to extend their public powers. Although the popes sometimes treated rulers as if they were their servants, by the thirteenth century, monarchs themselves were developing the machinery of government that would enable them to challenge these exalted claims of papal power and become the centers of political authority in Europe. Although they could not know it then, the actions of these medieval monarchs laid the foundation for the European kingdoms that in one form or another have dominated the European political scene ever since.

NOTES

1. Quoted in Jean Gimpel, *The Medieval Machine* (Harmondsworth, 1977), p. 92.
2. Quoted in Joseph and Frances Gies, *Life in a Medieval Castle* (New York, 1974), p. 175.
3. Quoted in Robert Delort, *Life in the Middle Ages*, trans. Robert Allen (New York, 1972), p. 218.
4. Quoted in Marvin Perry, Joseph Peden, and Theodore Von Laue, *Sources of the Western Tradition* (Boston, 1987), 1:218.
5. Quoted in Brian Tierney and Joan Scott, eds., *Western Societies: A Documentary History* (New York, 1984), 1:277.
6. Ibid., p. 278.
7. Jean de Joinville, *The Life of Saint Louis*, trans. M. R. B. Shaw (Harmondsworth, 1963), p. 167.
8. Ibid., p. 177.

SUGGESTIONS FOR FURTHER READING

On the revival of trade, see R. S. Lopez, *The Commercial Revolution of the Middle Ages: 950–1350* (Englewood Cliffs, N.J., 1971); and A. Sapori, *The Italian Merchant in the Middle Ages* (New York, 1970). Urban history is covered in E. Ennen, *The Medieval Town* (Amsterdam, 1978); H. A. Miskimin, D. Herlihy, and A. L. Udovich, eds., *The Medieval City* (New Haven, Conn., 1977); and the classic work of H. Pirenne, *Medieval Cities* (Princeton, N.J., 1925). There is an extensive section on medieval cities in M. Girouard, *Cities and People: A Social and Architectural History* (New Haven, Conn., 1985). A popular, readable study is J. and F. Gies, *Life in a Medieval City* (New York, 1969).

Works on the function and activities of the nobility in the High Middle Ages include S. Reynolds, *Kingdoms and Communities in Western Europe 900–1300* (Oxford, 1984); T. A. Reuter, ed., *The Medieval Nobility* (Amsterdam and Oxford, 1978); M. Keen, *Chivalry* (London, 1984); P. Contamine, *War in the Middle Ages* (Oxford, 1984); G. Duby, *The Chivalrous Society* (Berkeley, 1977); and the classic work by M. Bloch, *Feudal Society* (London, 1961). G. Duby discusses the theory of medieval social order in *The Three Orders* (Chicago, 1980). Various aspects of the social history of the nobility can be found in G. Duby, *The Knight, the Lady, and the Priest* (London, 1984), on noble marriages; R. Barber and J. Barker, *Tournaments: Jousts, Chivalry and Pageants in the Middle Ages* (New York, 1989), on tournaments; W. Anderson, *Castles of Europe* (London, 1970); C. B. Bouchard, *Life and Society in the West: Antiquity and the Middle Ages* (San Diego, 1988), Ch. 6; and Robert Delort, *Life in the Middle Ages*, trans. Robert Allen (New York, 1972). Also enjoyable is the popular study by J. and F. Gies, *Life in a Medieval Castle* (New York, 1974). On women, see R. T. Morewedge, ed., *The Role of Women in the Middle Ages* (Albany, N.Y., 1975); and S. M. Stuard, ed., *Women in Medieval Society* (Philadelphia, 1976).

There are numerous works on the different feudal principalities: On England, see R. R. Davies, *Domination and Conquest: The Experience of Scotland and Wales, 1100–1300* (Cambridge, 1990); F. Barlow, *The Feudal Kingdom of England, 1042–1216*, 3d ed. (New York, 1972); D. C. Douglas, *William the Conqueror: The Norman Impact upon England* (Berkeley, 1964); R. Frame, *The Political Development of the British Isles, 1100–1400* (Oxford, 1990); and W. L. Warren, *Henry II* (Berkeley, 1973). On Germany, see A. Haverkamp, *Medieval Germany* (Oxford, 1988); B. Arnold, *German Knighthood 1050–1300* (Oxford, 1985); H. Fuhrmann, *Germany in the High Middle Ages c. 1050–1250* (Cambridge, 1986), an excellent account; B. Arnold, *Princes and Territories in Medieval Germany* (Cambridge, 1991); and P. Munz's biography, *Frederick Barbarossa* (London, 1969). On France, see J. Dunbabin, *France in the Making 843–1180* (Oxford, 1985); and E. M. Hallam, *Capetian France 987–1328* (London, 1980), a well-done general account. On the Normans, see J. le Patourel, *The Norman Empire* (Oxford, 1976); and D. C. Douglas, *The Norman Achievement* (London, 1969), and *The Norman Fate* (Berkeley, 1977). On Spain, see G. Jackson, *The Making of Medieval Spain* (London, 1972); A. Mackay, *Spain in the Middle Ages* (London, 1977); J. F. Powers, *A Society Organized for War* (Berkeley, 1988); and H. Dillard, *Daughters of the Reconquest* (Cambridge, 1984). On Italy, see D. J. Herlihy, *Cities and Society in Medieval Italy* (London, 1980); J. K. Hyde, *Society and Politics in Medieval Italy* (London, 1973); and G. Tabacco, *The Struggle for Power in Medieval Italy* (New York, 1989). On eastern Europe and Scandinavia, see N. Davies, *God's Playground: A History of Poland*, vol. 1 (Oxford, 1981); T. K. Derry, *A History of Scandinavia* (London, 1979); J. Fennell, *The Crisis of Medieval Russia, 1200–1304* (New York, 1983); and the books listed for Chapter 8.

For specialized studies in the political history of the thirteenth century, see J. C. Holt, *Magna Carta* (Cambridge, 1965); T. C. Van Cleve, *The Emperor Frederick the Second of Hohenstaufen* (Oxford, 1973); D. Abulafia, *Frederick II. A Medieval Emperor* (London, 1987); M. W. Labarge, *St. Louis: The Life of Louis IX of France* (London, 1968); J. R. Strayer, *The Reign of Philip the Fair* (Princeton, 1980); and J. F. O'Callaghan, *A History of Medieval Spain* (Ithaca, N.Y., 1975), and *The Cortes of Castile-Leon* (Philadelphia, 1989).

CHAPTER

11

Crusades and Culture in the High Middle Ages

The economic, religious, and political growth of the High Middle Ages gave European society a new confidence that enabled it to look beyond its borders to the lands and empires of the east. Only a confident Europe could have undertaken the crusades, the military effort to recover the Holy Land of the Near East from the Muslims. The crusades gave the revived papacy of the High Middle Ages yet another opportunity to demonstrate its influence over European society. The crusades were a curious mix of God and warfare, two of the chief concerns of the Middle Ages. In the first crusade, a band of French knights under Bohemund managed to capture the city of Antioch in 1098, but a Muslim relief force counterattacked, surrounding the French knights in their newly conquered city. Bohemund's forces seemed doomed until a "miraculous discovery" was made in an Antioch church—the Holy Lance, the spear allegedly used to pierce Christ's body at the crucifixion. To prove the authenticity and power of the lance, its discoverer, Peter Bartholomew, agreed to a test. According to the chronicler Raymond of Aguilers, the crusaders set two piles of dry olive branches on fire. When the bonfires were burning fiercely, Peter Bartholomew, dressed only in his tunic but armed with the Holy Lance, stepped into the flames. He emerged a few minutes later unscathed, with no injuries, a sure sign to the onlookers of the special qualities of the lance. Inspired, the French troops marched out, defeated the Muslim forces, and lifted the siege of Antioch. The leaders of the army wrote to the pope, saying: "After firmly ordering our battle-lines, of both foot and horse, we boldly sought the place where their valor and bravery were greatest. The Holy Lance was with us, and from the very first engagement of the battle we forced the enemy to flee." The crusading knights then went on to capture the Holy City of Jerusalem.

Western assurance and energy, so crucial to the crusades, were also evident in a burst of intellectual and artistic activity. A rebirth of classical learning, new educational institutions known as universities, a

Timeline

1000	1050	1100	1150	1200	1250	1300

•••• First crusade

•• Second crusade

• Sack of Constantinople

•• Third crusade

• Saladin's conquest of Jerusalem

• Children's crusade

• Battle of Manzikert

• End of Christian presence in the Holy Land

• The Song of Roland

•••••••••••••••••••• The rise of universities

•••••••••••• Work of Thomas Aquinas

•••••••••••••••••••• Age of Gothic cathedrals

---

systematic approach to the study of theology and law, the development of science and technology, and a growing and diverse vernacular literature all gave witness to a vibrant intellectual life. At the same time, a religious building spree—especially evident in the great Romanesque and Gothic cathedrals of the age—left the landscape bedecked with churches that were the visible symbols of Christian Europe's vitality.

Background to the Crusades

Although European civilization developed in relative isolation, it had never entirely lost contact with the lands and empires of the east. At the end of the eleventh century, that contact increased, in part because developments in the Byzantine and Islamic worlds prompted the first major attempt of that new European civilization to expand beyond Europe proper.

The Islamic Empire

By the mid-tenth century, the Islamic empire led by the Abbasid caliphate in Baghdad was in the process of disintegration. An attempt was made in the tenth century to unify the Islamic world under the direction of a Shi'ite dynasty known as the Fatimids. Their origins lay in North Africa, but they managed to conquer Egypt and establish the new city of Cairo as their capital. In establishing a Shi'ite caliphate, they became rivals to the Sunni caliphate of Baghdad. Although the Fatimids did move into Syria and Arabia, they were unable to overcome the Abbasids in Mesopotamia, and the Islamic world remained divided.

As Egypt grew into an important center of eastern trade, the Fatimid dynasty prospered and surpassed the Abbasid caliphate as the dynamic center of the Islamic world. From their luxurious court in Cairo, the Fatimids pursued a religious policy based on toleration and created a strong military by using nonnative peoples as mercenaries. One of these peoples, the Seljuk Turks, soon posed a threat to the Fatimids themselves.

The Seljuk Turks were a nomadic people from central Asia who had been converted to Islam and flourished as military mercenaries for the Abbasid caliphate. Moving gradually into Iran and Armenia, they grew in number until by the eleventh century they were able to take over the eastern provinces of the Abbasid empire. In 1055, a Turkish leader captured Baghdad and assumed command of the Abbasid empire with the title of sultan. While the Abbasid caliph remained as the chief Sunni religious authority, the real military and political power of the state was in the hands of the Seljuk Turks. By the last quarter of the eleventh century, the Seljuk Turks were exerting military pressure on Egypt and the Byzantine Empire. When the Byzantine emperor foolishly challenged the Turks, the latter routed the Byzantine army at Manzikert in 1071. In dire straits, the Byzantines turned to the west for help, setting in motion the papal pleas that led to the crusades. To understand the complexities of the situation, however, we need to look first at the Byzantine Empire.

The Byzantine Empire

The Macedonian dynasty of the tenth and eleventh centuries had restored much of the power of the Byzantine Empire; its incompetent successors, however, reversed most of the gains. After the Macedonian dynasty was extinguished in 1056, the empire was beset by internal struggles for power between ambitious military leaders and aristocratic families who attempted to buy the support of the great landowners of Anatolia by allowing them greater control over their peasants. This policy was self-destructive, however, since the peasant-warrior was the traditional backbone of the Byzantine state.

The growing division between the Catholic church of the west and the Eastern Orthodox church of the Byzantine Empire had also weakened the Byzantine state. Although theological differences were an important cause of this rift, the question of authority came to overshadow all others. The Eastern Orthodox church was unwilling to accept the pope's claim that he was the sole head of the church. In the mid-eleventh century, this dispute reached a climax. To resolve the situation, Pope Leo IX sent Cardinal Humbert, a dedicated reformer, as his legate to Constantinople. The envoy was not a wise choice. Closed-minded and intense, he was a great champion of papal rights and did not believe that the issue could be compromised or even negotiated. His opponent in Constantinople was the head of the Byzantine church, the Patriarch Michael Cerularius, who was equally dogmatic and unwilling to come to terms. Unable to agree whatsoever, the two church leaders formally excommunicated each other in 1054, initiating a schism between the two great branches of Christianity that has not been completely healed to this day.

The Byzantine Empire faced external threats to its security as well. The establishment of the Normans in southern Italy had eliminated Byzantine influence from that region; now the Normans invaded Greece, threatening Byzantine control of the Balkans. The greatest challenge to Byzantium, however, came from the Seljuk Turks who had moved into Asia Minor—the heartland of the empire and its main source of food and manpower. In 1071, the Byzantine forces under Emperor Romanus IV Diogenes were disastrously defeated at Manzikert by a Turkish army. The Turks then advanced into Anatolia where many peasants, already disgusted by their exploitation at the hands of Byzantine landowners, readily accepted Turkish control.

A new dynasty, however, soon breathed new life into the Byzantine Empire. The Comneni, under Alexius I Comnenus (1081–1118), were victorious on the Greek Adriatic coast against the Normans, defeated the Pechenegs in the Balkans, and stopped the Turks in Anatolia. Lacking the resources to undertake additional campaigns against the Turks, Emperor Alexius I turned to the west for military assistance. It was the positive response of the west to the emperor's request that led to the crusades. The Byzantine Empire lived to regret it.

The Crusades

The crusades were based upon the idea of a holy war against the infidel or unbelievers. Although the concept of unbeliever was eventually broadened to include other groups, Christendom's wrath was directed initially against the Muslims. It had already found some expression in the attempt to reconquer Spain from the Muslims and the success of the Normans in reclaiming Sicily (see Chapter 10). At the end of the eleventh century, Christian Europe found itself with a glorious opportunity to attack the Muslims.

The immediate impetus for the crusades came when the Byzantine emperor Alexius I asked Pope Urban II (1088–1099) for help against the Seljuk Turks. Alexius's request was for financial aid to enable him to recruit mercenaries, but Urban II took a different perspective. Christian forces had recently captured Toledo in Spain, and the Normans had completed their conquest of Sicily. The pope saw a golden opportunity to provide papal leadership for a great cause: to rally the warriors of Europe for the liberation of Jerusalem and the Holy Land from the infidel. Urban also perceived an opportunity to reunite the Christian church under Rome's leadership. At the Council of Clermont in southern France near the end of 1095, Urban challenged Christians to take up their weapons against the infidel and participate in a holy war to recover the Holy Land (see the box on p. 345). The pope promised remission of sins: "All who die by the way, whether by land or by sea, or in battle against the pagans, shall have immediate remission of sins. This I grant them through the power of God with which I am invested."[1]

The initial response to Urban's speech reveals how appealing many people found this combined call to military arms and religious fervor. The first crusade was preceded by an exercise in religious fanaticism and futility. A self-appointed leader Peter the Hermit, who preached of his visions of the Holy City of Jerusalem, convinced a large mob, most of them poor and many of them peasants, to undertake a crusade to the east. This

❧ Pope Urban II Proclaims a Crusade ❧

Toward the end of the eleventh century, the Byzantine emperor Alexius I sent Pope Urban II a request for aid against the Seljuk Turks. At the Council of Clermont, Urban II appealed to a large crowd to take up weapons and recover Palestine from the Muslims. This description of Urban's appeal is taken from an account by Fulcher of Chartres.

Pope Urban II

Pope Urban II . . . addressed them [the French] in a very persuasive speech, as follows: "O race of the Franks, O people who live beyond the mountains [that is, reckoned from Rome], O people loved and chosen of God, as is clear from your many deeds, distinguished over all other nations by the situation of your land, your catholic faith, and your regard for the holy church, we have a special message and exhortation for you. For we wish you to know what a grave matter has brought us to your country. The sad news has come from Jerusalem and Constantinople that the people of Persia, an accursed and foreign race [the Seljuk Turks], enemies of God, . . . have invaded the lands of those Christians and devastated them with the sword, rapine, and fire. Some of the Christians they have carried away as slaves, others they have put to death. The churches they have either destroyed or turned into mosques. They desecrate and overthrow the altars. They circumcise the Christians and pour the blood from the circumcision on the altars or in the baptismal fonts. Some they kill in a horrible way by cutting open the abdomen, taking out a part of the entrails and tying them to a stake; they then beat them and compel them to walk until all their entrails are drawn out and they fall to the ground. Some they use as targets for their arrows. They compel some to stretch out their necks and then they try to see whether they can cut off their heads with one strike of the sword. It is better to say nothing of their horrible treatment of the women. They have taken from the Greek empire a tract of land so large that it takes more than two months to walk through it. Whose duty is to avenge this and recover that land, if not yours? For to you more than to any other nations the Lord has given the military spirit, courage, agile bodies, and the bravery to strike down those who resist you. Let your minds be stirred to bravery by the deeds of your forefathers, and by the efficiency and greatness of Karl the Great [Charlemagne], . . . and of the other kings who have destroyed Turkish kingdoms, and established Christianity in their lands. You should be moved especially by the holy grave of our Lord and Savior which is now held by unclean peoples, and by the holy places which are treated with dishonor and irreverently befouled with their uncleanness. . . ."

"O bravest of knights, descendants of unconquered ancestors, do not be weaker than they, but remember their courage. . . . Set out on the road to the holy sepulchre, take the land from that wicked people, and make it your own. . . . Jerusalem is the best of all lands, more fruitful than all others. . . . This land our Savior made illustrious by his birth, beautiful with his life, and sacred with his suffering. . . . This royal city is now held captive by her enemies, and made pagan by those who know not God. She asks and longs to be liberated and does not cease to beg you to come to her aid. . . . Set out on this journey and you will obtain the remission of your sins and be sure of the incorruptible glory of the kingdom of heaven."

When Pope Urban had said this and much more of the same sort, all who were present were moved to cry out with one accord, "It is the will of God, it is the will of God." When the pope heard this he raised his eyes to heaven and gave thanks to God, and commanding silence with a gesture of his hand, he said: "My dear brethren, today there is fulfilled in you that which the Lord says in the Gospel, 'Where two or three are gathered together in my name, there am I in the midst.' For unless the Lord God had been in your minds you would not all have said the same thing. . . . So I say unto you, God, who put those words into your hearts, has caused you to utter them. Therefore let these words be your battle cry, because God caused you to speak them. Whenever you meet the enemy in battle, you shall all cry out, 'It is the will of God, it is the will of God. . . .' Whoever therefore shall determine to make this journey and shall make a vow to God and shall offer himself as a living sacrifice, holy, acceptable to God, shall wear a cross on his brow or on his breast. And when he returns after having fulfilled his vow he shall wear the cross on his back."

✦ **Peasant's Crusade.** Before the aristocracy could organize a crusade in response to the call of Pope Urban II, a large group of peasants joined the fanatical Peter the Hermit and Walter the Penniless in an attempt to free the Holy Land. When they could not buy food, the poorly armed peasants ravaged the countryside and looted towns. This illustration shows a group of Hungarians attacking the peasants and reclaiming their goods.

"Peasant's Crusade" or "Crusade of the Poor" comprised a ragtag rabble that moved through the Balkans, terrorizing natives and looting for their food and supplies. Their misplaced religious enthusiasm led to another tragic by-product as well, the persecution of the Jews, long branded by the church as the murderers of Christ. As a contemporary chronicler described it, ". . . while passing through the cities along the Rhine, Main, and Danube, led by their zeal for Christianity, they persecuted the hated race of the Jews wherever they were found, and strove either to destroy them completely or to compel them to become Christians."[2] Two bands of peasant crusaders led by Peter the Hermit and Walter the Penniless managed to reach Constantinople. Emperor Alexius I wisely shipped them over to Asia Minor where the undisciplined and poorly armed rabble was massacred by the Turks.

The Early Crusades

Pope Urban II did not share the wishful thinking of the peasant crusaders but was more inclined to trust knights who had been well trained in the art of war. The first crusading armies were recruited from the warrior class of western Europe, particularly France. Urban also appointed a bishop, Adhemar of Le Puy, to lead the crusading host. Although the knights who made up this first serious crusading host were motivated by religious fervor, there were other attractions as well. Some sought adventure and welcomed a legitimate opportunity to pursue their favorite pastime—fighting. Others saw an opportunity to gain territory, riches, status, possibly a title, and even salvation—had the pope not offered a full remission of sins for those who participated in these "armed pilgrimages"? From the perspective of the pope and the European monarchs, the crusades offered a way to rid Europe of contentious young nobles who disturbed the peace and wasted lives and energy fighting each other.

Three organized crusading bands of noble warriors, most of them French, made their way to Constantinople by 1097. Emperor Alexius was not pleased with their arrival and greatly distrusted their motives. Bohemund, for example, the son of Robert Guiscard, had been one of the invaders of the Greek lands of the Byzantine Empire. The emperor's daughter was acutely suspicious of the true designs of the crusaders: ". . . in their dreams of capturing the capital [they] had come to the same decision . . . that while in appearance making the journey to Jerusalem, in reality their object was to dethrone the Emperor and to capture the capital [Constantinople]."[3] Instead of a band of mercenaries that he could pay to fight on his behalf, Alexius got a group of French nobles who wanted to conquer the Holy Land for their own purposes. The emperor entered into negotiations with the crusaders who eventually agreed to take an oath of allegiance to him.

The crusading army probably numbered several thousand cavalry and as many as 10,000 foot soldiers. After the capture of Antioch in 1098, much of the crusading host proceeded down the coast of Palestine, evading the garrisoned coastal cities, and reached Jerusalem in June 1099. After a five-week siege, the Holy City was taken amidst a horrible massacre of the inhabitants, men, women, and children. As executed by the crusaders, "God's judgment" on the infidel was indeed a frightful one (see the box on p. 348).

After further conquest of Palestinian lands, the crusaders largely ignored their promises to the Byzantine emperor and proceeded to organize four crusader states: the principality of Antioch under Bohemund, son of Robert Guiscard of Sicily; the county of Edessa under

Baldwin, the brother of Godfrey de Bouillon; the county of Tripoli under Count Raymond of Toulouse; and the kingdom of Jerusalem under Godfrey de Bouillon, but he died within a year and was succeeded by his brother, Baldwin of Edessa (1100–1118). In keeping with their own traditional practices, the crusading leaders created organized feudal states. Antioch, Edessa, and Tripoli were all held as fiefs from the ruler of the kingdom of Jerusalem.

Since the Latin states existed in a world surrounded by Muslim enemies, they grew increasingly dependent upon the Italian commercial cities for supplies from Europe. Some Italian cities, such as Genoa, Pisa, and, above all, Venice, waxed rich and powerful in the process. The role of supplier might logically have fallen to the Byzantine Empire, but relations between Byzantium and the crusader states deteriorated steadily. The presence of the Latin states in territory that the Byzantines believed belonged to them added to the hostility generated by religious differences. Moreover, commercial competition from the Italian cities hurt the Byzantines deeply at a time when they were experiencing a loss of lands and manpower and a shrinking tax base.

THE MILITARY RELIGIOUS ORDERS

An important part of the military force available to defend the crusader states came from a new institution, the military monastic orders. A product of the religious enthusiasm that accompanied the crusades, these orders combined the two greatest ideals of the High Middle Ages—the monk and the warrior—into a single person. Two such orders arose to defend the Latin states. The Knights of the Temple came into existence when a group of French knights took a religious oath and began to serve as escorts for pilgrims to the Holy City of Jerusalem. They settled in a house near the Temple of Solomon and soon became known as the Templars. In 1128, they were officially recognized by the pope as a monastic order. In addition to the regular monastic vows of poverty, chastity, and obedience, the brothers took a fourth vow to help and defend people making pilgrimages to Jerusalem. The Knights of St. John of Jerusalem made their debut when they organized a hospital to help sick pilgrims in the Holy Land. Their fourth vow was to take care of the sick, and they were soon acknowledged as a military religious order called the Hospitallers. Both of these monastic orders were given tracts of land in Palestine by the kings of Jerusalem, which they guarded with formidable fortresses. Since both orders also re-

ceived bequests of territories throughout Europe to support their missions in the Holy Land, they eventually became enormously wealthy. Many of their recruits stemmed from the nobility. At their high point, the Templars and Hospitallers together provided almost one thousand knights to defend the kingdom of Jerusalem.

The ideals of these two monastic orders spread from the east to the rest of Europe. The Templars served as models for three Spanish military orders as well as the order of Teutonic Knights founded in Germany in 1198. The Teutonic Knights conquered territory along the eastern coast of the Baltic from the pagan Lithuanians, Livonians, and Prussians. From their conquests eventually came the duchy of Prussia, which played an important role in European history.

THE SECOND CRUSADE

It was not easy for the crusader states to maintain themselves in the east. Already by the 1120s, the Muslims had begun to strike back. In 1144, Edessa became the first of the four Latin states to be recaptured. Its fall led to renewed calls for another crusade. This time, the moral exhortations to destroy the infidel came not from the pope, but from the monastic firebrand Saint Bernard of Clairvaux (see Chapter 9), who exclaimed: "Now, on account of our sins, the sacrilegious enemies of the cross have begun to show their faces. . . . What are you doing, you servants of the cross? Will you throw to the dogs that which is most holy? Will you cast pearls before swine?" But it was not beneath even the holy man to mix spiritual injunction with the language of commerce to encourage the enlistment of crusaders:

⇒ *The Christian Capture of Jerusalem* ⇐

The first crusade was the most successful of the Christian world's numerous efforts to seize the Holy Land from the Muslims. The crusading host of Christian knights laid siege to Jerusalem in June 1099. After five weeks, the city capitulated, whereupon the crusaders enacted a horrible vengeance upon the city's inhabitants. This excerpt is taken from an account by Fulcher of Chartres who accompanied the crusaders to the Holy Land.

Fulcher of Chartres, *Chronicle of the First Crusade*
Then the Franks entered the city magnificently at the noonday hour on Friday, the day of the week when Christ redeemed the whole world on the cross. With trumpets sounding and with everything in an uproar, exclaiming: "Help, God!" they vigorously pushed into the city, and straightway raised the banner on the top of the wall. All the heathen, completely terrified, changed their boldness to swift flight through the narrow streets of the quarters. The more quickly they fled, the more quickly were they put to flight.

Count Raymond and his men, who were bravely assailing the city in another section, did not perceive this until they saw the Saracens jumping from the top of the wall. Seeing this, they joyfully ran to the city as quickly as they could, and helped the others pursue and kill the wicked enemy.

Then some, both Arabs and Ethiopians, fled into the Tower of David; others shut themselves in the Temple of the Lord and of Solomon, where in the halls a very great attack was made on them. Nowhere was there a place where the Saracens could escape the swordsmen.

On the top of Solomon's Temple, to which they had climbed in fleeing, many were shot to death with arrows and cast down headlong from the roof. Within this Temple, about ten thousand were beheaded. If you had been there, your feet would have been stained up to the ankles with the blood of the slain. What more shall I tell? Not one of them was allowed to live.

They did not spare the women and children.

Or are you a shrewd businessman, a man quick to see the profits of this world? If you are, I can offer you a splendid bargain. . . . Take the sign of the cross. At once you will have indulgence for all the sins which you confess with a contrite heart. It does not cost you much to buy and if you wear it with humility you will find that it is the kingdom of heaven.[4]

Bernard aimed his message at knights and even managed to enlist two powerful rulers, King Louis VII of France and Emperor Conrad III of Germany.

The second crusade seemed destined for failure. The two crusading armies of king and emperor were not well organized and failed to cooperate in coordinating their efforts against the Muslims. They were even incapable of cooperating with the Byzantines. The French knights contemplated an attack on Constantinople, but the French king dissuaded them from such a dastardly act against a Christian city. Finally, the new crusading hosts found little cooperation from the crusader lords of the kingdom of Jerusalem. These local lords had found ways to live with local Muslim leaders and were quite unwilling to destroy the symbiotic relationship they had developed (see the box on p. 349). They, too, undermined the efforts of the two crusading monarchs. The

second crusade proved to be a total failure. Saint Bernard attributed its lack of success to the loss of God's favor due to human sinfulness; the French king simply blamed the wickedness of the people involved.

THE THIRD CRUSADE

The third crusade was a reaction to the renewal of Muslim energies and the fall of the Holy City of Jerusalem. In 1169, the Sunni Muslims of Syria invaded Egypt and, under the leadership of the warrior known to the west as Saladin, demolished the Fatimid caliphate. Eventually, Saladin established control over Syria, and the Latin states faced a unified Muslim power on two frontiers. Saladin's forces invaded the kingdom of Jerusalem and at the Battle of Hattin in 1187 destroyed the Latin forces gathered there. Saladin now began the reconquest of Palestine, and while Tripoli, Antioch, and Tyre were able to resist, Jerusalem fell in October 1187. Unlike the Christians, Saladin did not permit a massacre of the civilian population and even tolerated the continuation of Christian religious services. To the Christians, however, his enlightened policies were overshadowed by the actual fall of Jerusalem to the Muslims.

❧ The Crusaders in Muslim Eyes ❧

Usamah, an early twelfth-century Muslim warrior, had close associations with the crusaders. When he was ninety years old, he wrote his memoirs, including some entertaining observations on the Franks (the French). Here Usamah expresses his astonishment at the Franks' rudeness to Muslims and at their bizarre approach to justice.

Usamah, *Book of Reflections*

1. Everyone who is a fresh emigrant from the Frankish lands is ruder in character than those who have become acclimatized and have held long association with the Muslims. Here is an illustration of their rude character.

   Whenever I visited Jerusalem I always entered the Aqsa Mosque, beside which stood a small mosque which the Franks had converted into a church. When I used to enter the Aqsa Mosque, which was occupied by the Templars [see p. 347], who were my friends, the Templars would evacuate the little adjoining mosque so that I might pray in it. One day I entered this mosque, repeated the first formula, "Allah is great," and stood up in the act of praying, upon which one of the Franks rushed on me, got hold of me and turned my face eastward saying, "This is the way you should pray!" A group of Templars hastened to him, seized him and repelled him from me. I resumed my prayer The same man, while the others were otherwise busy, rushed once more on me and turned my face eastward, saying, "This is the way you should pray!" The Templars again came in to him and expelled him. They apologized to me, saying, "This is a stranger who has only recently arrived from the land of the Franks and he has never before seen anyone praying except eastward." Thereupon I said to myself, "I have had enough prayer." So I went out, and have ever been surprised at the conduct of this devil of a man. . . .

2. In the army of King Fulk, son of Fulk, was a Frankish reverend knight who had just arrived from their land in order to make the holy pilgrimage and then return home. He was of my intimate fellowship and kept such constant company with me that he began to call me "my brother." Between us were mutual bonds of amity and friendship. When he resolved to return by sea to his homeland, he said to me:

   "My brother, I am leaving for my country and I want you to send with me your son (my son, who was then fourteen years old, was at that time in my company) to our country, where he can see the knights and learn wisdom and chivalry. When he returns, he will be like a wise man."

   Thus there fell upon my ears words which would never come out of the head of a sensible man; for even if my son were to be taken captive, his captivity could not bring him a worse misfortune than carrying him into the lands of the Franks.

3. I inquired about this man and was informed that his mother had been married to a Frank whom she had killed. Her son used to practice ruses against the Frankish pilgrims and cooperate with his mother in assassinating them. They finally brought charges against him and tried his case according to the Frankish way of procedure.

   They installed a huge cask and filled it with water. Across it they set a board of wood. They then bound the arms of the man charged with the act, tied a rope around his shoulders, and dropped him into the cask, their idea being that in case he was innocent, he would sink in the water and they would then lift him up with the rope so that he might not die in the water; and in case he was guilty, he would not sink in the water. This man did his best to sink when they dropped him into the water, but he could not do it. So he had to submit to their sentence against him—may Allah's curse be upon them! They pierced his eyeballs with red-hot awls.

Now all of Christendom was ablaze with calls for a new crusade in the east. Rulers levied special taxes to raise troops, and three major monarchs agreed to lead their forces in person: Emperor Frederick Barbarossa of Germany (1152–1190), Richard I the Lionhearted of England (1189–1199), and Philip II Augustus, king of France (1180–1223). This overwhelming response seemed auspicious for the successful recovery of the Holy Land.

The crusaders, however, soon encountered the problems that had plagued their predecessors: the difficulties and expenses of either overland or sea travel to the east; conflict with the Byzantines and the leaders of the remaining crusader states; constant infighting, especially

♦ Richard the Lionhearted Executes Muslims at Acre.
The third crusade was organized in response to the capture of
the Kingdom of Jerusalem by the Sunni Muslims under the
leadership of Saladin. Though Saladin forbade the massacre of
Christians, his Christian foes were more harsh. Here Richard
the Lionhearted (at right with crown) watches the execution of
2,700 Muslims at Acre.

between Richard and Philip (kings were notoriously
unwilling to accept advice from anyone, especially fellow kings); and debilitating sickness for large numbers of
the crusaders in a hostile climate.

After overcoming the initial difficulties, some of the
crusaders finally arrived in the east by 1189 only to
encounter more problems. Frederick Barbarossa experienced stunning successes in Asia Minor, but then
drowned accidentally while swimming in a local river.
Without his strong leadership, his army quickly disintegrated. The English and French arrived by sea and met
with success against the coastal cities where they had
the support of their fleets. When they moved inland,
they failed miserably. Eventually, after Philip went
home, Richard the Lionhearted without more fighting
negotiated a settlement whereby Saladin agreed to allow
Christian pilgrims free access to Jerusalem.

The Crusades of the Thirteenth Century

Once again, in the thirteenth century, the popes, now at
the height of their power, took the initiative in calling
for a crusade. Although it may be apparent in retrospect
that the crusading energy of the twelfth century had
largely dissipated by the beginning of the thirteenth, at
the time, both monarchs and nobles felt compelled to

take up the crusading cross. The fourth crusade quickly
indicated, however, that greed was beginning to sup-
plant religious motives.

It was the great pope Innocent III who inaugurated
the fourth crusade. The death of Saladin in 1193 and
the subsequent disintegration of his empire had created
new opportunities. Innocent judged the moment auspicious and encouraged the nobility of Europe to put on
the crusader's mantle. The nobles of France and the
Netherlands responded in great numbers. The Venetians
agreed to transport the crusading army to the east, but
subverted it from its goal by using it first to capture Zara,
a port on the Dalmatian coast and a Christian city. The
crusading army next became entangled in Byzantine
politics, an involvement that soon had tragic results.

At the beginning of the thirteenth century, the
Byzantine Empire was experiencing yet another struggle
for the imperial throne. One contender, Alexius, son of
the overthrown Emperor Isaac II, appealed to the crusaders in Zara for assistance, offering them 200,000
marks in silver (the Venetians were getting 85,000 as a
transport fee) and reconciliation of the Greek church
with the Roman Catholic church. The leaders of the
crusaders now diverted their forces to Constantinople.
When the crusading army arrived, the deposed Isaac II
was reestablished with his son Alexius IV as co-emperor.
Unfortunately, the co-emperors were unable to pay the
promised sum. Relations between the crusaders and the
Byzantines deteriorated, leading to an attack on Constantinople by the crusaders in the spring of 1204. On
April 12, they stormed and sacked the city (see the box
on p. 353). Christian crusaders took gold, silver, jewelry,
and precious furs while the Catholic clergy accompanying the crusaders stole as many relics as they could find.

The Byzantine Empire now disintegrated into a series
of petty states ruled by crusading barons and Byzantine
princes. The chief state was the new Latin Empire of
Constantinople led by Count Baldwin of Flanders as
emperor. The Venetians seized the island of Crete and
secured domination of Constantinople's trade. Why had
the western crusaders succeeded so easily when Persians,
Bulgars, and Arabs had failed for centuries to conquer
Constantinople? Although the crusaders were no doubt
motivated by greed and a lust for conquest, they were
also convinced that they were acting on behalf of God's
cause. After all, a Catholic patriarch (a Venetian) had
now been installed in Constantinople and the reconciliation of Eastern Orthodoxy with Catholic Christianity
had been put in force. Nor should we overlook the
military superiority of the French warriors and the
superb organizational skills of the Venetians; together,
they formed a union of great effectiveness and power.

Map 11.1 The Crusades.

Conviction, military prowess, and the organizational skill of the mercantile element comprised a combination that eventually enabled Europe to make conquests around the world.

Although he protested the diversion of the crusade from the Holy Land, Pope Innocent III belatedly accepted as "God's work" the conversion of Greek Byzantium to Latin Christianity. But the use of force to reunite the churches virtually guaranteed that the reunion would not be permanent. The west was unable to maintain its Latin Empire for the western rulers of the newly created principalities were soon fighting each other. Some parts of the Byzantine Empire had managed to survive under Byzantine princes. In 1259, Michael Paleologus, a Greek military leader, took control of the kingdom of Nicaea in western Asia Minor, recaptured Constantinople two years later with a Byzantine army, and then established a new Byzantine dynasty, the Paleologi.

The Byzantine Empire had been saved, but it was no longer a great Mediterranean power. The restored empire was a badly truncated one comprising the city of Constantinople and its surrounding territory, some lands in Asia Minor, and part of Thessalonika. Even in its reduced size, however, the empire limped along for another 190 years until the Ottoman Turks brought about its final capitulation in 1453.

Despite the cynical diversion of the fourth crusade to Constantinople, the crusading ideal and the religious enthusiasm that inspired it were not completely lost. In Germany in 1212, a youth known as Nicholas of Cologne announced that God had inspired him to lead a "children's crusade" to the Holy Land. Thousands of young people joined Nicholas and made their way down the Rhine and across the Alps to Italy where the pope told them to go home. Most tried to do so. At about the same time, a group of about 20,000 French children, also inspired by the desire to free the Holy Land from the Muslims, made their way to Marseilles where two shipowners agreed to transport them to the Holy Land. Seven ships packed with hymn-singing youths soon left the port. Two of the ships perished in a storm near Sardinia; the other five sailed to North Africa where the children were sold into slavery. The next crusade of adult warriors was hardly more successful. The fifth crusade (1219–1221) attempted to recover the Holy Land by way of the powerful Muslim state of Egypt. The crusade achieved some early successes, but its ultimate failure marked an end to papal leadership of the western crusaders.

The sixth crusade, which was led by the German emperor Frederick II, took place without papal support

◆ **Siege and Capture of Constantinople.** This thirteenth-century miniature depicts the siege and capture of Constantinople by the fourth crusade in 1204. At the right, soldiers use a catapult to shower the city with stones while knights use a tower to attack the walls. Shown above the battle are scenes from the Passion of Christ, a deliberate and ironic reminder that the purpose of the crusades was to capture the holy city of Jerusalem.

❧ Christian Crusaders Capture Constantinople ❧

Pope Innocent III inaugurated the fourth crusade after Saladin's empire began to disintegrate. Tragically, however, the crusading army of mostly French nobles was diverted to Constantinople to intervene in Byzantine politics. In 1204, the Christian crusaders stormed and sacked one of Christendom's greatest cities. This description of the conquest of Constantinople is taken from a contemporary account by a participant in the struggle.

Villehardouin, *The Conquest of Constantinople*

The moment the knights aboard the transports saw this happen, they landed, and raising their ladders against the wall, climbed to the top, and took four more towers. Then all the rest of the troops started to leap out of warships, galleys, and transports, helter-skelter, each as fast as he could. They broke down about three of the gates and entered the city. The horses were then taken out of the transports; the knights mounted and rode straight towards the place where the Emperor had his camp. He had his battalions drawn up in front of the tents; but as soon as his men saw the knights charging towards them on horseback, they retreated in disorder. The Emperor himself fled through the streets of the city to the castle of Bucoleon.

Then followed a scene of massacre and pillage: on every hand the Greeks [Byzantines] were cut down, their horses, palfreys, mules, and other possessions snatched as booty. So great was the number of killed and wounded that no man could count them. A great part of the Greek nobles had fled towards the gate of Blachernae; but by this time it was past six o'clock, and our men had grown weary of fighting and slaughtering. The troops began to assemble in a great square inside Constantinople . . . [and] decided to settle down near the walls and towers they had already captured. . . .

That night passed, and the next day came. . . . Early that morning all the troops, knights and sergeants alike, armed themselves, and each man went to join his division. They left their quarters thinking to meet with stronger resistance than they had encountered the day before, since they did not know that the Emperor had fled during the night. But they found no one to oppose them.

The Marquis de Montferrat rode straight along the shore to the palace of Bucoleon. As soon as he arrived there the place was surrendered to him, on condition that the lives of all the people in it should be spared. Among these were very many ladies of the highest rank who had taken refuge there. . . . . Words fail me when it comes to describing the treasures found in the palace, for there was such a store of precious things that one could not possibly count them. . . .

The rest of the army, scattered throughout the city, also gained much booty; so much, indeed, that no one could estimate its amount or its value. It included gold and silver, table-services and precious stones, satin and silk, mantles of squirrel fur, ermine and miniver, and every choicest thing to be found on this earth. Geoffrey de Villehardouin here declares that, to his knowledge, so much booty had never been gained in any city since the creation of the world.

Everyone took quarters where he pleased, and there was no lack of fine dwellings in that city. So the troops of the Crusaders and the Venetians were duly housed. They all rejoiced and gave thanks to our Lord for the honor and the victory He had granted them, so that those who had been poor now lived in wealth and luxury. Thus they celebrated Palm Sunday and the Easter Day following, with hearts full of joy for the benefits our Lord and Savior had bestowed on them. And well might they praise Him; since the whole of their army numbered no more than twenty thousand men, and with His help they had conquered four hundred thousand, or more, and that in the greatest, most powerful, and most strongly fortified city in the world.

because the emperor had been excommunicated by the pope for starting late. In 1228, Frederick sailed to Palestine where his army paraded around while the emperor negotiated with the sultan of Egypt. The sultan finally caved in and agreed to return Jerusalem to the crusaders. Frederick marched into Jerusalem and accepted the crown as king of Jerusalem. The Holy City had been taken without a fight and without papal support. Although he was denounced for his agreement with the Muslims, Frederick had at least achieved the crusaders' major goal. Once Frederick left, the Christian barons regained control, and the city fell once again, this time to a group of Turks allied with the sultan of Egypt.

The last two major crusades were organized by the saintly king of France, Louis IX. In 1248, Louis attacked

✦ **Louis IX Departs for Tunis.** The pious French king Louis IX organized the last two major crusades of the thirteenth century. Both failed miserably. This illustration shows a robust Louis IX setting out for Tunis in 1270. In truth, the king was so weak that he had to be carried to the ship.

Egypt, pursuing a plan to regain Palestine by first seizing Egypt. The idea might have been sound, but its execution was pitiful. Although possessed of considerable daring and piety, Louis was an abysmal strategist. He and his army were defeated, taken prisoner, and forced to pay an enormous ransom to gain their freedom.

Not content with his failure, Louis tried again in 1270, leading a contingent of troops on an ill-planned and ill-fated expedition to Tunis in North Africa. Louis's contemporary and noble friend, Jean de Joinville, expressed his contempt for the effort:

> I considered that all those who had advised the king to go on this expedition committed mortal sin. For at that time the state of the country was such that there was perfect peace throughout the kingdom, and between France and her neighbors, while ever since King Louis went away the state of the kingdom has done nothing but go from bad to worse.[5]

Louis and much of his army died from plague without conquering any territory.

Slowly, the Christian possessions in the east were retaken. Acre, the last foothold of the crusaders, surrendered in 1291. All in all, the crusades had failed to accomplish their primary goal of holding the Holy Land for the Christian west.

Effects of the Crusades

Whether the crusades had much effect on European civilization is debatable. The crusaders made little long-term impact on the east where the only visible remnants of their conquests were their castles. There may have been some broadening of perspective that comes from the exchange between two cultures, but the interaction of Christian Europe with the Muslim world was actually both more intense and more meaningful in Spain and Sicily than in the Holy Land.

Did the crusades help to stabilize European society by removing large numbers of young warriors who would have fought each other in Europe? Some historians think so and believe that western monarchs established their control more easily as a result. There is no doubt that the crusades did contribute to the economic growth of the Italian port cities, especially Genoa, Pisa, and Venice. But it is important to remember that the growing wealth and population of eleventh-century Europe had made the crusades possible in the first place. The crusades may have enhanced the revival of trade, but they certainly did not cause it. Even without the crusades, Italian merchants would have pursued new trade contacts with the eastern world.

The crusades did have unfortunate side effects that would haunt European society for generations. The first widespread attacks on the Jews began with the crusades. As some Christians argued, to undertake holy wars against infidel Muslims while the "murderers of Christ" ran free at home was unthinkable. The massacre of Jews became a regular feature of medieval European life.

The Intellectual and Artistic World of the High Middle Ages

The High Middle Ages was a time of tremendous intellectual and artistic vitality. The period witnessed the growth of educational institutions, a quickening of theological thought, the revival of law, a rebirth of interest in ancient culture, the development of a vernacular literature, and a burst of activity in art and architecture. While monks continued to play an important role in intellectual life, increasingly the secular clergy, cities, and courts, whether of kings, princes, or high church officials, began to exert a newfound influence.

The Rise of Universities

The university as we know it with faculty, students, and degrees was a product not of ancient Greece or Rome, but of the High Middle Ages. The word *university* is derived from the Latin word *universitas,* meaning a corporation or guild, and referred to either a guild of teachers or a guild of students. Medieval universities were educational guilds or corporations that produced educated and trained individuals. Since a guild of students or a guild of teachers was formed without official sanction, there is no clear date for the founding of Europe's oldest universities.

ORIGINS

Education in the Early Middle Ages rested primarily with the clergy, especially the monks. Although monastic schools were the centers of learning from the ninth to the early eleventh century, they were surpassed in the course of the eleventh century by the cathedral schools organized by the secular clergy. The great cathedrals were managed by legal corporations called chapters, which were composed of canons who were priests or candidates for the priesthood. Canons assisted bishops in the administration of their dioceses and bore responsibility for their educational establishments.

Cathedral schools expanded rapidly in the eleventh century. There were twenty of them in 900, but by 1100 the number had grown to at least two hundred since every cathedral city felt compelled to establish one. The most famous were Chartres, Reims, Paris, Laon, and Soissons, all located in France, which was truly the intellectual center of Europe by the twelfth century. The primary purpose of the cathedral school was to educate priests to be more literate men of God, especially those aspiring to play an important role in the cathedral chapter and perhaps even become bishops. Cathedral schools also attracted other individuals who desired some education but did not want to become priests. Many university administrators today carry titles, such as chancellor, provost, and dean, that were originally used for the officials of cathedral chapters. Yet universities represented a novel development that moved beyond the sphere of cathedral schools.

The first European university appeared in Bologna, Italy (unless one accords this distinction to the first medical school established earlier at Salerno, Italy). The emergence of the University of Bologna coincided with the revival of interest in Roman law, especially the rediscovery of Justinian's *Body of Civil Law* (see The Revival of Roman Law later in this chapter). In the twelfth century, a great teacher, such as Irnerius (1088–1125), attracted students from all over Europe. Most of them were laymen, usually older individuals who served as administrators to kings and princes and were particularly eager to learn more about law so they could apply it in their jobs. To protect themselves, students at Bologna formed a guild or *universitas,* which was recognized by Emperor Frederick Barbarossa and given a charter in 1158. Although the faculty also organized itself as a group, the *universitas* of students at Bologna was far more influential. It obtained a promise of freedom for students from local authorities, regulated the price of books and lodging, and determined the curriculum, fees, and standards for the masters. Teachers were fined if they missed a class, began their lectures late, or failed to complete their scheduled program for the term. The University of Bologna remained the greatest law school in Europe throughout the Middle Ages.

In northern Europe, the University of Paris became the first recognized university. A number of teachers or masters who had received licenses to teach from the cathedral school of Notre Dame in Paris began to take on extra students for a fee. By the end of the twelfth century, these masters teaching at Paris had formed a *universitas* or guild of masters. By 1200, the king of France, Philip Augustus, officially acknowledged the existence of the University of Paris. The University of Oxford in England, organized on the Paris model, first appeared in 1208. A migration of scholars from Oxford in 1209 led to the establishment of Cambridge University. In the Late Middle Ages, kings, popes, and princes vied to found new universities. By the end of the Middle Ages, there were eighty universities in Europe, most of them located in England, France, Italy, and Germany.

Despite variations, most early universities shared similar characteristics. Almost all universities sought to gain independence from both church and lay authorities. All masters and students were regarded as clerics of a "lower order" and wore clerical garb. This is why academic gowns, even today, still look like priests' robes. Since women were not allowed to be priests, they were also excluded from universities. As clerics in minor orders, students and their masters shared the "clerical privilege"—they were not subject to arrest by the secular authorities, but could be tried only in ecclesiastical courts. As a result, university authorities sought and obtained widespread secular authority for themselves. The chancellor of Oxford, for example, received from the king of England complete authority over teachers and students, including the granting of degrees, which became a regular feature of most universities.

TEACHERS AND TEACHING IN THE MEDIEVAL UNIVERSITY

To gain admission to a medieval university, students were expected to read and write Latin although apparently exams were not rigorous and some students were not all that well prepared. Nevertheless, all classes were conducted in Latin, which provided a common means of communication for students, regardless of their country of origin.

A student's initial studies at a medieval university centered around the traditional liberal arts curriculum. The trivium consisted of grammar, rhetoric, and logic, and the quadrivium was comprised of arithmetic, geometry, astronomy, and music. Basically, medieval university instruction was done by a lecture method. The word

lecture is derived from the Latin and means "to read." Before the development of the printing press in the fifteenth century, books were expensive, and few students could afford them, so masters read from a text (such as a collection of law if the subject were law or a textbook such as the *Sentences* of Peter the Lombard if the subject were theology) and then added commentaries, which came to be known as glosses. A law professor at Bologna described his method, which was not unlike those followed in other fields at other universities:

Concerning the method of teaching the following order was kept by ancient and modern doctors and especially by my own master, which method I shall observe: First, I shall give you summaries of each title before I proceed to the text; second, I shall give you as clear and explicit a statement as I can of the purport of each law; third, I shall read the text with a view to correcting it; fourth, I shall briefly repeat the contents of the law; fifth, I shall solve apparent contradictions, adding any general principles of law . . . and any distinctions or subtle and useful problems

Map 11.2 Intellectual Centers of Medieval Europe.

... arising out of the law with their solutions, as far as the Divine Providence shall enable me. . . .[6]

No exams were given after a series of lectures, but when a student applied for a degree, he was given a comprehensive oral examination by a committee of teachers. These were taken after a four- or six-year period of study. The first degree a student could earn was an A.B., the *artium baccalarius,* or bachelor of arts; later, he might receive an A.M., *artium magister,* a master of arts. All degrees were technically licenses to teach, although most students receiving them did not become teachers.

After completing the liberal arts curriculum, a student could go on to study law, medicine, or theology. As we have seen, Bologna was known for the study of law. Salerno, in southern Italy, specialized in medical studies, although it was eventually overshadowed by French centers, such as Montpellier. The University of Paris was most famous for the study of theology, the most highly regarded subject of the medieval curriculum. The study of law, medicine, or theology was a long process that could take a decade or more. A student who passed his final oral examinations was granted a doctor's degree, which officially enabled him to teach his subject. Most students who pursued advanced degrees received their master's degrees first and taught the arts curriculum while continuing to pursue their advanced degrees. Students who received degrees from medieval universities could pursue other careers besides teaching that proved to be much more lucrative. A law degree was deemed essential for those who wished to serve as advisers to kings and princes. The growing administrative bureaucracies of popes and kings also demanded a supply of clerks with a university education who could keep records and draw up official documents.

The development of residence halls known as colleges was another feature of medieval universities. Wealthy benefactors provided these houses where poor students could live and be fed for modest fees. Eventually, masters also took up residence there to provide guidance for the students. The most famous college at the University of Paris was the Sorbonne, founded by Robert de Sorbon, chaplain of King Louis IX in 1258. The colleges of Merton and Balliol were founded at Oxford a few years later.

STUDENTS IN THE MEDIEVAL UNIVERSITY

Students at medieval universities stemmed predominantly from the middle groups of medieval society, the

◆ **University Classroom.** This illustration shows a university classroom in fourteenth-century Germany. As was customary in medieval classrooms, the master is reading from a text. The students obviously vary considerably in age and in the amount of attention they are willing to give the lecturer.

families of lesser knights, merchants, and artisans. All were male; many were poor, but ambitious and upwardly mobile. Many medieval students started when they were fourteen to eighteen years old and received their bachelor's or master's degrees by their early twenties. Study for a doctorate in one of the specialized schools of law, medicine, or theology entailed at least another ten years. It was not unusual for men to receive their doctorates in their late thirties or early forties.

There are obvious similarities between medieval and modern students. Then, as now, many students took their studies seriously and worked hard. Then, as now, alcohol, sex, and appeals for spending money were all too common. In medieval universities, handbooks provided form letters that students could use in requesting money from their fathers, guardians, or patrons. This is an example from Oxford:

> B. to his venerable master A., greeting. This is to inform you that I am studying at Oxford with the greatest diligence, but the matter of money stands greatly in the way of my promotion, as it is now two months since I spent the last of what you sent me. The city is expensive and makes many demands; I have to rent lodgings, buy necessaries, and provide for many other things which I cannot now specify. Wherefore I respectfully beg your paternity that by the promptings of divine pity you may assist me, so that I may be able to complete what I have well begun.[7]

⇒ *University Students and Violence at Oxford* ⇐

Medieval universities shared in the violent atmosphere of their age. Town and gown quarrels often resulted in bloody conflicts, especially during the universities' formative period. This selection is taken from an anonymous description of a student riot at Oxford at the end of the thirteenth century.

A Student Riot at Oxford

They [the townsmen] seized and imprisoned all scholars on whom they could lay hands, invaded their inns, made havoc of their goods and trampled their books under foot. In the face of such provocation the Proctors [university officials] sent their assistants about the town, forbidding the students to leave their inns. But all commands and exhortations were in vain. By nine o'clock next morning, bands of scholars were parading the streets in martial array. If the Proctors failed to restrain them, the mayor was equally powerless to restrain his townsmen. The great bell of St. Martin's rang out an alarm; oxhorns were sounded in the streets; messengers were sent into the country to collect rustic allies. The clerks [students and teachers], who numbered three thousand in all, began their attack simultaneously in various quarters. They broke open warehouses in the Spicery, the Cutlery and elsewhere. Armed with bows and arrows, swords and bucklers, slings and stones, they fell upon their opponents. Three they slew, and wounded fifty or more. One band . . . took up a position in High Street between the Churches of St. Mary and All Saints', and attacked the house of a certain Edward Hales. This Hales was a longstanding enemy of the clerks. There were no half measures with him. He seized his crossbow, and from an upper chamber sent an unerring shaft into the eye of the pugnacious rector. The death of their valiant leader caused the clerks to lose heart. They fled, closely pursued by the townsmen and country-folk. Some were struck down in the streets, and others who had taken refuge in the churches were dragged out and driven mercilessly to prison, lashed with thongs and goaded with iron spikes.

Complaints of murder, violence and robbery were lodged straightway with the King by both parties. The townsmen claimed three thousand pounds' damage. The commissioners, however, appointed to decide the matter, condemned them to pay two hundred marks, removed the bailiffs, and banished twelve of the most turbulent citizens from Oxford.

Lack of studiousness is not just a modern phenomenon as this letter from a medieval father to his son illustrates:

> To his son G. residing at Orleans, P. of Besançon sends greetings with paternal zeal. It is written, 'He also that is slothful in his work is brother to him that is a great waster.' I have recently discovered that you live dissolutely and slothfully, preferring license to restraint and play to work and strumming a guitar while the others are at their studies, whence it happens that you have read but one volume of law while your more industrious companions have read several. Wherefore I have decided to exhort you herewith to repent utterly of your dissolute and careless ways, that you may no longer be called a waster and your shame may be turned to good repute.[8]

We have no idea whether the letter convinced the student to change his ways.

Medieval universities shared in the violent atmosphere of the age. Records from courts of law reveal numerous instances of disturbances at European universities. One German professor was finally dismissed for stabbing one too many of his colleagues in faculty meetings. A student in Bologna was attacked in the classroom by another student armed with a sword. Oxford regulations attempted to dampen the violence by forbidding students to bring weapons to class. The University of Leipzig initiated a series of graded penalties for students who picked up objects to throw at professors, those who threw and missed, and those who threw and hit their target. Not uncommonly, town and gown struggles (gown refers to the academic robe worn by teachers and students) escalated into bloody riots between townspeople and students (see the box above).

Despite the violence, universities proved important to medieval civilization, not only for the growth of learning, which, after all, is the main task of the university, but also by providing a mechanism for training the personnel who served as teachers, administrators, lawyers, and doctors in an increasingly specialized society.

The Renaissance of the Twelfth Century

Another aspect of the intellectual revival of the High Middle Ages was a resurgence of interest in the works of classical antiquity. The renaissance (or rebirth) of classical antiquity in the twelfth century has been compared to the more famous Renaissance in Italy in the fifteenth century. While the renaissance of the twelfth century was not as deep or far-reaching as the latter, it was a significant step forward in the European recovery and understanding of the classical heritage, and it generated tremendous intellectual optimism. Western Europe, and particularly France, became the center of this intellectual renewal. The Latin language served as an international language for both speaking and writing.

In the twelfth century, western Europe was introduced to a large number of Greek scientific and philosophical works, including those of Galen and Hippocrates on medicine, Ptolemy on geography and astronomy, and Archimedes and Euclid on mathematics. Above all, the west now had available the complete works of Aristotle. (Greek drama and poetry, however, would not be recovered until the Italian Renaissance of the fifteenth century.) Before the twelfth century, only Aristotle's elementary works on logic (known as the "Old Logic") were available through the earlier translation of Boethius (see Chapter 7). By 1160, Aristotle's remaining works on logic (known as the "New Logic") were in use in European universities, especially at Paris. During the second half of the twelfth century, all of Aristotle's scientific works were translated into Latin. This great influx of Aristotle's works had an overwhelming impact on the west. He came to be viewed as the "master of those who know," the man who seemed to have understood every field of knowledge. Philosophers and theologians of the thirteenth century would expend much energy trying to assimilate and reconcile Aristotelian thought with Christian doctrines.

The recovery of Greek scientific and philosophical works was not a simple process, however. Little knowledge of Greek had survived in Europe. It was through the Muslim world that the west recovered Aristotle and other Greek authors. The translation of Greek works into Arabic had formed but one aspect of a brilliant Muslim civilization. In the twelfth century, these writings were now translated from Arabic into Latin, mak-

ing them available to the west. No doubt, much became garbled in this roundabout recovery of the Greek works (Greek to Arabic to Latin). Wherever Muslim and Christian cultures met—in the Norman kingdom of Sicily, southern Italy, and above all Spain—the work of translation was carried on by both Arabic and Jewish scholars. Some Christian scholars also learned Arabic and made their own translations.

The Islamic world had more to contribute intellectually to the west than translations, however. Scientific work in the ninth and tenth centuries had enabled it to forge far ahead of the western world, and in the twelfth and thirteenth centuries, Arabic works on physics, mathematics, medicine, and optics became available to the west in Latin translations. In addition, when Aristotle's works were brought into the west in the second half of the twelfth century, they were accompanied by commentaries written by outstanding Arabic and Jewish philosophers. Their works proved highly influential on western intellectuals.

Especially important was Ibn-Rushd or Averroës (1126–1198), a jurist and physician who lived in Córdoba. He studied virtually all of Aristotle's surviving works and composed a systematic commentary on them. There was no doubt in his mind that Aristotle had been the master of all knowledge:

> I consider that that man [Aristotle] was a rule and exemplar which nature devised to show that final perfection of man. . . . The teaching of Aristotle is the supreme truth, because his mind was the final expression of the human mind. Wherefore it has been well said that he was created and given to us by divine providence that we might know all there is to be known. Let us praise God, who set this man apart from all others in perfection, and made him approach very near to the highest dignity humanity can attain.[9]

Translated into Latin, the work of Averroës, with its emphasis on the differences between faith and reason, posed a problem for western scholars of the thirteenth century.

The west was also receptive to the works of Jewish scholars living in the Islamic world. Perhaps the best known is Moses ben Maimon or Maimonides (1135–1204), who also lived in Córdoba. He was conversant with Greek and Arabic traditions and interested in the problem of reconciling faith and reason. In his *Guide for the Perplexed*, written in Arabic, Maimonides attempted to harmonize the rational and natural philosophy of Aristotle with the basic truths of Judaism (see the box

⇒ *The Guide for the Perplexed* ⇐

Maimonides (1135–1204) was the most famous Jewish *philosopher of the Middle Ages. Born in Córdoba, Spain, he studied Aristotle and Greek medicine under the best Arab teachers. He and his family migrated to Egypt where he became a physician to the sultan's palace in Cairo. Maimonides' philosophical works were highly regarded by western scholars in the thirteenth century, especially his greatest work,* The Guide for the Perplexed. *In this section, Maimonides discusses a problem still debated by modern thinkers—the role of free will versus divine determinism.*

Maimonides, *The Guide for the Perplexed*

There are five different theories concerning Divine Providence; they are all ancient, known since the time of the Prophets, when the true Law was revealed to enlighten these dark regions.

First Theory—There is no Providence at all for anything in the Universe; all parts of the Universe, the heavens and what they contain, owe their origin to accident and chance; there exists no being that rules and governs them or provides for them. This is the theory of Epicurus, who assumes also that the Universe consists of atoms, that these have combined by chance, and have received their various forms by mere accident. . . .

Second Theory—While one part of the Universe owes its existence to Providence, and is under the control of a ruler and governor, another part is abandoned and left to chance. This is the view of Aristotle about Providence. . . .

Third Theory—This theory is the reverse of the second. According to this theory, there is nothing in the whole Universe, neither a class nor an individual being, that is due to chance; everything is the result of will, intention, and rule. It is a matter of course that he who rules must know [that which is under his control]. . . .

Fourth Theory—Man has free will; it is therefore intelligible that the Law contains commands and prohibitions, with announcements of reward and punishment. All acts of God are due to wisdom; no injustice is found in Him, and He does not afflict the good.

Fifth Theory—This is our theory, or that of our Law [Hebrew Law]. . . . The theory of man's perfectly free will is one of the fundamental principles of the Law of our Teacher Moses, and of those who follow the Law. According to this principle man does what is in his power to do, by his nature, his choice, and his will; and his action is not due to any faculty created for the purpose. All species of irrational animals likewise move by their own free will. This is the Will of God; that is to say, it is due to the external divine will that all living beings should move freely, and that man should have power to act according to his will or choice within the limits of his capacity. . . .

My opinion on this principle of Divine Providence I will now explain to you. . . . It is this: In the lower . . . portion of the Universe Divine Providence does not extend to the individual members of species except in the case of mankind. It is only in this species that the incidents in the existence of the individual beings, their good and evil fortunes, are the result of justice, in accordance with the words, "For all His ways are judgment." But I agree with Aristotle as regards all other living beings, . . . plants and all the rest of earthly creatures. For I do not believe that it is through the interference of Divine Providence that a certain leaf drops [from a tree], nor do I hold that when a certain spider catches a certain fly, that this is the direct result of a special decree and will of God in that moment. . . .

above). Although Maimonides' work was attacked by some orthodox Jews, western scholars in the thirteenth century paid close attention to it after its translation into Latin.

The great influx of Greek and Arabic works in the twelfth century brought a formidable challenge to western intellectuals. The application of reason to Catholic doctrine raised questions and new uncertainties. Aristotle's works, for example, questioned the soul's immortality and God's role in the universe, both direct challenges to Catholic thought. It was left to thirteenth-century theologians to reconcile the Aristotelian corpus with Christian doctrines.

The Development of Scholasticism

Medieval intellectuals were strongly influenced by a propensity for order. Their desire to introduce a systematic approach to knowledge greatly affected the formal study of religion that we call theology. Christianity's importance in medieval society probably made inevitable theology's central role in the European intellectual world. Whether in monastic or cathedral schools or the new universities, theology reigned as "queen of the sciences."

Beginning in the eleventh century, the effort to apply reason or logical analysis to the church's basic theological doctrines had a significant impact on the study of theology. The word *scholasticism* is used to refer to the philosophical and theological system of the medieval schools. A primary preoccupation of scholasticism was the attempt to reconcile faith and reason, to demonstrate that what was accepted on faith was in harmony with what could be learned by reason. The scholastic method came to be the basic instructional mode of the universities. In essence, this method consisted of posing a question, presenting contradictory authorities on that question, and then arriving at conclusions. It was a system that demanded rigorous analytical thought. Although scholasticism reached its high point in the thirteenth century, it had its beginnings in the theological world of the eleventh and twelfth centuries, especially in the work of two theologians, Anselm and Abelard.

Anselm (c. 1033–1109) was born in northern Italy but became a monk in France. Serving first as schoolmaster and then as abbot of the monastery of Bec in Normandy, he eventually left the monastery to become archbishop of Canterbury in England. Anselm began his theological inquiry by stressing the importance of faith as the starting point of all wisdom: "Nor do I seek to understand that I may believe, but I believe that I may understand. For this too I believe, that unless I first believe, I shall not understand."[10] For Anselm the emphasis on faith did not diminish the significance of reason or the use of logic. Although subordinate to faith, reason could, he thought, be used to further illuminate the truth already known by faith. In his major work, the *Proslogion*, Anselm tried to demonstrate how the truths of faith are compatible with reason.

Peter Abelard was even more responsible than Anselm for applying logic in a systematic fashion to church doctrines, greatly furthering the development of scholasticism. Between the time of Anselm and Abelard, however, was the important transformative period during which learning passed from isolated monasteries to the new schools of the urban world.

Abelard (1079–1142) studied in northern France with Anselm of Laon, a pupil of Anselm of Bec. He scorned his teachers as insignificant, however, and took up the teaching of theology in Paris. Possessed of a colorful personality, Abelard was a very popular teacher who attracted many students. A man with a strong ego, he became known for the zest with which he entered into arguments with fellow scholars as well as for his affair with Heloise (see the box on p. 362).

Above all others, Peter Abelard was responsible for furthering the new scholastic approach to theology. In his most famous work, *Sic et Non (Yes and No)*, he listed passages from Scripture and the Church Fathers that stood in direct contradiction to one another and stressed the need to use logic or dialectical reasoning to reconcile the apparent differences systematically. He summed up his method with the words, "By doubting we come to enquiry, through enquiry to the truth."

Abelard became one of the best-known thinkers in Europe, although his method of applying logic to church doctrine was not highly regarded by all churchmen. He was, in fact, persecuted for a while on the charge of failing to adhere to church teachings. But Abelard was not a skeptic hungering to overthrow established teachings. He, too, accepted church doctrines, yet felt that reason or "dialectical method" must be used to defend them since church authorities could and did disagree on fundamental points of theology.

Both Anselm and Abelard took positions on a major scholastic controversy of the twelfth and succeeding centuries involving the problem of universals. The basic issue involved the nature of reality itself: what constitutes what is real? Theologians were divided into two major schools of thought reflecting the earlier traditions of Greek thought, especially the divergent schools of Plato and Aristotle.

Following Plato, the scholastic realists took the position that the individual objects that we perceive with our senses, such as trees, are not real but merely manifestations of universal ideas (hence treeness) that exist in the mind of God. All knowledge, then, is based on the ideas implanted in human reason by the Creator. Truth, according to the realists, can only be discovered by contemplating universals.

The other school, the nominalists, were adherents of Aristotle's ideas and believed that only individual objects are real. In their view, universal ideas or concepts were simply names (Latin *nomina*—hence nominalism) created by humans. Truth could be discovered only by examining individual objects. Peter Abelard attempted to reconcile the two positions by maintaining that while universal ideas are real, they cannot be separated from the individual objects in which they inhere; universal ideas do not exist separately from individual objects. The struggle between realists and nominalists remained

The Misfortunes of Peter Abelard

Peter Abelard was a dynamic teacher at Paris and one of the founders of scholasticism. He was also one of the first persons in the Middle Ages to write an autobiographical account of his life, entitled History of My Misfortunes, *that revealed much of his personality. In this excerpt, he describes the unfortunate consequences of his affair with Heloise, the niece of Fulbert, a canon of the cathedral of Notre Dame and Abelard's landlord. Heloise bore a child by Abelard and secretly married him, but Fulbert, feeling betrayed by his tenant's behavior, sought revenge.*

Peter Abelard, *History of My Misfortunes*

At once we secretly parted [Abelard and Heloise after their secret marriage], nor did we see each other more, unless rarely and hiddenly, greatly concealing what we had done. But her uncle and his servants, seeking solace for their shame, began to divulge the marriage we had entered, and to violate the faith they had given me in this regard. She, on the other hand, denied it and swore that it was most false. From this the uncle was violently moved, and attacked her with frequent abuse. When I learned this, I sent her to a certain abbey of nuns near Paris, which is called Argenteuil, where she herself once as a young girl had been brought up and instructed. I had prepared for her the habit of a religious, suitable to the convent life, and had her wear it, except the veil. When they heard this, her uncle and his relatives and friends thought that I had now very much deceived them, and had conveniently rid myself of her, by making her a nun. They were greatly disturbed by this,

and conspired against me. They bribed one of my servants with money, and one night they took from me a most cruel and shameful vengeance, as I was resting and sleeping in the inner room of my lodging. This punishment the world has learned with the greatest astonishment. For they cut off those parts of my body, by which I had committed the deed which sorrowed them. They turned at once in flight, but two who could be caught lost their eyes and genitals. . . .

At morning, the entire city turned out about me. What shock the populace experienced, what sorrow it suffered, with what shouts they annoyed me, . . . it is difficult, or rather impossible, to express. The clerics above all, and especially our students, tormented me with unbearable laments and groans, so that I suffered more for their compassion than from the pain of the cut. I felt the embarrassment more than the wound, and was more afflicted by shame than by suffering. It occurred to my mind how great my glory once had been, how easily and in a brief incident it had been cast down, or rather entirely extinguished. How I had by the just judgment of God been punished in that part of my body in which I had sinned. . . .

The confusion, I admit, of my shame, rather than the devotion of my life compelled me, caught up in so wretched a sorrow, to the recesses of the monastic cloisters. She, who had taken the veil willingly at our command, had first entered a monastery. We thus received at the same time the sacred habit, I in the abbey of Saint-Denis, and she in the monastery of Argenteuil we have mentioned.

a fundamental issue in western philosophical and theological studies until the new scientific categories of thought in the seventeenth century.

The first successful attempt to apply the new dialectical method of Abelard was made by Peter the Lombard, a teacher at Paris and later bishop of the same city. Peter authored the *Four Books of Sentences* around 1150. In this work, he divided theological problems into topical areas, such as the Creation, Trinity, and Incarnation, and then proceeded to summarize and systematically reconcile scriptural passages and the works of Church Fathers on these topics. The *Sentences* became a fundamental textbook for the study of theology. As the

dialectical method became firmly entrenched in the schools, the study of theology became more and more an exercise in systematic explanation and definition. This gave rise to attempts to formulate precise definitions of the sacraments, grace, sin, and salvation.

By the thirteenth century, the scholastics were confronted by a new challenge—how to harmonize Christian revelation with the work of Aristotle. The great influx of Aristotle's works into the west in the High Middle Ages threw many theologians into consternation. Aristotle was so highly regarded that he was called "the philosopher," yet he had arrived at his conclusions by rational thought—not revelation—and some of his doctrines, such as the mortality of the individual soul, contradicted the teachings of the church. Many of the attempts of Muslim and Jewish scholars to reconcile their religious traditions with Aristotle had been rejected by Muslim and Jewish fundamentalists who clung rigidly to their spiritual traditions. The initial reaction in the west had also been one of repression. In 1210, Aristotle's books on natural science had been banned from the University of Paris. Fortunately for the west, papal bans were largely ignored. Different approaches were used to reconcile Aristotle and the doctrines of Christianity; the most famous was that of Saint Thomas Aquinas.

Thomas Aquinas (1225–1274) came from the aristocratic class of southern Italy. He began his studies at the University of Naples and became a Dominican monk in 1244. He studied theology at Cologne and Paris under Albertus Magnus (1193–1280), one of the most prominent theologians of the age, who tried to assimilate Aristotle's works on natural philosophy into the body of Christian education. Aquinas taught at both Naples and Paris, and it was at the latter that he finished his famous *Summa Theologica* (*A Summa of Theology*).

This masterpiece was organized according to the dialectical method of the scholastics. Aquinas first posed a question, cited sources that offered opposing opinions on the question, and then resolved them by arriving at his own conclusions. In this fashion, Aquinas raised and discussed some six hundred articles or issues (see the box on p. 364).

Aquinas's reputation derives from his masterful attempt to reconcile faith and reason. He took it for granted that there were truths derived by reason and truths derived by faith. He was certain, however, that the two truths could not be in conflict with each other:

> The light of faith that is freely infused into us does not destroy the light of natural knowledge [reason] implanted in us naturally. For although the natural light of the human mind is insufficient to show us these things made manifest by faith, it is nevertheless impossible that these things which the divine principle gives us by faith are contrary to these implanted in us by nature [reason]. Indeed, were that the case, one or the other would have to be false, and, since both are given to us by God, God would have to be the author of untruth, which is impossible . . . it is impossible that those things which are of philosophy can be contrary to those things which are of faith.[11]

The natural mind, unaided by faith, could arrive at truths concerning the physical universe. Without the help of God's grace, however, unaided reason alone could not grasp spiritual truths such as the Trinity or the Incarnation.

It is important to remember that Aquinas was a thoroughgoing rationalist who viewed human reason as the connecting point between the natural and spiritual worlds. He is well known for his attempts to argue five propositions for the existence of God from sense experience. For example, in his fourth argument, he reasoned that the existence of various levels of perfection in material things meant that there must be an absolute standard of perfection. Therefore, "there is something which is to all beings the cause of their being, and their goodness, and any other perfection. And this being we call God."[12]

The theological system that Aquinas created eventually came to be viewed by the Catholic church as its official philosophy and used as the basis for theological education in its schools, but not in the thirteenth century. Aquinas's work was subjected to close examination and found wanting by other theologians, notably the Franciscans, who supported the Platonic traditions of Augustine against what they considered the fervent Aristotelianism of the Dominicans. Although they did not accept their failure, thirteenth-century theologians, like twentieth-century scientists, seemed incapable of providing a harmonious synthesis of all knowledge that satisfied everyone.

The Revival of Roman Law

The development of a systematic approach to knowledge was also expressed in the area of law. Of special importance was the rediscovery of the great legal work of Justinian, the *Corpus Iuris Civilis* (*Body of Civil Law*), known to the medieval west before 1100 only in second-hand fashion. At first, famous teachers of law, such as Irnerius at Bologna, were content simply to explain the meaning of Roman legal terms to their students. Gradually, they became more sophisticated so that by the mid-twelfth century, "doctors of law" had developed commentaries and systematic treatises on the legal texts. Since these medieval teachers believed that Roman law was still applicable to Italy and the Holy Roman Empire, Italian cities, above all Pavia and Bologna, became prominent centers for the study of Roman law. By the thirteenth century, Italian jurists were systematizing the various professional commentaries on Roman law into a single commentary known as the ordinary gloss (*glossa ordinaria*). Study of Roman law at the universities came

⇒ The Dialectical Method of Thomas Aquinas ⇐

In his masterpiece of scholastic theology, the Summa Theologica, Thomas Aquinas attempted to resolve some six hundred theological issues by the dialectical method. This method consisted of posing a question, stating the objections to it, and then replying to the objections. This selection from the Summa Theologica focuses on Article 4 of Question 92, "The Production of the Woman."

Aquinas, *Summa Theologica*
Question 92: The Production of the Woman
(In Four Articles)

We must next consider the production of the woman. Under this head there are four points of inquiry: (1) Whether the woman should have been made in that first production of things? (2) Whether the woman should have been made from man? (3) Whether of man's rib? (4) Whether the woman was made immediately by God? . . .

Fourth Article: Whether the Woman Was Formed Immediately by God?

We proceed thus to the Fourth Article:—

Objection 1. It would seem that the woman was not formed immediately by God. For no individual is produced immediately by God from another individual alike in species. But the woman was made from a man who is of the same species. Therefore she was not made immediately by God.

Objection 2. Further, Augustine says that corporeal things are governed by God through the angels. But the woman's body was formed from corporeal matter. Therefore it was made through the ministry of the angels, and not immediately by God.

Objection 3. Further, those things which preexist in creatures as to their causal virtues are produced by the power of some creature, and not immediately by God. But the woman's body was produced in its causal virtues among the first created works, as Augustine says. Therefore it was not produced immediately by God.

On the contrary, Augustine says, in the same work: *God alone, to Whom all nature owes its existence, could form or build up the woman from the man's rib.*

I answer that, As was said above, the natural generation of every species is from some determinate matter. Now the matter whence man is naturally begotten is the human semen of man or woman. Wherefore from any other matter an individual of the human species cannot naturally be generated. Now God alone, the Author of nature, can produce an effect into existence outside the ordinary course of nature. Therefore God alone could produce either a man from the slime of the earth, or a woman from the rib of man.

Reply Objection 1. This argument is verified when an individual is begotten, by natural generation, from that which is like it in the same species.

Reply Objection 2. As Augustine says, we do not know whether the angels were employed by God in the formation of the woman; but it is certain that, as the body of man was not formed by the angels from the slime of the earth, so neither was the body of the woman formed by them from the man's rib.

Reply Objection 3. As Augustine says, The first creation of things did not demand that women should be made thus; it made it possible for her to be thus made. Therefore the body of the woman did indeed preexist in these causal virtues, in the things first created; not as regards active potentiality, but as regards a potentiality passive in relation to the active potentiality of the Creator.

to consist of learning the text of the law along with this gloss.

This revival of Roman law occurred in a world dominated by a body of law quite different from that of the Romans. European law comprised a hodgepodge of Germanic law codes, feudal customs, and urban regulations. The desire to know a more orderly world, already evident in the study of theology, perhaps made it inevitable that Europeans would enthusiastically welcome the more systematic approach of Roman law.

Indeed, while elements of Roman law were incorporated into the various legal systems of western Europe, even more significant was the indirect impact Roman law had on these traditional legal practices. Medieval jurists attempted to systematize and codify their traditional law in imitation of the Roman system. In England, Ranulf de Glanvill wrote a treatise *On the Laws and Customs of the Realm of England* (1189), showing how English law could be explained in a rational fashion. In practice, King Henry II was attempting the same thing by imposing the law of the royal courts upon all of England as the common law. Moreover, Roman law made it possible again for Europeans to think of the state as a public authority possessing the right to create new legislation. In feudal law, governmental functions had become largely vested in private hands (see Chapter 8).

The training of students in Roman law at medieval universities led to further application of its principles as these students became judges, lawyers, scribes, and councillors for the towns and monarchies of western Europe. By the beginning of the thirteenth century, the old system of ordeal was being replaced by a rational, decision-making process based on the systematic collection and analysis of evidence, a clear indication of the impact of Roman law on the European legal system.

The application of a systematic approach to a body of materials was also evident in the growth of canon law in the twelfth century. The Catholic church possessed a large number of canons or ecclesiastical laws and decrees relating to church affairs, but no authoritative collection of them. A Bolognese monk named Gratian began to right this lack. Around 1140 he authored a book called *A Concord of Discordant Canons,* known informally as the *Decretum,* in which he attempted a systematic codification of church canons, including a reconciliation of those that seemed to be in conflict. His *Decretum* became a model for later officially authorized collections of canon law. After Gratian, popes and scholars created a body of canon law affecting all clerical matters, church property, and lay people. Church law came to regulate numerous aspects of the latter's lives, including contracts, wills, marriages, education, and heresy.

Medieval Science and Technology

In the area of science as in many others, medieval intellectuals considered Aristotle the master of all knowledge. Aristotle had taught that natural science should be based on observations that could then lead to generalizations. In following Aristotle as their master, most medieval philosophers were content to accept his results without question. Even when new empirical observations were made, people were reluctant to question Aristotle's conclusions.

Some natural philosophers, however, furthered the scientific methodology of their day. The Englishman Robert Grosseteste (1168–1253), the chancellor of Oxford University, stressed the need for students to observe the world of nature and was especially interested in the study of light or the science of optics. He was persuaded that a deeper knowledge of physical light would serve to penetrate the nature of the universe. Believing that physical laws could be expressed mathematically, he attempted to show how the radiation of light could be demonstrated geometrically.

Grosseteste's pupil, Roger Bacon (1220–1292), carried on his master's work. Although Bacon achieved no scientific breakthroughs of his own, he is still remembered for his imaginative visions of flying machines, submarines, and powered ships and for emphasizing the importance of mathematics for the study of both "natural" and "divine" philosophy.

What modern authors call the pseudosciences seemed to hold considerably more attraction than the sciences in the High Middle Ages. Especially popular were astrology and alchemy. Despite the church's attempt to downplay it, astrology was widely studied and used by many people. Many rulers, including Frederick II, would not think of being without their court astrologers. This interest in the movement of planetary bodies, which was of great importance in the construction of astrological charts, did have the side effect of furthering interest in astronomy as well. The increasing knowledge of Arabic mathematics also promoted astronomical studies.

Alchemy was a "spiritual science," commonly regarded as an attempt to transmute base metals into pure ones, such as gold. While alchemists devised elaborate chemical devices to achieve their goal—and are therefore credited with being the first chemists—the more knowledgeable alchemists had a rather different goal, the transmutation of the soul from its baseness into pure

◆ **Mechanical Clock.** The Middle Ages was an era of technological advances. This illustration from a medieval manuscript shows a mechanical clock, one of the more inventive creations of the High Middle Ages.

spirit. Alchemists devised an elaborate system of symbols to disguise their true aims.

Despite what some historians regard as a lack of growth in science in the Middle Ages, it is important to remember that this was a period of many technological advances. Medieval machines, powered by wind and water, were used in such diverse areas as textile production, the grinding of grains, and iron-smelting forges. The development of machines eliminated many tasks previously done by hand. The medieval period was also highly inventive. Both eyeglasses and the first mechanical clocks were invented near the end of the thirteenth century.

Literature in the High Middle Ages

Latin was the universal language of medieval civilization. Used in the church and schools, it enabled learned men to communicate anywhere in Europe. The intellectual revival of the High Middle Ages included an outpouring of Latin literature. The cathedral school at

Chartres, where masters used literary models from Roman antiquity, became the literary center of western Europe.

Much of medieval Latin poetry was religious verse that did not follow classical models, but used rhyme and a meter based on accent. *Dies Irae* (*Day of Wrath*), whose theme is the Last Judgment, illustrates these characteristics as well as the profound religious feeling of the Middle Ages:

> *Day of wrath, that day of burning!*
> *Earth shall end, to ashes turning:*
> *Thus sing saint and seer, discerning.*
>
> *Ah, the dread beyond expression*
> *When the Judge in awful session*
> *Searcheth out the world's transgression.*
>
> *Then is heard a sound of wonder:*
> *Mighty blasts of trumpet-thunder*
> *Rend the sepulchers asunder. . . .*
>
> *On his throne the Judge is seated,*
> *And our sins are loud repeated,*
> *And to each is vengeance meted.*[13]

There was also a large body of Latin verse dedicated to themes of love and nature. Many of these poems constitute the so-called Goliardic poetry written by vagabond students and teachers. Goliardic poetry was highly irreverent and focused on wine, women, and song:

> *My intention is to die*
> *   In the tavern drinking;*
> *Wine must be at hand, for I*
> *   Want it when I'm sinking.*
> *Angels when they come shall cry,*
> *   At my frailties winking:*
> *"Spare this drunkard, God, he's high,*
> *   Absolutely stinking!"*[14]

The writing of history was yet another aspect of medieval Latin literature. Until the twelfth century, much historical writing had been done in the form of monastic annals, basically records of events pertinent to the monastery. Often narrow in scope and confined to local events, these annals can hardly be called histories. But in the twelfth century, some sound historical narratives appeared that transcended the monastic annals. Orderic Vitalis, a Norman monk of the early twelfth century, wrote an *Ecclesiastical History* that provided a rather unsystematic, yet considerably detailed account of Normandy in the eleventh and twelfth centuries. William of Malmesbury's *History of the Kings of England,* although still in the tradition of the monastic annals, presented a skillful narrative and relatively balanced evaluation of historical events.

While Latin continued to be used for literary purposes, by the twelfth century much of the creative literature was being written in the vernacular tongues. Throughout the Middle Ages, there had been a popular vernacular literature, especially manifest in the Germanic, Celtic, Old Icelandic, and Slavonic sagas. But a new market for vernacular literature appeared in the twelfth century when educated lay people at courts and in the new urban society sought fresh avenues of entertainment.

Perhaps the most popular vernacular literature of the twelfth century was troubadour poetry, chiefly the product of nobles and knights. This poetry focused on themes of courtly love, the love of a knight for a lady, generally a married noble lady, who inspires him to become a braver knight and a better poet. A good example is found in the laments of the crusading noble Jaufré Rudel, who cherished a dream lady from afar whom he said he would always love, but feared he would never meet:

> Most sad, most joyous shall I go away,
> Let me have seen her for a single day,
> My love afar,
> I shall not see her, for her land and mine
> Are sundered, and the ways are hard to find,
> So many ways, and I shall lose my way,
> So wills it God.
>
> Yet shall I know no other love but hers,
> And if not hers, no other love at all.
> She has surpassed all.
> So fair she is, so noble, I would be
> A captive with the hosts of paynimrie [the Muslims]
> In a far land, if so be upon me
> Her eyes might fall.[15]

Troubadour poetry reached its high point by the mid-twelfth century and declined in originality thereafter. Though it originated in southern France, it also spread to northern France, Italy, and Germany.

Troubadour poetry was also set to music. Songs were written for solo voice accompanied by a stringed instrument, the lute. Most troubadour songs consist of a number of stanzas or verses of the same length and meter and are strophic in character, meaning that they use basically the same music for each verse.

Another type of vernacular literature, known as the *chanson de geste,* or the heroic epic, appeared at the end of the eleventh century. The earliest and finest example is the *Chanson de Roland* (*The Song of Roland*), which appeared around 1100 and was written in a dialect of French, a Romance language derived from Latin (see the box on p. 368).

The *chansons de geste* were written for a male-dominated society. The chief events described in these poems, as in *The Song of Roland,* are battles and political contests. Their world is one of combat in which knights fight courageously for their kings and lords. Women play little or no role in this literary genre.

Chansons de geste would continue into the thirteenth century, a period that also saw the final written versions of the old sagas. The most famous of the latter was the *Nibelungenlied* (*Song of the Nibelungs*), an epic poem written by an unknown author between 1190 and 1205. Although based on stories from as far back as the sixth century, it was highly popular in thirteenth-century Germany. The story revolves around the deeds of the warrior Siegfried: "Goodly was this knight, . . . his body without blemish, a strong and valiant man of great worship; abroad, through the whole earth, went his fame . . . he rode boldly into many lands."[16] The main motif of the poem is loyalty, not the simple loyalty of a knight like Roland to Charlemagne, but the divided loyalties and attendant human choices that lead to tragedy.

Despite the persistence of the *chansons de geste,* a different kind of long poem, the courtly romance, emerged during the twelfth century and continued to be popular throughout the thirteenth century. The courtly romance was composed in rhymed couplets and dwelt on a romantic subject matter: brave knights, virtuous ladies, evil magicians, bewitched palaces, fairies, talking animals, and strange forests. Unlike the *chanson de geste,* in which the chief character engages in physical battle and embodies the values of his people, the medieval romance focused on the internal psychological development of the main character. The story of King Arthur, the legendary king of the fifth-century Britons, became a popular subject for the courtly romance. The best versions of the Arthurian legends survive in the works of Chrétien de Troyes, whose courtly romances in the second half of the twelfth century were viewed by contemporaries as the works of a master storyteller.

One of the best-known romances of the thirteenth century was *The Romance of the Rose,* a French poem that focused on one of the deep and abiding interests of

≥ The Song of Roland ≤

The Song of Roland *is one of the best examples of the medieval chanson de geste or heroic epic. Inspired by a historical event, it recounts the ambush of the rear guard of Charlemagne's Frankish army in the Pyrenees Mountains. It was written three hundred years after the event it supposedly describes, however, and reveals more about the eleventh century than about the age of Charlemagne. The Basques who ambushed Charlemagne's army have been transformed into Muslims; the Frankish soldiers into French knights. This selection describes the death of Roland, Charlemagne's nephew, who was the commander of the decimated rear guard.*

The Song of Roland

Now Roland feels that he is at death's door;
Out of his ears the brain is running forth.
Now for his peers he prays God call them all,
And for himself St. Gabriel's aid implores;
Then in each hand he takes, lest shame befal,
His Olifant and Durendal his sword.
Far as a quarrel flies from a cross-bow drawn,
Toward land of Spain he goes, to a wide lawn,
And climbs a mound where grows a fair tree tall,
And marble stones beneath it stand by four.

Face downward there on the green grass he falls,
And swoons away, for he is at death's door. . . .
Now Roland feels death press upon him hard;
It's creeping down from his head to his heart.
Under a pine-tree he hastens him apart,
There stretches him face down on the green grass,
And lays beneath him his sword and Olifant.
He's turned his head to where the Paynims [Muslims] are,
And this he does for the French and for Charles,
Since fain is he that they should say, brave heart,
That he has died a conqueror at the last.
He beats his breast full many a time and fast,
Gives, with his glove, his sins into God's charge.

Now Roland feels his time is at an end;
On the steep hill-side, toward Spain he's turned his head,
And with one hand he beats upon his breast;
Saying: "Mea culpa; Thy mercy, Lord, I beg
For all the sins, both the great and the less,
That e'er I did since first I drew my breath
Unto this day when I'm struck down by death."
His right-hand glove he unto God extends;
Angels from Heaven now to his side descend.

courtly society, love. *The Romance of the Rose* was an allegory on courtly love written by two different authors. Guillaume de Lorris wrote the first part around 1240. In it, he presented the dream-vision of a lover who sets out to win his lady. His quest leads him to a garden filled with personifications of human traits; Sir Mirth and Lady Gladness are the lord and lady of the garden. The lover is attracted to a rose, symbol of a young woman, and is aided by Courtesy, Gladness, Wealth, and other qualities personified as allegorical figures, but he is hindered by Shame, Jealousy, and Danger. Guillaume had an idealistic view of love and reflected the courtly manners of polite society. When the god of Love instructs the lover on the manners he must develop if his lady is to find him desirable, Guillame has him say:

Then, take care that you never say
Those vulgar words or smutty jokes.

To name a vulgar thing,
Never let your mouth be opened.
I don't call that man courteous,
Who mentions what's nasty and bad.
All women serve and honor,
Spare no pain and effort in their service;
And if you hear one speaking ill,
Who mouths contempt for women,
Rebuke him, and bid him be quiet.[17]

The second part was written by Jean de Meun around 1280. Jean was deeply versed in university learning, and his work is virtually a summary of contemporary learned opinion and knowledge. Although he continues the theme of love begun earlier by Guillaume de Lorris, he approaches it in a new way with a new intensity. Jean held a low opinion of women, and his advice on love is more sexually oriented than Guillaume's. As this selection on how a woman can win a man demonstrates, the innocence that dominated courtly love is gone:

> If her neck be lovely and white her throat,
> See to it that her seamstress so cuts her dress,
> And so reveals a décolletage,
> That her skin appears white and clear,
> Six inches in back and front,
> If she would be the more seductive.[18]

Both the *Song of the Nibelungs* and the *Romance of the Rose* found favor in courtly society.

Whereas the *chansons de geste* and courtly romances were most popular with the nobility, the *fabliaux* appealed to both knights and the urban middle classes. The *fabliaux* were fables or short stories in rhymed verse that usually related how a wandering clerk had outsmarted nobles, merchants, and clergy. Priests and monks, in particular, were portrayed as fools and hypocrites. Emerging by the end of the twelfth century, the *fabliaux* continued to be popular through the thirteenth century.

While Latin remained the universal language for intellectual debate, theological treatises, and state and church documents, the vernacular became popular not only for poetry, but also for the writing of history. Two major historical works were written in French in the thirteenth century. Geoffrey de Villehardouin (c. 1150–1213), a French nobleman, wrote an eyewitness narrative account of the fourth crusade and the capture of Constantinople (see the box on p. 353). Called the "first great monument of French prose," Geoffrey's work was used as a model for other chronicles and histories.

Another French nobleman, Jean de Joinville (1225–1317), wrote a biography of Saint Louis. Written toward the end of the thirteenth century, it was not completed until 1309. Joinville's account of Louis was responsible for embellishing an already positive image of the pious French ruler that lasted for centuries.

The Romanesque Style: "A White Mantle of Churches"

The eleventh and twelfth centuries witnessed an explosion of building, both private and public. The construction of castles and churches absorbed most of the surplus resources of medieval society and at the same time reflected its basic preoccupations, God and warfare. The churches were by far the most conspicuous of the public

♦ **King Arthur and His Knights.** The story of King Arthur was a favorite subject for authors of courtly romances. This fourteenth-century French manuscript shows the king and his knights gathered around the Round Table. Sir Galahad is about to take his seat.

buildings. As a chronicler of the eleventh century commented:

> As the year 1003 approached, people all over the world, but especially in Italy and France began to rebuild their churches. Although most of them were well built and in little need of alterations, Christian nations were rivalling each other to have the most beautiful edifices. One might say the world was shaking herself, throwing off her old garments, and robing herself with a white mantle of churches. Then nearly all the cathedrals, the monasteries dedicated to different saints, and even the small village chapels were reconstructed more beautifully by the faithful.[19]

Hundreds of new cathedrals and abbey and pilgrimage churches, as well as thousands of parish churches in rural villages, were built in the eleventh and twelfth centuries. A dramatic increase occurred, not only in the number of churches, but also in their size. The building spree was a direct reflection of a revived religious culture and the increased wealth of the period produced by agriculture, trade, and the growth of cities.

The cathedrals of the eleventh and twelfth centuries were built in a truly international style—the Romanesque. The construction of churches required the services of professional master builders, whose employment throughout Europe guaranteed an international unity in basic features. Prominent examples of Romanesque churches can be found in Germany (no church of the eleventh century is more massive or impressive than the cathedral at Speyer); France (the church of the Madeleine at Vézelay, dedicated to Saint Mary Magdalene, is certainly one of the most exquisite Romanesque churches); and Spain (where the Romanesque cathedral of Saint James in Santiago de Compostela was a favorite goal of pilgrims).

Romanesque churches were normally built in the basilica shape utilized in the construction of churches in the late Roman Empire. Basilicas were simply rectangular buildings with flat wooden roofs. While using this basic plan, Romanesque builders made a significant innovation by replacing the flat wooden roof with a long, round stone vault called a barrel vault or a cross vault where two barrel vaults intersected (a vault is simply a curved roof made of masonry). The latter was used when a transept was added to create a church plan in the shape of a cross. Although barrel and cross vaults were technically difficult to construct, they were considered aesthetically more pleasing and technically more proficient and were also less apt to catch fire.

Since stone roofs were extremely heavy, Romanesque churches required massive pillars and walls to hold them up. This left little space for windows, and Romanesque churches were correspondingly dark on the inside. Their massive walls and pillars gave Romanesque churches a sense of solidity and almost the impression of a fortress. Indeed, massive walls and slit windows were also characteristic of the castle architecture of the period.

This age also witnessed a revival of sculpture, especially ornamental sculpture in stone used primarily to adorn the exteriors of cathedrals and churches. Entranceways and the spaces above them were filled with figures of humans and animals to illustrate scenes from the Bible. There was little attempt at naturalism since the goal of such sculpture was didactic: to teach illiterate people the biblical stories.

The Romanesque style was also evident in the development of polyphonic music (music for two or more simultaneous voices). Early polyphony had been formed by merely adding a second line of music to be performed simultaneously with the existing line of chant. This doubling quoted the original tune exactly. But in the Romanesque period, the chant melody was not merely repeated note-for-note on a different pitch level by the additional voices, but rather experienced true melodic independence, controlled only by the need to produce sounds pleasing to the ear. In other words, music was moving away from parallel motion into a truer form of polyphonic music in which the voices became independent, adding harmony rather than merely mimicking the original chant. The new polyphony provided the music of the church with an expansiveness and massiveness that reflected the new height of the vaulted ceilings and the heavily reinforced walls of Romanesque architecture.

The Gothic Cathedral

Begun in the twelfth century and brought to perfection in the thirteenth, the Gothic cathedral remains one of

✦ **Barrel Vaulting.** The eleventh and twelfth centuries witnessed an enormous amount of church construction. Utilizing the basilica shape, master builders replaced flat wooden roofs with long, round stone vaults, known as barrel vaults. As this illustration of a Romanesque church in Vienne, France, indicates, the barrel vault limited the size of a church and left little room for windows.

the greatest artistic triumphs of the High Middle Ages. Soaring skyward, almost as if to reach heaven, it was a fitting symbol for medieval people's preoccupation with God.

Two fundamental innovations of the twelfth century made Gothic cathedrals possible. The combination of ribbed vaults and pointed arches replaced the barrel vault of Romanesque churches and enabled builders to make Gothic churches higher than their Romanesque counterparts. The use of pointed arches and ribbed vaults created an impression of upward movement, a sense of weightless upward thrust that implied the energy of God. Another technical innovation was also important. The flying buttress, basically a heavy arched

◆ **The Gothic Cathedral.** The Gothic cathedral was one of the great artistic triumphs of the High Middle Ages. Shown here is the cathedral of Notre Dame in Paris. Begun in 1163, it was not completed until the beginning of the fourteenth century.

◆ **Interior of a Gothic Cathedral.** The use of ribbed vaults and pointed arches gave the Gothic cathedral a feeling of upward movement. Moreover, due to the flying buttress, the cathedral could have thin walls with stained glass windows that filled the interior with light. The flying buttress was a heavy pier of stone built onto the outside of the walls to bear the brunt of the weight of the church's vaulted ceiling.

pier of stone built onto the outside of the walls, made it possible to distribute the weight of the church's vaulted ceilings outward and down and thus eliminate the heavy walls used in Romanesque churches to hold the weight of the massive barrel vaults. Gothic cathedrals were built, then, with thin walls that were filled with magnificent stained glass windows, which created a play of light inside that varied with the sun at different times of the day.

Medieval craftsmen of the twelfth and thirteenth centuries perfected the art of stained glass. Small pieces of glass were stained in glowing colors that craftsmen to this day have been unable to duplicate. This preoccupation with colored light in Gothic cathedrals was not accidental, but was executed by people inspired by the belief that natural light was a symbol of the divine light of God. Light is invisible but enables people to see; so too is God invisible, but the existence of God allows the world of matter to be. Those impressed by the mystical significance of light were also impressed by the mystical significance of number. The proportions of Gothic cathedrals were based on mathematical ratios that their

◆ **Construction of a Cathedral.** A Gothic cathedral was the work of an entire urban community and gave rise to an enormous building industry. This illustration from a medieval manuscript shows some of the steps involved in constructing a cathedral. At the right, two masons lay stone while other workers heighten the scaffold. At the left, workers building a tower raise a block of stone by means of a primitive crane.

◆ **Chartres Cathedral: Stained Glass Window.** The stained glass of Gothic cathedrals is remarkable for the beauty and variety of its colors. Stained glass windows depicted a remarkable variety of scenes. The windows of Chartres cathedral, for example, present the saints, views of the everyday activities of ordinary men and women, and, as in this panel, scenes from the life of Christ.

builders believed were derived from the ancient Greek school of Pythagoras and expressed the intrinsic harmony of the world as established by its creator.

The first fully Gothic church was the abbey church of Saint-Denis near Paris, inspired by Suger, the famous abbot of the monastery from 1122 to 1151, and built between 1140 and 1150. Although the Gothic style was a product of northern France, by the mid-thirteenth century, French Gothic architecture had spread to England, Spain, and Germany—indeed, to virtually all Europe. By the mid-thirteenth century, French Gothic architecture was seen most brilliantly in cathedrals in Paris (Notre Dame), Reims, Amiens, and Chartres.

The facades of Gothic cathedrals were covered with a mass of sculpture that served didactic as well as decorative purposes. Visual images, it was believed, helped ordinary people understand religious truths. The human figures were much more lifelike than the sculptures on Romanesque churches. Other objects, such as animals and flowers, were all carved with remarkable naturalism. An element of fantasy also crept in, with sculptures of mythical monsters, such as dragons, unicorns, and griffins.

A Gothic cathedral was the work of an entire community. Although the bishop and cathedral clergy initiated the plans to build a new cathedral, all classes contributed to its construction. Money was raised from wealthy townspeople who had profited from the new trade and industries as well as kings and nobles. Master masons who were both architects and engineers designed the cathedrals. They drew up the plans and supervised the work of construction. Stonemasons and other craftsmen were paid a daily wage and provided the skilled labor to build the cathedrals. Indeed, these buildings were the first monumental structures of consequence built by free, salaried labor.

The building of cathedrals often became highly competitive as communities vied with one another to build the highest tower, a rivalry that sometimes ended in disaster. The cathedral of Beauvais in northern France collapsed in 1284 after reaching the height of 157 feet. Gothic cathedrals also depended on a community's faith. After all, it often took two or more generations to complete a cathedral, and the first generation of builders must have begun with the knowledge that they would not live to see the completed project. Most importantly, a Gothic cathedral symbolized the chief preoccupation of a medieval Christian community, its dedication to a spiritual ideal. As we have observed before, the largest buildings of an era reflect the values of its society. The Gothic cathedral with its towers soaring toward heaven gave witness to an age when a spiritual impulse still underlay most of existence.

Conclusion

The High Middle Ages gave birth to an intellectual and spiritual revival that transformed European society. The intellectual revival led to a rediscovery of important aspects of the classical heritage, to new centers of learning in the cathedral schools and universities, and to the use of reason to systematize the study of theology and law and develop whole new ways of thought. Spiritual renewal in the High Middle Ages led to numerous and even divergent paths. While it produced a dramatic increase in the number and size of churches and added new dimensions to the religious life of the clergy and laity, it also gave rise to the crusading "holy warrior" who killed for God.

Growth and optimism seemed to characterize the High Middle Ages, but underneath the calm exterior lay seeds of discontent and change. Dissent from church teaching and practices grew in the thirteenth century, leading to a climate of fear and intolerance as the church responded with inquisitorial instruments to enforce conformity to its teachings. Minorities of all kinds suffered intolerance and, worse still, persecution at the hands of people who worked to maintain the image of an ideal Christian society. The breakdown of the old manorial system and the creation of new relationships between lords and peasants led to local peasant uprisings in the late thirteenth century. The crusades ended ignominiously with the fall of the last crusading foothold in the east in 1291. By that time, more and more signs of ominous troubles were appearing. The fourteenth century would prove to be a time of crisis for European civilization.

NOTES

1. Oliver J. Thatcher and Edgar H. McNeal, eds., *A Source Book for Medieval History* (New York, 1905), p. 517.
2. Ibid., p. 523.
3. Anna Comnena, *Alexiad*, trans. E. A. S. Dawes (London, 1928), p. 252.
4. Quoted in Hans E. Mayer, *The Crusades*, trans. John Gillingham (New York, 1972), pp. 99–100.
5. Jean de Joinville, *The Life of Saint Louis*, trans. M. R. B. Shaw (Harmondsworth, 1963), p. 346.
6. Quoted in John W. Baldwin, *The Scholastic Culture of the Middle Ages, 1000–1300* (Lexington, Mass., 1971), p. 60.
7. Quoted in Charles H. Haskins, *The Rise of Universities* (Ithaca, N.Y., 1957), pp. 77–78.
8. Ibid., pp. 79–80.
9. Quoted in David Knowles, *The Evolution of Medieval Thought* (New York, 1964), p. 200.
10. Quoted in Henry O. Taylor, *The Medieval Mind* (Cambridge, Mass., 1949), 1:278.
11. Quoted in John Mundy, *Europe in the High Middle Ages, 1150–1309* (New York, 1973), pp. 474–75.
12. Quoted in David Herlihy, ed., *Medieval Culture and Society* (New York, 1968), p. 227.
13. Ibid., p. 306.
14. *The Goliard Poets*, trans. George Whicher (Cambridge, Mass., 1949), p. 111.
15. Helen Waddell, *The Wandering Scholars* (New York, 1961), p. 222.
16. Charles W. Jones, ed., *Medieval Literature in Translation* (New York, 1950), p. 438.
17. Herlihy, *Medieval Culture and Society*, p. 237.
18. Ibid., p. 242.
19. Quoted in Baldwin, *The Scholastic Culture of the Middle Ages, 1000–1300*, p. 15.

SUGGESTIONS FOR FURTHER READING

Two good general surveys of the crusades are H. E. Mayer, *The Crusades* (New York, 1972); and J. Riley-Smith, *The Crusades: A Short History* (New Haven, Conn., 1987). Other works of value are J. Riley-Smith, ed., *The Oxford Illustrated History of the Crusades* (New York, 1995); J. Riley-Smith, *The First Crusade and the Idea of Crusading* (London, 1986); and J. Prawer, *The Latin Kingdom of Jerusalem* (London, 1972). On the background to the crusades, see B. Z. Kedar, *Crusade and Mission: European Approaches towards the Muslim* (Princeton, N.J., 1984). For works on the Byzantine and Islamic Empires, see the bibliography at the end of Chapter 8 and M. Angold, *The Byzantine Empire: 1025–1204* (London, 1984); and P. M. Holt, *The Age of the Crusades* (London, 1986). An excellent, beautifully illustrated collection of firsthand accounts can be found in E. Hallam, ed., *Chronicles of the Crusades* (New York, 1989). The disastrous fourth crusade is examined in J. Godfrey, *1204: The Unholy Crusade* (Oxford, 1980); and D. Queller, *The Fourth Crusade* (Philadelphia, 1977).

General works on medieval intellectual life are A. Murray, *Reason and Society in the Middle Ages* (Oxford, 1978); and D. Knowles, *The Evolution of Medieval Thought* (New York, 1962). For a good general introduction to the intellectual and artistic renewal of the eleventh and twelfth centuries, see C. N. L. Brooke, *The Twelfth Century Renaissance* (London, 1969); see also the classic work by C. H. Haskins, *The Renaissance of the Twelfth Century* (Cleveland, 1957). The development of universities is covered in the classic work by H. Rashdall, *The Universities of Europe in the Middle Ages*, 3 vols. (Oxford, 1936); S. Ferruolo, *The Origin of the University* (Stanford, 1985); A. B. Cobban, *The Medieval Universities* (London, 1975); and the brief, older work by C. H. Haskins, *The Rise of Universities* (Ithaca, N.Y., 1957). Various aspects of the intellectual and literary developments of the High Middle Ages are examined in J. W. Baldwin, *The Scholastic Culture of the Middle Ages,*

1000–1300 (Lexington, Mass., 1971); C. Morris, *The Discovery of the Individual, 1060–1200* (London, 1972); R. W. Southern, *St. Anselm, A Portrait in a Landscape* (Cambridge, 1990); D. E. Luscombe, *The School of Peter Abelard* (Cambridge, 1969); B. Smalley, *Historians in the Middle Ages* (London, 1974); and H. Waddell, *The Wandering Scholars* (London, 1934). A good biography of Thomas Aquinas is J. Weisheipl, *Friar Thomas d'Aquino: His Life, His Thought and Work* (New York, 1974). Aspects of medieval science are examined in R. C. Dales, *The Scientific Achievement of the Middle Ages* (Philadelphia, 1973); and S. E. Easton, *Roger Bacon* (Oxford, 1952).

For a good introduction to the art and architecture of the Middle Ages, see A. Shaver-Crandell, *The Middle Ages*, in the Cambridge Introduction to Art Series (Cambridge, 1982). A good introduction to Romanesque style is G. Künstler, *Romanesque Art in Europe* (New York, 1973). On the Gothic movement, see G. Henderson, *Gothic* (Baltimore, 1967); O. von Simson, *The Gothic Cathedral* (New York, 1964); E. Panofsky, *Gothic Architecture and Scholasticism* (New York, 1957); C. Wilson, *The Gothic Cathedral* (London, 1990); and J. Bony, *French Gothic Architecture of the Twelfth and Thirteenth Centuries* (Berkeley, 1983). Good books on the construction of Gothic cathedrals are J. Gimpel, *The Cathedral Builders* (New York, 1961); and A. Erlande-Brandenburg, *Cathedrals and Castles: Building in the Middle Ages* (New York, 1995). On music, see R. H. Hoppin, *Medieval Music* (London, 1978).

CHAPTER
12

The Late Middle Ages: Crisis and Disintegration in the Fourteenth Century

The High Middle Ages of the eleventh, twelfth, and thirteenth centuries had been a period of great innovation, evident in significant economic, social, political, religious, intellectual, and cultural changes. And yet, by the end of the thirteenth century, certain tensions had begun to creep into European society. In the course of the next century, these tensions became a torrent of troubles. At mid-century, one of the most destructive natural disasters in history erupted—the Black Death. One contemporary observer named Henry Knighton, a canon of Saint Mary-of-the-Meadow Abbey in Leicester, England, was simply overwhelmed by the magnitude of the catastrophe. Knighton began his account of the great plague with these words: "In this year [1348] and in the following one there was a general mortality of people throughout the whole world." Few were left untouched; the plague struck even isolated monasteries: "At Montpellier, there remained out of a hundred and forty friars only seven." Animals, too, were devastated: "During this same year, there was a great mortality of sheep everywhere in the kingdom; in one place and in one pasture, more than five thousand sheep died and became so putrefied that neither beast nor bird wanted to touch them." Knighton was also stunned by the economic and social consequences of the Black Death. Prices dropped: "And the price of everything was cheap, because of the fear of death; there were very few who took any care for their wealth, or for anything else." Meanwhile laborers were scarce, so their wages increased: "In the following autumn, one could not hire a reaper at a lower wage than eight pence with food, or a mower at less than twelve pence with food. Because of this, much grain rotted in the fields for lack of harvesting." So many people died that some towns were deserted and some villages disappeared altogether: "Many small villages and hamlets were completely deserted; there was not one house left in them, but all those who had lived in them were dead." Some people thought the end of the world was at hand.

| 1300 | 1325 | 1350 | 1400 | 1425 | 1450 |

Outbreak of Hundred Years' War

Golden Bull in Germany

Battle of Agincourt

Joan of Arc inspires the French

The popes at Avignon

Peasant revolts in France •

The Great Schism

Outbreak of the Black Death

Peasant revolt in England

Work of Giotto

Giovanni di Dondi's clock

Dante, *The Divine Comedy*

Chaucer, *The Canterbury Tales*

Plague was not the only disaster in the fourteenth century, however. Signs of disintegration were everywhere: famine, economic depression, war, social upheaval, a rise in crime and violence, and a decline in the power of the universal Catholic church. Periods of disintegration, however, are often fertile grounds for change and new developments. Out of the dissolution of medieval civilization came a rebirth of culture that many historians have labeled the Renaissance.

A Time of Troubles: Black Death and Social Crisis

Well into the thirteenth century, Europe had experienced good harvests and an expanding population. By the end of the thirteenth century, however, a period of disastrous changes had begun.

Famine and Population

By the end of the thirteenth and beginning of the fourteenth centuries, there were noticeable changes in weather patterns as Europe entered a period that has been called a "little ice age." Although the shift in overall temperature patterns was relatively small, even that small variation resulted in shortened growing seasons and disastrous weather conditions, including heavy storms and constant rain. Between 1315 and 1317, northern Europe experienced heavy rains that destroyed harvests and caused serious food shortages, resulting in extreme hunger and starvation. The great famine of

1315–1317 in northern Europe became an all-too-familiar pattern. Southern Europe, for example, seems to have been struck by similar conditions, especially in the 1330s and 1340s. Hunger became widespread, and the scene described by this chronicler became common:

> We saw a larger number of both sexes, not only from nearby places but from as much as five leagues away, barefooted and maybe even, except for women, in a completely nude state, together with their priests coming in procession at the Church of the Holy Martyrs, their bones bulging out, devoutly carrying bodies of saints and other relics to be adorned hoping to get relief.[1]

Some historians think famine may have caused as much as a 10 percent decline in the European population in the first half of the fourteenth century.

Europe had experienced a great increase in population in the High Middle Ages. By 1300, however, indications are that Europe had reached the upper limit of its population, not in an absolute sense, but in the number of people who could be supported by existing agricultural production and technology. Virtually all productive land was being farmed, including many marginal lands that needed intensive cultivation and proved easily susceptible to changing weather patterns. We know that there was also a distinct movement from overpopulated rural areas to urban locations. Eighteen percent of the people in the village of Broughton in England, for example, migrated between 1288 and 1340. There is no certainty that these migrants found better economic opportunities in urban areas. We might, in fact, conclude the opposite based on the reports of increasing numbers of poor people in the cities. In 1330, for example, one chronicler estimated that of the 100,000 inhabitants of Florence, 17,000, or almost 20 percent of the population, were paupers. Moreover, evidence suggests that because of the increase in population, individual peasant holdings by 1300 were shrinking in size to an acreage that could no longer support a peasant family. Europe seemed to have reached an upper limit to population growth, and the number of poor appeared to have increased noticeably.

Although the extent to which famine contributed to the decline of population in the early fourteenth century is unclear, some historians have pointed out that it could have had other effects on the surviving population. Famine may have led to chronic malnutrition, which in turn contributed to increased infant mortality, lower birthrates, and higher susceptibility to disease since malnourished people are less able to resist infection. This, they argue, helps to explain the virulence of the great plague known as the Black Death.

The Black Death

The Black Death of the mid-fourteenth century was the most devastating natural disaster in European history. It ravaged Europe, wiping out 25 to 50 percent of the population and causing economic, social, political, and cultural upheaval. A Sienese chronicler wrote that "father abandoned child, wife husband, one brother another, for the plague seemed to strike through breath and sight. And so they died. And no one could be found to bury the dead, for money or friendship."[2] People were horrified by an evil force they could not understand and by the subsequent breakdown of all normal human relations.

Epidemic disease had occurred earlier in Western history. Athens was struck by plague in the early years of the Peloponnesian War (431–404 B.C.); the Roman Empire had been devastated when the troops of Marcus Aurelius brought smallpox back to Italy toward the end of the second century A.D. and then from 251 to 260 by the "Antonine Plague," believed to be a virulent form of measles. Moreover, a great plague had caused considerable loss of life in Justinian's empire in the sixth century and recurred in the seventh century. But from the eighth to the mid-fourteenth century, European civilization was mostly free from epidemic diseases. The absence of major epidemic diseases undoubtedly aided medieval Europe's remarkable demographic expansion after 900.

The Black Death, then, struck Europe after a period of considerable freedom from epidemic diseases. This great plague originated in central Asia. It was spread, it is believed, both by the Mongols as they expanded across Asia and by ecological changes that caused central Asian rodents to move westward. These rodents, especially the Asian black rat, became the most active carriers of the plague bacillus known as *Yersinia pestis*.

The Black Death was actually a mixture of bubonic, pneumonic, and septicaemic plague strains. Bubonic plague was the most common and most important form of plague in the diffusion of the Black Death. It was spread by black rats infested with fleas who were host to the deadly bacterium *Yersinia pestis*. Symptoms of bubonic plague include high fever, aching joints, swelling of the lymph nodes, and dark blotches caused by bleeding beneath the skin. Bubonic plague was actually the least toxic of the three forms of plague, but nevertheless killed 50 to 60 percent of its victims. In pneumonic plague, the bacterial infection spreads to the lungs,

◆ **Mass Burial of Plague Victims.** The Black Death spread to northern Europe by the end of 1348. Shown here is a mass burial of victims of the plague in Tournai, located in modern Belgium. As is evident in the illustration, at this stage of the plague, there was still time to make coffins for the victims' burial. Later, as the plague intensified, the dead were thrown into open pits.

�֎ Map 12.1 Spread of the Black Death.

resulting in severe coughing, bloody sputum, and the relatively easy spread of the bacillus from human to human by coughing. Fortunately, since it was more deadly, this form of the plague occurred less frequently than bubonic plague. Ninety-five to 100 percent of the people with pneumonic plague died. Very rare was septicaemic plague, which was carried by insects. It was extremely lethal—a victim usually died within one day of the initial infection.

There is general agreement that the plague began in Europe when Genoese merchants brought it from the Middle East to the island of Sicily off the coast of southern Italy in October of 1347. It spread quickly, reaching southern Italy and southern France and Spain by the end of 1347. Usually, the diffusion of the Black Death followed commercial trade routes. In 1348, the

plague spread through France and the Low Countries and into Germany. By the end of that year, it had reached England, which it ravaged in 1349. By the end of 1349, it had expanded to northern Europe and Scandinavia. Eastern Europe and Russia were affected by 1351, although mortality rates were never as high in eastern Europe as they were in western and central Europe.

Mortality figures for the Black Death were incredibly high. Italy was especially hard hit. As the commercial center of the Mediterranean, Italy possessed scores of ports where the plague could be introduced. Italy's crowded cities, whether large, such as Florence, Genoa, and Venice with populations near 100,000, or small, such as Orvieto and Pistoia, suffered losses of 50 to 60 percent (see the box on p. 380). Only the northern

⋟ The Black Death ⋞

*T*he Black Death was the most terrifying natural calamity of the entire Middle Ages. It has been estimated that 25 to 50 percent of the population died as the plague spread throughout Europe between 1347 and 1351. This contemporary description of the great plague is taken from the preface to The Decameron *by the fourteenth-century Italian writer Giovanni Boccaccio.*

Giovanni Boccaccio, *The Decameron*

In the year of Our Lord 1348 the deadly plague broke out in the great city of Florence, most beautiful of Italian cities. Whether through the operation of the heavenly bodies or because of our own iniquities which the just wrath of God sought to correct, the plague had arisen in the East some years before, causing the death of countless human beings. It spread without stop from one place to another, until, unfortunately, it swept over the West. Neither knowledge nor human foresight availed against it, though the city was cleansed of much filth by chosen officers in charge and sick persons were forbidden to enter it, while advice was broadcast for the preservation of health. Nor did humble supplications serve. Not once but many times they were ordained in the form of processions and other ways for the propitiation of God by the faithful, but, in spite of everything, toward the spring of the year the plague began to show its ravages. . . .

It did not manifest itself as in the East, where if a man bled at the nose he had certain warning of inevitable death. At the onset of the disease both men and women were afflicted by a sort of swelling in the groin or under the armpits which sometimes attained the size of a common apple or egg. Some of these swellings were larger and some smaller, and were commonly called boils. From these two starting points the boils began in a little while to spread and appear generally all over the body. Afterwards, the manifestation of the disease changed into black or livid spots on the arms, thighs, and the whole person. In many these blotches were large and far apart, in others small and closely clustered. Like the boils, which had been and continued to be a certain indication of coming death, these blotches had the same meaning for everyone on whom they appeared.

Neither the advice of physicians nor the virtue of any medicine seemed to help or avail in the cure of these diseases. Indeed, . . . not only did few recover, but on the contrary almost everyone died within three days of the appearance of the signs—some sooner, some later. . . . The virulence of the plague was all the greater in that it was communicated by the sick to the well by contact, not unlike fire when dry or fatty things are brought near it. But the evil was still worse. Not only did conversation and familiarity with the diseased spread the malady and even cause death, but the mere touch of the clothes or any other object the sick had touched or used, seemed to spread the pestilence. . . .

More wretched still were the circumstances of the common people and, for a great part, of the middle class, for, confined to their homes either by hope of safety or by poverty, and restricted to their own sections, they fell sick daily by thousands. There, devoid of help or care, they died almost without redemption. A great many breathed their last in the public streets, day and night; a large number perished in their homes, and it was only by the stench of their decaying bodies that they proclaimed their death to their neighbors. Everywhere the city was teeming with corpses. . . .

So many bodies were brought to the churches every day that the consecrated ground did not suffice to hold them, particularly according to the ancient custom of giving each corpse its individual place. Huge trenches were dug in the crowded churchyards and the new dead were piled in them, layer upon layer, like merchandise in the hold of a ship. A little earth covered the corpses of each row, and the procedure continued until the trench was filled to the top.

Italian city of Milan miraculously escaped such devastation, suffering a loss of only 15 percent. France and England were also particularly devastated. In northern France, farming villages suffered mortality rates of 30 percent, while cities such as Rouen were more severely affected and experienced losses of 30 to 40 percent. In England and Germany, entire villages simply disappeared from history. In Germany, of approximately 170,000 inhabited locations, only 130,000 were left by the end of the fourteenth century. Overall, however, Germany suffered less than France and England.

It has been estimated that the European population declined by 25 to 50 percent between 1347 and 1351. If we accept the recent scholarly assessment of a European population of 75 million in the early fourteenth century, this means a death toll of 19 to 38 million people in four years. Moreover, the plague did not end in 1351. There were major outbreaks again in 1361–1362 and 1369 and then recurrences every five or six to ten or twelve years depending on climatic and ecological conditions during the remainder of the fourteenth century and all of the fifteenth century. Recent estimates are that the European population declined between 60 and 75 percent between 1347 and 1450 and did not begin to recover until the end of the fifteenth century; not until the mid-sixteenth century did Europe begin to regain its thirteenth-century population levels. Even then, recurrences of the plague did not end until the beginning of the eighteenth century when a new species of brown rat began to replace the black rat.

LIFE AND DEATH: REACTIONS TO THE PLAGUE

Natural disasters of the magnitude of the great plague produce extreme psychological reactions. There were acts of heroism and great courage. Stories abound of monks and nuns who stayed with the suffering until they themselves died of the plague. Equally large numbers of clergymen fled for their lives as fast as they could. Living for the moment, some people threw themselves with abandon into sexual and alcoholic orgies. The fourteenth-century Italian writer Giovanni Boccaccio gave a classic description of this kind of reaction to the plague in the preface to his famous work *The Decameron:*

> Others, arriving at a contrary conclusion, held that plenty of drinking and enjoyment, singing and free living and the gratification of the appetite in every possible way, letting the devil take the hindmost, was the best preventative of such a malady; and as far as they could, they suited the action to the word. Day and night they went from one tavern to another drinking and carousing

unrestrainedly. At the least inkling of something that suited them, they ran wild in other people's houses, and there was no one to prevent them, for everyone had abandoned all responsibility for his belongings as well as for himself, considering his days numbered.[3]

Wealthy and powerful people fled to their country estates, as Boccaccio recounted: "Still others . . . maintained that no remedy against plagues was better than to leave them miles behind. Men and women without number . . . caring for nobody but themselves, abandoned the city, their houses and estates, their own flesh and blood even, and their effects, in search of a country place."[4]

The attempt to explain the Black Death and mitigate its harshness led to extreme sorts of behavior. To many, the plague had either been sent by God as a punishment for humans' sins or caused by the evil one, the devil. Some resorted to extreme asceticism to cleanse themselves of sin and gain God's forgiveness. Such were the flagellants who became a popular movement in 1348, especially in Germany. Flagellants were not a new phenomenon, having already appeared in large numbers amidst the intense religious atmosphere of the thirteenth century. The Black Death gave them a new urgency, however. Groups of flagellants, both men and women, wandered from town to town, flogging each other with whips to win the forgiveness of a God whom they felt had sent the plague to punish humans for their sinful ways. One contemporary chronicler described a flagellant procession:

> The penitents went about, coming first out of Germany. They were men who did public penance and scourged

◆ The Flagellants. Reactions to the plague were extreme at times. Believing that asceticism could atone for humankind's sins and win God's forgiveness, flagellants wandered from town to town flogging themselves with whips, as in this illustration.

themselves with whips of hard knotted leather with little iron spikes. Some made themselves bleed very badly between the shoulder blades and some foolish women had cloths ready to catch the blood and smear it on their eyes, saying it was miraculous blood. While they were doing penance, they sang very mournful songs about the nativity and the passion of Our Lord. The object of this penance was to put a stop to the mortality, for in that time . . . at least a third of all the people in the world died.[5]

The flagellants attracted attention and created mass hysteria wherever they went. The Catholic church, however, became alarmed when flagellant groups began to kill Jews and attack the clergy who opposed them. Some groups also developed a millenarian aspect, placing their emphasis on the coming end of the world, the return of Christ, and the establishment of a thousand-year kingdom under Christ's governance. Pope Clement VI condemned the flagellants in October 1349 and urged the public authorities to crush them. By the end of 1350, most of the flagellant movements had been destroyed.

An outbreak of virulent anti-Semitism also accompanied the Black Death. Jews were accused of causing the plague by poisoning town wells. Although Jews were persecuted in Spain, the worst pogroms against this helpless minority were carried out in Germany; more than sixty major Jewish communities in Germany had been exterminated by 1351 (see the box on p. 383). Many Jews fled eastward to Russia and especially to Poland where the king offered them protection. Eastern Europe became home to large Jewish communities.

The prevalence of death because of the plague and its recurrences affected people in profound ways. Some survivors apparently came to treat life as something cheap and passing. Modern research has confirmed the impression of late medieval chroniclers: violence and violent death appeared to be more common after the plague than before. In England, the number of murders apparently doubled in the decade of the 1350s despite the drastic decline in population.

Postplague Europe also demonstrated a morbid preoccupation with death. In their sermons, priests reminded parishioners that each night's sleep might be their last. Greater emphasis came to be placed on elaborate funerals and detailed funerary monuments. Tombstones were decorated with macabre scenes of naked corpses in various stages of decomposition with snakes entwined in their bones and their innards filled with worms.

Economic Dislocation and Social Upheaval

The population collapse of the fourteenth century had dire economic and social consequences. Economic dislocation was accompanied by social upheaval. Between 1000 and 1300, Europe had been relatively stable. The tripartite division of society into the three estates of clergy (those who pray), nobility (those who fight), and laborers (those who work) had already begun to disintegrate in the thirteenth century, however. In the fourteenth century, a series of urban and rural revolts rocked European society.

NOBLE LANDLORDS AND PEASANTS

Both peasants and landlords were affected by the demographic crisis of the fourteenth century. Most noticeably, Europe experienced a serious labor shortage that caused a dramatic rise in the price of labor. At Cuxham manor in England, for example, a farm laborer who had received two shillings a week in 1347 was paid seven in 1349 and almost eleven by 1350. At the same time, the decline in population depressed or held stable the demand for agricultural produce, resulting in stable or falling prices for output (although in England prices remained high until the 1380s). The chronicler Henry Knighton observed: "And the price of everything was cheap. . . . For a man could buy a horse for half a mark [six shillings], which before was worth forty shillings. . . ."[6] Since landlords were having to pay more for labor at the same time that their rents or income was declining, they began to experience considerable adversity and lower standards of living. In England, aristocratic incomes dropped more than 20 percent between 1347 and 1353. The wealthiest aristocrats could still afford their privileged lifestyle, but lesser lords faced impoverishment.

Aristocrats responded to adversity in a variety of ways. Some shifted their estates from labor-intensive to land-intensive products. In England, sheep raising increased as landowners perceived that there was still a relatively good market for both raw wool and mutton. Moreover, lords found that though the demand for basic foodstuffs had declined, the demand for certain other products remained stable. Then, as now, wine and ale remained in constant demand, so wheat fields were converted to vines for making wine and to barley for producing ale.

Another response to adversity was to seek assistance from the monarchy and their fellow aristocrats by enacting legislation to lower the wage rate artificially.

A Medieval Holocaust: The Cremation of the Strasbourg Jews

In their attempt to explain the widespread horrors of the Black Death, medieval Christian communities looked for scapegoats. As at the time of the crusades, the Jews were blamed for poisoning wells and hence spreading the plague. This selection by a contemporary chronicler, written in 1349, gives an account of how Christians in the town of Strasbourg in the Holy Roman Empire dealt with their Jewish community. It is apparent that financial gain was also an important motive in killing the Jews.

Jacob von Königshofen, "The Cremation of the Strasbourg Jews"

In the year 1349 there occurred the greatest epidemic that ever happened. Death went from one end of the earth to the other.... And from what this epidemic came, all wise teachers and physicians could only say that it was God's will.... This epidemic also came to Strasbourg in the summer of the above-mentioned year, and it is estimated that about sixteen thousand people died.

In the matter of this plague the Jews throughout the world were reviled and accused in all lands of having caused it through the poison which they are said to have put into the water and the wells—that is what they were accused of—and for this reason the Jews were burnt all the way from the Mediterranean into Germany....

[The account then goes on to discuss the situation of the Jews in the city of Strasbourg.]

On Saturday ... they burnt the Jews on a wooden platform in their cemetery. There were about two thousand people of them. Those who wanted to baptize themselves were spared. [Some say that about a thousand accepted baptism.] Many small children were taken out of the fire and baptized against the will of their fathers and mothers. And everything that was owed to the Jews was canceled, and the Jews had to surrender all pledges and notes that they had taken for debts. The council, however, took the cash that the Jews possessed and divided it among the working-men proportionately. The money was indeed the thing that killed the Jews. If they had been poor and if the feudal lords had not been in debt to them, they would not have been burnt....

Thus were the Jews burnt at Strasbourg, and in the same year in all the cities of the Rhine, whether Free Cities or Imperial Cities or cities belonging to the lords. In some towns they burnt the Jews after a trial, in others, without a trial. In some cities the Jews themselves set fire to their houses and cremated themselves.

It was decided in Strasbourg that no Jew should enter the city for a hundred years, but before twenty years had passed, the council and magistrates agreed that they ought to admit the Jews again into the city for twenty years. And so the Jews came back again to Strasbourg in the year 1368 after the birth of our Lord.

The English Parliament passed the Statute of Laborers (1351), which attempted to limit wages to preplague levels and forbid the mobility of peasants as well. Although such laws proved largely unworkable, they did keep wages from rising as high as they might have in a free market. Overall, the position of noble landlords continued to deteriorate during the late fourteenth and early fifteenth centuries. At the same time, the position of peasants improved, though not uniformly throughout Europe.

The decline in the number of peasants after the Black Death accelerated the process of converting labor services to rents, freeing peasants from the obligations of servile tenure and weakening the system of manorialism. But there were limits to how much the peasants could advance. They faced the same economic hurdles as the lords. Moreover, peasants were faced with the attempts of lords to impose wage restrictions, reinstate old forms of labor service, and create new obligations. New gov-ernmental taxes also hurt. Peasant complaints became widespread and soon gave rise to rural revolts that were largely socioeconomic in character.

PEASANT REVOLTS

In 1358, a peasant revolt, known as the *Jacquerie*, broke out in northern France. The destruction of normal order by the Black Death and the subsequent economic dislocation were important factors in causing the revolt, but the situation of the French peasantry was complicated by the ravages created by the Hundred Years' War (see War and Political Instability later in this chapter). Both sides followed a deliberate policy of laying waste to peasants' lands while bands of mercenaries lived off the land by taking peasants' produce as well. Thus, the *Jacquerie* was a revolt of desperation; it was linked to the political ambitions of townspeople in Paris who were also upset with the conduct of the war and wished to limit monarchical power. The leader of the peasants was actually a bourgeois draper, Etienne Marcel.

Peasant anger was also exacerbated by growing class tensions. Landed nobles were eager to hold onto their politically privileged position and felt increasingly threatened in the new postplague world of higher wages and lower prices. Aristocrats looked upon peasants with utter contempt. A French tale related to upper-class audiences contained this remarkable passage:

> Tell me, Lord, if you please, by what right or title does a villein [peasant] eat beef? . . . Should they eat fish? Rather let them eat thistles and briars, thorns and straw and hay on Sunday and peapods on weekdays. They should keep watch without sleep and have trouble always; that is how villeins should live. Yet each day they are full and drunk on the best wines, and in fine clothes. The great expenditures of villeins comes as a high cost, for it is this that destroys and ruins the world. It is they who spoil the common welfare. From the villein comes all unhappiness. Should they eat meat? Rather should they chew grass on the heath with the horned cattle and go naked on all fours.[7]

The peasants reciprocated this contempt for their so-called social superiors.

◆ **Peasant Rebellion.** The fourteenth century witnessed a number of revolts of the peasantry against noble landowners. Although the revolts were initially successful, they were soon crushed. This illustration shows nobles massacring the rebels in the French *Jacquerie*.

The outburst of peasant anger led to savage confrontations. Castles were burned and nobles murdered (see the box on p. 385). Such atrocities did not go unanswered, however. The *Jacquerie* soon failed as the privileged classes closed ranks, savagely massacred the rebels, and ended the revolt.

The English Peasants' Revolt of 1381 was the most famous of all. It was a product not of desperation but of rising expectations. After the Black Death, the condition of the English peasants had improved as they enjoyed greater freedom and higher wages or lower rents. Aristocratic landlords had fought back with legislation to depress wages and an attempt to reimpose old feudal dues. The most immediate cause of the revolt, however, was the monarchy's attempt to raise revenues by imposing a poll tax or a flat charge on each adult member of the population. Three such poll taxes were levied between 1377 and 1381. The last one was met by a revolt of peasants in eastern England, the wealthiest part of the country. They refused to pay the tax and expelled the collectors forcibly from their villages.

This action produced a widespread rebellion of both peasants and townspeople led by a well-to-do peasant called Wat Tyler and a preacher named John Ball. The latter preached an effective message against the noble class, as recounted by the chronicler Froissart:

> Good people, things cannot go right in England and never will, until goods are held in common and there are no more villeins and gentlefolk, but we are all one and the same. In what way are those whom we call lords greater masters than ourselves? How have they deserved it? Why do they hold us in bondage? If we all spring from a single father and mother, Adam and Eve, how can they claim or prove that they are lords more than us, except by making us produce and grow the wealth which they spend?[8]

The movement developed a famous jingle based on Ball's preaching: "When Adam delved and Eve span, who was then a gentleman?"

The revolt was initially successful. The manor houses of aristocrats, lawyers, and government officials were burned down, and several important officials, including the archbishop of Canterbury, were murdered. The peasants marched on London, demanding an end to serfdom and immunity from prosecution for acts undertaken during the rebellion. The young king Richard II promised to accept the rebels' demands if they returned to their homes. They accepted the king's word and began to disperse, but the king reneged and with the assistance of the aristocrats brutally crushed the rebels. The poll tax was eliminated, however.

A Revolt of French Peasants

In 1358, French peasants rose up in a revolt known as the Jacquerie. The relationship between aristocrats and peasants had degenerated as a result of the social upheavals and privations caused by the Black Death and the Hundred Years' War. This excerpt from the chronicle of an aristocrat paints a horrifying picture of the barbarities that occurred during the revolt.

Jean Froissart, *Chronicles*

Not long after the King of Navarre had been set free, there were very strange and terrible happenings in several parts of the kingdom of France. . . . They began when some of the men from the country towns came together in the Beauvais region. They had no leaders and at first they numbered scarcely a hundred. One of them got up and said that the nobility of France, knights and squires, were disgracing and betraying the realm, and that it would be a good thing if they were all destroyed. At this they all shouted: "He's right! He's right! Shame on any man who saves the gentry from being wiped out!"

They banded together and went off, without further deliberation and unarmed except for pikes and knives, to the house of a knight who lived near by. They broke in and killed the knight, with his lady and his children, big and small, and set fire to the house. Next they went to another castle and did much worse; for, having seized the knight and bound him securely to a post, several of them violated his wife and daughter before his eyes.

Then they killed the wife, who was pregnant, and the daughter and all the other children, and finally put the knight to death with great cruelty and burned and razed the castle.

They did similar things in a number of castles and big houses, and their ranks swelled until there were a good six thousand of them. Wherever they went their numbers grew, for all the men of the same sort joined them. The knights and squires fled before them with their families. They took their wives and daughters many miles away to put them in safety, leaving their houses open with their possessions inside. And those evil men, who had come together without leaders or arms, pillaged and burned everything and violated and killed all the ladies and girls without mercy, like mad dogs. Their barbarous acts were worse than anything that ever took place between Christians and Saracens. Never did men commit such vile deeds. They were such that no living creature ought to see, or even imagine or think of, and the men who committed the most were admired and had the highest places among them. I could never bring myself to write down the horrible and shameful things which they did to the ladies. But, among other brutal excesses, they killed a knight, put him on spit, and turned him at the fire and roasted him before the lady and her children. After about a dozen of them had violated the lady, they tried to force her and the children to eat the knight's flesh before putting them cruelly to death.

REVOLTS IN THE CITIES

The economic effects of the Black Death varied from sector to sector and region to region. Most economic historians believe that European trade and industry experienced a severe economic recession. Some, indeed, have also spoken of an economic depression, at least in certain regions of Europe.

Commercial and industrial activity suffered almost immediately from the Black Death. An oversupply of goods and an immediate drop in demand led to a decline in trade after 1350. Some industries suffered greatly. Florence's woolen industry, one of the giants, produced 70,000 to 80,000 pieces of cloth in 1338; in 1378, it was yielding only 24,000 pieces. In Ypres, Flanders, cloth production fell an incredible 85 percent. Bordeaux wine exports fell by 50 percent.

Statistics can be misleading, however. The production of woolen cloth in England rose after the Black Death at the same time that production was falling elsewhere. England now exported woolen cloth abroad. In addition, luxury industries flourished temporarily after the Black Death since the survivors initially experienced a rise in per capita wealth through inheritance and were often willing to spend it on luxury goods. Prices rose as did the wages of skilled artisans whose products were much desired. Cities with luxury industries enjoyed a temporary affluence.

Bourgeois merchants and manufacturers responded to adversity in ways similar to landlords, namely, with attempts to restrict competition and resist the demands of the lower classes. Some asked the monarchs for protection. In England, for example, the government granted the Merchants of the Staple, a group of wool

✦ **Harbor Scene at Hamburg.** This illustration from a fifteenth-century treatise on the laws of Hamburg shows a busy port with ships of all sizes. At the left, a crane is used to unload barrels. In the building at the right, customs officials collect their dues. Merchants and townspeople are shown talking at dockside.

exporters, a monopoly on the wool trade in return for loans. In the cities, wealthy bourgeoisie tried to eliminate competition by imposing greater restrictions on guild membership.

In urban areas where capitalist industrialists paid low wages and managed to prevent workers from forming organizations to help themselves, industrial revolts broke out throughout Europe. Ghent experienced one in 1381, Rouen in 1382. Most famous, however, was the revolt of the *ciompi* in Florence in 1378. The *ciompi* were wool workers in Florence's most prominent industry. In the 1370s, the woolen industry was depressed, and wool workers saw their real wages decline when the coinage

in which they were paid was debased. Their revolt won them some concessions from the communal government, including the right to form guilds and be represented in the government. But their newly won rights were short-lived. A counterrevolution by government authorities brought an end to *ciompi* participation in the government by 1382.

The urban and rural revolts of the fourteenth century contained some common elements. As a result of the Black Death, both workers and peasants had sustained some basic improvements in wages and living conditions. The privileged classes, whether noble landlords or wealthy bourgeoisie, wished to retain their old advantages and deny workers and peasants their newfound gains. Peasants and workers simply fought back. They did so at a time when normal law and order were breaking down anyway as a result of the upheaval fostered by the Black Death.

Although the revolts sometimes resulted in short-term gains for the participants, it is also true that the uprisings were relatively easily crushed and their gains quickly lost. Geographically dispersed, rural and urban revolters were not united and had no long-range goals. Immediate gains were uppermost in their minds. Accustomed to ruling, the established classes easily combined and crushed dissent when faced with social uprisings. But after the fourteenth century, the harmony theoretically implicit in the medieval hierarchy of the classes was never the same again. The rural and urban revolts of the fourteenth century ushered in an age of social conflict that characterized much of later European history.

War and Political Instability

Famine, plague, economic turmoil, social upheaval, and violence were not the only problems of the fourteenth century. War and political instability must also be added to the list. Of all the struggles that ensued in the fourteenth century, the Hundred Years' War was the most famous and the most violent. It was not a single war between England and France, but a protracted series of conflicts with interludes of peace. Although its origins lay in a typical feudal dispute, the Hundred Years' War marked a transition from the use of feudal armies to mercenary levies hired by monarchs. The lengthy struggle also resulted in a growth of cultural nationalism that enabled the French monarchy to consolidate its position in France.

Causes of the Hundred Years' War

In 1259, the English king, Henry III, had relinquished his claims to all the French territories previously held by the English monarchy except for one relatively small possession known as the duchy of Gascony. As duke of Gascony, the English king pledged loyalty as a vassal to the French king. But this territory gave rise to numerous disputes between the kings of England and France. By the thirteenth century, the Capetian monarchs had greatly increased their power over their more important vassals, the great lords of France. Royal officials interfered regularly in the affairs of the vassals' fiefs, especially in matters of justice. Although this policy irritated all the vassals, it especially annoyed the king of England who considered himself the peer of the French king.

An economic problem involving the county of Flanders was a second factor contributing to the Hundred Years' War. Urban revolts in Flanders pitted artisans against wealthy merchants and threatened to disrupt the lucrative shipments of English wool to Flanders. Flanders was England's chief market for raw wool, and the English king received huge revenues from export duties on wool. When the French monarchy began to intervene in Flanders on the side of the merchants, the English felt threatened. If the French were to gain control of Flanders, they could play havoc with the wool trade. Accordingly, the English king began to support the Flemish artisans.

A dispute over the right of succession to the French throne also complicated the struggle between the French and English. In the fourteenth century, the Capetian dynasty failed to produce a male heir for the first time in almost four hundred years. In 1328, the senior branch of the Capetian dynasty became extinct in the male line with the death of Charles IV. As the son of the daughter of King Philip IV, King Edward III of England had a claim to the French throne as a close male relative. French practice, however, emphasized descent through the male line, and a cousin of the Capetians, Philip, duke of Valois, became king as Philip VI (1328–1350).

The immediate cause of the war between France and England was the seizure of Gascony by Philip VI in 1337. This action prompted the duke of Gascony, King Edward III of England (1327–1377), to declare war on Philip, the "so-called King of France." There is no doubt that the personalities of the two monarchs also had much to do with the outbreak of the Hundred Years' War. Both Edward and Philip loved luxury and shared a desire for the glory and prestige that came from military engagements. Both were only too willing to use their

CHRONOLOGY

The Hundred Years' War

Outbreak of hostilities	1337
Battle of Crécy	1346
Battle of Poitiers	1356
Peace of Brétigny	1359
Death of Edward III	1377
Twenty-year truce	1396
Henry V (1413–1422) renews the war	1415
Battle of Agincourt	1415
French recovery under Joan of Arc	1429–1431
End of the war	1453

nation's resources to satisfy their own desires. Moreover, for many nobles, the promise of plunder and territorial gain was an incentive to follow the disruptive path of their rulers.

Conduct and Course of the War

The Hundred Years' War began in a burst of knightly enthusiasm. Knights were trained to be warriors; they viewed the clash of battle as the ultimate opportunity to demonstrate their chivalric qualities. The Hundred Years' War proved to be an important watershed, however, since the feudal way of life was on the decline. This would become most evident when peasant foot soldiers instead of knights determined the outcomes of the chief battles of the Hundred Years' War.

It was the English, more than the French, who moved beyond the traditional feudal levy. The French army of 1337 with its heavily armed noble cavalry resembled its twelfth- and thirteenth-century forebears. The noble cavalry considered themselves the fighting elite and looked with contempt upon foot soldiers and crossbowmen since they were peasants or other social inferiors. Such attitudes cost the French dearly in the early battles.

The English army, however, had evolved differently and had included peasants as paid foot soldiers since at least Anglo-Saxon times. Armed with pikes, many of these foot soldiers had also adopted the longbow, invented by the Welsh. The longbow had greater striking power, longer range, and more rapid speed of fire than the crossbow. Although the English made use of heavily armed cavalry, they relied even more on large numbers of foot soldiers.

Edward III's early campaigns in France achieved little. When Edward renewed his efforts in 1346 with an invasion of Normandy, Philip responded by raising a large force to crush the English army and met Edward's forces at Crécy, just south of Flanders. Although historians disagree on the numbers involved, the undoubtedly larger French army followed no battle plan but simply attacked the English lines in a disorderly fashion.

The arrows of the English archers decimated the French cavalry. As the chronicler Froissart described it, "[with their longbows] the English continued to shoot into the thickest part of the crowd, wasting none of their arrows. They impaled or wounded horses and riders, who fell to the ground in great distress, unable to get up again [because of their heavy armor] without the help of several men."[9] It was a stunning victory for the English. Edward followed up his victory by capturing the French port of Calais to serve as a staging ground for future invasions.

Map 12.2 The Hundred Years' War.

The Hundred Years' War

In his account of the Hundred Years' War, the fourteenth-century chronicler Jean Froissart described the sack of the fortified French town of Limoges by the Black Prince, Edward, the prince of Wales. It provides a vivid example of how noncombatants fared during the war.

Jean Froissart, *Chronicles*

For about a month, certainly not longer, the Prince of Wales remained before Limoges. During that time he allowed no assaults or skirmishes, but pushed on steadily with the mining. The knights inside and the townspeople, who knew what was going on, started a countermine in the hope of killing the English miners, but it was a failure. When the Prince's miners who, as they dug, were continually shoring up their tunnel, had completed their work, they said to the Prince: "My lord, whenever you like now we can bring a big piece of wall down into the moat, so that you can get into the city quite easily and safely."

The Prince was very pleased to hear this. "Excellent," he said. "At six o'clock tomorrow morning show me what you can do."

When they knew it was the right time for it, the miners started a fire in their mine. In the morning, just as the Prince had specified, a great section of the wall collapsed, filling the moat at the place where it fell. For the English, who were armed and ready waiting, it was a welcome sight. Those on foot could enter as they liked, and did so. They rushed to the gate, cut through the bars holding it and knocked it down. They did the same with the barriers outside, meeting with no resistance. It was all done so quickly that the people in the town were taken unawares. Then the Prince, the Duke of Lancaster, the Earl of Cambridge, Sir Guichard d'Angle, with all the others and their men burst into the city, followed by pillagers on foot, all in a mood to wreak havoc and do murder, killing indiscriminately, for those were their orders. There were pitiful scenes. Men, women and children flung themselves on their knees before the Prince, crying: "Have mercy on us, gentle sir!" But he was so inflamed with anger that he would not listen. Neither man nor woman was heeded, but all who could be found were put to the sword, including many who were in no way to blame. I do not understand how they could have failed to take pity on people who were too unimportant to have committed treason. Yet they paid for it, and paid more dearly than the leaders who had committed it.

There is no man so hard-hearted that, if he had been in Limoges on that day, and had remembered God, he would not have wept bitterly at the fearful slaughter which took place. More than three thousand persons, men, women and children, were dragged out to have their throats cut. May God receive their souls, for they were true martyrs.

The Battle of Crécy was not decisive, however. The English simply did not possess the resources to subjugate all France. Truces, small-scale hostilities, and some major operations were combined in an orgy of seemingly incessant struggle. The English campaigns were waged by Edward III and his son Edward, the prince of Wales, known as the Black Prince. The Black Prince's campaigns in France were devastating (see the box above). Avoiding pitched battles, his forces deliberately ravaged the land, burning crops and entire unfortified villages and towns and stealing anything of value. For the English, such campaigns were profitable; for the French people, they meant hunger, deprivation, and death. When the army of the Black Prince was finally forced to do battle, the French, under their king John II (1350–1364), were once again defeated. This time even the king was captured. This Battle of Poitiers (1356) ended the first phase of the Hundred Years' War. Under the Peace of Brétigny (1359), the French agreed to pay a large ransom for King John, the English territories in Gascony were enlarged, and Edward renounced his claims to the throne of France in return for John's promise to give up any feudal control over English lands in France. This first phase of the war made it clear that, despite their victories, the English were not really strong enough to subdue all of France and make Edward III's claim to the French monarchy a reality.

Monarchs, however, could be slow learners. The Treaty of Brétigny was never really executed. In the next phase of the war, under the capable hands of John's son Charles V (1364–1380), the French recovered what they had previously lost. The English returned to plundering the French countryside and avoiding pitched battles. That pleased Charles, who did not want to engage in set battles, preferring to use armed bands to reduce the English fortresses systematically. By 1374, the French had recovered their lost lands, although France itself continued to be plagued by "free companies" of

◆ **Battle of Crécy.** This manuscript illustration depicts the Battle of Crécy, the first of several military disasters suffered by the French in the Hundred Years' War, and shows why the longbow was superior to the crossbow. At the left, the French crossbowmen stop firing and prime their weapons by cranking the handle, while English archers continue to fire their longbows (a skilled archer could fire ten arrows a minute).

mercenaries, who, no longer paid by the English, simply lived off the land by plunder and ransom. Nevertheless, for the time being, the war seemed over, especially when a twenty-year truce was negotiated in 1396.

In 1415, however, the English king, Henry V (1413–1422), renewed the war. At the Battle of Agincourt (1415), the French suffered a disastrous defeat and 1,500 French nobles died when the heavy, armor-plated French knights attempted to attack across a field turned to mud by heavy rain. Henry went on to reconquer Normandy and forge an alliance with the duke of Burgundy, making the English masters of northern France.

The seemingly hopeless French cause fell into the hands of Charles the dauphin (the title given to the heir to the throne), who governed the southern two-thirds of French lands from Bourges. Charles was weak and timid and was unable to rally the French against the English, who, in 1428, had turned south and were besieging the city of Orléans to gain access to the valley of the Loire. The French monarch was saved, quite unexpectedly, by a French peasant woman.

Joan of Arc was born in 1412, the daughter of well-to-do peasants from the village of Domrémy in Champagne. Deeply religious, Joan experienced visions and came to believe that her favorite saints had com-

manded her to free France and have the dauphin crowned as king. In February 1429, Joan made her way to the dauphin's court, where her sincerity and simplicity persuaded Charles to allow her to accompany a French army to Orléans. Apparently inspired by the faith of the peasant woman who called herself "the Maid," the French armies found new confidence in themselves and liberated Orléans, changing the course of the war. Within a few weeks, the entire Loire valley had been freed of the English. In July 1429, fulfilling Joan's other task, the dauphin was crowned king of France and became Charles VII (1422–1461). In accomplishing the two commands of her angelic voices, Joan had brought the war to a decisive turning point.

Joan, however, did not live to see the war concluded. She was captured by the Burgundian allies of the English in 1430. Wishing to eliminate the "Maid" for obvious political reasons, the English turned Joan over to the Inquisition on charges of witchcraft (see the box on p. 391). In the fifteenth century, spiritual visions were

◆ **Joan of Arc.** Pictured here in a suit of armor, Joan of Arc is holding aloft a banner that shows Christ and two angels. This miniature portrait is believed to be a good likeness of Joan.

⇒ The Trial of Joan of Arc ⇐

Feared by the English and Burgundians, Joan of Arc was put on trial on charges of witchcraft and heresy after her capture. She was condemned for heresy and burned at the stake on May 30, 1431. This excerpt is taken from the records of Joan's trial, which presented a dramatic confrontation between the judges, trained in the complexities of legal questioning, and a nineteen-year-old woman who relied only on the "voices" of saints who gave her advice. In this selection, Joan describes what these voices told her to do.

The Trial of Joan of Arc

Afterward, she declared that at the age of thirteen she had a voice from God to help her and guide her. And the first time she was much afraid. And this voice came toward noon, in summer, in her father's garden. . . . She heard the voice on her right, in the direction of the church; and she seldom heard it without a light. This light came from the same side as the voice, and generally there was a great light. . . .

Asked what instruction this voice gave her for the salvation of her soul: she said it taught her to be good

and to go to church often. . . . She said that the voice told her to come, and she could no longer stay where she was; and the voice told her again that she should raise the siege of the city of Orléans. She said moreover that the voice told her that she, Joan, should go to Robert de Baudricourt, in the town of Vaucouleurs of which he was captain, and he would provide an escort for her. And the said Joan answered that she was a poor maid, knowing nothing of riding or fighting. She said she went to an uncle of hers, and told him she wanted to stay with him for some time; and she stayed there about eight days. And she told her uncle she must go to the said town of Vaucouleurs, and so her uncle took her.

Then she said that when she reached Vaucouleurs she easily recognized Robert de Baudricourt, although she had never seen him before; and she knew him through her voice, for the voice had told her it was he. . . . The said Robert twice refused to hear her and repulsed her; the third time he listened to her and gave her an escort. And the voice had told her that it would be so.

thought to be inspired either by God or the devil. Since Joan dressed in men's clothing, it was relatively easy to convince others that she was in league with the "prince of darkness." She was condemned to death as a heretic and burned at the stake in 1431. To the end, as the flames rose up around her, she declared "that her voices came from God and had not deceived her." Twenty-five years later, a new ecclesiastical court exonerated her of these charges. In 1920, she was made a saint of the Roman Catholic church.

Joan of Arc's accomplishments proved decisive. Although the war dragged on in desultory fashion for another two decades, defeats of English armies in Normandy and Aquitaine led to French victory. The ability of the French to use artillery, which had first made its appearance in Europe in the fourteenth century, played an important role in their success. By 1453, the only part of France that was left in England's hands was the coastal town of Calais, which remained English for another century.

Political Instability

The fourteenth century was a period of adversity for the internal political stability of European governments.

Although government bureaucracies grew ever larger, at the same time the question of who should control the bureaucracies led to internal conflict and instability. This instability was part of a general breakdown of customary feudal institutions. Traditional feudal loyalties were disintegrating rapidly and had not yet been replaced by the national loyalties of the future. Like the lord and serf relationship, the lord and vassal relationship based on land and military service was being replaced by a contract based on money. Especially after the Black Death, money payments called scutage were increasingly substituted for military service. Monarchs welcomed this development since they could now hire professional soldiers who tended to be more reliable anyway. As lord and vassal relationships became less personal and less important, new relationships based on political advantage began to be formed, opening up new avenues for political influence—and for corruption as well. Especially noticeable, as the landed aristocrats suffered declining rents and social uncertainties with the new relationships, was the formation of factions of nobles who looked for opportunities to advance their power and wealth at the expense of other noble factions and of their monarchs. At the same time, two other developments, related to the rise of factions, added to the instability of governments in the fourteenth century.

First, dynasties of the fourteenth century seemed unable to produce direct male heirs. By the mid-fifteenth century, reigning monarchs in many European countries were actually not the direct male descendants of those ruling in 1300. The founders of these new dynasties had to struggle for their positions as factions of nobles vied to gain material advantages for themselves. At the end of the fourteenth century and beginning of the fifteenth, there were two claimants to the throne of France, and two aristocratic factions fought for control of England; in Germany, three princes struggled to be recognized as emperor.

Fourteenth-century monarchs, whether of old or new dynasties, found themselves with financial problems as well. The shift to using mercenary soldiers left monarchs perennially short on cash. Under the customs of the feudal monarchy, kings were usually expected to pay for their royal governments. But traditional revenues, especially rents from property, increasingly proved insufficient to meet their needs. Monarchs attempted to generate new sources of revenues, especially through taxes, which often meant going through parliaments. This opened the door for parliamentary bodies to gain more power by asking for favors first. Although unsuccessful in most cases, the parliaments simply added another element of uncertainty and confusion to fourteenth-century politics. By turning now to a survey of western and central European states (eastern Europe will be examined in Chapter 13), we can see how these disruptive factors worked in each country.

The Growth of England's Political Institutions

In the fourteenth century, the lengthy reign of Edward III (1327–1377) was an important one for the evolution of English political institutions. Parliament increased in prominence and developed its basic structure and functions during Edward's reign. Due to his constant need for money to fight the Hundred Years' War, Edward came to rely upon Parliament to levy new taxes. In return for regular grants, Edward made several concessions, including a commitment to levy no direct tax without Parliament's consent and to allow committees of Parliament to examine the government accounts to ensure that the money was being spent properly. By the end of Edward's reign, Parliament had become an important component of the English governmental system. Indeed, Parliament even impeached and condemned several royal ministers for acting contrary to its wishes.

During this same period, Parliament began to assume the organizational structure it has retained to this day.

The Great Council of barons became the House of Lords and evolved into a body composed of the chief bishops and abbots of the realm and aristocratic peers whose position in Parliament was hereditary. The representatives of the shires and boroughs, who were considered less important than the lay and ecclesiastical lords, held collective meetings to decide policy and soon came to

◆ **Richard II.** By aspiring to absolute power, Richard II caused a baronial revolt that led to his deposition as king of England. Richard commissioned this life-size portrait of himself in the early 1390s to be placed in Westminster Abbey. The artist's use of realistic details in the portrayal of the face ensured a genuine likeness of the king.

be regarded as the House of Commons. Together, the House of Lords and House of Commons constituted Parliament. Although the House of Commons did little beyond approving measures proposed by the Lords, during Edward's reign, the Commons did begin the practice of drawing up petitions, which, if accepted by the Lords and king, became law. Although the king and the Lords could amend or reject these petitions, this new procedure marked the beginning of the Commons' role in initiating legislation.

Edward's reign also saw the establishment of justices of the peace, officials appointed by the king from the members of the nobility and lesser aristocracy, who came to control the administration of justice in their counties and to be the chief powers of local government. Since they were appointed by the king, they were royal officials, but they were not paid and were primarily concerned with their own class interests.

After Edward III's death, England began to experience the internal instability of aristocratic factionalism that was wracking other European countries. The early years of the reign of Edward's grandson, Richard II (1377–1399), began inauspiciously with the Peasants' Revolt that ended only when the king made concessions. Richard's reign was troubled by competing factions of aristocrats who managed for a while to establish a balance of power. When Richard began to aspire to absolute power, however, by persuading Parliament to grant him taxes for life and to delegate its authority to a committee established by the king, a baronial revolt ensued.

After the barons had defeated the king's forces, a session of Parliament was convened. Richard II was deposed and soon killed, and the leader of the baronial revolt, Henry of Lancaster, was made king. Although Henry IV (1399–1413) proved to be a competent ruler, factions of nobles soon rose to take advantage of the new situation. In the fifteenth century, this factional conflict led to a devastating series of civil wars known as the War of the Roses.

The Problems of the French Kings

At the beginning of the fourteenth century, France was the most prosperous and best ruled monarchy in Europe. By the end of the fourteenth century, much of its wealth had been dissipated, and rival factions of aristocrats had made effective monarchical rule a virtual impossibility.

The French monarchical state had always had an underlying, inherent weakness that proved its undoing in difficult times. Although Capetian monarchs had found ways to enlarge their royal domain and extend their control by developing a large and effective bureaucracy, the various feudal territories that made up France still maintained their own princes, customs, and laws. The parliamentary institutions of France provide a good example of France's basic lack of unity. The French parliament, known as the Estates-General and composed of representatives of the clergy, nobility, and the Third Estate (everyone else), usually represented only the north of France, not the entire kingdom. The southern provinces had their own estates while local estates existed in other parts of France. Unlike the English Parliament, which was evolving into a crucial part of the English government, the French Estates-General was simply one of many such institutions.

When Philip VI (1328–1350) became involved in the Hundred Years' War with England, he found it necessary to devise new sources of revenue, including a tax on salt known as the *gabelle* and a hearth tax eventually called the *taille*. These taxes weighed heavily upon the French peasantry and middle class. Consequently, when additional taxes had to be raised to pay for the ransom of King John II after the fiasco at the Battle of Poitiers, the middle-class inhabitants of the towns tried to use the Estates-General to reform the French government and tax structure.

At the meeting of the Estates-General in 1357, under the leadership of the Parisian provost Etienne Marcel, representatives of the Third Estate granted taxes in exchange for a promise from King John's son, the dauphin Charles, not to tax without the Estates-General's permission and to allow the Estates-General to meet on a regular basis and participate in important political decisions. After Marcel's movement was crushed in 1358, this attempt to make the Estates-General a functioning part of the French government collapsed. The dauphin became King Charles V (1364–1380) and went on to recover much of the land lost to the English. His military successes underscored his efforts to reestablish strong monarchical powers. He undermined the role of the Estates-General by getting them to grant him taxes with no fixed time limit. Charles's death in 1380 soon led to a new time of troubles for the French monarchy, however.

The insanity of Charles VI (1380–1422), which first became apparent in 1392, opened the door to rival factions of French nobles aspiring to power and wealth. The dukes of Burgundy and Orléans competed to control Charles and the French monarchy. Their struggles created chaos for the French government and the French people. Many nobles supported the Orléanist faction while Paris and other towns favored the Burgundians. By the beginning of the fifteenth century, France seemed hopelessly mired in a civil war. When the English renewed the Hundred Years' War in 1415, the Burgundians supported the English cause and the English monarch's claim to the throne of France.

The German Monarchy

England and France had developed strong national monarchies in the High Middle Ages. By the end of the fourteenth century, they seemed in danger of disintegrating due to dynastic problems and the pressures generated by the Hundred Years' War. In contrast, the Holy Roman Empire, whose core consisted of the lands of Germany, had already begun to fall apart in the High Middle Ages. Northern Italy, which the German emperors had tried to include in their medieval empire, had been free from any real imperial control since the end of the Hohenstaufen dynasty in the thirteenth century. In Germany itself, the failure of the Hohenstaufens ended any chance of centralized monarchical authority, and Germany became a land of hundreds of virtually independent states. These varied in size and power and included princely states, such as the duchies of Bavaria and Saxony; free imperial city-states (self-governing cities directly under the control of the Holy Roman Emperor rather than a German territorial prince), such as Nuremberg; modest territories of petty imperial knights; and ecclesiastical states, such as the archbishopric of Cologne. In the latter states, an ecclesiastical official, such as a bishop, archbishop, or abbot, served in a dual capacity as an administrative official of the Catholic church and secular lord over the territories of his ecclesiastical state. Although all of the rulers of these different states had some obligations to the German king and Holy Roman Emperor, increasingly they acted independently of the German ruler.

Because of its unique pattern of development in the High Middle Ages, the German monarchy had become established on an elective rather than hereditary basis. This principle of election was standardized in 1356 by the Golden Bull issued by Emperor Charles IV (1346–1378). This document stated that four lay princes (the count palatine of the Rhine, the duke of Saxony, the margrave of Brandenburg, and the king of Bohemia) and three ecclesiastical rulers (the archbishops of Mainz, Trier, and Cologne) would serve as electors with the legal power to elect the "king of the Romans and future emperor, to be ruler of the world and of the Christian people."[10] "King of the Romans" was the official title of the German king; after his imperial coronation, he would also have the title emperor. The Golden Bull effectively eliminated any papal influence from the election of an emperor.

In the fourteenth century, the electoral principle further ensured that kings of Germany were generally weak. Their ability to exercise effective power depended upon the extent of their own family possessions. Two different families held the title of emperor in the fourteenth century; at the beginning of the fifteenth century, three emperors claimed the throne. Although the dispute was quickly settled, Germany entered the fifteenth century in a condition that verged on anarchy. Princes fought princes and leagues of cities. The emperors were virtually powerless to control any of them.

The States of Italy

By the fourteenth century, Italy, too, had failed to develop a centralized monarchical state. Papal opposition to the rule of the Hohenstaufen emperors in northern Italy had virtually guaranteed that. Moreover, southern Italy was divided into the kingdom of Naples, ruled by the house of Anjou, and Sicily, whose kings came from the Spanish house of Aragon. The center of the peninsula remained under the rather shaky control of the papacy. Lack of centralized authority had enabled numerous city-states in northern Italy to remain independent of any political authority.

In the fourteenth century, then, Italy was divided into a host of petty states operating independently of one another. The numerous northern city-states engaged in constant quarrels and petty wars as cities fought each other for control of trade routes or other commercial advantages. Within the cities, classes and parties fought for control of the government. In the midst of this confusion, two general tendencies can be discerned in the fourteenth century: the replacement of republican governments by tyrants and the expansion of the larger city-states at the expense of the less powerful ones.

Nearly all the cities of northern Italy began their existence as free communes with republican governments. But in the fourteenth century, they were subjected to intense internal strife, often caused by rivalry among socioeconomic groups, such as the wealthier merchant-industrialists, the lesser artisans and shopkeepers, and a growing body of hired laborers, an incipient proletariat. In their desperation to maintain law and order, city-states resorted to temporary expedients, allowing rule by one man with dictatorial powers, known either as a *podestá* or *capitano del popolo* (captain of the people), for a limited time. Limited rule, however, soon became long-term despotism, as tyrants proved willing to use whatever force and cunning were necessary to maintain themselves in power. Eventually, such tyrants tried to legitimize their power by purchasing titles from the emperor (still nominally ruler of northern Italy as Holy Roman Emperor). In this fashion, the Visconti became the dukes of Milan, the Gonzaga the marquises of Mantua, and the d'Este the dukes of Ferrara. With the major exceptions of Florence and Venice, most of the northern Italian city-states lost their republicanism to the rule of the *signore* (lords or despots).

Another change of great significance was the development of larger, regional states as the larger states expanded at the expense of the smaller ones. To fight their battles, city-states came to rely on mercenary soldiers, whose leaders, called *condottieri*, sold the services of their bands to the highest bidder. These mercenaries wreaked havoc on the countryside, living by blackmail and looting when they were not actively engaged in battles. Many were foreigners who flocked to Italy during the periods of truce of the Hundred Years' War. By the end of the fourteenth century and beginning of the fifteenth, three major states came to dominate northern Italy, the despotic state of Milan and the republican states of Florence and Venice.

Milan had been the chief center of opposition to the Holy Roman Emperors in the twelfth and thirteenth centuries. Located in the rich land of the Po valley where the chief trade routes from Italian coastal cities to the Alpine passes crossed, Milan was one of the richest city-states in Italy. Politically, it was also one of the most agitated. Constant rivalry between the nobles who possessed rich estates in the surrounding countryside and the wealthy merchant class within the city enabled a family known as the Visconti to enhance their own power. Already by 1322, the Visconti had established themselves as hereditary despots of Milan. Giangaleazzo Visconti, who ruled from 1385 to 1402, transformed this despotism into an hereditary duchy by purchasing the title of duke from the emperor in 1395. Under Giangaleazzo's direction, the duchy of Milan extended its power over all of Lombardy and even threatened to conquer much of northern Italy until the duke's untimely death before the gates of Florence in 1402.

Florence, like the other Italian towns, was initially a free commune dominated by a patrician class of nobles known as the *grandi*. But the rapid expansion of Florence's economy made possible the development of a wealthy merchant-industrialist class known as the *popolo grasso*—literally the "fat people." In 1293, the *popolo grasso* assumed a dominant role in government by establishing a new constitution known as the Ordinances of Justice. It provided for a republican govern-

ment controlled by the seven major guilds of the city, which represented the interests of the wealthier classes. Executive power was vested in the hands of a council of elected priors (the *signoria*) and a standard-bearer of justice called the *gonfaloniere*, assisted by a number of councils with advisory and overlapping powers. Near the mid-fourteenth century, revolutionary activity by the *popolo minuto*, the small shopkeepers and artisans, won them a share in the government. Even greater expansion occurred briefly when the *ciompi*, or industrial wool workers, were allowed to be represented in the government after their revolt in 1378. Only four years later, however, a counterrevolution brought the "fat people" back into virtual control of the government. After 1382, the Florentine government was controlled by a small merchant oligarchy that manipulated the supposedly republican government. By that time,

Florence had also been successful in a series of wars against its neighbors. It had conquered most of Tuscany and established itself as a major territorial state in northern Italy.

The other major northern Italian state was the republic of Venice, which had grown rich from commercial activity throughout the eastern Mediterranean and into northern Europe. A large number of merchant families became extremely wealthy. In the constitution of 1297, these patricians took control of the republic. In this year, the Great Council, the source of all political power, was closed to all but the members of about two hundred families. Since all other magistrates of the city were either chosen from or by this council, these families now formed an hereditary patriciate that completely dominated the city. Although the doge (or duke) had been the executive head of the republic since the Early Middle Ages, by 1300 he had become largely a figurehead. Actual power was vested in the hands of the Great Council and the legislative body known as the Senate, while an extraordinary body known as the Council of Ten, first formed in 1310, came to be the real executive power of the state. Venetian government was respected by contemporaries for its stability. A sixteenth-century Italian historian noted that Venice had "the best government of any city not only in our own times but also in the classical world."[11] It should be noted, however, that the relative secrecy in which the government of Venice was run gave an impression of harmony that sometimes belied the intense rivalry for power and subsequent discord that existed within the patrician class itself.

In the fourteenth century, Venice also embarked on a policy of expansion. By the end of the fourteenth century, it had created a commercial empire by establishing colonies and trading posts in the eastern Mediterranean and Black Sea as well as continuing its commercial monopolies in the Byzantine Empire. At the same time, Venice began to conquer the territory adjoining it in northern Italy.

The Decline of the Church

The papacy of the Roman Catholic church reached the height of its power in the thirteenth century. Theories of papal supremacy included a doctrine of "fullness of power" as the spiritual head of Christendom and claims to universal temporal authority over all secular rulers. But the growing secular monarchies of Europe presented a challenge to papal claims of temporal supremacy. The papacy competed with these states by centralizing its administration, developing a competent bureaucracy, and instituting a system of taxation to support the bureaucracy. Its repeated claims of temporal authority, however, led the papacy into a conflict with these territorial states that it was unable to win. Papal defeat, in turn, led to other crises that brought into question and undermined not only the pope's temporal authority over all Christendom, but his spiritual authority as well.

Boniface VIII and the Conflict with the State

The struggle between the papacy and the secular monarchies began during the pontificate of Pope Boniface VIII (1294–1303). On the surface, two issues appeared to be at stake between the pope and King Philip IV (1285–1314) of France. The king, in his desire to acquire new revenues, insisted that he had the right to tax the French clergy. Boniface VIII claimed that the clergy of any state could not pay taxes to their secular ruler without the pope's consent. A second issue arose over the clergy's claim of immunity from royal (or secular) courts. Philip claimed that he had the right to judge clerics in royal courts on certain crimes, such as treason against the king.

These two issues were secondary, however. Underlying them was a basic conflict between the claims of the papacy to universal authority over both church and state, which necessitated complete control over the clergy, and the claims of the king that all subjects, including the clergy, were under the jurisdiction of the crown and subject to the king's authority on matters of taxation and justice. In short, the fundamental issue was the universal sovereignty of the papacy versus the royal sovereignty of the monarch.

Boniface VIII attempted to assert his position by issuing a series of papal bulls or letters, the most important of which was *Unam Sanctam*, issued in 1302. It was the strongest statement ever made by a pope on the supremacy of the spiritual authority over the temporal authority (see the box on p. 398). Its statements, such as "The temporal authority ought to be subject to the spiritual power," and "If the earthly power errs it shall be judged by the spiritual power," made clear papal claims to temporal supremacy. When it became apparent that the pope had decided to act upon these principles by excommunicating Philip IV, the latter decided to preempt the pope's action.

To resolve the conflict, Philip had the French clergy issue a summons for Boniface VIII to appear on charges of heresy. A small contingent of French forces under the royal lawyer William de Nogaret was sent to capture Boniface and bring him back to France for trial. The pope was captured in Anagni, although Italian nobles from the surrounding countryside soon rescued him from Nogaret's clutches. The shock of this experience, however, soon led to the pope's death. Philip's strong-arm tactics had produced a clear victory for the national monarchy over the papacy since no later pope dared renew the extravagant claims of Boniface VIII. To ensure his position and avoid any future papal threat, Philip IV brought enough pressure to bear on the college of cardinals to achieve the election of a Frenchman as pope in 1305, Clement V (1305–1314). Using the excuse of turbulence in the city of Rome, the new pope took up residence in Avignon on the east bank of the Rhone River. Although Avignon was located in the Holy Roman Empire and was not a French possession, it lay just across the river from the territory of King Philip IV. Clement may have intended to return to Rome, but he and his successors remained in Avignon for the next seventy-five years, which created yet another crisis for the church.

The Papacy at Avignon (1305–1378)

The residency of the popes in Avignon for almost three-quarters of the fourteenth century led to a decline in papal prestige and a growing antipapal sentiment. The city of Rome was the traditional capital of the universal church. The pope was the bishop of Rome, and his position was based upon being the successor to the apostle Peter, the first bishop of Rome. It was quite unseemly that the head of the Catholic church should reside in Avignon instead of Rome. Although the Avignonese popes frequently announced their intention to return to Rome, the political turmoil in the Papal States in central Italy always gave them an excuse to postpone their departure. In the decades of the 1330s, the popes began to construct a stately palace in Avignon, a clear indication that they intended to stay for some time.

Other factors also led to a decline in papal prestige during the Avignonese residency. It was widely believed that the popes at Avignon were captives of the French monarchy. Although questionable, since Avignon did not belong to the French monarchy, it was easy to believe in view of Avignon's proximity to French lands. Moreover, during the seventy-three years of the Avignonese papacy, of the 134 new cardinals created by the popes, 113 of them were French. Understandably, then, others viewed the papacy as captive to French interests. It would appear, however, that papal policy in the fourteenth century was consistent in itself and not simply an instrument of the kings of France.

The papal residency at Avignon was also an important turning point in the church's attempt to adapt itself to the changing economic and political conditions of Europe. Like the growing monarchical states, the popes centralized their administration by developing a specialized bureaucracy. In fact, the papal bureaucracy in the fourteenth century became the most sophisticated administrative system in the medieval world. Under the leadership of the pope and college of cardinals, it was divided into four major units: the papal penitentiary oversaw ecclesiastical discipline and issued papal pardons; the chancery prepared and sent out papal letters and documents; the Roman rota was responsible for judicial affairs and served as a court of appeals for cases referred to it by the pope; and the papal chamber or treasury encompassed the various departments dealing with the collection and dispersal of the vast revenues of the church. Together, these administrative units constituted an increasingly specialized and efficient bureaucratic machine.

At the same time, the popes extended their right of provision, or the power to appoint officials to vacant benefices. A benefice was a church position that consisted of a sacred office and the right of the holder to the annual revenues from the endowment. The Avignonese popes enlarged the categories of benefices reserved for papal provision to include most major elective offices (archbishops, bishops, abbots) and a large number of

♦ **Pope Boniface VIII.** The conflict between church and state in the Middle Ages reached its height in the struggle between Pope Boniface VIII and Philip IV of France. This fourteenth-century miniature depicts Boniface VIII presiding over a gathering of cardinals.

lesser offices (canons and parish rectors). This right of provision came to be used in a manipulative way and led to serious abuses. Popes paid cardinals for their services by giving them a number of benefices (a practice known as pluralism). Since pluralists were frequently absent and simply paid substitutes to perform their duties, the practice led to low levels of performance. Widespread pluralism and absenteeism caused a decline in effective pastoral work.

The right of papal provision was closely related to the raising of new revenues. Popes streamlined tax collection by dividing Christendom into districts and instituted new taxes as well. Although steady revenues from ecclesiastical offices meant a drastic increase in papal income, such taxes and payments were often hard on the clergy, especially in light of fourteenth-century economic conditions. Nevertheless, payment of the taxes was enforced by the threat of excommunication.

The use of excommunication to force clerics to pay taxes did not improve people's opinion of the pope's use of his spiritual authority. Furthermore, the splendor in which the pope and cardinals were living in Avignon led to a highly vocal criticism of both clergy and papacy in the fourteenth century. Avignon had become a powerful symbol of abuses within the church. At last, Pope Gregory XI, perceiving the disastrous decline in papal prestige, returned to Rome in 1377. His untimely death shortly afterward, however, soon gave rise to an even greater crisis for the Catholic church.

The Great Schism

Gregory XI (1370–1378) died in Rome in the spring of 1378. When the college of cardinals met in conclave to elect a new pope, the citizens of Rome, fearful that the French majority would choose another Frenchman who would return the papacy to Avignon, threatened that the cardinals would not leave Rome alive unless a Roman or Italian were elected pope. Indeed, the guards of the conclave warned the cardinals that they "ran the risk of being torn in pieces" if they did not choose an Italian. Wisely, the terrified cardinals duly elected the

Italian archbishop of Bari, who was subsequently crowned as Pope Urban VI (1378–1389) on Easter Sunday. Following his election, Urban VI made clear his plans to reform the papal curia and even to swamp the college of cardinals with enough new Italian cardinals to eliminate the French majority. After many of the cardinals (the French ones) withdrew from Rome in late summer and were finally free of the Roman mob, they issued a manifesto, saying that they had been coerced by the mob and that Urban's election was therefore null and void. The dissenting cardinals thereupon chose one of their number, a Frenchman, who took the name Clement VII and promptly returned to Avignon. Since Urban remained in Rome, there were now two popes, initiating what has been called the Great Schism of the church. Europe's loyalties became divided: France, Spain, Scotland, and southern Italy supported Clement, while England, Germany, Scandinavia, and most of Italy supported Urban. These divisions generally followed political lines and reflected the bitter division between the English and the French in the Hundred Years' War. Since the French supported the Avignonese pope, so did their allies; their enemies, particularly England and its allies, supported the Roman pope. The need for political support caused both popes to subordinate their policies to the policies of these states.

The Great Schism lasted for nearly forty years and had a baleful effect upon the Catholic church and Christendom in general. The schism greatly aggravated the financial abuses that had developed within the church during the Avignonese papacy. Two papal administrative systems (with only one-half the accustomed revenues) worked to increase taxation. At the same time, the schism badly damaged the faith of Christian believers. The pope was widely believed to be the leader of Christendom and, as Boniface VIII had pointed out, held the keys to the kingdom of heaven. Since both lines of popes denounced the other as the Antichrist, such a spectacle could not help but undermine the institution that had become the very foundation of the church. The Great Schism introduced uncertainty into the daily lives of ordinary Christians.

New Thoughts on Church and State and the Rise of Conciliarism

The conflict between church and state in the pontificate of Boniface VIII and the crises caused by the Avignonese papacy and Great Schism led to radical critiques of papal power and revolutionary approaches to solving the church's institutional problems. One of the most system-

CHRONOLOGY

The Decline of the Church

Pope Boniface VIII	1294–1303
Unam Sanctam	1302
The papacy at Avignon	1305–1378
Pope Gregory XI returns to Rome	1377
The Great Schism begins	1378
Pope Urban VI	1378–1389
Failure of Council of Pisa to end schism; election of Alexander V	1409
Council of Constance	1414–1418
End of schism; election of Martin V	1417

atic was provided by Marsiglio of Padua (1270?–1342), rector of the University of Paris and author of the remarkable book, *Defender of the Peace*.

Marsiglio denied that the temporal authority was subject to the spiritual authority as popes from Innocent III to Boniface VIII had maintained. Instead, he argued that the church was only one element of society, part of the secular state with respect to temporal affairs, and must confine itself solely to spiritual functions. Furthermore, Marsiglio argued, the church was a community of the faithful in which all authority is ultimately derived from the entire community. The clergy hold no special authority from God, but serve only to administer the affairs of the church on behalf of all Christians. Final authority in spiritual matters must reside not with the pope but with a general church council representing all members. As Marsiglio stated it: "Doubtful sentences of divine law, especially on those matters which are called articles of the Christian faith, . . . must be defined only by the general council of the believers, . . . no partial group or individual person of whatever status [the pope], has the authority to make such definitions."[12]

As dissatisfaction with the papacy grew, so also did the number of people who espoused the conciliar idea. It was the Great Schism, however, that led large numbers of serious churchmen to take up the theory of conciliarism in the belief that only a general council of the church could end the schism and bring reform to the church in its "head and members." The only serious issue left to be decided was who should call the council. Canon law held that only a pope could convene a council. Professors of theology and canon law argued, however, that since the competing popes would not do so, either members of the church hierarchy or even secular princes, especially the Holy Roman Emperor, could convene a council to settle all relevant issues.

In desperation, a group of cardinals from both lines of popes finally heeded these theoretical formulations and convened a general council on their own. This Council of Pisa, which met in 1409, deposed the two popes and elected a new one, Alexander V. The council's action proved disastrous when the two deposed popes refused to step down. There were now three popes, and the church seemed more hopelessly divided than ever.

After the Council of Pisa had only worsened the schism, leadership in convening a new council passed to the Holy Roman Emperor Sigismund. As a result of his efforts, a new ecumenical church council met at Constance from 1414 to 1418. Ending the schism proved to be the Council of Constance's easiest task. After the three competing popes either resigned or were deposed, a new conclave elected Cardinal Oddone Colonna, a member of a prominent Roman family, as Pope Martin V (1417–1431). The Great Schism had finally been ended.

Popular Religion in an Age of Adversity

The concern of popes and leading clerics with finances and power during the struggles of Boniface VIII, the Avignonese papacy, and the Great Schism could not help but lead to a decline in prestige and respect for the institutional church, especially the papacy. At the same time, in the fourteenth century, the Black Death and its recurrences made an important impact on the religious life of ordinary Christians by heightening their preoccupation with death and salvation. The church often failed to provide sufficient spiritual comfort as many parish priests fled from the plague. In some English dioceses, for example, as many as 20 percent of the parish clergy abandoned their parishes.

Christians responded in different ways to the adversities of the fourteenth century. First of all, there was a tendency to stress the performance of good works, including acts of charity, as a means of assuring salvation. This was visible in wills where bequests to hospitals and other charitable foundations increased. In London, 5 percent of the wills registered in court before 1348 left a bequest to hospitals. From 1350 to 1360, 15 percent did so, while the average bequest increased by 40 percent. Another sign of the heightened concern for salvation was the establishment of family chapels served by priests whose primary responsibility was to say masses

for the good of the deceased's soul. These became even more significant as the importance of purgatory rose. Purgatory came to be defined by the church as the state in which souls existed after death so that they could be purged of the punishment due to the consequences of sin. In effect, the soul was purified in purgatory before it ascended into heaven. It was believed that, like indulgences, prayers and private masses for the dead could shorten the amount of time souls spent in purgatory.

All of these developments are part of a larger trend—a new emphasis in late medieval Christianity on a mechanical path to salvation. Chalking up good deeds to ensure salvation was done in numerous ways, but was nowhere more evident than in the growing emphasis on indulgences. We should also note that pilgrimages, which became increasingly popular, and charitable contributions were good works that could be accomplished without the involvement of clerics, a reflection of the loss of faith in the institutional church and its clergy and another noticeable feature of popular religious life. But while there was an evident loss of faith in the hierarchical or institutional church, interest in Christianity itself did not decline. Indeed, people sought to play a more active role in their own salvation. This is particularly evident in the popularity of mysticism and lay piety in the fourteenth century.

MYSTICISM AND LAY PIETY

The mysticism of the fourteenth century was certainly not new, for Christians throughout the Middle Ages had claimed to have had mystical experiences. Mysticism did have a particularly strong impact in the fourteenth century, however, especially along the Rhine River in Germany and in the Low Countries.

Simply defined, mysticism is the immediate experience of oneness with God (see the box on p. 401). It is this experience that characterized the teaching of Meister Eckhart (1260–1327), who sparked a mystical movement in western Germany. Eckhart was a well-educated Dominican theologian who wrote learned Latin works on theology, but he was also a popular preacher whose message on the union of the soul with God was typical of mysticism. According to Eckhart, such a union was attainable for those who pursued it wholeheartedly. He referred to this spiritual encounter as the "birth of Christ" in the soul.

Eckhart's mystical teachings were carried on by his disciples and pupils. One in particular, Johannes Tauler (c. 1300–1361), was significant in channeling German mysticism into a practical direction as an inspiration to

⇛ *A Mystical Visionary of the Fourteenth Century* ⇚

The fourteenth century witnessed a significant outpouring of mystical literature that, in turn, sparked a popular movement of lay piety, especially in the Low Countries and along the Rhine River. This selection is taken from the work of Richard Rolle, probably the most influential of the fourteenth-century English mystics. Rolle taught that the soul is capable of achieving a mystical union with God by surrendering to the Divine Being, which he called pure love.

Richard Rolle, *The Fire of Love*
Chapter 5

In all our actions and thoughts let us give greater weight to divine love than to learning and argument. For love delights the soul and sweetens the conscience, drawing it away from the attraction of lesser delights and the appetite for personal distinction. Learning without charity contributes nothing to eternal salvation but blows a man up to miserable perdition. May our spirit therefore be strong in taking upon itself hard labors for God; may it yearn to glow with wisdom eternal and to burn with that sweet flame which excites man to love and desire solely his Maker and be given powerful strength to despise all transitory things. Thus [the soul] puts away trust in the solace of things which do not endure, as one having there no dwelling place, but incessantly seeks that place to come which is not made by hands, and cries "For to me to live is Christ and to die is gain."

Chapter 13

There have been some men, and perhaps they still exist, who altogether prefer the communal to the solitary life; they hold that we must run in crowds if we desire to reach the highest perfection. One cannot seriously argue with such men because they praise only that kind of life which they would wish to follow or at least have known a little. They fail to praise the solitary life simply because they do not know it. For it is a life which no one living in the flesh can know except he to whom God grants that he live it, and no one assuredly judges rightly of this matter who remains uncertain what it is and how it works. I know beyond doubt that if they knew it they would praise it more to others. Others err more dangerously by unceasingly denouncing and slandering the solitary life. They say, "Woe to the solitary," meaning not only "man without God" but "man without fellows." For he is alone with whom God is not. When he shall fall into death he shall at once be taken to the torments and shall for ever be cut off from the sight of God's glory and the saints'. Indeed, he who chooses the solitary life for God and lives it rightly shall be full not of "Woe" but of "Wonderful Virtue" and shall continuously delight in thinking of the name of Jesus.

inner piety or an inwardness of religious feeling. Tauler's sermons concentrated on the same idea of the union of the soul with God, but they also focused on the need to prepare the soul for the mystical encounter by expressing the love of God in the ordinary activities of everyday life. Tauler's ideas deepened the religious life of clerics and lay folk and connected mysticism to the development of the lay piety that became more visible as Eckhart's and Tauler's movement spread from Germany into the Low Countries.

In the Low Countries, German mysticism was transformed into a new form called the Modern Devotion, whose founder was Gerard Groote (1340–1384). Groote was a canon lawyer, but after a religious conversion, he entered a monastery for several years of contemplation before reentering the world. Although he never became a priest, he was ordained as a deacon, entitling him to preach. His messages were typical of a practical mysticism. To achieve true spiritual communion with God, people must imitate Christ and lead lives dedicated to serving the needs of their fellow human beings. Groote emphasized a simple piety and morality based on scripture and an avoidance of the complexities of theology.

Eventually, Groote attracted a group of followers who came to be known as the Brothers of the Common Life. From this small beginning, a movement developed that spread through the Netherlands and back into Germany. Houses of the Brothers, as well as separate houses for women (Sisters of the Common Life), were founded in one city after another. The Sisters and Brothers of the Common Life did not constitute regular religious orders. They were lay people who took no formal monastic vows, but were nevertheless regulated by quasi-monastic rules that they imposed on their own communities. They also established schools throughout Germany and the Netherlands in which they stressed their message of imitating the life of Christ by serving others. The

Brothers and Sisters of the Common Life attest to the vitality of spiritual life among lay Christians in the fourteenth century. It is interesting to note, however, that popes feared the movement since it was not closely controlled by the ecclesiastical establishment.

The Intellectual and Cultural World of the Fourteenth Century

The intellectual world of the fourteenth century was also characterized by ferment, especially evidenced in the questioning of the grand synthesis attempted by Thomas Aquinas.

Changes in Theology

In the thirteenth century, Thomas Aquinas's grand synthesis of faith and reason was not widely accepted outside his own Dominican order. At the same time, differences with Aquinas were kept within a framework of commonly accepted scholastic thought. In the fourteenth century, however, the philosopher William of Occam (1285–1329) posed a severe challenge to the scholastic achievements of the High Middle Ages.

Occam posited a radical interpretation of nominalism. He asserted that all universals or general concepts were simply names and that only individual objects perceived by the senses were real. Although the mind was capable of analyzing individual objects or observable phenomena, it could not establish any truths about the nature of external, higher reality. Reason could not be used to substantiate spiritual truths. It could not, for example, prove the statement that "God exists." For William of Occam as a Christian believer, this did not mean that God did not exist, however. It simply indicated that the truths of religion were not demonstrable by reason, but could only be known by an act of faith. The acceptance of Occam's nominalist philosophy at the University of Paris brought an element of uncertainty to late medieval theology by seriously weakening the synthesis of faith and reason that had characterized the theological thought of the High Middle Ages. Nevertheless, Occam's emphasis on using reason to analyze the observable phenomena of the world had an important impact on the development of physical science by creating support for rational and scientific analysis. Some late medieval theologians came to accept the compatibility of rational analysis of the material world with mystical acceptance of spiritual truths.

The Development of Vernacular Literature

Although Latin remained the language of the church liturgy and the official documents of both church and state, the fourteenth century witnessed the rapid growth of vernacular literature, especially in Italy. Spoken vernacular tongues had been used in Europe for centuries, and some notable literature in French and German had appeared during the High Middle Ages, but in Italy a vernacular literature had been largely lacking until the second half of the thirteenth century.

The development of an Italian vernacular literature was mostly the result of the efforts of three writers in the fourteenth century, Dante, Petrarch and Boccaccio. Their use of the Tuscan dialect common in Florence and its surrounding countryside ensured that it would become the basis of the modern Italian language.

Dante (1265–1321) came from an old Florentine noble family that had fallen upon hard times. Although he had held high political office in republican Florence, factional conflict led to his exile from the city in 1302. Until the end of his life, Dante hoped to return to his beloved Florence, but his wish remained unfulfilled.

Dante's masterpiece in the Italian vernacular was his *Divine Comedy*, written between 1313 and 1321. Cast in a typical medieval framework, the *Divine Comedy* is basically the story of the soul's progression to salvation, a fundamental medieval preoccupation. The lengthy poem was divided into three major sections corresponding to the realms of the afterworld: hell, purgatory, and heaven or paradise. In the "Inferno" (see the box on p. 403), Dante is led by his guide, the classical author Virgil, who is a symbol of human reason. But Virgil (or reason) can only lead the poet so far on his journey. At the end of "Purgatory," Beatrice (the true love of Dante's life), who represents revelation—which alone can explain the mysteries of heaven—becomes his guide into "Paradise." Here, Beatrice presents Dante to Saint Bernard, a symbol of mystical contemplation. The saint turns Dante over to the Virgin Mary since grace is necessary to achieve the final step of entering the presence of God, where one beholds "The love that moves the sun and the other stars."[13] Symbolically, the "Inferno" represents despair, while "Purgatory," the second stage of the journey, represents hope. "Paradise" represents perfection or salvation.

Some scholars have considered the *Divine Comedy* a synthesis of medieval Christian thought. Like the Gothic cathedrals and the *Summa Theologica*, it reminds us that Christian faith was, after all, the basic foundation of medieval culture. The theology of the *Divine*

⇒ Dante's Vision of Hell ⇐

The Divine Comedy of Dante Alighieri is regarded as one of the greatest literary works of all time. Many consider it the supreme summary of medieval thought. It combines allegory with a remarkable amount of contemporary history. Indeed, forty-three of the seventy-nine people consigned to hell in the "Inferno" were Florentines. This excerpt is taken from Canto XVIII of the "Inferno," in which Dante and Virgil visit the eighth circle of hell, which is divided into ten trenches containing those who had committed malicious frauds upon their fellow human beings.

Dante, "Inferno," The Divine Comedy

We had already come to where the walk
crosses the second bank, from which it lifts
another arch, spanning from rock to rock.

Hear we heard people whine in the next chasm,
and knock and thump themselves with open palms,
and blubber through their snouts as if in a spasm.

Steaming from that pit, a vapor rose
over the banks, crusting them with a slime
that sickened my eyes and hammered at my nose.

That chasm sinks so deep we could not sight
its bottom anywhere until we climbed
along the rock arch to its greatest height.

Once there, I peered down; and I saw long lines
of people in a river of excrement
that seemed the overflow of the world's latrines.

I saw among the felons of that pit
one wraith who might or might not have been tonsured—
one could not tell, he was so smeared with shit.

He bellowed: "You there, why do you stare at me
more than at all the others in this stew?"
And I to him: "Because if memory

serves me, I knew you when your hair was dry.
You are Alessio Interminelli da Lucca.
That's why I pick you from this filthy fry."

And he then, beating himself on his clown's head:
"Down to this have the flatteries I sold
the living sunk me here among the dead."

And my Guide prompted then: "Lean forward a bit
and look beyond him, there—do you see that one
scratching herself with dungy nails, the strumpet

who fidgets to her feet, then to a crouch?
It is the whore Thäis who told her lover
when he sent to ask her, 'Do you thank me much?'

'Much? Nay, past all believing!' And with this
Let us turn from the sight of this abyss."

Comedy is that of Saint Thomas Aquinas; its science is that of Aristotle; and its politics centers on the Holy Roman Emperor as the savior of Italy. At the same time, some observers believe elements of Dante's work foreshadow the coming new age of the Renaissance. Dante, after all, is a layman describing theology in the vernacular, not Latin. The popes who turn up in hell have been consigned there by a layman. Moreover, using Virgil as his guide emphasizes the role of the classical tradition in providing wisdom, a theme that became increasingly important in the Renaissance. In addressing Virgil, Dante says, "Can you be Virgil? . . . You are my master. . . . From you alone I learned the singing strain, the noble style, that does me honor now."[14]

Like Dante, Petrarch was a Florentine who spent much of his life outside his native city. Petrarch's role in the revival of the classics made him a seminal figure in the literary Italian Renaissance (see Chapter 13). His primary contribution to the development of the Italian vernacular was made in his sonnets. He is considered to be one of the greatest European lyric poets. His sonnets were inspired by his love for a married lady named Laura, whom he had met in 1327. While honoring an idealized female figure was a longstanding medieval tradition, Laura was very human and not just an ideal. She was a real woman with whom Petrarch was involved for a long time. He poured forth his lamentations in sonnet after sonnet:

I am as tired of thinking as my thought
Is never tired to find itself in you,
And of not yet leaving this life that brought
Me the too heavy weight of signs and rue;

And because to describe your hair and face
And the fair eyes of which I always speak,
Language and sound have not become too weak
And day and night your name they still embrace.

And tired because my feet do not yet fail
After following you in every part,
Wasting so many steps without avail,

From whence derive the paper and the ink
That I have filled with you; if I should sink,
It is the fault of Love, not of my art.[15]

Petrarch's lamentations over his inability to gain his lady's love were in the medieval tradition. Yet in analyzing every aspect of the unrequited lover's feelings, he appeared less concerned to sing his lady's praise than to immortalize his own thoughts. This "psychology of love" and interest in his own personality reveal a sense of individuality stronger than in any previous medieval literature.

Although he too wrote poetry, Boccaccio (1313–1375) is primarily known for his contributions to the development of Italian prose. Another Florentine, he also used the Tuscan dialect. While working for the Bardi banking house in Naples, he fell in love with a noble lady whom he called his Fiammetta, his Little Flame. Under her inspiration, Boccaccio began to write prose romances. His best-known work, *The Decameron*, however, was not written until after he had returned to Florence. *The Decameron* is set at the time of the Black Death. Ten young people flee to a villa outside Florence to escape the plague and decide to while away the time by telling stories. Although the stories are not new and still reflect the acceptance of basic Christian values, Boccaccio does present the society of his time from a secular point of view. Boccaccio stresses cleverness and wit rather than piety and devotion. It is the seducer of women, not the knight or philosopher or pious monk, who is the real hero. Perhaps, as some historians have argued, *The Decameron* reflects the immediate easygoing, cynical postplague values. Boccaccio's later work certainly became gloomier and more pessimistic; as he grew older, he even rejected his earlier work as irrelevant. He commented in a 1373 letter that "I am certainly not pleased that you have allowed the illustrious women in your house to read my trifles. . . . You know how much in them is less than decent and opposed to modesty, how much stimulation to wanton lust, how many things that drive to lust even those most fortified against it."[16]

In the fourteenth century, one of the world's truly gifted poets, Geoffrey Chaucer (c. 1340–1400), brought a new level of sophistication to the English vernacular language in his famous work *The Canterbury Tales*. His beauty of expression and clear, forceful language were important in transforming his East Midland dialect into the chief ancestor of the modern English language. Although Chaucer's materials were taken from a typically medieval literary tradition, he placed much emphasis on individual characters.

The Canterbury Tales constitute a group of stories told by twenty-nine pilgrims journeying from Southwark to the tomb of Saint Thomas at Canterbury. This format gave Chaucer the chance to portray an entire range of English society, both high and low born. Among others, he presented the Knight, the Yeoman, the Prioress, the Monk, the Merchant, the Student, the Lawyer, the Carpenter, the Cook, the Doctor, the Plowman, and, of course, "A Good Wife was there from beside the city of Bath—a little deaf, which was a pity." The stories these pilgrims told to while away the time on the journey were just as varied as the storytellers themselves: knightly romances, fairy tales, saints' lives, sophisticated satires, and crude anecdotes.

Chaucer also used some of his characters to criticize the corruption of the church in the late medieval period. His portrayals of the Monk, the Friar, and the Pardoner leave no doubt of Chaucer's disdain for the corrupt practices of clerics. Of the Friar, he says:

He knew the taverns well in every town.
The barmaids and innkeepers pleased his mind
Better than beggars and lepers and their kind.

The Pardoner, too:

Well could he read the Scripture or saint's story,
But best of all he sang the offertory,
For he understood that when this song was sung,
Then he must preach, and sharpen up his tongue
To rake in cash, as well he knew the art,
And so he sang out gaily, with full heart.

And yet, Chaucer was still a pious Christian, never doubting basic Christian doctrines and remaining optimistic that the church could be reformed. The Parson was his model for what others should imitate:

I doubt there was a priest in any place
His better. He did not stand on dignity
Nor affect in conscience too much nicety,

But Christ's and his disciples' word he sought
To teach, and first he followed what he taught.[17]

Dante, Petrarch, Boccaccio, and Chaucer all contributed to the growth of written vernacular languages in the fourteenth century. Despite the revival of classical languages in the Renaissance of the fifteenth century, the future belonged not to Latin and Greek, but to the vernacular languages of the emerging European states.

Art and the Black Death

The fourteenth century produced an artistic outburst in new directions as well as a large body of morbid work influenced by the Black Death and the recurrence of the plague. The city of Florence witnessed the first dramatic break with medieval tradition in the work of Giotto (1266–1337), often considered a forerunner of Italian Renaissance painting. Born into a peasant family, Giotto acquired his painting skills in a workshop in Florence. Although he worked throughout Italy, his most famous works were done in Padua and Florence. Coming out of the formal Byzantine school, Giotto transcended it with a new kind of realism, a desire to imitate nature that Renaissance artists later identified as the basic component of classical art. Giotto's figures were solid and rounded and, placed realistically in relationship to each other and their background, provided a sense of three-dimensional depth. The expressive faces and physically realistic bodies gave his sacred figures human qualities with which spectators could identify. Although Giotto had no immediate successors, Florentine painting in the early fifteenth century pursued even more dramatically the new direction his work represents.

The Black Death made a visible impact on art. For one thing, it wiped out entire guilds of artists. At the same time, survivors, including the newly rich who patronized artists, were no longer so optimistic. Some were more guilty about enjoying life and more concerned about gaining salvation. Postplague art began to concentrate on pain and death. A fairly large number of artistic works came to be based on the *ars moriendi*, the art of dying. A morbid concern with death is particularly evident in Francesco Traini's fresco, *The Triumph of Death* in Pisa. On the left, three young nobles encounter three coffins containing decomposing bodies, while on the right young aristocrats engaged in pleasant pursuits are threatened by a grim figure of Death in the form of a witch flying through the air swinging a large scythe. Beneath her lie piles of dead citizens and clergy cut down in the prime of life.

✦ **Giotto, *Pietà*.** The work of Giotto marked the first clear innovation in fourteenth-century painting, making him a forerunner of the Early Renaissance. In this fresco, which was part of an elaborate series in the Arena chapel in Padua begun in 1305, the solidity of Giotto's human figures gives them a three-dimensional sense.

Society in an Age of Adversity

In the midst of disaster, the fourteenth century proved creative in its own way. New inventions made an impact on daily life at the same time that the effects of plague were felt in many areas of medieval urban life.

Changes in Urban Life

One immediate by-product of the Black Death was a greater regulation of urban activities. Authorities tried to keep cities cleaner by enacting new ordinances against waste products in the streets. Viewed as unhealthy places, bathhouses were closed down, leading to a noticeable decline in cleanliness. Efforts at regulation also affected the practice of female prostitution.

Medieval society had tolerated prostitution as a lesser evil; it was better for males to frequent prostitutes than to seduce virgins or have sex with married women. Since many males in medieval towns married late, the demand for prostitutes was high and was met by a regular supply, derived no doubt from the need of many poor girls and women to survive. The recession of the fourteenth century probably increased the supply of prostitutes while the new hedonism prevalent after the Black Death also increased demand. As a result, in the later fourteenth century, cities intensified their regulation of prostitution.

By organizing brothels, city authorities could supervise as well as tax prostitutes. Officials granted charters to citizens who were allowed to set up brothels, provided they were located only in certain areas of town. Prostitutes were also expected to wear special items of clothing—such as red hats—to distinguish them from other women. In some towns, church officials forced prostitutes to sit in special areas if they wished to attend church services.

FAMILY LIFE AND GENDER ROLES IN LATE MEDIEVAL CITIES

The basic unit of the late medieval urban environment was the nuclear family of husband, wife, and children. Especially in wealthier families, there might also be servants, apprentices, and other relatives, including widowed mothers and the husband's illegitimate children.

Before the Black Death, late marriages were common for urban couples. It was not unusual for husbands to be in their late thirties or forties and wives in their early twenties. The expense of setting up a household prob-

ably necessitated the delay in marriage. But the situation changed dramatically after the plague, reflecting new economic opportunities for the survivors and a new reluctance to postpone living in the presence of so much death. The economic difficulties of the fourteenth century also had a tendency to strengthen the development of gender roles created by thirteenth-century scholastic theologians and to set new limits on employment opportunities for women. Thomas Aquinas and others had offered rigid conceptions of men and women that were unthinkable in earlier centuries when some women had played important roles. Based on the authority of Aristotle, Aquinas had advanced the belief that according to the natural order, men were active and domineering while women were passive and submissive. As more and more lawyers, doctors, and priests, who had been trained in universities where these notions were taught, entered society, these ideas about the different natures of men and women became widely accepted. Increasingly, women were expected to eschew any active functions in society and remain subject to direction from males. A fourteenth-century Parisian provost commented that among glass cutters "no master's widow who keeps working at his craft after her husband's death may take on apprentices, for the men of the craft do not believe that a woman can master it well enough to teach a child to master it, for the craft is a very delicate one."[18] Although this statement suggests that some women

◆ Francesco Traini, *The Triumph of Death.* The plague gave rise to a morbid fascination with death that was reflected in the art of the period. At the left, several young nobles encounter three coffins with corpses in various stages of decomposition. At the right, young men and women are seated in a forest grove, oblivious to the figure of death, flying through the air in the guise of an old witch holding a huge scythe, who is about to wreak havoc on their world.

were, in fact, running businesses, it also reveals that they were viewed as incapable of undertaking all of men's activities. Based on a pattern of gender, Europeans created a division of labor roles between men and women that continued until the Industrial Revolution of the eighteenth and nineteenth centuries.

MEDIEVAL CHILDREN

Although historians' interpretations differ, there seems to be sufficient evidence to indicate that medieval parents of both the High and Later Middle Ages invested considerable resources and affection in rearing their children. The dramatic increase in specialized roles that accompanied the spread of commerce and the growth of cities demanded a commitment to educating children in the marketable skills needed for the new occupations. Philip of Navarre noted in the twelfth century that boys ought to be taught a trade "as soon as possible. Those who early become and long remain apprentices ought to be the best masters."[19] Some cities provided schools to educate the young. A Florentine chronicler related that between eight and ten thousand boys and girls between the ages of six and twelve attended the city's grammar schools, a figure that probably represented half of school-aged children. Although grammar school completed education for girls, around 1,100 boys proceeded into six secondary schools that

prepared them for business careers while another 600 studied Latin and logic in four other schools that readied them for university training and a career in medicine, law, or the church. In the High Middle Ages, then, urban communities demonstrated a commitment to the training of the young.

As a result of the devastating effects of the plague and its recurrences, these same communities became concerned about investing in the survival and health of children. Although a number of hospitals existed in both Florence and Rome in the fourteenth century, it was not until the 1420s and 1430s that hospitals were established that catered only to the needs of foundlings, supporting them until boys could be taught a trade and girls could marry.

New Directions in Medicine

The Black Death made a significant impact upon the existing medieval medical system, and some authorities think it created "the stirrings of modern medicine." The medical community comprised a number of different functionaries. At the top of the medical hierarchy were the physicians, usually clergymen, who received their education in the medieval universities where they studied ancient authorities, such as Hippocrates and Galen. As a result, physicians were highly trained in theory, but had little or no clinical practice. They were educated in six chief medical schools by the fourteenth century, Salerno, Montpellier, Bologna, Oxford, Padua, and Paris. The latter was regarded as the most prestigious by the time of the Black Death.

The preplague medicine of university-trained physicians was theoretically grounded in the classical theory of the "four humors," each connected to a particular organ: blood (from the heart), phlegm (from the brain), yellow bile (from the liver), and black bile (from the spleen). The four humors, in turn, corresponded to the four elemental qualities of the universe, earth (black bile), air (blood), fire (yellow bile), and water (phlegm), making a human being a microcosm of the cosmos. Good health resulted from a perfect balance of the four humors; sickness meant that the humors were out of balance. The task of the medieval physician was to restore proper order by a number of cures, such as rest, diet, herbal medicines, or bloodletting.

Beneath the physicians in the hierarchy of the medical profession stood the surgeons, whose activities included performing operations, setting broken bones, and bleeding patients. Their knowledge was largely based on practical experience. Below surgeons were the barber-surgeons, who were less trained and performed menial tasks such as bloodletting and setting simple bone fractures. They supplemented their incomes by shaving

and cutting hair. Apothecaries also constituted part of the medical establishment. They filled herbal prescriptions recommended by physicians and also prescribed drugs on their own authority.

All of these medical practitioners proved unable to deal with the plague. When King Philip VI of France requested the opinion of the medical faculty of the University of Paris on the plague, their advice proved worthless. This failure to understand the Black Death, however, produced a crisis in medieval medicine that resulted in some new approaches to health care.

One result was the rise of surgeons to greater prominence because of their practical knowledge. Surgeons were now recruited by universities, which placed them on an equal level with physicians and introduced a greater emphasis on practical anatomy into the university curriculum. Connected to this was a rise in medical textbooks, often written in the vernacular and stressing practical, "how to" approaches to medical and surgical problems. Hospitals also took on a new role. Before the plague, they were designed to isolate the sick from the rest of the population. After the Black Death, hospitals expressed a stronger interest in curing patients. New techniques in organization and management provided better facilities. Many hospitals developed associations with doctors or medical students from nearby universities to encourage them to practice there.

♦ **Birth of a Child.** This scene from the *Birth of the Virgin* by an unknown German artist is actually a painting of a wealthy fourteenth-century mother who has just given birth to a child. Female attendants prepare the water for the child's first bath while the mother holds her newborn in her canopied bed.

Finally, as a result of the plague, cities gave increased attention to public health and sanitation. Public health laws were instituted, and municipal boards of health came into being. The primary concern of the latter was to prevent plague, but gradually they came to control almost every aspect of health and sanitation. Boards of public health, consisting of medical practitioners and public officials, were empowered to enforce sanitary conditions, report on and attempt to isolate epidemics by quarantine (rarely successful), and regulate the activities of doctors. Some communities even began to hire "plague doctors," or municipal physicians and surgeons who were paid to treat victims.

Inventions and New Patterns

Despite its problems, the fourteenth century witnessed a continuation of the technological innovations that had characterized the High Middle Ages. The most extraordinary of these inventions, and one that made a visible impact on European cities, was the clock. There had been earlier experiments with waterpowered clocks, but they had obvious limitations, particularly in northern Europe where they froze in winter. The mechanical clock was invented at the end of the thirteenth century, but not perfected until the fourteenth. The time-telling clock was actually a by-product of a larger astronomical clock. The best-designed one was constructed by Giovanni di Dondi in the mid-fourteenth century. Dondi's clock contained the signs of the zodiac, but also struck on the hour. Since clocks were expensive, they were usually installed only in the towers of churches or municipal buildings. The first clock striking equal hours was in a church in Milan; in 1335, a chronicler described it as "a wonderful clock, with a very large clapper which strikes a bell twenty-four times according to the twenty-four hours of the day and night and thus at the first hour of the night gives one sound, at the second two strikes . . . and so distinguishes one hour from another, which is of greatest use to men of every degree."[20]

Clocks introduced a wholly new conception of time into the lives of Europeans; they revolutionized how people thought about and used time. Throughout most of the Middle Ages, time was determined by natural rhythms (daybreak and nightfall) or church bells that were rung at more or less regular three-hour intervals, corresponding to the ecclesiastical offices of the church. Clocks made it possible to plan one's day and organize one's activities around the regular striking of bells. This brought a new regularity into the life of workers and merchants, defining urban existence and enabling mer-

◆ **A Medical Textbook.** This illustration is taken from a fourteenth-century medical textbook that stressed a "how-to" approach to medical problems. *Top left*, a surgeon shows how to remove an arrow from a patient; *top right*, how to open a patient's chest; *bottom left*, how to deal with an injury to the intestines; *bottom right*, how to diagnose an abscess.

chants and bankers to see the value of time in a new way. Indeed, it was a conception that ultimately led them to believe that "time is money."

Like clocks, eyeglasses were introduced in the thirteenth century, but not refined until the fourteenth. Even then they were not overly effective by modern standards and were still extremely expensive. The high cost of parchment forced people to write in extremely small script; doubtlessly, eyeglasses made it more readable. At the same time, a significant change in writing materials occurred in the fourteenth century when parchment was supplemented by much cheaper paper made from cotton rags. Although it was more subject to insect and water damage than parchment, medieval paper was actually superior to modern papers made of high-acid wood pulp.

Invented earlier by the Chinese, gunpowder also made its appearance in the west in the fourteenth century. The use of gunpowder eventually brought drastic changes to European warfare. Its primary use was in cannons, although early cannons were prone to blow up, making them as dangerous to those firing them as to the enemy. Even as late as 1460, an attack on a castle using the "Lion," an enormous Flemish cannon, proved disastrous for the Scottish king James II when the "Lion" blew up, killing the king and a number of his retainers. Continued improvement in the construction of cannons, however, soon made them extremely valuable in reducing both castles and city walls.

Conclusion

In the eleventh, twelfth, and thirteenth centuries, European civilization developed many of its fundamental features. Territorial states, parliaments, capitalist trade and industry, banks, cities, and vernacular literatures were all products of that fertile period. During the same time, the Catholic church under the direction of the papacy reached its apogee. Fourteenth-century European society, however, was challenged by an overwhelming number of crises. Devastating plague, decline in trade and industry, bank failures, peasant revolts pitting lower classes against the upper classes, seemingly constant warfare, aristocratic factional conflict that undermined political stability, the absence of the popes from Rome, and even the spectacle of two popes condemning each other as the antichrist all seemed to overpower Europeans in this "calamitous century." Not surprisingly, much of the art of the period depicted the Four Horsemen of the Apocalypse described in the New Testament book of Revelation: Death, Famine, Pestilence, and War. No doubt, to some people the last days of the world appeared to be at hand.

The new European society, however, proved remarkably resilient. Periods of crisis are usually paralleled by the emergence of new ideas and new practices. Intellectuals of the period saw themselves as standing on the threshold of a new age or rebirth of the best features of classical civilization. It is their perspective that led historians to speak of a Renaissance in the fifteenth century.

NOTES

1. Quoted in H. S. Lucas, "The Great European Famine of 1315, 1316, and 1317," *Speculum* 5 (1930): 359.
2. Quoted in Robert Gottfried, *The Black Death: Natural and Human Disaster in Medieval Europe* (New York, 1983), p. xiii.
3. Giovanni Boccaccio, *The Decameron*, trans. Frances Winwar (New York, 1955), p. xxv.
4. Ibid., p. xxvi.
5. Jean Froissart, *Chronicles*, ed. and trans. Geoffrey Brereton (Harmondsworth, 1968), p. 111.
6. Quoted in James B. Ross and Mary M. McLaughlin, *The Portable Medieval Reader* (New York, 1949), pp. 218–19.
7. Quoted in Barbara W. Tuchman, *A Distant Mirror* (New York, 1978), p. 175.
8. Froissart, *Chronicles*, p. 212.
9. Ibid., p. 89.
10. Oliver J. Thatcher and Edgar H. McNeal, eds., *A Source Book for Medieval History* (New York, 1905), p. 288.
11. Quoted in D. S. Chambers, *The Imperial Age of Venice, 1380–1580* (London, 1970), p. 30.
12. Marsiglio of Padua, *The Defender of the Peace*, trans. Alan Gewirth (New York, 1956), 2:426.
13. Dante Alighieri, *The Divine Comedy*, trans. Dorothy Sayers (New York, 1962), "Paradise," Canto XXXIII, line 145.
14. Ibid., "Hell," Canto I, lines 79–87.
15. Petrarch, *Sonnets and Songs*, trans. Anna Maria Armi (New York, 1968), No. LXXIV, p. 127.
16. Quoted in Millard Meiss, *Painting in Florence and Siena after the Black Death* (Princeton, N.J., 1951), p. 161.
17. Geoffrey Chaucer, *The Canterbury Tales*, in *The Portable Chaucer*, ed. Theodore Morrisoon (New York, 1949), pp. 67, 81, 75.
18. Quoted in Susan Stuard, "Dominion of Gender: Women's Fortunes in the High Middle Ages," in Renate Bridenthal, Claudia Koonz, and Susan Stuard, eds., *Becoming Visible: Women in European History*, 2d ed. (Boston, 1987), p. 169.
19. Quoted in David Herlihy, "Medieval Children," in Bede K. Lackner and Kenneth R. Philp, eds., *Essays on Medieval Civilization* (Austin, 1978), p. 121.
20. Quoted in Jean Gimpel, *The Medieval Machine* (New York, 1976), p. 168.

SUGGESTIONS FOR FURTHER READING

For a general introduction to the fourteenth century, see D. Hay, *Europe in the Fourteenth and Fifteenth Centuries* (New York, 1966); G. Holmes, *Europe: Hierarchy and Revolt, 1320–1450* (New York, 1975); and the well-written popular history by B. Tuchman, *A Distant Mirror* (New York, 1978).

On the Black Death, see R. S. Gottfried, *The Black Death: Natural and Human Disaster in Medieval Europe* (New York, 1983); P. Ziegler, *The Black Death* (New York, 1969); and W. H. McNeill, *Plagues and People* (New York, 1976). On the peasant and urban revolts of the fourteenth century, see M. Mollat and P. Wolff, *The Popular Revolutions of the Late Middle Ages* (Winchester, Mass., 1973).

The classic work on the Hundred Years' War is E. Perroy, *The Hundred Years War* (New York, 1951). A more recent account is C. Allmand, *The Hundred Years's War: England and France at War, c. 1300–1450* (New York, 1988). The social impact of the war is described in J. Barnie, *War in Medieval English Society* (Ithaca, N.Y., 1974). On Joan of Arc, see M. Warner, *Joan of Arc: The Image of Female Heroism* (New York, 1981). On the political history of the period, see B. Guenée, *States and Rulers in Later Medieval Europe*, trans. J. Vale (Oxford, 1985); and D. Waley, *Later Medieval Europe* (New York, 1964). Works on individual countries include P. S. Lewis, *Later Medieval France: The Polity* (London, 1968); F. Pegues, *The Lawyers of the Last Capetians* (Princeton, N.J., 1962); A. R. Myers, *England in the Late Middle Ages* (Harmondsworth, 1952); and F. R. H. Du Boulay, *Germany in the Later Middle Ages* (London, 1983). On the Italian political scene, see D. P. Waley, *The Italian City-Republics* (London, 1978); and J. Larner, *Italy in the Age of Dante and Petrarch, 1216–1380* (London, 1980). Some good specialized studies include M. Mallet, *Mercenaries and Their Masters* (London, 1974); and F. C. Lane, *Venice: A Maritime Republic* (Baltimore, 1973).

Good general studies of the church in the fourteenth century can be found in F. P. Oakley, *The Western Church in the Later Middle Ages* (Ithaca, N.Y., 1980); and

S. Ozment, *The Age of Reform, 1250–1550: An Intellectual and Religious History of Late Medieval and Reformation Europe* (New Haven, Conn., 1980). A good, readable biography is T. S. R. Boase, *Boniface VIII* (London, 1933). On the Avignonese papacy, see Y. Renouard, *The Avignon Papacy, 1305–1403* (London, 1970); and G. Mollat, *The Popes at Avignon* (New York, 1965). Other facets of the religious scene are examined in L. E. Boyle, *Pastoral Care, Clerical Education and Canon Law, 1200–1400* (London, 1981); J. M. Clark, *The Great German Mystics* (Oxford, 1949); and A. Hyma, *The Christian Renaissance: A History of the Devotio Moderna* (Hamden, Conn., 1965).

A classic work on the life and thought of the Later Middle Ages is J. Huizinga, *The Waning of the Middle Ages* (New York, 1949). On the impact of the plague on culture, see the brilliant study by M. Meiss, *Painting in Florence and Siena after the Black Death* (New York, 1964).

A wealth of material on everyday life is provided in the second volume of *A History of Private Life* edited by G. Duby, *Revelations of the Medieval World* (Cambridge, Mass., 1988). On women in the Late Middle Ages, see S. Shahar, *The Fourth Estate: A History of Women in the Middle Ages*, trans. C. Galai (London, 1983). On childhood, see the work by P. Ariés, *Centuries of Childhood*, trans. R. Baldick (New York, 1962); and the article by D. Herlihy cited in the notes. The subject of medieval prostitution is examined in L. L. Otis, *Prostitution in Medieval Society* (Chicago, 1984). For late medieval townspeople, see J. F. C. Harrison, *The Common People of Great Britain* (Bloomington, Ind., 1985). Poor people are discussed in M. Mollat, *The Poor in the Middle Ages* (New Haven, Conn., 1986). For a general introduction to the changes in medicine, see T. McKeown, *The Role of Medicine* (Princeton, N.J., 1979). The importance of inventions is discussed in J. Gimpel, *The Medieval Machine* (New York, 1976). Another valuable discussion of medieval technology can be found in J. Le Goff, *Time, Work and Culture in the Middle Ages* (Chicago, 1980).

Recovery and Rebirth: The Age of the Renaissance

Medieval and Renaissance historians have argued interminably over the significance of the fourteenth and fifteenth centuries. Did they witness a continuation of the Middle Ages or the beginning of a new era? Obviously, both positions contain a modicum of truth. Although the disintegrative patterns of the fourteenth century continued into the fifteenth, at the same time there were elements of recovery that made the fifteenth century a period of significant political, economic, artistic, and intellectual change. The humanists or intellectuals of the age called their period (from the mid-fourteenth to the mid-sixteenth century) an age of rebirth, believing that they had restored arts and letters to new glory after they had been "neglected" or "dead" for centuries. The humanists also saw their age as one of great individuals who dominated the landscape of their time. Michelangelo, the great Italian artist of the early sixteenth century, and Pope Julius II, the "warrior pope," were two such titans. The artist's temperament and the pope's temper led to many lengthy and often loud quarrels between the two. Among other commissions, the pope had hired Michelangelo to paint the ceiling of the Sistine Chapel in Rome, a difficult task for a man long accustomed to being a sculptor. Michelangelo undertook the project but refused for a long time to allow anyone, including the pope, to see his work. Julius grew anxious, pestering Michelangelo on a regular basis about when the ceiling would be finished. Exasperated by the pope's requests, Michelangelo once replied, according to Giorgio Vasari, his contemporary biographer, that the ceiling would be completed "when it satisfies me as an artist." The pope responded, "and we want you to satisfy us and finish it soon," and then threatened that if Michelangelo did not "finish the ceiling quickly he would have him thrown down from the scaffolding." Fearing the pope's anger, Michelangelo "lost no time in doing all that was wanted" and quickly completed the ceiling, one of the great masterpieces in the history of Western art.

Rule of Cosimo de' Medici in Florence   Marriage of Ferdinand and Isabella

Fall of Constantinople   War of the Roses   Sack of Rome

Civic humanism in Florence   Machiavelli's *The Prince*

Invention of printing   Castiglione's *Book of the Courtier*

Masaccio's frescoes in Florence   Leonardo da Vinci's *The Last Supper*

Botticelli's *Primavera*   Michelangelo's Sistine Chapel ceiling

The humanists' view of their age as a rebirth of the classical civilization of the Greeks and Romans ultimately led historians to use the word Renaissance *to identify this age. Although recent historians have emphasized the many elements of continuity between the Middle Ages and the Renaissance, the latter age was also distinguished by its own unique characteristics.*

Meaning and Characteristics of the Italian Renaissance

The word *Renaissance* means "rebirth." A number of people who lived in Italy between c. 1350 and c. 1550 believed that they had witnessed a rebirth of antiquity or Greco-Roman civilization, which marked a new age. To them, the approximately thousand years between the end of the Roman Empire and their own era was a middle period (hence the "Middle Ages"), characterized by darkness because of its lack of classical culture. Historians of the nineteenth century later used similar terminology to describe this period in Italy. The Swiss historian and art critic Jacob Burckhardt created the modern concept of the Renaissance in his celebrated work, *Civilization of the Renaissance in Italy*, published in 1860. He portrayed Italy in the fourteenth and fifteenth centuries as the birthplace of the modern world (the Italians were "the firstborn among the sons of modern Europe") and saw the revival of antiquity, the "perfecting of the individual," and secularism ("worldliness of the Italians") as its distinguishing features. No doubt, Burckhardt exaggerated the individuality and secularism of the Renaissance and failed to recognize the depths of

its religious sentiment. Nevertheless, he established the framework for all modern interpretations of the Renaissance. Although contemporary scholars do not believe that the Renaissance represents a sudden or dramatic cultural break with the Middle Ages (as Burckhardt argued)—there was after all much continuity in economic, political, and social life between the two periods—the Renaissance can still be viewed as a distinct period of European history that manifested itself first in Italy and then spread to the rest of Europe. What, then, are the characteristics of the Italian Renaissance?

Renaissance Italy was largely an urban society. As a result of its commercial preeminence and political evolution, northern Italy by the mid-fourteenth century was mostly a land of independent cities that dominated the country districts around them. These city-states became the centers of Italian political, economic, and social life. Within this new urban society, a secular spirit emerged as increasing wealth created new possibilities for the enjoyment of worldly things.

Above all, the Renaissance was an age of recovery from the "calamitous fourteenth century." Italy and Europe began a slow process of recuperation from the effects of the Black Death, political disorder, and economic recession. By the end of the fourteenth and beginning of the fifteenth centuries, Italians were using the words *recovery* and *revival* and were actively involved in a rebuilding process.

Recovery was accompanied by rebirth, specifically, a rebirth of the culture of classical antiquity. Increasingly aware of their own historical past, Italian intellectuals became intensely interested in the Greco-Roman culture of the ancient Mediterranean world. This new revival of classical antiquity (the Middle Ages, after all, had preserved much of ancient Latin culture) affected activities as diverse as politics and art and led to new attempts to reconcile the pagan philosophy of the Greco-Roman world with Christian thought, as well as new ways of viewing human beings.

Though not entirely new, a revived emphasis on individual ability became characteristic of the Italian Renaissance. As the fifteenth-century Florentine architect, Leon Battista Alberti, expressed it, "Men can do all things if they will."[1] A high regard for human dignity and worth and a realization of individual potentiality created a new social ideal of the well-rounded personality or universal person (*l'uomo universale*) who was capable of achievements in many areas of life.

These general features of the Italian Renaissance were not characteristic of all Italians, but were primarily the preserve of the wealthy upper classes who constituted a small percentage of the total population. The achievements of the Italian Renaissance were the product of an elite, rather than a mass, movement. Nevertheless, indirectly it did have some impact on ordinary people, especially in the cities where so many of the intellectual and artistic accomplishments of the period were most apparent and visible.

The Making of Renaissance Society

The cultural flowering that we associate with the Italian Renaissance actually began in an era of severe economic difficulties. The commercial revolution of the twelfth, thirteenth, and early fourteenth centuries had produced great wealth and given rise to a money economy and the development of a capitalist system. Under this system, the capital or liquid wealth accumulated by private entrepreneurs was used to make further profits in trade, industry, and banking. After three centuries of economic expansion, in the second half of the fourteenth century, Europeans experienced severe economic reversals and social upheavals (see Chapter 12). By the middle of the fifteenth century, a gradual economic recovery had begun with an increase in the volume of manufacturing and trade. Economic growth varied from area to area, however, and despite the recovery Europe did not experience the economic boom of the High Middle Ages.

Economic Recovery

By the fourteenth century, Italian merchants were carrying on a flourishing commerce throughout the Mediterranean and had also expanded their lines of trade north along the Atlantic seaboard. The great galleys of the Venetian Flanders Fleet maintained a direct sea route from Venice to England and the Netherlands, where Italian merchants came into contact with the increasingly powerful Hanseatic League of merchants. Hard hit by the plague, the Italians lost their commercial preeminence while the Hanseatic League continued to prosper.

The Hanseatic League or Hansa had been formed as early as the thirteenth century, when some north German coastal towns, such as Lübeck, Hamburg, and Bremen, began to cooperate to gain favorable trading rights in Flemish cities. To protect themselves from pirates and competition from Scandinavian merchants, these and other northern towns formed a commercial and military league. By 1500, more than eighty cities belonged to the league, which enjoyed full navigational rights between the Baltic and North Seas and had established settlements and commercial bases in many cities in England and northern Europe, including the chief towns of Denmark, Norway, and Sweden. For almost two hundred years, the Hansa had a monopoly on northern European trade in timber, fish, grain, metals, honey, and wines. Its southern outlet in Flanders, the city of Bruges, became the economic crossroads of Europe in the fourteenth century since it served as the meeting place between Hanseatic merchants and the Flanders Fleet of Venice. In the fifteenth century, however, Bruges slowly began to decline. So, too, did the Hanseatic League as it proved increasingly unable to compete with the developing larger territorial states.

Overall, trade recovered dramatically from the economic contraction of the fourteenth century. The Italians and especially the Venetians, despite new restrictive pressures on their eastern Mediterranean trade from the Ottoman Turks (see The Ottoman Turks and the End of Byzantium later in this chapter), continued to maintain a wealthy commercial empire. Not until the sixteenth century, when the overseas discoveries gave new importance to the states facing the Atlantic, did the petty Italian city-states begin to suffer from the competitive advantages of the ever-growing and more powerful national territorial states.

The economic depression of the fourteenth century also affected patterns of industrial development. The woolen industries of Flanders and the northern Italian cities had been particularly devastated. By the beginning of the fifteenth century, however, the Florentine woolen industry was experiencing a recovery. At the same time, the Italian cities began to develop and expand luxury industries, especially lace and silk, glassware, and hand-

Florence: "Queen City of the Renaissance"

Florence has long been regarded by many historians as the "queen city of the Renaissance." It was the intellectual and cultural center of Italy in the fifteenth century. In a letter written to a Venetian in 1472, Benedetto Dei, a Florentine merchant, gave a proud and boastful description of Florence's economy under the guidance of Lorenzo de' Medici.

Benedetto Dei, Florence

Florence is more beautiful and five hundred years older than your Venice. We spring from triply noble blood. We are one-third Roman, one-third Frankish, and one-third Fiesolan [an ancient Etruscan town three miles northeast of Florence]. . . . We have round about us thirty thousand estates, owned by noblemen and merchants, citizens and craftsmen, yielding us yearly bread and meat, wine and oil, vegetables and cheese, hay and wood, to the value of nine hundred thousand ducats in cash, as you Venetians, Genoese, Chians, and Rhoadians who come to buy them know well enough. We have two trades greater than any four of yours in Venice put together—the trades of wool and silk. . . .

Our beautiful Florence contains within the city in this present year two hundred seventy shops belonging to the wool merchants' guild, from whence their wares are sent to Rome and the Marches, Naples and Sicily, Constantinople and Pera, Adrianople, . . . and the whole of Turkey. It contains also eighty-three rich and splendid warehouses of the silk merchants' guild, and furnishes gold and silver stuffs, velvet, brocade, damask, taffeta, and satin to Rome, Naples, Catalonia, and the whole of Spain, especially Seville, and to Turkey and Barbary. The principal fairs to which these wares go are those of Genoa, the Marches, Ferrara, Mantua, and the whole of Italy; Lyons, Avignon, Montpellier, Antwerp, and London. The number of banks amount to thirty-three; the shops of the cabinet-makers, whose business is carving and inlaid work, to eighty-four; and the workshops of the stonecutters and marble workers in the city and its immediate neighborhood, to fifty-four. There are forty-four goldsmiths' and jewelers' shops, thirty gold-beaters, silver wire-drawers, and a wax-figure maker [wax images were used in all churches]. . . . Go through all the cities of the world, nowhere will you ever be able to find artists in wax equal to those we now have in Florence. . . . Another flourishing industry is the making of light and elegant gold and silver wreaths and garlands, which are worn by young maidens of high degree, and which have given their names to the artist family of Ghirlandaio. Sixty-six is the number of the apothecaries' and grocer shops; seventy that of the butchers, besides eight large shops in which are sold fowls of all kinds, as well as game and also the native wine called Trebbiano, from San Giovanni in the upper Arno Valley; it would awaken the dead in its praise.

---

worked items in metal and precious stones. Unfortunately, these luxury industries employed fewer people than the woolen industry and contributed less to overall prosperity.

Other new industries, especially printing, mining, and metallurgy, began to rival the textile industry in importance in the fifteenth century. New machinery and techniques for digging deeper mines and for separating metals from ore and purifying them were put into operation. When rulers began to transfer their titles to underground mineral rights to financiers as collateral for loans, these entrepreneurs quickly developed large mining operations to produce copper, iron, and silver. Especially valuable were the rich mineral deposits in central Europe, Hungary, the Tyrol, Bohemia, and Saxony. Expanding iron production and new skills in metal working, in turn, contributed to the development of firearms that were more effective than the crude weapons of the fourteenth century.

The city of Florence regained its preeminence in banking in the fifteenth century, primarily due to the Medici family (see the box above). The Medici had expanded from cloth production into commerce, real estate, and banking. In its best days (in the fifteenth century), the House of Medici was the greatest banking house in Europe, with branches in Venice, Milan, Rome, Avignon, Bruges, London, and Lyons. Moreover, the family had controlling interests in industrial enterprises for wool, silk, and the mining of alum, used in the dyeing of textiles. Except for a brief interruption, the Medici were also the principal bankers for the papacy, a position that produced big profits and influence at the papal court. Despite its great success in the early and middle part of the fifteenth century, the Medici bank suffered a rather sudden decline at the end of the century, in part because of the lack of interest and financial ability of Lorenzo de' Medici, the head of the family from 1469 to 1492. A series of bad loans, especially uncollectible loans to rulers, put the entire structure in jeopardy. The final blow came in 1494 when the French expelled the Medici from Florence (see The Italian States in the Renaissance later in this chapter) and confiscated their property, bringing about the complete collapse of the Medici's financial edifice.

Social Changes in the Renaissance

The Renaissance inherited a tripartite division of society from the Middle Ages. Society was fundamentally divided into three estates: the clergy, whose preeminence was grounded in the belief that people should be guided to spiritual ends; the nobility, whose privileges were based on the principle that the nobles provided security and justice for society; and the third estate, which consisted of the peasants and inhabitants of the towns and cities. This social order experienced certain adaptations in the Renaissance, which we can see by examining the second and third estates (the clergy will be examined in Chapter 14).

THE SOCIAL CLASSES: THE NOBILITY

Throughout much of Europe, the landholding nobles were faced with declining real incomes during the greater part of the fourteenth and fifteenth centuries, while the expense of maintaining noble status was rising. It was once assumed that this decline of the nobility in the Late Middle Ages led to the triumph of the middle class, whose fortunes were made in trade, banking, and industry. But, in fact, members of the old nobility survived, while new blood infused its ranks. A reconstruction of the aristocracy was well underway by 1500.

As a result of this reconstruction, the nobles, old and new, who constituted between 2 and 3 percent of the population in most countries, managed to dominate society as they had done in the Middle Ages, serving as military officers and holding important political posts as well as advising the king. Increasingly in the sixteenth century, members of the aristocracy pursued education as the means to maintain their role in government. One noble in the Low Countries, in a letter outlining how his son should be formally educated, stated that, due to his own lack of learning, he dared not express his

opinions in the king's council and often "felt deep shame and humiliation" at his ignorance.

In northern Europe, the fifteenth century also saw the final flourishing of chivalry. Nobles played at being great warriors, but their tournaments were now characterized less by bloodshed than by flamboyance and a display of brilliant costumes that showed off an individual's social status.

THE DEVELOPMENT OF A COURTLY SOCIETY IN ITALY

One of the more interesting social developments during the Renaissance was the change that occurred in Italian society. In the Early Renaissance, old noble families had moved into the cities and generally merged with the merchant middle classes to form the upper classes in these new urban societies. Consequently, Italy seemed to lose the notion of nobility or aristocracy. In the fifteenth century, this began to change as the tenor of Italian upper-class urban society became more aristocratic. Although this was especially evident in the princely states, such as the duchy of Milan where a courtly society emerged around the duke, even in the Italian republics the behavior of the upper class took on an aristocratic appearance (see the box on p. 417).

By 1500, certain ideals came to be expected of the noble or aristocrat. These were best expressed in The Book of the Courtier by the Italian Baldassare Castiglione (1478–1529). First published in 1528, Castiglione's work soon became popular throughout Europe, and it remained a fundamental handbook for European aristocrats well into the twentieth century.

In The Book of the Courtier, Castiglione described the three basic attributes of the perfect courtier. First, nobles should possess fundamental native endowments, such as impeccable character, grace, talents, and noble birth. The perfect courtier must also cultivate certain achievements. Primarily, he should participate in military and bodily exercises since the principal profession of a courtier was arms. But unlike the medieval knight who had only been required to have military skill, the Renaissance courtier was also expected to have a classical education and to adorn his life with the arts by playing a musical instrument, drawing, and painting. In Castiglione's hands, the Renaissance ideal of the well-developed personality became a social ideal of the aristocracy. Finally, the aristocrat was expected to follow a certain standard of conduct. Nobles were expected to make good impressions; while being modest, they should not hide their accomplishments, but show them with grace.

A Renaissance Banquet

As in Greek and Roman society, the Renaissance banquet was an occasion for good food, interesting conversation, music, and dancing. In Renaissance society, it was also a symbol of status and an opportunity to impress people with the power and wealth of one's family. Banquets were held to celebrate public and religious festivals, official visits, anniversaries, and weddings. The following menu lists the foods served at a grand banquet given by Pope Pius V in the sixteenth century.

A Sixteenth-Century Banquet

First Course: Cold Delicacies from the Sideboard
Pieces of marzipan and marzipan balls
Neapolitan spice cakes
Malaga wine and Pisan biscuits
Fresh grapes
Prosciutto cooked in wine, served with capers
and grape pulp
Salted pork tongues cooked in wine, sliced
Spit-roasted songbirds, cold, with their tongues
sliced over them
Sweet mustard

Second Course: Hot Foods from the Kitchen, Roasts
Fried veal sweetbreads and liver
Spit-roasted skylarks with lemon sauce
Spit-roasted quails with sliced aubergines
Stuffed spit-roasted pigeons with capers
sprinkled over them
Spit-roasted rabbits, with sauce and crushed pine nuts
Partridges larded and spit-roasted, served with lemon
Heavily seasoned poultry with lemon slices

Slices of veal, spit-roasted, with a sauce made
from the juices
Leg of goat, spit-roasted with a sauce made
from the juices
Soup of almond paste, with the flesh of three
pigeons to each serving

Third Course: Hot Foods from the Kitchen, Boiled

Meats and Stews
Stuffed fat geese, boiled Lombard style and covered
with sliced almonds
Stuffed breast of veal, boiled, garnished with flowers
Very young calf, boiled, garnished with parsley
Almonds in garlic sauce
Turkish-style rice with milk, sprinkled with cinnamon
Stewed pigeons with mortadella sausage and
whole onions
Cabbage soup with sausages
Poultry pie, two chickens to each pie
Fricasseed breast of goat dressed with fried onions
Pies filled with custard cream
Boiled calves' feet with cheese and egg

Fourth Course: Delicacies from the Sideboard
Bean tarts
Quince pastries
Pear tarts, the pears wrapped in marzipan
Parmesan cheese and Riviera cheese
Fresh almonds on vine leaves
Chestnuts roasted over the coals and served
with salt and pepper
Milk curds
Ring-shaped cakes
Wafers made from ground corn

But what was the purpose of these courtly standards? Castiglione said:

> Therefore, I think that the aim of the perfect Courtier, which we have not spoken of up to now, is so to win for himself, by means of the accomplishments ascribed to him by these gentlemen, the favor and mind of the prince whom he serves that he may be able to tell him, and always will tell him, the truth about everything he needs to know, without fear or risk of displeasing him; and that when he sees the mind of his prince inclined to a wrong action, he may dare to oppose him . . . so as to dissuade him of every evil intent and bring him to the path of virtue.[2]

This ideal of service to the prince reflected the secular ethic of the active life espoused by the earlier civic humanists (see Italian Renaissance Humanism later in this chapter). Castiglione put the new moral values of the Renaissance into a courtly, aristocratic form that was now acceptable to the nobility throughout Europe.

Nobles would adhere to his principles for hundreds of years while they continued to dominate European life socially and politically.

THE SOCIAL CLASSES: THE THIRD ESTATE OF PEASANTS AND TOWNSPEOPLE

Traditionally, peasants made up the overwhelming mass of the third estate and indeed continued to constitute as much as 85 to 90 percent of the total European population, except in the highly urbanized areas of northern Italy and Flanders. The most noticeable trend produced by the economic crisis of the fourteenth century was the decline of the manorial system and the continuing elimination of serfdom. This process had already begun in the twelfth century when the introduction of a money economy made possible the conversion of servile labor dues into rents paid in money, although they also continued to be paid in kind or labor. The contraction of the peasantry after the Black Death simply accelerated this process since lords found it convenient to deal with the peasants by granting freedom and accepting rents. Demesne lands were then tilled by hired workers or rented out. By the end of the fifteenth century, serfdom was declining, and more and more peasants were becoming legally free, although in many places lords were able to retain many of the fees they charged their peasants. Lords, then, became rentiers, and the old manorial system was replaced by a new arrangement based on cash. It is interesting to note that while serfdom was declining in western Europe, eastern Europe experienced a reverse trend. The weakness of eastern rulers enabled nobles to tie their peasants to the land and use servile labor in the large-scale production of grain for an ever-growing export market.

The remainder of the third estate centered around the inhabitants of towns and cities, originally the merchants and artisans who formed the burghers. The Renaissance town or city of the fifteenth century actually possessed a multitude of townspeople widely separated socially and economically.

At the top of urban society were the patricians, whose wealth from capitalistic enterprises in trade, industry, and banking enabled them to dominate their urban communities economically, socially, and politically. Below them were the petty burghers, the shopkeepers, artisans, guildmasters, and guildsmen who were largely concerned with providing goods and services for local consumption. Below these two groups were the propertyless workers earning pitiful wages and the unemployed, living squalid and miserable lives. These people constituted as much as 30 or 40 percent of the urban population. Everywhere in Europe in the late fourteenth and fifteenth centuries, urban poverty had increased dramatically. One rich merchant of Florence wrote:

> Those that are lazy and indolent in a way that does harm to the city, and who can offer no just reason for their condition, should either be forced to work or expelled from the Commune. The city would thus rid itself of that most harmful part of the poorest class. . . . If the lowest order of society earn enough food to keep them going from day to day, then they have enough.[3]

But even this large group was not at the bottom of the social scale; beneath them were the slaves, especially in the Italian cities.

SLAVERY IN THE RENAISSANCE

Agricultural slavery had continued to exist in the Early Middle Ages, but had declined for economic reasons and been replaced by serfdom by the ninth century. Although some domestic slaves remained, slavery in European society had largely disappeared by the eleventh century. It reappeared first in Spain, where both Christians and Muslims used captured prisoners as slaves during the lengthy *reconquista*. In the second half of the fourteenth century, after the Black Death, the shortage of workers led Italians to introduce slavery on a fairly large scale. In 1363, for example, the government of Florence authorized the unlimited importation of foreign slaves.

In the Italian cities, slaves were used as skilled workers, making handcrafted goods for their masters, or as household workers. Girls served as nursemaids and boys as playmates. Fiammetta Adimari wrote to her husband in 1469: "I must remind you that when Alfonso is weaned we ought to get a little slave-girl to look after him, or else one of the black boys to keep him company."[4] In Florence, wealthy merchants might possess two or three slaves.

Slaves for the Italian market were obtained primarily from the eastern Mediterranean and the Black Sea region and included Tartars, Russians, Albanians, and Dalmatians. There were also slaves from Africa, either Moors or Ethiopians, and Muslims from Spain. Because of the lucrative nature of the slave trade, Italian merchants became involved in the transportation of slaves. Between 1414 and 1423, 10,000 slaves were sold on the Venetian market. Most slaves were females, many of them young girls.

By the end of the fifteenth century, slavery had declined dramatically in the Italian cities. Many slaves had been freed by their owners for humanitarian reasons, while the major source of slaves dried up as the Black Sea slave markets were closed to Italian traders after the Turks conquered the Byzantine Empire. Although some other sources remained, prices rose dramatically, further cutting demand. Moreover, a general feeling had arisen that slaves—the "domestic enemy" as they were called—were dangerous and not worth the effort. By the sixteenth century, slaves were in evidence only at princely courts where they were kept as curiosities; this was especially true of black slaves.

In the fifteenth century, the Portuguese had imported increasing numbers of African slaves for southern European markets. It has been estimated that between 1444 and 1505, 140,000 slaves were shipped from Africa. The presence of blacks in European society was not entirely new. Saint Maurice, a Christian martyr of the fourth century, was portrayed by medieval artists as a black knight and became the center of a popular cult in the twelfth and thirteenth centuries. The number of blacks in Europe was small, however, until their importation as slaves.

THE FAMILY IN RENAISSANCE ITALY

The family played an important role in Renaissance Italy. Family meant, first of all, the extended household of parents, children, and servants (if the family was wealthy) and could also include grandparents, widowed mothers, and even unmarried sisters. Families that were related and bore the same surname often lived near each other and might dominate an entire urban district. Old family names, such as the Strozzi, Rucellai, and Medici, conferred great status and prestige. The family bond was a source of great security in a dangerous and violent world, and its importance helps explain the vendetta in the Italian Renaissance. A crime committed by one family member fell on the entire family, ensuring that retaliation by the offended family would be a bloody affair involving large numbers of people.

To maintain the family, careful attention was given to marriages, which were arranged by parents, often to strengthen business or family ties. Details were worked out well in advance, sometimes when children were only two or three, and reinforced by a legally binding marriage contract (see the box on p. 420). The important aspect of the contract was the size of the dowry, a sum of money presented by the wife's family to the husband upon marriage. The dowry could involve large sums of money and was expected of all families. The size of the dowry was an indication of whether the bride was moving upward or downward in society. With a large dowry, a daughter could marry a man of higher social status, thereby enabling her family to move up in society; if the daughter married a man of lower social status, however, then her dowry would be smaller since the reputation of her family would raise the status of the husband's family. Since poor families often had difficulty providing a dowry, wealthy families established societies to provide dowries for poor girls.

◆ **Wedding Banquet.** Parents arranged marriages in Renaissance Italy to strengthen business or family ties. A legally binding marriage contract was considered a necessary part of the marital arrangements. So, too, was a wedding feast. This painting by Botticelli shows the wedding banquet in Florence that celebrated the marriage of Nastagio degli Onesti and the daughter of Paulo Traversaro.

Marriage Negotiations

Marriages were so important in maintaining families in Renaissance Italy that much energy was put into arranging them. Parents made the choices for their children, most often for considerations that had little to do with the modern notion of love. This selection is taken from the letters of a Florentine matron of the illustrious Strozzi family to her son Filippo in Naples. The family's considerations were complicated by the fact that the son was in exile.

Alessandra Strozzi to Her Son Filippo in Naples

[April 20, 1464] . . . Concerning the matter of a wife [for Filippo], it appears to me that if Francesco di Messer Tanagli wishes to give his daughter, that it would be a fine marriage. . . . Now I will speak with Marco [Parenti, Alessandra's son-in-law], to see if there are other prospects that would be better, and if there are none, then we will learn if he wishes to give her [in marriage]. . . . Francesco Tanagli has a good reputation, and he has held office, not the highest, but still he has been in office. You may ask: "Why should he give her to someone in exile?" There are three reasons. First, there aren't many young men of good family who have both virtue and property. Secondly, she has only a small dowry, 1,000 florins, which is the dowry of an artisan [although not a small sum, either—senior officials in the government bureaucracy earned 300 florins a year]. . . . Third, I believe that he will give her away, because he has a large family and he will need help to settle them. . . .

[July 26, 1465] . . . Francesco is a good friend of Marco and he trusts him. On S. Jacopo's day, he spoke to him discreetly and persuasively, saying that for several months he had heard that we were interested in the girl and . . . that when we had made up our minds, she will come to us willingly. [He said that] you were a worthy man, and that his family had always made good marriages, but that he had only a small dowry to give her, and so he would prefer to send her outside of Florence to someone of worth, rather than to give her to someone here, from among those who were available, with little money. . . . We have information that she is affable and competent. She is responsible for a large family (there are twelve children, six boys and six girls), and the mother is always pregnant and isn't very competent. . . .

[August 31, 1465] . . . I have recently received some very favorable information [about the Tanagli girl] from two individuals. . . . They are in agreement that whoever gets her will be content. . . . Concerning her beauty, they told me what I had already seen, that she is attractive and well-proportioned. Her face is long, but I couldn't look directly into her face, since she appeared to be aware that I was examining her . . . and so she turned away from me like the wind. . . . She reads quite well . . . and she can dance and sing. . . .

So yesterday I sent for Marco and told him what I had learned. And we talked about the matter for a while, and decided that he should say something to the father and give him a little hope, but not so much that we couldn't withdraw, and find out from him the amount of the dowry. . . . May God help us to choose what will contribute to our tranquility and to the consolation of us all.

[September 13, 1465] . . . Marco came to me and said that he had met with Francesco Tanagli, who had spoken very coldly, so that I understand that he had changed his mind. . . .

[Filippo Strozzi eventually married Fiametta di Donato Adimari in 1466.]

The father-husband was the center of the Italian family. He gave it his name, was responsible for it in all legal matters, managed all finances (his wife had no share in his wealth), and made the crucial decisions that determined his children's lives. A father's authority over his children was absolute until he died or formally freed his children. In Renaissance Italy, children did not become adults on reaching a certain age; instead adulthood came only when the father went before a judge and formally emancipated them. The age of emancipation varied from early teens to late twenties.

The mother managed the household, a position that gave women a certain degree of autonomy in their daily lives. Considering that marriages had been arranged, marital relationships ran the gamut from deep emotional attachments to purely formal ties. The lack of emotional attachment from arranged marriages did encourage extramarital relationships, especially for those groups whose lifestyle offered special temptations. While sexual license for males was the norm for princes and their courts, women were supposed to follow different guidelines. The first wife of Duke Filippo Maria Visconti of

Milan had an affair with the court musician and was executed for it.

The great age difference between husbands and wives that was noticeable in Italian Renaissance marriage patterns also heightened the need for sexual outlets outside marriage. In Florence in 1427–1428, the average difference was thirteen years. While females married before the ages of sixteen and eighteen, factors of environment, wealth, and demographic trends favored relatively late ages for the first marriages of males, who were usually in their thirties or even early forties. The existence of large numbers of young, unmarried males encouraged extramarital sex as well as prostitution. Prostitution was viewed as a necessary vice; since it could not be eliminated, it should be regulated. In Florence in 1415, the city fathers established communal brothels:

> Desiring to eliminate a worse evil by means of a lesser one, the lord priors . . . have decreed that the priors . . . may authorize the establishment of two public brothels in the city of Florence, in addition to the one which already exists. . . . [They are to be located] in suitable places or in places where the exercise of such scandalous activity can best be concealed, for the honor of the city and of those who live in the neighborhood in which these prostitutes must stay to hire their bodies for lucre. . . .[5]

A prostitute in Florence was required to wear a traditional garb of "gloves on her hands and a bell on her head."

The Italian States in the Renaissance

In the fourteenth century, Italy had experienced two major developments: the rise of despots in place of republican governments and the expansion of the larger city-states at the expense of the less powerful ones. By the fifteenth century, five major powers dominated the Italian peninsula—the duchy of Milan, Venice, Florence, the Papal States and the kingdom of Naples.

Northern Italy was divided between the duchy of Milan and Venice. After the death of the last Visconti ruler of Milan in 1447, Francesco Sforza, one of the leading *condottieri* (see Chapter 12) of the time, turned on his Milanese employers, conquered the city, and became its new duke. Both the Visconti and Sforza rulers worked to create a highly centralized territorial state. They were especially successful in devising systems of taxation that generated enormous revenues for the government. The maritime republic of Venice remained

an extremely stable political entity governed by a small oligarchy of merchant-aristocrats. Its commercial empire brought in enormous revenues and gave it the status of an international power. At the end of the fourteenth century, Venice embarked upon the conquest of a territorial state in northern Italy to protect its food supply and its overland trade routes. Although expansion on the mainland made sense to the Venetians, it frightened Milan and Florence, which worked to curb what they perceived as the expansionary designs of the Venetians.

The republic of Florence dominated the region of Tuscany. By the beginning of the fifteenth century, Florence was governed by a small merchant oligarchy that manipulated the apparently republican government. In 1434, Cosimo de' Medici took control of this oligarchy. Although the wealthy Medici family maintained republican forms of government for appearance' sake, it ran the government from behind the scenes. Through their lavish patronage and careful courting of political allies, Cosimo (1434–1464), and later his grandson Lorenzo the Magnificent (1469–1492), were successful in dominating the city at a time when Florence was the center of the cultural Renaissance.

The Papal States lay in central Italy. Nominally under the political control of the popes, papal residence in Avignon and the Great Schism had enabled individual cities and territories, such as Urbino, Bologna, and Ferrara, to become independent of papal authority. The Renaissance popes of the fifteenth century directed much of their energy toward reestablishing their control over the Papal States (see The Renaissance Papacy later in this chapter).

The kingdom of Naples, which encompassed most of southern Italy and usually the island of Sicily, was fought over by the French and the Aragonese until the latter established their domination in the mid-fifteenth century. Throughout the Renaissance, the kingdom of Naples remained a largely feudal monarchy with a population consisting largely of poverty-stricken peasants dominated by unruly barons. It shared little in the cultural glories of the Renaissance.

Besides the five major states, there were a number of independent city-states under the control of powerful ruling families that became brilliant centers of Renaissance culture in the fifteenth century. These included Mantua under the enlightened rule of the Gonzaga lords, Ferrara governed by the flamboyant d'Este family, and perhaps the most famous, Urbino, ruled by the Montefeltro dynasty.

Federigo da Montefeltro, who ruled Urbino from 1444 to 1482, received a classical education typical of the famous humanist school in Mantua run by Vittorino

da Feltre. He had also learned the skills of fighting, since the Montefeltro family compensated for the poverty of Urbino by hiring themselves out as *condottieri*. Federigo was not only a good ruler, but a rather unusual *condottiere* by fifteenth-century standards. Although not a brilliant general, he was reliable and honest. He did not break his promises, even when urged to do so by a papal legate. His employers included two kings of Naples, three popes, and two dukes of Milan. At the same time, Duke Federigo was one of the greatest patrons of Renaissance culture. Under his direction, Urbino became a well-known cultural and intellectual center. Though a despot, he was also benevolent. It was said of him that he could walk safely through the streets of Urbino unaccompanied by a bodyguard, a feat few Renaissance rulers dared to emulate.

A noticeable feature of these smaller Renaissance courts was the important role played by women. Battista Sforza, niece of the ruler of Milan, was the wife of Federigo da Montefeltro. The duke called his wife "the

Map 13.1 Renaissance Italy.

◆ **Piero della Francesca, *Duke and Duchess of Urbino*.** Federigo da Montefeltro and his wife, Battista Sforza, ruled the small central Italian principality of Urbino. These profile portraits by Piero della Francesca gave a realistic rendering of the two figures. Visible in the background are the hills and valleys of Urbino.

delight of both my public and my private hours." An intelligent woman, she was well versed in both Greek and Latin and did much to foster art and letters in Urbino. As a prominent *condottiere*, Federigo was frequently absent, and like earlier feudal wives, Battista Sforza was respected for governing the state "with firmness and good sense."

Perhaps the most famous of the Renaissance ruling women was Isabella d'Este (1474–1539), daughter of the duke of Ferrara, who married Francesco Gonzaga, marquis of Mantua. Their court was another important center of art and learning in the Renaissance. Educated at the brilliant court of Ferrara, Isabella was known for her intelligence and political wisdom. Called the "first lady of the world," she attracted artists and intellectuals to the Mantuan court and was responsible for amassing one of the finest libraries in all of Italy. Her numerous letters to friends, family, princes, and artists all over Europe disclose her political acumen as well as a good sense of humor (see the box on p. 424). Both before and after the death of her husband Francesco, she effectively ruled Mantua and won a reputation as a clever negotiator.

The frenzied world of the Italian territorial states gave rise to a political practice that was later used on a larger scale by competing European states. This was the concept of a balance of power, designed to prevent the aggrandizement of any one state at the expense of the others. This system was especially evident after 1454 when the Italian states signed the Peace of Lodi, which ended almost a half-century of war and inaugurated a relatively peaceful era in Italy until 1494. An alliance system (Milan, Florence and Naples versus Venice and the papacy) was then created that led to a workable balance of power within Italy. It failed, however, to establish lasting cooperation among the major powers or a common foreign policy.

The Letters of Isabella d'Este

Many Italian and European rulers at the beginning of the sixteenth century regarded Isabella d'Este as an important political figure. These excerpts from her letters reveal Isabella's political skills and her fierce determination. After her husband was taken prisoner by the Venetians in 1509, she refused to accept the condition for his release—namely, that her son Federico be kept as a hostage by the Venetians or the Holy Roman Emperor. She wrote to both the emperor and her husband, refusing to do as they asked.

Letter of Isabella d'Este to the Imperial Envoy

As to the demand for our dearest first-born son Federico, besides being a cruel and almost inhuman thing for any one who knows the meaning of a mother's love, there are many reasons which render it difficult and impossible. Although we are quite sure that his person would be well cared for and protected by His Majesty [the Holy Roman Emperor], how could we wish him to run the risk of this long and difficult journey, considering the child's tender and delicate age? And you must know what comfort and solace, in his father's present unhappy condition, we find in the presence of this dear son, the hope and joy of all our people and subjects. To deprive us of him, would be to deprive us of life itself, and of all we count good and precious. If you take Federico away you might as well take away our life and state. . . . Once for all, we will suffer any loss rather than part from our son, and this you may take to be our deliberate and unchanging resolution.

Letter of Isabella d'Este to her Husband [who had ordered her to send the boy to Venice]

If in this matter Your Excellency were to despise me and deprive me of your love and grace, I would rather endure such harsh treatment, I would rather lose our State, than deprive us of our children. I am hoping that in time your own prudence and kindness will make you understand that I have acted more lovingly toward you than you have to yourself.

Have patience! You can be sure that I think continuously of your liberation and when the time comes I will not fail you, as I have not relaxed my efforts. As witness I cite the Pope, the Emperor, the King of France, and all the other reigning heads and potentates of Christendom. Yes, and the infidels as well [she had written to the Turkish sultan for help]. If it were *really* the only means of setting you free, I would not only send Federico but all the other children as well. I will do everything imaginable. Some day I hope I can make you understand. . . .

Pardon me if this letter is badly written and worse composed, but I do not know if I am dead or alive.

> Isabella, who desires the
> best for Your Excellency,
> written with her own hand

[Isabella's husband was not pleased with her response and exclaimed angrily: "That whore of my wife is the cause of it all. Send me into battle alone, do what you like with me. I have lost in one blow my state, my honor and my freedom. If she does not obey, I'll cut her vocal cords."]

The growth of powerful monarchical states (see The "New Monarchies" later in this chapter) led to trouble for the Italians. Italy soon became a battlefield for the great power struggle between the French and Spanish monarchies. Italian wealth and splendor would probably have been inviting to its northern neighbors under any circumstances, but it was actually the breakdown of the Italian balance of power that encouraged the invasions and began the Italian wars. Feeling isolated, Ludovico Sforza, the duke of Milan, foolishly invited the French to intervene in Italian politics. The French king Charles VIII (1483–1498) was eager to do so and in 1494, with an army of 30,000 men, advanced through Italy and occupied the kingdom of Naples. Other Italian states turned to the Spanish for help, and Ferdinand of Aragon indicated his willingness to intervene. For the next

fifteen years, the French and Spanish competed to dominate Italy. Beginning in the decade of the 1510s, the war was continued by a new generation of rulers, Francis I of France and Charles I of Spain (see Chapter 14). This war was part of a long struggle for power throughout Europe between the Valois and Habsburg dynasties. Italy was only a pawn for the two great powers, a convenient arena for fighting battles. The terrible sack of Rome in 1527 by the armies of the Spanish king Charles I brought a temporary end to the Italian wars. Hereafter, the Spaniards dominated Italy; the Renaissance in Italy was at an end.

Although some Italians had developed a sense of national consciousness and differentiated between Italians and "barbarians" (all foreigners), few Italians conceived of creating an alliance or confederation of states that could repel foreign invaders. Italians remained fiercely loyal to their own petty states, making invasion a fact of life in Italian history for all too long. Italy would not achieve unification and nationhood until 1870.

The Birth of Modern Diplomacy

The modern diplomatic system was a product of the Italian Renaissance. There were ambassadors in the Middle Ages, but they were used only on a temporary basis. Moreover, an ambassador, regardless of whose subject he was, regarded himself as the servant of all Christendom, not just of his particular employer. As a treatise on diplomacy stated: "An ambassador is sacred because he acts for the general welfare." Since he was the servant of all Christendom, "the business of an ambassador is peace."[6]

This concept of an ambassador changed during the Italian Renaissance because of the political situation in Italy. A large number of states existed, many so small that their security was easily threatened by their neighbors. To survive, the Italian states began to send resident diplomatic agents to each other to ferret out useful information. During the Italian wars, the practice of resident diplomats spread to the rest of Europe, and in the course of the sixteenth and seventeenth centuries, Europeans developed the diplomatic machinery still in use today, such as the rights of ambassadors in host countries and the proper procedures for conducting diplomatic business.

With the use of permanent resident agents or ambassadors, the conception of the purpose of the ambassador also changed. A Venetian diplomat attempted to define the function of an ambassador in a treatise written at the end of the fifteenth century. He wrote: "The first duty of an ambassador is exactly the same as that of any other servant of a government, that is, to do, say, advise and think whatever may best serve the preservation and aggrandizement of his own state."[7] An ambassador was now simply an agent of the territorial state that sent him, not the larger body of Christendom. He could use any methods that were beneficial to the political interests of his own state. We are at the beginning of modern politics when the interests of the state supersede all other considerations.

Machiavelli and the New Statecraft

No one gave better expression to the Renaissance preoccupation with political power than Niccolò Machiavelli (1469–1527). He entered the service of the

◆ **Machiavelli.** In *The Prince*, Machiavelli gave concrete expression to the Renaissance preoccupation with political power. This slender volume remains one of the most famous Western treatises on politics. Machiavelli is seen here in a portrait by Santi di Tito.

Florentine republic in 1498, four years after the Medici family had been expelled from the city. As a secretary to the Florentine Council of Ten, he made numerous diplomatic missions, including trips to France and Germany, and saw the workings of statecraft firsthand. Since Italy had been invaded in 1494, Machiavelli was active during a period of Italian tribulation and devastation. In 1512, French defeat and Spanish victory led to the reestablishment of Medici power in Florence. Staunch republicans, including Machiavelli, were sent into exile. Forced to give up politics, the great love of his life, Machiavelli now reflected on political power and wrote books, including *The Prince* (1513), one of the most famous treatises on political power in the Western world.

Machiavelli's ideas on politics stemmed from two major sources, his preoccupation with Italy's political problems and his knowledge of ancient Rome. His major concerns in *The Prince* were the acquisition and expansion of political power as the means to restore and maintain order in his time. Machiavelli was aware that his own approach to political power was different from previous political theorists. Late medieval political theory conceived of the state as a necessary creation for humankind's spiritual, material, and social well-being. A ruler was justified in exercising political power only if it contributed to the common good of the people he served. The ethical side of a prince's activity—how a ruler ought to behave based on Christian moral principles—was the focus of many late medieval treatises on politics. Machiavelli bluntly contradicted this approach:

> But my hope is to write a book that will be useful, at least to those who read it intelligently, and so I thought it sensible to go straight to a discussion of how things are in real life and not waste time with a discussion of an imaginary world. . . . for the gap between how people actually behave and how they ought to behave is so great that anyone who ignores everyday reality in order to live up to an ideal will soon discover he had been taught how to destroy himself, not how to preserve himself.[8]

Machiavelli considered his approach far more realistic than that of his medieval forebears.

From Machiavelli's point of view, a prince's attitude toward power must be based on an understanding of human nature, which he perceived as basically self-centered: "For of men one can, in general, say this: They are ungrateful, fickle, deceptive and deceiving, avoiders of danger, eager to gain." Political activity, therefore, could not be restricted by moral considerations. The prince acts on behalf of the state and for the sake of the state must be willing to let his conscience sleep. As Machiavelli put it:

> You need to understand this: A ruler, and particularly a ruler who is new to power, cannot conform to all those rules that men who are thought good are expected to respect, for he is often obliged, in order to hold on to power, to break his word, to be uncharitable, inhumane, and irreligious. So he must be mentally prepared to act as circumstances and changes in fortune require. As I have said, he should do what is right if he can; but he must be prepared to do wrong if necessary.[9]

Machiavelli found a good example of the new Italian ruler in Cesare Borgia, the son of Pope Alexander VI, who used ruthless measures to achieve his goal of carving out a new state in central Italy. As Machiavelli said, "So anyone who decides that the policy to follow when one has newly acquired power is to destroy one's enemies, to secure some allies, to win wars, whether by force or by fraud, to make oneself both loved and feared by one's subjects, . . . cannot hope to find, in the recent past, a better model to imitate than Cesare Borgia." Machiavelli was among the first to abandon morality as the basis for the analysis of political activity (see the box on p. 427).

Because of the ideas in *The Prince*, Machiavelli is often considered the founder of modern, secular power politics, but we should note that Machiavelli himself was primarily concerned with Italy's tragic political condition. If it hoped to free itself from the "barbarous cruelties and outrages" perpetrated by the monarchical territorial states to the north, Italy needed "someone who could bind her wounds and . . . heal her sores which long ago became infected." If any person undertook the task, "What Italian would refuse to pledge him allegiance?"[10] If he followed the principles enunciated in *The Prince*, he would succeed. Machiavelli's own sympathies for a republican form of government were clearly evident in *The Discourses*, a political treatise written a few years after *The Prince*. In this work, Machiavelli reflected on the many lessons people of his age could learn from examining the institutions of the Roman Republic. And yet, Machiavelli doubted whether it was possible, in the turbulent politics of his age, to establish a republic. He said in *The Discourses*: "If any one wanted to establish a republic at the present time, he would find it much easier with the simple mountaineers, who are almost without any civilization, than with such as are accustomed to live in cities, where civilization is already corrupt."[11]

The Intellectual Renaissance in Italy

The emergence and growth of individualism and secularism as characteristics of the Italian Renaissance are most noticeable in the intellectual and artistic realms. Italian culture had matured by the fourteenth century. For the next two centuries, Italy was the cultural leader of Europe. This new Italian culture was primarily the product of a relatively wealthy, urban lay society. The most important literary movement we associate with the Renaissance is humanism.

Italian Renaissance Humanism

The word *humanism* has many meanings. It can refer to a tradition of classical scholarship, anything humanitarian, or a philosophy focusing on the significance of human activity. Renaissance humanism encompassed these definitions but above all was a form of education

≽ Machiavelli: "Is It Better to Be Loved Than Feared?" ≼

In 1513, Niccolò Machiavelli wrote a short treatise on political power that, justly or unjustly, has given him a reputation as a political opportunist. In this passage from Chapter 17 of The Prince, *Machiavelli analyzes whether it is better for a ruler to be loved than feared.*

Machiavelli, *The Prince*

This leads us to a question that is in dispute: Is it better to be loved than feared, or vice versa? My reply is one ought to be both loved and feared; but, since it is difficult to accomplish both at the same time, I maintain it is much safer to be feared than loved, if you have to do without one of the two. For of men one can, in general, say this: They are ungrateful, fickle, deceptive and deceiving, avoiders of danger, eager to gain. As long as you serve their interests, they are devoted to you. They promise you their blood, their possessions, their lives, and their children, as I said before, so long as you seem to have no need of them. But as soon as you need help, they turn against you. Any ruler who relies simply on their promises and makes no other preparations, will be destroyed. For you will find that those whose support you buy, who do not rally to you because they admire your strength of character and nobility of soul, these are people you pay for, but they are never yours, and in the end you cannot get the benefit of your investment. Men are less nervous of offending someone who makes himself lovable, than someone who makes himself frightening. For love attaches men by ties of obligation, which, since men are wicked, they break whenever their interests are at stake. But fear restrains men because they are afraid of punishment, and this fear never leaves them. Still, a ruler should make himself feared in such a way that, if he does not inspire love, at least he does not provoke hatred. For it is perfectly possible to be feared and not hated. You will only be hated if you seize the property or the women of your subjects and citizens. Whenever you have to kill someone, make sure you have a suitable excuse and an obvious reason; but, above all else, keep your hands off other people's property; for men are quicker to forget the death of their father than the loss of their inheritance. Moreover, there are always reasons why you might want to seize people's property; and he who begins to live by plundering others will always find an excuse for seizing other people's possessions; but there are fewer reasons for killing people, and one killing need not lead to another.

When a ruler is at the head of his army and has a vast number of soldiers under his command, then it is absolutely essential to be prepared to be thought cruel; for it is impossible to keep an army united and ready for action without acquiring a reputation for cruelty.

and culture based upon the study of the classics. Humanism was not so much a philosophy of life as it was an educational program that revolved around a clearly defined group of intellectual disciplines or "liberal arts"—grammar, rhetoric, poetry, moral philosophy or ethics, and history—all based on an examination of classical writers.

But what impelled the Italian literary world to cultivate classical Latin and Greek so diligently? The basic cause can be found in Italy's social development. With their new urban society and culture, Italians found little to emulate in the literary traditions of the High Middle Ages, based as they were on the interests of either feudal aristocrats or churchmen. Greco-Roman society, which had also been urban and secular, held far more interest for these Italian urbanites. Then, too, the Italians, living in the heart of the old Roman Empire, were surrounded by the remains of Latin civilization.

The central importance of literary preoccupations in Renaissance humanism is evident in the professional status or occupations of the humanists. Some of them were teachers of the humanities in secondary schools and universities, where they either gave occasional lectures or held permanent positions, often as professors of rhetoric. Others served as secretaries in the chancelleries of Italian city-states or at the courts of princes or popes. All of these occupations were largely secular, and most humanists were laymen rather than members of the clergy.

THE EMERGENCE OF HUMANISM

Petrarch (1304–1374) has often been called the father of Italian Renaissance humanism (see Chapter 12 on Petrarch's use of the Italian vernacular). Petrarch had rejected his father's desire that he become a lawyer and took up a literary career instead. Although he lived in Avignon for a time, most of his last decades were spent in Italy as the guest of various princes and city governments. With his usual lack of modesty, Petrarch once exclaimed, "Some of the greatest kings of our time have loved me and cultivated my friendship. . . . When I was their guest it was more as if they were mine."[12]

Petrarch did more than any other individual in the fourteenth century to foster the development of Renaissance humanism. He was the first intellectual to characterize the Middle Ages as a period of darkness, promoting the mistaken belief that medieval culture was ignorant of classical antiquity. Petrarch condemned the scholastic philosophy of the Middle Ages for its "barbarous" Latin and use of logic, rather than rhetoric, to harmonize faith and reason. Philosophy, he argued, should be the "art of virtuous living," not a science of logic chopping. Petrarch's interest in the classics led him on a quest for forgotten Latin manuscripts and set in motion a ransacking of monastic libraries throughout Europe. In his preoccupation with the classics and their secular content, Petrarch doubted at times whether he was sufficiently attentive to spiritual ideals (see the box on p. 429). His qualms, however, did not prevent him from inaugurating the humanist emphasis on the use of pure classical Latin, making it fashionable for humanists to use Cicero as a model for prose and Virgil for poetry. As Petrarch said, "Christ is my God; Cicero is the prince of the language." Humanists would always have a tendency to emphasize style, often at the expense of content.

The humanistic pursuits of Petrarch were best received in Florence. By the end of the fourteenth century, a whole circle of humanistic scholars had emerged in that city. Although some were connected to monastic orders, many were laymen. In fact, the latter were responsible for humanism gaining a powerful momentum at the beginning of the fifteenth century when it became closely tied to Florentine civic spirit and pride, giving rise to what one modern scholar has labeled "civic humanism."

HUMANISM IN FIFTEENTH-CENTURY ITALY

Fourteenth-century humanists such as Petrarch had glorified intellectual activity pursued in a life of solitude and had rejected a life of action in the community and family. In the busy civic world of Florence, intellectuals began to take a new view of their role, a trend that intensified when the city's liberty was threatened at the beginning of the fifteenth century by the Milanese

tyrant, Giangaleazzo Visconti. Florentine intellectuals responded to Visconti's aggression with a passionate defense of their city-state's independence. The Roman statesman and intellectual Cicero became their model. Leonardo Bruni (1370–1444), a humanist, Florentine patriot, and chancellor of the city, wrote a biography of Cicero, entitled the *New Cicero*, in which he waxed enthusiastically about the fusion of political action and literary achievement in Cicero's life: "No one seeing Cicero's literary legacy would believe that he had any time for dealing with men; anyone reviewing his political deeds, his speeches, his occupations and his struggles both in public and private life, would imagine he could ever have had leisure for reading and writing."[13] How could this be? The answer was that Cicero's literary and political activities were simply two sides of the same task, the work of a Roman citizen on behalf of his state. From Bruni's time on, Cicero served as the inspiration for the Renaissance ideal that one must live an active life for one's state, and everything, including riches, must be considered good if it increases one's power of action. An active civic life not only does not distract from the highest intellectual energies, but it actually stimulates them. An individual only "grows to maturity—both intellectually and morally—through participation" in the life of the state.

Civic humanism emerged in Florence but soon spread to other Italian cities and beyond. It reflected the values of the urban society of the Italian Renaissance. Civic humanism intensified the involvement of humanist intellectuals in government and guaranteed that the rhetorical discipline they praised would be put to the service of the state. It is no accident that humanists served the state as chancellors, councillors, and advisers. Rhetoricians had become diplomats.

Also evident in the humanism of the first half of the fifteenth century was a growing interest in Greek. One of the first Italian humanists to gain a thorough knowledge of Greek was Leonardo Bruni, who became an enthusiastic pupil of the Byzantine scholar Manuel Chrysoloras, who taught in Florence from 1396 to 1400 (see the box on p. 430). Humanists eagerly perused the works of Plato as well as Greek poets, dramatists, historians, and orators, such as Thucydides, Euripides, and Sophocles, all of whom had been ignored by the scholastics of the High Middle Ages as irrelevant to the theological questions they were examining.

By the fifteenth century, a consciousness of being humanists had emerged. This was especially evident in the career of Lorenzo Valla (1407–1457). Valla was brought up in Rome and educated in both Latin and

Petrarch: Mountain Climbing and the Search for Spiritual Contentment

Petrarch has long been regarded as the father of Italian Renaissance humanism. One of his literary masterpieces was The Ascent of Mt. Ventoux. *Its colorful description of an attempt to climb a mountain and survey the world from its top has unwisely led some to see it as a vivid example of the humanists' rediscovery of nature after the medieval period's concentration on the afterlife. Of course, medieval people had been aware of the natural world. Moreover, Petrarch's primary interest is in presenting an allegory of his own soul's struggle to achieve a higher spiritual state. The work is addressed to a professor of theology in Paris who had initially led Petrarch to read Augustine. The latter had experienced a vivid conversion to Christianity almost a thousand years earlier.*

Petrarch, *The Ascent of Mt. Ventoux*

Today I ascended the highest mountain in this region, which, not without cause, they call the Windy Peak. Nothing but the desire to see its conspicuous height was the reason for this undertaking. For many years I have been intending to make this expedition. You know that since my early childhood, as fate tossed around human affairs, I have been tossed around in these parts, and this mountain, visible far and wide from everywhere, is always in your view. So I was at last seized by the impulse to accomplish what I had always wanted to do. . . .

[After some false starts, Petrarch finally achieves his goal and arrives at the top of Mt. Ventoux.]

I was glad of the progress I had made, but I wept over my imperfection and was grieved by the fickleness of all that men do. In this manner I seemed to have somehow forgotten the place I had come to and why, until I was warned to throw off such sorrows, for which another place would be more appropriate. I had better look around and see what I had intended to see in coming here. The time to leave was approaching, they said. . . . Like a man aroused from sleep, I turned back and looked toward the west. . . . one could see most distinctly the mountains of the province of Lyons to the right and, to the left, the sea near Marseilles as well as the waves that break against Aigues Mortes. . . . The Rhone River was directly under our eyes.

I admired every detail, now relishing earthly enjoyment, now lifting up my mind to higher spheres after the example of my body, and I thought it fit to look in the volume of Augustine's *Confessions* which I owe to your loving kindness and preserve carefully, keeping it always in my hands, in remembrance of the author as well as the donor. It is a little book of smallest size but full of infinite sweetness. I opened it with the intention of reading whatever might occur to me first: nothing, indeed, but pious and devout sentences could come to hand. I happened to hit upon the tenth book of the work. . . . Where I fixed my eyes first, it was written: "And men go to admire the high mountains, the vast floods of the sea, the huge streams of the rivers, the circumference of the ocean, and the revolutions of the stars—and desert themselves." I was stunned, I confess. I bade my brother [who had accompanied him], who wanted to hear more, not to molest me, and closed the book, angry with myself that I still admired earthly things. Long since I ought to have learned, even from pagan philosophers, that "nothing is admirable besides the soul; compared to its greatness nothing is great."

I was completely satisfied with what I had seen of the mountain and turned my inner eye toward myself. From this hour nobody heard me say a word until we arrived at the bottom. These words occupied me sufficiently. I could not imagine that this had happened to me by chance: I was convinced that whatever I had read there was said to me and to nobody else. I remembered that Augustine once suspected the same regarding himself, when, while he was reading the Apostolic Epistles, the first passage that occurred to him was, as he himself relates: "Not in banqueting and drunkenness, not in chambering and wantonness, not in strife and envying; but put you on the Lord Jesus Christ, and make no provision for the flesh to fulfill your lusts."

Greek. Eventually, during the pontificate of Nicholas V (1447–1455), he achieved his chief ambition of becoming a papal secretary. It was Valla, above all others, who turned his attention to the literary criticism of ancient texts. His most famous work was his demonstration that the Donation of Constantine, a document used by the popes, especially in the ninth and tenth centuries (see Chapter 8), to claim temporal sovereignty over all the west, was a forgery written in the eighth century. Valla's other major work, *The Elegances of the Latin Language*, was an effort to purify medieval Latin and restore Latin to its proper position over the vernacular. The treatise

A Humanist's Enthusiasm for Greek

One of the first humanists to have a thorough knowledge of both Latin and Greek was the Florentine chancellor Leonardo Bruni. Bruni was fortunate to be instructed by the Greek scholar Manuel Chrysoloras, who was persuaded by the Florentines to come to Florence to teach Greek. As this selection illustrates, Bruni seized the opportunity to pursue his passion for Greek letters.

Leonardo Bruni, *History of His Own Times in Italy*

Then first came the knowledge of Greek letters, which for seven hundred years had been lost among us. It was the Byzantine, Chrysoloras, a nobleman in his own country and most skilled in literature, who brought Greek learning back to us. Because his country was invaded by the Turks, he came by sea to Venice; but as soon as his fame went abroad, he was cordially invited and eagerly besought to come to Florence on a public salary to spread his abundant riches before the youth of the city [1396]. At that time I was studying Civil Law. But my nature was afire with the love of learning and I had already given no little time to dialectic and rhetoric. Therefore at the coming of Chrysoloras I was divided in my mind, feeling that it was a shame to desert the Law

and no less wrong to let slip such an occasion for learning Greek. And often with youthful impulsiveness I addressed myself thus: "When you are privileged to gaze upon and have converse with Homer, Plato, and Demosthenes as well as the other poets, philosophers, and orators of whom such wonderful things are reported, and when you might saturate yourself with their admirable teachings, will you turn your back and flee? Will you permit this opportunity, divinely offered you, to slip by? For seven hundred years now no one in Italy has been in possession of Greek and yet we agree that all knowledge comes from that source. What great advancement of knowledge, enlargement of fame, and increase of pleasure will come to you from an acquaintance with this tongue! There are everywhere quantities of doctors of the Civil Law and the opportunity of completing your study in this field will not fail you. However, should the one and only doctor of Greek letters disappear, there will be no one from whom to acquire them."

Overcome at last by these arguments, I gave myself to Chrysoloras and developed such ardor that whatever I learned by day, I revolved with myself in the night while asleep.

examined the proper use of classical Latin and created a new literary standard. Early humanists had tended to take as classical models any author (including Christians) who had written before the seventh century A.D. Valla identified different stages in the growth of the Latin language and accepted only the Latin of the last century of the Roman Republic and the first century of the empire.

Another significant humanist of this period was Poggio Bracciolini (1380–1459), who reflected the cult of humanism at its best. Born and educated in Florence, he went on to serve as a papal secretary for fifty years, a position that enabled him to become an avid collector of classical manuscripts. He was responsible for finding all of the writings of fifteen different authors. Poggio's best-known literary work was the *Facetiae,* a light-hearted collection of jokes, which included a rather cynical criticism of the clergy:

> A friar of Tivoli, who was not very considerate of the people, was once thundering away with many words about the detestability of adultery. Among other things,

he declared that this sin was so grave that he would prefer to lie with ten virgins than with one married woman. And many of those present shared his opinion.[14]

Poggio and other Italian humanists were very critical of the Catholic church at times, but fundamentally they accepted the church and above all wished only to restore a simpler, purer, and more ethical Christianity. To the humanists, the study of the classics was perfectly compatible with Christianity.

HUMANISM AND PHILOSOPHY

In the second half of the fifteenth century, a new generation of thinkers became preoccupied with philosophies derived from the Greeks. This shift was particularly apparent in Florence. As the Medici family strengthened its rule over the city, the humanists' interest in civic life waned. At the same time, there appeared a renewed concern for Greek letters, especially the writings of Plato and a series of works known as the *Corpus Hermeticum.* These interests gave rise to the development of two new philosophies called Neoplatonism and Hermeticism.

By the mid-fifteenth century, there had been a dramatic upsurge of interest in the works of Plato, especially evident among the members of the Florentine Platonic Academy. This academy was not a formal school, but rather an informal discussion group. Cosimo de' Medici, the de facto ruler of Florence, became its patron and commissioned a translation of Plato's dialogues by Marsilio Ficino (1433–1499), one of the academy's leaders. Ficino dedicated his life to the translation of Plato and the exposition of the Platonic philosophy known as Neoplatonism.

In two major works, Ficino undertook the synthesis of Christianity and Platonism into a single system. His Neoplatonism was based upon two primary ideas, the Neoplatonic hierarchy of substances and a theory of spiritual love. Drawing upon the Neoplatonists of the ancient world, Ficino restated the idea of a hierarchy of substances or great chain of being from the lowest form of physical matter (plants) to the purest spirit (God), in which humans occupied a central or middle position. They were the link between the material world (through the body) and the spiritual world (through the soul), and their highest duty was to ascend toward that union with God that was the true end of human existence. Ficino's theory of spiritual or Platonic love maintained that just as all people are bound together in their common humanity by love, so too are all parts of the universe held together by bonds of sympathetic love.

Renaissance Hermeticism was another product of the Florentine intellectual environment of the late fifteenth century. Upon the request of Cosimo de' Medici, Ficino translated into Latin a Greek work entitled the *Corpus Hermeticum*. The Hermetic manuscripts contained two kinds of writings. One type stressed the occult sciences with emphasis on astrology, alchemy, and magic. The other focused on theological and philosophical beliefs and speculations. Some parts of the Hermetic writings were distinctly pantheistic, seeing divinity embodied in all aspects of nature, in the heavenly bodies as well as in earthly objects. As Giordano Bruno, one of the most prominent of the sixteenth-century Hermeticists stated, "God as a whole is in all things."[15] For Renaissance intellectuals, the Hermetic revival offered a new view of humankind. They believed that human beings had been created as divine beings endowed with divine creative power, but had freely chosen to enter the material world (nature). Humans could recover their divinity, however, through a regenerative experience or purification of the soul. Thus regenerated, they became true sages or magi,

as the Renaissance called them, who had knowledge of God and of truth. In regaining their original divinity, they reacquired an intimate knowledge of nature and the ability to employ the powers of nature for beneficial purposes.

In Italy, the most prominent magi in the late fifteenth century were Ficino and his friend and pupil, Giovanni Pico della Mirandola (1463–1494). Pico produced one of the most famous writings of the Renaissance, the *Oration on the Dignity of Man*, a preface to his 900 *Conclusions*, which were meant to be a summation of all learning and were offered as theses for a public debate. Pico combed diligently through the writings of many philosophers of different backgrounds for the common "nuggets of universal truth" that he believed were all part of God's revelation to humanity. In the *Oration* (see the box on p. 432), Pico offered a ringing statement of unlimited human potential: "To him it is granted to have whatever he chooses, to be whatever he wills."[16] Like Ficino, Pico took an avid interest in Hermetic philosophy, accepting it as the "science of the Divine," which "embraces the deepest contemplation of the most secret things, and at last the knowledge of all nature."[17]

Education in the Renaissance

The humanist movement had a profound effect on education. Genuinely optimistic about the educability of human beings, Renaissance humanists produced treatises on educational theory and developed secondary schools based on their educational philosophy. Most famous was the one founded in 1423 by Vittorino da Feltre (1378–1446) at Mantua, where the ruler of that small Italian state, Gian Francesco I Gonzaga, wished to provide a humanist school for his children. Vittorino based much of his educational system on the ideas of classical authors, particularly Cicero and Quintilian.

At the core of the academic training Vittorino offered were the "liberal studies." The Renaissance view of the value of the liberal arts was most strongly influenced by a treatise on education called *Concerning Character* by Pietro Paolo Vergerio (1370–1444). This work stressed the importance of the liberal arts as the key to true freedom, enabling individuals to reach their full potential. According to Vergerio, "we call those studies liberal which are worthy of a free man; those studies by which we attain and practice virtue and wisdom; that education which calls forth, trains, and develops those highest gifts of body and mind which ennoble men, and which are rightly judged to rank next in dignity to virtue

⧽ Pico della Mirandola and the Dignity of Man ⧼

Giovanni Pico della Mirandola was one of the foremost intellects of the Italian Renaissance. Pico boasted that he had studied all schools of philosophy, which he tried to demonstrate by drawing up nine hundred theses for public disputation at the age of twenty-four. As a preface to his theses, he wrote his famous oration, On the Dignity of Man, in which he proclaimed the unlimited potentiality of human beings.

Pico della Mirandola, Oration on the Dignity of Man
At last the best of artisans [God] ordained that that creature to whom He had been able to give nothing proper to himself should have joint possession of whatever had been peculiar to each of the different kinds of being. He therefore took man as a creature of indeterminate nature, and assigning him a place in the middle of the world, addressed him thus: "Neither a fixed abode nor a form that is yours alone nor any function peculiar to yourself have we given you, Adam, to the end that according to your longing and according to your judgment you may have and possess what abode, what form, and what functions you yourself desire. The nature of all other beings is limited and constrained within the bounds of laws prescribed by Us. You, constrained by no limits, in accordance with your own free will, in whose hand We have placed you, shall ordain for yourself the limits of your nature. We have set you at the world's center that you may from there more easily observe whatever is in the world. We have made you neither of heaven nor of earth, neither mortal nor immortal, so that with freedom of choice and with honor, as though the maker and molder of yourself, you may fashion yourself in whatever shape you shall prefer. You shall have the power to degenerate into the lower forms of life, which are brutish. You shalt have the power, out of your soul's judgment, to be reborn into the higher forms, which are divine."

O supreme generosity of God the Father, O highest and most marvelous felicity of man! To him it is granted to have whatever he chooses, to be whatever he wills. Beasts as soon as they are born bring with them from their mother's womb all they will ever possess. Spiritual beings, either from the beginning or soon thereafter, become what they are to be for ever and ever. On man when he came into life the Father conferred the seeds of all kinds and the germs of every way of life. Whatever seeds each man cultivates will grow to maturity and bear in him their own fruit. If they be vegetative, he will be like a plant. If sensitive, he will become brutish. If rational, he will grow into a heavenly being. If intellectual, he will be an angel and the son of God.

---

only. . . ."[18] What, then, are the "liberal studies"?

> Amongst these I accord the first place to History, on grounds both of its attractiveness and of its utility, qualities which appeal equally to the scholar and to the statesman. Next in importance ranks Moral Philosophy, which indeed is, in a peculiar sense, a "Liberal Art," in that its purpose is to teach men the secret of true freedom. History, then, gives us the concrete examples of the precepts inculcated by Philosophy. The one shows what men should do, the other what men have said and done in the past, and what practical lessons we may draw therefrom for the present day. I would indicate as the third main branch of study, Eloquence. . . . By philosophy we learn the essential truth of things, which by eloquence we so exhibit in orderly adornment as to bring conviction to differing minds.[19]

The remaining liberal studies included letters (grammar and logic), poetry, mathematics, astronomy, and music ("as to Music," said Vergerio, "the Greeks refused the title of 'Educated' to anyone who could not sing or play"). Crucial to all liberal studies was the mastery of Greek and Latin since it enabled students to read the great classical authors who were the foundation stones of the liberal arts. In short, the purpose of a liberal education was to produce individuals who followed a path of virtue and wisdom and possessed the rhetorical skills to persuade others to take it.

Following the Greek precept of a sound mind in a sound body, Vittorino's school at Mantua stressed the need for physical education. Pupils were taught the arts of javelin throwing, archery, and dancing and encouraged to run, wrestle, hunt, and swim frequently. Nor was Christianity excluded from Vittorino's school. His students were taught the Scriptures and the works of the Church Fathers, especially Augustine. A devout Christian, Vittorino required his pupils to attend mass daily and be reverent in word and deed.

Although a small number of children from the lower classes were provided free educations, humanist schools such as Vittorino's were primarily geared for the education of an elite, the ruling classes of their communities. Also largely absent from such schools were females.

Vittorino's only female pupils were the two daughters of the Gonzaga ruler of Mantua. While these few female students studied the classics and were encouraged to know some history and to ride, dance, sing, play the lute, and appreciate poetry, they were discouraged from learning mathematics and rhetoric. In the educational treatises of the time, religion and morals were thought to "hold the first place in the education of a Christian lady."

The humanist schools of the Renaissance aimed to develop the human personality to the fullest extent and underscored the new social ideal of the Renaissance, the creation of the universal being known to us as the "Renaissance man." We should also note that Vittorino and other humanist educators considered a humanist education to be a practical preparation for life. The aim of humanist education was not to create great scholars but rather to produce complete citizens who could participate in the civic life of their communities. As Vittorino said, "Not everyone is obliged to excel in philosophy, medicine, or the law, nor are all equally favored by nature; but all are destined to live in society and to practice virtue."[20] Humanist schools, combining the classics and Christianity, provided the model for the basic education of the European ruling classes until the twentieth century.

Humanism and History

Humanism had a strong impact on the writing of history. Influenced by Roman and Greek historians, the humanists approached the writing of history differently from the chroniclers of the Middle Ages. The humanists' belief that classical civilization had been followed by an age of barbarism (the Middle Ages), which, in turn, had been succeeded by their own age with its rebirth of the study of the classics, enabled them to think in terms of the passage of time, of the past as past. Their division of the past into ancient world, dark ages, and their own age provided a new sense of chronology or periodization in history.

The humanists were also responsible for secularizing the writing of history. Humanist historians reduced or eliminated the role of miracles in historical interpretation, not because they were anti-Christian, but because they took a new approach to sources. They wanted to use documents and exercised their newly developed critical skills in examining them. Greater attention was paid to the political events and forces that affected their city-states or larger territorial units. Thus, Leonardo Bruni wrote a *History of the Florentine People;* the German scholar Jacob Wimpheling penned *On the*

Excellence and Magnificence of the Germans. The new emphasis on secularization was also evident in the humanists' conception of causation in history. In much medieval historical literature, historical events were often portrayed as being caused by God's active involvement in human affairs. Humanists deemphasized divine intervention in favor of human motives, stressing political forces or the role of individuals in history.

The high point of Renaissance historiography was achieved at the beginning of the sixteenth century in the works of Francesco Guicciardini (1483–1540). He has been called by some Renaissance scholars the greatest historian between Tacitus in the first century A.D. (see Chapter 6) and Voltaire and Gibbon in the eighteenth century (see Chapter 18). His *History of Italy* and *History of Florence* represent the beginning of "modern analytical historiography." To Guicciardini, the purpose of writing history was to teach lessons, but he was so impressed by the complexity of historical events that he felt those lessons were not always obvious. From his extensive background in government and diplomatic affairs, he developed the political skills that enabled him to analyze political situations precisely and critically. Emphasizing political and military history, his works relied heavily on personal examples and documentary sources.

The Impact of Printing

The period of the Renaissance witnessed the invention of printing, one of the most important technological innovations of Western civilization. The art of printing made an immediate impact on European intellectual life and thought.

Printing from hand-carved wooden blocks had been present in the west since the twelfth century. What was new in the fifteenth century was multiple printing with movable metal type. The development of printing from movable type was a gradual process that culminated some time between 1445 and 1450; Johannes Gutenberg of Mainz played an important role in bringing the process to completion. Gutenberg's Bible, completed in 1455 or 1456, was the first real book produced from movable type.

The new printing spread rapidly throughout Europe in the last half of the fifteenth century. Printing presses were established throughout the Holy Roman Empire in the 1460s and within ten years had spread to Italy, France, the Low Countries, Spain, and eastern Europe. Especially well known as a printing center was Venice, home by 1500 to almost one hundred printers who had produced almost two million volumes.

By 1500, there were more than a thousand printers in Europe who had published almost 40,000 titles (between eight and ten million copies). Probably 50 percent of these books were religious in character—Bibles and biblical commentaries, books of devotion, and sermons. Next in importance were the Latin and Greek classics, medieval grammars, legal handbooks, works on philosophy, and an ever-growing number of popular romances.

Printing became one of the largest industries in Europe, and its effects were soon felt in many areas of European life. Although some humanists condemned printing because they believed that it vulgarized learning, the printing of books actually encouraged the development of scholarly research and the desire to attain knowledge. Moreover, printing facilitated cooperation among scholars and helped produce standardized and definitive texts. Printing also stimulated the development of an ever-expanding lay reading public, a development that had an enormous impact on European society. Indeed, the new religious ideas of the Reformation would never have spread as rapidly as they did in the sixteenth century without the printing press.

The Artistic Renaissance

Leonardo da Vinci, one of the great Italian Renaissance artists, once explained: "Hence the painter will produce pictures of small merit if he takes for his standard the pictures of others, but if he will study from natural objects he will bear good fruit . . . those who take for their standard any one but nature . . . weary themselves in vain."[21] Renaissance artists considered the imitation of nature to be their primary goal. Their search for naturalism became an end in itself: to persuade onlookers of the reality of the object or event they were portraying. At the same time, the new artistic standards reflected a new attitude of mind as well, one in which human beings became the focus of attention, the "center and measure of all things," as one artist proclaimed.

Leonardo and other Italians maintained that it was Giotto in the fourteenth century (see Chapter 12) who began the imitation of nature. But what Giotto had begun was not taken up again until the work of Masaccio (1401–1428) in Florence. Masaccio's cycle of frescoes in the Brancacci Chapel has long been regarded as the first masterpiece of Early Renaissance art. With his use of monumental figures, the demonstration of a more realistic relationship between figures and landscape, and the visual representation of the laws of perspective, a new realistic style of painting was born. Onlookers become aware of a world of reality that appears to be a continuation of their own world. Masaccio's massive, three-dimensional human figures provided a model for later generations of Florentine artists.

This new or Renaissance style was absorbed and modified by other Florentine painters in the fifteenth century. Especially important was the development of an experimental trend that took two directions. One emphasized the mathematical side of painting, the working out of the laws of perspective and the organization of outdoor space and light by geometry and perspective. In the work of Paolo Uccello (1397–1475), figures became merely stage props to show off his mastery of the laws of perspective. The other aspect of the experimental trend involved the investigation of movement and anatomical structure. *The Martyrdom of St. Sebastian* by Antonio Pollaiuolo (c. 1432–1498) revels in classical motifs and attempts to portray the human body under stress. Indeed, the realistic portrayal of the human nude became one of the foremost preoccupations of Italian Renaissance art. The fifteenth century, then, was a period of experimentation and technical mastery.

During the last decades of the fifteenth century, a new sense of invention emerged in Florence, especially in the circle of artists and scholars who formed part of the court of the city's leading citizen, Lorenzo the Magnificent. One of this group's prominent members

was Sandro Botticelli (1445–1510), whose interest in Greek and Roman mythology was well reflected in one of his most famous works, *Primavera* or *Spring*. The painting is set in the garden of Venus, a garden of eternal spring. While Botticelli's figures are well defined, they also possess an otherworldly quality that is far removed from the realism that characterized the painting of the Early Renaissance.

The revolutionary achievements of Florentine painters in the fifteenth century were matched by equally stunning advances in sculpture and architecture. Donato di Donatello (1386–1466) spent time in Rome, studying and copying the statues of antiquity. His subsequent work in Florence reveals how well he had mastered the essence of what he saw. Among his numerous works was a statue of David, which is the first known

◆ **Botticelli,** *Primavera.* This work reflects Botticelli's strong interest in classical antiquity. At the center of the painting is Venus, the goddess of love. At her left stands Flora, a Roman goddess of flowers and fertility, while the Three Graces dance playfully at her right. Cupid, the son of Venus, aims his arrow at the Three Graces. At the far left of the picture is Mercury, the messenger of the gods. Later in his life, Botticelli experienced a profound religious crisis, leading him to reject his earlier preoccupation with pagan gods and goddesses. He burned many of his early paintings and then produced only religious works.

"lifesize freestanding bronze nude in European art since antiquity." With the severed head of the giant Goliath beneath David's feed, Donatello's statute celebrated Florentine heroism in the triumph of the Florentines over the Milanese in 1428. Like Donatello's other statues, *David* also radiated a simplicity and strength that reflected the dignity of humanity.

Filippo Brunelleschi (1377–1446) was a friend of Donatello and accompanied him to Rome. Brunelleschi drew much inspiration from the architectural monuments of Roman antiquity, and when he returned to

✦ **Donatello, *David*.** Donatello's *David* first stood in the courtyard of the Medici Palace. On its base was an inscription praising Florentine heroism and virtue, leading art historians to assume that the statue was meant to commemorate the victory of Florence over Milan in 1428.

✦ **Filippo Brunelleschi, Interior of San Lorenzo.** Cosimo de' Medici contributed massive amounts of money to the rebuilding of the church of San Lorenzo. As seen in this view of the nave and choir of the church, Brunelleschi's architectural designs were based on the basilica plan borrowed by early Christians from pagan Rome. San Lorenzo's simplicity, evident in its rows of slender Corinthian columns, created a human-centered space.

Florence, he poured his new insights into the creation of a new architecture. When the Medici commissioned him to design the church of San Lorenzo, Brunelleschi, inspired by Roman models, created a church interior very different from that of the great medieval cathedrals. San Lorenzo's classical columns, rounded arches, and coffered ceiling created an environment that did not overwhelm the worshiper, materially and psychologically, as Gothic cathedrals did, but comforted as a space created to fit human, not divine, measurements. Like painters and sculptors, Renaissance architects sought to reflect a human-centered world.

The new assertion of human individuality, evident in Early Renaissance art, was also reflected in the new emphasis on portraiture. Patrons appeared in the corners of sacred pictures, and monumental tombs and portrait statues honored many of Florence's prominent citizens. By the mid-fifteenth century, artists were giving an accurate rendering of their subjects' facial features while revealing the inner qualities of their personalities. The portraits of the duke and duchess of Urbino by Piero della Francesca (c. 1410–1492) provide accurate representations as well as a sense of both the power and the wealth of the rulers of Urbino.

By the end of the fifteenth century, Italian painters, sculptors, and architects had created a new artistic environment. Many artists had mastered the new techniques for a scientific observation of the world around them and were now ready to move into individualistic forms of creative expression. This final stage of Renaissance art, which flourished between 1480 and 1520, is called the High Renaissance. The shift to the High Renaissance was marked by the increasing importance of Rome as a new cultural center of the Italian Renaissance.

The High Renaissance was dominated by the work of three artistic giants, Leonardo da Vinci (1452–1519), Raphael (1483–1520), and Michelangelo (1475–1564). Leonardo represents a transitional figure in the shift to High Renaissance principles. He carried on the fifteenth-century experimental tradition by studying everything and even dissecting human bodies to better see how nature worked. But Leonardo stressed the need to advance beyond such realism and initiated the High Renaissance's preoccupation with the idealization of nature, or the attempt to generalize from realistic portrayal to an ideal form. Leonardo's *Last Supper,* painted in Milan, is a brilliant summary of fifteenth-century trends in its organization of space and use of perspective to depict subjects three-dimensionally in a two-dimensional medium. But it is also more. The figure of Philip is idealized, and there are profound psychological dimensions to the work. The words of Christ that "one of you shall betray me" are experienced directly as each of the apostles reveals his personality and his relationship to the Savior. In one of his notebooks, Leonardo wrote that the highest and most difficult aim of painting is to depict "the intention of man's soul." Through gestures and movement, Leonardo hoped to reveal a person's inner life.

Raphael blossomed as a painter at an early age; at twenty-five, he was already regarded as one of Italy's best painters. Well-known for his frescoes in the Vatican Palace, Raphael was especially acclaimed for his numerous madonnas, in which he attempted to achieve an ideal of beauty far surpassing human standards. His *Alba Madonna* reveals a world of balance, harmony, and order—basically, the underlying principles of the art of the classical world of Greece and Rome.

Michelangelo, an accomplished painter, sculptor, and architect, was another giant of the High Renaissance. Fiercely driven by his desire to create, he worked with great passion and energy on a remarkable number of projects. Michelangelo was influenced by Neoplatonism, especially evident in his figures on the ceiling of the Sistine Chapel in Rome. These muscular figures reveal an ideal type of human being with perfect proportions. In good Neoplatonic fashion, their beauty is meant to be a reflection of divine beauty; the more beautiful the body, the more God-like the figure.

Another manifestation of Michelangelo's search for ideal beauty was his *David,* a colossal marble statue

Leonardo da Vinci, *The Last Supper.* Leonardo da Vinci was the impetus behind the High Renaissance concern with the idealization of nature, moving from a realistic portrayal of the human figure to an idealized form. Evident in Leonardo's *Last Supper* is his effort to depict a person's character and inner nature by the use of gesture and movement. Unfortunately, Leonardo used an experimental technique in this fresco, which soon led to its physical deterioration.

◆ **Raphael, *The Alba Madonna.*** Although he died at the age of thirty-seven, Raphael achieved in his own lifetime a fame comparable to that of Michelangelo and Leonardo da Vinci. In his madonnas, Raphael sought an idealized beauty that was typical of the High Renaissance. His serene *Alba Madonna* illustrates his mastery of the classical principles of balance harmony, clarity, and rational composition.

commissioned by the Florentine government in 1501 and completed in 1504. Michelangelo maintained that the form of a statue already resided in the uncarved piece of stone: "I only take away the surplus, the statue is already there."[22] Out of a piece of marble that had remained unused for fifty years, Michelangelo created a fourteen-foot-high figure, the largest piece of sculpture in Italy since the time of Rome. An awe-inspiring hero, Michelangelo's *David* proudly proclaims the beauty of the human body and the glory of human beings.

A High Renaissance in architecture was also evident, especially in the work of Donato Bramante (1444–1514). He came from Urbino but took up residence in Rome, where he designed a small temple on the supposed site of Saint Peter's martyrdom. The Tempietto—or little temple—with its Doric columns surrounding a sanctuary enclosed by a dome, summarized the architectural ideals of the High Renaissance. Columns, dome, and sanctuary form a monumental and harmonious whole. Inspired by antiquity, Bramante had recaptured the grandeur of ancient Rome. His achievement led Pope Julius II to commission him to design a

new basilica for Rome, which eventually became the great St. Peter's.

The Artist and Social Status

Early Renaissance artists began their careers as apprentices to masters in craft guilds. Apprentices with unusual talent might eventually become masters and run their own workshops. As in the Middle Ages, artists were still largely viewed as artisans. Since guilds depended on commissions for their projects, patrons played an impor-

◆ **Michelangelo, *David.*** This statue of David, cut from an eighteen-foot-high piece of marble, exalts the beauty of the human body and is a fitting symbol of the Italian Renaissance's affirmation of human power. Completed in 1504, the *David* was moved by Florentine authorities to a special location in front of the Palazzo Vecchio, the seat of the Florentine government.

✦ **Michelangelo, *Creation of Adam*.** In 1508, Pope Julius II recalled Michelangelo to Rome and commissioned him to decorate the ceiling of the Sistine Chapel. This colossal project was not completed until 1512. Michelangelo attempted to tell the story of the Fall of Man by depicting nine scenes from the biblical book of Genesis. In this scene, the well-proportioned figure of Adam, meant by Michelangelo to be a reflection of divine beauty, awaits the divine spark.

tant role in the art of the Early Renaissance. The wealthy upper classes determined both the content and purpose of the paintings and pieces of sculpture they commissioned.

By the end of the fifteenth century, a transformation in the position of the artist had occurred. Especially talented individuals, such as Leonardo, Raphael, and Michelangelo, were no longer seen as artisans, but as artistic geniuses with creative energies akin to the divine (see the box on p. 440). Artists were heroes, individuals who were praised more for their creativity than for their competence as craftsmen. Michelangelo, for example, was frequently addressed as "Il Divino"—the Divine One. As society excused their eccentricities and valued their creative genius, the artists of the High Renaissance became the first to embody the modern concept of the artist.

As respect for artists grew, so too did their ability to profit economically from their work and to rise on the social scale. Now welcomed as equals into the circles of the upper classes, they mingled with the political and intellectual elite of their society and became more aware of new intellectual theories, which they then embodied in their art. The Platonic Academy and Renaissance Neoplatonism had an especially important impact on Florentine painters.

✦ **Bramante, Tempietto.** Ferdinand and Isabella of Spain commissioned Donato Bramante to design a small building in Rome that would commemorate the place at which Saint Peter was supposedly crucified. Completed in 1502, the temple reflected Bramante's increasing understanding of ancient Roman remains.

The Genius of Leonardo da Vinci

During the Renaissance, artists came to be viewed as creative geniuses with almost divine qualities. One individual who helped to create this image of the Renaissance artist was himself a painter. Giorgio Vasari was an avid admirer of Italy's great artists and wrote a series of brief biographies of them. This excerpt is taken from his account of Leonardo da Vinci.

Giorgio Vasari, *Lives of the Artists*

In the normal course of events many men and women are born with various remarkable qualities and talents; but occasionally, in a way that transcends nature, a single person is marvelously endowed by heaven with beauty, grace, and talent in such abundance that he leaves other men far behind, all his actions seem inspired, and indeed everything he does clearly comes from God rather than from human art.

Everyone acknowledged that this was true of Leonardo da Vinci, an artist of outstanding physical beauty who displayed infinite grace in everything he did and who cultivated his genius so brilliantly that all problems he studied he solved with ease. He possessed great strength and dexterity; he was a man of regal spirit and tremendous breadth of mind; and his name became so famous that not only was he esteemed during his lifetime but his reputation endured and became even greater after his death. . . .

He was marvelously gifted, and he proved himself to be a first-class geometrician in his work as a sculptor and architect. In his youth Leonardo made in clay several heads of women, with smiling faces, of which plaster casts are still being made, as well as some children's heads executed as if by a mature artist. He also did many architectural drawings both of ground plans and of other elevations, and, while still young, he was the first to propose reducing the Arno River to a navigable canal between Pisa and Florence. He made designs for mills, fulling machines, and engines that could be driven by waterpower; and as he intended to be a painter by profession he carefully studied drawing from life. . . . Altogether, his genius was so wonderfully inspired by the grace of God, his powers of expression were so powerfully fed by a willing memory and intellect, and his writing conveyed his ideas so precisely, that his arguments and reasonings confounded the most formidable critics. In addition, he used to make models and plans showing how to excavate and tunnel through mountains without difficulty, so as to pass from one level to another; and he demonstrated how to lift and draw great weights by means of levers and hoists and ways of cleaning harbors and using pumps to suck up water from great depths.

The Northern Artistic Renaissance

In trying to provide an exact portrayal of their world, the artists of the north (especially the Low Countries) and Italy took different approaches. In Italy, the human form became the primary vehicle of expression as Italian artists sought to master the technical skills that allowed them to portray humans in realistic settings. The large wall spaces of Italian churches had given rise to the art of fresco painting, but in the north, the prevalence of Gothic cathedrals with their stained glass windows resulted in more emphasis on illuminated manuscripts and wooden panel painting for altarpieces. The space available in these works was limited, and great care was required to depict each object, leading northern painters to become masters at rendering details.

The most influential northern school of art in the fifteenth century was centered in Flanders. Jan van Eyck (1390?–1441) was among the first to use oil paint, a medium that enabled the artist to use a varied range of colors and make changes to create fine details. In the famous *Giovanni Arnolfini and His Bride*, van Eyck's attention to detail is staggering: precise portraits, a glittering chandelier, a mirror reflecting the objects in the room, and the effects of light filtering through the window. Although each detail was rendered as observed, it is evident that van Eyck's comprehension of perspective was still uncertain. His work is truly indicative of northern Renaissance painters, who, in their effort to imitate nature, did so not by mastery of the laws of perspective and proportion, but by empirical observation of visual reality and the accurate portrayal of details. Moreover, northern painters placed great emphasis on the emotional intensity of religious feeling and created great works of devotional art, especially in their altarpieces. Michelangelo summarized the difference between northern and Italian Renaissance painting in these words:

> In Flanders, they paint, before all things, to render exactly and deceptively the outward appearance of things. The painters choose, by preference, subjects provoking transports of piety, like the figures of saints or of prophets. But most of the time they paint what are called landscapes with plenty of figures. Though the eye is agreeably impressed, these pictures have neither choice of values nor grandeur. In short, this art is without power and without distinction; it aims at rendering minutely many things at the same time, of which a single one would have sufficed to call forth a man's whole application.[23]

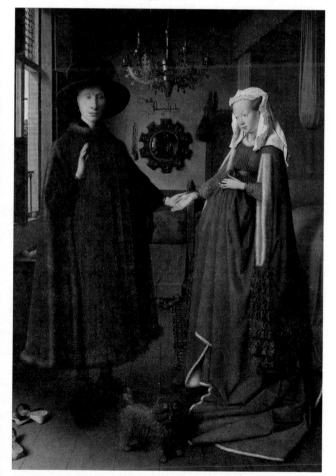

◆ **Jan van Eyck, *Giovanni Arnolfini and His Bride.***
Northern painters took great care in depicting each object and became masters in rendering details. This emphasis on a realistic portrayal is clearly evident in this oil painting, supposedly a portrait of Giovanni Arnolfini, an Italian merchant who had settled in Bruges, and his wife, Giovanna Cenami.

◆ **Albrecht Dürer, *Adoration of the Magi.*** By the end of the fifteenth century, northern artists began studying in Italy and adopting many of the techniques used by Italian painters. As is evident in this painting, which was the central panel for an altarpiece done for Frederick the Wise in 1504, Albrecht Dürer masterfully incorporated the laws of perspective and the ideals of proportion into his works. At the same time, he did not abandon the preoccupation with detail typical of northern artists.

By the end of the fifteenth century, however, artists from the north began to study in Italy and were visually influenced by what artists were doing there.

One northern artist of this later period who was greatly affected by the Italians was Albrecht Dürer (1471–1528) from Nuremberg. Dürer made two trips to Italy and absorbed most of what the Italians could teach, as is evident in his mastery of the laws of perspective and Renaissance theories of proportion. He wrote detailed treatises on both subjects. At the same time, as in his famous *Adoration of the Magi,* Dürer did not reject the use of minute details characteristic of northern artists. He did try, however, to integrate those details more harmoniously into his works and, like the Italian artists of the High Renaissance, tried to achieve a standard of ideal beauty by a careful examination of the human form.

Music in the Renaissance

For much of the fifteenth century, an extraordinary cultural environment was fostered in the domains of the dukes of Burgundy in northern Europe. The court of the dukes attracted some of the best artists and musicians of the time. Among them was Guillaume Dufay (c. 1400–1474), perhaps the most important composer of his time. Born in northern France, Dufay lived for a few years in Italy and was thus well suited to combine the late medieval style of France with the early Renaissance style of Italy. One of Dufay's greatest contributions was a change in the composition of the Mass. He was the first to use secular tunes to replace Gregorian chants as the fixed melody that served as the basis for the Mass. Dufay also composed a number of secular songs, an important reminder that during the Renaissance music ceased to be used chiefly in the service of God and moved into the secular world of courts and cities. In Italy and France, the chief form of secular music was the madrigal.

The Renaissance madrigal was a poem set to music, and its origins were in the fourteenth-century Italian courts. The texts were usually twelve-line poems written in the vernacular, and their theme was emotional or erotic love. By the mid-sixteenth century, most madrigals were written for five or six voices and employed a technique called text painting, in which the music tried to portray the literal meaning of the text. Thus, the melody would rise for the word "heaven" or use a wavelike motion to represent the word "water." By the mid-sixteenth century, the madrigal had also spread to England, where the most popular form was characterized by the fa-la-la refrain like that found in the English carol "Deck the Halls."

The European State in the Renaissance

The High Middle Ages had witnessed the emergence of territorial states that began to develop the administrative machinery of centralized government. Professional bureaucracies, royal courts, and parliamentary assemblies were all products of the twelfth and thirteenth centuries. Strong monarchy had provided the organizing power for the development of these states, but in the fourteenth century, the internal stability of European governments had been threatened by financial and dynastic problems as well as challenges from their nobilities. By the fifteenth century, rulers began to rebuild their states by checking the violent activities of their nobles and maintaining internal order. Some territorial units, such as the Holy Roman Empire and Italy, failed to develop strong national monarchies, but even in these areas, strong princes and city councils managed to centralize their authority within their smaller territorial states. In Italy, Milan, Venice, and Florence managed to become fairly well centralized territorial states.

Some historians believe that the Italian Renaissance states, with their preoccupation with political power, were the first true examples of the modern secular state.

The "New Monarchies"

In the first half of the fifteenth century, European states continued the disintegrative patterns of the previous century. In the second half of the fifteenth century, however, recovery set in, and attempts were made to reestablish the centralized power of monarchical governments. To characterize the results, some historians have used the label "Renaissance states"; others have spoken of the "new monarchies," especially those of France, England, and Spain at the end of the fifteenth century. Although appropriate, the term "new monarch" can also be misleading. These Renaissance monarchs were new in their concentration of royal authority, their attempts to suppress the nobility, their efforts to control the church in their lands, and their insistence upon having the loyalty of people living within definite territorial boundaries. Like the rulers of fifteenth-century Italian states, the "new monarchs" were often crafty men obsessed with the acquisition and expansion of political power. Of course, none of these characteristics was entirely new in that a number of medieval monarchs, especially in the thirteenth century, had also exhibited them. Nevertheless, the Renaissance period does mark the further extension of centralized royal authority. Of course, the degree to which monarchs were successful in extending their political authority varied from area to area. In central and eastern Europe, decentralization rather than centralization of political authority remained a fact of life.

THE GROWTH OF THE FRENCH MONARCHY

The Hundred Years' War had left France prostrate. Depopulation, desolate farmlands, ruined commerce, and independent and unruly nobles had made it difficult for the kings to assert their authority. But the war had also developed a strong degree of French national feeling toward a common enemy that the kings could use to reestablish monarchical power. The need to prosecute the war provided an excuse to strengthen the authority of the king, already evident in the policies of Charles VII (1422–1461) after he was crowned king at Reims. With the consent of the Estates-General, Charles established a royal army composed of cavalry and archers. He received from the Estates-General the right to levy the *taille*, an annual direct tax usually on

Map 13.2 Europe in the Renaissance.

land or property, without any need for further approval from the Estates-General. Losing control of the purse meant less power for this parliamentary body. Charles VII also secured the Pragmatic Sanction of Bourges (1438), an agreement with the papacy that strengthened the liberties of the French church administratively at the expense of the papacy and enabled the king to begin to assume control over the church in France.

The process of developing a French territorial state was greatly advanced by King Louis XI (1461–1483), known as the Spider because of his wily and devious ways. Some historians have called this "new monarch" the founder of the French national state. By retaining the *taille* as a permanent tax imposed by royal authority, Louis secured a sound, regular source of income. Louis was not, however, completely successful in repressing the French nobility whose independence posed a threat

to his own state building. A major problem was his supposed vassal, Charles the Bold, duke of Burgundy (1467–1477). Charles attempted to create a middle kingdom between France and Germany, stretching from the Low Countries in the north to Switzerland. Louis opposed his action, and when Charles was killed in 1477 fighting the Swiss, Louis added part of Charles's possessions, the duchy of Burgundy, to his own lands. Three years later, the provinces of Anjou, Maine, Bar, and Provence were brought under royal control. Louis the Spider also encouraged the growth of industry and commerce in an attempt to bolster the French economy. For example, he introduced new industries, such as the silk industry to Lyons.

Many historians believe that Louis created a base for the later development of a strong French monarchy. In any case, the monarchy was at least well enough estab-

The "New Monarchies"

France	
Charles VII	1422–1461
Pragmatic Sanction of Bourges	1438
Louis XI the Spider	1461–1483
Charles VIII	1483–1498
Louis XII	1498–1515
England	
War of the Roses	1450s–1485
Richard III	1483–1485
Henry VII	1485–1509
Spain	
Isabella of Castile	1474–1504
Ferdinand of Aragon	1479–1516
Marriage of Ferdinand and Isabella	1469
Introduction of Inquisition	1478
Expulsion of the Jews	1492
Expulsion of the Muslims	1502
Holy Roman Empire	
Frederick III	1440–1493
Maximilian I	1493–1519
Eastern Europe	
Creation of Lithuanian-Polish state	1386
Hungary: Matthias Corvinus	1458–1490
Russia: Ivan III	1462–1505
Fall of Constantinople and Byzantine Empire	1453

lished to weather the policies of the next two monarchs, Charles VIII (1483–1498) and Louis XII (1498–1515), whose attempts to subdue parts of Italy initiated a series of Italian wars. Internally, France survived these wars without too much difficulty.

ENGLAND: CIVIL WAR AND A NEW MONARCHY

The Hundred Years' War had also strongly affected the other protagonist in that conflict. The cost of the war in its final years and the losses in manpower strained the English economy. Moreover, the end of the war brought even greater domestic turmoil to England when the War of the Roses broke out in the 1450s. This civil war pitted the ducal house of Lancaster, whose symbol was a red rose, against the ducal house of York, whose symbol was a white rose. Many aristocratic families of England were drawn into the conflict. Finally, in 1485, Henry Tudor, duke of Richmond, defeated the last Yorkist king, Richard III (1483–1485), at Bosworth Field and established the new Tudor dynasty.

As the first Tudor king, Henry VII (1485–1509) worked to reduce internal dissension and establish a strong monarchical government. The English aristocracy had been much weakened by the War of the Roses since many nobles had been killed. Henry eliminated the private wars of the nobility by abolishing "livery and maintenance," the practice by which wealthy aristocrats maintained private armies of followers dedicated to the service of their lord. Since England, unlike France and Spain, did not possess a standing army, the king relied on special commissions to trusted nobles to raise troops for a specific campaign, after which the troops were disbanded. Henry also controlled the irresponsible activity of the nobles by establishing the Court of Star Chamber, which did not use juries and allowed torture to be used to extract confessions.

Henry VII was particularly successful in extracting income from the traditional financial resources of the English monarch, such as the crown lands, judicial fees and fines, and customs duties. By using diplomacy to avoid wars, which are always expensive, the king avoided having to call Parliament on any regular basis to grant him funds. By not overburdening the landed gentry and middle class with taxes, Henry won their favor, and they provided much support for his monarchy.

Henry also encouraged commercial activity. By increasing wool exports, royal export taxes on wool rose. Henry's thriftiness as well as his domestic and foreign policies enabled him to leave England with a stable and prosperous government and an enhanced status for the monarchy itself.

THE UNIFICATION OF SPAIN

During the Middle Ages, several independent Christian kingdoms had emerged in the course of the long reconquest of the Iberian peninsula from the Muslims. Aragon and Castile were the strongest Spanish kingdoms; in the west was the independent monarchy of Portugal; in the north the small kingdom of Navarre, oriented toward France; and in the south the Muslim kingdom of Granada. Few people at the beginning of the fifteenth century could have predicted the unification of the Iberian kingdoms.

A major step in that direction was taken with the marriage of Isabella of Castile (1474–1504) and Ferdinand of Aragon (1479–1516) in 1469. This marriage was a dynastic union of two rulers, not a political union. Both kingdoms maintained their own parliaments (Cortes), courts, laws, coinage, speech, customs, and political organs. Nevertheless, the two rulers worked to strengthen royal control of government, especially in Castile. The royal council, which was supposed to supervise local administration and oversee the implementation of government policies, was stripped of aristocrats and filled primarily with middle-class lawyers. Trained in the principles of Roman law, these officials operated on the belief that the monarchy embodied the power of the state.

The towns were also enlisted in the policy of state building. Medieval town organizations known as *hermandades* ("brotherhoods"), which had been organized to maintain law and order, were revived. Ferdinand and Isabella transformed them into a kind of national militia whose primary goal was to stop the wealthy landed aristocrats from disturbing the peace, a goal also favored by the middle class. The *hermandades* were disbanded by 1498 when the royal administration became strong enough to deal with lawlessness. The appointment of *corregidores* by the crown to replace corrupt municipal officials enabled the monarchs to extend the central authority of royal government into the towns.

Ferdinand and Isabella reorganized the military forces of Spain, seeking to replace the undisciplined feudal levies they had inherited with a more professional royal army. The development of a strong infantry force as the heart of the new Spanish army made it the best in Europe by the sixteenth century.

Because of its vast power and wealth, Ferdinand and Isabella recognized the importance of controlling the Catholic church. They secured from the pope the right to select the most important church officials in Spain, virtually guaranteeing the foundation of a Spanish Catholic church in which the clergy became an instrument for the extension of royal power. The monarchs, who were sincere Catholics, also used their authority over the church to institute reform. Isabella's chief minister, the able and astute Cardinal Ximenes, restored discipline and eliminated immorality among the monks and secular clergy.

The religious zeal exhibited in Cardinal Ximenes's reform program was also evident in the policy of strict religious uniformity pursued by Ferdinand and Isabella. Of course, it served a political purpose as well: to create unity and further bolster royal power. Spain possessed two large religious minorities, the Jews and Muslims, both of whom had been largely tolerated in medieval Spain. Although anti-Semitism had become a fact of life in medieval Europe, Spain had remained tolerant. In some areas of Spain, Jews exercised much influence in economic and intellectual affairs. Increased persecution in the fourteenth century, however, led the majority of Spanish Jews to convert to Christianity. Although many of these *conversos* came to play important roles in

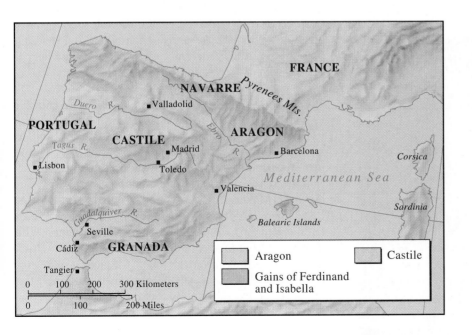

✂ **Map 13.3** Iberian Peninsula.

Spanish society, complaints that they were secretly reverting to Judaism prompted Ferdinand and Isabella to ask the pope to introduce the Inquisition into Spain in 1478. Under royal control, the Inquisition worked with cruel efficiency to guarantee the orthodoxy of the *conversos*, but had no authority over practicing Jews. Consequently, in 1492, flush with the success of the conquest of Muslim Granada, Ferdinand and Isabella took the drastic step of expelling all professed Jews from Spain. It is estimated that 150,000 out of possibly 200,000 Jews fled.

Muslims, too, were "encouraged" to convert to Christianity after the conquest of Granada. In 1502, Isabella issued a decree expelling all professed Muslims from her kingdom. To a very large degree, the "Most Catholic" monarchs had achieved their goal of absolute religious orthodoxy as a basic ingredient of the Spanish state. To be Spanish was to be Catholic, a policy of uniformity enforced by the Inquisition.

During the reigns of Ferdinand and Isabella, Spain (or the union of Castile and Aragon) began to emerge as an important power in European affairs. Both Granada and Navarre had been conquered and incorporated into the royal realms. Nevertheless, Spain remained divided in many ways. Only the royal dynasty provided the centralizing force, and when a single individual, the grandson of Ferdinand and Isabella, succeeded both rulers as Charles I in 1516, he inherited lands that made him the most powerful monarch of his age.

THE HOLY ROMAN EMPIRE: THE SUCCESS OF THE HABSBURGS

Unlike France, England, and Spain, the Holy Roman Empire failed to develop a strong monarchical authority. After 1438, the position of Holy Roman Emperor remained in the hands of the Habsburg dynasty. Having gradually acquired a number of possessions along the Danube, known collectively as Austria, the house of Habsburg had become one of the wealthiest landholders in the empire and by the mid-fifteenth century began to play an important role in European affairs.

Much of the Habsburg success in the fifteenth century was due not to military success, but to a well-executed policy of dynastic marriages. As the old Habsburg motto said: "Leave the waging of wars to others! But you, happy Austria, marry; for the realms which Mars [god of war] awards to others, Venus [goddess of love] transfers to you." Although Frederick III (1440–1493) lost the traditional Habsburg possessions of Bohemia and Hungary, he gained Franche-Comté in east central France, Luxembourg, and a large part of the Low Countries by marrying his son Maximilian to Mary, the daughter of Duke Charles the Bold of Burgundy. The addition of these territories made the Habsburg dynasty an international power and brought them the undying opposition of the French monarchy because the rulers of France feared they would be surrounded by the Habsburgs.

Much was expected of the flamboyant Maximilian I (1493–1519) when he became emperor. Through the Reichstag, the imperial diet or parliament, Maximilian attempted to centralize the administration by creating new institutions common to the entire empire. Opposition from the German princes doomed these efforts, however. Maximilian's only real success lay in his marriage alliances. Philip of Burgundy, the son of Maximilian's marriage to Mary, was married to Joanna, the daughter of Ferdinand and Isabella. Philip and Joanna produced a son, Charles, who, through a series of unexpected deaths, became heir to all three lines, the Habsburg, Burgundian, and Spanish, making him the leading monarch of his age (see Chapter 14).

✦ **Emperor Maximilian I.** Although the Holy Roman Emperor possessed little power in Germany, the Habsburg dynasty, which held the position of emperor after 1438, steadily increased its wealth and landholdings through dynastic marriages. This portrait of Emperor Maximilian I reflects well the description by a Venetian ambassador: "He is not very fair of face, but well proportioned, exceedingly robust, of sanguine and choleric complexion and very healthy for his age."

Although the Holy Roman Empire did not develop along the lines of a centralized monarchical state, within the empire the power of the independent princes and electors increased steadily. In numerous German states, such as Bavaria, Hesse, Brandenburg, and the Palatinate, princes built up bureaucracies, developed standing armies, created fiscal systems, and introduced Roman law, just like the national monarchs of France, England, and Spain. They posed a real threat to the church, the emperor, and other smaller independent bodies in the Holy Roman Empire, especially the free imperial cities.

THE STRUGGLE FOR STRONG MONARCHY IN EASTERN EUROPE

In eastern Europe, rulers struggled to achieve the centralization of their territorial states but faced serious obstacles. Although the population was mostly Slavic, there were islands of other ethnic groups that caused untold difficulties. Religious differences also troubled the area, as Roman Catholics, Greek Orthodox Christians, and pagans confronted each other.

Much of Polish history revolved around the bitter struggle between the crown and the landed nobility. The dynastic union of Jagiello, grand prince of Lithuania, with the Polish queen Jadwiga resulted in a large Lithuanian-Polish state in 1386. Jagiello and his immediate successors were able to control the landed magnates, but by the end of the fifteenth century, the preoccupation of Poland's rulers with problems in Bohemia and Hungary as well as war with the Russians and Turks enabled the aristocrats to reestablish their power. Through their control of the *Sejm* or national diet, the magnates reduced the peasantry to serfdom by 1511 and established the right to elect their kings. The Polish kings proved unable to establish a strong royal authority.

Bohemia, Poland's neighbor, was part of the Holy Roman Empire, but distrust of the Germans and close ethnic ties to the Poles and Slovaks encouraged the Czechs to associate with their northeastern Slavic neighbors. The Hussite wars (see The Problems of Heresy and Reform later in this chapter) led to further dissension and civil war. Because of a weak monarchy, the Bohemian nobles increased their authority and wealth at the expense of both crown and church.

The history of Hungary had been closely tied to that of central and western Europe by its conversion to Roman Catholicism by German missionaries. The church became a large and prosperous institution. Wealthy bishops, along with the great territorial lords, became powerful, independent political figures. For a brief while, Hungary developed into an important European state, the dominant power in eastern Europe. King Matthias Corvinus (1458–1490) broke the power of the wealthy lords and created a well-organized bureaucracy. Like a typical Renaissance prince, he patronized the new humanist culture, brought Italian scholars and artists to his capital at Buda, and made his court one of the most brilliant outside Italy. After his death, Hungary returned to weak rule, and the work of Corvinus was largely undone.

Since the thirteenth century, Russia had been under the domination of the Mongols. Gradually, the princes of Moscow rose to prominence by using their close relationship to the Mongol khans to increase their wealth and expand their possessions. In the reign of the great prince Ivan III (1462–1505), a new Russian state was born. Ivan III annexed other Russian principalities and took advantage of dissension among the Mongols to throw off their yoke by 1480. He invaded the lands of the Lithuanian-Polish dynasty and added the territories around Kiev, Smolensk, and Chernigov to his new Muscovite state.

THE OTTOMAN TURKS AND THE END OF BYZANTIUM

Eastern Europe was increasingly threatened by the steadily advancing Ottoman Turks. The Byzantine Empire had, of course, served as a buffer between the Muslim Middle East and the Latin West for centuries. It was severely weakened by the sack of Constantinople in 1204 and its occupation by the west. Although the Palaeologus dynasty (1260–1453) had tried to reestablish Byzantine power in the Balkans after the overthrow of the Latin Empire, the threat from the Turks finally doomed the long-lasting empire.

Beginning in northeastern Asia Minor in the thirteenth century, the Ottoman Turks spread rapidly, seizing the lands of the Seljuk Turks and the Byzantine Empire. In 1345, they bypassed Constantinople and moved into the Balkans, which they conquered by the end of the century. Finally in 1453, the great city of Constantinople fell to the Turks after a siege of several months. After consolidating their power, the Turks prepared to exert renewed pressure on the west, both in the Mediterranean and up the Danube valley toward Vienna. By the end of the fifteenth century, they were threatening Hungary, Austria, Bohemia, and Poland. The Holy Roman Emperor, Charles V, became their bitter enemy in the sixteenth century.

Our survey of European political developments makes it clear that, although individual German or especially

Map 13.4 Southeastern Europe.

Italian princes had developed culturally brilliant states, the future belonged to territorial states organized by national monarchies. They possessed superior resources and were developing institutions that represented the interests of much of the population. Nevertheless, the Renaissance states were still only dynastic-states, not nation-states. The interests of a state were the interests of its ruling dynasty. Loyalty was owed to the ruler, not the state. Residents of France considered themselves subjects of the French king, not citizens of France. Moreover, although Renaissance monarchs were strong rulers centralizing their authority, they were by no means absolute monarchs. Some chance of representative government still remained in the form of Parliament, Estates-General, Cortes, or Reichstag. Kings were strongest in the west and, with the exception of the Russian rulers, weakest in the east.

The Church in the Renaissance

As a result of the efforts of the Council of Constance, the Great Schism had finally been brought to an end in 1417 (see Chapter 12). The council had had three major objectives: to end the schism, to eradicate heresy, adn to reform the church in "head and members." The ending of the schism proved to be the council's easiest task; it was much less successful in dealing with the problems of heresy and reform.

The Problems of Heresy and Reform

Heresy was, of course, not a new problem, and in the thirteenth century, the church had developed inquisitorial machinery to deal with it. But two widespread movements in the fourteenth and early fifteenth centuries—Lollardy and Hussitism—posed new threats to the church.

English Lollardy was a product of the Oxford theologian John Wyclif (c. 1328–1384), whose disgust with clerical corruption led him to a far-ranging attack on papal authority and medieval Christian beliefs and practices. Wyclif alleged that there was no basis in Scripture for papal claims of temporal authority and advocated that the popes be stripped of both their authority and property. At one point, he even denounced the pope as the Antichrist. Believing that the Bible should be a Christian's sole authority, Wyclif urged that it be made available in the vernacular languages so that every Christian could read it. Rejecting all practices not mentioned in Scripture, Wyclif condemned pilgrimages, the veneration of saints, and a whole series of rituals and rites that had developed in the medieval church.

Wyclif has sometimes been viewed as a forerunner of the Reformation of the sixteenth century because his arguments attacked the foundations of the medieval Catholic church's organization and practices. His attacks on church property were especially popular, and he attracted a number of followers who came to be known as Lollards. Persecution by royal and church authorities who feared the socioeconomic consequences of Wyclif's ideas forced the Lollards to go underground after 1400.

A connection between the royal families of England and Bohemia enabled Lollard ideas to spread to Bohemia, where they reinforced the ideas of a group of Czech reformers led by the chancellor of the university at Prague, John Hus (1374–1415). In his call for reform, Hus urged the elimination of the worldliness and corruption of the clergy and attacked the excessive power of the papacy within the Catholic church. Hus's objections fell on receptive ears, since the Catholic church as one of the largest landowners in Bohemia was already widely criticized. Moreover, many clergymen were German, and the native Czechs' strong resentment of the Germans who dominated Bohemia also contributed to Hus's movement.

The Council of Constance attempted to deal with the growing problem of heresy by summoning John Hus to the council. Granted a safe conduct by Emperor Sigismund, Hus went in the hope of a free hearing of his ideas. Instead he was arrested, condemned as a heretic (by a narrow vote), and burned at the stake in 1415. This action turned the unrest in Bohemia into revolutionary upheaval. The resulting Hussite wars combined religious, social, and national issues and wracked the Holy Roman Empire until a truce was arranged in 1436.

CHRONOLOGY

The Church in the Renaissance

Council of Constance	1414–1418
Burning of John Hus	1415
End of the Great Schism	1417
Pius II issues the papal bull *Execrabilis*	1460
The Renaissance papacy	
Sixtus IV	1471–1484
Alexander VI	1492–1503
Julius II	1503–1513
Leo X	1513–1521

The reform of the church in "head and members" was even less successful than the attempt to eradicate heresy. Two reform decrees were passed by the Council of Constance. *Sacrosancta* stated that a general council of the church received its authority from God; hence, every Christian, including the pope, was subject to its authority. The decree *Frequens* provided for the regular holding of general councils to ensure that church reform would continue. Taken together, *Sacrosancta* and *Frequens* provided for an ecclesiastical legislative system within the church superior to the popes.

Decrees alone, however, proved insufficient to reform the church. Councils could issue decrees, but popes had to execute them and popes would not cooperate with councils that diminished their authority. Beginning as early as Martin V in 1417, successive popes worked steadfastly for the next thirty years to defeat the conciliar movement. The victory of the popes and the final blow to the conciliar movement came when Pope Pius II issued the papal bull *Execrabilis* in 1460, condemning appeals to a council over the head of a pope as heretical.

By the mid-fifteenth century, the popes had reasserted their supremacy over the Catholic church. No longer, however, did they have any possibility of asserting supremacy over temporal governments as the medieval papacy had. Furthermore, to gain support during their struggles with the councils, some popes had granted the rulers of territorial states the right to appoint high ecclesiastical officials and tax the clergy. Although these were practical concessions, in truth they limited the pope's exercise of spiritual supremacy. Nevertheless, through all its adversities, the papal monarchy had been maintained, although it had lost much moral prestige.

♦ **A Renaissance Pope: Sixtus IV.** The Renaissance popes allowed secular concerns to overshadow their spiritual duties. They became concerned with territorial expansion, finances, and Renaissance culture. Pope Sixtus IV built the Sistine Chapel and later had it decorated by some of the leading artists of his day. This fresco by Melozzo da Forlì shows the pope on his throne receiving the humanist Platina (kneeling), who was keeper of the Vatican Library.

By the mid-fifteenth century, it was incumbent upon the popes to try to regain that prestige by fostering the reforms the church badly needed. Instead, the papacy turned, almost as if in compensation for the loss of its temporal supremacy in Europe, to regaining secular authority in central Italy. The Renaissance papacy provided little spiritual leadership and contributed to a further decline in the moral leadership of the popes.

The Renaissance Papacy

Historians use the phrase "Renaissance papacy" to refer to the line of popes from the end of the Great Schism (1417) to the beginnings of the Reformation in the early sixteenth century. The primary concern of the papacy is governing the Catholic church as its spiritual leader. But as heads of the church, popes had temporal preoccupations as well, and the story of the Renaissance papacy is really an account of how the latter came to overshadow the popes' spiritual functions. In the process, the Renais-

sance papacy and the Catholic church became noticeably secularized.

The preoccupation of the popes with the territory of the Papal States and Italian politics was not new to the Renaissance. Popes had been temporal as well as spiritual rulers for centuries. The manner in which Renaissance popes pursued their temporal interests, however, especially their use of intrigue, deceit, and open bloodshed, was shocking. Undoubtedly, the popes were motivated in part by the desire to maintain their independence. One papal supporter expressed it this way: "I used to think that it would be well to separate completely religious authority from temporal power, but now I see that virtue without power is only ridiculous. The Pope of Rome, without the papal realm, could only be the lackey of kings and princes."[24] In the world of Renaissance politics, maintaining a political state was not easy. It demanded a ruthlessness unbecoming to the spiritual leader of Christendom. Of all the Renaissance popes, Julius II (1503–1513) was most involved in war and politics. The fiery "warrior-pope" personally led armies against his enemies, much to the disgust of pious Christians who viewed the pope as a spiritual leader. The great humanist Erasmus (see Chapter 14) witnessed the triumphant entry of Julius II into Bologna at the head of his troops and later wrote scathing indictments of the papal proclivity for warfare. With Julius II in mind, he proclaimed in *The Complaint of Peace:* "How, O bishop standing in the room of the Apostles, dare you teach the people the things that pertain to war?"

To further their territorial aims in the Papal States, the popes needed financial resources and loyal servants. Preoccupation with finances was not new, but its grossness received considerable comment: "Whenever I entered the chambers of the ecclesiastics of the Papal court, I found brokers and clergy engaged and reckoning money which lay in heaps before them."[25] Since they were not hereditary monarchs, popes could not build dynasties over several generations and came to rely on the practice of nepotism to promote their families' interests. Pope Sixtus IV (1471–1484), for example, made five of his nephews cardinals and gave them an abundance of church offices to build up their finances (the word *nepotism* is, in fact, derived from *nepos*, meaning nephew). Alexander VI (1492–1503), a member of the Borgia family who was known for his debauchery and sensuality, raised one son, one nephew, and the brother of one mistress to the cardinalate. A Venetian envoy stated that Alexander, "joyous by nature, thought of nothing but the aggrandizement of his children." Alexander scandalized the church by encouraging his son Cesare to carve a territorial state in central Italy out of the territories of the Papal States.

The Renaissance popes were great patrons of Renaissance culture, and their efforts made Rome the focal point of the High Renaissance at the beginning of the sixteenth century. For the warrior-pope Julius II, the patronage of Renaissance culture was mostly a matter of policy as he endeavored to add to the splendor of his pontificate by tearing down the basilica of Saint Peter and beginning construction of the greatest building in Christendom, Saint Peter's Basilica. Julius's successor, Leo X (1513–1521), was also a patron of Renaissance culture, not as a matter of policy, but as a deeply involved participant. Such might be expected of the son of Lorenzo de' Medici. Made an archbishop at the age of eight and a cardinal at thirteen, he was raised in the lap of Renaissance luxury. He acquired a refined taste in art, manners, and social life among the Florentine Renaissance elite. He became pope at the age of thirty-seven, supposedly remarking to the Venetian ambassador, "Let us enjoy the papacy, since God has given it to us." Humanists were made papal secretaries, Raphael was commissioned to do paintings, and the construction of Saint Peter's was accelerated as Rome became the literary and artistic center of the Renaissance.

Of course, the popes' cultivation of Renaissance culture was not blameworthy in itself. But it did have adverse effects. It was expensive and led to ever more dubious methods of increasing revenue. It is no secret that to raise money to build the new Saint Peter's, Leo X authorized the sale of a special jubilee indulgence in Germany, an indulgence that led indirectly to Luther's Ninety-Five Theses and his defiance of the Catholic church. With all of his political skills and refined taste, Leo X, the acknowledged spiritual leader of Christendom, was unable to comprehend the depth of Luther's religious feeling.

Conclusion

Whether the Renaissance represents the end of the Middle Ages or the beginning of a new era, a frequently debated topic among medieval and Renaissance historians, is perhaps an irrelevant question. The Renaissance was a period of transition that witnessed a continuation of the economic, political, and social trends that had begun in the High Middle Ages. It was also a movement in which intellectuals and artists proclaimed a new vision of humankind and raised fundamental questions about the value and importance of the individual. Of course, intellectuals and artists wrote and painted for the upper classes, and the brilliant intellectual, cultural, and artistic accomplishments of the Renaissance were really products of and for the elite. The ideas of the Renaissance did not have a broad base among the masses of the people. As Lorenzo the Magnificent, ruler of Florence, once commented, "Only men of noble birth can obtain perfection. The poor, who work with their hands and have no time to cultivate their minds, are incapable of it."

The Renaissance did, however, raise new questions about medieval traditions. In advocating a return to the early sources of Christianity and criticizing current religious practices, the humanists raised fundamental issues about the Catholic church, which was still an important institution. In the sixteenth century, the intellectual revolution of the fifteenth century gave way to a religious renaissance that touched the lives of people, including the masses, in new and profound ways. After the Reformation, Europe would never again be the unified Christian commonwealth it once believed it was.

NOTES

1. Quoted in Jacob Burckhardt, *The Civilization of the Renaissance in Italy*, trans. S. G. C. Middlemore (London, 1960), p. 81.
2. Baldassare Castiglione, *The Book of the Courtier*, trans. Charles S. Singleton (Garden City, N.Y., 1959), pp. 288–89.
3. Quoted in De Lamar Jensen, *Renaissance Europe* (Lexington, Mass., 1981), p. 94.
4. Quoted in Iris Origo, "The Domestic Enemy: The Eastern Slaves in Tuscany in the Fourteenth and Fifteenth Centuries," *Speculum* 30 (1955): 333.

5. Gene Brucker, ed., *The Society of Renaissance Florence* (New York, 1971), p. 190.

6. Quoted in Garrett Mattingly, *Renaissance Diplomacy* (Baltimore, 1964), p. 42.

7. Ibid., p. 95.

8. Niccolò Machiavelli, *The Prince*, trans. David Wootton (Indianapolis, 1995), p. 48.

9. Ibid., p. 55.

10. Ibid., pp. 27, 77, 80.

11. Niccolò Machiavelli, *The Discourses*, trans. Christian Detmold (New York, 1950), p. 148.

12. Petrarch, "Epistle to Posterity," *Letters from Petrarch*, trans. Morris Bishop (Bloomington, Ind., 1966), pp. 6–7.

13. Quoted in Hans Baron, "Cicero and the Roman Civic Spirit in the Middle Ages and Early Renaissance," *Bulletin of the John Rylands Library* 22 (1938): 90.

14. Bernhardt J. Hurwood, trans., *The Facetiae of Giovanni Francesco Poggio Bracciolini* (New York, 1968), p. 57.

15. Quoted in Frances Yates, *Giordano Bruno and the Hermetic Tradition* (Chicago, 1964), p. 211.

16. Giovanni Pico della Mirandola, *Oration on the Dignity of Man*, in E. Cassirer, P. O. Kristeller, J. H. Randall, Jr., eds., *The Renaissance Philosophy of Man* (Chicago, 1948), p. 225.

17. Ibid., pp. 247–49.

18. W. H. Woodward, *Vittorino da Feltre and Other Humanist Educators* (Cambridge, 1897), p. 102.

19. Ibid., pp. 106–7.

20. Quoted in Iris Origo, "The Education of Renaissance Man," *The Light of the Past* (New York, 1959), p. 136.

21. Quoted in Elizabeth G. Holt, ed., *A Documentary History of Art* (Garden City, N.Y., 1957), 1:286.

22. Quoted in Rosa M. Letts, *The Cambridge Introduction to Art: The Renaissance* (Cambridge, 1981), p. 86.

23. Quoted in Johan Huizinga, *The Waning of the Middle Ages* (Garden City, N.Y., 1956), p. 265.

24. Quoted in Emil Lucki, *History of the Renaissance* (Salt Lake City, 1964), 2:46.

25. Quoted in Alexander C. Flick, *The Decline of the Medieval Church* (London, 1930), 1:180.

SUGGESTIONS FOR FURTHER READING

The classic study of the Italian Renaissance is J. Burckhardt, *The Civilization of the Renaissance in Italy*, trans. S. G. C. Middlemore (London, 1960), first published in 1860. General works on the Renaissance in Europe include De Lamar Jensen, *Renaissance Europe* (Lexington, Mass., 1981); E. Breisach, *Renaissance Europe, 1300–1517* (New York, 1973); J. Hale, *The Civilization of Europe in the Renaissance* (New York, 1994); and the classic work by M. P. Gilmore, *The World of Humanism, 1453–1517* (New York, 1962). Although many of its interpretations are outdated, W. Ferguson's *Europe in Transition, 1300–1520* (Boston, 1962), contains a wealth of information. The brief study by P. Burke, *The Renaissance* (Atlantic Highlands, N.J., 1987), is a good summary of recent literature on the Renaissance.

Brief, but basic works on Renaissance economic matters are H. A. Miskimin, *The Economy of Early Renaissance Europe, 1300–1460* (New York, 1975) and *The Economy of Later Renaissance Europe, 1460–1600* (New York, 1978). Numerous facets of social life in the Renaissance are examined in J. R. Hale, *Renaissance Europe: The Individual and Society* (London, 1971); J. Gage, *Life in Italy at the Time of the Medici* (New York,

1968); B. Pullan, *Rich and Poor in Renaissance Venice* (Cambridge, Mass., 1971); J. H. Langbein, *Prosecuting Crime in the Renaissance* (Cambridge, Mass., 1974); and G. Ruggiero, *The Boundaries of Eros: Sex Crime and Sexuality in Renaissance Venice* (Oxford, 1985). On family and marriage, see D. Herlihy, *The Family in Renaissance Italy* (St. Louis, 1974); R. Kelso, *Doctrine of the Lady of the Renaissance*, 2d ed. (Urbana, Ill., 1978); and the valuable C. Klapisch-Zuber, *Women, Family, and Ritual in Renaissance Italy* (Chicago, 1985). On women, see M. L. King, *Women of the Renaissance* (Chicago, 1991).

The best overall study of the Italian city-states is L. Martines, *Power and Imagination: City-States in Renaissance Italy* (New York, 1979), although D. Hay and J. Law, *Italy in the Age of the Renaissance* (London, 1989), is also a good survey. A new approach to the culture of Renaissance Italy can be found in P. Burke, *The Italian Renaissance* (Princeton, N.J., 1986). There is an enormous literature on Renaissance Florence. The best introduction is G. A. Brucker, *Renaissance Florence*, rev. ed. (Berkeley and Los Angeles, 1983). On the Medici period, see J. R. Hale, *Florence and the Medici: The*

Pattern of Control (London, 1977). Works on other Italian states and rulers include D. S. Chambers, *The Imperial Age of Venice, 1380–1580* (New York, 1970); and W. L. Gundersheimer, *Ferrara: The Style of a Renaissance Despotism* (Princeton, N.J., 1973). A popular biography of Isabella d'Este is G. Marek, *The Bed and the Throne* (New York, 1976). On the *condottieri,* see M. Mallett, *Mercenaries and Their Masters: Warfare in Renaissance Italy* (Totowa, 1974). The work by G. Mattingly, *Renaissance Diplomacy* (Boston, 1955) remains the basic one on the subject. Machiavelli's life can be examined in J. R. Hale, *Machiavelli and Renaissance Italy* (New York, 1960); and his thought in F. Gilbert, *Machiavelli and Guicciardini: Politics and History in Sixteenth-Century Florence* (Princeton, N.J., 1965).

Brief introductions to Renaissance humanism can be found in D. R. Kelley, *Renaissance Humanism* (Boston, 1991); C. G. Nauert, Jr., *Humanism and the Culture of Renaissance Europe* (Cambridge, 1995); and F. B. Artz, *Renaissance Humanism, 1300–1550* (Oberlin, Ohio, 1966). An important collection of essays can be found in P. O. Kristeller, *Renaissance Thought: The Classic, Scholastic and Humanist Strains* (New York, 1961). The fundamental work on fifteenth-century civic humanism is H. Baron, *The Crisis of the Early Italian Renaissance,* 2d ed. (Princeton, N.J., 1966). The classic work on humanist education is W. H. Woodward, *Vittorino da Feltre and Other Humanist Educators* (New York, 1963), first published in 1897. A basic work on the writing of history in the Italian Renaissance is E. Cochrane, *Historians and Historiography in the Italian Renaissance* (Chicago, 1981). On Guicciardini, see M. Philips, *Francesco Guicciardini: The Historian's Craft* (Toronto, 1977). The impact of printing is exhaustively examined in E. Eisenstein, *The Printing Press as an Agent of Change,* 2 vols. (New York, 1978).

For brief introductions to Renaissance art, see R. M. Letts, *The Cambridge Introduction to Art: The Renaissance* (Cambridge, 1981); and B. Cole and A. Gealt, *Art of the Western World* (New York, 1989), Chapters 6–8. Good surveys of Renaissance art include M. Levy, *Early Renaissance* (Harmondsworth, 1967); A. Smith, *The Renais-* *sance and Mannerism in Italy* (New York, 1971); and L. Murray, *The High Renaissance* (New York, 1967). For studies of individual artists, see R. Jones and N. Penny, *Raphael* (New Haven, Conn., 1983); M. Kemp, *Leonardo da Vinci: The Marvellous Works of Nature and of Man* (London, 1981); and D. Summers, *Michelangelo and the Language of Art* (Princeton, N.J., 1981). Also of value is B. Cole, *The Renaissance Artist at Work from Pisano to Titian* (London, 1983). On music, see the general work by S. Sadie and A. Latham, *Music Guide* (Englewood Cliffs, N.J., 1987); and the specialized work by H. M. Brown, *Music in the Renaissance* (Englewood Cliffs, N.J., 1976).

For a general work on the political development of Europe in the Renaissance, see J. H. Shennan, *The Origins of the Modern European State, 1450–1725* (London, 1974). On France, see J. R. Major, *Representative Institutions in Renaissance France, 1421–1559* (Madison, Wis., 1960); and P. M. Kendall's biography, *Louis XI: The Universal Spider* (New York, 1971). Early Renaissance England is examined in J. R. Lander, *Crown and Nobility, 1450–1509* (London, 1976). On the first Tudor king, see S. B. Chrimes, *Henry VII* (Berkeley, 1972). Good coverage of Renaissance Spain can be found in J. N. Hillgarth, *The Spanish Kingdoms, 1250–1516,* vol. 2, *Castilian Hegemony, 1410–1516* (New York, 1978). Some good works on eastern Europe include P. W. Knoll, *The Rise of the Polish Monarchy* (Chicago, 1972); and C. A. Macartney, *Hungary: A Short History* (Edinburgh, 1962). On the Ottomans and their expansion, see H. Inalcik, *The Ottoman Empire: The Classical Age, 1300–1600* (London, 1973); and the classic work by S. Runciman, *The Fall of Constantinople, 1453* (Cambridge, 1965).

On problems of heresy and reform, see C. Crowder, *Unity, Heresy and Reform, 1378–1460* (London, 1977). Aspects of the Renaissance papacy can be examined in E. Lee, *Sixtus IV and Men of Letters* (Rome, 1978); and M. Mallett, *The Borgias* (New York, 1969). On Rome, see especially P. Partner, *Renaissance Rome, 1500–1559: A Portrait of a Society* (Berkeley, 1976).

CHAPTER
14

The Age of Reformation

On April 18, 1520, a lowly monk stood before the emperor and princes of Germany in the city of Worms. He had been called before this august gathering to answer charges of heresy, charges that could threaten his very life. The monk was confronted with a pile of his books and asked if he wished to defend them all or reject a part. Courageously, Martin Luther defended them all and asked to be shown where any part was in error on the basis of "Scripture and plain reason." The emperor was outraged by Luther's response and made his own position clear the next day: "Not only I, but you of this noble German nation, would be forever disgraced if by our negligence not only heresy but the very suspicion of heresy were to survive. After having heard yesterday the obstinate defense of Luther, I regret that I have so long delayed in proceeding against him and his false teaching. I will have no more to do with him." Luther's appearance at Worms set the stage for a serious challenge to the authority of the Catholic church. This was by no means the first crisis in the church's fifteen-hundred-year history, but its consequences were more far-reaching than anyone at Worms in 1520 could have imagined.

Throughout the Middle Ages, the Catholic church continued to assert its primacy of position. It had overcome defiance of its temporal authority by emperors while challenges to its doctrines had been crushed by the Inquisition and combated by new religious orders that carried its message of salvation to all the towns and villages of medieval Europe. The growth of the papacy had paralleled the growth of the church, but by the end of the Middle Ages challenges to papal authority from the rising power of monarchical states had resulted in a loss of papal temporal authority. An even greater threat to papal authority and church unity arose in the sixteenth century when the unity of Christendom was shattered by the Reformation.

The movement begun by Martin Luther when he made his dramatic stand quickly spread across Europe, a clear indication of dissatisfaction with Catholic

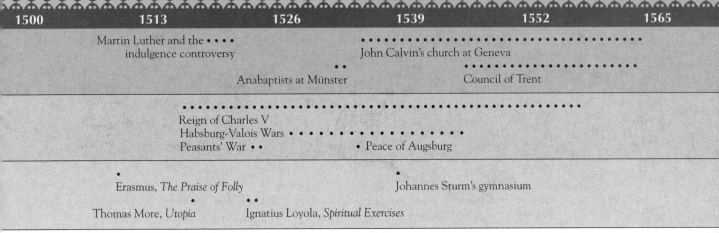

1500	1513	1526	1539	1552	1565

Martin Luther and the • • • •
indulgence controversy

John Calvin's church at Geneva

Anabaptists at Münster

Council of Trent

Reign of Charles V
Habsburg-Valois Wars • • • • • • • • • • • • • •
Peasants' War • • ● Peace of Augsburg

Erasmus, *The Praise of Folly*

Johannes Sturm's gymnasium

Thomas More, *Utopia*

Ignatius Loyola, *Spiritual Exercises*

practices. Within a short time, new forms of religious practices, doctrines, and organizations, including Zwinglianism, Calvinism, Anabaptism, and Anglicanism, were attracting adherents all over Europe. Although seemingly helpless to stop the new Protestant churches, the Catholic church also underwent a religious renaissance and managed by the mid-sixteenth century to revive its fortunes. Those historians who speak of the Reformation as the beginning of the modern world exaggerate its importance, but there is no doubt that the splintering of Christendom had consequences that ushered in new ways of thinking and at least prepared the ground for modern avenues of growth.

$\mathcal{P}$relude to Reformation: The Northern Renaissance

Martin Luther's reform movement was not the first in sixteenth-century Europe. Christian or northern Renaissance humanism, which evolved as Italian Renaissance humanism spread to northern Europe, had as one of its major goals the reform of Christendom. The new classical learning of the Italian Renaissance did not spread to the European countries north of the Alps until the second half of the fifteenth century. Northern Europe had fewer ties to the classical past than Italy and was initially less interested in recovering Greco-Roman culture. Gradually, however, a number of intellectuals and artists from the cities north of the Alps went to Italy and returned home enthusiastic about the new education and the recovery of ancient thought and literature that we associate with Italian Renaissance humanism. In this manner, Italian humanism spread to the north, but with some noticeable differences. What, then, are the distinguishing characteristics of northern Renaissance humanism, a movement that flourished from the late fifteenth century until it was overwhelmed by the Reformation in the 1520s?

Christian or Northern Renaissance Humanism

Like their Italian counterparts, northern humanists cultivated a knowledge of the classics, the one common bond that united all humanists into a kind of international fellowship. The northern humanists brought out translations or scholarly editions of the classics for the printing press and sought to reconcile the ethical content of those works with Christian ethics. In the classics, northern humanists felt they had found a morality more humane than the theological arguments of the medieval scholastics.

In returning to the writings of antiquity, northern humanists (who have been called Christian humanists by historians because of their profound preoccupation with religion) also focused on the sources of early Christianity, the Holy Scriptures and the writings of such Church Fathers as Augustine, Ambrose, and Jerome. In these early Christian writings, they discovered a simple religion that they came to feel had been distorted by the complicated theological arguments of the Middle Ages. Their interest in Christian writings also led them to master Greek for the express purpose of reading the Greek New Testament and such early Greek

Church Fathers as John Chrysostom. Some northern humanists even mastered Hebrew to study the Old Testament in its original language.

Although Christian humanists sought positions as teachers and scholars, the influence of scholastic theologians in the universities often made it difficult for them to do so. So long as they stuck to the classics, Christian humanists coexisted amicably with the scholastic theologians, but when they began to call for radical change in the methods and aims of theological study, they ran into bitter opposition. On the other hand, northern Renaissance humanists had opportunities to serve as secretaries to kings, princes, and cities, where their ability to write good prose and deliver orations made them useful. Support for humanism came from other directions as well, notably from patricians, lawyers, and civic officials, especially in the south German cities.

The most important characteristic of northern humanism was its reform program. With their belief in the ability of human beings to reason and improve themselves, the northern humanists felt that through education in the sources of classical, and especially Christian, antiquity, they could instill a true inner piety or an inward religious feeling that would bring about a reform of the church and society. For this reason, Christian humanists supported schools, brought out new editions of the classics, and prepared new editions of the Bible and writings of the Church Fathers. In the preface to his edition of the Greek New Testament, the famous humanist Erasmus wrote:

> Indeed, I disagree very much with those who are unwilling that Holy Scripture, translated into the vulgar tongue, be read by the uneducated, as if Christ taught such intricate doctrines that they could scarcely be understood by very few theologians, or as if the strength of the Christian religion consisted in men's ignorance of it ... I would that even the lowliest women read the Gospels and the Pauline Epistles. And I would that they were translated into all languages so that they could be read and understood not only by Scots and Irish but also by Turks and Saracens.... Would that, as a result, the farmer sing some portion of them at the plow, the weaver hum some parts of them to the movement of his shuttle, the traveler lighten the weariness of the journey with stories of this kind![1]

This belief in the power of education would remain an important characteristic of European civilization. Like later intellectuals, Christian humanists believed that to change society they must first change the human beings who compose it. While some have viewed the Christian humanists as naive, they themselves were very optimistic. Erasmus proclaimed in a letter to Pope Leo X: "I congratulate this our age—which bids fair to be an age of gold, if ever such there was—wherein I see ... three of the chief blessings of humanity are about to be restored to her. I mean, first, that truly Christian piety, ... secondly, learning of the best sort, ... and thirdly, the public and lasting concord of Christendom...."[2] This belief that a golden age could be achieved by applying the new learning to the reform of church and society proved to be a common bond among the Christian humanists. The turmoil of the Reformation shattered much of this intellectual optimism, as the lives and careers of two of the most prominent Christian humanists, Desiderius Erasmus and Thomas More, illustrate.

ERASMUS

The most influential of all the Christian humanists, and in a way the symbol of the movement itself, was Desiderius Erasmus (1466–1536), who formulated and popularized the reform program of Christian humanism. Born in Holland, Erasmus was educated at one of the schools of the Brothers of the Common Life. He wandered to France, England, Italy, Germany, and Switzerland, conversing everywhere in the classical Latin that might be called his mother tongue. By 1500, he had turned seriously toward religious studies where he concentrated on reconciling the classics and Christianity through their common ethical focus.

In 1500, Erasmus published the *Adages*, an anthology of proverbs from ancient authors that showed his ability in the classics. The *Handbook of the Christian Knight*, printed in 1503, reflected his preoccupation with religion. He called his conception of religion "the philosophy of Christ," by which he meant that Christianity should be a guiding philosophy for the direction of daily life rather than the system of dogmatic beliefs and practices that the medieval church seemed to stress. In other words, he emphasized inner piety and deemphasized the external forms of religion (such as the sacraments, pilgrimages, fasts, veneration of saints, and relics). To return to the simplicity of the early church, people needed to understand the original meaning of the Scriptures and early Church Fathers. Since Erasmus thought that the standard Latin edition of the Bible, known as the Vulgate, contained errors, he edited the Greek text of the New Testament from the earliest available manuscripts and published it, along with a new Latin translation, in 1516.

To Erasmus, the reform of the church meant spreading an understanding of the philosophy of Christ, providing enlightened education in the sources of early Christianity, and making commonsense criticism of the abuses in the church. The latter is especially evident in his work, *The Praise of Folly*, written in 1511. It is a satirical view of his contemporary society in which folly, personified as a woman, shows how she dominates the affairs of humankind. Through this scheme, Erasmus was able to engage in a humorous, yet effective criticism of the most corrupt practices of his own society. He was especially harsh on the abuses within the ranks of the clergy (see the box on p. 458).

Erasmus's reform program was not destined to effect the reform of the church that he so desired. His moderation and his emphasis on education were quickly overwhelmed by the violence unleashed by the passions of the Reformation. Undoubtedly, though, his work helped to prepare the way for the Reformation; as contemporaries proclaimed, "Erasmus laid the egg that Luther hatched." Yet Erasmus eventually disapproved of Luther and the Protestant reformers. He had no intention of destroying the unity of the medieval Christian church, since his whole program was based on reform within the church.

THOMAS MORE

Born the son of a London lawyer, Thomas More (1478–1535) received the benefits of a good education. Although trained in the law, he took an avid interest in the new classical learning and became proficient in both Latin and Greek. Like the Italian humanists who believed in putting their learning at the service of the state, More entered upon a public career that ultimately took him to the highest reaches of power as lord chancellor of England.

His career in government service, however, did not keep More from the intellectual and spiritual interests that were so dear to him. He was well acquainted with other English humanists and became an intimate friend of Erasmus. He made translations from Greek authors and wrote both prose and poetry in Latin. A deeply devout man, he spent many hours in prayer and private devotions. Many praised his household as a shining model of Christian family life.

More's most famous work, and one of the most controversial of his age, was *Utopia*, written in 1516. This literary masterpiece is an account of the idealistic life and institutions of the community of Utopia (literally "nowhere"), an imaginary island in the vicinity of the New World. It reflects More's own concerns with the economic, social, and political problems of his day. He presented a new social system in which cooperation

◆ **Erasmus.** Desiderius Erasmus was the most influential of the Northern Renaissance humanists. He sought to restore Christianity to the early simplicity found in the teachings of Christ. This portrait of Erasmus was painted in 1523 by Hans Holbein the Younger, who had formed a friendship with the great humanist while they were both in Basel.

and reason replaced power and fame as the proper motivating agents for human society. Utopian society, therefore, is based on communal ownership rather than private property. All persons work but six hours a day, regardless of occupation, and are rewarded according to their needs. Possessing abundant leisure time and relieved of competition and greed, Utopians were free to do wholesome and enriching things. As More stated in Book II: "All the rest of the twenty-four [hours] they're free to do what they like—not to waste their time in idleness or self-indulgence, but to make good use of it in some congenial activity."[3] More envisioned Utopia as an orderly world where social relations, recreation, and even travel were carefully controlled for the moral welfare of society and its members.

In serving King Henry VIII, More came face to face with the abuses and corruption he had criticized in

The Praise of Folly is one of the most famous pieces of literature of the sixteenth century. Erasmus, who wrote it in a short period of time during a visit to the home of Thomas More, considered it a "little diversion" from his "serious work." Yet both contemporaries and later generations have appreciated "this laughing parody of every form and rank of human life." In this selection, Erasmus belittles one of his favorite objects of scorn—the monks.

Erasmus, *The Praise of Folly*

Those who are the closest to these [the theologians] in happiness are generally called "the religious" or "monks," both of which are deceiving names, since for the most part they stay as far away from religion as possible and frequent every sort of place. I cannot, however, see how any life could be more gloomy than the life of these monks if I [Folly] did not assist them in many ways. Though most people detest these men so much that accidentally meeting one is considered to be bad luck, the monks themselves believe that they are magnificent creatures. One of their chief beliefs is that to be illiterate is to be of a high state of sanctity, and so they make sure that they are not able to read. Another is that when braying out their gospels in church they are making themselves very pleasing and satisfying to God, when in fact they are uttering these psalms as a matter of repetition rather than from their hearts. . . .

Moreover, it is amusing to find that they insist that everything be done in fastidious detail, as if employing the orderliness of mathematics, a small mistake in which would be a great crime. Just so many knots must be on each shoe and the shoelace may be of only one specified color; just so much lace is allowed on each habit; the girdle must be of just the right material and width; the hood of a certain shape and capacity; their hair of just so many fingers' length; and finally they can sleep only the specified number of hours per day. Can they not understand that, because of a variety of bodies and temperaments, all this equality of restrictions is in fact very unequal? Nevertheless, because of all this detail that they employ they think that they are superior to all other people. And what is more, amid all their pretense of Apostolic charity, the members of one order will denounce the members of another order clamorously because of the way in which the habit has been belted or the slightly darker color of it. . . .

Many of them work so hard at protocol and at traditional fastidiousness that they think one heaven hardly a suitable reward for their labors; never recalling, however, that the time will come when Christ will demand a reckoning of that which he had prescribed, namely charity, and that he will hold their deeds of little account. One monk will then exhibit his belly filled with every kind of fish; another will profess a knowledge of over a hundred hymns. Still another will reveal a countless number of fasts that he has made, and will account for his large belly by explaining that his fasts have always been broken by a single large meal. Another will show a list of church ceremonies over which he has officiated so large that it would fill seven ships.

Utopia. But he did not allow the idealism of Utopia to outweigh his own ultimate realism, and in *Utopia* itself he justified his service to the king:

> If you can't completely eradicate wrong ideas, or deal with inveterate vices as effectively as you could wish, that's no reason for turning your back on public life altogether. You wouldn't abandon ship in a storm just because you couldn't control the winds. On the other hand, it's no use attempting to put across entirely new ideas, which will obviously carry no weight with people who are prejudiced against them. You must go to work indirectly. You must handle everything as tactfully as you can, and what you can't put right you must try to make as little wrong as possible. For things will never be perfect, until human beings are perfect—which I don't expect them to be for quite a number of years.[4]

More's religious devotion and belief in the universal Catholic church proved even more important than his service to the king, however. Always the man of conscience, More willingly gave up his life opposing England's break with the Roman Catholic church over the divorce of King Henry VIII.

*P*relude to Reformation: Church and Religion on the Eve of the Reformation

The institutional problems of the Catholic church in the fourteenth and fifteenth centuries, especially the failure of the Renaissance popes to provide spiritual leadership, were bound to affect the spiritual life of all Christendom. The general impression of the tenor of religious life on the eve of the Reformation is one of much deterioration, coupled with evidence of a continuing desire for meaningful religious experience from millions of devout lay people.

The Clergy

The economic changes of the Late Middle Ages and Renaissance and the continuing preoccupation of the papal court with finances had an especially strong impact upon the clergy. One need only read the names of the cardinals in the fifteenth century to realize that the highest positions of the clergy were increasingly held by either the nobility or the wealthier members of the bourgeoisie. At the same time, to enhance their revenues, high church officials accumulated church offices in ever-larger numbers. This practice of pluralism (the holding of many church offices) led, in turn, to the problem of absenteeism, as church officeholders neglected their episcopal duties and delegated the entire administration of their dioceses to priests, who were often underpaid and little interested in performing their duties.

At the same time, these same economic forces led to a growing division between the higher and lower clergy. While cardinals, archbishops, bishops, and abbots vied for church offices and accumulated great wealth, many members of the lower clergy—the parish priests—tended to exist at the same economic level as their parishioners. Social discontent grew, especially among those able and conscientious priests whose path to advancement was blocked by the nobles' domination of higher church offices. By the same token, pluralism on the lower levels left many parishes without episcopal direction of any kind. Such a lack of leadership often resulted in lower clergy of poor quality. The fifteenth century was rife with complaints about the ignorance and incapacity of parish priests, as well as their greed and sexual offenses.

Popular Religion

The atmosphere of the Late Middle Ages and Renaissance, with its uncertainty of life and immediacy of death, brought a craving for meaningful religious expression and certainty of salvation. This impulse, especially strong in Germany, expressed itself in two ways that often seemed contradictory.

One manifestation of religious piety in the fifteenth century was the almost mechanical view of the process of salvation. Collections of relics grew as more and more people sought certainty of salvation through their veneration. By 1509, Frederick the Wise, elector of Saxony and Luther's prince, had amassed over 5,000 relics to which were attached indulgences that could officially reduce one's time in purgatory by 1,443 years (an indulgence is a remission of all or part of the temporal punishment due to sin). Despite the physical dangers, increasing numbers of Christians made pilgrimages to such holy centers as Rome and Jerusalem to gain spiritual benefits.

Another form of religious piety, the quest for a tranquil spirituality, was evident in the popular mystical movement known as the Modern Devotion (see Chapter 12), which spawned the lay religious order, the Brothers and Sisters of the Common Life, and a reform of monastic life in Germany and the Low Countries. The best-known member of the Brothers of the Common Life in the fifteenth century was Thomas à Kempis (1380–1471), to whom most scholars ascribe the writing of the great mystical classic of the Modern Devotion, *The Imitation of Christ*.

One notable feature of *The Imitation of Christ* was its deemphasis of religious dogma. A life of inner piety, totally dedicated to the moral and ethical precepts of Christ, was preferable to dogma and intellectual speculation. As Thomas à Kempis stated, "Truly, at the day of judgment we shall not be examined by what we have read, but what we have done; not how well we have spoken, but how religiously we have lived." This portrayal of formal theology as secondary to living a good life had deep roots in an emphasis on the Bible as a Christian's primary guide to the true Christian life. In the New Testament, one could find models for the imitation of Christ that even the uneducated could understand. The copying and dissemination of the Bible, as well as its exposition, played an important role in the work of the Brothers of the Common Life.

Popular mysticism, then, as seen in the Modern Devotion, bears an important relationship to the Reformation. Although adherents of the Modern Devotion did not question the traditional beliefs or practices of the church, their deemphasis of them in favor of the inner life of the spirit and direct communion with God minimized the importance of the formal church and undermined the position of the church and its clergy in Christians' lives. At the same time, the movement gained its strength through its appeal to lay people, especially townspeople who liked its direct personal approach to religion.

What is striking about the revival of religious piety in the fifteenth century—whether expressed through such external forces as the veneration of relics and the buying of indulgences or the mystical path—was its adherence to the orthodox beliefs and practices of the Catholic church. The agitation for certainty of salvation and spiritual peace was done within the framework of the "holy mother Church." But disillusionment grew as the devout experienced the clergy's inability to live up to their expectations. The deepening of religious life, especially in the second half of the fifteenth century, found little echo among the worldly-wise clergy, and it is this environment that helps to explain the tremendous and immediate impact of Luther's ideas.

Martin Luther and the Reformation in Germany

The Protestant Reformation had its beginning in a typical medieval question—what must I do to be saved? Martin Luther, a deeply religious man, found an answer that did not fit within the traditional teachings of the late medieval church. Ultimately, he split with that church, destroying the religious unity of western Christendom. That other people were concerned with the same question is evident in the rapid spread of the Reformation. But religion was so entangled in the social, economic, and political forces of the period that the Protestant reformers' hope of transforming the church quickly proved illusory.

The Early Luther

Martin Luther was born on November 10, 1483, into a peasant family, although his father raised himself into the ranks of the lower bourgeoisie by going into mining. His father wanted him to become a lawyer, so Luther enrolled at the University of Erfurt where he received his bachelor's degree in 1502. In 1505, after becoming a master in the liberal arts, the young Martin began to study law. Luther was not content with the study of law and all along had shown religious inclinations. In the summer of 1505, en route back to Erfurt after a brief visit home, he was caught in a ferocious thunderstorm and vowed that, if he were spared, he would become a monk. He then entered the monastic order of the Augustinian Hermits in Erfurt, much to his father's disgust. While in the monastery, Luther focused on his major concern, the assurance of salvation. The traditional beliefs and practices of the church seemed unable to relieve his obsession with this question, especially evident in his struggle

with the sacrament of penance or confession. The sacraments were a Catholic's chief means of receiving God's grace; that of confession offered the opportunity to have one's sins forgiven. Luther spent hours confessing his sins, but he was always doubtful. Had he remembered all of his sins? Even more, how could a hopeless sinner be acceptable to a totally just and all-powerful God? Luther threw himself into his monastic routine with a vengeance:

> I was indeed a good monk and kept my order so strictly that I could say that if ever a monk could get to heaven through monastic discipline, I was that monk. . . . And yet my conscience would not give me certainty, but I always doubted and said, "You didn't do that right. You weren't contrite enough. You left that out of your confession." The more I tried to remedy an uncertain, weak and troubled conscience with human traditions, the more I daily found it more uncertain, weaker and more troubled.[5]

Despite his herculean efforts, Luther achieved no certainty and even came, as he once expressed it, to hate "this just God who punishes sinners."

To help overcome his difficulties, his superiors recommended that the intelligent, yet disturbed monk study theology. He received his doctorate in 1512 and then became a professor in the theological faculty at the University of Wittenberg, lecturing on the Bible. Probably sometime between 1513 and 1516, through his study of the Bible, he arrived at an answer to his problem.

Luther's dilemma had derived from his concept of the "justice of God," which he interpreted as a punitive justice in which God weighs the merits or good works performed by humans as a necessary precondition for salvation. To Luther it appeared that the church was saying that one must earn salvation by good works. In Luther's eye, human beings, weak and powerless in the sight of an almighty God, could never do enough to justify salvation in these terms. Through his study of the Bible, especially his work on Paul's Epistle to the Romans, Luther rediscovered another way of viewing the justice of God:

> Night and day I pondered until I saw the connection between the justice of God and the statement that "the just shall live by his faith." Then I grasped that the justice of God is that righteousness by which through grace and sheer mercy God justifies us through faith. Thereupon I felt myself to be reborn and to have gone through open doors into paradise.[6]

To Luther, the "justice of God" was now not a punitive justice but the grace of God that bestows salvation freely to humans, not through their good works, but through the sacrifice of Christ on the cross. Even faith or the power of belief is a product of divine grace or a gift of God. Humans do nothing to merit grace; it is purely God's decision. The doctrine of justification by grace through faith alone became the primary doctrine of the Protestant Reformation (justification is the act by which a person is made deserving of salvation). Since Luther had arrived at this doctrine from his study of Scripture, the Bible became for Luther as for all other Protestants the chief guide to religious truth. Justification by faith and the Bible as the sole authority in religious affairs were the twin pillars of the Protestant Reformation.

The event that propelled Luther into an open confrontation with church officials and forced him to see the theological implications of justification by faith alone was the indulgence controversy. In 1517, Pope Leo X had issued a special jubilee indulgence to finance the ongoing construction of the new Saint Peter's Basilica (see Chapter 13). This special indulgence was connected to political and ecclesiastical affairs in Germany through one Albrecht of Brandenburg. Though he was already both bishop of Halberstadt and archbishop of Magdeburg, Albrecht purchased a special dispensation from Pope Leo X to obtain yet another church office, the archbishopric of Mainz. To get the money, Albrecht borrowed from the Fugger banking firm in Augsburg, which paid the pope. Albrecht was then given the rights to sell the special jubilee indulgence in Germany for ten years, with half of the proceeds going to the Fuggers to pay off his debt and the other half to Rome to rebuild Saint Peter's. Johann Tetzel, a rambunctious Dominican, hawked the indulgences with the slogan, "As soon as the coin in the coffer rings, the soul from purgatory springs."

Luther was greatly distressed by the sale of indulgences, certain that people were simply guaranteeing their eternal damnation by relying on these pieces of paper to assure themselves of salvation. In response, he issued his Ninety-Five Theses, although scholars are unsure whether he nailed them to a church door in Wittenberg, as is traditionally alleged, or mailed them to his ecclesiastical superior. In either case, his theses were a stunning indictment of the abuses in the sale of indulgences (see the box on p. 462). If the pope had the power to grant indulgences, "Why does not the Pope empty purgatory for the sake of most holy love and the supreme need of souls?" It is doubtful that Luther intended any break with the church over the issue of

◆ **Luther and the Wittenberg Reformers.** This painting by Lucas Cranach the Younger shows the reformers of Wittenberg with their prince, Elector John Frederick of Saxony. Luther is at the far left; Philip Melanchthon is at the far right. The powerful presence of John Frederick in the center foreground reminds us of how much Luther's reform movement depended upon the support of German rulers.

indulgences. If the pope had clarified the use of indulgences, as Luther wished, then he would probably have been satisfied and the controversy closed. But the Renaissance pope Leo X did not take the issue seriously and is even reported to have said that Luther was simply "some drunken German who will amend his ways when

≈ *Luther and the Ninety-Five Theses* ≈

To most historians, the publication of Luther's Ninety-Five Theses marks the beginning of the Reformation. To Luther, they were simply a response to what he considered to be the blatant abuses of Johann Tetzel's selling of indulgences. Although written in Latin, the theses were soon translated into German and disseminated widely across Germany. They made an immense impression on Germans already dissatisfied with the ecclesiastical and financial policies of the papacy.

Martin Luther, Selections from the Ninety-Five Theses

5. The Pope has neither the will nor the power to remit any penalties beyond those he has imposed either at his own discretion or by canon law.

20. Therefore the Pope, by his plenary remission of all penalties, does not mean "all" in the absolute sense, but only those imposed by himself.

21. Hence those preachers of Indulgences are wrong when they say that a man is absolved and saved from every penalty by the Pope's Indulgences.

27. It is mere human talk to preach that the soul flies out [of purgatory] immediately the money clinks in the collection-box.

28. It is certainly possible that when the money clinks in the collection-box greed and avarice can increase; but the intercession of the Church depends on the will of God alone.

45. Christians should be taught that he who sees a needy person and passes him by, although he gives money for pardons, wins for himself not Papal Indulgences but the wrath of God.

50. Christians should be taught that, if the Pope knew the exactions of the preachers of Indulgences, he would rather have the basilica of St. Peter reduced

to ashes than built with the skin, flesh and bones of his sheep.

81. This wanton preaching of pardons makes it difficult even for learned men to redeem respect due to the Pope from the slanders or at least the shrewd questionings of the laity.

82. For example: "Why does not the Pope empty purgatory for the sake of most holy love and the supreme need of souls? This would be the most righteous of reasons, if he can redeem innumerable souls for sordid money with which to build a basilica, the most trivial of reasons."

86. Again: "Since the Pope's wealth is larger than that of the crassest Crassi of our time, why does he not build this one basilica of St. Peter with his own money, rather than with that of the faithful poor?"

88. Again: "What greater good would be done to the Church if the Pope were to bestow these remissions and dispensations, not once, as now, but a hundred times a day, on any believer whatever."

90. To suppress these most conscientious questionings of the laity by authority only, instead of refuting them by reason, is to expose the Church and the Pope to the ridicule of their enemies, and to make Christian people unhappy.

91. If, therefore, pardons were preached in accordance with the spirit and mind of the Pope, all these difficulties would be easily overcome, or rather would never have arisen.

94. Christians should be exhorted to seek earnestly to follow Christ, their Head, through penalties, deaths, and hells.

95. And let them thus be more confident of entering heaven through many tribulations rather than through a false assurance of peace.

he sobers up." But the development of printing prevented such a speedy resolution. A German translation of the Ninety-Five Theses was quickly printed in thousands of copies and received sympathetically in a Germany that had a long tradition of dissatisfaction with papal policies and power.

The controversy reached an important turning point with the Leipzig Debate in July 1519. There Luther's opponent, the capable Catholic theologian Johann Eck, forced Luther to move beyond indulgences and deny the

authority of popes and councils. In effect, Luther was compelled to see the consequences of his new theology. At the beginning of 1520, he proclaimed: "Farewell, unhappy, hopeless, blasphemous Rome! The Wrath of God has come upon you, as you deserve. We have cared for Babylon, and she is not healed: let us then, leave her, that she may be the habitation of dragons, spectres, and witches."[7] At the same time, Luther was convinced that he was doing God's work and had to proceed regardless of the consequences. To a friend who had urged moderation, he exclaimed: "Let there be a new and great conflagration, who can resist the counsel of God? Who knows whether these insensate men are not predestined by Him as the means of revealing the truth? . . . God alone is in this business. We are carried away by Him. We are led rather than lead."[8]

In three pamphlets published in 1520, Luther moved toward a more definite break with the Catholic church. The *Address to the Nobility of the German Nation* was a political tract written in German. The papacy, Luther declared, had used three claims to prevent reform: that the church is superior to the state, that only the pope can interpret Scripture, and that only the pope can call a council. Luther believed that all three were false, and he called upon the German princes to overthrow the papacy in Germany and establish a reformed German church. *The Babylonian Captivity of the Church*, written in Latin for theologians, attacked the sacramental system as the means by which the pope and church had held the real meaning of the Gospel in captivity for a thousand years. He called for the reform of monasticism and for the clergy to marry. While virginity is good, Luther argued, marriage is better, and freedom of choice is best. *On the Freedom of a Christian Man* was a short treatise on the doctrine of salvation. It is faith alone, not good works, which justifies, frees, and brings salvation through Christ. Being saved and freed by his faith in Christ, however, does not free the Christian from doing good works. Rather, he performs good works out of gratitude to God. "Good works do not make a good man, but a good man does good works." From faith flows love and from love a free spirit that is disposed to serve one's neighbor voluntarily. Hence, "a Christian man is the most free lord of all, and subject to none; a Christian man is the most dutiful servant of all, and subject to everyone."[9]

Unable to countenance Luther's forcefully worded dissent from traditional Catholic teachings, the church excommunicated him in January 1521. He was also summoned to appear before the imperial diet or Reichstag of the Holy Roman Empire in Worms, convened by the newly elected emperor Charles V (1519–1556). Expected to recant the heretical doctrines he had espoused, Luther refused and made the famous reply that became the battle cry of the Reformation:

> Since then Your Majesty and your lordships desire a simple reply, I will answer without horns and without teeth. Unless I am convicted by Scripture and plain reason—I do not accept the authority of popes and councils, for they have contradicted each other—my conscience is captive to the Word of God. I cannot and I

will not recant anything, for to go against conscience is neither right nor safe. Here I stand, I cannot do otherwise. God help me. Amen.[10]

Luther's heroic stand at Worms was once viewed as a step in the development of religious freedom, but that interpretation overlooked an important consideration. While Luther clearly placed his conscience above the authority of the church, he also believed that he had arrived at the truth, from which others were not allowed to deviate. As Luther once expressed it: "I have neither the power nor the will to deny the Word of God. If any man has a different opinion concerning me, he does not think straight or understand what I have actually said."

The young emperor Charles was outraged at Luther's audacity and gave his opinion that "a single friar who goes counter to all Christianity for a thousand years must be wrong." By the Edict of Worms, Martin Luther was made an outlaw within the empire. His works were to be burned and Luther himself captured and delivered to the emperor. Because of his religious conviction, Luther had been forced to defy both church and emperor and was now forced to depend on the German princes and people. As he did so, his religious movement became a revolution.

The Development of Lutheranism

After a brief period of hiding, Luther returned to Wittenberg at the beginning of 1522 and began to organize a reformed church. In the decade of the 1520s, Lutheranism had much appeal and spread rapidly. The University of Wittenberg served as a center for the diffusion of Luther's ideas. Between 1520 and 1560, 16,000 students from all over Germany matriculated at the university and returned home to spread Luther's teachings. The preaching of evangelical sermons, based on a return to the original message of the Bible, found favor throughout Germany. In city after city, the arrival of preachers presenting Luther's teachings was soon followed by a public debate in which the new preachers proved victorious. A reform of the church was then instituted by state authorities. Also useful to the spread of the Reformation were pamphlets illustrated with vivid woodcuts portraying the pope as a hideous Antichrist and titled with catchy phrases, such as "I Wonder Why There Is No Money in the Land" (which, of course, was an attack on papal greed). Luther also insisted on the use of music as a means to teach the Gospel, and his own "A Mighty Fortress Is Our God"

◆ **Woodcut: Luther versus the Pope.** In the 1520s, after Luther's return to Wittenberg, his teachings began to spread rapidly, ending ultimately in a reform movement supported by state authorities. Pamphlets containing picturesque woodcuts were important in the spread of Luther's ideas. In the woodcut shown here, the crucified Jesus attends Luther's service on the left, while on the right the pope is at a table selling indulgences.

became the battle hymn of the Reformation:

> *Standing alone are we undone, the Fiend would soon*
> *   enslave us;*
> *but for us fights a mighty One whom God has sent to save*
> *   us.*
> *Ask you who is this? Jesus Christ is He, Lord God of*
> *   Hosts*
> *There is no other God; He can and will uphold us.*

Lutheranism spread to both princely and ecclesiastical states in northern and central Germany as well as to two-thirds of the free imperial cities, especially those of southern Germany, where prosperous burghers, for both religious and secular reasons, became committed to Luther's cause. Nuremberg, where an active city council led by the dynamic city secretary Lazarus Spengler brought a conversion as early as 1525, was the first imperial city to convert to Lutheranism. At its outset, the Reformation in Germany was largely an urban phenomenon.

A series of crises in the mid-1520s made it apparent, however, that spreading the word of God was not as easy as Luther had originally envisioned, the usual plight of most reformers. Luther experienced dissent within his own ranks in Wittenberg from people such as Andreas Carlstadt, who wished to initiate a more radical reform by abolishing all relics, images, and the mass. Luther had no sooner dealt with them when he was faced with defection from the Christian humanists. Many had initially supported Luther, believing that he shared their goal of reforming the abuses within the church. But after 1521, when it became apparent that Luther's movement threatened the unity of Christendom, the older generation of Christian humanists, including Erasmus, broke with the reformer. A younger generation of Christian

Luther and the "Robbing and Murdering Hordes of Peasants"

The Peasants' War of 1524–1525 encompassed a series of risings by German peasants who were suffering from economic changes they did not comprehend. In a sense, it was part of a century of peasant discontent. Led by radical religious leaders, the revolts quickly became entangled with the religious revolt set in motion by Luther's defiance of the church. But it was soon clear that Luther himself did not believe in any way in social revolution. This excerpt is taken from Luther's pamphlet written in May 1525 at the height of the peasants' power, but not published until after their defeat.

Martin Luther, *Against the Robbing and Murdering Hordes of Peasants*

The peasants have taken on themselves the burden of three terrible sins against God and man, by which they have abundantly merited death in body and soul. In the first place they have sworn to be true and faithful, submissive and obedient, to their rulers, as Christ commands, when he says, "Render unto Caesar the things that are Caesar's," and in *Romans* XIII, "Let everyone be subject unto the higher powers." Because they are breaking this obedience, and are setting themselves against the higher powers, willfully and with violence, they have forfeited body and soul, as faithless, perjured, lying, disobedient knaves and scoundrels are wont to do. . . .

In the second place, they are starting a rebellion, and violently robbing and plundering monasteries and castles which are not theirs, by which they have a second time deserved death in body and soul, if only as highwaymen and murderers. . . . For rebellion is not simple murder, but is like a great fire, which attacks and lays waste a whole land. . . . Therefore, let everyone who can, smite, slay and stab, secretly or openly, remembering that nothing can be more poisonous, hurtful or devilish than a rebel. . . .

In the third place, they cloak this terrible and horrible sin with the Gospel, call themselves "Christian brothers," receive oaths and homage, and compel people to hold with them to these abominations. Thus they become the greatest of all blasphemers of God and slanderers of his holy Name, serving the devil, under the outward appearance of the Gospel, thus earning death in body and soul ten times over. . . . It does not help the peasants, when they pretend that, according to Genesis I and II, all things were created free and common, and that all of us alike have been baptized. . . . For baptism does not make men free in body and property, but in soul; and the Gospel does not make goods common. . . . Since the peasants, then, have brought both God and man down upon them and are already so many times guilty of death in body and soul, . . . I must instruct the worldly governors how they are to act in the matter with a clear conscience.

First, I will not oppose a ruler who, even though he does not tolerate the Gospel, will smite and punish these peasants without offering to submit the case to judgment. For he is within his rights, since the peasants are not contending any longer for the Gospel, but have become faithless, perjured, disobedient, rebellious murderers, robbers and blasphemers, whom even heathen rulers have the right and power to punish; nay, it is their duty to punish them, for it is just for this purpose that they bear the sword, and are "the ministers of God upon him that doeth evil. . . ."

---

humanists, however, played a significant role in Lutheranism. Philip Melanchthon (1497–1560) arrived in Wittenberg in 1518 (at the age of twenty-one) to teach Greek and Hebrew, was immediately attracted to Luther's ideas, and became his staunch supporter.

It was the Peasants' War that constituted Luther's greatest challenge in the mid-1520s. Peasant dissatisfaction in Germany stemmed from several sources. Many peasants had not been touched by the gradual economic improvement of the early sixteenth century. In some areas, especially southwestern Germany, influential local lords continued to abuse their peasants while new demands for taxes and other services caused them to wish for a return to "the good old days." Social discontent soon became entangled with religious revolt as peasants looked to Martin Luther for support. It was not Luther, however, but one of his ex-followers, the radical Thomas Müntzer, who inflamed the peasants against their rulers with his fiery language: "Strike while the iron is hot!" Revolt first erupted in southwestern Germany in June 1524 and spread northward and eastward.

Luther reacted quickly and vehemently against the peasants. In his pamphlet, *Against the Robbing and Murdering Hordes of Peasants*, he called upon the German princes to "stab, smite, and slay" the stupid and stubborn peasantry (see the box above). The issue was clear to Luther. Although convinced that he himself was compelled by the word of God to rebel against church authorities, he did not believe in social revolution. To Luther, the state and its rulers were ordained by God, who had given them the authority to maintain the peace and order necessary for the spread of the Gospel. It was the responsibility of subjects to obey these authorities, and it was the duty of princes to suppress all revolt. But Luther was no political thinker, and he certainly knew how much his reformation of the church depended upon the full support of the German princes and magistrates. Luther was fully prepared to lend religious dignity to the rulers in return for their ongoing support. In May 1525, the German princes ruthlessly massacred the remaining peasant hordes in a bloodbath at Frankenhausen. By this time, Luther found himself ever more dependent on state authorities for the growth and maintenance of his reformed church.

Church and State

Justification by faith alone was the starting point for most of Protestantism's major doctrines. Since Luther downplayed the role of good works in salvation, the sacraments also had to be redefined. No longer were they merit-earning works, but divinely established signs signifying the promise of salvation. Based on his interpretation of scriptural authority, Luther kept only two of the Catholic church's seven sacraments, baptism and the Lord's Supper. Baptism signified rebirth through grace. As to the sacrament of the Lord's Supper, Luther denied the Catholic doctrine of transubstantiation, which taught that the substance of the bread and wine is miraculously transformed into the body and blood of Christ. Yet he continued to insist upon the real presence of Christ's body and blood in the bread and wine given as a testament to God's forgiveness of sin.

Luther's emphasis on the importance of Scripture led him to reject the Catholic belief that the authority of Scripture must be supplemented by the traditions and decrees of the church. The word of God as revealed in the Bible was sufficient authority in religious affairs. A hierarchical priesthood was thus unnecessary since all Christians who followed the word of God were their own priests ("priesthood of all believers"). While Luther thus considered the true church to be an invisible one, the difficulties of actually creating a reformed church led him to believe that a visible, organized church was needed. Since the Catholic ecclesiastical hierarchy had been scrapped, Luther came to rely increasingly on the princes or state authorities to organize and guide the new Lutheran reformed churches. He had little choice. By the sixteenth century, secular authorities in Germany as elsewhere were already playing an important role in church affairs. By 1530, in the German states that had converted to Lutheranism, both princes and city councils appointed officials who visited churches in their territories and regulated matters of worship. The Lutheran churches in Germany (and later in Scandinavia) quickly became territorial or state churches in which the state supervised and disciplined church members.

As part of the development of these state-dominated churches, Luther also instituted new religious services to replace the mass. These featured a worship service consisting of a German liturgy that focused on Bible reading, preaching the word of God, and song. Following his own denunciation of clerical celibacy, Luther married a former nun, Katherina von Bora, in 1525. His union provided a model of married and family life for the new Protestant minister.

Germany and the Reformation: Religion and Politics

From its very beginning, the fate of Luther's movement was closely tied to political affairs. In 1519, Charles I, king of Spain and the grandson of the Emperor Maximilian, was elected Holy Roman Emperor as Charles V (1519–1556). Charles V ruled over an immense empire, consisting of Spain and its overseas possessions, the traditional Austrian Habsburg lands, Bohemia, Hungary, the Low Countries, and the kingdom of Naples in southern Italy. The extent of his possessions was reflected in the languages he used: "I speak Spanish to God, Italian to women, French to men, and German to my horse." Politically, Charles wanted to maintain his dynasty's control over his enormous empire; religiously, he hoped to preserve the unity of the Catholic faith throughout his empire. Despite his strengths, Charles spent a lifetime in futile pursuit of his goals. Four major problems—the French, the Turks, the papacy, and Germany's internal situation—cost him both his dream and his health. At the same time, the emperor's problems gave Luther's movement time to grow and organize before facing the concerted onslaught of the Catholic forces.

The chief political concern of Charles V was his rivalry with the king of France. Francis I (1515–1547), the benevolent despot of the Valois dynasty, proved a worthy adversary. Encircled by the possessions of the Habsburg empire, Francis became embroiled in conflict with Charles over disputed territories in southern France, the Netherlands, the Rhineland, northern Spain, and Italy. These conflicts, known as the Habsburg-Valois Wars, were fought intermittently over twenty-four years (1521–1544), preventing Charles from concentrating his attention on the Lutheran problem in Germany.

Meanwhile, Charles was faced with two other enemies. The Habsburg emperor expected papal cooperation in dealing with the Lutheran heresy. Papal policy, however, was guided by political considerations, not religious ones. Fearful of Charles's power in Italy, Pope Clement VII (1523–1534) joined the side of Francis I in the second Habsburg-Valois War (1527–1529), but with catastrophic results. In April 1527, the Spanish-imperial army of Charles V went berserk while attacking

♦ **Charles V.** Charles V sought to create religious unity throughout his vast empire by keeping all his subjects within the bounds of the Catholic church. Due to his conflict with Francis I as well as difficulties with the Turks, the papacy, and the German princes, Charles was never able to check the spread of Lutheranism. This is a portrait of Charles V by the Venetian painter Titian.

♦ **Francis I.** The conflict between Francis I of France and Emperor Charles V prevented Charles from effectively dealing with the Lutheran problem in Germany. Feeling surrounded by Charles's possessions, Francis initiated a series of Habsburg-Valois Wars, which were fought over a period of twenty-five years. Pictured here is a portrait of Francis I attributed to Jean Clouet.

Rome and subjected the capital of Catholicism to a fearful and bloody sack. Sobered by the experience, Clement came to terms with the emperor, and by 1530 Charles V stood supreme over much of Italy.

In the meantime, a new threat to the emperor's power had erupted in the eastern part of his empire. The Ottoman Turks, under the competent Suleiman the Magnificent (1520–1566), had defeated and killed King Louis of Hungary, Charles's brother-in-law, at the Battle of Mohács in 1526. Subsequently, the Turks overran most of Hungary, moved into Austria, and advanced as far as Vienna, where they were finally repulsed in 1529.

First Habsburg-Valois War	1521–1525
Battle of Mohács	1526
Second Habsburg-Valois War	1527–1529
Defeat of the Turks at Vienna	1529
Diet of Augsburg	1530
Formation of Schmalkaldic League	1531
Third Habsburg-Valois War	1535–1538
Fourth Habsburg-Valois War	1542–1544
Schmalkaldic Wars	1546–1555
Peace of Augsburg	1555

By the end of 1529, Charles was ready to deal with Germany. The second Habsburg-Valois War had ended, the Turks had been defeated temporarily, and the pope subdued. The internal political situation in the Holy Roman Empire was not in his favor, however. Germany was a land of several hundred territorial states: princely states, ecclesiastical principalities, and free imperial cities (see Chapter 13). While all owed loyalty to the emperor, Germany's medieval development had enabled these states to become quite independent of imperial authority. They had no desire to have a strong emperor. Although those states that had become Lutheran were most concerned about that possibility, even Catholic authorities that might approve of the emperor's anti-Lutheran policies had no real desire to strengthen the emperor's hand politically.

Charles's attempt to settle the Lutheran problem at the Diet of Augsburg in 1530 proved completely inadequate, and the emperor wound up demanding that the Lutherans return to the Catholic church by April 15, 1531. In February 1531, fearful of Charles's intentions, eight princes and eleven imperial cities—all Lutheran—formed a defensive alliance known as the Schmalkaldic League. These Protestant German states vowed to assist each other "whenever any one of us is attacked on account of the Word of God and the doctrine of the Gospel." Religion was dividing the empire into two armed camps.

The renewed threat of the Turks against Vienna forced Charles once again to seek compromise instead of war with the Protestant authorities. From 1532 to 1535, Charles was forced to fight off a Turkish, Arab, and Barbary attack on the Mediterranean coasts of Italy and Spain. Two additional Habsburg-Valois Wars (1535–1538 and 1542–1544) soon followed and kept Charles preoccupied with military campaigns in southern France and the Low Countries. Finally, Charles made peace with Francis in 1544 and the Turks in 1545. Fifteen years after the Diet of Augsburg, Charles was finally free to resolve his problem in Germany.

By the time of Luther's death in February 1546, all hopes of a peaceful compromise had faded. Charles brought a sizable imperial army of Germans, Dutch, Italian, and Spanish troops to do battle with the Protestants. In the first phase of the Schmalkaldic Wars (1546–1547), the emperor's forces decisively defeated the Lutherans at the Battle of Mühlberg. Charles V was at the zenith of his power, and the Protestant cause seemed doomed.

Appearances proved misleading, however. The Schmalkaldic League was soon reestablished, and the German Protestant princes allied themselves with the new French king, Henry II (1547–1559)—a Catholic—to revive the war in 1552. This time, Charles was less fortunate and was forced to negotiate a truce. Exhausted by his efforts to maintain religious orthodoxy and the unity of his empire, Charles abandoned German affairs to his brother Ferdinand, abdicated all of his titles in 1556, and retired to his country estate in Spain to spend the remaining two years of his life in solitude.

An end to religious warfare in Germany came in 1555 with the Peace of Augsburg, which marks an important turning point in the history of the Reformation. The division of Christianity was formally acknowledged, with Lutheranism being granted the same legal rights as Catholicism. Although the German states were now free to choose between Catholicism and Lutheranism, the peace settlement did not recognize the principle of religious toleration for individuals; the right of each German ruler to determine the religion of his subjects was accepted, but not the right of the subjects to choose their religion.

The Peace of Augsburg was a victory for the German princes. The independence of the numerous German territorial states guaranteed the weakness of the Holy Roman Empire and the continued decentralization of Germany. Charles's hope for a united empire had been completely dashed. At the same time, what had at first been merely feared was now confirmed: the ideal of medieval Christian unity was irretrievably lost. The rapid proliferation of new Protestant groups served to underscore the new reality.

✂ Map 14.1 The Empire of Charles V.

The Spread of the Protestant Reformation

To Catholic critics, Luther's heresy had opened the door to more extreme forms of religious and social upheaval. For both Catholics and Protestant reformers, it also raised the question of how to determine what constituted the correct interpretation of the Bible. The inability to agree on this issue led not only to theological confrontations but also to bloody warfare as each Christian group was unwilling to admit that it could be wrong.

Lutheranism in Scandinavia

In 1397, the Union of Kalmar had brought about the unification of Denmark, Norway, and Sweden under the rule of one monarch, the king of Denmark. This union, however, failed to achieve any real social or political unification of the three states, particularly since the independent-minded, landed nobles worked to frustrate any increase in monarchical centralization. By the beginning of the sixteenth century, the union was on the brink of disintegration. In 1520, Christian II (1513–1523) of Denmark, ruler of the three Scandinavian

◆ **Zwingli.** Ulrich Zwingli began the Reformation in Switzerland through his preaching in Zürich. Zwingli's theology was accepted in Zürich and soon spread to other Swiss cities. This portrait of Zwingli was done by Hans Asper, probably in 1531.

kingdoms, was overthrown by Swedish barons led by Gustavus Vasa. Three years later, Vasa became king of an independent Sweden (1523–1560) and took the lead in establishing a Lutheran Reformation in his country. Swedish nobles supported his efforts, while Olavus Petri, who had studied at Wittenberg, wrote treatises based on Luther's writings and published the first Swedish New Testament in 1526. By the 1530s, a Swedish Lutheran National Church had been created.

Meanwhile, Christian II had also been deposed as the king of Denmark by the Danish nobility and succeeded by his uncle, who became Frederick I (1523–1533). Frederick encouraged Lutheran preachers to spread their evangelical doctrines and to introduce a Lutheran liturgy into the Danish church service. In the 1530s, under Frederick's successor, Christian III (1534–1559), a Lutheran state church was installed with the king as the supreme authority in all ecclesiastical affairs. Christian was also instrumental in spreading Lutheranism to Norway. By the 1540s, Scandinavia had become a Lutheran stronghold. Like the German princes, the Scandinavian monarchs had been the dominant force in establishing state-run churches.

The Zwinglian Reformation

Switzerland, which has played little role in our history to date, was home to two major Reformation movements, Zwinglianism and Calvinism. In the sixteenth century, the Swiss Confederation was a loose association of thirteen self-governing states called cantons. Theoretically part of the Holy Roman Empire, they had become virtually independent after the Swiss defeated the forces of Emperor Maximilian in 1499. The six forest cantons were democratic republics while the seven urban cantons, which included Zürich, Bern, and Basel, were mostly governed by city councils controlled by narrow oligarchies of wealthy citizens. Perennially troubled by a weak economy, the Swiss had grown accustomed to selling their warriors as mercenary soldiers and had become the principal exporters of mercenaries in the sixteenth century. All in all, the Swiss Confederation was a loose conglomeration of states that possessed no common institutions and worked together only for survival and gain.

Ulrich Zwingli (1484–1531) was a product of the Swiss rural cantons. The precocious son of a relatively prosperous peasant, the young Zwingli eventually obtained both the bachelor of arts and master of arts degrees. During his university education at Vienna and Basel, Zwingli was strongly influenced by Christian humanism. Ordained a priest in 1506, he accepted a parish post in rural Switzerland until his appointment as a cathedral priest in the Great Minster of Zürich in 1518. Through his preaching there, Zwingli began the Reformation in Switzerland.

Zwingli always maintained that he came to his evangelical theology independently of Luther: "I began to preach the Gospel of Christ in 1516, long before anyone in our region had ever heard of Luther. . . . Why don't you call me a Paulinian since I am preaching as St. Paul preached. . . . If Luther preaches Christ, he does just what I do." Modern scholars doubt Zwingli's protestation, believing that he was influenced by Luther's writings, beginning at least in 1519. In any case, Zwingli's evangelical preaching caused such unrest that in 1523 the city council held a public disputation or debate in the town hall. The disputation became a standard method of spreading the Reformation to many cities. It gave an advantage to reformers since they had the power of new ideas and Catholics were not used to defending their teachings. Zwingli's party was accorded the victory, and the council declared that "Mayor, Council and Great Council of Zürich, in order to do away with disturbance and discord, have upon due deliberation and consultation decided and resolved that Master Zwingli should continue as heretofore to proclaim the Gospel and the pure sacred Scripture."[11] City magistrates were not always motivated solely by religious considerations. By removing the Catholic church—a rival for authority in their town—the secular authorities enhanced their own power.

Over the next two years, evangelical reforms were promulgated in Zürich by a city council strongly influenced by Zwingli. Zwingli looked to the state to supervise the church. "A church without the magistrate is mutilated and incomplete," he declared. Relics and images were abolished; all paintings and decorations were removed from the churches and replaced by whitewashed walls. The mass was replaced by a new liturgy consisting of Scripture reading, prayer, and sermons. Music was eliminated from the service as a distraction from the pure word of God. Monasticism, pilgrimages, the veneration of saints, clerical celibacy, and the pope's authority were all abolished as remnants of papal Christianity. Zwingli's movement soon spread to other cities in Switzerland, including Bern in 1528 and Basel in 1529.

By 1528, Zwingli's reform movement faced a serious political problem as the forest cantons remained staunchly Catholic. Zürich feared an alliance between them and the Habsburgs. To counteract this danger, Zwingli attempted to build a league of evangelical cities by seeking an agreement with Luther and the German reformers. An alliance between them seemed possible, since the Reformation had spread to the south German cities, especially Strasbourg, where a moderate reform movement containing characteristics of both Luther's and Zwingli's movements had been instituted by Martin Bucer (1491–1551). Both the German and the Swiss reformers realized the need for unity to defend against imperial and conservative opposition. Protestant political leaders, especially Landgrave Philip of Hesse, fearful of Charles V's ability to take advantage of the division between the reformers, attempted to promote an alliance of the Swiss and German reformed churches by persuading the leaders of both groups to attend a colloquy (or conference) at Marburg to resolve their differences. Able to agree on virtually everything else, the gathering splintered over the interpretation of the Lord's Supper (see the box on p. 472). Zwingli believed that the scriptural words "This is my Body, This is my blood" should be taken figuratively, not literally, and refused to accept Luther's insistence on the real presence of the body and blood of Christ "in, with, and under the bread and wine." The Marburg Colloquy of 1529 produced no agreement and no evangelical alliance. While this failure to reach an accord was a setback for Lutheranism and Philip of Hesse, it proved even more harmful to Zwingli.

In October 1531, war erupted between the Swiss Protestant and Catholic cantons. Zürich's army was routed, and Zwingli was found wounded on the battlefield. His enemies killed him, cut up his body, and burned the pieces, scattering the ashes. Although Zwingli was succeeded by the able Heinrich Büllinger, the momentum of the Zwinglian reform movement was slowed. This Swiss civil war of 1531 provided an early indication of what religious passions would lead to in the sixteenth century. Unable to find peaceful ways to agree on the meaning of the Gospel, the disciples of Christianity resorted to violence and decision by force. When he heard of Zwingli's death, Martin Luther, who had not forgotten the confrontation at Marburg, is supposed to have remarked that Zwingli got what he deserved.

The Radical Reformation: The Anabaptists

Since the Reformation had broken down traditional standards and relationships, reformers such as Luther sought a new authority by allowing the state to play an important, if not dominant, role in church affairs. But some people favored a far more radical approach. Collectively called the Anabaptists, these radicals actually formed a large variety of different groups who, nevertheless, shared some common characteristics. Although some middle-class intellectuals participated in this movement, Anabaptism was especially attractive to those peasants, weavers, miners, and artisans who had been adversely affected by the economic changes of the age. The upper classes were aware of the obvious link between social dissatisfaction and religious radicalism, which was particularly evident in commercial and industrial cities like Zürich, Strasbourg, Nuremberg, and Augsburg. All of these cities initiated a Lutheran or Zwinglian Reformation early on, but, thanks to their relatively large lower classes affected by economic upheavals, also became centers for radical religious groups.

Anabaptists everywhere shared some common ideas. To them, the true Christian church was a voluntary association of believers who had undergone spiritual rebirth and had then been baptized into the church. Anabaptists advocated adult rather than infant baptism. They also tried to return literally to the practices and spirit of early Christianity. Adhering to the accounts of early Christian communities in the New Testament,

A Reformation Debate: The Marburg Colloquy

Debates played a crucial role in the Reformation period. They were a primary instrument in introducing the Reformation into innumerable cities as well as a means of resolving differences among like-minded Protestant groups. This selection contains an excerpt from the vivacious and often brutal debate between Luther and Zwingli over the sacrament of the Lord's Supper at Marburg in 1529. The two protagonists failed to reach agreement.

The Marburg Colloquy, 1529

THE HESSIAN CHANCELLOR FEIGE: My gracious prince and lord [Landgrave Philip of Hesse] has summoned you for the express and urgent purpose of settling the dispute over the sacrament of the Lord's Supper. . . . And let everyone on both sides present his arguments in a spirit of moderation, as becomes such matters. . . . Now then, Doctor Luther, you may proceed.

LUTHER: Noble prince, gracious lord! Undoubtedly the colloquy is well intentioned. . . . Although I have no intention of changing my mind, which is firmly made up, I will nevertheless present the grounds of my belief and show where the others are in error. . . . Your basic contentions are these: In the last analysis you wish to prove that a body cannot be in two places at once, and you produce arguments about the unlimited body which are based on natural reason. I do not question how Christ can be God and man and how the two natures can be joined. For God is more powerful than all our ideas, and we must submit to his word.

Prove that Christ's body is not there where the Scripture says, "This is my body!" Rational proofs I will not listen to. . . . God is beyond all mathematics and the words of God are to be revered and carried out in awe. It is God who commands, "Take, eat, this is my body." I request, therefore, valid scriptural proof to the contrary.

Luther writes on the table in chalk, "This is my body," and covers the words with a velvet cloth.

OECOLAMPADIUS [leader of the reform movement in Basel and a Zwinglian partisan]: The sixth chapter of John clarifies the other scriptural passages. Christ is not speaking there about a local presence. "The flesh is of no avail," he says [John 6:63]. It is not my intention to employ rational, or geometrical, arguments—neither am I denying the power of God—but as long as I have the complete faith I will speak from that. For Christ is risen; he sits at the right hand of God; and so he cannot be present in the bread. Our view is neither new nor sacrilegious, but is based on faith and Scripture. . . .

ZWINGLI: I insist that the words of the Lord's Supper must be figurative. This is ever apparent, and even required by the article of faith: "taken up into heaven, seated at the right hand of the Father." Otherwise, it would be absurd to look for him in the Lord's Supper at the same time that Christ is telling us that he is in heaven. One and the same body cannot possibly be in different places. . . .

LUTHER: I call upon you as before: your basic contentions are shaky. Give way, and give glory to God!

ZWINGLI: And we call upon you to give glory to God and to quit begging the question! The issue at stake is this: Where is the proof of your position? I am willing to consider your words carefully—no harm meant! You're trying to outwit me. I stand by this passage in the sixth chapter of John, verse 63 and shall not be shaken from it. You'll have to sing another tune.

LUTHER: You're being obnoxious.

ZWINGLI: (*excitedly*): Don't you believe that Christ was attempting in John 6 to help those who did not understand?

LUTHER: You're trying to dominate things! You insist on passing judgment! Leave that to someone else!. . . . It is your point that must be proved, not mine. But let us stop this sort of thing. It serves no purpose.

ZWINGLI: It certainly does! It is for you to prove that the passage in John 6 speaks of a physical repast.

LUTHER: You express yourself poorly and make about as much progress as a cane standing in a corner. You're going nowhere.

ZWINGLI: No, no, no! This is the passage that will break your neck!

LUTHER: Don't be so sure of yourself. Necks don't break this way. You're in Hesse, not Switzerland. . . .

they followed a strict sort of democracy in which all believers were considered equal. Each church chose its own minister, who might be any member of the community since all Christians were considered priests (though women were often excluded). Those chosen as ministers had the duty to lead services, which were very simple and contained nothing not found in the early church. Anabaptists rejected theological speculation in favor of simple Christian living according to what they believed was the pure word of God. The Lord's Supper was interpreted as a remembrance, a meal of fellowship celebrated in the evening in private houses according to Christ's example. Finally, unlike the Catholics and other Protestants, most Anabaptists believed in the complete separation of church and state. Not only was government to be excluded from the realm of religion, it was not even supposed to exercise political jurisdiction over real Christians. Anabaptists refused to hold political office or bear arms since many took literally the commandment "Thou shall not kill," although some Anabaptist groups did become quite violent. Their political beliefs as much as their religious beliefs caused the Anabaptists to be regarded as dangerous radicals who

threatened the very fabric of sixteenth-century society. Indeed, the chief thing Protestants and Catholics could agree on was the need to persecute Anabaptists.

One early group of Anabaptists known as the Swiss Brethren arose in Zürich. Their ideas frightened Zwingli, and they were soon expelled from the city. As their teachings spread through southern Germany, the Austrian Habsburg lands, and Switzerland, Anabaptists suffered ruthless persecution, especially after the Peasants' War of 1524–1525, when the upper classes resorted to repression. To Catholics and Lutherans alike, the Anabaptists threatened not only religious peace but also secular authority because of their political ideas (see the box on p. 474). Virtually stamped out in Germany, Anabaptist survivors emerged in Moravia, Poland, and the Netherlands. In the latter, Anabaptism took on a strange form.

In the 1530s, the city of Münster in Westphalia in northwest Germany near the Dutch border was the site of an Anabaptist uprising that determined the fate of Dutch Anabaptism. Seat of a powerful Catholic prince-bishop, Münster had experienced severe economic disasters, including crop failure and plague. Although con-

◆ **An Anabaptist Execution in the Netherlands.** The Anabaptists were the radicals of the Reformation. They advocated adult baptism and believed that the true Christian should not actively participate in or be governed by the secular state. Due to their radical ideas, the Anabaptists were persecuted and put to death by Catholics and Protestants alike. This sixteenth-century woodcut depicts the execution of Anabaptist reformers.

The Trial of Michael Sattler

Michael Sattler had been prior of a Benedictine monastery before abandoning Catholicism for Lutheranism and then Anabaptism. He was responsible for drawing up a set of seven articles (the Schleitheim Articles) in 1527, which constituted the "first formal Anabaptist confession of faith." Both Catholics and other Protestant sects viewed Anabaptists as dangerous radicals, subversive of both church and state. This excerpt, taken from a contemporary account of Sattler's trial for heresy by Austrian authorities, begins after Sattler has given a speech detailing his beliefs. As his sentence indicates, Anabaptists were subjected to cruel and unusual punishments.

The Trial of Michael Sattler

Upon this speech the judges laughed and put their heads together, and the town clerk of Ensisheim said, "Yes, you infamous, desperate rascal of a monk, should we dispute with you? The hangman will dispute with you, I assure you!"

Michael said: "God's will be done."

The town clerk said: "It were well if you had never been born."

Michael replied: "God knows what is good."

The town clerk: "You archheretic, you have seduced pious people. If they would only now forsake their error and commit themselves to grace!"

Michael: "Grace is with God alone."

The town clerk: "Yes, you desperate villain, you archheretic, I say, if there were no hangman here, I would hang you myself and be doing God a good service thereby."

Michael: "God will judge aright."

The town clerk than admonished the judges and said: "He will not cease from this chatter anyway. Therefore, my Lord Judge, you may proceed with the sentence. I call for a decision of the court."

The judge asked Michael Sattler whether he too committed it to the court. He replied: "Ministers of God, I am not sent to judge the Word of God. We are sent to testify and hence cannot consent to any adjudication, since we have no command from God concerning it. But we are not for that reason removed from being judged and we are ready to suffer and to await what God is planning to do with us. We will continue in our faith in Christ so long as we have breath in us, unless we be dissuaded from it by the Scriptures."

The town clerk said: "The hangman will instruct you, he will dispute with you, archheretic."

Michael: "I appeal to the Scriptures."

Then the judges arose and went into another room where they . . . determined on the sentence. . . .

The judges having returned to the room, the sentence was read. It was as follows: "In the case of the attorney of His Imperial Majesty [Holy Roman Emperor] vs. Michael Sattler, judgment is passed that Michael Sattler shall be delivered to the executioner, who shall lead him to the place of execution and cut out his tongue, then forge him fast to a wagon and thereon with red-hot tongs twice tear pieces from his body; and after he has been brought outside the gate, he shall be plied five times more in the same manner. . . ."

verted to Lutheranism in 1532, Münster experienced a more radical mass religious hysteria that led to legal recognition for the Anabaptists. Soon, Münster became a haven for Anabaptists from the surrounding neighborhood, especially the more wild-eyed variety known as Melchiorites who adhered to a vivid millenarianism. They believed that the end of the world was at hand and that they would usher in the Kingdom of God with Münster as the New Jerusalem. By the end of February 1534, these millenarian Anabaptists had taken control of the city, driven out those they considered godless or unbelievers, burned all books except the Bible, and proclaimed communal ownership of all property. Eventually, the leadership of this New Jerusalem fell into the hands of one man, John of Leiden, who proclaimed himself king of the New Jerusalem. As king, he would lead out the elect from Münster to cover the entire world and purify it of evil by the sword in preparation for Christ's Second Coming and the creation of a New Age. In this new kingdom, John of Leiden believed, all goods would be held in common and the saints would live without suffering.

But it was not to be. As the Catholic prince-bishop of Münster gathered a large force and laid siege to the city, the new king repeatedly had to postpone the ushering forth from Münster. Finally, after many inhabitants had starved, a joint army of Catholics and Lutherans recaptured the city in June 1535 and executed the radical Anabaptist leaders in a gruesome fashion. The New Jerusalem had ceased to exist.

Purged of its fantasies and more extreme elements, Dutch Anabaptism reverted to its pacifist tendencies, especially evident in the work of Menno Simons (1496–1561), the man most responsible for rejuvenating Dutch Anabaptism. A popular leader, Menno dedicated his life to the spread of a peaceful, evangelical Anabaptism that stressed separation from the world in order to live a truly Christ-like life. Simons imposed strict discipline on his followers and banned those who refused to conform to the rules. The Mennonites, as his followers were called, spread from the Netherlands into northwestern Germany and eventually into Poland and Lithuania as well as the New World. Both the Mennonites and the Amish, who are also descended from the Anabaptists, can be found in the United States today.

The Reformation in England

At one time, a Reformation in England would have been unthinkable. Had not Henry VIII penned an attack against Martin Luther in 1521, the *Defense of the Seven Sacraments*, and been rewarded for it by the pope with the title "Defender of the Faith"? Nevertheless, there were elements of discontent in England. Antipapal feeling ran high as many of the English resented papal influence in English affairs, especially in matters of taxation and justice. Anticlericalism (opposition to and criticism of the activities of the clergy) was rife as people denounced greedy clerics who flaunted their great wealth in ostentatious extravagance. One layman charged that "These [the clergy] are not the shepherds, but the ravenous wolves going in shepherds' clothing, devouring the flock."

Anticlericalism and antipapal feelings were not the only manifestations of religious sentiment in early sixteenth-century England. A craving for spiritual expression fostered the spread of Lutheran ideas, encouraged in part by two different traditions of dissent. Heretical Lollardy, stressing the use of the Bible in the vernacular and the rejection of papal supremacy, continued to exert influence among the lower classes, while Christian humanism, with its calls for reform, influenced the English middle and upper classes. People influenced by Lollardy and Christian humanism were among the first to embrace Lutheran writings when they began to arrive in England in the 1520s.

Despite these factors, there might not have been a Reformation in England had it not been for the king's desire to divorce his first wife Catherine of Aragon. Henry VIII's reasons were twofold. Catherine had produced no male heir, an absolute essential if his Tudor dynasty were to flourish. At the same time, Henry had fallen in love with Anne Boleyn, a lady-in-waiting to Queen Catherine. Her unwillingness to be only the king's mistress, as well as the king's desire to have a legitimate male heir, made a new marriage imperative. The king's first marriage stood in the way, however.

Henry relied upon Cardinal Wolsey, the highest ranking English church official and lord chancellor to the king, to obtain an annulment of his marriage from Pope Clement VII. Normally, the pope might have been willing to oblige, but the sack of Rome in 1527 had made the pope dependent upon the Holy Roman Emperor Charles V, who happened to be the nephew of Queen Catherine. Discretion dictated delay in granting the English king's request. Impatient with the process, Henry dismissed Wolsey in 1529.

Two new advisers now became the king's agents in fulfilling his wishes. These were Thomas Cranmer (1489–1540), who became archbishop of Canterbury in 1532, and Thomas Cromwell (1485–1540), the king's principal secretary after the fall of Wolsey. They advised the king to obtain an annulment of his marriage in England's own ecclesiastical courts. The most important step toward this goal was the promulgation by Parliament of an act cutting off all appeals from English church courts to Rome, a piece of legislation that essentially abolished papal authority in England. Henry no longer needed the pope to attain his annulment. He was now in a hurry, since Anne Boleyn had become pregnant and he had secretly married her in January 1533 to legitimize the expected heir. Now, as archbishop of Canterbury and head of the highest ecclesiastical court in England, Thomas Cranmer ruled in May that the king's marriage to Catherine was "null and absolutely void," and then validated Henry's marriage to Anne. At the beginning of June, Anne was crowned queen. Three months later a child was born. Much to the king's disappointment, the baby was a girl, the future Queen Elizabeth I.

In 1534, Parliament completed the break of the Church of England with Rome by passing the Act of Supremacy, which declared that the king was "taken, accepted, and reputed the only supreme head on earth of the Church of England." This meant that the English monarch now controlled the church in all matters of doctrine, clerical appointments, and discipline. In addition, Parliament passed a Treason Act making it punishable by death to deny that the king was the supreme head of the church. The Act of Supremacy and the Treason Act went beyond religious issues in their implications, for they asserted that there could be no higher authority over England than laws made by the king and Parliament.

Few challenged the new order. One who did was Thomas More, the humanist and former lord chancellor,

◆ **Henry VIII, His Wife, and Children.** The desire of Henry VIII for a male heir played a significant role in his break with the Catholic church. Pictured here in the central panel of this 1545 portrait by an unknown artist are Henry VIII, Jane Seymour, his third wife, and Prince Edward, who became King Edward VI in 1547. On the far left is Princess Mary and on the far right is Princess Elizabeth.

who saw clearly to the heart of the issue: loyalty to the pope in Rome was now treason in England. More refused to publicly support the new laws and was duly tried for treason. At his trial, he asked, rhetorically, what the effect of the actions of the king and Parliament would be: "Therefore am I not bound . . . to conform my conscience to the Council of one realm [England] against the general Council of Christendom?"[12] Because his conscience could not accept the victory of the national state over the church, nor would he, as a Christian, bow his head to a secular ruler in matters of faith, More was beheaded in London on July 6, 1535.

Thomas Cromwell worked out the details of the Tudor government's new role in church affairs based on the centralized power exercised by the king and Parliament. Cromwell also came to his extravagant king's financial rescue with a daring plan for the dissolution of the monasteries. About four hundred religious houses were closed in 1536, and their land and possessions confiscated by the king. Many were sold to nobles, gentry, and some merchants. The king received a great boost to his treasury, as well as creating a group of supporters who now had a stake in the new Tudor order.

Although Henry VIII had broken with the papacy, little change occurred in matters of doctrine, theology, and ceremony. Some of his supporters, such as Arch-bishop Thomas Cranmer, wished to have a religious reformation as well as an administrative one, but Henry was unyielding. To counteract a growing Protestant sentiment, the king had Parliament pass the Six Articles Act of 1539, which reaffirmed transubstantiation, clerical celibacy, and other aspects of Catholic doctrine. No doubt, Henry's conservatism helped the English accept the basic changes he had made; since religious doctrine and worship had changed very little, most people were indifferent to the transformation that had occurred. Popular acceptance was also furthered by Henry's strategy of involving Parliament in all the changes.

The last decade of Henry's reign was preoccupied with foreign affairs, factional intrigue, and a continued effort to find the perfect wife. Henry had soon tired of Anne Boleyn and had had her beheaded in 1536 on a charge of adultery. His third wife, Jane Seymour, produced the long-awaited male heir but died during childbirth. His fourth marriage to Anne of Cleves, a German princess, was arranged for political reasons and on the basis of a painted portrait. Henry was shocked at her physical appearance when he first saw her in person and soon divorced her. His fifth wife, Catherine Howard, was more attractive but less moral. When she committed adultery, Henry had her beheaded. His last wife was Catherine Parr, who married the king in 1543 and outlived him. Henry was succeeded by the underage and sickly Edward VI (1547–1553), the son of his third wife.

Since the new king was only nine years old at the time of his accession to the throne, real control of England passed to a council of regency. During Edward's reign, Archbishop Cranmer and others inclined toward Protestant doctrines were able to move the Church of England in more of a Protestant direction. New acts of Parliament instituted the right of the clergy to marry, the elimination of images, and the creation of a revised Protestant liturgy that was elaborated in a new prayer book and liturgical guide known as the Book of Common Prayer. These rapid changes in doctrine and liturgy aroused much opposition and prepared the way for the reaction that occurred when Mary, Henry's first daughter by Catherine of Aragon, came to the throne.

There was no doubt that Mary (1553–1558) was a Catholic who intended to restore England to Roman Catholicism. But she understood little about the practical nature of politics and even less about the changes that had swept over England in the past thirty years.

Mary's restoration of Catholicism, achieved by joint action of the monarch and Parliament, aroused much opposition. Although the new owners of monastic lands were assured otherwise, many feared that the lands confiscated by Henry would be restored to the church. Moreover, there was widespread antipathy to Mary's unfortunate marriage to Philip II, the son of Charles V and the future king of Spain. Philip was strongly disliked in England, and Mary's foreign policy of alliance with Spain aroused further hostility, especially when her forces lost Calais, the last English possession from the Hundred Years' War. The burning of more than three hundred Protestant heretics roused further ire against "bloody Mary." As a result of her policies, Mary managed to achieve the opposite of what she had intended: England was more Protestant by the end of her reign than it had been at the beginning. When she came to power, Protestantism had become identified with church destruction and religious anarchy. Now people identified it with English resistance to Spanish interference. The death of Mary in 1558 ended the restoration of Catholicism in England.

John Calvin and the Development of Calvinism

Of the second generation of Protestant reformers, one stands out as the systematic theologian and organizer of the Protestant movement—John Calvin (1509–1564). Born a generation later than Luther, Calvin reached

manhood when Christian unity had for all intents and purposes already disappeared.

John Calvin began his academic training in humanistic studies in 1523 at the University of Paris, but switched to the study of law at Orléans and Bourges from 1528 to 1531, while simultaneously studying Greek. In 1531, he returned to Paris to concentrate on his humanistic pursuits. In his early development, Calvin was also influenced by Luther's writings, which were being circulated and read by French intellectuals as early as 1523. By 1533, then, Calvin had received a remarkably diverse education. In that same year, he experienced a religious crisis that determined the rest of

◆ **John Calvin.** After a conversion experience, John Calvin abandoned his life as a humanist and became a reformer. In 1536, Calvin began working to reform the city of Geneva, where he remained until his death in 1564. This sixteenth-century portrait of Calvin pictures him near the end of his life.

his life's work. He described it in these words:

> God, by a sudden conversion, subdued and brought my mind to a teachable frame, which was more hardened in such matters than might have been expected from one at my early period of life. Having thus received some taste and knowledge of true godliness, I was immediately inflamed with so intense a desire to make progress therein, although I did not leave off other studies, I yet pursued them with less ardor.[13]

Calvin's conversion was solemn and straightforward. He was so convinced of the inner guidance of God that he became the most determined of all the Protestant reformers.

After his conversion and newfound conviction, Calvin was no longer safe in Paris, since King Francis I periodically persecuted Protestants. Eventually, Calvin made his way to Basel, where in 1536, he published the first edition of the *Institutes of the Christian Religion,* a masterful synthesis of Protestant thought, a manual for ecclesiastical organization, and a work that immediately secured his reputation as one of the new leaders of Protestantism. Although the *Institutes* were originally written in Latin, Calvin published a French edition in 1541, facilitating the spread of his ideas in French-speaking lands.

On most important doctrines, Calvin stood very close to Luther. He adhered to the doctrine of justification by faith alone to explain how humans achieved salvation. But Calvin also placed much emphasis on the absolute sovereignty of God or the "power, grace, and glory of God." Thus, "God asserts his possession of omnipotence, and claims our acknowledgment of this attribute; not such as is imagined by sophists, vain, idle, and almost asleep, but vigilant, efficacious, operative and engaged in continual action."[14]

One of the ideas derived from his emphasis on the absolute sovereignty of God—predestination—gave a unique cast to Calvin's teachings. Although it was but one aspect of his doctrine of salvation, predestination became the central focus of succeeding generations of Calvinists. This "eternal decree," as Calvin called it, meant that God had predestined some people to be saved (the elect) and others to be damned (the reprobate). According to Calvin, "He has once for all determined, both whom he would admit to salvation, and whom he would condemn to destruction."[15] Calvin identified three tests that might indicate possible salvation: an open profession of faith, a "decent and godly life," and participation in the sacraments of baptism and communion. In no instance did Calvin ever suggest that

worldly success or material wealth was a sign of election. Most importantly, although Calvin stressed that there could be no absolute certainty of salvation, some of his followers did not always make this distinction. The practical psychological effect of predestination was to give some later Calvinists an unshakable conviction that they were doing God's work on earth. Thus, Calvinism became a dynamic and activist faith. It is no accident that Calvinism became the militant international form of Protestantism.

To Calvin, the church was a divine institution responsible for preaching the word of God and administering the sacraments. Calvin kept only two sacraments, baptism and the Lord's Supper. Baptism was a sign of the remission of sins. Calvin believed in the real presence of Christ in the sacrament of the Lord's Supper, but only in a spiritual sense. Christ's body is at the right hand of God and thus cannot be in the sacrament, but to the believer, Christ is spiritually present in the Lord's Supper. Finally, Calvin agreed with other reformers that the church had the power to discipline its members. This element of his thought was apparent when Calvin finally had the opportunity to establish his church in Geneva.

Up to 1536, John Calvin had essentially been a scholar. But in that year, he took up a ministry in Geneva that lasted until his death in 1564. Calvin achieved a major success in 1541 when the city council accepted his new church constitution known as the Ecclesiastical Ordinances. This document established four orders or offices: pastors, teachers (or doctors), elders, and deacons. The duties of the pastors or ministers were to preach the Gospel, administer the sacraments, and correct un-Christian behavior. To the teachers was given the responsibility to "instruct the faithful in sound doctrine, in order that the purity of the Gospel may not be corrupted." The elders or presbyters were laymen, chosen from and by the city magistrates; their function was to maintain discipline: "to have oversight of the life of everyone, to admonish amicably those whom they see to be erring or to be living a disordered life, and . . . to enjoin fraternal corrections." The deacons were also laymen who were responsible for the care of the poor, widows, and orphans and the administration of the city's hospitals.

The Ecclesiastical Ordinances created a special body for enforcing moral discipline. Consisting of five pastors and twelve elders, the Consistory functioned as a court to oversee the moral life, daily behavior, and doctrinal orthodoxy of Genevans and to admonish and correct deviants (see the box on p. 479). As its power increased,

The Role of Discipline in the "Most Perfect School of Christ on Earth"

To John Calvin's followers, the church that the French reformer had created in Geneva was, in the words of John Knox, "the most perfect school of Christ on earth." Calvin had emphasized in his reform movement that the church should have the ability to enforce proper behavior. Consequently, the Ecclesiastical Ordinances of 1541, the constitution of the church in Geneva, provided for an order of elders whose function was to cooperate with the pastors in maintaining discipline, "to have oversight of the life of everyone," as Calvin expressed it. These selections from the official records of the Consistory show the nature of its work.

Reports of the Genevan Consistory

Donna Jane Peterman is questioned concerning her faith and why she does not receive communion and attend worship. She confesses her faith and believes in one God and wants to come to God and the holy Church and has no other faith. She recited the Lord's Prayer in the vernacular. She said that she believes what the Church believes. Is questioned why she never participates in communion when it is celebrated in this town, but goes to other places. She answers that she goes where it seems good to her. Is placed outside the faith.

The sister of Sr. Curtet, Lucresse, to whom remonstrances have been made on account of her going with certain monies to have masses said at Nessy by the monks of St. Claire. Questioned whether she has no scruples as to what she says. Replied that her father and mother have brought her up to obey a different law from the one now in force here. However, she does not desire the present law. Asked as to when was the festival of St. Felix, she replied that it was yesterday. Asked if she had not fasted, she replied that she fasted when it pleased her. Asked if she did not desire to pray to a single God; said that she did. Asked if she did not pray to St. Felix; said that she prayed to St. Felix and other saints who interceded for her. She is very obstinate. Decision that she be sent to some minister of her choice every sermon day and that the Lord's Supper be withheld from her.

At about this time, by resolution of the Consistory . . . the marriage contracted between the widow of Jean Achard, aged more than 70, and a servant of hers, aged about 27 or 28, was dissolved because of the too great inequality of age. The Consistory resolved further that Messieurs should be requested to make a ruling on this matter for the future.

the Consistory went from "fraternal corrections" to the use of public penance and excommunication. More serious cases could be turned over to the city council for punishments greater than excommunication. During Calvin's last years, stricter laws against blasphemy were enacted and enforced with banishment and public whippings. Although Calvin's detractors felt that Geneva was an example of religious fanaticism, to visitors of similar inclination, it presented a glorious sight. John Knox, the Calvinist reformer of Scotland, called it "the most perfect school of Christ on earth."

Calvin's success in Geneva enabled the city to become a vibrant center of Protestantism. Following Calvin's lead, missionaries trained in Geneva were sent to all parts of Europe. Calvinism became established in France, the Netherlands, Scotland, and central and eastern Europe. By the mid-sixteenth century, Calvinism had replaced Lutheranism as the international form of Protestantism while Calvin's Geneva stood as the fortress of the Reformation.

The Social Impact of the Protestant Reformation

Since Christianity was such an integral part of European life, it was inevitable that the Reformation would have an impact on the family, education, and popular religious practices.

The Family

For centuries, Catholicism had praised the family and sanctified its existence by making marriage a sacrament. But the Catholic church's high regard for abstinence from sex as the surest way to holiness made the celibate state of the clergy preferable to marriage. Nevertheless, since not all men could remain chaste, marriage offered the best means to control sexual intercourse and give it a purpose, the procreation of children. To some extent, this attitude persisted among the Protestant reformers; Luther, for example, argued that sex in marriage allowed

A Protestant Woman

In the initial zeal of the Protestant Reformation, women were frequently allowed to play unusual roles. Catherine Zell of Germany (c. 1497–1562) first preached beside her husband in 1527. After the death of her two children, she devoted the rest of her life to helping her husband and their Anabaptist faith. This selection is taken from one of her letters to a young Lutheran minister who had criticized her activities.

Catherine Zell to Ludwig Rabus of Memmingen

I, Catherine Zell, wife of the late lamented Mathew Zell, who served in Strasbourg, where I was born and reared and still live, wish you peace and enhancement in God's grace. . . .

From my earliest years I turned to the Lord, who taught and guided me, and I have at all times, in accordance with my understanding and His grace, embraced the interests of His church and earnestly sought Jesus. Even in youth this brought me the regard and affection of clergymen and others much concerned with the church, which is why the pious Mathew Zell wanted me as a companion in marriage; and I, in turn, to serve the glory of Christ, gave devotion and help to my husband, both in his ministry and in keeping his house. . . . Ever since I was ten years old I have been a student and a sort of church mother, much given to attending sermons. I have loved and frequented the company of learned men, and I conversed much with them, not about dancing, masquerades, and worldly pleasures but about the kingdom of God. . . .

Consider the poor Anabaptists, who are so furiously and ferociously persecuted. Must the authorities everywhere be incited against them, as the hunter drives his dog against wild animals? Against those who acknowledge Christ the Lord in very much the same way we do and over which we broke with the papacy? Just because they cannot agree with us on lesser things, is this any reason to persecute them and in them Christ, in whom they fervently believe and have often professed in misery, in prison, and under the torments of fire and water?

Governments may punish criminals, but they should not force and govern belief, which is a matter for the heart and conscience not for temporal authorities. . . . When the authorities pursue one, they soon bring forth tears, and towns and villages are emptied.

one to "make use of this sex in order to avoid sin," and Calvin advised that every man should "abstain from marriage only so long as he is fit to observe celibacy." If "his power to tame lust fails him," then he must marry.

But the Reformation did bring some change to the conception of the family. Both Catholic and Protestant clergy preached sermons advocating a positive view of family relationships. The Protestants were especially important in developing this new idea of the family. Since Protestantism had eliminated any idea of special holiness for celibacy, abolishing both monasticism and a celibate clergy, the family could be placed at the center of human life, and a new stress on "mutual love between man and wife" could be extolled. But were doctrine and reality the same? For more radical religious groups, at times they were (see the box above). One Anabaptist wrote to his wife before his execution: "My faithful helper, my loyal friend. I praise God that he gave you to me, you who have sustained me in all my trial."[16] But more often reality reflected the traditional roles of husband as the ruler and wife as the obedient servant whose chief duty was to please her husband. Luther stated it clearly:

> The rule remains with the husband, and the wife is compelled to obey him by God's command. He rules the home and the state, wages war, defends his possessions, tills the soil, builds, plants, etc. The woman on the other hand is like a nail driven into the wall . . . so the wife should stay at home and look after the affairs of the household, as one who has been deprived of the ability of administering those affairs that are outside and that concern the state. She does not go beyond her most personal duties.[17]

But obedience to her husband was not her only role; her other important duty was to bear children. To Calvin and Luther, this function of women was part of the divine plan. God punishes women for the sins of Eve by the burdens of procreation and feeding and nurturing their children, but, said Luther, "it is a gladsome punishment if you consider the hope of eternal life and the honor of motherhood which had been left to her."[18] Although the Protestant reformers sanctified this role of woman as mother and wife, viewing it as a holy vocation, Protestantism also left few alternatives for women. Since monasticism had been destroyed, that career avenue was no longer available; for most Protestant women, family life was their only destiny. At the same time, by emphasizing the father as "ruler" and hence the center of household religion, Protestantism even removed the woman from her traditional role as controller of religion in the home.

Protestant reformers called upon men and women to read the Bible and participate in religious services together. In this way, the reformers provided a stimulus for the education of girls so they could read the Bible and other religious literature. The city council of Zwickau, for example, established a girls' school in 1525. But these schools were designed to encourage proper moral values rather than intellectual development and really did little to improve the position of women in society. Likewise, when women attempted to take more active roles in religious life, reformers—Lutheran and Calvinist alike—shrank back in horror. To them, the equality of the Gospel did not mean overthrowing the inequality of social classes or the sexes. Overall, the Protestant Reformation did not noticeably transform women's subordinate place in society.

Education in the Reformation

The Reformation had an important effect upon the development of education in Europe. Renaissance humanism had significantly altered the content of education (see Chapter 13), and Protestant educators were very successful in implementing and using humanist methods in Protestant secondary schools and universities. Unlike the humanist schools, however, which had been mostly for an elite, the sons and a few daughters of the nobility and wealthier bourgeoisie, Protestant schools were aimed at a much wider audience. Protestantism created an increased need for at least a semiliterate body of believers who could read the Bible for themselves.

While adopting the classical emphasis of humanist schools, Protestant reformers broadened the base of those being educated. Convinced of the need to provide the church with good Christians and good pastors as well as the state with good administrators and citizens, Martin Luther advocated that all children should have the opportunity of an education provided by the state. To that end, he urged the cities and villages of Saxony to establish schools paid for by the public. Luther's ideas were shared by his Wittenberg co-worker, Philip Melanchthon, whose educational efforts earned him the title of *Praecepter Germaniae*, the Teacher of Germany. In his scheme for education in Saxony, Melanchthon divided students into three classes or divisions based on their age or capabilities.

Following Melanchthon's example, the Protestants in Germany were responsible for introducing the gymnasium, or secondary school, where the humanist emphasis on the liberal arts based on instruction in Greek and Latin was combined with religious instruction. Most famous was the school in Strasbourg founded by Johannes Sturm in 1538, which served as a model for

◆ **A Sixteenth-Century Classroom.** Protestants in Germany developed secondary schools that combined instruction in the liberal arts with religious education. This scene from a painting by Hans Holbein shows a schoolmaster instructing a pupil in the alphabet while his wife helps a little girl.

other Protestant schools. John Calvin's Genevan Academy, founded in 1559, was organized in two distinct parts. The "private school" or gymnasium was divided into seven classes for young people who were taught Latin and Greek grammar and literature as well as logic. In the "public school," students were taught philosophy, Hebrew, Greek, and, most importantly, theology. The Genevan Academy, which eventually became a university, came to concentrate on preparing ministers to spread the Calvinist view of the Gospel.

Catholics also perceived the importance of secondary schools and universities in educating people to Catholic perspectives. The Jesuits (see The Society of Jesus later in this chapter) were especially proficient in combining humanist educational methods with religious instruction. Although both Catholic and Protestant secondary schools and universities were influenced by humanism, some humanists attacked them for misusing humanist methods. No doubt, as the Reformation progressed, confessional struggles made education increasingly serve the religious goal of producing zealous Protestants or Catholics. Virtually everywhere, teachers and professors were expected to follow the creeds of their ruling authorities.

Religious Practices and Popular Culture

Although Protestant reformers were conservative in their political and social attitudes, their attacks on the Catholic church led to radical changes in religious practices. The Protestant Reformation abolished or severely curtailed such customary practices as indulgences, the veneration of relics and saints, pilgrimages, monasticism, and clerical celibacy. In Protestant cities, attacks on the veneration of saints brought an end to popular religious processions that had been an important focus of religious devotion and often served as rituals to placate nature. The elimination of saints put an end to the numerous celebrations of religious holy days and changed a community's sense of time. Thus, in Protestant communities, religious ceremonies and imagery, such as processions and statues, tended to be replaced with individual private prayer, family worship, and collective prayer and worship at the same time each week on Sunday.

Many religious practices that had played an important role in popular culture were criticized by Protestant reformers as superstitious or remnants of pagan culture. Smarting under pressure from these Protestant attacks, even Catholic leaders sought to eliminate the more frivolous aspects of popular practices, although they never went as far as the Protestants. In addition to abolishing saints' days and religious carnivals, some Protestant reformers even tried to eliminate customary forms of entertainment. English Puritans (as English Calvinists were called), for example, attempted to ban drinking in taverns, dramatic performances, and dancing. Dutch Calvinists denounced the tradition of giving small presents to children on the feast of Saint Nicholas, near Christmas. Many of these Protestant attacks on popular culture were unsuccessful, however. The importance of taverns in English social life made it impossible to eradicate them while celebrating at Christmas time persisted in the Dutch Netherlands.

The Catholic Reformation

By the mid-sixteenth century, Lutheranism had become established in parts of Germany and Scandinavia, and Calvinism in parts of Switzerland, France, the Netherlands, and eastern Europe. In England, the split from Rome had resulted in the creation of a national church. The situation in Europe did not look particularly favorable for the Roman Catholic church. But even at the beginning of the sixteenth century, constructive, positive forces were at work for reform within the Catholic church, and by the mid-sixteenth century, they came to be directed by a revived and reformed papacy, giving the Catholic church new strength. By the second half of the sixteenth century, Catholicism had regained much that it had lost, especially in Germany and eastern Europe, and was able to make new conversions as well, particularly in the New World. We call the story of the revival of Roman Catholicism the Catholic Reformation, although some historians prefer to use the term Counter-Reformation, especially for those elements of the Catholic Reformation that were directly aimed at stopping the spread of the Protestant Reformation.

The Catholic Reformation was a mixture of old and new elements. The best features of medieval Catholicism were revived and then adjusted to meet new conditions, a situation most apparent in the revival of mysticism and monasticism. The emergence of a new mysticism, closely tied to the traditions of Catholic piety, was especially evident in the life of the Spanish mystic, Saint Teresa of Avila (1515–1582). A nun of the Carmelite order, Teresa experienced a variety of mystical visions that she claimed resulted in the ecstatic union of her soul with God. But Teresa also believed that mystical experience should lead to an active life of service on behalf of her Catholic faith. Consequently, she founded a new order of barefoot Carmelite nuns and worked to foster their mystical experiences.

The regeneration of religious orders also proved invaluable to the reform of Catholicism. Old orders, such as the Benedictines and Dominicans, were reformed and renewed. The Capuchins emerged when a group of Franciscans decided to return to the simplicity and poverty of Saint Francis of Assisi, the medieval founder of the Franciscan order. In addition to caring for the sick and the poor, the Capuchins focused on preaching the Gospel directly to the people and emerged as an effective force against Protestantism.

New religious orders and brotherhoods were also created. The Theatines, founded in 1524, placed their emphasis on reforming the secular clergy and encouraging those clerics to fulfill their duties among the laity. The Theatines also founded orphanages and hospitals to care for the victims of war and plague. The Ursulines, a new order of nuns founded in Italy in 1535, focused their attention on establishing schools for the education of girls.

The Oratory of Divine Love, first organized in Italy in 1497, was not a new religious order but an informal group of clergy and laymen who worked to foster reform by emphasizing personal spiritual development and outward acts of charity. The "philosophy of Christ," advo-

Map 14.2 Catholics and Protestants in Europe by 1560.

cated by the Christian humanist Erasmus, was especially appealing to many of them. The Oratory's members included a number of cardinals who favored the reform of the Catholic church.

The Society of Jesus

Of all the new religious orders, the most important was the Society of Jesus, known as the Jesuits, who became the chief instrument of the Catholic Reformation. The Society of Jesus was founded by a Spanish nobleman, Ignatius of Loyola (1491–1556), whose injuries in battle cut short his military career. Loyola experienced a spiritual torment similar to Luther's but, unlike Luther, resolved his problems not by a new doctrine, but by a decision to submit his will to the will of the church. Unable to be a real soldier, he vowed to be a soldier of God. Over a period of twelve years, Loyola prepared for his life work by mortification, prayer, pilgrimages, going to school, and working out a spiritual program in his brief, but powerful book, *The Spiritual Exercises*. This was a training manual for spiritual development emphasizing exercises by which the human will could be strengthened and made to follow the will of God as manifested through his instrument, the Catholic church (see the box on p. 485).

Gradually, Loyola gathered together a small group of individuals who shared his single-minded devotion and were eventually recognized as a religious order, the Society of Jesus, by a papal bull in 1540. The new order was grounded on the principles of absolute obedience to the papacy, a strict hierarchical order for the society, the use of education to achieve its goals, and a dedication to engage in "conflict for God." Jesuit organization came to resemble the structure of a military command. A two-year novitiate weeded out all but the most dedicated. Executive leadership was put in the hands of a general, who nominated all important positions in the order and was to be revered as the absolute head of the order. Loyola served as the first general of the order until his death in 1556. A special vow of absolute obedience to the pope made the Jesuits an important instrument for papal policy.

The Jesuits pursued three major activities. They established highly disciplined schools, borrowing freely from humanist schools for their educational methods. To the Jesuits, the thorough education of young people was crucial to combat the advance of Protestantism. In the course of the sixteenth century, the Jesuits took over the

✦ **Ignatius Loyola.** The Jesuits became the most important new religious order of the Catholic Reformation. Shown here in a sixteenth-century painting by an unknown artist is Ignatius Loyola, founder of the Society of Jesus. Loyola is seen kneeling before Pope Paul III, who officially recognized the Jesuits in 1540.

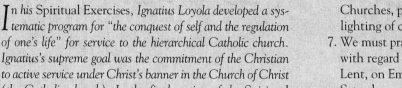

Loyola and Obedience to "Our Holy Mother, the Hierarchical Church"

In his Spiritual Exercises, Ignatius Loyola developed a systematic program for "the conquest of self and the regulation of one's life" for service to the hierarchical Catholic church. Ignatius's supreme goal was the commitment of the Christian to active service under Christ's banner in the Church of Christ (the Catholic church). In the final section of the Spiritual Exercises, Loyola explained the nature of that commitment in a series of "Rules for Thinking with the Church."

Ignatius Loyola, "Rules for Thinking with the Church"

The following rules should be observed to foster the true attitude of mind we ought to have in the Church militant.

1. We must put aside all judgment of our own, and keep the mind ever ready and prompt to obey in all things the true Spouse of Jesus Christ, our holy Mother, the hierarchical Church.
2. We should praise sacramental confession, the yearly reception of the Most Blessed Sacrament [the Lord's Supper], and praise more highly monthly reception, and still more weekly Communion. . . .
3. We ought to praise the frequent hearing of Mass, the singing of hymns, psalmody, and long prayers whether in the church or outside. . . .
4. We must praise highly religious life, virginity, and continency; and matrimony ought not be praised as much as any of these.
5. We should praise vows of religion, obedience, poverty, chastity, and vows to perform other works of supererogation conducive to perfection. . . .
6. We should show our esteem for the relics of the saints by venerating them and praying to the saints. We should praise visits to the Station

Churches, pilgrimages, indulgences, jubilees, the lighting of candles in churches.
7. We must praise the regulations of the Church, with regard to fast and abstinence, for example, in Lent, on Ember Days, Vigils, Fridays, and Saturdays.
8. We ought to praise not only the building and adornment of churches, but also images and veneration of them according to the subject they represent.
9. Finally, we must praise all the commandments of the Church, and be on the alert to find reasons to defend them, and by no means in order to criticize them.
10. We should be more ready to approve and praise the orders, recommendations, and way of acting of our superiors than to find fault with them. Though some of the orders, etc., may not have been praiseworthy, yet to speak against them, either when preaching in public or in speaking before the people, would rather be the cause of murmuring and scandal than of profit. As a consequence, the people would become angry with their superiors, whether secular or spiritual. But while it does harm in the absence of our superiors to speak evil of them before the people, it may be profitable to discuss their bad conduct with those who can apply a remedy.
13. If we wish to proceed securely in all things, we must hold fast to the following principle: What seems to me white, I will believe black if the hierarchical Church so defines. For I must be convinced that in Christ our Lord, the bridegroom, and in His spouse the Church, only one Spirit holds sway, which governs and rules for the salvation of souls.

premier academic posts in Catholic universities, and by 1600, they were the most famous educators in Europe. Another prominent Jesuit activity was the propagation of the Catholic faith among non-Christians. Francis Xavier (1506–1552), one of the original members of the Society of Jesus, carried the message of Catholic Christianity to the Far East, ministering to India and Japan before dying of fever. Although conversion efforts in Japan proved short-lived, Jesuit activity in China, espe-

cially that of the Italian Matteo Ricci, was more long lasting. Finally, the Jesuits were determined to carry the Catholic banner and fight Protestantism. Jesuit missionaries proved singularly successful in restoring Catholicism to parts of Germany and eastern Europe. Poland was, in fact, largely won back for the Catholic church through Jesuit efforts. As the "shock troops of the papacy," the Jesuits proved invaluable allies of papal policies.

A Revived Papacy

The involvement of the Renaissance papacy in dubious finances and Italian political and military affairs had created numerous sources of corruption. The meager steps taken to control corruption left the papacy still in need of serious reform, and it took the jolt of the Protestant Reformation to bring it about. Indeed, the change in the papacy in the course of the sixteenth century was one of the more remarkable aspects of the Catholic Reformation.

The pontificate of Pope Paul III (1534–1549) proved to be a turning point in the reform of the papacy. Raised in the lap of Renaissance luxury, Paul III continued Renaissance papal practices by appointing his nephews as cardinals, involving himself in politics, and patronizing arts and letters on a lavish scale. Nevertheless, he perceived the need for change and expressed it decisively. Advocates of reform, such as Gasparo Contarini and Gian Pietro Caraffa, were made cardinals. In 1535, Paul took the audacious step of appointing a Reform Commission to study the church's condition. The commission's report in 1537, which blamed the church's problems on the corrupt policies of popes and cardinals, was used even by Protestants to demonstrate that their criticisms of Catholic corruption had been justified. Paul III also formally recognized the Jesuits and summoned the Council of Trent.

A decisive turning point in the direction of the Catholic Reformation and the nature of papal reform came in the 1540s. In 1541, a colloquy had been held at Regensburg in a final attempt to settle the religious division peacefully. Here Catholic moderates, such as Cardinal Contarini, who favored concessions to Protestants in the hope of restoring Christian unity, reached a compromise with Protestant moderates on a number of doctrinal issues. When Contarini returned to Rome with these proposals, Cardinal Caraffa and other hardliners, who regarded all compromise with Protestant innovations as heresy, accused him of selling out to the heretics. It soon became apparent that the conservative reformers were in the ascendancy when Caraffa was able to persuade Paul III to establish a Roman Inquisition or Holy Office in 1542 to ferret out doctrinal errors. There was to be no compromise with Protestantism.

When Cardinal Caraffa was chosen pope as Paul IV (1555–1559), he so increased the power of the Inquisition that even liberal cardinals were silenced. This "first true pope of the Catholic Counter-Reformation," as he has been called, also created an Index of Forbidden Books, a list of books that Catholics were not allowed to read. It included all the works of Protestant theologians as well as authors considered "unwholesome," a category general enough to include the works of Erasmus. Rome, the capital of Catholic Christianity, was rapidly becoming fortress Rome; any hope of restoring Christian unity by compromise was fast fading. The activities of the Council of Trent made compromise virtually impossible.

The Council of Trent

In 1542, Pope Paul III took the decisive step of calling for a general council of Christendom to resolve the religious differences created by the Protestant revolt. It was not until March 1545, however, that a group of cardinals, archbishops, bishops, abbots, and theologians met in the city of Trent on the border between Germany and Italy. This Council of Trent met intermittently from 1545 to 1563 in three major sessions. Two fundamental struggles determined its outcome. While the pope hoped to focus on doctrinal issues, the Holy Roman Emperor Charles V wanted church reform to be the chief order of business, since he realized that defining doctrine first would only make the split in the church permanent. A second conflict focused on the division between Catholic moderates and conservatives. While the former believed that compromises would have to be made in formulating doctrinal definitions, the latter favored an uncompromising restatement of Catholic doctrines in strict opposition to Protestant positions. The latter group won, although not without a struggle. The Protestants were invited to attend the council, but since they were not permitted to participate, they refused the meaningless invitation. By and large, the popes controlled the council.

The final doctrinal decrees of the Council of Trent reaffirmed traditional Catholic teachings in opposition to Protestant beliefs. Scripture and tradition were affirmed as equal authorities in religious matters; only the church could interpret Scripture. Both faith and good works were declared necessary for salvation. The seven sacraments, the Catholic doctrine of transubstantiation, and clerical celibacy were all upheld. Belief in purgatory and in the efficacy of indulgences was affirmed, although the hawking of indulgences was prohibited. Of the reforming decrees that were passed, the most important established theological seminaries in every diocese for the training of priests.

After the Council of Trent, the Roman Catholic church possessed a clear body of doctrine and a unified church under the acknowledged supremacy of the popes who had triumphed over bishops and councils. The

Roman Catholic church had become one Christian denomination among many with an organizational framework and doctrinal pattern that would not be significantly altered until Vatican Council II four hundred years later. With a new spirit of confidence, the Catholic church entered a militant phase, as well prepared as the Calvinists to do battle for the Lord. An era of religious warfare was about to unfold.

Conclusion

When the Augustinian monk Martin Luther entered the public scene with a series of theses on indulgences, few people in Europe, or Germany for that matter, suspected that they would eventually produce a division of Europe along religious lines. But the yearning for reform of the church and meaningful religious experience caused a seemingly simple dispute to escalate into a powerful movement. Clearly, the papacy and other elements in the Catholic church underestimated the strength of Martin Luther and the desire for religious change.

Although Luther felt that his revival of Christianity based on his interpretation of the Bible should be acceptable to all, others soon appeared who also read the Bible but interpreted it in different ways. Protestantism split into different sects, which, though united in their dislike of Catholicism, were themselves divided over the interpretation of the sacraments and religious practices. As reform ideas spread, religion and politics became ever more intertwined. Political support played a crucial role in the spread of the Reformation.

Although Lutheranism was legally acknowledged in the Holy Roman Empire by the Peace of Augsburg in 1555, it had lost much of its momentum and outside of Scandinavia had scant ability to attract new supporters. Its energy was largely replaced by the new Protestant form of Calvinism, which had a clarity of doctrine and a fervor that made it attractive to a whole new generation of Europeans. But while Calvinism's militancy enabled it to expand across Europe, Catholicism was also experiencing its own revival and emerged as a militant faith, prepared to do combat for the souls of the faithful. An age of religious passion would tragically be followed by an age of religious warfare.

NOTES

1. Erasmus, *The Paraclesis,* in John Olin, ed., *Christian Humanism and the Reformation: Selected Writings of Erasmus,* 3d ed. (New York, 1987), p. 101.
2. Quoted in James B. Ross and Mary M. McLaughlin, eds., *The Portable Renaissance Reader* (New York, 1953), p. 83.
3. Thomas More, *Utopia,* trans. Paul Turner (Harmondsworth, 1965), p. 76.
4. Ibid., pp. 63–64.
5. Quoted in Alister E. McGrath, *Reformation Thought: An Introduction* (Oxford, 1988), p. 72.
6. Quoted in Roland Bainton, *Here I Stand: A Life of Martin Luther* (New York, 1950), pp. 49–50.
7. Quoted in Gordon Rupp, *Luther's Progress to the Diet of Worms* (New York, 1964), p. 82.
8. Quoted in ibid., p. 81.
9. *On the Freedom of a Christian Man,* quoted in E. G. Rupp and Benjamin Drewery, eds., *Martin Luther* (New York, 1970), p. 50.
10. Quoted in Bainton, *Here I Stand: A Life of Martin Luther,* p. 144.
11. Quoted in De Lamar Jensen, *Reformation Europe* (Lexington, Mass., 1981), p. 83.
12. Quoted in A. G. Dickens and Dorothy Carr, eds., *The Reformation in England to the Accession of Elizabeth I* (New York, 1968), p. 72.
13. Quoted in Lewis W. Spitz, *The Renaissance and Reformation Movements* (Chicago, 1971), p. 414.
14. John Calvin, *Institutes of the Christian Religion,* trans. John Allen (Philadelphia, 1936), 1:220.
15. Ibid., 1:228; 2:181.
16. Quoted in Roland Bainton, *Women of the Reformation in Germany and Italy* (Minneapolis, 1971), p. 154.
17. Quoted in Bonnie S. Anderson and Judith P. Zinsser, *A History of Their Own: Women in Europe from Prehistory to the Present* (New York, 1988), 1:259.
18. Quoted in John A. Phillips, *Eve: The History of an Idea* (New York, 1984), p. 105.

SUGGESTIONS FOR FURTHER READING

Basic surveys of the Reformation period include H. J. Grimm, *The Reformation Era, 1500–1650*, 2d ed. (New York, 1973); P. J. Klassen, *Europe in the Reformation* (Englewood Cliffs, N.J., 1979); D. L. Jensen, *Reformation Europe* (Lexington, Mass., 1981); G. R. Elton, *Reformation Europe, 1517–1559* (Cleveland, 1963); and E. Cameron, *The European Reformation* (New York, 1991). L. W. Spitz, *The Protestant Reformation, 1517–1559* (New York, 1985), is a sound and up-to-date history. The significance of the Protestant Reformation is examined in S. Ozment, *Protestants: The Birth of a Revolution* (New York, 1992). A brief but very useful introduction to the theology of the Reformation can be found in A. McGrath, *Reformation Thought: An Introduction*, 2d ed. (Oxford, 1993). For an overview of how European religious life in the Late Middle Ages affected the Reformation, see J. Bossy, *Christianity in the West: 1400–1700* (Oxford, 1987).

The development of humanism outside Italy is examined in C. G. Nauert, Jr., *Humanism and the Culture of Renaissance Europe* (Cambridge, 1995). On Thomas More, see R. Marius, *Thomas More: A Biography* (New York, 1984); and E. E. Reynolds, *The Life and Death of St. Thomas More* (New York, 1978). The best general biography of Erasmus is still R. Bainton, *Erasmus of Christendom* (New York, 1969), although the shorter works by J. K. Sowards, *Desiderius Erasmus* (Boston, 1975); and J. McConica, *Erasmus* (Oxford, 1991), are also good.

On religious conditions in Europe on the eve of the Reformation, see T. N. Tentler, *Sin and Confession on the Eve of the Reformation* (Princeton, N.J., 1977); and on Germany, G. Strauss, *Manifestations of Discontent in Germany on the Eve of the Reformation* (Bloomington, Ind., 1971).

The Reformation in Germany can be examined in H. Holborn, *A History of Modern Germany: The Reformation* (New York, 1959), still an outstanding survey of the entire Reformation period in Germany; and J. Lortz, *The Reformation in Germany*, trans. R. Walls, 2 vols. (New York, 1968), a detailed Catholic account. The classic account of Martin Luther's life is R. Bainton, *Here I Stand: A Life of Martin Luther* (New York and Nashville, 1950). More recent works include H. A. Oberman,

Luther (New York, 1992); W. von Loewenich, *Martin Luther: The Man and His Work* (Minneapolis, 1986); J. M. Kittelson, *Luther the Reformer: The Story of the Man and His Career* (Minneapolis, 1986); and H. G. Haile, *Luther: An Experiment in Biography* (Garden City, N.Y., 1980). An interesting psychoanalytical approach to Luther can be found in E. H. Erikson, *Young Man Luther: A Study in Psychoanalysis and History* (New York, 1962). Luther's relations with early Protestant dissenters from his ideas can be examined in M. Edwards, Jr., *Luther and the False Brethren* (Stanford, 1975); and E. G. Rupp, *Patterns of Reformation* (London, 1969). On the Peasants' War, see especially P. Blickle, *The Revolution of 1525: The German Peasants' War from a New Perspective* (Baltimore, Md., 1981). The spread of Luther's ideas in Germany can be examined in M. Hannemann, *The Diffusion of the Reformation in Southwestern Germany, 1518–1534* (Chicago, 1975); B. Moeller, *Imperial Cities and the Reformation* (Durham, N.C., 1982); S. Ozment, *The Reformation in the Cities* (New Haven, Conn., 1975); G. Strauss, *Nuremberg in the Sixteenth Century* (Bloomington, Ind., 1978); T. Brady, *Ruling Class, Regime and Reformation at Strassburg* (Leiden, 1978); and R. Po-Chia Hsia, ed., *The German People and the Reformation* (Ithaca, N.Y., 1988).

The best account of Ulrich Zwingli is G. R. Potter, *Zwingli* (Cambridge, 1976). One aspect of the spread of the Reformation in Switzerland is examined in J. M. Kittelson, *Wolfgang Capito: From Humanist to Reformer* (Leiden, 1975).

The most comprehensive account of the various groups and individuals who are called Anabaptists is G. H. Williams, *The Radical Reformation* (Philadelphia, 1962). Other valuable studies include C.-P. Clasen, *Anabaptism: A Social History, 1525–1618* (Ithaca, N.Y., 1972); M. Mullett, *Radical Religious Movements in Early Modern Europe* (London, 1980); and C. Krahn, *Dutch Anabaptism: Origin, Spread, Life and Thought, 1450–1600* (The Hague, 1968). Also see R. Po-Chia Hsia, *Society and Reformation in Münster, 1535–1618* (New Haven, Conn., 1984).

Two worthwhile surveys of the English Reformation are A. G. Dickens, *The English Reformation* (New York, 1964); and G. R. Elton, *Reform and Reformation: En-*

gland, 1509–1558 (Cambridge, Mass., 1977). Good biographies of the leading personalities of the age include J. J. Scarisbrick, *Henry VIII* (Berkeley, 1968); B. W. Beckensgale, *Thomas Cromwell, Tudor Minister* (Totowa, N.J., 1978); J. Ridley, *Thomas Cranmer* (Oxford, 1962); W. K. Jordan, *Edward VI, the Young King* (Cambridge, Mass., 1968), and *Edward VI, the Threshold of Power* (Cambridge, Mass., 1970); and D. M. Loades, *The Reign of Mary Tudor* (London, 1979). Other specialized works on the period include the controversial classic by G. R. Elton, *The Tudor Revolution in Government*, 2d ed. (Cambridge, 1973); D. Knowles, *Bare Ruined Choirs: The Dissolution of the English Monasteries* (New York, 1976); and W. R. D. Jones, *The Mid-Tudor Crisis, 1539–1563* (New York, 1973).

For a good biography of Calvin, see the recent work by W. J. Bouwsma, *John Calvin* (New York, 1988). The best account of Calvin's work in the city of Geneva is W. Monter, *Calvin's Geneva* (New York, 1967).

The best overall account of the impact of the Reformation on the family is S. Ozment, *When Fathers Ruled: Family Life in Reformation Europe* (Cambridge, Mass., 1983). M. E. Wiesner's *Working Women in Renaissance Germany* (New Brunswick, N.J., 1986), covers primarily the sixteenth century. Also of value is R. Bainton, *Women of the Reformation in Germany and Italy* (Minneapolis, 1971). Broader perspectives are available in L. Stone, *The Family, Sex and Marriage in England: 1500–1800* (New York, 1979); and N. Z. Davis, *Society and Culture in Early Modern France* (Stanford, 1975). On education, see G. Strauss, *Luther's House of Learning* (Baltimore, 1978). R. W. Scribner's *For the Sake of Simple Folk* (Cambridge, 1981) deals with a number of issues on the popular culture of the German Reformation.

A good introduction to the Catholic Reformation can be found in the beautifully illustrated brief study by A. G. Dickens, *The Counter Reformation* (New York, 1969). Also valuable is M. R. O'Connell, *The Counter Reformation, 1559–1610* (New York, 1974). The work by J. Brodrick, *The Origin of the Jesuits* (Garden City, N.Y., 1960) offers a clear discussion of the founding of the Jesuits. A more critical approach is available in R. Fülöp-Miller, *The Jesuits: A History of the Society of Jesus* (New York, 1963). The most detailed study of the Council of Trent is H. Jedin, *History of the Council of Trent*, trans. E. Graf, 2 vols. (London, 1957–61).

Discovery and Crisis in the Sixteenth and Seventeenth Centuries

By the middle of the sixteenth century, it was apparent that the religious passions of the Reformation era had brought an end to the religious unity of medieval Europe. The religious division (Catholics versus Protestants) was instrumental in beginning a series of wars that dominated much of European history between 1560 and 1650. The struggles fought in Germany at the beginning of the seventeenth century (known as the Thirty Years' War) were especially brutal and devastating. When the Catholic general Johann Tilly captured Neubrandenburg, his forces massacred the 3,000 defenders. A month later, the army of the Protestant leader Gustavus Adolphus retaliated by slaughtering the entire garrison of 2,000 men at Frankfurt-an-der-Oder. Noncombatants suffered as well, as is evident from the contemporary description by Otto von Guericke of the sack of Magdeburg. Once the city had been captured, Tilly's forces were let loose: "Then there was nothing but beating and burning, plundering, torture, and murder." All the buildings were looted of anything valuable, and then the city was "given over to the flames, and thousands of innocent men, women, and children, in the midst of a horrible noise of heartrending shrieks and cries, were tortured and put to death in so cruel and shameful a manner that no words would suffice to describe." Thus, "in a single day this noble and famous city, the pride of the whole country, went up in fire and smoke, and the remnant of its citizens, with their wives and children, were taken prisoners and driven away by the enemy."

The wars, in turn, worsened the economic and social crises that were besetting Europe. Wars, rebellions and constitutional crises, economic depression, social disintegration, a witchcraft craze, and a demographic crisis all afflicted Europe and have led some historians to speak of the ninety years between 1560 and 1650 as an age of crisis in European life.

Periods of crisis, however, are frequently ages of opportunities, nowhere more apparent than in the geographical discoveries that made this an era of Eu-

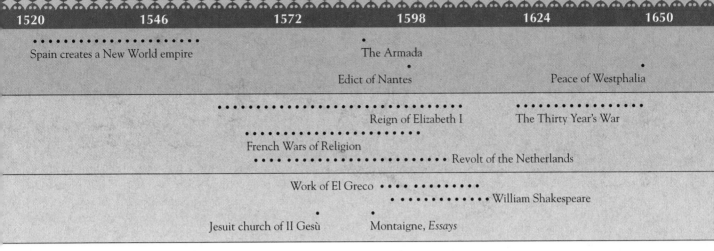

1520	1546	1572	1598	1624	1650

Spain creates a New World empire

The Armada

Edict of Nantes

Peace of Westphalia

Reign of Elizabeth I

The Thirty Year's War

French Wars of Religion

Revolt of the Netherlands

Work of El Greco

William Shakespeare

Jesuit church of II Gesù

Montaigne, *Essays*

---

ropean expansion into new worlds. Although the discovery of new territories began before the sixteenth century, it was not until the sixteenth and seventeenth centuries that Europeans began to comprehend the significance of their discoveries and to exploit them for their material gain.

An Age of Discovery and Expansion

Nowhere has the dynamic and even ruthless energy of Western civilization been more apparent than in its expansion into the rest of the world. By the sixteenth century, the Atlantic seaboard had become the center of a commercial activity that raised Portugal and Spain and later the Dutch Republic, England, and France to prominence. The age of expansion was a crucial factor in the European transition from the agrarian economy of the Middle Ages to a commercial and industrial capitalistic system.

The Motives

For almost a millennium, Catholic Europe had been confined to one geographical area. Its one major attempt to expand beyond those frontiers, the crusades, had largely failed. Of course, Europe had never completely lost touch with the outside world: the goods of Asia and Africa made their way into medieval castles; the works of Muslim philosophers were read in medieval universi-

ties; and in the ninth and tenth centuries the Vikings had even made their way to the eastern fringes of North America. But in all cases, contacts with non-European civilizations remained limited until the end of the fifteenth century, when Europeans embarked upon a remarkable series of overseas journeys. What caused Europeans to undertake such dangerous voyages to the ends of the earth?

Europeans had long had an attraction to the Far East. In the Middle Ages, myths and legends of an exotic Far East of great riches and magic were widespread. Although Muslim control of central Asia cut Europe off from the east, Mongol conquests in the thirteenth century reopened the doors. The most famous medieval travelers to the east were the Polos of Venice. Niccolò and Maffeo, merchants from Venice, accompanied by Niccolò's son Marco, undertook the lengthy journey to the court of the great Mongol ruler Kublai Khan (1259–1294) in 1271. As one of the great Khan's ambassadors, Marco traveled to Japan as well and did not return to Italy until 1295. An account of his experiences, the *Travels*, proved to be the most informative of all the descriptions of Asia by medieval European travelers. Others followed the Polos, but in the fourteenth century, the conquests of the Ottoman Turks and then the overthrow of the Mongols by the first of the Ming Chinese emperors halted Western traffic to the east. With the closing of the overland routes to the Far East, a number of people became interested in the possibility of reaching Asia by sea to gain access to eastern spices and other precious items.

An economic motive thus looms large in Renaissance European expansion. There were high hopes of finding precious metals and new areas of trade, in particular, more direct sources for the spices of the east. The latter continued to come to Europe via Arab middlemen but were outrageously expensive. Many European explorers and conquerors did not hesitate to express their desire for material gain. One Spanish conquistador explained that he and his kind went to the New World to "serve God and His Majesty, to give light to those who were in darkness, and to grow rich, as all men desire to do."[1]

This statement expresses another major reason for the overseas voyages—religious zeal. A crusading mentality was particularly strong in Portugal and Spain where the Muslims had largely been driven out in the Middle Ages. Contemporaries of Prince Henry the Navigator of Portugal (see the next section) said that he was motivated by "his great desire to make increase in the faith of our Lord Jesus Christ and to bring him all the souls that should be saved." While most scholars believe the religious motive was secondary to economic considerations, it would be foolish to overlook the genuine desire on the part of both explorers and conquistadors, let alone missionaries, to convert the heathen to Christianity. Hernan Cortés, the conqueror of Mexico, asked his Spanish rulers if it was not their duty to ensure that the native Mexicans "are introduced into and instructed in the holy Catholic faith," and predicted that if "the devotion, trust and hope which they now have in their idols turned so as to repose with the divine power of the true God ... they would work many miracles."[2] Spiritual and secular affairs were closely intertwined in the sixteenth century. No doubt, grandeur and glory as well as plain intellectual curiosity and spirit of adventure also played some role in European expansion.

If "God, glory, and gold" were the motives, what made the voyages possible? First of all, the expansion of Europe was connected to the growth of centralized monarchies during the Renaissance. Although historians still debate the degree of that centralization, the reality is that Renaissance expansion was a state enterprise. By the second half of the fifteenth century, European monarchies had increased both their authority and their resources and were in a position to turn their energies beyond their borders. For France, that meant the invasion of Italy, but for Portugal, a state not strong enough to pursue power in Europe, it meant going abroad. The Spanish situation was more complex since by the sixteenth century the strength of the Spanish monarchy enabled it to pursue power on both the continent and beyond.

At the same time, by the end of the fifteenth century, European states had achieved a level of wealth and technology that enabled them to undertake a regular series of voyages beyond Europe. Although the highly schematic and symbolic medieval maps were of little help to sailors, the portolani or detailed charts made by medieval navigators and mathematicians in the thirteenth and fourteenth centuries, featuring details on coastal shapes, distances between ports, and compass readings, proved of great value. By the end of the fifteenth century, cartography had developed to the point that Europeans possessed fairly accurate maps of the known world. Moreover, Europeans had developed remarkably seaworthy ships as well as navigational aids, such as the compass and astrolabe (an instrument used to determine the position of heavenly bodies). Much of the geographical knowledge learned in the early phase of expansion was passed on to succeeding generations. Indeed, one of the most immediate results of the age of expansion was an enormous increase in knowledge of the physical proportions of the world.

The Development of a Portuguese Maritime Empire

Portugal took the lead in exploring the coast of Africa under the leadership of Prince Henry the "Navigator" (1394–1460), whose motives were a blend of seeking a Christian kingdom as an ally against the Muslims, acquiring trade opportunities for Portugal, and extending Christianity. In 1419, Prince Henry founded a school for navigators on the southwestern coast of Portugal. Shortly thereafter, Portuguese fleets began probing southward along the western coast of Africa in search of gold, which had been carried northward from south of the Atlas Mountain in central Morocco for centuries. In 1441, Portuguese ships reached the Senegal River, just north of Cape Verde, and brought home a cargo of black Africans, most of whom were then sold as slaves to wealthy buyers elsewhere in Europe. Within a few years, an estimated thousand slaves were shipped annually from the area back to Lisbon.

Through regular expeditions, the Portuguese gradually crept down the African coast, and in 1471, they discovered a new source of gold along the southern coast of the hump of West Africa (an area that would henceforth be known to Europeans as the Gold Coast). A few years later, they established contact with the state of Bakongo, near the mouth of the Zaire (Congo) River in Central Africa. To facilitate trade in gold, ivory, and slaves (some of the latter were brought back to Lisbon while others were bartered to local merchants for gold), the Portuguese leased land from local rulers and built stone forts along the coast.

Hearing reports of a route to India around the southern tip of Africa, Portuguese sea captains continued their probing, and in 1487, Bartholomew Diaz rounded the Cape of Good Hope. Vasco da Gama surpassed that accomplishment by rounding the cape, skirting the eastern coast of Africa, and cutting across the Indian Ocean to the southwestern coast of India. At the port of Calicut, he took on a cargo of pepper and precious stones and then returned to Portugal, where he made a handsome profit on his valuable goods. Da Gama's successful voyage marked the beginning of an all-water route to India.

After da Gama's return, Portugal sent a larger fleet to the east. Despite opposition from Muslim traders in west India, the ships managed to return to Portugal with valuable cargo. One contemporary described their contents: "Cinnamon, fresh and dried ginger, much pepper, cloves, nutmegs, mace, musk, porcelains, incense, myrrh, red and white sandalwood, opium, India paper, and a great variety of drugs. . . . I saw many diamonds, rubies, and pearls." By 1501, annual Portuguese fleets to India were making serious inroads into the Mediterranean trade of the Venetians and Turks.

Under the direction of officials known as viceroys, Portugal now created an overseas empire. Most important was Alfonso d'Albuquerque (c. 1462–1515), a

Map 15.1 Discoveries and Possessions in the Fifteenth and Sixteenth Centuries.

Principal Voyages of Discovery

A Portuguese expeditions 1430s–1480s
B Diaz 1487–1488
C Da Gama 1497–1499
D Portuguese voyages to the Far East 1509–1514
E Columbus's first voyage 1492
F Columbus's three successive voyages 1493–1504
G Voyages attended by Vespucci 1499–1502
H Magellan—Del Cano 1519–1522
I Cabot 1497

Areas under Spanish control
Areas under Portuguese control
Line of Demarcation, Treaty of Tordesillas 1492
Spanish trading cities
Portuguese trading cities
Independent trading cities
Spanish routes
Portuguese routes
Other routes

✦ **Two-Masted Ocean-Going Ship.** Numerous overseas voyages to both North and South America were made in the first two decades of the sixteenth century. This detail from Pieter Brueghel's *Landscape with the Fall of Icarus* depicts a two-masted ocean-going ship of the type used in the voyages of the mid-sixteenth century.

heavily armed and were able not only to intimidate but also to inflict severe defeats if necessary on local naval and land forces. The Portuguese by no means possessed a monopoly on the use of firearms and explosives, but their effective use of naval technology, heavy guns, and tactics gave them a military superiority over lightly armed rivals that they were able to exploit until the arrival of other European forces—the English, Dutch, and French—in the seventeenth century.

Voyages to the New World

While the Portuguese sought access to the spice trade of the Indies by sailing eastward through the Indian Ocean, the Spanish attempted to reach the same destination by sailing westward across the Atlantic. Although the Spanish came to overseas discovery and exploration after the initial efforts of Henry the Navigator, their resources enabled them to establish an overseas empire that was far grander and quite different from the Portuguese enclaves.

An important figure in the history of Spanish exploration was an Italian, Cristoforo Colombo, more commonly known as Christopher Columbus (1451–1506). Knowledgeable Europeans were aware that the world was round, but had little understanding of its circumference or the extent of the continent of Asia. Convinced that the circumference of the earth was less than contemporaries believed and that Asia was larger than people thought, Columbus felt that Asia could be reached by sailing west instead of around Africa. Queen Isabella of Spain was finally persuaded to finance Columbus's exploratory expedition, which reached the Americas in October 1492, exploring the Bahamas, the coastline of Cuba, and the northern shores of Hispaniola (present-day Haiti and the Dominican Republic). Columbus believed that he had reached Asia, and in three subsequent voyages (1493, 1498, 1502), he sought in vain to find a route through the outer lands to the Asian mainland. In his four voyages, Columbus reached all the major islands of the Caribbean and the mainland of Central America.

Although Columbus clung to his belief until his death, other explorers soon realized that he had discovered a new frontier altogether. State-sponsored explorers joined the race to the New World. A Venetian seaman, John Cabot, explored the New England coastline of the Americas under a license from King Henry VII of England. The continent of South America was discovered accidentally by the Portuguese sea captain Pedro

tough nobleman who took the lead in establishing a ring of commercial-military bases centered at Goa, an island off the Malabar Coast of India. The Portuguese also reached beyond India by taking the island of Macao at the mouth of the Pearl River in China. The Portuguese empire remained a limited empire of enclaves or trading posts on the coasts of India and China. The Portuguese possessed neither the power nor the desire to colonize the Asian regions.

Why were the Portuguese so successful? Basically, their success was a matter of guns and seamanship. The first Portuguese fleet to arrive in Indian waters was relatively modest in size, consisting of three ships and twenty guns, a force sufficient for self-defense and intimidation, but not for serious military operations. Later Portuguese fleets, which began to arrive with regularity by the end of the sixteenth century, were more

Cabral in 1500. Amerigo Vespucci, a Florentine, accompanied several voyages and wrote a series of letters describing the geography of the New World. The publication of these letters led to the use of the name "America" (after Amerigo) for the new lands.

The first two decades of the sixteenth century witnessed numerous overseas voyages that explored the eastern coasts of both North and South America. Vasco Nuñez de Balboa, a Spanish explorer, led an expedition across the Isthmus of Panama and reached the Pacific Ocean in 1513. Perhaps the most dramatic of all these expeditions was the journey of Ferdinand Magellan (1480–1521) in 1519. After passing through the Straits named after him at the bottom of South America, he sailed across the Pacific Ocean and reached the Philippines (named after King Philip of Spain by Magellan's crew) where he met his death at the hands of the natives. Although only one of his original fleet of five ships survived and returned to Spain, Magellan's name is still associated with the first known circumnavigation of the earth.

The newly discovered territories were called the New World, although they possessed flourishing civilizations populated by millions of people when the Europeans arrived. The Americas were, of course, new to the Europeans who quickly saw opportunities for conquest and exploitation. The Spanish, in particular, were interested because in 1494 the Treaty of Tordesillas had divided up the newly discovered world into separate Portuguese and Spanish spheres of influence. Hereafter the route east around the Cape of Good Hope was to be reserved for the Portuguese while the route across the Atlantic (except for the eastern hump of South America) was assigned to Spain.

The Spanish Empire

The Spanish conquistadors were hardy individuals motivated by a typical sixteenth-century blend of glory, greed, and religious crusading zeal. Although sanctioned by the Castilian crown, these groups were financed and outfitted privately, not by the government. Their superior weapons, organizational skills, and determination brought the conquistadors incredible success. They also benefited from rivalries among the native peoples.

In 1519, a Spanish expedition under the command of Hernan Cortés landed at Veracruz, on the Gulf of Mexico. Marching to the city of Tenochtitlań (see the box on p. 496) at the head of a small contingent of troops, Cortés received a friendly welcome from the

Aztec monarch Moctezuma Xocoyotzin (often called simply Montezuma), who initially believed his visitor was a representative of Quetzacoatl, a godlike being who had departed from his homeland centuries before. But tensions soon erupted between the Spaniards and the Aztecs, provoked in part by demands by Cortés that the Aztecs denounce their native beliefs and accept Christianity. When the Spanish took Moctezuma hostage and began to destroy Aztec religious shrines, the local population revolted and drove the invaders from the city. With the assistance of other Indians, Cortés managed to

◆ **Christopher Columbus.** Columbus was an Italian explorer who worked for the queen of Spain. He has become a symbol for two entirely different perspectives. To some, he was a great and heroic explorer who discovered the New World; to others, especially in Latin America, he was responsible for beginning a process of invasion that led to the destruction of an entire way of life. This painting by the Italian Sebastiano del Piombo in 1519 is the earliest known portrait of Columbus, but it was done thirteen years after his death and reveals as much about the painter's conception of Columbus as it does about the explorer himself.

The Spanish Conquistador: Cortés and the Conquest of Mexico

Hernan Cortés was a minor Spanish nobleman who came to the New World in 1504 to seek his fortune. Contrary to his superior's orders, Cortés waged an independent campaign of conquest and overthrew the Aztec empire of Mexico (1519–1521). Cortés wrote a series of five reports to Emperor Charles V to justify his action. The second report includes a description of Tenochtitlán, the capital of the Aztec empire. The Spanish conquistador and his men were obviously impressed by this city, awesome in its architecture yet built by people who lacked European technology, such as wheeled vehicles and tools of hard metal.

Cortés's Description of an Aztec City

The great city Tenochtitlán is built in the midst of this salt lake, and it is two leagues from the heart of the city to any point on the mainland. Four causeways lead to it, all made by hand and some twelve feet wide. The city itself is as large as Seville or Córdoba. The principal streets are very broad and straight, the majority of them being of beaten earth, but a few and at least half the smaller thoroughfares are waterways along which they pass in their canoes. Moreover, even the principal streets have openings at regular distances so that the water can freely pass from one to another, and these openings which are very broad are spanned by great bridges of huge beams, very stoutly put together, so firm indeed that over many of them ten horsemen can ride at once. Seeing that if the natives intended any treachery against us they would have every opportunity from the way in which the city is built, for by removing the bridges from the entrances and exits they could leave us to die of hunger with no possibility of getting to the mainland, I immediately set to work as soon as we entered the city on the building of four brigs, and in a short space of time had them finished, so that we could ship three hundred men and the horses to the mainland whenever we so desired.

The city has many open squares in which markets are continuously held and the general business of buying and selling proceeds. One square in particular is twice as big as that of Salamanca and completely surrounded by arcades where there are daily more than sixty thousand folk buying and selling. Every kind of merchandise such as may be met with in every land is for sale there, whether of food and victuals, or ornaments of gold and silver, or lead, brass, copper, tin, precious stones, bones, shells, snails and feathers; limestone for building is likewise sold there, stone both rough and polished, bricks burnt and unburnt, wood of all kinds and in all stages of preparation. . . . There is a street of herb-sellers where there are all manner of roots and medicinal plants that are found in the land. There are houses as it were of apothecaries where they sell medicines made from these herbs, both for drinking and for use as ointments and salves. There are barbers' shops where you may have your hair washed and cut. There are other shops where you may obtain food and drink. . . .

Finally, to avoid prolixity in telling all the wonders of this city, I will simply say that the manner of living among the people is very similar to that in Spain, and considering that this is a barbarous nation shut off from a knowledge of the true God or communication with enlightened nations, one may well marvel at the orderliness and good government which is everywhere maintained.

The actual service of Moctezuma and those things which call for admiration by their greatness and state would take so long to describe that I assure your Majesty I do not know where to begin with any hope of ending. For as I have already said, what could there be more astonishing than that a barbarous monarch such as he should have reproductions made in gold, silver, precious stones, and feathers of all things to be found in his land, and so perfectly reproduced that there is no goldsmith or silversmith in the world who could better them, nor can one understand what instrument could have been used for fashioning the jewels; as for the featherwork its like is not to be seen in either wax or embroidery; it is so marvelously delicate.

---

fight his way back into the city. Meanwhile the Aztecs were beginning to suffer the first effects of the diseases brought by the Europeans, which would eventually wipe out the majority of the local population. In a climactic battle, the Aztecs were finally vanquished. Within months, their magnificent city and its temples, believed by the conquerors to be the work of Satan, had been destroyed, and within three years, the mighty Aztec empire on mainland Mexico was no more. Between 1531 and 1550, the Spanish gained control of northern Mexico.

The Inca empire high in the Peruvian Andes was still in existence when the first Spanish expeditions arrived in the area. The leader of the Spanish invaders, Francisco Pizarro, was accompanied by only a few hundred companions, but like Cortés he possessed steel weapons, gunpowder, and horses, none of which were familiar to his hosts. In the meantime, internal factionalism, combined with the onset of contagious diseases spread unknowingly by the Europeans, had weakened the ruling elite, and the empire fell rapidly to the Spanish forces in 1532. The last Inca ruler was tried by the Spaniards and executed. Although it took another three decades before the western part of Latin America was brought under Spanish control (the Portuguese took over Brazil), already by 1535, the Spanish had created a system of colonial administration that made the New World an extension of the old.

ADMINISTRATION OF THE SPANISH EMPIRE IN THE NEW WORLD

The desires and actions of the conquistadors determined the early features of the colonial empire established by Spain in the Western Hemisphere. One primary goal guided many of these sixteenth-century Spanish adventurers—the desire to become nobles by gaining riches, land, and dominion over the inhabitants of the New World. Thus, the conquistadors searched for sources of gold and silver and tried to exploit the Indians as a regular source of labor.

While the conquistadors made decisions based on expediency and their own interests, Queen Isabella declared the natives to be subjects of Castile and instituted the Spanish *encomienda*, a system that permitted the conquering Spaniards to collect tribute from the natives and use them as laborers. In return, the holders of an *encomienda* were supposed to protect the Indians, pay them wages, and supervise their spiritual needs. In practice, this meant that the settlers were free to implement the paternalistic system of the government as they pleased. Three thousand miles from Spain, Spanish settlers largely ignored their government and brutally used the Indians to pursue their own economic interests. Indians were put to work on plantations and in the lucrative gold and silver mines. Forced labor, starvation, and especially disease took a fearful toll of Indian lives. With little or no natural resistance to European diseases, the Indians of America were ravaged by smallpox, measles, and typhus. These diseases came with the explorers and the conquistadors. Although scholarly estimates of native populations vary drastically, a rea-

✦ **World Map of the Early Sixteenth Century.** Overseas expansion affected not only the inhabitants of the New World, but also their European conquerors. New sources of gold and silver were discovered, and tensions grew between the European states as they competed for the products of the New World and Asia. Pictured here is a world map drawn by Girolamo Verrazano in 1529 showing the coastlines that had been charted by that time.

Las Casas and the Spanish Treatment of the American Natives

Bartolomé de Las Casas (1474–1566) participated in the conquest of Cuba and received land and Indians in return for his efforts. But in 1514 he underwent a radical transformation and came to believe that the Indians had been cruelly mistreated by his fellow Spaniards. He became a Dominican monk and spent the remaining years of his life (he lived to the age of ninety-two) fighting for the Indians. This selection is taken from his most influential work, which is known to English readers as The Tears of the Indians. *This work was largely responsible for the "black legend" of the Spanish as inherently "cruel and murderous fanatics." Most scholars feel that Las Casas may have exaggerated his account in order to shock his contemporaries into action.*

Bartolomé de Las Casas, *The Tears of the Indians*

There is nothing more detestable or more cruel, than the tyranny which the Spaniards use toward the Indians for the getting of pearl. Surely the infernal torments cannot much exceed the anguish that they endure, by reason of that way of cruelty; for they put them under water some four or five ells deep, where they are forced without any liberty of respiration, to gather up the shells wherein the pearls are; sometimes they come up again with nets full of shells to take breath, but if they stay any while to rest themselves, immediately comes a hangman row'd in a little boat, who as soon as he has well beaten them, drags them again to their labor. Their food is nothing but filth, and the very same that contains the pearl, with a small portion of that bread which that country affords; in the first whereof there is little nourishment; and as for the latter, it is made with great difficulty, besides that they have not enough of that neither for sustenance; they lie upon the ground in fetters, lest they should run away; and many times they are drown'd in this labor, and are never seen again till they swim upon the top of the waves: oftentimes they also are devoured by certain sea monsters, that are frequent in those seas. Consider whether this hard usage of the poor creatures be consistent with the precepts which God commands concerning charity to our neighbour, by those that cast them so undeservedly into the dangers of a cruel death, causing them to perish without any remorse or pity, or allowing them the benefit of the sacraments, or the knowledge of religion; it being impossible for them to live any time under the water; and this death is so much the more painful, by reason that by the coarctation of the breast, while the lungs strive to do their office, the vital parts are so afflicted that they die vomiting the blood out of their mouths. Their hair also, which is by nature black, is hereby changed and made of the same color with that of the sea wolves; their bodies are also so besprinkled with the froth of the sea, that they appear rather like monsters than men.

---

sonable guess is that 30 to 40 percent of the natives died. On Hispaniola alone, out of an initial population of 100,000 natives when Columbus arrived in 1493, only 300 Indians survived by 1570. In 1542, largely in response to the publications of Bartolomé de Las Casas, a Dominican monk who championed the Indians (see the box above), the government abolished the *encomienda* system and provided more protection for the natives.

The Spanish created a formal administrative system for their new empire. While a board of trade known as the *Casa de Contratación* supervised all economic matters related to the New World, the Council of the Indies, established in 1524, became the chief organ of colonial administration. The council nominated colonial officials (actual appointments were made by the crown), oversaw their New World activities, and kept an eye on ecclesiastical affairs in the colonies.

As disorder persisted in the New World possessions, the Spanish crown sought to affirm its authority by creating a new administrative system based on viceroys. Spanish possessions were divided into two major administrative units: New Spain (Mexico, Central America, and the Caribbean islands), with its center in Mexico City, and Peru (western South America), governed by a viceroy in Lima. The two viceroyalties in turn were subdivided into *presidencias* and captaincies-general, administered by presidents and captains-general who were theoretically, but not always practically, subordinate to the viceroys. *Audiencias* or royal courts provided advice and even laws to assist the viceroys in governing.

By papal agreement, the Catholic monarchs of Spain were given extensive rights over ecclesiastical affairs in the New World. They could appoint all bishops and clergy, build churches, collect fees, and supervise the affairs of the various religious orders who sought to

Christianize the heathen. Catholic missionaries—especially the Dominicans, Franciscans, and Jesuits—fanned out across the Spanish empire where they converted and baptized hundreds of thousands of Indians in the early years of the conquest. To facilitate their efforts, the missionaries brought Indians together into villages where they could be converted, taught trades, and encouraged to grow crops. Removing the Indians from their homes to these villages helped the missionaries not only to gain control over the Indians' lives but also to ensure that they would be docile subjects of the empire.

The mass conversion of the Indians brought the organizational and institutional structures of Catholicism to the New World. Dioceses, parishes, cathedrals, schools, and hospitals—all the trappings of civilized European society—soon appeared in the Spanish empire. So, too, did the Spanish Inquisition, established first in Peru in 1570 and then in Mexico in 1571.

The Impact of Expansion

European expansion made an enormous impact on both the conquerors and the conquered. The native American civilizations, which had their own unique qualities and a degree of sophistication not much appreciated by Europeans, were virtually destroyed. Ancient social and political structures were ripped up and replaced by European institutions, religion, language, and culture. The Portuguese trading posts in the Far East, on the other hand, had much less impact on native Asian civilizations.

European expansion also affected the conquerors, perhaps most notably in the economic arena. Wherever they went in the New World, Europeans sought to find sources of gold and silver. One Aztec commented that the Spanish conquerors "longed and lusted for gold. Their bodies swelled with greed, and their hunger was ravenous; they hungered like pigs for that gold."[3] Rich silver deposits were found and exploited in Mexico and southern Peru (modern Bolivia). When the mines at Potosí in Peru were opened in 1545, the value of precious metals imported into Europe quadrupled. It has been estimated that between 1503 and 1650 sixteen million kilograms (over thirty-five million pounds) of silver and 185,000 kilograms (407,000 pounds) of gold entered the port of Seville and helped to create a price revolution that affected the Spanish economy.

But gold and silver were only two of the products sent to Europe from the New World. Into Seville flowed sugar, dyes, cotton, vanilla, and hides from livestock raised on the grass-covered plains of South America.

New agricultural products such as potatoes, coffee, corn, and tobacco were also imported. Because of its trading posts in Asia, Portugal soon challenged the Italian states as the chief entry point of the eastern trade in spices, jewels, silk, carpets, ivory, leather, and perfumes, although the Venetians clung tenaciously to the spice trade until they lost out to the Dutch in the seventeenth century. Economic historians believe that the increase in the volume and area of European trade as well as the rise in fluid capital due to this expansion were crucial factors in producing a new era of commercial capitalism that represented the first step toward the world economy that has characterized the modern historical era.

European expansion, which was in part a product of European rivalries, also deepened those rivalries and increased the tensions among European states. Bitter conflicts arose over the cargoes coming from the New World and Asia. Although the Spanish and Portuguese were first to enter the competition, the Dutch, French, and English soon became involved on a large scale and by the seventeenth century were challenging the Portuguese and Spanish monopolies.

Finally, how does one evaluate the psychological impact of colonization on the colonizers? The relatively easy European success in dominating native peoples reinforced Christian Europe's belief in the inherent superiority of European civilization. The Scientific Revolution of the seventeenth century (see Chapter 17), the Enlightenment of the eighteenth (see Chapter 18), and the imperialism of the nineteenth (see Chapter 25) would all strengthen this Eurocentric perspective that has pervaded Western civilization's relationship with the rest of the world.

Politics and the Wars of Religion in the Sixteenth Century

The so-called wars of religion were a product of Reformation ideologies that allowed little room for compromise or toleration of differing opinions. By the middle of the sixteenth century, Calvinism and Catholicism had become highly militant religions dedicated to spreading the word of God as they interpreted it. While their struggle for the minds and hearts of Europeans is at the heart of the religious wars of the sixteenth century, economic, social, and political forces also played an important role in these conflicts. Of the sixteenth-century religious wars, none were more momentous or shattering than the French civil wars known as the French Wars of Religion.

The French Wars of Religion (1562–1598)

France seemed an unlikely place for a religious war. The Valois monarchs Francis I (1515–1547) and Henry II (1547–1559) had been strong rulers aided by royal officials, a permanent mercenary army, the power to tax, and the ability to control the French church by nominating bishops. But when Henry II was killed accidentally in a tournament in 1559 and was succeeded by a series of weak, feeble, and neurotic sons, two of whom were dominated by their mother, Catherine de' Medici, as regent, the forces held in check by the strong monarchy broke loose, beginning a series of intermittent and confused civil wars. Religious, political, economic, and social forces all contributed to these wars.

The religious forces were the most important. The growth of Calvinism led to persecution by Francis I that intensified under Henry II but did little to stop the spread of Calvinism. Huguenots (as the French Calvinists were called) came from all levels of society: artisans and shopkeepers hurt by rising prices and a rigid guild system; merchants and lawyers in provincial towns whose local privileges were tenuous; and members of the nobility. Possibly 40 to 50 percent of the French nobility became Huguenots, including the house of Bourbon, which stood next to the Valois in the royal line of succession and ruled the southern French kingdom of Navarre. The conversion of so many nobles made the Huguenots a potentially dangerous political threat to monarchical power. Though the Calvinists constituted only about 7 percent of the population, they were a strong-willed and well-organized minority. When civil war came in 1562, the Calvinists were ready for combat.

The Calvinist minority was greatly outnumbered by the Catholic majority. The Valois monarchy was staunchly Catholic, and its control of the Catholic church gave it little incentive to look favorably upon Protestantism. As regent for her sons, the moderate Catholic Catherine de' Medici (1519–1589) looked to religious compromise as a way to defuse the political tensions, but found to her consternation that both sides possessed their share of religious fanatics unwilling to make concessions. The extreme Catholic party—known as the ultra-Catholics—favored strict opposition to the Huguenots and were led by the Guise family. Possessing the loyalty of Paris and large sections of northern and northwestern France through their client-patronage system, they could recruit and pay for large armies and received support abroad from the papacy and Jesuits who favored the Guises' uncompromising Catholic position. Ironically, the allegiance of the Catholic Guises to their own dynasty and international Catholicism posed a strong threat to the Catholic Valois monarchy.

The religious issue was not the only factor that contributed to the French civil wars. Towns and provinces, which had long resisted the growing power of monarchical centralization, were only too willing to join a revolt against the monarchy. This was also true of the nobility, and the fact that so many of them were Calvinists created an important base of opposition to the crown. The French Wars of Religion, then, constituted a major constitutional crisis for France. At the same time, they were complicated by foreign intervention. The devout Catholic king of Spain, Philip II,

◆ **The Saint Bartholomew's Day Massacre.** Although the outbreak of religious war seemed unlikely in France, the collapse of the strong monarchy with the death of Henry II unleashed forces that created a series of civil wars. Pictured here is the Saint Bartholomew's Day massacre of 1572. This contemporary painting by the Huguenot artist François Dubois depicts a number of the incidents of that day when approximately three thousand Huguenots were murdered in Paris.

supported the policies of the ultra-Catholic Guise family while Elizabeth I of England supported the Huguenots for political reasons.

The French Wars of Religion temporarily halted the development of the French centralized territorial state. The claim of the ruling dynasty of the state to a person's loyalties was temporarily superseded by loyalty to one's religious belief. The remark of a close friend of the Guises to the Spanish ambassador in 1565 went to the heart of the problem:

> Nowadays Catholic princes must not proceed as they once did. At one time friends and enemies were distinguished by the frontiers of provinces and kingdoms, and were called Italians, Germans, French, Spaniards, English, and the like; now we must say Catholics and heretics, and a Catholic prince must consider all Catholics of all countries as his friends, just as the heretics consider all heretics as friends and subjects, whether they are their own vassals or not.[4]

For some people, the unity of France was less important than religious truth. But there also emerged in France a group of politiques who placed politics before religion and believed that no religious truth was worth the ravages of civil war. The politiques ultimately prevailed, but not until both sides were exhausted by bloodshed.

The wars erupted in 1562 when the powerful duke of Guise massacred a peaceful congregation of Huguenots at Vassy. In the decade of the 1560s, the Huguenots held their own. Too small a group to conquer France, their armies were so good at defensive campaigns that they could not be defeated either, even with the infamous Saint Bartholomew's Day massacre.

This massacre of Huguenots on August 24, 1572, occurred at a time when the Catholic and Calvinist parties had apparently been reconciled through the marriage of Henry of Navarre, the Bourbon ruler of Navarre and acknowledged political leader of the Huguenots, to the sister of the reigning Valois king Charles IX (1560–1574). Many Huguenots traveled to Paris for the wedding. But the Guise family persuaded the king and his mother, Catherine de' Medici, that this gathering of Huguenots was a threat to them. The subsequent massacre on the night of August 24 left three thousand Huguenots dead, although not Henry of Navarre who saved his life by promising to turn Catholic. Thousands more were killed in provincial towns. The massacre boomeranged, however, since it discredited the Valois dynasty without ending the conflict.

The fighting continued. The Huguenots rebuilt their strength while the ultra-Catholics formed a Holy League in 1576, vowing to exterminate heresy and seat a true

CHRONOLOGY

The French Wars of Religion (1562–1598)

Francis I	1515–1547
Henry II	1547–1559
Charles IX	1560–1574
Duke of Guise massacres Huguenot congregation at Vassy	1562
Saint Bartholomew's Day massacre	1572
Henry III	1574–1589
Formation of the Holy League	1576
War of the Three Henries	1588–1589
Assassination of Henry III	1589
Coronation of Henry IV	1594
Edict of Nantes	1598

Catholic champion—Henry, duke of Guise—on the French throne in place of the ruling king, Henry III (1574–1589), who had succeeded his brother Charles IX in 1574. The turning point in the conflict came in the War of the Three Henries in 1588–1589. Henry, duke of Guise, in the pay of Philip II of Spain, seized Paris and forced King Henry III to make him his chief minister. To rid himself of Guise influence, Henry III assassinated the duke of Guise and then joined with Henry of Navarre (who had once again returned to Calvinism), who was next in line to the throne, to crush the Catholic Holy League and retake the city of Paris. Although successful, Henry III in turn was assassinated in 1589 by a monk who was repelled by the spectacle of a Catholic king cooperating with a Protestant. Henry of Navarre now claimed the throne. Realizing, however, that he would never be accepted by Catholic France, Henry took the logical way out and converted once again to Catholicism. With his coronation in 1594, the Wars of Religion finally came to an end. It remained only to solve the religious problem, which was accomplished by the Edict of Nantes in 1598. While Catholicism was acknowledged as the official religion of France, the Huguenots were guaranteed the right to worship in selected places in every district and were allowed to retain a number of fortified towns for their protection. In addition, Huguenots were allowed to enjoy all political privileges, including the holding of public offices.

≫ *Philip II, the Most Catholic King of Spain* ≪

After the abdication of Charles V in 1556, his son Philip II became king of Spain at the age of twenty-nine. Modern historical opinions of Philip II have varied widely. Some Protestant historians have viewed him as a moral monster while Catholic apologists have commended him for his sincerity and sense of responsibility. These selections include an assessment of Philip II by a contemporary, the Venetian ambassador to Spain, and a section from a letter by Philip II to his daughters, revealing the more loving side of the king.

Suriano, An Estimate of Philip II

The Catholic king was born in Spain, in the month of May, 1527, and spent a great part of his youth in that kingdom. Here, in accordance with the customs of the country and the wishes of his father and mother, . . . he was treated with all the deference and respect which seemed due to the son of the greatest emperor whom Christendom had ever had, and to the heir to such a number of realms and to such grandeur. As a result of this education, when the king left Spain for the first time and visited Flanders, passing on his way through Italy and Germany, he everywhere made an impression of haughtiness and severity, so that the Italians liked him but little, the Flemings were quite disgusted with him, and the Germans hated him heartily. But when he had been warned by the cardinal of Trent and his aunt, and above all by his father, that this haughtiness was not in place in a prince destined to rule over a number of nations so different in manners and sentiment, he altered his manner so completely that on his second journey,

when we went to England, he everywhere exhibited such distinguished mildness and affability that no prince has ever surpassed him in these traits. . . .

In the king's eyes no nation is superior to the Spaniards. It is among them that he lives, it is they that he consults, and it is they that direct his policy; in all this he is acting quite contrary to the habit of his father. He thinks little of the Italians and Flemish and still less of the Germans. Although he may employ the chief men of all the countries over which he rules, he admits none of them to his secret counsels, but utilizes their services only in military affairs, and then perhaps not so much because he really esteems them, as in the hope that he will in this way prevent his enemies from making use of them.

A Letter of Philip II to His Daughters

It is good news for me to learn that you are so well. It seems to me that your little sister is getting her eye teeth pretty early. Perhaps they are in place of the two which I am on the point of losing and which I shall probably no longer have when I get back. But if I had nothing worse to trouble me, that might pass. . . .

I am sending you also some roses and an orange flower, just to let you see that we have them here [Lisbon]. Calabrés brings me bunches of both these flowers every day, and we have had violets for a long time. . . . After this rainy time I imagine that you will be having flowers, too, by the time my sister arrives, or soon after. God keep you as I would have him!

Although the Edict of Nantes recognized the rights of the Protestant minority and ostensibly the principle of religious toleration, it did so only out of political necessity, not out of conviction. The French Wars of Religion also demonstrated once again to many French people the necessity for strong government, laying a foundation for the growth of monarchy in the seventeenth century.

Philip II and the Cause of Militant Catholicism

The greatest advocate of militant Catholicism and the most important political figure in the second half of the sixteenth century was King Philip II of Spain (1556–

1598), the son and heir of Charles V (see the box above). Philip's reign ushered in an age of Spanish greatness, both politically and culturally. A tremendous price was paid, however, for the political and military commitments that Philip made, and we can see in retrospect that the Golden Age of Spain was also the period in which Spain's decline began.

The first major goal of Philip II was to consolidate and secure the lands he had inherited from his father, Charles V. These included Spain, the Netherlands, and the possessions in Italy and the New World. For Philip this meant a strict conformity to Catholicism, enforced by aggressive use of the Spanish Inquisition, and the establishment of strong, monarchical authority. The latter was not an easy task because Philip had inherited a governmental structure in which each of the various states and territories of his empire stood in an individual relationship to the king. Philip did manage, however, to expand royal power in Spain by making the monarchy less dependent on the traditional landed aristocracy, especially in the higher echelons of government. He enlarged the system of administrative councils first developed by Ferdinand and Isabella and broadened by his father. Although Philip found that his ability to enforce his will was restricted by local legal traditions, lack of rapid communication, and an inadequate bureaucracy, he tried to be the center of the whole system and supervised the work of all departments, even down to the smallest details. His meticulousness was tragic for both Philip and Spain. Unwilling to delegate authority, he failed to distinguish between important and trivial matters and fell weeks behind on state correspondence, where he was inclined to make marginal notes and even correct spelling. One Spanish official said, "If God used the Escorial [the royal palace where Philip worked] to deliver my death sentence, I would be immortal." Philip's administrative machinery enabled him to do little more than maintain the status quo.

One of Philip's aims was to make Spain a dominant power in Europe. To a great extent, Spain's preeminence depended upon a prosperous economy fueled by its importation of gold and silver from its New World possessions, its agriculture, its commerce, and its industry, especially in textiles, silk, and leather goods. The importation of silver had detrimental effects as well, however, as it helped set off a spiraling inflation that disrupted the Spanish economy, eventually hurting both textile production and agriculture. Moreover, the expenses of war, especially after 1580, proved devastating to the Spanish economy. American gold and silver never constituted more than 20 percent of the royal revenue, leading the government to impose a crushing burden of direct and indirect taxes, especially on the people of Castile. Even then the government was forced to borrow. Philip repudiated his debts seven times; still two-thirds of state income went to pay interest on the debt by the end of his reign. The attempt to make Spain a great power led to the decline of Spain after Philip's reign.

Crucial to an understanding of Philip II is the importance of Catholicism to the Spanish people and their ruler. Driven by a heritage of crusading fervor, the Spanish had little difficulty seeing themselves as a nation of people divinely chosen to save Catholic Christianity from the Protestant heretics. Philip II, the "Most Catholic King," became the champion of Ca-

tholicism throughout Europe. To Philip, as to other European rulers, church and state were inextricably intertwined, a fact beautifully symbolized in Philip's new palace known as the Escorial, which served as a seat of government, church, and mausoleum for Charles V. Philip's activities on behalf of Catholicism were not done to please the papacy, however. Despite his devotion to Catholicism, Philip allowed the popes little say in the Spanish Catholic church and did not hesitate to disagree with papal religious and political policies.

Philip's role as the champion of Catholicism led to spectacular victories and equally spectacular defeats for the Spanish king. Spain's leadership of a Holy League against Turkish encroachments in the Mediterranean, especially the Muslim attack on the island of Cyprus, led to a stunning victory over the Turkish fleet in the Battle of Lepanto in 1571. But Philip was to experience few other such successes. His intervention in France on

◆ **Philip II of Spain.** This portrait depicts Philip II of Spain at the age of fifty-two. The king's attempts to make Spain a great power led to large debts and crushing taxes, and his military actions in defense of Catholicism ended in failure and misfortune in both France and the Netherlands.

CHRONOLOGY

◆◆◆◆◆◆◆◆◆◆◆◆◆◆◆◆◆◆◆◆◆◆◆◆◆

Philip II and Militant Catholicism

Philip II	1556–1598
Outbreak of revolt in the Netherlands	1566
Battle of Lepanto	1571
Recall of the Duke of Alva	1573
Pacification of Ghent	1576
Union of Arras	1579
The Spanish Armada	1588
Twelve-year truce (Spain and Netherlands)	1609
Independence of the United Provinces	1648

behalf of the ultra-Catholics in the decade of the 1580s led only to failure. But the major thrust of his foreign policy was aimed at the Netherlands and England. Philip's attempt to crush the revolt in the Netherlands and his tortured relations with the English queen Elizabeth led to his greatest misfortunes.

The Revolt of the Netherlands

One of the richest parts of Philip's empire, the Spanish Netherlands was of great importance to the "Most Catholic King." The Netherlands consisted of seventeen provinces (modern Netherlands, Belgium, and Luxembourg). The seven northern provinces were largely Germanic in culture and Dutch speaking, while the French- and Flemish-speaking southern provinces were closely tied to France. Situated at the commercial crossroads of northwestern Europe, the Netherlands had become prosperous through commerce and a flourishing textile industry. Because of its location, the Netherlands was open to the religious influences of the age. While some inhabitants had adopted Lutheranism or Anabaptism, by the time of Philip II, Calvinism was also making inroads. These provinces had no real political bond holding them together except their common ruler, and that ruler was Philip II, a foreigner who was out of touch with the situation in the Netherlands.

Philip II hoped to strengthen his control in the Netherlands, regardless of the traditional privileges of the separate provinces. This was strongly opposed by the nobles, towns, and provincial states, which stood to lose politically if their jealously guarded privileges and freedoms were weakened. Resentment against Philip was also aroused when the residents of the Netherlands realized that the taxes they paid were being used for Spanish interests. Finally, religion became a major catalyst for rebellion when Philip attempted both to reorganize the ecclesiastical structure of the Dutch Catholic church and to crush heresy. Calvinism continued to spread, especially among the nobility and artisans in the towns. Philip's policy of repression alienated the Calvinists without halting the spread of the movement. Resistance against the king's policies increased, especially from the aristocrats led by William of Nassau, the prince of Orange, also known as William the Silent. Violence erupted in 1566 when Calvinists—especially nobles—began to destroy statues and stained glass windows in Catholic churches. Philip responded by sending the duke of Alva with 10,000 veteran Spanish and Italian troops to crush the rebellion.

The repressive policies of the duke proved counterproductive. The levying of a permanent sales tax alienated many merchants and commoners who now joined the nobles and Calvinists in the struggle against Spanish rule. A special tribunal, known as the Council of Troubles (nicknamed by the Dutch the Council of Blood), inaugurated a reign of terror in which even powerful aristocrats were executed. As a result, the revolt now became organized, especially in the northern provinces where William of Orange and Dutch pirates known as the "Sea Beggars" mounted growing resistance. In 1573, Philip removed the duke of Alva and shifted to a more conciliatory policy to bring an end to the costly revolt.

William of Orange wished to unify all seventeen provinces, a goal seemingly realized in 1576 with the Pacification of Ghent. This agreement stipulated that all the provinces would stand together under William's leadership, respect religious differences, and demand that Spanish troops be withdrawn. But religious differences proved too strong for any lasting union. When the duke of Parma, the next Spanish leader, arrived in the Netherlands, he astutely played upon the religious differences of the provinces and split their united front. The southern provinces formed a Catholic union—the Union of Arras—in 1579 and accepted Spanish control. To counter this, William of Orange organized the northern, Dutch-speaking states into a Protestant union—the Union of Utrecht—determined to oppose Spanish rule. The Netherlands was now divided along religious, geographical, and political lines into two hostile camps. Unwilling to rule themselves, the northern provinces sought to place themselves under the French king and then the English queen Elizabeth. Both refused, although Elizabeth further antagonized Philip II by continuing military assistance. The struggle went on until 1609, after both Philip and Elizabeth had died; then the war ended with a twelve-year truce that virtually recognized the independence of the northern provinces. These "United Provinces" soon emerged as the Dutch Republic, although the Spanish did not formally recognize them as independent until 1648. The southern provinces remained a Spanish possession.

The England of Elizabeth

After the death of Queen Mary in 1558, her half-sister Elizabeth ascended the throne of England. During Elizabeth's reign, England rose to prominence as the relatively small island kingdom became the leader of the Protestant nations of Europe, laid the foundations for a world empire, and experienced a cultural renaissance.

The daughter of King Henry VIII and Anne Boleyn, Elizabeth had had a difficult early life. During Mary's reign, she had even been imprisoned for a while and had learned early to hide her true feelings from both private and public sight. While appearing irresolute in avoiding confrontation as long as possible, she was capable of decisive action when it was finally forced upon her. Intelligent and self-confident, she moved quickly to solve the difficult religious problem she had inherited from Mary, who had become extremely unpopular when she tried to return England to the Catholic fold.

Elizabeth's religious policy was based on moderation and compromise. Although she had some deep religious feelings, the changes she had experienced had taught her caution and tolerance. As a ruler, she wished to prevent England from being torn apart over matters of religion. Interests of state and personal choice combined to favor a temperate approach to religious affairs. As the Scottish Calvinist reformer John Knox remarked, "Elizabeth was neither a good Protestant nor yet a resolute Papist." Nor did she care what her subjects believed privately as long as they did not threaten the state's power.

Parliament cooperated with the queen in initiating the Elizabethan religious settlement in 1559. The Catholic legislation of Mary's reign was repealed, and a new Act of Supremacy designated Elizabeth as "the only supreme governor of this realm, as well in all spiritual or

 Map 15.2 Philip II and the Height of Spanish Power.

ecclesiastical things or causes, as temporal." An Act of Uniformity restored the church service of the Book of Common Prayer from the reign of Edward VI with some revisions to make it more acceptable to Catholics. Elizabeth's religious settlement was basically Protestant but a moderate Protestantism that avoided overly subtle distinctions and extremes.

The new religious settlement worked, at least to the extent that it smothered religious differences in England in the second half of the sixteenth century. Two groups, however, the Catholics and Puritans, continued to oppose the new religious settlement. By the end of Elizabeth's reign, the Catholics had dwindled to a tiny minority, a process aided by the identification of Catholicism in English minds with the Spanish King Philip II, but earlier they appeared to pose a significant threat. One of Elizabeth's greatest challenges came from her Catholic cousin, Mary, queen of Scots, who was next in line to the English throne. Mary was ousted from Scotland by rebellious Calvinist nobles in 1568 and fled for her life to England. There Elizabeth placed her under house arrest and for fourteen years tolerated her involvement in a number of ill-planned Catholic plots designed to kill Elizabeth and replace her on the throne with the Catholic Mary. Finally, in 1586 when Mary became embroiled in a far more serious plot, Elizabeth had her cousin beheaded to end the threats to her regime.

Potentially more dangerous to Anglicanism in the long run were the Puritans. The word *Puritanism* first appeared in 1564 when it was used to refer to those Protestants within the Anglican church who, inspired by Calvinist theology, wanted to remove any trace of Catholicism from the Church of England. Elizabeth managed to contain the Puritans during her reign, but the indefatigible Puritans would dominate the English scene in the middle part of the seventeenth century.

Elizabeth proved as adept in government and foreign policy as in religious affairs. She was well served administratively by the principal secretary of state, an office created by Thomas Cromwell during the reign of Henry VIII. The talents of Sir William Cecil and Sir Francis Walsingham, who together held the office for thirty-two years, ensured much of Elizabeth's success in foreign and domestic affairs. Elizabeth also handled Parliament with much skill; it met only thirteen times during her entire reign (see the box on p. 508).

Elizabeth's foreign policy was also dictated by caution, moderation, and expediency. Fearful of other countries' motives, Elizabeth realized that war could be disastrous for her island kingdom and her own rule. Unofficially, however, she encouraged English seamen to raid Spanish ships and colonies. Francis Drake was especially adept at plundering Spanish fleets loaded with gold and silver from Spain's New World empire. While encouraging English piracy and providing clandestine aid to French Huguenots and Dutch Calvinists to weaken France and Spain, Elizabeth pretended complete aloofness and avoided alliances that would force her into war with any major power.

Gradually, however, Elizabeth was drawn into more active involvement in the Netherlands and by 1585 had reluctantly settled upon a policy of active military intervention there. This move accelerated the already mounting friction between Spain and England. After years of resisting the idea of invading England as too impractical, Philip II of Spain was finally persuaded to do so by advisers who assured him that the people of England would rise against their queen when the Spaniards arrived. Moreover, Philip was easily convinced that the revolt in the Netherlands would never be crushed as long as England provided support for it. In any case, a successful invasion of England would mean the overthrow of heresy and the return of England to Catholicism, surely an act in accordance with the will of God. The execution of Mary, queen of Scots, in 1587 reinforced the king's decision, especially when the pope, angered by Mary's beheading, offered to provide financial support for the undertaking. Accordingly, Philip ordered preparations for an Armada that would rendezvous with the army of the duke of Parma in Flanders and escort his troops across the English Channel for the invasion.

The Armada proved to be a disaster. The Spanish fleet that finally set sail had neither the ships nor the manpower that Philip had planned to send. A conversation between a papal emissary and an officer of the Spanish fleet before the Armada departed reveals the fundamental flaw:

> "And if you meet the English armada in the Channel, do you expect to win the battle?" "Of course," replied the Spaniard.
>
> "How can you be sure?" [asked the emissary]
>
> "It's very simple. It is well known that we fight in God's cause. So, when we meet the English, God will surely arrange matters so that we can grapple and board them, either by sending some strange freak of weather or, more likely, just by depriving the English of their wits. If we can come to close quarters, Spanish valor and Spanish steel (and the great masses of soldiers we shall have on board) will make our victory certain. But unless God helps us by a miracle the English, who have faster and handier ships than ours, and many more long-range guns, and who

know their advantage just as well as we do, will never close with us at all, but stand aloof and knock us to pieces with their culverins, without our being able to do them any serious hurt. So," concluded the captain, and one fancies a grim smile, "we are sailing against England in the confident hope of a miracle."[5]

The hoped-for miracle never materialized. The Spanish fleet, battered by a number of encounters with the English, sailed back to Spain by a northward route around Scotland and Ireland where it was further battered by storms. Although the English and Spanish would continue their war for another sixteen years, the defeat of the Armada guaranteed for the time being that England would remain a Protestant country. Although Spain made up for its losses within a year and a half, the defeat was a psychological blow to the Spaniards.

Economic and Social Crises

The period of European history from 1560 to 1650 witnessed severe economic and social crises as well as political upheaval. Economic uncertainties, intensified by wildly fluctuating boom and bust cycles, were accom-panied by social uncertainties and stark contrasts between the living standards of the rich and the poor. Although historians commonly refer to a sixteenth-century price revolution and a seventeenth-century economic crisis, the lack of concrete data has made it difficult to be precise in these areas, leading to numerous historical controversies.

Inflation and Economic Stagnation

Inflation was a major economic problem in the six-teenth and early seventeenth centuries. This so-called price revolution was a Europeanwide phenomenon, al-though different areas were affected at different times. While the inflation rate was probably a relatively low 2 to 3 percent a year, it was noticeable in a Europe accustomed to stable prices. Foodstuffs were most sub-ject to price increases, especially evident in the price of wheat. An upward surge in wheat prices was first noticed in the Mediterranean area—in Spain, southern France, and Italy—and reached its peak there in the 1590s. By the 1620s and 1630s, wheat prices in northern Europe had undergone similar increases.

Although precise data are lacking, economic histori-ans believe that as a result of the price revolution, wages

◆ **Procession of Queen Elizabeth I.** Intelligent and learned, Elizabeth Tudor was familiar with Latin and Greek and spoke several European languages. Served by able administrators, Elizabeth ruled for nearly forty-five years and generally avoided open military action against any major power. Her participation in the revolt of the Netherlands, however, brought England into conflict with Spain. This picture painted near the end of her reign shows the queen on a ceremonial procession.

❧ *Queen Elizabeth Addresses Parliament (1601)* ❧

Queen Elizabeth I ruled England from 1558 to 1603 with a consummate skill that contemporaries considered unusual in a woman. Though shrewd, calculating, and paternalistic, Elizabeth, like other sixteenth-century monarchs, depended for her power upon the favor of her people. This selection is taken from her speech to Parliament in 1601, when she had been forced to retreat on the issue of monopolies after vehement protests by members of Parliament. Although the speech was designed to make peace with Parliament, some historians also feel that it was a sincere expression of the rapport that existed between the queen and her subjects.

Queen Elizabeth I, "The Golden Speech"

I do assure you there is no prince that loves his subjects better, or whose love can countervail our love. There is no jewel, be it of never so rich a price, which I set before this jewel: I mean your love. For I do esteem it more than any treasure or riches. . . . And, though God has raised me high, yet this I count the glory of my crown, that I have reigned with your loves. This makes me that I do not so much rejoice that God has made me to be a Queen, as to be a Queen over so thankful a people. . . .

Of myself I must say this: I never was any greedy, scraping grasper, nor a strait, fast-holding Prince, nor yet a waster. My heart was never set on any worldly goods, but only for my subjects' good. What you bestow on me, I will not hoard it up, but receive it to bestow on you again. Yea, mine own properties I account yours, to be expended for your good. . . .

I have ever used to set the Last-Judgment Day before mine eyes, and so to rule as I shall be judged to answer before a higher Judge, to whose judgment seat I do appeal, that never thought was cherished in my heart that tended not unto my people's good. And now, if my kingly bounties have been abused, and my grants turned to the hurt of my people, contrary to my will and meaning, and if any in authority under me neglected or perverted what I have committed to them, I hope God will not lay their culps [crimes] and offences to my charge; who, though there were danger in repealing our grants, yet what danger would I not rather incur for your good, than I would suffer them still to continue?

There will never Queen sit in my seat with more zeal to my country, care for my subjects, and that will sooner with willingness venture her life for your good and safety, than myself. For it is my desire to live nor reign no longer than my life and reign shall be for your good. And though you have had and may have many princes more mighty and wise sitting in this seat, yet you never had nor shall have any that will be more careful and loving. . . .

---

failed to keep up with price increases. Wage earners, especially agricultural laborers and salaried workers in urban areas, began to experience a lower standard of living. At the same time, landed aristocrats who could raise rents managed to prosper. To contemporaries, in fact, the rent increases imposed by the landed nobility were responsible for the problem, as the English Bishop Latimer proclaimed in a sermon preached before King Edward VI in 1549:

> You landlords, you rent-raisers, I may say you step-lords, you have for your possessions yearly too much. For what here before went for twenty or forty pound by year (which is an honest portion to be had gratis in one lordship of another man's sweat and labor), now is let for fifty or an hundred pound by year. Of this "too much" comes this monstrous and portentous dearth made by man . . . that poor men, which live by their labor cannot with the sweat of their face have a living, all kinds of victuals is so dear. . . .[6]

Wealthy commercial and industrial entrepreneurs also benefited from the price revolution because of rising prices, expanding markets, and relatively cheaper labor costs. Some historians regard this profit inflation as a valuable stimulus to investment and the growth of capitalism, helping to explain the economic expansion and prosperity of the sixteenth century. Governments were likewise affected by inflation. They borrowed heavily from bankers and placed new tax burdens on their subjects, often creating additional discontent.

The causes of the price revolution are a subject of much historical debate. Already in the 1560s European intellectuals had associated the rise in prices with the great influx of precious metals from the New World. Although this view was accepted for a long time, many economic historians now believe that the increase in population in the sixteenth century played an important role in creating inflationary pressures. A growing population increased the demand for land and food and drove up prices for both.

But the inflation-fueled prosperity of the sixteenth century showed signs of slackening by the beginning of the seventeenth century. Economic contraction began to be evident in some parts of Europe by the 1620s. In the 1630s and 1640s, as imports of silver declined, economic recession intensified, especially in the Mediterranean area. The industrial and financial center of Europe in the age of the Renaissance, Italy was now becoming an economic backwater. Spain's economy was also seriously failing by the decade of the 1640s.

Trade, Industry, Banking, and Agriculture

The flourishing European trade of the sixteenth century revolved around three major areas: the Mediterranean in the south, the Low Countries and the Baltic region in the north, and central Europe, whose inland trade depended on the Rhine and Danube Rivers. As overseas trade expanded, however, the Atlantic seaboard began to play a more important role, linking the Mediterranean, Baltic, and central European trading areas together and making the whole of Europe into a more integrated market that was all the more vulnerable to price shifts. With their cheaper and faster ships, the Dutch came to monopolize both European and world trade, although they were increasingly challenged by the English and French in the seventeenth century.

The commercial expansion of the sixteenth and seventeenth centuries was made easier by new forms of commercial organization, especially the joint-stock trading company. Individuals bought shares in a company and received dividends on their investment while a board of directors ran the company and made the important business decisions. The return on investments could be spectacular. During its first ten years, investors received 30 percent on their money from the Dutch East India Company, which opened the Spice Islands and Southeast Asia to Dutch activity. The joint-stock company made it easier to raise large amounts of capital for world trading ventures.

Enormous profits were also being made in shipbuilding and in mining and metallurgy, where technological innovations, such as the use of pumps and new methods of extracting metals from ores, proved highly successful. The mining industry was closely tied to sixteenth-century family banking firms. In exchange for arranging large loans to Charles V, Jacob Fugger was given a monopoly over silver, copper, and mercury mines in the Habsburg possessions of central Europe that produced profits in excess of 50 percent per year. While these close relationships between governments and entrepre-

◆ **Jacob Fugger the Rich.** Jacob Fugger, head of one of the wealthiest banking firms of the sixteenth century, is pictured here with his faithful secretary, Matthaus Schwartz, who painted this scene in 1516. The cabinet in the background lists the names of the cities where Fugger's firm had branch offices, including Milan, Innsbruck, Nuremberg, and Lisbon.

neurs could lead to stunning successes, they could also be precarious. The House of Fugger went bankrupt at the end of the sixteenth century when the Habsburgs defaulted on their loans.

By the seventeenth century, the traditional family banking firms were no longer able to supply the numerous services needed for the commercial capitalism of the seventeenth century. New institutions arose to take their place. The city of Amsterdam created the Bank of Amsterdam in 1609 as both a deposit and a transfer institution and the Amsterdam Bourse or Exchange where the trading of stocks replaced the exchange of goods. By the first half of the seventeenth century, the

Amsterdam Exchange had emerged as the hub of the European business world, just as Amsterdam itself had replaced Antwerp as the greatest commercial and banking center of Europe.

Despite the growth of commercial capitalism, most of the European economy still depended on an agricultural system that had experienced few changes since the thirteenth century. At least 80 to 90 percent of Europeans still worked on the land. Almost all of the peasants of western Europe were free of serfdom, although many still owed a variety of feudal dues to the nobility. Despite expanding markets and rising prices, increased rents, fees, and higher taxes imposed by the state meant little or no improvement in the lot of the European peasants. In eastern Europe, their position had even worsened as peasants were increasingly tied to the land in a new serfdom enforced by powerful landowners (see Chapter 16).

Population and the Growth of Cities

The sixteenth century was a period of expanding population, possibly related to a warmer climate and increased food supplies. It has been estimated that the population of Europe increased from 60 million in 1500 to 85 million by 1600, the first major recovery of the European population since the devastation of the Black Death in the mid-fourteenth century. However, records also indicate that the population had leveled off by 1620 and even begun to decline by 1650, especially in central and southern Europe. Only the Dutch, English, and, to a lesser degree, the French grew in number in the first half of the seventeenth century. Europe's longtime adversaries, war, famine, and plague, continued to affect population levels. In 1630, for example, northern Italy was hit by a devastating recurrence of bubonic plague; Verona and Mantua lost 60 to 70 percent of their populations. Europe's entry into another "little ice age" after the middle of the sixteenth century, when average temperatures fell and glaciers even engulfed small Alpine villages, affected harvests and gave rise to famines. Historians have noted the parallels between population increase and economic prosperity in the sixteenth century and population decline and economic recession in the seventeenth century.

The rise in population was reflected in the growth of cities. In 1500, Paris, Constantinople, and four cities in Italy (Naples, Venice, Milan, Genoa) had populations above 100,000 people. By 1600, Naples had grown to 300,000, while Rome, Palermo, and Messina reached 100,000. Cities along coasts and well-traveled trade routes grew the most, reflecting the close ties between commerce and urban growth. Naples became the largest port in Italy while Seville in Spain, the port of entry for the wealth of the New World, and Lisbon in Portugal had populations over 100,000 by 1600. Across the English Channel, London's domination of the commercial and financial life of England pushed its population to 250,000 by 1600. By that year, Europe's greatest and most populous city was Paris with its 500,000 people.

Seventeenth-century cities visibly reflected the remarkable disparity in wealth during the seventeenth century. The beautiful houses and palaces of rich nobles and wealthy merchants contrasted sharply with the crowded tenements and dirty hovels of the lower classes. Crime, pollution, filth, and lack of sanitation, fresh water, and food were accompanied by social tensions between landed nobles who moved into the cities and the wealthy merchants who resented their presence.

Seventeenth-Century Crises: War and Rebellions

Although many Europeans responded to the upheavals of the second half of the sixteenth century with a desire for peace and order, the first fifty years of the seventeenth century continued to be a period of crisis. A devastating war that affected much of Europe and rebellions seemingly everywhere protracted an atmosphere of disorder and violence.

The Thirty Years' War

Religion, especially the struggle between a militant Catholicism and a militant Calvinism, certainly played an important role in the outbreak of the Thirty Years' War, often called the "last of the religious wars." As the war progressed, however, it became increasingly clear that secular, dynastic-nationalist considerations were far more important.

Although much of the fighting in the Thirty Years' War (1618–1648) took place in the Germanic lands of the Holy Roman Empire, the war became a European-wide struggle. In fact, some historians view it as part of a larger conflict between the Bourbon dynasty of France and the Habsburg dynasties of Spain and the Holy Roman Empire for European leadership and date it from 1609 to 1659. A brief look at the motives of the European states and the situation in the Holy Roman Empire provides the background necessary to understand the war.

Since the beginning of the sixteenth century, France had worked to break out of what it perceived as its encirclement by the house of Habsburg. The situation had eased in 1556 when Charles V abdicated and divided his empire. His son Philip inherited Spain, the Netherlands, Italy, and the New World while his brother Ferdinand became Holy Roman Emperor and received the Habsburg possessions in Austria and eastern Europe. France felt threatened by the Spanish Habsburgs and feared the consolidation of the Holy Roman Empire by the Habsburg emperor.

Spain, which viewed the twelve-year truce negotiated with the Dutch in 1609 as only temporary, was determined to regain control of the Netherlands, specifically, the northern Dutch provinces. English and Dutch control of the seas, however, forced the Spanish to seek an alternative route for shipping supplies and men to the Dutch provinces by way of Italy and western Germany. Although in retrospect it might be easy to recognize that Spain's economic decline made it foolish to undertake the reconquest of the Dutch, to contemporaries, Spain was still the greatest power in the Christian world.

The Austrian Habsburgs wished to consolidate their holdings in Austria and Bohemia by eliminating Protestantism and establishing stronger central authority. At the same time, as Holy Roman Emperors, they remained frustrated by their lack of real authority over the lands of Germany where hundreds of individual states still pro-

Map 15.3 The Thirty Years' War.

The Protestant Union	1608
The Catholic League	1609
Election of Habsburg Archduke Ferdinand as king of Bohemia	1617
Bohemian revolt against Ferdinand	1618
The Bohemian phase	1618–1625
Battle of White Mountain	1620
Spanish conquest of Palatinate	1622
The Danish phase	1625–1629
Edict of Restitution	1629
The Swedish phase	1630–1635
Battle of Lützen	1632
Battle of Nördlingen	1634
The Franco-Swedish phase	1635–1648
Battle of Rocroi	1643
Peace of Westphalia	1648
Peace of the Pyrenees	1659

vided the real basis of political power. It was among these German states that the Thirty Years' War had its immediate beginnings.

The Peace of Augsburg in 1555 had brought an end to the religious warfare between German Catholics and Lutherans. Religion, however, continued to play a divisive role in German life as Lutherans and Catholics persisted in vying for control of various principalities. In addition, although the treaty had not recognized the rights of Calvinists, a number of German states had adopted Calvinism as their state church. At the beginning of the seventeenth century, the Calvinist ruler of the Palatinate, the Elector Palatine Frederick IV, assumed the leadership in forming a league of German Protestant states called the Protestant Union. To counteract it, a Catholic League of German states was organized by Duke Maximilian of the south German state of Bavaria. This division of Germany into two armed camps was made even more dangerous by the involvement of foreign states. The Protestant Union gained the support of the Dutch, English, and French, while Spain and the Holy Roman Emperor aided the Catholic League. By 1609, then, Germany was dividing into two armed camps in anticipation of religious war.

The religious division was exacerbated by a constitutional issue. The desire of the Habsburg emperors to

consolidate their authority in the Holy Roman Empire was resisted by the princes who fought for their "German liberties," their constitutional rights and prerogatives as individual rulers. To pursue their policies, the Habsburg emperors looked to Spain for assistance while the princes turned to the enemies of Spain, especially France, for help against the emperor. The divisions in the Holy Roman Empire and Europe made it almost inevitable that if war did erupt, it would be widespread and difficult to stop. Events in Bohemia in 1617 and 1618 finally brought the outbreak of the war everyone dreaded.

Historians have traditionally divided the Thirty Years' War into four major phases. The Bohemian phase (1618–1625) began in one of the Habsburgs' own territories. In 1617, the Bohemian Estates (primarily the nobles) accepted the Habsburg Archduke Ferdinand as their king but soon found themselves unhappy with their choice. While many of the nobles were Calvinists, Ferdinand was a devout Catholic who began a process of re-Catholicizing Bohemia and strengthening royal power. The Protestant nobles rebelled against Ferdinand in May 1618 and proclaimed their resistance by throwing two of the Habsburg governors and a secretary out of the window of the royal castle in Prague, the seat of Bohemian government. The Catholic side claimed that their seemingly miraculous escape from death in the seventy-foot fall from the castle was due to the intercession of the Virgin Mary, while Protestants pointed out that they fell into a manure pile. The Bohemian rebels now seized control of Bohemia, deposed Ferdinand, and elected as his replacement the Protestant ruler of the Palatinate, Elector Frederick V, who was also head of the Protestant Union.

Ferdinand, who in the meantime had been elected as Holy Roman Emperor, refused to accept his deposition. Aided by the imposing forces of Maximilian of Bavaria and the Catholic League, the imperial forces defeated Frederick and the Bohemian nobles at the Battle of White Mountain outside Prague on November 8, 1620. Spanish troops meanwhile took advantage of Frederick's predicament by invading the Palatinate and conquering it by the end of 1622. The unfortunate Frederick who had lost two crowns—Bohemia and the Palatinate—fled into exile in Holland. The Spanish took control of the western part of the Palatinate (to gain the access route from Italy to the Netherlands that they had wanted), and Duke Maximilian of Bavaria took the rest of the territory. Reestablished as king of Bohemia, Emperor Ferdinand declared Bohemia a hereditary Habsburg possession, confiscated the land of the Protestant nobles, and established Catholicism as the sole religion. Some

30,000 Protestant families emigrated to Saxony and Hungary. The Spanish renewed their attack on the Dutch, and the forces of Catholicism seemed on the road to victory. But the war was far from over.

The second phase of the war, the Danish phase (1625–1629), began when King Christian IV of Denmark (1588–1648), a Lutheran, intervened on behalf of the Protestant cause by leading an army into northern Germany. Most likely, he also wished to annex territories in northern Germany that would give him control of the southern Baltic. His campaign turned out to be a complete fiasco.

The imperial forces were now led by a brilliant and enigmatic commander, Albrecht von Wallenstein, a Bohemian nobleman who had taken advantage of Ferdinand's victory to become the country's wealthiest landowner. Wallenstein marched the imperial army north, utterly defeated the Danes, and occupied parts of northern Germany, including the Baltic ports of Hamburg, Lübeck, and Bremen. Christian IV's total defeat ended Danish involvement in the Thirty Years' War and even meant the end of Danish supremacy in the Baltic.

After the success of the imperial armies, the emperor Ferdinand II was at the height of his power and took this opportunity to issue the Edict of Restitution in March 1629. His proclamation prohibited Calvinist worship and restored to the Catholic church all property taken by Protestant princes or cities during the past seventy-five years. But this sudden growth in the power of the Habsburg emperor frightened many German princes who feared for their independent status and reacted by forcing the emperor to dismiss Wallenstein. At the same time, Ferdinand was faced with another intervention by foreign powers as the war entered its third phase.

The Swedish phase (1630–1635) marked the entry of Gustavus Adolphus, king of Sweden (1611–1635), into the war. Gustavus Adolphus was responsible for reviving Sweden and making it into a great Baltic power. The French, disturbed by the Habsburg consolidation of power, provided financial support to Gustavus, a military genius who brought a disciplined and well-equipped Swedish army to northern Germany. Gustavus had no desire to see the Habsburgs in northern Germany since he wanted the Baltic Sea to be a Swedish lake. At the same time, Gustavus Adolphus was a devout Lutheran who felt compelled to aid his coreligionists in Germany.

Gustavus's army swept the imperial forces out of the north and moved into the heart of Germany. In despera-

✦ **Soldiers Pillaging a Farm.** This painting shows a group of soldiers running amok on a French peasant's farm. This scene was typical of many that occurred during the Thirty Years' War, especially in Germany where the war caused enormous destruction.

tion, the imperial side recalled Wallenstein, who was given command of the imperial army that met Gustavus Adolphus's troops near Leipzig. At the Battle of Lützen (1632), the Swedish forces prevailed but paid a high price for the victory when the Swedish king was killed in the battle. Although the Swedish forces remained in Germany, they proved much less effective. Despite the loss of Wallenstein, who was assassinated in 1634 by one of his own captains, the imperial army decisively defeated the Swedes at the Battle of Nördlingen at the end of 1634 and drove them out of southern Germany. This imperial victory guaranteed that southern Germany would remain Catholic. The emperor used this opportunity to make peace with the German princes by agreeing to annul the Edict of Restitution of 1629. But peace failed to come to war-weary Germany. The Swedes wished to continue while the French, under the direction of Cardinal Richelieu, the chief minister of King Louis XIII (see Chapter 16), entered the war directly, beginning the fourth and final phase of the war, the Franco-Swedish phase (1635–1648).

By this time, religious issues were losing their significance as dynastic power politics came to the fore. The Catholic French, after all, were now supporting the Protestant Swedes against the Catholic Habsburgs of Germany and Spain. This phase of the war was fought by Sweden in northern Germany and by France in the Netherlands and along the Rhine in western Germany. The Battle of Rocroi in 1643 proved decisive as the French beat the Spanish and brought an end to Spanish military greatness. The French then moved on to victories over the imperialist-Bavarian armies in southern Germany. By this time all parties were ready for peace, and after five years of protracted negotiations, the war in Germany was officially ended by the Peace of Westphalia in 1648. The war between France and Spain, however, continued until the Peace of the Pyrenees in 1659. By that time, Spain had become a second-class power, and France had emerged as the dominant nation in Europe.

What were the results of this "basically meaningless conflict," as one historian has called it? The Peace of Westphalia ensured that all German states, including the Calvinist ones, were free to determine their own religion. Territorially, France gained parts of western Germany, part of Alsace and the three cities of Metz, Toul, and Verdun, giving the French control of the Franco-German border area and excellent bases for future military operations in Germany. While Sweden and the German states of Brandenburg and Bavaria gained some territory in Germany, the Austrian Habs-

burgs did not really lose any, but did see their authority as rulers of Germany further diminished. The more than three hundred states that made up the Holy Roman Empire were virtually recognized as independent states, since each received the power to conduct its own foreign policy; this brought an end to the Holy Roman Empire as a political entity and ensured German disunity for another two hundred years. The Peace of Westphalia also made it clear that religion and politics were now separate worlds. The pope was completely ignored in all decisions at Westphalia, and political motives became the guiding forces in public affairs as religion moved closer to becoming primarily a matter of personal conviction and individual choice.

The economic and social effects of the Thirty Years' War on Germany are still debated. An older view pictured a ruined German economy and a decline in German population from 21 to 13 million between 1600 and 1650, but more recent opinions have estimated that Germany's population grew from 16 to 17 million while a redistribution of economic activity rather than an overall decline took place. Both views contain some truth. Some areas of Germany were completely devastated while others remained relatively untouched and even experienced economic growth. In any case, the Thirty Years' War was undoubtedly the most destructive conflict Europeans had yet experienced (see the box on p. 515). Unfortunately, it was not the last.

A Military Revolution?

By the seventeenth century, war played an increasingly important role in European affairs. One historian has calculated that between 1562 and 1721 there were only four years in which all Europe was at peace. Military power was considered essential to a ruler's reputation and power; thus, the pressure to build an effective military machine was intense. Although some would disagree, some historians believe that the changes that occurred in the science of warfare between 1560 and 1650 warrant the title of military revolution.

Medieval warfare, with its mounted knights and supplementary archers, had been transformed in the Renaissance by the employment of infantry armed with pikes and halberds and arranged in massed rectangles, known as squadrons or battalions. The squadron of pikemen became a crucial element in sixteenth-century armies and helps to explain the success of the Spanish who perfected its use. The utilization of firearms required adjustments to the size and shape of the massed infantry while the cavalry declined in effectiveness.

The Face of War in the Seventeenth Century

The Thirty Years' War was the most devastating war Europeans had experienced since the Hundred Years' War. Destruction was especially severe in Germany. We have a firsthand account of the face of war in Germany from a picaresque novel called Simplicius Simplicissimus, written by Jakob von Grimmelshausen. The author's experiences as a soldier in the Thirty Years' War give his descriptions of the effect of the war on ordinary people a certain vividness and reality. This selection describes the fate of a peasant farm, an experience all too familiar to thousands of German peasants between 1618 and 1648.

Jakob von Grimmelshausen,
Simplicius Simplicissimus

The first thing these horsemen did in the nice back rooms of the house was to put in their horses. Then everyone took up a special job, one having to do with death and destruction. Although some began butchering, heating water, and rendering lard, as if to prepare for a banquet, others raced through the house, ransacking upstairs and down; not even the privy chamber was safe, as if the golden fleece of Jason might be hidden there. Still others bundled up big packs of cloth, household goods, and clothes, as if they wanted to hold a rummage sale somewhere. What they did not intend to take along they broke and spoiled. Some ran their swords into the hay and straw, as if there hadn't been hogs enough to stick. Some shook the feathers out of beds and put bacon slabs, hams, and other stuff in the ticking, as if they might sleep better on these. Others knocked down the hearth and broke the windows, as if announcing an everlasting summer. They flattened out copper and pewter dishes and baled the ruined goods. They burned up bedsteads, tables, chairs, and benches, though there were yards and yards of dry firewood outside the kitchen. Jars and crocks, pots and casseroles all were broken, either because they preferred their meat broiled or because they thought they'd eat only one meal with us. In the barn, the hired girl was handled so roughly that she was unable to walk away, I am ashamed to report. They stretched the hired man out flat on the ground, stuck a wooden wedge in his mouth to keep it open, and emptied a milk bucket full of stinking manure drippings down his throat; they called it a Swedish cocktail. He didn't relish it and made a very wry face. By this means they forced him to take a raiding party to some other place where they carried off men and cattle and brought them to our farm. Among these were my father, mother, and Ursula [sister].

Then they used thumbscrews, which they cleverly made out of their pistols, to torture the peasants, as if they wanted to burn witches. Though he had confessed to nothing as yet, they put one of the captured hayseeds in the bake-oven and lighted a fire in it. They put a rope around someone else's head and tightened it like a tourniquet until blood came out of his mouth, nose, and ears. In short, every soldier had his favorite method of making life miserable for peasants, and every peasant had his own misery. My father was, as I thought, particularly lucky because he confessed with a laugh what others were forced to say in pain and martyrdom. No doubt because he was the head of the household, he was shown special consideration; they put him close to a fire, tied him by his hands and legs, and rubbed damp salt on the bottoms of his feet. Our old nanny goat had to lick it off and this so tickled my knan [father] that he could have burst laughing. This seemed so clever and entertaining to me—I had never seen or heard my knan laugh so long—that I joined him in laughter, to keep him company or perhaps to cover up my ignorance. In the midst of such glee he told them the whereabouts of hidden treasure much richer in gold, pearls, and jewelry than might have been expected on a farm.

I can't say much about the captured wives, hired girls, and daughters because the soldiers didn't let me watch their doings. But I do remember hearing pitiful screams from various dark corners and I guess that my mother and our Ursula had it no better than the rest.

It was Gustavus Adolphus, the king of Sweden, who developed the first standing army of conscripts, notable for the flexibility of its tactics. The infantry brigades of Gustavus's army were composed of equal numbers of musketeers and pikemen, standing six men deep. They employed the salvo in which all rows of the infantry fired at once instead of row by row. These salvos of fire, which cut up the massed ranks of the opposing infantry squadrons, were followed by a pike charge, giving the infantry a primarily offensive deployment. Gustavus also used the cavalry in a more mobile fashion. After shooting a pistol volley, they charged the enemy with their swords. Additional flexibility was obtained by utilizing lighter artillery pieces that were more easily moved during battle. All of these changes required coordination, careful training, and better discipline, forcing rulers to move away from undisciplined mercenary forces. Naturally, the success of Gustavus Adolphus led to imitation. Perhaps the best example was the New Model Army of Oliver Cromwell (see Chapter 16). His army consisted of infantry (two-thirds musketeers and one-third pikemen), cavalry, mounted infantry known as dragoons, and artillery units. A well-integrated and disciplined army, it was known for its mobility and flexibility.

The military changes between 1560 and 1650 included an increased use of firearms and cannon, greater flexibility and mobility in tactics, and better disciplined and trained armies. These innovations necessitated standing armies, based partly on conscription, which grew ever larger and more expensive as the seventeenth century progressed. Such armies could only be maintained by levying heavier taxes, making war an economic burden and an ever more important part of the early modern European state. To some historians, the creation of large bureaucracies to supervise the military resources of the state was the real reason for the rise of royal absolutism in the seventeenth century (see Chapter 16).

Rebellions

Before, during, and after the Thirty Years' War, a series of rebellions and civil wars stemming from the discontent of both nobles and commoners rocked the domestic stability of many European governments. To strengthen their power, monarchs attempted to extend their authority at the expense of traditional powerful elements who resisted the rulers' efforts. At the same time, to fight their battles, governments increased taxes and created such hardships that common people also rose in opposition. The resulting widespread revolts of subjects against their ruling princes have caused some historians to speak of a general crisis of authority in the first half of the seventeenth century.

Peasant and lower-class revolts occurred in central and southern France in 1593–1597, 1636–1637, and 1639; in Austria in 1595–1597, 1626–1627, and 1632–1636; and in Hungary in 1597, 1604–1607, and 1631–1632. In the decades of the 1640s and 1650s, even greater unrest occurred. Portugal and Catalonia rebelled against the Spanish government in 1640. The common people in Naples and Sicily revolted against both the

government and the landed nobility in 1647. Russia, too, was rocked by urban uprisings in 1641, 1645, and 1648. Nobles rebelled in France from 1648 to 1652 to halt the growth of royal power (see Chapter 16). The northern states of Sweden, Denmark, and Holland were also not immune from upheavals involving clergy, nobles, and mercantile groups. Even relatively stable Switzerland had a peasant rebellion in 1656. By far the most famous and wide-ranging struggle, however, was the civil war and rebellion in England, commonly known as the English Revolution (see Chapter 16).

The Witchcraft Craze

In the midst of the turmoil created by wars, rebellions, and economic and social uncertainties, yet another source of disorder arose as hysteria over witchcraft came to affect the lives of many Europeans in the sixteenth and seventeenth centuries. Witchcraft trials were prevalent in England, Scotland, Switzerland, Germany, some parts of France and the Low Countries, and even New England in America. As is evident from this list, the witchcraft craze affected both Catholic and Protestant countries.

Witchcraft was not a new phenomenon in the sixteenth and seventeenth centuries. Its practice had been part of traditional village culture for centuries, but it came to be viewed as both sinister and dangerous when the medieval church began to connect witches to the activities of the Devil, thereby transforming witchcraft into a heresy that had to be extirpated. After the creation of the Inquisition in the thirteenth century, some people were accused of a variety of witchcraft practices and, following the biblical injunction, "Thou shalt not suffer a witch to live," were turned over to secular authorities for burning at the stake or hanging (in England).

The search for scapegoats to explain the disaster of the Black Death in the fourteenth century led to a rise in the persecution of people accused of sorcery. In a papal bull of 1484, Pope Innocent VIII made official the belief of the Catholic church in such pernicious practices:

> It has recently come to our ears, not without great pain to us, that in some parts of upper Germany, . . . many persons of both sexes, heedless of their own salvation and forsaking the catholic faith, give themselves over to devils male and female, and by their incantations, charms, and conjurings, . . . ruin and cause to perish the

◆ **The Persecution of Witches.** Hysteria over witchcraft affected the daily lives of many Europeans in the sixteenth and seventeenth centuries. This picture by Frans Francken the Young, painted in 1607, shows a number of activities commonly attributed to witches. In the center, several witches are casting spells with their magic books and instruments while at the top, a witch on a post prepares to fly off on her broomstick.

offspring of women, the foal of animals, the products of the earth, the grapes of vines, and the fruits of trees, as well as men and women, cattle and flocks and herds and animals of every kind . . .; that they afflict and torture with dire pains and anguish, both internal and external, these men, women, cattle, flocks, herds, and animals, and hinder men from begetting and women from conceiving, and prevent all consummation of marriage; . . . that, moreover, at the instigation of the enemy of mankind [Satan], they do not fear to commit and perpetrate many other abominable offenses and crimes.[7]

To combat these dangers, Innocent sent two Dominican monks, Jacob Sprenger and Heinrich Krämer, to Germany to investigate and root out the witches. Based on their findings, they wrote the *Malleus Maleficarum (The Hammer of the Witches)*, which until the eighteenth century remained one of the standard handbooks on the practices of witchcraft and the methods that could be used to discover and try witches.

What distinguished witchcraft in the sixteenth and seventeenth centuries from these previous developments was the increased number of trials and executions of presumed witches. Although estimates have varied widely, the most recent figures indicate that more than 100,000 people were prosecuted throughout Europe on charges of witchcraft. As more and more people were brought to trial, the fear of witches as well as the fear of being accused of witchcraft escalated to frightening proportions. Approximately 25 percent of the villages in the English county of Essex, for example, had at least one witchcraft trial in the sixteenth and seventeenth centuries. Although larger cities were affected first, the trials also spread to smaller towns and rural areas as the hysteria persisted well into the seventeenth century (see the box on p. 518).

From an account of witch persecution in the German city of Trier, we get some glimpse of who the accused were: "Scarcely any of those who were accused escaped punishment. Nor were there spared even the leading men in the city of Trier." Although this statement makes it clear that the witchcraft trials had gone so far that even city officeholders were not immune from

A Witchcraft Trial in France

Persecutions for witchcraft reached their high point in the sixteenth and seventeenth centuries when tens of thousands of people were brought to trial. In this excerpt from the minutes of a trial in France in 1652, we can see why the accused witch stood little chance of exonerating herself.

The Trial of Suzanne Gaudry

28 May, 1652. . . . Interrogation of Suzanne Gaudry, prisoner at the court of Rieux. . . . [During interrogations on May 28 and May 29, the prisoner confessed to a number of activities involving the devil.]

Deliberation of the Court—June 3, 1652

The undersigned advocates of the Court have seen these interrogations and answers. They say that the aforementioned Suzanne Gaudry confesses that she is a witch, that she had given herself to the devil, that she had renounced God, Lent, and baptism, that she has been marked on the shoulder, that she has cohabited with the devil and that she has been to the dances, confessing only to have cast a spell upon and caused to die a beast of Philippe Cornié. . . .

Third Interrogation, June 27

This prisoner being led into the chamber, she was examined to know if things were not as she had said and confessed at the beginning of her imprisonment.

—Answers no, and that what she has said was done so by force.

Pressed to say the truth, that otherwise she would be subjected to torture, having pointed out to her that her aunt was burned for this same subject.

—Answers that she is not a witch. . . .

She was placed in the hands of the officer in charge of torture, throwing herself on her knees, struggling to cry, uttering several exclamations, without being able, nevertheless to shed a tear. Saying at every moment that she is not a witch.

The Torture

On this same day, being at the place of torture.

This prisoner, before being strapped down, was admonished to maintain herself in her first confessions and to renounce her lover.

—Says that she denies everything she has said, and that she has no lover. Feeling herself being strapped down, says that she is not a witch, while struggling to cry. . . . and upon being asked why she confessed to being one, said that she was forced to say it.

Told that she was not forced, that on the contrary she declared herself to be a witch without any threat.

—Says that she confessed it and that she is not a witch, and being a little stretched [on the rack] screams ceaselessly that she is not a witch. . . .

Asked if she did not confess that she had been a witch for twenty-six years.

—Says that she said it, that she retracts it, crying that she is not a witch.

Asked if she did not make Philippe Cornié's horse die, as she confessed.

—Answers no, crying Jesus-Maria, that she is not a witch.

The mark having been probed by the officer, in the presence of Doctor Bouchain, it was adjudged by the aforesaid doctor and officer truly to be the mark of the devil.

Being more tightly stretched upon the torture-rack, urged to maintain her confessions.

—Said that it was true that she is a witch and that she would maintain what she had said.

Asked how long she has been in subjugation to the devil.

—Answers that it was twenty years ago that the devil appeared to her, being in her lodgings in the form of a man dressed in a little cow-hide and black breeches. . . .

Verdict

July 9, 1652. In the light of the interrogations, answers and investigations made into the charge against Suzanne Gaudry, . . . seeing by her own confessions that she is said to have made a pact with the devil, received the mark from him, . . . and that following this, she had renounced God, Lent, and baptism and had let herself be known carnally by him, in which she received satisfaction. Also, seeing that she is said to have been a part of nocturnal carols and dances.

For expiation of which the advice of the undersigned is that the office of Rieux can legitimately condemn the aforesaid Suzanne Gaudry to death, tying her to a gallows, and strangling her to death, then burning her body and burying it here in the environs of the woods.

persecution, it also implies what is borne out in most witchcraft trials—that women of the lower classes were more likely to be accused of witchcraft. Indeed, where lists are given, those mentioned most often are milk-maids, peasant women, and servant girls. In the witchcraft trials of the sixteenth and seventeenth centuries, 80 percent of those accused were women, most of them single or widowed and many over fifty years old. Moreover, almost all victims belonged to the lower classes, the poor and propertyless.

The accused witches usually confessed to a number of practices. Many of their confessions were extracted by torture, greatly adding to the number and intensity of activities mentioned. But even when people confessed voluntarily, certain practices stand out. Many said that they had sworn allegiance to the devil and attended sabbats or nocturnal gatherings where they feasted, danced, and even copulated with the devil in sexual orgies. More common, however, were admissions of using evil incantations and special ointments and powders to wreak havoc on neighbors by killing their livestock, injuring their children, or raising storms to destroy their crops.

A number of contributing factors have been suggested to explain why the witchcraft craze became so widespread in the sixteenth and seventeenth centuries. Religious uncertainties clearly played some part. Many witchcraft trials occurred in areas where Protestantism had been recently victorious or in regions, such as southwestern Germany, where Protestant-Catholic controversies still raged. As religious passions became inflamed, accusations of being in league with the devil became common on both sides.

Recently, however, historians have emphasized the importance of social conditions, especially the problems of a society in turmoil, in explaining the witchcraft hysteria. At a time when the old communal values that stressed working together for the good of the community were disintegrating before the onslaught of a new economic ethic that emphasized that each person should look out for himself or herself, property owners became more fearful of the growing numbers of poor in their midst and transformed them psychologically into agents of the devil. Old women were particularly susceptible to suspicion. Many of them, no longer the recipients of the local charity available in traditional society, may even have tried to survive by selling herbs, potions, or secret remedies for healing. When problems arose—and there were many in this crisis-laden period—these same women were the most likely scapegoats at hand.

That women should be the chief victims of witchcraft trials was hardly accidental. Indeed, the authors of the *Malleus Maleficarum* (written in 1486) had argued that there was a direct link between witchcraft and women. According to them, women were inferior to men both mentally and morally. Women's moral weaknesses made them especially open to temptation and hence especially vulnerable to the allures of Satan. The strong beliefs of the authors of the *Malleus Maleficarum* were repeated in virtually all of the new witchcraft treatises written in the sixteenth and seventeenth centuries. Nicholas Rémy, a witchcraft judge in France in the 1590s, found it "not unreasonable that this scum of humanity, i.e., witches, should be drawn chiefly from the feminine sex." To another judge, it came as no surprise that witches would confess to sexual experiences with Satan: "The Devil uses them so, because he knows that women love carnal pleasures, and he means to bind them to his allegiance by such agreeable provocations."[8] Of course, not only witch hunters held such low estimates of women. Most theologians, lawyers, and philosophers in early modern Europe believed in the natural inferiority of women and thus would have found it plausible that women would be more susceptible to witchcraft.

By the mid-seventeenth century, the witchcraft hysteria began to subside. The destruction of the religious wars had at least forced people to accept a grudging toleration, causing religious passions to subside. Moreover, as governments began to stabilize after the period of crisis, fewer magistrates were willing to accept the unsettling and divisive conditions generated by the trials of witches. Finally, by the end of the seventeenth and beginning of the eighteenth centuries, more and more educated people were questioning altogether their old attitudes toward religion and finding it especially contrary to reason to believe in the old view of a world haunted by evil spirits.

Culture in a Turbulent World

Art and literature passed through two major stylistic stages between the Renaissance and 1650. These changes were closely linked to the religious, political, and intellectual developments of the period.

Art: Mannerism and the Baroque

The artistic Renaissance came to an end when a new movement called Mannerism emerged in Italy in the

◆ **El Greco, *Laocöon*.** Mannerism reached one of its highest expressions in the work of El Greco. Born in Crete, trained in Venice and Rome, and settling finally in Spain, El Greco worked as a church painter in Toledo. Pictured here is his version of the *Laocöon*, a famous piece of Hellenistic sculpture that had been discovered in Rome in 1506. The elongated, contorted bodies project a world of suffering while the somber background scene of the city of Toledo adds a sense of terror and doom.

decades of the 1520s and 1530s. The age of the Reformation had brought a revival of religious values accompanied by much political turmoil. Especially in Italy, the worldly enthusiasm of the Renaissance gave way to anxiety, uncertainty, suffering, and a yearning for spiritual experience. Mannerism reflected this environment in its deliberate attempt to break down the High Renaissance principles of balance, harmony, and moderation (the term *Mannerism* derives from critics who considered their contemporary artists to be second-rate imitators, painting in the "manner" of Michelangelo's

late style). Italian Mannerist painters deliberately distorted the rules of proportion by portraying elongated figures that conveyed a sense of suffering and a strong emotional atmosphere filled with anxiety and confusion.

Mannerism spread from Italy to other parts of Europe and perhaps reached its apogee in the work of El Greco (1541–1614). Doménikos Theotocópoulos (called "the Greek"—El Greco) was from Crete, but after studying in Venice and Rome, he moved to Spain in the 1570s where he became a church painter in Toledo. El Greco's elongated and contorted figures, portrayed in unusual shades of yellow and green against an eerie background of turbulent grays, reflect well the artist's desire to create a world of intense emotion.

Mannerism was eventually replaced by a new movement—the Baroque—that dominated the artistic world for another century and a half. The Baroque began in Italy in the last quarter of the sixteenth century and spread to the rest of Europe. Baroque artists sought to harmonize the classical traditions of Renaissance art with the intense religious feelings fostered by the revival of religion in the Reformation. The Baroque first appeared in Rome in the Jesuit church of Il Gesù, whose facade was completed in 1575. Although Protestants were also affected, the Baroque was most wholeheartedly embraced by the Catholic reform movement, as is evident at the Catholic courts, especially those of the Habsburgs in Madrid, Prague, Vienna, and Brussels. Although it was resisted in France, England, and Holland, eventually the Baroque style spread to all of Europe and to Latin America.

In large part, Baroque art and architecture reflected the search for power that was characteristic of much of the seventeenth century. Baroque churches and palaces featured richly ornamented facades, sweeping staircases, and an overall splendor that were meant to impress people. Kings and princes wanted other kings and princes as well as their subjects to be in awe of their power. The Catholic church, which commissioned many new churches, wanted people to see clearly the triumphant power of the Catholic faith.

Baroque painting was known for its use of dramatic effects to heighten emotional intensity. This style was especially evident in the works of Peter Paul Rubens (1577–1640), a prolific artist and an important figure in the spread of the Baroque from Italy to other parts of Europe. In his artistic masterpieces, bodies in violent motion, heavily fleshed nudes, a dramatic use of light and shadow, and rich sensuous pigments converge to show intense emotions. The restless forms and constant movement blend together into a dynamic unity.

Perhaps the greatest figure of the Baroque was the Italian architect and sculptor Gian Lorenzo Bernini (1598–1680), who completed Saint Peter's Basilica and designed the vast colonnade enclosing the piazza in front of it. Action, exuberance, profusion, and dramatic effects mark the work of Bernini in the interior of Saint Peter's, where Bernini's *Throne of Saint Peter* hovers in mid-air, held by the hands of the four great doctors of the Catholic church. Above the chair, rays of golden light drive a mass of clouds and angels toward the spectator. In his most striking sculptural work, the *Ecstasy of Saint Theresa*, Bernini depicts a moment of mystical experience in the life of the sixteenth-century Spanish saint. The elegant draperies and the expression on her face create a sensuously real portrayal of physical ecstasy.

♦ **Il Gesù.** The Jesuit church of Il Gesù in Rome was the first example of Baroque. Its facade, seen here, was completed in 1575. With its use of classical columns, entablatures, and pediments, it served as a model for later church designs done in the Baroque style.

✦ **Peter Paul Rubens, *The Landing of Marie de' Medici at Marseilles*.** Peter Paul Rubens played a key role in spreading the Baroque style from Italy to other parts of Europe. In *The Landing of Marie de' Medici at Marseilles*, Rubens made a dramatic use of light and color, bodies in motion, and luxurious nudes to heighten the emotional intensity of the scene. This was one of a cycle of twenty-one paintings dedicated to the queen mother of France.

✦ **Gian Lorenzo Bernini, *Ecstasy of St. Theresa*.** One of the greatest figures of the Baroque period was the Italian sculptor and architect Gian Lorenzo Bernini. The *Ecstasy of St. Theresa*, created for the Cornaro Chapel in the church of Santa Maria della Vittoria in Rome, was one of Bernini's most famous pieces of sculpture. Bernini sought to convey visually Theresa's own description of her mystical experience when an angel supposedly pierced her heart repeatedly with a golden arrow.

Thought: The World of Montaigne

The crises of the century between 1550 and 1650 produced challenges to the optimistic moral and intellectual premises of the Renaissance. The humanist emphasis on the dignity of man and the role of education in producing moral virtue seemed questionable in view of the often violent and irrational passions of dynastic and religious warfare. Intellectuals and writers began to adopt new approaches in criticizing tradition and authority. The concept of a positive skepticism is closely associated with the work of Michel de Montaigne (1533–1592).

Son of a prosperous French merchant, Montaigne received the kind of classical education advocated by Renaissance humanists. Montaigne served as a lawyer and magistrate in the Parlement of Bordeaux, but the religious wars so disgusted him that he withdrew to his country estate to think and write his *Essays*, the first two books of which were published in 1580. His aim was to "disclose himself," or to use self-knowledge as an instrument to understand the world. Montaigne questioned tradition and authority and attacked moral absolutists. He was especially critical of the Huguenot and ultra-Catholic fanatics of the French Wars of Religion who deluded themselves and took the easy way out of life's complexities by trying to kill each other: "instead of transforming themselves into angels, they transform themselves into beasts."

To counteract fanaticism, Montaigne preached moderation and toleration or the "middle way." In his *Essay on Experience*, he wrote: "It is much easier to go along the sides, where the outer edge serves as a limit and a guide, than by the middle way, wide and open, and to go by art than by nature; but it is also much less noble and less commendable. Greatness of soul is not so much pressing upward and forward as knowing how to set oneself in order."[9] Montaigne also brought his middle way and skeptical mind to bear on other subjects of the day. He wondered, for example, whether "civilized" Europeans were superior to the "savages" of the New World.

Montaigne was secular minded and discussed moral issues without reference to Christian truths. He was, in many ways, out of step with his own age of passionate religious truths and hatreds, but his ideas would be welcomed by many Europeans once Europe passed through this stage of intense intolerance. His maturity, experience, gentleness, and openness all made Montaigne one of the timeless writers of Western civilization.

A Golden Age of Literature: England and Spain

Periods of crisis often produce great writing, and so it was of this age, which was characterized by epic poetry, experimental verse, the first great chivalric novel, and, above all, a golden age of theater. In both England and Spain, writing for the stage reached new heights between 1580 and 1640. All of this impressive literature was written in the vernacular. Except for academic fields, such as theology, philosophy, jurisprudence, and the sciences, Latin was no longer a universal literary language.

The golden age of English literature is often called the Elizabethan Era because much of the English cultural flowering of the late sixteenth and early seventeenth centuries occurred during her reign. Elizabethan literature exhibits the exuberance and pride associated with English exploits under Queen Elizabeth (see the box on p. 524). Of all the forms of Elizabethan literature, none expressed the energy and intellectual versatility of the era better than drama. Of all the dramatists, none is more famous than William Shakespeare (1564–1616).

Shakespeare was the son of a prosperous glovemaker from Stratford-upon-Avon. When he appeared in London in 1592, Elizabethans were already addicted to the stage. By 1576, two professional theaters run by actors' companies were in existence. Elizabethan theater became a tremendously successful business. In or near London, at least four to six theaters were open six afternoons a week. London theaters ranged from the Globe, which was a circular unroofed structure holding 3,000, to the Blackfriars, which was roofed and held only 500. In the former, an admission charge of one or two pennies enabled even the lower classes to attend, while the higher prices in the latter ensured an audience of the well-to-do. Elizabethan audiences varied greatly, putting pressure on playwrights to write works that pleased nobles, lawyers, merchants, and even vagabonds. When the Puritans, who had long criticized the wickedness of the London stage, assumed power in 1642, one of their first actions was to close the theaters. They did not

◆ **William Shakespeare.** The golden age of English literature is identified with the Elizabethan era. Drama flourished during the period, and the greatest dramatist of the age was William Shakespeare. An actor and shareholder in a theatrical company as well as a playwright, Shakespeare wrote a number of tragedies, comedies, romances, and histories.

William Shakespeare: In Praise of England

William Shakespeare is one of the most famous playwrights of the Western world. He was a universal genius, outclassing all others in his psychological insights, depth of characterization, imaginative skills, and versatility. His historical plays reflected the patriotic enthusiasm of the English in the Elizabethan era, as this excerpt from Richard II illustrates.

William Shakespeare, *Richard II*

This royal throne of kings, this sceptered isle,
This earth of majesty, this seat of Mars,
This other Eden, demi-Paradise,
This fortress built by Nature for herself
Against infection and the hand of war,
This happy breed of men, this little world,
This precious stone set in the silver sea,
Which serves it in the office of a wall
Or as a moat defensive to a house
Against the envy of less happier lands—

This blessed plot, this earth, this realm, this England,
This nurse, this teeming womb of royal kings,
Feared by their breed and famous by their birth,
Renowned for their deeds as far from home,
For Christian service and true chivalry,
As is the sepulcher in stubborn Jewry [the Holy Sepulcher in Jerusalem]
Of the world's ransom, blessed Mary's Son—
This land of such dear souls, this dear dear land,
Dear for her reputation through the world,
Is now leased out, I die pronouncing it,
Like a tenement or pelting farm.
England, bound in with the triumphant sea,
Whose rocky shore beats back the envious siege
Of watery Neptune, is now bound in with shame,
With inky blots and rotten parchment bonds.
That England, what was wont to conquer others,
Hath made a shameful conquest of itself.
Ah, would the scandal vanish with my life,
How happy then were my ensuing death!

---

reopen until the monarchy was restored, eighteen years later.

William Shakespeare was a "complete man of the theater." Although best known for writing plays, he was also an actor and shareholder in the chief company of the time, the Lord Chamberlain's Company, which played in theaters as diverse as the Globe and the Blackfriars. Shakespeare has long been recognized as a universal genius. A master of the English language, he was instrumental in transforming a language that was still in a period of transition. His technical proficiency, however, was matched by an incredible insight into human psychology. Whether in his tragedies or comedies, Shakespeare exhibited a remarkable understanding of the human condition.

The theater was one of the most creative forms of expression during Spain's golden century. In the course of the sixteenth century, Spanish theater made the transition from religious morality plays to a popular form of dramatic art. The first professional theaters established in Seville and Madrid in the 1570s were run by actors' companies as in England. Soon, a public playhouse could be found in every large town, including Mexico City in the New World. Touring companies brought the latest Spanish plays to all parts of the Spanish empire.

Beginning in the 1580s, the agenda for playwrights was set by Lope de Vega (1562–1635). Like Shakespeare, he was from a middle-class background. He was an incredibly prolific writer; almost 500 of his 1,500 plays survive. They have been characterized as witty, charming, action-packed, and realistic. Lope de Vega made no apologies for the fact that he wrote his plays to please his audiences. In a treatise on drama written in 1609, he stated that the foremost duty of the playwright was to satisfy public demand. Shakespeare undoubtedly believed the same thing since his livelihood depended on public approval, but Lope de Vega was considerably more cynical about it: he remarked that if anyone thought he had written his plays for fame, "undeceive him and tell him that I wrote them for money."

One of the crowning achievements of the golden age of Spanish literature was the work of Miguel de Cervantes (1547–1616), whose *Don Quixote* has been acclaimed as one of the greatest literary works of all time. While satirizing medieval chivalric literature, Cervantes also perfected the chivalric novel and reconciled it with literary realism. The two main figures of his famous work represented the dual nature of the Spanish character. The knight Don Quixote from La Mancha is the visionary who is so involved in his lofty ideals that he is oblivious to the hard realities around him. To him, for example, windmills appear as four-armed giants. In contrast, the knight's fat and earthy squire, Sancho Panza, is the realist who cannot get his master to see the realities in front of him. But after adventures that took them to all parts of Spain, each came to see the value of the other's perspective. We are left with Cervantes's conviction that idealism and realism, visionary dreams and the hard work of reality, are both necessary to the human condition.

Conclusion

The period from 1560 to 1650 witnessed Europe's attempt to adjust to a whole range of change-laden forces. Population contracted as economic expansion gave way to economic recession. The discovery of new trade routes to the Far East and the "accidental" discovery of the Americas led Europeans to plunge outside the medieval world in which they had been enclosed for virtually a thousand years. The conquest of the Ameri-

cas brought out the worst and some of the best of European civilization. The greedy plundering of resources and the brutal repression, enslavement, and virtual annihilation of millions of Indians were hardly balanced by attempts to create new institutions, convert the natives to Christianity, and foster the rights of the indigenous peoples.

In the sixteenth century, the discoveries made little impact on Europeans preoccupied with the problems of dynastic expansion and, above all, religious division. It took one hundred years of religious warfare complicated by serious political, economic and social issues—the worst series of wars and civil wars since the collapse of the Roman Empire in the west—before Europeans finally admitted that they would have to tolerate different ways of worshiping God. That men who were disciples of the Apostle of Peace would kill each other—often in brutal and painful fashion—aroused skepticism about Christianity itself. As one German writer put it in 1650: "Lutheran, popish, and Calvinistic, we've got all these beliefs here; but there is some doubt about where Christianity has got to."[10] It is surely no accident that the search for a stable, secular order of politics and for order in the universe through natural laws played such important roles in the seventeenth century. The religious wars of the sixteenth and seventeenth centuries opened the door to the secular perspectives that have characterized modern Western civilization.

NOTES

1. Quoted in J. H. Parry, *The Age of Reconnaissance: Discovery, Exploration and Settlement, 1450 to 1650* (New York, 1963), p. 33.
2. Quoted in Richard B. Reed, "The Expansion of Europe," in Richard DeMolen, ed., *The Meaning of the Renaissance and Reformation* (Boston, 1974), p. 308.
3. Miguel Leon-Portilla, ed., *The Broken Spears: The Aztec Account of the Conquest of Mexico* (Boston, 1969), p. 51.
4. Quoted in E. Harris Harbison, *The Age of Reformation* (Ithaca, N.Y., 1955), p. 109.
5. Quoted in Garrett Mattingly, *The Armada* (Boston, 1959), pp. 216–17.

6. Quoted in H. G. Koenigsberger, *Early Modern Europe: 1500–1789* (London, 1987), pp. 29–30.
7. Quoted in Alan Kors and Edward Peters, eds., *Witchcraft in Europe, 1100–1700* (Philadelphia, 1972), p. 112.
8. Quoted in Joseph Klaits, *Servants of Satan: The Age of the Witch Hunts* (Bloomington, Ind., 1985), p. 68.
9. *The Complete Essays of Montaigne,* trans. Donald Frame (Stanford, 1958), p. 852.
10. Quoted in Theodore Schieder, *Handbuch der Europäischen Geschichte,* (Stuttgart, 1979), 3:579.

SUGGESTIONS FOR FURTHER READING

General works on the period from 1560 to 1650 include C. Wilson, *The Transformation of Europe, 1558–1648* (Berkeley, 1976); and H. Kamen, *The Iron Century: Social Change in Europe, 1550–1660* (New York, 1971). For an extremely detailed account of all aspects of life in the Mediterranean basin in the second half of the sixteenth century, see F. Braudel, *The Mediterranean and the Mediterranean World in the Age of Philip II*, trans. S. Reynolds, 2 vols. (New York, 1972–73).

The best general accounts of European discovery and expansion are G. V. Scammell, *The First Imperial Age* (London, 1989); J. H. Parry, *The Age of Reconnaissance: Discovery, Exploration and Settlement, 1450 to 1650* (New York, 1963); and B. Penrose, *Travel and Discovery in the Renaissance, 1420–1620* (New York, 1962). On the technological aspects of the subject, see C. M. Cipolla, *Guns, Sails, and Empires: Technological Innovation and the Early Phases of European Expansion, 1400–1700* (New York, 1965). On the Portuguese expansion, the fundamental work is C. R. Boxer, *The Portuguese Seaborne Empire: 1415–1825* (New York, 1969); but see also W. B. Diffie and G. D. Winius, *Foundations of the Portuguese Empire, 1415–1580* (Minneapolis, 1979). On Columbus, see the brief biography by J. S. Collis, *Christopher Columbus* (London, 1976); and F. Fernandez-Armesto, *Columbus* (New York, 1991). For a fundamental work on Spanish colonization, see J. H. Parry, *The Spanish Seaborne Empire* (New York, 1966). The standard work on the conquistadors is F. A. Kirkpatrick, *The Spanish Conquistadores* (Cleveland, 1968). Cortés is examined in W. W. Johnson, *Cortés* (Boston, 1975). The impact of expansion on European consciousness is explored in J. H. Elliott, *The Old World and the New, 1492–1650* (Cambridge, 1970). The human and ecological effects of the interaction of New World and Old World cultures are examined thoughtfully in A. W. Crosby, *The Columbian Exchange, Biological and Cultural Consequences of 1492* (Westport, Conn., 1972).

Two works by J. H. M. Salmon provide the best studies on the French Wars of Religion. They are *Society in Crisis: France in the Sixteenth Century* (New York, 1975) and *French Government and Society in the Wars of Religion* (St. Louis, 1976). Also valuable is N. M. Sutherland, *The Massacre of St. Bartholomew and the European Conflict, 1559–1572* (New York, 1973). An adequate popular biography of Henry of Navarre can be found in D. Seward, *The First Bourbon: Henry IV, King of France and Navarre* (Boston, 1971).

Two good histories of Spain in the sixteenth century are J. H. Elliott, *Imperial Spain, 1469–1716* (New York, 1964); and J. Lynch, *Spain under the Habsburgs*, vol. 1, *Empire and Absolutism, 1516–1598* (New York, 1964). The best biographies of Philip II are P. Pierson, *Philip II of Spain* (London, 1975); and G. Parker, *Philip II* (Boston and London, 1978). Economic aspects of sixteenth-century Spain are well discussed in the classic account of J. V. Vives, *An Economic History of Spain* (Berkeley, 1969). On the revolt of the Netherlands, see the classic work by P. Geyl, *The Revolt of the Netherlands, 1555–1609* (London, 1962); and the more recent work of G. Parker, *The Dutch Revolt* (London, 1977).

Elizabeth's reign can be examined in three good biographies, J. Ridley, *Elizabeth I* (New York, 1988); W. T. MacCaffrey, *Elizabeth I* (London, 1993); and L. B. Smith, *Elizabeth Tudor: Portrait of a Queen* (London, 1976). The role of the Catholic and Puritan minorities is discussed in A. Morey, *The Catholic Subjects of Elizabeth I* (Totowa, N.J., 1978); and P. Collinson, *The Elizabethan Puritan Movement* (Berkeley, 1967). The classic work on the Armada is the beautifully written *The Armada* by G. Mattingly (Boston, 1959).

The classic study on the Thirty Years' War is C. V. Wedgwood, *The Thirty Years War* (Garden City, N.Y., 1961), but it needs to be supplemented by the more recent works by S. H. Steinberg, *The Thirty Years' War and the Conflict for European Hegemony, 1600–1660* (New York, 1966), which emphasizes the wider context of the struggle; G. Parker, *The Thirty Years War* (London, 1984); and the brief study by S. J. Lee, *The Thirty Years War* (London, 1991). On Gustavus Adolphus, see M. Roberts, *Gustavus Adolphus and the Rise of Sweden* (London, 1973). The best biography of Wallenstein is G. Mann, *Wallenstein: His Life Narrated*, trans. C. Kessler (New York, 1976). The idea of a military revolution in the sixteenth and seventeenth centuries was first presented forcefully in M. Roberts, *The Military Revolution, 1560–1660* (London, 1956), although it has not gone unchallenged; see G. Parker, *The Military*

Revolution: Military Innovation and the Rise of the West 1500–1800 (Cambridge, 1988).

The story of the witchcraft craze can be examined in three recent works, J. Klaits, *Servants of Satan: The Age of the Witch Hunts* (Bloomington, Ind., 1985); J. B. Russell, *A History of Witchcraft* (London, 1980); and B. P. Levack, *The Witch-Hunt in Early Modern Europe* (London, 1987). Although narrower in scope, also of great value is C. Larner, *Enemies of God: The Witch-hunt in Scotland* (London, 1981).

For a brief, readable guide to Mannerism, see L. Murray, *The Late Renaissance and Mannerism* (New York, 1967). For a general survey of Baroque culture, see M. and L. Mainstone, *The Cambridge Introduction to Art: The Seventeenth Century* (Cambridge, 1981); and J. S. Held, *Seventeenth and Eighteenth Century Art: Baroque Painting, Sculpture, Architecture* (New York, 1971). The best biography of Montaigne remains D. M. Frame, *Montaigne: A Biography* (New York, 1965). On the Spanish golden century of literature, see R. O. Jones, *The Golden Age: Prose and Poetry*, which is volume 2 of *The Literary History of Spain* (London, 1971). The literature on Shakespeare is enormous. For a biography, see A. L. Rowse, *The Life of Shakespeare* (New York, 1963).

CHAPTER

16

*Response to Crisis:
State Building and
the Search for Order
in the Seventeenth
Century*

The age of crisis from 1560 to 1650 was accompanied by a decline in religious orientation and a growing secularization that affected both the political and the intellectual worlds of Europe (on the intellectual effect, see the Scientific Revolution in Chapter 17). Some historians like to speak of the seventeenth century as a turning point in the evolution of a modern state system in Europe. The idea of a united Christian Europe (the practice of a united Christendom had actually been moribund for some time) gave way to the practical realities of a system of secular states in which reason of state took precedence over the salvation of subjects' souls. Of course, these states had emerged and begun their development during the Middle Ages, but medieval ideas about statehood had still been couched in religious terms. By the seventeenth century, the credibility of Christianity had been so weakened in the religious wars that more and more Europeans could think of politics in secular terms.

One of the responses to the crises of the seventeenth century was a search for order. As the internal social and political rebellions and revolts died down, it became apparent that the privileged classes of society—the aristocrats—remained in control, although the various states exhibited important differences in political forms. The most general trend saw an extension of monarchical power as a stabilizing force. This development, which historians have called absolutism or absolute monarchy, was most evident in France during the flamboyant reign of Louis XIV, regarded by some as the perfect embodiment of an absolute monarch. In his memoirs, the duc de Saint-Simon, who had firsthand experience of French court life, said that Louis was "the very figure of a hero, so imbued with a natural but most imposing majesty that it appeared even in his most insignificant gestures and movements." The king's natural grace gave him a special charm as well: "He was as dignified and majestic in his dressing gown as when dressed in robes of state, or on horseback at the head of his troops." He excelled at exercise and was never affected by the

Rule by Cardinal Richelieu

Reign of Louis XIV

Frederick William the Great Elector   Peter the Great

English, French, Dutch settle North America

The Glorious Revolution

Official recognition of the Dutch Republic

English Civil War

Paintings of Rembrandt

John Locke, *Two Treatises of Government*

Thomas Hobbes, *Leviathan*

Plays of Racine

weather: "Drenched with rain or snow, pierced with cold, bathed in sweat or covered with dust, he was always the same." He spoke well and learned quickly. He was naturally kind and "he loved truth, justice, order, and reason." His life was orderly: "Nothing could be regulated with greater exactitude than were his days and hours." His self-control was impeccable: "He did not lose control of himself ten times in his whole life, and then only with inferior persons." But even absolute monarchs had imperfections, and Saint-Simon had the courage to point them out: "Louis XIV's vanity was without limit or restraint," which led to his "distaste for all merit, intelligence, education, and, most of all, for all independence of character and sentiment in others," as well as "to mistakes of judgment in matters of importance."

But absolutism was not the only response to crisis in the seventeenth century. Other states, such as England, reacted differently to domestic crisis, and another very different system emerged where monarchs were limited by the power of their representative assemblies. Absolute and limited monarchy were the two poles of seventeenth-century state building.

The Theory of Absolutism

Absolute monarchy or absolutism meant that the sovereign power or ultimate authority in the state rested in the hands of a king who claimed to rule by divine right. But what did sovereignty mean? The late sixteenth-century political theorist Jean Bodin believed that sovereign power consisted of the authority to make laws, tax, administer justice, control the state's administrative system, and determine foreign policy. These powers made a ruler sovereign.

One of the chief theorists of divine-right monarchy in the seventeenth century was the French theologian and court preacher Bishop Jacques Bossuet (1627–1704), who expressed his ideas in a book entitled *Politics Drawn from the Very Words of Holy Scripture*. Bossuet argued first that government was divinely ordained so that humans could live in an organized society. Of all forms of government, monarchy, he averred, was the most general, most ancient, most natural, and the best, since God established kings and through them reigned over all the peoples of the world. Since kings received their power from God, their authority was absolute. They were responsible to no one (including parliaments) except God. Nevertheless, Bossuet cautioned, although a king's authority was absolute, his power was not since he was limited by the law of God. Bossuet believed there was a difference between absolute monarchy and arbitrary monarchy. The latter contradicted the rule of law and the sanctity of property and was simply lawless tyranny. Bossuet's distinction between absolute and arbitrary government was not always easy to maintain. There was also a large gulf between the theory of absolutism as expressed by Bossuet and the practice of absolutism. As we shall see in our survey of seventeenth-century states, a monarch's absolute power was often limited greatly by practical realities.

Absolutism in Western Europe

An examination of seventeenth-century absolutism must begin with western Europe since France during the reign of Louis XIV (1643–1715) has traditionally been regarded as the best example of the practice of absolute monarchy in the seventeenth century.

France and Absolute Monarchy

By the end of the seventeenth century, France had come to play a dominant role in European affairs. French culture, language, and manners influenced all levels of European society. French diplomacy and wars shaped the political affairs of western and central Europe. The court of Louis XIV seemed to be imitated everywhere in Europe. In his desire to emulate Louis XIV, the elector of Brandenburg, although a happily married German prince, added to his court "a lady who had the title and court functions, though not the pleasures, of being his mistress." Of course, French greatness depended upon a treasury filled by imposing ever-increasing tax burdens on the people while the stability of Louis's reign was magnified by the instability that had preceded it.

FOUNDATIONS OF FRENCH ABSOLUTISM

The history of France before the reign of Louis XIV was hardly the story of steady, unbroken progress toward the ideal of absolute monarchy that many historians have tended to portray. During the fifty years or so before Louis, royal and ministerial governments had to struggle to avoid the breakdown of the state. The line between order and anarchy was often a narrow one. Nevertheless, the French monarchy gradually succeeded in overcoming the threats to its power and establishing a strong monarchical authority.

Thirty years of bloody civil war had ceased at the end of the sixteenth century when Henry IV established the Bourbon dynasty (see Chapter 15). Henry began the task of reconstructing a badly shattered France, aided by a forceful group of ministers, including the astute minister of finances, the duke of Sully. The accumulation of debts from the wars and a lack of sufficient revenue constituted the government's most serious problems. Sully took steps to remedy them. Tax collectors, who paid the government a fixed percentage of the taxes they collected in their districts (a system known as tax farming), were forced to take smaller shares for themselves. More efficiently administered direct taxes were imposed. The *gabelle*, the much-hated tax on salt, a crucial necessity for preserving food in the seventeenth century, was raised to even higher levels. Furthermore, by the end of Henry's reign, sales of government offices had increased. By 1608, half of the government's debt had been paid, and a reservoir of funds had even been accumulated in the state treasury. Sully's expenditures on roads, land drainage, and agricultural improvements helped to stimulate and improve economic growth.

Another major problem was the government's need to restore the central authority of the monarchical government in France after thirty years of civil war. Henry IV began the process by taking numerous trips through the provinces and exercising more control over the appointment of officials in the town governments. While these steps hardly constituted a "master plan for creating absolute monarchy," they did boost the role of the central government in the life of the country. But monarchical authority was still precarious when the king was unexpectedly assassinated in 1610 and succeeded by his nine-year-old son, Louis XIII. Could the new royal government survive under the regency of Henry's wife, the Italian Marie de' Medici?

At first the issue proved problematic. Marie's policy of bribing the great nobles into submission failed to prevent them from rebelling against her authority, to which she responded—successfully—by giving them more money and new positions of power. Marie's palace clique managed to remain in power until her son, Louis XIII, took personal charge of the government in 1617. Louis's problems seemed only to mount, however, until the king's council fell under the control of the cunning, competent, and clever Cardinal Richelieu in 1624. As leader of the royal council and hence the king's chief minister, Richelieu initiated policies that eventually strengthened the power of the monarchy.

It has usually been assumed that Cardinal Richelieu had a clear plan to create an absolute monarchy at home and expand French power abroad. In his *Political Testament*, he claimed to have promised the king to "use all my industry and all the authority it has pleased you to give me to ruin the Huguenot party, to humble the pride of the great men, to bring your subjects to their duty and to raise your name abroad to the place that is its due."[1] But it is just as likely that Richelieu's primary aims were to keep himself in power and to extend the central government's authority by any means possible.

One of the dangers to royal authority came from the Huguenots (see Chapter 15). Richelieu's policy toward them was dictated by political, not religious motives, despite his position as a cardinal of the Catholic church. Richelieu realized the potential danger the fortified cities of the Huguenots posed to the authority of the king, especially if the Huguenots attracted foreign support as they had in the sixteenth century. Just such a situation occurred in 1627, when the Huguenot city of La Rochelle, with English aid, rebelled against the crown. One year after the rebellion was finally crushed and the city occupied by French troops, Richelieu capitalized on his success by issuing the Peace of Alais (1629), which allowed the Huguenots to keep their religious and civil rights from the Edict of Nantes, but stripped them of their private armies and fortified cities. By eliminating their political and military rights while preserving their religious ones, the Peace of Alais helped transform the Huguenots into more reliable subjects.

Richelieu acted more cautiously in "humbling the pride of the great men," the important French nobility. He understood the influential role the nobles played in the French state. The dangerous ones were those who asserted their territorial independence when they were excluded from participating in the central government. Proceeding slowly but determinedly, Richelieu developed an efficient network of spies to uncover noble plots and then crushed the conspiracies and executed the conspirators, thereby eliminating a major threat to royal authority. Richelieu even issued edicts against dueling as a remnant of the private warfare reminiscent of medieval nobles. To Richelieu, private warfare was as bad as armed rebellion; both repudiated central state authority.

To reform and strengthen the central administration, initially for financial reasons, Richelieu sent out royal officials called intendants to the provinces to execute the orders of the central government. As the functions of the intendants grew, they came into conflict with provincial governors. Since the intendants were victorious in most of these disputes, they further strengthened the power of the crown. Richelieu proved less capable in financial matters, however. Not only was the basic system of state finances corrupt, but so many people benefited from the system's inefficiency and injustice that the government faced strong resistance when it tried to reform it. The *taille* (an annual direct tax usually levied on land or property) was increased—in 1643 it was two and a half times what it had been in 1610—and crown lands were mortgaged again. Expenditures, especially the cost of war preparations, soon outstripped the additional revenues, however, and French debt continued its upward spiral under Richelieu.

The general success of Richelieu's domestic policy in strengthening the central role of the monarchy was mirrored by a successful foreign policy. That policy was dictated, first of all, by opposition to Spain, which led in turn to further anti-Habsburg activity in the Holy Roman Empire to France's east. Eventually, the Catholic cardinal of France was led to subsidize Protestant Sweden and then in 1635 to intervene directly with French troops to support the Protestant cause against the Habsburgs (see Chapter 15). Although both Richelieu and Louis XIII died before the Thirty Years' War ended, French policy had proved successful at one level since France emerged as Europe's leading power by 1648.

Richelieu died in 1642, followed five months later by King Louis XIII, who was succeeded by his son Louis XIV, then but four years old. This necessitated a regency under Anne of Austria, wife of the dead king. But she allowed Cardinal Mazarin, Richelieu's trained successor, to dominate the government. An Italian who had come to France as a papal legate and then become naturalized,

◆ **Cardinal Richelieu.** A key figure in the emergence of a strong monarchy in France was Cardinal Richelieu, pictured here in a portrait by Philippe de Champagne. Chief minister to Louis XIII, Richelieu strengthened royal authority by eliminating the private armies and fortified cities of the Huguenots and by crushing aristocratic conspiracies.

Mazarin attempted to carry on Richelieu's policies until his death in 1661.

The most important event during Mazarin's rule was a revolt known as the Fronde, which can be viewed as the last serious attempt to limit the growing power of the crown until the French Revolution. As a foreigner, Mazarin was greatly disliked by all elements of the French population. The nobles, who particularly resented the centralized administrative power being built up at the expense of the provincial nobility, temporarily allied with the members of the Parlement of Paris, who opposed the new taxes levied by the government to pay the costs of the Thirty Years' War, and with the masses of Paris, who were also angry at the additional taxes. The Parlement of Paris was the most important court in France with jurisdiction over half of the kingdom, and its members formed the nobles of the robe, the service nobility of lawyers and administrators. These nobles of the robe led the first Fronde (1648–1649), which broke out in Paris and was ended by compromise. The second Fronde, begun in 1650, was led by the nobles of the sword, whose ancestors were medieval nobles. They were interested in overthrowing Mazarin for their own purposes: to secure their positions and increase their own power. The second Fronde was crushed by 1652, a task made easier when the nobles began fighting each other instead of Mazarin. With the end of the Fronde, the vast majority of the French concluded that the best hope for stability in France lay in the crown. When Mazarin died in 1661, the greatest of the seventeenth-century monarchs, Louis XIV, took over supreme power.

THE REIGN OF LOUIS XIV (1643–1715)

The day after Cardinal Mazarin's death, Louis XIV, at the age of twenty-three, expressed his determination to be a real king and the sole ruler of France:

> Up to this moment I have been pleased to entrust the government of my affairs to the late Cardinal. It is now time that I govern them myself. You [secretaries and ministers of state] will assist me with your counsels when I ask for them. I request and order you to seal no orders except by my command, ... I order you not to sign anything, not even a passport ... without my command; to render account to me personally each day and to favor no one.[2]

His mother, who was well aware of Louis's proclivity for fun and games and getting into the beds of the maids in the royal palace, laughed aloud at these words. But Louis was quite serious.

Louis proved willing to pay the price of being a strong ruler (see the box on p. 534). He established a conscientious routine from which he seldom deviated, but he did not look upon his duties as drudgery since he judged his royal profession to be "grand, noble, and delightful." Eager for glory (in the French sense of achieving what was expected of one in an important position), Louis created a grand and majestic spectacle at the court of Versailles (see Daily Life at the Court of Versailles later in this chapter). Consequently, Louis and his court came to set the standard for monarchies and aristocracies all over Europe. Less than fifty years after his death, the great French writer Voltaire selected the title "Age of Louis XIV" for his history of Europe from 1661 to 1715. Historians have tended to use it ever since.

Although Louis may have believed in the theory of absolute monarchy and consciously fostered the myth of himself as the Sun King, the source of light for all of his people, historians are quick to point out that the realities fell far short of the aspirations. Despite the centralizing efforts of Cardinals Richelieu and Mazarin, seventeenth-century France still possessed a bewildering system of overlapping authorities. Provinces had their own regional parlements, their own local Estates, their own sets of laws. Members of the high nobility with their huge estates and clients among the lesser nobility still exercised much authority. Both towns and provinces possessed privileges and powers seemingly from time immemorial that they would not easily relinquish. Much of Louis's success rested less on the modernization of administrative machinery, as is frequently claimed, than on his clever and adroit manipulation of the traditional priorities and values of French society.

One of the keys to Louis's power was that he was able to restructure the central policy-making machinery of government because it was part of his own court and household. The royal court was an elaborate structure that served three purposes simultaneously: it was the personal household of the king, the location of central governmental machinery, and the place where powerful subjects came to find favors and offices for themselves and their clients as well as the main arena where rival aristocratic factions jostled for power. The greatest danger to Louis's personal rule came from the very high nobles and princes of the blood (the royal princes) who considered it their natural function to assert the policy-making role of royal ministers. Louis eliminated this threat by removing them from the royal council, the chief administrative body of the king and overseer of the central machinery of government, and enticing them to his court where he could keep them preoccupied with court life and out of politics.

Instead of the high nobility and royal princes, Louis relied for his ministers on nobles who came from relatively new aristocratic families. Such were François Michel Le Tellier, secretary of state for war; Hugues de Lionne, secretary for foreign affairs; and Nicholas Fouquet, superintendent of finances. His ministers were expected to be subservient; said Louis, "I had no intention of sharing my authority with them." When Fouquet began to flaunt the enormous wealth and power he had amassed in the king's service, Louis ordered his arrest and imprisoned him for life. Fouquet was replaced in the king's council by Colbert, another noble of bourgeois origin. Louis's domination of his ministers and secretaries gave him control of the central policy-making machinery of government and thus authority over the traditional areas of monarchical power: the formulation of foreign policy, the making of war and peace, the assertion of the secular power of crown against any religious authority, and the ability to levy taxes to fulfill these functions.

According to recent historical scholarship, however, Louis had considerably less success with the internal administration of the kingdom. The traditional groups and institutions of French society—the nobles, officials, town councils, guilds, and representative Estates in some provinces—were simply too powerful for the king to have direct control over the lives of his subjects. Louis had three ways of ruling the provinces. Officially, he worked through hereditary officeholders, usually aristocrats, who were untrustworthy since they were always inclined to balance the king's wishes against their own interests. The king also had his intendants as direct royal agents, but they, too, proved unreliable and their actions often provoked disturbances in the provinces. The intendants were not so much the instruments by which the central government carried out decisions, but simply the "eyes and ears of the ministers" in the provinces. Finally, the king had an informal system of royal patronage, which Louis used successfully. The king and his ministers enlisted the aid of nobles and senior churchmen and their clients by granting them offices and pensions. Thus, the central government exercised its control over the provinces and the people by carefully bribing the important people to ensure that the king's policies were executed. Nevertheless, local officials could still obstruct the execution of policies they disliked, indicating clearly that a so-called absolute monarch was not always that absolute.

The maintenance of religious harmony had long been considered an area of monarchical power. The desire to keep it led Louis into conflict with the French Huguenots. Louis XIV did not want to allow Protestants to

◆ **Louis XIV.** Louis XIV was determined to be the sole ruler of France. Louis eliminated the threat of the high nobility by removing them from the royal council and replacing them with relatively new aristocrats whom he could dominate. This portrait by Hyacinth Rigaud captures the king's sense of royal dignity and grandeur.

practice their faith in largely Catholic France. Perhaps he was motivated by religion, but it is more likely that Louis, who believed in the motto, "one king, one law, one faith," felt that the existence of this minority undermined his own political authority. His anti-Protestant policy, aimed at converting the Huguenots to Catholicism, began mildly by offering rewards, but escalated by 1681 to a policy of forced conversions. The most favored method was to quarter French soldiers in Huguenot communities and homes with the freedom to misbehave so that their hosts would "see the light quickly." This approach did produce thousands of immediate conversions. In October 1685, Louis issued the Edict of Fontainebleau. In addition to revoking the

Louis XIV: Kingly Advice

Throughout his reign, Louis XIV was always on stage, acting the role of the wise "Grand Monarch." In 1661, after he became a father, Louis began his Memoirs for the Dauphin, *a frank collection of precepts for the education of his oldest son and heir to the throne. He continued to add to these* Memoirs *over the next twenty years.*

Louis XIV, *Memoirs for the Dauphin*

Kings are often obliged to do things which go against their inclinations and offend their natural goodness. They should love to give pleasure and yet they must often punish and destroy persons on whom by nature they wish to confer benefits. The interest of the state must come first. One must constrain one's inclinations and not put oneself in the position of berating oneself because one could have done better in some important affair but did not because of some private interest, because one was distracted from the attention one should have for the greatness, the good and the power of the state. Often there are troublesome places where it is difficult to make out what one should do. One's ideas are confused. As long as this lasts, one can refrain from making a decision. But as soon as one has fixed one's mind upon something which seems best to do, it must be acted upon. This is what enabled me to succeed so often in what I have done. The mistakes which I made, and which gave me infinite trouble, were the result of the desire to please or of allowing myself to accept too carelessly the opinions of others. Nothing is more danger-ous than weakness of any kind whatsoever. In order to command others, one must raise oneself above them and once one has heard the reports from every side one must come to a decision upon the basis of one's own judgment, without anxiety but always with the concern not to command anything which is of itself unworthy either of one's place in the world or of the greatness of the state. Princes with good intentions and some knowledge of their affairs, either from experience or from study and great diligence in making themselves capable, find numerous cases which instruct them that they must give special care and total application to everything. One must be on guard against oneself, resist one's own tendencies, and always be on guard against one's own natural bent. The craft of a king is great, noble and delightful when one feels worthy of doing well whatever one promises to do. But it is not exempt from troubles, weariness and worries. Sometimes uncertainty causes despair, and when one has spent a reasonable time in examining an affair, one must make a decision and take the step which one believes to be best. When one has the state in view, one works for one's self. The good of the one constitutes the glory of the other. When the former is fortunate, eminent and powerful, he who is the cause thereof becomes glorious and consequently should find more enjoyment than his subjects in all the pleasant things of life for himself and for them. When one has made a mistake, it must be corrected as soon as possible, and no other consideration must stand in the way, not even kindness.

Edict of Nantes, the new edict provided for the destruction of Huguenot churches and the closing of their schools. Although they were forbidden to leave France, it is estimated that 200,000 Huguenots left for shelter in England, the United Provinces, and the German states. Through their exodus, France lost people who had commercial and industrial skills, although some modern scholars have argued this had only a minor impact on the French economy. Perhaps a more important effect of the Huguenot dispersal was the increased hatred of France that the Huguenot émigrés stirred up in their adopted Protestant countries.

The cost of building Versailles and other palaces, maintaining his court, and pursuing his wars made finances a crucial issue for Louis XIV. He was most fortunate in having the services of Jean-Baptiste Colbert (1619–1683) as controller-general of finances. Colbert sought to increase the wealth and power of France through general adherence to that loose collection of economic policies called mercantilism, which stressed government regulation of economic activities to benefit the state (see Mercantilism later in this chapter). To decrease the need for imports and increase exports, Colbert attempted to expand the quantity and improve the quality of French manufactured goods. He founded new luxury industries, such as the royal tapestry works at Beauvais; invited Venetian glassmakers and Flemish clothmakers to France; drew up instructions regulating the quality of goods produced; oversaw the training of workers and granted special privileges, including tax exemptions, loans, and subsidies to those who established new industries. To improve communications and the transportation of goods internally, he built roads and canals. To decrease imports directly, he raised tariffs on foreign manufactured goods, especially English and Dutch cloth, and created a merchant marine to facilitate the conveyance of French goods.

Colbert was not really much of an innovator, especially in his financial policies. France still depended on the system of tax farming. Moreover, the sale of offices, which remained a common practice, absorbed huge revenues as officeholders sought to take financial advantage of their positions to recoup the money they had spent purchasing them. As one judge expressed it: "The ministry of the judges, their jurisdiction and distribution of justice are nothing but a shop where the offices they have purchased wholesale are sold at retail." Vast exemptions for clergy and nobility as well as towns and provinces made the collection of revenue highly irrational. Colbert was unable or unwilling to change the basic system, although he attempted to correct the most obvious abuses and eliminate some of the tax exemptions. While Colbert's policies are given much credit for fostering the development of manufacturing, some historians are dubious about the usefulness of many of his mercantilistic policies. Regulations were often evaded, and the imposition of high tariffs brought foreign retaliation. French trading companies entered the scene too late to be really competitive with the British and the Dutch. And above all, Colbert's economic policies, which were geared to making his king more powerful, were ultimately self-defeating. The more revenue Colbert collected to enable the King to make war, the faster Louis depleted the treasury. At the same time, the burden of taxes fell increasingly upon the peasants who still constituted the overwhelming majority of the French population.

DAILY LIFE AT THE COURT OF VERSAILLES

The court of Louis XIV at Versailles set a standard that was soon followed by other European rulers. In 1669, Louis, who disliked Paris as a result of his humiliating experiences at the hands of Parisian mobs during the Fronde, decided to convert a hunting lodge at Versailles, located near Paris, into a chateau. Not until 1688, after untold sums of money had been spent and tens of thousands of workers had labored incessantly, was most of the construction completed on the enormous palace that housed thousands of people.

Versailles served many purposes. It was the residence of the king; a reception hall for state affairs; an office building for the members of the king's government; and the home of thousands of royal officials and aristocratic courtiers. Versailles became a symbol for the French

absolutist state and the power of the Sun King, Louis XIV. As a visible manifestation of France's superiority and wealth, this lavish court was intended to overawe subjects and impress foreign powers. If an age's largest buildings reflect its values, then Versailles is a reminder of the seventeenth-century preoccupation with monarchical authority and magnificence.

Versailles also served a practical political purpose. It became home to the high nobility and princes of the blood (the royal princes), those powerful figures who had aspired to hold the policy-making role of royal ministers. By keeping them involved in the myriad activities that made up daily life at the court of Versailles, Louis excluded them from real power while allowing them to share in the mystique of power as companions of the king.

Life at Versailles became a court ceremony with Louis XIV at the center of it all. The king had little privacy; only when he visited his wife or mother or mistress or met with ministers was he free of the noble courtiers who swarmed about the palace. Most daily ceremonies were carefully staged, such as those attending Louis's rising from bed, dining, praying, attending mass, and going to bed. A mob of nobles aspired to assist the king in carrying out these solemn activities. It was considered a great honor for a noble to be chosen to hand the king his shirt while dressing. But why did nobles participate in so many ceremonies, some of which were so obviously demeaning? Active involvement in the activities at

✦ **Palace of Versailles.** Louis XIV spent untold sums of money in the construction of a new royal residence at Versailles. The enormous palace of Versailles also housed the members of the king's government and served as home for thousands of French nobles. As the largest royal residence in Europe, Versailles impressed foreigners and became a source of envy for other rulers.

◆ **Interior of Versailles: Hall of Mirrors.** Pictured here is the exquisite Hall of Mirrors at Versailles. A number of daily and occasional ceremonies dominated the lives of the residents of Versailles. Rules of etiquette became so complex that they guided virtually every aspect of behavior.

Versailles was the king's prerequisite for obtaining the offices, titles, and pensions that only he could grant. This policy reduced great nobles and ecclesiastics, the "people of quality," to a plane of equality, allowing Louis to exercise control over them and prevent them from interfering in the real lines of power. To maintain their social prestige, the "people of quality" were expected to adhere to rigid standards of court etiquette appropriate to their rank.

Indeed, court etiquette became a complex matter. Nobles and royal princes were arranged in an elaborate order of seniority and expected to follow certain rules of precedence. Who could sit down and on what kind of chair was a subject of much debate. Who could sit where at meals with the king was also carefully regulated. On one occasion, when the wife of a minister sat closer to the king than a duchess at dinner, Louis XIV became so angry that he did not eat for the rest of the evening. Another time, Louis reproached his talkative brother for the sin of helping himself to a dish before Louis had touched it with the biting words: "I perceive that you are no better able to control your hands than your tongue."[3]

Besides the daily and occasional ceremonies that made up the regular side of court life at Versailles and the many hours a day Louis spent with his ministers on affairs of state, daily life at Versailles included numerous forms of entertainment. While he was healthy, Louis and his courtiers hunted at least once a week; members of the royal family nearly every day. Walks through the Versailles gardens, boating trips, performances of tragedies and comedies, ballets, and concerts all provided sources of pleasure (see the box on p. 537). Three evenings a week, from seven to ten, Louis also held an *appartement* where he was at "home" to his court. The *appartement* was characterized by a formal informality. Relaxed rules of etiquette even allowed people to sit down in the presence of their superiors. The evening's entertainment began with a concert, followed by games of billiards or cards, and ended with a sumptuous buffet.

One form of entertainment—gambling—became an obsession at Versailles. Although a few of the courtiers made a living by their gambling skill, many others were simply amateurs. This did not stop them from playing regularly and losing enormous sums of money. One princess described the scene: "Here in France as soon as people get together they do nothing but play [cards]; they play for frightful sums, and the players seem bereft of their senses. . . . One shouts at the top of his voice, another strikes the table with his fist, a third blasphemes. . . . it is horrible to watch them."[4] Louis did not share the princess's sensibilities; he was not horrified by an activity that kept the Versailles nobles busy and out of mischief.

THE WARS OF LOUIS XIV

The increase in royal power that Louis pursued as well as his desire for military glory had an effect on the development of the military. During Louis's reign, the French army was transformed from a host of small armies dominated by provincial nobles to a state activity, a standing army subject to the monarch's command. In itself, the standing army was neither new nor a product of absolute monarchy—the first real standing armies had been organized earlier by Venice and the United Provinces. But French resources enabled Louis to develop one larger than Europe had ever seen.

Under the secretary of war, François Michel Le Tellier, the marquis of Louvois, France developed a professional army numbering 100,000 men in peacetime and 400,000 in time of war. Unable to fill the ranks with

➤ *Travels with the King* ➤

The duc de Saint-Simon was one of many noble courtiers who lived at Versailles and had firsthand experience of court life there. In this Memoirs, *he left a controversial and critical account of Louis XIV and his court. In this selection, he describes the price court ladies paid for the "privilege" of riding with the great king.*

Duc de Saint-Simon, *Memoirs*

The King always traveled with his carriage full of women: His mistresses, his bastard daughters, his daughters-in-law, sometimes Madame [the wife of the king's brother], and the other ladies of the court when there was room. This was the case for hunts, and trips to Fontainebleau, Chantilly, Compiégne, and the like. . . . In his carriage during these trips there was always an abundance and variety of things to eat: meats, pastries, and fruit. Before the carriage had gone a quarter league the King would ask who was hungry. He never ate between meals, not even a fruit, but he enjoyed watching others stuff themselves. It was mandatory to eat, with appetite and good grace, and to be gay; otherwise; he

showed his displeasure by telling the guilty party she was putting on airs and trying to be coy. The same ladies or princesses who had eaten that day at the King's table were obliged to eat again as though they were weak from hunger. What is more, the women were forbidden to mention their personal needs, which in any case they could not have relieved without embarrassment, since there were guards and members of the King's household in front and in back of the carriage, and officers and equerries riding alongside the doors. The dust they kicked up choked everyone in the carriage, but the King, who loved fresh air, insisted that all the windows remain open. He would have been extremely displeased if one of the ladies had pulled a curtain to protect herself from the sun, the wind, or the cold.

He pretended not to notice his passengers' discomfort, and always traveled very fast, with the usual number of relays. Sickness in the carriage was a demerit which ruled out further invitations. . . . When the king had to relieve himself he did not hesitate to stop the carriage and get out; but the ladies were not allowed to budge.

volunteers, the French resorted to conscription, a practice that led to other problems as unwilling soldiers were eager to desert. But the new standing armies did not exist to be admired. Louis and other monarchs used them to make war an almost incessant activity of the seventeenth and eighteenth centuries.

Louis XIV had a great proclivity for war. Historians have debated the assertion that Louis pursued war to expand his kingdom to its "natural frontiers"—the Alps, Pyrenees, and Rhine River. But few doubt his desire to achieve the prestige and military glory befitting a Sun King as well as his dynastic ambition, his desire to ensure the domination of his Bourbon dynasty over European affairs. His ends soon outstripped his means, however, as his ambitions roused much of Europe to form coalitions that even he could not overcome.

In 1667, Louis began his first war by invading the Spanish Netherlands to his north and Franche-Comté to the east. But a Triple Alliance of the Dutch, English, and Swedes forced Louis to sue for peace in 1668 and accept a few towns in the Spanish Netherlands for his efforts. He never forgave the Dutch for arranging the Triple Alliance, and in 1672, after isolating the Dutch, France invaded the United Provinces with some initial

success. But the French victories led Brandenburg, Spain, and the Holy Roman Emperor to form a new coalition that forced Louis to end the Dutch War by making peace at Nimwegen in 1678. While Dutch territory remained intact, France received Franche-Comté from Spain, which served merely to stimulate Louis's appetite for even more land.

This time, Louis moved eastward against the Holy Roman Empire, which he perceived from his previous war as feeble and unable to resist. The gradual annexation of the provinces of Alsace and Lorraine was followed by the occupation of the city of Strasbourg, a move that led to widespread protest and the formation of a new coalition. The creation of this League of Augsburg, consisting of Spain, the Holy Roman Emperor, the United Provinces, Sweden, and England led to Louis's third war, the War of the League of Augsburg (1689–1697). This bitterly contested eight-year struggle brought economic depression and famine to France. The Treaty of Ryswick ending the war forced Louis to give up most of his conquests in the empire, although he was allowed to keep Strasbourg and part of Alsace. The gains were hardly worth the bloodshed and misery he had caused the French people.

Louis's fourth war, the War of the Spanish Succession (1702–1713), was over bigger stakes, the succession to the Spanish throne. Charles II, the sickly and childless Habsburg ruler, left the throne of Spain in his will to a grandson of Louis XIV. When the latter became King Philip V of Spain after Charles's death, the suspicion that Spain and France would eventually be united in the same dynastic family caused the formation of a new coalition, determined to prevent a Bourbon hegemony that would mean the certain destruction of the European balance of power. This coalition of England, Holland, Habsburg Austria, and German states opposed France and Spain in a war that dragged on in Europe and the colonial empires in North America from 1702 to 1713. In a number of battles, including the memorable defeat of the French forces at Blenheim in 1704 by allied troops led by the English commander, John Churchill, duke of Marlborough, the coalition wore down Louis's forces. An end to the war finally came with the Peaces of Utrecht in 1713 and Rastatt in 1714. Although these peace treaties confirmed Philip V as the Spanish ruler, initiating a Spanish Bourbon dynasty that would last into the twentieth century, they also affirmed that the thrones of Spain and France were to remain separated. The Spanish Netherlands, Milan, and Naples were given to Austria while the newly emerging Brandenburg-Prussia gained additional territories. The real winner at Utrecht, however, was England, which received Gibraltar as well as the French possessions in America of Newfoundland, Hudson's Bay Territory, and Nova Scotia. While France, by its sheer size and position, remained a great power, England had emerged as a formidable naval power.

Map 16.1 The Wars of Louis XIV.

Only two years after the treaty, the Sun King was dead, leaving France impoverished and surrounded by enemies. On his deathbed, the seventy-six-year-old monarch seemed remorseful when he told his successor:

> Soon you will be King of a great kingdom. I urge you not to forget your duty to God; remember that you owe everything to Him. Try to remain at peace with your neighbors. I loved war too much. Do not follow me in that or in overspending. Take advice in everything; try to find the best course and follow it. Lighten your people's burden as soon as possible, and do what I have had the misfortune not to do myself.[5]

Did Louis mean it? Did Louis ever realize how tarnished the glory he had sought had become? One of his subjects wrote ten years before the end of his reign: "Even the people ... who have so much loved you, and have placed such trust in you, begin to lose their love, their trust, and even their respect. ... They believe you have no pity for their sorrows, that you are devoted only to your power and your glory."[6] In any event, the advice to his successor was probably not remembered; his great-grandson was only five years old.

The Decline of Spain

At the beginning of the seventeenth century, Spain possessed the most populous empire in the world, controlling almost all of South America and a number of settlements in Asia and Africa. To most Europeans, Spain still seemed the greatest power of the age, but the reality was quite different. The rich provinces of the Netherlands were lost. The treasury was empty; Philip II went bankrupt in 1596 from excessive expenditures on the Armada while his successor Philip III did the same in 1607 by spending a fortune on his court. The armed forces were out-of-date; the government inefficient; and the commercial class weak in the midst of a suppressed peasantry, a luxury-loving class of nobles, and an over-supply of priests and monks. Spain continued to play the role of a great power, but appearances were deceiving.

During the reign of Philip III (1598–1621), many of Spain's weaknesses became only too apparent. Interested only in court luxury or miracle-working relics, Philip III allowed his first minister, the greedy duke of Lerma, to run the country. The aristocratic Lerma's primary interest was accumulating power and wealth for himself and his family. While important offices were filled with his relatives, crucial problems went unsolved. His most drastic decision was to expel all remaining Moriscos (see

Chapter 13) from Spain, a spectacular blunder in view of their importance to Spain's economy. The loss of labor and rents in the province of Valencia, for example, brought immediate economic disaster there. During Lerma's misrule, the gap between privileged and unprivileged grew wider. Notably absent was a prosperous urban middle class, as an astute public official observed in 1600. Spain, he said, had come "to be an extreme contrast of rich and poor, ... we have rich who loll at ease, or poor who beg, and we lack people of the middling sort, whom neither wealth nor poverty prevents from pursuing the rightful kind of business enjoined by natural law."[7] An apparent factor in this imbalance was the dominant role played by the Catholic church. While maintaining strict orthodoxy by efficient inquisitorial courts, the church prospered and attracted ever-larger numbers of clerics to its ranks. The Castilian Cortes (parliament) was informed in 1626 that Castile alone possessed 9,000 monasteries for men. The existence of so many official celibates offered little help to Spain's declining economy or its declining population.

At first, the reign of Philip IV (1621–1665) seemed to offer hope for a revival of Spain's energies, especially in the capable hands of his chief minister, Gaspar de Guzman, the count of Olivares. This clever, hard-working, and power-hungry statesman dominated the king's every move and worked to revive the interests of the monarchy. A flurry of domestic reform decrees, aimed at curtailing the power of the church and the landed aristocracy, was soon followed by a political reform program whose purpose was to further centralize the government of all Spain and its possessions in monarchical hands. All of these efforts met with little real success, however, since both the number (estimated at one-fifth of the population) and power of the Spanish aristocrats made them too strong to curtail in any significant fashion. At the same time, most of the efforts of Olivares and Philip were undermined by their desire to pursue Spain's imperial glory and by a series of internal revolts.

During the 1620s, 1630s, and 1640s, Spain's involvement in the Thirty Years' War led to a series of frightfully expensive military campaigns that intensified the economic misery of the overtaxed Spanish subjects. Unfortunately for Spain, the campaigns also failed to produce victory. As Olivares wrote to King Philip IV, "God wants us to make peace; for He is depriving us visibly and absolutely of all the means of war."[8] At the same time, increasingly heavy financial exactions to fight the wars led to internal revolts, first in Catalonia, the northeastern province, in 1640, then in the same

Absolutism in Western Europe

France	
Henry IV	1589–1610
Louis XIII	1610–1643
Cardinal Richelieu as chief minister	1624–1642
Peace of Alais	1629
Ministry of Cardinal Mazarin	1642–1661
First Fronde	1648–1649
Second Fronde	1650–1652
Louis XIV	1643–1715
First war (vs. Triple Alliance)	1667–1668
Dutch War	1672–1678
Edict of Fontainebleau	1685
War of the League of Augsburg	1689–1697
War of the Spanish Succession	1702–1713
Spain	
Philip III	1598–1621
Philip IV	1621–1665
Revolts in Catalonia and Portugal	1640
Revolt in Naples	1647
Charles II	1665–1700

year in Portugal, which had been joined to Spain in 1580 by Philip II, and finally in the Italian dependency of Naples in 1647. Despite years of civil war, the Spanish government regained control of all these territories except for Portugal, which successfully reestablished the monarchy of the old ruling house of Braganza when Duke John was made King John IV in 1640.

The defeats in Europe and the internal revolts of the 1640s ended any illusions about Spain's greatness. The actual extent of Spain's economic difficulties is still a much debated historical topic, but there is no question about Spain's foreign losses. Dutch independence was formally recognized by the Peace of Westphalia in 1648, and the Peace of the Pyrenees with France in 1659 meant the surrender of Artois and the outlying defenses of the Spanish Netherlands as well as certain border regions, such as the Catalan province of Roussillon, which went to France. It did not augur well for the

future of Spain that the king who followed Philip IV, Charles II (1665–1700), perhaps unfairly characterized by historians as a "moribund half-wit," was only of interest to the rest of Europe because he had no heirs. The French and Austrians anxiously awaited his death in the hope of placing a member of their royal houses on the Spanish throne. When he died in 1700, the War of the Spanish Succession soon followed.

Absolutism in Central, Eastern, and Northern Europe

During the seventeenth century, a development of great importance for the modern Western world took place in central and eastern Europe, the appearance of three new powers: Prussia, Austria, and Russia.

The German States

The Peace of Westphalia, which officially ended the Thirty Years' War in 1648, left each of the three hundred or more German states comprising the Holy Roman Empire virtually autonomous and sovereign. After 1648, the Holy Roman Empire was largely a diplomatic fiction; as the French intellectual Voltaire said in the eighteenth century, the Holy Roman Empire was neither holy, nor Roman, nor an empire. Properly speaking, there was no German state, but over three hundred "Germanies." Of these states, two emerged as great European powers in the seventeenth and eighteenth centuries.

THE RISE OF BRANDENBURG-PRUSSIA

For much of the seventeenth century, little about the German state of Brandenburg would have led one to think it would ever be a prosperous and powerful state. Indeed, the German states of Bavaria and Saxony would have seemed better candidates for a brilliant future. The development of Brandenburg as a state was largely the story of the Hohenzollern dynasty, which in 1415 had come to rule the rather insignificant principality in northeastern Germany. In 1609, the Hohenzollerns inherited some lands in the Rhine valley in western Germany; nine years later, they received the duchy of Prussia (or east Prussia). By the seventeenth century, then, the dominions of the house of Hohenzollern, now called Brandenburg-Prussia, consisted of three disconnected masses in western, central, and eastern Germany. Although it would appear that Hohenzollern long-range policy would seek to connect the three lands, the Hohenzollerns' more immediate concern was to establish their power in these diverse territories. Each had its own privileges, customs, and loyalties; only the person of the Hohenzollern ruler connected them. Unlike France, an old kingdom possessing a reasonably common culture based on almost a thousand years of history, Brandenburg-Prussia was an artificial creation, highly vulnerable and dependent upon its ruling dynasty to create a state where one simply did not exist.

The first important Hohenzollern ruler and the one who laid the foundation for the Prussian state was Frederick William the Great Elector (1640–1688), who came to power in the midst of the Thirty Years' War. Realizing that Brandenburg-Prussia was a small, open territory with no natural frontiers for defense, Frederick William built a competent and efficient standing army. By 1678, he possessed a force of 40,000 men that absorbed more than 50 percent of the state's revenues.

To sustain the army and his own power, Frederick William needed a regular source of income. The Estates of old Brandenburg and the new territories jealously guarded their prerogatives, however, especially their right to raise taxes. The Great Elector broke the power of the Estates and freed himself to raise money by establishing the General War Commissariat to levy taxes for the army and oversee its growth and training. The Commissariat soon evolved into an agency for civil government as well, collecting the new excise tax in the towns and overseeing the foundation of new industrial and commercial enterprises. Directly responsible to the elector, the new bureaucratic machine became his chief instrument for governing the state. Many of its officials were members of the Prussian landed aristocracy, the Junkers, who also served as officers in the all-important army.

The nobles' support for Frederick William's policies derived from the tacit agreement that he made with them. In order to eliminate the power that the members of the nobility could exercise in their provincial Estates-General, Frederick William made a deal with the nobles. In return for a free hand in running the government (in other words, for depriving the provincial Estates of their power), he gave the nobles almost unlimited power over their peasants, exempted them from taxation, and awarded them the highest ranks in the army and the Commissariat with the understanding that they would not challenge his political control. As for the peasants, the nobles were allowed to appropriate their land and bind them to the soil as serfs.

To build Brandenburg-Prussia's economy, Frederick William followed the fashionable mercantilist policies, using high tariffs, subsidies, and monopolies for manufacturers to stimulate domestic industry and the construction of roads and canals. Wisely, Frederick William invited people from other countries to settle in Brandenburg-Prussia and, in 1685, issued an edict encouraging the dispossessed Huguenots from Louis XIV's France to come to Prussia. Almost 20,000 did. At the same time, however, Frederick William continued to

✖ **Map 16.2** The Growth of Brandenburg-Prussia.

Brandenburg (1415)

Prussian acquisitions to 1740

Conquest of Silesia by 1748

From Poland as result of first partition (1792)

favor the interests of the nobility at the expense of the commercial and industrial middle classes in the towns.

In these ways, Frederick William the Great Elector laid the foundations for the Prussian state, although it would be misleading to think that he had a modern conception of that state. He thought nothing of amending his will to give pieces of his supposedly unified state as independent principalities to his younger sons. He was succeeded by his son Frederick III (1688–1713), who, less rigid and militaristic than his father, spent much of the treasury building palaces, establishing a university, and imitating the splendors of the court of Louis XIV. He did make one significant contribution to the development of Prussia. In return for aiding the Holy Roman Emperor in the War of the Spanish Succession, he received officially the title of king in Prussia. Elector Frederick III was transformed into King Frederick I, and Brandenburg-Prussia became simply Prussia. In the eighteenth century, Prussia emerged as a great power on the European stage.

THE EMERGENCE OF AUSTRIA

The Austrian Habsburgs had long played a significant role in European politics. They were Holy Roman Emperors and had important family connections with the wealthier Habsburgs of Spain. In the seventeenth century, these two bastions of their power collapsed. By the end of the Thirty Years' War, the Habsburg hopes of creating an empire in Germany had been dashed. At the same time, Spain's decline made that relationship less rewarding, and it ended completely at the beginning of the eighteenth century when Spain came into the hands of the French house of Bourbon. In the seventeenth century, then, the house of Austria made an important transition; the German empire was lost, but a new empire was created in eastern and southeastern Europe.

The nucleus of the new Austrian Empire remained the traditional Austrian hereditary possessions: Lower and Upper Austria, Carinthia, Carniola, Styria, and Tyrol. To these had been added the kingdom of Bohemia, which had been reclaimed by the Habsburgs during the Thirty Years' War. Since 1526, the Habsburg ruler had also been king of Hungary, although he exercised little real power except in northwestern Hungary. The eastern Hungarian principality of Transylvania remained independent while the central parts of Hungary were controlled by the Ottoman Turks.

Leopold I (1658–1705) encouraged the eastward movement of the Austrian Empire, but he was sorely

Map 16.3 The Growth of the Austrian Empire.

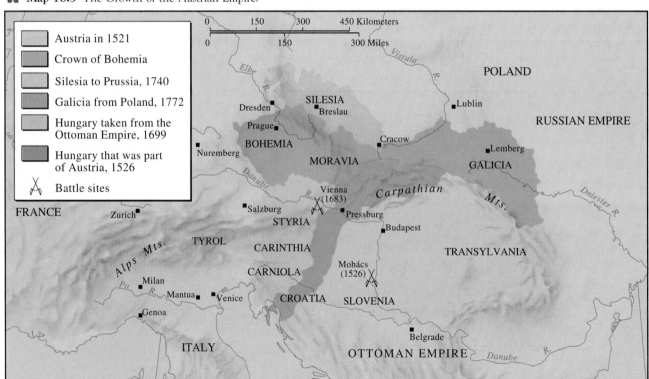

challenged by the revival of Turkish power in the seventeenth century. Having moved into Transylvania, the Turks eventually pushed westward and laid siege to Vienna in 1683. Only a dramatic rescue by a combined army of Austrians, Saxons, Bavarians, and Poles saved the Austrian city. A European army, led by the Austrians, counterattacked and decisively defeated the Turks in 1687. By the Treaty of Karlowitz in 1699, Austria took control of Hungary, Transylvania, Croatia, and Slovenia, thus establishing an Austrian Empire in southeastern Europe. At the end of the War of the Spanish Succession, Austria gained possession of the Spanish Netherlands and received formal recognition of its occupation of the Spanish possessions in Italy, namely, Milan, Mantua, Sardinia, and Naples. By the beginning of the eighteenth century, the house of Austria had acquired a new empire of considerable size.

The Austrian monarchy, however, never became a highly centralized, absolutist state, primarily because it contained so many different national groups. The Austrian Empire remained a collection of territories held together by a personal union. The Hapburg emperor was archduke of Austria, king of Bohemia, and king of Hungary. Each of these areas had its own laws, Estates-General, and political life. The landed aristocrats throughout the empire were connected by a common bond of service to the house of Habsburg, whether as military officers or government bureaucrats, but no other common sentiment tied the regions together. The nobles in the Austrian Empire remained quite strong and were also allowed to impose serfdom on their peasants. By the beginning of the eighteenth century, Austria was a populous empire in central Europe of great potential military strength.

Italy: From Spanish to Austrian Rule

By 1530, Emperor Charles V had managed to defeat the French armies in Italy and become the arbiter of Italy (see Chapter 14). Initially, he was content to establish close ties with many native Italian rulers and allow them to rule, provided that they recognize his dominant role. But in 1540, he gave the duchy of Milan to his son Philip II and transferred all imperial rights over Italy to the Spanish monarchy.

From the beginning of Philip II's reign in 1559 to 1713, the Spanish presence was felt everywhere in Italy. Only the major states of Florence, the Papal States, and Venice managed to maintain relatively independent policies. At the same time, the influence of the papacy became oppressive in Italy as the machinery of the

Catholic Counter-Reformation—the Inquisition, Index, and the Jesuits—was used to stifle any resistance to the Catholic orthodoxy created by the Council of Trent (see Chapter 14). While artistic and intellectual activity continued in post-Renaissance Italy, it often exacted a grievous cost. Some intellectuals, such as Galilei Galileo and Giordano Bruno (see Chapter 17), found themselves imprisoned or executed by the Inquisition.

At the beginning of the eighteenth century, Italy suffered further from the struggles between France and Spain. But it was Austria, not France, that benefited the most from the War of the Spanish Succession. By gaining Milan, Mantua, Sardinia, and Naples, Austria supplanted Spain as the dominant power in Italy. It was a mixed blessing. Austrian rule would eventually galvanize Italians into a desire for freedom from all foreign domination.

From Muscovy to Russia

Since its origins in the Middle Ages, Russia had existed only on the fringes of European society, remote and isolated from the Western mainstream. But in the seventeenth century, the energetic Peter the Great pushed Russia westward and raised it to the status of a great power.

A new Russian state had emerged in the fifteenth century under the leadership of the principality of Muscovy and its grand dukes (see Chapter 13). In the sixteenth century, Ivan IV the Terrible (1533–1584), who was the first ruler to take the title of tsar, expanded the territories of Russia eastward, after finding westward expansion blocked by the powerful Swedish and Polish states. Ivan also extended the autocracy of the tsar by crushing the power of the Russian nobility, known as the boyars.

Ivan's dynasty came to an end in 1598 and was followed by a resurgence of aristocratic power in a period of anarchy known as the Time of Troubles. It did not end until the Zemsky Sobor, or national assembly, chose Michael Romanov (1613–1645) as the new tsar, beginning a dynasty that lasted until 1917.

In the seventeenth century, Muscovite society was highly stratified. At the top was the tsar, who claimed to be a divinely ordained autocratic ruler, assisted by two consultative bodies, a Duma, or council of boyars, and the Zemsky Sobor, a landed assembly begun in 1550 by Ivan IV to facilitate support for his programs. Russian society was dominated by an upper class of landed aristocrats who, in the course of the seventeenth century, managed to bind their peasants to the land. An abundance of land and a shortage of peasants made serfdom desirable to the landowners, who killed another's serf simply had to replace him. Townspeople were also stratified and controlled. Artisans were sharply separated from merchants, and many of the latter were not allowed to move from their cities without government permission or to sell their businesses to anyone outside their class. In the seventeenth century, merchant and peasant revolts as well as a schism in the Russian Orthodox church created very unsettled conditions. In the midst of these political and religious upheavals, seventeenth-century Muscovy was experiencing more frequent contacts with the West while Western ideas also began to penetrate a few Russian circles. When Peter the Great came on the scene, Muscovy was already undergoing changes. While neither his aims nor his solutions were new, Peter did

◆ **Peter the Great.** Peter the Great wished to westernize Russia, especially in the realm of technical skills. His foremost goal was the creation of a strong army and navy in order to make Russia a great power. A Dutch painter created this portrait of the armored tsar during his visit to the West in 1697.

accelerate the process with a ruthlessness that accomplished much, but at a great price.

THE REIGN OF PETER THE GREAT (1689–1725)

Peter was only four years old when his father died so his sister Sophia acted as regent for him and his feeble-minded brother as joint tsars. At the age of seventeen (in 1689), Peter seized power from his sister. Peter the Great was an unusual character. A strong man, towering six feet, nine inches tall, Peter was coarse in his tastes and rude in his behavior. He enjoyed a low kind of humor—belching contests, crude jokes, comical funerals—and vicious punishments—floggings, impalings, roastings, and beard burnings (see the box on p. 545). At the same time, he was capable of tender feelings, especially toward his family.

Peter gained his initial knowledge of Western ideas in the "German suburb," a section of Moscow where Europeans of different nationalities resided. He received a firsthand view of the West when he made a trip there in 1697–1698 and returned to Russia with a firm determination to westernize or Europeanize Russia. Perhaps too much has been made of Peter's desire to westernize a "backward country." Peter's policy of Europeanization was largely technical. He admired European technology and gadgets and desired to transplant these to Russia. Only this kind of modernization could give him the army and navy he needed to make Russia a great power. His only consistent purpose was to win military victories.

As could be expected, one of his first priorities was the reorganization of the army and the creation of a navy. Employing both Russians and Europeans as officers, he conscripted peasants for twenty-five-year stints of service to build a standing army of 210,000 men. Peter has also been given credit for forming the first Russian navy.

Peter reorganized the central government, partly along Western lines. What remained of the consultative bodies disappeared; neither the Duma of boyars nor the Zemsky Sobor was ever summoned. In 1711, Peter created a Senate to supervise the administrative machinery of the state while he was away on military campaigns. In time the Senate became something like a ruling council, but its ineffectiveness caused Peter to borrow the Western institution of "colleges," or boards of administrators entrusted with specific functions, such as foreign affairs, war, and justice. To impose the rule of the central government more effectively throughout the land, Peter divided Russia into eight provinces and later,

≫ *Peter the Great Deals with a Rebellion* ≪

During his first visit to the West in 1697–1698, Peter received word that the streltsy, an elite military unit stationed in Moscow, had revolted against his authority. Peter hurried home and crushed the revolt in a very savage fashion. This selection is taken from an Austrian account of how Peter dealt with the rebels.

Peter and the Streltsy

How sharp was the pain, how great the indignation, to which the tsar's Majesty was mightily moved, when he knew of the rebellion of the Streltsy, betraying openly a mind panting for vengeance! He was still tarrying at Vienna, quite full of the desire of setting out for Italy; but, fervid as was his curiosity of rambling abroad, it was, nevertheless, speedily extinguished on the announcement of the troubles that had broken out in the bowels of his realm. Going immediately to Lefort. . ., he thus indignantly broke out: "Tell me, Francis, how I can reach Moscow by the shortest way, in a brief space, so that I may wreak vengeance on this great perfidy of my people, with punishments worthy of their abominable crime. Not one of them shall escape with impunity. Around my royal city, which, with their impious efforts, they planned to destroy, I will have gibbets and gallows set upon the walls and ramparts, and each and every one of them will I put to a direful death." Nor did he long delay the plan for his justly excited wrath; he took the quick post, as his ambassador suggested, and in four weeks' time he had got over about three hundred miles without accident, and arrived the 4th of September, 1698,—a monarch for the well deposed, but an avenger for the wicked.

His first anxiety after his arrival was about the rebellion—in what it consisted, what the insurgents meant, who dared to instigate such a crime. And as nobody could answer accurately upon all points, and some pleaded their own ignorance, others the obstinacy of the Streltsy, he began to have suspicions of everybody's loyalty. . . . No day, holy or profane, were the inquisitors idle; every day was deemed fit and lawful for torturing. There was as many scourges as there were accused, and every inquisitor was a butcher. . . . The whole month of October was spent in lacerating the backs of culprits with the knout and with flames; no day were those that were left alive exempt from scourging or scorching; or else they were broken upon the wheel, or driven to the gibbet, or slain with the ax. . . .

To prove to all people how holy and inviolable are those walls of the city which the Streltsy rashly meditated scaling in a sudden assault, beams were run out from all the embrasures in the walls near the gates, in each of which two rebels were hanged. This day beheld about two hundred and fifty die that death. There are few cities fortified with as many palisades as Moscow has given gibbets to her guardian Streltsy.

---

in 1719, into fifty. Although he hoped to create a "police state," by which he meant a well-ordered community governed in accordance with law, few of his bureaucrats shared his concept of honest service and duty to the state. One of his highest officials even stated: "Would your Majesty like to be a ruler without any subjects? We all steal, only some do it on a bigger scale, and in a more conspicuous way, than others."[9] Peter hoped for a sense of civic duty, but his own forceful personality created an atmosphere of fear that prevented it. He wrote to one administrator, "According to these orders act, act, act. I won't write more, but you will pay with your head if you interpret orders again." But when others were understandably cautious in interpreting his written instructions, he stated: "This is as if a servant, seeing his master drowning, would not save him until he had satisfied himself as to whether it was written down in his contract that he should pull him out of the water."[10] Peter wanted his administrators to be slaves and free men at the same time, and it did not occur to him that the task was impossible.

To further his administrative aims, Peter demanded that all members of the landholding class serve in either military or civil offices. Moreover, in 1722, Peter instituted a Table of Ranks to create opportunities for nonnobles to serve the state and join the ranks of the nobility. All civil offices were ranked according to fourteen levels; a parallel list of fourteen grades was also created for all military offices. Every official was then required to begin at level one and work his way up the ranks. When a nonnoble reached the eighth rank, he acquired the status of nobility. This attempt by Peter to create a new nobility based on merit was not carried on by his successors.

� **Map 16.4** From Muscovy to Russia.

To satisfy his insatiable need of money for an army and navy that absorbed as much as four-fifths of the state revenue, Peter adopted Western mercantilistic policies to stimulate economic growth. He tried to increase exports and develop new industries while exploiting domestic resources like the iron mines in the Urals. But his military needs were endless, and he came to rely on the old expedient of simply raising taxes, imposing additional burdens upon the hapless peasants who were becoming ever more oppressed in Peter's Russia.

Peter also sought to gain state control of the Russian Orthodox church. In 1721, he abolished the position of patriarch and created a body called the Holy Synod to make decisions for the church. At its head stood a procurator, a layman who represented the interests of the tsar and assured Peter of effective domination of the church.

Already after his first trip to the West in 1697–1698, Peter began to introduce Western customs, practices, and manners into Russia. He ordered the preparation of the first Russian book of etiquette to teach Western manners. Among other things, it pointed out that it was not polite to spit on the floor or scratch oneself at dinner. Since westerners did not wear beards or the traditional long-skirted coat, Russian beards had to be shaved and coats shortened, a reform Peter personally enforced at court by shaving off his nobles' beards and cutting their coats at the knees with his own hands. Outside the court, the edicts were enforced by barbers and tailors planted at town gates with orders to cut the beards and cloaks of those who entered or left. Anyone who failed to conform was to be "beaten without mercy." For the nobles, who were already partly westernized, these changes were hardly earth-shattering. But to many others who believed that shaving the beard was a "defacement of the image of God," the attack was actually blasphemous.

One group of Russians benefited greatly from Peter's cultural reforms—women. Having watched women mixing freely with men in Western courts, Peter shattered the seclusion of upper-class Russian women and demanded that they remove the traditional veils that covered their faces. Peter also decreed that social gatherings be held three times a week in the large houses of St. Petersburg where men and women could mix for conversation, card games, and dancing, which Peter had learned in the West. The tsar also now insisted that women could marry of their own free will.

The object of Peter's domestic reforms was to make Russia into a great state and military power; an examination of his foreign policy reveals how well he succeeded. His primary goal was to "open a window to the west," meaning an ice-free port easily accessible to Europe. This could only be achieved on the Baltic, but at that time the Baltic coast was controlled by Sweden, the most important power in northern Europe. Desirous of these lands, Peter, with the support of Poland and Denmark, attacked Sweden in the summer of 1700, believing that the young king of Sweden, Charles XII, could easily be defeated. Charles, however, proved to be a brilliant general. He smashed the Danes, flattened the Poles, and, with a well-disciplined force of only 8,000 men, routed the Russian army of 40,000 at the Battle of Narva (1700). The Great Northern War (1701–1721) had begun.

While Charles wasted valuable time in an inconclusive war in Poland, Peter took the opportunity to reorganize his army along Western lines. In 1702, he overran the Swedish Baltic provinces while Charles was preoccupied elsewhere. When the Swedish king turned his attention to Peter again in 1708, he decided to invade Russia and capture Moscow, the capital, but Russian weather and scorched-earth tactics devastated his army. In July 1709, at the Battle of Poltava, Peter's forces defeated Charles's army decisively. Although the war dragged on for another twelve years, the Peace of Nystadt in 1721 gave formal recognition to what Peter had already achieved: the acquisition of Estonia, Livonia, and Karelia. Sweden became a second-rate power while Russia was now the great European state Peter had wanted.

Already in 1703, in these northern lands on the Baltic, Peter had begun to construct a new city, St. Petersburg, his window on the west and a symbol that Russia was looking westward to Europe. Built on marshland, its construction cost the lives of thousands of peasants. Finished during Peter's lifetime, St. Petersburg remained the Russian capital until 1917.

It is difficult to assess the work of Peter the Great. He modernized and westernized Russia to the extent that it became a great military power and, by his death in 1725, an important member of the European state system. But his policies were also detrimental to Russia. Westernization was a bit of a sham, since Western culture reached only the upper classes while the real object of the reforms, the creation of a strong military, only added more burdens to the masses of the Russian people. The forceful way in which Peter the Great imposed westernization led to a distrust of Europe and Western civilization. Russia was so strained by Peter the Great that after his death an aristocratic reaction undid much of his work.

The Growth of Monarchy in Scandinavia

As the economic link between the products of eastern Europe and the West, the Baltic Sea bestowed special importance on the lands surrounding it. In the sixteenth century, Sweden had broken its ties with Denmark and emerged as an independent state (see Chapter 14). Despite their common Lutheran religion, Denmark's and Sweden's territorial ambitions in northern Europe kept them in rather constant rivalry in the seventeenth century.

Under Christian IV (1588–1648), Denmark seemed the likely candidate for expansion, but it met with little success. The system of electing monarchs forced the kings to share their power with the Danish nobility who exercised strict control over the peasants who worked their lands. Danish ambitions for ruling the Baltic were severely curtailed by the losses they sustained in the Thirty Years' War and later in the so-called Northern War (1655–1660) with Sweden. Danish military losses led to a constitutional crisis in which a meeting of Denmark's Estates brought to pass a bloodless revolution in 1660. The power of the nobility was curtailed, a hereditary monarchy reestablished, and a new, absolutist constitution proclaimed in 1665. Under Christian V (1670–1699), a centralized administration was instituted with the nobility as the chief officeholders.

Compared to Denmark, Sweden seemed a relatively poor country, and historians have had difficulty explaining why it played such a large role in European affairs in the seventeenth century. Sweden's economy was weak while the monarchy was still locked in conflict with the powerful Swedish nobility. During the reign of Gustavus Adolphus (1611–1632), his wise and dedicated chief minister, Axel Oxenstierna, persuaded the king to adopt a new policy in which the nobility formed a "first estate" occupying the bureaucratic positions of an expanded central government. This created a stable monarchy and freed the king to raise a formidable army and participate in the Thirty Years' War, only to be killed in battle in 1632.

Sweden experienced a severe political crisis after the death of Gustavus Adolphus. His daughter Christina (1633–1654) proved to be far more interested in philosophy and religion than ruling. Her tendency to favor the interests of the nobility led the other estates of the Riksdag, Sweden's parliament—the burghers, clergy, and

Absolutism in Central, Eastern, and Northern Europe

Brandenburg-Prussia	
Hohenzollerns established in Brandenburg	1415
Hohenzollerns acquire lands along the Rhine	1609
Hohenzollerns acquire east Prussia	1618
Frederick William the Great Elector	1640–1688
Elector Frederick III (King Frederick I)	1688–1713
The Austrian Empire	
Leopold I	1658–1705
Turkish siege of Vienna	1683
Treaty of Karlowitz	1699
Russia	
Ivan IV the Terrible	1533–1584
Time of Troubles	1598–1613
Michael Romanov	1613–1645
Peter the Great	1689–1725
First trip to the West	1697–1698
Great Northern War	1701–1721
Battle of Poltava	1709
Construction of St. Petersburg begins	1703
Holy Synod	1721
Denmark	
Christian IV	1588–1648
"Bloodless Revolution"	1660
Christian V	1670–1699
Sweden	
Gustavus Adolphus	1611–1632
Christina	1633–1654
Charles X	1654–1660
Charles XI	1660–1697
Charles XII	1697–1718
The Ottoman Empire	
Suleiman I the Magnificent	1520–1566
Battle of Lepanto	1571
Turkish defeat at Vienna	1683

peasants—to protest. In 1654, tired of ruling and wishing to become a Catholic, which was forbidden in Sweden, Christina abdicated in favor of her cousin, who became King Charles X (1654–1660). His accession to the throne defused a potentially explosive peasant revolt against the nobility.

Charles X reestablished domestic order, but it was his successor, Charles XI (1660–1697), who did the painstaking work of building the Swedish monarchy along the lines of an absolute monarchy. By resuming control of the crown lands and the revenues attached to them from the nobility, Charles managed to weaken the independent power of the nobility. He built up a bureaucracy, subdued both the Riksdag and the church, improved the army and navy, and left to his son, Charles XII (1697–1718), a well-organized Swedish state that dominated northern Europe. In 1693, he and his heirs were acclaimed as "absolute, sovereign kings, responsible for their actions to no man on earth."

Charles XII was primarily interested in military affairs. Energetic and regarded as a brilliant general, his grandiose plans and strategies, which involved Sweden in conflicts with Poland, Denmark, and Russia, proved to be Sweden's undoing. By the time he died in 1718, Charles XII had lost much of Sweden's northern empire to Russia, and Sweden's status as a first-class northern power had proved to be short-lived.

The Ottoman Empire

After their conquest of Constantinople in 1453, the Ottoman Turks tried to complete their conquest of the Balkans, where they had been established since the fourteenth century. Although they were successful in taking the Romanian territory of Wallachia in 1476, the resistance of the Hungarians kept them from advancing up the Danube valley. From 1480 to 1520, internal problems and the need to consolidate their eastern frontiers kept the Turks from any further attacks on Europe.

The reign of Sultan Suleiman I the Magnificent (1520–1566), however, brought the Turks back to Europe's attention. Advancing up the Danube, the Turks seized Belgrade in 1521 and Hungary by 1526, although their attempts to conquer Vienna in 1529 were repulsed. At the same time, Turkish power was extended into the western Mediterranean, which they threatened to turn into a Turkish lake until a large Turkish fleet was destroyed by the Spanish at Lepanto in 1571. Despite the defeat, the Turks continued to hold nominal suzerainty over the southern shores of the Mediterranean.

Although Europeans frequently spoke of new Christian crusades against the infidel Turks, by the beginning of the seventeenth century the Ottoman Empire was being treated like another European power by European rulers seeking alliances and trade concessions. The Ottoman Empire possessed a highly effective governmental system, especially when it was led by strong sultans or powerful grand viziers (prime ministers). The splendid capital Constantinople possessed a population far larger than any European city. Nevertheless, Ottoman politics periodically degenerated into bloody intrigues as factions fought each other for influence and the throne. In one particularly gruesome practice, a ruling sultan would murder his brothers to avoid challenges to his rule. Despite the periodic bouts of civil

chaos, a well-trained bureaucracy of civil servants continued to administer state affairs efficiently.

A well-organized military system also added to the strength of the Ottoman Empire. Especially outstanding were the Janissaries, composed of Christian boys who had been taken from their parents, converted to the Muslim faith, and subjected to rigid military discipline to form an elite core of 8,000 troops personally loyal to the sultan. Like other praetorian guards, however, the Janissaries came to play an important role in making and unmaking sultans.

In the first half of the seventeenth century, the Ottoman Empire was a "sleeping giant." Occupied by domestic bloodletting and severely threatened by a challenge from Persia, the Ottomans were content with

⚔ Map 16.5 The Ottoman Empire.

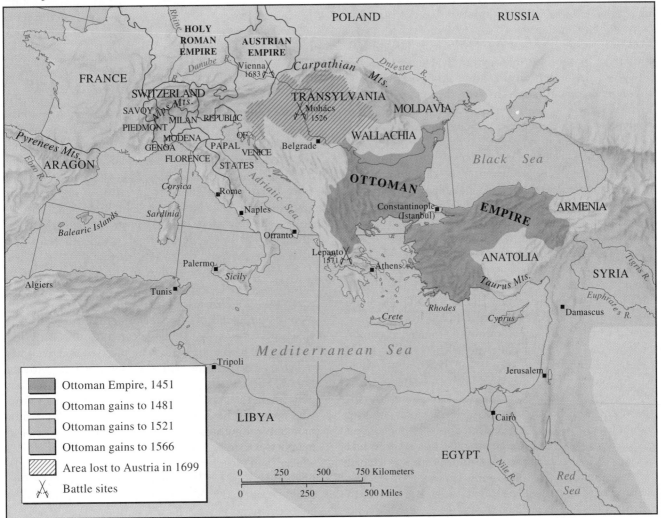

the status quo in eastern Europe. But under a new line of grand viziers in the second half of the seventeenth century, the Ottoman Empire again took the offensive. By mid-1683, the Ottomans had marched through the Hungarian plain and laid siege to Vienna. Repulsed by a mixed army of Austrians, Poles, Bavarians, and Saxons, the Turks retreated and were pushed out of Hungary by a new European coalition. Although they retained the core of their empire, the Ottoman Turks would never again be a threat to Europe. Although the Ottoman Empire held together for the rest of the seventeenth and eighteenth centuries, it would be faced with new challenges from the ever-growing Austrian Empire in southeastern Europe and the new Russian giant to the north.

The Limits of Absolutism

In recent decades, historical studies of local institutions have challenged the traditional picture of absolute monarchs. Control of the administrative machinery of state did not enable rulers to dominate the everyday lives of their subjects, as was once thought. The centralization of power was an important element in the growth of the seventeenth-century state, however, and the most successful monarchs were those who managed to restructure the central policy-making machinery of government to give them a certain amount of control over the traditional areas of monarchical power: formulation of foreign policy, making of war and peace, the church, and taxation. Seventeenth-century governments also intervened in economic affairs to strengthen their war-making capacities. In all of these areas, absolute monarchy meant rulers extending their power or at least resisting challenges to their authority.

It is misleading, however, to think that so-called absolute monarchs actually controlled the lives of their subjects. In 1700, government for most people still meant the local institutions that affected their lives: local courts, local tax collectors, and local organizers of armed forces. Kings and ministers might determine policies and issue guidelines, but they still had to function through local agents and had no guarantee whatever that their wishes would be carried out. A mass of urban and provincial privileges, liberties, and exemptions (including from taxation) and a whole host of corporate bodies and interest groups—provincial and national Estates, clerical officials, officeholders who had bought or inherited their positions, and provincial nobles—limited what monarchs could achieve. The most successful rulers were not those who tried to destroy the old system, but those like Louis XIV who

knew how to use the old system to their advantage. Above all other considerations stood the landholding nobility. Everywhere in the seventeenth century, the landed aristocracy played an important role in the European monarchical system. As military officers, judges, officeholders, and landowners in control of vast, untaxed estates, their power remained immense. In some places, their strength even put severe limits on how effectively monarchs could rule.

Limited Monarchy and Republics

Almost everywhere in Europe in the seventeenth century, kings and their ministers were in control of central governments. But not all European states followed the pattern of absolute monarchy. In eastern Europe, the Polish aristocracy controlled a virtually powerless king. In western Europe, two great states—the Dutch Republic and England—successfully resisted the power of hereditary monarchs.

The Weakness of the Polish Monarchy

Poland had played a major role in eastern Europe in the fifteenth century and had ruled over Lithuania and much of the Ukraine by the end of the sixteenth. After the elective throne of Poland had been won by the Swede Sigismund III (1587–1631), Poland had a king who even thought seriously of creating a vast Polish empire that would include at least Russia and possibly Finland and Sweden. Poland not only failed to achieve this goal, but by the end of the seventeenth century, it had become a weak, decentralized state.

It was the elective nature of the Polish monarchy that reduced it to impotence. The *Sejm*, or Polish diet, was a two-chamber assembly in which landowners completely dominated the few townsmen and lawyers who were also members. To be elected to the kingship, prospective monarchs (who were mostly foreigners) had to agree to share power with the *Sejm* (in effect with the nobles) in matters of taxation, foreign and military policy, and the appointment of state officials and judges. The power of the *Sejm* had disastrous results for central monarchical authority since the real aim of most of its members was to ensure that central authority would not affect their local interests. The acceptance of the liberum veto in 1652, whereby the meetings of the *Sejm* could be stopped by a single dissenting member, reduced government to virtual chaos.

Poland, then, was basically a confederation of semi-independent estates of landed nobles. By the late seventeenth century, it also became a battleground for foreign powers who found it easy to invade, but difficult to rule. The continuation of Polish weakness into the eighteenth century eventually encouraged its more powerful neighbors—Prussia, Austria, and Russia—to dismember it.

The "Golden Age" of the Dutch Republic

The seventeenth century has often been called the "Golden Age" of the Dutch Republic as the United Provinces held center stage as one of Europe's great powers. Like France and England, the United Provinces was an Atlantic power, underlining the importance of the shift of political and economic power from the Mediterranean basin to the countries on the Atlantic seaboard. As a result of the sixteenth-century revolt of the Netherlands, the seven northern provinces, which began to call themselves the United Provinces of the Netherlands in 1581, became the core of the modern Dutch state. The new state was officially recognized by the Peace of Westphalia in 1648.

With independence came internal dissension. There were two chief centers of political power in the new state. Each province had an official known as a stadholder who was responsible for leading the army and maintaining order. Beginning with William of Orange and his heirs, the house of Orange occupied the stadholderate in most of the seven provinces and favored the development of a centralized government with themselves as hereditary monarchs. The States General, an assembly of representatives from every province, opposed the Orangist ambitions and advocated a decentralized or republican form of government. A requirement of complete unanimity of the delegates tended to weaken the effectiveness of this body, however, causing the States General to refer all issues back to the provincial assemblies and permitting the latter to retain much power. Moreover, as the largest and richest province, Holland exercised the greatest influence in the States General; in fact, an oligarchy of wealthy merchants and financiers, especially from Amsterdam, tended to control this representative body.

The political rivalry between the monarchical and republican blocs was intensified by religious division within the Calvinist church, which remained the official church of the Dutch Republic. But other religious groups were tolerated as long as they worshiped in private. Catholics, other Protestants, and even Jewish communities felt relatively free in Holland, especially in Amsterdam. In their religious toleration, the Dutch were truly unique in the seventeenth century.

During the first half of the seventeenth century, the Orangist stadholders continued to pursue one fundamental aim—the conversion of the Dutch Netherlands into a monarchy under the house of Orange—but met with little success. Indeed, for twenty-two years after 1650, the seven Dutch provinces became accustomed to their republican existence without a stadholder. But in 1672, burdened with war against both France and England, the United Provinces turned once again to the house of Orange and restored it to the stadholderate in the person of William III (1672–1702). Seventeenth-century Dutch history is remarkable for the relative ease with which the Dutch shifted from one power base to the other in accordance with their external and internal needs. From that year on, William III worked consciously to build up his pseudo-royal power. When he succeeded to the throne of England in 1688 (see England and the Emergence of Constitutional Monarchy later in the chapter), it strengthened his position in the Netherlands as well. However, his death in 1702, without direct heirs, enabled the republican forces to gain control once more. The Dutch Republic would not be seriously threatened again by the monarchical forces.

Underlying Dutch prominence in the seventeenth century was its economic prosperity, fueled by the Dutch role as carriers of European trade. But war proved disastrous to the Dutch Republic. The two Anglo-Dutch wars of the 1650s and 1660s, the war with France and England in the 1670s, and their support of England against France in the War of the Spanish Succession placed heavy burdens on Dutch finances and manpower. English shipping began to challenge what had been Dutch commercial supremacy, and by 1715, the Dutch were experiencing a serious economic decline.

LIFE IN SEVENTEENTH-CENTURY AMSTERDAM

By the beginning of the seventeenth century, Amsterdam had replaced Antwerp as the financial and commercial capital of Europe. In 1570, Amsterdam had 30,000 inhabitants; by 1610, that number had doubled as refugees poured in, especially from the Spanish Netherlands. Intellectuals and Jews drawn by the city's reputation for toleration, as well as merchants and workers attracted by the city's prosperity, added to the number of new inhabitants. In 1613, this rapid growth caused the city government to approve an "urban expansion plan" that expanded the city's territory from 500 to 1,800

The Economic Superiority of the Dutch

Europeans were astonished by the apparent prosperity of the Dutch in the first half of the seventeenth century. This selection is taken from a treatise entitled Observations Touching Trade and Commerce with the Hollanders, and Other Nations. *It was written by an Englishman named John Keymer who believed that the Dutch economy could serve as a guide for the English.*

John Keymer, Observations Touching Trade and Commerce with the Hollanders, and Other Nations

I have diligently in my travels, observed how the countries herein mentioned [mainly Holland] do grow potent with abundance of all thing to serve themselves and other nations, where nothing grows; and that their never dried fountains of wealth, by which they raise their estate to such an admirable height, [so] that they are . . . [now] a wonder to the world, [come] from your Majesty's seas and lands.

I thus moved, began to delve into the depth of their policies and circumventing practices, whereby they drain, and still covet to exhaust, the wealth and coin of this kingdom, and so with our own commodities to weaken us, and finally beat us quite out of trading in other countries. I found that they more fully obtained these their purposes by their convenient privileges, and settled constitutions, than England with all the laws, and superabundance of home-bred commodities which God has vouchsafed your sea and land. . . .

To bring this to pass they have many advantages of us; the one is, by their fashioned ships . . . that are made to hold great bulk of merchandise, and to sail with a few men for profit. For example . . . [Dutch ships] do serve the merchant better cheap by one hundred pounds [English money] in his freight than we can, by reason he has but nine or ten mariners, and we near thirty; thus he saves twenty men's meat and wages in a voyage; and so in all other their ships according to their burden, by which means they are freighted wheresoever they come, to great profit, while our ships lie still and decay. . . .

Thus they and others glean this wealth and strength from us to themselves; and these reasons following procure them this advantage to us.

1. The merchants . . . which make all things in abundance, by reason of their store-houses continually replenished with all kind of commodities.
2. The liberty of free traffic for strangers to buy and sell in Holland, and other countries and states, as if they were free-born, makes great intercourse.
3. The small duties levied upon merchants, draws all nations to trade with them.
4. Their fashioned ships continually freighted before ours, by reason of their few mariners and great bulk, serving the merchant cheap.
5. Their forwardness to further all manner of trading.
6. Their wonderful employment of their busses [herring boats] for fishing, and the great returns they make.
7. Their giving free custom inward and outward, for any new-erected trade, by means whereof they have gotten already almost the sole trade into their hands.

acres through the construction of three large concentric canals. Builders prepared plots for the tall, narrow-fronted houses that were characteristic of the city by hammering wooden columns through the mud to the firm sand underneath. The canals in turn made it possible for businessmen to utilize the upper stories of their houses as storerooms for their goods. Wares carried by small boats were hoisted to the top windows of these dwellings by block and tackle beams fastened to the gables of the roofs. Amsterdam's physical expansion was soon matched by its population as the city grew to 100,000 people in 1610 and then to 200,000 by 1660.

The exuberant expansion of Amsterdam in the seventeenth century was based upon the city's new role as the commercial and financial center of Europe (see the box above). But what had made this possible? For one thing, Amsterdam merchants possessed vast fleets of ships, many of which were used for the lucrative North Sea herring catch. Amsterdam ships were also important carriers for the products of other countries. The Dutch invention of the fluyt, a shallow-draft ship of large capacity, enabled them to transport enormous quantities of cereals, timber, and iron. The Dutch produced large ships for ocean voyages as well.

Amsterdam merchants unloaded their cargoes at Dam Square, where all goods above fifty pounds in weight were recorded and tested for quality. The quantity of goods brought to Amsterdam soon made the city a crossroads for many of Europe's chief products. Amsterdam was, of course, the chief port for the Dutch

West and East Indian trading companies (see Overseas Trade and Colonies later in this chapter). Moreover, city industries turned imported raw materials into finished goods, making Amsterdam an important producer of woolen cloth, refined sugar and tobacco products, glass, beer, paper, books, jewelry, and leather goods. Some of the city's great wealth came from war profits: by 1700, Amsterdam was the principal supplier of military goods in Europe; its gun foundries had customers throughout the continent.

A third factor in Amsterdam's prosperity was its importance as a financial center. Trading profits provided large quantities of capital for investment. As a haven for religious minorities, Amsterdam housed a number of wealthy refugees with money to invest. Its financial role was greatly facilitated by the foundation in 1609 of the Exchange Bank of Amsterdam, long the greatest public bank in northern Europe. As an English gentleman noted, the reputation of the bank was "another invitation for People to come, and lodge here what part of their Money they could transport, and knew no way of securing at home."[11] The city also founded the Amsterdam Stock Exchange for speculating in commodities.

Amsterdam's prosperity (it possessed the highest per capita income in Europe) did not prevent it from having enormous social differences. At the bottom of the social ladder were the beggars, unskilled day laborers, and poor immigrants attracted by Amsterdam's riches. The upper classes disliked and feared the poor, which created much ambivalence in the way city authorities treated them. Militia forces made up of upper-class volunteers stood ready to crush lower-class revolts, while wealthy individuals founded orphanages and almshouses to care for their needs. Many of these poor people were forcefully recruited as ordinary sailors, especially for dangerous overseas voyages. Above this lower class stood the artisans and manual laborers, who belonged to the guilds or worked for guild members. Since widows were allowed to take their husbands' places in the craft guilds, Amsterdam was known for its high number of businesswomen. The artisans lived in a district called the Jordaan, built outside the three new canals. Its crowded quarters and small streets crisscrossed by canals created a quaint atmosphere and sense of fellowship that appealed to many of Amsterdam's artists.

Above the craftspeople stood a professional class of lawyers, teachers, bureaucrats, and wealthier guild mem-

◆ **Dam Square.** This work by J. van der Ulft, done in 1659, shows Dam Square in Amsterdam. Merchants unloaded their cargoes here, making Dam Square one of the busiest centers of the city.

bers, but above them were the landed nobles who intermarried with the wealthier burghers and built more elaborate town houses. At the very top of Amsterdam's society stood a select number of very prosperous manufacturers, shipyard owners, and merchants, whose wealth enabled them to control the city government of Amsterdam as well as the Dutch Republic's States General.

In the first half of the seventeenth century, the Calvinist background of the wealthy Amsterdam burghers led them to adopt a simple lifestyle. They wore dark clothes and lived in substantial, but simply furnished houses, known for their steep, narrow stairways. The oft-quoted phrase that "cleanliness is next to Godliness" was literally true for these self-confident Dutch burghers. Their houses were clean and orderly; foreigners often commented that Dutch housewives always seemed to be scrubbing. But in the second half of the seventeenth century, the wealthy burghers began to reject their Calvinist heritage, a transformation that is especially evident in their more elaborate and colorful clothes.

England and the Emergence of Constitutional Monarchy

One of the most prominent examples of resistance to absolute monarchy came in seventeenth-century England where king and Parliament struggled to determine the role each should play in governing England. But the struggle over this political issue was complicated by a deep and profound religious controversy. With the victory of Parliament came the foundation for constitutional monarchy by the end of the seventeenth century.

REVOLUTION AND CIVIL WAR

With the death of Queen Elizabeth in 1603, the Tudor dynasty became extinct, and the Stuart line of rulers was inaugurated with the accession to the throne of Elizabeth's cousin, King James VI of Scotland (son of Mary, queen of Scots), who became James I (1603–1625) of England. Although used to royal power as king of Scotland, James understood little about the laws, institutions, and customs of the English. He espoused the divine right of kings, the belief that kings receive their power directly from God and are responsible to no one except God. This viewpoint alienated Parliament, which had grown accustomed under the Tudors to act on the premise that monarch and Parliament together ruled England as a "balanced polity." Parliament expressed its displeasure with James's claims by refusing his requests for additional monies needed by the king to

meet the increased cost of government. Parliament's power of the purse proved to be its trump card in its relationship with the king.

Some members of Parliament were also alienated by James's religious policy. The Puritans—those Protestants within the Anglican church inspired by Calvinist theology—wanted James to eliminate the episcopal system of church organization used in the Church of England (in which the bishop or *episcopos* played the major administrative role) in favor of a Presbyterian model (used in Scotland and patterned after Calvin's church organization in Geneva, where ministers and elders—also called presbyters—played an important governing role). James refused because he realized that the Anglican church, with its bishops appointed by the crown, was a major support of monarchical authority. But the Puritans were not easily cowed and added to the rising chorus of opposition to the king. Many of England's gentry, mostly well-to-do landowners below the level of the nobility, had become Puritans, and these Puritan gentry not only formed an important and substantial part of the House of Commons, the lower house of Parliament, but also held important positions locally as justices of the peace and sheriffs. It was not wise to alienate them.

The conflict that had begun during the reign of James came to a head during the reign of his son Charles I (1625–1649). In 1628, Parliament passed a Petition of Right that the king was supposed to accept before being granted any taxes. This petition prohibited taxes without Parliament's consent, arbitrary imprisonment, the quartering of soldiers in private houses, and the declaration of martial law in peacetime. Although he initially accepted it, Charles later reneged on the agreement because of its limitations on royal power. In 1629, Charles decided that since he could not work with Parliament, he would not summon it to meet. From 1629 to 1640, Charles pursued a course of "personal rule," which forced him to find ways to collect taxes without the cooperation of Parliament. One expedient was a tax called Ship Money, a levy on seacoast towns to pay for coastal defense, which was now collected annually by the king's officials throughout England and used to finance other goverment operations besides defense. This use of Ship Money aroused opposition from middle-class merchants and landed gentry who believed the king was attempting to tax without Parliament's consent.

The king's religious policy also proved disastrous. His marriage to Henrietta Maria, the Catholic sister of King Louis XIII of France, aroused suspicions about the king's own religious inclinations. Even more important, however, the efforts of Charles and William Laud, the archbishop of Canterbury, to introduce more ritual into the Anglican church struck the Puritans as a return to Catholic popery. Grievances mounted, yet Charles might have survived unscathed if he could have avoided calling Parliament, which alone could provide a focus for the many cries of discontent throughout the land. But when the king and Archbishop Laud attempted to impose the Anglican Book of Common Prayer upon the Scottish Presbyterian church, the Scots rose up in rebellion against the king. Financially strapped and unable to raise troops to defend against the Scots, the king was forced to call Parliament into session. Eleven years of frustration welled up to create a Parliament determined to deal with the King.

In its first session from November 1640 to September 1641, the so-called Long Parliament (because it lasted in one form or another from 1640 to 1660) took a series of steps that placed severe limitations upon royal authority. These included the abolition of arbitrary courts, the abolition of taxes that the king had collected without Parliament's consent, such as Ship Money, and the passage of the revolutionary Triennial Act, which specified that Parliament must meet at least once every three years, with or without the king's consent. By the end of 1641, one group within Parliament was prepared to go no further, but a group of more radical parliamentarians pushed for more change, including the elimination of bishops in the Anglican church. When the king tried to take advantage of the split by arresting some members of the more radical faction in Parliament, a large group in Parliament led by John Pym and his fellow Puritans decided that the king had gone too far. England now slipped into civil war (1642).

Parliament proved victorious in the first phase of the English Civil War (1642–1646), aided by two significant factors. The Scots came into the war on Parliament's side when Parliament agreed in 1643 to consider a Presbyterian church organization for England. Even more important, however, was the creation of the New Model Army by Oliver Cromwell. The New Model Army was composed primarily of more extreme Puritans known as the Independents, who believed they were doing battle for the Lord. It is striking to read in Cromwell's military reports such statements as "Sir, this is none other but the hand of God; and to Him alone belongs the glory." We might also attribute some of the credit to Cromwell himself since his crusaders were well disciplined and trained in the new continental military tactics. Supported by the New Model Army, Parliament

✦ **Oliver Cromwell.** Oliver Cromwell was a dedicated Puritan who formed the New Model Army and defeated the forces supporting King Charles I. Unable to work with Parliament, he came to rely on military force to rule England. Cromwell is pictured here in 1649, on the eve of his ruthless military campaign in Ireland.

ended the first phase of the civil war with the capture of King Charles I in 1646.

A split now occurred in the parliamentary forces. A Presbyterian majority wanted to disband the army and restore Charles I with a Presbyterian state church. The army, composed mostly of the more radical Independents, who opposed an established Presbyterian church, marched on London in 1647 and began negotiations with the king. Charles took advantage of this division to flee and seek help from the Scots. Enraged by the king's treachery, Cromwell and the army engaged in a second civil war (1648) that ended with Cromwell's victory and the capture of the king. This time Cromwell was determined to achieve a victory for the army's point of view. The Presbyterian members of Parliament were purged, leaving a Rump Parliament of fifty-three members of the House of Commons who then tried and condemned the king on a charge of treason and adjudged that "he, the said Charles Stuart, as a tyrant, traitor, murderer, and public enemy to the good people of this nation, shall be put to death by the severing of his head from his body." On January 30, 1649, Charles was beheaded, a most uncommon act in the seventeenth century. The revolution had triumphed, and the monarchy in England had been destroyed, at least for the moment.

After the death of the king, the Rump Parliament abolished the monarchy and the House of Lords and proclaimed England a republic or Commonwealth (1649–1653). This was not an easy period for Cromwell. As commander-in-chief of the army, he had to crush a Catholic uprising in Ireland, which he accomplished with a brutality that earned him the eternal enmity of the Irish people, as well as an uprising in Scotland on behalf of the son of Charles I. He also faced opposition at home, especially from more radically minded groups who took advantage of the upheaval in England to push their agendas. The Levellers, for example, advocated such advanced ideas as freedom of speech, religious toleration, and a democratic republic. Cromwell, a country gentleman, defender of property and the ruling classes, smashed the radicals by force. At the same time, Cromwell found it difficult to work with the Rump Parliament and finally dispersed it by force. As the members of Parliament departed (April 1653), he shouted after them: "It's you that have forced me to do this, for I have sought the Lord night and day that He would slay me rather than put upon me the doing of this work." With the certainty of one who is convinced he is right, Cromwell had destroyed both king and Parliament.

The army provided a new goverment when it drew up the Instrument of Government, England's first and last written constitution. Executive power was vested in the Lord Protector (a position held by Cromwell) and legislative power in a Parliament. But the new system also failed to work. Cromwell found it difficult to work with the Parliament, especially when its members debated his authority and advocated once again the creation of a Presbyterian state church. In 1655, Cromwell dissolved Parliament and divided the country into eleven regions, each ruled by a major general who served virtually as a military governor. To meet the cost of military government, Cromwell levied a 10 percent land tax on all former Royalists. Unable to establish a constitutional basis for a working government, Cromwell had resorted to military force to maintain the rule of the Independents, ironically using even more arbitrary policies than those of Charles I.

Oliver Cromwell died in 1658. After floundering for eighteen months, the military establishment decided that arbitrary rule by the army was no longer feasible and reestablished the monarchy in the person of Charles II, the son of Charles I. The restoration of the Stuart monarchy ended England's time of troubles, but it was not long before England experienced yet another constitutional crisis.

RESTORATION AND A GLORIOUS REVOLUTION

After eleven years of exile, Charles II (1660–1685) returned to England. As he entered London amid the acclaim of the people, he remarked sardonically, "I never knew that I was so popular in England." The restoration of the monarchy and the House of Lords did not mean, however, that the work of the English Revolution was undone. Parliament kept much of the power it had won; arbitrary courts were still abolished; Parliament's role in government was acknowledged; and the necessity for its consent to taxation was accepted. Yet Charles continued to push his own ideas, some of which were clearly out of step with many of the English people.

A serious religious problem disturbed the tranquillity of Charles II's reign. After the restoration of the monarchy, a new Parliament (the Cavalier Parliament) met in 1661 and restored the Anglican church as the official church of England. In addition, laws were passed to force everyone, particularly Catholics and Puritan Dissenters, to conform to the Anglican church and even to exclude these people from holding positions in local government.

Charles was not pleased with this legislation. He was sympathetic to and perhaps even inclined to Catholicism. By the secret Treaty of Dover of 1670 with King Louis XIV of France, Charles had promised, in return for a substantial subsidy, to become Catholic and make England a Catholic commonwealth at the appropriate opportunity. Moreover, Charles's brother James, heir to the throne, did not hide the fact that he was a Catholic. Parliament's suspicions were therefore aroused in 1672 when Charles took the audacious step of issuing a Declaration of Indulgence that suspended the laws that Parliament had passed against Catholics and Puritans. By linking Catholics to Puritan Dissenters, Charles hoped to succeed with his religious policy, but Parliament would have none of it and induced the king to suspend the declaration. Propelled by a strong anti-Catholic sentiment, Parliament then passed a Test Act in 1673, specifying that only Anglicans could hold military and civil offices.

A supposed Catholic plot to assassinate King Charles and place his brother James on the throne, although shown to be imaginary, inflamed Parliament to attempt to pass an Exclusion Bill between 1678 and 1681 that would have barred James from the throne as a professed Catholic. Although these attempts failed, the debate over the bill created two political groupings: the Whigs, who wanted to exclude James and establish a Protestant king with toleration of Dissenters, and the Tories, who supported the king, despite their dislike of James as a Catholic, because they did not believe Parliament should tamper with the lawful succession to the throne. To foil these efforts, Charles dismissed Parliament in 1681, relying on French subsidies to rule alone. When he died in 1685, his Catholic brother came to the throne.

The accession of James II (1685–1688) to the crown virtually guaranteed a new constitutional crisis for England, for the stubborn and uncompromising James II was more reminiscent of his father, Charles I, than his brother. An open and devout Catholic, his attempt to further Catholic interests made religion once more a primary cause of conflict between king and Parliament.

After some initial successes, James took advantage of his newfound popularity to seek advantages for his fellow Catholics. Contrary to the Test Act, he named Catholics to high positions in the government, army, navy, and universities. In 1687, he issued a Declaration of Indulgence, which suspended all laws barring Catholics and Dissenters from office. Parliamentary outcries against James's policies stopped short of rebellion because members knew that he was an old man and his successors were his Protestant daughters Mary and Anne, born to his first wife. But on June 10, 1688, a son was born to James II's second wife, also a Catholic. Suddenly the specter of a Catholic hereditary monarchy loomed large. A group of seven prominent English noblemen invited William of Orange, husband of James's daughter Mary, to invade England. An inveterate foe of Louis XIV, William welcomed this opportunity to fight France with England's resources. William and Mary raised an army and invaded England while James, his wife, and infant son fled to France. With almost no bloodshed, England had undergone a "Glorious Revolution," not over the issue of whether there would be a monarchy, but rather over who would be monarch.

The events of late 1688 constituted only the initial stage of the Glorious Revolution. The second, and far more important part, was the Revolution Settlement that confirmed William and Mary as monarchs. In January 1689, a Convention Parliament asserted that James had tried to subvert the constitution "by breaking

◆ **William and Mary.** As a result of the Glorious Revolution, William of Orange and his wife Mary, daughter of King James II, became rulers of England in January 1689. William and Mary are shown here in a cameo portrait by Peter Hoadley.

the original contract between king and people," and declared the throne of England vacant. It then offered the throne to William and Mary, who accepted it along with the provisions of a Declaration of Rights, later enacted into law as a Bill of Rights in 1689 (see the box on p. 558). The Bill of Rights affirmed Parliament's right to make laws and levy taxes and made it impossible for kings to oppose or do without Parliament by stipulating that standing armies could be raised only with the consent of Parliament. Both elections and debates of Parliament had to be free, meaning that the king could not interfere. The rights of citizens to petition the sovereign, keep arms, have a jury trial, and not be subject to excessive bail were also confirmed. The Bill of Rights helped to fashion a system of government based on the rule of law and a freely elected Parliament, thus laying the foundation for a constitutional monarchy.

The Bill of Rights did not settle the religious questions that had played such a large role in England's troubles in the seventeenth century. The Toleration Act of 1689 granted Puritan Dissenters the right of free public worship (Catholics were still excluded), although

⇒ *The Bill of Rights* ⇐

In 1688, the English experienced yet another revolution, a rather bloodless one in which the Stuart king James II was replaced by Mary, James's daughter, and her husband, William of Orange. After William and Mary had assumed power, Parliament passed a Bill of Rights that specified the rights of Parliament and laid the foundation for a constitutional monarchy.

The Bill of Rights

Whereas the said late King James II having abdicated the government, and the throne being thereby vacant, his Highness the prince of Orange (whom it has pleased Almighty God to make the glorious instrument of delivering this kingdom from popery and arbitrary power) did (by the device of the lords spiritual and temporal, and diverse principal persons of the Commons) cause letters to be written to the lords spiritual and temporal, being Protestants, and other letters to the several counties, cities, universities, boroughs, and Cinque Ports, for the choosing of such persons to represent them, as were of right to be sent to parliament, to meet and sit at Westminster upon the two and twentieth day of January, in this year 1689, in order to such an establishment as that their religion, laws, and liberties might not again be in danger of being subverted; upon which letters elections have been accordingly made.

And thereupon the said lords spiritual and temporal and Commons, pursuant to their respective letters and elections, being now assembled in a full and free representation of this nation, taking into their most serious consideration the best means for attaining the ends aforesaid, do in the first place (as their ancestors in like case have usually done), for the vindication and assertion of their ancient rights and liberties, declare:

1. That the pretended power of suspending laws, or the execution of laws, by regal authority, without consent of parliament is illegal.

2. That the pretended power of dispensing with the laws, or the execution of law by regal authority, as it has been assumed and exercised of late, is illegal.

3. That the commission for erecting the late court of commissioners for ecclesiastical causes, and all other commissions and courts of like nature, are illegal and pernicious.

4. That levying money for or to the use of the crown by pretense of prerogative, without grant of parliament, for longer time or in other manner than the same is or shall be granted, is illegal.

5. That it is the right of the subjects to petition the king, and all commitments and prosecutions for such petitioning are illegal.

6. That the raising or keeping a standing army within the kingdom in time of peace, unless it be with consent of parliament, is against law.

7. That the subjects which are Protestants may have arms for their defense suitable to their conditions, and as allowed by law.

8. That election of members of parliament ought to be free.

9. That the freedom of speech, and debates or proceedings in parliament, ought not to be impeached or questioned in any court or place out of parliament.

10. That excessive bail ought not to be required, nor excessive fines imposed, nor cruel and unusual punishments inflicted.

11. That jurors ought to be duly impaneled and returned, and jurors which pass upon men in trials for high treason ought to be freeholders.

12. That all grants and promises of fines and forfeitures of particular persons before conviction are illegal and void.

13. And that for redress of all grievances, and for the amending, strengthening, and preserving of the laws, parliament ought to be held frequently.

they did not yet have full civil and political equality since the Test Act was not repealed. Although the Toleration Act did not mean complete religious freedom and equality, it marked a departure in English history since few people would ever again be persecuted for religious reasons.

Many historians have viewed the Glorious Revolution as the end of the seventeenth-century struggle between king and Parliament. By deposing one king and establishing another, Parliament had destroyed the divine-right theory of kingship (William was, after all, king by grace of Parliament, not God) and confirmed its right to participate in the government. Parliament did not have complete control of the government, but it now had an unquestioned right to participate in affairs of state. Over the next century, it would gradually prove to be the real authority in the English system of constitutional monarchy.

RESPONSES TO REVOLUTION

The English revolutions of the seventeenth century prompted very different responses from two English political thinkers—Thomas Hobbes and John Locke (see the box on p. 560). Thomas Hobbes (1588–1679), who lived during the English Civil War, was alarmed by the revolutionary upheavals in his contemporary England. "The state of man," he wrote, "can never be without some incommodity or other"; nevertheless, "the greatest, that in any form of government can possibly happen to the people in general, is scarce sensible in respect of the miseries, and horrible calamities, that accompany a civil war, or that dissolute condition of masterless men, without subject to laws, and a coercive power to tie their hands from rapine and revenge." Hobbes's name has since been associated with the state's claim to absolute authority over its subjects, which he elaborated in his major treatise on political thought known as the *Leviathan*, published in 1651.

Hobbes claimed that in the state of nature, before society was organized, human life was "solitary, poor, nasty, brutish, and short." Humans were guided not by reason and moral ideals, but by animalistic instincts and a ruthless struggle for self-preservation. To save themselves from destroying each other (the "war of every man against every man"), people contracted to form a commonwealth, which Hobbes called "that great Leviathan (or rather, to speak more reverently, that mortal god) to which we owe our peace and defense." This commonwealth placed its collective power into the hands of a sovereign authority, preferably a single ruler, who served as executor, legislator, and judge. This absolute ruler possessed unlimited power. In Hobbes's view, subjects may not rebel; if they do, they must be suppressed.

John Locke (1632–1704) viewed the exercise of political power quite differently from Hobbes and argued against the absolute rule of one man. Locke's experience of English politics during the Glorious Revolution was incorporated into a political work called *Two Treatises of Government*. Like Hobbes, Locke began with the state of nature before human existence became organized socially. But, unlike Hobbes, Locke believed humans lived then in a state of equality and freedom rather than a state of war. In this state of nature, humans had certain inalienable natural rights—to life, liberty, and property.

Like Hobbes, Locke did not believe all was well in the state of nature. Since there was no impartial judge in the state of nature, people found it difficult to protect these natural rights. So they mutually agreed to establish a government to ensure the protection of their rights. This agreement established mutual obligations: government would protect the rights of the people while the people would act reasonably toward government. But if a government broke this agreement—if a monarch, for example, failed to live up to his obligation to protect the natural rights or claimed absolute authority and made

CHRONOLOGY

Limited Monarchy and Republics

Poland	
Sigismund III	1587–1631
Beginning of liberum veto	1652
The United Provinces	
Official recognition of United Provinces	1648
House of Orange	
William III	1672–1702
England	
James I	1603–1625
Charles I	1625–1649
Petition of Right	1628
First Civil War	1642–1646
Second Civil War	1648
Execution of Charles I	1649
Commonwealth	1649–1653
Death of Cromwell	1658
Restoration of monarchy—Charles II	1660
Charles II	1660–1685
Cavalier Parliament	1661
Treaty of Dover	1670
Declaration of Indulgence	1672
Test Act	1673
James II	1685–1688
Declaration of Indulgence	1687
Glorious Revolution	1688
Bill of Rights	1689

⇒ Hobbes and Locke: Two Views of Political Authority ⇐

The seventeenth-century obsession with order and power was well reflected in the political thought of the Englishmen Thomas Hobbes and John Locke. In his Leviathan, *Hobbes presented the case for the state's claim to absolute authority over its subjects. John Locke, on the other hand, argued for limiting government power in his* Two Treatises of Government.

Thomas Hobbes, *Leviathan*

The only way to erect a Common Power, as may be able to defend them from the invasion of foreigners and the injuries of one another, and thereby to secure them in such sort, as that by their own industry, and by the fruits of the Earth, they may nourish themselves and live contentedly; is, to confer all their power and strength upon one Man, or upon one Assembly of men, that may reduce all their Wills, by plurality of voices, unto one Will . . . and therein to submit their Wills, every one to his Will, and their Judgments, to his Judgment. This is more than Consent, or Concord; it is a real Unity of them all, in one and the same Person, made by Covenant of every man with every man. . . . This done, the Multitude so united in one Person, is called a COMMONWEALTH. . . .

They that have already instituted a Commonwealth, being thereby bound by Covenant cannot lawfully make a new Covenant, among themselves, to be obedience to any other, in any thing whatsoever, without his permission. And therefore, they that are subjects to a Monarch, cannot without his leave cast off Monarchy, and return to the confusion of a disunited Multitude; nor transfer their Person from him that bears it, to another Man, or other Assembly of men: for they . . . are bound, every man to every man, to acknowledge that he that already is their Sovereign, shall do, and judge fit to be done; so that those who do not obey break their Covenant made to that man, which is injustice. . . . Consequently, none of the sovereign's Subjects, by any pretense of forfeiture, can be free from his Subjection.

John Locke, *The Second Treatise of Government*

There is, therefore, another way whereby governments are dissolved, and that is when the legislative or the prince, either of them, act contrary to their trust. . . . Whenever the legislators endeavor to take away and destroy the property of the people, or to reduce them to slavery under arbitrary power, they put themselves into a state of war with the people who are thereupon absolved from any further obedience, and are left to the common refuge which God has provided for all men against force and violence. Whensoever, therefore, the legislative shall transgress this fundamental rule of society, and either by ambition, fear, folly, or corruption, endeavor to grasp themselves, or put into the hands of any other, an absolute power over the lives, liberties, and estates of the people, by this breach of trust they forfeit the power the people had put into their hands for quite contrary ends, and it devolves to the people, who have a right to resume their original liberty and, by the establishment of a new legislative, such as they shall think fit, provide for their own safety and security, which is the end for which they are in society. What I have said here concerning the legislative in general holds true also concerning the supreme executor, who having a double trust put in him—both to have a part in the legislative and the supreme execution of the law—acts against both when he goes about to set up his own arbitrary will as the law of the society.

laws without the consent of the community—the people might form a new government. "The community perpetually retains a supreme power," Locke claimed. For Locke, however, the community of people was primarily the landholding aristocracy who were represented in Parliament, not the landless masses. Locke was hardly an advocate of political democracy, but his ideas proved important to both Americans and French in the eighteenth century and were used to support demands for constitutional government, the rule of law, and the protection of rights.

*E*conomic Trends: Mercantilism and European Colonies in the Seventeenth Century

The sixteenth century had witnessed a rising population, severely escalating prices, and a growing economy. The seventeenth century, however, as recent economic studies have demonstrated, was characterized more by economic contraction, if not depression, although variations existed depending on the country or region. Trade, industry, and agriculture all felt the pinch of a depression, which some historians believe bottomed out between 1640 and 1680, while others argue that the decade of the 1690s was still bad, especially in France. Translated into everyday life, for many people the economic contraction of the seventeenth century meant scarce food, uncertain employment, and high rates of taxation.

Climate, too, played a factor in this economic reversal as Europeans experienced worsening weather patterns. In this "little ice age," extending from the sixteenth well into the eighteenth century, average temperatures fell, winters were colder, summers were wetter, and devastating storms seemed more frequent. Although the exact impact of climatic changes is uncertain, there were numerous reports of crop failures, the worst in 1649, 1660–1661, and the 1690s.

Population was also affected. Based on the birthrate of the seventeenth century, demographers would expect the European population to have doubled every twenty-five years. In reality, the population either declined or increased only intermittently as a result of a variety of factors. Infant mortality rates were high, 30 percent in the first year of life and 50 percent before the age of ten. Epidemics and famines were again common experiences in European life. The last great epidemic of bubonic plague spread across Europe in the middle and late years of the seventeenth century. The Mediterranean region suffered from 1646 to 1657, when the plague killed off 130,000 persons in Naples alone. In 1665, it struck England and devastated London, killing 20 percent of its population. France and Spain experienced outbreaks in the 1690s. The last major outburst of bubonic plague struck Poland, Germany, and Scandinavia between 1708 and 1713, southern France in 1720, and Sicily in 1755.

Mercantilism

Mercantilism is the name historians use to identify a set of economic principles that dominated economic thought in the seventeenth century. Fundamental to mercantilism was the belief that the total volume of trade was unchangeable. Therefore, as Colbert, the French practitioner of mercantilism, stated: "Trade causes perpetual conflict, both in war and in peace, among the nations of Europe, as to who should carry off the greatest part. The Dutch, the English and the French are the actors in this conflict."[12] Since one nation could expand its trade and hence its prosperity only at the expense of others, to mercantilists, economic activity was war carried on by peaceful means.

According to the mercantilists, the prosperity of a nation depended upon a plentiful supply of bullion, or gold and silver. For this reason, it was desirable to achieve a favorable balance of trade in which goods exported were of greater value than those imported, promoting an influx of gold and silver payments that would increase the quantity of bullion. Furthermore, to encourage exports, governments should stimulate and protect export industries and trade by granting trade monopolies, encouraging investment in new industries through subsidies, importing foreign artisans, and improving transportation systems by building roads, bridges, and canals. By placing high tariffs on foreign goods, they could be kept out of the country and prevented from competing with domestic industries. Colonies were also deemed valuable as sources of raw materials and markets for finished goods.

As a system of economic principles, mercantilism focused on the role of the state, believing that state intervention in some aspects of the economy was desirable for the sake of the national good. Government regulations to ensure the superiority of export goods, the construction of roads and canals, and the granting of subsidies to create trade companies were all predicated on government involvement in economic affairs.

Overseas Trade and Colonies

Mercantilist theory on the role of colonies was matched in practice by Europe's overseas expansion. With the development of colonies and trading posts in the Americas and Far East, Europeans entered into an age of international commerce in the seventeenth century. While some historians speak of a world economy, we should remember that local, regional, and intra-European trade still dominated the scene. At the end of the seventeenth century, for example, English imports totaled 360,000 tons, but only 5,000 tons came from the East Indies. About one-tenth of English and Dutch exports were shipped across the Atlantic; slightly more went to the Far East. What made the transoceanic trade rewarding, however, was not the volume, but the value of its goods. Dutch, English, and French merchants were bringing back products that were still consumed largely by the wealthy, but were beginning to make their way into the lives of artisans and merchants. Pepper and spices from the Indies, West Indian and Brazilian sugar, and Asian coffee and tea were becoming more readily available to European consumers. The first coffee and tea houses opened in London in the 1650s and spread rapidly to other parts of Europe.

In 1600, much overseas trade was still carried by the Spanish and Portuguese, who alone possessed colonies of any significant size. But war and steady pressure from their Dutch and English rivals eroded Portuguese trade in both the west and the east, although Portugal continued to profit from its large colonial empire in Brazil. The Spanish also maintained an enormous South American empire, but Spain's importance as a commercial power declined rapidly in the seventeenth century because of a drop in the output of the silver mines, the poverty of the Spanish monarchy, and the stifling hand of the Spanish aristocracy as well as the pressure of its English rivals.

Although the Dutch became the leading carriers of European products within Europe, they faced more severe competition when they moved into Asian and American markets. The Dutch East India Company was formed in 1602 to consolidate the gains made at the expense of the Portuguese and exploit the riches of the Far East. Since the wealthy oligarchy that controlled the company also dominated the Dutch government, this joint-stock company not only had a monopoly on all Asian trade but also possessed the right to make war, sign treaties, establish military and trading bases, and appoint governing officials. Gradually, the Dutch East India Company took control of most of the Portuguese bases in the Far East and opened trade with China and Japan. Its profits were spectacular in the first ten years.

Although the Dutch West India Company was created in 1621 along lines similar to its eastern counterpart, it was less successful. Its efforts were aimed against Portuguese and Spanish trade and possessions, and though it made some inroads in Portuguese Brazil and the Caribbean, they were not enough to compensate for its expenditures. Dutch settlements were also established on the North American continent. The mainland colony of New Netherlands stretched from the mouth of the Hudson as far north as Albany, New York. Present-day names, such as Manhattan, Staten Island, Harlem, and the Catskills, remind us that it was the Dutch who initially settled the Hudson River valley. In the second half of the seventeenth century, rivalry and years of warfare with the English and French brought the decline of the Dutch commercial empire. In 1664, the English seized the colony of New Netherlands and renamed it New York while the Dutch West India Company soon went bankrupt. By the end of the seventeenth century, the Dutch Golden Age was beginning to tarnish.

The Dutch overseas trade and commercial empire faced two major rivals in the seventeenth century—the English and French. The English had founded their own East India Company in 1601 and proceeded to create a colonial empire in the New World along the Atlantic seaboard of North America. The failure of the Virginia Company made it evident that the colonizing of American lands was not necessarily conducive to quick profits.

◆ **The Dutch East India Company in India.** Pictured here is the Dutch trading post known as Hugly, founded in Bengal in 1610. This 1665 painting shows warehouses laid out in precise patterns surrounded by protective walls. Hugly was an important link in the network of bases that constituted Holland's trading empire in the Far East.

West Meets East: An Exchange of Royal Letters

Economic gain was not the only motivation of Western rulers who wished to establish a European presence in the Far East. In 1681, King Louis XIV of France wrote a letter to the king of Tonkin asking permission for Christian missionaries to proselytize in Vietnam. The king of Tonkin politely declined the request.

A Letter to the King of Tonkin

Most high, most excellent, most mighty and most magnanimous Prince, our very dear and good friend, may it please God to increase your greatness with a happy end!

We hear from our subjects who were in your Realm what protection you accorded them. We appreciate this all the more since we have for you all the esteem that one can have for a prince as illustrious through his military valor as he is commendable for the justice which he exercises in his Realm. . . . Since the war which we have had for several years, in which all of Europe had banded together against us, prevented our vessels from going to the Indies, at the present time, when we are at peace after having gained many victories and expanded our Realm through the conquest of several important places, we have immediately given orders to the Royal Company to establish itself in your kingdom as soon as possible. . . . We have given orders to have brought to you some presents which we believe might be agreeable to you. But the one thing in the world which we desire most, both for you and for your Realm, would be to obtain for your subjects who have already embraced the law of the only true God of heaven and earth, the freedom to profess it, since this law is the highest, the noblest, the most sacred and especially the most suitable to have kings reign absolutely over the people.

We are even quite convinced that, if you knew the truths and the maxims which it teaches, you would give first of all to your subjects the glorious example of embracing it. We wish you this incomparable blessing together with a long and happy reign, and we pray God that it may please Him to augment your greatness with the happiest of endings.

Your very dear and good friend,
Louis

Answers from the King of Tonkin to Louis XIV

The King of Tonkin sends to the King of France a letter to express to him his best sentiments. . . . Your communication, which comes from a country which is a thousand leagues away, and which proceeds from the heart as a testimony of your sincerity, merits repeated consideration and infinite praise. Politeness toward strangers is nothing unusual in our country. There is not a stranger who is not well received by us. How then could we refuse a man from France, which is the most celebrated among the kingdoms of the world and which for love of us wishes to frequent us and bring us merchandise? These feelings of fidelity and justice are truly worthy to be applauded. As regards your wish that we should cooperate in propagating your religion, we do not dare to permit it, for there is an ancient custom, introduced by edicts, which formally forbids it. Now, edicts are promulgated only to be carried out faithfully; without fidelity nothing is stable. How could we disdain a well-established custom to satisfy a private friendship? . . . This then is my letter. We send you herewith a modest gift which we offer you with a glad heart.

This letter was written at the beginning of winter and on a beautiful day.

But the desire to practice one's own religion combined with economic interests could lead to successful colonization, as the Massachusetts Bay Company demonstrated. The Massachusetts colony had 4,000 settlers in its early years, but by 1660 had swelled to 40,000. Although the English had established control over most of the eastern seaboard by the end of the seventeenth century, the North American colonies were still of only minor significance to the English economy.

French commercial companies in the Far East experienced much difficulty. Though due in part to a late start, French problems also demonstrated the weakness of a commerce dependent on political rather than economic impetus (see the box above). The East Indian companies set up by Henry IV and Richelieu all failed. Colbert established a new East India Company in 1664 that only barely managed to survive. The French had greater success in North America where in 1663 Canada was made the property of the crown and administered like a French province. But the French failed to provide adequate men or money, allowing their continental wars to take precedence over the conquest of the North

American continent. Already in 1713, by the Treaty of Utrecht, the French began to cede some of their American possessions to their English rival.

The World of Seventeenth-Century Culture

The seventeenth century was a remarkably talented one. In addition to the intellectuals responsible for the Scientific Revolution (see Chapter 17), the era was blessed with a number of prominent thinkers, artists, and writers. Some historians have even labeled it a century of genius.

Art: French Classicism and Dutch Realism

In the second half of the seventeenth century, France replaced Italy as the cultural leader of Europe. Rejecting the Baroque style as overly showy and passionate, the French remained committed to the classical values of the High Renaissance. French late classicism with its emphasis on clarity, simplicity, balance, and harmony of design was, however, a rather austere version of the High Renaissance style. Its triumph reflected the shift in seventeenth-century French society from chaos to order.

The nature of French classicism was evident in the principles of the French Academy of Painting and Sculpture. These included an imitation of the artists of

antiquity, an emphasis on geometric shapes and the use of definite lines to clearly delineate objects, a deemphasis on color because of its sensuousness, and the idealization of nature. While rejecting the emotionalism and high drama of the Baroque, French classicism continued the Baroque's conception of grandeur in the portrayal of noble subjects, especially those from classical antiquity. Nicholas Poussin (1594–1665) exemplified these principles in his paintings. His choice of scenes from classical mythology, the orderliness of his landscapes, the postures of his figures copied from the sculptures of antiquity, and his use of brown tones all reflect the classical principles of the French Academy.

The supremacy of Dutch commerce in the seventeenth century was parallelled by a brilliant flowering of Dutch painting. Since the Dutch possessed no real royal court or rich aristocracy, it was the wealthy patricians and burghers of Dutch urban society who commissioned works of art for their guild halls, town halls, and private dwellings. The interests of this burgher society were reflected in the subject matter of many Dutch paintings: portraits of themselves, group portraits of their military companies and guilds, landscapes, seascapes, genre scenes, still lifes, and the interiors of their residences. Neither classical nor Baroque, Dutch painters were primarily interested in the realistic portrayal of secular, everyday life. To a great extent, they turned away from the religious themes that had dominated art for so long.

The finest example of the golden age of Dutch painting was Rembrandt van Rijn (1606–1669). Rem-

◆ **Nicholas Poussin, *Landscape with the Burial of Phocian.*** France became the new cultural leader of Europe in the second half of the seventeenth century. French classicism upheld the values of High Renaissance style, but in a more static version. In Nicholas Poussin's work, we see the emphasis of French classicism on the use of scenes from classical sources and the creation of a sense of grandeur and noble strength in both human figures and landscape.

◆ **Rembrandt van Rijn, *Syndics of the Cloth Guild.*** The Dutch experienced a Golden Age of painting during the seventeenth century. The burghers and patricians of Dutch urban society commissioned works of art, and these quite naturally reflected the burghers' interests, as this painting by Rembrandt illustrates.

brandt's early career was reminiscent of Rubens in that he painted opulent portraits and grandiose scenes in often colorful fashion. Like Rubens, he was prolific and successful; unlike Rubens, he turned away from materialistic success and public approval to follow his own artistic path. In the process, he lost public support and died bankrupt.

Although Rembrandt shared the Dutch predilection for realistic portraits, he became more introspective as he grew older. He refused to follow his contemporaries whose pictures were largely secular in subject matter; half of his paintings focused on scenes from biblical tales. Since the Protestant tradition of hostility to religious pictures had discouraged artistic expression, Rembrandt stands out as the one great Protestant painter of the seventeenth century. Rembrandt's religious pictures, however, avoided the monumental sub-

jects, such as the Creation and Last Judgment, that were typical of Catholic artists. Instead, he favored pictures that focused on the individual's relationship with God and depicted people's inward suffering in quiet, evocative scenes.

The Theater: The Triumph of French Neoclassicism

As the great age of theater in England and Spain was drawing to a close around 1630, a new dramatic era began to dawn in France that lasted into the 1680s. Unlike Shakespeare in England and Lope de Vega in Spain, French playwrights wrote more for an elite audience and were forced to depend upon royal patronage. Louis XIV used theater as he did art and architecture—to attract attention to his monarchy.

French Comedy: The Would-Be Gentleman

The comedy writer Jean-Baptiste Moliére has long been regarded as one of the best playwrights of the age of Louis XIV. Moliére's comedy, The Would-Be Gentleman, focuses on Monsieur Jourdain, a vain and pretentious Parisian merchant who aspires to become a gentleman (at that time, a term for a member of the nobility who possessed, among other things, a title, fine clothes, and good taste). Jourdain foolishly believes that he can buy these things and hires a number of teachers to instruct him. In this scene from Act II, Jourdain learns from his philosophy teacher that he has been speaking prose all his life.

Jean-Baptiste Moliére, *The Would-Be Gentleman*

PHILOSOPHY MASTER: I will explain to you all these curiosities to the bottom.

M. JOURDAIN: Pray do. But now, I must commit a secret to you. I'm in love with a person of great quality, and I should be glad you would help me to write something to her in a short *billet-doux* [love letter], which I'll drop at her feet.

PHILOSOPHY MASTER: Very well.

M. JOURDAIN: That will be very gallant, won't it?

PHILOSOPHY MASTER: Without doubt. Is it verse that you would write to her?

M. JOURDAIN: No, no, none of your verse.

PHILOSOPHY MASTER: You would only have prose?

M. JOURDAIN: No, I would neither have verse nor prose.

PHILOSOPHY MASTER: It must be one or the other.

M. JOURDAIN: Why so?

PHILOSOPHY MASTER: Because, sir, there's nothing to express one's self by, but prose, or verse.

M. JOURDAIN: Is there nothing then but prose, or verse?

PHILOSOPHY MASTER: No, sir, whatever is not prose, is verse; and whatever is not verse, is prose.

M. JOURDAIN: And when one talks, what may that be then?

PHILOSOPHY MASTER: Prose.

M. JOURDAIN: How? When I say, Nicole, bring me my slippers, and give me my nightcap, is that prose?

PHILOSOPHY MASTER: Yes, sir.

M. JOURDAIN: On my conscience, I have spoken prose above these forty years without knowing anything of the matter; and I have all the obligations in the world to you for informing me of this. I would therefore put into a letter to her: Beautiful marchioness, your fair eyes make me die with love; but I would have this placed in a gallant manner; and have a gentle turn.

PHILOSOPHY MASTER: Why, add that the fire of her eyes has reduced your heart to ashes: that you suffer for her night and day all the torments—

M. JOURDAIN: No, no, no, I won't have all that—I'll have nothing but what I told you. Beautiful marchioness, your fair eyes make me die with love.

PHILOSOPHY MASTER: You must by all means lengthen the thing out a little.

M. JOURDAIN: No, I tell you, I'll have none but those very words in the letter: but turned in a modish way, ranged handsomely as they should be. I desire you'd show me a little, that I may see the different manners in which one may place them.

PHILOSOPHY MASTER: One may place them first of all as you said: Beautiful marchioness, your fair eyes make me die for love. Or suppose: For love die me make, beautiful marchioness, your fair eyes. Or perhaps: Your eyes fair, for love me make, beautiful marchioness, die. Or suppose: Die your fair eyes, beautiful marchioness, for love me make. Or however: Me make your eyes fair die, beautiful marchioness, for love.

M. JOURDAIN: But of all these ways, which is the best?

PHILOSOPHY MASTER: That which you said: Beautiful marchioness, your fair eyes make me die for love.

M. JOURDAIN: Yet at the same time, I never studied it, and I made the whole of it at the first touch. I thank you with all my heart, and desire you would come in good time tomorrow.

PHILOSOPHY MASTER: I shall not fail.

French dramatists cultivated a classical style in which the Aristotelian rules of dramatic composition, observing the three unities of time, place, and action, were closely followed. French neoclassicism emphasized the clever, polished, and correct over the emotional and imaginative. Many of the French works of the period derived both their themes and their plots from Greek and Roman sources, especially evident in the works of Jean-Baptiste Racine (1639–1699). In *Phédre*, which has been called his best play, Racine followed closely the plot of the Greek tragedian Euripides' *Hippolytus*. Like the ancient tragedians, Racine, who perfected the

French neoclassical tragic style, focused on conflicts, such as between love and honor or inclination and duty, that characterized and revealed the tragic dimensions of life.

Jean-Baptiste Molière (1622–1673) enjoyed the favor of the French court and benefited from the patronage of the Sun King. He wrote, produced, and acted in a series of comedies that often satirized the religious and social world of his time (see the box on p. 566). In *The Misanthrope*, he mocked the corruption of court society, while in *Tartuffe*, he ridiculed religious hypocrisy. Molière's satires, however, sometimes got him into trouble. The Paris clergy did not find *Tartuffe* funny and had it banned for five years. Only the protection of Louis XIV saved Molière from more severe harassment.

Conclusion

To many historians, the seventeenth century has assumed extraordinary proportions. The divisive effects of the Reformation had been assimilated and the concept of a united Christendom, held as an ideal since the Middle Ages, had been irrevocably destroyed by the religious wars, making possible the emergence of a system of nation-states in which power politics took on an increasing significance. The growth of political thought focusing on the secular origins of state power reflected the changes that were going on in seventeenth-century society.

Within those states, there slowly emerged some of the machinery that made possible a growing centralization of power. In those states called absolutist, strong monarchs with the assistance of their aristocracies took the lead in providing the leadership for greater centralization. But in England, where the landed aristocracy gained power at the expense of the monarchs, the foundations were laid for a constitutional government in which Parliament provided the focus for the institutions of centralized power. In all the major European states, a growing concern for power and dynastic expansion led to larger armies and greater conflict. The growth of international law represented an attempt to create a rational system for this conflict, but it did nothing to achieve a peaceful solution to human problems. War remained an endemic feature of Western civilization.

But the search for order and harmony continued, evident in art and literature. At the same time, while it would be misleading to state that Europe had become a secular world, we would have to say that religious preoccupations and values were losing ground to secular considerations. The seventeenth century was a transitional period to a more secular spirit that has characterized modern Western civilization until the present time. No stronger foundation for this spirit could be found than in the new view of the universe that was created by the Scientific Revolution of the seventeenth century, and it is to that story that we must now turn.

NOTES

1. Quoted in D. H. Pennington, *Europe in the Seventeenth Century*, 2d ed. (London and New York, 1989), p. 313.
2. Quoted in John B. Wolf, *Louis XIV* (New York, 1968), p. 134.
3. Quoted in W. H. Lewis, *The Splendid Century* (Garden City, N.Y., 1953), pp. 39–40.
4. Quoted in Wolf, *Louis XIV*, p. 284.
5. Quoted in ibid., p. 618.
6. Quoted in Pennington, *Europe in the Seventeenth Century*, p. 494.
7. Quoted in J. H. Elliott, *Imperial Spain, 1469–1716* (New York, 1963), p. 306.
8. Quoted in ibid., p. 338.
9. Quoted in Vasili Klyuchevsky, *Peter the Great*, trans. Liliana Archibald (New York, 1958), p. 244.
10. Quoted in B. H. Sumner, *Peter the Great and the Emergence of Russia* (New York, 1962), p. 122.
11. Quoted in Violet Barbour, *Capitalism in Amsterdam in the 17th Century* (Ann Arbor, Mich., 1963), p. 46.
12. Quoted in H. G. Koenigsberger, *Early Modern Europe: 1500–1798* (London, 1987), p. 172.

SUGGESTIONS FOR FURTHER READING

In addition to the general works listed in Chapter 15, see also D. H. Pennington, *Europe in the Seventeenth Century*, 2d ed. (London and New York, 1989); T. Munck, *Seventeenth Century Europe 1598–1700* (London, 1990); and R. S. Dunn, *The Age of Religious Wars, 1559–1715*, 2d ed. (New York, 1979).

For a brief account of seventeenth-century French history, see R. Briggs, *Early Modern France, 1560–1715* (Oxford, 1977). More detailed studies on France during the periods of Henry IV and Cardinals Richelieu and Mazarin are M. Greengrass, *France in the Age of Henri IV: The Struggle for Stability* (London, 1984); R. Bonney, *Society and Government in France under Richelieu and Mazarin, 1624–1662* (London, 1985); and J. Bergin, *Cardinal Richelieu: Power and the Pursuit of Wealth* (London, 1985). A solid and very readable biography of Louis XIV is J. B. Wolf, *Louis XIV* (New York, 1968). Also of value are the works by G. R. R. Treasure, *Seventeenth Century France* (Garden City, N.Y., 1967); O. Bernier, *Louis XIV* (New York, 1988); and P. Goubert, *Louis XIV and Twenty Million Frenchmen*, trans. A. Carter (New York, 1970). A now classic work on life in Louis XIV's France is W. H. Lewis, *The Splendid Century* (Garden City, N.Y., 1953). Well-presented summaries of revisionist views on Louis's monarchical power are R. Mettam, *Power and Faction in Louis XIV's France* (Oxford, 1988); and W. Beik, *Absolutism and Society in Seventeenth-Century France* (Cambridge, 1985). C. W. Cole, *Colbert and a Century of French Mercantilism*, 2 vols. (London, 1939), is still the fundamental study.

Good general works on seventeenth-century Spanish history include the relevant sections of J. H. Elliott, *Imperial Spain, 1469–1716* (New York, 1963; rev. ed. 1977); H. Kamen, *Spain 1469–1716: A Society of Conflict* (London, 1983); and R. A. Stradling, *Europe and the Decline of Spain, 1580–1720* (London, 1981). On the last half of the seventeenth century, see the more detailed work by H. Kamen, *Spain in the Later Seventeenth Century, 1665–1700* (London, 1980). The important minister Olivares is examined in J. H. Elliott, *The Count-Duke of Olivares: The Statesman in an Age of Decline* (London, 1986).

An older, but still valuable survey of the German states in the seventeenth century can be found in H. Holborn, *A History of Modern Germany, 1648–1840*

(London, 1965). An important recent work is M. Hughes, *Early Modern Germany, 1477–1806* (Philadelphia, 1992). On the creation of an Austrian state, see R. J. W. Evans, *The Making of the Habsburg Monarchy, 1550–1700* (Oxford, 1979). The older work by F. L. Carsten, *The Origins of Prussia* (Oxford, 1954), remains an outstanding study of early Prussian history. On aspects of seventeenth-century Swedish history, see the work by M. Roberts, *Sweden's Age of Greatness* (London, 1973). A good biography of the dynamic Charles XII is R. Hatton, *Charles XII of Sweden* (London, 1968). For an introduction to Polish history, see N. Davies, *God's Playground: A History of Poland*, vol. 1, *The Origins to 1795* (Oxford, 1981).

On Russian history before Peter the Great, see the classic work by V. O. Klyuchevsky, *A Course in Russian History: The Seventeenth Century* (Chicago, 1968); and R. Nellie, *Enserfment and Military Change in Muscovy* (Chicago, 1971). Works on Peter the Great include V. O. Klyuchevsky, *Peter the Great*, trans. L. Archibald (New York, 1958); M. S. Anderson, *Peter the Great* (London, 1978); B. H. Sumner, *Peter the Great and the Emergence of Russia* (New York, 1962); and the massive popular biography by R. K. Massie, *Peter the Great* (New York, 1980). For an introduction to Ottoman history, see P. Coles, *The Ottoman Impact on Europe, 1350–1699* (London, 1968).

Good general works on the period of the Revolution include G. E. Aylmer, *Rebellion or Revolution? England, 1640–1660* (New York, 1986); L. Stone, *Causes of the English Revolution, 1529–1642* (New York, 1972); and the brief study by R. Howell, Jr., *The Origins of the English Revolution* (St. Louis, 1975). On the war itself, see C. Hill, *God's Englishman: Oliver Cromwell and the English Revolution* (New York, 1970); and R. Ashton, *The English Civil War: Conservatism and Revolution, 1604–1649* (London, 1976). On Oliver Cromwell, see R. Howell, Jr., *Cromwell* (Boston, 1977); and the beautifully written popular account by A. Fraser, *Cromwell: The Lord Protector* (New York, 1974). For a general survey of the post-Cromwellian era, see J. R. Jones, *Country and Court: England, 1658–1714* (London, 1978). A more specialized study is J. R. Jones, *The Revolution of 1688 in England* (London, 1972). On Charles II, see the scholarly biography by R. Hutton,

Charles II (Oxford, 1989). Locke's political ideas are examined in J. H. Franklin, *John Locke and the Theory of Sovereignty* (London, 1978). On Thomas Hobbes, see D. D. Raphael, *Hobbes* (London, 1977).

On the United Provinces, see two short, but sound introductions, K. H. D. Haley, *The Dutch in the Seventeenth Century* (London, 1972); and C. Wilson, *The Dutch Republic and the Civilisation of the Seventeenth Century* (London, 1968). On Amsterdam, see J. J. Murray, *Amsterdam in the Age of Rembrandt* (Norman, Okla., 1967). Of much value is S. Schama, *The Embarrassment of Riches: An Interpretation of Dutch Culture in the Golden Age* (New York, 1987).

On the economic side of the seventeenth century, there are the three volumes by F. Braudel, *Civilization and Capitalism in the 15th to 18th Century*, which obviously cover much more than just the seventeenth century: *The Structures of Everyday Life* (London, 1981); *The Wheels of Commerce* (London, 1982); and *The Perspective of the World* (London, 1984). Two single-volume comprehensive surveys are J. de Vries, *The Economy of Europe in an Age of Crisis* (Cambridge, 1976); and H. Kellenbenz, *The Rise of the European Economy: An Economic History of Continental Europe from the Fifteenth to the Eighteenth Century* (London, 1976). On overseas trade and colonial empires, see C. R. Boxer, *The Dutch Seaborne Empire, 1600–1800* (New York, 1965); and R. Davis, *English Overseas Trade, 1500–1700* (London, 1973). Although frequently criticized, the standard work on mercantilism remains E. Hecksher, *Mercantilism*, 2 vols. (London, 1935).

French theater and literature are examined in A. Adam, *Grandeur and Illusion: French Literature and Society, 1600–1715*, trans. J. Tint (New York, 1972). For an examination of French and Dutch art, see A. Blunt, *Art and Architecture in France, 1500–1700* (London, 1953); J. Rosenberg, S. Silve, and E. H. ter Kuele, *Dutch Art and Architecture, 1600–1800* (London, 1966); and C. White, *Rembrandt and His World* (London, 1964).

CHAPTER
17

Toward a New Heaven and a New Earth: The Scientific Revolution and the Emergence of Modern Science

In addition to the political, economic, social, and international crises of the seventeenth century, we need to add an intellectual one. The Scientific Revolution questioned and ultimately challenged conceptions and beliefs about the nature of the external world and reality that had crystallized into a rather strict orthodoxy by the Late Middle Ages. Derived from the works of ancient Greeks and Romans and grounded in Christian thought, the medieval worldview had become a formidable one. No doubt, the breakdown of Christian unity during the Reformation and the subsequent religious wars had created an environment in which Europeans had become accustomed to challenging both the ecclesiastical and political realms. Should it surprise us that a challenge to intellectual authority soon followed?

The Scientific Revolution brought Europeans a new way of viewing the universe and their place in it. The shift from an earth-centered to a sun-centered cosmos had an emotional as well as an intellectual effect upon those who understood it. Thus, the Scientific Revolution, popularized in the eighteenth-century Enlightenment, stands as the major force in the transition to the largely secular, rational, and materialistic perspective that has defined the modern Western mentality since its full acceptance in the nineteenth and twentieth centuries.

The transition to a new worldview was not an easy one, however. In the seventeenth century, the Italian scientist Galileo, an outspoken advocate of the new worldview, found that his ideas were strongly opposed by the authorities of the Catholic church. Galileo's position was clear: "I hold the sun to be situated motionless in the center of the revolution of the celestial bodies, while the earth rotates on its axis and revolves about the sun." Moreover, "nothing physical that sense-experience sets before our eyes . . . ought to be called in question (much less condemned) upon the

• Copernicus, *On the Revolutions of the Heavenly Spheres*

• • • Kepler's laws

Galileo, *The Starry Messenger*

Newton, Law of universal gravitation

• Vesalius, *On the Fabric of the Human Body*

Harvey's theory of circulation

Descartes, *Discourse on Method*

Pascal, *Pensées*

• Cavendish, *Grounds of Natural Philosophy*

Spinoza, *Ethics* •

Bacon, *The Great Instauration*

• • • Beginnings of English Royal Society

Establishment of French Royal Academy of Sciences

testimony of Biblical passages." But the church had a different view, and in 1633, Galileo, now sixty-eight and in ill health, was called before the dreaded Inquisition in Rome. He was kept waiting for two months before he was tried and found guilty of heresy and disobedience. Completely shattered by the experience, he denounced his errors: "With a sincere heart and unfeigned faith I curse and detest the said errors and heresies contrary to the Holy Church, and I swear that I will nevermore in future say or assert anything that may give rise to a similar suspicion of me." Legend holds that when he left the trial room, Galileo muttered to himself: "And yet it does move!" In any case, Galileo had been silenced, but his writings remained, and they began to spread through Europe. The Inquisition had failed to stop the spread of the new ideas of the Scientific Revolution.

In one sense, the Scientific Revolution was not a revolution. It was not characterized by the explosive change and rapid overthrow of traditional authority that we normally associate with the word revolution. The Scientific Revolution did overturn centuries of authority, but only in a gradual and piecemeal fashion. Nevertheless, its results were truly revolutionary. The Scientific Revolution was a key factor in setting Western civilization along its modern secular and material path.

$\mathcal{B}$ackground to the Scientific Revolution

To say that the Scientific Revolution brought about a dissolution of the medieval worldview is not to say that the Middle Ages was a period of scientific ignorance. Many educated Europeans took an intense interest in the world around them since it was, after all, "God's handiwork" and therefore an appropriate subject for study. Late medieval scholastic philosophers had advanced mathematical and physical thinking in many ways, but the subjection of these thinkers to a strict theological framework and their unquestioning reliance on a few ancient authorities, especially Aristotle and Galen, limited where they could go. Many "natural philosophers," as medieval scientists were called, preferred refined logical analysis to systematic observations of the natural world. A number of historians have argued, however, that some of the natural philosophers developed ideas that came to fruition in the seventeenth century. These historians have pointed out, for example, that Galileo's development of the science of mechanics was grounded upon the work of fourteenth-century scholastics. And yet, as other scholars have noted, there was still a great contrast between the "theoretical" approach of the scholastics and the "hands-on" experiments of Galileo that enabled him to make his case.

The historical debate over the issue of late medieval influence on the Scientific Revolution reminds us that historians have had a difficult time explaining the causes of the Scientific Revolution. They have pointed out, however, that a number of changes and advances in the fifteenth and sixteenth centuries may have played a major role in helping natural philosophers abandon their old views and develop new ones.

While medieval scholars had made use of Aristotle, Galen, and Ptolemy in Latin translations to develop many of their positions in the fields of physics, medicine, and astronomy, the Renaissance humanists had mastered Greek as well as Latin and made available new works of Galen, Ptolemy, and Archimedes as well as Plato and the pre-Socratics. These writings made it apparent that even the unquestioned authorities of the Middle Ages, Aristotle and Galen, had been contradicted by other thinkers. The desire to discover which school of thought was correct stimulated new scientific work that sometimes led to a complete rejection of the classical authorities. We know that Copernicus, for example, founder of the heliocentric theory, had read in Plutarch (discovered by the Renaissance) that Philolaus and a number of other ancients had believed that it was the earth and not the sun that moved.

Renaissance artists have also been credited with making an impact on scientific study. Their desire to imitate nature led them to rely upon a close observation of nature. Their accurate renderings of rocks, plants, animals, and human anatomy established new standards for the study of natural phenomena. At the same time, the "scientific" study of the problems of perspective and correct anatomical proportions led to new insights. "No painter," one Renaissance artist declared, "can paint well without a thorough knowledge of geometry."[1] Renaissance artists were frequently called upon to be practicing mathematicians as well. Leonardo da Vinci devised "war machines" while Albrecht Dürer made designs for the fortifications of cities.

Although most of these artistic designs for technical innovations were not intended for actual use and remained on paper, mathematicians, military engineers, naval architects, and navigators were having to deal with such practical problems as how to navigate in unknown seas, how to compute the trajectories of cannonballs for more effective impact, and how to calculate the tonnage of ships accurately. These technical problems served to stimulate scientific activity since all of them required careful observation and accurate measurements. The fifteenth and sixteenth centuries witnessed a proliferation of books dedicated to machines and technology, all of which espoused the belief that innovation in techniques was necessary. The relationship between technology and the Scientific Revolution is not a simple one, however, for many technological experts did not believe in abstract or academic learning.

Indeed, many of the technical innovations of the Middle Ages and Renaissance were accomplished outside the universities by people who emphasized practical rather than theoretical knowledge. In any case, the invention of new instruments and machines, such as the telescope and microscope, often made new scientific discoveries possible. Above all, the printing press had an indirect, but crucial role in spreading innovative ideas quickly and easily.

Mathematics, which played such a fundamental role in the scientific achievements of the sixteenth and seventeenth centuries, was promoted in the Renaissance by the rediscovery of the works of ancient mathematicians and the influence of Plato (see Chapter 13), who had emphasized the importance of mathematics in explaining the universe. While mathematics was applauded as the key to navigation, military science, and geography, the Renaissance also held the widespread belief that mathematics was the key to understanding the nature of things. According to Leonardo da Vinci, since God eternally geometrizes, nature is inherently mathematical: "Proportion is not only found in numbers and measurements but also in sounds, weights, times, positions, and in whatsoever power there may."[2] Moreover, mathematical reasoning was seen as promoting a degree of certainty that was otherwise impossible. In the words of Leonardo da Vinci: "There is no certainty where one can neither apply any of the mathematical sciences nor any of those which are based upon the mathematical sciences."[3] Copernicus, Kepler, Galileo, and Newton were all great mathematicians who believed that the secrets of nature were written in the language of mathematics.

A final factor in the origins of the Scientific Revolution, the role of magic, has been the object of heated scholarly debate. Renaissance magic (see Chapter 13) was the preserve of an intellectual elite from all of Europe (see the box on p. 573). By the end of the sixteenth century, Hermetic magic had become fused with alchemical thought into a single intellectual framework. This tradition believed that the world was a living embodiment of divinity. Humans, who it was believed also had that spark of divinity within, could use magic, especially mathematical magic, to understand and dominate the world of nature or employ the powers of nature for beneficial purposes. Was it Hermeticism, then, that inaugurated the shift in consciousness that made the Scientific Revolution possible, since the desire to control and dominate the natural world was a crucial motivating force in the Scientific Revolution? One scholar has argued:

Magic and Science: The Case of Girolamo Cardano

Girolamo Cardano or Jerome Cardan (1501–1576) was a very important figure in the history of mathematics. He also became a physician and professor of medicine at Pavia in 1547. Like many other intellectuals of the sixteenth century, Cardano was a student of magic and astrology. In this selection taken from his autobiography, The Book of My Life, Cardano discusses the presence in his life of what we would call paranormal powers, including prescient dreams, extrasensory perception, and intuitive flashes of direct understanding.

Girolamo Cardano, The Book of My Life

I am conscious that some influence from without seems to bring a murmuring sound to my ear from precisely that direction or region where some one is discussing me. If this discussion be fair, the sound seems to come to rest on the right side; or, if perchance it approaches from the left, it penetrates to the right and becomes a steady hum. If, however, the talk be contentious, strangely conflicting sounds are heard; when evil is spoken, the noise rests in the left ear, and comes from the quarter exactly whence the voices of my detractors are making disturbance, and, accordingly, may approach from any side of my head. . . . Very often when the discussion about me has taken place in the same city, it has happened that the vibration has scarcely ceased before a messenger has appeared who addresses me in the name of my detractors. But if the conversation has taken place in another state and the messenger should appear, one has but to compute the space of time which had elapsed between the discussion and the beginning of the messenger's journey, and the moment I heard the voices and the time of the discussion itself will fall out the same. . . .

A few years later, eight perhaps, that is, about 1534, I began to see in my dreams the events shortly to come to pass. If these events were due to happen on the day following the dream, I used to have clear and defined visions of them just after sunrise, so that even on occasion I saw the motion for my admission to the College of Physicians straightway brought to vote, to a decision, and the motion lost. I dreamed, as well, that I was about to obtain my appointment to the professorship at Bologna. This manifestation by dreams ceased in the year just preceding the cessation of the former manifestation, that is, about 1567. . . . And so it had lasted about thirty-three years.

A third peculiarity is an intuitive flash of direct knowledge. This I employed with gradually increasing advantage. It originated about the year 1529; its effectiveness was increased but it could never be rendered infallible, except toward the close of 1573. For a period between the end of August of that year and the beginning of September 1574, and particularly, as it seems to me, now in this year 1575, I have considered it infallible. It is, moreover, a gift which has not deserted me, and it replaces the powers of those two latter faculties which did; it prepares me to meet my adversaries, and for any pressing necessity. Its component parts are an ingeniously exercised employment of the intuitive faculty, and an accompanying lucidity of understanding.

It is a movement of the will which really originates an intellectual movement. A new center of interest arises, surrounded by emotional excitement; the mind turns where the will has directed it and new attitudes, new discoveries follow. Behind the emergence of modern science there was a new direction of the will toward the world, its marvels, and mysterious workings, a new longing and determination to understand those workings and to operate with them.[4]

"This time," the author continues, "the return to the occult [Hermetic tradition] stimulates the genuine science."[5] Histories of the Scientific Revolution frequently overlook the fact that the great names we associate with the revolution in cosmology—Copernicus, Kepler, Galileo, and Newton—all had a serious interest in Hermetic ideas and the fields of astrology and alchemy. The mention of these names also reminds us of one final consideration in the origins of the Scientific Revolution: it largely resulted from the work of a handful of great intellectuals.

Toward a New Heaven: A Revolution in Astronomy

The greatest achievements in the Scientific Revolution of the sixteenth and seventeenth centuries came in those fields most dominated by the ideas of the Greeks—astronomy, mechanics, and medicine. The cosmological views of the Late Middle Ages had been built upon a synthesis of the ideas of Aristotle, Claudius Ptolemy (the greatest astronomer of antiquity who lived in the second century A.D.), and Christian theology. In the resulting Ptolemaic or geocentric conception, the universe was seen as a series of concentric spheres with a fixed or motionless earth as its center. Composed of the material substances of earth, air, fire, and water, the earth was imperfect and constantly changing. The spheres that surrounded the earth were made of a crystalline, transparent substance and moved in circular orbits around the earth. Circular movement, according to Aristotle, was the most "perfect" kind of motion and hence appropriate for the "perfect" heavenly bodies thought to consist of a nonmaterial, incorruptible "quintessence." These heavenly bodies, pure orbs of light, were embedded in the moving, concentric spheres and in 1500 numbered ten. Working outward from the earth, eight spheres contained the moon, Mercury, Venus, the sun, Mars, Jupiter, Saturn, and the fixed stars. The ninth sphere imparted to the eighth sphere of the fixed stars its motion while the tenth sphere was frequently described

as the prime mover that moved itself and imparted motion to the other spheres. Beyond the tenth sphere was the Empyrean Heaven—the location of God and all the saved souls. This Christianized Ptolemaic universe, then, was a finite one. It had a fixed end in harmony with Christian thought and expectations.

This medieval, geocentric conception of the universe was one that accorded well with both Christianity and common sense at that time. God and the saved souls were at one end of the universe while humans were at the center. They had been given power over the earth, but their real purpose was to achieve salvation. To ordinary people, this conception of the universe also appeared sensible as they looked up at the night sky. The huge earth could easily be seen as motionless and surrounded by ethereal heavenly bodies circling around it.

This conception, however, did not satisfy professional astronomers who wished to ascertain the precise paths of the heavenly bodies across the sky. Finding that their observations did not always correspond to the accepted

◆ **Medieval Conception of the Universe.** As this sixteenth-century illustration shows, the medieval cosmological view placed the earth at the center of the universe, surrounded by a series of concentric spheres. The earth was imperfect and constantly changing while the heavenly bodies that surrounded it were perfect and incorruptible. Beyond the tenth and final sphere was heaven where God and all the saved souls were located.

scheme, astronomers tried to "save appearances" by developing an elaborate system of devices. They proposed, for example, that the planetary bodies traveled on epicycles, concentric spheres within spheres, that would enable the paths of the planets to correspond more precisely to observations while adhering to Aristotle's ideas of circular planetary movement.

Copernicus

Although Nicolaus Copernicus (1473–1543) received a doctorate in canon law and spent the last thirty years of his life as canon of a cathedral, mathematics and astronomy occupied most of his time. He had studied both subjects first at Cracow in his native Poland and later at the Italian universities of Bologna and Padua. Before he left Italy in 1506, he had become aware of ancient views that contradicted the Ptolemaic, earth-centered conception of the universe. Between 1506 and 1530, he completed the manuscript of his famous book, *On the Revolutions of the Heavenly Spheres*, but his own

timidity and fear of ridicule from fellow astronomers kept him from publishing it until May 1543, shortly before his death.

Copernicus was not an accomplished observational astronomer and relied for his data on the records of his predecessors. But he was a mathematician who felt that Ptolemy's geocentric system was too complicated and failed to accord with the observed motions of the heavenly bodies (see the box on p. 576). Copernicus hoped that his heliocentric or sun-centered conception would offer a simpler, more accurate, and more elegant explanation for previously observed phenomena.

Using elaborate astronomical and mathematical calculations, Copernicus argued in his book that the universe consisted of eight spheres with the sun motionless at the center and the sphere of the fixed stars at rest in the eighth sphere. The planets revolved around the sun in the order of Mercury, Venus, the earth, Mars, Jupiter, and Saturn. The moon, however, revolved around the earth. Moreover, according to Copernicus, what appeared to be the movement of the sun and the fixed stars

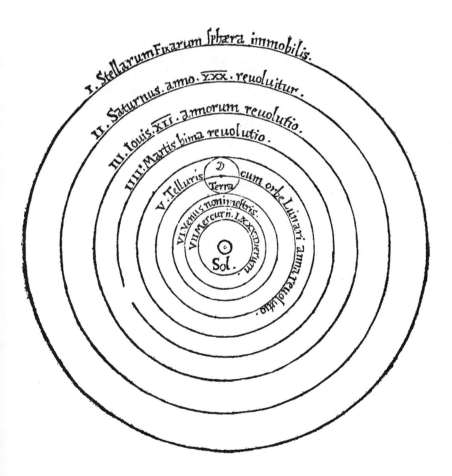

✦ **The Copernican System.** The Copernican system was presented in *On the Revolutions of the Heavenly Spheres*, published shortly before Copernicus's death. As shown in this illustration from the first edition of the book, Copernicus maintained that the sun was the center of the universe while the planets, including the earth, revolved around it. Moreover, the earth rotated daily on its axis.

Nicolaus Copernicus began a revolution in astronomy when he argued that it was the sun and not the earth that was at the center of the universe. Expecting controversy and scorn, Copernicus hesitated to publish the work in which he put forth his heliocentric theory. He finally relented, however, and managed to see a copy of it just before he died.

Nicolaus Copernicus, *On the Revolutions of the Heavenly Spheres*

For a long time, then, I reflected on this confusion in the astronomical traditions concerning the derivation of the motions of the universe's spheres. I began to be annoyed that the movements of the world machine, created for our sake by the best and most systematic Artisan of all, were not understood with greater certainty by the philosophers, who otherwise examined so precisely the most insignificant trifles of this world. For this reason I undertook the task of rereading the works of all the philosophers which I could obtain to learn whether anyone had ever proposed other motions of the universe's spheres than those expounded by the teachers of astronomy in the schools. And in fact first I found in Cicero that Hicetas supposed the earth to move. Later I also discovered in Plutarch that certain others were of this opinion. I have decided to set his words down here, so that they may be available to everybody:

> Some think that the earth remains at rest. But Philolaus the Pythagorean believes that, like the sun and moon, it revolves around the fire in an oblique circle. Heraclides

of Pontus and Ecphantus the Pythagorean make the earth move, not in a progressive motion, but like a wheel in a rotation from the west to east about its own center.

Therefore, having obtained the opportunity from these sources, I too began to consider the mobility of the earth. And even though the idea seemed absurd, nevertheless I knew that others before me had been granted the freedom to imagine any circles whatever for the purpose of explaining the heavenly phenomena. Hence I thought that I too would be readily permitted to ascertain whether explanations sounder than those of my predecessors could be found for the revolution of the celestial spheres on the assumption of some motion of the earth.

Having thus assumed the motions which I ascribe to the earth later on in the volume, by long and intense study I finally found that if the motions of the other planets are correlated with the orbiting of the earth, and are computed for the revolution of each planet, not only do their phenomena follow therefrom but also the order and size of all the planets and spheres, and heaven itself is so linked together that in no portion of it can anything be shifted without disrupting the remaining parts and the universe as a whole. . . .

Hence I feel no shame in asserting that this whole region engirdled by the moon, and the center of the earth, traverse this grand circle amid the rest of the planets in an annual revolution around the sun. Near the sun is the center of the universe. Moreover, since the sun remains stationary, whatever appears as a motion of the sun is really due rather to the motion of the earth.

around the earth was really explained by the daily rotation of the earth on its axis and the journey of the earth around the sun each year.

Copernicus, however, was basically conservative. He did not reject Aristotle's principle of the existence of heavenly spheres moving in circular orbits. As a result, when he put forth the calculations to prove his new theory, he retained Ptolemy's epicycles and wound up with a system almost as complicated as that of the Alexandrian astronomer.

Nevertheless, the shift from an earth-centered to a sun-centered system was significant and raised serious questions about Aristotle's astronomy and physics despite Copernicus's own adherence to Aristotle. It also seemed to create uncertainty about the human role in

the universe as well as God's location. Protestant reformers, adhering to a literal interpretation of Scripture, were the first to attack the new ideas. Martin Luther thundered against "the new astrologer who wants to prove that the earth moves and goes round. . . . The fool wants to turn the whole art of astronomy upside down. As Holy Scripture tells us, so did Joshua bid the sun stand still and not the earth." Luther's cohort at Wittenberg, Philip Melanchthon condemned Copernicus as well:

> The eyes are witness that the heavens revolve in the space of twenty-four hours. But certain men, either from the love of novelty, or to make a display of ingenuity, have concluded that the earth moves, and they maintain

that neither the eighth sphere [of the fixed stars] nor the sun revolves. . . . Now it is a want of honesty and decency to assert such notions publicly, and the example is pernicious. It is the part of a good mind to accept the truth as revealed by God and to acquiesce in it.[6]

The Catholic church remained silent for the time being; it did not denounce Copernicus until the work of Galileo appeared. The denunciation came at a time when an increasing number of astronomers were being attracted to Copernicus's ideas.

Brahe and Kepler

Copernicus did not have a great impact immediately, however—no revolution occurred overnight. Nevertheless, although most people were not yet ready to accept the theory of Copernicus, doubts about the Ptolemaic system were growing. The next step in destroying the geocentric conception and supporting the Copernican system was taken by Johannes Kepler. It has been argued, however, that Kepler's work would not have occurred without the material provided by Tycho Brahe.

Although Tycho Brahe (1546–1601) advanced a new model of the solar system based on a compromise between Copernicus and Ptolemy—the sun and planets revolved around the earth while the other planets revolved around the sun—his real fame rests on a less spectacular contribution. A Danish nobleman, Brahe was granted possession of an island near Copenhagen by King Frederick II. Here Brahe built the elaborate Uraniborg castle, which he outfitted with a library, observatories, and instruments he had designed for more precise astronomical observations. For twenty years, Brahe patiently concentrated on compiling a detailed record of his observations of the positions and movements of the stars and planets, a series of observations that have been described as the most accurate up to that time. This body of data led him to reject the Aristotelian-Ptolemaic system, but at the same time he was unable to accept Copernicus's suggestion that the earth actually moved. Brahe's last years were spent in Prague as imperial mathematician to Emperor Rudolf II, who took a keen interest in astronomy, astrology, and the Hermetic tradition. While he was in Prague, Brahe took on an assistant by the name of Johannes Kepler.

Johannes Kepler (1571–1630) had been destined by his parents for a career as a Lutheran minister. While studying theology at the university at Tübingen, however, he fell under the influence of Michael Mästlin, Germany's best-known astronomer, and spent much time pursuing his real interests, mathematics and as-

tronomy. He abandoned theology and became a teacher of mathematics and astronomy at Graz in Austria.

Kepler's work illustrates well the narrow line that often separated magic and science in the early Scientific Revolution. An avid astrologer, Kepler possessed a keen interest in Hermetic thought and Neoplatonic mathematical magic. In a book written in 1596, he elaborated upon his theory that the universe was constructed on the basis of geometric figures, such as the pyramid and the cube (see the box on p. 578). Believing that the harmony of the human soul (a divine attribute) was mirrored in the numerical relationships existing between the planets, he focused much of his attention upon discovering the "music of the spheres." Kepler was also a brilliant mathematician and astronomer and, after Brahe's death, succeeded him as imperial mathematician

◆ **Johannes Kepler.** Abandoning theology in favor of mathematics and astrology, Kepler was a key figure in the rise of the new astronomy. Building upon Tycho Brahe's vast astronomical data, Kepler discovered the three laws of planetary motion that both confirmed and modified the Copernican theory. They also eliminated the Ptolemaic-Aristotelian ideas of uniform circular motion and crystalline spheres moving in circular orbits.

Kepler and the Emerging Scientific Community

The exchange of letters between intellectuals was an important avenue for scientific communication. Through letters, they could provide practical assistance to each other as well as offer encouragement when their innovative work was received negatively. After receiving a copy of Johannes Kepler's first major work, the Italian Galileo Galilei wrote to Kepler, inaugurating a correspondence between them. This selection contains samples of their letters to each other as well as Kepler's letter to his teacher at Tübingen.

Galileo to Kepler, Padua, August 4, 1597

Your book, highly learned gentleman, which you sent me through Paulus Amberger, reached me not days ago but only a few hours ago, and as this Paulus just informed me of his return to Germany, I should think myself indeed ungrateful if I should not express to you my thanks by this letter. I thank you especially for having deemed me worthy of such a proof of your friendship. . . . So far I have read only the introduction, but have learned from it in some measure your intentions and congratulate myself on the good fortune of having found such a man as a companion in the exploration of truth. For it is deplorable that there are so few who seek the truth and do not pursue a wrong method of philosophizing. But this is not the place to mourn about the misery of our century but to rejoice with you about such beautiful ideas proving the truth. . . . I would certainly dare to approach the public with my ways of thinking if there were more people of your mind. As this is not the case, I shall refrain from doing so. . . . I shall always be at your service. Farewell, and do not neglect to give me further good news of yourself.

Yours in sincere friendship,
Galilaeus Galilaeus
Mathematician at the Academy of Padua

Kepler to Michael Mästlin, Graz, September 1597

. . . Lately I have sent two copies of my little book to Italy. They were received with gladness by a mathematician named Galileo Galilei, as he signs himself. He has also been attached for many years to the Copernican heresy.

Kepler to Galileo, Graz, October 13, 1597

I received your letter of August 4 on September 1. It was a double pleasure to me. First because I became friends with you, the Italian, and second because of the agreement in which we find ourselves concerning Copernican cosmography. As you invite me kindly at the end of your letter to enter into correspondence with you, and I myself feel greatly tempted to do so, I will not let pass the occasion of sending you a letter with the present young nobleman. For I am sure, if your time has allowed it, you have meanwhile obtained a closer knowledge of my book. And so a great desire has taken hold of me, to learn your judgment. For this is my way, to urge all those to whom I have written to express their candid opinion. Believe me, the sharpest criticism of one single understanding man means much more to me than the thoughtless applause of the great masses.

I would, however, have wished that you who have such a keen insight into everything would choose another way to reach your practical aims. By the strength of your personal example you advise us, in a cleverly veiled manner, to go out of the way of general ignorance and warn us against exposing ourselves to the furious attacks of the scholarly crowd. (In this you are following the lead of Plato and Pythagoras, our true masters.) But after the beginning of a tremendous enterprise has been made in our time, and furthered by so many learned mathematicians, and after the statement that the earth moves can no longer be regarded as something new, would it not be better to pull the rolling wagon to its destination with united effort. . . . For it is not only you Italians who do not believe that they move unless they feel it, but we in Germany, too, in no way make ourselves popular with this idea. Yet there are ways in which we protect ourselves against these difficulties. . . . Be of good cheer, Galileo, and appear in public. If I am not mistaken there are only a few among the distinguished mathematicians of Europe who would dissociate themselves from us. So great is the power of truth. If Italy seems less suitable for your publication and if you have to expect difficulties there, perhaps Germany will offer us more freedom. But enough of this. Please let me know, at least privately if you do not want to do so publicly, what you have discovered in favor of Copernicus.

to Rudolf II. There he gained possession of Brahe's detailed astronomical data and, using them, arrived at his three laws of planetary motion. These laws may have confirmed Kepler's interest in the "music of the spheres," but more importantly, they confirmed Copernicus's heliocentric theory while modifying it in some ways. Above all, they drove another nail into the coffin of the Aristotelian-Ptolemaic system.

Kepler published his first two laws of planetary motion in 1609. Although at Tübingen he had accepted Copernicus's heliocentric ideas, in his first law he rejected Copernicus by showing that the orbits of the planets around the sun were not circular but elliptical in shape with the sun at one focus of the ellipse rather than at the center. In his second law, he demonstrated that the speed of a planet is greater when it is closer to the sun and decreases as its distance from the sun increases. This proposition destroyed a fundamental Aristotelian tenet that Copernicus had shared—that the motion of the planets was steady and unchanging. Published ten years later, Kepler's third law established that the square of a planet's period of revolution is proportional to the cube of its average distance from the sun. In other words, planets with larger orbits revolve at a slower average velocity than those with smaller orbits.

Kepler's three laws effectively eliminated the idea of uniform circular motion as well as the idea of crystalline spheres revolving in circular orbits. The basic structure of the traditional Ptolemaic system had been disproved, and people had been freed to think in new terms of the actual paths of planets revolving around the sun in elliptical orbits. By the end of Kepler's life, the Ptolemaic system was rapidly losing ground to the new ideas. Important questions remained unanswered, however: What were the planets made of? And how does one explain motion in the universe? It was an Italian scientist who achieved the next important breakthrough to a new cosmology by answering the first question and making important strides toward answering the second.

Galileo

Galileo Galilei (1564–1642) came from a lesser noble Pisan family. Knowing that his son was obviously gifted, his father encouraged him to study medicine, which at that time was a financially rewarding career. Before long Galileo abandoned medicine for his true love, mathematics, and was soon teaching this subject, first at Pisa and later at Padua, one of the most prestigious universities in Europe.

Galileo was the first European to make systematic observations of the heavens by means of a telescope, thereby inaugurating a new age in astronomy. He had heard of a Flemish lens grinder who had created a "spyglass" that magnified objects seen at a distance and soon constructed his own after reading about it. Instead of peering at terrestrial objects, Galileo turned his telescope to the skies and made a remarkable series of discoveries: mountains and craters on the moon, four moons revolving around Jupiter, the phases of Venus, and sunspots. Galileo's observations seemed to destroy yet another aspect of the traditional cosmology in that the universe seemed to be composed of material sub-

◆ **Galileo's Sketch of the Phases of the Moon.** Galileo Galilei was the first European scientist to use a telescope in making systematic observations of the heavens. Galileo discovered mountains on the moon, sunspots, and the phases of Venus. Shown here are drawings of the moon from Galileo's notes for one of his books.

The Starry Messenger

The Italian Galileo Galilei was the first European to use a telescope to make systematic observations of the heavens. His observations, as reported in The Starry Messenger *in 1610, stunned European intellectuals by revealing that the celestial bodies were not perfect and immutable, as had been believed, but were apparently composed of material substance similar to the earth. In this selection, Galileo describes how he devised a telescope and what he saw with it.*

Galileo Galilei, *The Starry Messenger*

About ten months ago a report reached my ears that a certain Fleming had constructed a spyglass by means of which visible objects, though very distant from the eye of the observer, were distinctly seen as if nearby. Of this truly remarkable effect several experiences were related, to which some persons gave credence while others denied them. A few days later the report was confirmed to me in a letter from a noble Frenchman at Paris, Jacques Badovere, which caused me to apply myself wholeheartedly to inquire into the means by which I might arrive at the invention of a similar instrument. This I did shortly afterwards, my basis being the theory of refraction. First I prepared a tube of lead, at the ends of which I fitted two glass lenses, both plane on one side while on the other side one was spherically convex and the other concave. Then placing my eye near the concave lens I perceived objects satisfactorily large and near, for they appeared three times closer and nine times larger than when seen with the naked eye alone. Next I constructed another one, more accurate, which represented objects as enlarged more than sixty times. Finally, sparing neither labor nor expense, I succeeded in constructing for myself so excellent an instrument that objects seen by means of it appeared nearly one thousand times larger and over thirty times closer than when regarded without natural vision.

It would be superfluous to enumerate the number and importance of the advantages of such an instrument at sea as well as on land. But forsaking terrestrial observations, I turned to celestial ones, and first I saw the moon from as near at hand as if it were scarcely two terrestrial radii. After that I observed often with wondering delight both the planets and the fixed stars, and since I saw these latter to be very crowded, I began to seek (and eventually found) a method by which I might measure their distances apart. . . .

Now let us review the observations made during the past two months, once more inviting the attention of all who are eager for true philosophy to the first steps of such important contemplations. Let us speak first of that surface of the moon which faces us. For greater clarity I distinguish two parts of this surface, a lighter and a darker; the lighter part seems to surround and to pervade the whole hemisphere, while the darker part discolors the moon's surface like a kind of cloud, and makes it appear covered with spots. . . . From observation of these spots repeated many times I have been led to the opinion and conviction that the surface of the moon is not smooth, uniform, and precisely spherical as a great number of philosophers believe it (and the other heavenly bodies) to be, but is uneven, rough, and full of cavities and prominences, being not unlike the face of the earth, relieved by chains of mountains and deep valleys.

---

stance similar to that of the earth rather than ethereal or perfect and unchanging substance.

Galileo's revelations, published in *The Starry Messenger* in 1610, stunned his contemporaries and probably did more to make Europeans aware of the new picture of the universe than the mathematical theories of Copernicus and Kepler (see the box above). The English ambassador in Venice wrote to the chief minister of King James I in 1610:

> I send herewith unto His Majesty the strangest piece of news . . . that he has ever yet received from any part of the world; which is the annexed book of the Mathematical Professor at Padua [Galileo], who by the help of an optical instrument . . . has discovered four new planets rolling about the sphere of Jupiter. . . . So upon the whole subject he has first overthrown all former astronomy. . . . By the next ship your Lordship shall receive from me one of the above instruments [a telescope], as it is bettered by this man.[7]

During a trip to Rome, Galileo was received by cardinals and scholars as a conquering hero. Grand Duke Cosimo II of Florence offered him a new position as his court mathematician, which Galileo readily accepted. But even in the midst of his newfound acclaim, Galileo found himself increasingly suspect by the authorities of the Catholic church.

In *The Starry Messenger*, Galileo had revealed himself as a firm proponent of Copernicus's heliocentric system. Encouraged by the Dominicans, who held strongly to Aristotelian ideas, and the Jesuits, who feared that any dissension would weaken Catholicism in its struggle with Protestantism, the Roman Inquisition (or Holy Office) of the Catholic church condemned Copernicanism and ordered Galileo to reject the Copernican thesis. As one cardinal commented, "the intention of the Holy Spirit is to teach us not how the heavens go, but how to go to heaven." The report of the Inquisition ran: "That the doctrine that the sun was the center of the world and immovable was false and absurd, formally heretical and contrary to Scripture, whereas the doctrine that the earth was not the center of the world but moved, and has further a daily motion, was philosophically false and absurd and theologically at least erroneous."[8] Galileo was told, however, that he could continue to discuss Copernicanism as long as he maintained that it was not a fact but a mathematical supposition. It is apparent from the Inquisition's response that the church attacked the Copernican system because it threatened not only Scripture, but also an entire conception of the universe. The heavens were no longer a spiritual world, but a world of matter. Humans were no longer at the center and God was no longer in a specific place. The new system raised such uncertainties that it seemed prudent simply to condemn it.

Galileo, however, never really accepted his condemnation. In 1632, he published his most famous work, *Dialogue on the Two Chief World Systems: Ptolemaic and Copernican.* Unlike most scholarly treatises, it was written in Italian rather than Latin, making it more widely available to the public, which no doubt alarmed the church authorities. The work took the form of a dialogue among Simplicio, a congenial but somewhat stupid supporter of Aristotle and Ptolemy; Sagredo, an open-minded layman; and Salviati, a proponent of Copernicus's ideas. There is no question who wins the argument, and the *Dialogue* was quickly perceived as a defense of the Copernican system. Galileo was dragged once more before the Inquisition in 1633, found guilty of teaching the condemned Copernican system, and forced to recant his errors. Placed under house arrest on his estate near Florence, he spent the remaining eight years of his life studying mechanics, a field in which he made significant contributions.

One of the problems that fell under the heading of mechanics was the principle of motion. The Aristotelian conception, which dominated the late medieval world, held that an object remained at rest unless a force was applied against it. If a force was constantly exerted, then the object moved at a constant rate, but if it was removed, then the object stopped. This conception encountered some difficulties, especially with a projectile thrown out of a cannon. Late medieval theorists had solved this problem by arguing that the rush of air behind the projectile kept it in motion. The Aristotelian principle of motion also raised problems in the new Copernican system. In the Ptolemaic system, the concentric spheres surrounding the earth were weightless, but in the Copernican system, if a constant force had to be applied to objects to cause movement, then what power or force kept the heavy earth and other planets in motion?

Galileo made two contributions to the problem of motion. First, he demonstrated by experiments that if a uniform force was applied to an object, it would move at an accelerated speed rather than a constant speed. Moreover, Galileo discovered the principle of inertia when he argued that a body in motion continues in motion forever unless deflected by an external force. Thus, a state of uniform motion is just as natural as a state of rest. Before Galileo, natural philosophers had tried to explain motion; now their task was to explain changes in motion. Historians agree that Galileo's work on inertia was important, but differ on whether his work was merely the culmination of the medieval tradition or pointed the way to Newton's law of dynamics.

The condemnation of Galileo by the Inquisition seriously hampered further scientific work in Italy, which had been at the forefront of scientific innovation. Leadership in science now passed to the northern countries, especially England, France, and the Dutch Netherlands. By the 1630s and 1640s, no reasonable astronomer could deny that Galileo's discoveries combined with Kepler's mathematical laws had made nonsense of the Ptolemaic-Aristotelian world system and clearly established the reasonableness of the Copernican model. Despite Galileo's theories of dynamics, the problem of explaining motion in the universe and tying together the ideas of Copernicus, Galileo, and Kepler had not yet been done. This would be the work of an Englishman who has long been considered the greatest genius of the Scientific Revolution.

Newton

Born in the little English village of Woolsthorpe in 1642, the young Isaac Newton showed little brilliance until he attended Cambridge University and fell under the influence of the mathematician Isaac Barrow. Newton experienced his first great burst of creative energy in 1666 when the fear of plague closed Cambridge and forced him to return to Woolsthorpe for eighteen months. There Newton discovered his creative talents: "In those days I was in the prime of my life for invention and minded mathematics and philosophy more than at any time since."[9] During this period he invented the calculus, a mathematical means of calculating rates of change, began his investigations into the composition of light, and inaugurated his work on the law of universal gravitation. Two years after his return to Cambridge, in 1669, he accepted a chair of mathematics at the university. During a second intense period of creativity from 1684 to 1686, he wrote his famous *Principia* (see the box on p. 583). After a nervous breakdown in 1693, he sought and received an administrative post as warden of the royal mint and was advanced to master of the mint by 1699, a post he held until his death in 1727. Made president of the Royal Society (see The Scientific Societies later in this chapter) in 1703 and knighted in 1705 for his great achievements, Sir Isaac Newton wound up the only English scientist to be buried in Westminster Abbey.

Although Isaac Newton occupies a very special place in the history of modern science, we need to remember that he, too, remained extremely interested in aspects of the occult world. He left behind hundreds of manuscript pages of his studies of alchemy, and, in fact, his alchemical experiments were a major feature of his life until he moved to London in 1696 to become warden of the royal mint. The British economist John Maynard Keynes said of Newton after examining his manuscripts in 1936:

> Newton was not the first of the age of reason. He was the last of the magicians. . . . He looked on the whole universe and all that is in it as a riddle, as a secret which could be read by applying pure thought to certain evidence, certain mystic clues which God had laid about the world to allow a sort of philosopher's treasure hunt to the esoteric brotherhood. He believed that these clues were to be found partly in the evidence of the heavens and in the constitution of elements, . . . but also partly in certain papers and traditions handed down by the brethren in an unknown chain back to the original cryptic revelation in Babylonia.[10]

Although Newton may have considered himself a representative of the Hermetic tradition, he chose, it has been recently argued, for both political and psychological reasons to repress that part of his being, and it is as the "symbol of Western science" that Newton came to be viewed.

Newton's major work, the "hinge point of modern scientific thought," was his *Mathematical Principles of Natural Philosophy*, known simply as the *Principia* by the first word of its Latin title. In this work, the last, highly influential book in Europe to be written in Latin, Newton spelled out the mathematical proofs demonstrating his universal law of gravitation. Newton's work was the culmination of the theories of Copernicus, Kepler, and Galileo. While each had undermined some part of the Ptolemaic-Aristotelian cosmology, until Newton no one had pieced together a coherent synthesis for a new cosmology.

In the first book of the *Principia*, Newton defined the basis concepts of mechanics by elaborating the three laws of motion: every object continues in a state of rest or uniform motion in a straight line unless deflected by a force; the rate of change of motion of an object is proportional to the force acting upon it; and to every action there is always an equal and opposite reaction. In

◆ **Isaac Newton.** Pictured here is a portrait of Isaac Newton by Sir Godfrey Kneller. With a single law, that of universal gravitation, Newton was able to explain all motion in the universe. His great synthesis of the work of his predecessors created a new picture of the universe, one in which the universe was viewed as a great machine operating according to natural laws.

⇒ *Newton's Rules of Reasoning* ⇐

In 1687, Isaac Newton published his masterpiece, the Mathematical Principles of Natural Philosophy. In this work, Newton demonstrated the mathematical proofs for his universal law of gravitation and completed the new cosmology begun by Copernicus, Kepler, and Galileo. Newton's work demonstrated that the universe was one huge, regulated, and uniform machine operating according to natural laws. He also described the rules of reasoning by which he arrived at his universal law.

Isaac Newton, *Rules of Reasoning in Philosophy*

Rule 1
We are to admit no more causes of natural things than such as are both true and sufficient to explain their appearances.

To this purpose the philosophers say that Nature does nothing in vain, and more is in vain when less will serve; for Nature is pleased with simplicity, and affects not the pomp of superfluous causes.

Rule 2
Therefore to the same natural effects we must, as far as possible, assign the same causes.

As to respiration in a man and in a beast; the descent of stones in Europe and in America; the light of our culinary fire and of the sun; the reflection of light in the earth, and in the planets.

Rule 3
The qualities of bodies, which admit neither intensification nor remission of degrees, and which are found to belong to all bodies within the reach of our experiments, are to be esteemed the universal qualities of all bodies whatsoever.

For since qualities of bodies are only known to us by experiments, we are to hold for universal all such as universally agree with experiments; and such as are not liable to diminution can never be quite taken away.

Rule 4
In experimental philosophy we are to look upon propositions inferred by general induction from phenomena as accurately or very nearly true, notwithstanding any contrary hypotheses that may be imagined, till such time as other phenomena occur, by which they may either be made more accurate, or liable to exceptions.

This rule we must follow, that the argument of induction may not be evaded by hypotheses.

Book Three, Newton applied his theories of mechanics to the problems of astronomy by demonstrating that these three laws of motion govern the planetary bodies as well as terrestrial objects. Integral to his whole argument was the universal law of gravitation, which explained why the planetary bodies did not go off in straight lines but continued in elliptical orbits about the sun. In mathematical terms, Newton explained that every object in the universe was attracted to every other object with a force (that is, gravity) that is directly proportional to the product of their masses and inversely proportional to the square of the distances between them.

The implications of Newton's universal law of gravitation were enormous, even though it took another century before they were widely recognized. Newton had demonstrated that one universal law mathematically proved could explain all motion in the universe, from the movements of the planets in the celestial world to an apple falling from a tree in the terrestrial world. The secrets of the natural world could be known by human investigations. At the same time, the Newtonian synthesis created a new cosmology in which the world was seen largely in mechanistic terms. The universe was one huge, regulated, and uniform machine that operated according to natural laws in absolute time, space, and motion. Although Newton believed that God was "everywhere present" and acted as the force that moved all bodies on the basis of the laws he had discovered, later generations dropped his spiritual assumptions. Newton's world-machine, conceived as operating absolutely in time, space, and motion, dominated the Western worldview until the twentieth century, when the Einsteinian revolution based on a concept of relativity superseded the Newtonian mechanistic concept.

Newton's ideas were soon accepted in England, possibly out of national pride, conviction, and, as has been argued recently, for political reasons (see Science and Society later in this chapter). Natural philosophers on the continent resisted Newton's ideas, and it took much of the eighteenth century before they were generally accepted everywhere in Europe. They were also reinforced by developments in other fields, especially medicine.

Important Works of the Scientific Revolution

Copernicus, *On the Revolutions of the Heavenly Spheres*	1543
Vesalius, *On the Fabric of the Human Body*	1543
Galileo, *The Starry Messenger*	1610
Harvey, *On the Motion of the Heart and Blood*	1628
Galileo, *Dialogue on the Two Chief World Systems*	1632
Cavendish, *Grounds of Natural Philosophy*	1668
Newton, *Principia*	1687

Advances in Medicine

Although the Scientific Revolution of the sixteenth and seventeenth centuries is associated primarily with the dramatic changes in astronomy and mechanics that precipitated a new perception of the universe, a third field that had been dominated by Greek thought in the Late Middle Ages, that of medicine, also experienced a transformation. Late medieval medicine was dominated not by the teachings of Aristotle, but by those of the Greek physician Galen who had lived in the second century A.D.

Galen's influence on the medieval medical world was pervasive in anatomy, physiology, and disease. Galen had relied on animal, rather than human, dissection to arrive at a picture of human anatomy that was quite inaccurate in many instances. Even when Europeans began to practice human dissection in the Late Middle Ages, instruction in anatomy still relied on Galen. While a professor read a text of Galen, an assistant dissected a cadaver for illustrative purposes. Physiology or the functioning of the body was also dominated by Galenic hypotheses, including the belief that there were two separate blood systems. One controlled muscular activities and contained bright red blood moving upward and downward through the arteries; the other governed the digestive functions and contained dark red blood that ebbed and flowed in the veins.

Treatment of disease was highly influenced by Galen's doctrine of four bodily humors: blood, considered warm and moist; yellow bile, warm and dry; phlegm, cold and moist; and black bile, cold and dry. Since disease was supposedly the result of an imbalance of humors that could be discerned from the quantity and color of urine, the examination of a patient's urine became the chief diagnostic tool. Although purging and bleeding to remedy the imbalance were often harmful to patients, treatment with traditional herbal medicines sometimes proved beneficial.

Three figures are associated with the changes in medicine in the sixteenth and seventeenth centuries: Paracelsus, Andreas Vesalius, and William Harvey. Philippus Aureolus von Hohenheim (1493–1541), who renamed himself Paracelsus (or greater than Celsus, the ancient physician), was born in a small town near Zürich, the son of a country physician who dabbled in astrology. After leaving home at the age of fourteen, Paracelsus traveled widely and may have been awarded a medical degree from the University of Ferrara. He achieved a moment of glory when he was appointed city physician and professor of medicine at Basel in 1527. But this, like so many other appointments, proved short-lived due to his vanity, cantankerous nature, and quick temper. He could never disguise his contempt for universities and physicians who did not agree with his new ideas:

> I am *monarcha medicorum*, monarch of physicians, and I can prove to you what you cannot prove. . . . It was not the constellations that made me a physician: God made me . . . I need not don a coat of mail or a buckler against you, for you are not learned or experienced enough to refute even one word of mine. I wish I could protect my bald head against the flies as effectively as I can defend my monarchy. . . . Let me tell you this: every little hair on my neck knows more than you and all your scribes, and my shoebuckles are more learned than your Galen and Avicenna, and my beard has more experience than all your high colleges.[11]

Paracelsus was not easy to get along with, and he was forced to wander from one town to another until his death in 1541.

Paracelsus rejected the work of both Aristotle and Galen and attacked the universities as centers of their moribund philosophy. He and his followers hoped to replace the traditional system with a new chemical philosophy that was based upon a new understanding of nature derived from fresh observation and experiment. This chemical philosophy was, in turn, closely connected to a view of the universe based on the macrocosm-microcosm analogy. According to this view, a human being was a small replica (microcosm) of the larger world (macrocosm) about him. All parts of the universe were represented within each person. As Paracelsus said: "For the sun and the moon and all planets, as well as the stars and the whole chaos, are in man. . . . For what is outside is also inside; and what is not outside man is not inside. The outer and the inner are one thing."[12] In accordance with the macrocosmic-microcosmic principle, Paracelsus believed that the chemical reactions of the universe as a whole were reproduced in human beings on a smaller scale. Disease, then, was not caused by an imbalance of the four humors (as Galen had argued), but was due to chemical imbalances that were localized in specific organs and could be treated by chemical remedies.

Although others had used chemical remedies, Paracelsus and his followers differed from them in giving careful attention to the proper dosage of their chemically prepared metals and minerals. Gauging the proper amount was especially important because Paracelsus had turned against the Galenic principle that "contraries cure" in favor of the ancient Germanic folk principle that "like cures like." The poison that caused a disease would be its cure if used in proper form and quantity. This use of toxic substances to cure patients was, despite its apparent effectiveness (Paracelsus did have a strong reputation for actually curing his patients), viewed by Paracelsus's opponents as the practice of a "homicide Physician." Later generations came to view Paracelsus more favorably, and historians who have stressed Paracelsus's concept of disease and recognition of "new drugs" for medicine have viewed him as a father of modern medicine. Others have argued that his macrocosmic-microcosmic philosophy and use of "like cures like" drugs make him the forerunner of both homeopathy and the holistic medicine of the postmodern era.

Historians usually associate the name of Paracelsus with the diagnosis and treatment of disease. The new anatomy of the sixteenth century, however, was the work of Andreas Vesalius (1514–1564). His study of medicine at Paris involved him in the works of Galen, the great ancient authority. Especially important to him was a recently discovered text of Galen, *On Anatomical Procedures*, that led Vesalius to emphasize practical research as the principal avenue for understanding human anatomy. After receiving a doctorate in medicine at the University of Padua in 1536, he accepted a position there as professor of surgery. In 1543, he published his masterpiece, *On the Fabric of the Human Body*.

This book was based on his Paduan lectures, in which he deviated from traditional practice by personally

✦ Paracelsus. An extremely arrogant man, Paracelsus was one of the chief figures in the revision of late medieval medicine, which had been dominated by the ideas of the Greek physician Galen. Paracelsus embraced a chemical philosophy that held that disease was the result of chemical influences and could be treated by chemical remedies.

dissecting a body to illustrate what he was discussing. Vesalius's anatomical treatise presented a careful examination of the individual organs and general structure of the human body. The book would not have been feasible without both the artistic advances of the Renaissance and technical developments in the art of printing. Together, they made possible the creation of illustrations superior to any hitherto produced.

Vesalius's "hands-on" approach to teaching anatomy enabled him to overthrow some of Galen's most glaring errors. He did not hesitate, for example, to correct Galen's assertion that the great blood vessels originated from the liver since his own observations made it apparent that they came from the heart. Nevertheless, Vesalius still clung to a number of Galen's erroneous assertions, including the Greek physician's ideas on the ebb and flow of two kinds of blood in the veins and arteries. It was not until William Harvey's work on the circulation of the blood that this Galenic misperception was corrected.

William Harvey (1578–1657) attended Cambridge University and later Padua where he received a doctorate of medicine in 1602. Appointed physician to St. Bartholomew's Hospital in 1609, he later became physician to King James I and Charles I. His reputation, however, rests upon his book, *On the Motion of the Heart and Blood,* published in 1628.

Although questions had been raised in the sixteenth century about Galen's physiological principles, no major break from his system had occurred. Harvey's work, which was based upon meticulous observations and experiments, led him to demolish the ancient Greek's work. Harvey demonstrated that the heart and not the liver was the beginning point of the circulation of blood in the body, that the same blood flows in both veins and arteries, and, most importantly, that the blood makes a complete circuit as it passes through the body. Although Harvey's work dealt a severe blow to Galen's theories, his ideas did not begin to achieve general recognition until the 1660s, when the capillaries, which explained how the body's blood passed from the arteries to the veins, were discovered. Harvey's theory of the circulation of the blood laid the foundation for modern physiology.

$\mathcal{W}$omen in the Origins of Modern Science

During the Middle Ages, except for members of religious orders, women who sought a life of learning were severely hampered by the traditional attitude that a woman's proper role was as a daughter, wife, and mother. But in the late fourteenth and early fifteenth centuries, new opportunities for elite women emerged as enthusiasm for the new secular learning called humanism encouraged Europe's privileged and learned men to encourage women to read and study classical and Christian texts. The daughters and sisters of prominent Christian humanists, for example, were known for their learning. In northern Italy, a number of educated families allowed their young women to pursue a life of scholarship. The ideal of a humanist education for some of the daughters of Europe's elite persisted into the seventeenth century, but only for some privileged women.

In the same fashion as they were drawn to humanism, women were also attracted to the Scientific Revolution.

Unlike females educated formally in humanist schools, women attracted to science had to obtain a largely informal education. Female contributions to science were even more remarkable when we consider that women were largely excluded from universities and the new scientific societies. This was not quite the handicap that it would be today, however. Since science in the seventeenth century was not the preserve of universities, there was often no real dividing line between popular science and professional science, creating chances for women to enter scientific circles. Opportunities for women as well as alternatives to formal humanistic education could often be found in aristocratic and princely courts and in artisan workshops.

European nobles had the leisure and resources that gave them easy access to the world of learning. This door was also open to noblewomen who could participate in the informal scientific networks of their fathers and brothers. One of the most prominent female scientists of the seventeenth century, Margaret Cavendish (1623–1673), came from an aristocratic background. Cavendish was not a popularizer of science for women but a participant in the crucial scientific debates of her time. She also corresponded with important people on these issues. Despite her achievements, however, she was excluded from membership in the Royal Society (see The Scientific Societies later in this chapter), although she was once allowed to attend a meeting. She wrote a number of works on scientific matters including *Observations upon Experimental Philosophy* and *Grounds of Natural Philosophy.* In these works she did not hesitate to attack what she considered the defects of the rationalist and empiricist approaches to scientific knowledge and was especially critical of the growing belief that through science humans would be masters of nature: "We have no power at all over natural causes and effects. . . . for man is but a small part, . . . his powers are but particular actions of Nature, and he cannot have a supreme and absolute power."[13]

As an aristocrat, the duchess of Cavendish was a good example of the women in France and England who worked in science. Women interested in science who lived in Germany came from a different background. There the tradition of female participation in craft production enabled some women to become involved in observational science, especially entomology and astronomy. Between 1650 and 1710, 14 percent of all German astronomers were women.

A good example of female involvement in the Scientific Revolution stemming from the craft tradition was Maria Sibylla Merian (1647–1717), who had established a reputation as an important entomologist by the beginning of the eighteenth century. Merian's training came from working in her father's workshop where she learned the art of illustration, a training of great importance since her exact observation of insects and plants was only demonstrated through the superb illustrations she made. Her first work was the *Wonderful Metamorphosis and Special Nourishment of Caterpillars*, an illustrated study of caterpillars showing every stage in their development, which she had carefully observed and rendered in her drawings. In 1699, she undertook an expedition into the wilds of the Dutch colony of Surinam to collect and draw samples of plants and insect life. This led to her major scientific work, the *Metamorphosis of the Insects of Surinam*, in which she used sixty illustrations to show the reproductive and developmental cycles of Surinam's insect life.

The craft organization of astronomy also gave women opportunities to become involved in science. Those who did worked in family observatories; hence, daughters and wives received training as apprentices to fathers or husbands. The most famous of the female astronomers in Germany was Maria Winkelmann (1670–1720). She was educated by her father and uncle and received advanced training in astronomy from a nearby self-taught astronomer. Her opportunity to be a practicing astronomer came when she married Gottfried Kirch, Germany's foremost astronomer. She became his assistant at the astronomical observatory operated in Berlin by the Academy of Science. She made some original contributions, including a hitherto undiscovered comet, as her husband related:

> Early in the morning (about 2:00 A.M.) the sky was clear and starry. Some nights before, I had observed a variable star, and my wife (as I slept) wanted to find and see it for herself. In so doing, she found a comet in the sky. At which time she woke me, and I found that it was indeed a comet ... I was surprised that I had not seen it the night before.[14]

Moreover, Winkelmann corresponded with the famous scientist Gottfried Leibniz (who invented the calculus independently of Newton), who praised her effusively as "a most learned woman who could pass as a rarity." When her husband died in 1710, she applied for a position as assistant astronomer for which she was highly qualified. As a woman—with no university degree—she was denied the post by the Berlin Academy, which feared that it would establish a precedent by hiring a woman ("mouths would gape"). Winkelmann

managed, nevertheless, to continue her astronomical work a while longer at the private observatory of Baron Friederich von Krosigk in Berlin.

Winkelmann's difficulties with the Berlin Academy reflect the obstacles women faced in being accepted in scientific work, which was considered a male preserve. Although no formal statutes excluded women from membership in the new scientific societies, no woman was invited to join either the Royal Society of England or the French Academy of Sciences until the twentieth century. All of these women scientists were exceptional women since a life devoted to any kind of scholarship was still viewed as being at odds with the domestic duties women were expected to perform.

The nature and value of women had been the subject of an ongoing, centuries-long debate known as the *querelles des femmes*—arguments about women. Male opinions in the debate were largely a carryover from medieval times and were not favorable. Women were portrayed as inherently base, prone to vice, easily swayed, and "sexually insatiable." Hence, men needed to control them. Learned women were viewed as having overcome female liabilities to become like men. One man in praise of a woman scholar remarked that her writings were so good that you "would hardly believe they were done by a woman at all."

In the early modern era, women joined this debate by arguing against these male images of women. They argued that women also had rational minds and could grow from education. Further, since most women were pious, chaste, and temperate, there was no need for male authority over them. These female defenders of women in the *querelles des femmes* emphasized education as the key to women's ability to move into the world. How, then, did the era of the Scientific Revolution affect this debate over the nature of women? As an era of intellectual revolution in which traditional authorities were being overthrown, we might expect significant change in men's views of women. But by and large, instead of becoming an instrument for liberation, science was used to find new support for the old, traditional views about a woman's place in the scheme of things. This was done in a variety of ways.

One approach is evident in the work of William Harvey who was renowned for his work on the circulation of the blood. In his 1651 book on human reproduction, he argued that a woman provided "matter" but it was the man who gave it life and form from his semen. Harvey regarded semen as the active agent, and in his view it was so powerful that it was "vivifying, endowed with force and spirit and generative influence." By the end of the century, however, some scientists were arguing that males and females influenced the generative process equally. Likewise, new views on anatomy also appeared, but interestingly enough were used to perpetuate old stereotypes about women.

From the work of Galen until late in the sixteenth century, the male and female genitals had been portrayed as not significantly different. The uterus, for example, had been pictured as an internal and inadequate penis. According to Galen, "All parts that men have, women have too . . . the difference between them lies in only one thing . . . that in women the parts are within the body, whereas in men they are outside."[15] But this perspective was radically reevaluated in the seventeenth century, and the uterus was now presented as a perfect instrument for childbearing. It was not long before this view was used to reinforce the traditional argument that women were designed for their role as bearer of their husband's children.

An important project in the new anatomy of the sixteenth centuries was the attempt to illustrate the human body and skeleton. For Vesalius, the portrayal of physical differences between males and females was limited to external bodily form (the outlines of the body) and the sexual organs. Vesalius saw no difference in skeletons and portrayed them as the same for men and women. It was not until the eighteenth century, in fact, that a new anatomy finally prevailed. Drawings of female skeletons between 1730 and 1790 varied, but females tended to have a larger pelvic area, and, in some instances, female skulls were portrayed as smaller than those of males. Eighteenth-century studies on the anatomy and physiology of sexual differences provided "scientific evidence" to reaffirm the traditional inferiority of women. The larger pelvic area "proved" that women were meant to be childbearers while the larger skull "demonstrated" the superiority of the male mind. Male-dominated science had been used to "prove" male social dominance.

At the same time, during the seventeenth and eighteenth centuries, women even lost the traditional spheres of influence they had possessed, especially in the science-related art of midwifery. Women serving as midwives had traditionally been responsible for birthing. Similar to barber-surgeons or apothecaries (see Chapter 18), midwives had acquired their skills through apprenticeship. But the impact of the Scientific Revolution caused traditional crafts to be upgraded and then even professionalized as males took over. When medical men entered this arena, they also began to use devices and techniques derived from the study of anatomy. These were increasingly used to justify the male takeover of the traditional role of midwives. By the end of the eighteenth century, midwives were simply accessories to the art they had once controlled, except for the poor. Since little money was to be made in serving them, midwives were allowed to continue to practice their traditional art for the lower classes.

Overall the Scientific Revolution reaffirmed traditional ideas about women's nature. Male scientists used the new science to spread the view that women were inferior by nature, subordinate to men, and suited by nature to play a domestic role as nurturing mothers. The widespread distribution of books ensured the continuation of these ideas (see the box on p. 589). Jean de La Bruyère, the seventeenth-century French moralist, was typical when he remarked that an educated woman was like a gun that was a collector's item "which one shows to the curious, but which has no use at all, any more than a carousel horse."[16]

Toward a New Earth: Descartes, Rationalism, and a New View of Humankind

The fundamentally new conception of the universe contained in the cosmological revolution of the sixteenth and seventeenth centuries inevitably had an impact on the Western view of humankind. Nowhere is this more evident than in the work of René Descartes (1596–1650), an extremely important figure in Western history. Descartes began by reflecting the doubt and uncertainty that seemed pervasive in the confusion of the seventeenth century and ended with a philosophy that dominated Western thought until the twentieth century.

René Descartes was born into a family of the French lower nobility. After a Jesuit education, he studied law at Poitiers but traveled to Paris to study by himself. As far as can be deduced, he spent much of this period absorbed in the skeptical works of Montaigne. In 1618, at the beginning of the Thirty Years' War, Descartes volunteered for service in the army of Maurice of Nassau, but his motives seem to have been guided less by the desire for military action than for travel and leisure time to think. On the night of November 10, 1619, Descartes underwent what one historian has called an experience comparable to the "ecstatic illumination of the mystic." Having perceived in one night the outlines of a new rational-mathematical system,

The "Natural" Inferiority of Women

Despite the shattering of old views and the emergence of a new worldview in the Scientific Revolution of the seventeenth century, attitudes toward women remained tied to traditional perspectives. In this selection, the philosopher Benedict de Spinoza argues for the "natural" inferiority of women to men.

Benedict de Spinoza, *A Political Treatise*

But, perhaps, someone will ask, whether women are under men's authority by nature or institution? For if it has been by mere institution, then we had no reason compelling us to exclude women from government. But if we consult experience itself, we shall find that the origin of it is in their weakness. For there has never been a case of men and women reigning together, but wherever on the earth men are found, there we see that men rule, and women are ruled, and that on this plan, both sexes live in harmony. But on the other hand, the Amazons, who are reported to have held rule of old, did not suffer men to stop in their country, but reared only their female children, killing the males to whom they gave birth. But if by nature women were equal to men, and were equally distinguished by force of character and ability, in which human power and therefore human right chiefly consist; surely among nations so many and different some would be found, where both sexes rule alike, and others, where men are ruled by women, and so brought up, that they can make less use of their abilities. And since this is nowhere the case, one may assert with perfect propriety, that women have not by nature equal right with men: but that they necessarily give way to men, and that thus it cannot happen, that both sexes should rule alike, much less that men should be ruled by women. But if we further reflect upon human passions, how men, in fact, generally love women merely from the passion of lust, and esteem their cleverness and wisdom in proportion to the excellence of their beauty, and also how very ill-disposed men are to suffer the women they love to show any sort of favor to others, and other facts of this kind, we shall easily see that men and women cannot rule alike without great hurt to peace.

---

with a sense of divine approval he made a new commitment to mind, mathematics, and a mechanical universe. For the rest of his life, Descartes worked out the details of his vision.

The starting point for Descartes's new system was doubt, as he explained at the beginning of his most famous work, *Discourse on Method*, written in 1637:

> From my childhood I have been familiar with letters; and as I was given to believe that by their means a clear and assured knowledge can be acquired of all that is useful in life, I was extremely eager for instruction in them. As soon, however, as I had completed the course of study, at the close of which it is customary to be admitted into the order of the learned, I entirely changed my opinion. For I found myself entangled in so many doubts and errors that, as it seemed to me, the endeavor to instruct myself had served only to disclose to me more and more of my ignorance.[17]

Descartes decided to set aside all that he had learned and begin again. Having rejected the senses, since they easily deceived, one fact seemed to Descartes beyond doubt—his own existence:

> But I immediately became aware that while I was thus disposed to think that all was false, it was absolutely necessary that I who thus thought should be something; and noting that this truth *I think, therefore I am*, was so steadfast and so assured that the suppositions of the skeptics, to whatever extreme they might all be carried, could not avail to shake it, I concluded that I might without scruple accept it as being the first principle of the philosophy I was seeking.[18]

With this emphasis on the mind, Descartes asserted that he would accept only those things that his reason said were true.

From his first postulate, Descartes deduced two additional principles, the existence of God and the separation of mind and matter. Since he—an imperfect being—had conceived of the idea of perfection, it could only have come from a perfect being, that is, God:

> And since it is no less contradictory that the more perfect should result from, and depend on, the less perfect than that something should proceed from nothing, it is equally impossible I should receive it from myself. Thus we are committed to the conclusion that it has been placed in

♦ **Descartes with Queen Christina of Sweden.** René Descartes was one of the primary figures in the Scientific Revolution. Claiming to use reason as his sole guide to truth, Descartes posited a sharp distinction between mind and matter. He is shown here, standing to the right of Queen Christina of Sweden. The queen had a deep interest in philosophy and invited Descartes to her court.

me by a nature which is veritably more perfect than I am, and which has indeed within itself all the perfections of which I have any idea, that is to say, in a single word, that is God.[19]

Secondly, Descartes argued that since "the mind cannot be doubted but the body and material world can, the two must be radically different." From this came an absolute dualism between mind and body, or what has also been called Cartesian dualism.

According to Descartes, the universe contains two things, both of which God has created. One is thinking substance, what we call the mind. It is essentially spiritual and not composed of matter. Everything in the universe except the thinking substance or mind is extended substance, what we call matter. The material world is the most fundamental thing in the universe and displays two primary characteristics: extension (it occupies space) and motion (it moves). Using mind or human reason, the path to certain knowledge, and its best instrument, mathematics, humans can understand the material world because it is pure mechanism, a machine that is governed by its own physical laws because it was created by God—the great geometrician.

Descartes's conclusions about the nature of the universe and human beings had important implications. His separation of mind and matter allowed scientists to view matter as dead or inert, as something that was totally separate from themselves and could be investigated independently by reason. The split between mind and body led Westerners to equate their identity with mind and reason rather than with the whole organism. Descartes has rightly been called the father of modern rationalism (see the box on p. 591). His books were placed on the papal Index of Forbidden Books and condemned by many Protestant theologians. The radical Cartesian split between mind and matter, and between mind and body, had devastating implications not only for traditional religious views of the universe, but for how Westerners viewed themselves.

The Scientific Method

In the course of the Scientific Revolution, attention was also paid to the problem of establishing the proper means to examine and understand the physical realm. This development of a scientific method was crucial to the evolution of science in the modern world.

Curiously enough, it was an Englishman with few scientific credentials who attempted to put forth a new method of acquiring knowledge that made an impact on the Royal Society in England in the seventeenth century and other European scientists in the eighteenth century. Francis Bacon (1561–1626), a lawyer and lord chancellor, rejected Copernicus and Kepler and misunderstood Galileo. And yet in his unfinished work, *The Great Instauration* (*The Great Restoration*), he called for his contemporaries "to commence a total reconstruction of sciences, arts, and all human knowledge, raised upon the proper foundations." According to Bacon, two attitudes had held people back from this project. Some men had foolishly continued to rely on the ancients, especially Aristotle: "And for its value and utility it must be plainly avowed that that wisdom which we have derived principally from the Greeks is but like the boyhood of knowledge, and has the characteristic property of boys: it can talk, but it cannot generate; for it is fruitful of controversies but barren of works." Equally harmful was the attitude that it was beyond "the powers of man" to understand what God had created in the world. Bacon

⧽ The Father of Modern Rationalism ⧼

René Descartes has long been viewed as the founder of modern rationalism and modern philosophy because he believed that human beings could understand the world—itself a mechanical system—by the same rational principles inherent in mathematical thinking. In his Discourse on Method, *he elaborated upon his approach to discovering truth.*

René Descartes, *Discourse on Method*

In place of the numerous precepts which have gone to constitute logic, I came to believe that the four following rules would be found sufficient, always provided I took the firm and unswerving resolve never in a single instance to fail in observing them.

The first was to accept nothing as true which I did not evidently know to be such, that is to say, scrupulously to avoid precipitance and prejudice, and in the judgments I passed to include nothing additional to what had presented itself to my mind so clearly and so distinctly that I could have no occasion for doubting it.

The second, to divide each of the difficulties I examined into as many parts as may be required for its adequate solution.

The third, to arrange my thoughts in order, beginning with things the simplest and easiest to know, so that I may then ascend little by little, as it were step by step, to the knowledge of the more complex, and in doing so, to assign an order of thought even to those objects which are not of themselves in any such order of precedence.

And the last, in all cases to make enumerations so complete, and reviews so general, that I should be assured of omitting nothing.

Those long chains of reasonings, each step simple and easy, which geometers are wont to employ in arriving even at the most difficult of their demonstrations, have led me to surmise that all the things we human beings are competent to know are interconnected in the same manner, and that none are so remote as to be beyond our reach or so hidden that we cannot discover them—that is, provided we abstain from accepting as true what is not thus related, i.e., keep always to the order required for their deduction one from another. And I had no great difficulty in determing what the objects are with which I should begin, for that I already knew, namely, that it was with the simplest and easiest. Bearing in mind, too, that of all those who in time past have sought for truth in the sciences, the mathematicians alone have been able to find any demonstrations, that is to say, any reasons which are certain and evident, I had no doubt that it must have been by a procedure of this kind that they had obtained them.

---

did not doubt humans' ability to know the natural world, but believed that they had proceeded incorrectly: "The entire fabric of human reason which we employ in the inquisition of nature is badly put together and built up, and like some magnificent structure without foundation."

Bacon's new foundation—a correct scientific method—was to be built upon inductive principles. Rather than beginning with assumed first principles from which logical conclusions could be deduced, he urged scientists to proceed from the particular to the general. From carefully organized experiments and thorough, systematic observations, correct generalizations could be developed. Bacon's method—to seek knowledge by experiment and observation—has frequently been criticized for emphasizing the empirical, experimental side while lacking any foundation in mathematics and intuition.

Bacon was clear about what he believed his method could accomplish. His concern was more for practical than for pure science. He stated that "the true and lawful goal of the sciences is none other than this: that human life be endowed with new discoveries and power." He wanted science to contribute to the "mechanical arts" by creating devices that would benefit industry, agriculture, and trade. Bacon was prophetic when he said that "I am laboring to lay the foundation, not of any sect or doctrine, but of human utility and power." And how would this "human power" be used? To "conquer nature in action."[20] The control and domination of nature became a central proposition of modern science and the technology that accompanied it. Only in the twentieth century have some scientists asked whether this assumption might not be at the heart of the twentieth-century ecological crisis.

René Descartes proposed a different approach to scientific methodology by emphasizing deduction and mathematical logic. As Descartes explained in *Discourse on Method*, each step in an argument should be as sharp and well founded as a mathematical proof:

These long chains of reasonings which geometers are accustomed to using to reach their most difficult demonstrations, had given me cause to imagine that everything which can be encompassed by man's knowledge is linked in the same way, and that provided only that one abstains from accepting any for true which is not true, and that one always keeps the right order for one thing to be deduced from that which precedes it, there can be nothing so distant that one does not reach it eventually, or so hidden that one cannot discover it.[21]

Descartes believed then that one could start with self-evident truths, comparable to geometrical axioms, and deduce more complex conclusions. His emphasis on deduction and mathematical order complemented Bacon's stress on experiment and induction. It was Sir Isaac Newton who synthesized them into a single scientific methodology by uniting Bacon's empiricism with Descartes's rationalism. This scientific method began with systematic observations and experiments, which were used to arrive at general concepts. New deductions derived from these general concepts could then be tested and verified by precise experiments.

The scientific method, of course, was valuable in answering the question "how" something works, and its success in doing this gave others much confidence in the method. It did not attempt to deal with the question of "why" something happens or the purpose and meaning behind the world of nature. This allowed religion still to be important in the seventeenth century.

Science and Religion in the Seventeenth Century

In Galileo's struggle with the inquisitorial Holy Office of the Catholic church, we see the beginning of the conflict between science and religion that has marked the history of modern Western civilization and ultimately led to much grief for the organized religions. Since time immemorial, theology had seemed to be the queen of the sciences. It was natural that the churches would continue to believe that religion was the final measure of all things. To the emerging scientists, however, it often seemed that theologians knew not of what they spoke. These "natural philosophers" then tried to draw lines between the knowledge of religion and the knowledge of "natural philosophy" or nature. Galileo had clearly felt that it was unnecessary to pit science against religion:

In discussions of physical problems we ought to begin not from the authority of scriptural passages, but from sense-experiences and necessary demonstrations; for the holy Bible and the phenomena of nature proceed alike from the divine word, the former as the dictate of the Holy Ghost and the latter as the observant executrix of God's commands. It is necessary for the Bible, in order to be accommodated to the understanding of every man, to speak many things which appear to differ from the absolute truth so far as the bare meaning of the words is concerned. But Nature, on the other hand, is inexorable and immutable; she never transgresses the laws imposed upon her, or cares a whit whether her abstruse reasons and methods of operation are understandable to men.[22]

To Galileo it made little sense for the church to determine the nature of physical reality on the basis of biblical texts that were subject to radically divergent interpretations. The church, however, decided otherwise in Galileo's case and lent its great authority to one scientific theory, the Ptolemaic-Aristotelian cosmology, no doubt because it fit so well with its own philosophical views of reality. But the church's decision had tremendous consequences, just as the rejection of Darwin's ideas did in the nineteenth century. For educated individuals, it established a dichotomy between scientific investigations and religious beliefs. As the scientific beliefs triumphed, it became almost inevitable that religious beliefs would suffer, leading to a growing secularization in European intellectual life, precisely what the church had hoped to combat by opposing Copernicanism. Many seventeenth-century intellectuals were both religious and scientific and believed that the implications of this split would be tragic. Some believed that the split was largely unnecessary while others felt the need to combine God, humans, and a mechanistic universe into a new philosophical synthesis. Two individuals—Spinoza and Pascal—illustrate some of the wide diversity in the response of European intellectuals to the implications of the cosmological revolution of the seventeenth century.

Benedict de Spinoza (1632–1677) was a philosopher who grew up in the relatively tolerant atmosphere of Amsterdam. He was excommunicated from the Amsterdam synagogue at the age of twenty-four for rejecting the tenets of Judaism. Ostracized by the local Jewish community and major Christian churches alike, Spinoza lived a quiet, independent life, earning a living by grinding optical lenses and refusing to accept an academic position in philosophy at the University of Heidelberg for fear of compromising his freedom of thought. Spinoza read a great deal of the new scientific literature and was influenced by Descartes.

Although he followed Descartes's rational approach to knowledge, Spinoza was unwilling to accept the implications of Descartes's ideas, especially the separation of mind and matter and the apparent separation of an infinite God from the finite world of matter. God was not simply creator of the universe, he was the universe. All that is is in God, and nothing can be apart from God. This philosophy of pantheism (others have labeled it panentheism or monism) was set out in Spinoza's book, *Ethics Demonstrated in the Geometrical Manner,* which was not published until after his death.

To Spinoza, human beings are not "situated in nature as a kingdom within a kingdom," but are as much a part of God or nature or the universal order as other natural objects. The failure to understand God had led to many misconceptions; for one, that nature exists only for one's use:

> As they find in themselves and outside themselves many means which assist them not a little in their search for what is useful, for instance, eyes for seeing, teeth for chewing, herbs and animals for yielding food, the sun for giving light, the sea for breeding fish, they come to look on the whole of nature as a means for obtaining such conveniences.[23]

Furthermore, unable to find any other cause for the existence of these things, they attributed them to a creator-God who must be worshiped to gain their ends: "Hence also it follows, that everyone thought out for himself, according to his abilities, a different way of worshiping God, so that God might love him more than his fellows, and direct the whole course of nature for the satisfaction of his blind cupidity and insatiable avarice." Then, when nature appeared unfriendly in the form of storms, earthquakes, and diseases, "they declared that such things happen, because the gods are angry at some wrong done them by men, or at some fault committed in their worship," rather than realizing "that good and evil fortunes fall to the lot of pious and impious alike."[24] Likewise, human beings made moral condemnations of others since they failed to understand that human emotions, "passions of hatred, anger, envy and so, considered in themselves, follow from the same necessity and efficacy of nature" and "nothing comes to pass in nature in contravention to her universal laws." To explain human emotions, like everything else, we need to analyze them as we would the movements of planets: "I shall, therefore, treat of the nature and strength of my emotions according to the same method as I employed heretofore in my investigations concerning God and the mind. I shall consider human actions and desires in exactly the same manner as though I were concerned with lines, planes, and solids."[25] Everything has a ratio-

nal explanation and humans are capable of finding it. In using reason, people can find true happiness. Their real freedom comes when they understand the order and necessity of nature and achieve detachment from passing interests.

Spinoza's complex synthesis of God, humans, and the universe was not easily accepted by his contemporaries, and his pantheism was mistakenly condemned as "hideous atheism." Others were upset by his attitude toward morality since he viewed it as found in nature and known by reason, not revealed to people through the Bible. Even Spinoza declared that some would find strange his attempt to treat of human desires "in exactly the same manner as though I were concerned with lines, planes, and solids."

Blaise Pascal (1623–1662) was a French scientist who sought to keep science and religion united. He had a brief, but checkered career. He was for a short time a reader of Montaigne and a companion of freethinkers. He was an accomplished scientist and brilliant mathematician, who excelled at both the practical, by inventing a calculating machine, and the abstract, by

✦ **Pascal.** Blaise Pascal was a brilliant scientist and mathematician who hoped to keep science and Christianity united. In the *Pensées,* he made a passionate argument on behalf of the Christian religion. He is pictured here in a posthumous portrait by Quesnel.

❧ Pascal: "What Is a Man in the Infinite?" ❧

Perhaps no intellectual in the seventeenth century gave greater expression to the uncertainties generated by the cosmological revolution than Blaise Pascal. Himself a scientist, Pascal's mystical vision of God's presence caused him to pursue religious truths with a passion. His work, the Pensées, *consisted of notes for a larger, unfinished work justifying the Christian religion. In this selection, Pascal presents his musings on the human place in an infinite world.*

Blaise Pascal, *Pensées*

Let man then contemplate the whole of nature in her full and exalted majesty. Let him turn his eyes from the lowly objects which surround him. Let him gaze on that brilliant light set like an eternal lamp to illumine the Universe; let the earth seem to him a dot compared with the vast orbit described by the sun, and let him wonder at the fact that this vast orbit itself is no more than a very small dot compared with that described by the stars in their revolutions around the firmament. But if our vision stops here, let the imagination pass on; it will exhaust its powers of thinking long before nature ceases to supply it with material for thought. All this visible world is no more than an imperceptible speck in nature's ample bosom. No idea approaches it. We may extend our conceptions beyond all imaginable space; yet produce only atoms in comparison with the reality of things. It is an infinite sphere, the center of which is everywhere, the circumference nowhere. In short, it is the greatest perceptible mark of God's almighty power that our imagination should lose itself in that thought.

Returning to himself, let man consider what he is compared with all existence; let him think of himself as lost in his remote corner of nature; and from this little dungeon in which he finds himself lodged—I mean the Universe—let him learn to set a true value on the earth, its kingdoms, and cities, and upon himself. What is a man in the infinite? . . .

For, after all, what is a man in nature? A nothing in comparison with the infinite, an absolute in comparison with nothing, a central point between nothing and all. Infinitely far from understanding these extremes, the end of things and their beginning are hopelessly hidden from him in an impenetrable secret. He is equally incapable of seeing the nothingness from which he came, and the infinite in which he is engulfed. What else then will he perceive but some appearance of the middle of things, in an eternal despair of knowing either their principle or their purpose? All things emerge from nothing and are borne onward to infinity. Who can follow this marvelous process? The Author of these wonders understands them. None but He can.

---

devising a theory of chance or probability and doing work on conic sections. After a profound mystical vision on the night of November 23, 1654, which assured him that God cared for the human soul, he devoted the rest of his life to religious matters. He planned to write an "Apology for the Christian Religion" but died before he could do so. He did leave a set of notes for the larger work, however, which in published form became known as *Pensées* or *The Thoughts*.

In the *Pensées*, Pascal tried to convert rationalists to Christianity by appealing both to their reason and to their emotions. Humans were, he argued, frail creatures, often deceived by their senses, misled by reason, and battered by their emotions. And yet they were beings whose very nature involved thinking: "Man is but a reed, the weakest in nature; but he is a thinking reed. . . . Our whole dignity consists, therefore, in thought. By thought we must raise ourselves. . . . Let us endeavor, then, to think well; this is the beginning of morality."[26]

Pascal was determined to show that the Christian religion was not contrary to reason: "If we violate the principles of reason, our religion will be absurd, and it will be laughed at." Christianity, he felt, was the only religion that recognized people's true state of being as both vulnerable and great. To a Christian, a human being was both fallen and at the same time God's special creation. But it was not necessary to emphasize one at the expense of the other—to view humans as only rational or only hopeless. Thus, "Knowledge of God without knowledge of man's wretchedness leads to pride. Knowledge of man's wretchedness without knowledge of God leads to despair. Knowledge of Jesus Christ is the middle course, because by it we discover both God and our wretched state." Pascal even had an answer for skeptics in his famous wager. God is a reasonable bet; it is worthwhile to assume that God exists. If he does, then we win all; if he does not, we lose nothing.

Despite his background as a scientist and mathematician, Pascal refused to rely on the scientist's world of order and rationality to attract people to God: "If we submit everything to reason, there will be no mystery and no supernatural element in our religion." In the new cosmology of the seventeenth century, "finite man," Pascal believed, was lost in the new infinite world, a realization that frightened him: "The eternal silence of those infinite spaces strikes me with terror" (see the box on p. 594). The world of nature, then, could never reveal God: "Because they have failed to contemplate these infinites, men have rashly plunged into the examination of nature, as though they bore some proportion to her. . . . Their assumption is as infinite as their object." A Christian could only rely on a God who through Jesus cared for human beings. In the final analysis, after providing reasonable arguments for Christianity, Pascal came to rest on faith. Reason, he believed, could take people only so far: "The heart has its reasons of which the reason knows nothing." As a Christian, faith was the final step: "The heart feels God, not the reason. This is what constitutes faith: God experienced by the heart, not by the reason."[27]

In retrospect, it is obvious that Pascal failed to achieve his goal of uniting Christianity and science. Increasingly, the gap between science and traditional religion grew wider as Europe continued along its path of secularization. Of course, traditional religions were not eliminated, nor is there any evidence that churches had yet lost their numbers. That would happen later. Nevertheless, more and more of the intellectual, social, and political elites began to act on the basis of secular rather than religious assumptions.

The Spread of Scientific Knowledge

In the course of the seventeenth century, scientific learning and investigation began to increase dramatically. Major universities in Europe established new chairs of science, especially in medicine. Royal and princely patronage of individual scientists became an international phenomenon. The king of Denmark constructed an astronomical observatory for Tycho Brahe; Emperor Rudolf II hired Tycho Brahe and Johannes Kepler as imperial mathematicians; the grand duke of Tuscany appointed Galileo to a similar post. Of greater importance to the work of science, however, was the emergence of new learned societies and journals that enabled the new scientists to communicate their ideas to each other and to disseminate them to a wider, literate public.

The Scientific Societies

The first of these scientific societies appeared in Italy and included the Academy of Experiments, founded in Florence in 1657 by two of Galileo's pupils under the patronage of the Medicean grand duke of Tuscany. Its laboratory facilities enabled research to be carried out along the new experimental lines. This Florentine Academy was short-lived, however, and came to an end when its Medici supporters discontinued their funding in 1667.

Ultimately of more significance were the scientific societies of England and France. The English Royal Society evolved out of informal gatherings of scientists at London and Oxford in the 1640s, although it did not receive a formal charter from King Charles II until 1662. The French Royal Academy of Sciences also arose out of informal scientific meetings in Paris during the 1650s. In 1666, urged on by his minister Colbert, Louis XIV formally recognized the group. The French Academy received abundant state support and remained under government control; its members were appointed and paid salaries by the state. In contrast, the Royal Society

✦ **Louis XIV and Colbert Visit the Academy of Sciences.** In the seventeenth century, individual scientists received royal and princely patronage, and a number of learned societies were established. In France, Louis XIV, urged on by his minister Colbert, gave formal recognition to the French Academy in 1666. In this painting by Henri Testelin, Louis XIV is shown seated, surrounded by Colbert and members of the French Royal Academy of Sciences.

of England received little government encouragement, and its fellows simply co-opted new members.

Early on, both the English and French scientific societies formally emphasized the practical value of scientific research. The Royal Society established a committee to investigate technological improvements for industry while the French Academy collected tools and machines. This concern with the practical benefits of science proved short-lived, however, as both societies came to focus their primary interest on theoretical work in mechanics and astronomy. The construction of observatories at Paris in 1667 and at Greenwich, England, in 1675 greatly facilitated research in astronomy by both

groups. The French Academy, however, since it was controlled by the state, was forced by the war minister of France, the marquis de Louvois, to continue its practical work to benefit both the "king and the state." The French example was especially important as a model for the scientific societies established in neighboring Germany. German princes and city governments encouraged the foundation of small-scale scientific societies of their own. Most of them, such as the Scientific Academy created in 1700 by the elector of Brandenburg, as well as the scientific academies established in most European countries in the eighteenth century, were sponsored by governments and were mainly devoted to the betterment of the state. While both the English and French societies made useful contributions to scientific knowledge in the second half of the seventeenth century, their true significance arose from their example that science should proceed as a cooperative venture.

Scientific journals furthered this concept of cooperation. The French *Journal des Savants*, published weekly beginning in 1665, printed results of experiments as well as general scientific knowledge. Its format appealed to both scientists and the educated public interested in the new science. The *Philosophical Transactions* of the Royal Society, however, also initiated in 1665, published papers of its members and learned correspondence and was aimed at practicing scientists. It became a prototype for the scholarly journals of later learned and academic

◆ **The Royal Observatory at Greenwich.** To facilitate their astronomical investigations, both the English and the French constructed observatories, such as the one pictured here, which was built at Greenwich, England, in 1675. Here the royal astronomer works at the table while his two assistants make observations.

societies and a crucial instrument for circulating news of scientific and academic activities.

Science and Society

The importance of science in the history of modern Western civilization is usually taken for granted. No doubt the Industrial Revolution of the nineteenth century provided tangible proof of the effectiveness of science and ensured its victory over Western minds. But how did science become such an integral part of Western culture in the seventeenth and eighteenth centuries? Recent research has stressed that one cannot simply assert that people perceived that science was a rationally superior system. Two important social factors, however, might help to explain the relatively rapid acceptance of the new science.

It has been argued that the literate mercantile and propertied elites of Europe were soon attracted to a new science that offered new ways to exploit resources for profit. Some of the early scientists made it easier for these groups to accept the new ideas by showing how they could be applied directly to specific industrial and technological needs. Galileo, for example, consciously sought an alliance between science and the material interests of the educated elite when he assured his listeners that the science of mechanics would be quite useful "when it becomes necessary to build bridges or other structures over water, something occurring mainly in affairs of great importance." At the same time, Galileo stressed that science was fit for the "minds of the wise" and not for "the shallow minds of the common people." This made science part of the high culture of Europe's wealthy elites at a time when that culture was being increasingly separated from the popular culture of the lower classes (see Chapter 18). This merger of scientists with the literate and propertied elites occurred first in England and later in France and the Low Countries.

It has also been argued that political interests used the new scientific conception of the natural world to bolster social stability. One scholar has recently argued that "no single event in the history of early modern Europe more profoundly shaped the integration of the new science into Western culture than did the English Revolution (1640–1660)."[28] Fed by their millenarian expectations that the end of the world would come and usher in a thousand-year reign of the saints, Puritan reformers felt it was important to reform and renew their society. They seized on the new science as a socially useful instrument to accomplish this goal. The Puritan Revolution's role in the acceptance of science, however, stemmed even more from the reaction to the radicalism spawned by the revolutionary ferment. The upheavals of the Puritan Revolution gave rise to groups, such as the Levellers, Diggers, and Ranters, who advocated not only radical political ideas, but also a new radical science based on Paracelsus and the natural magic associated with the Hermetic tradition. The chaplain of the New Model Army said that the radicals wanted "the philosophy of Hermes, revived by the Paracelsian schools." The propertied and educated elites responded vigorously to these challenges to the established order by supporting the new mechanistic science and appealing to the material benefits of science. Hence, the founders of the Royal Society were men who wanted to pursue an experimental science that would remain detached from radical reforms of church and state. Although willing to make changes, they now viewed those changes in terms of an increase in food production and commerce. By the eighteenth century, the Newtonian world-machine had been readily accepted, and Newtonian science would soon be applied to trade and industry by a mercantile and landed elite that believed that they "could retain a social order that primarily rewarded and enriched themselves while still improving the human condition."

Conclusion

The Scientific Revolution represents a major turning point in modern Western civilization. In the Scientific Revolution, the Western world overthrew the medieval, Ptolemaic-Aristotelian worldview and arrived at a new conception of the universe: the sun at the center, the planets as material bodies revolving around the sun in elliptical orbits, and an infinite rather than finite world. With the changes in the conception of "heaven" came changes in the conception of "earth." The work of Bacon and Descartes left Europeans with the separation of mind and matter and the belief that by using only reason they could, in fact, understand and dominate the world of nature. The development of a scientific method furthered the work of scientists while the creation of scientific societies and learned journals spread its results. Although traditional churches stubbornly resisted the new ideas and a few intellectuals pointed to some inherent flaws, nothing was able to halt the replacement of the traditional ways of thinking by new ways of thinking that created a more fundamental break with the past than that represented by the breakup of Christian unity in the Reformation.

The Scientific Revolution forced Europeans to change their conception of themselves. At first, some were appalled and even frightened by its implications. Formerly, humans on earth had been at the center of the universe. Now the earth was only a tiny planet revolving around a sun that was itself only a speck in a boundless universe. Most people remained optimistic despite the apparent blow to human dignity. After all, had Newton not demonstrated that the universe was a great machine governed by natural laws? Newton had found one—the universal law of gravitation. Could others not find other laws? Were there not natural laws governing every aspect of human endeavor that could be found by the new scientific method? Thus, the Scientific Revolution leads us logically to the age of the Enlightenment of the eighteenth century.

NOTES

1. Quoted in Alan G. R. Smith, *Science and Society in the Sixteenth and Seventeenth Centuries* (London, 1972), p. 59.
2. Edward MacCurdy, *The Notebooks of Leonardo da Vinci* (London, 1948), 1:634.
3. Ibid., p. 636.
4. Frances Yates, *Giordano Bruno and the Hermetic Tradition* (New York, 1964), p. 448.
5. Ibid., p. 450.
6. Quoted in Smith, *Science and Society in the Sixteenth and Seventeenth Centuries*, p. 97.
7. Logan P. Smith, *Life and Letters of Sir Henry Wotton* (Oxford, 1907), 1:486–87.
8. Quoted in John H. Randall, *The Making of the Modern Mind* (Boston, 1926), p. 234.
9. Quoted in Smith, *Science and Society in the Sixteenth and Seventeenth Centuries*, p. 124.
10. Quoted in Betty J. Dobbs, *The Foundations of Newton's Alchemy* (Cambridge, 1975), pp. 13–14.
11. Jolande Jacobi, ed., *Paracelsus: Selected Writings* (New York, 1965), pp. 5–6.
12. Ibid., p. 21.
13. Quoted in Londa Schiebinger, *The Mind Has No Sex? Women in the Origins of Modern Science* (Cambridge, Mass., 1989), pp. 52–53.
14. Ibid., p. 85.
15. Galen, *On the Usefulness of the Parts of the Body*, trans. Margaret May (Ithaca, N.Y., 1968), 2:628–29.
16. Quoted in Phyllis Stock, *Better Than Rubies: A History of Women's Education* (New York, 1978), p. 16.
17. René Descartes, *Philosophical Writings*, ed. and trans. Norman K. Smith (New York, 1958), p. 95.
18. Ibid., pp. 118–19.
19. Ibid., p. 120.
20. Francis Bacon, *The Great Instauration*, trans. Jerry Weinberger (Arlington Heights, Ill., 1989), pp. (in order of quotations) 2, 8, 2, 16, 21.
21. Descartes, *Discourse on Method*, in *Philosophical Writings*, p. 75.
22. Stillman Drake, ed. and trans., *Discoveries and Opinions of Galileo* (New York, 1957), p. 182.
23. Benedict de Spinoza, *Ethics*, trans. R. H. M. Elwes (New York, 1955), pp. 75–76.
24. Ibid., p. 76.
25. Benedict de Spinoza, *Letters*, quoted in Randall, *The Making of the Modern Mind*, p. 247.
26. Blaise Pascal, *The Pensées*, trans. J. M. Cohen (Harmondsworth, 1961), p. 100.
27. Ibid., pp. (in order of quotations) 31, 45, 31, 52–53, 164, 165.
28. Margaret C. Jacob, *The Cultural Meaning of the Scientific Revolution* (New York, 1988), p. 73.

SUGGESTIONS FOR FURTHER READING

Three general surveys of the entire Scientific Revolution are A. G. R. Smith, *Science and Society in the Sixteenth and Seventeenth Centuries* (London, 1972); M. Boas, *The Scientific Renaissance: 1450–1630* (London, 1962); and H. Butterfield, *The Origins of Modern Science* (New York, 1962). A more detailed and technical introduction can be found in A. R. Hall, *The Revolution in Science, 1500–1750* (London, 1983). Also of much value is A. G. Debus, *Man and Nature in the Renaissance* (Cambridge, 1978), which covers the period from the mid-fifteenth through the mid-seventeenth century. The importance of mathematics to the Scientific Revolution is brought out in P. L. Rose, *The Italian Renaissance of Mathematics: Studies on Humanists and Mathematicians from Petrarch to Galileo* (Geneva, 1975). On the relationship of magic to the beginnings of the Scientific Revolution, see the pioneering works by F. Yates, *Giordano Bruno and the Hermetic Tradition* (New York, 1964), and *The Rosicrucian Enlightenment* (London, 1975). Some criticism of this approach is provided in R. S. Westman and J. E. McGuire, eds., *Hermeticism and the Scientific Revolution* (Los Angeles, 1977). An important book on magic in the early modern period is K. Thomas, *Religion and the Decline of Magic* (London, 1971).

A good introduction to the transformation from the late medieval to the early modern worldview is A. Koyré, *From the Closed World to the Infinite Universe* (New York, 1958). Also still of value are A. Koestler, *The Sleepwalkers: A History of Man's Changing Vision of the Universe* (New York, 1959); and E. A. Burtt, *The Metaphysical Foundations of Modern Physical Science* (London, 1942). On the important figures of the revolution in astronomy, see E. Rosen, *Copernicus and the Scientific Revolution* (New York, 1984); M. Sharratt, *Galileo: Decisive Innovator* (Oxford, 1994); S. Drake, *Galileo* (New York, 1980); M. Casper, *Johannes Kepler*, trans. C. D. Hellman (London, 1959), the standard biography; and R. S. Westfall, *The Life of Isaac Newton*

(New York, 1993). On Newton's relationship to alchemy, see the invaluable study by B. J. Dobbs, *The Foundations of Newton's Alchemy* (Cambridge, 1975).

The worldview of Paracelsus and his followers can be examined in W. Pagel, *Paracelsus: An Introduction to Philosophical Medicine in the Era of the Renaissance* (New York, 1958); and A. G. Debus, *The Chemical Philosophy: Paracelsian Science and Medicine in the Sixteenth and Seventeenth Centuries*, 2 vols. (New York, 1977). The standard biography of Vesalius is C. D. O'Malley, *Andreas Vesalius of Brussels, 1514–1564* (Berkeley, 1964). The work of Harvey is discussed in G. Whitteridge, *William Harvey and the Circulation of the Blood* (London, 1971). A good general account of the development of medicine can be found in W. P. D. Wightman, *The Emergence of Scientific Medicine* (Edinburgh, 1971).

The importance of Francis Bacon in the early development of science is underscored in P. Rossi, *Francis Bacon: From Magic to Science* (Chicago, 1968); and C. Webster, *The Great Instauration: Science, Medicine, and Reform, 1620–1660* (London, 1975). A good introduction to the work of Descartes can be found in A. Kenny, *Descartes* (New York, 1968). The standard biography of Spinoza in English is S. Hampshire, *Spinoza* (New York, 1961).

For histories of the scientific academies, see R. Hahn, *The Anatomy of a Scientific Institution: The Paris Academy of Sciences, 1666–1803* (Berkeley, 1971); and M. Purver, *The Royal Society, Concept and Creation* (London, 1967).

On the subject of women and early modern science, see the comprehensive and highly informative work by L. Schiebinger, *The Mind Has No Sex? Women in the Origins of Modern Science* (Cambridge, Mass., 1989). The social and political context for the triumph of science in the seventeenth and eighteenth centuries is examined in M. Jacobs, *The Cultural Meaning of the Scientific Revolution* (New York, 1988), and *The Newtonians and the English Revolution, 1689–1720* (Ithaca, N.Y., 1976).

Index

Photo credits continued

CHAPTER 3

64 © Michael Holford, London; **67** © Dimitrios Harissiadis, Athens; **68** Erich Lessing/Art Resource, NY; **69** Black Figure Hydria; *Achilles Dragging the Body of Hector around the Walls of Troy*, William Francis Warden Fund; Courtesy, Museum of Fine Arts, Boston; **72** Scala/Art Resource, NY; **79** The Metropolitan Museum of Art, New York, Fletcher Fund, 1932(32.11.1), Photograph by Schechter Lee; **85** © British Museum, London, reproduced by Courtesy of the Trustees of the British Museum; **87** Courtesy of William M. Murray; **91** Sonia Halliday Photographs; **94** © Michael Holford, London; **95** Scala/Art Resource, NY; **98** © A. F. Kersting, London; **100** The Metropolitan Museum of Art, Fletcher Fund, 1931(31.11.10)

CHAPTER 4

104 *Bust of Alexander*, Musee du Louvre, © Photo R.M.N.; **105** American Numismatic Society, New York; **107** *Bust of Alexander*, Musee du Louvre, © Photo R.M.N.; **109** Scala/Art Resource, NY; **112** Giraudon/Art Resource, NY; **114** Scala/Art Resource, NY; **117** The Metropolitan Museum of Art, New York, Rogers Fund, 1920(20.2.21); **122** Scala/Art Resource, NY; **123** The Metropolitan Museum of Art, Rogers Fund, 1909(09.39); **125** The Metropolitan Museum of Art, Rogers Fund, 1911(11.90); **128** © Leonard von Matt/Photo Researchers, Inc.

CHAPTER 5

132 British Museum, Photo © Michael Holford, London; **135** Art Resource, NY; **137** Alinari; **143** SEF/Art Resource, NY; **144** British Museum, Photo © Michael Holford, London; **150** Scala/Art Resource, NY; **151** © Leslye and Roy Adkins Picture Library; **154** The Metropolitan Museum of Art, Rogers Fund, 1903(03.14.5); **156** © Leonard von Matt/Photo Researchers, Inc.; **157** Scala/Art Resource, NY; **162** (Left) The Ny Carlsberg Glyptotek; (Right) Scala/Art Resource, NY; **164** Scala/Art Resource, NY

CHAPTER 6

170 © British Museum, London, reproduced by Courtesy of the Trustees of the British Museum; **172** Photo Vatican Museums; **173** *Relief of Praetorian Guards*, Musee du Louvre, © Photo R.M.N.-H.Lewandowski; **181** Courtesy of James R. Spencer; **182** © British Museum, London, reproduced by Courtesy of the Trustees of the British Museum; **183** © Brian Brake/Photo Researchers, Inc.; **184** Photo © Eberhard Thiem, Lotos-Film, Kaufbeuren, Germany; **188** SEF/Art Resource, NY; **191** (Top) © Thomas S. England/Photo Researchers, Inc.; (Bottom) Roger Wood/© Corbis; **195** Scala/Art Resource, NY; **200** Scala/Art Resource, NY

CHAPTER 7

206 Bibliotheque Nationale, Paris, Ms. Nouv. Acq. Fr. 1098; **214** Vat. Lat. 1202F.80r, Foto Biblioteca Vaticana; **219** © G. Dagli Orti; **221** Bibliotheque Nationale, Paris, Ms. Nouv. Acq. Fr. 1098; **225** Kunsthistorisches Museum, Vienna; **227** The Board of Trinity College Dublin; **230** Scala/Art Resource, NY; **233** Sonia Halliday Photographs; **234** © Erich Lessing/Art Resource, NY; **236** Edinburgh University Library (Or. Ms. 161, f.10v); **239** Bibliotheque Nationale, Paris

CHAPTER 8

244 The Granger Collection; **248** *Statue of Charlemagne*, Musee du Louvre, © Photo R.M.N.; **249** © Ronald Sheridan/Ancient Art and Architecture; **251** The Granger Collection; **253** © J. L. Charmet, from Chroniques de Saint-Denis. XV Eme, MS2028, Bibliotheque Mazarine; **256** MS Hunter 252, f.70, Courtesy of the Librarian, Glasgow University Library; **260** The Pierpont Morgan Library/Art Resource, NY, M.736, f.9v; **261** Leiden, University Library, BPL20, f.60r; **265** E.T. Archive, London, from the collections of the British Library, Psalter, Calendar, c1250–1260; **270** Byzantine Visual Resources, Dumbarton Oaks, Washington, D.C., ©1996; **274** Scala/Art Resource, NY

CHAPTER 9

278 The Pierpont Morgan Library/Art Resource, NY, MS399, f.5v, c. 1515, Bruges (Detail); **281** Bridgeman Art Library/ Art Resource, NY; **283** The Pierpont Morgan Library/Art Resource, NY, MS399, f.5v, c. 1515, Bruges; **285** Bibliotheque Nationale, Paris; **290** Scala/Art Resource, NY; **291** Giraudon/Art Resource, NY; **293** (Left) Scala/Art Resource, NY; (Right) British Library, London, Ms. Arundel 83, Part II, f. 132r; **294** (Left) © Bibliotheque royale Albert ler (Ms IV 119, fol. 72 verso); (Right) Giraudon/Art Resource, NY; **298** (Left) Bibliotheque Nationale, Paris; (Right) British Library, London, Cotton, Nero, C.IV, f. 39; **299** Map adapted from *Revelations: The Medieval World* by James Harpur (London: Marshall Editions, 1995) p. 76; **301** Bridgeman Art Library/Art Resource, NY

CHAPTER 10

306 Bibliotheque Nationale, Paris; **310** Bibliotheque Nationale, Paris; **312** © Wysocki/Explorer/Photo Researchers, Inc.; **314** British Library, London, Harley 4379, f.64; **315** Bibliotheque Nationale, Paris; **317** British Library, London, Ms. Royal 15 E.II, f.269; **319** Giraudon/Art Resource, NY; **320** Giraudon/Art Resource, NY; **322** Bibliotheque Nationale, Paris; **323** Bibliotheque Nationale, Paris; **324** Tapisserie de Bayeux et avec autorisation speciale de la Ville de Bayeux; **333** Hirmer Fotoarchiv, Munich

CHAPTER 11

342 Bibliotheque Nationale, Paris; **346** Bibliotheque Nationale, Paris; **350** Bibliotheque Nationale, Paris; **352** Bibliotheque Nationale, Paris; **354** The Granger Collection; **357** Staatliche Museen, Berlin, Photo © Bildarchiv Preussischer Kulturbesitz; **366** Bibliotheque Nationale, Paris; **369** Bibliotheque Nationale, Paris/Art Resource, NY; **370** © G. Dagli Orti; **371** (Top) © G. Dagli Orti; (Bottom) © Sylvain Grandadam/Photo Researchers, Inc.; **372** (Left) Sonia Halliday Photographs; (Right) British Library, London, Ms. Hours, Add. 35313, f.34

CHAPTER 12

376 © Bibliotheque royale Albert ler, Bruxelles (Ms. 13076-77, f. 16v); **378** © Bibliotheque royale Albert ler, Bruxelles (Ms. 13076-77, f. 12v); **381** © Bibliotheque royale Albert ler, Bruxelles (Ms. 13076-77, f. 16v); **384** Bibliotheque Nationale, Paris; **386** Staatliche Landesbildstelle Hamburg; **390** (Left) Froissart's Chronicle, Fr2643, f.165v, Bibliotheque Nationale, Paris, Bridgeman/Art Resource, NY; (Right) Giraudon/Art Resource, NY; **392** The Granger Collection; **397** British Library, London, Ms.

Add. 23923, f.2; **405** Scala/Art Resource, NY; **406-7** Scala/Art Resource, NY; **408** Meister des Marienlebens, "Geburt Mariae," Alte Pinakothek, Munich, Photo © Artothek; **409** British Library, London, Ms. Sloane 1977, f.7

CHAPTER 13

412 Michelangelo, *Creation of Adam*, (Detail), Photo Vatican Museums; **419** Private Collection/The Bridgeman Art Library; **423** (Left) Scala/Art Resource, NY; (Right) Scala/Art Resource, NY; **425** © ARCHIV/Photo Researchers, Inc.; **434** Scala/Art Resource, NY; **435** Erich Lessing/Art Resource, NY; **436** (Left) Scala/Art Resource, NY; (Right) Scala/Art Resource, NY; **437** Scala/Art Resource, NY; **438** (Left) *The Alba Madonna*, Raphael, National Gallery of Art, Washington, Andrew W. Mellon Collection; (Right) Scala/Art Resource, NY; **439** (Top) Michelangelo, *Creation of Adam*, Photo Vatican Museums; (Bottom) Art Resource, NY; **441** (Left) Jan van Eyck, *Giovanni Arnolfini and His Bride*, reproduced by Courtesy of the Trustees, The National Gallery, London; (Right) Alinari/Art Resource, NY; **446** Kunsthistorisches Museum, Vienna; **450** Photo Vatican Museums

CHAPTER 14

454 Staatliche Museen Preussischer Kulturbesitz, Kupferstichkabinett, Berlin (West), Photo: Jorg P. Anders; **457** Oeffentliche Kunstsammlung Basel, Kunstmuseum: Colorphoto Hans Hinz; **461** Cranach the Younger, *Martin Luther and the Wittenberg Reformers*, The Toledo Museum of Art, Toledo, Ohio: Gift of Edward Drummond Libbey; **464** Staatliche Museen Preussischer Kulturbesitz, Kupferstichkabinett, Berlin (West), Photo: Jorg P. Anders; **467** (Bottom) Jean Clouet, *Francis I*, Musee du Louvre, © Photo R.M.N.; (Top) Alte Pinakothek, Munich; **470** Hans Asper, *Zwingli*, Kunstmuseum Winterthur; **473** © British Museum, London, reproduced by Courtesy of the Trustees of the British Museum; **476** The Royal Collection © Her Majesty Queen Elizabeth II; **477** © Bibliotheque Publique et Universitaire, Geneva; **481** Oeffentliche Kunstsammlung Basel, Kunstmuseum: Colorphoto Hans Hinz; **484** Scala/Art Resource, NY

CHAPTER 15

490 Private Collection (Detail of the work); **494** Musees Royaux des Beaux-Arts de Belgique, Bruxelles (Photo by G. Cussac); **495** The Metropolitan Museum of Art, Gift of J. Pierpont Morgan, 1900(00.18.2); **497** National Maritime Museum, Greenwich; **500**

Francois Dubois D'Amiens, *The St. Bartholomew's Day Massacre*, Musee Cantonal des Beaux-Arts, Lausanne; **503** Derechos Reservados, © Museo del Prado, Madrid; **507** Private Collection; **509** Herzog Anton Ulrich Museum, Braunschweig; **513** Giraudon/Art Resource, NY; **517** Kunsthistorisches Museum, Vienna; **520** *Laocoon*, El Greco, National Gallery of Art, Washington: Samuel H. Kress Collection; **521** Scala/Art Resource, NY; **522** (Left) Peter Paul Rubens, *The Landing of Marie de Medicis at Marseilles*, Musee du Louvre, © Photo R.M.N.; (Right) Scala/Art Resource, NY; **523** John Taylor, *William Shakespeare*, By courtesy of the National Portrait Gallery, London, England

CHAPTER 16

528 Hyacinthe Rigaud, *Louis XIV*, Musee du Louvre, © Photo R.M.N.; **531** Reproduced by Courtesy of the Trustees, The National Gallery, London; **533** Hyacinthe Rigaud, *Louis XIV*, Musee du Louvre, © Photo R.M.N.; **535** Giraudon/Art Resource, NY; **536** Giraudon/Art Resource, NY; **544** Russian School, *Czar Peter the Great*, Rijksmuseum, Amsterdam; **553** Jacob van der Ulft, *The square of the Dam at Amsterdam*, 1659, Musee Conde, Chantilly, Photo Giraudon/Art Resource, NY; **555** Robert Walker, *Oliver Cromwell*, 1649, By courtesy of the National Portrait Gallery, London; **557** Peter Hoadley, *William III and Mary Stuart*, Rijksmuseum, Amsterdam; **562** H. v. Schuylenburgh, *Head Office of the Dutch East India Company at Hugly in Bengal, 1665*, Rijksmuseum, Amsterdam; **564** Nicholas Poussin, *Landscape with the Burial of Phocion*, Musee du Louvre, © Photo R.M.N.; **565** Rembrandt, *The Syndics of the Cloth Guild*, Rijksmusuem, Amsterdam

CHAPTER 17

570 National Portrait Gallery, London; **574** Courtesy of the Lilly Library, Indiana University, Bloomington, Indiana; **575** Courtesy of the Lilly Library, Indiana University, Bloomington, Indiana; **577** Deutsches Musuem, Munich; **579** Biblioteca Nazionale Centrale, Firenze; **582** National Portrait Gallery, London; **585** Metsys, *Paracelsus*, Musee du Louvre, © Photo R.M.N.; **590** Dumesnil, *Queen Christina of Sweden with Descartes*, Musee du Louvre, © Photo R.M.N.; **593** Ecole francaise (17e siecle), *Blaise Pascal*, Versailles et Trianon, © Photo R.M.N.; **595** Giraudon/Art Resource, NY; **596** Reproduced by Courtesy of the Science Museum (neg. 4534)